the World

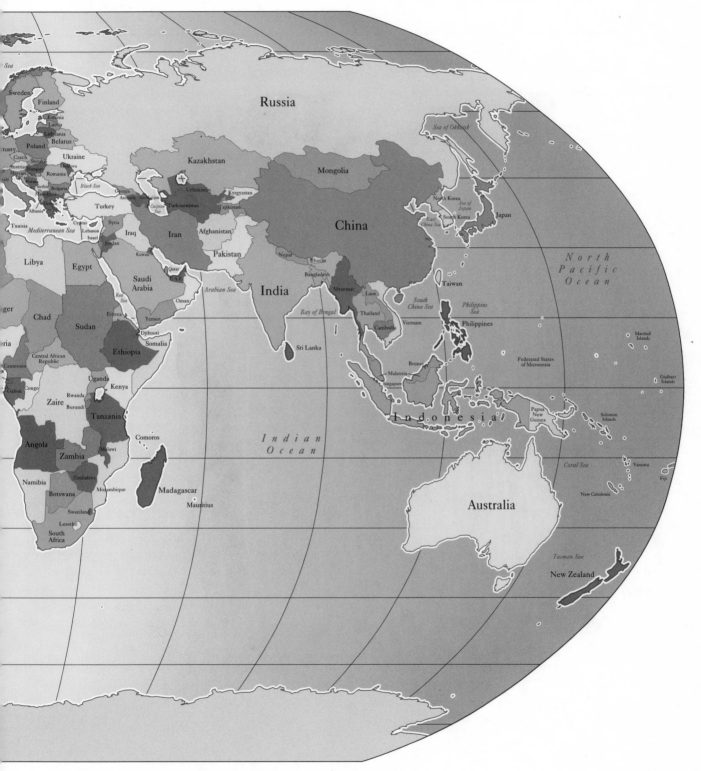

ENCYCLOPEDIA OF U.S. FOREIGN RELATIONS

ENCYCLOPEDIA OF
U.S. FOREIGN
RELATIONS

SENIOR EDITORS

Bruce W. Jentleson   Thomas G. Paterson

PREPARED UNDER THE AUSPICES OF THE

Council on Foreign Relations

SENIOR CONSULTING EDITOR

Nicholas X. Rizopoulos

VOLUME 1

Oxford University Press
New York   Oxford
1997

OXFORD UNIVERSITY PRESS

Oxford   New York
Athens Auckland Bangkok Bogotá Bombay Buenos Aires
Calcutta Cape Town Dar es Salaam Delhi Florence Hong Kong
Istanbul Karachi Kuala Lumpur Madras Madrid Melbourne
Mexico City Nairobi Paris Singapore Taipei Tokyo Toronto

and associated companies in
Berlin   Ibadan

Published by Oxford University Press, Inc.,
198 Madison Avenue, New York, New York 10016

Oxford is a registered trademark of Oxford University Press

Library of Congress Cataloging-in-Publication Data
Encyclopedia of U.S. foreign relations / senior editors, Bruce W.
Jentleson, Thomas G. Paterson.
p. cm.
Includes bibliographical references and index.
1. United States—Foreign relations—Encyclopedias. 2. United
States—Relations—Encyclopedias. I. Jentleson, Bruce W., 1951-.
II. Paterson, Thomas G., 1941-.
E183.7.E53   1997   96-8159   327.73—dc20   CIP
ISBN 0-19-511055-2 (4-vol. set)
ISBN 0-19-511056-0 (vol. 1)

PROJECT STAFF FOR AMERICAN REFERENCE PUBLISHING, INC.
PUBLISHER: Richard Gottlieb
MANAGING EDITOR: Laura Mars
EDITORIAL ASSISTANTS: Alexcia Fales, Mary Massey, Betsy Trotta
COMPOSITOR: Chestnut Hill Enterprises, Inc.
INDEXER: Alexandra Nickerson
CARTOGRAPHERS: Cartographic Research Corporation, Magellan Geographix

Printing (last digit): 9 8 7 6 5 4 3 2 1

Printed in the United States of America
on acid-free paper

Foreword

The Council on Foreign Relations was born in the wake of World War I and in the midst of a heated national debate over America's role and obligations as a world leader. Seventy-five years ago, the small group of our founding members dedicated this non-partisan institution to pursuing one principal task: improving America's understanding of international affairs in general and of U.S. foreign policy concerns in particular.

In the debates of the late 1990s over America's evolving international leadership in what is now a far more complicated world, we hear echoes of those of the 1920s. But there is one marked difference. In 1921, both the number of leaders and the variety of U.S. interests engaged in international relations was limited. Today, Americans in greater numbers and variety than ever before participate in the world, and never before has the world been so much a part of America. The idea of growing mutual interdependence has underpinned so much of what the Council has done and dedicated itself to.

It is therefore most fitting that the Council be associated with the publication of the first comprehensive, multivolume reference work on the history of America's foreign relations—all the more so since a central element of the Council's mission is to identify and encourage the next generation of foreign policy leaders, who will have to confront the varied challenges of the world we live in.

There has never been a time that was more important for experts and laymen alike to better know the basic facts and information that bind together our common history—and destiny.

Leslie H. Gelb
President, Council on Foreign Relations

Editorial Board

Contents

Preface

The veteran foreign-service officer George F. Kennan, commenting in 1950 on U.S. foreign policy found "utter confusion in the public mind.... The President doesn't understand it; Congress doesn't understand it; nor does the public, nor does the press."* This kind of critical comment could be dismissed as the sour musings of a disgruntled diplomat who was just leaving the Department of State to pursue a new career if similar utterances had not been spoken by countless others since the birth of the United States in 1776.

Kennan went on to a life of writing history—in fact, a life largely dedicated to reducing "confusion" about American foreign relations. Many have debated whether Kennan succeeded, but few have disputed the importance of the task he undertook. The *Encyclopedia of U.S. Foreign Relations (EUSFR)*, like Kennan, seeks in its own way to clarify U.S. foreign relations by providing general readers and scholars alike with a comprehensive survey that examines the myriad ways in which Americans and their government have interacted with the world. In these four volumes the reader will find the many dimensions of international relations: political, economic, military, cultural, ideological, environmental, and more. Diplomatic crises, treaties and agreements, wars, international conferences; the activities of leaders, nations, and organizations; movements, doctrines, and concepts—all are treated in detail and in broad historical context.

The encyclopedia's authoritative articles, by both American and foreign scholars, explore the people who influenced and shaped policies, the ideas that drove their decisions, and the key events that compelled change. With appropriate attention to history, the articles explain how U.S. foreign relations developed over time. The multilayered story is brought forward to the present: the contributors do not predict what comes next, but their articles provide the information necessary for reasoned thought about the future.

This encyclopedia presents 1,024 articles. One of the distinctive features of the *EUSFR* is the in-depth treatment given to major topics. Such subjects as the American Revolution, World Wars I and II, the Cold War, the U.S. Constitution, the Congress, Immigration, and the Environment, for example, receive extended coverage. Biographical profiles link leaders to significant foreign-policy issues. Articles about countries, and about regions such as the Middle East, identify the key characteristics and themes of U.S. relations. There are 756 articles in the 150–1,000-word range, 217 in the 1,000–5,000-word range, and 51 in the 5,000–10,000-word range. Most entries carry cross-references as well as bibliographical suggestions for further reading and research. Blind entries, alphabetically listed, provide additional guidance to the reader. Numerous maps, charts, and figures are included to highlight the text. The last volume contains a unique three-part appendix: a detailed chronology covering U.S. foreign relations since independence in 1776; a comprehensive table of the countries of the world with significant data on each; and an extensive master bibliography of reference works. A comprehensive index rounds out the encyclopedia.

---

*George F. Kennan, *Memoirs, 1925–1950* (Boston: Little, Brown, 1967), p. 500.

The encyclopedia's articles were written by 373 contributors. Although each article was reviewed and edited by members of the editorial board, individual contributors bear final responsibility for an entry's content and the views expressed therein. Every article carries its contributor's name. The contributors (with their professional affiliations) are listed alphabetically at the beginning of volume 1.

Scholars and teachers will discover in the *EUSFR* an instructive reference source. Students, both high school and college, will find these volumes valuable for definitions, data, and ideas for research papers. Policymakers, government officials, and others in the United States and abroad who follow international affairs can rely upon the *EUSFR* for quick reference, incisive analysis, and historical perspective.

ACKNOWLEDGMENTS

Senior Editor Bruce W. Jentleson thanks the University of California, Davis, and the UC Davis Washington Center for their institutional support, Melody Johnson and Lori Renard for their able and reliable staff assistance, and especially Rebecca Britton for her conscientious and creative research assistance.

Senior Editor Thomas G. Paterson thanks Jerry Padula, Michael Reno, Shane Maddock, Michael Donoghue, and Aaron M. Paterson for their research assistance and office management of the project.

The senior editors and the American Reference Publishing Company thank Senior Consulting Editors Nicholas X. Rizopoulos and Gaddis Smith and Associate Editors Caroline A. Hartzell, Ole R. Holsti, Howard Jones, and Henry R. Nau. The senior editors also thank Richard Gottlieb, president of American Reference Publishing, for initiating this project, and especially Laura Mars, managing editor of American Reference Publishing, for her expert handling of this complex project.

The members of the editorial board thank all the contributors of the *EUSFR* for accepting assignments, meeting deadlines, making revisions, and writing articles that are truly accessible to a general audience.

The Council on Foreign Relations, the principal institutional sponsor of the *EUSFR*, and its Senior Studies Editor Nicholas X. Rizopoulos (also one of *EUSFR*'s two senior consulting editors) acknowledge the thoughtful encouragement given to the project at its inception by the then president of the Council, Peter Tarnoff, as well as the continuing support provided by the Council's current president, Leslie Gelb, and by the director of publications, David Kellogg.

American Reference Publishing, which produced the encyclopedia for Oxford University Press, thanks its staff: Managing Editor Laura Mars, her dedicated assistants Alexcia Fales, and Mary Massey, and its former staff members, including former managing editors Karen Christensen and Leslie Kelley and assistants Lee Kennedy, Diane Marchiona, Penni Martorell, and Betsy Trotta.

Additionally, American Reference Publishing would like to express its thanks to the many librarians, historians, and archivists at the following agencies and departments for their assistance with this project: the Arms Control and Disarmament Agency, Central Intelligence Agency Public Affairs Office, Department of Commerce, Department of State, Department of the Treasury, Energy Information Administration, International Olympic Committee (Switzerland), National Archives, National Security Council, Office of the Joint Chiefs of Staff, Office of the Secretary of Defense (Public Affairs) Directorate of Public Communication, Office of Science and Technology Policy, Office of the U.S. Trade Representative, United Nations, U.S. Air Force, U.S. Navy, U.S. House of Representatives, and U.S. Senate.

Last, American Reference Publishing expresses its appreciation to Oxford University Press for its support in completing this work, especially President Edward Barry and senior members of the staff of the Scholarly and Professional Reference Department: Editorial Director Claude Conyers, Senior Editor Christopher Collins, and Managing Editor Jeffrey Edelstein.

Introduction

The foreign relations of the United States encompass the many interactions—political, economic, military, cultural, and more—of the federal government and the American people with other nations and peoples. Problems of war and peace; reassuring foreign friends and discomfiting foes; the encouragement of democratic forms of government and respect for human rights; arms competition and arms control; covert operations and other intelligence activities; commerce in goods, services, and ideas; the immigration of people across borders; the regulation of international environmental conditions; humanitarian concerns—all are examples of central issues in U.S. foreign relations. Behind the policies addressing such issues are debates and sometimes serious conflict within the United States: between Congress and the president; within Congress; within the bureaucracy; and among advocacy groups and individuals with different views of the nation's principal interests. The domestic story is as much a part of American foreign relations as the interplay with international actors and the constant attention paid to external developments.

There has never been a single foreign-relations consciousness—or personality—known as "the United States," an actor thinking with one mind, deciding on clear, unconflicted policies, and carrying them out as would an individual. The reality is that the nation's foreign relations spring from shifting factors and relationships within the United States, events in other countries, and international conditions as a whole.

Entries in an encyclopedia such as this are of necessity limited to specific subjects: a concrete event; a seminal idea; the significant achievements of an individual; the development and particular function of an institution; the nature of a policy process. For example, the entries in these volumes are designed to describe: Jay's Treaty and why it was significant; isolationism; William H. Seward and what he did; how relations with Mexico have changed over time; the changing role of the U.S. Congress in the conduct of foreign policy; what happened during the Suez Crisis of 1956; how nuclear weapons have affected international relations; how the United States has sought to confront the issue of environmental degradation; how concepts of human rights have been promoted internationally by the United States. But individual articles cannot by themselves convey a sense of the broad nature of American foreign relations or the intricate interconnectedness of its many elements. That sense must be supplied by the questioning mind of a reader motivated by a desire to trace such connections. The purpose of this introduction is to provide a brief overview of the nature of U.S. foreign relations and to suggest at least some of the questions that must inform a searching examination of this complicated subject.

Because the activity of the federal government reflects all the interests and internal arguments of American society, there is no sharp dividing line between foreign and domestic policy. The international activity of the government, especially in the military realm, is expensive, and expense translates into taxes. Military action usually costs lives and inflicts wounds both physical and psychological on members of society. Political parties seeking to win seats in Congress or the office of the president influence foreign policy as do individuals with distinctive systems of belief and traits of character. So do economic interest groups—organized labor, farmers, manufacturers, bankers, importers, and exporters. They contend with each other and help shape the foreign-policy agenda. Groups promoting particular causes—such as respect for human rights, protection of the physical environment, humane treatment for minorities in another country, withdrawal of American troops from a particular conflict, or intervention abroad to support or overthrow a regime—also figure in the making of foreign policy.

At the official level, specific governmental institutions develop and carry out the nation's foreign policies: the presidency and certain organizations within the White House such as the National Security Council and its staff; the Department of State, and its consulates and embassies overseas; the Central Intelligence Agency and the rest of the intelligence-gathering community; the Pentagon—meaning, the military, itself never a monolithic institution given both the principle and the practice of civilian control and the reality of interservice rivalries; and federal departments and agencies dealing with trade, finance, immigration, health, propaganda, and a score of other foreign-affairs related issues. Every aspect of foreign policy is at least potentially influenced by public opinion—that is, by views and arguments directed at the government from outside. Public opinion is itself dependent on the flow of relevant information—clear or confused, complete or restricted. Thus, the press and ever-changing forms of communication—from the eighteenth century weekly newspaper reporting months after the event to instant pictures available today via satellite—are essential components of the American foreign-relations story.

Some Key Questions to Understanding Foreign Relations

The first question is *what* happened—for example, a war was won or lost, a peace concluded, a territory gained, an alliance forged or dissolved, economic relationships flourished or languished, an environmental disaster occurred, people migrated. This first question leads automatically to the concept (sometimes nebulous) of "the national interest." Was what happened seen by contemporaries to have been in "the national interest"? To answer this question one must deal with the views of influential people, functioning within specific time frames.

The *who* question, then, explores the attitudes and pronouncements (public and private) of presidents, members of Congress, and cabinet officers, diplomats and thousands of other functionaries, members of the judiciary (rarely but sometimes crucially), political party leaders, ethnic and racial groups, advocates for particular interests from particular geographical regions, farmers and industrialists, environmental and health advocates, military enthusiasts and pacifists, journalists and editorial writers, and lobbyists for foreign governments.

Next come questions dealing with *where* and *when* that would appear to be relatively straightforward examinations of matters of fact. Indeed, it is easy enough to state that the United States signed a peace treaty with Great Britain on 3 September 1783, or that the Japanese attacked Pearl Harbor on 7 December 1941. But inquiring about "where" and "when" involves more than looking at a treaty map or a chronological table. It also requires familiarity with the larger historical context, including the availability (and reliability) of sources of information. Thus, as in the case of the Cold War, even where and when questions can become matters of serious historical disputes.

Why and *how* are the most difficult and challenging questions of all. Answers to why and how can never avoid a certain degree of subjectivity because they are inevitably connected with value judgments, themselves leading to explanations of consequences or to rhetorical and at times counter-factual questions. For example, an isolationist and an interventionist arguing in 1940–1941 about events in Europe and Asia would offer very different explanations of the threats posed to American interests and recommend radically different courses of action for the United States to follow.

None of these leading questions can be answered with absolute precision. Most answers depend in large measure on the historical prism through which an event is viewed. A writer can aim, in good conscience, at "factual" accuracy and yet (unintentionally) subvert historical "truth" by excluding this piece of information or overemphasizing that one, or even as a matter of honest interpretation. For example, the European policy advocated by President Woodrow Wilson in 1917–1919 can be seen simultaneously as one aspect of the struggle between Congress and the president, as a first chapter in the development of the notion of collective security, as a belated effort to deny Germany continental hegemony, as a forceful defense of neutral rights, as a calculated (and largely ideological) response to the Bolshevik Revolution, or simply as a significant section of a president's political biography. Similarly, did an episode of armed U.S. intervention in the affairs of another country necessarily end with the withdrawal of U.S. troops, or did the memory and continuing impact of that intervention—in that country, if not in the United States—become inseparable from the original episode?

Understanding a nation's ongoing foreign relations thus also calls for a grasp of the lessons people choose to draw from the remembered past. As the novelist William Faulkner said, "the past is never dead; it is not even past." The greater a nation's freedom of action in the international arena, the less it is a slave to overwhelming force of circumstances—and the more such "lessons" of the past influence contemporary policy decisions and arguments over present and future courses of action. Thus, in 1919 the United States was in principle free to enter the League of Nations and in the process assume long-term European responsibilities under the umbrella of collective security. The opponents of membership in the League predictably invoked the traditional U.S. attachment to isolationism, American detachment from "corrupt" European politics and entanglements, and the wisdom of the Founding Fathers in prescribing an "independent" foreign policy. Advocates of membership invoked the more recent history of international affairs and the failure of the old world order either to prevent the horrendous carnage of the Great War of 1914–1918 or to protect American interests through neutrality or continuing reliance on the Atlantic "moat."

In the 1960s, President Lyndon B. Johnson and his closest advisers took the United States into the Vietnam War in significant part by invoking the memory of appeasement of Hitler's Germany in the 1930s, arguing (above and beyond the seductive theory of "falling dominoes") that the early acceptance of Nazi aggression inevitably led to global war—and American participation in it. Opponents of the war in Vietnam identified instead previous episodes of American military power used unadvisedly—for selfish economic or misguided political reasons—against the people of Asia or Latin America, and excoriated U.S. intervention in Vietnam partly for being more of the same, only on a more horrendous scale. A generation later, moreover, "lessons" drawn from the painful experience in Indochina may have restrained the U.S. military, Congress, the president, and public opinion from forceful interventions abroad out of fears of engendering yet "another Vietnam."

Finally, there is a more mundane reason why definitive answers are hard to come by: governments traditionally act and negotiate in secret, and they guard the detailed record of the most important diplomatic transactions against the probing eye of journalists and historians, often for many decades after the event. Disinformation and the loss of archival sources also play havoc with honest attempts at reconstructing past events. Even more, the historical record requires constant refinement and revision as new sources—a diplomat's private letters or heretofore secret government documents—are discovered or declassified.

Eight Historical Periods

Periodization helps organize the study of foreign relations. The history of American foreign relations from independence in 1776 to the end of the twentieth century can be conveniently broken into seven segments—and the beginning of an eighth.

(1) 1776–1815. The first period, from 1776 to 1815, saw a new, sparsely populated, economically developing, militarily weak nation win and retain independence and expand territorially by exploiting opportunities provided by the almost continuous "world war" waged by the two superpowers of that era, Great Britain and France, against each other, and by defeating those Native Americans who resisted white encroachment on their lands. When the thirteen colonies effectively went to war against Britain and then declared their independence in 1776, France seized the opportunity to weaken its great foe by aiding the United States. Without French military, naval, and economic support, the war for independence could not have been won.

Two decades later Napoleon Bonaparte aimed to occupy the Mississippi valley, thus restricting the future growth of the United States while recreating a French empire in North America. The threat to American national security was enormous. But the mercurial Napoleon changed his mind and sold the vast Louisiana territory to the United States in 1803 largely because he had decided to focus all his energies on the resumption of war with Britain.

Disputes over British treatment of U. S. nationals and commercial and neutral rights, along with an unrealistic ambition by some Americans to conquer Canada, led to a second Anglo-American war in 1812. The British had sufficient naval and military might to crush the United States and impose draconian terms. But once again, in Samuel Flagg Bemis's classic statement, there came "American's advantage from Europe's distress": the British in 1814 still faced a serious French threat on the continent. London accepted what amounted to a draw, demanding no painful concessions from the United States.

The key to understanding American foreign relations in this first, post-independence period is the reality of constant warfare in Europe that spilled into the high seas and threatened U.S. sovereignty and trade. This struggle continued until the final defeat of Napoleon at Waterloo in 1815, providing a fortuitous setting that American leaders came to appreciate and managed to exploit.

(2) 1815–1840s. The second period, from 1815 to the 1840s, saw the U.S. government and people concentrate on pursuing economic growth and territorial (largely transcontinental) expansion. A salient characteristic of this period was, in the words of the historian C. Vann Woodward, "free security"—free in the economic sense of minuscule expenditures needed for national defense, and free in the psychological sense of a nation without fear of foreign attack or of suffering a devastating injury to any of its vital interests. This was also a time when the great powers of Europe themselves avoided large-scale wars, generally cooperated in putting out the fires of smaller regional conflicts, and (more important for our purposes) did little to threaten the security of the United States—with one notable exception. The remote possibility of a monarchical Franco-Spanish attempt to undo the newly won independence of various Latin American republics was taken seriously enough in Washington in 1823 to help produce (with tacit British support) the famous, end-of-year message by President James Monroe enunciating the doctrine stating that the United States would view any European attempt to impose its political system on the new world as a threat to its own vital interests.

While lecturing Europe, the U.S. government launched an Indian removal policy to end Indian resistance to westward expansion. The greatest American expansionist surge took place in the 1840s with the annexation of Texas, the resulting war with

Mexico, the acquisition of California and the southwest, and the near simultaneous drawing of the new boundary between the United States and Canada along the 49th parallel to the Pacific. During this period the United States continued expansion of its foreign commerce, development of its market economy, removal of Native Americans from the path of new white settlement, and the gradual articulation and embellishment of the notion of American exceptionalism—to wit, Manifest Destiny.

(3) 1840s–1865. The middle decades of the nineteenth century saw the issue of slavery in the southern States come to the fore and become explosively entangled with the even larger problem of competition between North and South and with how the benefits accruing from territorial expansion and economic growth would be distributed. Attempts to move into Cuba collided with fears that new slave states would be added to the Union. Victory in the war with Mexico increased the size of the United States by almost a third but also intensified the burgeoning internal conflict, contributing to the Civil War of 1861 to 1865.

Americans fought each other without any significant intervention from abroad. The British wisely resisted any serious temptation to "divide and rule"—all the more so once the military balance began to swing to the North's advantage, as well as in light of the south's ineffective "King Cotton" diplomacy. Only the French emperor, Napoleon III, tried to take advantage of American domestic distractions by backing a foolish scheme to impose a European monarch on Mexico. The scheme collapsed thanks both to Mexican resistance and to the U.S. threat of sending its forces into Mexico following the Union's victory.

(4) 1865–1900. In the immediate post-bellum period, the reunified nation turned its attention again to domestic concerns, although America's tremendous economic growth increasingly fueled overseas activities. Interest in the Pacific region intensified as international competition for strategic and economic outposts increased. Samoa and Hawai'i soon entered the U.S. empire, as did Alaska. U.S. influence in the Western Hemisphere grew and Washington lectured the European powers that the United States considered the hemisphere a U.S. sphere of influence. To protect its growing overseas interests, the United States built a steel navy—the "New Navy." Meanwhile American "cultural imperialism" manifested itself principally through Protestant missionary activity abroad.

In 1898, the United States went to war against Spain ostensibly in order to bring the latest Cuban revolution to an acceptable conclusion. In the process the United States seized the Philippines and Puerto Rico and annexed the Hawai'ian islands. Across America, imperialists and anti-imperialists engaged in a major debate over the benefits and disadvantages of the acquisition of overseas territorial empire—even a relatively puny one compared to the colonial possessions of the European great powers. More to the point, to protect its commercial interests with a gradually disintegrating China, Washington issued the Open Door Notes, declaring sacrosanct the principles of equal trade opportunity and of China's territorial integrity.

(5) 1900–1914. In the first years of the twentieth century, the United States took on the task of managing its farflung possessions, warned other powers to respect U.S. interests (especially in the Western Hemisphere), and quelled an insurrection in the Philippines. Under the exuberant leadership of President Theodore Roosevelt, the United States consolidated its role as a newly emerged colonial power, with directly governed islands in the Caribbean and the Pacific and through temporary occupations and indirect controls over nominally independent countries in Central America and the Caribbean. Roosevelt "showed the flag" by his theatrical mediation of the Russo-Japanese war, by launching the Panama Canal project, and by accelerating the construction of a modern U.S. navy with global range. He anointed the United States as the "policeman" of the Western Hemisphere; and he argued—like few presidents before him—that major political developments in Europe and Asia were of vital interest to the United States. Yet, ironically, his most significant long-term contribution in the area of foreign affairs may have been the help he (unintentionally) provided in securing Woodrow Wilson's election in 1912 by running as a third-party candidate.

(6) 1914–1945. The momentous sixth period, covering the years from Sarajevo to Hiroshima, encompasses the two world wars, the continued expansion of American global power, and increasingly sharp domestic debates over foreign-policy priorities, intervention abroad, and the overall role the United States should play in maintaining international stability. This period saw stark fluctuations in America's relationship to the world: initial neutrality in the European conflict between 1914 and 1917; momentary assumption of a world leadership role in contributing mightily to the final defeat of the Central Powers while also setting the terms of peace in 1918–1919; dramatic diminution of this role when the domestic opponents of U.S. membership in the League of Nations prevailed in 1919–1920; two decades of limited international commitments while the forces that eventually led to World War II gathered strength; and, following the Japanese attack on Pearl Harbor in December 1941, the assumption of commanding world leadership once again—militarily, economically, diplomatically— as the principal ally of Britain and the Soviet Union in the war against the Axis, triumphantly concluded in August 1945, after the atomic bombings of two Japanese cities, Hiroshima and Nagasaki.

(7) 1945–Late 1980s. The seventh period, from 1945 to the late 1980s, was dominated by the Cold War, and by a competition on many fronts—not least in the Third World—between the United States and the Soviet Union, whose interests, global aspirations, and ideologies repeatedly clashed. The Cold War resulted from a confluence of several important developments growing out of World War II: the emergence of the United States not only as the supreme world power eager to exert its influence as never before but also as the unquestioned leader of the "Free World," and thus in direct competition with a totalitarian Soviet Union, dominant (at least as a local power) in Eurasia and eager to promote communist revolutionaries worldwide; the economic and political disarray left by the war's massive destruction and loss of life; the crumbling of the old European colonial empires and the simultaneous birth of what became known as the Third World; the proliferation of new weaponry, above all nuclear arsenals and delivery systems of intercontinental range and great accuracy; and the gradual emergence of a broad consensus in the United States in favor of this country's almost unconditional assumption of responsibility to lead a global crusade aimed at averting economic instability, political upheavals thought to be fueled by communist propaganda, and a third world war. The process of decolonization—and the so-called wars of national liberation—in Asia, the Middle East and Africa inevitably produced zones of instability, competition over the control of strategic raw materials, and the ingrained perception both in Moscow and in Washington that the future of the world, and the "ideological" victory of one superpower, could be determined by the political orientation of these new nations.

In the initial phase of the Cold War (1945–1949), any serious efforts at diplomatic compromise were abandoned as the Soviet Union consolidated its control over Eastern Europe and seemed poised to seek to expand it, and the United States launched foreign-aid programs, cultivated allies, and developed its doctrine of "containment." The most dangerous and confrontational years ran from the outbreak of war in Korea in 1950 through the Suez and Hungarian crises of 1956 and to the crisis over Soviet missiles in Cuba in 1962. Greater cooperation and some relaxation of tensions ("détente"), notably in Europe and on issues of nuclear-arms control followed. But wrenching conflicts continued to afflict world politics, most notably the Vietnam War. The Soviet invasion of Czechoslovakia in 1968 chilled the limited progress that had been made in the mid-1960s. Even amidst the détente developed in the early 1970s, the United States and the Soviet Union came close toconfrontations during the 1973 Arab-Israeli war, a crisis that threatened to escalate into nuclear war. Indeed, competition for influence in the Third World both spread and intensified, with the Soviet invasion of Afghanistan in December 1979 marking the culmination of this trend. Tensions again rose, diplomacy again became confrontational, nuclear-arms competition outstripped arms control, and more Third World proxy wars were fought. The beginning of the end came in 1985 when Mikhail Gorbachev became leader of the Soviet Union. And while debate continues to rage about who gets what share of the credit, few are those who genuinely can claim to have foreseen the speed and sweep with which the Cold War ended.

(8) **1990s–Present.** Once again the United States has entered a new era. Once again American foreign policy must deal with the uncertainties of historic transition. The United States does not face any one single adversary such as an Adolf Hitler or a Joseph Stalin, no single danger that is convincingly clear and present. And once again the combination of weariness after years of mobilization and wariness over what lies ahead is prompting, for some, sentiments of "isolationism." Yet the key question is not whether the international threats and challenges the United States faces are more or less than before, but rather how they have changed. In 1994–1995, for example, the United States saw its interests and values severely enough threatened to have deployed its military forces on an emergency or combat basis to more countries than in any other two-year period since World War II. And, in so many different areas of policy—for example, the economy, the environment, urban crime, and drugs—the very distinctions between "foreign" and "domestic" are becoming increasingly blurred, making foreign policy, however distant or less pressing it now may seem to many, even more pertinent to an even wider range of issues that affect the daily lives of the American people.

The initial euphoria that greeted the fall of the Berlin Wall in 1989 and the demise of the Soviet Union marking the end of the Cold War did receive some reinforcement from the overwhelming military victory over Iraq in 1990–1991 in the Persian Gulf War. But the euphoria did not last. Ethnic violence has raged and spread in the Balkans, in Africa, and elsewhere. Democratic institution-building has proven problematic in many ex-communist countries. Global efforts to cope with environmental degradation have made but limited progress. The stability of the global economy has been called into question by increasingly tough trade battles among the G-7 countries, and by currency crises and other economic instabilities. Given these and other uncertainties, it is little wonder that, as of this writing, we have as yet not progressed beyond terms such as the "post–Cold War era" for the current period. We know what it is not, but we are not yet sure what it is—other than the beginning of yet another distinct period in the history of the foreign relations of the United States.

Core U.S. Goals

(1) **Survival and Independence.** The foreign relations of any nation deal in the first instance with issues of national security: the definition and protection of interests deemed necessary for the nation's well-being. Survival is the irreducible, fundamental security objective of every nation—survival both in the material sense of avoiding the decimation of population and resources, and in the political sense of preserving

national independence. Independence and survival were this nation's consuming concerns in the early years of the history of the republic; they have remained significant concerns ever since.

The roots of the foreign relations of the United States reach back to the first English settlements along the Atlantic coast in the seventeenth century. From the beginning the settlers had needs, interests, and dreams of a future different from the mother country's. But as part of the British empire, the colonies were barred from dealing directly with foreign countries. They had no voice in the foreign-policy decisions made in London. When England was at war, the American colonists were at war; indeed, they had no alternative but to look to British imperial power against potential enemies of their own, principally France by virtue of its colonial possessions in neighboring Canada. The year 1763 was a major turning point in North America. France, defeated in the Seven Years' War (known in North America as the French and Indian War), relinquished Canada and thereby removed one great threat to British colonial security. At the same time, the British decided that it was time to make the American colonists pay a fair share of the cost of imperial defense and also to enforce long-neglected laws regulating colonial trade. The stage was thus set for the American Revolution.

From 1765, with the American protest against the Stamp Act (a tax on business transactions in the colonies), until 1775, the colonists pressed their grievances through political argument and the sporadic adoption of economic measures meant to scare the metropolis—such as the refusal to purchase certain British goods. During the first decade of this Anglo-American contretemps the colonists sought the redress of specific grievances leading to a larger degree of self-government but not to independence per se. The British responded with ever more punishing coercive measures leading to the first serious armed conflict with the battles of Lexington and Concord in 1775. Henceforth, neither the London government nor colonial leaders were willing to compromise. George III and his key advisors believed that the principle of colonial subordination to central imperial rule had to be enforced. The Americans, in turn, decided that continued adherence to imperial regulations had become insufferable and that full independence was therefore essential—as a goal in itself, as the only clear way of avoiding British repression, and as a necessary condition for dealing freely with other nations. Thus, the Declaration of Independence of 4 July 1776, must be seen both as an eloquent "philosophical" statement (deeply rooted in the Enlightenment) and as the first, formal pronouncement of an *American* foreign policy. In the words of the closing paragraph of the Declaration, the United States would "have full Power to levy War, conclude Peace, contract Alliances, establish Commerce, and do all other Acts and Things which Independent States may of right do."

Preserving that independence became the overriding objective of U.S. foreign policy during the war with Britain and for two generations thereafter, until the conclusion of the War of 1812, also with Britain, left independence no longer in doubt. As a small country seeking its independence from a world-class power, initially the United States had to turn for military and economic assistance to the enemies of its foe—France, Spain, and the Netherlands. As astute observers of international politics, American leaders knew that the European powers were motivated by their own selfish goals and their dislike for Great Britain, not by any sentimental attachment to American liberty. For the young nation, then, ties of alliance had to be entered into cautiously, with eyes open to changing geographical circumstances. Thus, the alliance of 1778 with France certainly helped the colonists win independence from Great Britain, but at the risk that in the future American freedom of action might be constrained by certain commitments to France. During the administrations of George Washington and John Adams, the United States sought to separate itself from this French bind. The goal was achieved only after a brief undeclared naval war, and the alliance was canceled by mutual agreement in 1800. Not until 1949 (in the North Atlantic Treaty Organization, or NATO) did the United States enter into another permanent alliance with any European powers.

Preserving American independence was the fundamental issue at stake that led to the second war with Great Britain in 1812. Seen from the U.S. end, the ever haughty British, admittedly engaged in a life-and-death struggle with Napoleonic France, sought unfairly to control American merchant shipping and trade and repeatedly seized (impressed) American seamen, forcing them to serve in the undermanned Royal Navy as if they were British citizens. Some of the young members of Congress, known as "War Hawks," who had already seen American rights disregarded with impunity by Great Britain, now declared that the United States had a clear choice to make between servile acquiescence or proud defiance worthy of an independent nation. The United States neither won nor lost the war—although the British occupied Washington, D.C., and burned the White House. But for fully one hundred years American notions of the freedom of the seas were not to be challenged, nor was the nation's territorial integrity seriously threatened. American independence became secure.

(2) Territorial Integrity and Expansion. The preservation of a nation's territorial integrity is the mirror image to survival, once independence is formally achieved, and therefore always a national-security priority. For the young American nation, the first internationally recognized boundary was contained in the 1783 treaty of peace with Britain, but it was quickly deemed less than satisfactory by most Americans. Benjamin Franklin, chief American negotiator of the treaty, had made a bold play to acquire all of Canada, but had to be content with a boundary giving the United States the area east of the Mississippi River (south of present-day Canada, and north of the northern boundary of Spanish-held territory). Spain owned the Floridas, the Gulf coast, New Orleans, and the vast Louisiana territory west of the Mississippi. Moreover, U.S. boundaries were not secure. The British continued to retain military posts on U.S. territory and to encourage Indians in their resistance to white American expansion. Also, the Spanish did not recognize the boundaries in the south and west and hoped to coop up the United States east of the Appalachian Mountains.

The difficulty faced by the weak government (operating under the Articles of Confederation) in dealing with two threats to its territory helped lead the way to the calling of a constitutional convention, the writing of the Constitution, and the establishment of a centralized, *national* government. In due course, under President George Washington, the United States succeeded in settling some of the more important boundary disputes to its satisfaction—through Jay's Treaty with Britain and Pinckney's Treaty with Spain.

As direct threats to its territorial integrity diminished, the United States gradually sought and obtained vast new territories in the west and south, and expansionary wars were justified by the government in part as being essential for the nation's security as well as the fulfillment of national greatness. This extraordinary expansion was achieved partly through negotiation (the Louisiana Purchase from France, the Floridas and other western territory from Spain, the Pacific northwest settlement dividing the Oregon Territory with Britain, the purchase of Alaska from Russia) and partly through the war against Mexico in the 1840s.

The acquisition of new territory was not applauded by all Americans. Some New Englanders opposed the Louisiana Purchase out of fear that the new territories, eventually admitted to the Union as states, would upset the precarious political balance of power achieved by maritime interests in the east coast. The greatest controversy, however, swirled around the annexation of Texas, the consequent war with Mexico, and the acquisition of California and the southwest. Here, of course, the burning issue was whether the new territories would be open to slavery and, if so, whether that would give the slave-owning states of the South an inordinate amount of power. Nevertheless, transcontinental expansion continued unabated, and, with the nightmare of the Civil War behind it, by the end of the century led in no small measure to the emergence of the United States as a great power.

(3) **Military Security.** For any nation, military security depends at any given moment on a variety of factors: the nature of weaponry; the capabilities and intentions of other nations, friends and foes alike; advantages and disadvantages due to geography, resources, and demographic trends. Until the twentieth century most Americans correctly believed that the nation's fortunate geographical position—separated by the Atlantic Ocean from Europe, with only sparsely populated Canada to the north and weak Latin American countries to the south—allowed it the luxury of a small military and naval establishment. Before 1861, the Navy consisted of a very few sailing ships capable of "showing the flag" in distant ports—for example, Commodore Matthew Perry's expedition to Japan in 1853—and of chasing pirates, and patrolling against the illegal slave trade. The Union navy expanded during the Civil War in order to blockade Confederate ports, chase Confederate commerce raiders, and lend support to the land operations of the Union armies. The standing army of the United States was minuscule during most of the nineteenth century and was used primarily for expeditions against Indian tribes. Most of the men who fought in the war with Mexico were volunteers. The huge Union and Confederate forces that fought in the Civil War were raised specifically for that purpose, and the survivors returned to civilian life after 1865.

Real American concerns over military security—or at least for the need of a stronger military establishment—did not surface until the end of the nineteenth century, and focused largely on naval power—building the New Navy. The growing concern was prompted both by the emergence of the modern, steam-powered, armored warship with dramatic new range and firepower, and to the escalating Great Power competition for control of colonial possessions around the globe—in which "game" the United States was a latecomer, but an active latecomer at that: gaining colonial possessions in Asia and hegemonic control in the Caribbean through military victory in the Spanish-American-Cuban-Filipino War; flexing its diplomatic muscle in Asia, both as an interested party (the Boxer Rebellion, the Open Door Notes) and as an impartial, third-party peacemaker (the Russo-Japanese War); building a trans-isthmian canal in Panama, among the benefits of which was the much-facilitated ocean-to-ocean deployment of the New Navy; and, as a new and enthusiastic advocate of "gunboat diplomacy," launching numerous military interventions in Latin America and the Caribbean on behalf of U. S. economic interests.

Serious threats to its own security and independence did not emerge until the outbreak of the Great War in 1914. The United States tried to stay out of the European conflict, but the scope of its maritime and business interests (including loans to the allies) and the challenge posed by unrestricted German submarine warfare ensured that it could not. Having contributed mightily to Germany's military defeat, the United States then tried everything from creating a "new world order" through the League of Nations, to naval arms-control treaties, to restructuring war debts and reparations payments, in efforts to ensure long-term peace internationally and security for itself. None of these steps worked, in part because the United States wished to help with moral suasion rather than direct military guarantees, despite new security dangers posed by fascist dictators both in Europe and Asia. Thus again the United States was obliged to participate in world war, after American national security had been searingly breached by the Japanese bombers that attacked Pearl Harbor. This time the United States would mount an even more massive military effort, in both Europe and the Pacific, capped by the development and use of the atomic bomb.

Notwithstanding America's unequaled status as the world's greatest military and economic power in 1945, the next 45 years were dominated by a fundamental feeling of military insecurity in the United States. The specter of the global spread of communism, the adversarial intentions of the Soviet Union and its allies, and above all the Soviets' own advances in military technology were generally seen as posing direct threats to all major U.S. interests—potentially even to the very survival of the nation and its political culture. Ongoing peacetime military alliances were forged for the first time in the nation's history. Overseas military bases were established to a greater extent than ever before. A peacetime draft was maintained. Client-state conflicts multiplied. More and more weapons of greater and greater technological sophistication and destructive capability were developed, including intercontinental ballistic missiles carrying multiple nuclear warheads. In all, a general sense of quasi-permanent, general mobilization pertained over the American public in what was viewed by most as the functional and moral equivalent of another global war—the Cold War. Despite ebbs and flows, the requisites of military security by and large dominated U.S. foreign relations until the first real thawing of the Cold War in the late 1980s, followed by the collapse of the Soviet Union in 1991.

Nevertheless, the end of the Cold War has not guaranteed U.S. security. The safe dismantling of nuclear arsenals built up over four decades by both the United States and the Soviets remains incomplete. The threat of proliferation of nuclear weapons, as well as of other weapons of mass destruction (chemical, biological), among so-called rogue states, other potential aggressors, and terrorist organizations, persists and has arguably become worse of late. "Resource" wars (partly spurred by environmental degradation) and vicious ethnic conflicts constantly loom on the horizon, threatening regional stability in most parts of the world, and with it the very security that the end of the East-West conflict was expected to produce.

(4) Economic Security. Even before the Declaration of Independence, Americans engaged in two conflicting courses of economic foreign policy. On the one hand, they sought maximum commercial profit by trading with the West Indies in violation of certain prohibitions imposed by the British imperial system. On the other, they occasionally used boycotts against British products as an economic weapon designed to force the British metropolis to lift its restrictions, special taxes, and punitive orders-in-council. Thus were born two persistent themes of U.S. economic foreign policy: the effort to have the door open for trade wherever profit beckoned *and* a readiness to employ costly (that is, potentially self-defeating) economic measures in the hope of hurting the adversary more than the Americans themselves (Jefferson's ill-fated embargo at the time of the Napoleonic wars being the classic case in point). Economic advantage—"global competitiveness" in late twentieth-century parlance—has long stood as an objective of U.S. foreign policy.

A tension has long existed between the ideal of the Open Door for the freest possible exercise of trade everywhere in the world, and the reality of domestic pressures to protect American industries and workers from foreign competition. This tension also reflects the fact that "laissez-faire" foreign-economic policy will, at different times, benefit some Americans more than others, and may indeed even inflict injury on some. This conundrum stood at the center of the original debate between Jeffersonian agrarian traders and the Hamiltonian infant manufacturing-industry protectionists, as well as in the great "tariff debates" of the 1880s and 1890s, when presidential election campaigns often revolved around trade issues. The infamous Smoot-Hawley tariff of 1930 provided neither "protection" nor economic security, and hurt both Americans and foreigners alike as it fed the tariff wars of the pre–World War II period, deepening and spreading the global Great Depression. The free-trade policies nurtured by Secretary of State Cordell Hull in the 1930s and institutionalized in the General Agreement on Tariffs and Trade (GATT) after World War II were supposed to resolve this tension once and for all. But while the GATT achieved a great deal, the combination of the global oil shocks of the 1970s, the intensification of international economic competition from a dramatically reconstructed western Europe and Japan as well as newly emerging industrialized countries in Southeast Asia, and the increasing volatility of markets engendered renewed public pressure in favor of protectionism. This pressure has been kept somewhat contained, as reflected in the approval by Congress in 1993 of the North American Free Trade Agreement (NAFTA). But it surely has not gone away.

Issues of economic security often also have raised the old question of how closely the flag should follow the dollar, particularly with regard to foreign direct investments in raw materials by U.S. multinational corporations (MNCs). In many instances there has been a close consonance between the MNCs' interests and both the broader interests of the U.S. economy and larger American geopolitical interests—for example, in procuring the stability of friendly (though not necessarily democratic) regimes. Economic calculations have often led to U.S. military interventions and covert activities abroad in clear opposition to the liberal values ostensibly at the heart of U.S. foreign policy priorities. These tensions between political ideals and economic interests became more pronounced in efforts to balance human-rights concerns and emerging market opportunities—with the Soviet Union in the 1970s, South Africa in the 1980s, and China in the 1990s.

International economic issues, too often relegated to the sphere of "low politics" during the years of the Cold War, once again have emerged as serious considerations of American national security. And the relationship between issues of the natural environment, economic development, and political stability have increasingly sparked debate, such as at the Earth Summit in 1992 and over the Biodiversity and Climate Change treaties.

(5) Democratic Values and Ideals. U.S. foreign relations have never strictly revolved around traditional political, strategic, or economic interests. For better or worse, the promotion of democratic values and ideals worldwide has also defined the "national purpose" from the early days of the republic, and thus too the special role the United States should play in world affairs.

Much of this history has been rooted in the self-image of "American exceptionalism," the sense that the United States was different from—indeed, superior to—all other modern nation-states, because of its republican foundations and peaceable predilections, and that it was Americans' destiny to play a unique role on the world's stage. "We shall be as a City upon a Hill," wrote Massachusetts Bay Colony Governor John Winthrop more than three centuries ago. "The eyes of all people are upon us." From the "City on the Hill" to the American Revolution, to nineteenth-century Manifest Destiny, to early twentieth-century Wilsonianism, to Henry Luce's vision of the "American Century," to the Truman Doctrine, to Jimmy Carter's promotion of human rights, to Ronald Reagan's explicit evocation of Thomas Paine that "We have it in our power to begin the world over again": the line of argumentation has been rather straightforward even if not always crystal-clear or entirely convincing to outsiders. Moreover, precisely how the United States should best play its exceptionalist role, with what specific objectives in mind and by what means, has always been the subject of heated debate among American themselves. In those instances where democratic ideals and strategic and/or economic interests could be mutually served, the circle was squared. But it often has been the case that ideals and self-interest have clashed, that trade-offs have had to be considered and compromises taken. How can America continue to glorify its own revolutionary origins, for example, while excoriating (and combating) almost all "leftist" revolutions of the twentieth century? Moreover, if in John Quincy Adams's famous words America's "purpose" was to lead by example, at home, rather than constantly to venture forth "seeking monsters to destroy" abroad, how could a proper balance be reached and sustained between the advocates of "internationalism" and the various proponents of "isolationism," however much *both* sides might be devoted to the notion of American exceptionalism and indeed to the ideals of American democracy?

* * *

These and many other difficult questions will long continue to infuse debate into the making and execution of American foreign policy. The editors of this encyclopedia invite readers to enter the debate by informing themselves about the whats, whos, wheres, whys, and hows of U.S. foreign relations, the periods of history that mark the nation's relations with the rest of the world, and the core goals that the United States has pursued.

List of Entries

Aberdeen, Fourth Earl
Kenneth R. Stevens
Texas Christian University

Abrams, Elliott
Stephen G. Rabe
University of Texas, Dallas

Acheson, Dean Gooderham
Douglas Brinkley
University of New Orleans

Acheson-Lilienthal Report
Martin J. Sherwin
Tufts University

Acquired Immune Deficiency
Syndrome (AIDS) Pandemic
Daniel Tarantola
Harvard School of Public Health
Sara Finklestein
Writer, Cambridge, Massachusetts

Adams, Charles Francis
Norman B. Ferris
Middle Tennessee State University

Adams, John
Clifford L. Egan
University of Houston

Adams, John Quincy
Richard C. Rohrs
Oklahoma State University

Adams-Onís Treaty
Richard C. Rohrs
Oklahoma State University

Addams, Jane
Harriet Hyman Alonso
Fitchburg State College

Adenauer, Konrad
Thomas A. Schwartz
Vanderbilt University

Aerospace
Jeffrey A. Hart
Indiana University

Afghanistan
Dennis Merrill
University of Missouri

Africa
Donald Rothchild
University of California, Davis

Agency for International
Development
Steven H. Arnold
American University

Agriculture
Jeffrey L. Anderson
St. John's University

Aguinaldo, Emilio
Glenn Anthony May
University of Oregon

Air Force, U.S. Department of
Vincent Davis
University of Kentucky

Airline Companies
Jonathan D. Aronson
University of Southern California

Alabama Claims
Norman B. Ferris
Middle Tennessee State University

Alaska Boundary Dispute
Louis R. Smith, Jr.
University of West Alabama

Alaska Purchase
Paul S. Holbo
University of Oregon

Albright, Madeleine K.
Harold K. Jacobson
University of Michigan

Alexander I
Carol A. Jackson
Salt Lake Community College

Algeria
Catherine Elkins
Duke University

Alien and Sedition Acts
Clifford L. Egan
University of Houston

Allen, Horace Newton
Bruce D. Mactavish
University of Alabama

Allende (Gossens), Salvador
Paul E. Sigmund
Princeton University

Alliance for Progress
Stephen G. Rabe
University of Texas, Dallas

Ambassadors and Embassies
Gaddis Smith
Yale University

America First Committee
Janet M. Manson
Clemson University

American China Development
Company
Noel H. Pugach
University of New Mexico

American Civil War
Norman B. Ferris
Middle Tennessee State University

American Federation of Labor-
Congress of Industrial Organizations
Jerel A. Rosati
University of South Carolina

American Legion
Jerel A. Rosati
University of South Carolina

American Revolution
Rebecca G. Goodman
Hunter College of the City University of New York

Amiens, Treaty of
Ronald L. Hatzenbuehler
Idaho State University

Amistad Affair
Donald A. Rakestraw
Georgia Southern University

Amnesty International
James David Barber
Duke University

Directory of Contributors

Philip Abbott
Wayne State University
Morgenthau, Henry, Jr.

Bernhard J. Abrahamsson
University of Wisconsin, Superior
Shipping Companies

Morton I. Abramowitz
Carnegie Endowment for International Peace
Carnegie Endowment for International Peace

Irwin Abrams
Antioch University
Nobel Peace Prize

Victor Aikhionbare
Salt Lake Community College
Nigeria

Henry S. Albinski
Penn State University
Anzus Treaty

John H. Aldrich
Duke University
Elections and Foreign Policy

Harriet Hyman Alonso
Fitchburg State College
Addams, Jane; Kellogg-Briand Pact

David Alvarez
St. Mary's College of California
Vatican

Lloyd E. Ambrosius
University of Nebraska, Lincoln
Bernstorff, Johann Heinrich; La Follette, Robert Marion

Jeffrey L. Anderson
St. John's University
Agriculture

Terry H. Anderson
Texas A & M University
Stettinius, Edward Reilly, Jr.

George Andreopoulos
Yale University
Humanitarian Intervention and Relief

Thom M. Armstrong
Mt. Hood Community College
Burr, Aaron; Gallatin, Albert; Hamilton, Alexander; Jay, John; Jay's Treaty; Logan Act; Nootka Sound Affair; Pinckney's Treaty; Rush-Bagot Agreement; Smith, Robert; Washington, George; Washington's Farewell Address

Steven H. Arnold
American University
Agency for International Development; Food for Peace

Jonathan D. Aronson
University of Southern California
Airline Companies; Broadcast and Film Companies; Computer Companies; Telecommunication Companies

LeRoy Ashby
Washington State University
Church, Frank Forrester III

David P. Augustyn
Center for Strategic and International Studies
Denmark; Finland; Greenland; Iceland; Norway; Sweden

Andrew J. Bacevich
Johns Hopkins University, SAIS
Defense Reorganization Act; Powell, Colin Luther

Timothy W. Baker
Johns Hopkins University, SAIS
Hungary

James David Barber
Duke University
Amnesty International

Michael A. Barnhart
State University of New York, Stony Brook
Javits, Jacob

Jeffrey D. Bass
University of Connecticut
Kim Il Sung; Piracy; Rhee, Syngman

James L. Baughman
University of Wisconsin, Madison
Murrow, Edward (Egbert) Roscoe

Michael Baum
University of Connecticut
Portugal

Jules R. Benjamin
Ithaca College
Radio Martí

Edward H. Berman
University of Louisville
Philanthropic Foundations, Overseas Programs of; Soros, George

Larry Berman
University of California, Davis
Presidency; Vietnam War

Barton J. Bernstein
Stanford University
Cuban Missile Crisis

Gary K. Bertsch
University of Georgia
Extraterritoriality; Jackson-Vanik Amendment; Technology Transfer

Thomas Borstelmann
Cornell University
De Klerk, Frederik Willem; Mandela, Nelson Rolihlahla; Mobutu, Sese Seko; Race and Racism; Young, Andrew Jackson, Jr.

Robert Bothwell
University of Toronto
Trudeau, Pierre Elliott

William W. Boyer, Jr.
University of Delaware
Danish West Indies, Acquisition of

Paul F. Braim
Embry-Riddle University
Army, U.S. Department of

H. William Brands
Texas A & M University
Henderson, Loy Wesley; Revisionism; Sukarno

Kinley J. Brauer
University of Minnesota
Benjamin, Judah Philip; Confederate States of America; Davis, Jefferson; Slave Trade and Slavery

Aimee Breslow
Johns Hopkins University, SAIS
Slovenia

Douglas Brinkley
University of New Orleans
Acheson, Dean Gooderham; Forrestal,
James Vincent; Rockefeller, Nelson Aldrich

Rebecca Britton
University of California, Davis
Belgium; Netherlands; Switzerland

MacAlister Brown
Williams College
Myanmar; Singapore; Southeast Asia Treaty
Organization; Thailand

Lester H. Brune
Bradley University
Conant, James Bryant

Bernard V. Burke
Portland State University
Chamberlain, Arthur Neville; Coughlin,
Charles Edward; Munich Conference;
Mussolini, Benito

James D. Calder
University of Texas, San Antonio
Angleton, James Jesus; Central Intelligence
Agency Act; Colby, William Egan; Dulles,
Allen Welsh; Foreign Intelligence Advisory
Board; Helms, Richard McGarrah; McCone,
John Alex

Dan Caldwell
Pepperdine University
Antiballistic Missile Treaty; Arms Control
and Disarmament Agency; Massive
Retaliation; Mutual Assured Destruction;
Strategic Arms Limitation Talks and
Agreements; Strategic Arms Reduction
Treaties

Thomas Carothers
Carnegie Endowment For International Peace
National Endowment for Democracy

John E. Carroll
University of New Hampshire
International Joint Commission

W. Seth Carus
Washington Institute for Near East Policy
Biological Weapons

John Whiteclay Chambers II
Rutgers University
Ridgway, Matthew Bunker; Weinberger,
Caspar Willard

Gordon H. Chang
Stanford University
China Hands; China Lobby; Jiang Jieshi;
Jinmen-Mazu Crises; Sun Zhongshan; Zhou
Enlai

Jonathan I. Charney
Vanderbilt University
Law of the Sea

Charles Chatfield
Wittenberg University
Peace Movements and Societies, 1914 to
Present

Anthony Q. Cheeseboro
Southern University of Illinois, Edwardsville
Ghana; Sierra Leone; Swaziland; Tanzania,
United Republic of; Zambia; Zimbabwe

Nazli Choucri
Massachusetts Institute of Technology
Biodiversity Treaty; Earth Summit, Rio de
Janeiro; Montreal Protocol; United Nations
Conference on the Human Environment,
Stockholm; United Nations Environment
Program

Lawrence A. Clayton
University of Alabama
Ecuador; Peru

Kendrick A. Clements
University of South Carolina
Bryan, William Jennings; Grey, Edward;
Lusitania; Wilson, Thomas Woodrow; World
War I; Zimmermann Telegram

J. Garry Clifford
University of Connecticut
Connally, Thomas Terry; Coolidge, Calvin;
Davis, Elmer Holmes; Ford, Gerald
Rudolph; Haig, Alexander Meigs, Jr.;
Hoover, Herbert; Hopkins, Harry Lloyd;
Hurley, Patrick Jay; Isolationism; Kellogg,
Frank Billings; Leahy, William Daniel;
London Naval Conferences of 1930 and
1935-1936; McCarthy, Eugene Joseph;
McCarthyism; McFarlane, Robert Carl;
Reagan, Ronald Wilson; Roosevelt, Anna
Eleanor; Stilwell, Joseph; Stimson, Henry
Lewis; Taft, Robert A.; Willkie, Wendell
Lewis

Kenton J. Clymer
University of Texas, El Paso
Missionaries

Benjamin J. Cohen
University of California, Santa Barbara
Dollar Diplomacy; International Debt;
Third World Debt

Stephen D. Cohen
American University
Caribbean Basin Initiative; Commerce, U.S.
Department of; General Agreement on
Tariffs and Trade; Generalized System of
Preferences; International Monetary Fund;
Most-Favored-Nation Principle; North
American Free Trade Agreement; Overseas
Private Investment Corporation; Treasury,
U.S. Department of; United States Trade
Representative; World Trade Organization

Wayne S. Cole
University of Maryland, Emeritus
Lindbergh, Charles Augustus; Ludlow
Amendment

Richard H. Collin
University of New Orleans
Bunau-Varilla, Philippe; Gentlemen's
Agreements; Roosevelt, Theodore; Roosevelt
Corollary; Root, Elihu; Root-
Takahira Agreement

Jerald A. Combs
San Francisco State University
Bemis, Samuel Flagg

John W. Coogan
Michigan State University
Submarine Warfare

Steven A. Cook
Washington Institute for Near East Policy
Uganda

Anthony H. Cordesman
Center for Strategic and International Studies
Gulf War of 1990-1991; Hussein, Saddam

Maria Courtis
University of California, Davis
Overseas Military Bases

John M. Craig
Slippery Rock University
Bourne, Randolph Silliman; Croly, Herbert
David; Knox, Philander Chase; Taft,
William Howard; Taft-Katsura Agreement

Edward P. Crapol
College of William and Mary
Cushing, Caleb; Opium Wars; Turner,
Frederick Jackson; Tyler, John; Upshur,
Abel Parker

Martha Crenshaw
Wesleyan University
Assassination

Jill Crystal
Journalist, Auburn, Alabama
Kuwait

Donna Tully Cummings
University of Connecticut
Luce, Henry Robinson

Ivo H. Daalder
University of Maryland
Conventional Armed Forces in Europe,
Treaty on; Intermediate-Range Nuclear
Forces Treaty

Calvin D. Davis
Duke University
Arbitration Treaties of 1911; Drago
Doctrine; Hague Peace Conferences; Peace
Movements and Societies to 1914

Paul K. Davis
RAND Corporation
Rapid Deployment Force

Vincent Davis
University of Kentucky
Air Force, U.S. Department of; Defense,
U.S. Department of; Marine Corps, U.S.;
War, U.S. Department of

Alexander DeConde
University of California, Santa Barbara
Ethnic Groups

Michael J. Devine
University of Wyoming
Arthur, Chester Alan; Bayard, Thomas
Francis; Blaine, James Gillespie; Carnegie,
Andrew; Darwinism; Evarts, William
Maxwell; Fletcher, Henry Prather; Foster,
John Watson; Gresham, Walter Quintin;
Harriman, Edward Henry; Harrison,
Benjamin; Hayes, Rutherford Birchard;
Salisbury, Third Marquess of; Sanford,
Henry Shelton; Sherman, John

David L. DiLeo
Saddleback College
Ball, George Wildman

Wilson Dizard, Jr.
Center for Strategic and International Studies
Communications Policy

Alan P. Dobson
University College of Swansea
Civil Aviation

John M. Dobson
Iowa State University
Boxer Rebellion; Hay, John Milton;
McKinley, William; McKinley Tariff Act;
Open Door Policy

Justus D. Doenecke
New College, University of South Florida
Carr, Wilbur John; Cleveland, Stephen
Grover; Frelinghuysen, Frederick Theodore;
Garfield, James Abram; Olney, Richard;
Venezuelan Boundary Dispute

Jaime Domínguez
Autonomous University of Santo Domingo
Trujillo Molina, Rafael Leónidas

Jorge I. Domínguez
Harvard University
Batista y Zaldívar, Fulgencio; Castro, Fidel;
Díaz (José de la Cruz), Porfirio; Huerta,
Victoriano; Juárez, Benito Pablo; Mexico;
Villa, Pancho

Jack Donnelly
University of Denver
Helsinki Accords; Human Rights

Michael E. Donoghue
University of Connecticut
Bundy, McGeorge; Colonialism

Kurk Dorsey
University of New Hampshire
Boutros-Ghali, Boutros; Continental
Expansion; Environment; Environmental
Protection Agency; Fisheries; Fur Trade;
Gadsden Purchase; Lie, Trygve;
Newfoundland; Saint Lawrence Seaway;
Sealing; Thant, U; Waldheim, Kurt;
Whaling; Wildlife

Sina Dubovoy
Woodrow Wilson House Museum
Bliss, Tasker Howard; Clemenceau,
Georges; Lloyd George, David; Paris Peace
Conference of 1919; Pershing, John;
Versailles Treaty of 1919

Arthur Power Dudden
Bryn Mawr College
Japan

William J. Duiker
Pennsylvania State University
Vietnam

Kenneth A. Duncan
U.S. Department of State
Terrorism *[The views and opinions expressed are
solely those of the author and do not represent those of
the U.S. government or of the Department of State.]*

Robert M. Dunn, Jr.
George Washington University
Balance of Payments and Balance of Trade;
Brady Plan; Copyright and Intellectual
Property; Export-Import Bank; Federal
Reserve Bank of New York; Free Trade;
Gold Standard; Group of Seven;
International Trade Commission

Nicholas Eberstadt
American Enterprise Institute
Foreign Aid

Clifford L. Egan
University of Houston
Adams, John; Alien and Sedition Acts;
Barbary States; Convention of 1800;
Federalist Party; Marshall, John; Pickering,
Timothy; XYZ Affair

Michael Eisenstadt
Washington Institute for Near East Policy
Chemical Weapons

Catherine Elkins
Duke University
Algeria; Morocco; Somalia; Sudan; Tunisia

Jean Bethke Elshtain
Vanderbilt University
Women, War, Peace, and Foreign Relations

John English
House of Commons, Canada
Pearson, Lester Bowles

Paul M. Evans
York University, Toronto
Fairbank, John King

Judith Ewell
College of William and Mary
Kirkpatrick, Jeane Duane

Dean Fafoutis
Salisbury State University
Clayton, John Middleton; Taylor, Zachary;
Young America

Robert H. Ferrell
Indiana University
Hoover, Herbert

Norman B. Ferris
Middle Tennessee State University
Adams, Charles Francis; Alabama Claims;
American Civil War; Johnson, Andrew;
Lincoln, Abraham; Seward, William Henry;
Slidell, John; Sumner, Charles

James A. Fetzer
State University of New York, Maritime College
Davies, John Paton, Jr.

Sara Finklestein
Writer, Cambridge, Massachusetts
Acquired Immune Deficiency Syndrome
(AIDS) Pandemic

Richard B. Finnegan
Stonehill College
Ireland; Northern Ireland

William J. Foltz
Yale University
Chad

Benjamin Fordham
Princeton University
Atomic Energy Commission; Atoms for
Peace; Joint Chiefs of Staff; Mutual
Security Act; National Security Act;
National Security Agency; National
Security Council; Strategic Air Command

Edward R. Fried
Brookings Institution
International Bank for Reconstruction and
Development

Joseph A. Fry
University of Nevada, Las Vegas
Anti-Imperialist League; Beveridge, Albert
Jeremiah; Hoar, George Frisbie; Mahan,
Alfred Thayer

Marguerite Galaty
Johns Hopkins University, SAIS
Tito

Raymond L. Garthoff
Brookings Institution
Brezhnev, Leonid Ilyich; Brezhnev
Doctrine; Détente

Mark J. Gasiorowski
Louisiana State University
Iran; Khomeini, Ruhollah; Mosaddeq,
Mohammad; Shah of Iran

F. Gregory Gause III
University of Vermont
Middle East; Yemen

Jeffrey Gedmin
American Enterprise Institute
Sonnenfeldt Doctrine

James N. Giglio
Southwest Missouri State University
Johnson, Ural Alexis; Kennedy, Joseph
Patrick

Mark T. Gilderhus
Colorado State University
Clark Amendment

Richard Gilmore
GIC Trade, Inc.
Food and Agricultural Companies

Robert G. Gilpin, Jr.
Princeton University
Realism

Roy H. Ginsberg
Center for European Policy Studies
European Union

Abbott Gleason
Brown University
Russia and the Soviet Union

Emily O. Goldman
University of California, Davis
Distant Early Warning (DEW) Line;
Gunboat Diplomacy; Open Skies;
Verification; Washington Conference on the
Limitation of Armaments

Donald Goldstein
University of Pittsburgh
Pearl Harbor, Attack on

Rebecca G. Goodman
*Hunter College of the City University of New
York*
American Revolution; Articles of
Confederation; Beaumarchais, Pierre
Augustin Caron de; Federalist Papers;
George III; Lafayette, Marie Joseph Paul
Yves Roch Gilbert du Motier; Loyalists;
Morris, Gouverneur; Northwest Ordinance;
Paine, Thomas; Talleyrand, Charles
Maurice; Vergennes, Duc de

James L. Gormly
Washington and Jefferson College
Durbrow, Elbridge; White, Harry Dexter

Norman A. Graebner
University of Virginia
Manifest Destiny; Mexico, War with; Trist,
Nicholas Philip

Edward M. Graham
Institute for International Economics
Foreign Direct Investment; Multinational
Corporations

J. L. Granatstein
York University
Canada; King, William Lyon Mackenzie

Paul R. Grass
Valley Springs Middle School
California; Frémont, John Charles; Larkin,
Thomas Oliver; Mississippi River;
Portsmouth, Treaty of; Russo-Japanese War;
Sino-Japanese War

Marshall Green
Writer, Washington, D.C.
Population Policy

Kenneth J. Grieb
University of Wisconsin, Oshkosh
Bucareli Agreements; Daniels, Josephus, Jr.;
Davis, Norman Hezekiah; Harding, Warren;
Morrow, Dwight Whitney

Ann Griffiths
Dalhousie University
International Trade and Commerce

Brandon Grove, Jr.
U.S. Ambassador, Retired
Zaire

Peter L. Hahn
Ohio State University
Egypt; McGhee, George Crews; Nasser,
Gamal Abdel; Sadat, Anwar El-

Gerald K. Haines
National Reconnaissance Office Historian
Brazil

P. Edward Haley
Claremont McKenna College
Libya

Lee H. Hamilton
United States Congress
Iran-Contra Affair

Wolfram F. Hanrieder
University of California, Santa Barbara
Germany

Joyce Hanson
University of Connecticut
DuBois, William Edward Burghardt;
Garvey, Marcus Moziah; Washington,
Booker T.

Fraser J. Harbutt
Emory University
British Loan of 1946; Churchill, Winston
Leonard Spencer

Jeffrey A. Hart
Indiana University
Aerospace

Caroline A. Hartzell
Gettysburg College
Grenada; Guatemala; Guinea-Bissau;
Honduras; Nonaligned Movement; Third
World

Robert M. Hathaway
*Foreign Affairs Committee, U.S. House of
Representatives*
Attlee, Clement Richard; Bevin, Ernest

Ronald L. Hatzenbuehler
Idaho State University
Amiens, Treaty of; French Revolution;
Livingston, Robert R.; Louisiana Purchase;
Madison, James; Napoleon Bonaparte;
Napoleonic Wars; Toussaint-L'Ouverture,
François-Dominque

Barbara Heep-Richter
Council on Foreign Relations
Schmidt, Helmut

David C. Hendrickson
Colorado College
Jefferson, Thomas; Morgenthau, Hans

Louis Henkin
Columbia University
International Law; Supreme Court and the
Judiciary

Alan K. Henrikson
Tufts University
Diplomatic Method

Charles F. Hermann
Ohio State University, Mershon Center
Bureaucracy

Robert Edwin Herzstein
University of South Carolina
Luce, Ann Clare Boothe

Gary R. Hess
Bowling Green State University
Bangladesh; India; Pakistan; Sri Lanka

Donald R. Hickey
Wayne State College
Chesapeake-Leopard Affair; Ghent, Treaty
of; Hartford Convention; Impressment;
Monroe-Pinkney Treaty; Orders in Council;
War of 1812; War Hawks

Robert C. Hilderbrand
University of South Dakota
Austin, Warren Robinson; Bunche, Ralph
Johnson; Johnson, Lyndon Baines

William I. Hitchcock
Yale University
France

Walter L. Hixson
University of Akron
Harriman, William Averell; Kennan, George
Frost

Joan Hoff
Center for the Study of the Presidency
Nixon, Richard Milhous; Nixon Doctrine

J. Michael Hogan
Indiana University
Panama and Panama Canal

A. William Hoglund
University of Connecticut
Immigration and Naturalization Service;
Passports and Visas

Paul S. Holbo
University of Oregon
Alaska Purchase; Grant, Ulysses Simpson

John D. Holm
Cleveland State University
Botswana

John W. Holmes
U.S. Diplomat, Retired
Italy

Ole R. Holsti
Duke University
Public Opinion

Frank X. J. Homer
University of Scranton
Bismarck, Otto Edward Leopold von

David A. Hubert
Salt Lake Community College
Shultz, George Pratt

Henry R. Huttenbach
City College of the City University of New York
Armenia; Azerbaijan

John O. Iatrides
Southern Connecticut State University
Containment; Cyprus; Greece; MacVeagh,
Lincoln

Richard H. Immerman
Temple University
Eisenhower, Milton Stover; Peurifoy, John
Emil

Akira Iriye
Harvard University
Cultural Diplomacy

Carol A. Jackson
Salt Lake Community College
Alexander I; Baldwin, Stanley; Balfour,
Arthur James; Balfour Declaration; Bolívar,
Simón; Canning, George; Castlereagh,
Robert Stewart; League to Enforce Peace;
Quadruple Alliance; Rankin, Jeannette;
Trieste

Harold K. Jacobson
University of Michigan
Albright, Madeleine K.; Mandates and
Trusteeships; United Nations

Bruce W. Jentleson
University of California, Davis
Communism; Formosa Resolution; Kurds

Loch K. Johnson
University of Georgia
Central Intelligence Agency; Covert Action;
Deutch, John M.; Intelligence; Turner,
Stansfield

Manfred Jonas
Union College
Neutral Rights; Neutrality Acts of the 1930s

Howard Jones
University of Alabama
Trent Affair

Christopher C. Joyner
Georgetown University
Arbitration; Boycotts; Dumbarton Oaks
Conference; Freedom of the Seas;
Permanent Court of Arbitration (Hague
Tribunal); Permanent Court of International
Justice

David Kahn
Newsday
Cryptology

William Kamman
University of North Texas
Walker, William

Lawrence S. Kaplan
Kent State University, Emeritus
Clay, Lucius Dubignon; Kohl, Helmut;
Mitterrand, François; Monnet, Jean

Ethan B. Kapstein
Harvard University
Armament Companies

Thomas H. Karas
Sandia National Laboratories
Nuclear Nonproliferation

Margaret P. Karns
University of Dayton
European Bank for Reconstruction and
Development; Hammarskjöld, Dag Hjalmar
Agne Carl; Inter-American Development
Bank; International Atomic Energy Agency;
International Labor Organization;
International Trade Organization;
Organization for Economic Cooperation and
Development; Organization of American
States; Organization of Petroleum
Exporting Countries; Pérez de Cuéllar,
Javier; United Nations Conference on Trade
and Development; United Nations Relief
and Rehabilitation Administration

Burton I. Kaufman
Virginia Polytechnic Institute & State University
Camp David Accords; Carter, James Earl; Carter Doctrine

Charles W. Kegley, Jr.
University of South Carolina
Idealism

LeeAnna Y. Keith
University of Connecticut
El Salvador; Moynihan, Daniel Patrick; Nicaragua; Phillips, William; Sandino, Augusto César; Vanderbilt, Cornelius

Catherine Kelleher
Brookings Institution
Berlin

Scott D. Keller
University of Alabama
Bullitt, William Christian; Castle, William Richards, Jr.; Colby, Bainbridge; Davies, Joseph Edward; Kelley, Robert; Lenin, Vladimir Ilyich

Thomas C. Kennedy
University of Wyoming
Beard, Charles Austin

James P. Ketterer
Johns Hopkins University
Saudi Arabia

Ben Kiernan
Yale University
Cambodia

Linda Killen
Radford University
Gorbachev, Mikhail Sergeevich; Yeltsin, Boris Nikolayevich

Benedict W. Kingsbury
Duke University
Asylum; Chadha Decision; Curtiss-Wright Case; Extradition; Geneva Conventions

Deborah Kisatsky
University of Connecticut
Bruce, David Kirkpatrick Este; Gates, Robert Michael; Grady, Henry Francis; Lansdale, Edward Geary; Mayaguez Incident; Pueblo Incident; Schuman, Robert

Stephen Kneeshaw
College of the Ozarks
Gibson, Hugh Simons

Thomas J. Knock
Southern Methodist University
Hughes, Charles Evans; McGovern, George Stanley

Harold Hongju Koh
Yale University
Constitution

Edward A. Kolodziej
University of Illinois
Arms Transfers and Trade

Julia Cosentino Konmaz
University of California, Los Angeles
Macedonia, Former Yugoslav Republic of

Lawrence J. Korb
Brookings Institution
Perry, William

Michael Krepon
Henry L. Stimson Center
Comprehensive Test Ban Treaty

Bruce R. Kuniholm
Duke University
Aspin, Leslie (Les), Jr.; Baker, James Addison III; Brown, Harold; Central Treaty Organization; Cheney, Richard Bruce; Christopher, Warren Minor; Eagleburger, Lawrence Sydney; Turkey

Diane B. Kunz
Yale University
Economic Sanctions; Eden, Robert Anthony; Habib, Philip Charles; McDonald, James Grover; Perkins, Edward J.; Suez Crisis

Walter LaFeber
Cornell University
North, Oliver Lawrence; Rusk, David Dean; Williams, William Appleman

Sanford Lakoff
University of California, San Diego
Strategic Defense Initiative

Chris Lamb
Georgetown University
Guerrilla Warfare

Dimitri D. Lazo
Alverno College
Lansing, Robert; Lansing-Ishii Agreement

Rensselaer W. Lee III
Global Advisory Services
Narcotics, International

Jeffrey A. LeFebvre
University of Connecticut
Bahrain; Diego Garcia; Eritrea; Ethiopia; Kenya; Mozambique; Oman; United Arab Emirates

Joseph Lepgold
Georgetown University
Azores; North Atlantic Treaty Organization; Spheres of Influence

James E. Lewis, Jr.
Los Angeles State University
Fox, Charles James; French and Indian War; Pitt, William

Roy Licklider
Rutgers University
Oil and World Politics; Oil Companies

Anatol Lieven
The Times
Estonia; Latvia; Lithuania

Douglas Little
Clark University
Bowers, Claude Gernade; Eisenhower Doctrine; Franco, Francisco

Fredrik Logevall
University of California, Santa Barbara
de Gaulle, Charles André Joseph Marie; Diem, Ngo Dinh

John M. Logsdon
George Washington University
National Aeronautics and Space Administration; Space Policy

Timothy J. Lomperis
U.S. Military Academy
Bipolarity; Brinkmanship; Dien Bien Phu; Ho Chi Minh; My Lai Incident; Taylor, Maxwell Davenport; Tet Offensive; Thieu, Nguyen Van; Westmoreland, William

William J. Long
Georgia Institute of Technology
Technology Transfer

Mark M. Lowenthal
Library of Congress
Casey, William Joseph

Alan W. Lukens
U.S. Ambassador, Retired
Congo

Michael Lund
Creative Associates International, Inc.
Preventive Diplomacy

Mark H. Lytle
Bard College
Clifford, Clark McAdams; Helms, Jesse Alexander, Jr.

Scott MacLeod
Time Magazine
Arafat, Yassir; Palestine Liberation
Organization

Bruce D. Mactavish
University of Alabama
Allen, Horace Newton; Filibusters; Harris,
Townsend; Hawai'i; Marcy, William
Learned; Rogers Act; Shidehara, Kijuro

Shane J. Maddock
University of Connecticut
Crocker, Chester Arthur; Jessup, Philip
Caryl; King, Martin Luther, Jr.; Lovett,
Robert Abercrombie; Nitze, Paul Henry;
Olympic Games; Rogers, William Pierce;
Smith, Gerard C.; Sputnik I; Strauss, Robert

Janet M. Manson
Clemson University
America First Committee; Borah, William
Edgar; Great Britain; League of Nations;
Lodge, Henry Cabot, Sr.; Nye, Gerald
Prentice; Straight, Willard Dickerman

Jocelyn M. Nash Marinescu
Writer, Chaplin, Connecticut
Mongolia

Luis Martínez-Fernández
Rutgers University
Dominican Republic

Teresita Martínez-Vergne
Macalester College
Puerto Rico

Michael Mastanduno
Dartmouth College
Coordinating Committee for Multilateral
Export Controls; Export Controls

Gale A. Mattox
U.S. Naval Academy
Organization on Security and Cooperation
in Europe

Henry E. Mattox
North Carolina State University
Energy, U. S. Department of; Foreign
Service; Freedom of Information Act;
Fulbright Program; Justice, U. S.
Department of

Glenn Anthony May
University of Oregon
Aguinaldo, Emilio; Aquino, Benigno S. and
Corazon C.; Marcos, Ferdinand; Philippines

Robert E. May
Purdue University
Buchanan, James; Pierce, Franklin

James M. McCormick
Iowa State University
Bipartisanship; Bricker Amendment; Case-
Zablocki Act; Congress; Earmarking;
Executive Agreements; Executive Privilege;
Jackson, Henry Martin; Legislative Veto;
Nunn, Samuel; Pentagon Papers;
Prohibition

Roderick A. McDonald
Rider University
Antigua and Barbuda; Bahamas; Barbados;
Jamaica; Trinidad and Tobago

David W. McFadden
Fairfield University
Sakharov, Andrei; Solzhenitsyn, Aleksandr
Isayevich; Stalin, Joseph

Charles D. McGraw
University of Connecticut
Donovan, William Joseph; International
Red Cross and Red Crescent Movement;
Office of Strategic Services; Pan Am Flight
103; Ridgway, Rozanne Lejeanne; Walters,
Vernon Anthony

John McLean
Three Rivers Technical College
Fenians

Thomas L. McNaugher
RAND Corporation
Iran-Iraq War

Richard A. Melanson
National Defense University
Vance, Cyrus Roberts

Natalie Melnyczuk
U.S. Institute of Peace
Ukraine

Dennis Merrill
University of Missouri, Kansas City
Afghanistan; Galbraith, John Kenneth;
Gandhi, Indira Priyadarshini; Nehru,
Jawaharlal; Rostow, Walt Whitman

Robert L. Messer
University of Illinois, Chicago
Byrnes, James Francis; Clayton, William
Lockhart; Vandenberg, Arthur Hendrick

Raymond F. Mikesell
University of Oregon
Oil and Foreign Policy

H. Lyman Miller
Johns Hopkins University, SAIS
Deng Xiaoping

Patrick M. Morgan
University of California, Irvine
Deterrence

Laurie Mylroie
Foreign Policy Research Institute
Iraq

Jonathan Nashel
Indiana University, South Bend
Domino Theory; French Indochina; Laos

James Nathan
Auburn University
Brzezinski, Zbigniew Kasimierz; U-2
Incident

Anna K. Nelson
American University
Carlucci, Frank Charles III

Charles E. Neu
Brown University
House, Edward Mandell

Rodney W. Nichols
New York Academy of Sciences
Science and Technology

Miroslav Nincic
University of California, Davis
Collective Security; National Security and
National Defense

Donald R. Norland
U.S. Ambassador, Retired
Namibia

Elizabeth Nuxoll
*Queens College of the City University of New
York*
Deane, Silas; Declaration of Independence;
Morris, Robert

Arnold A. Offner
Lafayette College
Truman, Harry S.; Truman Doctrine

John L. Offner
Shippensburg University
Day, William Rufus; Dewey, George;
Hearst, William Randolph; Maine, USS;
Spanish-American-Cuban-Filipino War,
1898; Teller Amendment

Edward A. Olsen
Naval Postgraduate School
Korea

Makram Ouaiss
Johns Hopkins University, SAIS
Lebanon

David S. Painter
Georgetown University
Cold War

Herbert S. Parmet
City University of New York, Emeritus
Scowcroft, Brent

Robert A. Pastor
Emory University
Latin America

Thomas G. Paterson
University of Connecticut
Bowles, Chester Bliss; Korean War;
Palestine (to 1948); Samoa, American; Self-
Determination; World Health Organization

Christopher M. Paulin
University of Connecticut
Lesotho; Macmillan, Maurice Harold;
Rwanda; Thatcher, Margaret Hilda

Neal Pease
University of Wisconsin, Milwaukee
Lane, Arthur Bliss; Walesa, Lech

Stephen E. Pelz
University of Massachusetts
Bundy, William Putnam; Bunker, Ellsworth;
Lodge, Henry Cabot, Jr.

William E. Pemberton
University of Wisconsin, LaCrosse
Hiss, Alger

Louis A. Pérez, Jr.
University of North Carolina
Cuba; Platt Amendment

Hugh D. Phillips
Western Kentucky University
Litvinov, Maksim Maksimovich; Long,
Breckinridge; Manchurian Crisis; Panay
Episode; Shandong Question

Daniel Pipes
Middle East Quarterly
Syria

Brenda Gayle Plummer
University of Wisconsin, Madison
Haiti

Ronald E. Powaski
Euclid High School
Nuclear Weapons and Strategy

Ronald W. Pruessen
University of Toronto
Dulles, John Foster; Eisenhower, Dwight
David; Herter, Christian Archibald

Noel H. Pugach
University of New Mexico
American China Development Company

George H. Quester
University of Maryland
Television and Foreign Policy

Stephen G. Rabe
University of Texas, Dallas
Abrams, Elliott; Alliance for Progress;
Betancourt, Rómulo; Caribbean Legion;
Chapultepec Conference; Mann, Thomas
Clifton; Rio Treaty; Venezuela

Donald A. Rakestraw
Georgia Southern University
Amistad Affair; Astor, John Jacob; Calhoun,
John Caldwell; Lewis and Clark
Expedition; McLane, Louis; Oregon
Question; Pacific Mail Steamship Company;
Palmerston, Third Viscount; Polk, James
Knox

Stephen J. Randall
University of Calgary
Calvo Clause; Colombia; Good Neighbor
Policy

Harry Howe Ransom
Vanderbilt University
Espionage

Alan R. Raucher
Wayne State University
Hoffman, Paul Gray

A. James Reichley
Georgetown University
Democratic Party; Republican Party

David M. Reimers
New York University
Immigration

Michael A. Reno
San Francisco, California
Foreign Corrupt Practices Act

Edward Rhodes
Rutgers University
Navy, U.S. Department of

James Richter
Bates College
Khrushchev, Nikita Sergeyevich

Barney J. Rickman III
Valdosta State University
Grew, Joseph Clark; Hornbeck, Stanley
Kuhl; Reischauer, Edwin Oldfather; Tòjo,
Hideki; Yoshida, Shigeru

Robert B. Marks Ridinger
Northern Illinois University
National Defense Education Act; Peace
Corps

Donald A. Ritchie
U.S. Senate, Office of the Secretary
Humphrey, Hubert Horatio

Horace B. Robertson
Duke University
Blockade

William R. Rock
Bowling Green State University
Appeasement

Bert A. Rockman
University of Pittsburgh
Bush, George Herbert Walker

Richard C. Rohrs
Oklahoma State University
Adams, John Quincy; Adams-Onís Treaty;
Florida

Jerel A. Rosati
University of South Carolina
American Federation of Labor-Congress of
Industrial Organizations; American Legion;
Committee on the Present Danger; Foreign
Policy Association; Hot Line Agreements;
Military-Industrial Complex; National
Association of Manufacturers; Rollback and
Liberation; Trilateral Commission; Veterans
of Foreign Wars; Warnke, Paul Culliton

Richard N. Rosecrance
University of California, Los Angeles
Balance of Power

Joel H. Rosenthal
*Carnegie Council on Ethics and International
Affairs*
Ethics

Martin Rossmann
Johns Hopkins University, SAIS
Austria; Bosnia-Herzegovina; Croatia;
Yugoslavia

Donald Rothchild
University of California, Davis
Africa

T. Michael Ruddy
Saint Louis University
Bohlen, Charles Eustis; Hammer, Armand;
Smith, Walter Bedell

Jeffrey J. Safford
Montana State University
Mansfield, Michael Joseph

Robert B. Satloff
Washington Institute for Near East Policy
Jordan

Michael Schaller

University of Arizona
Chennault, Claire Lee and Anna Chan; KAL-007 Incident; MacArthur, Douglas; Reagan Doctrine

Arthur M. Schlesinger, Jr.

City University of New York
Kennedy, John Fitzgerald; Kennedy, Robert Francis

Stephen A. Schuker

University of Virginia
Reparations

Robert D. Schulzinger

University of Colorado
Kissinger, Henry Alfred; Richardson, Elliot Lee; Watergate

Thomas A. Schwartz

Vanderbilt University
Adenauer, Konrad; European Defense Community; Nuremberg, International Military Tribunal at; McCloy, John Jay; Morgenthau Plan

Steven Schwartzberg

Yale University
Berle, Adolf Augustus, Jr.; Messersmith, George Strausser

Deborah Shapley

Journalist, Washington, D.C.
McNamara, Robert Strange

David Sheinin

Trent University
Argentina; Bolivia; Braden, Spruille; Dependency; Grenada Invasion; Pan-Americanism; Perón, Juan Domingo

Martin J. Sherwin

Tufts University
Acheson-Lilienthal Report; Baruch, Bernard Mannes; Einstein, Albert; Hiroshima and Nagaski Bombings of 1945; Hyde Park Aide-Mémoire Agreement; Lilienthal, David; Oppenheimer, Julius Robert; Strauss, Lewis

Kenneth E. Shewmaker

Dartmouth College
Cass, Lewis; Harrison, William Henry; Parker, Peter; Perry, Matthew Calbraith; Wangxia, Treaty of; Webster, Daniel; Webster-Ashburton Treaty

Holly Cowan Shulman

University of Maryland, College Park
Propaganda; Radio Free Europe and Radio Liberty

Mark Russell Shulman

Air War College
Navy League

Paul E. Sigmund

Princeton University
Allende (Gossens), Salvador; Chile; Pinochet (Ugarte), Augusto

William E. Simons

RAND Corporation
Coercive Diplomacy

Timothy D. Sisk

U.S. Institute of Peace
Angola; Congo Crisis; South Africa

Thomas Michael Slopnick

University of Connecticut
Heritage Foundation

Melvin Small

Wayne State University
Journalism and Foreign Policy

Edwin M. Smith

University of Southern California
Genocide Convention; War Powers Resolution

Gaddis Smith

Yale University
Ambassadors and Embassies; Antarctica; Cairo Conference; Clark Memorandum; Executive Agents; Falkland Islands; Fourteen Points; Johnson Act; Monroe, James; Monroe Doctrine; No-Transfer Principle; Potsdam Conference; Privateering; Recognition; Roosevelt, Franklin Delano; Strong, Josiah; Unconditional Surrender; World War II; Yalta Conference

Geoffrey S. Smith

Queen's University, Kingston
Wilkes, Charles

Louis R. Smith, Jr.

University of West Alabama
Alaska Boundary Dispute; Burlingame, Anson; Dawes Plan; Dodd, William Edward; Fillmore, Millard; Mellon, Andrew William; Ostend Manifesto

Thomas G. Smith

Nichols College
Douglas, Lewis Williams

Michael Smitka

Washington and Lee University
Automotive Companies

W. R. Smyser

Conrad Hilton Foundation
Refugees

Robert Mark Spaulding, Jr.

University of North Carolina, Wilmington
Brandt, Willy

Donald Spivey

University of Miami
DuBois, William Edward Burghardt; Garvey, Marcus Moziah; Washington, Booker T.

Sheldon L. Stanton

Culver-Stockton College
Spain

Ronald L. Steel

University of Southern California
Lippmann, Walter

John D. Stempel

University of Kentucky, Patterson School of Diplomacy and International Commerce
State, U.S. Department of

Kenneth R. Stevens

Texas Christian University
Aberdeen, Fourth Earl; Ashburton, First Baron; Caroline Affair; Clay, Henry; Creole Affair; Everett, Edward; Forsyth, John; Jackson, Andrew; Livingston, Edward; Poinsett, Joel Roberts; Van Buren, Martin

Robert L. Stevenson

University of North Carolina, Chapel Hill
Cable News Network; Committee on Public Information; Foreign Broadcast Information Service; United States Information Agency; Voice of America

Kendall W. Stiles

Loyola University, Chicago
Bretton Woods System; Dillon, Clarence Douglas; Hegemony; London Economic Conference; New International Economic Order; Point Four; Reciprocal Trade Agreement Act; War Debt of World War I; Webb-Pomerene Act; Welles, Benjamin Sumner

Mark A. Stoler

University of Vermont
Lend-Lease; Marshall, George Catlett, Jr.; Murphy, Robert Daniel; Muskie, Edmund Sixtus

Stephen M. Streeter

Wilfrid Laurier University
Cabot, John Moors; Noriega, Manuel

John J. Stremlau
Carnegie Commission on Preventing Deadly Conflict
Nongovernmental Organizations

Robert G. Sutter
Library of Congress, Congressional Research Service
Australia; East Timor; Hong Kong; Indonesia; Malaysia; New Zealand; Okinawa; Pacific Island Nations and U.S. Territories; Taiwan

Donald Swainson
Queen's University, Kingston
Macdonald, John Alexander

John Temple Swing
Foreign Policy Association
Council on Foreign Relations

Daniel Tarantola
Harvard School of Public Health
Acquired Immune Deficiency Syndrome (AIDS) Pandemic

Arnold H. Taylor
Howard University
Liberia

Nathaniel Thayer
International University of Japan
Hirohito

William F. Theobald
Purdue University
Tourism

James C. Thomson, Jr.
Boston University
Bowles, Chester Bliss

Seth P. Tillman
Georgetown University
Fulbright, James William

Jonathan B. Tucker
Monterey Institute of International Studies
Flexible Response

Nancy Bernkopf Tucker
Georgetown University
China

Robert W. Tucker
Johns Hopkins University, Emeritus
Jefferson, Thomas

Ogwo Jombo Umeh
California State University, Hayward
Nigeria

Jonathan G. Utley
University of Tennessee, Knoxville
Hull, Cordell

Linda O. Valenty
San Jose State University
Presidency

Lucien S. Vandenbroucke
U.S. Department of State
Bay of Pigs Invasion

Richard Vengroff
University of Connecticut
Senegal

J. Samuel Walker
U.S. Nuclear Regulatory Commission
Wallace, Henry Agard

Thomas W. Walker
Ohio University
Contadora Group; Contras; Esquipulas II; Somoza Debayle, Anastasio

William O. Walker III
Ohio Wesleyan University
Drug Enforcement Agency

Harold M. Waller
McGill University
Begin, Menachem; Ben-Gurion, David; Israel

William T. Warner
Attorney at Law, Writer, Arlington, Virginia
Status of Forces Agreements

R. Kent Weaver
Brookings Institution
Think Tanks

Philip Weeks
Kent State University
Native Americans

Edmund S. Wehrle
University of Connecticut
Hitler, Adolf; Imperialism; Stuart, John Leighton

Samuel F. Wells, Jr.
Woodrow Wilson Center
NSC-68

Christopher Welna
Duke University
Costa Rica; Paraguay; Uruguay; Virgin Islands

Imanuel Wexler
University of Connecticut, Emeritus
Marshall Plan

David L. Wilson
Southern Illinois University
Fish, Hamilton

Theodore A. Wilson
University of Kansas
Atlantic Charter; Destroyers-for-Bases Deal; Saint Pierre-Miquelon Affair

Gilbert R. Winham
Dalhousie University
International Commodity Agreements; International Trade and Commerce; Tariffs

Sharon L. Wolchik
George Washington University
Beneš, Eduard; Bulgaria; Czech Republic; Eastern Europe; Havel, Václav; Poland; Romania

Stephen D. Wrage
U.S. Naval Academy
Warsaw Pact

David S. Wyman
University of Massachusetts
Holocaust

Herbert F. York
University of California, San Diego
Hydrogen Bomb; Manhattan Project; Limited Nuclear Test Ban Treaty; Teller, Edward

Luke Zahner
Johns Hopkins University, SAIS
Serbia

Marvin R. Zahniser
Ohio State University
Franklin, Benjamin

Fareed Zakaria
Foreign Affairs
Clinton, William Jefferson

Jan Zaprudnik
Belarusan Institute of Arts and Sciences
Belarus

Thomas W. Zeiler
University of Colorado, Boulder
Goldwater, Barry; Stevenson, Adlai Ewing II; Thompson, Llewellyn E., Jr.; Trading with the Enemy Act

Shu Guang Zhang
University of Maryland
Mao Zedong

Vladislav M. Zubok
George Washington University
Gromyko, Andrei Andreyevich; Molotov, Vyacheslav Mikhailovich

A

ABERDEEN, FOURTH EARL
George Hamilton Gordon
(*b.* 28 January 1784; *d.* 14 December 1860)

British foreign secretary (1828–1830, 1841–1846), secretary for war and the colonies (1834–1835), and prime minister (1852–1855), who improved Anglo-American relations through patient and conciliatory diplomacy. He first served as foreign secretary during the Duke of Wellington's Conservative ministry from 1828 to 1830—a period that corresponded with the presidential administrations of John Quincy Adams and Andrew Jackson in the United States. The most important diplomatic issues between the United States and Great Britain during that time were U.S. trade with British colonies and the Maine–New Brunswick boundary controversy.

When Sir Robert Peel became prime minister in 1841, Aberdeen replaced Lord Palmerston at the Foreign Office and held that post until 1846. Relations with the United States had been tumultuous under Palmerston, but the accession of the conciliatory Aberdeen in England and the Anglophile Daniel Webster as U.S. secretary of state forecast improved relations between the nations. In 1842 Aberdeen sent Lord Ashburton on a special mission to Washington, with authority to settle all disputes with the United States: the Maine–New Brunswick boundary, the northwest boundary along the Great Lakes, the Oregon boundary, the *Caroline* and *Creole* affairs, and the African slave trade. Not every matter was resolved—notably the Oregon question—but the Webster-Ashburton Treaty of 1842 concluded several long-standing problems between the countries and significantly improved Anglo-American relations.

Aberdeen continued discussions on Oregon during the administration of James K. Polk, despite difficulties posed by the president's bellicose statements and those of a succession of U.S. secretaries of state. Just as the Peel ministry came to a close in 1846, Aberdeen achieved an Oregon boundary settlement at the 49th parallel, with Vancouver Island reserved for Great Britain.

Out of office during Lord Palmerston's third term as foreign secretary (1846–1851), Aberdeen returned to the government as prime minister in December 1852. Although his ministry negotiated in 1853 an Anglo-American agreement that established a commission for settling all claims between the countries, relations with the United States during his tenure as prime minister were turbulent.

In Central America, Great Britain had assumed since 1848 the responsibility of protecting the Mosquito Indians from encroachments by other Central American nations. In July 1854 the U.S. naval vessel *Cyane* bombarded the Mosquito port of Greytown in retaliation for an alleged insult to the United States. Preoccupied with the Crimean War, which had broken out in March 1854, Britain did nothing except protest. Later that year, however, when the United States announced its intention to annex Hawai'i, Great Britain increased its naval force in U.S. waters as a demonstration of its determination to resist such a move. One difficult issue involved the quest for a reciprocal trade agreement between the United States and Canada. When Great Britain adopted free trade in 1846, Canadians were forced to compete in an unprotected world market and their economy suffered. In June 1854, during the Franklin Pierce administration, the United States, Great Britain, and Canada agreed to a reciprocity treaty that provided for limited free trade, navigation rights on the Saint Lawrence and Saint John rivers, and U.S. fishing privileges in Canadian waters.

The Crimean War (1854–1856), in which Great Britain and France fought against Russia, most frustrated Aberdeen's foreign policy. The war effort was hobbled by a series of military disasters. When a call was made, in January 1855, for a Parliamentary inquiry into the conduct of the war, Aberdeen's ministry fell, to be replaced with one headed by Lord Palmerston.

KENNETH R. STEVENS

See also Ashburton, Alexander Baring; Canada; Fisheries; Great Britain; Hawai'i; Nicaragua; Oregon Question; Polk, James Knox ; Webster, Daniel; Webster-Ashburton Treaty

FURTHER READING
Jones, Wilbur Devereux. *The American Problem in British Diplomacy.* Athens, Ga., 1974.
Newton, A. P. "United States and Colonial Developments, 1815–1846." In *The Cambridge History of British Foreign Policy, 1783–1919,* edited by A.W. Ward and G.P. Gooch. New York, 1923.
Stuart, Reginald. *United States Expansionism and British North America, 1775–1871.* Chapel Hill, N.C., 1988.

ABM TREATY

See Antiballistic Missile Treaty

ABRAMS, ELLIOTT

(*b.* 24 January 1948)

Assistant secretary of state for international organizations (1981), assistant secretary of state for human rights and humanitarian affairs (1981–1985), and assistant secretary of state for inter-American affairs (1985–1989). In the 1970s Abrams worked for Democratic Senators Henry M. Jackson and Daniel Patrick Moynihan, but by 1980, as a neoconservative, he supported Ronald Reagan for president, claiming that the Democratic party was no longer sufficiently anticommunist. As director of the State Department's human rights office, Abrams carried out President Reagan's policy of withholding public criticism of human rights violations committed by anticommunist governments and relentlessly denouncing communist societies. As assistant secretary for inter-American affairs, Abrams devoted himself to aiding the Contras, a Nicaraguan exile group waging war against the leftist Sandinista government. Abrams became entangled in the Iran-Contra scandal. In October 1986 he testified to Congress that he was unaware of secret U.S. government efforts to supply the Contras, but in 1991 Abrams pleaded guilty to two misdemeanor counts of failing to give "full and complete testimony" to Congress during those congressional appearances.

STEPHEN G. RABE

See also Contras; Iran-Contra Affair; Reagan, Ronald Wilson

FURTHER READING

Abrams, Elliott. *Undue Process: A Story of How Political Differences Are Turned into Crimes.* New York, 1993.
Arnson, Cynthia J. *Crossroads: Congress, the Reagan Administration, and Central America.* New York, 1993.
Carothers, Thomas. *In the Name of Democracy: U.S. Policy Toward Latin America in the Reagan Years.* Berkeley, Calif., 1991.
Shultz, George P. *Turmoil and Triumph: My Years as Secretary of State.* New York, 1993.

ACDA

See Arms Control and Disarmament Agency

ACHESON, DEAN GOODERHAM

(*b.* 11 April 1893; *d.* 12 October 1971)

Undersecretary of state (1945–1947), secretary of state (1949–1953), and the president's closest and the principal architect of U.S. foreign policy in the decade following World War II. During the Truman administration, he served as most influential adviser on foreign affairs. Acheson significantly shaped foreign policy regarding control of atomic weapons Greece, Iran and Turkey; the Truman Doctrine and the Marshall Plan, the Berlin blockade; the North Atlantic Treaty (1949); and its subsequent organization (NATO) with a permanent U.S. military presence in Europe. He influenced the forming of the West German government and that nation's rearmament, the 1949 decision not to recognize the People's Republic of China, the decision to develop the hydrogen bomb, the drafting of National Security Council document 68 (NSC-68), the Japanese peace treaty, the U.S. response when British oil interests were nationalized in Iran in the early 1950s, and aid for the French in their effort to retain colonial control of Indochina.

When the Chinese Communists emerged victorious in the civil war with Jiang Jieshi's (Chiang Kai-Shek's) Nationalists in 1949, the decision to provide Jiang with only lukewarm support left the administration open to fierce domestic political attacks from its conservative critics. Dean Acheson became a lightning rod for groundless charges by Republican Senator Joseph McCarthy that Acheson was protecting communists in the Department of State. After the Truman presidency, Acheson never again held full-time public office, although he continued to devote his energies toward influencing U.S. foreign policy.

Born in Middletown, Connecticut, to British-born Edward Campion Acheson and Canadian-born Eleanor Gertrude Gooderham Acheson, Dean Acheson came of age during the ascendancy of a U.S. patriciate, an elite that was primarily, but not exclusively, white, Anglo-Saxon, and Protestant, and which contributed in sizeable numbers to a remarkable generation of leaders and public servants during the Roosevelt and Truman administrations. His father was the Episcopal bishop of Connecticut, and Acheson was born into comfortable circumstances. His memoirs paint an idyllic childhood growing up in Connecticut, with family life centered around his father's church. Acheson attended Groton, the exclusive private academy that has served to incubate many of the nation's leaders. There he developed an interest in public service.

Graduating from Yale University in 1915 and Harvard Law School in 1918, Acheson served briefly in the U.S. Navy as a junior officer during World War I prior to becoming private secretary to Supreme Court Justice Louis D. Brandeis. In 1921, he joined the prestigious law firm of Covington and Burling, and for the next half century divided his time between government service and the private practice of law in Washington, D.C.

At the recommendation of Felix Frankfurter, a Brandeis protégé and unofficial talent scout of the Roosevelt administration, President Franklin D. Roosevelt appointed Acheson undersecretary of the treasury in 1933, a post Acheson resigned six months later in protest against Roosevelt's decision to reduce the gold content of the dollar. He spent the next eight years in the private practice of law.

With the outbreak of war in Europe in 1939, Acheson once again returned to public affairs. He became an active member of the Committee to Defend America by Aiding the Allies, emerging as an articulate advocate of U.S. intervention on the side of Great Britain against Hitler's Germany. In 1940, he played an instrumental role in the initial steps toward intervention through his collaboration with presidential aide Ben Cohen. The two drafted the constitutional justification for the destroyer-base agreement with the British, under which the president transferred—without seeking congressional approval—fifty superannuated destroyers to the British Navy in exchange for leases on British naval and air bases off the Atlantic coast of Canada and in the Caribbean.

Impressed by this demonstration of legal draftsmanship tied to deft political instincts, Roosevelt asked Acheson to rejoin the administration as assistant secretary of state for economic affairs. He served in that capacity from 1941 to 1944, first under Cordell Hull and then under Edward Stettinius. During this wartime period, he was involved in coordinating the Lend-Lease program, acted as a liaison with Congress, contributed to the development of such postwar organizations as the United Nations Relief and Rehabilitation Administration, the World Bank, the International Monetary Fund (IMF), and the Food and Agriculture Organization (FAO). He even lobbied Congress on behalf of the United Nations Charter, although he personally regarded the organization as impractical and of marginal importance. During the war years, Acheson's view that the economic reconstruction of Europe was an essential component to the maintenance of postwar peace dominated U.S. foreign policy for the next decade; in the immediate postwar years he played a leading role in pressing for U.S. economic aid to Europe.

By the end of the Roosevelt era, the Acheson who had a decade earlier aborted his budding government career over a matter of principle had grown more pragmatic in the rough and tumble where principle and politics intersect. Acheson viewed foreign policy in terms of power politics and was impatient with, and an opponent of, the Wilsonian school of internationalism as well as of any attempt to base foreign policy on appeals to abstract principles of right and wrong, which he saw as an attempt to avoid the responsibilities inherent in the exercise of power. And yet he occasionally adopted a moralistic, ideological rhetoric in a crusade against world communism that some scholars have found exaggerated and counterproductive.

Undersecretary of State: 1945–1947

By Achesonian standards, the culmination of his foreign-policy achievements came not when he was secretary of state during Truman's second term but when he held the number two post at State during Truman's first term. It was during this period that he persuaded the president and Congress to adopt his Eurocentric world view and to build institutional ties and programs of foreign aid that would shape U.S. foreign relations for the next decade. Acheson saw a profound connection between America's destiny and its European heritage; it was in this context that he considered the rebuilding and rehabilitation of the war-torn industrial nations of Europe as crucial to securing the gains of the Allied military victory and peace in the postwar world. Initially his objectives were to ensure stable, pro-U.S. governments in Europe, while simultaneously securing new markets for surplus U.S. industrial products. When communist insurgencies in Europe and elsewhere appeared on the horizon, his objectives enlarged to thwarting and containing communist expansion at every opportunity and to developing a strong military presence so that the United States could force the Soviet Union to negotiate on U.S. terms. That Acheson's influence was greatest when he did not hold the top job at State grew out of a fortuitous convergence of circumstance and personality.

In 1945, as the Cold War began to develop, President Truman appointed his former political rival James F. Byrnes secretary of state, and Byrnes appointed Acheson to the number two position, undersecretary. Truman had narrowly defeated Byrnes for the Democratic vice-presidential nomination in 1944, and the rivalry between the men continued to smolder after Byrnes's appointment, even though much of Byrnes's eighteen months in office was spent abroad. There were continual conflicts between the White House and the Department of State, and Acheson was regularly called upon to act as buffer and mediator between the president and his former rival. The formidable and talented Acheson was able to capitalize on his daily access to the president to win Truman's complete confidence on foreign-policy matters, thereby becoming one of the most powerful undersecretaries ever to hold the post.

As Acheson skillfully navigated the shoals of the Truman-Byrnes relationship, the sophisticated, urbane member of the East Coast establishment was able to forge a close relationship with Truman, a Midwestern small businessman and product of Democratic machine politics. Despite their differences in background and temperament, Acheson and Truman worked well together. Each day, Acheson would set out the foreign-policy issues in a crisp, no-nonsense fashion and then make sure that the president's decision was carried out. Both men were in complete agreement on the necessity of "negotiating from strength" and of containing Soviet expansionism, and on the special role Western Europe played in U.S. security. The only significant foreign-policy issue on which they did not see eye-to-eye was the new state of Israel, which Truman insisted on recognizing in 1948. Acheson believed that Truman's policies should have taken greater account of U.S. interests in maintaining warm relations with the Arab states. During this period, Acheson was not only responsible for day-to-day operations, but streamlined the functioning of State's bureaucracy. Acheson's reforms included the introduction of a clear chain of command that ended with his office. Girded by the strong personal support of the president, Acheson effectively became acting secretary.

As a principal formulator of Cold War tactics and U.S. foreign policymaking, Acheson was intimately involved in shaping U.S. policy on atomic weapons. During Truman's first term, policymakers were divided on how to deal with nuclear issues. One group, which included Secretary of State Byrnes and Secretary of the Navy James Forrestal, wanted the United States to maintain a nuclear monopoly as an important weapon to extract concessions from the Soviet Union. Another group, including Acheson and Henry Stimson, secretary of war from 1940 to 1945, opposed making policy on the basis of a nuclear monopoly, because they saw the ability to maintain a monopoly as a pipe dream. Based on information from knowledgeable nuclear scientists, they believed that the Soviet Union would soon possess its own nuclear capability. They proposed instead the establishment of an international agency with a world monopoly on uranium. In this way, it might be possible to establish some control over the Soviets and to avoid a mutually destructive arms race.

In 1946, Byrnes appointed Acheson to chair a committee, which included David Lilienthal, chairman of the Tennessee Valley Authority (TVA), and J. Robert Oppenheimer, distinguished physicist and a progenitor of the atomic bomb, to draft a report to be presented to the United Nations (UN) on the Soviet Union's buildup of a nuclear arsenal and a plan to establish some control over it. The Acheson-Lilienthal report of 28 March 1946 proposed the establishment of an international atomic development agency jointly staffed by the United States, Great Britain, and the Soviet Union that would coordinate the exchange of information on nuclear weapons, survey nuclear raw materials, and assume control of nuclear material and production plants. The agency would control, license, and monitor all nuclear weapons to the United Nations for appropriate action by member states. The report offered to end the U.S. atomic weapons program.

The Acheson-Lilienthal report became the foundation of the Baruch Plan presented to the United Nations later that year. Byrnes had assigned Bernard Baruch, the U.S. delegate to the UN Atomic Energy Commission, the responsibility of presenting the arms control plan to the United Nations. Baruch, adamant about insuring Soviet compliance, amended the Acheson-Lilienthal report by inserting a provision prohibiting UN Security Council members from exercising their veto on atomic energy issues. Acheson opposed the amendment, warning that the Soviets would find the provision unacceptable, and, indeed, the Soviet Union rejected the plan in June 1946. Acheson was again involved in nuclear issues in Truman's second term after the Soviets successfully tested an atom bomb on 23 September 1949. Acheson actively advocated a policy which led to a crash program to develop the hydrogen bomb.

During Acheson's final six months as undersecretary, he served under Secretary of State George C. Marshall. Truman had appointed as secretary of state a distinguished military figure highly respected both domestically and internationally. Marshall saw his role at State as managerial—to delegate work to his experienced diplomatic subordinates. Acheson, one of the most talented men at the Department of State, became responsible for much of the policymaking. With his continuing support from the president and control of the bureaucracy, Acheson, always an effective and articulate advocate, a skillful diplomat, and wielder of bureaucratic power, became the principal voice in foreign affairs during the Truman years.

Early in his tenure as undersecretary, Acheson had tried to carry forward the Roosevelt policy of conciliation toward America's wartime ally, the Soviet Union. But the growing perception in Washington of Soviet interference in Greek and Turkish affairs, seemingly calculated to gain Moscow a foothold in the eastern Mediterranean as well as in Iran, caused him to reverse his position. By spring 1946, he had joined George F. Kennan in warning about Soviet expansionism and became a staunch advocate of a policy of containment toward the USSR. There was vigorous debate within the administration about the nature of Soviet ideology, intentions, and military capabilities and thus on what form containment should take. Kennan had alerted the policymakers' attention to the problems with the Soviets, but also saw the solutions in a series of nuanced political, economic, and military responses. Acheson came to view the Soviet Union as an expansionary power bent on world domination. This led Acheson to a rigid policy of refusing to negotiate with the Soviets and a containment policy conceived primarily in a bipolar, military framework.

By 1947, the Achesonian interpretation of containment had become a cornerstone of U.S. foreign policy. When the British announced their impending withdrawal from Greece in February 1947, Acheson became one of the prime movers in convincing the president to take up

Great Britain's traditional responsibilities in Greece. Acheson urged the immediate extension of U.S. military and economic assistance to a conservative Athens government in the throes of a renewed guerrilla war mounted by communist insurgents—aided and abetted by Greece's northern communist neighbors. Acheson formulated the proposal for submission to Congress and won the backing of congressional leaders. Against a domestic backdrop of general war weariness and resurgent forces of prewar isolationism, Acheson was able to convince the president and Congress that political, military, and economic links forged between North America and Western Europe should form the foundation of U.S. foreign policy structure. In the process, the Truman Doctrine of March 1947 was forged, and the nation made its first postwar military commitment to protect Western Europe—albeit conveniently redefined to include Greece and Turkey—from a perceived communist threat.

Besides his day-to-day operational responsibilities, Acheson was heavily involved in foreign-policy planning for Europe's economic recovery. He was assigned to flesh out a program to rebuild Europe's economies so that they could withstand political and military aggression from the Soviet Union. With Marshall often away from Washington, Acheson had considerable latitude to leave his mark on the economic aspects of containment. Acheson outlined the basic tenets of what would become the Marshall Plan in a memorandum to President Truman on 5 March 1947. The details were debated within the administration that spring and publicly floated by Acheson in a speech on 8 May 1947, delivered in Mississippi. Acheson proposed a massive program of European assistance. Marshall, who had been at the Moscow foreign ministers conference of 1947 during most of the preliminary planning stages of the aid plan, had likewise become more convinced that the Soviets had aggressive intentions toward Western Europe, but he objected to the strongly ideological tone of Acheson's speech. Nevertheless, Marshall ratified the essentials of the Acheson trial balloon in his famous commencement address at Harvard University on 4 June 1947.

The Marshall Plan was spread over a four-year period and led to $12.5 billion being directed toward the reconstruction of Western Europe. By 1952, the Marshall Plan had played a vital role in boosting European industrial and agricultural output significantly above prewar levels. But if the Marshall Plan was a significant factor in rebuilding Europe's economies after World War II, it also accelerated the political and economic rifts between East and West. The plan was positively received by the French and the British, but the Soviets saw it as a form of financial imperialism. Even with Western European agreement, the Truman administration still had to win acceptance from the U.S. Congress. Marshall encoun-

tered vehement opposition from Republican conservatives, unwilling to allow the Democratic administration a major diplomatic triumph during an election year. But Marshall's substantial prestige and Acheson's persuasive case enabled the administration to prevail.

Acheson returned to his private law practice in the summer of 1947, although he continued his public service as vice chairman of the Hoover Commission, which proposed reform of the civil service system, and lobbying on behalf of the Marshall Plan. In November 1948, President Truman asked Acheson to replace the ailing Marshall as secretary of state, and Acheson was sworn into office on 21 January 1949.

Secretary of State: 1949–1953

By the time Acheson assumed the top job at State, economic and military containment had become the hallmarks of U.S. foreign policy. The Truman Doctrine had checked the communist insurgency in Greece, the Marshall Plan was in full swing, and Europe's nascent economic recovery was providing less fertile ground for communist inroads. Acheson thus turned his attention to forging and maintaining the stronger political and military bonds within the Atlantic Community and to building a strong military alliance in Europe.

To counter the Soviet Union's overwhelming superiority in conventional military forces vis-à-vis Western Europe, Acheson pressed, ultimately without success, for a European Defense Community (EDC), essentially a European defense structure, with assistance from the United States. Such a structure had several advantages: it would help buttress the thinly stretched U.S. forces in the postwar era and would provide the means to rearm Germany that was politically acceptable to the Europeans.

In the immediate aftermath of World War II, the Allied powers, especially the Soviet Union, were resolute that Germany's warmaking ability should be destroyed and permanently constrained. The military end game of World War II had left Germany divided, and in 1949 the Truman administration pressed for the creation of the Federal Republic of Germany, an accommodation to the status quo. By the early 1950s, however, the United States came to view a rearmed West Germany integrated into the fabric of Europe as the fulcrum of a strategy of maintaining Western unity and containing communist expansion. Germany's strategic position in Europe's industrial heartland could not be ignored.

Convinced of the need for German rearmament, Acheson journeyed to Paris and London to assess how European fears of a revived German military might be allayed. At a governmental level the French and British were open to discussions of the issue as long as they remained private, because European public opinion still reflected strong anti-German sentiment. The start of the

Korean War just six weeks later strongly affected the political climate in Europe, where the communist offensive in Korea was viewed as a means of diverting U.S. troops away from the defense of Europe and ignited European fears that the Red Army would soon be sweeping across the plains of Germany. The Europeans eventually bracketed their anti-German concerns to approve a unified European army that would include German units. The whole enterprise began to founder, however, when it became clear that British political parties were unprepared to commit British troops to a common European army. Enthusiasm for the EDC dwindled, and the focus turned to the creation in 1949 of NATO, with a permanent U.S. military presence in Europe.

Acheson was emphatically Eurocentric, and his foreign-policy positions on other global issues were filtered through the lens of Europe. For example, in the early 1950s his support for U.S. intervention on behalf of French colonists in Indochina against the procommunist Vietminh was seen as a means to make the French more amenable to U.S. plans for the economic and military recovery of Germany, as well as to contain the People's Republic of China. U.S. commitment to the French began on a small scale in May 1950 and increased rapidly after the outbreak of the Korean War a month later. Acheson was uneasy at the time over the growing U.S. involvement in Indochina, but neither he nor anyone else foresaw its ultimate disastrous consequences for the United States.

When Acheson assumed the post of secretary of state in 1949, the Nationalist Chinese led by Jiang Jieshi were on the verge of defeat in their civil war with the communists. Conservative Republican members of Congress demanded increased aid to Jiang, who they believed was being ignored because of the administration's European orientation. Acheson opposed these demands on the grounds that Jiang had lost the support of the Chinese people. In August 1949 Acheson defended his position in a Department of State White Paper on China, arguing that nothing short of direct U.S. military intervention would change the outcome in China. When the communist victory came in December 1949, U.S. conservatives condemned the Department of State for failing to contain communism in the world's largest nation, for "selling out" Jiang, and for "losing" China. In this highly charged political atmosphere, baseless charges that the communist victory in China stemmed from a communist conspiracy within the U.S. Department of State were hurled against Acheson.

Acheson had sown seeds of ideological anticommunist rhetoric when it suited his Eurocentric policies, and he reaped the whirlwind when this same rhetoric was applied to the administration's policies in Asia. His Eurocentrism left him unprepared for just how incendiary the domestic political fallout over China would become. His

Asia policy was shaped in part by his recognition of the limits of U.S. military intervention on the Asian mainland, as well as by his tendency to relegate to the margins events he regarded as unrelated to Europe. His failure to take into account just how vitriolic the blame game would become when it came to assigning responsibility for the communist takeover in China contributed to his fall from political grace.

Acheson spoke at the National Press Club in Washington, D.C., in January 1950, a month after the communist victory in China, and his speech addressed future U.S. responsibilities in Asia. Korea was not mentioned as part of America's "defense perimeter." Although the Soviets and the United States had been sparring for several years on the fate of the divided Korean peninsula, the Truman administration was ambivalent about the South Korean government of Syngman Rhee and its violent repression of political opponents. Acheson's speech also reflected his assessment that the United States was unwilling and unprepared to secure the entire Pacific against military attack. However, six months later, when North Korea invaded the South, administration critics charged that Acheson's omission of South Korea in this speech had been an open invitation for the communists to invade.

At the end of 1949, soon after Mao Zedong's forces won in China, the Soviets had exploded an atomic device. Acheson ordered a reassessment of U.S. foreign policy and defense capabilities known as NSC-68. The report, completed in the spring of 1950, was the first comprehensive review of U.S. national security policy. Against the context of the conservative political backlash, NSC-68 called for a massive military buildup to meet the challenge of Soviet expansionism, and called on the United States, as the world's major nuclear power, to assume unilateral defense of the noncommunist world rather than rely on a multinational force. To support America's role as world policeman, NSC-68 proposed an increase in U.S. defense spending to $35 billion a year, or 20 percent of the gross national product (GNP). This emphasis on military superiority brought criticism of Acheson from within the administration as too hard-line, and President Truman was initially reluctant to back the study's proposals. With the outbreak of war in Korea in June 1950, Acheson renewed his push for increased defense spending, a move that some analysts believe exacerbated the Cold War by forcing the Soviet Union into a similar hard-line stance to meet tit for tat.

With the Soviet-supported invasion of South Korea by North Korean troops on 25 June 1950, Acheson recommended that the United States commit itself to a war to save South Korea, primarily to reassure the nations of Western Europe of U.S. willingness and ability to defend them. Within the week, Truman dispatched ground divisions to support South Korea's forces and sent the Seventh Fleet to the Formosa Straits. By dint of U.S. diplomatic maneuvering within the United Nations, the Korean War was conducted under color of a UN military operation commanded by General Douglas MacArthur. When it became clear that the UN troops would push North Korean units from the South, Acheson advocated the liberation of North Korea. Neither Acheson nor General MacArthur nor any other member of the Truman administration took seriously the Chinese Communist threat to intervene should the UN troops cross the 38th parallel. Thus China's intervention in the war in November 1950 caught the administration off guard.

The enlargement of the Korean War and the domestic fallout of the communist victory in China had poisoned relations between Congress and the Truman administration in general, and with Acheson in particular. These events also provided fuel for Republican Senator Joseph McCarthy. In 1950, the senator publicly condemned a number of prominent diplomats in the Department of State by name, charging they were communists or communist sympathizers who had been using their positions to influence Acheson's Asia policies. In vain, Acheson tried to protect some of these men, only succeeding in fueling a campaign to oust Acheson himself for "the loss of China." Acheson was slandered by the rancorous Wisconsin senator as the "Red Dean."

When the Truman presidency ended in January 1953, Acheson returned once more to the private practice of law. He had left office at the height of McCarthyism and under a hail of criticism for his China policy. But by his objectives, Acheson's foreign policy had accomplished what he intended. Western Europe had recovered from the devastation of war, its democracies and economies flourishing under the protective umbrella of U.S. military support should it ever be needed.

Writer, Adviser, Critic

Though Acheson never again returned to public service on a full-time basis, he maintained an active correspondence on the political issues of the day with Truman and became a prolific writer on foreign policy. Acheson emerged as an outspoken critic of the Eisenhower administration and its foreign policy under Secretary of State John Foster Dulles. He criticized Dulles's massive retaliation strategy and the administration's reliance on nuclear weapons rather than on conventional forces. From 1957 to 1960, Acheson served as chairman of the Foreign Policy Committee of the Democratic Party when the party regained the presidency.

During the early 1960s, Acheson served as an official adviser to President John F. Kennedy on the Berlin and Cuban crises. In some cases, his views were highly influential; in others he was ignored. In October 1962 he was appointed to the Executive Committee of the National Security Council (NSC), a special bipartisan group created by President Kennedy during the Cuban missile crisis. The hard-line Acheson recommended immediate, decisive action against Cuba, including air strikes to destroy the Soviet missile sites. The president finally concluded that the Acheson proposal left him too little room to maneuver and followed the ultimately successful course of action proposed by Secretary of Defense Robert McNamara: a naval blockade of the island that helped persuade Soviet premier Nikita Khrushchev to agree to dismantle and remove the missiles.

In the 1950s, the Eurocentric Acheson could justify supporting French intervention in Indochina as the necessary price to pay to secure French support for U.S. policies and to contain communism. But, by 1968, when Lyndon Johnson asked Acheson, who had generally supported Johnson's Vietnam intervention, to reassess U.S. military policy in Southeast Asia, this most hawkish of Johnson's senior advisers concluded that the United States could not achieve military victory. He advised Johnson to withdraw as quickly as possible to avoid further erosion of the administration's domestic support. Acheson's assessment contributed to Johnson's announcement on 31 March 1968 that U.S. intervention in Vietnam would be de-escalated, and was instrumental in Johnson's decision not to run for reelection.

Even though Acheson eventually turned against the Vietnam War, he was disheartened and disillusioned by the antiwar protests and the rioting that spread through inner city ghettos during the 1960s, so disillusioned that the life-long Democrat saw in Republican Richard M. Nixon the best hope for the restoration of domestic tranquillity and rapid and honorable disengagement from the morass of Vietnam. With Henry Kissinger acting as liaison, Acheson advised the Nixon administration on NATO policy and African affairs. But his relationship with the Nixon administration soured over Acheson's opposition to the 1970 incursion in Cambodia, which expanded the Vietnam War.

Acheson wrote six books after he left office. Three of them (*A Democrat Looks at His Party*, 1955; *A Citizen Looks at Congress*, 1957; and *Power and Diplomacy*, 1958) fall into the category of political tracts designed to make a new and better world and garner votes for the Democratic Party. The other three (*Sketches from Life of Men I Have Known*, 1961, *Morning and Noon*, 1965; and his magisterial memoir, *Present at the Creation*, 1969; which won a Pulitzer Prize) are still highly regarded for their literary style and the compelling portrait of Acheson's life from earliest childhood until he stepped down as secretary of state.

DOUGLAS BRINKLEY

See also Baruch, Bernard Mannes; Berlin; Byrnes, James Francis; China; Cold War; Containment; Cuban Missile

Crisis; Destroyers-for-Bases Deal; European Defense Community; French Indochina; Germany; Greece; International Monetary Fund; Israel; Jiang Jieshi; Kennan, George Frost; Korean War; Lend-Lease; Lilienthal, David; Mao Zedong; Marshall, George Catlett, Jr.; Marshall Plan; McCarthyism; Nixon, Richard Milhous; North Atlantic Treaty Organization; NSC-68; Nuclear Weapons and Strategy; Russia and the Soviet Union; Truman, Harry S.; Truman Doctrine; Turkey; United Nations Relief and Rehabilitation Administration; Vietnam War; World War II

FURTHER READING

Acheson, Dean. *Acheson County.* New York, 1994.
———. *Present at the Creation: My Years in the State Department.* New York, 1969.
———. *Morning and Noon.* Boston, 1965.
———. *Sketches from Life of Men I Have Known.* New York, 1961.
Brinkley, Douglas. *Dean Acheson: The Cold War Years 1953–1971.* New Haven, 1993.
Brinkley, Douglas, ed., *Dean Acheson and the Making of the U.S. Foreign Policy.* New York, 1993.
Isaacson, Walter, and Evan Thomas. *The Wise Men: Six Friends and The World They Made.* New York, 1986.
McLellan, David S. *Dean Acheson: The State Department Years.* New York, 1976.
Smith, Gaddis. *Dean Acheson.* Totowa, N.J., 1972.

ACHESON-LILIENTHAL REPORT

Issued in March 1946 by the Department of State as "A Report on the International Control of Atomic Energy," it was drafted by a Board of Consultants to the Department of State appointed only two months earlier by Undersecretary of State Dean Acheson. Its members were Chester I. Barnard (president of the New Jersey Bell Telephone Company), Dr. J. Robert Oppenheimer (wartime director of the Los Alamos nuclear weapons laboratory), Dr. Charles A. Thomas (vice president and technical director of the Monsanto Chemical Company), Harry A. Winne (vice president in charge of engineering policy at General Electric Co.), and the Board's chairman, David E. Lilienthal (attorney and chairman of the Tennessee Valley Authority). Not surprisingly, most of the ideas that shaped the report were contributed by Oppenheimer, the only member who had any first-hand knowledge of atomic energy. The Report was the U.S. government's first nuclear-arms control proposal. Though hastily assembled, its complex conceptual framework of international control had begun to take shape during the war in conversations initiated by the Danish physicist Niels Bohr. Seeking to develop an international arrangement acceptable to the United States, Great Britain, and the Soviet Union, the Board created a plan designed to promote nuclear research and the development of

nuclear power while simultaneously preventing a nuclear arms race. The heart of the plan was a powerful international Atomic Development Authority (ADA) that would own, control, inspect, and license all mining, research, and manufacturing associated with fissionable material. The plan stipulated that research and development facilities would be distributed equitably among the concerned parties, the United States would maintain its nuclear monopoly during a period of transition, fundamental scientific information on nuclear energy would be published, the ADA would be organized to control "dangerous" nuclear research and development, and an international inspection regime would be agreed upon by the principal nations. The Report was forwarded to the Secretary of State "not as a final plan, but as a place to begin, a foundation on which to build." Whether or not the Soviets would have found the Acheson-Lilienthal proposal acceptable will remain uncertain since it was significantly transformed by Ambassador Bernard Baruch before he presented it to the United Nations in June 1946 as the Baruch Plan.

MARTIN J. SHERWIN

See also Acheson, Dean Gooderham; Baruch, Bernard Mannes; Lilienthal, David; Nuclear Weapons and Strategy; Oppenheimer, Julius Robert

FURTHER READING

Bundy, McGeorge. *Danger and Survival: Choices About the Bomb in the First Fifty Years.* Palo Alto, Calif., "1997."
Hewlett, Richard E., and Oscar Anderson, Jr. *The New World, 1939–1946: A History of the United States Atomic Energy Commission,* vol. I. University Park, Pa., 1962.
Lilienthal, David E. *The Journals of David E. Lilienthal: The Atomic Energy Years, 1945–1950,* vol. II. New York, 1964.

ACQUIRED IMMUNE DEFICIENCY SYNDROME (AIDS) PANDEMIC

The global spread of a virus that has caused millions of infections and deaths since the early 1980s. AIDS is caused by the human immunodeficiency virus (HIV). The virus is transmitted through intimate sexual contact, through blood exchange via transfusions or sharing of needles, and from mother to fetus/infant. HIV affects the immune system over a period of several years, through mechanisms which lead to the disablement and destruction of host cells. AIDS will follow a latency period which, in industrialized countries, may exceed ten years for more than half of the persons infected. The latency period may be much shorter in developing countries. A wide variety of illnesses may appear in the course of HIV infection, including opportunistic viral, bacterial or fungal infections and certain types of cancers. Tuberculosis is often the first opportunistic infection to appear in the course of HIV infection. The prevention and early treatment of opportunistic infections and appropriate medical and social support can extend the survival of people with AIDS to several years and improve considerably the quality of their lives.

AIDS is diagnosed according to case definitions which differ from one world region to another depending on the ease with which defining conditions can be diagnosed and on the availability of biomedical tests.

Two HIV viruses are currently identified with the global HIV/AIDS pandemic: HIV-1 and HIV-2. Found in almost every country around the world since its discovery in 1983, HIV-1 has been extensively researched and its high variability established. Several sub-types of HIV-1 have now been recognized. They differ by their genetic structure and biological and serological properties, as well as geographic distribution. In contrast to the widely spread HIV-1, the second virus, HIV-2, identified in 1985, is mostly prevalent in West Africa and in countries linked to that region through patterns of population mobility. In addition to structural, serological and pathogenic differences, epidemiological studies have shown that HIV-1 transmits more efficiently than HIV-2. Thus, in areas where HIV-2 was initially involved in the majority of infections, the spread of this virus is being overtaken by HIV-1. Several diagnostic tests are widely available to detect HIV-1 and HIV-2 antibodies. More complex and expensive, HIV antigen detection tests are used mostly in research.

From the beginning of the pandemic in the early 1980s until 1 January 1996, the Harvard-based Global AIDS Policy Coalition estimates that 30.6 million people worldwide had been infected with HIV. Of these, 27.5 million were adults (15.8 million men and 11.7 million women) and 3.2 million were children. The largest numbers of HIV-infected people were in sub-Saharan Africa (19.2 million; 63 percent of global total) and Southeast Asia (6.9 million; 23 percent). Since the beginning of the pandemic, the large majority of HIV infections (over 28 million; 93 percent) have occurred in the developing world.

An estimated 10.4 million people developed AIDS from the beginning of the pandemic until 1 January 1996, including: 8.4 million (81 percent) in sub-Saharan Africa; 0.7 million in Latin America and the Caribbean (7 percent), and 0.7 million in North America, Western Europe, and Oceania combined (7 percent). In Southeast Asia, where the pandemic gained intensity more recently, it is estimated that 0.5 million people have already developed AIDS. Of the 2.4 million children with AIDS, the large majority (2 million; 87 percent) were in sub-Saharan Africa. By 1 January 1996, some 9.2 million people are estimated to have died from AIDS worldwide, or 89 percent of all people with AIDS. The total number of people having died from AIDS includes 7.6 million people in sub-Saharan Africa (83 percent of those infected),

0.5 million in Latin America; 0.4 million in Southeast Asia; 358,000 in North America, 144,000 in Western Europe, and 168,000 in the rest of the world.

The number of adults becoming infected each year seemed to have reached a plateau in the early 1990s in Western Europe, the Caribbean, and sub-Saharan Africa. The annual number of new infections appears to have decreased, at least temporarily, in North America, Oceania, and the Southeast Mediterranean. However, in recently affected areas, such as Southeast and Northeast Asia, HIV incidence (new infections per year) is rising steeply.

On 1 January 1996, an estimated 21.4 million people worldwide were living with HIV or AIDS. Of these, 11.6 million (54 percent) were in sub-Saharan Africa; about 6.4 million (30 percent) were in Southeast Asia; one million (5 percent) were in Latin America; 928,000 (4 percent) were in North America; 694,000 (3 percent) were in Western Europe; and 583,000 (3 percent) were in the rest of the world. The majority of people living with HIV/AIDS were in the developing world (including 92 percent of all infected adults, 97 percent of all infected women, and 98 percent of all infected children.)

If current epidemic trends persist through the end of the century, the World Health Organization (WHO) predicts conservatively that, by the end of the year 2000, more than 38 million adults will have become infected with HIV since the beginning of the pandemic. The Global AIDS Policy Coalition sets the figure at between 60 million and 70 million. Of these adults, about 50 percent will be in Southeast Asia and about 40 percent in sub-Saharan Africa. In the later part of the decade, India is expected to be the site of an HIV/AIDS epidemic of unprecedented magnitude.

In 1987, WHO created a special program to lead and coordinate the global response to the AIDS pandemic. The WHO Global Programme on AIDS (WHO/GPA), funded at an annual level averaging US-$70 million, had three main objectives: (1) to lead and coordinate the global response to HIV/AIDS; (2) to support research and information exchange; and (3) to support the development and implementation of national HIV/AIDS prevention and control programs.

Globally, international funding for HIV/AIDS prevention, care, and research grew steadily from less than US-$1 million in 1986 to more than US-$212 million in 1990, at which point it leveled off. By 1994, more than half of these funds were channeled directly from donor to governmental or non-governmental AIDS programs in recipient countries. In that year, the U.S. Agency for International Development contributed over US-$117 million (over half of the global aid on AIDS) to the developing world and international organizations in support of AIDS programs. African nations received more than half of the global aid on AIDS, the rest being distributed among countries in Asia, Latin America, and the Caribbean. The vast majority of funds allocated to AIDS research—estimated at over US-$3 billion in 1995—are spent by, in and for industrialized countries: the United States accounts for over 85 percent of this global total.

By 1995, there were clear signs that HIV was responding to effective prevention. In industrialized countries, as well as in certain populations in Africa and Southeast Asia, the incidence of HIV infection began to decline in communities which had appropriate access to information, education, diagnostic, and treatment services for other sexually transmitted diseases, and social support. However, the global HIV/AIDS pandemic was by no means under control in the mid-1990s and the demand for medical care for people living with HIV/AIDS in the developing world was skyrocketing, already overwhelming the coping capacity of most local health systems in Africa. Particularly vulnerable to HIV/AIDS were individuals and communities who are stigmatized and marginalized. Relevant factors in marginalizing people can include lower economic status, ethnicity, race, gender, sexual orientation, drug injecting behavior, and political or religious affiliation.

In the early 1990s, growing criticism was expressed by both industrialized and developing countries against the WHO/GPA for its insufficient effort on AIDS, in particular for its reluctance to broaden the scope of the response to the pandemic and to enroll the participation of other UN agencies. In January 1996, the Joint United Nations Programme on HIV/AIDS (UNAIDS), co-sponsored by six international agencies—WHO, the United Nations Development Programme (UNDP), the United Nations Children's Fund (UNICEF), the United Nations Population Fund (UNFPA), the United Nations Educational, Scientific and Cultural Organization (UNESCO), and the World Bank—was launched with the objective of expanding the world's response to HIV/AIDS through improved leadership and coordination, as well as through the promotion of a broader vision of HIV/AIDS as a combined health and human development issue. Provided the UNAIDS is able to surmount initial difficulties arising from the divergence of its six co-sponsors' institutional missions, structures, and styles, it may play a critical role in revitalizing the global response to HIV/AIDS, at a time when the demographic, economic, and social impacts of the pandemic begin to be felt at the macro level.

Since 1987 the United States government has maintained a policy of excluding foreigners wishing to travel or immigrate to this country if they are infected with (HIV). The vigorous condemnation of this policy by prestigious international health organizations and foreign governments spurred the U.S. Immigration and Naturalization Service to establish two waiver policies for short-term travelers to the United States. The first is a 30-day waiver that allows an infected person to enter the country to attend health conferences, conduct short-term business, visit family members, or seek medical treatment. Travelers applying for such a waiver must declare their HIV status. A separate 10-day waiver allows travelers into the country without declaring their HIV status if they are attending a conference designated in the public interest.

HIV-infected immigrants are barred outright and must submit to an HIV test before entering the United States. Exceptions may be made under certain circumstances. The basis for restricting HIV-positive people from the country is a clause in the Immigration and Nationality Act of 1952 which bans prospective immigrants or travelers who have a "communicable disease of public health significance." The U.S. Public Health Service (PHS), a branch of the Department of Health and Human Services, maintains the list of diseases covered by this clause. The list includes HIV, active tuberculosis, leprosy, infectious syphilis, gonorrhea, and three other treatable sexually transmitted diseases (STDs).

In 1990, PHS reevaluated the entire medical exclusions list and recommended eliminating everything except active tuberculosis, which is the only casually contagious disease on the list. By 1993, the Clinton administration seemed poised to accept the new PHS guidelines. However, Congress overwhelmingly passed a measure mandating that HIV remain on the medical exclusions list, overriding PHS's authority to regulate immigration policy for those infected with this disease.

In 1996 the United States was one of the countries of the world that applied entry restrictions on the basis of HIV status and/or banned the entry of prospective long-term residents who carry the virus.

DANIEL TARANTOLA
SARA FINKELSTEIN

See also Agency for International Development; Immigration; World Health Organization

FURTHER READING

Bayer, Ronald. *Private Acts, Social Consequences: AIDS and the Politics of Public Health.* New York, 1989.
De Vita, V., S. Hellman, and S. Rosenberg, eds. *AIDS: Etiology, Diagnosis, Treatment and Prevention,* 3rd ed. Philadelphia, Pa., 1992.
Jarvis, Robert, Michael Closen, Donald Hermann, and Arthur Leonard. *AIDS Law in a Nutshell.* Saint Paul, Minn., 1991.
Mann, J., Daniel Tarantola, and T. Netter, eds. *AIDS in the World,* vol. 1. Cambridge, Mass. and London, 1992.
———, and Daniel Tarantola, eds. *AIDS in the World,* vol. 2. New York and Oxford, Eng., 1996.

ADAMS, CHARLES FRANCIS

(*b.* 18 August 1807; *d.* 21 November 1886)

U.S. minister to Great Britain (1861–1868). As the grandson of the second U.S. president and son of the sixth,

Adams was immersed from birth in politics and international relations. After spending most of his childhood in Europe, Adams graduated from Harvard University (1825), studied law with Daniel Webster, spent five years in the Massachusetts legislature (1841–1845), and served a term in Congress (1859–1861). Shortly after Abraham Lincoln became president in 1861, Secretary of State William H. Seward persuaded him to designate Adams minister to Great Britain. Adams soon won the trust and ultimately the admiration of most of the political leaders of Great Britain as a forceful but reliable diplomat of strong intellect and great good sense.

During the American Civil War, Adams confronted a series of diplomatic challenges, any one of which, if mismanaged in London, might have erupted into an Anglo-American war. Among these were the *Trent* Affair in 1861, in which two Confederate commissioners traveling to Europe were taken by a Union navy ship, and crises in 1862 and 1863 involving the federal blockade and European recognition of the Confederacy. Adams relentlessly opposed the construction by the British of Confederate warships that devastated the American merchant fleet. His complaints eventually led the British government to impound or purchase three of the most formidable vessels destined for Confederate service: the *Alexandra* and two Laird rams. The documentation Adams accumulated on the shipbuilding issue led to the payment of substantial damages to the United States by Great Britain in 1872, following Adams's appointment in 1871 as the principal U.S. negotiator at the Geneva arbitration conference and his masterly presentation of his country's case before that tribunal. During the summer of 1872 liberal Republicans, hoping to deny reelection to President Ulysses S. Grant, sought to make Adams their presidential nominee, but he gave them little encouragement and retired to private life in Boston.

NORMAN B. FERRIS

See also Alabama Claims; American Civil War; Confederate States of America; Seward, William Henry; Trent Affair

FURTHER READING

Adams, Charles Francis, Jr. *Charles Francis Adams, 1807–1886, by His Son.* Boston, 1900. Reprinted. Edited by John T. Morse, Jr. Boston, 1972.

Duberman, Martin B. *Charles Francis Adams, 1807–1886.* Stanford, Calif., 1968.

Ford, Worthington C., ed. *A Cycle of Adams Letters, 1861–1865,* 2 vols. Boston, 1920.

ADAMS, JOHN

(*b.* 19 October 1735; *d.* 4 July 1826)

First vice president (1789–1797) and second president of the United States (1797–1801) following years of service as a lawyer, revolutionary leader, and diplomat. John Adams was descended from English Puritans who settled in Braintree, Massachusetts, in 1640. Graduating from Harvard College in 1755, Adams taught school and studied law in Worcester, Massachusetts. Returning to Braintree, Adams was admitted to the Massachusetts bar in the fall of 1758, and he rapidly became a prominent attorney. Adams played a significant role in the colonial struggle against Great Britain in the years prior to the American Revolution. He prepared Braintree's Instructions concerning the town's noncompliance with the Stamp Act (1765); he helped defend British soldiers accused of murder in the Boston Massacre of 5 March 1770; he served in the Massachusetts General Court (legislature); and as "Novanglus" he defended colonial rights against the mother country (1775). As a delegate to the First and Second Continental Congresses, Adams was instrumental in the selection of George Washington to command the United States' revolutionary forces and he served on the committee to draft the Declaration of Independence. On 12 June 1776, Adams, who was widely regarded as a leading expert on foreign affairs, was appointed to a committee to create a plan of treaties to be offered to foreign nations; and the Model Treaty of 1776 was largely his creation. In essence, the Model Treaty proposed opening U.S. commerce on an equal basis to all nations with the intent of avoiding "perpetual alliances" with any state or league of states.

Adams spent most of the years between 1778 and 1788 abroad. Late in 1777, the 42-year-old Adams, who was acutely self-conscious about his ignorance of France and its language, was appointed a commissioner to France (replacing Silas Deane). On 17 February 1778, Adams and his ten-year-old son, John Quincy, departed Marblehead, Massachusetts, for Louis XVI's France on what turned out to be an utterly fruitless journey. Well-meaning French citizens mistook him for his celebrated cousin, Sam Adams. "I was a man of whom nobody had ever heard before, a perfect cipher, a man who did not know a word of French; awkward in his figure—awkward in his dress—no abilities—a perfect bigot—and fanatic," he ruefully recorded. More important, Adams's mission had been made superfluous by the signing of the Franco-American Alliance of 6 February 1778. Another man might have traveled through Europe, but the indefatigable politician-turned-diplomat was cut from a different cloth. Equating idleness with sinfulness, he busied himself straightening out the tangled records of the mission (blaming Benjamin Franklin for the chaos); he observed the French close-up, happily realizing that they were not the Catholic devils he had feared; and he witnessed the bitter wrangling between fellow convoys Deane and Arthur Lee. Late in 1778 a chagrined Adams discovered that Franklin had been appointed sole U.S. representative to France. Adams, who had gone from being an admirer to jealous critic of the elderly Pennsylvanian, could not leave for the United States fast enough. Maddening delays followed one another so it was only early in August 1779 that he and John Quincy were on U.S. soil again.

A scant eight weeks later the Continental Congress chose Adams to be minister plenipotentiary to negotiate treaties of peace and commerce with Great Britain. Convinced that his position was the most significant of the war, Adams returned to Paris on 9 February 1780, via Spain and a winter crossing of the Pyrenees. Adams spent five and one-half months in the French capital sniping at Franklin and infuriating Charles Gravier, Comte de Vergennes, the French foreign minister. Adams concluded that France was putting its interest first and that Franklin had become a willing agent of the foreign power. Vergennes was dumbfounded by Adams's arrogance and was mystified by Adams's flouting of congressional instructions which ordered the New Englander to work in concert with the United States' French ally. By late June, Vergennes had grown weary of Adams.

At this juncture, 27 July 1780, Adams left Paris for what he hoped would be a friendlier venue, the Netherlands. Adams resided more than two years among the Dutch. Early enthusiasm and hope turned to criticisms and despair: the United Provinces, caught between two powerful neighbors (Great Britain and France) were divided politically and in no rush to recognize the United States or to loan significant sums to the U.S. rebels. Adams made his job more difficult by steadfastly shunning France's ambassador—though the French representative favored Dutch recognition of U.S. independence. Adams's despair may even have triggered a nervous breakdown in August 1781 that incapacitated him for months. In fact, the Netherlands only moved to admit Adams as a representative from the United States in April 1782, six months after the decisive Battle of Yorktown. A treaty of friendship and commerce followed on 8 October 1782.

An exultant Adams, crowing that he was the George Washington of negotiators, rushed to Paris to join John Jay and Franklin in negotiating a peace with Great Britain. Still suspicious of France and Franklin, Adams worked closely with Jay lest the French with Franklin's aid betray the United States. With both the British and the Americans disposed to peace, the two sides refused to let complicated and difficult issues—the Loyalists or prewar debts—block accord. Adams played a key role in the discussions; he protected New England fishing rights in the Gulf of St. Lawrence and the Grand Banks of Newfoundland. A preliminary treaty was signed on 30 November 1782; the definitive agreement (Treaty of Paris) was signed on 3 September 1783.

With peace won, Adams campaigned vigorously to become the first U.S. minister to Great Britain, and on 24 February 1785, Congress named Adams to the post. Adams presented his credentials to King George III on 1 June 1785, informing His Majesty of his desire to foster an Anglo-American rapprochement. Three years later a disappointed Adams left Great Britain with his goal unfulfilled. The British had reacted with incredulity to the appearance of a U.S. diplomat; they did not send an envoy of equal rank to the United States until 1791. Implementing the peace accords proved particularly arduous; the British would not surrender control of a string of posts on U.S. soil. They found it next to impossible to collect old debts in the United States. The hated Loyalists remained a thorn in Anglo-American relations, too, pestering officialdom in London and being greeted hostilely in the new nation. Americans expressed surprise and anger when the former mother country discriminated against U.S. shipping in the West Indies. Some Americans even believed that the British incited attacks on their vessels by the Barbary corsairs in the Mediterranean.

By the time Adams sailed for America, the old form of government—the Articles of Confederation—was being replaced by the Constitution, a change Adams favored. Indeed, Adams was chosen to be the nation's first vice president, spending eight years in that office. In George Washington's shadow and seldom consulted by the illustrious leader, Adams became disturbed by the insignificance of his position. Yet he cast twenty tiebreaking votes in the Senate and he became identified with the political faction called the Federalists that governed the United States and lent its name to the era from 1789 to 1801. Adams was too independent, too much a loner, to be, in Alexander Hamilton's words, a party man. Political sentiments were very much influenced by the French Revolution in the 1790s, and the conservative Adams had doubts about the great upheaval from the beginning. He worried about the Revolution's impact on the United States and he worried about an apocalyptic event domestically. Years later, for example, he recalled the turbulence surrounding citizen Edmond Genet's mission to curry French favor with the United States and he spoke erroneously of mobs numbering in the thousands rampaging through Philadelphia's streets intimidating the government.

The Presidential Years

France's revolution was over by the time John Adams took the reins of government from Washington's hands on 4 March 1797, but Franco-American relations stood as the central issue of Adams's presidency because of incidents associated with that historical event. Angered by its ally's acceptance of Jay's Treaty and U.S. commercial activities in the rebellious colony of Haiti, France had seized several hundred U.S. vessels in the West Indies in 1796–1797. The French had intrigued in the presidential campaign of 1796, promoting Thomas Jefferson's candidacy, and they had also refused to receive Charles Cotesworth Pinckney, Washington's last appointment to France. Adams, who wanted a peaceful resolution of outstanding issues between the two countries as well as termination of the two-decade-old alliance of 1778, named a three-man delegation to negotiate with the Directory, as the French government was called, though he was uncertain if the French would receive the trio. The three—Pinckney, Elbridge Gerry, and John Marshall—rendezvoused in Paris in October and immediately sought to open discussions. To their disgust, the French insisted upon money being advanced before official talks commenced, a demand the three Americans rejected. Rather than leaving, however, Gerry, Marshall, and Pinckney remained in Paris hoping for some kind of accommodation. Meanwhile, the despatch describing the failed October meeting reached the United States in early March 1798, and upon becoming public caused a firestorm of protest.

Adams stood at a crossroads in the middle of 1798. Basking in the popularity born of the intensely nationalistic response to the XYZ Affair, as the attempted shakedown of the U.S. envoys became known, Adams knew that war with the French would appease militant Federalists and probably assure a victory for the party's candidates in the 1798 elections. On the other hand, a considerable body of evidence existed that France wanted peace. For a time, Adams seemed to incline towards hostilities: he created the navy department; launched an ambitious ship construction program; expanded the army; and laid plans to augment regulars with a huge militia call-up in war. The Congress approved a series of measures popularly known as the Alien and Sedition Acts, measures designed to control the population in general and immigrants and aliens in particular. Finally, Congress scrapped the 1778 alliance. Adams refrained from requesting a declaration of war, however, and as evidence accumulated of France's desire to avoid conflict, chose to renew negotiations, nominating William Vans Murray, a Maryland Federalist and diplomat, to be minister to France. Murray's nomination in February 1799 enraged passionate Federalists who disagreed with Adams's decision. Trying to placate his critics, Adams asked two regular Federalists, Oliver Ellsworth and William R. Davie, to join Murray in France. Months passed before Davie and Ellsworth sailed. Meanwhile, the country grew restive because of the sharply increased tax burden necessitated by a doubling of the federal budget to pay for the defense buildup. Navigation problems and Napoleon's seizure of power further retarded Davie's and Ellsworth's arrival in Paris until 7 March. The two

and Murray found the French agreeable to negotiations, but progress hinged on the presence of Napoleon (designated the First Consul), and because the youthful French leader was absent for extended periods, it was only at the end of September 1800 that an accord styled the Convention of 1800 (or Convention of Mortefontaine) was signed to end the alliance with France.

In the United States, meanwhile, Adams had finally realized that two cabinet members, Timothy Pickering and James McHenry, had been working to undermine him politically. McHenry resigned without trouble. Pickering had to be dismissed. Thus Adams went into the 1800 presidential campaign the nominal leader of a fractured political party. In retrospect it is astonishing he ran such a close race in the contest with his erstwhile friend, Thomas Jefferson. Embittered in defeat, Adams appointed numerous Federalists to judicial posts (the "midnight appointments") and left the new capital of Washington before Jefferson's inaugural. It was Jefferson and his Republican followers who approved the Convention of 1800 that ended the Quasi-War with France.

John Adams lived another quarter century. He delighted in the political rise of John Quincy Adams. Like his son, he supported Jefferson's and Madison's foreign policies. He renewed his friendship with Jefferson. With the end of the War in 1812 and the demise of Federalism, Adams's stature rose steadily. He survived until the fiftieth anniversary of the Declaration of Independence.

CLIFFORD L. EGAN

See also Alien and Sedition Acts; Adams, John Quincy; American Revolution; Barbary States; Convention of 1800; Federalist Party; France; Franklin, Benjamin; French Revolution; Great Britain; Jay, John; Jay's Treaty; Jefferson, Thomas; Loyalists; Vergennes, Duc de; Washington, George; XYZ Affair

FURTHER READING

Brown, Ralph Adams. *The Presidency of John Adams*. Lawrence, Kans., 1975.

Ferling, John. *John Adams*. 1992.

Handler, Edward. *Europe and America in the Political Thought of John Adams*. Cambridge, Mass., 1964.

Haraszti, Zoltan. *John Adams and the Prophets of Progress*. Cambridge, Mass., 1952.

Hutson, James H. *John Adams and the Diplomacy of the American Revolution*. Lexington, Ky., 1980.

Shaw, Peter. *The Character of John Adams*. Chapel Hill, N.C., 1976.

Smith, Page. *John Adams*, 2 vols. Garden City, N.Y., 1962.

ADAMS, JOHN QUINCY

(*b.* 11 July 1767; *d.* 23 February 1848)

President of the United States (1825–1829) and generally acknowledged as one of the greatest secretaries of state in U.S. history. Adams served for six decades in a variety of important state, national, and international posts. Through an examination of his career, one can observe the evolution of early U.S. foreign policy. In the decades after the Treaty of Paris of 1783, the maintenance of independence, competition with Europe over the Western Hemisphere, freedom of the seas, commercial relations, territorial expansion, and the determination and security of international boundaries preoccupied the nation. By the time of Adams's death, slavery and its potential expansion had begun to dominate U.S. foreign policy. Although he was initially a vocal advocate of continental expansion, his enthusiasm waned by the 1830s, when the addition of new territory often could mean extending the area of slavery. The foreign policy principles Adams helped to identify and implement served as the foundation of U.S. foreign policy for most of the remainder of the nineteenth century and some even continued into the next century.

Adams was an arrogant and independent man. While his nominal affiliation with the Federalist, Republican, and Whig parties perhaps best exemplified this aspect of his character, it also manifested itself in his response to foreign and domestic issues. He frequently adopted positions at variance with many of his contemporaries. He also exhibited certain human frailties; occasionally, he manipulated information and events to further the interests of his country and his own political ambitions, but the anglophobic Adams trusted in the practice of diplomacy, even with the British.

Adams was born in Braintree (now Quincy), Massachusetts, to John and Abigail (Smith) Adams. As the first son of a renowned politician and of one of the most fascinating women of that generation, John Quincy Adams had a childhood uniquely suited for a diplomat-in-training. In 1778 he accompanied his father to Paris while he served as U.S. commissioner to France. During that stay and subsequent ones, John Quincy Adams was educated in several European academies and universities. Before his twentieth birthday he served as a personal secretary to Francis Dana, the U.S. minister to Russia, and to his father during the negotiations that produced the Treaty of Paris of 1783. John Quincy Adams later returned to the United States and entered Harvard College, graduating in 1787. He then studied law and was admitted to the bar in July 1790.

His interest in law never flourished; he was much better suited to politics and representing his country abroad. His knowledge of foreign languages, his familiarity with the capitals, leaders, and culture of Europe, and his education made him especially well qualified for a diplomatic career. In 1794 President George Washington recognized these special attributes and appointed Adams, still in his twenties, U.S. minister to the Netherlands. During

his father's term as president, Adams served in that same capacity in Prussia before returning to the United States in 1801. During his tenure in the latter post he negotiated a new treaty of amity and commerce (1799) with the Prussian government. After being defeated in his bid to represent Massachusetts in the House of Representatives, Adams was elected to the state senate (1802) and later to the U.S. Senate.

While in the Senate (1803–1808), Adams struggled with major foreign policy issues, including the Louisiana Purchase of 1803. Although Adams did not reach the capital in time to vote on the purchase itself, he generally supported the administration of President Thomas Jefferson in subsequent votes to implement the purchase. Adams did, however, have some reservations. For example, he favored the passage of a constitutional amendment that would have empowered Congress to extend citizenship to and pass laws for the inhabitants of any territory purchased by the United States. He also believed that the United States could not constitute a government for the inhabitants of the Louisiana Territory without their consent. To the extent that he approved of the purchase, Adams was the sole New England Federalist in either house of Congress to back the Jefferson administration on this issue.

Adams's subsequent support of Jefferson's economic sanctions against the British, including the Embargo Act of 1807, further alienated him from Massachusetts Federalists. Perhaps sensing the decline of that party, Adams cooperated with the Republicans on some occasions, apparently placing national interests above party loyalty. Federalists in Massachusetts then forced him to resign his Senate seat in June 1808 by selecting his successor before the end of Adams's term.

In 1809 President James Madison appointed Adams minister to Russia. Adams spent the next eight years observing and reporting on the remarkable events in Europe. He was in Russia when Napoleon attacked that country and in Paris in 1815 when Napoleon returned during the Hundred Days. He also served as the head of the U.S. delegation appointed to negotiate an end to the War of 1812. During these deliberations at Ghent, Belgium, Adams had the first of several clashes with Henry Clay—another emerging force in U.S. politics. The most obvious difference between the men was in their lifestyles. A studious and introspective man, Adams was unlike Clay, who was more apt to enjoy the social occasions available during their stay in Ghent. They also frequently differed on important policy issues. One such example was Adams's willingness to allow British navigation of the Mississippi River in return for the right of U.S. citizens to fish and dry their catch along the Atlantic coast of Canada. This was the type of concession that angered westerners such as Clay but was important to

New Englanders. The Treaty of Ghent, signed by representatives of the United States and Great Britain on 24 December 1814, established relations between the two countries on the basis of the status quo antebellum. In the treaty the British promised to withdraw from U.S. territory they had occupied during the war. Both nations also agreed to try to resolve their remaining disputes by specially constituted commissions. This solution provided the foundation for an extended period of cordial relations between the United States and Great Britain.

After the negotiation of the Treaty of Ghent in 1814, Adams's next diplomatic appointment was as U.S. minister to Great Britain. During his tenure at the Court of St. James's, Adams promoted improved relations between the United States and Great Britain as those two countries peacefully resolved some of the outstanding issues that had troubled their earlier relations. These successes included a commercial treaty negotiated by Adams (the Convention of 1815), which prohibited the placement of discriminatory duties on either country's commerce and opened several ports in the East Indies to U.S. trade. Although Great Britain was at this time unwilling to grant the United States direct commercial access to all British colonies worldwide, the prohibition on discriminatory duties was a significant achievement, and the United States and other nations used it as a model for subsequent treaties. Adams also pushed to completion a treaty that reduced U.S. and British naval strength on the Great Lakes and Lake Champlain (the Rush-Bagot Agreement of 1817), and a treaty that identified the boundary between the United States and Canada from the Lake of the Woods westward to the crest of the Rockies and allowed for the joint occupation of the Oregon Territory (the Convention of 1818).

Secretary of State, 1817–1825

Upon his election to the presidency in 1816, James Monroe invited John Quincy Adams to return to the United States and join his cabinet as secretary of state. Few men have been as well prepared to assume that responsibility. Adams's appointment marked the culmination of his career in foreign relations and offered the possibility of even higher political office (Thomas Jefferson, James Madison, and James Monroe all had been secretary of state before being elected president). During his tenure as secretary of state, Adams reorganized the State Department. Upon his arrival in Washington in 1817, he found that office in considerable disarray. He instituted several changes that included the establishment of an index and register of all correspondence, the creation of a departmental library, and the drafting of standard instructions to all new diplomatic appointees. He also ended the practice of U.S. diplomats accepting gifts from the countries to which they were accredited. Adams

believed that this custom was contrary to the best interests of the United States and was unconstitutional.

Perhaps the most pressing foreign policy issue facing the country when Adams was appointed secretary of state was the resolution of several territorial disputes with Spain. The Spanish had never recognized the U.S. purchase of the Louisiana Territory; Spain in 1800 had retroceded the territory to the French with the assurance that it would never be sold to any other country. Other outstanding issues included the determination of the boundaries of the Louisiana Territory and the status of East and West Florida. As Spanish control in the Floridas weakened, marauding Indians and runaway slaves used this area as a safe haven after crossing the border and attacking settlements in the United States. In 1812 the United States annexed most of West Florida and, during the War of 1812, seized East Florida only to return it to Spain after the war.

Realizing that its control of the Floridas and its other colonial possessions in the New World was tenuous, and facing isolation in Europe, the Spanish government initiated negotiations on all these outstanding issues with the United States. The Spanish minister to the United States, Luis de Onís, initially proposed a very restricted definition of the territorial extent of the Louisiana Territory. During the winter of 1817–1818, Onís made several concessions that gradually moved the western border of the territory farther to the west, and he agreed to the cession of the Floridas to the United States. Adams introduced a new and important element into the negotiations in July 1818, when he suggested that the two countries agree on a boundary that extended all the way to the Pacific Ocean. Prior to this suggestion even Adams had limited the territorial claims of the United States to the front range of the Rocky Mountains. This was a notable departure from the previous stance of both countries because it suggested a transcontinental boundary that would significantly strengthen U.S. claims to territory in the Pacific Northwest and would ultimately facilitate the expansion of trade relations with Asia.

Onís recognized the weakness of his government's position; by this time, the United States controlled both East and West Florida, and there did not seem to be any interest among the other European powers in supporting the Spanish. In addition, Onís feared that, if frustrated by these negotiations, the United States might assume a more aggressive policy in defense of the independence movements among the Spanish colonies in Latin America. Limited by his instructions, Onís stalled and made no further concessions. Disheartened by the lack of progress in its negotiations, the Monroe administration increased its pressure on the Spanish government. Adams's primary weapon was the threat that the United States would rescind its neutrality policy toward the emerging South

American republics and recognize or even aid them. Several other events then occurred that further strengthened the position of the United States. A new government in Spain recognized that it would have to make concessions to forestall the seizure of additional Spanish territory by the United States and a more sympathetic policy toward South America. The threat of territorial aggression seemed more plausible when, in early 1819, the U.S. Congress refused to censure Andrew Jackson for his incursion into East and West Florida. Coincidentally, the United States and Great Britain agreed to the Convention of 1818. Aware that the United States had, therefore, strengthened its title to the Pacific coast, the Spanish were now less hesitant to cede their claims in the area.

Confronting these obstacles, the Spanish government made further concessions, and by February 1819 Adams and Onís signed the Adams-Onís Treaty (also known as the Transcontinental Treaty) of 1819. Under the provisions of that agreement, Spain recognized U.S. control of West Florida and the United States returned East Florida to the Spanish, who then immediately ceded it back. In addition, the treaty identified a boundary between the U.S. and Spanish territory in the Southwest that extended from the Sabine River in the Gulf of Mexico to the intersection of the 42nd parallel and the Pacific Ocean. In return, the United States agreed to pay up to $5 million of claims by its citizens against Spain. Although most contemporaries emphasized the significance of the cession of the Floridas, in retrospect, Adams's major achievement was the establishment of a transcontinental boundary. Critics did, however, fault Monroe and Adams for failing to secure control of Texas. The administration had, in effect, traded the U.S. claim to Texas for Spanish territorial claims north of the 42nd parallel.

During the negotiations between Adams and Onís, related events occurred that threatened a swift resolution of the territorial issues dividing the two countries. The most troubling was General Andrew Jackson's invasion of East and West Florida in 1818. His action had been a blatant display of military aggression against a weakened European power. Although there was some question about whether President Monroe's administration had sanctioned Jackson's incursion in advance, Adams was the general's lone defender in the cabinet. The secretary of state wanted to ensure that the invasion of Florida did not jeopardize his negotiations with Onís. It was during the debate over Jackson's invasion that Adams demonstrated his commitment to territorial expansion and whatever tactics were necessary to achieve it.

In a dispatch addressed to George Erving, the U.S. minister to Spain, Adams aggressively defended Jackson specifically and territorial expansionism by the United States generally. At times basing his argument more on fiction than on fact, Adams argued that British influence in

Florida posed a significant threat to the United States. Adams, therefore, justified the invasion of Florida, seizure of Spanish territory, and execution of British subjects. Instead of suggesting that the Monroe administration punish Jackson, Adams demanded that the Spanish government discipline its colonial officials in Florida. The Erving dispatch suggests that Adams would do whatever was necessary to further the foreign policy interests of his country and his own political ambitions. Adams was aware of the incongruity of his conduct; his diary entries during this period reveal his anxiety about manipulating the facts to justify the actions of his country.

During the negotiations with Onís, Adams also had to temper U.S. public opinion on the revolutions in the Spanish colonies in Latin America. There was considerable sympathy in the United States with these revolutionaries; in a situation similar to that in the United States several decades earlier, these revolutionaries were attempting to end their colonial status by establishing their independence from a European power. Some in the United States, such as Henry Clay (now a member of the House of Representatives from Kentucky), insisted that the Monroe administration support the revolutionaries by recognizing the new republics and appointing diplomatic representatives.

Adams realized that any policy other than neutrality might jeopardize his negotiations with Onís. There were also other reasons to delay. Adams had some reservations about the abilities of the new South American republics to emulate the governmental model of the United States. In addition, he rejected the notion, popular with many of his contemporaries, that the United States should serve as more than just a passive model of the virtues of republicanism. He consequently attempted to influence public opinion in the United States and undermine Clay's popularity through a series of anonymous letters to the *National Intelligencer* written under the pseudonym "Phocion."

As he did again later in his dispatch to Erving, Adams manipulated the facts to achieve the result he endorsed. To reduce public support for the South American revolutionaries, the secretary of state offered several reasons why the United States should remain neutral. First, he argued that there were few similarities between those rebellions and the United States' own war for independence. He predicted that the South American revolutions would fail. He also hinted that the British hoped that the United States would interfere. Aware that there was still considerable anti-British sentiment as a result of the War of 1812, Adams anticipated that public opinion in the United States would reject any policy proposed by the British. Moreover, he exploited the racism of the era and southern paranoia about potential slave revolts by informing the readers of the *National Intelligencer* that many of the South American revolutionaries were black.

Only after signing the Transcontinental Treaty did Adams willingly accept a less cautious policy in support of the South American republics. At first, however, the Monroe administration remained neutral; most of the former Spanish colonies had not yet solidified their independence or ensured domestic stability. By 1822 conditions had improved significantly and the United States recognized several of the new republics. As the policies of Adams and Clay now began to coincide, the rift between them narrowed.

The Monroe Doctrine

The threat of possible European intervention to reestablish Spanish control over its former colonies was not the only foreign policy crisis confronting the Monroe administration in the early 1820s. There were also indications that both Great Britain and Russia intended to establish new colonies in the Western Hemisphere. In his December 1823 annual message, President Monroe pledged that the United States would not intervene in European affairs and demanded that Europeans not intervene in the internal affairs of the Western Hemisphere. In addition, Monroe warned that the United States would oppose the creation of any new European colonies in the New World. As secretary of state, Adams was instrumental in helping to formulate the principles enunciated in the Monroe Doctrine. Fearful that the Holy Alliance (Russia, Austria, and Prussia) might attempt to reassert European control over the former Spanish colonies, George Canning, the British foreign minister, suggested to the Monroe administration that the United States and Great Britain jointly declare their opposition to such an eventuality. Most members of the Monroe cabinet and former presidents Jefferson and Madison urged Monroe to accept the Canning proposal, believing that it would help guarantee the independence of the South American republics and deter any action on the part of the Holy Alliance. In addition, the United States would benefit by cooperating with the one nation—Great Britain—that posed the greatest threat to its independence.

Adams resisted these arguments. Concerned that his country do nothing that would jeopardize its ability to act independently, he maintained that the United States should never subordinate itself to Great Britain or interfere in any way in the internal affairs of Europe. Instead, he advocated a policy of neutrality and isolation from the political and military affairs of Europe. He also argued that the British insistence that both countries deny any intent of acquiring territory in the Spanish colonial empire in the New World would impede the territorial ambitions of the United States for, at least, Cuba and Texas.

Adams suggested that the United States issue a unilateral proclamation that considered not only the potential threat to the former Spanish colonies, but also the possibility of renewed European colonization in the Western Hemisphere. The latter principle was in response to British activity in the Northwest and interest in Cuba and a recent Russian proclamation. In 1821 the Russian government claimed territory southward along the Pacific coast down to the 51st parallel and denied all naval vessels access to these waters for 100 miles off the coast. Arguing that there was little reason to fear intervention by the Holy Alliance and that the interests of Great Britain and the United States were identical, Adams believed that the Monroe administration could unilaterally issue a proclamation that would pose no danger to itself and that British naval power would enforce. Adams successfully persuaded Monroe and the president incorporated these ideas in his 1823 annual message.

Another manifestation of Adams's belief in the importance of the separation of spheres arose over the issue of Greek independence. As early as 1821 the inhabitants of what is today modern Greece began to fight for their independence from the Ottoman Empire. As had been the case with the South American revolutionaries, there was considerable sympathy in the United States for the Greek efforts. Some in the United States wanted to recognize the newly proclaimed Greek government and appoint a diplomatic representative or possibly aid the revolutionaries in an even more direct manner. Adams, however, counseled delay. Just as he had insisted that Europeans not interfere in the internal affairs of the Western Hemisphere, he maintained that the United States should not interfere in European internal affairs. Given that the Greek revolt occurred simultaneously with the insistence by the United States that the Holy Alliance not intervene to reassert European control over the former Spanish colonies in South America, Adams believed it inappropriate for the United States to take any action on behalf of the Greeks.

This legacy of John Quincy Adams was rediscovered in the late twentieth century by those who admired his support of self-government, opposition to slavery, and commitment to human rights without regard to race. Others embraced his philosophy as an argument against intervention abroad, especially in Vietnam. One passage in particular—from his famous Fourth of July address in 1821—is often quoted: "Wherever the standard of freedom and independence has been or shall be unfurled, there will her [America's] heart, her benedictions, and her prayers be. But she goes not abroad in search of monsters to destroy. She is the well-wisher to the freedom and independence of all—she is the champion and vindicator only of her own."

President of the United States, 1825–1829

As the end of President Monroe's second term approached, many politicians, including Adams, hoped to become the next president of the United States. The demise of the Federalist party and the factionalization of the Republican party ensured that the Republicans would be unable to agree on a candidate. The leading candidates, both within and outside the Monroe administration, had spent years maneuvering and advocating positions to enhance their chances in the presidential election of 1824. When none of the four candidates—Adams, Clay, William Crawford, and Jackson—achieved a majority in the electoral college, the House of Representatives determined the election. Although Jackson had received the greatest number of electoral votes and the highest percentage of the popular vote, the House elected Adams to be the sixth president of the United States. The nature of the election, the disappointment of Jackson's supporters, and rumors of a bargain between Adams and Clay (arising because Adams appointed Clay secretary of state) did not bode well for the Adams presidency.

Although the major focus of Adams's one term as president was domestic affairs, he did preside during the Panama Congress, a conference called by South American leaders to devise a plan for the defense of the Western Hemisphere against any European attempt to reestablish control over the former Spanish colonies. Adams hoped that a delegation representing the United States would observe the proceedings and promote commercial relations with the emerging South American nations based on the principle of free ships, free goods. Domestic opponents of the administration used the appointment of the delegation as an opportunity to express their displeasure with Adams. Many in the United States opposed sending representatives to the Panama Congress because they believed that their government should adhere to Washington's admonition about entangling alliances. Southerners, in particular, grew apprehensive about the inclusion of such agenda items as the abolition of the slave trade. Although the Senate ultimately approved the appointment of a two-person delegation, various delays ensued and the United States never fully participated in the proceedings.

Later Career

After his presidency, Adams did not retire permanently to the solitude of Massachusetts as his father had done. Instead, after a brief respite, he returned to public life as a member of the House of Representatives from Massachusetts. Reelected eight times, he served in that capacity from 1831 until his death in 1848. A major foreign policy issue faced by Adams during his tenure as a member of the House was the Jackson administration's attempt to annex Texas. Increasingly worried about the expansion of slavery, Adams adopted a far less aggressive position on territorial expansion than he had as secretary of state or president. Although not an abolitionist, Adams consistently opposed expanding the area of slavery beyond where it already existed. If Texas was able to establish its independence from Mexico, Adams suspected that southerners would then reintroduce slavery there and divide the area into several slave states before requesting admission into the Union. He again challenged the notion that the Constitution granted authority to either Congress or the president to annex the territory of another country. As the Constitution did not specifically delegate that power to either the executive or the legislative branch, it must, therefore, be a power reserved to the people. If the Jackson administration insisted on annexing Texas, Adams urged his fellow citizens "to resist."

Adams demonstrated his antislavery position in two later incidents involving the slave trade. The first concerned a Spanish ship named the *Amistad*. In 1839, after successfully overthrowing the ship's crew, the slaves on board gained control of the *Amistad* in the Caribbean and, probably because of the prevailing current in the Gulf Stream, landed in New York City. There, government officials seized the ship and detained the slaves; in time, the Spanish government petitioned for the return of the slaves under the provisions of Pinckney's Treaty of 1795. Adams subsequently represented the slaves and argued for their release before the U.S. Supreme Court. Although the court freed the blacks on a technicality unrelated to Adams's human rights arguments, he had introduced important issues before the U.S. public that would intensify in succeeding years. Private funds eventually facilitated the return of the blacks to Africa. A similar case involved the *Creole*, another slave ship, which was taken over by slaves in 1841. After the mutiny the *Creole* landed in Nassau in the Bahamas, where British authorities freed the slaves. At the time Adams was the chair of the House Foreign Affairs Committee, and the divisive issue of the *Creole* affair split the committee along sectional lines and hindered Adams's effectiveness. Despite his extensive experience and expertise in foreign relations, Adams was not reappointed as chair during the next session. His position on these two cases and his repeated attempts to rescind the gag rule—a parliamentary practice during the 1830s and 1840s that precluded debate of antislavery petitions—established his reputation as an outspoken antislavery advocate in the House of Representatives.

Adams's changing attitudes toward territorial expansion became evident during the period of Manifest Destiny in the 1840s. His opposition to the expansion of slavery made him one of the most ardent and consistent critics of the administrations of Presidents John Tyler and James K. Polk on the proposed annexation of Texas and the conduct of the War with Mexico. Adams did, however, promote Polk's attempt at commercial expansion into the Pacific. Adams was, therefore, an ardent supporter of the annexation of "All Oregon." In this instance, he enthusiastically supported President Polk's confrontation with Great Britain over the Oregon Territory. Adams's opposition to the annexation of Texas and call for all of Oregon were not the inconsistencies of an elder statesman. For Adams the crucial difference was the status of slavery in the two areas. Annexation of the Oregon Territory by the United States would not expand the area of slavery because no one at the time anticipated that slavery would thrive in the Oregon Territory. In addition, Oregon's coast was essential to the expansion of commercial opportunities for the United States in the Pacific and Asia. Adams's support for all of Oregon reflected his earlier dream of a commercial empire for the United States.

Adams continued to serve in the House through the 1840s. In November 1846 he suffered a stroke, but recovered and returned to his seat in Congress. On 21 February 1848 Adams suffered a second stroke and died two days later.

RICHARD C. ROHRS

See also Adams-Onís Treaty; Amistad Affair; Creole Affair; Ghent, Treaty of; Great Britain; Greece; Latin America; Louisiana Purchase; Manifest Destiny; Mexico, War with; Monroe, James; Monroe Doctrine; Napoleonic Wars; Oregon Question; Rush-Bagot Agreement; Russia and the Soviet Union; Slave Trade and Slavery; Spain; War of 1812

FURTHER READING

Bemis, Samuel Flagg. *John Quincy Adams and the Foundations of American Foreign Policy*. New York, 1949.
———. *John Quincy Adams and the Union*. New York, 1956.
Brooks, Philip Coolidge. *Diplomacy and the Borderlands: The Adams-Onís Treaty of 1819*. Berkeley, Calif., 1939.
Hargreaves, Mary W. M. *The Presidency of John Quincy Adams*. Lawrence, Kans., 1985.
Hecht, Marie B. *John Quincy Adams: A Personal History of an Independent Man*. New York, 1972.
Jones, Howard. *Mutiny on the Amistad: The Saga of a Slave Revolt and Its Impact on American Abolition, Law, and Diplomacy*. New York, 1987.
May, Ernest R. *The Making of the Monroe Doctrine*. Cambridge, Mass., 1975.
Perkins, Bradford. *Castlereagh and Adams: England and the United States, 1812–1823*. Berkeley, Calif., 1964.
———. *The Creation of a Republican Empire, 1776–1865*. New York, 1993. Vol. 1 of Warren I. Cohen, ed., *The Cambridge History of American Foreign Relations*, 4 vols. New York, 1993.
Perkins, Dexter. *The Monroe Doctrine, 1823–1826*. Cambridge, Mass., 1927.
Richards, Leonard L. *The Life and Times of Congressman John Quincy Adams*. New York, 1986.
Russell, Greg. *John Quincy Adams and the Public Virtues of Diplomacy*. Columbia, Mo., 1995.
Weeks, William Earl. *John Quincy Adams: American Global Empire*. Lexington, Ky., 1992.

ADAMS-ONÍS TREATY

(1819)

Also known as the Transcontinental Treaty, was a significant triumph for Secretary of State John Quincy Adams

and the administration of President James Monroe because it resolved several territorial disputes between the United States and Spain. The acquisition of the Louisiana Territory from France in 1803 had imperiled relations between the United States and Spain. What was the boundary to be between the United States and Spanish territory in the Southwest? Did the Louisiana Territory include Texas and West Florida? Would Spain recognize the purchase? The Spanish rejected the earlier attempts of Presidents Thomas Jefferson and James Madison to settle these issues. The annexation of West Florida by the United States in 1812, the invasion of East Florida by U.S. troops under the command of Andrew Jackson in 1818, and revolts by Latin American revolutionaries against Spain's colonial rule in the New World forced the Spanish government to seek a peaceful settlement. Negotiations between Adams and Luis de Onís, Spanish minister to the United States, resulted in a treaty signed in February 1819, in which the United States returned East Florida to Spain, which then ceded it back, and Spain acknowledged U.S. control of West Florida. The treaty also identified the boundary between the United States and Spanish territory from the mouth of the Sabine River in the Gulf of Mexico northwestward to the 42nd parallel on the Pacific Coast. In return the United States agreed to assume claims of its citizens against Spain up to $5 million. Although the exclusion of Texas from U.S. jurisdiction caused difficulties for subsequent administrations, the willingness of Spain to abandon its claims to the Pacific Northwest strengthened the U.S. position in later negotiations with England on the Oregon Territory.

RICHARD C. ROHRS

See also Adams, John Quincy; Florida; Louisiana Purchase

FURTHER READING

Bemis, Samuel Flagg. *John Quincy Adams and the Foundations of American Foreign Policy*. New York, 1949.
Brooks, Philip Coolidge. *Diplomacy and the Borderlands: The Adams-Onís Treaty of 1819*. Berkeley, Calif., 1939.
Weeks, William Earl. *John Quincy Adams: American Global Empire*. Lexington, Ky., 1992.

ADDAMS, JANE

(*b.* 6 September 1860; *d.* 21 May 1935)

Social reformer, pacifist-feminist, Nobel Peace Prize recipient. Born into an upper-middle-class, politically active Illinois family, Addams enjoyed a privileged upbringing and education, receiving a B.A. from Rockford Seminary in 1881, but a chronic condition caused by childhood spinal tuberculosis disrupted her medical studies. While on a European trip in 1887–1888, she and a friend, Ellen Gates Starr, made plans to replicate Toynbee Hall, a London settlement house, in the United States, and in February 1889 the two women opened Hull House in Chicago. Hull House made Addams famous. The settlement boasted an array of clubs and functions, a day nursery, a gymnasium, and a cooperative boarding house for single working women. Addams's experiences at the settlement house turned her toward pacifism. Having observed how people from disparate ethnic groups could learn to cooperate and to build a caring and peaceful community, Addams came to believe that international relations could work the same way. In particular, she identified poverty, starvation, unemployment, and homelessness as the causes of conflict. If such conditions could be alleviated, she believed, war would cease to exist. Addams expressed these ideas in such works as *Democracy and Social Ethics* (1902), *The Newer Ideals of Peace* (1907), and *Peace and Bread in Time of War* (1922).

In 1915 Addams and other woman suffragists formed the Woman's Peace Party, the U.S. Section of the International Committee of Women for Permanent Peace, which had been founded in The Hague that same year to push for an end to World War I. Addams traveled throughout Europe to speak with national leaders and then returned to the United States, where between July and December 1915 she met with President Woodrow Wilson six times. When the United States finally entered the war, Addams volunteered to work for Herbert Hoover's federal Department of Food Administration. The U.S. government and prowar patriots harassed Addams for her antiwar views. The Woman's Peace Party office in Chicago was vandalized repeatedly. In 1919, the year the Woman's Peace Party became the U.S. Section of the Women's International League for Peace and Freedom (WILPF), an international organization of pacifist women, Addams's name appeared on the Overman Senate Subcommittee's list of dangerous citizens (nicknamed by the press the "Who's Who of Pacifists and Radicals"), in the 1920 Lusk Committee Report of New York State on Revolutionary Radicalism, and on the 1923 War Department's "Spider Web Chart." Because of such publicity, Addams's membership in the Daughters of the American Revolution was terminated, and she was blacklisted from many speaking engagements. Between 1919 and 1935 Addams continued her work on behalf of both Hull House and WILPF. She traveled around the world to speak on peace and attempted to combat conservatism at home by helping to found the American Civil Liberties Union (ACLU) in 1920. As the U.S. political climate became less restrictive, she returned to a position of respect. In 1931 she received the Nobel Peace Prize in recognition of her work as a humanitarian and a pacifist; in 1932, in a poll

taken by the National Council of Women, she was ranked second among the twelve U.S. women named as the greatest in the twentieth century.

HARRIET HYMAN ALONSO

See also Peace Movements and Societies, 1914 to Present; Wilson, Thomas Woodrow; Women, War, Peace, and Foreign Relations; World War I

FURTHER READING

Addams, Jane. *Twenty Years at Hull-House*. New York, 1910; reprinted, New York, 1981.
———, Emily Greene Balch, and Alice Hamilton. *Women at The Hague: The International Congress of Women and Its Results*. New York, 1915.
Davis, Allen F. *American Heroine: The Life and Legend of Jane Addams*. New York, 1973.

ADENAUER, KONRAD

(*b.* 5 January 1876; *d.* 19 April 1967)

First chancellor of the Federal Republic of Germany (1949–1963) and architect of West Germany's membership in the North Atlantic Treaty Organization (NATO) and the European Community. A devout Catholic from the Rhineland, Adenauer served as the mayor of Cologne from 1917 to 1933, when he was dismissed by the Nazis. After World War II he cofounded the conservative Christian Democratic Union (CDU) in 1945 and was its president from 1946 to 1966. He won a narrow victory for chancellor in 1949, the first postwar election. Throughout his career as chancellor, Adenauer suffered from his "Potsdam nightmare," the fear that the West and the Soviet Union would negotiate agreements at the expense of West Germany. For this reason Adenauer sought to end Germany's isolation through an unreserved commitment to alliance with the United States and European integration. Critics charged that he abandoned the goal of German reunification, but Adenauer argued that he would reach this objective through a "policy of strength" with the West. In cooperation with U.S. High Commissioner John J. McCloy, in the early 1950s Adenauer supported such initiatives as the Schuman Plan, which led to the establishment of the European Coal and Steel Community, and the failed European Defense Community, which was designed to merge the armed forces of France and Germany. These policies, along with Germany's rapid economic revival, resulted in an impressive electoral triumph for the CDU in 1953. Adenauer's success in steering Germany in a pro-Western and democratic direction led to NATO membership and a restored sovereignty in May 1955.

During most of President Dwight D. Eisenhower's administration, Adenauer enjoyed considerable prestige and influence in Washington. He shared a strong religious and anticommunist perspective with Secretary of State John Foster Dulles, along with an opposition to negotiations with the Soviet Union. Increasing Soviet pressure on the Berlin question, however, beginning in November 1958, coupled with the death of Dulles in May 1959, led Adenauer to detect correctly a weakening of U.S. support for his policy and an increasing U.S. interest in negotiations with the Soviet Union. He then aligned himself with French President Charles de Gaulle, a critic of U.S. alliance policy. Relations between Adenauer and President John F. Kennedy were strained by the Soviet and East German construction of the Berlin Wall in August 1961, which put an end to German hopes for an early reunification of the country and led to the loss of the parliamentary majority for Adenauer's CDU in the September 1961 elections. Adenauer was forced by his political opponents to resign halfway through his term in October 1963.

THOMAS A. SCHWARTZ

See also Berlin; European Defense Community; Germany; McCloy, John Jay; North Atlantic Treaty Organization; Schuman, Robert

FURTHER READING

Adenauer, Konrad. *Memoirs 1945–1953*, translated by Beate Ruhm von Oppen. Chicago, 1966.
Ninkovich, Frank. *Germany and the United States: The Transformation of the German Question Since 1945*. New York, 1994.
Schwartz, Thomas Alan. *America's Germany: John J. McCloy and the Federal Republic of Germany*. Cambridge, Mass., 1991.

AEROSPACE

The multibillion-dollar global industry that develops and produces commercial and military aircraft and spacecraft. The aerospace industry is of great importance in contemporary foreign affairs. Aerospace technology has vital military applications in military aviation, rocketry, space satellites, and space weaponry. In addition, large industrialized nations feel a need to have a presence in the civilian aerospace industry because of its high-wage jobs, revenues, profits, and export receipts; the aerospace industry generated $40 billion in annual export revenues in the United States in the early 1990s (one aerospace firm, Boeing, is the largest single earner of export revenues). Some underlying technologies in aerospace are generic technologies that have applications outside of the aerospace complex, including, for example, the development of Plexiglas for aircraft cockpits, charge-coupled devices (CCDs) for digital imaging, solar cells and solar arrays, advanced radars, and new composite materials. The use of satellites for earth observation and broadcasting of data and video images makes the satellite and launcher industries important for an increasingly wide range of economic activities. The next generation of low-orbiting satellites promises to turn the earth into a single cellular telephone market.

The aircraft industry accounts for a large part of the aerospace industry's total revenues and employment. It is particularly vulnerable to strategic trade policies because of the high research and development (R&D) costs required for the invention of new aircraft and because of the steep learning curves in their subsequent production. A commercial aircraft company developing a new wide-body jet, for example, may have to sell seventy aircraft or more at a loss before breaking even. But once the break-even point has been attained, profits are typically quite high. There is substantial risk, however, that a particular new aircraft will not meet the needs of purchasers and that the company will never make a profit on its substantial investment, sometimes reaching billions of dollars. Military aircraft manufacturers face similar economic requirements. It has been estimated that from 1972 to 1988, General Dynamics spent somewhere between $5 and $7 billion to develop and improve the F-16, at least half of which went into the electronics (called "avionics" in the aircraft industry) for the plane. Such large and risky investments are not likely to be made without assurances that there will be, in the end, a big customer like the U.S. government.

One reason the commercial aircraft industry is of considerable interest to governments is that many aircraft, with the exception of supersonic fighters and the like, are dual-use products utilizing dual-use technologies. (The term "dual-use" means that the product or technology can have either military or civilian applications.) A jet engine, for example, can be used in either a military or a civilian aircraft. A missile can be used to carry either civilian communications satellites or nuclear warheads into space. In the past, there has been considerable "spin-off" from military technologies to civilian ones because there were many military technologies that could be applied to commercial products. The early commercial airline industry was made possible because of investments by the military and the U.S. Postal Service in aircraft technology for the military and other governmental uses, and the turbofan engine that is used for commercial wide-body jet aircraft was developed initially for military transports.

Spin-off may be limited, however, by the exotic and highly expensive nature of new military technologies—it is not likely that a commercial aircraft needs to have "stealth" radar profiles or special radar-absorbing coatings. As a result, attention has increasingly been paid to the opportunities for "spin-on" applications from civilian to military technologies. A good example of spin-on is the current ability of military products to take advantage of greatly improved performance and lower unit costs of microelectronic circuits built mainly for civilian applications. Because of increased concern about spin-on, many members of the defense community no longer consider it sufficient simply to maintain defense-oriented industries by subsidizing R&D and products for military weapons systems. Increasingly, these individuals are willing to provide governmental support to civilian industries where dual-use products and technologies are created, arguing that the United States would otherwise be less able to afford needed high-technology weapons systems. This issue was a topic of rather heated debates during the 1992 presidential election campaign, in which the administration of President George Bush defended its policies of supporting only military-use technologies, while Bill Clinton's forces argued for stronger support of dual-use technologies.

Global Aerospace Production

World sales of aircraft totaled $220 billion in 1990. Military aircraft accounted for 70 percent of global sales in that year, civilian aircraft for only 30 percent. U.S. shipments of aerospace products peaked at over $133.6 billion in 1992 but were projected to decline to $101.9 billion in 1994. Shipments of complete aircraft totaled $41.8 billion in 1992: $30.3 billion in civilian large transports, $1.8 billion in civilian general aviation, $0.1 billion in civilian rotocraft, and $9.6 billion in military aircraft. In 1992, shipments of aircraft engines totaled $24.1 billion, aircraft parts and equipment shipments were $23.3 billion, guided missiles and space vehicle shipments were $22.1 billion, space propulsion units and parts were $3.5 billion, and space vehicle equipment shipments were $1.8 billion. Demand for large transports and military aircraft, a substantial chunk of the total demand for aerospace products, was projected to drop sharply in 1993 and 1994, while demand for other aerospace products were projected to be flat or increasing.

The ten largest companies in aerospace by revenue in 1992 were Boeing, McDonnell-Douglas, General Electric, Rockwell, United Technologies, British Aerospace, General Dynamics, Lockheed, Deutsche Aerospace, and Airbus Industrie. Of these, only British Aerospace, Deutsche Aerospace and Airbus Industrie were not U.S. firms. The U.S. aerospace industry has traditionally had strong competitive advantages over its overseas competitors (in 1992, for example, U.S. exports of aerospace vehicles and equipment totaled $45 billion and imports were $14.5 billion, producing a trade surplus of $30.5 billion). The U.S. aerospace trade surplus declined during the 1990s, mainly as a result of the increasing competitiveness of the European commercial aircraft industry.

One reason for the stiffer foreign aerospace competition was the formation in 1969 of Airbus Industrie, a European consortium which eventually had four principal members, British Aerospace, Deutsche Aerospace, Aerospatiale of France, and CASA of Spain. The attempt to establish a European consortium for civilian aircraft had begun in the 1960s. By the end of 1990, the governments of Western Europe had spent at least $5.6 billion and possibly as much as $26 billion in support of the efforts of the Airbus consortium to challenge successfully the two other major producers of wide-body jet aircraft, Boeing and McDonnell-Douglas.

Aside from the threat from Europe, the U.S. commercial aircraft industry has suffered from the long-term effects of governmental deregulation. Beginning in 1978, deregulation has had the effect of increasing the number of passenger miles and carriers but at the expense of the profit margins and hence the investment capability of the major airlines. When there is a round of price competition, the airlines tend to cancel or defer orders for new aircraft. Hence, one source of competitive advantage of the period before 1978, strong and steady domestic demand for new aircraft, has been weakened. U.S. aircraft producers are increasingly dependent, as are the Europeans, on demand for aircraft in third markets.

The production of aircraft outside the major industrialized regions has been increasing since the 1970s. This is partly driven by increased domestic demand for aircraft in those countries and the desire to limit foreign imports. Through tariff protections or state-run enterprises, some newly industrializing countries in the Third World have built local commuter aircraft businesses and have even been able to export some of their domestic production of aircraft in order to earn hard currencies. For example, the Brazilian state-owned aerospace firm, Embraer, was quite successful in selling turboprop aircraft both for military uses and for commuter airlines.

As a result of the rapid drop in demand for military aircraft worldwide, U.S. military aircraft manufacturers shipped only $8.4 billion in complete aircraft in 1993. Historically, the U.S. government has accounted for 80 percent of U.S. military aircraft purchases. The rest is sold through direct exports and the Department of Defense's Foreign Military Sales program.

International Cooperation in Aerospace

U.S. dominance in the aerospace industry has created some tensions with its major allies. The U.S. government has tried to deal with these tensions by promoting international cooperative ventures. For example, the U.S. position in NATO has been to favor cooperation in defense matters. During the 1970s, U.S. policy recognized the desire and the necessity for European countries to build up their own defense production capabilities by adopting the idea of a "two-way street" in defense contracting and procurement. The United States supported the creation of the Independent European Program Group (IEPG) in 1976, which was a forum for meetings by European defense ministers to harmonize national policies toward promoting defense industries. In addition, the United States favored within NATO a policy of Rationalization, Standardization, and Interoperability (RSI) which would redress the unwillingness of NATO member countries to standardize production of major weapons systems. The lack of standards in military production not only reduced the combat readiness of NATO troops but also may have added $10–15 billion to annual defense procurement costs. The U.S. government encouraged coproduction of military aircraft by firms in major allied countries. Coproduction agreements took the form of memoranda of understanding (MOUs) negotiated among governments and firms. Examples include a U.S.-European agreement to coproduce F-16 fighters; a U.S.-German agreement to coproduce AIM 9L air-to-air missiles; and a U.S.-U.K. agreement to coproduce Harrier "jump-jet" fighters.

The response of the European governments to these U.S. initiatives was somewhat disappointing in that the United States expected to be a partner in a much wider variety of agreements than were actually obtained. The U.S. government remains concerned that a "fortress Europe" mentality is developing in this sector, with a pronounced tendency to favor intra-European cooperation over cooperation between the United States and Europe. It has been U.S. government policy not to allow key aerospace technologies to be transferred to foreign countries. One example is the great effort made by the U.S. government to prevent foreign firms or governments from acquiring the capability to use high-definition satellite imaging technologies for "spy-in-the-sky" satellites. Another is the policy of not revealing the source code for the software controlling avionics computers in advanced fighter aircraft (even to allies in coproduction agreements).

Aerospace issues rose to the top of the policy agenda of U.S. presidential administrations in the 1980s and 1990s. The "Strike Force" of President Ronald Reagan's administration wrote a report on the threat to the U.S. civilian aerospace industry posed by European subsidies for Airbus a decade earlier. There was insufficient consensus at that time for the recommendations of the report to be carried out. President Reagan and his advisers pushed hard for new efforts in aerospace technology through their advocacy of the Strategic Defense Initiative (SDI or Star Wars). They tried to win support for SDI in Europe by allowing European firms to bid for SDI contracts.

The administration of George Bush focused its attention on both military and civilian aerospace issues after the Department of Defense announced, and the U.S. Senate attacked, the agreement with Japan to build a modified F-16 fighter plane called the FSX (Fighter Support Experimental). Critics of the deal claimed that it represented a precedent for the transfer of avionics source code and other vital technologies. The FSX conflict was an embarrassment for both governments and may have done great long-term damage to U.S.-Japanese relations. The Bush administration was responsible for negotiating the U.S.-E.C. Commercial Aircraft Subsidy Agreement (1992), which was designed to end the dispute between the United States and the European Community over Airbus. This agreement helped to dampen what was becoming a very serious trade dispute.

At an appearance at a Boeing Aircraft plant in February 1993, just after taking office, President Bill Clinton presented his ideas for promoting high technology in the United States, but in a highly publicized aside he commented that Boeing's current financial difficulties were due to "the $26 billion that the U.S. sat by and let Europe plow into Airbus…" and promised to "change the rules of the game" so that this would not continue. Shortly after this, President Clinton reaffirmed his support of the 1992 Aircraft Subsidy Agreement, but the underlying tensions created by the efforts of Europe, Japan, and even some Third World nations like the Republic of China (Taiwan) to challenge the United States in commercial aircraft markets did not appear likely to go away.

Jeffrey A. Hart

See also North Atlantic Treaty Organization; Strategic Defense Initiative

FURTHER READING

Bright, Charles D. *The Jet Makers: The Aerospace Industry from 1945 to 1972.* Lawrence, Kans., 1978.

March, Artemis. "The U.S. Commercial Aircraft Industry and Its Foreign Competitors." In *The Working Papers of the MIT Commission on Industrial Productivity.* Cambridge, Mass., 1989.

Matthews, Ron. *European Armaments Collaboration: Policy, Problems, and Prospects.* Philadelphia, 1992.

Moran, Theodore H., and David C. Mowery. "Aerospace." In *Defense and Dependence in a Global Economy,* edited by Raymond Vernon and Ethan Kapstein. Washington, D.C., 1992.

Mowery, David C. *Alliance Politics and Economics: Multinational Joint Ventures in Commercial Aircraft.* Cambridge, Mass., 1987.

Newhouse, John. *The Sporty Game.* New York, 1982.

Phillips, Almarin. *Technology and Market Structure: A Study of the Aircraft Industry.* Lexington, Mass., 1971.

Tyson, Laura D'Andrea. *Who's Bashing Whom? Trade Conflicts in High-Technology Industries.* Washington, D.C., 1992.

Vander Meulen, Jacob A. *The Politics of Aircraft: Building an American Military Industry.* Lawrence, Kans., 1991.

AFGHANISTAN

A predominantly Muslim country located in southern Asia, bordered by Iran, Pakistan, and the former Soviet republics of Turkmenistan, Uzbekistan, and Tajikistan; it was long a territory where Great Britain and Russia competed for influence. Beginning in the 1950s, Afghanistan became a Cold War issue when the country moved toward alignment with the Soviet Union. Taking form as a nation-state in the 1740s under the leadership of Ahmad Shah Durrani, Afghanistan was governed by him and his descendants until 1978. During the nineteenth century, Russia and Great Britain (from its imperial position in India) basically set the boundaries of a country they viewed as a buffer between empires. On three occasions (1839–1842, 1878–1880, and 1919), British troops marched into Afghanistan, maintaining it as a British sphere of influence. The United States accorded Afghanistan official recognition in 1934, the same year that Afghanistan joined the League of Nations, but has rarely sought close ties to the government in Kabul.

Afghanistan's chief exports of wool, carpets, tea, and natural gas have accorded it only marginal economic importance. Cold War geopolitics, however, increasingly gave Afghanistan strategic significance, drawing U.S. attention. Although Kabul remained nonaligned during most of the Cold War, geographic proximity and Russia's long-standing quest for influence pulled Afghanistan toward the Soviet orbit. Washington's military alliance with Afghanistan's neighboring rival Pakistan also increased Kabul's reliance on Moscow beginning in the 1950s. From the early 1950s through the late 1970s the United States extended $500 million in economic aid to Afghanistan, compared to Soviet aid of more than $2.5 billion. In 1973 the monarchy was abolished and a republic inaugurated. In April 1978 a military coup toppled the government, and a Marxist regime under the People's Democratic Party soon came to power. Within months the new pro-Soviet regime challenged Islamic traditions, setting off antigovernment demonstrations and resistance, much of it engineered by Islamic fundamentalists.

In December 1979 the Soviet Union ordered 75,000 troops into Afghanistan to prop up its besieged client regime. Concerned by the aggression and its possible consequences for the security of the oil-rich Persian Gulf region, President Jimmy Carter proclaimed the Carter Doctrine, which pledged the deployment of U.S. military force to ward off outside aggression in the Persian Gulf area. Tensions developed between the superpowers, and the withdrawal of the Soviet-American Strategic Arms Limitation Treaty (SALT II) from Senate ratification, the U.S. boycott of the 1980 Moscow Olympics, economic sanctions against the Soviet Union, and increased U.S. aid to Pakistan soon followed. Covert Central Intelligence Agency (CIA) support, begun under Carter and expanded under President Ronald Reagan, assisted a determined coalition of Afghan resistance fighters known as the Mujahadeen. Overwhelmed by the costs of the invasion, both in terms of lives and rubles, Premier Mikhail Gorbachev in 1988 and 1989 withdrew Soviet troops. The Kremlin's former client regime of Mohammed Najibullah was overthrown in April 1992, but the various elements within the Mujahadeen, divided by ethnic, religious, and linguistic differences, continued to fight a bloody and indecisive civil war.

DENNIS MERRILL

See also Carter Doctrine; Cold War; Gorbachev, Mikhail Sergeevich; Pakistan; Reagan, Ronald Wilson; Russia and the Soviet Union

FURTHER READING

Dupree, Louis. *Afghanistan*. Princeton, N.J., 1973.
Kakar, M. Hassar. *Afghanistan: The Soviet Invasion and the Afghan Response, 1979–1982*. Berkeley, 1995.
Klass, Rosanne, ed. *Afghanistan: The Great Game Revisited*, 2nd ed. New York, 1990.
Poullada, Leon B. *The Kingdom of Afghanistan and the United States: 1828–1973*. Lincoln, Neb., 1995.
Rubin, Barnett Richard. *The Search for Peace in Afghanistan: From Buffer State to Failed State*. New Haven, 1995.
Urban, Mark. *War in Afghanistan*, 2nd ed. New York, 1991.
Wolpert, Stanley A. *Roots of Confrontation in South Asia: Afghanistan, Pakistan, India, and the Superpowers*. New York, 1982.

AFL-CIO

See American Federation of Labor–Congress of Industrial Organizations

AFRICA

The world's second largest continent, Africa is bounded by the Mediterranean Sea and the Atlantic and Indian Oceans, and connected with Asia by the Sinai Peninsula. U.S. contacts with the continent through trade, religious missionary activity, and naval patrols developed minimally before the twentieth century, although the flourishing slave trade in black Africans during the American colonial and early national periods established commerce and race as significant questions in American-African relations. As the Cold War has receded into history, observers have become increasingly aware of the extent to which U.S. foreign policy in Africa was formulated through a Soviet-centric prism in the decades following World War II. Consciously or unconsciously, U.S. foreign policymakers adopted a narrowly ideological view, playing down regional concerns over poverty, human rights, democracy, and self-determination, and concentrating instead on strategic advantages in their rivalry with the Soviet Union. The United States often withheld criticism from conservative "friends"—anticommunist strongmen, some of whom were highly authoritarian leaders known for their corrupt and repressive practices, such as Zairian President Mobutu Sese

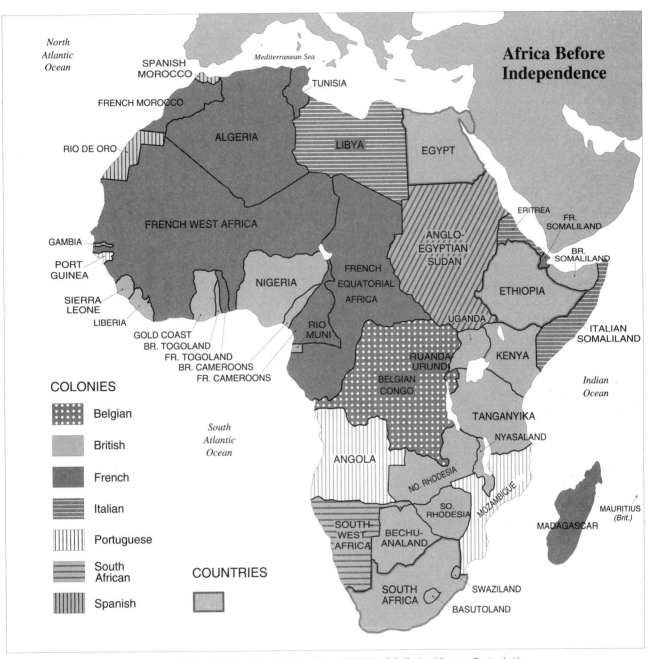

Africa Before Independence

North
Atlantic
Ocean

Mediterranean Sea

SPANISH
MOROCCO

TUNISIA

FRENCH MOROCCO

RIO DE ORO

ALGERIA

LIBYA

EGYPT

ERITREA

FR.
SOMALILAND

FRENCH WEST AFRICA

ANGLO-
EGYPTIAN
SUDAN

BR.
SOMALILAND

GAMBIA

PORT
GUINEA

SIERRA
LEONE

LIBERIA

NIGERIA

FRENCH
EQUATORIAL
AFRICA

ETHIOPIA

GOLD COAST
BR. TOGOLAND
FR. TOGOLAND
BR. CAMEROONS
FR. CAMEROONS

RIO
MUNI

UGANDA

KENYA

ITALIAN
SOMALILAND

RUANDA
URUNDI

BELGIAN
CONGO

Indian
Ocean

COLONIES

South
Atlantic
Ocean

TANGANYIKA

NYASALAND

Belgian

British

French

Italian

Portuguese

South
African

Spanish

ANGOLA

NO. RHODESIA

SO.
RHODESIA

MOZAMBIQUE

MADAGASCAR

MAURITIUS
(Brit.)

COUNTRIES

SOUTH-
WEST
AFRICA

BECHU-
ANALAND

SWAZILAND

SOUTH
AFRICA

BASUTOLAND

Seko, Kenyan President Daniel arap Moi, Angolan insurgent leader Jonas Savimbi—while being too hard at times on such perceived "enemies" as the Marxist-oriented Popular Movement for the Liberation of Angola (MPLA) and, in the mid-1980s, South Africa's African National Congress (ANC). In adopting this hard-line view, the U.S. squandered an opportunity to identify with independent-minded heads of state intent on resisting corruption and prepared to experiment with democratic reforms.

U.S. Relations Through the Cold War

Before World War II and the Cold War, Africa ranked low among vital U.S. interests, and the European colonial powers dominated the continent. Still, Americans had long interacted with Africans. In the late eighteenth century, the United States signed treaties with several North African states, paying tribute to protect American merchant vessels from the so-called Barbary Pirates. Because the marauding did not abate, in 1803–1805, U.S. war-

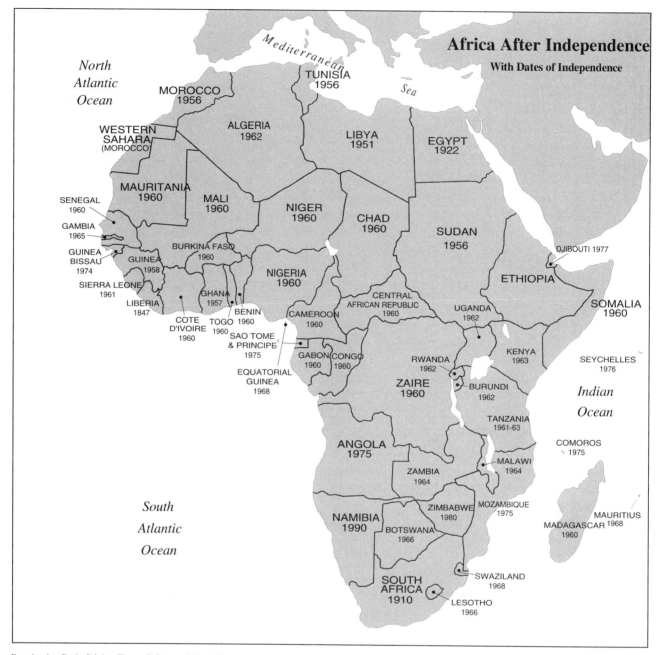

Africa After Independence

With Dates of Independence

Mediterranean Sea

North Atlantic Ocean

TUNISIA 1956

MOROCCO 1956

WESTERN SAHARA (MOROCCO)

ALGERIA 1962

LIBYA 1951

EGYPT 1922

MAURITANIA 1960

MALI 1960

NIGER 1960

CHAD 1960

SUDAN 1956

DJIBOUTI 1977

SENEGAL 1960

GAMBIA 1965

GUINEA BISSAU 1974

GUINEA 1958

BURKINA FASO 1960

NIGERIA 1960

ETHIOPIA

SIERRA LEONE 1961

LIBERIA 1847

GHANA 1957

BENIN 1960

CAMEROON 1960

CENTRAL AFRICAN REPUBLIC 1960

UGANDA 1962

SOMALIA 1960

COTE D'IVOIRE 1960

TOGO 1960

SAO TOME & PRINCIPE 1975

GABON 1960

CONGO 1960

RWANDA 1962

KENYA 1963

SEYCHELLES 1976

EQUATORIAL GUINEA 1968

ZAIRE 1960

BURUNDI 1962

Indian Ocean

TANZANIA 1961-63

COMOROS 1975

ANGOLA 1975

ZAMBIA 1964

MALAWI 1964

South Atlantic Ocean

NAMIBIA 1990

BOTSWANA 1966

ZIMBABWE 1980

MOZAMBIQUE 1975

MAURITIUS 1968

MADAGASCAR 1960

SWAZILAND 1968

SOUTH AFRICA 1910

LESOTHO 1966

ships battled pirate vessels in the Mediterranean Sea. In 1815 the United States extracted new, more favorable treaties from Tripoli, Algiers, and Tunis.

The slave trade became the United States' major contact with sub-Saharan Africa, especially the western coastal region. As slavery expanded in North America, the demand for slaves intensified. The boom years of the Yankee slave trade were 1700–1750. The Constitution set 1808 as the date to end the slave trade, but it proved difficult to halt, despite the creation of the U.S. Navy's African Squadron in 1843. In 1862 the United States and Great Britain signed a treaty to clamp down on the African slave trade, and by the end of the American Civil War in 1865 the slave trade to the United States had stopped.

One African nation with which the United States developed unique relations was Liberia. In 1821 the American Colonization Society, with the assistance of the U.S. Navy, took possession of land in Liberia in order to settle freed American slaves. Although the colonization effort faltered (only some 15,000 freed slaves went there), the United States essentially became Liberia's protector in the face of growing European colonialism on the continent after Liberia's independence in 1847. Liberia developed strong commercial ties with the United States.

As for the rest of Africa in the nineteenth century, the United States largely developed trade relations and appealed for an open trade door. But discriminatory tariffs imposed by the colonial powers often impeded commerce. Religious missionaries of the American Board of Commissioners for Foreign Missions established stations in South Africa, Mozambique, and Angola. Baptists sought converts in Nigeria, whereas Lutherans opened missions in Madagascar. Dramatic stories out of Africa sometimes stirred the American popular imagination, as when Henry Stanley, working for the New York *Herald*, arrived in Zanzibar in 1871, trekked into and mapped central Africa, and found the missing Dr. David Livingstone, the missionary-explorer. Stanley next went to work for King Leopold of Belgium, who sought a colonial empire in the Congo. The United States sent a delegation to an international conference in Berlin in 1884; an agreement confirmed Belgian authority over the Congo. By 1895 most of Africa had been partitioned by the Europeans.

At the Versailles peace conference following World War I, the United States helped strip Germany of its African colonies, which entered the mandate system of the League of Nations. During the 1920s the Firestone company built its huge rubber business in Liberia, shipping lines began to operate between the United States and Africa, and U.S.-African trade in manganese, industrial diamonds, and cobalt expanded. Still, by 1930 U.S. trade with Africa represented only two and a half percent of total American exports and imports. In 1938, on the eve of World War II, the U.S. Department of State for the first time created a "desk" for African affairs, although official U.S. representation consisted of only four consulates in tropical Africa.

World War II changed America's relationship with Africa, which now loomed larger as a strategic site guarding the shipping lanes of the South Atlantic, as a bridge to Allied forces in the Middle East and elsewhere, as a staging area for the Allied invasion of Italy, as a supplier of vital raw materials (including uranium), and as a region of growing anticolonial nationalism. In 1944 the Department of State demonstrated its heightened interest in Africa by creating the Division of African Affairs.

Direct American relations with colonial territories in Africa remained minimal. Even as self-government and independence became imminent in the late 1950s, American spokesmen encouraged African leaders to retain close ties with Europe after the transfer of power, and the Dwight Eisenhower administration remained aloof from the new African leadership. U.S. policy concerns in Africa during the 1960s and 1970s were largely limited to containment of the Soviet Union and maintenance of the world economic order and international stability. President John F. Kennedy strove to build effective independent relations with African nationalist leaders, because of his belief that nationalism would overcome the attraction of communism. American engagement in Africa remained minimal during the Lyndon Johnson, Richard Nixon, and Gerald Ford administrations, and might be characterized as "benign neglect."

The competition for strategic advantage with the Soviet Union narrowed the agenda and gave a sense of purpose and coherence to U.S. foreign policy toward Africa in the 1960–1987 period. It was relatively easy to set priorities, ranking choices in terms of their relative effectiveness in achieving U.S. objectives on such critical issues as alliances, security, and access to raw materials. By contrast, the end of the Cold War and resulting lack of superpower rivalry brought new uncertainties about U.S. purposes in Africa. It no longer was necessary to engage in the embarrassing trade-offs of the past, in particular, supporting dictatorial and racist regimes in the name of a more pressing objective: the defeat of international communism. Moreover, there now was no overriding political logic to make the ordering of contemporary objectives self-evident. Unable to rank its purposes, the United States seemed inclined to look inward and to adopt a passive stance at a time of unfolding economic and social crisis. Unwilling to act in advance of a crisis, the United States seemed prone to underreact to challenges (repression in the southern Sudan; deteriorating state-society relations in Zaire; genocide in Rwanda; the ongoing civil strife in Liberia) or to overreact (unilaterally dispatching military forces to Somalia, even though under U.N. auspices).

Clinton Administration Policies

The end of the Cold War gave the Bill Clinton administration a fresh opportunity to pull back from the reactive, ideologically driven approach of the past and to rethink its African priorities. As it did so a number of objectives presented themselves, including the promotion of democracy, respect for human rights, the ending of racial discrimination and apartheid, efforts to deal with internally displaced peoples and international refugees, measures to cope with the AIDS epidemic, more effective management of intra- and interstate conflicts, assistance for sustainable development, aid to disaster victims, encouragement of regional integration, and the suppression of the international drug trade.

With respect to promoting democracy and human rights in Africa, then Governor Clinton declared in an address at Georgetown University on 12 December,

1991, "we must align America with the rising tide of democracy." In a subsequent article in *Africa Report* in September/October 1992 he returned to this theme and described the promotion of democracy as "our top priority." Many Africans agreed with this sentiment. Some (Botswana, Mauritius, Senegal [after 1976]) have been practicing democracy since independence; others subscribe to democratic norms and have been struggling, with some success in the 1990s, for multiparty elections and governmental accountability. In Benin, Zambia, Cape Verde, and São Tomé and Principe, regimes have met what many consider to be the critical test of democracy: the replacement of one set of rulers by another following an open, competitive election.

The case has been made that it is in U.S. interests to back the forces working for democratization and human rights on the continent. Improved "governance" is likely to facilitate the achievement of many of the goals supported by American officials, such as state and regional stability, respect for civil liberties, governmental accountability, effective management of conflict, and economic development. In emphasizing the value of democracy, what is essential is open, party contestation; the availability of information on which to base choices; and respect for the rules of encounter. But it is important to stress that democracy is a set of procedures for dealing with power, not a specific outcome. Hence there is a wide latitude as to acceptable formulas—unitary or federal, centralized or decentralized, presidential or parliamentary, majoritarian or elite power-sharing, liberal or populist. So long as governments respect the democratic procedures they have agreed upon, they have earned U.S. support. This was one factor in the Clinton administration's decision to recognize the legitimacy of the MPLA government in Angola which had played by the 1992 election rules. However, where democratic norms have been violated (such as Savimbi's resumption of the civil war in 1992 after his election defeat in Angola), the United States did not always act consistently to send a clear signal of U.S. disapproval, because Savimbi once represented an important Cold War ally. U. S. diplomats have played important roles in Malawi and Kenya, pressuring the government of former President Hastings Banda and President arap Moi to move toward multiparty democracy and to respect the civil liberties of their countrymen. By placing conditions on aid to such authoritarian-inclined regimes, the U.S. has used its leverage to identify with political leaders who champion political reforms in line with basic American values.

Because sustained democracy also depends upon a stable political environment capable of coping effectively with separatist demands and destructive regional conflicts, diplomacy and conflict management also have been critical components of U.S. foreign policy in Africa.

The appeals of a stable international order have long been recognized as essential by American officials who have responded relatively quickly to the need for promoting the peaceful settlement of Africa's internal and external conflicts. U.S. involvement in Africa's conflict resolution processes has taken many forms. These include behind-the-scenes support for the mediation of disputes (Zimbabwe); backing a regional organization (ECOMOG in Liberia; OAU in Rwanda); endorsement of an extra-continental actor (support for Portugal in negotiating the internal settlement in Angola, and for Italy and various unofficial mediators in the Mozambican negotiations); pressure on local parties to negotiate (South Africa; Sudan); humanitarian intervention (Somalia); the facilitation of a transition (Ethiopia); and mediation among internal parties (Zaire) and between international parties (Angola/Namibia).

Somalia, South Africa, and Angola

The efforts made by U.S. diplomats to promote a peaceful resolution of the conflicts in Somalia, South Africa, and Angola are illustrative of the range of intervention initiatives already undertaken. In Somalia, dismantling the old, authoritarian order led to a breakdown of the civil order—with terrifying consequences. The world community watched from afar as helpless civilian bystanders starved and gang warfare made normal life impossible. By late 1992, American officials, dismayed over the social distress unfolding in Somalia, decided to launch an American-led humanitarian intervention endorsed by the United Nations. Asserting a moral obligation, the U.S. Congress enacted Concurrent Resolution 132 of 1992 urging the President, working through the United Nations (UN), to deploy security guards to protect those engaged in the relief effort. Operation Restore Hope, then, had a limited mission: to create a secure environment for the delivery of humanitarian relief. In a relatively brief period, an American force of some 25,000 troops were deployed, being withdrawn in stages as replacements arrived from other countries (some 15,000 soldiers from other lands by April 1993). This international force ensured that relief convoys could move about the countryside unimpeded and reduced the intensity of the fighting by standing as a buffer between the warring factions.

Acknowledging that the problems in Somalia were essentially political in nature, the intervening force quickly recognized that it had to go beyond pacification to assist in creating a framework for good governance. The U.S.-led force used its momentary opportunity to create the conditions in which diplomacy could operate, allowing local leaders to develop ties of reciprocity and patterns of political exchange. This task of facilitation proved a difficult assignment in circumstances where state institutions have collapsed. The U.S.-led peace-keeping force started by empowering various groups in civil society—traditional leaders, professionals, women's groups, and so forth—to organize for local relief and security roles. Working within a framework grounded on the regions, these groups were encouraged to assume political and administrative responsibilities, leading in time to the creation of a national council of seventy-four representatives. Although some of the warlords continued to feud among themselves, the fifteen Somali factions meeting in Addis Ababa indicated their general support for this regionally based arrangement. In the subsequent months, heavy fighting broke out in Mogadishu between General Mohammed Farah Aidid's force and UN units. Peacekeeping had been enlarged into peace enforcement, with fatal consequences for U.S. and other troops. The upshot was increasing pressure in Congress to withdraw the remaining American contingents. In response, the Clinton administration removed the main elements of its military force in late 1993. With the UN unable to forge a new regime its peacekeeping force was withdrawn from the country early in 1995, with U.S. units protecting the rear flank of the UN contingents as they left Somalia. America's commitment to peacekeeping initiatives was adversely affected by the Somali experience. The Clinton administration issued Presidential Decision Directive 25 calling for a more selective and effective approach to peacekeeping. The effects of this were soon to become apparent. In 1994, as waves of genocidal destruction swept Rwanda, the U.S. stood on the sidelines while the killing was at its peak.

In the case of South Africa, the American mood was one of general support for negotiated change. By the time of the Ronald Reagan administration, the struggle for a progressive transformation in that country had become a domestic American concern. Despite administration resistance to placing sanctions on South African trade and access to certain technology and services, the Congress passed the 1986 Comprehensive Anti-Apartheid Act into law, backing the acceptance of the South African government as a legitimate member of the world community conditional upon its reevaluation of the need for political reform. To a limited extent at least, international sanctions had an impact upon the country's economy. The ban on new loans and investment was damaging, as was the loss of access to world markets for certain goods, technology, and services. Real growth slackened, leading to a rise in unemployment and an estimated fall in average incomes of some 15 percent. The George Bush administration, ambivalent from the outset over applying sanctions to South Africa, reacted positively to the news of African National Congress (ANC) leader Nelson Mandela's release, the lifting of the ban on party activity, the freeing of political prisoners, and ending of the state of

emergency to ease restrictions in 1990 on iron and steel exports and the sale of Boeing 747s. Then in 1991, as Bush became convinced that the transition process was irreversible, he terminated federal (but not state and local) economic sanctions.

In the period that followed, the U.S. seemed increasingly indecisive on South African policy. When the talks in the Convention for a Democratic South Africa were suspended and, in the wake of this breakdown, the ANC announced a program of mass action in mid-1992, the U.S. administration encouraged the parties to reach a compromise to put the negotiating process back on track. But other than such efforts to maintain confidence in the peace process, the U.S. seemed to have a minimal direct role to play. The negotiations had become an internally driven dialogue between the main South African parties, and both of these parties rejected the idea of external intervention, particularly as mediator.

Clinton's words in his major policy address during the campaign were most hopeful: "Today," he declared in 1991 at Georgetown, "we should concentrate our attention on insuring that the process toward dismantling apartheid and constructing an open society is irreversible….The Administration and our states and cities should only relax our remaining sanctions as it becomes clearer that the day of democracy and guaranteed individual rights is at hand." In line with ANC leader Mandela's guidelines, it was regarded as too soon for Western friends to ease up on sanctions; American pressure was necessary, Mandela contended, to ensure that no backsliding took place. It was not until September 1993 that Mandela became convinced that sufficient political progress had been made to warrant a call for the termination of international sanctions. Following elections in April 1994, Mandela assumed the presidency, bringing about an easing of internal political tensions and South Africa's acceptability by the world community.

Finally, in Angola, U.S. diplomats were prominent participants in the peace process, successfully mediating the international conflict in 1988 and then helping to facilitate the Portuguese-mediated intrastate negotiations in 1991 as well as the UN-mediated Lusaka Protocol of 1994. What began as a struggle by Angolan nationalist movements in the early 1960s against a colonial power, Portugal, became, by the time of independence in 1975, a war characterized by conflict on both the interstate and intrastate levels. After the MPLA, aided by Cuban troops, won the battle for Luanda in 1975, it began the process of consolidating its control over the country. The period from 1976 to 1987 was one of continuing military encounters between the Popular Armed Forces for the Liberation of Angola (FAPLA) and both Savimbi's National Union for the Total Independence of Angola (UNITA) insurgents and the South African

Defense Forces (SADF). The intensity of this conflict rose noticeably during the 1980s, as SADF troops advanced deep into southern Angola and their UNITA allies pushed outward toward the western and northwestern parts of the country. An American-mediated disengagement of forces was negotiated between the Angolans and the South Africans in 1984, followed soon after by a resumption of skirmishing and then large-scale battles between heavily armed FAPLA and UNITA combat troops. With war-weariness evident on the part of all the combatants and little chance of a decisive military victory by either side, the prospect of a negotiated end to the war became a somewhat more attractive option to all contenders by 1988.

Although a party to the conflict by dint of supplying sophisticated military equipment to Savimbi, the U.S. nonetheless had sought to promote a negotiated Angola-Namibia settlement throughout the 1980s. Its chance to play an effective role increased in 1988, as both sides came to perceive the war as costly and unwinnable and as the two superpowers moved from antagonistic to pragmatic relations. What followed was a determined initiative, with important behind-the-scenes support from Soviet diplomats, to link Namibia's independence to a redeployment and phased withdrawal of Cuban troops from Angola. In what amounts to a casebook example of tacit superpower cooperation, sufficient pressure was brought to bear on the two sets of combatants to bring about an agreement in 1988 between the MPLA government and the various international actors. This left the internal conflict between the MPLA and UNITA still to be negotiated, something that was achieved in 1991 under the auspices of the Portuguese, with the U.S. and the Russians playing a highly important behind-the-scenes supporting role. As scheduled under the resulting Bicesse Accords, national elections were held in Angola in 1992. After these elections, Savimbi, infuriated by the outcome, refused to abide by the results and resumed the civil war. Following sharp military encounters, the rearmed Angolan government forces seized the initiative, threatening UNITA in its home base area. Faced with the prospect of heavy losses, Savimbi bowed to the inevitable and agreed to the UN-mediated Lusaka Protocol in November 1994. With distrust between the two parties remaining apparent, the resulting peace appears fragile.

Another important issue concerns assistance for African development. Although it is difficult to be precise about the link between democracy and economic well-being, it seems clear that expectations of economic progress act to stabilize reforms in the political arena. The key, though, is that aid not just be extended generously, but that it also be used effectively. In this respect, President Clinton's call in an article in *Africa Report* in September-October 1992 for a reform of aid programs "to ensure that the assistance we provide truly benefits Africans and encourages the development of democratic institutions and free market economies" was aimed to foster sustainable, broad-based development linked to his political and economic reform agenda. While praising the Reagan and Bush administrations for providing record amounts of aid to Africa (between $1 billion and $1.6 billion annually through a variety of programs), he criticized the use of that aid to support corrupt, dictatorial regimes in many instances. Many observers and officials consider U.S. aid, which is responsible for less than 10 percent of the official development assistance allocated to Africa, as patently insufficient; nevertheless, in times of grave economic stringency at home, Congress appears unwilling to maintain aid to Africa at former levels. The result is tragic in terms of lost opportunities to promote livable societies in much of the continent.

In sum, the end of the Cold War has left the U.S. relatively free to pursue African policies that play down the importance of strategic concerns and allow U.S. policymakers to emphasize political reforms roughly in line with the country's own basic values. In addition to the basic thrust toward democracy and human rights, U.S. officials also place a heavy emphasis upon such related objectives as conflict management and assistance for sustainable economic development. If the shift in primary goals and objectives seems appropriate to a new era in which superpower competition no longer seems meaningful, it nonetheless is unclear whether what Africans perceive as a financially overburdened American government will have the determination and ability to deliver on its promises of support for democratic reforms, the facilitation of conflict management, and assistance for development. U.S. diplomats in Africa must compete vigorously with claimants from other regions (especially Eastern Europe, Latin America, and Asia) at a time of diminishing financial resources. Unless the advocates for Africa in the United States and elsewhere can gain broad support for their pressing policy concerns, Africa may give vent to its despair and sense of global marginalization by turning inward and at the same time looking outward with indignation, even animosity.

DONALD ROTHCHILD

See also countries of Africa; Acquired Immune Deficiency Syndrome (AIDS) Pandemic; Barbary States; Clinton, William Jefferson; Cold War; Colonialism; Mandates and Trusteeships; Mandela, Nelson Rolihlahla; Slave Trade and Slavery

FURTHER READING

Chester, Edward. *Clash of Titans: Africa and American Foreign Policy.* Maryknoll, N.Y., 1974.

Duignan, Peter, and Lewis H. Gann. *The United States and Africa: A History*. New York, 1984.

Goldschmidt, Walter. *The United States and Africa*. New York, 1963.

Hickey, Dennis. *An Enchanted Darkness: The American Vision of Africa in the Twentieth Century*. East Lansing, Mich., 1993.

Howe, Russell W. *Along the African Shore*. New York, 1975.

Jackson, Henry F. *From Congo to Soweto: U.S. Foreign Policy Toward Africa Since 1960*. New York, 1982.

McKinley, Edward H. *The Lure of Africa: American Interests in Tropical Africa, 1919–1939*. Indianapolis, Ind., 1974.

Noer, Thomas J. *Cold War and Black Liberation: The United States and White Rule in Africa, 1948–1968*. Columbia, Mo., 1985.

Rothchild, Donald, and John Ravenhill. "Retreat from Globalism: U.S. Policy Toward Africa in the 1990s." In *Eagle in a New World*, edited by Kenneth A. Oye, Robert J. Lieber, and Donald Rothchild. New York, 1992.

Schraeder, Peter J. *United States Foreign Policy Toward Africa*. New York, 1994.

Smock, David R., and Chester A. Crocker, eds. *African Conflict Resolution: The U.S. Role in Peacemaking*. Washington, D.C., 1995.

Ungar, Sanford J. *Africa: The People and Politics of an Emerging Continent*. New York, 1985.

Whitaker, Jennifer Seymour. *Africa and the United States: Vital Interests*. New York, 1978.

AGENCY FOR INTERNATIONAL DEVELOPMENT

The U.S. agency primarily responsible for administering bilateral nonmilitary development assistance programs, created by executive order of President John F. Kennedy in 1961. Although the United States had been operating a variety of foreign aid programs since the 1940s, the creation of AID marked an important milestone by giving Third World development increasing prominence in the national agenda. By 1994 AID administered an annual budget in excess of $8 billion and had programs in more than 100 countries, including the newly independent states of the former Soviet Union. AID's activities included the provision of both technical and financial assistance and spanned a wide range: agricultural and rural development; nutrition, health, and population and child survival; education and human resource development; private sector and microenterprise development; environmental and energy development; governance and the building of democratic institutions; and relief aid during famines and following earthquakes and other natural disasters.

Despite the publicity often given to the foreign aid programs, AID is a relatively small and vulnerable agency whose authority is circumscribed by a variety of factors. It has always had an uneasy relationship with the Department of State, and the extent to which that department influences AID policy and programs changes with each presidential administration. In 1979 Congress created The International Development Cooperation Agency (IDCA), which was to report directly to the President.

The initial intention was for it to control all development-related activities (including the section of the Department of Treasury that worked with multilateral development banks, and the Peace Corps), but ultimately it only supervised AID, OPIC, and maybe one other small agency. IDCA quickly turned into nothing more than a hollow shell. Technically speaking, IDCA and AID are completely separate from the State Department, but the reality is that, particularly in areas where the United States has strong national security interests, the State Department does play an important, if informal, role in determining how money is used. For its part, however, AID strongly resists being controlled by State. For this reason, the proposal introduced by Republican Senator Jesse Helms, in the mid-1990s, to integrate State, AID, and other international agencies into a new Department of International Relations is being strongly opposed by AID, which sees it this as a way to make the agency more subordinate to the interests of what is now the State Department. The Food for Peace program is jointly administered with the Department of Agriculture. Other agencies have their own programs with developing countries completely apart from AID, the most prominent being the Department of Defense, which funds and administers various forms of military assistance. Under its mandate as a bilateral aid agency, AID is not in charge of formulating U.S. policy toward multilateral development agencies, such as the World Bank and the three regional development banks, which are the responsibility of the Department of the Treasury.

AID's budget, which is broken down into detailed country and functional accounts, requires annual congressional approval that gives Congress considerable influence over the specifics of the program. Congress also affects AID programs by earmarking funds for specified purposes and by requiring annual compliance reports from the agency on particular activities. Most of these specific requirements have been added over time in a piecemeal fashion, leading to a diffuse and confusing mandate under which AID had more than thirty major objectives in the 1990s .

Unlike development assistance agencies in most other donor nations, AID is organized so that it maintains a significant portion of its staff overseas in AID missions, which can be quite influential in determining AID policy on the ground. In its early years AID officials were often directly responsible for carrying out specific projects and programs, but following reductions in the size and scope of the agency after the 1980s, more activities were contracted out to private voluntary organizations and private contractors, which were supported by AID officials.

AID's development policy changed dramatically over the years, responding to changing circumstances and development theories. In the 1960s the agency focused primarily on large capital outlays for infrastructure and industry. In the 1970s it concentrated more directly on helping the poor with what came to be called a "basic needs" strategy. The focus shifted in the 1980s toward reforming national policies to promote a vigorous private sector and an open economy. In the 1990s, the focus on creating an open economy has continued, along with an emphasis on the promotion of democratic political systems, under the general goal of promoting "broad based" sustainable development. Since its creation, however, AID was always expected to serve three goals simultaneously: a humanitarian goal, to improve the quality of life for people in developing countries; an economic goal, to help promote U.S. commercial interests; and a national security goal, which focused largely on anticommunism and efforts to ensure the acceptance of Israel in the Middle East. The way in which these goals have been implemented has varied from administration to administration, but it has proved virtually impossible to find a strategy that would enable AID to pursue all three simultaneously without controversy. For example, the pursuit of the national security objective has meant that between 40 and 50 percent of the AID budget has been allocated to the Economic Support Fund (ESF). ESF funds were officially designated for development purposes, but the recipient countries were selected on the basis of their strategic significance to U.S. interests, and ESF money often was not as carefully programmed and supervised as that in the regular development budget; these programming and supervision inconsistencies put a strong bias in the country selection process. From all accounts, the two largest recipients of AID resources have been Israel and Egypt. Less than 25 percent of the total budget was usually allocated for the poorest nations where the need is presumably greatest. The fall of the Soviet Union opened an opportunity in the 1990s to rethink the idea of national security. Indications in 1995 suggested that there would be increased programs in Eastern Europe, Russia, and the newly independent states of the former USSR, and fewer for Africa, the poorest continent. A focus on less poor nations was often supported by U.S. farmers and businesses, which saw them as potential customers.

Beyond the problem of conflicting goals, AID was considered by many to be increasingly marginal to both foreign policy and international development. Unlike the 1960s, when it was the predominant global donor, accounting for more than 60 percent of all development aid from all bilateral donors, AID in 1995 accounted for considerably less than 20 percent of development aid and was only one of many donors. In fact, AID was no longer even the single largest donor; by 1995 the largest donor was Japan. AID's reduced role was explained not only by the increased economic strength of other donor countries

since the 1960s, but also by what is referred to as "donor fatigue." Since the 1960s the amount of aid contributed by the United States, when measured as a percentage of gross national product, has gradually declined to its 1994 level of about 0.2 percent. This was not only far below the United Nations goal of 0.7 percent, but also placed the United States at the bottom of the list of all major donors. The fact that as of 1995 Congress had not passed a foreign aid bill since 1985 (it simply extended the previous bill) was a telling indication of the low priority to which the issue had been relegated. Furthermore, there were increasing indications that, unlike the 1960s, foreign aid in general was no longer the dominant instrument for promoting development. Issues such as trade, private investment, and other international economic policies in which AID played virtually no role assumed increasing importance.

STEVEN H. ARNOLD

See also Bowles, Chester Bliss; Defense, U.S. Department of; Earmarking; Food for Peace; Foreign Aid; Peace Corps; State, U.S. Department of

FURTHER READING
Hellinger, Stephen, Douglas Hellinger, and Fred M. O'Regan. *Aid for Just Development.* Boulder, Colo., 1988.
Morrison, Elizabeth, and Randall B. Purcell, eds. *Players and Issues in U.S. Foreign Aid.* West Hartford, Conn., 1988.
Organization for Economic Cooperation and Development. *Development Cooperation: Efforts and Policies of the Members of the Development Assistance Committee.* Paris, annual.
Porter, D. *U.S. Economic Foreign Aid: A Case Study of the United States Agency for International Development.* New York, 1990.
Ruttan, Vernon W. *United States Development Assistance Policy: The Domestic Politics of Foreign Economic Aid.* Baltimore, 1995.
Zimmerman, Robert F. *Dollars, Diplomacy and Dependency: Dilemmas of U.S. Economic Aid.* Boulder, Colo., 1993.

AGRICULTURAL COMPANIES
See Food and Agricultural Companies

AGRICULTURE

The numerous and varied techniques for producing crops from the earth. The United States occupies a dominant position in agricultural science and trade, ranking first in the world for exporting corn, wheat, oilseeds, and cotton. However, the emergence of a positive trade balance in U.S. agriculture is a relatively recent event, with agricultural exports not surpassing agricultural imports on a consistent basis until 1960. Recently, rapid growth in the export of services and manufactures has sharply diminished agriculture's share of total U.S. exports. Despite this fact, trade disputes of an agricultural nature continue

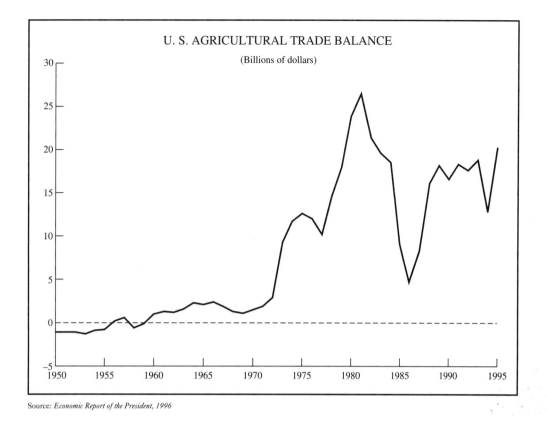

U. S. AGRICULTURAL TRADE BALANCE

(Billions of dollars)

Source: *Economic Report of the President, 1996*

to complicate U.S. foreign relations. In part, agriculture remains so contentious in the international arena because of longstanding government intervention on behalf of agriculture.

Agricultural issues have occupied a central, though evolving, position in U.S. foreign relations. In the pre-revolutionary era, the mercantilist policies of the British required the colonists to ship certain products (such as tobacco) to England and not to a foreign market. Additional restrictions on production attempted to ensure that the colonies would complement rather than compete with British industry. The infamous tea tax, although it generated little revenue for the British, served as justification for rebellious action by the colonists during the "tea parties" of 1773.

At the time of U.S. independence, agriculture was the leading industry and involved roughly 90 percent of the population. From this strongly agrarian beginning, the percentage of U.S. citizens engaged in agriculture fell to 50 percent in the late 1800s, and by the mid-1990s only 2 percent of the U.S. population lived on farms. Despite this decline, the influence of domestic farm groups on U.S. foreign agricultural relations remains strong. In part, this is due to Thomas Jefferson's incantation of the yeoman farmer as the backbone of U.S. society, which has left a legacy of broad public support for farmers and their values of independence and individualism. Jefferson's

arguments, and similar ones made in Europe and Japan, have provided valuable moral justification for a potent agricultural lobby intent on resisting both domestic and foreign threats to its sector.

From the colonial era through the early twentieth century, U.S. foreign agricultural relations were fairly simple. Until the mechanical advances of the mid-1800s, such as McCormick's mechanical reaper, most farmers' production schemes involved a number of crops. This, along with the fact that agricultural trade was not as developed as at present, hindered the development of a strong farm lobby demanding protection from foreign competition. Thus, tariffs on imported commodities were used mainly as a key revenue producer for the government in the pre-income-tax era.

A notable exception to this generally quiet environment surrounding agricultural trade was cotton, which soared in importance after the introduction of Eli Whitney's cotton gin in 1793. On a value basis, cotton accounted for half of all U.S. exports after 1840 and the South produced over half of the entire global supply. The South, proclaiming "Cotton is King," believed that Great Britain would intervene on behalf of the Confederacy in order to ensure an uninterrupted supply of cotton for its factories. Yet Great Britain remained officially neutral due to the following factors: huge prewar exports left Great Britain with an oversupply of cotton; Egypt and

India increased their output of cotton; captured cotton was shipped by the Union; poor grain harvests in Great Britain left them dependent on Northern wheat and corn; and the British public opposed intervention in support of the Southern slave states.

Cotton, like every other crop associated with U.S. pre-eminence, is an "immigrant." Of the crops currently grown in the United States, only the cranberry, blueberry, sunflower, pecan, and Jerusalem artichoke are indigenous. Native Americans added corn, beans, and squash to the list of plants that were available to the colonists. Not surprisingly, early U.S. leaders strongly encouraged that foreign seeds be introduced from abroad. In 1770, while serving as the colony of Pennsylvania's ambassador to England, Benjamin Franklin sent certain Chinese seeds to a friend in the colonies. These soybeans, as they would later be called, did not become a major U.S. crop until the late 1920s, yet by the 1980s the United States would produce roughly 60 percent of the world's soybeans. During the 1800s, diplomats were directed to send seeds home from their foreign posts and congressional members liberally used their "franking" privileges to mail seeds to interested constituents at government expense. From 1839 until the creation of the United States Department of Agriculture (USDA) in 1862, the U.S. Patent Office was responsible for the collection and distribution of seeds and plants. The initial mandate of USDA was to expand the collection and dissemination of valuable plants, seeds, and information to farmers. With the rediscovery of the Mendelian principles of genetics in the early 1900s, a more scientific approach to plant introduction emerged. The study of genetics also provided the basis for breeding breakthroughs that significantly contributed to a six-fold increase in the average corn yield per acre by 1985.

The Age of Surplus: 1920–1970

Many current tensions in U.S. foreign agricultural relations have their origins in the events of the 1920s and 1930s. Technological advances in agriculture and the return of foreign agricultural production in the wake of World War I led to surplus conditions in the 1920s. The U.S. tariff policy of this era reflected the plight of farmers burdened by surplus production. The tariff reductions achieved with the Underwood Tariff of 1913, which reduced tariff levels to under 15 percent, were sharply reversed in the 1920s. The culmination of this tariff escalation was the Smoot-Hawley Tariff Act (1930) which raised the average tariff level to 60 percent by 1932. Recognizing that interest group pressures jeopardized the creation of an effective international trade policy, Congress delegated its responsibility for setting tariffs to the executive branch in the Reciprocal Trade Agreements Act (RTA) of 1934. This delegation of power to the exec-

utive has continued to be a key aspect of multilateral trade liberalization efforts, as evidenced in the negotiating rounds of the General Agreement on Tariffs and Trade (GATT) and the North American Free Trade Agreement (NAFTA).

In addition to raising tariffs, the government instituted price supports, quotas, and export subsidies to reduce the plight of U.S. farmers, which was thought to be feeding the Great Depression. Up until 1933, government support for agriculture was mostly of an indirect character (for example, public research, agricultural extension). The nature of this support changed to direct market intervention with the Agricultural Adjustment Act (AAA) of 1933, instituting minimum price guarantees and acreage controls, and authorizing the secretary of agriculture to use import quotas to reduce supplies and raise farm incomes. In 1935, Section 32 of the act was added, enabling the government to provide export subsidies in order to dispose of excess production. Direct market interventions, such as these, continue to be key components of the farm policies of industrialized countries and are at the core of most agricultural trade disputes.

Events surrounding the Great Depression also highlight another important issue in U.S. foreign relations: agricultural guest workers. The Mexican Revolution (1913–1920) reduced the employment opportunities for Mexican farmhands and consequently many Mexicans looked northward. Farming practices in the western states had developed an insatiable hunger for seasonal farmhands willing to work for low wages. During the Depression, widespread concern developed that the Mexican migrant workers were contributing to an oversupply of labor, driving down wages, and impeding attempts to unionize and improve conditions for farmworkers. As a result, many Mexicans were returned to Mexico and Senate hearings were held to investigate western farmers' manipulation of immigration policy and enforcement.

World War II brought a speedy demise to efforts designed to reform farm labor and immigration policies. Asserting that farm labor shortages would lead to crop losses, farmers used the war effort to persuade the U.S. government to conclude with Mexico, in August of 1942, an agreement to import Mexican *Braceros* (farmhands). In the largest foreign laborer program in U.S. history, roughly five million *Braceros* were contracted over the next two decades. The *Bracero* Program was unilaterally terminated by the United States in 1964 when the growers' arguments that without immigrants crops would rot and food prices soar no longer prevailed. The *Bracero* Program was effectively portrayed by civil rights advocates as inhibiting the ability of our own agricultural workers to improve their lot, many of whom were themselves Hispanic. Despite the termination of the *Bracero*

Program, the agricultural sector remains an important factor in the legal and illegal migration of Mexicans to the United States. For example, during the 1996 House. debate over an immigration reform bill, agricultural interests proposed to import 250,000 Mexican guest workers if the Immigration and Naturalization Service (INS) "succeeded" in reducing illegal Mexican immigration. This amendment was rejected by the House.

World War II, in addition to derailing efforts to reform immigration and farm labor policies, solved the agricultural surplus crisis of the 1930s thanks to the disruption of agricultural production in Europe. However, high price supports, improved breeding techniques, and the application of newly available agrichemicals in the form of fertilizers and pesticides heralded a new age of surplus soon to come. In the immediate postwar years, the negative effects of war on the European economies and the extensive aid given through the Marshall Plan in order to contain the spread of communism, kept agricultural surpluses at bay. However, declining aid and the revival of European agricultural production marked the return of detrimental surpluses.

The farm lobby's pressure on the government to deal with the agricultural surplus problem had two important effects on U.S. foreign relations. First, record production levels paired with weakened demand contributed to the approval of the Food for Peace program, also called Public Law 480. This program was designed to protect U.S. farmers's income from the negative effects of overproduction through the sale of surplus grain to developing nations. The foreign currency earned from these sales would then be reinvested into the economies of those countries, thus, in theory, strengthening the market for U.S. exports and at the same time contributing to humanitarian and national security goals.

The second result of domestic agrarian pressure was the exclusion of the agricultural sector from GATT negotiations. While the United States played a hegemonic role in liberalizing trade in manufactured products, it failed to act similarly in agriculture. The existence of extensive government intervention and well-organized agricultural interest groups explains why the United States supported the drafting of GATT rules to be in accordance with agricultural policies rather than the reverse. The clearest example of U.S. farmers' ability to pressure the United States to pursue illiberal practices regarding agriculture is the GATT waiver granted to the United States in 1955. In this case, the United States threatened to withdraw from GATT unless they were granted a waiver allowing them to impose import quotas on agricultural products that adversely affected the operation of a domestic price-support program. This waiver, which technically applies only to the United States, has been a source of resentment from other GATT members

and has served as justification for other nations to pursue illiberal trade practices.

While the United States was significantly responsible for the preferential treatment agriculture received from the GATT, escalating costs for domestic farm programs and a desire to pursue a perceived comparative advantage in agriculture led the United States to pursue stronger liberalization efforts in the 1960s. Yet by this time, the European Community (EC) was basing its political stability and economic integration on a Common Agricultural Policy (CAP) that relied heavily on agricultural protectionism. As a result, progress on bringing agriculture within the international norms that applied to other areas of trade would be extremely limited during the first seven GATT negotiating rounds. Only with the eighth GATT round, the Uruguay Round (1986–1993), would agriculture emerge as a significant focus of multilateral trade negotiations.

The Export Boom: 1970–1981

The rising costs of domestic farm support programs and U.S.-EC trade friction would be temporarily alleviated with the export boom and record high prices for agricultural commodities in the 1970s. Every year, from 1969 to 1981, U.S. agricultural exports grew. U.S. farmers became more reliant on export sales which by the 1970s comprised 25 percent of farm cash receipts as compared with only 10 percent in the 1950s. This heyday for agricultural exports appears to have resulted from a unique set of circumstances. First, oil-exporting countries relied on the massive price increase of oil to increase their food imports fourfold. Second, Western banks dramatically increased their lending to the Third World, which contributed to a doubling of food imports into developing countries during the 1970s. Finally, the Soviet Union suffered disappointing grain harvests and looked to the world market to offset the shortfalls.

The United States captured a significant portion of the increased agricultural trade opportunities of the 1970s. In the area of grain exports, which nearly doubled over the 1970s, the United States was particularly impressive, capturing 80 percent of the increase. In part, this was due to the United States's willingness, for primarily economic reasons, to initiate agricultural sales to China and the Soviet Union. The political-security implications of these sales were not a major issue until the Soviets invaded Afghanistan in December 1979. As one component of his overall response to the Soviet aggression, President Carter initiated an embargo on seventeen million metric tons of grain to the Soviet Union. This action initiated a contentious debate over the effectiveness of using agricultural trade disruptions as an economic sanction.

Critics of the embargo found it to be ineffective, expensive, and ironically, more harmful to U.S. citizens than Russian citizens. Their argument was bolstered by the fact that the Soviets were largely able to replace the embargoed grain with purchases from other suppliers. Viewing the economic sanctions as more costly to the United States than to the Soviets, skeptics felt the embargo communicated weakness and a lack of capacity to punish and deter.

Others, however, strongly disagreed with the critics' disparagement of the embargo because of its perceived cost to the United States, arguing that the willingness of the United States to impose economic hardship upon itself was instrumental in communicating the serious implications of the invasion. In such analysis, it was the perceived costliness of the embargo at the time President Carter announced it which made it an effective symbol of U.S. resolve. Ironically, the same factors that helped the Soviet Union to avoid many of the costs of the embargo also eased the burden of the embargo on U.S. farmers. In fact, during the first year of the embargo, U.S. farmers saw a 22 percent increase in grain exports and actually increased their share of world sales of wheat and coarse grain.

Collapse of the Export Market

U.S. farmers suffered economic hardship and farm support costs soared, not as a result of the grain embargo, but because of the combination of several economic events. The tight U.S. monetary policy adopted by the Federal Reserve Board in 1979 raised real interest rates and contributed to a worldwide recession. Worse still for exporters, these same monetary policies propelled the dollar exchange rate up by seventy percent between 1980 and 1985. Further compounding the crisis was the fact that U.S. exporters had grown increasingly dependent on exports to developing countries. The debt crisis of the 1980s hit Latin American countries particularly hard. From 1981 to 1987 U.S. agricultural exports to Latin America fell by nearly 50 percent. The austerity programs undertaken by these countries suppressed their demand for U.S. imports. In certain cases, most notably Brazil's soybean production program, their quest to earn foreign exchange to pay off their debt intensified export competition with U.S. agricultural products.

Along with the return of vexing surpluses, a sharp decline in prices and export earnings occurred. Wheat stocks, for example, increased by 70 percent from 1981 to 1987, while the price of wheat fell by 45 percent. What distinguished this period of surplus from the surplus of the 1950s and 1960s was that the United States no longer occupied a hegemonic trade position. The EC had emerged as a potent trade competitor and trade frictions characterized this period, including a costly export subsidy war. Mounting surpluses and the soaring economic costs of farm programs required that farm trade be fixed.

Efforts to counteract farm programs implemented by trading partners increased the cost of domestic farm programs to the point where, in 1988, an estimated $288 billion was transferred from consumers and taxpayers to farmers in the OECD countries.

The 1980s exemplify the connection between domestic farm interests and U.S. foreign relations. The manipulation of U.S. sugar import quotas provides a good illustration of how domestic pressures can impede foreign policy. The protection of domestic sugar producers by the United States and other developed nations has been fiercely contested by Third World sugar exporters whose economies have languished as a result of sharply lower prices. Moreover, these exporters recognize that their quota allocation could be suspended at any time for political reasons, as the United States did to Cuba in 1960. The United States, which was purchasing in excess of half of Cuba's sugar under a preferential quota arrangement, suspended Cuba's quota as an economic reprisal for their radicalization and nationalization of U.S. companies under Fidel Castro. In response, the Soviets stepped in and purchased the sugar on terms favorable to the Cubans for the duration of the Cold War.

Again during the 1980s, manipulation of the sugar quota punished several Latin American countries. However, the economic hardship induced by changes in the sugar quota were intentional in some cases and unintentional in others. In two instances, Nicaragua in 1983 and Panama in 1987, the U.S. government suspended the sugar quota to punish the country. In Nicaragua's case, the United States attempted to weaken the Nicaraguan economy and delegitimize the Sandinista government because of its pro-Soviet and pro-Cuban relations. The suspension of the sugar quota, worth only $18.5 million, probably had more significance as a sign that the United States was proceeding towards the severance of trade relations. The quota was restored in 1990 after the Sandinistas lost the presidential election. In Panama's case, the quota was suspended in December 1987 in an attempt to contribute to the demise of General Manuel Noriega. The quota was restored in early 1990, shortly after the U.S. invasion of Panama and the removal of Noriega.

The irony of U.S. sugar policy in the 1980s is that the United States inadvertently imposed economic hardship on a number of Latin American allies. The economic destabilization resembled that which was purposefully enacted against Nicaragua and Panama. The Dominican Republic faced a severe decline in sugar revenue, earning only $136 million in 1988 when it had earned $513 million seven years earlier. President Reagan did not support a reduction in the size of the sugar quota because of the negative effects it would have on regional allies; however, he acquiesced to the tightening because of the budgetary ramifications of not doing so. In essence, Reagan's foreign policy goal of political security in the Caribbean Basin was seriously threatened by the need to support producer prices.

The same farm support programs that were constraining Reagan's ability to bolster his Caribbean allies's economies were also creating budgetary difficulties. The perception among U.S. leaders was that farm policies in most OECD countries, including the United States, were inducing high-cost surplus production that had to be protected through import restrictions or else dumped on the international market with the help of export subsidies. Both interventions generated constant trade friction and cost the taxpayer and consumer. The farm problem could only be resolved in a multilateral fashion because it was connected to distorting farm policies in other countries.

This realization led the United States to become a vocal advocate of bringing agriculture within the GATT at the upcoming Uruguay Round (1986–1993). Driven by budgetary difficulties and the promise of U.S. farm exports, the United States indicated that the whole of its agricultural policy was on the table, assuming others would do likewise. U.S. leaders stressed the need to share the difficulties of farm reform through multilateral concessions. The fact that EC and Japanese farmers are more heavily subsidized than their U.S. counterparts meant that they would bear more of the cost of trade liberalization. Moreover, the mushrooming Japanese trade surplus with the United States strengthened the sentiment that Japan must open its lucrative agricultural market. As an added benefit, Reagan officials perceived an opportunity to circumvent domestic opposition by elevating farm policy reform negotiations to the international level.

Ironically, as noted by Robert L. Paarlberg, a contributor to the book *World Agriculture and the GATT*, the Reagan administration's attempt to create a two-level game was effectively countered by the farm lobby's creation of their own two-level game. The farm lobby took advantage of the Reagan administration's first position on agricultural reform in the Uruguay Round, which called for the elimination of all subsidies that cause distortions in agricultural trade within ten years. Recognizing that this "zero option" proposal would be far too threatening to the heavily-protected European and Japanese economies, farm lobbyists began to support the "zero option" as the only acceptable position. U.S. farm groups successfully lobbied for more subsidies so that U.S. negotiators would have more to work with at the multilateral talks. Unilateral measures, such as the U.S. acreage reduction programs of the 1980s, would simply allow the EC to wrest export markets away from the United States

This examination of the domestic/foreign policy linkages clarifies why U.S. leaders did not view their proposal for a radical liberalization of agricultural trade as inconsistent with the launching of the subsidy policy called the Export Enhancement Program (EEP) in 1985 as part of the ongoing subsidy war. While the United States has subsidized exports since the Depression era, export subsidies were not employed from 1973 to 1983. EEP, however, is similar to the export subsidies offered by the EC and other countries, though on a smaller scale. EEP became problematic when it was extended to exports to China and the Soviet Union. This upset competitors of the United States, failed to lead to additional purchases, and produced an ironic situation in which U.S. citizens were paying more for U.S. grain than were their Soviet counterparts.

Judging the extent to which the United States achieved its objectives in agriculture in the Uruguay Round is difficult. The U.S. position had four basic objectives: (1) that export subsidies be phased out over five years and domestic subsidies over ten years; (2) that non-tariff barriers (NTBs) be converted to tariffs which are more transparent and thus more easily reduced over time through negotiation; (3) that scientifically-based guidelines be prepared for sanitary and phytosanitary restrictions on trade; and (4) that the developing nations adopt the reforms, though possibly under a slightly delayed schedule.

The actual agricultural agreement, while ending a forty-year exclusion of agriculture from GATT rules, was certainly more modest than what the United States had proposed. Future changes in agricultural trade relations will occur slowly and substantial government intervention will remain the norm for quite some time. Regarding the specifics, export subsidies are to be reduced by 36 percent and domestic subsidies by 20 percent over a six-year period, with 1986–1990 serving as the base period. Additionally, no new export subsidies are allowed. All NTBs, such as quotas, voluntary export restraints (VERs), and variable levies are to be converted to tariffs and reduced by an average of 36 percent for developed countries and 24 percent for developing countries over a ten-year period. In a related agreement, a significant step toward harmonizing sanitary and phytosanitary measures was achieved requiring the use of international and scientifically-based principles.

Future Issues in U.S. Agricultural Relations

The success of the newly-formed World Trade Organization (WTO) in implementing the Uruguay Round will have important implications for future U.S. foreign agricultural relations. The agreement on agriculture calls for further negotiations beginning in the fifth year of implementation with the goal of further reduction of trade distortions. Since the agreement on agriculture provides improved rules in lieu of any significant immediate liberalization of agricultural trade, the success of future negotiations will weigh heavily in history's assessment of the Uruguay Round.

Developing countries are an increasingly common destination for U.S. farm exports. By 1990, more than 40 percent of U.S. agricultural exports were consumed by developing countries, as compared with only 20 percent in the 1960s. This constitutes the most attractive growth market for U.S. agricultural exporters for three key reasons. First, the sheer size of the population means that even modest consumption gains could translate into a significantly larger market. Second, when poor people's incomes rise, they tend to spend a large amount of the increase on upgrading their diet, thus creating increased demand for agricultural products. Finally, since many people in developing countries are employed in a relatively unproductive agricultural sector, there are opportunities to improve productivity and incomes with technical assistance.

To many U.S. farmers it seems counterintuitive to suggest that we are helping ourselves by exporting our production technologies and assisting farmers in developing countries. Instead, many commodity groups suggest that it is simply creating more competition in an already fiercely competitive global market. In such cutthroat eras it is difficult to convince farmers that the potential market growth depends on income gains being widespread, and that since agriculture remains the primary sector in many developing countries, development assistance must focus on helping raise farmer incomes. As the African experience over the 1980s has shown, rapid population growth and persistent hunger do not create strong export markets. Nonetheless, it remains an arduous task to persuade struggling U.S. farmers that their salvation depends on increased foreign agricultural assistance.

Assisting Third World farmers has the added benefit of helping U.S. scientists gain access to genetic material. Control over germplasm became a contentious North-South issue during the 1980s and agricultural assistance is likely to be required for continued access. In part, the control of genetic material became a source of North-South friction because of the promise of biotechnology. As the major producer of agricultural biotechnology, the United States has taken several steps to ensure a global environment conducive to its development. First, the United States continues to fund bilateral and multilateral agricultural assistance efforts for developing countries so as to maintain access to germplasm. Second, the United States has taken steps to extend its own strong intellectual property rights for agricultural biotechnology to the global arena. Technology producers, like the United States, tend to favor strong international protection of intellectual property rights, whereas technology consumers prefer much less stringent protection. The United States has aggressively targeted countries with weak patent protection. Additionally, an agreement on Trade-Related Intellectual Property Rights (TRIPS), successfully concluded during the Uruguay Round, established minimum standards for intellectual property rights. Finally, the United States has consistently opposed attempts by the Food and Agricultural Organization (FAO) to take control of germplasm collection and dissemination. Despite these efforts, access to germplasm is likely to remain contentious in the foreseeable future.

Government leaders increasingly view the complex system of import barriers and agricultural regulations as the source of, rather than the solution to, the difficulties facing the agricultural sector. Classical economic analyses suggest that many economic benefits for both the developed and the developing countries could be gained by exposing protected domestic agricultural production to the discipline of the international market. However, there exists an underestimation of the importance of social, political, and ideological factors in determining agricultural reform. The extensive government intervention in the industrialized countries has received key support from two noneconomic arguments: (1) the Jeffersonian image of the farmers providing fundamental values for liberal democracy; and (2) the desirability of some measure of food security, even at a significant economic cost. These arguments, as well as political systems in Japan, the United States, and the EC that generally remain responsive to the agricultural lobby, will not vanish in the wake of the GATT agreement on agriculture. Therefore, despite agriculture's declining share of domestic production and foreign trade, the agricultural sector will remain a contentious aspect of U.S. foreign relations and WTO negotiations for years to come.

JEFFREY L. ANDERSON

See also Economic Sanctions; Food for Peace; General Agreement on Tariffs and Trade; Immigration; International Trade and Commerce

FURTHER READING

Anania, Giovanni, Colin A. Carter, and Alex F. McCalla, eds. *Agricultural Trade Conflicts and GATT: New Dimensions in U.S.-European Agricultural Trade Relations*. Boulder, Colo., 1994.
Avery, William P., ed. *World Agriculture and the GATT*. Boulder, Colo., 1993.
Baldwin, David A. *Economic Statecraft*. Princeton, N.J., 1985.
MacDonald, Scott B., and Georges A. Fauriol, eds. *The Politics of the Caribbean Basin Sugar Trade*. New York, 1991.
Marlin-Bennett, Renee. *Food Fights: International Regimes and the Politics of Agricultural Trade Disputes*. Langhorne, Pa., 1993.
Martin, Philip L. *Trade and Migration: NAFTA and Agriculture*. Washington, D.C., 1993.
Persley, Gabrielle J. *Beyond Mendel's Garden: Biotechnology in the Service of World Agriculture*. Wallingford, Great Britain, 1990.
Skogstad, Grace, and Andrew Fenton Cooper, eds. *Agricultural Trade: Domestic Pressures and International Tensions*. Halifax, Nova Scotia, 1990.

Swegle, Wayne E., Denise Felton Bryant, and Dick Lee, eds. *The Globalization of Agriculture: Promises and Pressures for U.S. Farmers and Agribusinesses.* Morrilton, Ark., 1991.

AGRICULTURE, U.S. DEPARTMENT OF

See Agriculture

AGRICULTURE TRADE DEVELOPMENT AND ASSISTANCE ACT OF 1954

See Food for Peace

AGUINALDO, EMILIO

(*b.* 22 March 1869; *d.* 6 February 1964)

A key figure in the Philippine revolution against Spain (1896–1898), president of the independent Philippine government established in 1898, and commander of the Filipino forces in the Philippine-American War (1899–1902). A member of the gentry of Cavite province, south of Manila, Aguinaldo attended secondary school and then turned to local politics, winning election to the top municipal post of his hometown, Kawit. Increasingly dissatisfied with Spanish colonial rule, he was inducted in 1895 into the *Katipunan*, a secret society that aimed to liberate the Philippines. After the outbreak of the Philippine Revolution in August 1896, Aguinaldo came into conflict with Andres Bonifacio, the head of the *Katipu-nan*, and emerged as leader of the revolutionary movement.

At first the revolutionaries failed on the battlefield, and in December 1897 Aguinaldo went into exile in Hong Kong. In May 1898, however, following the outbreak of war between Spain and the United States, Aguinaldo returned from exile and resumed leadership of the revolution. With Spain now distracted by the war with the United States, the Filipino forces took control over most of Luzon by the end of June. In the same month, Aguinaldo established a government with himself as president.

Aguinaldo's victory was short-lived. Although he initially believed (based on conversations with U.S. officials) that the United States had no designs on the Philippines, Aguinaldo discovered that he was mistaken. A U.S. Army expeditionary force reached the Philippines in June 1898, and relations between it and Filipino troops soon became tense. Aguinaldo tried without success to negotiate. Inevitably, in February 1899, a collision occurred between the two armies; the Philippine-American War had begun.

Aguinaldo has often been celebrated as the leader of a popular struggle against the United States, but he did not have mass support. As president of the Philippine government, he had earlier pursued policies palatable to his social class while ignoring the poor. As the fighting went on, the lack of popular enthusiasm for the war effort proved fatal. Aguinaldo's choice of tactics also hurt his chances. Having decided to fight a conventional war, he suffered an unbroken series of defeats. Only in November 1899, after his best units had been decimated, did he switch to guerrilla warfare, and only then did the Filipinos began to experience modest success.

Captured in March 1901, Aguinaldo quickly issued a manifesto encouraging Filipino troops to surrender, but guerrilla warfare continued without him for more than a year. Held under house arrest until mid-1902, Aguinaldo then returned to Cavite. In later years, he acquired large landholdings and played a dominant role in provincial politics, always behind the scenes. His two forays into national politics were disastrous. In 1935 he made an unsuccessful bid to become Commonwealth president. During World War II, he held several important posts in the Japanese administration, and because of his open collaboration, he emerged from the war as a discredited figure.

GLENN ANTHONY MAY

See also Philippines; Spanish-American-Cuban-Filipino War, 1898

FURTHER READING

Agoncillo, Teodoro. *Malolos: The Crisis of the Republic.* Quezon City, 1960.

Aguinaldo, Emilio. *Mga Gunita ng Himagsikan [Recollections of the Rebellion].* Manila, 1964.

Saulo, Alfredo B. *Emilio Aguinaldo: Generalissimo and President of the First Philippine Republic—First Republic in Asia.* Quezon City, 1983.

Sidel, John. "Walking in the Shadow of the Big Man: Justiniano Montano and Failed Dynasty Building in Cavite, 1935–1972." In *An Anarchy of Families: State and Family in the Philippines,* edited by Alfred W. McCoy. Madison, Wis., 1993.

AID

See Agency for International Development

AIDS

See Acquired Immune Deficiency Syndrome (AIDS) Pandemic

AIR FORCE, U.S. DEPARTMENT OF

The civilian administrative department in charge of the U.S. Air Force (USAF), which was formally chartered as a new third branch of the American armed services by the National Security Act of 1947. This act also rechartered the constitutionally mandated departments of the Army (formally Department of War) and the Navy (which includes the Marine Corps). In 1949 these three were combined as structurally parallel and nearly identical subordinate units within the new Department of Defense when it was chartered by amendments to the 1947 act. The organizational structure of the Department of the Air Force is parallel to and nearly identical to that of the other two primary services. The department is headed by a civilian secretary of the air force appointed by the president, who reports to the secretary of defense. A large bureaucracy, partly career personnel and partly political appointees, works for the secretary. Also working for the secretary in an administrative sense are the chief of staff of the air force, its senior uniformed officer, and his bureaucracy. In military matters, however, the chief of staff represents the USAF as a member of the Joint Chiefs of Staff (JCS), reporting to the chairman of the JCS and upward through the secretary of defense to the president as commander in chief. The secretary and chief of staff work together to recruit, train, and equip USAF personnel—within budgetary allowances and policy guidance from above—to have available for use by the joint "unified" and "specified" commands (under the JCS chairman) when so directed by higher authority in war or warlike situations.

This simple outline of organizational history masks the far larger issues raised by the origins and evolution of the USAF, which lay near the heart of decisions as to how the United States would fight its wars in the 20th century, and by the impact of ever-more-overwhelming technological innovations. The invention of the airplane raised major questions about its potential military uses. Received military wisdom prescribed how to organize and use armed forces, according to whether the fighting was to be done largely by armies on the dry side of a coastline or navies on the wet side. The airplane did not respect this coastline principle. The controversies this raised beset U.S. leaders, both military and civilian, beginning with the appearance of Samuel Pierpont Langley's first aircraft at the beginning of the century. What became the U.S. Air Force began in 1907 as one officer and two soldiers assigned to the Army's Signal Corps within the War Department. Radically expanded to 100,000 men and 3,500 aircraft a decade later when the U.S. entered World War I, it was separated from the Signal Corps at the end of the war and named the Air Service. In 1926 its name was changed to the Army Air Corps. In 1935 it was further strengthened and separated from the army in all but final language when it was renamed as General Headquarters, Air Force. Thinking about missions for the air force evolved over the decades. After the first combat application of powered flight in

World War I, inconclusively featuring flimsy little fighters mainly engaged in trying to shoot one another down, Army General Billy Mitchell led zealots in arguing that the true use of air power in war must take the form of long-range strategic bombing, and that this would render obsolete virtually all forms of surface warfare. Numerous efforts to support this contention failed; substantial ground and naval units remained vital to virtually all subsequent military endeavors. It was nevertheless widely agreed that strategic bombing could be a useful component of large-scale, complex military encounters. In World War II the USAF took this as its principle mission, developing large bombers for this purpose, augmented by tactical missions for smaller aircraft. After the war ended, Congress perceived a strategic bombing capability as the best way to exploit the new U.S. nuclear weapons. The newly emerging concept of deterrence held that virtually no adversary would attack the United States as long as it appeared that the United States possessed a capacity for what Secretary of State John Foster Dulles called "massive retaliation." During the two Eisenhower administrations roughly half of the defense budget was devoted to building this capability within the air force, leaving the army and navy to scrap over the remaining funds. President John F. Kennedy was the first commander in chief to harbor doubts about the all-purpose effectiveness of strategic bombing, taking into account the question of credibility in the face of the growing nuclear arsenals of the Soviet Union and several other countries. Accordingly, the army and navy received increasing shares of the defense budget during the 1960s, reinforced by requirements for fighting the Vietnam War. The air force remained in business, but the overall mission of deterrence began to be shared by a triad featuring not only the big air force bombers but also sea-based and land-based missiles. The air force succeeded, however, in getting itself assigned the primary responsibility for any military missions in space.

Interactions between national and international politics and technological developments during the 1970s and 1980s led to changes in emphasis regarding mission assignments for all of the armed services, including the air force. The Goldwater-Nicholas Act of 1986 further downgraded the significance of each individual service while reinforcing the trend toward improvised force mixtures tailored to specific situations. The collapse of the Soviet Union at the end of 1991 removed the main threat against which long-range strategic strike capabilities had been designed. Continuing arms control efforts, and the increasing length of time since the first and only use of nuclear weapons at the end of World War II, persuaded many Americans that nuclear war, which had once seemed a looming threat, was almost inconceivable. The conflicts in Korea and Vietnam represented the high-water marks of the concept of "limited war" as the use of

SECRETARY OF THE AIR FORCE

ADMINISTRATION	SECRETARY	PERIOD OF APPOINTMENT
Truman	W. Stuart Symington	1947–1950
	Thomas K. Finletter	1950–1953
Eisenhower	Harold E. Talbott	1953–1955
	Donald A. Quarles	1955–1957
	James H. Douglas, Jr.	1957–1959
	Dudley C. Sharp	1959–1961
Kennedy	Eugene M. Zuckert	1961–1965
L. Johnson		
	Harold Brown	1965–1969
Nixon	Robert C. Seamans, Jr.	1969–1973
	John L. McLucas	1973–1975
Ford	James W. Plummer	1975–1976
	Thomas C. Reed	1976–1977
Carter		
	John C. Stetson	1977–1979
	Hans M. Mark	1979–1981
Reagan	Verne Orr	1981–1985
	Russell A. Rourke	1985–1986
	Edward C. Aldridge, Jr.	1986–1988
Bush	Donald B. Rice	1989–1993
Clinton	Sheila E. Widnall	1993–Present

Source: U.S. Department of the Air Force

U.S. military capabilities gradually became more frequent but substantially smaller in scale.

Operations called "low-intensity conflict" and often-related missions dubbed "humanitarian intervention" became more prominent, and these seemed to require the types of smaller tactical airplanes and helicopters emphasized by the army and navy during the years when the air force was concentrating on large strategic bombers. Huge "strategic lift" cargo planes nevertheless continued to be needed and were often operated by the air force, but on behalf of joint forces directed by the chairman of the JCS.

The military aviation establishment peaked during World War II, with 2.3 million men and women with 63,175 aircraft. At its post-Vietnam Cold War height in 1985, the USAF had a budget of $116 billion, which was then projected to increase to $138 billion by 1993. But when fiscal year 1993 arrived, after the collapse of the Soviet Union and the end of the Cold War, the actual budget turned out to be only $68 billion. By 1994 it had dropped to $63 billion, and air force missions were scheduled to include only minimum-level strategic deterrence capabilities and a dwindling assortment of other tasks. Manpower numbers flesh out the story. In 1986 the air force had 608,000 uniformed personnel on active duty.

The number had dropped to 434,000 by 1993, and was slated to be further reduced to 375,000 by the year 2000. President George Bush anticipated a base force of 1.6 million uniformed personnel in all services when his post-Cold War downsizing program was completed. President Bill Clinton reduced this to a base force of 1.4 million, and many military authorities expect the base force to be even further reduced, possibly to a total as low as 1.1 or 1.2 million. All of this repeated a pattern that has occurred after every war and major warlike crisis in the twentieth century: the United States has repeatedly undertaken a form of disarmament while taking on complicated new global responsibilities which could conceivably require substantial military capabilities. As of the fiscal year 1995, the American defense budget had experienced ten straight years of real decline in constant dollars. Unabating political pressures to cut taxes, cut expenses, and cut the national deficit, and indications of re-emerging isolationist tendencies, came into conflict with competing demands to increase arms-related expenditures as long as presidents considered stretching U.S. military capabilities in connection with situations as diverse as those in Somalia, Haiti, Panama, Cuba, and Bosnia in the 1990s.

These problems faced all services, but the Department of the Air Force faced an additional threat to organizational coherence and integrity in the renewed controversies, present since the very invention of the airplane, over the proper roles and missions of manned aircraft in future military involvements. The air force is the only armed service built around a particular technology, and this lies at the heart of the controversies because of a propensity of all technologies to become obsolete with time.

VINCENT DAVIS

See also Aerospace; Cold War; Cuban Missile Crisis; Defense, U.S. Department of; Defense Reorganization Act; Deterrence; Goldwater, Barry; Joint Chiefs of Staff; National Aeronautics and Space Administration; North Atlantic Treaty Organization; Strategic Air Command; Vietnam War; World War I; World War II

FURTHER READING

Emme, Eugene M., ed. *The Impact of Air Power.* Princeton, 1959.
Hurley, Alfred F., and Robert C. Ehrhart, eds. *Air Power and Warfare.* U.S. Air Force Academy, Colorado, 1979.
Legere, Lawrence J. *Unification of the Armed Forces.* New York, 1989.
Millis, Walter, Harvey C. Mansfield, and Harold Stein. *Arms and the State.* New York, 1958.
Sigaud, Louis A. *Douhet and Aerial Warfare.* New York, 1941.
Smith, Dale O. *U.S. Military Doctrine.* New York, 1955.
Thayer, Frederick C., Jr. *Air Transport Policy and National Security.* Chapel Hill, N.C., 1965.

AIRLINE COMPANIES

Regulated commercial entities that use aircraft to carry persons, property and mail on scheduled flights within the United States and abroad. The United States pressed for an open, multilateral regime for postwar international air services at the 1944 Chicago Conference on International Civil Aviation. The conference created the International Civil Aviation Organization (ICAO) which was forced to focus on technical and safety matters because negotiators failed to reach an agreement for a liberal exchange of route rights on a multilateral basis. Many countries, led by the United Kingdom, worried that airlines from the United States would dominate a liberal, multilateral regime and were unwilling to grant foreign airlines unlimited access to their markets. When the Chicago conference failed, bilateral air service agreements became the basis for international air service operations. The U.S.-U.K. Agreement (Bermuda I) was the model for most bilateral air service agreements. Such agreements govern access to and competition within international air service routes and define the exchange of economic rights, including entry, capacity, routes, and pricing.

Airline technology, demographics, and economics changed steadily in the three decades after the Chicago Conference, but policy change lagged until the mid-1970s. The revised U.S.-U.K. Agreement (Bermuda II), signed in 1977, cut back services and increased political pressure in the United States for a more open international air services regime. The United States resolved thereafter to seek to trade "opportunities for opportunities, not restrictions for restrictions." The passage of the Airline Deregulation Act of 1978 pushed this process along. This act led to increases in competition and major structural changes in the U.S. airline industry. New commercial airlines entered the U.S. market and began to compete for business. U.S. domestic deregulation and competitive international aviation policy forced airlines in other countries to accept more market liberalization. (Fifteen years later most of these airlines were gone, as were some established carriers such as Pan Am. Talk of partial airline reregulation proliferated.) In the United States, American Airlines, United Airlines, and Delta Airlines are the three dominant carriers with comprehensive national networks and extensive international coverage. Northwest, US Air, Continental, and TWA are second-tier players. The wild card is the efficient, low-cost, no-frills Southwest Airlines which has the best cost structure in the industry and a strong balance sheet.

The biggest problem for the airline industry is that airline companies consistently lose money. In aggregate, U.S. carriers have lost money since the Wright brothers first flew at Kitty Hawk in 1903. Often airlines expanded capacity to serve marginal passengers, creating overcapacity. The price of aircraft increased dramatically, pushing capital requirements for airlines skyward. Union success at the bargaining table created high cost labor forces in many airlines. Price competition often is fierce in markets that are contested. In addition, when fuel costs rise, the industry suffers because higher fuel costs cannot easily be passed along to customers. In short, the cost structure and the price structure are out of balance at most U.S. airlines and are forcing them to evolve so that they might thrive.

As a result, the international airline industry is in transition. Traditionally, air services were provided by a collection of local monopolies connected by a set of equally protected international routes. In the future most global air services probably will be provided by fifteen to twenty-five multinational airlines competing on a global scale. To prepare, the big three U.S. airlines and some of the other U.S. and European carriers are creating, on their own or in alliance with other domestic and foreign airlines, seamless global networks that allow customers to travel between any two points in North America, Europe, and Asia on the same integrated system. The major airlines have built sophisticated computerized reservation systems and elaborate frequent flyer programs to try to lock in customers, enhance brand name loyalty, and provide a steady stream of passengers to fill flights.

U.S. airlines and the U.S. government face two ongoing foreign policy issues. The first is structural and has inhibited U.S. efforts to export competition in air services. The United States has about fifteen desirable destinations for international traffic. Most other countries have only one or two attractive destinations. In addition, there are more international carriers based in the United States than in other countries. U.S. carriers complain that foreign carriers seek landing rights at numerous U.S. destinations, but consistently try to limit the number of U.S. carriers that may enter their market and make it difficult for U.S. carriers to get adequate access to gates and desirable landing slots. Second, in Europe, Asia, and throughout the developing world many government-owned or -dominated carriers still are treated as national treasures that bring prestige and tourist dollars to the state. Usually there is little or no competition on domestic routes. National carriers often are subsidized by taxpayers, and prices, particularly on domestic or intra-European routes, are set high. U.S. carriers complain that the playing field is not level. These barriers to access and subsidies hamper the globalization of networks, making it hard for U.S. carriers to compete in many markets. Furthermore, the traditional bilateral structure of airline negotiations provides the United States with little leverage to gain market access, increase route competition, and thereby promote price competition.

JONATHAN D. ARONSON

See also Aerospace

FURTHER READING

Kasper, Daniel. *Deregulation and Globalization: Liberalizing International Trade in Air Services.* , New York, 1988.
Taneja, Nawal. *The International Airline Industry.* Lexington, Ky., 1988.

ALABAMA CLAIMS

(1871–1872)

U.S. damage claims against Great Britain for providing the Confederacy with warships during the American Civil War. Between March 1862 and late 1864, British officials allowed five warships built or purchased by Confederate agents to put to sea. The *Alabama, Florida, Georgia, Rappahannock,* and *Shenandoah* sank or captured well over 150 civilian vessels, decimating the U.S. merchant fleet. Vigorous protests by Secretary of State William H. Seward and the U.S. minister in London, Charles Francis Adams, persuaded the British government to detain three additional warships, the *Alexandra* and two formidable Laird rams, and also laid the foundation for future damage claims, based on the contention that the British Foreign Enlistment Act, which prohibit-

ed the equipping, fitting out, or arming of ships for belligerent warfare, had been repeatedly violated. British local authorities, sanctioned by the highest officials of the Admiralty, War, and Foreign offices, had, either through connivance with Confederate agents or through negligence, allowed the departure from, and later the sustenance in, British ports of Confederate commerce raiders from British ports and their subsequent resupply there.

In 1871 the Treaty of Washington, which included a British expression of regret for the sponsorship of the Confederate cruisers, acknowledged that neutral governments must use "due diligence" to prevent the building, arming, equipping, or supplying by their citizens of belligerent warships. The treaty also created a commission to determine by arbitration the final disposition of what were now universally called the "*Alabama* Claims." Convening in mid-December 1871 in Geneva, the tribunal in 1872 rejected U.S. Secretary of State Hamilton Fish's demand for "indirect damages" and agreed upon the sum of $15.5 million to be paid by Great Britain to the United States in full satisfaction of the *Alabama* Claims. Thus did the first arbitration treaty ever entered into by the United States establish a solid foundation for Anglo-American rapprochement.

NORMAN B. FERRIS

See also Adams, Charles Francis; American Civil War; Arbitration; Confederate States of America; Fish, Hamilton; Seward, William Henry

FURTHER READING

Cook, Adrian. *The* Alabama *Claims: American Politics and Anglo-American Relations, 1865–1872.* Ithaca, N.Y., 1975.
Duberman, Martin B. *Charles Francis Adams, 1807–1886.* Stanford, Calif., 1961.

ALASKA BOUNDARY DISPUTE

(1896–1903)

The controversy over the boundary line between Alaska and Canada. Following the discovery of gold in the Klondike region of Canada in 1896, the Canadians, using the vague wording of the Anglo-Russian Treaty of 1825 that divided Alaska from Canada, claimed that the boundary of the Alaska panhandle, from Yakutat Bay south along the coast to the Portland Channel (Portland Inlet), gave Canada control of the important harbors leading to the goldfields. The Anglo-Russian Treaty, which had formed the basis for the boundaries of Alaska when the United States purchased the territory in 1867, stated that the boundary line in the panhandle extended inland approximately thirty miles. The Canadians claimed that this line should follow a straight line marking the outer coastal areas, whereas the United States countered that it should follow the convoluted coastline.

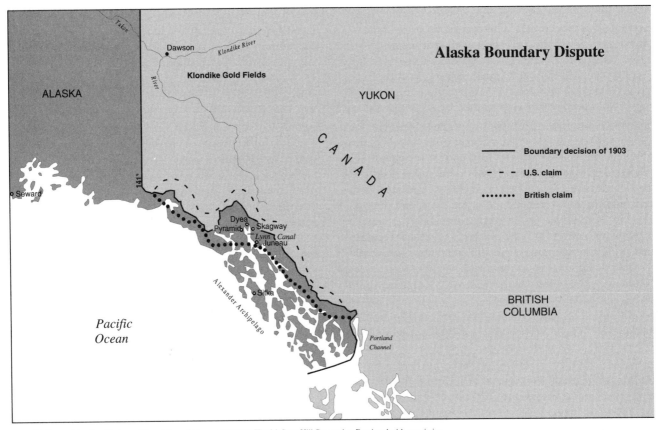

Alaska Boundary Dispute

ALASKA

Dawson
Klondike River
Klondike Gold Fields

YUKON

River

Talca

141°

C
A
N
A
D
A

———— Boundary decision of 1903

– – – U.S. claim

•••••• British claim

Seward

Dyea
Pyramid
Skagway
Lynn Canal
Juneau

Alexander Archipelago

Sitka

Pacific
Ocean

Portland
Channel

BRITISH
COLUMBIA

From *The Course of American Diplomacy*, Howard Jones, Volume I. ©1992 by The McGraw-Hill Companies. Reprinted with permission of The McGraw-Hill Companies.

In 1902 President Theodore Roosevelt, fearing that the discovery of gold in the disputed territory would spark further conflict between U.S. and Canadian miners, ordered U.S. troops into the territory to keep peace. After Canada appeared willing to make concessions, the United States and Great Britain agreed to Secretary of State John Hay's proposal in January 1903 to establish a tribunal of six "impartial jurists"—three from the United States and three from Great Britain, which, at the time, conducted Canada's foreign relations—to settle the dispute. The British group consisted of two prominent Canadians, Sir Louis A. Jetté and Allen B. Aylesworth, and Lord Alverstone, Lord Chief Justice of England. Roosevelt selected Elihu Root, his secretary of war; former Senator George Turner of Washington; and Senator Henry Cabot Lodge, Sr., of Massachusetts to represent the United States. British leaders worried that the dispute might undermine the recent Anglo-American rapprochement. As the tribunal was debating the question, President Roosevelt let it be known that he was willing to order U.S. troops to occupy the disputed area if the decision was unfavorable to the United States. When the tribunal voted in October 1903, Lord Alverstone sided with the U.S. members. Although the decision reduced the territory claimed by the United States, it ranked as a

victory for the United States. Anglo-American rapprochement survived, but Canadian nationalists, including Prime Minister Sir Wilfred Lanier, believed that Great Britain had sacrificed Canada's interests.

LOUIS R. SMITH, JR.

See also Alaska Purchase; Canada; Great Britain; Hay, John Milton; Roosevelt, Theodore; Root, Elihu

FURTHER READING

Beale, Howard K. *Theodore Roosevelt and the Rise of America to World Power.* Baltimore, 1984.

Bothwell, Robert. *Canada and the United States: Politics of Partnership.* New York, 1992.

Esthus, Raymond A. *Theodore Roosevelt and the International Rivalries.* Claremont, Calif., 1982.

Gould, Lewis L. *The Presidency of Theodore Roosevelt.* Lawrence, Kans., 1991.

Munro, John A., ed. *The Alaska Boundary Dispute.* Toronto, 1970.

ALASKA PURCHASE

(1867)

The acquisition of the northwestern extension of the North American continent from Russia. Russian traders, organized as the Russian-American Company, established posts in northwest North America in the late eighteenth century. In 1823 Secretary of State John Quincy Adams contested Russia's right to any "territorial establishment" on this continent. During the 1840s the Oregon Question put Alaska on the horizon of U.S. expansionists, and in the 1850s the administration of President James Buchanan offered to buy the territory from the Russians. During the Civil War the expansionist Democrat and former Senator Robert J. Walker revived the idea, which appealed to like-minded Republican Secretary of State William H. Seward. Russia, which had withdrawn its small presence from California in 1824, recognized by the 1850s that Russian America was defenseless and the Russian-American Company unprofitable. In 1866 the Russian crown decided to cede the area for $5 million in order to thwart her Crimean War enemy and rival Great Britain and maintain good relations with the United States. During secret negotiations the Russian envoy Edouard Stoeckl asked for $7 million and Seward eagerly agreed. Private Russian claims raised the payment to $7.2 million.

The chairman of the Senate Foreign Relations Committee, Charles Sumner, championed Seward's treaty of cession because he believed that the acquisition of Alaska would facilitate an even greater achievement—-the annexation of Canada by the United States. After a 4-to-2 committee vote and delaying efforts by Senator William Fessenden of Maine, the Senate on 9 April 1867 approved the treaty by a margin of 37 to 2. A majority of newspaper editors favored annexation, but Horace Greeley's *New York Tribune* suspected corruption involving Seward, his lobbyist friend Thurlow Weed, and California senators. With Russian approval, U.S. forces occupied Sitka in October 1867. President Andrew Johnson's impeachment trial and reports that Seward also wanted Greenland and Iceland delayed payment to Russia. A frustrated Stoeckl hired Walker as "counsel" for $20,000 in gold and spent another $200,000 to influence members of Congress and reporters. Congress finally passed the appropriation in July 1868 following debates over private claims and the House's authority in matters relative to treaties. Several newspapers alleged that payoffs totaling millions of dollars had changed hands to win congressional approval of the treaty. A lengthy House investigation focused on Walker, his shadowy associates, and Seward, but avoided implicating any members of Congress in scandal. The widely publicized hearings tarnished Seward's purchase and contributed to the suspicion that surrounded the interest of President Ulysses S. Grant's administration in acquiring the Dominican Republic.

PAUL S. HOLBO

See also Russia and the Soviet Union; Seward, William Henry

FURTHER READING

Holbo, Paul S. *Tarnished Expansion: The Alaska Scandal, the Press, and Congress, 1867–1871.* Knoxville, Tenn., 1983.
Jensen, Ronald J. *The Alaska Purchase and Russian-American Relations.* Seattle, Wash., 1975.
Saul, Norman E. *Distant Friends: The United States and Russia, 1763–1867.* Lawrence, Kans., 1991.

ALBANIA

See Appendix 2

ALBRIGHT, MADELEINE K.

(*b.* 15 May 1937)

Twentieth U.S. ambassador and permanent representative to the United Nations (UN), appointed in January 1993 by President William Clinton at the rank of cabinet officer. Born in Prague, Czechoslovakia, and educated at Wellesley College (B.A., 1959) and Columbia University (Ph.D., 1976), she served as chief legislative assistant for Senator Edmund Muskie (1976–1978) and as a member of the National Security Council (1978–1981) during the Carter administration. Prior to assuming the ambassadorship to the UN, she was research professor at Georgetown University and president of the Center for National Policy. Revival of the practice, dropped in the 1980s, of giving the U.S. permanent representative cabinet rank symbolized the Clinton administration's intention of elevating the place of the UN in U.S. foreign policy. Ambassador Albright played a major part in efforts to expand the UN's role in international security issues and peacekeeping. Initially these efforts brought some successes, but as time went on some UN operations, especially those in Somalia and Bosnia, encountered difficulties in altering political conditions and became highly controversial, raising questions about the feasibility and desirability of an expanded UN role.

HAROLD K. JACOBSON

See also Bosnia-Herzegovina; Clinton, William Jefferson; Somalia; United Nations

ALEXANDER I

(*b.* 12 December 1777; *d.* 19 November 1825)

Czar of Russia from 1801 to 1825, who led Russia to victory in the Napoleonic Wars, played a major role at the Congress of Vienna (1814–1815), and pursued territorial claims along the Pacific Coast of North America that brought him into conflict with the United States. Alexander's grandmother, Catherine the Great, had planned his Westernized education, particularly in the ideals of the Enlightenment. After his ascension to the Russian throne in 1801, he improved education and relaxed censorship, but his liberalism stopped short of approving a proposed constitution or otherwise fundamentally compromising autocratic rule. After leading Russian forces to victory over Napoleon (1814) and capturing Paris, Alexander was one of the leading advocates at the Congress of Vienna (and after) of the principle of legitimacy, as well as cooperation among the European dynasties to suppress revolutions against them and, in the case of the Greek War of Independence, against the Ottoman Empire. Alexander desired a large Polish kingdom under his sovereignty, but protests from the other representatives forced him to divide control over Polish territory with Austria and Prussia. During the congress, Alexander proposed the formation of the Holy Alliance as the basis for maintaining order; it was also the culmination of his growing interest in mysticism and religion. Initially signed on 26 September 1815 by the sovereigns of Russia, Austria, and Prussia, and later by other continental princes (but not the British king), the document pledged members to rule in accordance with Christian ideals and to preserve peace. It failed, however, to provide any means of implementing such ideals.

In the early 1820s the U.S. government became worried about possible interference in parts of South America by the members of the Quadruple Alliance (Great Britain, Russia, Austria, and Prussia), originally created in 1814 in opposition to Napoleonic expansionism. U.S. officials also became alarmed by Russia's expansion in the northwest sector of North America in 1821. Alexander issued a ukase (imperial decree) claiming exclusive Russian control from the Bering Straits to the 51st parallel, thus extending Russian claims into much of the Oregon Territory then under shared American and British control. Alexander's attempt in 1821 to expand Russian territorial claims southward from Alaska prompted the declaration from Secretary of State John Quincy Adams that the United States would oppose any expansion of European colonies on the American continents. Although Alexander had suspended the ukase by August 1822, the U.S. noncolonization principle became part of the Monroe Doctrine in 1823. At the same time, Washington perceived Alexander's celebration of monarchy and denunciation of the republican form of government as part of a threat to the newly won independence of the Latin American republics. This concern contributed to the doctrine's warning to Europe to stay out of the political affairs of the Western Hemisphere. In 1824 Alexander agreed to a southern boundary of Alaska at the 54° 40' line.

CAROL A. JACKSON

See also Adams, John Quincy; Monroe Doctrine; Napoleonic Wars; Quadruple Alliance; Russia and the Soviet Union

FURTHER READING

Kushner, Howard I. *Conflict on the Northwest Coast: American-Russian Rivalry in the Pacific Northwest, 1790–1867.* Westport, Conn., 1975.

McConnell, Allen. *Tsar Alexander I: Paternalistic Reformer.* New York, 1978.

Perkins, Dexter. *The Monroe Doctrine.* Cambridge, Mass., 1927.

Saul, Norman E. *Distant Friends: The United States and Russia, 1763–1867.* Lawrence, Kans., 1991.

ALGERIA

Located in North Africa, along the Mediterrean Sea between Morocco and Tunisia, the second largest country in Africa. The evolution of three issue areas has shaped U.S. relations with Algeria: Algeria's historical and contemporary relationship with France, Algeria's post-independence international militancy, and U.S.-Algerian disagreements with respect to regional controversies.

Although some sources refer to Algeria as a former French colony, for over eighty years the French government considered the territory not a colony but an integral part of France. French control of Algeria began with the 1830 conquest of Algiers, an important Mediterranean port. France established control over the rest of the territory only gradually, and rebellions in the interior continued to challenge the colonial authorities throughout the nineteenth century. Nonetheless, many French citizens and other Europeans took advantage of land grants and other incentives to settle in Algeria; these settlers, or *piedsnoirs* "*black feet,*" had great influence in the administration of this overseas *département* of France from 1871 through the late 1950s.

After World War II, Arab and Berber Algerians mobilized politically toward the goal of national independence. However, the settlers' long-standing political influence, French interests in the productivity of the settler economy, and the trauma the French were experiencing as they lost colonial control over Indochina (Vietnam) combined to complicate negotiations regarding Algeria's future with respect to France. In 1956, Algerian nationalists began terrorist campaigns in pursuit of independence from France, and by 1958 civil war ravaged the territory. The crisis in Algeria contributed to the collapse of the Fourth French Republic, and the settlers worked to return Charles de Gaulle to power as the Fifth Republic was created. President de Gaulle, however, moved against the European settlers, granting the independence demands of the nationalists in 1962.

Despite the civil war, since 1962 Algeria's relationship with France has continued to outweigh most other factors in its foreign relations with other countries, including the United States. Trade relations, financial agreements, and immigration levels indicate the continued closeness of France and Algeria. U.S. interests in maintaining cooperative relations with France typically influence U.S. policy toward all of France's former territories to some degree; the intensity of the French experience in Algeria has tended to heighten that influence in U.S.-Algerian relations. (On the other hand, U.S. trade with Algeria has exceeded French levels in some recent years.)

Algeria's militancy after independence, as its leaders achieved Third World and United Nations prominence with their fiery anti-imperialist and anti-Israel rhetoric, eventually led to a rupture in U.S.-Algerian diplomatic relations which lasted from 1967 to 1974. Specific disagreements over U.S. policy in Vietnam, OPEC production and pricing policies, and Algeria's leadership in the Third World movement for nonalignment contributed to the tensions.

In 1975, a new disagreement emerged as a regional dispute among Morocco, Mauritania, and Algeria developed into war over the future international status of Western Sahara (formerly the Spanish colony of Rio de Oro). U.S. support for the Moroccan plan to annex the phosphate-rich territory directly challenged Algeria's interest in establishing Western Sahara as an independent state. This tension continued until the late 1980s, when cooperation among the North African Maghreb countries began to increase.

Algerian-U.S relations did begin to improve somewhat in the late 1970s, notably through the crucial intermediary role Algeria played in U.S.-Iranian negotiations for the release of the U.S. hostages in 1981. Moreover, pragmatic leadership in the face of a worsening economy further encouraged Algeria to improve its relations with the United States. Natural gas and oil reserves in Algeria (fifth and fourteenth largest in the world, respectively) also provide the United States and other Western countries with economic incentives to maintain stable and friendly relations with Algeria. Thus, despite Algerian leaders' lingering propensity for revolutionary attitudes and socialist economic policies, U.S.-Algerian relations generally improved through the early 1990s. The Algerian government did enact a number of partial political and economic reforms over this period, following Western and international advice.

Recent Developments

The United States supported Algeria's internal political reforms as the 1980s ended, including movements toward a competitive multiparty system. However, one of the most popular parties in Algerian politics after 1989, the Islamic Salvation Front (FIS), advocated the establishment of a more activist Islamic state. The FIS captured even more votes than expected in the first round of a general election for delegates to the National People's Assembly (December 1991); shortly before the second round could take place, the government cancelled further voting until elections could be rescheduled. The government leaders created a committee backed by the military, the High Council of State, to rule in the interim. Widespread violence ensued. The state of emergency declared by the government granted the military extraordinary powers to use in its efforts to restore order.

The effect of these events on the Algerian government's relations with the United States and the West has been ambiguous. Simultaneously concerned over the government's abuse of human and civil rights and also over the potential dangers feared from a fundamentalist or activist Muslim takeover in Algeria, U.S. and Western European reaction has been cautious support for the government's political goals, tempered by occasional condemnation of its tactics. Economically, the interests of the United States and other Western nations are similarly ambivalent. Amid the political turmoil, many market reforms paradoxically have become easier to enact, but the toll which terrorist violence and violent state suppression exacts on stable economic performance slows and distorts the measurable impact of those reforms. International lenders and donors, including the United States, continued to demonstrate in the mid-1990s, through rescheduling debt repayments and providing additional monies, that they consider the Algerian government to be an acceptable international partner.

CATHERINE ELKINS

See also Africa; France; Middle East; Third World

FURTHER READING

Ageron, Charles-Robert. *Modern Algeria: A History from 1830 to the Present*. London, 1992.
Entelis, John P., and Phillip C. Naylor, eds. *State and Society in Algeria*. Boulder, 1992.
Smith, Tony. *The French Stake in Algeria 1945–1962*. Cornell, 1978.

ALIEN AND SEDITION ACTS
(1798)

Four laws designed to safeguard the United States against French and Irish aliens and suspected home-grown treasonous elements. The measures were enacted amid hysteria sparked by news from France that America's former ally would not negotiate outstanding issues until bribes had been paid (the XYZ Affair). Many observers consider these four laws the first major infringement on civil liberties in the country's history. With the failure of the U.S. mission to France and the arrival of diplomatic dispatches describing the abortive negotiations in the spring of 1798, fear gripped the American populace. Speaker of the House Jonathan Dayton of New Jersey reported French troops massing to invade the United States, and Secretary of State Timothy Pickering spoke of French-inspired slave revolts in the southern states. Dayton and Pickering were members of the Federalist party, a political faction filled with Francophobes and Hibernophobes. Capitalizing on the war sentiment sweeping the nation, the Federalists saw an opportunity to strike a blow at their political foes, the Republicans, who enjoyed solid support from French and Irish residing in the United States. First, on 18 June President John Adams signed the Naturalization Act, which extended residency requirements for citizenship from five to fourteen years. The Alien Friends Act of 25 June allowed the president to deport aliens deemed a threat to the United States. Little more than a week later, on 6 July, the Alien Enemies Act became law, allowing the president a range of options in treating enemy aliens in wartime. Finally, the Sedition Act (formally the Act for the Punishment of Certain Crimes) was passed on 14 July and sought to define sedition and establish punishment for violators. Although the national government did not vigorously enforce them, the Alien and Sedition Acts stifled dissent. The people supported the legislation, although Republican dissent was registered in Thomas Jefferson, and James Madison's famous Virginia and Kentucky Resolutions.

CLIFFORD L. EGAN

See also Adams, John; Convention of 1800; France; Jefferson, Thomas; Madison, James; Marshall, John; Pickering, Timothy; XYZ Affair

FURTHER READING

Miller, John Chester. *Crisis in Freedom: The Alien and Sedition Acts.* Boston, 1951.
Smith, James Morton. *Freedom's Fetters: The Alien and Sedition Laws and American Civil Liberties.* Ithaca, N.Y., 1956.

ALLEN, HORACE NEWTON

(*b.* 23 April 1858; *d.* 11 December 1932)

American doctor, missionary, and diplomat who promoted closer U.S.-Korean relations. Born in Ohio, Allen graduated from Ohio Wesleyan University (1881) and earned a medical degree from Miami Medical School (1883). In 1883 the Presbyterian Board of Foreign Missions assigned Allen to Nanking and Shanghai, China. After a brief stay in China, Allen moved to Seoul, Korea, with the title of American Legation Doctor. At the time, the Kingdom of Korea was trying to steer a neutral course between two competing neighbors, Japan and China, and looked to the United States for help. Allen quickly gained the favor of, and access to, the king and queen of Korea for successfully treating Prince Min Yong Ik for wounds received in the Kapsin Coup, and for later advis-

ing the government on methods to deal with the disease cholera. In 1887 Allen went to Washington, D.C., as secretary and interpreter to the Korean Embassy. From 1890 to 1905, Allen played a prominent role in the development of U.S.-Korean relations as a representative for both the Korean king and the U.S. government, a negotiator and broker who aided U.S. companies in gaining access to Korean markets and resources, and a strong advocate of U.S. Protestant missionaries. In 1890 Allen was appointed secretary of the U.S. legation in Seoul. Four years later he began a long term as U.S. minister to Korea (1894–1902). Allen consistently and vocally advocated greater U.S. involvement in Korea. He argued that a strong U.S. presence would provide the United States with a foothold in Asia and allow Korea to remain independent from ever-increasing pressures from China and Japan. Later, with little support from Washington forthcoming, he urged Korea to ally with Japan.

Allen used his longstanding palace influence to aid numerous U.S. businesses (James R. Morse's American Trading Company and Collbran and Bostick, in particular) in gaining franchises in Korea in banking and finance, railroad lines, transportation, communication, electricity, mineral resources, timber, and pearls. Although he never completely agreed with U.S. Protestant missionary leaders in Korea, his support of their work proved useful in establishing hospitals and schools and in gaining tacit permission for U.S. missionary efforts among the Korean people. During the final decades of his life Allen lived in Toledo, Ohio, lobbied unsuccessfully to halt the U.S. abandonment of Korea to Japanese control, wrote numerous books and articles on Korean culture and politics, and devoted himself to a successful medical practice.

BRUCE D. MACTAVISH

See also Korea; Missionaries

FURTHER READING

Chay, Jongsuk. *Diplomacy of Asymmetry: Korean-American Relations to 1910.* Honolulu, 1990.
Harrington, Fred Harvey. *God, Mammon, and the Japanese: Dr. Horace N. Allen and Korean American Relations, 1885–1905.* Madison, Wis., 1944.
Lee, Yur-Bok, and Wayne Patterson, eds. *One Hundred Years of Korean-American Relations, 1882–1982.* Alabama, 1986.

ALLENDE (GOSSENS), SALVADOR

(*b.* 26 July 1908; *d.* 11 September 1973)

A leader of the Socialist party of Chile and president of Chile from November 1970 until his overthrow and death during a military coup in 1973. Allende was born in Valparaíso to a family of doctors and lawyers. A committed Marxist from his days as a student leader at the Medical

School of the University of Chile, he helped found the Socialist party in 1933. He was elected to the Chilean Chamber of Deputies in 1937 and, in 1945, to the Senate, where he served for the following twenty-five years. Allende ran unsuccessfully for president of Chile in 1952, 1958, and 1964. In 1964, when he ran on the ticket of a Socialist-Communist coalition, the administration of President Lyndon B. Johnson, through the Central Intelligence Agency (CIA), covertly spent $2.6 million to defeat him. This action was probably not necessary because rightist parties in Chile had already thrown their support to the ultimately victorious center-left Christian Democratic candidate, Eduardo Frei.

In 1970 the Chilean right, angry with the Christian Democrats for adopting, with U.S. backing, a strong agrarian reform law, ran its own candidate, former President Jorge Alessandri. Running in a three-way race, Allende won the popular vote by a margin of 1.2 percent, but because he did not win an absolute majority the election went to a runoff vote in the Chilean Congress, where the candidate with the highest popular vote traditionally was selected. According to CIA Director Richard Helms, before the congressional vote President Richard M. Nixon ordered the CIA to do everything possible ("make the economy scream") to prevent Allende from becoming president, which included not only economic pressures but also, it was later revealed, an unsuccessful effort to instigate a military coup.

Once Allende was elected, the CIA was authorized to use covert funds to support Chilean opposition parties, radio stations, and newspapers. The CIA spent an estimated $7 million for these purposes between 1970 and 1973. Allende took over most U.S.-owned properties in Chile by either nationalization with little or no compensation (such as the U.S.-owned copper mines that had been partially "Chileanized" under the Frei administration), purchase, or "intervention" using legal loopholes. The United States demanded compensation for the nationalized U.S. companies and ceased providing new economic aid, although humanitarian assistance in the "pipeline" and loans to the anticommunist military continued. Allende called the U.S. economic pressure on his regime an "invisible blockade," but economic and diplomatic relations were not cut off. The International Telephone and Telegraph Company (ITT) had urged a trade embargo, but this drastic step was opposed by the other U.S. companies whose holdings had been taken over.

Economic conditions in Chile deteriorated during the Allende administration because of the dislocations resulting from the wholesale government takeovers in industry and agriculture, rising political polarization, and violence by extremists of the left and right. Fearing economic collapse, increasing Marxist domination, and the loss of control over the instruments of coercion, in September 1973 the Chilean armed forces staged a coup in which the presidential palace was bombed. Allende, evidence indicates, took his own life rather than surrender.

In the years that followed, the U.S. role in the breakdown of Chilean democracy became the subject of heated debate. In 1975 a special report, "Covert Action in Chile," published by the U.S. Senate Select Committee on Intelligence Activities, recommended increased congressional control over covert intelligence activities. Despite his ambivalence as a Marxist about the possibilities of peaceful change under capitalism, Allende became an international martyr to democracy. The U.S. sense of culpability for the death of Chilean democracy contributed to rising support for a stronger U.S. commitment to democracy and human rights around the world.

PAUL E. SIGMUND

See also Central Intelligence Agency; Chile; Latin America; Nixon, Richard Milhous

FURTHER READING

Davis, Nathaniel. *The Last Two Years of Salvador Allende.* Ithaca, N.Y., 1985.
Debray, Regis. *Conversations with Allende: Socialism in Chile.* Translated by Peter Beglan. New York, 1971.
Falcoff, Mark. *Modern Chile, 1970–1989: A Critical History.* New Brunswick, N.J., 1989.
Israel, Ricardo. *Politics and Ideology in Allende's Chile.* Tempe, Ariz., 1989.
Sigmund, Paul E. *The Overthrow of Allende and the Politics of Chile, 1964–1976.* Pittsburgh, Pa., 1977.
———. *The United States and Democracy in Chile.* Baltimore, Md., 1993.
Valenzuela, Arturo. *The Breakdown of Democratic Regimes: Chile.* Baltimore, Md., 1978.

ALLIANCE FOR PROGRESS

A U.S. commitment in the 1960s to a long-term economic assistance program to facilitate economic growth, social modernization, and political democratization in Latin America. In a speech on 13 March 1961, President John F. Kennedy pledged that the United States would work to satisfy the basic human needs of Latin Americans and that these socioeconomic improvements would be accomplished within the framework of democratic institutions. The Kennedy administration gave substance to those words at an inter-American conference held in August 1961 at Punta del Este, Uruguay, when U.S. representatives announced that during the 1960s Latin Americans could expect more than $20 billion in public and private capital from the United States and international lending authorities. They predicted that this new money, when combined with an expected $80 billion in internal investment, would produce a real economic growth rate of not less than 2.5 percent a year.

The United States developed this so-called Marshall Plan for Latin America because it feared that the region had become vulnerable to social revolution and communist expansion. Fidel Castro had overthrown Cuba's pro-U.S. dictator and in 1959–1960 transformed the Cuban Revolution into a bitterly anti-U.S. movement. Officials in Washington worried that the impoverished, politically oppressed masses of Latin America might follow a similar radical course.

The Alliance for Progress helped generate the promised $20 billion in outside capital, but the program failed to transform Latin America. Latin American economies performed poorly, registering an unimpressive annual growth rate of 1.5 percent during the 1960s. Imperceptible progress was made in health, education, and welfare, and Latin American societies remained grossly inequitable and undemocratic. During the decade sixteen extraconstitutional changes of government, including several military coups, rocked Latin America. The Alliance fell short of its enumerated goals because Latin America's problems were daunting and because Latin American elites and middle-income groups resisted meaningful reforms, such as a progressive income tax. The United States also proved timid about pursuing meaningful change in land, tax, or education policies, fearing that communists might take advantage of the inevitable instability engendered by progressive social change. Through extensive counterinsurgency, internal security, and military aid programs, the United States demonstrably bolstered regimes and groups, such as the Latin American military, that were undemocratic, conservative, and frequently repressive. Aid to the Alliance for Progress was reduced in the 1970s and the program came to a gradual end.

STEPHEN G. RABE

See also Kennedy, John Fitzgerald; Latin America

FURTHER READING

Levinson, Jerome, and Juan de Onís. *The Alliance that Lost Its Way.* Chicago, 1970.

Rabe, Stephen G. "Controlling Revolutions: Latin America, the Alliance for Progress, and Cold War Anti-Communism." In *Kennedy's Quest for Victory: American Foreign Policy, 1961–1963,* edited by Thomas G. Peterson. New York, 1989.

Scheman, L. Ronald, ed. *The Alliance for Progress: A Retrospective.* New York, 1988.

Walker, William O., III. "Mixing the Sweet with the Sour: Kennedy, Johnson, and Latin America." In *The Diplomacy of the Crucial Decade: American Foreign Relations During the 1960s,* edited by Diane B. Kunz. New York (1994) 42–79.

AMBASSADORS AND EMBASSIES

Ambassadors are diplomatic officers of the highest rank assigned to represent one nation in another, who conduct their activities in official headquarters called embassies. States send accredited envoys to reside in each other's capitals to become the official conduits of communication and agents of negotiation. Ambassadors and other diplomats are in principle immune from harm and even arrest, although the host government can expel them from the country. Embassies possess some of the qualities of the territory of the ambassador's own country and cannot be entered by officials of the host country without permission.

Until the early part of the twentieth century the diplomats of the world were divided by rank. The great powers of Europe exchanged ambassadors, persons accredited by one sovereign to the court of the other. Lesser countries, including the United States, sent and received ministers, envoys of lower rank. Ministers operated out of a legation, ambassadors out of an embassy. The United States did not send or receive an ambassador until 1893 when ambassadors were exchanged with Great Britain, France, Germany, and Italy. Diplomatic relations were next raised to the ambassadorial level with Russia (1898), Mexico (1898), Brazil (1913), Japan (1913), Argentina (1914), and Chile (1914). But after World War II all countries, no matter how small, sent and received ambassadors as chiefs of mission.

The ambassador is the chief of mission in the country to which he or she is accredited. Their responsibility is to represent the interests of their country, deliver messages and conduct negotiations under instructions, convey messages from the host government, and provide their own government with the best possible information about political conditions, economic opportunities, and foreign policy issues. Permanent heads of missions to the United Nations have carried the rank of ambassador as have the chief delegates to special conferences.

In U.S. practice, the ambassador is head of the "country team" (all the lower ranking diplomats and specialists attached to the embassy). Large embassies at the end of the twentieth century have staffs numbering in the hundreds: specialists on political reporting, economic issues, culture and education, communications, agriculture, intelligence, and military affairs, as well as a contingent of marines for security. In the second half of the twentieth century the Central Intelligence Agency maintained stations connected to most U.S. embassies. But the existence of the stations was not publicly acknowledged. In fact, CIA agents frequently carried the titles of ordinary embassy personnel as "cover."

U.S. ambassadors are both "career" and "noncareer." Career ambassadors rise through the professional Foreign Service and their appointments represent distinguished service. Noncareer ambassadors are appointed by the president from outside the Foreign Service. This category has included over the years wealthy contributors to the president's political party or election campaign, former members of Congress or governors, leaders from education and literature, and military officers. Noncareer ambassadors are usually supported by an experienced senior foreign service officer as deputy chief of mission (DCM). The DCM usually holds the rank of minister. Other officers are designated first, second, or third secretary of the embassy. In the absence of the ambassador, the DCM is normally in charge and is called the chargé d'affaires. Sometimes an ambassador is recalled by the sending government as a mark of displeasure and the embassy is headed for a prolonged period by a chargé d'affaires.

Until the Rogers Act of 1924, the Foreign Service and the Consular Service were separate entities, both under the supervision of the Department of State. The Foreign Service provided the political officers and diplomats for embassies and legations. The Consular Service provided officials to handle the routine business of U.S. citizens overseas and foreign individuals involved with the United States, regulation of shipping and seamen, commercial documentation, licenses, passports, and visas. Since 1924 a single foreign service has staffed both the consular and the political side and many Foreign Service personnel during their careers have both kinds of experience.

In the age of sailing ships and before the introduction of global communication by telegraph, the chiefs of mission—whether ambassadors or ministers—had considerable responsibility for conducting negotiations. It could take months to send a message home and receive a reply. But instant communication by cable, fully established around 1900, and rapid air transportation beginning in the 1950s, inevitably reduced the importance of the individual ambassador. Instructions could be sent and updated by the minute. During a crisis, high officials—foreign ministers and even heads of government—could fly halfway around the world to negotiate crucial matters directly. U.S. secretaries of state, for example, have spent months every year flying from conference to conference and shuttling between foreign capitals. Ambassadors nonetheless have remained in special circumstances, especially in small countries in time of crisis or when, through experience and time in service, they acquired unusual access both to the host and home governments.

Another change tending to downgrade the importance of the resident ambassador has been the increasing importance after World War II of multilateral international organizations, beginning with the United Nations and including the North Atlantic Treaty Organization, regional entities such as the Organization of American States, and specialized conferences dealing with arms control and reduction, the law of the sea, environment, food, trade, and other issues.

GADDIS SMITH

See also Central Intelligence Agency; Diplomatic Method; Foreign Service; Rogers Act

FURTHER READING

Anderson, M.S. *The Rise of Modern Diplomacy, 1919–1950.* New York, 1993.

Feltham, R.S. *Diplomatic Handbook.* London, 1988.

Kennedy, Charles Stuart. *The American Consul: A History of the United States Consular Service 1776–1914.* New York, 1990.

Steigman, Andrew L. *The Foreign Service of the United States.* Boulder, Colo., 1985.

Sweeny, Jerry K., and Margaret B. Denning. *A Handbook of American Diplomacy.* Boulder, Colo., 1993.

AMERICA FIRST COMMITTEE
(1940–1942)

Noninterventionist organization whose goal was to keep the United States out of World War II. Originally named the Emergency Committee to Defend America First, the committee was established in July 1940 by prominent Americans who were convinced that the U.S. entry into the war would destroy the nation's democratic institutions and who advocated staying out of the war and increasing U.S. defense expenditures. Its objectives were to promote a strong military defense, to oppose the "aid short of war" that it detected in Lend-Lease military aid shipments in the belief that such aid undermined U.S. defense capabilities, and to publicize the organization's views to the president and Congress.

America First was founded by Robert Douglas Stuart, Jr., son of the first vice president of the Quaker Oats Company in Chicago; General Robert E. Wood, chairman of the board of Sears Roebuck; Jay C. Hormel, president of the Hormel Meat Packing Company; Hanford Mac-Nider, an Iowa manufacturer and a former national commander of the American Legion; Philip La Follette, former governor of Wisconsin; and others. Stuart took over as the organization's national director. General Wood became one of the most powerful members of America First because he presided over both national and executive committee meetings. The executive committee set political and financial policies and made virtually all major policy decisions, and its members also served on the national committee. The national committee authorized the formation of America First chapters, which numbered approximately 450 by 7 December 1941, and orchestrated their activities. The organization was financed almost exclusively through donations. Business leaders such as William H. Regnery, president of the Western Shade Cloth Company and a member of the executive committee; H. Smith Richardson of the Vick Chemical Company; General Wood; and others provided most of the financial support, yet the average contributor donated a small amount of money. The majority of America First members were midwestern Republicans; approximately two-thirds of the members lived in the region centered around Chicago. Prominent Democrats, such as Chester Bowles, General Hugh S. Johnson, Mrs. Burton K. Wheeler, and Mrs. Bennett Champ Clark served on the national committee.

The America First Committee soon became the most powerful isolationist organization in the country. President Franklin D. Roosevelt more than once adjusted his strategy of pressing Congress for adjustments in neutrality legislation in response to the group's influence. In the spring and fall of 1941, for example, Roosevelt decided against requesting congressional authorization for bolder measures against Germany in the Atlantic because he believed that he would be defeated by isolationists, backed by America First. The committee's broadcasts and meetings featured well-known speakers, including senators Gerald P. Nye and Burton K. Wheeler, Colonel Charles A. Lindbergh, Lillian Gish, John T. Flynn, Kathleen Norris, and the Reverend John A. O'Brien. After Japan's attack on Pearl Harbor, America First discontinued all isolationist activities and pledged its support for the war. Organization leaders officially dissolved America First on 22 April 1942.

JANET M. MANSON

See also Bowles, Chester Bliss; Isolationism; Lend-Lease; Lindbergh, Charles Augustus; Nye, Gerald Prentice; Roosevelt, Franklin Delano; World War II

FURTHER READING

Cole, Wayne S. *America First: The Battle Against Intervention, 1940–1941*. Madison, Wis., 1953.
————. *Charles A. Lindbergh and the Battle Against American Intervention in World War II*. New York, 1974.
Jonas, Manfred. *Isolationism in America, 1935–1941*. Ithaca, N.Y., 1966.

AMERICAN CHINA DEVELOPMENT COMPANY

An enterprise incorporated in New Jersey in 1895, with the backing of leading U.S. financiers, to obtain major construction projects in China. The ACDC was symptomatic of rising U.S. interest in overseas investments and markets in the late nineteenth century. In 1898 the syndicate won a valuable contract to build the Hankow-Canton Railroad, linking central and southern China. The Chinese, alarmed by the scramble by foreign powers to secure spheres of influence and concessions (contracts for various projects) in China, had turned to U.S. investors precisely because they believed that the United States did not harbor aggressive ambitions. The ACDC venture was a fiasco, however, and over the next seven

years the ACDC engaged in inconclusive negotiations with Chinese authorities and in complex dealings with international interests. Worried about financial losses, intense international rivalries, and Chinese instability, U.S. investors sold most of their shares at a handsome profit to a rival Belgian syndicate linked to France and Russia, which had political as well as financial motives.

What the Chinese saw as U.S. betrayal and duplicity led the imperial government in 1904 to threaten to invoke a provision allowing it to cancel the contract if the shares were sold to other nationals. Angry Chinese officials had other grievances against the ACDC as well: the construction of less than thirty miles of railroad track, extravagant spending, and gross mismanagement caused by the company's inability to monitor its agents in China. Chinese officials also faced strong local opposition to foreign management of the project. In response to the Chinese threat, U.S. investors, led by J. P. Morgan and Company, repurchased a majority of the company's shares. The Chinese, however, decided to buy out the ACDC contract. President Theodore Roosevelt pressed both Morgan and the Chinese to retain the concession, but the Chinese terminated the ACDC contract in 1905. The ACDC case demonstrated to the Chinese that a considerable gap existed between the promises of U.S. financiers and their capacity to deliver. The ACDC experience also showed the limits of using the United States to counter the economic and political pressure of other nations. Painfully conscious of their nation's growing vulnerability, some Chinese officials continued to look to the United States to neutralize the other powers in Manchuria and China proper, but to no avail.

NOEL H. PUGACH

See also China

FURTHER READING

Braisted, William R. "The United States and the American China Development Company." *Far Eastern Quarterly* 11 (February 1952): 147–165.
Hunt, Michael H. *The Making of a Special Relationship: The United States and China to 1914*. New York, 1983.

AMERICAN CIVIL WAR
(1861–1865)

The bloody clash of arms between the Confederate States of America and the Union, which threatened to expand into an international conflict. Taking office on 4 March 1861 with a civil war impending, President Abraham Lincoln declared that inasmuch as he was entirely ignorant of diplomacy he planned to entrust the conduct of foreign relations during his presidency to his secretary of state, William H. Seward. Having traveled extensively abroad and served during the 1850s as an active member of the Senate Foreign Relations Committee, Seward seemed well-suited to direct the Department of State; in any case, most Americans who had actual diplomatic experience had opposed Lincoln's election and had thus rendered themselves politically ineligible for service in his cabinet.

Seward primarily sought to fend off European intervention in the American Civil War, which could prevent national reunification. Ever since the formation of the Holy Alliance, created to maintain the global hegemony of the antidemocratic European aristocracies in the aftermath of the Napoleonic Wars, the proclivities of the continental Great Powers of Europe to meddle in the affairs of weaker nations had been well understood in the United States. Even the political leaders of Great Britain, while exhibiting a paternalistic disposition toward their former colony, shared the distaste for American democracy characteristic of the ruling nobility in Europe. Most members of that privileged class appeared eager to grasp at any opportunity to assist in bringing about the destruction of the American Union, even if that meant sponsoring the nationhood of the Southern slaveholders. Seward's task, then, was to convince European statesmen that the liabilities of intervention in the U.S. conflict outweighed any advantages. Against him were arrayed a formidable coalition of European leaders, continually lobbied by Confederate agents and envoys. Supporting him were U.S. ministers and consuls whose overseas experience varied greatly, from the sophisticated and prudent Charles Francis Adams in London to the indiscreet Kentucky duelist Cassius Clay in Saint Petersburg.

A serious problem arose from the arrogant intrusiveness of the radical Republicans in Congress, particularly in the Senate. Many members of that faction had worked assiduously in 1860 to defeat Seward, the popular favorite in the North for the Republican presidential nomination; they had preferred a lesser known politician whom they believed would be more malleable. Charles Sumner of Massachusetts—the most radical member of the cabal—sought from the beginning of the Lincoln administration to undermine Seward's credibility so as to force him out of the cabinet, in order that Sumner himself might become secretary of state. Sumner had plenty of collaborators, including the intensely ambitious Secretary of the Treasury Salmon P. Chase. The radicals and their allies in the Northern press lambasted Seward as Lincoln's evil genius—an impulsive warmonger and deceptive opportunist who lacked principle. This did not enhance the secretary of state's credibility in Europe, where suspicion of his motives and purposes, much of it fueled by Sumner and his radical allies, came close to paranoia during crucial moments of the Civil War.

Seward faced other handicaps. European diplomats in Washington had recommended recognition of Confederate independence even before the Lincoln administration took office. Influential journalists like Horace Greeley of the *New York Times* had declared good riddance to the seceders, and Southerners in Europe, some still employed as official representatives of the United States, encouraged the notion that the Union was irrevocably divided. On 13 May, only two weeks after news reached Europe of the surrender of Fort Sumter to the South Carolina insurrectionists that opened the armed conflict, the British government hastened to issue a proclamation of neutrality granting a belligerent status under international law to the embryonic Southern Confederacy. Full diplomatic recognition seemed only a short step away.

Well before Lincoln announced a Northern blockade of southern seaports, the British had threatened forcibly to resist any such interference with their cotton imports from the American South. Lord Lyons, the British minister in Washington, continuously issued dire warnings of Great Power intervention should the incoming administration attempt to interdict Southern commerce with Europe. Lyons also recommended that British Foreign Secretary Lord John Russell not rebuff Confederate commissioners sent to Europe to obtain diplomatic recognition. Meanwhile, the French and Russian envoys in Washington recommended that their governments join Great Britain in opening diplomatic relations with the new Confederacy. The Spanish government was known to be planning to occupy Santo Domingo; and rumors of a combined British, French, and Spanish military expedition against Mexico had also begun to circulate in Washington. Soon, word of a pact between the British and French governments to act jointly in regard to the American question led Seward to conclude that no such agreement would have been entered into without an intention to intervene on the side of the Southern secessionists.

Seward's Desperate Diplomacy

Meanwhile, even before alerting the president on 1 April to the existence of a rapidly developing crisis requiring energetic resistance, Seward was informing diplomats and journalists at every opportunity that the Lincoln administration would not shrink from a foreign war, if one became necessary to restore the Union. If Southern commissioners were received officially in Europe, Seward declared, the government at Washington would break off diplomatic relations with the offending regime. Yet what Lord Lyons described as Seward's obtuse refusal to conciliate the European powers began to show dividends. Despite Lincoln's imposition of a naval blockade, the British government backed away from intervention and Lord Russell announced that he had no intention of holding official meetings with Confederate

The American Civil War 1861-1865

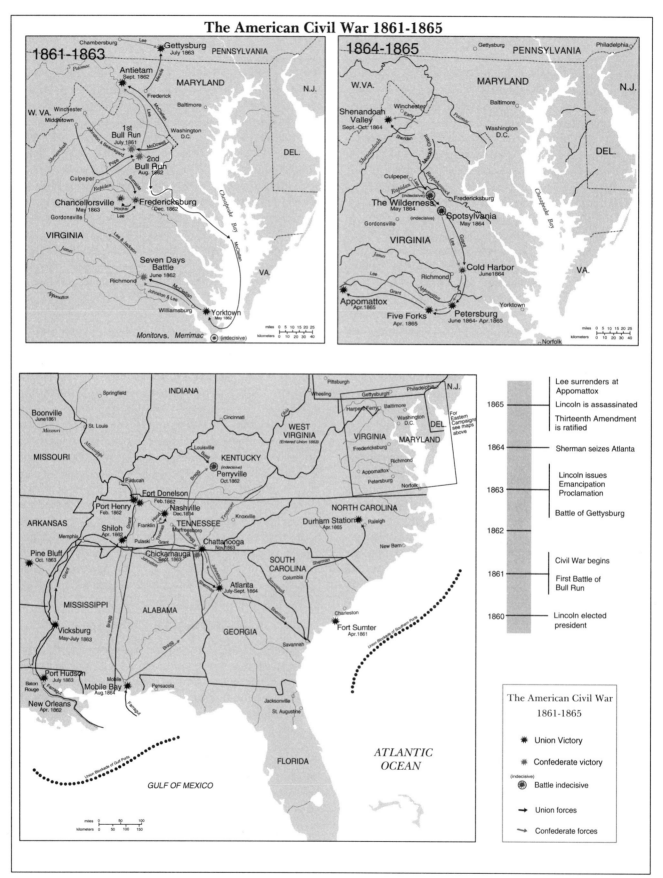

commissioners. Although Lyons's repeated warnings about Seward's alleged bellicosity, fueled by Sumner's fulminations against the secretary of state, had evoked caution in London, Russell and the prime minister, Lord Palmerston, were both so worried by the danger in the event of war with the United States that they obtained cabinet approval to rush a large force of British regulars across the Atlantic Ocean to Canada and have the West Indian Fleet reinforced. They also drew closer to the regime of the Emperor Napoleon III of France, believing that Lincoln and Seward would hesitate to make war on England and France simultaneously.

Realizing that both the British and French leaders thought the American Union permanently divided and that diplomatic recognition of Confederate independence was merely a question of economic need, opportunity, and time, Seward declared in an instruction sent to Adams in London, dated 21 May 1861, that any overt British attempt to assist the Southern rebellion would bring about a war of self-preservation on the part of the Union.

When Seward asked for an explanation of British policy toward the American Civil War, he was confronted on 15 June by Lyons and the French minister to Washington, Henri Mercier, who insisted on jointly delivering the official announcements of British and French neutrality. Seward refused to receive these communications and declared that he would only meet with Lyons and Mercier separately. He would not concede that the Southern rebellion was anything more than treason, making the Union naval blockade a legitimate means of quelling it, and leaving the rebels unentitled to belligerent rights provided for under international law. Any foreign alliance formed to uphold those alleged rights, he warned, would evidence ill intentions toward the United States.

Lyons retreated, much as he had done two months earlier when his efforts to dissuade Lincoln and Seward from proclaiming the blockade had proven ineffectual. He complained to Russell of Seward's recklessness and possible desire to provoke a war with England, but he did not insist that the U.S. secretary of state officially recognize the Anglo-French initiative or acquiesce in the bestowal of belligerent rights upon the Southerners. Nor did his superiors in London fault him for his caution; equally cautious, they dealt Confederate strategy a smashing setback by announcing that belligerent privateers and warships would not be allowed to take prizes into British ports anywhere in the world. They also forced the withdrawal on 7 June of a motion by William Gregory, a leading Southern sympathizer in Parliament, to recognize Confederate independence.

Gregory had been in close touch with the Southern commissioners, Dudley Mann, Pierre Rost, and William Yancey, who reached Europe in April with instructions to obtain recognition of and military aid for the Confederate government. The King Cotton argument—that England and France were so dependent upon a continuous supply of cotton to feed their textile industries that they would have to support the South's cause—had thus far not prevailed, but officials in Richmond, the Confederate capital, remained optimistic that the passage of the time would render the notion irresistible.

Soon Seward sent word to the British and French governments through the U.S. envoys—Adams in London and William Dayton in Paris—that he was eager to avoid any misunderstanding that might endanger peaceful relations. Warned by Adams how thoroughly Lyons, coached by Senator Sumner, had discredited him in England, Seward retorted that to be unyielding on the issue of unbroken American sovereignty over the entire federal union did not mean that he was hostile to any foreign nation. The British, he believed, had been very close to recognizing the Confederacy and to trying to break the Union blockade of the southern coast when his remonstrances caused them to reconsider. When the Russian, British, Prussian, and French ministers proposed mediation during the first two months of the war, Seward declared that the dispute between the Northerners and Southerners would never be decided by outsiders and warned that any attempt by foreigners to force a solution on the combatants would meet vigorous resistance. Thus thwarted in their attempts to decide the outcome of the American rebellion through direct diplomacy, the Old World aristocracies, deferring to the leadership of Great Britain and France, embarked upon a more indirect course.

In 1856, in the aftermath of the Crimean War, the former belligerents had signed a document known as the Declaration of Paris, which recognized the legitimacy of naval blockades as a belligerent right, prohibited the capture of noncontraband belligerent private property aboard neutral ships or similar neutral property aboard belligerent ships, and condemned privateering as piracy. The U.S. government had refused an invitation to accede to the declaration unless a fifth clause was added banning the seizure of belligerent private property on belligerent ships.

Seward was worried that European governments would precipitously grant the Confederates belligerent rights, soon followed by full diplomatic recognition. He hurriedly instructed his ministers in London and Paris to propose treaties by which the United States would accede to the Declaration of Paris, thereby gaining European acceptance in Europe of the Union blockade of southern seaports, while the United States would assume the responsibility of guarding foreign ships against attacks by Southern privateers. He was too late. Russell and Edouard Thouvenel, the French foreign minister, had already instructed their representatives in Washington to act together to procure American acceptance of the first three articles of the Declaration of Paris, omitting the fourth one prohibiting privateering. They were willing to permit the Confederates to use privateering as a potent instrument of destruction against the rival Northern merchant marine. The Confederacy, lacking a navy, was already commissioning privateers by issuing letters of marque and reprisal.

Russell and Thouvenel also instructed their consuls at Charleston, South Carolina, to transmit an identical proposal to the Confederate government in Richmond. The British consul, Robert Bunch, boasted that he was conducting a diplomatic negotiation with Jefferson Davis's government as a preliminary step toward full diplomatic recognition. Having learned this, Seward had no choice other than to revoke Bunch's exchequer, his license to represent England as an official economic agent in Charleston. Although the British and French obtained substantially what they desired of both the Lincoln and the Davis administrations, namely acquiescence in three of the four Paris declaration articles, they had been forced to disclaim any design to negotiate officially with the rebellious slaveholders. The Declaration of Paris and Bunch affairs, therefore, while increasing British and French apprehensions about Seward's irritability, also reduced the likelihood of a transatlantic war growing out of European intervention in the American Civil War.

The *Trent* Affair

In July 1861, despite strenuous objections from Lyons and Mercier, Congress passed and Lincoln signed an act authorizing the president to declare any southern port no longer a legitimate port of entry to foreign commerce. The British and French ministers immediately announced that if Lincoln activated such an illegal "paper" blockade, it would be vigorously opposed by the European powers, even at the risk of armed conflict with the United States. Despite the defiant disposition of the radicals in Congress and the administration—an attitude that Seward momentarily seemed to emulate in a widely publicized request of Northern governors to fortify their borders against possible foreign attacks—the secretary of state convinced Lincoln not to proclaim the blockaded ports of the South closed by decree, thus averting a crisis.

A new danger soon materialized. Late in 1861, under heavy pressure from French manufacturing and shipping interests already suffering from the American conflict, Thouvenel besieged Seward for a relaxation of the Northern blockade in order to let Southern cotton out of and French manufactured goods into, Confederate ports. Had the British not evidenced reluctance to join in disputing the legitimacy of the blockade, a serious Franco-American dispute might have occurred before Spring; but growing British dependence on Northern wheat to make up for poor European grain crops, and increasing

profits from selling arms to both sides, helped to restrain British intervention. Then, suddenly, the *Trent* Affair erupted and peace hung by a thread.

Confederate authorities, impatient with the failure of the original commissioners in Europe to win diplomatic recognition, decided to send former U.S. Senators James Mason of Virginia and John Slidell of Louisiana to England and France. Successfully evading federal blockaders off Charleston, the Southern envoys arrived in Cuba, where they eventually took passage on a British mail steamer, the *Trent*. On 8 November 1861 Captain Charles Wilkes of the USS *San Jacinto* waylaid the *Trent* in the Bahama Channel and abducted Mason, Slidell, and their two secretaries. In the North, the seizure of four men considered archtraitors to the Union constituted the first notable success of the war, and Wilkes was viewed as a national hero—banqueted, promoted, and officially commended by the House of Representatives. The British had been forced to gulp down a draught of their own medicine, dating back to the hated practice of impressment that had played a major role in bringing on the War of 1812.

In England, however, the *Trent* seizure was universally viewed as an outrage, perhaps ordered by Seward to provoke armed conflict. The Palmerston ministry prepared at once to send more troops to Canada and warships to the West Indies and approved an ultimatum (softened at the last moment by the Prince Consort) requiring the Lincoln administration to apologize and relinquish the four captives within seven days. Otherwise, the British government would sever diplomatic relations as a preliminary step to more serious measures. Senator Sumner urged Lincoln to counter the British demand with a call for arbitration, but Seward successfully made the case for compliance during a two-day session of the cabinet that began on Christmas Day. The prisoners were released, and Seward wrote a diplomatic note expressing satisfaction that the British had at last accepted principles of international law for which Americans had fought in the War of 1812. The *Trent* Affair left a residue of resentment in the North, where it appeared that the English had been unjustifiably hasty in assuming a pugnacious posture before receiving any official explanation from Washington. In Great Britain, however, officials like Lord Russell finally realized that Lincoln and Seward had no desire to incite a war, and expressions of relief at the peaceful settlement of the controversy were virtually universal. From then on, the British were less contentious when Anglo-American disputes occurred, although the risk of European involvement in the American Civil War was far from over.

The Blockade Attacked in Parliament

For the first two years of the Civil War, European aristocrats (and their allies) were restrained from trying to dictate the outcome of the contest by the following factors: a strong conviction that the breakup of the United States was inevitable; the knowledge that many textile mills could run on warehoused cotton until at least late 1862; the large profits being made from shipping munitions of war to the belligerents; the desire not to jeopardize access to Northern wheat; British concern for the safety of Canada and a French wish to be unhampered in Mexico; and, at the outset, an apprehension that Seward might be seeking a pretext to widen the war into a worldwide social upheaval to fulfill his well-known prediction of an "irrepressible conflict" between aristocracy and democracy.

Nevertheless, the *Trent* Affair had hardly ended in January 1862 when Adams warned Seward that Napoleon would soon urge the British to join France in demanding a relaxation of the federal naval blockade of Confederate cotton ports, with the intention of recognizing Southern independence should the North refuse to comply. Adams hoped that the *Trent* affair had so sobered the British leaders that they would oppose any effort at intervention when Parliament met in February. Meanwhile, he suggested, Northern military victories and an expression of a determination by the Lincoln administration to end slavery had become essential to prevent armed intervention by the Great Powers of Europe.

Those powers had vigorously opposed the sinking expendable old whaling ships filled with heavy rocks in ship channels off Charleston. The very stridency of their complaints (inasmuch as the British had done the same thing in the past) betokened an itch to intervene. The Palmerstonian press in London and the imperialistic papers in Paris cooperated in denouncing what they characterized as a sordid act directed against the peaceful commerce of the world. Then, just as British and French officials were beginning to realize near the end of February that the "stone boats" were unlikely to do any lasting damage to shipping in southern waters, the Confederacy's supporters in Parliament, notably William Gregory and William Lindsay, instituted a debate in the House of Commons about the alleged ineffectiveness and therefore illegality of the federal blockade. Backed by the wealthy industrialist James Spence and urged on by James Mason, they hoped that the discussion would culminate in British recognition of Confederate independence. The pro-Southern members believed that their statistical evidence—hundreds of examples of blockade violations—was conclusive and pressed their case in the House of Commons on 7 March and in the House of Lords on 10 March, but William Forster and other Union supporters used arguments and figures supplied by Adams to demolish Mason's claims that the blockade was so ineffective that it was illegal under international law.

Months earlier Lyons had written grudgingly from Washington that the blockade was creating considerable consternation in the South and that had it really been ineffective, there would not have been such a desperate desire to get rid of it. Russell and Palmerston understood that naval blockades would be vital weapons of war for Great Britain in future conflicts and did not want to uphold absolute standards of effectiveness as a binding precedent. They made sure that the Lindsay-Gregory initiative was thwarted, with Russell warning in the House of Lords on 10 March that if Great Britain interfered with the Northern blockade, the Lincoln administration would probably initiate a slave insurrection that would devastate the cotton-growing regions of the South. A patient adherence to a hands-off policy, he advised, would probably result, perhaps as soon as June, in Confederate independence.

Disappointed, Lindsay sought help in Paris. In April he had three interviews with Napoleon, in the course of which the French emperor expressed a desire to act with Great Britain to break the Northern blockade and recognize Southern independence. Napoleon's disposition to meddle, coupled with a well-publicized journey by Mercier from Washington to Richmond that same month to seek Southern support for European mediation, portended renewed efforts to induce the British to join in some act of intervention. In mid-May, however, Europe learned of the fall of New Orleans to the Union, the Confederate retreat from Shiloh into Mississippi, and the repulse of the ironclad *Virginia* by the USS *Monitor* at Hampton Roads. The news of these events created caution in London and eventually in Paris. Statesmen there awaited the fate of Richmond, toward which General George McClellan's army was advancing, before taking up the question of intervention once more.

Seward's Counterattack

Determined to thwart intervention, Seward once again adopted an aggressive posture. The succession of Northern victories at Forts Henry and Donelson near the Tennessee-Kentucky border in February and at New Orleans near the end of April already had provided a pretext for asking France and England to rescind their neutrality proclamations. These announcements, Seward declared, had precipitously elevated the Southern insurgents to the status of lawful belligerents, thus engendering hopes of further European assistance in accomplishing their independence. As early as February, Seward had pointed out that practically all of the vessels violating the blockade had been furnished by the British. The resulting incursions, he declared, would not have been permitted if Her Majesty's government had not granted the Southern rebels belligerent rights. It was not until early May, however, that Seward instructed Adams in London and Dayton in Paris to seek the withdrawal of that concession, in order, he said, to avoid needlessly prolonging the war, because it had only been European sympathy and assistance that had given the Confederates sufficient heart to persist in their ill-fated rebellion for thirteen long months.

Adams, however, responded that he did not think the time propitious for pressing the British government to retract its neutrality proclamation. Both Palmerston and Russell, he maintained, still contemplated recognizing the secessionist states and the final division of the Union. Despairing of any retrograde action by the British government, Adams had begun to establish a documentary record to show in later years that nearly all the outside help received by the insurgent slaveholders had come from Great Britain, particularly in the form of warships to prey on vulnerable Northern merchantmen and benefit the British carrying trade. What Adams termed the "perpetuating of testimony" for the "verdict of posterity" became a regular occupation of the Americans at the London legation. The record thus accumulated became the basis for the postwar *Alabama* Claims, which resulted in an 1872 arbitration award of damages to the United States.

Seward, however, desired more than the favorable judgment of future generations. He wanted to exert immediate pressure on the British government not only to withdraw its concession of belligerent rights to the secessionists but also to intervene actively to prevent its subjects from continuing to run supplies through the blockade into southern seaports. Adams warned Seward in mid-May, however, that British sentiment in favor of breaking the blockade was actually growing, despite the news of Northern military successes, and that only continued victories in battle, coupled with a growing realization in Europe that the sooner the rebellion was put down the faster cotton would be available, were likely to fend off intervention.

As the summer of 1862 slowly passed, Adams uneasily awaited some sudden act of interposition on the part of the Great Powers. He was especially worried by a testy note from Palmerston objecting to an order issued by General Benjamin Butler at New Orleans, threatening to jail local women who treated federal soldiers with disrespect. Palmerston had expressed disgust at hearing of an act that, he said, was unmatched for infamy in the entire history of civilized nations. The note led Adams to speculate that Palmerston sought a pretext to precipitate a quarrel with the United States. Russell reassured him, however, that the government intended no change in policy, and a conciliatory note from Palmerston received on 19 June diminished Adams's concern about the chances of a recognition motion, authored by Lindsay and scheduled to be taken up by Parliament the following day. As it turned out, Lindsay postponed his motion, which was not debated until 11 July, when it was opposed by Palmerston himself, thus forcing its withdrawal.

Adams was not deceived, however, into thinking that intervention was a dead issue. British public opinion, as reflected both in the parliamentary speeches during the session just ending and in the London press, appeared to contemplate tangible movement in that direction. The Lancashire textile industry was expected to have used up all stocks of cotton on hand by the end of 1862, after which the rapid growth of already serious unemployment would result in widespread destitution if something were not done to obtain a fresh supply. Alternative sources such as India and Egypt were inadequate. Seward had successfully persuaded Lincoln to reopen several captured southern seaports, including New Orleans, but, because of a boycott by Confederate cotton growers, not much cotton had been shipped.

News of McClellan's retreat from Richmond, which reached London in mid-July, led to a growing conviction in Europe that the North could never conquer the South. Seward's remonstrances against blockade-running and his insistence that Great Britain and France revoke their neutrality proclamations now seemed merely desperate measures. Adams's official objections to the construction in a Liverpool dockyard of a formidable warship (the future *Alabama*) for the insurrectionists, which he first registered near the end of June, evoked little more than perfunctory responses from Russell.

Warships for the South

Adams had complained in February about the construction at Liverpool of the ship *Oreto*, being readied to make war upon the United States, and had declared that if it were allowed to put to sea, Anglo-American amity would be endangered. Nevertheless, the *Oreto*, soon transformed into the Confederate raider *Florida*, was allowed to sail on 22 March, confirming Adams's belief that British neutrality was a sham. Now, in July, Adams was making every effort, including legal action, to stop the warship *290* from following the *Florida* to sea, but the British authorities were unresponsive. This led Seward to warn that Lincoln might issue letters of marque and reprisal, allowing shipowners of any nation to combat Southern piracy, seemingly sponsored by the British, in return for substantial prize money from the U.S. government. Such a step would substantially increase the chances of serious maritime incidents, but with most Union warships occupied with blockade duties, privateering appeared the only effective way to counteract the Confederate cruisers.

On 29 July the *290*, soon to become the *Alabama*, escaped to sea a few hours before a belated order arrived from the Foreign Office to detain the ship for a court hearing on its status. By October, months of protests had failed to induce the British authorities to prosecute or even to investigate the responsibility of Southern agents and their English associates for the destruction of Northern merchant ships by the *Florida* and the *Alabama*. Adams wrote Seward that he could do little more than amass documentary evidence of British connivance in constructing the Confederate corsairs. Seward visualized using that material to gain credibility for future complaints directed at the construction of similar vessels, which both he and Adams knew were already being built in England. If more ships like the *Alabama* were allowed to escape, he wrote Adams in late October, there would be little hope of averting an armed clash with Great Britain. Adams would have to do his best to keep what were later called the Laird rams from becoming operational Confederate warships.

Seward had begun to warn European governments of social convulsions, not only in the form of a slave uprising in the South but perhaps also in the shape of an equivalent in Europe to the French Revolution, that would inevitably accompany a transatlantic war following interference with the blockade. All chances of obtaining substantial supplies of cotton for British and French factories would end. He also made sure that President Lincoln was aware that Adams, joined by most of the other American envoys in Europe, had repeatedly urged that a proclamation emancipating the slaves be issued, in order to identify the Union cause in the minds of Europeans with that of human freedom rather than that of military domination.

In a last-ditch effort to prevent secession, the 1860 Republican Party platform had upheld the right of every state to control its own domestic institutions, and Lincoln had endorsed that sentiment. He had even declared in his inaugural address that he had no intention of interfering with slavery in the fifteen states where it already existed. Congress had ratified this position in July 1861, when it asserted by joint resolution that the Civil War was not being waged to overthrow the established institutions of the slave states. Many federal officials, including Lincoln and Seward, believed that noninterference with slavery was necessary to hold the border slave states, especially Lincoln's home state of Kentucky, within the Union, and to prevent an outbreak of violent political opposition elsewhere in the North, where few whites desired to expend blood and treasure to liberate Southern slaves. With these considerations in mind, Seward had informed U.S. diplomats that even if the slaveholders' insurrection failed, the Constitution prohibited both the president and the Congress from disturbing the slave system in the South.

Slavery and Diplomacy

Abroad, however, this disposition not to touch slavery created the widespread impression that, as the British foreign secretary had declared in a public address in October 1861, the combatants were not struggling over the slavery question at all, but were fighting on the Northern side for empire and on the Southern side for independence. This idea had been reinforced by Lincoln's instructions to Generals John C. Fremont and David Hunter in September 1861 and May 1862, respectively, overruling military orders designed to emancipate slaves in Missouri and three southeastern states. Pro-Southern Europeans therefore continued to deprecate the Northern cause and exalt that of the Confederacy, maintaining that the Lincoln administration was motivated solely by the sordid ambition of armed conquest, whereas the Southerners sought to be free and independent. The same Southern sympathizers, however, had also insisted that the Civil War was becoming a crusade for emancipation, which would inevitably bring about a slave revolt, the barbarities of which would shatter many innocent lives and interfere with the production and export of American cotton to European textile mills for many years to come. They managed to create a widespread impression in Europe that orderly emancipation would come more quickly within an independent Confederacy than within a restored American Union.

Although he continued to resist the importunities of U.S. envoys to transform the Civil War into a contest for human freedom, Lincoln had nevertheless approved the enactment by Congress in 17 February 1862 of a measure authorizing military commanders to free the slaves of rebels. He also approved the execution on 21 February of the captain of a slave ship, the passage of a law on 13 March prohibiting U.S. military commanders from restoring fugitive slaves to their owners, and the signing on 2 April of a Seward-Lyons treaty that abruptly ended the centuries-old transatlantic slave trade. On 16 April Lincoln signed into law an act abolishing slavery in the District of Columbia. Previously, on 6 March, he had delivered a special message to Congress recommending voluntary compensated emancipation as a justifiable war measure—a step that Congress had quickly approved, as it did the president's recommendation that the black republics of Haiti and Liberia be recognized as sovereign nations (and therefore appropriate places to send newly freed slaves from the United States). Meanwhile, Congress enacted a new law outlawing slavery in federal territories. All of these indications of an accelerating antislavery effort on the part of the U.S. government served as the foundation for an announcement by Seward on 28 May in which the secretary of state lifted his gag order of more than a year's duration and granted permission to his overseas envoys officially to discuss abolition as a war issue; this they began eagerly to do.

Only a handful of European statesmen, however, were willing to concede that the longer the American Civil War dragged on, the more inevitable it was that slavery would end in North America. Even those Europeans who favored reunification were almost unanimous in believing that it could be achieved neither by military conquest nor by negotiation. In their view, a continuation of the contest would only reinforce slavery. Meanwhile, the production and transport of American cotton to European textile factories had dwindled to a trickle, with the restoration of the cotton trade to prewar levels appearing impossible unless the fighting ended with Confederate independence.

In Great Britain, Queen Victoria, Prime Minister Palmerston, Foreign Secretary Russell, Chancellor of the Exchequer William E. Gladstone, and most of the other high officials in the Liberal government, as well as the leaders of the Conservative opposition, shared this perspective. On the Continent, from King Leopold I of Belgium to the pope in Rome, the ruling aristocracies also viewed reunion in America as impossible and slavery as regrettable but virtually irrelevant compared with the adverse impact of the war on key elements of the European economy. In France, Emperor Napoleon and both of his foreign ministers, first Thouvenel and later Drouyn de Lhuys, believed that the sooner the American war ended in separation, the better for all concerned. Only Russia, among the great powers of the day, was inclined to favor a restoration of the American Union. The Russians wanted to see a strong maritime power develop in the West to counterbalance France and Great Britain, the Czar's enemies in the recent Crimean War and Russia's rivals for hegemony in the eastern Mediterranean region. Nevertheless, Edouard Stoeckl, the Russian envoy in Washington, joined his colleagues in the diplomatic corps in deprecating any chance of reunion and in recommending the early recognition of the Southern confederacy. Mercier, in particular, urged active European intervention to hasten this result. His British counterpart, Lyons, was much more cautious and disposed at least to appear neutral until the combatants had worn themselves out.

Many political leaders in England, feeling frustrated in part because the bumptious Yankees, and especially Seward, were not sufficiently defcreatial to their Old World superiors, were seemingly eager to further the failure of an experiment in democratic government so threatening to European aristocracy. Although there is no general agreement on this subject, a number of scholars believe that Russell and Gladstone—among other members of Palmerston's cabinet—now began to consider what action the British government might take to hasten the downfall of democracy in America and the triumph there, through Confederate independence, of oligarchy if not of aristocracy.

With the federal armies failing to produce the victories that might give the European interventionists pause, Lincoln decided to play the emancipation card. In mid-July Seward sent word to Europe that the president had just signed into law a confiscation act granting freedom to the slaves of all persons in rebellion against the United States. Then, on 22 July, Lincoln informed his cabinet that, as a matter of military necessity, he intended to use his constitutional powers as commander in chief of the armed forces to issue an emancipation proclamation. On Seward's advice, however, the public announcement of this measure was delayed, pending a significant military victory over the South. Seward had pointed out that Europeans might interpret such a proclamation as primarily designed to compensate for military weakness by instigating a slave uprising, which would indefinitely deprive them of cotton.

Following the summer adjournment of the British Parliament on 17 August, Confederate agents abroad redoubled their efforts to broker a European intervention. Slidell was convinced that the French emperor was prepared to join in breaking the blockade if the British would assist. Napoleon, indeed, had already asked Thouvenel to inquire whether the moment had come for recognition. Both Mercier and William Stuart, who was substituting for Lyons in Washington during the British minister's summer holiday in England, were advocating intervention in October. Russell, who had condemned the federal Confiscation Act of mid-July as likely to incite a slave rebellion, sent a note to Palmerston on 6 August, saying that he agreed with Mercier in favoring at least a mediation proposal in early October. Gladstone, too, became convinced that mediation should not be delayed much longer.

News of the Union debacle at the second Battle of Bull Run reached London in mid-September and led Russell and Palmerston promptly to issue a memorandum advocating a European effort at mediation in October. If the North objected, which appeared certain, recognition would follow. Russell began contacting the French, Russian, Austrian, and Prussian governments to seek their cooperation in the venture. Lyons, who was scheduled to return to duty in Washington, was detained in London while these preparations took place. By the end of September, Palmerston, Russell, and Gladstone had agreed to hold a cabinet meeting in early October to gain final approval for the Anglo-French mediation-recognition initiative. Except for Thouvenel, who now advocated postponing action until the results of the November elections in the North were known, and Lyons, who feared a declaration of war by Lincoln and Seward if the Europeans officially meddled in the American conflict, the major players in Europe now all appeared committed to some sort of intervention. With Confederate General Robert E. Lee's army advancing into Maryland, the timing seemed opportune. As soon as the outcome of Lee's campaign was known, Palmerston averred, the cabinet should meet and decide.

The Decline of Interventionism

On 17 September, Lee met McClellan at Antietam Creek, and, after the bloodiest single day of the war, the Confederate forces retreated back into Virginia. Five days later Lincoln issued his preliminary Emancipation Proclamation, announcing to the world his assumption of responsibility, as military commander in chief, for doing what Congress had already dictated on 17 July—freeing the slaves of all insurrectionists as of 1 January 1863. Stuart hurriedly wrote from Washington that he and Mercier no longer favored any step that might lead to recognition of the Confederacy as a separate nation. They now recommended an armistice as a means of beginning peace negotiations.

Influential members of the British Cabinet, especially Lord Granville and Sir George Cornewall Lewis, declared their opposition to intervention in any form. Nevertheless, Russell wrote Palmerston on 6 October suggesting that perhaps Stuart's idea of confining Anglo-French action to a request for an armistice should be submitted to the cabinet. The foreign secretary was supported by Gladstone, who announced in an electioneering speech at Newcastle on 7 October that the Southerners had already "made a nation," and then followed at York on 11 October with a plea for Southern independence. When Russell circulated a cabinet memorandum on 13 October calling for an armistice to be proposed by the Great Powers, Lewis responded with a powerful rejoinder that carried the majority of the cabinet with him, including the prime minister. The British, declared Palmerston, should continue as mere onlookers until the outcome of the American war became clear. On 23 October an informal cabinet meeting unattended by Palmerston upheld his anti-interventionist position. Lyons left for Washington on the 24th, with instructions to maintain a posture of strict neutrality. Russell, however, had not entirely capitulated. He wrote Palmerston on 25 October that he now looked forward to recognition in May or June of 1863.

A strong interventionist push from France might possibly have affected the decision in England, but in October 1862 growing difference, within the emperor's government over Italian affairs had produced the dismissal of Foreign Minister Thouvenel and the enforced retirement of Count Auguste Flahault, the venerable French ambassador to London. October was therefore a time of reorganization for the emperor's government. It was not until the end of the month that Napoleon expressed renewed interest in the American question. He then recommended that Great Britain and Russia join France in cosponsoring a proposal to the American belligerents of an armistice for six months, coupled with a suspension of the Northern naval blockade, so that European textile manufacturers could more easily obtain cotton. Although

Russell and Gladstone favored the emperor's project, and even Palmerston gave it tepid support, the Russians would have no part of it, and a large majority of the remaining members of the British cabinet, led by Lewis, rejected it on 12 November. Napoleon, who was already beginning to sink into the quicksand of his Mexican adventure, shrank from confronting the Lincoln administration alone.

Had the midterm U.S. elections of November 1862 taken place a few weeks earlier, there might have been some impetus to European intervention. The Republicans suffered huge losses in both congressional and state elections in key states, barely maintaining control of Congress. Lincoln's own state of Illinois went heavily Democratic. The impression created in Europe was that of a widespread distrust of the president's policies and considerable frustration over the lack of progress in prosecuting the war against the South. News of the election results did not cross the Atlantic Ocean until after the British had rejected Napoleon's armistice project, and the Lincoln administration, therefore, was granted a few months more to reverse its political decline in the North by winning military victories in the South.

When the U.S. Congress reconvened in December 1862, Lincoln sent it a lengthy annual message recommending that Congress initiate a constitutional amendment providing for voluntary compensated emancipation, with federal assistance for the colonization of freed slaves abroad. Adoption of this measure, Lincoln declared, would end the Civil War and save the Union, but a sizeable majority of Congress now consisted of Lincoln's political opponents and severe critics, who rejected his plea. Instead, a clique of Republican radicals in the Senate, outraged over Lee's humiliating pummeling of General Ambrose Burnside's army at Fredericksburg on 12 December, called a party caucus and persuaded their colleagues at that meeting that Lincoln should be told to replace all nonradicals in his cabinet with several of those same senators or their political friends. Sumner might replace Seward, and Chase would become in effect Lincoln's prime minister, acting with his radical associates to determine administration policies. Here was a taste of what Andrew Johnson was later to experience from many of the same intriguers, but Lincoln managed the crisis so astutely that he was able to keep both Chase and Seward in the cabinet, with the Senate radicals frustrated at their failure to bend the president to their collective will. Had this cabal succeeded, it is doubtful whether a foreign policy dictated by Sumner and his radical colleagues would have averted foreign intervention, followed by a transatlantic war that probably would have ensured the permanent dissolution of the Union

The initial reactions in Europe to Lincoln's September 1862 preliminary Emancipation Proclamation ranged from cynicism to hostility. Both press and public in England appeared to share the suspicions of Palmerston and Russell that declaring slaves prospectively free only in parts of the former Union not under federal control was at best an act of desperation by a foundering government, and at worst an attempt to incite a barbarous slave rebellion. The British decision in October not to intrude in the American Civil War, though influenced by the Battle of Antietam, was in no way a result of the Emancipation Proclamation, which had actually (as Seward had feared) ended by encouraging the interventionists. In December, however, British and French public opinion, influenced not a little by the strenuous efforts of pro-Union orators and journalists, futilely fought by Confederate propaganda agents Henry Hotze and Edwin de Leon, shifted dramatically in favor of the idea of freeing the slaves. When news arrived in mid-January 1863 of Lincoln's final version of the Emancipation Proclamation, issued on New Year's Day, a series of massive public meetings endorsed the step and praised the administration that had taken it. Many British newspapers and even some French journals began to characterize the Northern war effort as a struggle on behalf of human freedom. A barrier of public opinion was thus erected against future intervention on the side of the South. In vain, therefore, did Russell, Gladstone, and other proponents of interposition pursue their chimera of abruptly halting the war through foreign intervention. Lacking some serious incident equivalent to the *Trent* affair that might inadvertently draw Europeans into the war in America, that conflict would now be allowed to continue without outside interference.

There was no greater potential interventionist than Napoleon. In January 1863 he ordered Mercier to propose European mediation to Seward, who promptly rejected the idea. The fact that Mercier received no support for his government's proposal from the other European envoys in Washington indicated that the Old World anti-American entente was beginning to crumble. In March, when accused in the House of Lords of diverging from the French alliance regarding America by declining to participate in Mercier's overture, Russell merely reiterated the British government's nonintervention position. This disheartened the partisans of the insurrectionists in Europe, whose morale was not improved when a disagreement arose that spring between the governments at London and Paris over how to react to the Polish insurrection against Russia, thus further endangering the chances of an Anglo-French intervention in America.

In May 1863, however, Lee's victory at Chancellorsville led John Roebuck, an independent member of Parliament who strongly favored the breakup of the American Union, to give notice of a motion for recognition of the Confederacy. In June, Roebuck and Lindsay obtained a promise from Napoleon at Paris that the emperor would formally request the British to join in announcing recognition. Napoleon, however, did not keep his promise, and Roebuck was forced to keep postponing parliamentary consideration of his motion while he vainly awaited the arrival of an overture from across the channel, which never came.

Lee's invasion of Pennsylvania and Grant's prolonged failure to capture Vicksburg inspired Confederate sympathizers in England to push for a vote on recognition before Parliament adjourned for the summer vacation, even if the French proposal did not arrive by that time. Palmerston, however, preferred to await the outcome of Lee's offensive, especially to see whether his army could capture Washington. The prime minister's opposition doomed Roebuck's recognition motion, which he reluctantly withdrew on 13 July, just before Parliament disbanded. By 20 July news of the Union victory at Gettysburg and the surrender of Vicksburg had arrived, further dashing Southern hopes for intervention. The last straw for Richmond was news that the British government had impounded the warship *Alexandria*, destined for the Confederacy, which resulted in a rapid decline in the value of Southern cotton bonds in Europe. In response, Confederate Secretary of State Judah Benjamin angrily expelled the remaining British consuls in the South and ordered Mason to leave England.

The Laird Rams Crisis

Mason decided to linger in London to observe the outcome of a serious clash of wills between Adams and Russell. Russell had been so chagrined by the escape of the *Alabama* and its subsequent spoliation that he had suggested parliamentary legislation to prevent any repetition, but in February 1863 he wrote to Lyons that the cabinet saw no way to improve the law. Hence, Adams warned, trouble could be expected from the existence of contracts since the early summer of 1862 with John Laird and Sons, a shipbuilding firm at Liverpool, to construct two large warships designed to smash the Northern blockade and even threaten northern coastal cities. A similar project existed to construct Confederate warships in France. Reacting to this state of affairs, the U.S. Congress in March 1863 passed a privateering act designed to procure fighting ships capable of destroying the *Alabama* and hunting down future Confederate warships. Lyons notified Seward that actually sending such vessels to sea might well produce maritime incidents that could ignite a transatlantic war.

Secretary of the Navy Gideon Welles sent special agents William Aspinwall and John Forbes to England to try to purchase the Laird rams, and Seward sent William M. Evarts to assist Adams in filing legal proceedings against them, but all were unsuccessful. Meanwhile, friends of the North in Parliament tried to persuade the Palmerston ministry to stop the rams from sailing, but they only succeeded in antagonizing Palmerston and Russell, who proceeded to vindicate the government's hands-off conduct regarding the *Alabama* and the *Florida* in the past and the rams in the present.

Lyons wrote from Washington that the rams must not be allowed to sail. Anxiety increased almost daily, with Seward threatening privateering. On 3 September, with the rams almost ready to sail, Russell ordered them impounded, but his failure to inform Adams of that fact elicited an exasperated exclamation that "this is war," a dramatic but actually inconsequential epilogue to a crisis already over. Thus had the steadily increasing pressure for more than a year from Seward, ably seconded in London by Adams, and reinforced by Northern military victories in July, produced an altered British policy on the launching of Confederate warships from English dockyards.

James D. Bulloch, the capable Confederate naval agent in England who had arranged for the construction of the *Florida*, *Alabama*, and the Laird rams, as well as the purchase of many other vessels for the South, had decided as early as January 1863 that the British government would probably prohibit the delivery to the Confederacy of any more warships built in England. He therefore shifted Confederate naval activities largely to France. Encouraged by Lucien Armand, that country's largest shipbuilder and a friend of Napoleon, Slidell and Bullock signed a contract in April 1863 for the construction of four vessels of the *Alabama* class, and in July an additional contract was approved for two ironclad rams. When William Dayton, the U.S. minister in Paris, learned of these projects, he immediately launched a series of complaints that by early 1864 resulted in orders from Foreign Minister Drouyn de Lhuys to keep the ships out of Confederate hands. (The Confederacy managed to acquire one of the rams, renamed the *Stonewall*, but it did not reach North America until the Civil War was over.) Bulloch also purchased a British Navy relic, the *Victor*, in September 1863, and sailed it to France, where at year's end it became the Confederate cruiser *Rappahannock*. By early 1864, however, the French government had been so sensitized by Dayton to such violations of its neutrality that it ordered the ship held at Calais under conditions that forced it to become a floating rendezvous for Southern agents in Europe until it was sold to a British buyer later that year.

Early in 1863 another purchase by Bulloch had resulted in a six-month long voyage of destruction by the Confederate commerce raider *Georgia*. That vessel had sailed from Greenock, Scotland, despite belated orders from Russell to detain it after Adams and Thomas Dudley, the U.S. consul at Liverpool, had bombarded him with complaints. The *Georgia* captured nine Northern merchantmen before it was trapped refitting at Liverpool by the USS *Kearsarge*, which was hunting for the *Alabama* in English waters. In May 1864 the *Georgia* was sold to an English buyer, while the *Kearsarge* sailed into the English Channel finally to confront the *Alabama* and, on 19 June 1864, to sink it off Cherbourg, France. Meanwhile, the *Florida* and its satellites destroyed some sixty vessels before it was captured by the USS *Wachusett* in October 1864 in the Brazilian harbor of Bahia. On 28 November the *Florida* was sunk near Hampton Roads while in federal custody awaiting adjudication. The last of the Confederate raiders was the *Sea King*, a majestic vessel purchased by Bulloch late in 1864 and converted into the CSS *Shenandoah*. Under the command of Lieutenant James Waddell it roamed the icy waters of the North Pacific and Arctic Oceans, preying on Northern whaling vessels until well after the Confederate armies in the South had surrendered. In November 1865 it finally appeared at an English port to surrender.

France in Mexico

Drouyn de Lhuys had reluctantly prevented warships constructed for the Confederacy in France from escaping to sea largely because of the adverse effect offending the Lincoln administration might have on a shaky French enterprise in Mexico. In January 1862, in fulfillment of a tripartite treaty signed by Great Britain, France, and Spain the previous October, a large army landed on the Mexican east coast, ostensibly to force Benito Juarez's government to meet its overdue financial obligations to European creditors. Seward had attempted to avert this violation of the Monroe Doctrine by negotiating a treaty whereby the United States would assume the Mexican debt in exchange for a mortgage on portions of northern Mexico, but the complications of internal rebellions both there and in the United States precluded final agreement until it was too late to stop the European expedition.

In May 1862, as British and Spanish troops were withdrawn from Mexico, a reinforced French army pushed inland in what was now clearly a campaign of conquest. By June 1863 this army occupied Mexico City. In September, immediately after Seward learned that the Laird rams would not be allowed by the British government to join the Confederate navy, he began to issue a steady stream of protests against the French presence in Mexico. This did not, however, prevent the French from installing Archduke Ferdinand Joseph Maximilian, the younger brother of Emperor Francis Joseph of Austria, as the emperor of Mexico on 28 March 1864. Seward's remonstrances subsided somewhat that summer, as Lee held Grant away from Richmond and Lincoln awaited what he believed would be his defeat by General McClellan in the November presidential election.

Following Lincoln's re-election, however, with Grant pounding Lee mercilessly and General William T. Sherman well along on his "march to the sea" in Georgia, the secretary of state renewed his insistence that the French and their puppet ruler, Maximilian, evacuate Mexico. Napoleon began to realize that he was overextended. Faced with the complications of the Danish and Italian questions, the growing probability of war with Prussia, and rumors that the North and South might end the Civil War in America with a joint attack on the Maximilian regime to "liberate" Mexico, he decided to evacuate French forces from that troubled country. (The final withdrawal took place in February 1867, and four months later Maximilian was executed by a Mexican firing squad as Juarez returned to power.)

Early in 1864 Lyons had warned Russell in London that the burgeoning military might of the federal government was contributing to the growing arrogance of officials like Secretary of the Navy Welles, whose belligerence toward England Seward was having trouble holding in check. As early as the previous summer the British minister had confessed that he had come to the realization that it was Seward's influence over Lincoln that held out the best hope for continued transatlantic peace. Problems with Canada over trade restrictions and military recruiting for the Union armies, compounded by personal differences between U.S. Consul General Joshua R. Giddings and members of the Ottawa government, were exacerbated in March 1864 by the advent of a pro-Southern ministry that allowed Confederate agents full freedom to operate in Canada. The Confederates launched an armed attack on Saint Albans, Vermont, that October. Seward responded by giving notice of the termination of the 1817 Rush-Bagot Agreement limiting armaments along the Canadian-U.S. border and by warning that the Lincoln administration might also abrogate the U.S.-Canadian Reciprocity Treaty of 1854. He also informed Lyons that it was becoming difficult to hold back proponents of "hot pursuit" into Canada to hunt down rebel raiders like those who had invaded Vermont, or to restrain Irish Fenians from raiding across the Canadian border. Under this pressure, the British government arranged for closer policing of the north side of the border, approved an indemnity for Saint Albans, and ordered the arrest and expulsion of aliens suspected of trying to compromise British neutrality. Seward then abandoned his coercive approach and, as the Civil War ended, the fears in London of a U.S. attack on Canada gradually subsided.

Canada was not Palmerston's and Russell's only worry in 1864; the Liberal government also faced a no-confidence vote in Parliament over what the Conservatives alleged was their mishandling of the Danish question. Through June and July, as the prime minister sought to solidify support for his ministry in the House of Commons, he tantalized Lindsay and the other pro-Southern members with hints of support for a motion recognizing Confederate independence, but once the government had survived a close ballot on 8 July, Mason, Lindsay, and their associates discovered that the Palmerston ministry had entirely lost interest in their cause. Even a Confederate proposal to abolish slavery in return for diplomatic recognition carried to London by Louisiana legislator Duncan Kenner in March 1865 was rebuffed as too late. Shortly thereafter, the British received news that the American Civil War had ended with the surrender of the main Confederate armies. Effective diplomacy had succeeded in preventing the crisis of the Union from enlarging into an international conflict. All that remained were the diplomatic aftershocks.

NORMAN B. FERRIS

See also Adams, Charles Francis; Alabama Claims; Benjamin, Judah Philip; Canada; Confederate States of America; Davis, Jefferson; Evarts, William Maxwell; Fenians; France; Great Britain; Lincoln, Abraham; Mexico; Palmerston, Third Viscount; Privateering; Rush-Bagot Agreement; Seward, William Henry; Slave Trade and Slavery; Slidell, John; Spain; Sumner, Charles; Trent Affair; War of 1812; Wilkes, Charles

FURTHER READING

Adams, Ephraim D. *Great Britain and the American Civil War.* New York, 1925.
Case, Lynn M., and Warren F. Spencer. *The United States and France: Civil War Diplomacy.* Philadelphia, Pa., 1970.
Crook, David P. *The North, the South, and the Powers, 1861–1865.* New York, 1974.
Duberman, Martin B. *Charles Francis Adams, 1807–1886.* Boston, 1961.
Ferris, Norman B. *Desperate Diplomacy: William H. Seward's Foreign Policy, 1861.* Knoxville, Tenn., 1976.
———. *The Trent Affair: A Diplomatic Crisis.* Knoxville, Tenn., 1977.
Jenkins, Brian. *Britain and the War for the Union,* 2 vols. Montreal, 1980.
Jones, Howard. *Union in Peril: The Crisis Over British Intervention in the Civil War.* Chapel Hill, N.C., 1992.
Merli, Frank J. *Great Britain and the Confederate Navy, 1861–1865.* Bloomington, Ind., 1970.
Owsley, Frank L. *King Cotton Diplomacy: Foreign Relations of the Confederate States of America,* 2nd ed. Chicago, 1959.
Spencer, Warren F. *The Confederate Navy in Europe.* Ala., 1983.

AMERICAN FEDERATION OF LABOR–CONGRESS OF INDUSTRIAL ORGANIZATIONS

The leading labor union in the United States involved in foreign and domestic policy. The American Federation of Labor (AFL) was founded in 1886 in Columbus, Ohio, as a national federation of trade unions designed to counter the economic power of large business enterprises. Under the leadership of Samuel Gompers, the AFL rejected the more radical and utopian positions of other labor organizations to promote major structural changes in the capitalist system. Instead, the AFL committed itself to improving the immediate condition of its members—skilled workers engaged in various trades and crafts. By the early twentieth century, more than a hundred unions were affiliated with the AFL, representing as much as 80 percent of organized labor. After World War II the AFL backed policies to contain the Soviet Union and counter communism.

The Congress of Industrial Organizations (CIO) emerged as a strong rival and competitor of the AFL in the 1930s. The CIO began as a splinter group of labor progressives within the AFL that formally organized the new union in 1938. Unlike the AFL, the CIO sought to organize largely unskilled and semiskilled workers in the mass-production industries (such as auto, steel, and chemical) that had grown since the turn of the century. The CIO was also much more active than the AFL in attempting to influence government, legislation, and partisan politics and in addressing racial discrimination.

After almost twenty years of often intense and bitter rivalry, the AFL and CIO were united in 1955 into the AFL–CIO, symbolizing the peak of organized labor in terms of union membership and influence in American society. Such factors as organized labor's growing legitimacy and moderation in goals, the postwar return of economic prosperity and probusiness attitudes, Republican and McCarthyite attacks against unionization and New Deal policies, and the national security demands of World War II and the Cold War caused unions to become more comfortable and supportive of the status quo. The leadership of the AFL–CIO, for example, tended to promote domestic legislation and programs often identified with the Democratic party. Although more than 14 million men and women were members of AFL–CIO unions in the early 1990s, the size and political clout of organized labor had declined since the 1950s.

During the Cold War the AFL–CIO, a strong proponent of anticommunism at home and abroad, supported the government's policies of containment and free trade. For example, it sought to influence the international labor movement through the International Confederation of Free Trade Unions—an organization that was particularly active in Europe, Asia, and Latin America. The AFL–CIO Institute for Free Labor Development supported anticommunist movements and unionization in Latin America, often working in conjunction with the Central Intelligence Agency (CIA). In the late 1970s, following the Vietnam War and as foreign economic competition increased, the anticommunist stance of the AFL–CIO began to soften. The group also turned increasingly against free trade to protect American jobs,

for example, opposing the North American Free Trade Agreement (NAFTA) negotiated from 1992 to 1993 by Canada, Mexico, and the United States under Presidents George Bush and Bill Clinton.

JEREL A. ROSATI

See also International Trade and Commerce; North American Free Trade Agreement; Public Opinion

FURTHER READING

Gershman, Carl. *The Foreign Policy of American Labor.* Beverly Hills, Calif., 1975.
Radosh, Ronald. *American Labor and United States Foreign Policy: The Cold War in the Unions from Gompers to Lovestone.* New York, 1969.
Sims, Beth. *Workers of the World Undermined: American Labor's Role in U.S. Foreign Policy.* Boston, 1992.

AMERICAN LEGION

The largest veterans organization in the United States; both a fraternal organization, with chapters (posts) throughout the country, and a prominent national political lobby in foreign and defense policy. All honorably discharged wartime veterans of the U.S. armed forces are eligible for membership; in the mid-1990s there were more than 3 million members. Founded in 1919 at Paris, France, by a group of Allied Expeditionary Forces staff officers to bolster soldier morale and represent the interests of veterans, the American Legion is headquartered in Indianapolis, Indiana, and maintains 7 regional, 51 state, and more than 16,000 local posts. Throughout its history the American Legion has run numerous programs and taken many initiatives to serve its members and to provide community services and projects. After World War I it helped more than one million veterans find jobs. After World War II it played a key role in winning passage of the GI Bill of Rights. It also has supported and lobbied for numerous other benefits and assistance for veterans. It may be best known for its community activity activities, its Boys and Girls State programs of civic education, its sponsorship of Boy Scout troops, and its American Legion baseball leagues. The Legion has also been heavily involved in many foreign and defense policy issues. It advocated military preparedness during the 1930s, when isolationism was the dominant national sentiment, and supported the rise of McCarthyism during the 1950s to fight the threat of communism abroad and at home. In the 1960s and 1970s the Legion supported the Vietnam War and opposed and often questioned the patriotism of those involved in the antiwar movement. During the 1980s, and especially with the end of the Cold War, its membership, influence, and conservatism began to wane.

JEREL A. ROSATI

See also Cold War; Public Opinion

FURTHER READING
Baker, Roscoe. *The American Legion and American Foreign Policy.* New York, 1954.
Severo, Richard, and Lewis Milford. *The Wages of War: When America's Soldiers Came Home: From Valley Forge to Vietnam.* New York, 1989.

AMERICAN REVOLUTION

(1775–1783)

The rebellion by thirteen North American colonies against Great Britain that won independence for the United States. The diplomacy of the American revolutionary war era is best understood within the larger context of international politics. The states of Europe were often at war in an effort to enhance their power and prestige, but these struggles occurred within a recognized framework that prevented any nation from becoming too powerful. To the end of maintaining an equilibrium, or balance of power, nations maintained armies and navies and frequently shifted alliances. If one nation made a bid for hegemony in Europe or attempted to acquire overseas territories (colonies), new alliances usually formed in order to reassert and maintain the status quo among the European powers in Europe and in other parts of the world.

The Struggle Between France and Great Britain

By the late seventeenth century, however, a titanic struggle between the empires of France and Great Britain developed that was difficult to contain. By that time the power of Spain and Portugal had suffered decline, and in 1678 Holland had been forced into an alliance with England that made it Great Britain's economic and diplomatic satellite. Then France's efforts to expand French territory and diplomatic position in Europe and America aroused Great Britain's anxiety. When King Louis XIV tried to extend the territory of New France (located to the north and west of Great Britain's North American colonies), conflicts developed between British and French fur traders on Hudson Bay and between their fishermen around Newfoundland, and each one raided the other's colonies in the West Indies. The rivalry in Europe and the rivalry in the New World soon intersected. Many colonists came to believe that they were little more than pawns in European battles on American soil.

By the end of Queen Anne's War (known in Europe as the War of the Spanish Succession, 1702–1713), the European balance of power remained marginally intact but the superiority of British economic and naval development became evident everywhere. Hudson Bay, New-

foundland, and Nova Scotia (mostly captured with colonial troops) had come under British sovereignty. Entrance to the Saint Lawrence River, so important for French control of their North American empire, lay in British hands. British commerce and the British navy dominated the seas and had secured Gibraltar at the entrance to the Mediterranean Sea from France's ally, Spain. During the next forty years Great Britain and France maneuvered to increase their positions in North America. England solidified its alliance with the Iroquois Confederacy in western New York, built forts along the frontier between British and French territorial claims, and planted the colony of Georgia in Spanish territory in 1733. France strengthened its alliance with the Huron (enemies of the Iroquois) and built frontier forts to prevent British expansion into the Ohio Valley.

Unlike earlier conflicts between the two nations that originated in dynastic rivalries in Europe, the final conflict before the American Revolution began in North America over colonial rivalries. Competition to control the interior of North America led to a French victory in western Pennsylvania in 1754. A subsequent French victory over British forces near what is now Pittsburgh the following year resulted in a British declaration of war against France in 1756.

The French and Indian War (known in Europe as the Seven Years' War, 1756–1763) began badly for the British. Not until William Pitt came to power in 1757 and focused the country's naval power effectively did the conflict shift in England's favor. By blockading the coast of France, the British prevented ships and supplies from reaching the West Indies and North America. In 1758 they captured Louisbourg, a French fortress in the Gulf of Saint Lawrence. In 1759 Quebec fell, and in 1760 the British took Montreal. France was defeated in North America as well as other parts of the world. The Treaty of Paris in 1763 reflected the new power of Great Britain. In North America, France lost New France (Canada) and only retained two small islands in the Gulf of the Saint Lawrence for fishing and three islands in the West Indies. The loss of Quebec meant an end to French territorial claims in the Ohio Valley and westward to the Mississippi River. France gave up New Orleans and the Louisiana Territory (between the Mississippi River and the Rocky Mountains) to its ally, Spain, as compensation for Spain's loss of the Floridas to the British and to use as a buffer against further British territorial advance. Great Britain thus controlled North America east of the Mississippi River from Hudson Bay to the Gulf of Mexico, with the exception of New Orleans.

The first British empire had reached its peak of power, and loyalty to the empire in British North America had never been stronger. The new imperial possessions, however, created problems. How were they to be governed and how was the expensive war to be paid for? Resentment against England's hegemony smoldered in France and in all Europe. Some observers in Great Britain wondered whether removal of France from North America would not encourage a colonial tendency to independent action now that the colonists no longer needed British protection from a French threat on their northern and western borders.

Colonial Resistance to British Rule

Strong American colonial attachment to the imperial connection with Great Britain did not long survive the war. No longer concerned with a foreign foe in North America, England turned its full attention to imperial responsibilities. To consolidate controls neglected during the first part of the eighteenth century and to bring some relief to British taxpayers, Parliament sought to shift part of the cost of the French and Indian War and the administration of British North America to the colonies. Between 1764 and 1775 the British government adopted controversial policies that prompted colonial protest. Parliamentary legislation designed to raise money to help administer Great Britain's new territorial possessions and to regulate more effectively colonial trade, either through internal taxes in the colonies (Stamp Act, 1765), or customs duties on goods entering colonial ports (Townshend Duties, 1767, and Tea Act, 1773), produced open defiance of British authority by a significant number of influential colonials.

Belief in the superiority of American society and politics also helped to fuel violent resistance to British policies in the 1760s and 1770s. For example, the concept of republicanism, deeply rooted in colonial thought, meant much more than government accountable to the male, propertied population. There was a pervasive fear that, as power in government increased, institutions would become more corrupt and inevitably pose a threat to the liberty of the people. The fear of this threat was widespread but was countered somewhat by the belief that a virtuous population could collectively maintain the people's liberty through its assemblies against the pervasive corruption British politics. In addition, the generally accepted political theory of John Locke—that all people are born free and that each individual has the right to life, liberty, and property—informed debate over British policy. While not dismissing the fear of corruption in society, Locke believed human beings were rational enough to protect their natural rights not by inherent virtue but through self-interest. Consequently, they would establish governments based on limited power under fixed laws. Most colonials also were aware of Locke's view that because government was an artificial creation, the people could alter or abolish it if it became oppressive.

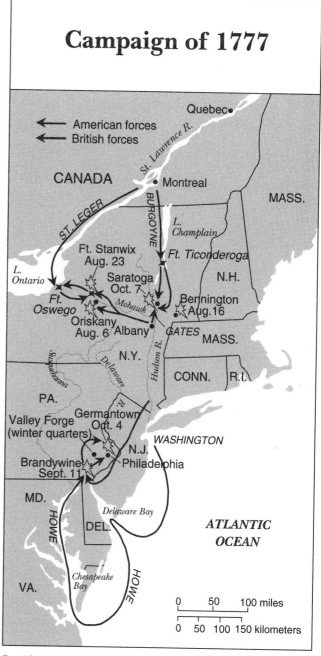

From *A People and A Nation: A History of the United States*, Mary Beth Norton et al., 4th Edition. ©1994 by Houghton Mifflin Company. Reprinted with permission

The crisis between Great Britain and its colonies came to a head in 1774. In March, Parliament passed the so-called Coercive Acts, which closed the port of Boston until the town paid for tea destroyed the year before and restricted the self-government of the colony of Massachusetts. Outraged Massachusetts leaders called for a colonywide meeting to discuss countermeasures. In September delegates from the thirteen colonies met in Philadelphia. This First Continental Congress created the Continental Association, a nonimportation, nonex-

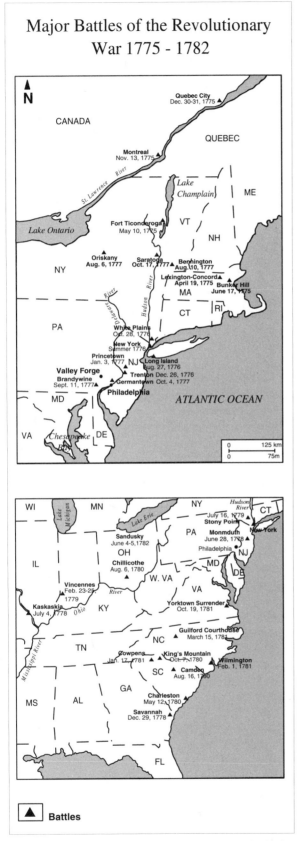

Major Battles of the Revolutionary War 1775 - 1782

N

CANADA

QUEBEC

Quebec City
Dec. 30-31, 1775 ▲

Montreal
Nov. 13, 1775 ▲

St. Lawrence River

Lake Champlain

ME

Fort Ticonderoga
May 10, 1775

VT

NH

Lake Ontario

Oriskany
Aug. 6, 1777 ▲

Saratoga
Oct. 17, 1777 ▲

Bennington
Aug. 10, 1777

NY

Lexington-Concord
April 19, 1775 ▲

Bunker Hill
June 17, 1775

MA

RI

CT

PA

White Plains
Oct. 28, 1776

New York
Summer 1776

Princetown
Jan. 3, 1777 NJ Long Island
Aug. 27, 1776

Valley Forge

Trenton Dec. 26, 1776

Brandywine
Sept. 11, 1777 ▲ Germantown Oct. 4, 1777

MD

Philadelphia

ATLANTIC OCEAN

VA   *Chesapeake Bay*   DE

0   125 km
0   75m

WI   MN   NY   *Hudson River*

Lake Michigan   *Lake Erie*   July 16, 1779
Stony Point   CT

Sandusky
June 4-5, 1782   PA   Monmouth
June 28, 1778 ▲   New York

OH   Philadelphia   NJ

IL   Chillicothe
Aug. 6, 1780   MD

W. VA   DE

Vincennes
Feb. 23-25,
1779   *River*   VA

Kaskaskia
July 4, 1778 *Ohio* KY   Yorktown Surrender
Oct. 19, 1781

Mississippi River

Guilford Courthouse
March 15, 1781

NC

TN

Cowpens
Jan. 17, 1781 ▲   King's Mountain
Oct. 7, 1780   Wilmington
Feb. 1, 1781

SC   Camden
Aug. 16, 1780

GA

MS   AL   Charleston
May 12, 1780

Savannah
Dec. 29, 1778

FL

▲ **Battles**

portation, and nonconsumption agreement against Great Britain. By the time the Second Continental Congress began meeting in May 1775, open warfare had erupted between British and American troops at Lexington and Concord in Massachusetts.

The Continental Congress did not back down. On 15 June it responded to the British use of force with the appointment of Virginia's George Washington as commander in chief of an American army, and on 6 July it issued the "Declaration of the Causes and Necessity of Taking Up Arms" against the mother country. For its part, on 23 August the Crown declared the colonies in a state of rebellion. Most congressional delegates, now convinced that independence was imminent, supported the creation on 29 November of the Committee of Secret Correspondence, with Benjamin Franklin as chair. Clearly, the Americans could not win a war against Great Britain's powerful army and navy without outside support; therefore, their main objective became the securing of military aid for the revolutionary cause from foreign countries.

The Quest for Aid from France

France seemed the nation most likely to take a serious interest in disrupting the British empire. A desire for revenge against its old rival and plans to reassert its primacy in Europe dominated the thinking of the French foreign office. Amid efforts to rebuild the French army and navy, France welcomed the news of American resistance to British imperial policy. The possibility of turmoil in the empire of its archenemy led Étienne-François, Duc de Choiseul, the minister of foreign affairs (1758–1770) under Louis XV, to send observers to America to report on Great Britain's military resources and on the state of unrest in British North America. His agents reported that a rebellion was imminent. In 1774 Charles Gravier, Comte de Vergennes, became foreign minister under Louis XVI. A man of intelligence, prudence, and subtlety, he sought to continue Choiseul's policy of seeking revenge against Great Britain. Pierre-Augustin Caron de Beaumarchais also advocated aid to Great Britain's American colonies. In mid-1775 a French political agent in London, this playwright, poet, musician, inventor, and politician learned from Americans in London that the colonies had launched an insurrection. Beaumarchais told Vergennes that aid to the rebellious colonists "will diminish the power of England and proportionately raise that of France."

The French government followed the advice of Beaumarchais and sent an agent, Julien-Alexandre Achard de Bonvouloir, to North America in September 1775. After meeting with the Committee of Secret Correspondence, he sent back favorable reports on the colonial determination to obtain independence. Beaumarchais recommended secret aid to avoid an immediate conflict with England. At this point Vergennes agreed, and in two April 1776 memoranda titled *Considerations* and *The Reflections*, Vergennes cautiously urged the king to support the American rebels with secret aid. He argued that the loss of the American colonies would immeasurably hurt the British empire and restore France to preeminence in Europe. France had to seize this opportunity to weaken its natural adversary, "a rapacious, unjust and faithless enemy." French aid might ensure American independence, leave England as a second-rate imperial power, damage British trade, and create strong commercial ties between France and the new nation. Assistance also could help France recover such possessions as the Newfoundland and Saint Lawrence fisheries.

On 2 May 1776, under the king's orders, France began undercover aid to the colonies. French (and some Spanish) arms and ammunition were channeled through a fictitious firm, Rodrigue Hortalez and Company, set up by Beaumarchais. While many ships went directly to the colonies, most sailed to Haiti, where American vessels picked up the cargoes. Thus began an operation that provided 90 percent of American arms, ammunition, tents, and clothing for the next two years. The well-developed British spy network in France learned about this project, but British ships could not stop the shipments because French warships stationed in the West Indies protected the vessels.

In March 1776, the Continental Congress chose Silas Deane, a Connecticut merchant with a reputation for devious financial practices but strong support for the revolution, as secret agent to France to secure arms for the rebel cause as well as to negotiate treaties of alliance and commerce with the French government. Deane soon procured supplies for the United States at a handsome commission; he also conducted a profitable personal trade. In these activities he formed a connection with an old friend, Edward Bancroft, a British spy and interpreter between Deane and Beaumarchais. Because Deane talked freely of his activities, the British became well informed of his operation. The Continental Congress, meanwhile, opened American ports to all nations on 6 April.

In June the Congress began discussing resolutions for American independence from Great Britain introduced by Richard Henry Lee of Virginia. The members voted for independence on 2 July and published its formal declaration thereof on 4 July. Then ensued a long debate on the subject of the nation's desire to remain independent of European politics, with its emphasis on maintaining a balance of power, and the possible need to seek more foreign aid and even military alliances to secure American independence from Great Britain. The initial desire for friendship and aid from foreign nations without entangling alliances appeared in the Plan of Treaties presented to the Congress by John Adams in July 1776. The plan outlined the American desire for freedom of commerce with other nations as the means for undermining Great Britain's commercial supremacy. It provided that noncontraband goods carried on neutral ships were not subject to interference by belligerent powers. It championed freedom of the seas as the means for creating internal economic prosperity (rather than acquisition of a colonial empire). Such a plan would not only aid America's independence from European politics but also expand its economic prosperity. The Continental Congress adopted Adams's plan in September.

After the Declaration of Independence, the armed conflict intensified in North America. The war did not go well for the Americans during the summer; Washington lost Long Island to the British army in August and occupied then Brandywine and Germantown in Pennsylvania the following month. To counter these setbacks, on 26 September the United States appointed a three-person commission to France—Deane, Arthur Lee, and Franklin. They had orders to press France for recognition of American independence, a treaty of commerce, and a continuation of military assistance. Foreign military assistance probably would mean political and military commitments by the United States in violation of the Plan of Treaties, but in the long run the newly declared nation had to compromise out of necessity.

Franklin arrived in Paris in December 1776. At age seventy he had extensive experience as an American colonial agent in England. Highly regarded as an author, scientist (inventor of the lightning rod, a stove, and bifocals), and a man of the Enlightenment, Franklin already had been elected to the French Academy. He seemed the embodiment of the colonial cause in his humble manner, fur hat, and homespun clothes. He quickly became America's chief diplomat in Paris, but his hint that without more French aid and recognition of American independence the United States might have to seek a reconciliation with England did not budge the government of Louis XVI. France did allow American privateers (armed merchant ships used to attack enemy shipping) to operate out of its ports but would not give diplomatic recognition to the new nation. When the war continued to go badly for the Americans into the fall of 1777, the Continental Congress reluctantly changed its policy and instructed Franklin to seek a military alliance with France.

Even Franklin's subtle diplomacy would not have won over Vergennes if America's military fortunes had not improved. Although General Sir William Howe had taken Philadelphia in September, on 17 October 1777 American forces defeated the British army under General John Burgoyne in the Battle of Saratoga in upstate New York.

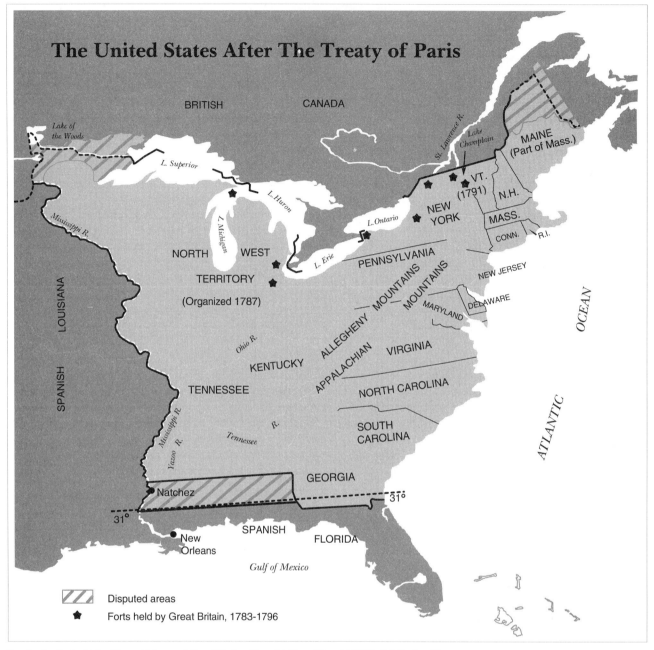

The United States After The Treaty of Paris

BRITISH CANADA

Lake of
the Woods

L. Superior

St. Lawrence R.

Lake Champlain

MAINE
(Part of Mass.)

Mississippi R.

L. Huron

L. Michigan

L. Ontario

VT.
(1791)

N.H.

NEW
YORK

MASS.

CONN.

R.I.

NORTH   WEST

L. Erie

PENNSYLVANIA

NEW JERSEY

TERRITORY

(Organized 1787)

ALLEGHENY MOUNTAINS

MOUNTAINS

MARYLAND

DELAWARE

Ohio R.

KENTUCKY

APPALACHIAN

VIRGINIA

TENNESSEE

NORTH CAROLINA

Tennessee   R.

SOUTH
CAROLINA

Yazoo R.

Mississippi R.

GEORGIA

31°

Natchez

31°

New
Orleans

SPANISH

FLORIDA

Gulf of Mexico

LOUISIANA

SPANISH

OCEAN

ATLANTIC

Disputed areas

★   Forts held by Great Britain, 1783-1796

From *American Foreign Relations*, Thomas G. Paterson, J. Garry Clifford, and Kenneth J. Hagan, Volume I. ©1995 by D.C. Heath and Company.
Reprinted with permission of Houghton Mifflin Company

The news reached Paris on 3 December, and the British quickly sent an agent, Paul Wentworth, to Paris to urge the Americans to stay within the empire. Franklin refused the overture but informed Vergennes of the British proposal. At this point an anxious Vergennes changed course under Franklin's prodding and decided on 17 December to offer the Americans recognition of independence and a treaty of alliance.

Negotiations began on 8 January and ended on 6 February 1778, when France and the United States signed the Treaty of Amity and Commerce. Its first article recognized American independence by establishing peace and friendship between France and the United States of America. In matters of commerce it generally reflected the model Plan of Treaties adopted by the Continental Congress on 17 September 1776. The treaty provided that both France and the United States would grant to each other the same trading opportunities in their ports as either one gave to its most-favored trading partner. The treaty also accepted the American, or small nation, position on the rights of neutral traders in wartime, a policy generally known as freedom of the seas. The United States could foresee the likelihood of being a prominent carrier of neutral goods during future European conflicts and gained French support for the following wartime protections: contraband of war must be limited to warlike equipment (arms and ammunition but not clothing, food, or naval stores); neutral ships could carry and trade in noncontraband goods with any belligerent (free ships, free goods); if either nation extended commercial benefits to other nations, both signers must extend this most-favored-nation status to each other; and neutrals were to be able to trade between the ports of a belligerent (such as between France and its West Indian islands).

The terms of the Treaty of Alliance, signed the same day, made it almost inevitable that France would become involved openly in the war within the British empire. The agreement stated that its purpose was "to maintain ...the liberty, sovereignty, and independence" of the United States and that the military alliance between the countries would go into effect in the event of a war between France and Great Britain. It also provided that "neither of the two parties shall conclude either truce or peace with Great Britain without the formal consent of the other first obtained." The two parties pledged that neither would lay down its arms until the independence of the United States was assured by a treaty ending the conflict. Finally, both nations agreed to a mutual guarantee of each other's possessions in North America. France guaranteed American independence and territory "forever" and renounced any design on territory in North America held by Great Britain before 1763, and the United States guaranteed French possessions in America "forever." These terms favored the United States. France asked for no special privileges and no additional territory in the Western Hemisphere.

Infuriated by the Franco-American alliance, Great Britain broke diplomatic relations with France in March 1778. At the same time, the British Parliament continued to try to bring the colonies back into the empire by offering them home rule. It also sent a commission under Frederick Howard, Lord Carlisle, to America to persuade members of Congress to accept the proposal. The Carlisle commission arrived a month too late. On 4 May the Continental Congress had approved the treaties. Six weeks later British warships attacked the French navy in the English Channel (17 June 1778). Fulfilling the terms of the alliance, France now formally entered the war on the side of the new nation and sent a naval squadron to North America to aid the Americans against the British navy. The French government also sent over Conrad Alexandre Gérard as the first French minister to the United States (the American representatives in Paris had been received by Louis XVI on March 20).

Revolutionary Diplomacy in Europe

Before signing the treaties with the United States, France had urged Spain, allied to France in the Family Compact of 1761, to support the American drive for independence from Great Britain. In fact, a secret article in the Franco-American alliance reserved the right of King Carlos III of Spain to become a party to the treaty. The Spanish perspective on the American Revolution, however, was very different from the French. In 1776 José Moñino y Redondo, Conde de Floridablanca, became principal minister. Floridablanca feared that representative government in British North America might appeal to Spain's colonies in the Western Hemisphere and that the American effort to gain independence from Great Britain might encourage revolt within the Spanish empire. An independent United States, moreover, would undoubtedly become an aggressively expansionist nation that could threaten Spain's American empire. Spain hoped that the British and Americans would fight each other for years and become exhausted. Spain, therefore, cut back aid to the Americans after the British defeat at Saratoga and refused to recognize American independence.

The key to Spanish policy was its determination to win back Gibraltar, lost to England in 1704. If Great Britain would give up its land at the southern tip of Spain, strategically located at the entrance to the western end of the Mediterranean Sea, Spain would remain neutral in the war. Floridablanca even proposed that Spain act as a mediator of the American rebellion on terms that would have left the Americans in the British empire. If Great Britain would not make such an agreement and France would help restore Gibraltar, Spain was prepared to enter the war against Great Britain. England vacillated, not wanting to give up the strategic real estate and turned down the Spanish offer to mediate the conflict. Spain then made a secret alliance with France on 12 April 1779. In the Convention of Aranjuez, Spain pledged to aid France in its war against England if Great Britain did not return Gibraltar; France honored Spain's determination not to become an ally of the United States and not to recognize American independence. France also pledged not to make peace with Great Britain until Spain had recovered Gibraltar. Spain hoped to get back the Floridas, which had fallen under British authority during the Seven Years' War. The Spanish and French fleets began joint maneuvers, and on 21 June Spain declared war on Great Britain. Thus, without American knowledge, the independence of the United States became tied to the French promise to recover Gibraltar for Spain. It was not until a year later (April 1780) that American diplomats learned the terms of the Franco-Spanish convention.

On hearing of the Spanish declaration of war on Great Britain, the pleased Continental Congress in

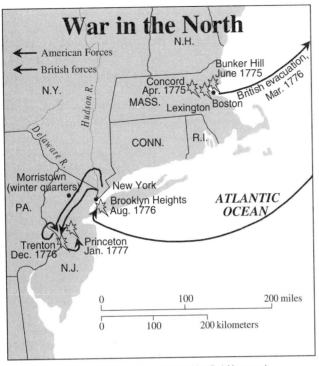

War in the North

← American Forces

← British forces

N.H.

Bunker Hill
June 1775

Concord
Apr. 1775

British evacuation, Mar. 1776

N.Y.

MASS.

Lexington Boston

Hudson R.

CONN.

R.I.

Delaware R.

Morristown
(winter quarters)

New York

Brooklyn Heights
Aug. 1776

PA.

ATLANTIC
OCEAN

Trenton
Dec. 1776

Princeton
Jan. 1777

N.J.

0   100   200 miles

0   100   200 kilometers

From *A People and A Nation: A History of the United States*, Mary Beth Norton et al., 4th Edition. ©1994 by Houghton Mifflin Company. Reprinted with permission

October 1779 appointed one of its former presidents, John Jay, the American minister plenipotentiary to Spain. Unaware of the real motives of Spanish policy, the U.S. government hoped that Jay would negotiate Spanish recognition of American independence, a loan of $5 million, and treaties of alliance and commerce with Spain similar to those Franklin had worked out with France. In addition, Jay was specifically instructed to secure free navigation of the Mississippi River to the Gulf of Mexico and the use of a free port on the river near the gulf in Spanish territory.

Jay's mission proved a disaster from beginning to end. He arrived in Spain in January 1780, but he soon received a cold note from the Spanish government saying that he might come to Madrid but not in "a public character." Floridablanca was determined to maintain exclusive control of the Mississippi River where it touched territory under Spanish jurisdiction. He also planned to regain the Floridas. With no intention of recognizing American independence, Floridablanca still hoped that if Great Britain did give the colonies their freedom the result would be a weak United States under French and Spanish protection. Jay had a few brief visits with Floridablanca, but he was never officially received at the Spanish court, and the Spanish government intercepted and read his correspondence. During the two and a half dreary years he spent in Spain, moreover, he found himself in a more and more desperate personal financial

position. He ultimately squeezed only $174,011 from the Spanish government for the American cause. Annoyed by Jay's persistence, Floridablanca finally told him in September 1780 that Spain would consider an alliance only if the United States gave up its demand for free navigation of the Mississippi River below the northern boundary of the Floridas (the 31st parallel) in return for a mutual guarantee of territory in North America. Jay wrote to the president of Congress, "There are a great many wheels in our business, and the machine won't move easily, unless the great wheel be turned by the waters of the Mississippi."

Although this concession met opposition from the state of Virginia and settlers in the Kentucky territory, so great was the American need for more financial and military aid that Congress agreed to the Spanish proposal in February 1781. Disgusted with Spain, Jay was not surprised when Floridablanca delayed discussion of specific treaty terms. Jay sensed that Spain still hoped to negotiate with rather than fight Great Britain, and that he was probably nothing more than a pawn in Floridablanca's strategy of trying to maneuver England into negotiation of Spain's grievances rather than deal openly with a representative of the United States. From November 1779 to March 1781, Thomas Hussey, an Irish priest working for Spain, and a British agent named Richard Cumberland tried without success to arrange a truce to bring Spain out of the war and leave Great Britain in control of a large part of the former colonies. Embittered and disillusioned, his dignity affronted, Jay welcomed Franklin's suggestion in April 1782 that he leave Spain for Paris, where his talents would be put to greater use in negotiating a peace treaty with Great Britain.

While Jay languished in Spain, events in the rest of Europe favored the American cause. Led by Catherine II of Russia, several countries in February 1780 formed the Armed Neutrality. It called for arming merchant ships for protection against attack and proclaimed a code for the protection of neutral shipping against seizures by all belligerents, especially Great Britain. The code included most of the same protections for neutrals as those embodied in the Treaty Plan of 1776 and the 1778 commercial treaty between France and the United States. In addition, a provision of the Armed Neutrality held that a blockade must be effective to be binding. Denmark, Norway, Sweden, Prussia, the Holy Roman Empire, Portugal, the Two Sicilies, and Holland soon joined the pact. Although Catherine II characterized the Armed Neutrality as an "armed nullity" of small-navy nations, it was successful for a while in isolating the British and in closing the Baltic Sea to their privateers. The Armed Neutrality also aided the American war effort by preventing Great Britain from finding allies on the European continent. At the same time, except for Holland, these nations grew uncomfortable with the cause of American independence. For example, Catherine II refused to receive an American minister to Russia, Francis Dana.

The Continental Congress had high hopes of securing financial support as well as supplies from the Dutch. Holland ranked as a great financial power as well as an important trading nation. At the beginning of the conflict, the Dutch government refused to lend money to the Americans because it wanted to remain neutral and profit from trade with both sides. One of the main sources of arms and gunpowder for the American cause was the Dutch Caribbean island of Saint Eustatius, an enormous warehouse for arms smuggling. To avoid antagonizing Great Britain, the Dutch government ordered the operation stopped but failed to enforce its laws. At the same time, Holland allowed its shippers to transport food and naval stores to French ports, where they were reloaded onto French vessels for shipment to America.

When France entered the war on the side of the United States in 1778, the Dutch saw an opportunity to continue the trade with France as a neutral (particularly in naval stores). This time Great Britain grew angry. In fall 1778 British naval vessels began detaining Dutch ships carrying naval stores to French ports. Not only were these actions a threat to Holland's lucrative trade, but the British also called for assistance by reminding the Dutch government of the inconveniently pertinent 1678 treaty of alliance between the two countries that obliged them to aid each other if either one were threatened by a third power. When the Dutch government protested that the pact only applied to European wars, England allowed its privateers to attack Dutch shipping. Holland's decision to join the Armed Neutrality and an American-Dutch commercial agreement based on the Treaty Plan of 1776, negotiated by William Lee of Virginia, alarmed London. The British navy fired on a convoy of Dutch trading vessels in December 1780, precipitating war between the two nations.

Peace Negotiations

As the conflict within the British empire expanded into world war, the belligerents began turning their thoughts to a diplomatic solution. The Continental Congress had appointed John Adams as principal American negotiator in September 1779. On arriving in Paris, Adams, a tough and often abrasive individual, angered Vergennes with his demands that the United States open direct negotiations with Great Britain. The French government, determined to keep control of events, wanted Adams recalled. Instead, at the end of 1780 Congress appointed him minister to Holland. At first he met resistance to his efforts to secure financial assistance, the Dutch still preferring the advantages of the profits from neutral trade; but after

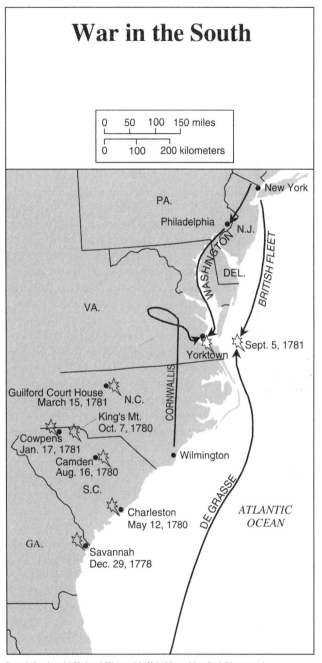

From *A People and A Nation: A History of the United States*, Mary Beth Norton et al., 4th Edition. ©1994 by Houghton Mifflin Company. Reprinted with permission

Holland went to war with Great Britain, the Dutch received Adams as minister in April 1782, thus recognizing American independence. His patience and persistence ultimately paid off when on 8 October he secured a commercial treaty and a large loan, the initial installment of which was about $1.7 million.

As the war dragged on in America, the Russian and Austrian governments in March 1781 tried to settle the conflict by mediation of the great powers. Vergennes at first approved of the idea, thinking it would put an end to the continuing negotiations between Great Britain and Spain. The Russian government proposed that Great Britain and the American colonies engage in direct negotiation of their dispute and accept a year's armistice while a settlement was being worked out. From Holland, Adams sent word that the United States would negotiate only as an independent power. As for the British, George III rejected the idea out of hand, calling it an interference with a domestic problem within the empire.

It was not European diplomacy, but disillusionment with the struggle within Great Britain itself and military defeat, that finally led to the opening of peace negotiations. In February 1781 the British navy had captured Saint Eustatius from the Dutch; that island had become the center of trade between Europeans and Americans, a large part of it contraband. The British also captured some 2,000 American merchants and seamen, but during the operation a French fleet under Admiral François Joseph de Grasse eluded the British commander, Admiral George B. Rodney, and joined other French ships sailing for the Chesapeake. Then on 19 October 1781 Great Britain met defeat at the hands of American and French forces at Yorktown, Virginia, General George Washington receiving the arms of the British army as a band played "The World Turned Upside Down." Military defeats in the East Indies, a sagging British economy, and growing sentiment for peace in Great Britain as the war depleted its resources and threatened its supremacy in the English Channel also bedeviled Great Britain. Unable to maintain its support in the House of Commons, the government of Lord North fell in March 1782 after being in power for twelve years.

A new government came to power under Lord Rockingham, a leader of one of the Whig political factions. Determined to put an end to the war, Rockingham had the king's grudging pledge to recognize the independence of the rebellious colonies. Foreign Secretary Charles James Fox supported independence but was opposed by the minister of colonial affairs, William Petty, the Earl of Shelburne. Shelburne wished to obtain peace and commercial ties with the Americans while still keeping British North America in the empire. In July Rockingham died, and when Shelburne was chosen by the king to succeed him as prime minister, Fox resigned. Shelburne only came to accept the idea of complete American independence after several months of negotiation; but as early as March 1782 he seized on a friendly note from his old friend Franklin to begin peace talks. He offered to renew his friendship with the Americans and in April sent over to Paris another old friend of Franklin's, Richard Oswald, to explore a framework for peace.

Patient and sensible but inexperienced, Oswald quickly fell under Franklin's influence. He dutifully reported to Shelburne that a treaty should include independence, evacuation of all British troops from the United States, western boundaries to the Mississippi River, a southern boundary adjacent to the Spanish Floridas (the 31st parallel), and the right of American fishermen to use the Newfoundland fisheries freely as in prewar days. Franklin added that to reestablish Anglo-American friendship it would be most "advisable" for Great Britain to provide payments to those Americans ruined by the war, acknowledge its error in using force against the Americans, establish commercial reciprocity between the nations, and cede Canada to the United States. Franklin hinted that sufficiently generous peace terms from Great Britain could lead the American negotiators to threaten France with a separate Anglo-American peace treaty. The Oswald talks with Franklin established the basis for a successful negotiation.

Wary of Adams, Vergennes used his influence with the Continental Congress to secure new instructions (15 June 1781) that enlarged the delegation to include men whom he believed to be more pro-French or of French ancestry. The full American delegation included Franklin, John Jay, Adams, Thomas Jefferson, and Henry Laurens. Adams was still in Holland, Jefferson did not set out from America soon enough to arrive for the negotiations, and Laurens, who had been captured by the British, was a prisoner in the Tower of London from October 1780 to December 1781. Although the intervention of friends in England secured Laurens's release in January 1782, by the time he arrived in Paris the preliminary articles of the peace treaty were almost ready for signature. In addition to the necessary proposals Franklin had made to Oswald, the new instructions placed the American diplomats under French supervision in any peace talks. Jay arrived in Paris on 23 June and immediately began to take part in new discussions with Oswald. While Franklin was easygoing and had formed a friendship with Vergennes, Jay was highly suspicious and quickly began to question both British and French motives. He told Oswald (as had Franklin) that the United States would negotiate a peace treaty only as an independent power. Jay also rejected Vergennes's claim that there was no need to rush into peace talks with Great Britain.

Jay resented the congressional instructions and began to believe that France might not even want the United States to achieve complete independence. Although this was not true, French policy sought to limit the new nation's boundaries so that they did not include territory between the Appalachian Mountains and the Mississippi River. It would suit French interests to have the British remain in control of Canada and the area between the Great Lakes and the Ohio River and for Spain to dominate the territory south of the Ohio between the Mississippi and the Appalachians as well as the Floridas, which Spain had retaken from Great Britain in February 1781. In addition, Vergennes hoped to keep the United States out of the Newfoundland fisheries and to remain weak and dependent on France for trade. Jay perceived Vergennes's attitude as an affront to American dignity and independence and refused to consult the French foreign minister further about the negotiation. Grasping the overriding goal of French policy, Jay saw that France wanted to delay American independence until it could secure Gibraltar for Spain. In his words, "Let us be grateful to the French for what they have done for us, but let us think for ourselves. And, if need be, let us act for ourselves." By late August Franklin's and Jay's demand that the British negotiate with the United States as an independent nation had led Shelburne to authorize Oswald to meet with the representatives of the "thirteen United States."

At the same time, Franklin was stricken with kidney stones and painful attacks of gout, leaving Jay on his own to negotiate with Oswald until early October. Jay pressed Oswald for a change in his instructions that would grant American independence before the terms of the treaty were worked out. Jay's analysis of French policy toughened his stance, and three events further alienated Jay from the French foreign office. First, in discussions with the Spanish ambassador to France, Pedro Pablo Abarca de Bolea, Conde de Aranda, and Vergennes's private secretary, Joseph Matthias Gérard de Rayneval, Jay resented their united determination to prevent any American claim to the Mississippi Valley. On 6 September, Jay received a proposal from Rayneval suggesting that Great Britain maintain control of the area north of the Ohio River and that Spain and the United States divide the area below it as far as the border of the Floridas. Second, the British put in Jay's hands a letter intercepted from the secretary of the French legation to America, François de Barbé-Marbois, suggesting that the Americans be kept out of the Newfoundland fisheries. Jay now had support for his suspicion that the French government wanted to limit American rights to fish in that area. Third, on 9 September, Jay learned that Rayneval was setting out on a secret mission to England to talk with Shelburne. The purpose of the mission was much broader than Jay imagined, but he was correct in his fear that American and Spanish territorial demands would be discussed. During the talks, Shelburne, even more than Rayneval, stressed the need to prevent the Americans from obtaining too much land, and they both discussed the possibility of keeping them out of the Newfoundland fisheries. Shelburne rather disingenuously told the king that the French seemed "more jealous than partial to America."

Jay saw a need for quick action to preserve the American cause from being frustrated by European diplomatic intrigue. He completely defied the congressional instruc-

tions to act only with French "knowledge and concurrence." Without either Vergennes's or Franklin's knowledge, he immediately sent his own emissary to talk with Shelburne. Jay's proposal was simple: if the British government would alter Oswald's commission, giving him power to treat with the commissioners of the United States so that the United States could negotiate as an independent nation (American independence would be recognized in the first article of the peace treaty), the rest of the peace talks could go forward smoothly and without French advice. Shelburne hesitated. He did not want the negotiations in Paris to drag out, because he wanted a peace treaty ready to present to Parliament when it met in December. Negotiating with the Americans as representatives of an independent nation would be very unpopular with conservative members of the House of Commons, but Shelburne decided to take a chance that granting the American demand could be the means of breaking up the Franco-American alliance and laying the groundwork for future Anglo-American good will and economic ties.

On 27 September, Shelburne sent Oswald and two other representatives back to Paris with new instructions granting American independence in the first article of a peace treaty. The rest of the agreement would be worked out between Great Britain and the United States as two independent nations. The instructions accepted America's demands for a northern boundary to the southern end of Lake Nipissing (the southwest tip of Quebec before 1774), which would have granted the United States considerable territory north of Lakes Erie and Ontario. The instructions also gave up Great Britain's claim to the return of prewar debts to British merchants and confiscated Loyalist property. On 5 October, Franklin and Jay initialed this new draft and sent it to London, but after news arrived of the British naval victory at Gibraltar on 30 September, Shelburne decided to demand concessions on the northern boundary line and the prewar debts and Loyalist clauses.

Between mid-October and 30 November, when the preliminary peace treaty was signed, the discussions grew intense. One British diplomat remarked after the treaty was signed that "these Americans are the greatest quibblers I ever knew." By 16 October, Adams had arrived in Paris and agreed with Jay's views on all aspects of the negotiations. Outnumbered, Franklin accepted the independent approach and talked no further with Vergennes. Increased British confidence at the negotiating table encountered the toughness of the American diplomats. It became impossible for the British to obtain any significant concessions.

The Treaty of Paris and Independence

In addition to the first article establishing American independence, the treaty lowered the northern boundary of the United States from the original Lake Nipissing line to that of the Lake of the Woods on the west through the Great Lakes eastward to the St. Lawrence River and the Saint Croix River to the Atlantic Ocean. The southern boundary was determined at the 31st parallel (the northern boundary of the Spanish Floridas) and the western boundary at the Mississippi River. The article on the fisheries was essentially the work of New Englander Adams. In it the Americans gained the right to fish on the high seas around Newfoundland and the "liberty" to fish along the inshore Newfoundland coast as well as to dry and cure fish in unsettled areas of Nova Scotia, Labrador, and Magdalen Island. Article 8 provided for both nations to have free navigation of the Mississippi River from its source to its mouth at New Orleans. Laurens, who appeared at the end of the talks, secured the inclusion in Article 7 of a clause that forbade the carrying away of slaves by British troops evacuating the United States. Franklin was staunchly against any concessions to the Loyalists, "our bitterest enemies." In Article 5 the British secured only a paper pledge by the United States to "recommend" to state legislatures that those who had remained loyal to Great Britain be able to recover or be paid for property abandoned or confiscated in America. According to Article 4, British creditors would "meet no lawful impediment" to recovery of prerevolutionary war debts owed to them by Americans.

The terms of the Treaty of Paris were not to go into effect until a peace agreement was worked out between England and France; thus the treaty did not constitute a direct violation of the Franco-American alliance of 1778. An outstanding diplomatic achievement, it reflected the skill and tenacity of the American diplomats as well as their ability to take advantage of hostilities among the European powers. When he learned of the terms from Franklin, Vergennes, who probably knew what had been going on, expressed no surprise. As a formality, however, two weeks later he protested to Franklin that he and his colleagues had not followed their instructions to consult France during the negotiations. Franklin admitted that he and his colleagues had acted indiscreetly; but he expressed confidence that their actions would not undermine the Franco-American alliance. He confided that "[t]he English, I just now learn, flatter themselves they have already divided us. I hope…this little misunderstanding will therefore be kept secret, and that they will find themselves totally mistaken." He also had the audacity to ask the French government for another loan of 6 million livres. Even more surprising, Vergennes, who possibly feared the collapse of the American government before the treaties were safely signed, agreed to provide this amount despite the poor condition of the French treasury.

On 20 January 1783, Great Britain completed a peace treaty with Spain and France and a separate one with Holland. All treaties were formally signed on 3 September 1783, and the U.S. Congress approved the Anglo-American agreement on 14 January 1784. Although the House of Commons approved the treaty in February 1783, the terms were considered so humiliating to England that Lord Shelburne resigned under public attack. An effort to negotiate a commercial agreement between Great Britain and the United States that would have furthered Franklin's and Shelburne's ideas for freer trade ended in failure when hard-line mercantilists in the British government secured an Order in Council in July 1783 that closed the British West Indies to all American carrying trade.

Vergennes had exclaimed that "the English buy the peace more than they make it." If France felt misused during the Anglo-American peace negotiation, at least Paris had aided Vergennes in getting out of his commitment to obtain Gibraltar for Spain and had secured the disruption of the first British empire. France, however, actually lost more from the war than England. Great Britain had not really been humbled despite its losses. France had spent itself into near bankruptcy, which helped lead to the French Revolution of 1789 and its attendant internal upheaval and destruction. The British, in order to undermine the Franco-American connection, had made concessions to the United States that had not been achieved by the new nation's power and military actions. It took time and in some cases further negotiation for the new nation to implement some of the provisions of the peace treaty. The articles on the prewar debts and Loyalist property were difficult to enforce, the territory beyond the Appalachian Mountains and the Mississippi River was not in American hands, and the articles on the fisheries and navigation of the Mississippi River forced the United States into further negotiations with Great Britain and Spain, respectively. Nevertheless, independence had been won and, with its vast domain, the groundwork had been laid for the new nation's future political and economic expansion.

REBECCA G. GOODMAN

See also Adams, John; Beaumarchais, Pierre Augustin Caron de; Canada; Deane, Silas; Declaration of Independence; Fisheries; France; Franklin, Benjamin; French and Indian War; George III; Great Britain; Jay, John; Loyalists; Mississippi River; Netherlands; Neutral Rights; Russia and the Soviet Union; Spain; Vergennes, Duc de

FURTHER READING

Bemis, Samuel F. *The Diplomacy of the American Revolution*, 4th ed. New York, 1955.

Clark, Ronald W. *Benjamin Franklin: A Biography*. New York, 1983.

Cummins, Light Townsend. *Spanish Observers and the American Revolution, 1775–1783*. Baton Rouge, La., 1991.

Dull, Jonathan R. *A Diplomatic History of the American Revolution*. New Haven, Conn., 1985.

Ferling, John. *John Adams: A Life.* Knoxville, Tenn., 1992

Gilbert, Felix. *To the Farewell Address: Ideas of Early American Foreign Policy.* Princeton, N.J., 1961.

Hoffman, Ronald, and Peter J. Albert, eds. *Diplomacy and Revolution: The Franco-American Alliance of 1778.* Charlottesville, Va., 1981.

———. *Peace and the Peacemakers: The Treaty of 1783.* Charlottesville, Va., 1986.

Horsman, Reginald. *The Diplomacy of the New Republic, 1776–1815.* Arlington Heights, Ill., 1985.

Hutson, James H. *John Adams and the Diplomacy of the American Revolution.* Lexington, Ky., 1980.

Kaplan, Lawrence S. *Colonies into Nation: American Diplomacy, 1763–1801.* New York, 1972.

Kramnick, Isaac. *Republicanism and Bourgeois Radicalism: Political Ideology in Late 18th Century England and America.* Ithaca, N.Y., 1990.

Mackesy, Piers. *The War for America, 1775–1783.* Cambridge, Mass., 1964.

Middlekauff, Robert. *The Glorious Cause: The American Revolution, 1763–1789.* New York, 1982.

Morris, Richard Brandon. *The Peacemakers: The Great Powers and American Independence.* New York, 1965.

Perkins, Bradford. *The Creation of a Republican Empire, 1776–1865,* vol. 1 of *The Cambridge History of American Foreign Relations,* edited by Warren I. Cohen. Cambridge, 1993.

Savelle, Max. *The Origins of American Diplomacy: The International History of Anglo-America, 1492–1763.* New York, 1967.

Schulte Nordholt, Jan Willem. *The Dutch Republic and American Independence.* Chapel Hill, N.C., 1982.

Stinchcombe, William C. *The American Revolution and the French Alliance.* Syracuse, N.Y., 1969.

Stourzh, Gerald. *Benjamin Franklin and American Foreign Policy.* Chicago, 1954.

Tucker, Robert W., and David C. Hendrickson. *The Fall of the First British Empire: Origins of the War of American Independence.* Baltimore, 1982.

Van Alstyne, Richard Warner. *Empire and Independence: The International History of the American Revolution.* New York, 1965.

Louisiana and Saint Domingue (Haiti) failed because of a slave rebellion and disease among French troops. President Thomas Jefferson used this lull in the Napoleonic Wars to cut expenditures for the army, navy, and coastal fortifications and began dismantling Alexander Hamilton's financial program. The peace, however, also cut into the profitable U.S. carrying trade—the import of goods from the French West Indies into the United States and their reshipment to France. By 1803 the British were having second thoughts about the treaty. Napoleon had shown no interest in concluding a trade pact with Great Britain, and his annexation to France of the Piedmont region and Elba and naming himself president of the Italian (formerly Cisalpine) Republic threatened British interests in the Mediterranean. In March the British resumed their war effort against Napoleon, with mixed consequences for the United States. On the positive side, Napoleon needed money for the renewed fighting and a possible invasion of England. Thus, he agreed to sell Louisiana to the United States for $15 million. On the other hand, the renewed fighting quickly led to British mastery of the seas, French control of the continent of Europe, and increased difficulties for Americans who sought to trade equally with the two belligerents.

R<small>ONALD</small> L. H<small>ATZENBUEHLER</small>

See also France; Great Britain; Haiti; Louisiana Purchase; Spain

FURTHER READING

DeConde, Alexander. *This Affair of Louisiana.* New York, 1976.

Perkins, Bradford. *The First Rapprochement: England and the United States, 1795–1805.* Berkeley, Calif., 1967.

AMIENS, TREATY OF

(27 March 1802)

Signed by Great Britain and France after nine years of war, and best viewed as a temporary truce in the Napoleonic Wars. The British needed the peace to rebuild economically through an expansion of trade with the European continent. Napoleon used the lull in fighting to put into motion various plans for consolidating his control of France and for expanding French interests in Europe and North America. Napoleon instituted numerous projects, including buildings in Paris, promulgation of the Code Napoleon, installation of the Concordat (a compromise with the pope over the role of the Catholic Church in France), and a new constitution naming him consul for life. In Europe, he worked to deny to England markets across Europe and gained control of territory in Switzerland, Italy, and the Mediterranean. In North America, his dream of building a new French empire in

AMISTAD AFFAIR

(1839)

An incident arising from the rebellion of fifty-three African slaves aboard the Spanish schooner *Amistad* off the coast of Cuba. From 1839 to 1841 the event brought U.S., international, and natural law under scrutiny against a complex backdrop of domestic and international politics. Under the leadership of Joseph Cinqué, in June 1839 the slaves killed the crew and demanded that the two Spanish owners aboard navigate the ship back to Africa. The two Spaniards, however, deceptively meandered about the Caribbean until the vessel was drawn northward by the Gulf Stream. After about two months, it was sighted and seized by a U.S. naval vessel off the coast of Long Island, New York. When abolitionists heard of the affair, they decided to take the matter to court to expose the horrors of slavery and the slave trade. The crucial issue was whether or not the slaves were free men because they had been illegally brought from

Africa. The *Amistad* affair snaked through the U.S. court system and finally came before the Supreme Court in 1841. The case centered on the status of the Africans and of slavery, but it also involved diplomatic problems for President Martin Van Buren's administration. Almost immediately after the appearance of the *Amistad* in the United States, Spain evoked the reciprocity clause of Pinckney's Treaty (1795) and demanded that the "property" be returned. Van Buren sought to comply despite the fact that doing so would validate the assumption that the Africans were cargo and would create a particularly sticky situation because Anglo-Spanish treaties had long forbidden the international slave trade. If Spain was forced to prove that the *Amistad* Africans were property, it would be an admission that it had violated their anti-slave trade arrangement with Great Britain and provide a pretext for British intervention in Cuba, which could be damaging for U.S. hemispheric policy because the United States hoped to acquire Cuba. Despite the insistence of Attorney General Henry D. Gilpin that the U.S. government was bound by treaty to return the slaves to Spain, former President John Quincy Adams and attorney Roger S. Baldwin persuaded the court that Cinqué and the others were "kidnapped Africans," thereby winning their freedom.

DONALD A. RAKESTRAW

See also Pinckney's Treaty; Slave Trade and Slavery

FURTHER READING

Hoyt, Edwin P. *The "Amistad" Affair.* New York, 1970.
Jones, Howard. *Mutiny on the* Amistad: *The Saga of a Slave Revolt and Its Impact on American Abolition, Law, and Diplomacy.* New York, 1987.

AMNESTY INTERNATIONAL

A leading nongovernmental organization for advocating and defending human rights that won the Nobel Peace Prize in 1977. Founded in 1961 in Great Britain, Amnesty International (AI) has chapters in the United States (AIUSA) and more than 110 other countries; in the early 1990s AI had a worldwide membership of 330,000. It works for the release of political prisoners and other prisoners of conscience and victims of torture who neither use nor advocate violence. It also opposes the death penalty. AI does not accept any funding from governments. Its local chapters and members raise voluntary contributions. Through AIUSA it lobbies members of Congress and the executive branch of government and organizes grass-roots letter-writing campaigns among its members. AI keeps track of general human rights violations (for example, by issuing annual reports on the status of human rights in different countries) and of the status of individual prisoners of conscience, who are "adopted"

by local chapters. Among the issues in which AI has played a prominent role have been apartheid in South Africa, maltreatment of dissidents in the Soviet Union, the jailing of political dissidents in China, and the use of chemical weapons by Iraqi president Saddam Hussein against Iraqi Kurds.

JAMES DAVID BARBER

See also Human Rights

FURTHER READING

Amnesty International. *Report.* 1993.
Power, Jonathan. *Amnesty International: The Human Rights Story.* New York, 1981.

ANDORRA

See Appendix 2

ANGLETON, JAMES JESUS
(*b.* 9 December 1917; *d.* 11 May 1987)

Career secret-service and counterintelligence official. Born in Boise, Idaho, Angleton drew his middle name from his Mexican mother, Carmen Moreno, who married James H. Angleton. His father served with General John J. Pershing in Mexico during the search for Pancho Villa, a Mexican bandit and revolutionary leader. In the early 1920s the Angletons moved to Milan, Italy, where the elder Angleton expanded his business as an operations manager for National Cash Register Company. Returning to the United States, young James entered Yale in 1937, graduating in 1941. After studying law at Harvard from 1941 to 1943, Angleton was drafted into the army, then recruited into the X-2 counterintelligence (CI) branch of the Office of Strategic Services (OSS). Trained in the basics of CI work in the Maryland mountains, Angleton was sent to London in late 1943 to take advanced training from the British CI organization, MI6. Recognized for his superior work in London, he was promoted to captain, then transferred to Rome to head a special unit aimed at uncovering German spies. In May 1945 Angleton was asked to remain in Rome as commander of an army intelligence regiment. Returning to the United States in 1947, he joined the Central Intelligence Agency (CIA), shortly thereafter becoming the aide to the director of the CIA's Office of Special Operations.

From his office in the first CIA headquarters in downtown Washington, D.C., Angleton plotted, implemented, and controlled hundreds of counterespionage operations over the next few years. In 1948 he was directly involved in U.S. actions to prevent a widely rumored communist takeover of the Italian government. From his station in Italy, Angleton built an important relationship between the CIA and the Israeli secret service, Mossad, a bond that was sustained for more than twenty years. In 1954, following a decision by CIA Director Allen Dulles to reorganize the counterintelligence function, Angleton was made chief of counterintelligence and counterespionage. He was a principal force behind the acquisition of Soviet Premier Nikita Khrushchev's secret speech in 1956 to the Twentieth Communist Party Congress on the horrors of Joseph Stalin's government. Angleton's counterintelligence career crossed paths with notorious cases of Soviet espionage, such as H. A. R. (Kim) Philby's betrayal of British intelligence and the Soviet defections—to British and U.S. intelligence units—of Anatoly Golitsyn, Oleg Gordievsky, Oleg V. Penkovsky, Pyotr Popov, and Yuri Nosenko. Ironically, Angleton had befriended Philby in connection with field training in London during World War II and dined with him on numerous occasions after the war.

Increasingly fixated on the CIA's internal security, Angleton spent his last years in the agency searching for Soviet moles. Despite his conviction that Soviet intelligence acted logically in its desire to plant moles in the CIA, Angleton's methods for countering such logic produced staff divisiveness, a massive collection of questionable personnel files, and several destroyed careers. No Soviet mole was ever identified. Appointment of William Colby as CIA director in 1973 marked the beginning of the end of Angleton's career. Colby questioned the effectiveness of the mole hunt; in particular, he contested Angleton's belief that Nosenko was a Soviet mole and believed that Angleton's paranoia had paralyzed the agency's Soviet division.

Angleton's forced resignation from the CIA came in December 1974. He was permitted to remain as a special consultant until September 1975. Retirement from the CIA enabled Angleton, reclusive in professional and private life, to return to his hobbies of fly-fishing, growing orchids, collecting gems, and reading poetry. Abolition of key CI staff positions also hastened the retirement of two of Angleton's deputies, Raymond G. Rocca and Newton S. Miler. In August 1975 Senate hearings inquired into alleged domestic abuses of CIA authority and into Angleton's role in keeping files on CIA employees. Even after his death Angleton remains widely regarded—heralded by some, reviled by others—as the master of counterintelligence tradecraft. The 1994 espionage case of the CIA's former Soviet division's chief of counterintelligence, Aldrich Ames, lent credibility to Angleton's reasoning, but not his actions, concerning Soviet intentions to achieve a high-level penetration of the agency. Ames, found guilty of supplying the Soviets with volumes of CIA documents and the names of many CIA double agents, destroyed numerous U.S. and allied intelligence operations and contributed to the assassination of at least ten Soviets.

JAMES D. CALDER

See also Central Intelligence Agency; Colby, William Egan; Cold War; Covert Action; Intelligence

FURTHER READING

Grose, Peter. *Gentleman Spy: The Life of Allen Dulles.* Boston, 1994.
Mangold, Tom. *Cold Warrior: James Jesus Angleton.* New York, 1991.
Martin, David C. *Wilderness of Mirrors.* New York, 1980.
Riebling, Mark. *Wedge: The Secret War Between the FBI and the CIA.* New York, 1994.
Winks, Robin W. *Cloak and Gown: Scholars in the Secret War, 1939–1961.* New York, 1987.
Wise, David. *Molehunt: The Secret Search of Traitors that Shattered the CIA.* New York, 1992.

ANGOLA

A country located in southern Africa, bordering the South Atlantic Ocean, Zambia, Namibia, and Zaire, that was the scene of one of the primary Cold War proxy conflicts waged between the United States and the Soviet Union. Indirect superpower intervention in Angola's agonizing civil war, fought by deeply divided political factions since its abrupt independence from Portugal in 1975, was abetted by direct Cuban and South African intervention for nearly fifteen years. U.S. policy toward Angola and its conflict shifted with the changing winds of the larger global competition. Following superpower disengagement in the late 1980s, peacemaking among Angola's warring factions became the primary—albeit often elusive—U.S. policy goal.

Engagement

Sporadic uprisings by Angolans resisting centuries of Portuguese colonialism became organized guerrilla resistance by 1962, and the armed struggle against Portugal lasted until independence in 1975. The anticolonialists split into three factions. The Popular Movement for the Liberation of Angola (MPLA), backed in part by the Mbundu ethnic group and led by Agostinho Neto, espoused Marxism-Leninism; the Front for the Liberation of Angola (FNLA), led by Holden Roberto, had ties to the Bakongo group and proclaimed itself antisocialist; and the National Union for the Total Independence of Angola (UNITA), based among the Ovimbundu and headed by the fiery guerrilla leader Jonas Savimbi, turned pro-Western and anticommunist. U.S. policy during Angola's preindependence period was supportive of Portugal.

A coup in Portugal in 1974, which overthrew the right-wing dictatorship of Antonio Salazar and installed a leftist military leadership, brought rapid decolonization to

Angola by 1975. In the chaotic run-up to independence, with the Cold War in full swing but tempered by détente, the three anticolonialist parties, which were also fighting among themselves, aligned themselves with the superpowers and other ideological and regional allies. Despite ongoing violence, the parties concluded a doomed pact in 1975, the Alvor Accord, which created an interim coalition government and established ground rules for elections leading to independence in November 1975. The accord collapsed in an upsurge of fighting.

U.S. policy toward Angola during its troubled transition to independence, heavily influenced by the views of Secretary of State Henry Kissinger, was guided by two primary objectives—to halt expanding Soviet influence in the resource-rich country and region and to maintain a global strategic balance with its Cold War foe. The United States, along with its allies, initially supported the FNLA (and to a lesser extent, UNITA). In June 1974 the Central Intelligence Agency (CIA) began supporting Roberto's FNLA without the approval of the Forty Committee, a working group convened to supervise covert operations. Controversy continues over the timing of superpower intervention, kicking off the tit-for-tat escalation that became a hallmark of the proxy conflict in Angola. In any event, the Forty Committee authorized the CIA's support of the FNLA within weeks after the Alvor Accord in January 1975, further weakening the already deteriorating U.S.-Soviet détente. Soviet military supplies began arriving in March 1975, which had presumably been in the pipeline prior to the U.S. decision to support the FNLA.

During 1975 the MPLA gained the upper hand in renewed fighting with increased Soviet support. When the first Cuban advisers were dispatched to aid the FNLA in June, the Forty Committee asked the CIA for a comprehensive covert operations plan. Aid to the FNLA was upped, with the concurrence of President Gerald R. Ford, to $6 million, supplemented by an additional $8 million. When the MPLA remained ascendant, South African troops directly intervened in October 1975 on behalf of the FNLA and UNITA, which had formed an anti-MPLA alliance. The MPLA, with the help of a large infusion of Cuban troops and advanced Soviet weaponry, essentially defeated the FNLA near the capital city Luanda and successfully fought back South African and UNITA troops to win control of much of the country. The MPLA declared a one-party state, which the United States refused to recognize. The CIA sought to further aid the FNLA to defeat the MPLA's attempt to consolidate its control, but it needed congressional approval for new funds. In December 1975, in the wake of the Vietnam War and Watergate, Congress prohibited the administration from arming or assisting parties in the Angolan conflict through the adoption of the Clark Amendment.

The administration of President Jimmy Carter, legally constrained by the congressional prohibition on covert aid but also less ideologically disposed to intervene, continued to oppose the MPLA but was increasingly critical of South Africa. Carter continued Ford's policy of refusing to recognize the MPLA regime. UNITA continued to be supported by South Africa, and the conflict remained stalemated at a relatively low level until the early 1980s.

The administration of President Ronald Reagan significantly changed U.S. policy toward Angola. Assistant Secretary of State for African Affairs Chester Crocker pursued a regional policy of "constructive engagement." With fighting escalating and a new incursion by South Africa in 1983, Washington sought to link agreement on withdrawal of South African and Cuban troops from Angola with an agreement on Namibian independence from South Africa. The Reagan administration won repeal of the Clark Amendment in 1985, in order to aid UNITA against participation in the war by some 20,000 Cuban troops. The amendment's repeal was aided by a strong anti-Castro, anti-Cuban lobby in the United States. Aid for UNITA was part of the overall Reagan Doctrine, a policy to support anticommunist rebel movements as part of a global anti-Soviet strategy. In July 1985 the United States began covertly to deliver sophisticated antiaircraft and antitank weapons to UNITA, and Reagan hosted Savimbi in 1986 as if he were the Angolan head of state, lending political support. As the fighting intensified, key battles in 1987 and 1988 led to a costly military stalemate, with the United States and South Africa backing UNITA in the proxy war. All the while, however, U.S. oil companies were paradoxically exploring, pumping, and exporting oil from Angola's Cabinda province, with U.S. dollars the primary source of foreign exchange for the MPLA.

Disengagement

The easing of Cold War tensions following Soviet "new thinking" created a brief window of opportunity for joint U.S.-Soviet peacemaking in Angola in the late 1980s. Crocker pursued a disengagement agreement employing the linkage principle, and after a complex series of multilateral negotiations, involving the United States, the Soviet Union, South Africa, Cuba, and the Angolan parties, the United States clinched an accord in December 1988. The agreement linked Cuban and South African troop redeployment and withdrawal from Angola with independence for Namibia, a significant accomplishment for U.S. diplomats.

In 1989 the phased withdrawal of Cuban and South African troops began and the administration of President George Bush sought to facilitate peace between the MPLA and UNITA. The Angolan parties reached an agreement in 1991—the Estoril Accords—principally brokered by Portugal but backed by the United States and the Soviet Union. Despite progress in the peace talks, Congress voted to continue covert aid to UNITA, authorizing $30 million. The Estoril Accords led to a seventeen-month United Nations–sponsored peace process that climaxed with elections in September 1992, monitored by a small UN peacekeeping force and election observer mission. The MPLA won legislative and presidential majorities, with UNITA running a distant second. The UN declared the poll free and fair, but Savimbi contested the balloting and intense fighting soon resumed. For the remainder of 1992 and into 1993, the UN attempted to broker peace as the war spread and grew fiercer. The United States, essentially crediting UNITA with the new violence, limited its UNITA aid to humanitarian assistance.

Angola policy shifted considerably under the administration of President Bill Clinton. U.S. support for UNITA further diminished. With the MPLA showing flexibility in talks and UNITA remaining intransigent, the United States recognized the MPLA government in mid-1993 and later agreed to support UN economic sanctions in UNITA-controlled territory while mediation continued. UN mediation—backed by the United States, Portugal, Russia, and regional powers—led to an agreement in November 1994 to end the Angolan civil war and move toward new elections. A much larger UN peacekeeping force was deployed to oversee implementation of the accords, without the direct participation of any U.S. troops. With this agreement, most observers believe that Angola's tortuous civil war has finally come to an end. The United States emerged in 1995 and 1996 as the principal external party, along with the UN, committed to keeping the implementation of the 1994 agreements on track. Additionally, U.S. nongovernmental organizations have been active in providing post-war reconstruction aid and humanitarian relief.

TIMOTHY D. SISK

See also Clark Amendment; Portugal; Reagan Doctrine

FURTHER READING

Alfred, Lisa. "U.S. Foreign Policy and the Angola Peace Process." *Africa Today* 39 (1992).

Bender, Gerald J. "The Eagle and the Bear in Angola." *Annals of the AAPSS* 489 (1987).

Crocker, Chester A. *High Noon in Southern Africa: Making Peace in a Rough Neighborhood.* New York, 1992.

Laidi, Zaki. *The Superpowers and Africa: The Constraints of a Rivalry, 1960–1990.* Chicago, 1990.

Rothchild, Donald, and Caroline Hartzell. "The Case of Angola: Four Power Intervention and Disengagement." In *Foreign Military Intervention: The Dynamics of Protracted Conflict*, edited by Ariel E. Levite, Bruce W. Jentleson, and Larry Berman. New York, 1992.

Tvedten, Inge. "U.S. Policy Toward Angola Since 1975." *Journal of Modern African Studies* 30 (1992).

ANTARCTICA

An ice-covered continent located mostly south of the Antarctic Circle without permanent human habitation, governed by a unique international regime. First seen by European explorers and U.S. seal hunters in the early nineteenth century, Antarctica became an object of international rivalry in the first half of the twentieth century, after Norwegian explorer Roald Amundsen beat British explorer Robert F. Scott in the race to discover the South Pole (1911–1912). By the 1930s, seven nations—Great Britain, Australia, New Zealand, France, Argentina, Chile, and Norway—claimed wedge-shaped and overlapping slices of territory converging on the South Pole. The first significant U.S. exploration of Antarctica was the privately financed expedition of Admiral Richard E. Byrd in 1929. Ten years later Byrd persuaded President Franklin D. Roosevelt to establish the U.S. Antarctic Service and provide government backing for Byrd's 1939–1941 expedition. In 1946, at the start of the Cold War, Byrd commanded the U.S. Navy's Operation High Jump, involving 4,000 men and twelve vessels, including a submarine and an aircraft carrier. The purpose of the High Jump expedition was both scientific and military—to gain experience in extreme cold weather operations and to be prepared should the Soviet Union seek to establish itself on the continent.

Meanwhile, sharp disagreements developed, and even a few shots were fired (though nobody was hurt), between Great Britain and Argentina over their conflicting claims. Argentina and other Latin American governments wanted U.S. support for the argument, which Washington did not accept, that the British presence violated the Monroe Doctrine. In 1948 the United States proposed that the entire continent be governed under a condominium or United Nations trusteeship with the Soviet Union excluded. The territorial claimants rejected the idea. Some U.S. officials in the 1950s advocated that the United States make its own territorial claim, establish a military presence, and use the continent for nuclear tests. Others said that if the United States made a claim, so would the Soviet Union, already active in the scientific research. Still others argued that the United States should claim access to the entire continent and not lock itself into contests over territorial sovereignty.

President Dwight D. Eisenhower questioned arguments about Antarctica's military significance and listened instead to scientists who called for international cooperation. After the success of the 1957 International Geophysical Year with its focus on Antarctica, and with full Soviet cooperation, the United States took the lead in negotiating the Antarctic Treaty of 1959. The treaty, while neither affirming nor denying existing territorial claims, declared the continent and its surrounding waters north to sixty degrees south latitude a zone of peace in which all military activity, bases, and testing of weapons, especially nuclear weapons, were prohibited. This treaty represented the first post–World War II arms control agreement. All nations willing to invest in scientific research could establish stations on the continent and scientists could travel from place to place without regard to nationality. The treaty went into effect in June 1961, for thirty years' duration. The Cold War was thus banned from the coldest place on earth.

During the first thirty years of the treaty, environmental issues rose in importance for U.S. foreign policy and the world. In 1972 and 1980 the United States signed two conservation treaties protecting seals and other living marine resources. As the basic treaty came up for renewal, however, the most controversial issue was whether Antarctica should be open for the exploration and extraction of minerals—above all, oil. Environmental groups argued for banning all commercial mineral operations because the ecology of Antarctica was so fragile and so important for the world that a single oil spill could have terrible consequences. The initial U.S. government position was to permit exploration and exploitation but under safeguards designed to minimize damage. The environmentalist position, supported by France and Australia, prevailed. The renewed treaty contained the Protocol on Environmental Protection barring commercial mineral activity for fifty years and imposing strict regulations on all activity, including tourism. The protocol was signed in October 1991 and approved by the U.S. Senate in October 1992.

GADDIS SMITH

See also Environment; Science and Technology

FURTHER READING

Beck, Peter J. *The International Politics of Antarctica*. Cambridge, 1987.
Carter, Paul Allen. *Little America: Town at the End of the World*. New York, 1979.
National Research Council. *Science and Stewardship in the Antarctic*. Washington, D.C., 1993.
Triggs, Gilligan D., ed. *The Antarctic Treaty Regime: Law, Environment and Resources*. Cambridge, 1987.

ANTIBALLISTIC MISSILE TREATY

Signed in May 1972 by the United States and the Soviet Union. The advent of nuclear weapons, with their enormous destructive capabilities, increased the desire of national leaders to find effective defenses against attack. In the 1940s and 1950s both the United States and the Soviet Union developed and deployed air-defense systems designed to protect against attacks by bombers. When both superpowers deployed long-range missiles,

each began to search for an effective antiballistic missile (ABM). The United States initially developed the Nike-Zeus missile, which was succeeded by the Nike-X program. In 1967 the administration of President Lyndon B. Johnson announced that it would deploy a light nationwide ABM system, called Sentinel, to protect the U.S. population; then, two months after assuming the presidency in January 1969, Richard M. Nixon announced that he would reorient the ABM program to protect U.S. missile silos rather than the American people. Nixon dubbed this program Safeguard.

In May 1972 Nixon traveled to Moscow, where he signed a number of agreements with Soviet leader Leonid Brezhnev. Two of the most important were the first Strategic Arms Limitation Talks (SALT I) agreements: the ABM Treaty and the Interim Agreement on the Limitation of Strategic Offensive Arms. According to the terms of the ABM Treaty, the United States and the Soviet Union agreed that each country would deploy no more than 100 ABM launchers at each of two sites, one at the opposite's national capital and the other at a site at least 1,300 kilometers (800 miles) from the capital. In order to ensure compliance with the treaty's provisions, the agreement called for "national technical means of verification," a diplomatic euphemism for satellite reconnaissance and the monitoring of electronic signals. The United States and the Soviet Union agreed neither to interfere with these verification procedures nor to conceal deliberately any ABM components. The two signatories placed specific, technical restrictions on ABM radars and prohibited the deployment of new ABM systems based on new technologies such as lasers. The treaty was to be reviewed every five years, and either party retained the right to withdraw from it on six months' notice.

Because the ABM agreement was a treaty (unlike the Interim Agreement), the Nixon administration was required to submit it to the Senate for its advice and consent. That body approved the treaty by a vote of 88 to 2. In 1974 the United States and the Soviet Union signed a protocol to the ABM Treaty that decreased the number of ABM deployment sites from two to one. Most experts consider the ABM Treaty to be one of the most important arms control agreements ever signed because it strengthened strategic deterrence in a way consistent with the doctrine of mutual assured destruction. Because under the terms of the treaty neither superpower could be assured of its capacity to defend itself against a second-strike nuclear attack, neither had an incentive to launch a first-strike nuclear attack.

The observance of the treaty became an issue during President Ronald Reagan's administration when the president pushed for research and development of the Strategic Defense Initiative (also referred to as SDI or Star

Wars). During the first Reagan administration (1981–1985), because of its massive buildup of potentially offensive strategic weapons and its pursuit of strategic defense, the United States appeared to be shifting from a policy based on mutual assured destruction to a policy seeking damage limitation and a nuclear war–fighting capability, in violation of the ABM Treaty. This apparent shift challenged the view that strategic defense was destabilizing and that the mutual vulnerability of strong offenses was a stabilizing force in a nuclear world, a belief that had prevailed since the administration of President John F. Kennedy. The SDI program remained a research program, however, and the ABM Treaty remained in force.

DAN CALDWELL

See also Nuclear Weapons and Strategy; Strategic Arms Limitation Talks and Agreements; Strategic Arms Reduction Treaties; Strategic Defense Initiative

FURTHER READING

Bunn, Matthew. *Foundation for the Future: The ABM Treaty and National Security.* Washington, D.C., 1990.
Newhouse, John. *Cold Dawn: The Story of SALT.* New York, 1973.
Smith, Gerard C. *Doubletalk: The Story of the First Strategic Arms Limitation Talks.* New York, 1980.

ANTICOMMUNISM

See Cold War; McCarthyism

ANTIGUA AND BARBUDA

Two small islands, located in the Eastern Caribbean, about 650 kilometers east-southeast of Puerto Rico. They formed a nation on 1 November 1981 at the time they achieved independence from Great Britain. Columbus sighted the islands in 1493 during his second voyage, but no permanent European settlements were established until the seventeenth century. A lengthy imperial struggle over control of Antigua ended when the Treaty of Breda (1667) recognized the island as a British colony. In 1860, Antigua was formally united with Barbuda, its smaller northern neighbor.

Antigua and Barbuda is governed under a parliamentary system. The British monarch is titular head of state. Full diplomatic relations have been maintained with the United States since independence (in 1982, the United States upgraded its diplomatic presence in Antigua and Barbuda from consular to ambassadorial), as has membership in the United Nations, and in the British Commonwealth of Nations. Antigua and Barbuda joined the Organization of American States (OAS) in 1981, holds observer status with the Nonaligned Movement, and was a founding member of both the Caribbean Community and

Common Market (CARICOM) in 1973, and the Organization of Eastern Caribbean States (OECS) in 1981.

Antigua and Barbuda has been one of the Caribbean region's most consistent supporters of the United States, which occupies air force and naval facilities on Antigua. Tourism's growing importance to an economy that has benefited from significant levels of U.S. aid has been strengthening ties between the two countries, despite Washington's concern during the 1980s about allegations of government corruption. Antigua and Barbuda joined the other members of the OECS in providing troops for the 1983 U.S.-led invasion of Grenada. Antigua and Barbuda participated in the U.S.-financed Regional Security System from its inception in 1985, and under the U.S.-sponsored Caribbean Basin Initiative (CBI) received favorable trade terms. As a CARICOM member, Antigua and Barbuda supported, in 1994, the U.S.-led, UN-sanctioned invasion of Haiti to oust the military dictatorship and install democratically-elected President Jean-Bertrand Aristide.

RODERICK A. MCDONALD

See also Caribbean Basin Initiative; Grenada Invasion; Haiti; Nonaligned Movement; Organization of American States; Reagan, Ronald Wilson

FURTHER READING

Coram, Robert. *Caribbean Time Bomb: The United States' Complicity in the Corruption of Antigua.* New York, 1993.
Henry, Paget. *Peripheral Capitalism and Underdevelopment in Antigua.* New Brunswick, 1985.
Meditz, Sandra W., and Dennis M. Hanratty, eds. *Islands of the Commonwealth Caribbean: A Regional Study.* Washington D.C., 1989.
Peters, Donald C. *The Democratic System in the Eastern Caribbean.* Westport, Conn., 1992.

ANTI-IMPERIALIST LEAGUE
(1898–1920)

Organization opposed to the annexation of colonial territories, especially the Philippines. The league was founded in Boston in November 1898 by politically independent reformers and intellectuals, such as Edward Atkinson, Charles Eliot Norton, and Moorfield Storey. Although similar groups formed throughout the nation and in 1899 nominally consolidated into the American Anti-Imperialist League and claimed a membership of 700,000, the Boston chapter remained the center of U.S. anti-imperialist activities. The league's leadership was composed largely of older men from established families. Some had been active opponents of slavery in their youth. The league's most intense activity occurred between 1898 and 1900, when it unsuccessfully opposed the Treaty of Paris, which ended the Spanish-American-

Cuban-Filipino War and annexed the Philippines, and William McKinley's reelection to the presidency. Hampered by internal disagreements, the advanced age of its leadership, a dearth of political experience, and the long-term strength of the imperialist tradition in the United States, the league failed to achieve its immediate political goals. From a broader moral and educational perspective, however, it publicized the incompatibility between colonialism and the U.S. principle of government by the consent of the governed.

JOSEPH A. FRY

See also Imperialism; Philippines; Spanish-American-Cuban-Filipino War, 1898

FURTHER READING

Beisner, Robert L. *Twelve Against Empire: The Anti-Imperialists, 1898–1900*, repr. Chicago, 1992.
Tompkins, E. Berkeley. *Anti-Imperialism in the United States: The Great Debate: 1890–1920*. Philadelphia, 1970.

ANZUS TREATY

(1951)

A security agreement between Australia, New Zealand, and the United States, signed in September 1951 and in force from April 1952. The pact reflected Cold War fears of the Soviet Union and China, the disappearance of Great Britain's capacity to serve as a security guarantor in the Pacific, and, on Australia's and New Zealand's part, a desire to extract protection from the United States against the possible resurgence of Japan. The United States agreed to the alliance partly to ensure Australia, and New Zealand's adherence to the peace treaty concluding hostilities with Japan. Although ANZUS had no standing forces or secretariat, it developed elaborate defense cooperation between the three signatories. In 1986 the United States suspended its treaty obligations and special defense links with New Zealand because New Zealand legislation barred entry of nuclear-powered ships and nuclear weapons into that country's waters and ports. U.S. policy prohibited public disclosure about whether a U.S. ship carried nuclear weapons. The treaty remains formally tripartite, with close defense cooperation between the United States and Australia and between Australia and New Zealand.

HENRY S. ALBINSKI

See also Australia; New Zealand

FURTHER READING

Albinski, Henry S. *ANZUS, the United States, and Pacific Security*. Lanham, Md., 1987.
McIntyre, David W. *Background to the ANZUS Pact: Policymaking, Strategy, and Diplomacy 1945–1955*. N.Y. and Christchurch, 1995.
Starke, Joseph G. *The ANZUS Treaty Alliance*. Melbourne, 1965.
Young, Thomas-Durell. *Australian, New Zealand, and United States Security Relations, 1951–1986*. Boulder, Colo., 1992.

APPEASEMENT

The practice of granting concessions to an aggrieved nation in circumstances of general tension or specific crisis. This practice underwent dramatic change in popular meaning during the twentieth century. Before the mid-1930s appeasement primarily referred to timely concessions to disgruntled nations whose grievances had some legitimacy, in the hope of defusing difficulties and promoting peace and goodwill. Acting from a position of strength, the appeasing power was motivated not by fear or weakness but by a sense of statesmanship and a perception that limited concessions would not endanger its vital national interests. Appeasement did not constitute a broad, well-defined foreign-policy orientation but was a technique used to address specific problems of limited scope. Examples include some of President Woodrow Wilson's concessions to the Japanese at the Paris Peace Conference of 1919 and elements of President Franklin D. Roosevelt's Good Neighbor Policy toward Latin America in the 1930s.

During the turbulent 1930s, confronted with the aggressive foreign policies of authoritarian regimes in Germany, Italy, and Japan—nations driven by intense dissatisfaction with the division of spoils after World War I and by economic needs—-the war's victors sought to reduce tension by a new type of appeasement that included overlooking blatant violations of the peace settlement. Leadership fell to Great Britain and France as the primary guarantors of the Treaty of Versailles, given that the United States had failed to ratify the treaty or join the League of Nations and had assumed a position of neutrality toward European crises. British and French efforts were sporadic until Neville Chamberlain became prime minister of Great Britain in May 1937. Fearing another terrible war if something drastic were not done, he and a coterie of Conservative Party colleagues made appeasement into a clearly formulated, highly publicized foreign policy endeavor. The French tagged weakly along. The authoritarian leaders, however, especially Adolf Hitler in Germany, had ambitions that were not appeasable, and concessions invariably resulted in increased demands, heightened tensions, and threats of war. As successive failures strengthened the determination of the appeasers to succeed through intensification of their efforts, a policy that was conceived with honorable objectives degenerated into one of intrigues and machinations, and, at length, humiliating surrender. The Munich Agreement of September 1938, by which the disputed area called the Sudetenland was transferred from Czechoslovakia to Germany amid ominous threats from Berlin and extreme Anglo-French pressure on Prague to cede the territory, is generally considered the primary symbol of this development.

President Roosevelt, sympathetic to the objectives of British-French appeasement but skeptical that it would work, was enabled by the geographic separation of the United States from Europe and the U.S. posture of neutrality to be both supportive and critical as the turn of events seemed to warrant. Some historians believe that the United States, in Great Britain's place, would have acted similarly. Other scholars have concluded that Roosevelt, more perceptive than Chamberlain about the nature and dangers of Nazism, actually took steps in 1937 and early 1938 to bring U.S. weight to bear into the balance of forces in Europe. Rebuffed by Chamberlain, however, Roosevelt withdrew to a wait-and-see position from which he could do nothing effective. Meanwhile, Roosevelt hoped that vigorous protest against the rising tide of Japanese aggression in China, punctuated by occasional warning moves of various kinds, would suffice in Asia—-while Washington and London played a game of expecting stauncher initiatives from each other and assessing blame accordingly when they were not forthcoming. Roosevelt was not forced by events, or the public's perception of them, to take decisive actions until after war had begun in Europe. This aloofness in the face of increasing dangers, and the issuing of vague, ambiguous, and sometimes inconsistent policy statements, clearly implicated the United States in the appeasement policies of the 1930s. U.S. appeasement, however, was more a matter of procrastination and a denial of responsibility than a carefully crafted policy.

Having failed ignobly in the late 1930s, appeasement became a reviled term, connoting a policy of shameful weakness to be assiduously avoided. Every U.S. president in the Cold War era sought to avoid the appearance of condoning appeasement, although political critics often hurled the charge, especially at advocates of détente with the Soviet Union. The earlier failure of appeasement was a major factor in the development of the policy of containment (of the Soviet Union and communism) during the administration of President Harry S. Truman. President Dwight D. Eisenhower publicly rejected appeasement as the road to "surrender on the installment plan," and President John F. Kennedy bolstered his defense of Berlin and West Germany (1960) and his resolve in the Cuban missile crisis (1962) by invoking the specter of Czechoslovakia in 1938. Presidents Lyndon B. Johnson and Richard M. Nixon, in attempts to explain U.S. policy in Southeast Asia, regularly railed against appeasement, while Presidents Ronald Reagan and George Bush built foreign policy around a get-tough attitude that benefitted substantially from what was widely perceived as a weakened U.S. position of power in the world during the Jimmy Carter administration. Over many years, the term "appeasement" grew popular among government officials and

politicians as a means of stigmatizing policies of compromise. Invoking the appeasement (or Munich) analogy of 1938 became a ritual that was antagonistic toward efforts at international accommodation.

After the Cold War, some observers recognized appeasement as a vital element of diplomacy that ought not to be discarded just because it had been misused, in the wrong circumstances, in the late 1930s. In the new formulation, appeasement must emanate from a position of strength; the object of appeasement must show itself to be appeasable by the nature of its reaction to proffered concessions; and concessions must eschew the surrender of any fundamental principle upon which rests the claim to loyalty and respect of the government by its people. Of course, the distinction between wise and unwise concessions is always open to debate, and the practice of branding a posture of conciliation as "appeasement" in order to condemn it has not disappeared. An attitude of conciliation was present in elements of U.S. foreign policy during the early years of Bill Clinton's presidency, but insofar as it was equated with appeasement, it resembled the pre-1937 meaning of the term.

WILLIAM R. ROCK

See also Containment; Munich Conference; Paris Peace Conference of 1919; World War II

FURTHER READING

Dallek, Robert. *Franklin D. Roosevelt and American Foreign Policy, 1932–1945.* New York, 1979.
Gaddis, John L. *Strategies of Containment: A Critical Appraisal of Postwar American National Security Policy.* New York, 1982.
Levering, Ralph B. *The Cold War: A Post Cold-War History.* Arlington Heights, Ill., 1994.
Offner, Arnold A. *American Appeasement: United States Foreign Policy and Germany, 1933–1938.* Cambridge, Mass., 1969.
Reynolds, David. *The Creation of the Anglo-American Alliance, 1937–1941: A Study in Competitive Cooperation.* Chapel Hill, N.C., 1982.
Rock, William R. *Chamberlain and Roosevelt: British Foreign Policy and the United States, 1937–1940.* Columbus, Ohio, 1988.

AQUINO, BENIGNO S. AND CORAZON C.

(*b.* 27 November 1932; *d.* 21 August 1983)
(*b.* 25 January 1933)

Benigno S. Aquino was a Philippine senator and opposition leader (1967–1972), and Corazon Cojuanco was president of the Philippines (1986-1992). Elected to the Philippine Senate in 1967, Benigno ("Ninoy") Aquino emerged as President Ferdinand Marcos's chief rival and was widely expected to succeed Marcos as president. In 1972, however, claiming that the Philippines was threatened by a communist takeover, Marcos declared martial law, suspending civil liberties, arresting Aquino and other political opponents, and maintaining his hold on the presidency. Tried on trumped-up charges, Aquino was sentenced to execution, but the sentence was not carried out, and he was imprisoned from 1972 to 1980. During U.S. President Jimmy Carter's administration, the Department of State put mild pressure on Marcos to release Aquino. In 1980 Marcos allowed Aquino to travel to Dallas for a heart bypass operation. Aquino remained in the United States for three years, but in August 1983, informed that Marcos was close to death, he decided to return to the Philippines. Aquino was killed at Manila's international airport by soldiers from the Aviation Security Command. Overnight he became a martyr.

Aquino's widow, Corazon ("Cory"), had shown little interest in politics up to then; by her own admission, she had been a housewife for most of her adult life. Her husband's death propelled her into politics, however, and she became the symbol of opposition to the Marcos regime. In February 1986 she outpolled Marcos in presidential elections and became president. Aquino's principal accomplishments as president were to restore free elections and oversee the adoption of a new constitution. She made limited progress in rebuilding the economy, shattered by Marcos's misrule. Lauded by the U.S. media and championed by the Department of State and Congressman Stephen Solarz, Aquino hoped for a massive amount of U.S. aid, but her hopes were not fulfilled. Her administration was troubled by instability within the Philippine military; of several coup attempts that occurred, the most serious one, in December 1989, failed only because U.S. aircraft assisted Aquino. Limited by the new constitution to one six-year term of office, Aquino supported her ally Fidel Ramos (the eventual winner) in the 1992 presidential elections. Since leaving office, she has not played a prominent role in Philippine politics, choosing to focus on promoting the cause of women's rights inside and outside the Philippines.

GLENN ANTHONY MAY

See also Marcos, Ferdinand; Philippines

FURTHER READING
Burton, Sandra. *Impossible Dream: The Marcoses, the Aquinos, and the Unfinished Revolution.* New York, 1989.
Joaquin, Nick. *The Aquinos of Tarlac: An Essay on History as Three Generations*, third edition. Manila, 1986.
Komisar, Lucy. *Corazon Aquino: The Story of a Revolution.* New York, 1987.

ARAB-ISRAELI CONFLICT

See Israel; Middle East; Palestine to 1948

ARAB OIL EMBARGO

See Israel; Middle East; Organization of Petroleum Exporting Countries

ARAFAT, YASSIR

(*b.* 24 August 1929)

Chairman of the Palestine Liberation Organization (1969–), and the guerrilla leader who spearheaded the rise of Palestinian nationalism and became its symbol. Educated as an engineer in Cairo, Arafat was influenced by the successful Algerian rebellion against France (1954–1962) and by distant relatives Amin Husseini, the anti-Zionist mufti of Jerusalem, and Abdul Qadir Husseini, a guerrilla commander who died fighting Zionist forces in 1948. In 1958, Arafat co-founded the Palestine National Liberation Movement, known as Fatah, which seven years later launched sabotage attacks in Israel. After Israel defeated the Arab states in the 1967 Mideast war, Fatah's popularity rapidly increased and Arafat took over the PLO in 1969. Arafat, whose trademark is a *keffiyeh*, an Arab headdress, called for a peaceful settlement during a speech to the United Nations General Assembly in 1974. However, his aims and motives were repeatedly questioned because elements in the PLO carried out acts of terrorism against Israel. Arafat experienced further setbacks in 1982, when a fierce Israeli bombardment of Beirut, his base since 1971, caused him to evacuate the city. This led to factional violence within Fatah, which resulted in Arafat's forced expulsion from his last stronghold in Lebanon in 1983. Arafat survived, and the Palestine National Council, the PLO's "parliament-in-exile," elected him "president" of Palestine in 1988. For many years Arafat's diplomatic efforts were hampered by Israel's refusal to acknowledge Palestinian national rights. In 1993, through secret negotiations in Oslo, Norway, between PLO and Israeli government representatives which culminated in the signing of an initial peace agreement (Declaration of Principles), the Israeli government recognized the PLO and Arafat recognized Israel's right to exist and accepted limited self-rule in Israeli-occupied territories. The following year, Arafat shifted his headquarters from Tunis to Gaza as the Palestinian Authority (PA) was created with Arafat as its head. The peace process continued to progress with the signing of additional agreements, including "Oslo II" in 1995, and with elections in Gaza and the West Bank in January 1996 in which Arafat was elected president. In these elections Arafat and his Fatah supporters soundly defeated the challenge from the political wing of Hamas. But Hamas's challenge to Arafat runs deeper, both through its continuing anticorruption and social welfare campaigns among the Palestinian people and its continuing resort to terrorism against the PA and against Israel.

SCOTT MacLEOD

See also Israel; Middle East; Palestine Liberation Organization; Terrorism

FURTHER READING

Hart, Alan. *Arafat: Terrorist or Peacemaker?* London, 1984.
Wallach, John, and Janet Wallach. *Arafat: In the Eyes of the Beholder.* London, 1991.

ARBITRATION

A procedure involving the peaceful settlement of a dispute by a third party mutually chosen by both sides to hear pleadings of a case and hand down a legally binding decision. In U.S. foreign policy, arbitration was first incorporated into Jay's Treaty of 1794 to resolve disputes between the United States and Great Britain. Early U.S. interest in arbitration was fostered by the New York Society of Peace and the Massachusetts Peace Society, which encouraged Congress to promote arbitration in U.S. foreign policy. The efforts of these groups led to the inclusion of arbitration in the 1848 Treaty of Guadalupe-Hidalgo with Mexico and the 1953 Treaty of London with Great Britain. The landmark event underscoring the value of this procedure for U.S. foreign policy was the successful arbitration in 1872 of the *Alabama* Claims under the Treaty of Washington between the United States and Great Britain. The United States won a compensation award of $15.5 million for losses caused by Confederate warships unlawfully supplied to the South by British interests.

At the First International Conference of American States in 1890, a broad Plan of Arbitration was drafted but not ratified. Widespread acceptance of arbitration came at the Hague Peace Conference of 1899, including establishment of the Permanent Court of Arbitration under the Convention for the Pacific Settlement of International Disputes, which was revised in 1907. The United States played a key role in drafting the agreement. Among the most significant cases decided early on by the Hague procedure was the Newfoundland fisheries dispute between the United States and Great Britain in 1910. In the Western Hemisphere the 1975 Inter-American Convention on International Commercial Arbitration was still in force in the mid-1990s for many Latin American states, although the United States had not yet ratified that agreement.

The most active arbitration proceeding since the 1980s has been the Iranian–United States Claims Tribunal. Created in 1981 as part of the agreement to release American hostages, this panel has worked to arbitrate more than 4,000 commercial claims arising from the severance in 1979 of business relations between the two governments. The record of this tribunal is impressive: about 95 percent of all claims submitted have been resolved, more than $2 billion has changed hands in arbitral awards, and every award adjudicated in favor of a U.S. claimant has been paid in full by Iran.

U.S. policy regarding international arbitration is guided by the 1958 Convention on the Recognition and Enforcement of Foreign Arbitral Awards, the New York Convention, to which the United States is a party. The implementing legislation for this agreement, the United States Arbitration Act of 1970 makes enforcement of foreign arbitral awards a question arising under U.S. laws and treaties. Federal courts therefore have jurisdiction to enforce awards falling under the convention, irrespective of the nationality of the parties or the size of the controversy. Provisions to recognize and enforce arbitral awards in U.S. treaties of friendship, navigation, and commerce are generally consistent with the New York Convention. A valid agreement between the disputants to arbitrate is essential for jurisdiction of an arbitral tribunal. U.S. law requires only that an agreement be in writing, but the New York Convention also stipulates that parties must sign the agreement. Enforcement in the United States of agreements to arbitrate is done by the federal courts, in accordance with the U.S. Arbitration Act.

In the view of the United States, reciprocity is key to the convention, with the critical element being the place of the award. The United States has formally declared that the convention applies to the recognition and enforcement of awards made only in the territory of another contracting state. Further, the convention applies to all territories for which the United States is responsible, although only to differences arising out of legal relationships considered commercial under U.S. national law. Enforcement of foreign arbitral awards under the convention is an international obligation and in the United States is governed by federal law. Enforcement of other arbitral awards is a matter of local U.S. state law and is handled in the same manner as foreign judgments. Special arbitral institutions, such as the International Chamber of Commerce, the American Arbitration Association, the Society of Marine Arbitrators, and the United Nations Commission on International Trade Law, have enhanced opportunities for arbitration in U.S. foreign trade policy.

CHRISTOPHER C. JOYNER

See also Hague Peace Conferences; International Law; Iran

FURTHER READING

Brower, Charles N. "Lessons to be Drawn from the Iran-U.S. Claims Tribunal." *Journal of International Arbitration* 9 (March 1992): 51–58.

Schwebel, Stephen. *International Arbitration: Three Salient Problems.* Cambridge, 1987.

Stuyt, A. M., ed. *Survey of International Arbitrations 1794–1989.* Dordrecht, The Netherlands, 1990.

ARBITRATION TREATIES OF 1911

Treaties signed by the United States with France and Great Britain in an effort to improve the means of settling international disputes. President William Howard Taft in 1910 called for new arbitration treaties that did not include the reservations about vital interests and national honor found in the existing treaties negotiated by Secretary of State Elihu Root. Taft declared that the time had come to regard questions of national honor as suitable for arbitration. The French and British governments expressed interest, and Secretary of State Philander C. Knox on 3 August 1911 signed almost identical treaties with French ambassador Jean Jules Jusserand and British ambassador James Bryce.

Like other obligatory arbitration agreements, the Taft treaties were contradictory. On the one hand, they included pledges to refer disputes to arbitration; on the other, they included terms and procedures the signatory powers could use to limit their obligations. The treaties provided for referral to the Permanent Court of Arbitration at The Hague of all differences regarded as "justiciable," meaning that legal principles or equity could be used in deciding them. The word "justiciable" aroused criticism because it was new to the language of international arbitration, but Taft and Knox believed it expressed their hope establishing arbitration of international differences analogous to the referral of disputes between individuals to courts. As broad as the scope of the treaties appeared to be, they contained the Root Treaty provision for a special agreement for each arbitration and its approval by the Senate. They also included provisions for joint international commissions of inquiry to decide which disputes were justiciable.

The special agreements and commissions of inquiry notwithstanding, the treaties were both hailed as important contributions to the maintenance of peace and criticized as threats to traditional foreign policies. So inspired was Andrew Carnegie by Taft's proposals that he gave $10 million to found the Carnegie Endowment for International Peace. President Taft himself, whose purpose at the outset had been to quiet criticism of his naval building program, became an increasingly earnest advocate. When former President Theodore Roosevelt and several senators opposed the treaties, Taft went on a speaking tour to win popular support. The administration's efforts had little effect on the Senate. That body approved the treaties, but only with significant changes, on 7 March 1912. It replaced the word "may" with "shall" in the provision for special agreements. It deleted a provision referring questions to commissions despite disagreements between signatories. More important, it inserted several amendments, including one that excluded from arbitration questions about admission of aliens into the United States or the schools of any state. Another amendment excluded questions concerning the Monroe Doctrine or other policies of the United States. Learning of French and British dissatisfaction with the modifications made by the Senate, Taft did not ratify the treaties, but they continued to be a factor in the development of specific means for settling international disputes. The commissions of the "cooling-off" treaties negotiated by Secretary of State William Jennings Bryan in 1913 and 1914 were in part inspired by the Taft treaties. As President Woodrow Wilson in 1919 and 1920 struggled in vain to win Senate approval of the Versailles Treaty and the attached Covenant of the League of Nations, Taft and other supporters of the league recalled their experience with the arbitration treaties and persuaded Wilson to secure a provision in the covenant safeguarding the Monroe Doctrine.

Arbitration treaties negotiated by the United States during the late 1920s used the key word "justiciable" of the Taft treaties and provided for special arbitral agreements; conciliation treaties making use of commissions of inquiry were sometimes negotiated at the same time. Issues raised in 1911 no longer seemed so pressing, and later treaties easily won ratification.

CALVIN D. DAVIS

See also Arbitration; Carnegie, Andrew; France; Great Britain; Taft, William Howard

FURTHER READING

Campbell, John P. "Taft, Roosevelt, and the Arbitration Treaties of 1911." *Journal of American History* (September 1966):279–298.

Patterson, David S. *Toward a Warless World: The Travail of the American Peace Movement 1887–1914.* Bloomington, Ind., 1976.

Pringle, Henry F. *The Life and Times of William Howard Taft,* 2 vols. New York, 1939.

Scholes, Walter V., and Marie V. Scholes. *The Foreign Policies of the Taft Administration.* Columbia, Mo., 1970.

ARGENTINA

A South American republic bordering the South Atlantic Ocean, Chile, Uruguay, Paraguay, and Bolivia that has often contested U.S. influence in the Western Hemisphere. U.S.-Argentine relations began with eighteenth-century trade along the Atlantic coast, where New England whalers and merchants would stop at Buenos Aires, and Montevideo in Uruguay, to purchase goods. Argentine leaders credited American seamen with bringing the ideas of Thomas Jefferson and James Madison to South

America and, as a consequence, helping to inspire the Argentine independence struggle. During the first decade of the nineteenth century, the U.S. government refused repeated requests from Argentine independence fighters for support in their war against Spain, although each country sent diplomatic and trade missions to the other during the years leading up to Argentine independence. The United States recognized the new state in 1822.

Despite generally cordial bilateral relations complemented by a steady increase in trade through the nineteenth century, Argentine leaders grew repeatedly disappointed by the unwillingness of U.S. authorities to invoke the Monroe Doctrine. For example, Argentines expected the United States to protest the British seizure of the Falkland Islands in the 1830s. In addition, when the British and French fleets blockaded the River Plate at midcentury the United States refused to interfere. A new constitution promulgated in 1853 was based in significant measure on the U.S. Constitution and, in the same year, the two countries concluded a commercial treaty. Although the American Civil War created demand for Argentine wool, the U.S. tariff of 1867 and subsequent protective legislation blocked the expansion of export markets for many Argentine products. In 1889–1890, at the First International Conference of American States, held in Washington, D.C., Argentine diplomats accused the United States of trying to dominate Pan-American commerce. Argentine dismay over high U.S. tariff rates persisted until the administration of President Grover Cleveland ended duties on Argentine wool in 1893. As a result, Argentine exports to the United States reached a record high in 1895.

Between 1900 and 1930, the United States sought greater diplomatic influence in Argentina in conjunction with a rapid expansion of U.S. commercial and financial strength in South America. U.S. diplomats pressed for Argentine legislation that would protect U.S. patents and copyrights, allow the free movement of American salesmen, stabilize the Argentine currency, and provide open access to Argentine markets for American goods. Argentina responded favorably to the trade-based emphasis in U.S. foreign policy, thus contributing to the strengthening of U.S.-Argentine economic ties, but Argentine leaders suspected Americans of trying to dominate the Pan-American Union, established in 1890 in accordance with a resolution passed at the First International Conference. When Argentina remained neutral during World War I, the United States found the decision unacceptable; again during World War II bilateral relations deteriorated when Argentina refused to join the Allied cause. In both wars, however, Argentina was a vital supplier of foodstuffs and raw materials to the Allies.

The rise of Juan Domingo Perón in the military junta that came to power in 1943 also troubled U.S. officials.

Perón advanced economic nationalism and corporatist labor-reform legislation. U.S. officials became convinced that he represented a pro-Nazi faction within the Argentine military. When Perón ran for president in 1945 and 1946, U.S. Ambassador to Argentina Spruille Braden tried to undermine the campaign. He publicized the "Blue Book on Argentina," a State Department document released in January 1946 that labelled wartime Argentina pro-Nazi. Braden's criticisms may have backfired. Perón used the conflict with the United States to his advantage, persuading Argentines that the Americans had interfered in domestic Argentine affairs.

After Perón's election, U.S.-Argentine relations remained tense. The United States blocked funds from international agencies from reaching Argentina and restricted trade and investment opportunities for Americans interested in doing business in the country. Perón continued to confound U.S. observers by adopting a nonaligned stance in the evolving Cold War. During the 1950s, however, in response to failed economic policies, Perón reversed his hostility to foreign investors. U.S. multinational corporations were once again welcomed in Argentina. Before his ouster by the Argentine military in 1955, Perón made diplomatic overtures to the administration of President Dwight D. Eisenhower.

In 1959 President Arturo Frondizi became the first Argentine president to visit the United States. Bilateral relations during the 1960s and 1970s were cordial, as Argentina supported most U.S. policy initiatives in the Americas, including the Alliance for Progress, the Dominican invasion of 1965, and the isolation of Cuba. President Jimmy Carter's emphasis on human rights in U.S. foreign policy soured relations with Argentina's military dictatorship, which had seized power in 1976. Relations deteriorated further in 1982 when the United States backed British territorial claims in the South Atlantic during the Falklands War. The United States welcomed Argentina's return to democracy in 1983, and when renegade officers tried to topple the democratic government in 1987, President Ronald Reagan's administration voiced its confidence in the elected government. During President George Bush's administration (1989– 1993), the Argentine government announced that it would follow the terms of the Brady Plan, a Treasury Department initiative designed to assist large debtor nations in negotiating less restrictive borrowing terms with the International Monetary Fund and private financial institutions. Argentina did not meet Brady Plan requirements for U.S. government support of its international loan requests. Even so, Argentines abandoned decades-old protectionist trade policies and initiated a privatization program—policy shifts promoted by the U.S. government. In 1991 Argentina sent a battleship to the Persian Gulf in support of the war against Iraq, the first occasion on which the United States and Argentina fought as allies.

DAVID SHEININ

See also Braden, Spruille; Brady Plan; Falkland Islands; Gulf War of 1990–1991; Monroe Doctrine; Perón, Juan Domingo; World War I; World War II

FURTHER READING

McGann, Thomas F. *Argentina, the United States, and the Inter-American System, 1880–1914.* Cambridge, Mass., 1957.

Milenky, Edward S. *Argentina's Foreign Policies.* Boulder, Colo., 1978.

Peterson, Harold F. *Argentina and the United States, 1810–1960.* Albany, N.Y., 1964.

Sheinin, David. *Argentina and the United States at the Sixth Pan American Conference (Havana 1928).* London, 1991.

Tulchin, Joseph S. *Argentina and the United States: A Conflicted Relationship.* Boston, 1990.

ARIAS PLAN

See Esquipulas II

ARMAMENT COMPANIES

With the possible exception of the oil companies, no sector of the U.S. economy has traditionally been more intertwined with state policymaking. The major defense firms of a nation, or "prime contractors," sit on the cusp of economic and national security, making them subject to a unique constellation of state and societal pressures. It is within this crucible that defense industrial policy has been forged.

The political economy of the armaments industry is best understood by looking at two critical variables: the defense budget on the one hand, and the cost of building weapons on the other. Since 1986 defense budgets in most countries have been falling, with procurement accounts taking the largest share of the reductions. That means governments have less money to buy existing systems and to continue the development of new ones. At the same time, the costs of building weapons continue to rise, as defense officials demand the most advanced technology in each and every platform. The combination of lower budgets and higher costs inevitably means fewer purchases.

This situation could be offset to some degree by rising foreign sales; indeed, the U.S. share of world arms sales has increased substantially since the Soviet Union's collapse, and it now commands on the order of fifty percent of all sales. But the overall market for arms has also fallen since 1986, from about $45 billion to $25 billion, resulting in greater competition for the sales that occur. The largest markets for such sales are in East Asia—the only growing market as of the mid-1990s—and the Middle East, and the United States has a commanding share of both markets.

If the armaments sector is shrinking, along with the defense budget, it raises important questions about the future vitality of defense contractors. Driven by Cold War threats on the one hand, and competition for major weapons projects on the other, U.S. firms had a powerful incentive to find and maintain the best design teams. For most of the postwar period, defense firms could hire many of the "best and brightest" of the nation's scientists and engineers. Good career prospects, coupled with ample funds for research and development, meant that young graduates were attracted to the industry. As the industry decreases in size and rationalizes its research, development, and production facilities, there will be fewer opportunities available, and undoubtedly fewer young people will seek a career in this field. As a consequence, it is questionable whether the industry can retain its technological edge.

The armaments industries constitute a major but not the sole element in what is commonly referred to as the "defense-industrial base." The defense-industrial base encompasses the aggregate ability of a nation to provide itself with the weaponry required to arm its military services. Thus, in addition to armaments companies it includes such organizations as universities and government laboratories. Looking back at the expansion of this complex during the Cold War, President Dwight D. Eisenhower warned in his farewell address that "we must guard against the acquisition of unwarranted influence, whether sought or unsought, by the military-industrial complex. The potential for the disastrous rise of misplaced power exists, and will persist."

The privatization of the defense industry is a relatively recent phenomenon, at least in U.S. history. Until World War I, most weapons were produced by government-owned and operated armories. These armories themselves played an important role in U.S. economic history; consider the Springfield Armory, where many nascent mass-production techniques were introduced to U.S. industry. By World War I, however, the demands of modern warfare called for a marriage between the state and the private sector in defense research, development, and production. Aerospace firms in particular began to shift toward the design and production of military aircraft, supported largely by government contracts. After the carnage of World War I, a number of critics held that the arms industries were responsible for instigating international conflict—a theme also made popular by such novelists as Eric Ambler—and in many countries congressional or parliamentary bodies investigated their behavior in foreign countries. Nonetheless, in the United States these ties between government and the private sector were only strengthened during World War II and the Cold War, despite periodic findings throughout the postwar period of bribery of foreign officials by arms companies, and efforts to win unfair advantages over rivals in the procurement process. Like every industry, the armaments sector has its special characteristics. These include its relatively high degree of concentration (for example, only one firm produces aircraft carriers or submarines); the cyclical nature of demand for its products; its monopsonistic (sole) buyer; its high research and development (R&D) costs and systems integration requirements; the increasing cost structure of its products; its dependence on government budgeting; and its heavy government regulations. These characteristics, it should be noted, constitute an important barrier to entry in the business. Given the high capital costs, and the unique set of government regulations, it is very difficult for an entrepreneur to enter weapons manufacture.

Increasingly, defense enterprises are beginning to resemble their civilian counterparts in their reliance on foreign-made inputs. The U.S. defense industry now relies on foreign sources for computer memory chips, silicon for electronic switching, gallium-arsenide-based semiconductors for data processing, precision glass for reconnaissance satellites, and ball bearings for a wide array of equipment. In some cases, the cause of the shift is that U.S. firms have moved production facilities overseas in order to reduce their labor costs and gain access to foreign markets; in others it is simply that U.S. suppliers have lost their position in the face of foreign competition.

In production, too, one can begin to observe the dawn of the "global weapon." Several weapons projects have been launched among North Atlantic Treaty Organization members, and this trend is even more widespread among members of the European Union. Given the rising costs and declining budgets discussed above, arms collaboration offers nations a potential vehicle for maintaining high-technology programs while spreading the costs over a larger number of weapons systems.

For much of the postwar period, armaments industries were regarded as important generators of technology for the commercial side of the economy. These "spin-offs" seemed to justify the large share of government R&D funds that went to the defense-industrial complex. Radar, transistors, jet engines, and computer hardware and software—these are examples of technologies developed by the military which have had important commercial effects.

In recent years, however, some analysts have expressed skepticism over the defense industry's ability to generate spin-offs. Given the long life cycles required to build new weapons—the entire process from design to production can take twenty years or more—it is claimed that weapons systems often integrate obsolete technolo-

gy when compared to complex commercial systems. Further, given the constant demands by consumers for new products, commercial companies must have a short design-to-production time horizon. Thus, it has become popular to speak of "spin-ons" from the commercial to the military spheres, and the development of "dual-use" technology with applications in both areas. Recent U.S. administrations have encouraged the Department of Defense to finance the development of such technology through its Advanced Research Projects Agency, the Pentagon's equivalent of a venture capital fund. Executives from the armaments industry, however, have generally been skeptical of such an approach, pointing out that many contemporary military technologies (such as stealth radar) have no civilian application.

In the face of declining defense budgets, many observers also have promoted the "conversion" of defense enterprises to civilian manufacture, or the shifting of a firm from guns to butter production. These efforts to convert defense industries are especially notable in the former Soviet Union, where many multilateral and bilateral assistance programs have been devoted to this task. Since the defense sector consumed such a large share of the Soviet economy, and since many cities and towns were created around defense enterprises, both Russian and Western officials have seen the conversion of these enterprises as a central element in the economic transition.

Unfortunately, conversion has proved to be an elusive goal. The substantial differences between military and commercial production and markets mean that defense firms are rarely prepared to compete in the new economic environment. Rather than convert, defense firms are shutting down and their workers moving to new employment in other sectors of the economy. In the Russian case, many defense workers also have emigrated, bringing their skills to countries around the world.

In the United States, defense firms have responded to the post–Cold War shrinkage of the procurement budget through mergers and acquisitions. The most notable include Lockheed's acquisition of General Dynamics' F-16 jet aircraft production; the subsequent merger of Lockheed and Martin Marietta; and the merger of Northrop and Grumman. The result is the formation of enormous defense firms with significant capabilities across a wide array of technologies and platforms.

These mergers and acquisitions raise important questions for antitrust officials, as several companies will now monopolize the production of particular weapons; the United States government will thus find itself in a marketplace characterized by "bilateral monopoly," in which both the buyer and seller are monopolists. The end of effective competition for the industry means that the policy tools once used to promote the development of new technology will no longer be effective. Thus, new policies will be needed if the United States is to maintain an advanced armaments industry.

Defense firms also have placed greater emphasis on foreign sales. Traditionally, exports constituted less than ten percent of total sales for the major defense enterprises. Today, such sales may be twenty-five percent or more of the total. It is notable that, despite the overall shrinkage of global spending on armaments, the Paris Air Show—in which the major commercial and military aircraft producers show their wares—iof 1995 was the largest aerospace exhibition in history, with more companies participating than ever before.

This economic pressure to export will inevitably conflict in certain cases with the foreign-policy goals of the United States. Firms will wish to sell weapons to countries that traditionally have not been permitted to buy U.S. weaponry. The reconciliation of competing economic and foreign-policy objectives will challenge U.S. administrations for many years to come.

Another source of tension is found in the arms control arena. The United States has played a leading role in seeking to limit the transfer of nuclear and missile technology, and the development of chemical and biological weapons. In some cases, even commercial technology may be prohibited from export because of the ease of converting it to military production; this is especially the case with chemical and biological weapons. Should weapons technology increasingly become "dual-use," these tensions between the private sector and the state must rise.

In sum, the defense industry is in a period of profound transformation. Shrinking budgets, rising costs, rationalization, and decreasing competition are the primary factors shaping the industry. The response of the industry to these pressures—namely mergers and acquisitions and greater foreign sales—raises troubling questions for public policy. The question remains whether these various tendencies and trends can be shaped in such a way as to maintain a defense industry that meets the United States' national security requirements in the twenty-first century.

ETHAN B. KAPSTEIN

See also Arms Transfers and Trade; Military-Industrial Complex; Nye, Gerald Prentice

FURTHER READING

Kapstein, Ethan B. *The Political Economy of National Security.* New York, N.Y., 1992.
Kapstein Ethan B., ed. *Global Arms Production: Policy Dilemmas for the 1990's.* Lanham, Md., 1992.
Krause, Keith. *Arms and the State: Patterns of Military Productions and Trade.* New York, N.Y., 1992.
Malleret, Thierry. *Conversion of the Defense Industry in the Former Soviet Union.* New York, N.Y., 1992.
Mussington, David. *Arms Unbound: The Globalization of Defense Production.* Washington, D.C., 1994.

ARMENIA

A Soviet successor state, located in the southern Caucasus, whose capital is Yerevan. Armenia is bordered by Georgia, Azerbaijan, Iran, and Turkey. When the republic of Armenia declared its independence from the Soviet Union in August 1991, the United States recognized it in December of that year but Washington had no specific policy in mind for the new state or its ancient people. A U.S. embassy opened in Yerevan in February 1992.

Armenia had had a brief earlier bout with independence, following the collapse of the Russian Empire in 1917 and prior to its absorption into the USSR in 1920. Actually, between the Congress of Berlin (1878) and the end of World War I, a Greater Armenia had struggled—in vain—to emerge as an independent state that would have incorporated lands historically populated by Armenians that were located both in southern Russia and eastern Turkey. Accused by the Ottoman government (allied with the Central Powers) of "collaborating" with a Tsarist regime (at that point still fighting on the side of the Entente) set upon the dismemberment of the Ottoman Empire, somewhere between half a million to a million Turkish Armenians were massacred by Ottoman forces between 1915 and 1917. Later, even Soviet Armenia had to defend its territorial integrity against the claims of its two Transcaucasian neighbors, Georgia and Azerbaijan.

When an independent Armenia reemerged seventy years later, it again found itself in a state of undeclared war with Azerbaijan over control of Nagorno-Karabakh. This Armenian-populated enclave inside Azerbaijan has been a source of bitter dispute throughout the century, and one that erupted once again in 1988. The United States, while recognizing Armenia's independence, had no official position with regard to the Nagorno-Karabakh issue, except that it subscribed to the general principle of preserving the territorial status quo, namely, recognizing the legitimacy of the boundaries of all the ex-Soviet successor states. Pitted against this Department of State position was the pro-Armenian public sentiment generated by a powerful Armenian-American lobby in the U.S. Congress.

The Armenian-American community—well organized, relatively affluent, and highly political—strategically placed Op-Ed articles and advertisements in national newspapers between 1988 and 1991. Even though neither the Bush nor the Clinton administrations condoned the occupation of western Azerbaijan by Armenian forces, Washington muted its criticism. Blockaded by Azerbaijan, crucial supplies did not reach an Armenia suffering severe shortages of building supplies (as a result of an earthquake), fuel, and food. The United States became instrumental in flying nonmilitary supplies through Turkish airspace; this operation meant, at times, having to persuade Turkey not to impose an embargo. Turkey was a nonofficial ally of Azerbaijan and had sought to extract concessions from Armenia. Between 1992 and 1994, the United States provided $12 million for earthquake assistance, pledged $5 million to assist refugees fleeing from Armenia, sent $2 million in Department of Defense excess pharmaceuticals, $500,000 worth of medicine, $66 million in food from the Department of Agriculture, $5 million to cover transport costs of fuel from Russia, and $11 million for food for babies and their mothers. Operation Provide Hope, a private voluntary agency, also worked with the U.S. government to ship humanitarian supplies to Armenia.

Since 1922 U.S. policy has markedly changed to a more even-handed stance toward Armenia and Azerbaijan, when oil interests eager to exploit Azerbaijani deposits, in particular AMOCO, began to exert powerful pressure on both houses of Congress. As oil extraction and oil transportation (pipeline) politics in Central Asia and Caucasia came to the fore, the United States developed a more coordinated regional policy, in which it sought successful negotiations with the government in Azerbaijan, even if this meant a less-pronounced pro-Armenian position. This posture risked offending the highly sensitized Armenian-American constituency and its many sympathizers in Congress. By simplistically reducing the war in Transcaucasia to one between Christian Armenians and Azerbaijani Muslims, Armenians in the United States tapped large reservoirs of Christian support, and kept anti-Muslim prejudices alive and ahead of fears of oil shortages and high gas prices. Business interests, however, eventually overcame the tilt toward Armenia especially as they promoted U.S. projects—all oil connected—in Kazakhstan and Turkmenistan, the Central Asian states straddling the Caspian littoral, including Azerbaijan.

In April 1992, the United States and Armenia signed a trade agreement with a most-favored-nation (MFN) status clause. This agreement was followed in September with a bilateral investment treaty and an agreement with the Peace Corps aimed at developing small businesses so as to encourage Armenia's economy to make the transition from a command to a market economy. Underlying U.S. policy toward Armenia, as it had evolved by the mid-1990s, were two interrelated strategic goals: to foster democracy in order for the United States to remain a player in Armenia, where Russian influence, including the stationing of Russian troops, remained strong; and to exercise pressure on Armenia to end its hostilities with Azerbaijan over Nagorno-Karabakh so that U.S. oil politics in the Caspian region could overcome growing Russian competition.

HENRY R. HUTTENBACH

See also Azerbaijan; Humanitarian Intervention and Relief; Oil and Foreign Policy; Oil and World Politics; Peace Corps; Russia and the Soviet Union

FURTHER READING

Goldenberg, Suzanne. *The Pride of Small Nations: The Caucasus and Post-Soviet Disorder.* London, 1994.
Mesbahi, Mohiaddin, ed. *Central Asia and the Caucasus after the Soviet Union.* Tampa, 1994.
Suny, Ronald G. *Armenia in Modern History.* Indiana, 1993.

ARMS CONTROL

See Nuclear Weapons and Strategy

ARMS CONTROL AND DISARMAMENT AGENCY

Government agency established to serve as a focal point for the planning, negotiating, and implementation of arms control and disarmament agreements. Serving under the direction of the secretary of state, the Arms Control and Disarmament Agency (ACDA) director functions as the principal adviser to the president, the secretary of state, and the National Security Council on matters pertaining to arms control and disarmament. The agency was created by the Arms Control and Disarmament Act of 26 September 1961, with the support of Representative Thomas Morgan and Senator Hubert Humphrey. The legislation described the new organization as "an Agency of Peace," and President John F. Kennedy stated that its purpose was "to find an approach to disarmament which would be so far-reaching yet realistic, so mutually balanced and beneficial that it could be accepted by every nation." Kennedy intended ACDA to be a permanent agency within the U.S. government that would serve as a bureaucratic counterweight to the Department of Defense.

Underlying this seemingly smooth start, however, was a controversial beginning that has bedeviled ACDA throughout its history. During the congressional hearings on the agency in the summer of 1961, a number of witnesses were very critical. One went so far as to suggest that ACDA would become a haven for pacifists and "nutball people" who wanted to surrender to the Kremlin. Until the end of 1972 ACDA operated the way in which its supporters had intended, a fact in part attributable to the prominence of early ACDA directors and their close working relationships with the secretaries of state and presidents. Following the conclusion of the first Strategic Arms Limitation Talks agreement (SALT I) in May 1972, however, a group critical of SALT and ACDA led by Senator Henry Jackson pressured the administration of Presi-

DIRECTORS OF THE ARMS CONTROL AND DISARMAMENT AGENCY

ADMINISTRATION	DIRECTOR	PERIOD OF APPOINTMENT
Kennedy	William C. Foster	1961–1969
L. Johnson		
Nixon	Gerard C. Smith	1969–1973
	Fred C. Ikle	1973–1977
Ford		
Carter	Paul C. Warnke	1977–1978
	George C. Seignious	1978–1979
	Ralph Earle II	1979–1981
Reagan	Eugene V. Rostow	1981–1983
	Kenneth L. Adelman	1983–1987
	William F. Burns	1988–1989
Bush	Ronald F. Lehman II	1989–1993
Clinton	John D. Holum	1993–Present

Source: Arms Control and Disarmament Agency

dent Richard M. Nixon to weaken the agency significantly. The leaders of ACDA were forced to resign, the budget was cut by one-third, and overall staffing was reduced by one-fifth.

President Jimmy Carter supported the objectives and operation of ACDA, and during his administration (1977–1981) the agency experienced a renaissance. Paul Warnke, an eloquent, forceful supporter of arms control who had served in the Defense Department, was appointed director of ACDA and chief negotiator at the SALT II negotiations. International negotiations on the nuclear fuel cycle were begun, and the Mutual, Balanced Force Reduction Talks in Europe were continued. In addition, U.S.-Soviet working groups were established to discuss a wide variety of issues, including a comprehensive test ban, radiological weapons, conventional arms transfers, military deployments in the Indian Ocean, antisatellite weapons, missile test-flight limitations, and chemical weapons. When President Ronald Reagan took office in 1981, however, the agency's budget and personnel were once again cut significantly. Although several were quite knowledgeable about arms control, the directors who served during the twelve years of the Reagan and George Bush administrations, in general, were not as politically prominent as earlier directors. ACDA also faced increasing bureaucratic competition from both the Department of State's Bureau of Politico-Military Affairs and the Department of Defense's Bureau for Arms Control and Non-Proliferation.

After considering whether to abolish ACDA, integrate it into the Department of State, or to leave it as a semi-independent agency, President Bill Clinton chose the last option and appointed as director John Holum, who though a close political ally lacked substantial political stature. With the end of the Cold War, the major shift for ACDA was in its primary focus, moving to issues of nonproliferation. Work continued for the implementation and verification of the Strategic Arms Reduction Treaties (START) and other arms control agreements reached with the Soviet Union and its successor states, but strategic arms control no longer dominated the agenda to the extent it had during the Cold War. Preventing the spread of nuclear, chemical, and biological weapons, as well as ballistic missiles, long a U.S. foreign-policy objective, became an even higher priority, given the threats posed by "rogue" states and terrorists in the 1990s. In the post–Cold War era ACDA also became involved in negotiations for extension of the Nuclear Non-Proliferation Treaty and other nonproliferation measures. Despite the successes of ACDA, Senator Jesse Helms and other conservatives called for its abolition.

DAN CALDWELL

See also Nuclear Nonproliferation; Nuclear Weapons and Strategy; Strategic Arms Limitation Talks and Agreements; Strategic Arms Reduction Treaties

FURTHER READING
Clarke, Duncan L. *Politics of Arms Control: The Role and Effectiveness of the U.S. Arms Control and Disarmament Agency.* New York, 1979.
Funk, Sherman M. *New Purposes and Priorities for Arms Control.* Washington, 1992.
Krepon, Michael, Amy E. Smithson, and James A. Schear. *The U.S. Arms Control and Disarmament Agency: Restructuring for the Post–Cold War Era.* Washington, 1992.

ARMS TRANSFERS AND TRADE

Defined as the global process of arms production and exchanges, including the movement of weapons, components, and associated technologies across national borders. Patterns of U.S. arms transfers and trade policies can be explained only in the context of the international system within which the United States pursues its geopolitical and economic interests; the role of arms transfers as vehicle for political influence and for projecting U.S. power abroad; the domestic decision-making process and complex institutional structure within which U.S. arms sales policies are defined and approved; and the impact of arms sales on the U.S. arms industry, the defense budget, and the economy. Of these factors the systemic structure of global power has been decisive for U.S. arms transfer policies. While economic, technological, and domestic political considerations—societal and bureaucratic—have always influenced U.S. arms transfer policies, the dominant explanation for U.S. behavior, especially during the Cold War, was geopolitical. Successive Washington administrations used arms transfers as a major instrument of U.S. foreign policy to influence the behavior of other states in favorable ways, to support friendly governments (democratic and authoritarian), and to construct a global system of alliances and regional balances of power congenial to U.S. security interests.

The specific, varied, and changing aims of U.S. arms transfer policy may be divided into geopolitical and economic objectives. Geopolitical goals include assistance to allies, alliance burden sharing, political and strategic influence, competition with rivals (principally the Soviet Union during the Cold War), access to foreign elites and bases, and the political stabilization and internal security of friendly foreign governments. Economic concerns include promoting exports and rectifying trade balances, disposing of excess arms inventories and surplus output, economies of scale in long production runs, and creating underwriting of research and development of new weapons. Always a factor, economic concerns have become even more salient since the end of the Cold War as military spending has decreased along with the need for allies.

In the aftermath of the collapse of the Soviet Union and the end of the Cold War, the United States has emerged as the world's principal arms supplier. In the three-year period between 1991–1993, the United States accounted for 41 percent of the total value of all arms deliveries and 60 percent of arms sales agreements between states. The United Kingdom and the Russian Federation, the next largest arms suppliers, accounted, respectively, for 13 and 11 percent of the deliveries and 6 and 10 percent of the agreements. In this period, the United States was particularly dominant in arms transfers to Third World states. It accounted for 41 percent of the deliveries to these developing nations and over 50 percent of the agreements, reaching a high in the latter category of 73 percent in 1993. In this three-year period, all major West European suppliers, as a group, accounted for 28 percent of arms deliveries to these nations, but signed only 20 percent of future arms agreements. The American lead in arms agreements and the long leadtime normally needed to fill these orders, especially for advanced weapon systems, insures that the United States will be the undisputed leader in arms exports for the remainder of the 1990s.

Immediately after World War II, the United States was the world's primary supplier of arms, with most of its arms exports to allies in Europe and Asia. However, as the Cold War conflict evolved, as Eastern and Western Europe recovered after World War II, and as demand for weapons grew among newly independent states emerging from colonization, the United States gradually lost ground to the Soviet Union and to an increasing number of second- and third-tier suppliers in world arms markets. The U.S. share of global arms transfers fell from over 50 percent in 1966–1975 to approximately half that amount in the final years of the Cold War. The Soviet Union surpassed the United States during the mid-1970s and held this position until its collapse, reaching a peak of approximately 45 percent of the world market in the late 1970s and through much of the 1980s. Other U.S. competitors in world arms markets also arose both in Europe—principally France, Great Britain, West Germany and Italy—and in the developing world. By the early 1990s, there were sixty arms-exporting and 138 arms-importing states.

Even though the United States relinquished its primacy in arms sales during the latter stages of the Cold War, the economic value and sophistication of its arms transferred abroad were still significant. Between 1985 and 1989, the United States supplied arms, components, and military technologies to eighty-six states, more than half of the states importing arms from foreign suppliers. The list of principal recipients is impressive in terms of its length and geographical distribution. In Africa, recipients included Tunisia and Morocco (each in excess of $250 million); in NATO, Europe, the United Kingdom, West Germany, Turkey, Spain, and the Netherlands (each importing between $2 and $3 billion); in East Asia, Japan, Taiwan, and South Korea (each over $2.5 billion, with Japan as the second largest recipient of U.S. arms at $5.3 billion); in Latin America, Venezuela, Brazil, El Salvador, and Mexico (each between $300 and $500 million); in South Asia, Pakistan ($925 million); and in the Middle East, Israel ($6.1 billion, the largest importer of U.S. arms), Saudi Arabia ($5 billion), and Egypt ($2.9 billion). Other important recipients were Canada ($735 million) and Australia ($4.1 billion).

	US	SU RS	UK	GM	FR	Other W. Eur	CH	Other
1984	24	32	4	5	10	8	3	7
1985	26	32	3	3	13	7	1	5
1986	23	39	7	2	8	5	2	6
1987	26	37	8	2	5	6	3	6
1988	23	37	8	3	3	6	5	9
1989	30	36	9	2	4	3	4	8
1990	33	33	9	4	10	3	3	3
1991	41	21	14	7	5	4	4	3
1992	47	8	16	5	5	6	3	8
1993	49	11	16	6	3	4	4	6
1994	56	6	15	3	4	4	4	5

SHARE OF WORLD ARMS EXPORTS
(in percent)

From *World Military Expenditures and Arms Transfers, 1995*. U.S. Arms Control and Disarmament Agency.

Data bearing on arms transfers are essentially of two kinds, each having quite different policy implications. The first refers to the economic value of the arms that are sent or traded; the second identifies the actual military capabilities that are transferred. The first set of data is crucial for assessing the economic impact of arms production, transfers, and sales on the U.S. economy and the economies of foreign recipients. The second set of information focuses on the distribution of military capabilities and the repercussions of these transfers on regional and global balances of power, arms control and disarmament negotiations and accords, and security relations and the mutual dependencies of supplier and recipient states.

The term "arms" refers to all conventional end items (excluding nuclear, biological, and chemical weapons) that can be used for lethal purposes. Among the most important and prominent are large weapon systems, such as tanks and self-propelled guns, artillery, armored personnel carriers and cars, major and minor combatant ships (destroyers or patrol boats, respectively), submarines, supersonic and subsonic aircraft, helicopters, and all forms of missiles, ranging from surface-to-surface to air-to-surface and anti-shipping missiles. Conventional arms transfers, grants, or sales also extend to logistical equipment (trucks and transport vessels), small arms and motors, ammunition, ordnance, and uniforms.

Transfers also encompass important dual-use equipment and technologies associated with communications and electronic systems, like the U.S. airborne AWACS system that can direct air combat operations and deliver real-time intelligence of enemy capabilities and movements. Weapons components, such as computer process-ing chips or switching gear, are also included in arms transfers. Components are an especially important element in global arms production and transfers where, increasingly, national weapon systems are dependent for important components on foreign suppliers. Arms transfers can also include the construction of base facilities and the provision of after-sales service and training by supplier states.

Historical Background

U.S. arms transfer policies may be viewed within four time periods, corresponding to major changes in the structure of power in interstate relations and the axis of conflict among the major powers and regional states. The first covers the period from the end of World War I to the outbreak of World War II. The second is framed by U.S. entry into World War II and its role as the principal supplier of arms and equipment to the victorious allied powers. These two periods mark a fundamental systemic transition from the multipolar system of the interwar period—challenged by Nazi Germany and Japan—to the bipolar superpower conflict between the United States and the Soviet Union of the postwar period. This third and longest period is marked by the Cold War from the end of the 1940s to the breakup of the Soviet Union in December 1991. Following the schema developed by Edward Laurence, this period itself may be divided into three phases: the period of tight U.S.–Soviet bipolarity, 1946–1966; the period of looser multipolarity characterized by the expansion of the arms trade around the globe, particularly to the developing world, 1966–1980; and the progressive multilateralization of the arms trade,

1980–1992. In the last systemic period, the post-Cold War era, no state or even a group of states can challenge the United States as the premier supplier of advanced military weaponry and material to other states.

Prior to World War II, U.S. arms transfer policies were principally driven by economic and commercial aims. Geopolitical factors were less important because the United States decided to disengage from European power politics after the end of World War I and to resume its traditional isolationist policy toward Europe, as reflected in the Senate's rejection of the Versailles Treaty and refusal to join the League of Nations. Public outcries against commercial sales and the so-called "Merchants of Death" had little effect on the sales of arms, even to states that would later become opponents in World War II. Japan, for example, acquired U.S. military equipment, ammunition, and technology throughout the interwar period. According to one estimate (Harkavy, 1975), the United States supplied approximately 23 percent of the military aircraft, 54 percent of the transport aircraft, 26 percent of the trainer aircraft, 15 percent of the tanks, 18 percent of the armored cars, and 3–4 percent of naval vessels and patrol boats to foreign countries between 1930 and 1939.

U.S. policies paralleled the behavior of other arms suppliers in this period. The relatively low technological sophistication of most weapon systems and the modest costs of entry into arms markets created conditions favorable for the emergence of a decentralized and multipolar system of suppliers. Since early fighter aircraft cost as little as $20,000, numerous states, including less economically and technologically developed countries, like Poland, Lithuania, and Yugoslavia, were able to design and produce combat aircraft. Sales were made across emerging bloc lines, and recipients pursued multiple-supplier patterns of acquisition. Alliances were neither dependable nor ideologically coherent enough to define basic supplier-recipient relations. U.S. manufacturers were essentially permitted to sell abroad with little or no political constraints on their activities until the mid-1930s.

As war increasingly threatened in Europe, the laissez-faire arms policy came under increasing public and congressional scrutiny. Congress passed the Neutrality Act of 1935 in the wake of the Italian invasion of Ethiopia. The Neutrality Act of 1937 placed further restrictions on selling arms and munitions and on granting loans or credits to belligerents and forbade U.S. civilian travel on belligerent ships. Warring states could still purchase nonmilitary goods, but these had to be transported on their own ships and paid for on a cash-and-carry basis. The aim of these restrictions was to preclude any U.S. involvement in a European war arising from arms sales or from the provision of credits to purchase military equipment. Many believed that such

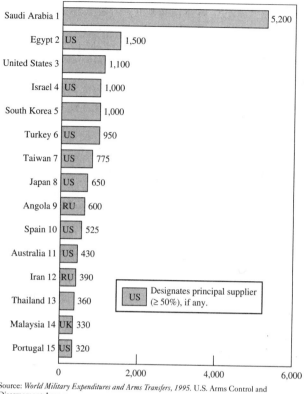

LEADING ARMS IMPORTERS, 1994

(in millions of dollars)

Country		Value
Saudi Arabia 1		5,200
Egypt 2	US	1,500
United States 3		1,100
Israel 4	US	1,000
South Korea 5	US	1,000
Turkey 6	US	950
Taiwan 7	US	775
Japan 8	US	650
Angola 9	RU	600
Spain 10	US	525
Australia 11	US	430
Iran 12	RU	390
Thailand 13		360
Malaysia 14	UK	330
Portugal 15	US	320

US Designates principal supplier (≥ 50%), if any.

Source: *World Military Expenditures and Arms Transfers, 1995.* U.S. Arms Control and Disarmament Agency.

economic and financial ties to Franco-British interests had drawn the United States into World War I.

Restrictions on the sale and financing of arms sales were swept away almost as rapidly as they had been put in place as the United States was drawn into the worldwide conflict. Paramount national security interests propelled the country into alliance with Great Britain and the Soviet Union to defeat Germany and Japan. In September 1940 President Franklin D. Roosevelt transferred fifty aging destroyers to Great Britain in return for basing rights in Newfoundland and Bermuda and for rent-free leases to six sites in the Caribbean and South Atlantic. The passage of the Lend-Lease act less than a year later reversed U.S. arms transfer policy and transformed the United States into what President Roosevelt called "the arsenal of democracy." The United States was now prepared "to lend" from its arsenal to its incipient allies, particularly Great Britain and the Soviet Union— whether or not they were democracies—needed arms and equipment that would purportedly be "returned" after the war. Once the United States entered World War II on 8 December 1941, the Lend-Lease act was transformed into a military assistance program to supply allied armies with the arms and material to win the war.

VALUE OF ARMS TRANSFER DELIVERIES, CUMULATIVE 1992–1994 BY MAJOR SUPPLIER AND RECIPIENT COUNTRY
(In Millions of Current Dollars)

Recipient	Total(a)	United States	United Kingdom	Russia	Germany	France	China	Canada	Other Western Europe	Middle East	Other Eastern Europe	Other East Asia	Others
World Totals	78,615	39,460(b)	12,450	6,550	3,695	3,125	2,795	2,160	3,940	1,420	1,320	630	1,070
-Developed(@)	33,090	20,005(b)	2,080	1,070	3,295	1,320	180	1,250	2,460	910	95	195	230
-Developing	45,525	19,455(b)	10,370	5,480	400	1,805	2,615	910	1,480	510	1,225	435	840
Africa	2,305	395	130	610	20	255	180	0	245	150	120	65	135
Central America & Caribbean	495	275	0	205	0	10	0	0	0	0	0	0	5
North America (NAFTA)	5,080	530	1,420	40	375	210	120	600	1,095	360	10	180	140
South America	1,095	365	55	10	50	180	25	0	100	140	0	10	160
Central Asia & Cauc.	185	0	0	95	0	0	0	0	0	0	70	0	20
Middle East	34,055	17,585	9,560	1,590	385	985	865	900	820	60	690	245	370
East Asia	12,210	6,580	800	1,855	1,315	155	580	0	325	230	235	85	50
South Asia	2,520	50	65	940	80	150	1,015	0	90	10	80	0	40
Eastern Europe	1,535	25	0	1,025	90	0	0	10	0	220	115	40	10
Western Europe	13,350	8,150	400	180	1,380	1,180	0	640	1,105	200	0	5	110
Oceania	1,195	915	20	0	0	0	0	10	160	50	0	0	40

0   Nil or negligible ($2.5 million or less).
@   Developed country (all others are "developing").
(a)   Totals are not precise due to the fact that rounding was done at different stages of aggregation.
(b)   U.S. arms transfers to the World, Developed, and Developing groupings include transfers to NATO agencies as such and to other international agencies and classified transfers, which are not attributed to individual recipient countries or regions.

Source: *World Military Expenditures and Arms Transfers, 1995*. U.S. Arms Control and Disarmament Agency.

U.S.–Soviet Bipolarity: 1945–1966

The Cold War completely transformed U.S. arms transfer policies. The laissez-faire stance of much of the interwar period was replaced by tightly controlled and geopolitically directed policy of military assistance and of weapons and technology transfers. After World War II, the United States abandoned its traditional isolationist position towards Europe and Asia and entered into a series of bilateral and multilateral security agreements with forty-two nations around the globe. Among the most important of these from the perspective of arms transfers were the North Atlantic Treaty Organization (NATO), which pledged the United States to defend its West European allies against external aggression, the Southeast Asian Treaty Organization (SEATO), and bilateral security pacts with Japan and South Korea in Northeast Asia. The rationale for these security pacts was the containment of the Soviet Union and Communist China and their allies. Arms transfers were a key U.S. foreign and strategic policy tool to deter communist attack on allies and to bolster governments friendly to the United States and the West.

The United States and the Soviet Union were the major suppliers of arms throughout most of the bipolar phase of the Cold War. The United States ranked first in the transfer of warships and combat aircraft and second in the number of tanks transferred to other states in the postwar period up to 1968. As Table 1 details, the Soviet Union was either a close second or first in combat aircraft and tanks, respectively, but a distant seventh in warships, where Great Britain was second. Some suppliers, like France, actually supplied used U.S. equipment to other states, principally its former colonies and protectorates in North Africa.

Even so, these data underestimate the amount of assistance supplied by the United States. In all military assistance programs, including outright grants, offshore foreign purchases, and sales, U.S. transfer or support for foreign arms production is far greater than a focus on major end items (tanks, aircraft, and warships) would suggest. Between 1950 and 1966, the United States signed military assistance agreements worldwide of $101 billion and delivered $89 billion in military material, measured in constant 1977 dollars.

Until the early 1960s, the principal recipients of U.S. military assistance were the European states of NATO, particularly France, Great Britain, and West Germany, and the states of Northeast Asia, principally Japan, South Korea, and the exiled Chinese Nationalist government of Taiwan. Between 1950 and 1966, Europe and Canada received military deliveries of approximately $51 billion in constant 1977 dollars, or approximately 58 percent of all deliveries during this period. In the early 1950s the United States provided indispensable arms, munitions, and equipment to assist French military operations in Indochina. From 1950 to 1954 the United States accounted for one-quarter of the French military budget. Of particular importance is U.S. assistance for the purchase of arms and equipment. In this period the United States covered about 50 percent of all French purchases. U.S. offshore arms purchases from its NATO allies accounted for additional billions in spending and contributed critically, along with U.S. economic assistance under the Marshall Plan, to the postwar creation of a European arms industry that in the 1970s would challenge U.S. dominance of world arms markets.

After Europe, Northeast and Southeast Asia, including Australia, were the next important regions for U.S. arms transfers. Between 1950 and 1966, these regions received approximately $24 billion in deliveries or 27 percent of the total of all arms sent abroad. The gradual buildup of U.S. forces in Southeast Asia to fight the communist insurgency in South Vietnam and to neutralize North Vietnamese assistance to the rebels accounts for much of this shift in priorities toward Asia. By the late 1960s Asia had overtaken Europe as the principal region for the receipt of U.S. arms.

Arms transfer policy toward the other major regions of the globe was much more restrictive. Africa received negligible amounts of U.S. arms during this period. Deliveries were generally around $20 million annually, reaching a peak in 1966 of $43 million. Similarly, the constant-dollar value of military deliveries to Latin America remained stable and low, relative to Europe and Asia. Annual deliveries to this region never exceeded $200 million, averaging slightly less than $127 million. In a tripartite accord reached in the early 1950s, the United States, France, and Great Britain also attempted to control the flow of arms to the Middle East. However, the allied policy of constraint was essentially undermined by the decision of the Soviet Union and Czechoslovakia to sell arms to Egypt in 1955. Thereafter, U.S., French, and British arms transfers to the Middle East gradually rose, eventually supplanting other regions as the primary regional market for U.S. arms.

In this first phase of the Cold War, there was a notable consensus between Congress and the president and among elites on the value and logic of arms transfers. The federal government absorbed the cost of these transfers through direct grants of military equipment and technology. However, the heavy costs of the Korean War and of U.S. rearmament, the progressive economic rehabilitation of NATO allies and Japan, domestic economic recession, and swelling U.S. balance-of-payment deficits led the administrations of Presidents Dwight D. Eisenhower and John F. Kennedy, pressed by Congress, to search for new ways to furnish arms to allies at less cost to the U.S. treasury and taxpayer. By the mid-1960s a policy of arms sales under the aegis of the Department of Defense through a program of Foreign Military Sales (FMS) replaced grants as the principal mode for the transfer of arms and equipment. Expanded U.S. transfers of arms to allies, particularly those in Europe, also met the concerns of military planners who stressed the need for standardization of alliance weapons systems and equipment to enhance military preparedness. From 1962 to 1966 military sales to NATO countries exceeded $3.5 billion, whereas they had never before topped $400 million in any one year and rarely more than $100 million throughout the 1950s.

The Loosening of Bipolarity: 1966–1980

By the late 1960s and early 1970s Europe stabilized and the U.S.–Soviet competition shifted primarily to the developing world. Arms transfers of both states reflected this strategic reorientation in their conflict. By 1967, thirty-nine new states had gained their independence. State building increased demand for arms to which Washington and Moscow and an increasing number of suppliers, particularly the Western and Eastern European allies of the superpowers, responded. Regional arms races expanded the number of recipients and suppliers, particularly in the Middle East, in South and Southeast Asia, and, to a lesser degree, in Latin America, where restricted U.S. arms policies were challenged by other suppliers for the first time. The dramatic rise in oil prices in the 1970s afforded oil-producing states, especially those heavily engaged in Middle East rivalries, the opportunity to purchase more and better arms from a wider array of ready suppliers.

As the superpowers' monopoly gradually relaxed and as new suppliers entered global arms markets, recipients tended to widen supplier sources and to become less dependent on weapons from a single country. The number of states dependent on a sole supplier (96 percent or more of its arms imports originating from a single state) fell from twenty-six to sixteen during this period. The same trend held for principal or dominant suppliers (56 to 96 percent of a recipient's arms originating from a single source). Meanwhile, states dependent on multiple suppliers more than doubled from twenty-nine to sixty-two states of the 144 countries receiving arms.

As the United States began to feel the effect of new suppliers in arms markets and reduced its transfer of arms abroad as a consequence of its defeat in Vietnam and of subsequent domestic and Congressional pressures, the superpower hold on world markets declined to 62 percent. The relative positions of the United States and the Soviet Union were reversed: The Soviet Union, which had increased its reliance on arms transfers to influence Third World countries, accounted for almost 40 percent of all military equipment that was transferred, while the U.S. total fell to below 25 percent, with Iraq as one of its major new clients. Among European suppliers, France rose to first rank, enlarging its share of the world market from 4.5 percent to almost 10 percent by the end of this period. Other suppliers as a group also improved their positions, increasing their share of global sales to approximately 10–15 percent annually.

In this buyer's market, recipients were able to bargain with suppliers over favorable economic and political conditions of sale. They also had greater freedom from political conditions or restraints. Playing on the heightened competition among suppliers, recipients also enjoyed more leverage in demanding increasingly more sophisticated weapons, including advanced jet aircraft, armor, missiles, and electronics. They also insisted on the transfer of technology and expertise along with major weapon systems and components.

Increased demand from an even larger number of states, competition among suppliers for these expanding markets, and the Cold War rivalry conspired to increase the quantity and quality of arms in state inventories around the globe. More destructive military power was at the disposal of states than ever before, and these arms were increasingly more efficient in their lethal and damaging power. These include main and medium tanks (MBTs and MTs), major naval combatants, jet aircraft, and all kinds of missiles. Between 1960 and 1980, the number of states acquiring these systems increased dramatically. Third World tank inventories grew from thirty to over sixty; naval combatants, from approximately twenty-two to thirty-eight; jet aircraft, from twenty to over seventy; and missiles, from less than five to seventy-five.

The regional pattern of U.S. arms transfers during this period of looser bipolarity also shifted in response to an increase in the number and intensity of regional armed conflicts. From 1966 to 1980, the United States sent an estimated $41.5 billion in arms and military equipment to Asia. This was approximately 42 percent of the total of $102 billion in arms sent abroad by Washington. Much of this assistance, transferred under the direction of several aid programs, was designated for South Vietnam. U.S. arms transfers to Asia peaked at $7.2 billion in 1973, the year of the U.S. military withdrawal from the Southeast Asian conflict.

As that conflict gradually slowed to a close with North Vietnam's victory in 1975, the Middle East ($34 billion in constant 1977 dollars or about 35 percent of the total arms sent abroad) replaced Asia as the major recipient of U.S. arms. Three reinforcing rivalries converged in the Middle East and the Persian Gulf to drive U.S. arms transfer policies in an upward spiral—the superpower rivalry, the continuing Arab-Israeli conflict, and the revolutionary forces of political change and division among Arab and Muslim states of the northern tier, most notably Iran and Afghanistan. The United States became Israel's principal supplier, supplanting France after the Six-Day War in 1967. After the brokered Camp David accords of 1978 led to the Israeli-Egyptian peace treaty of March 1979, the United States added Egypt to its list of major recipients. Over half of U.S. military and economic assistance has since been channeled to these two countries to underwrite the peace accord and to ensure the security of both states. The United States also began selling massive amounts of arms to its principal oil suppliers among the moderate Arab states, such as Saudi Arabia, and to Iran, to bolster the external and internal security of these states, to recycle petrodollars, to improve a sagging U.S. balance-of-payments position, to lower the unit price of producing arms, and to cover the mounting costs of research and development for new and improved arms.

With respect to Israel and Egypt, as the United States moved to assure one ally, it was confronted by demands from the other to match and enhance its arms commitment. To balance the sale of F-15s to Israel, the premier attack aircraft in the U.S. arsenal, Egypt was offered Phantom F-4Es and, later, F-16s, which Israel had already received. Both sides were supplied in proportionate measure with armor, artillery, and air-to-air, air-to-surface, and surface-to-surface missiles.

Washington was especially keen to court Iran and Saudi Arabia as regimes willing to staunch or moderate the spread of secular Arab nationalism as a destabilizing force in the region. Each received privileged access to U.S. arms and technology. Each was essentially exempted from restrictions imposed on other potential arms recipients. These included, for example, prohibitions decreed by President Jimmy Carter against human rights violators or the transfer of high-performance weapon systems into regions where they had not been introduced before. Between 1975 and 1978, a year before the shah of Iran was deposed, the United States delivered more than $7 billion in arms, including advanced F-14 air-superiority fighters, to Iran. The shah's government was also scheduled to receive hundreds of additional modern aircraft of all kinds (F-5Fs, Phantom F-4s, and F-16s), over 500 military helicopters, 25,000 antitank missiles, and four Spruance-class destroyers. At the height of the arms boom, an estimated 10,000 U.S. technicians were supporting Iran's arms buildup.

After the shah's fall, the United States redoubled efforts to strengthen the Saudi Arabian regime by selling even an even larger array of advanced weapon systems to Riyadh than had been sent to Teheran. President Carter's administration agreed to sell sixty advanced F-15 aircraft (but without bomb racks and extra fuel tanks to assure Israel) and other sophisticated military equipment. Over stiff congressional opposition and Israeli resistance, President Ronald Reagan's administration also consented to selling five AWACS advanced radar surveillance systems to Saudi Arabia. U.S. arms policy in the Middle East and the Persian Gulf was again drawn into a bidding war between Washington and its allies in the region. To match Soviet arms deliveries to its regional clients, U.S. allies demanded more and better arms of increasingly higher quality and sophistication. As one U.S. ally's request was granted, another would demand a pledge of equal treatment as a test of the U.S. security commitment and of Washington's resolve.

U.S. arms transfer policy was similarly held hostage both to revolutionary changes occurring in Africa and Latin America and to the competitive pressures exerted by the Soviet Union and new arms suppliers operating in these regions. The restrictive policies that the United States had unilaterally attempted to pursue in these regions no longer appeared viable. The introduction of Cuban troops into the Ethiopian and Angolan civil wars and the stepped-up transfer of Soviet arms to these areas prompted the United States to follow suit by sending arms to newly acquired allies such as the Siad Barre regime in Somalia to counter Soviet influence. Rebuffed by the United States, Peru bought tanks from the Soviet Union and Mirage jet aircraft from France. Leftist insurgencies in Central America, principally El Salvador, and the Sandinista victory in Nicaragua raised the specter of Cuban-style communist takeovers throughout the region. In response to these perceived security threats, Washington sent substantial amounts of arms and military assistance to the Salvadoran government and neighboring Honduras. At the same time, the conservative, military-dominated governments of Brazil, Argentina, and Chile embarked on the creation of their own arms industries and sought modern arms from other states, principally Western European arms suppliers. Unlike the United States, these states were prepared to waive human rights considerations and other political conditions to increase their sales abroad.

The terms of U.S. arms trade with Western Europe contrasted sharply with those in the developing world. The arms transfer issues dividing the United States and its allies turned principally on questions of military preparedness, on European resentment of the favorable U.S. balance of trade in the flow of arms and military technology between nations on the two continents, and on burdensharing within the alliance. U.S. policy was keyed to a policy of rationalization, standardization, and interoperability (RSI) within the alliance to decrease redundancy in weapons development and to maximize compatibility between the arsenals of NATO's national armed forces. The stance conflicted with the desire of European countries to develop their own arms industries, to increase sales among themselves and to the U.S. market, and to compete successfully on a global scale. These aims could not be easily reconciled with U.S. demands for greater burden-sharing and enhanced NATO preparedness through RSI, based on the supply of U.S. arms. These complex issues came to a head in the mid-1970s in the so-called "sale of the century" of F-16 fighter aircraft to Norway, Denmark, Belgium, and Holland. The United States finally won the contract over strong bids by France and Sweden to supply advanced fighter aircraft, but only after agreeing to significant coproduction and licensing concessions. Between 1966 and 1980, the United States delivered approximately $24.4 billion in arms to NATO Europe. This impressive showing, however, could not obscure growing European resistance to dependence on U.S. arms.

Fluctuations in the regional patterns of U.S. arms transfer policy reflected a deeper division within the country, and specifically between the president and Congress, over how U.S. geopolitical aims and interests could be served by selling arms and transferring military equipment and technology to other states or insurgent groups. In an effort to reduce U.S. commitments abroad, President Richard M. Nixon announced what became known as the Nixon Doctrine. It called on U.S. allies to shoulder a greater amount of cost and responsibility for their own defense. The president's redefinition of U.S. geopolitical strategy implied a readiness to sell arms to allies and to provide military assistance to meet local security needs. In contrast, Congress demanded a greater say in what arms and military technology would be sold or transferred and attempted to restrain sales or make them subject to an array of political conditions and human rights concerns. Throughout the 1970s, Congress also tried to restrain the introduction of advanced weapons into Latin America and other troubled regions. On different occasions it also prohibited military assistance or arms sales to Argentina, Brazil, Chile, El Salvador, Guatemala, and Uruguay due to human rights violations occurring in these nations.

President Carter, attempting to codify these restraints in a comprehensive overhaul of U.S. arms transfer policy announced in May 1977 a ceiling of the fiscal 1977 level of sales as the cap total dollar value of U.S. transfers. This ceiling was to be lowered in subsequent years. The development of arms solely for export, the promotion of arms sales abroad, the sale of arms to governments in violation of human rights, the transfer of advanced systems to regions where they had not been introduced before, and coproduction arrangements with states not specifically exempted from these blanket prohibitions were all forbidden. The president further called on other suppliers to enter into multilateral negotiations to curb global arms sales and military technology transfers.

President Carter's ambitious policy came under attack from a diverse coalition of critics. Interests closely associated with the U.S. military-industrial complex objected to constraints on their efforts to sell arms while their foreign competitors enjoyed the backing of their home governments. The Soviet Union's seeming successes in Africa and Central America, inspired and assisted by Cuba's Fidel Castro, also made President Carter's administration vulnerable to criticism for having allegedly failed to contain communist influence in the developing world. Even supporters of the president's restrictive policies complained about the exceptions made for Iran, Saudi Arabia, and Egypt.

Attempts to reach multilateral accords with other suppliers to dampen global arms sales also failed. The Soviet invasion of Afghanistan in December 1979 ended whatever hope existed for reaching multilateral accords on reducing global and regional arms transfers. The Soviet Union had little interest in restraining its use of arms transfers to gain influence with other states; other suppliers, most notably the NATO allies of the United States, were skeptical about U.S. motives and sought instead to increase, not decrease, arms sales. The U.S. security community itself was deeply split over the advisability of limiting arms transfers and sales as a preferred policy tool. The enlarged scope and increased intensity of the U.S.–Soviet struggle in the developing world ushered in the final phase of the Cold War. Also accelerated was the nuclear and conventional arms race between the United States and the Soviet Union. As Cold War tensions and arms expenditures rose, restraints on the transfer of U.S. arms abroad to friendly regimes and insurgent groups opposed to Moscow's clients were correspondingly lowered.

The Multilateralization of Arms Transfers 1980–1992

Several factors characterized this period. First, between 1981 and 1991, while less than in earlier periods, the superpowers continued to dominate world arms markets, accounting together for approximately 60 percent of the $528 billion of deliveries and agreements reached. Second, by the end of the 1970s and well into the 1980s, the Soviet Union became the world's leading arms supplier, principally to the developing world. Moscow's share of global transfers neared 40 percent; those of the United States were slightly more than half as large. Third, NATO European and neutral European states roughly equaled U.S. transfers. These states were able to capture almost 25 percent of sales. Western Europe, France, Great Britain, and West Germany led the others, trailed by Italy, Spain, and Sweden. Fourth, new suppliers arose in the developing world and gained upwards of 10–15 percent of the world market. Moreover, the number of weapon systems and arms platforms which these new suppliers were producing multiplied. Many of the same considerations that led developed states to expand their arms production industry encouraged developing states to adopt the same strategies. Some, like China, India, Pakistan, South Africa, and Israel, were deeply engaged in regional conflicts, and were largely driven by geopolitical aims in developing an increasingly autonomous weapons production capability. Others, like Brazil, appeared to be motivated more by commercial gain and the opportunities afforded by petrodollars, sustained world demand for arms due to new and continuing regional conflicts, and the interest of recipients to broaden their supplier base.

A three-tier global arms transfer system clearly emerged in the final phase of the Cold War. The system was primarily defined by the economic and technological development of the supplier states. At the top stood the United States and the Soviet Union. On the second tier were clustered the Western European states and, to a lesser and subordinate degree, the arms producers of the Warsaw Pact. On the bottom tier were an increasing number of developing states. This hierarchical structure and the increasing diffusion of technology were fostered by a progressively more complex set of coproduction and licensing agreements that have become a permanent feature of the international arms production and transfer system. From almost zero in 1960, almost half of the value of all weapons manufactured in developing states a generation later was produced largely under licensing or coproduction agreements with first- and second-tier suppliers.

The Post-Cold War

The disintegration of the Soviet Union in December 1991 and the subsequent end of the Cold War has had a profound effect on the global arms production and transfer system. These events also reinforced several other forces that have crystallized still another systemic structure within which arms are made and marketed. New patterns contrast sharply with the dominant patterns of the Cold War periods. First, the United States has once again become the primary supplier of advanced arms and military technology. Its present unassailable position arises from its ascendancy in the Cold War struggle as well as its decisive leadership and success in the use of high-tech arms, especially aerospace capabilities, in defeating Iraq and forcing its withdrawal from Kuwait.

Second, a buyer's market for arms has emerged. Developed states are cutting defense budgets now that the Cold War is over. Developing states also are likely to spend less on arms as they integrate these new weapons into their arsenals, spend more for a more highly trained professional military, meet debt payments on past large-scale borrowing, and respond to demands for greater domestic welfare.

Third, the costs of profitable entry into arms markets are rising. The increasing sophistication of new weapons research and development drive economic costs and technological requirements ever upward. The three-tier system of weapons suppliers is being reinforced, and the base of the pyramid is being narrowed. Russia can no longer compete with the United States as it struggles to reform its economy and downsize its military. European states are compelled either to develop new weapons jointly or to concede U.S. supremacy. France has already declared its intention to Europeanize its defense industry and cooperate with its partners in the European Union on joint acquisition projects for new weapons. Developing states are reduced to producing weapons of lower technological sophistication, and they will have to rely on licensing and coproduction to strengthen their technological base.

Fourth, these structural changes have reinforced the multilateralization of arms production. Coproduction, licensing, and commercial offsets are now common features of the global arms production and transfer system. In fiscal year 1992, U.S. sales of military equipment and services totaled $15.2 billion, while commercial licensing agreements reached $16 billion among more than thirty-four countries in all major regions of the world. For the first time, Turkish-produced U.S. F-16 fighters will be sold in Egypt.

This process of arms multilateralization is likely to deepen and widen in the absence of a geopolitical polarization of the kind that divided the world into two armed camps during the Cold War. Even the United States now depends on other states, like Japan, for critical components and technology to develop new weapon systems. Closely associated with the trend toward multilateralization is greater consolidation of defense industries in the United States and Europe.

Finally, the end of the global geopolitical struggle for world dominance between two continental powers along with the rising demand of national populations for economic growth, technological development, and employment have had a significant downward impact on arms production and transfers. U.S. transfer policies are also sensitive to these concerns. Increasingly, commercial aims are becoming the principal motivation for arms sales and military technology: to cut costs in developing weapons, to save jobs, to improve profit margins, to meet rising global trade competition, and to solve chronic balance-of-payments problems. Restrictions on the sale of dual-use technologies capable of being adapted to civilian purposes have been relaxed. COCOM, NATO's multilateral coordinating mechanism to restrict the transfer of advanced technologies to communist countries during the Cold War, has been disbanded; its successor, the Wassenaan Agreement, has had trouble even getting started. After almost half a century of war, corporate profits and commercial gain are again, as during the inter-war period, assuming increasing importance in U.S. arms sales policies. But this trend toward commercialization may again be overtaken by geopolitical and military strategic concerns if a new challenger to current American military predominance should arise or if regional conflicts where the U.S. has important interests at stake, as in Northeast Asia, should again erupt.

EDWARD A. KOLODZIEJ

See also Afghanistan; Armament Companies; Arms Control and Disarmament Agency; El Salvador; Iran; Iraq; Lend-Lease; Military-Industrial Complex; Neutrality Acts of the 1930s; North Atlantic Treaty Organization

FURTHER READING

Broszka, Michael, and Peter Lock, eds. *Restructuring of Arms Production in Western Europe.* New York, 1992.

Broszka, Michael, and Thomas Ohlson. *Arms Transfers to the Third World, 1971–1985.* Oxford, 1987.

Grimmett, Richard F. *Conventional Arms Transfers to the Third World, 1987–1994.* Washington, D.C., 1995.

Harkavy, Robert E. *The Arms Trade and International Systems.* Cambridge, Mass., 1975.

Hartung, William D. *And Weapons For All.* New York, 1994.

Klare, Michael. *American Arms Supermarket.* Austin, Tex., 1984.

Kolodziej, Edward. *Making and Marketing Arms: The French Experience and Its Implications for the International System.* Princeton, N.J., 1987.

———. "Arms Transfers and International Politics: The Interdependence of Independent." In *Arms Transfers in the Modern World,* edited by Stephanie G. Neuman and Robert E. Harkavy. New York, 1980.

Krause, Keith. *Arms and the State: Patterns of Military Production and Trade.* New York, 1992.

Laurence, Edward J. *The International Arms Trade.* New York, 1992.

Neuman, Stephanie G., and Robert E. Harkavy, eds. *The Arms Trade: Problems and Prospects in the Post-Cold War World.*

Pearson, Frederic F. *The Global Spread of Arms: The Political Economy of International Security.* Boulder, Colo., 1994.

Pierre, Andrew. *The Global Politics of Arms Sales.* Princeton, N.J., 1982.

U.S. Arms Control and Disarmament Agency. *World Military Expenditures and Arms Transfers.* Washington, D.C.: 1963–1973; 1968–1977; 1971–1980; 1972–1982; and annually 1985–1994.

U.S. Congress. Office of Technology Assessment. *Global Arms Trade: Commerce in Advanced Military Technology and Weapons.* Washington, D.C., June, 1991.

ARMY, U.S. DEPARTMENT OF

An agency of the Department of Defense with the general mission of conducting military operations on land. The Department of the Army originally was established under the U.S. Constitution by the creation of the Department of War on 7 August 1789. The secretary of war under the former Articles of Confederation government, Henry Knox, continued in that office, and the Commanding General of the Army of the Confederation, Brigadier General Josiah Harmar, was confirmed in his command; the army officers, the enlisted men, the weaponry, the forts, and the facilities were accepted in service to the new government of the United States. The total number of officers and soldiers in active service then reached approximately 800. Most were located in the Northwest Territory, where their primary duties were pacifying Indians and driving "squatters" out of Indian Territory. As President George Washington struggled to protect settlers pressing into the Ohio Valley and put down minor civil insurrections against federal authority, the army was expanded to 3,000, and assigned politico-military duties in enforcing civil law and order, negotiating with and "chastising" the Indians, and fighting when and where order could not be maintained. These peacetime missions continued through the nineteenth century.

The secretary of war was a cabinet officer, acting for the president in direction of the army. The Militia Act of 1792 authorized the president to call the states' militia into federal service for three months. This act remained the law for the civil components of the army until the twentieth century. Under President Thomas Jefferson, the Military Peace Establishment Act of 1802 authorized a small army, enjoined to remain "out of the purview of civilized society." This act created a military academy at West Point, New York, as a means of "republicanizing" the officer corps. With the purchase of the Louisiana Territory, army officers and detachments were sent to explore, map, and represent the government in this vast territory.

Victory in the War of 1812, despite poor military leadership and indecisive campaigns, confirmed in the minds of most citizens the adequacy of the militia system for insuring national security. Lack of a major foreign threat to the security of the United States in the ensuing years led to a state of military unpreparedness. The small regular army did serve as the agent of aggressive U.S. territorial expansion; it was charged with removing eastern Indians to the west, opening and protecting the western trails, and establishing governmental authority on the frontier. For the War with Mexico (1846), however, the strength of the U.S. Army had to be expanded to 78,000, including 50,000 volunteers. That war, which extended U.S. territory to the shores of the Pacific, also demonstrated the increasing professionalism of the army, especially of the officers trained at the military academy. After victory over Mexico in 1848, the small regular army occupied posts mainly in the west; army engineers explored, surveyed and engineered public projects. The Army also supervised elections in the territories and fought Indians.

SECRETARIES OF THE ARMY

ADMINISTRATION	SECRETARY	PERIOD OF APPOINTMENT
Truman	Kenneth C. Royall	1947–1949
	Gordon Gray	1949–1950
	Frank Pace, Jr.	1950–1953
Eisenhower	Robert T. Stevens	1953–1955
	Wilber M. Brucker	1955–1961
Kennedy	Elvis J. Stahr, Jr.	1961–1962
	Cyrus R. Vance	1962–1964
L. Johnson		
	Stephen Alles	1964–1965
	Stanley R. Resor	1965–1971
Nixon		
	Robert F. Froehlke	1971–1973
	Howard H. Callaway	1973–1975
Ford		
	Martin R. Hoffmann	1975–1977
Carter	Clifford L. Alexander, Jr. 1977–1981	
Reagan	John O. Marsh, Jr.	1981–1989
Bush	Michael P. W. Stone	1989–1993
Clinton	Togo D. West, Jr.	1993–Present

Source: U.S. Department of the Army

The American Civil War confirmed the unreadiness of the regular army to fight a modern war. Increased by conscription to more than a million men, the Union Army under the leadership of General Ulysses Grant gained victory over the Confederacy mainly by a strategy of attrition. After the Civil War, the peacetime regular army was committed to "Reconstruction" of the former Confederacy, to the pacification of the Plains Indians, and as the nation industrialized, to the quelling of labor disorders.

The Spanish-American-Cuban-Filipino War (1898) first committed the U.S. Army to overseas operations as an agent of U.S. foreign policy. The invasion of Cuba, the suppression the Philippine Insurrection, and occupation duties in Latin America and the Philippines spread the army in duties and stations worldwide. Public criticism, including denunciations of the army's conduct of the war in the Philippines, led to reorganization of the War Department beginning in 1899. Secretary of War Elihu Root appointed a chief of staff for the army (in lieu of a commanding general), established a general staff, and improved staff planning. Secretary Root also improved military education and training, and founded the Army War College.

The Militia Act of 1903 established the National Guard as a federal military force, and improved peacetime support of reserve forces. In 1909, the army acquired its first airplane. The army also supervised construction of the Panama Canal and, in the process, army doctors successfully identified and battled several tropical diseases. A bloody raid into the United States by the Mexican nationalist Pancho Villa provoked a "Punitive Expedition" into Mexico to capture Villa. The expedition by the U.S. Army failed to capture Villa, but gave the army some experience in command and support of a large combat organization.

Following the onset of World War I in Europe, the National Defense Act of 1916 authorized the president to call reserve forces into federal service for unlimited terms in times of national emergency; it also increased the regular army and organized an Officer and Enlisted Reserve Corps. During World War I, the army expanded, through enlistments and conscription, to more than four million men. The major mission of the army was to form the American Expeditionary Forces (AEF), to fight in France in cooperation with the Allies. In 1918, the AEF, under the command of General John J. Pershing, conducted successful offensives, which made a major contribution to the Allied victory over the Central Powers.

The National Defense Act of 1920 established the Army of the United States, consisting of the Regular Army, the National Guard, and the Organized Reserve Corps. Each of these components was to be organized, equipped, and trained so as to be able to contribute to national defense in time of emergency. Budgetary limitations, especially during the Great Depression, prevented all of these components from achieving readiness in peacetime to accomplish their missions. During the interwar period, the army provided civic assistance in disasters, flew the mail, and operated the Civilian Conservation Corps (CCC) program, which provided jobs for 300,000 young men in flood control and land conservation projects.

During World War II, the U.S. Army expanded tremendously, by enlistment and conscription, to more than eight million men and women. Organized and trained under the leadership of General George C. Marshall, the army was committed into coalition warfare with Allied nations on every continent of the world. The army also managed a broad array of politico-military cooperation and assistance programs, including Lend-Lease and Military Government of Liberated Peoples. Under General Dwight D. Eisenhower, the army participated in major land and air offensives, in cooperation with European Allies, which brought victory over Germany and Italy. In the Pacific, U.S. Army ground and air forces, under General Douglas MacArthur, conducted joint operations with the U.S. Navy, gaining a bloody victory over Japan after dropping atomic bombs on two Japanese cities, ending the war against the Axis Powers in 1945.

The Post–World War II Era

The postwar U.S. Army initially managed a massive demobilization, ultimately reducing its active strength to less than half a million. Army forces occupied and governed Germany and Japan, and provided civil relief and resettlement in war-torn areas. Demobilization included the processing for discharge of over seven million persons and their transportation to their homes of record. As the Cold War began, the army stationed in Europe was committed to the North Atlantic Treaty Organization; it also provided forces in execution of other mutual assistance treaties around the world.

The National Security Act of 1947 limited the mission of the Department of the Army to organizing, training, and equipping forces for the operational commands, consisting of members of all military services overseas. Removed from operational command, the army also lost its primary air mission, as the Air Force became a separate service. The secretary of war became the secretary of the army, losing cabinet rank when, under the National Security Act, the secretary of defense became the president's adviser on military affairs. The chief of staff of the army became a member of the Joint Chiefs of Staff; that group, consisting of the chiefs of all the U.S. armed services, provides military advice to the secretary of defense and the president.

During the undeclared Korean War, the U.S. Army provided the majority of the forces which served under the United Nations in a "police action" to defend South Korea. Under the command of General MacArthur, and later General Matthew Ridgway, these forces fought North Korean and Chinese forces to a bitter stalemate. U.S. Army forces in Korea were reduced over time, but in the mid-1990s a division still remained on alert in South Korea. In the 1950s the army reorganized to a "pentomic" structure, armed and equipped to fight limited nuclear warfare. The army was selected to carry out a Universal Military Training Program (UMT) to expand acceptance of individuals with limited skills into military service; it was called upon to enforce the civil rights of minorities in the United States, and also led the way in integrating racial minorities and women into military service.

The Vietnam War, a long, undeclared but bloody conflict, saw the U.S. Army committed in a broad skein of politico-military advisory duties under the rubric of "nation building." Responding to a strategy of "incremental escalation" established by Secretary of Defense Robert S. McNamara, the Army was "politicized" by the agreement of senior army leaders to a flawed military strategy of piecemeal commitment of army forces, in order to accommodate the demands of President Lyndon Johnson to limit U.S. operations in Vietnam, which he regarded as a sideshow to his major programs.

U.S. Army combat forces were first committed into Vietnam in 1965. Under General William C. Westmoreland, army strength in Vietnam rose to over 350,000 by 1969, the troops committed into a strategy of attrition against primarily native guerrillas. The communist Tet Offensive in 1969 was the high point for both sides, as the communists lost the military campaign but gained a propaganda victory in the United States. The long war had become a military and political stalemate, unpopular at home and deleterious to morale in the field. Indiscipline in the army increased, while the war became a lightning rod for increasing dissidence at home. In 1969, President Richard M. Nixon announced a strategy of "Vietnamization," gradually replacing U.S. forces with Vietnamese units. U.S. force withdrawals began in 1969; the last U.S. Army forces departed Vietnam in 1973. It was the first war the army, and the nation, had lost.

With the end of military conscription in the United States, the army became an "all-volunteer" service in 1973. Reduced in strength and appropriations, troubled with disciplinary problems and racial and generational strife, the "hollow army" reflected the fractured society it served in the 1970s. Army training and liaison missions to nations in the Third World were drastically reduced. The failed mission to rescue U.S. hostages held by the Islamic republic of Iran in 1979 capped a period in which army strength and morale reached a nadir.

President Ronald Reagan's strategy of "Peace through Strength" increased the modernization and readiness, as well as the morale, of the army. The army was the major force in the U.S. invasion of Grenada in 1983. Other counterinsurgency operations in Latin America, especially in El Salvador, Guatemala, and Honduras, sought to blunt revolutionary challenges to U.S.-backed regimes. The U.S. invasion of Panama in 1989, primarily by army forces deposed a military dictator who was involved in drug shipments to the U.S..

The army's resounding victory (in cooperation with Allies) over the land forces of Iraq in the Gulf War in 1991 restored the esprit de corps of U.S. forces and demonstrated the high-tech effectiveness of the "Modern Volunteer Army." In the 1990s, the U.S. Army participated in U.N. "peacekeeping" operations in Somalia, the Sinai, Rwanda, Kuwait, Macedonia, and Bosnia. The army was the major force committed into Haiti to restore its democratically elected president to office in 1994. In the mid-1990s, the U.S. Army was modernizing and reducing itself in size, to a planned strength of 495,000, while maintaining readiness under fiscal constraints.

PAUL F. BRAIM

See also American Civil War; Continental Expansion; Defense, U.S. Department of; Gulf War of 1990–1991; Korean War; Native Americans; Vietnam War; War, U.S. Department of; World War I; World War II

FURTHER READING

Abbott, Willis J. *The Story of Our Army: From Colonial Days to the Present.* New York, 1977.
Coffman, Edward M. *The Old Army: A Portrait of the American Army in Peacetime, 1784–1898.* New York: Oxford University Press, 1986.
Dupuy, Trevor N., and Paul F. Braim. *Military Heritage of America,* 3rd ed. 2 vols. Dubuque, Iowa, 1992.
Millett, Allan R., and Peter Maslowski. *For the Common Defense.* New York, 1984.
Weigley, Russell F. *History of the United States Army.* New York, 1967.

AROOSTOOK WAR

See Webster-Ashburton Treaty

ARTHUR, CHESTER ALAN

(*b.* 5 October 1830; *d.* 18 November 1886)

Twenty-first president of the United States (1881–1885). He was born in Franklin County, Vermont, and graduated from Union College in Schenectady, New York, in 1848. Arthur taught school, read law, and established a successful legal practice in New York City. During the Civil War, he held a series of administrative offices, including that of quartermaster-general for the New York Volunteers. In 1871 President Ulysses S. Grant appointed Arthur customs collector of the Port of New York, and even though no financial scandals tarnished his administration, the New York Customs House was overstaffed with Republican patronage workers from Senator Roscoe Conkling's political machine. In 1878 reform-minded President Rutherford B. Hayes replaced Arthur over Conkling's objections, but the New York "stalwarts" had their revenge in 1880, when they placed Arthur on the winning Republican presidential ticket headed by James A. Garfield. When Garfield died from an assassin's bullet, Arthur succeeded to the presidency on 19 September 1881. He frustrated his Republican backers in New York by refusing to install the spoils system in Washington and by backing civil service reform. Arthur undercut Secretary of State James G. Blaine's efforts to hold a Pan-American conference in Washington, encouraged Blaine's resignation in December 1881, and replaced him with Frederick T. Frelinghuysen. Arthur labored unsuccessfully to bring about tariff reform, vetoed a Chinese exclusion bill that would have violated existing treaty obligations, and took the initial steps to build a modern navy to replace the obsolete ships of the Civil War era. Arthur's support of civil service reform alienated party stalwarts but failed to win enough support from reformers to secure his party's nomination in 1884.

MICHAEL J. DEVINE

See also Blaine, James Gillespie

FURTHER READING

Doenecke, Justus D. *The Presidencies of James A. Garfield and Chester A. Arthur.* Lawrence, Kans., 1981.
Pletcher, David M. *The Awkward Years: American Foreign Relations Under Garfield and Arthur.* Columbia, Mo., 1962.

ARTICLES OF CONFEDERATION

(1781–1789)

The first U.S. constitution, which created the operational framework for the U.S. government and its diplomacy between 1781 and 1789. Even though the new United States had great potential for economic and political power, it began its history with significant weaknesses. Under the Articles of Confederation, ratified in 1781, the preponderance of power in the new government remained with the states, which retained "sovereignty, freedom, and independence." The central government was weak by comparison and lacked the authority to solve many of the problems created by the American Revolution. The powers to tax and to control interstate and foreign commerce, for example, remained with the states; each state was allowed to establish its own tariff and customs regulations and thus compete with the others for trade. On the other hand, the Continental Congress had created the Department of War, the Department of the Treasury, and the Department of Foreign Affairs. The articles gave the national government the power to make war and peace, send and receive ambassadors, make treaties (except commercial agreements) and alliances, and settle disputes among the states.

It was not immediately clear whether a national government of such limited power would be able to secure control of and maintain order within the country's vast domain or to gain the respect of foreign nations; but Congress was determined to try. It called on some of the most dedicated leaders of the Revolution to continue their diplomatic service to the fledgling nation. John Jay, on returning to the United States in 1784 from Paris, was appointed secretary for foreign affairs, replacing Robert R. Livingston. Congress in 1785 appointed John Adams to the difficult post of minister to Great Britain and in the same year named Thomas Jefferson to the more felicitous assignment of minister to France. Although the United States and France remained allies, Jefferson complained that the French did not treat his country with respect. The government in Paris made no effort to aid the United States in its disputes with Spain and Great Britain in the trans-Appalachian West. Moreover, France gave the United States only limited access to its West Indian islands and complained that the new nation had not paid its war debts.

The most difficult diplomatic challenges, however, came from Great Britain, which sent consuls to the United States but no minister and received John Adams coldly. The British felt humiliated by the loss of their North American colonies, and the Treaty of Paris, which had ended the Revolutionary War, was very unpopular. The mercantilists in the British Parliament, having succeeded in closing the British West Indies to U.S. trade, continued their dominance over imperial commerce. Merchants and shipowners who saw the United States as a potential commercial rival made sure that the newly independent nation received no favorable trading concessions. The chief spokesman for British mercantilism, Lord Sheffield, attacked U.S. pretensions to trading privileges in the British market in his pamphlet *Observations on the Commerce of the American States* (1783). He asked why Great Britain should make any concessions to a nation already tied to the British by trade and whose government was unable to control foreign commerce in any case.

Further British trade restrictions after the war hurt U.S. merchants even more. England bought only raw materials, such as tobacco, cotton, naval stores, and lumber, from the United States and allowed American ships to trade in Great Britain's home ports but not in those of its colonies. U.S. merchants nevertheless developed a fairly lucrative illicit trade with the British West Indies.

The legal trade between Great Britain and the United States also flourished. By the mid-1780s about 75 percent of U.S. exports went to England and 90 percent of U.S. imports came from there. Thus, despite U.S. merchants' annoyance at the restrictions imposed on their trade activities by the British, both nations benefited from the trade, with Great Britain providing the U.S. market with much-needed textiles and household manufactures. British products in fact dominated the American market, and U.S. merchants followed British business practices. Because about 60 percent of the population of the United States during that time claimed British ancestry, the ties of language and culture increased the new nation's economic dependence on its mother country. Throughout the Confederation era the United States unsuccessfully tried to change British trade policy. It proved impossible for the thirteen states of the Union to unite on a commercial policy toward England. Adams complained bitterly to Jay of the utter contempt expressed toward the United States in Great Britain and maintained that it would be necessary to strengthen the central government of the United States if commercial relations with Great Britain were to improve. He never succeeded in negotiating a more favorable trade agreement between the nations; deeply resenting British condescension, he returned to the United States in 1788.

More than trade disputes undermined Anglo-American relations in the 1780s. Each nation accused the other of violating the Peace Treaty of 1783. In violation of Article 7, British troops had taken away hundreds, perhaps thousands, of slaves, some of whom were eventually given their freedom and some of whom were sold to plantation owners in the British West Indies. Great Britain refused to compensate the United States on the ground that the United States had refused compliance with Article 4 of the treaty, under which British merchants were entitled to repayment of millions of dollars in debts contracted before the Revolutionary War. Because the debts dated from before the war, debtors in the United States believed that the Revolution had canceled the laws under which the debts had been incurred. Southern states defied the treaty and passed laws prohibiting creditors from using state courts to obtain redress. Collectors usually found it impossible to collect the debts, and Congress lacked the power to enforce the treaty's provisions.

The United States also could not fulfill Article 5 of the treaty, which called for restitution of property to loyalists. Although Congress recommended that the states return such property, anti-British feeling prevented their carrying out this provision. During the war every state had provided for confiscation of loyalist property or had taxed it heavily. Some loyalists who tried to return to their homes after the war were mobbed or even killed, while others ultimately did regain their estates; but the states did not repeal their confiscation laws.

At the same time, the British were violating Article 2 of the treaty, which specified that the boundary between British North America and the United States was to run through the Great Lakes to the Saint Lawrence River. British traders maintained a chain of eight trading posts on U.S. soil south of the Great Lakes. The British had decided on 7 April 1784, even before U.S. violations of the treaty began, to hold the posts because of their importance to the lucrative fur trade in the region. There was also a feeling among some in the British government that giving up the Old Northwest to the United States was a mistake and a violation of England's obligations to its Native American allies in the region. British military leaders feared a Native American uprising against Canada if the United States took over the territory. In 1786 the governor general of Canada received orders to continue holding the posts against any U.S. effort to seize them. Americans were angry about the British presence on U.S. soil because it prevented the peaceful opening of the territory for settlement and spread fear that the mother country was supplying Native Americans with arms and ammunition for use against settlers. There were even rumors that the British had offered to let the people of Vermont use the Saint Lawrence River to export goods as long as they remained outside the American Union.

Relations With Spain

Relations with Spain remained unfriendly during the Confederation era. Only after Great Britain and the United States signed the 1783 peace treaty did Spain recognize U.S. independence. Territorial boundaries and commercial relations between Spain and the United States were also in dispute. Conflict over navigation rights on the Mississippi River had further increased the animosity between the two nations. Controversy over the boundary line between the United States and the Spanish Floridas stemmed from the provision in the Peace Treaty of 1783 that placed the line at the thirty-first parallel. A secret article in the preliminary treaty of 1782, however, had placed the northern boundary of the Floridas at about 32°28', the English border established in 1764 at the mouth of the Yazoo River, should Great Britain retain control of the territory during the war. During the Revolutionary War, Spain had retaken the Floridas from Great Britain, including territory north of the thirty-first parallel. Great Britain had recognized Spain's control of the territory in its peace treaty with that nation, and as a result Spain did not believe itself bound by the terms of the Anglo-American treaty of 1783. In fact, Spain claimed land all the way to the Tennessee and Ohio Rivers. It kept military posts in Alabama, Mississippi, and Tennessee and supplied weapons to the Native American tribes in the

area for their use against the numerous American settlers (about 50,000 at war's end) swarming into the area between the Appalachian Mountains and the Mississippi River. Spain closed the Mississippi River to U.S. trade in 1784 in the midst of fierce frontier warfare.

Great Britain's right to use the Mississippi River for trade to the sea at New Orleans also stemmed from the Seven Years' War. England agreed to share the right to navigate the river "from its source to the ocean" in the Peace Treaty of 1783. Spain, however, refused to recognize any U.S. right to navigate the Mississippi River in Spanish territory. Western farmers believed that their livelihood depended on using the Mississippi River to get their products out to market through New Orleans. They found water transportation easier and less expensive than moving their goods overland through the mountains to the East Coast and wanted the federal government to force Spain to open the river to their trade. Spain, which had only a few hundred soldiers in Louisiana, was more worried about western settlers' demands than were merchants and shippers in the northeastern United States, who were interested primarily in securing trade in Spanish ports in Europe and in the Western Hemisphere; Spain attempted to forestall attacks by U.S. farmers on its forts or efforts to take New Orleans by force. At one time, Spain tried to create a separatist movement in the Kentucky Territory by offering the settlers special trading privileges on the Mississippi. It also attempted to negotiate solutions to U.S. grievances regarding trade. In return for recognition of its exclusive control of the lower Mississippi River, Spain proposed to modify its extensive boundary claims and to negotiate a commercial treaty granting the United States trading privileges in certain Spanish ports.

In 1785 Spain sent Don Diego de Gardoqui as envoy to the United States to discuss the disagreements between the nations. As the official in charge of shipping Spanish munitions to the United States, Gardoqui had met Jay in Spain during the American Revolution. He spoke excellent English and spent time entertaining Jay's wife, whom he thought dominated her husband. Despite his social activities, bribe money offered to members of Congress, and intense discussions with Jay, Gardoqui did not succeed in negotiating an agreement acceptable to his country. Not only did he misjudge Jay's character, but Jay was operating under strict instructions from Congress that left him no room to make an independent judgment. Congress insisted that Spain grant the United States navigation rights along the entire Mississippi River clear to New Orleans and accept a boundary between the United States and the Spanish Floridas at the thirty-first parallel. Gardoqui, bound by his instructions to reject both demands, instead offered commercial concessions that would satisfy U.S. merchants on the Atlantic seaboard in return for a temporary closing of the Mississippi to U.S. trade. Jay liked the idea, and the two men ignored their instructions and drew up a commercial agreement in 1786 under whose terms the United States would "forbear" use of the river in the area under Spanish control for twenty-five to thirty years while retaining the right to its navigation. In return, Spain would provide trading concessions in its home ports and in ports in the Canary Islands. Both nations also agreed to guarantee each other's territory in the Western Hemisphere.

In August, Jay asked Congress to change his instructions so that he could formally negotiate the agreement. He argued that the United States did not have the strength to establish navigation of the Mississippi by force and that it should therefore "consent to forbear to use what we know is not in our power to use." Congress agreed to change Jay's instructions to make the new treaty terms possible, but by a vote of only seven to five, less than the two-thirds majority needed to approve such an agreement; all the delegates from the Southern states, believing that their interests were being sacrificed to those of the merchant class, voted against changing the instructions. Residents of the western territories thought of either seeking British or Spanish protection or leaving the Union if such an agreement were ratified; some talked about seizing New Orleans.

Because Congress could not muster the votes to approve the agreement, it was never completed. Concern for international politics governed Jay's outlook, and he did not comprehend the intense nationalism of the western settlers. Fear of British power in North America almost certainly influenced his decision to ask for concessions to Spain. As for Gardoqui, he was instructed to use his talents to create a new state in the U.S. Southwest that would follow the bidding of Spain. A double agent, General James Wilkinson, who while in the pay of the United States also accepted bribes and swore allegiance to Spain, played an important role in this intrigue. His covert maneuvers with political leaders in Kentucky, however, did not succeed in detaching that territory from the United States. Even the opening of the Mississippi River to U.S. trade in December 1788 under a special license system and the granting to U.S. merchants of the right to land cargoes in New Orleans did not resolve the real issue of free use of the river or the boundary dispute with Spain.

The United States, now outside the British Empire and no longer protected by the British Navy, had to pay bribes to the Barbary states in the Mediterranean—Morocco, Algiers, Tunis, and Tripoli—to avoid attacks on U.S. ships by raiders or pirates. The Confederation government found it difficult to raise enough money to pay tribute to these states, and only in 1786 did it successfully negotiate a treaty with Morocco that contained no provision for payment of tribute.

The weakness imposed on the United States government by the Articles of Confederation as it engaged in diplomacy with other nations helped precipitate the calling of the Constitutional Convention in 1787. From this meeting emerged the U.S. Constitution, which among other changes gave the federal government control over the making of foreign policy.

REBECCA G. GOODMAN

See also Adams, John; American Revolution; Constitution; France; Great Britain; Jay, John; Jefferson, Thomas; Mississippi River; Northwest Ordinance; Spain

FURTHER READING

Bemis, Samuel F. *Jay's Treaty*, rev. ed. New Haven, Conn., 1962.
———. *Pinckney's Treaty: A Study of America's Advantage From Europe's Distress, 1783–1800.* Baltimore, Md., 1926.
Darling, Arthur B. *Our Rising Empire, 1763–1803.* Hamden, Conn., 1962.
Ferling, John. *John Adams: A Life.* Knoxville, Tenn., 1992.
Gilbert, Felix. *To the Farewell Address: Ideas of Early American Foreign Policy.* Princeton, N.J., 1961.
Hoffman, Ronald, and Peter J. Albert, eds. *Sovereign States in an Age of Uncertainty.* Charlottesville, Va., 1982.
Horsman, Reginald. *The Diplomacy of the New Republic, 1776–1815.* Arlington Heights, Ill., 1985.
———. *The Frontier in the Formative Years, 1783-1815.* Albuquerque, N.M., 1975.
Jensen, Merrill. *The New Nation.* New York, 1950.
Kaplan, Lawrence S. *Colonies Into Nation: American Diplomacy, 1763–1801.* New York, 1972.
———. *Thomas Jefferson and France.* New Haven, Conn., 1967.
Marks, Frederick W., III. *Independence on Trial: Foreign Affairs and the Making of the Constitution.* Baton Rouge, La., 1973.
Middlekauff, Robert. *The Glorious Cause: The American Revolution, 1763–1789.* New York, 1982.
Morris, Richard B. *The Forging of the Union, 1781–1789.* New York, 1987.
Onuf, Peter S. *Statehood and Union: A History of the Northwest Ordinance.* Bloomington, Ind., 1987.
Perkins, Bradford. *The Creation of a Republican Empire, 1776–1865,* vol. 1. *The Cambridge History of American Foreign Relations.* Cambridge, Mass., 1993.
Ritcheson, Charles R. *Aftermath of Revolution. British Policy Toward the United States, 1783–1795.* Dallas, Tex., 1969.
Tucker, Robert W., and David C. Hendrickson. *Empire of Liberty, The Statecraft of Thomas Jefferson.* New York, 1990.
Whitaker, Arthur P. *The Spanish-American Frontier: 1783–1795.* Lincoln, Nebr., 1969.

ASHBURTON, FIRST BARON
Alexander Baring

(b. 27 October 1774; *d.* 13 May 1848)

A partner in the financial House of Baring, Ashburton was named by the British foreign secretary, Lord Aberdeen, to head a special diplomatic mission to the United States in 1842 to negotiate differences between the United States and Great Britain. He was an excellent choice because the House of Baring was a major investor in U.S. securities, and Ashburton had a number of U.S. contacts stemming from an extended visit to the United States in 1795. On 23 August 1798, moreover, he had married Anne Louisa Bingham, daughter of Senator William Bingham of Pennsylvania.

Baring served in the House of Commons from 1806 to 1835 and, in Sir Robert Peel's first administration of 1834, as president of the Board of Trade and master of the Mint. He became Baron Ashburton in 1835. Although he changed from Whig to Tory and from an advocate to an opponent of free trade over the course of his political career, he consistently advocated good relations with the United States. The many notable Americans among his friends included John Quincy Adams, Albert Gallatin, Rufus King, Richard Rush, and Daniel Webster (who also served as U.S. counsel for the House of Baring).

When he arrived in Washington on 4 April 1842, Ashburton and Webster entered into cordial but earnest discussions on issues between the countries. While they did not resolve all differences between Great Britain and the United States—the Oregon boundary remained unsettled—the 1842 Treaty of Washington, as the Webster-Ashburton treaty is officially known, achieved a great deal. It established the northeastern boundary between Maine and Canada and the northwestern boundary along the Great Lakes. The treaty included an agreement that British and U.S. naval vessels would jointly cruise the coast of Africa to suppress slave trading, and provided for the extradition of fugitives. Webster and Ashburton also dealt with the *Caroline*, *Creole*, and other impressment controversies in supplemental correspondence. Despite their accomplishment, both Ashburton and Webster were later denounced by political opponents in their respective countries for making too many concessions. Yet the treaty that bears their name helped inaugurate an Anglo-American rapprochement that, with fits and starts, gradually emerged by the end of the nineteenth century.

KENNETH R. STEVENS

See also Aberdeen, Fourth Earl; Canada; Caroline Affair; Creole Affair; Great Britain; Impressment; Oregon Question; Webster, Daniel; Webster-Ashburton Treaty

FURTHER READING

Hidy, Ralph W. *The House of Baring in American Trade and Finance: English Merchant Bankers at Work, 1763–1861.* Cambridge, Mass., 1949.

Jones, Howard. *To the Webster-Ashburton Treaty: A Study in Anglo-American Relations, 1783–1843.* Chapel Hill, N.C., 1977.

Jones, Wilbur Devereux. *The American Problem in British Diplomacy, 1841–1861.* Athens, Ga., 1974.

Newton, A.P. "United States and Colonial Developments, 1815–1846." In *The Cambridge History of British Foreign Policy, 1783–1919*, vol. 2, edited by A. W. Ward and G. P. Gooch. New York, 1922–1923.

ASPIN, LESLIE (LES), JR.
(*b.* 21 July, 1938; *d.* 21 May 1995)

Secretary of defense (1993–1994). A graduate of Yale and Oxford universities and the Massachusetts Institute of Technology, Aspin taught economics at Marquette University, served in the U.S. Army, and was one of Secretary of Defense Robert S. McNamara's "whiz kids." From 1971 to 1993 he was a Democratic member of Congress from Wisconsin, and was chairman of the House Armed Services Committee from 1985 to 1993. A highly regarded defense intellectual, Aspin supported the MX missile and aid to the Nicaraguan Contras but opposed the B-2 bomber and the Strategic Defense Initiative. Aspin's backing of the January 1991 congressional resolution supporting the use of force against Iraq following Iraq's invasion of Kuwait was a crucial factor in gaining House approval; his prescient analysis of the manner in which a war with Iraq would be fought and his prediction that U.S. casualties could be kept low, questioned by many analysts at the time, were both borne out in the event. As secretary of defense for President Bill Clinton, he grappled with difficult social issues, such as the roles of homosexuals in the military and of women in combat; decisions on when and how to use military force in Somalia, Bosnia, and Haiti; and the budgetary cuts and force restructuring called for as part of the downsizing of the military in the post–Cold War era. Secretary Aspin's problems in office stemmed both from the difficulty of resolving these tough issues satisfactorily and from a perceived lack of managerial skills. The Clinton administration's need for a better interface with the military establishment contributed to his resignation under pressure.

BRUCE R. KUNIHOLM

See also Clinton, William Jefferson; Defense, U.S. Department of; McNamara, Robert Strange

FURTHER READING

Aspin, Les. *The Aspin Papers: Sanctions, Diplomacy, and War in the Persian Gulf.* Washington, D.C., 1991.

———. *Defense for a New Era: Lessons of the Persian Gulf War.* Washington, D.C., 1992.

ASSASSINATION

The murder of political leaders has been occasionally practiced by individuals and groups, and even covertly by governments, since the beginning of recorded history. The use of assassination by agents of the U.S. government was unthinkable until the height of the Cold War in the 1950s and 1960s, when the covert arm of the Central Intelligence Agency (CIA) was involved in the support or encouragement of several assassinations in Latin America, Asia, and Africa. After a Senate committee investigation into this practice, assassinations were prohibited in 1976 by an executive order of the president.

The rise to power of Fidel Castro in Cuba in 1959 prompted the first high-level consideration of a policy of assassination—a tactic that won the approval of President Dwight D. Eisenhower. The CIA conducted a series of attempts on Castro's life between 1961 and 1965; other assassination targets included Rafael Trujillo of the Dominican Republic and Patrice Lumumba of the Congo, both in 1966. In practice none of these plots, which included using such devices as poisoned cigars and toothpaste and exploding shells, succeeded. Castro escaped harm and Lumumba and Trujillo were probably assassinated independent of CIA help. The assassination of President John F. Kennedy in 1963 generated rumors that his death was an act of revenge for the CIA's involvement in assassination plots against Castro; the possible involvement of Castro has remained a staple of conspiracy theories about the murder. The assassination of South Vietnamese president Ngo Dinh Diem in 1963 was often mentioned in connection with the Kennedy presidency because Kennedy had authorized the assassination, but the plan was vetoed by CIA Director John McCone; the CIA's failure to investigate the murder was probably dictated by Vietnamese local politics.

In 1974 CIA-directed assassination attempts became front-page news as part of the more general controversy over covert action and the role of the CIA. Revelations in 1975 that the CIA had spied on U.S. citizens who opposed the Vietnam War prompted President Gerald Ford to appoint the Rockefeller Commission to investigate whether the CIA had broken any U.S. laws. The Senate formed a select committee, headed by Senator Frank Church of Idaho, to investigate covert operations abroad, and the House of Representatives followed with its own investigative committee. In this atmosphere of extreme suspicion, President Ford admitted publicly that the government had been involved in assassination plots. The Rockefeller Commission's scope of inquiry was broadened to cover the CIA's involvement in assassination attempts but its report did not calm criticism. The Church Committee, after hearing more than 100 witnesses and compiling 10,000 pages of testimony, unanimously approved a 349-page interim report titled *Alleged Assassination Plots Involving Foreign Leaders* (1975) and voted, with one abstention, to make the report public, despite White House objections. The committee agreed that the injury to the national reputation caused by the revelation of embarrassing secrets should not outweigh the requirements of democracy. It concluded that "assassination is an abhorrent practice that must never again be undertaken in times of peace by the U.S. government" and that "an absolute prohibition against assassination should be written into law." The

committee was particularly critical of the doctrine of "plausible deniability" by which democratic accountability was subverted. In 1976 and 1977 the Senate and House, respectively, established permanent intelligence oversight committees. In February 1976 President Ford issued an executive order outlawing assassination as an instrument of U.S. foreign policy. Presidents Jimmy Carter and Ronald Reagan repeated this step, but an executive order does not have the force of law.

Assassination became an issue again in October 1984 when press reports described a manual for psychological operations, including assassination, used by the U.S.-supported Contras against the Sandinista government in Nicaragua. The author was apparently a CIA agent. Although critics of the administration thought that the manual violated President Reagan's December 1981 executive order, the president claimed that the manual was not an official CIA document. Within the Reagan administration, proponents of a proactive response to terrorism abroad often argued that the ban on assassination should be rescinded or overridden. Suspicions were raised in March 1985, when a car bomb in Beirut, Lebanon, killed eighty people near the home of Mohammed Hussein Fadlallah, a Shi'ite cleric whom the United States suspected of having links with such anti-American terrorists as those who had carried out the bombing of the U.S. Marines barracks in Beirut in October 1983. The CIA had started training the Lebanese in counterterrorist operations, but the House Intelligence Committee uncovered no evidence of CIA participation in or encouragement of an assassination attempt against Fadlallah.

A related issue is whether or not assassination attempts within the context of military operations violate the presidential prohibition. The U.S. bombing raid against Libya in 1986 was perhaps meant to kill the Libyan leader Muammar al-Qaddafi, and the bombing of Baghdad during the Gulf War of 1990–1991 may have been intended to kill the Iraqi president, Saddam Hussein. The prevailing interpretation of the ban is that it does not apply to military actions in situations of armed conflict between states.

MARTHA CRENSHAW

See also Central Intelligence Agency; Church, Frank Forrester III; Covert Action

FURTHER READING
Jeffreys-Jones, Rhodri. *The CIA and American Democracy.* New Haven, Conn., 1989.

ASTOR, JOHN JACOB

(*b.* 17 July 1763; *d.* 29 March 1848)

Fur trader and financier whose commercial activities contributed to the expansion of U.S. borders. Emigrating to the United States from Germany in 1784, the opportunistic Astor exploited every opening to develop a fur empire in the hinterland of North America and, consequently, to extend the influence of the young republic. After Jay's Treaty of 1794 stabilized the northern border and loosened trade restrictions with Canada, Astor extended his activities into the Northwest Territory. Early in the nineteenth century he followed the Lewis and Clark Expedition (1804–1806) into the Louisiana Territory with hopes of tapping into the potentially lucrative trade in the Pacific. Although the trading post he established at Astoria on the Columbia River (in present-day Oregon) was short-lived, his lucrative projects established a considerable U.S. presence from the Mississippi Valley to the Oregon Territory, thereby enhancing U.S. territorial claims. As a man of tremendous wealth and property, Astor moved in powerful circles and wielded substantial influence on the U.S. government. In fact, when President James Madison's administration struggled under the fiscal strain of the War of 1812, Astor intervened with a critical loan.

DONALD A. RAKESTRAW

See also Fur Trade; Oregon Question

FURTHER READING

Graebner, Norman A. *Empire on the Pacific: A Study in American Continental Expansion.* New York, 1955.
Ronda, James P. *Astoria and Empire.* Lincoln, Nebr., 1990.

ASYLUM

Conferral of a place of safety by allowing a noncitizen to enter or remain in a country rather than return to persecution or other suffering. During the period of relatively unrestricted immigration, which lasted until the mid-1870s, most noncitizen whites wishing to enter the United States to escape persecution in their home countries did so without particular difficulty, although many states restricted entry of blacks, the poor, and other groups. As immigration controls intensified in subsequent decades, persons seeking asylum had to take their chances within the discriminatory and eventually quota-based immigration regime—no special asylum regime was established. Until World War II, Congress was generally unwilling to make exceptions to immigration controls, as shown by its reluctance to grant general asylum to persecuted groups fleeing Nazi Germany in the 1930s. Provision was made in the Displaced Persons Act of 1948 for refugees displaced by World War II. Other groups, usually fleeing regimes uncongenial to the United States, were subsequently accommodated by ad hoc provisions, including statutes opening the way to permanent resident status for Hungarians (1958), Cubans (1966), and Indochinese

(1977) who had earlier been paroled into the United States in large numbers under executive emergency authority. A limited preference category for refugees from communist and Middle Eastern countries was added to immigration law in 1965.

The first comprehensive statutory scheme was the Refugee Act of 1980, which together with subsequent regulations gave effect to basic obligations stated in the 1967 United Nations Protocol Relating to the Status of Refugees. The 1980 act shifted away from ideological classifications of refugees, tracking instead the definition of "refugee" under international law—persons unable or unwilling to return to their home countries "because of persecution or a well-founded fear of persecution on account of race, religion, nationality, membership in a particular social group, or political opinion." Persons outside the United States who fall within this definition may be admitted to the United States with refugee status under regional quotas. These quotas are determined by the president in consultation with Congress and have been heavily influenced by considerations of foreign policy and domestic politics, leading to criticisms that humanitarian need has not been the only consideration.

Persons actually in the United States or at a U.S. point of entry may apply for asylum, the granting of which requires that they fall within the above definition of "refugee," that they have not committed a particularly serious crime, that they have not had the possibility of permanent resettlement in a nonpersecuting country, and that the executive branch exercise its (legally controlled) discretion in their favor. Successful applicants become eligible for permanent residence one year after the grant of asylum. Critics demonstrated in the 1980s that asylum was being granted unevenly, with persons from countries with regimes favored by the United States, such as El Salvador, having vastly greater difficulty meeting the supposedly objective test. In 1990 a more independent and specialized Asylum Officer Corps was created by the Immigration and Naturalization Service, but its resources were insufficient to handle totals of some 200,000 adjudications per year, necessitated by rising application rates and a huge backlog of unprocessed applications. Many applicants continued to spend long periods in detention centers, and many more were paroled into the United States with work permits pending resolution of their cases.

Even where asylum has not been granted, the 1980 act mandates "withholding of deportation" where there is a clear probability of persecution (a threat to life or freedom) in the particular country. This implements the international law obligation of non-return. In 1993 the Supreme Court held that the statute does not confer rights on aliens who have not entered the United States, and that the controversial policy, under Presidents George

Bush and Bill Clinton, of interdicting and returning boatloads of Haitians without asylum screening was lawful.

Evaluating complex human motives and circumstances against the circumscribed definition of "refugee" is highly problematic. Interpretations have shifted somewhat with social values, such as encompassing some persons persecuted on grounds of sexual orientation or subject to extreme sexual harassment. The narrowness of the definition, however, raises serious problems of fairness to people fleeing civil war, endemic violence, natural disasters, famine, and other miseries that affect whole societies more or less indiscriminately. While the vast majority of such externally displaced persons continue to be accommodated with fairness in neighboring developing countries, in the United States, as in most industrialized countries, the political climate has tended to favor tightening controls rather than any widening of the definition. Nevertheless, the compromise category of Temporary Protected Status was introduced in 1990 to permit people from executive-designated countries who are already in the United States to stay while particular emergency conditions in their countries continue.

Widespread claims for asylum by people already in the United States challenge the political and legal control of immigration and may engage foreign policy interests. There are severe limits to the economic, political, military, and legal resources available to rich countries for the amelioration of conditions in home countries from which people flee. There remains no imminent resolution to the conundrum of treating meritorious applicants fairly and expeditiously in accordance with national traditions and commitments without either encouraging circumvention of immigration controls or attracting politically problematic numbers of applicants.

BENEDICT W. KINGSBURY

See also Immigration; Refugees

FURTHER READING

Aleinikoff, T. Alexander, and David A. Martin. *Immigration: Process and Policy*, 2nd ed. St. Paul, Minn., 1991.
Anker, Deborah E. *The Law of Asylum in the United States*. Washington, D.C., 1991.

ATLANTIC CHARTER

(1941)

Anglo-American statement of war and peace aims issued at an epochal secret meeting off Argentia, Newfoundland, in August 1941 at which President Franklin D. Roosevelt, British prime minister Winston S. Churchill, and their military and diplomatic advisers discussed the coordination of Anglo-American political and strategic policies. Although sharp differences arose over strategic priorities, the U.S. and British leaders were able to become

acquainted, and the shipboard meeting, christened the Atlantic Conference, proved a milestone in the creation of the wartime Allied coalition. The most enduring result of this Roosevelt-Churchill encounter proved to be the Atlantic Charter. Echoing the liberal internationalist stance of Woodrow Wilson's Fourteen Points and elaborating on Roosevelt's Four Freedoms address of 6 January 1941, this eight-point declaration proclaimed the desire of the two leaders "to make known certain common principles…on which they base their hopes for a better future for the world." The statement pledged the two governments to forswear "territorial aggrandizement," to protect the sovereignty and legitimate aspirations toward self-government of all peoples, to work for global prosperity and a postwar system of widespread disarmament, and to support "a wider and permanent system of general security." The document reflected hard bargaining over such issues as trade liberalization and a postwar world organization. The Atlantic Charter's lasting significance is derived from its pioneering espousal of individual human rights. Five of the declaration's points dealt in some sense with such individual or group rights as self-determination, freedom from fear, freedom from want, and freedom of movement. The statement, although officially no more than a press release by the leader of a belligerent power and the head of a neutral nation, strongly implied the general applicability of the ideas being enunciated. The Atlantic Charter's principles were incorporated in their totality into the United Nations Declaration, signed by twenty-six nations in January 1942.

THEODORE A. WILSON

See also Churchill, Winston Leonard Spencer; Colonialism; Fourteen Points; Human Rights; Roosevelt, Franklin Delano; United Nations; World War II

FURTHER READING

Brinkley, Douglas, and David Facey-Crowther, eds. *The Atlantic Charter*. New York, 1994.
Louis, William Roger. *Imperialism at Bay 1941–1945: The United States and the Decolonization of the British Empire*. New York, 1977.
Wilson, Theodore A. *The First Summit: Roosevelt and Churchill at Placentia Bay*, rev. ed. Lawrence, Kans., 1991.

ATOMIC BOMB

See Hiroshima and Nagasaki Bombings of 1945; Nuclear Weapons and Strategy

ATOMIC ENERGY COMMISSION

An agency established by the Atomic Energy Act of 1946 to provide for the civilian control of both atomic weapons and potential civilian uses of atomic power. The Atomic Energy Commission (AEC) consisted of a five members, all civilians appointed by the president. Its first chairman was David E. Lilienthal, the former head of the Tennessee Valley Authority. The AEC oversaw the activities of four operating units covering all areas of U.S. atomic energy policy for both military and civilian purposes and assumed control of the atomic weapons research and development activities formerly under War Department supervision as part of the Manhattan Project, which developed the first atomic bombs. As in the Manhattan Project, security in the AEC was extremely tight, and restrictions were placed on the ability of the agency to cooperate with foreign governments or to allow government patents to be used by private organizations. Given these restrictions, the AEC exercised a virtual monopoly on nuclear technology in the United States for much of the commission's history and owned many of the facilities that produced components using technologies developed under government auspices. The AEC's supervision of all phases of U.S. nuclear weapons production, testing, and stockpiling extended even to the loading of the bombs onto specially modified aircraft in the early days of the commission's existence. In 1975 the AEC was dissolved and its functions divided between the Nuclear Regulatory Commission and the Energy Research and Development Administration (ERDA). Two years later the ERDA was absorbed by the newly created Department of Energy. The secrecy surrounding the early days of the AEC also allowed it to fund and perform experiments with radioactive material on unwitting Americans without provoking a public outcry; these controversial experiments were not officially revealed until the early 1990s.

BENJAMIN FORDHAM

See also Atoms for Peace; Manhattan Project

FURTHER READING

Anders, Roger M. *Forging the Atomic Shield: Excerpts from the Diary of Gordon E. Dean.* Chapel Hill, N.C., 1987.

Hewlett, Richard G. *Atoms for Peace and War, 1953–1961: Eisenhower and the Atomic Energy Commission.* Berkeley, Calif., 1989.

————, and Francis Duncan. *Atomic Shield: A History of the United States Atomic Energy Commission.* University Park, Pa., 1969.

Lilienthal, David E. *The Journals of David E. Lilienthal,* vol. 2, *The Atomic Energy Years, 1945–1950.* New York, 1964.

Mazuzan, George T., and J. Samuel Walker. *Controlling the Atom: The Beginnings of Nuclear Regulation 1946–1962.* Berkeley, Calif., 1985.

Walker, J. Samuel. *Containing the Atom: Nuclear Regulation in a Changing Environment, 1963–1971.* Berkeley, Calif., 1992.

ATOMS FOR PEACE

A phrase from President Dwight D. Eisenhower's 8 December 1953 speech to the United Nations General Assembly. It usually refers to the program proposed by Eisenhower in that speech to establish the International Atomic Energy Agency (IAEA), which would be charged with overseeing a stockpile of fissionable materials for peaceful use. This stockpile was to be established through donations of atomic material from all the countries capable of producing such material. Although progress toward establishing the stockpile was slow, a treaty establishing the IAEA was signed in 1956. In 1954 the United States also allocated a small amount of uranium-235 for eventual use by the international organization. At a time when the nuclear arms race was accelerating and the doctrine of massive retaliation was damaging the image of the United States, the Atoms for Peace idea was designed to put the United States in a humanitarian light. The Atoms for Peace initiative, and the early history of the IAEA, were hampered by Cold War tensions between the United States and the Soviet Union. The United States first agreed to select a director-general for the new organization from a neutral country but then insisted that an American be named to fill the position. The Soviets responded by obstructing the new director-general's efforts through the IAEA board of governors, whose chairman they controlled. The program was also hampered by a general lack of public support in the United States for transferring control of nuclear technology to an international body. The IAEA sponsored a series of international conferences on the peaceful uses of nuclear technology but failed to accomplish the more ambitious goals originally set forth by Eisenhower. The organization survived, however, and acquired a greater international role after the signing of the 1968 Nuclear Nonproliferation Treaty, which assigned the IAEA responsibility for inspecting the nuclear power facilities of signatory countries to ensure that none of the nuclear material was being removed for military use.

BENJAMIN FORDHAM

See also Atomic Energy Commission; International Atomic Energy Agency

FURTHER READING

Cantelon, Philip L., Richard G. Hewlett, and Robert C. Williams, eds. *The American Atom: A Documentary History of Nuclear Policies from the Discovery of Fission to the Present.* Philadelphia, 1984.

Hewlett, Richard G., and Jack M. Holl. *Atoms for Peace and War, 1953–1961: Eisenhower and the Atomic Energy Commission.* Berkeley, Calif., 1989.

ATTLEE, CLEMENT RICHARD, 1st Earl

(*b.* 3 January 1883; *d.* 8 October 1967)

Prime minister of Great Britain (1945–1951). Elected to parliament by London's working classes in 1922, Attlee became leader of the Labour party in 1935, a position he held for twenty years. After serving as deputy prime minister in Winston S. Churchill's coalition government during World War II, Attlee and the Labour party defeated Churchill's Conservatives in the July 1945 general election, an electoral outcome Americans found inexplicable. As prime minister he presided over the creation of the welfare state in Great Britain and staunchly supported U.S. Cold War policies, including the Truman Doctrine, the Marshall Plan, the North Atlantic Treaty Organization, and participation in the Korean War. In December 1950, however, he cautioned President Harry S. Truman against the use of atomic weapons in Korea. Called on to lead his country at a time when Great Britain's resources no longer matched its commitments or aspirations, Attlee oversaw the British withdrawal from India, Burma, Ceylon, and Palestine, early steps in the dismantling of the old British empire. In October 1951 the British electorate, tired of austerity at home and a stalemated war in Korea, voted the Attlee government out of power and turned once more to Churchill and the Conservatives.

ROBERT M. HATHAWAY

See also Great Britain

FURTHER READING

Attlee, Clement. *As It Happened*. New York, 1954.
———, and Francis Williams. *Twilight of Empire*. New York, 1962.
Morgan, Kenneth O. *Labour in Power, 1945–1951*. Oxford, 1984.

AUSTIN, WARREN ROBINSON

(*b.* 12 November 1877; *d.* 25 December 1962),

Senator from Vermont and head of the U.S. mission to the United Nations (1947–1953) with the rank of ambassador. Born in Highgate Center, Vermont, Austin graduated from the University of Vermont in 1899. He was admitted to the bar in 1902, became active in the Republican party, and held various public offices in Vermont. He was elected to the U.S. Senate in a special election in March 1931 and held that office for fifteen years. An anti–New Deal Republican, Austin stood out as an internationalist in the Senate. He had a moralistic belief in a worldwide mission for the United States, based on his faith in the beneficent effects of democracy and capitalism. During World War II Austin was an early advocate of planning for a postwar international organization and was a charter member of the congressional foreign policy advisory group that the State Department established in 1942. Although his internationalism brought him into conflict with leading Senate Republicans, he worked for bipartisan support of an international organization as a member of the Senate Foreign Relations Committee. In 1947 President Harry S. Truman, in a bipartisan gesture,

appointed Austin to serve as ambassador to the UN. He had lofty ambitions for the UN as a peacekeeping body, ambitions that the Truman administration did not fully share and that he was powerless to realize. During the early years of the Cold War he was often placed in the uncomfortable position of explaining how the nationalistic policies of the Truman administration, which he played almost no part in formulating, served the UN's idealistic goals. His experiences dealing with communist nations during the Korean War undermined Austin's belief in the possibility of cooperation with the Soviet Union and its allies but did not shake his faith in the peacekeeping capabilities of the UN.

ROBERT C. HILDEBRAND

See also United Nations

FURTHER READING

Austin, Warren Robinson. Papers. University of Vermont.
George T. Mazuzan. *Warren R. Austin at the UN, 1946–1950*. Kent, Ohio, 1977.

AUSTRALIA

Island continent, which along with the island state of Tasmania comprises the Commonwealth of Australia. It is located in Southwestern Oceania between Indonesia and New Zealand. U.S. relations with Australia have been exceptionally close and friendly. Defense alliances, especially during World War II, similarities in culture and historical background, and shared democratic values link the two nations across the entire spectrum of international relations. Traditional friendship has been reinforced by the wide range of common interests and similar views on most major international questions. Before World War II, Australia, as part of the British Commonwealth, relied mainly on Great Britain for support. In return, the Australians supplied combat divisions to British forces in World War I and, proportionately, lost more men than Great Britain in that conflict; the 330,000 Australian troops that served overseas suffered 226,000 casualties, including almost 60,000 killed. During World War II, Australian airmen took part in the defense of Great Britain and the attack on German-occupied Europe. Australian divisions participated in the successful Allied defense against the German advance on Egypt and were withdrawn from the Middle East only when Australia's own national security was put in jeopardy in 1942 by the collapse of British imperial defenses in the face of Japan's quick drive through Southeast Asia. Unable to rely on Great Britain for defense aid, the Australian government turned to the United States. General Douglas MacArthur's retreat to Australia from the Philippines and combined U.S.-Australian efforts to drive the Japanese from New Guinea and the Pacific established a new strategic partnership. Throughout the war the Australian government continued to work closely with Great Britain but came to depend more heavily on the United States.

In the postwar period Australians looked increasingly to the United States as their most important shield in the struggle to contain first Chinese, then Soviet communist, expansionism in the region. U.S. assurances of support were vital to Australia's forward defense in Southeast Asia, an area where it felt directly or potentially threatened. From 1951 on these assurances were backed by the vibrant U.S.-Australian relationship in the tripartite ANZUS (Australia, New Zealand, United States) Treaty of 1951. Australia supported with troops the U.S.-led military actions in Korea and Vietnam and backed the adjustment in U.S. strategic deployment in Asia and the Pacific under the terms of President Richard M. Nixon's 1969 Guam Doctrine, also known as the Nixon Doctrine. Australia was quicker, however, than the United States in adjusting its policy toward China, recognizing the People's Republic of China before Nixon visited Beijing in 1972. It supported the Paris Peace Accord of January 1973, which signaled the end of the U.S. combat leadership in Vietnam. In the 1980s a series of issues prompted the United States and Australia to devote increased diplomatic, military, and other attention to bilateral relations and to developments in nearby areas of Oceania.

Australia was particularly important to the U.S. ability to maintain secure commercial and military access through the south and central Pacific to Southeast Asia, the Indian Ocean, and the Persian Gulf. In the 1980s this undisturbed access was called into question by uncertainty over continuing U.S. ability to maintain air and naval bases in the Philippines; growing regional opposition to U.S. policy regarding transit of nuclear weapons–capable ships and aircraft, which eventually led to the suspension of the U.S. military alliance with New Zealand; and increased Soviet and Libyan efforts to gain influence among small Pacific island states. Other sources of friction included regional opposition to U.S. farm, trade, and fishing policies and the perception in the region of U.S. association with French nuclear weapons testing and colonial administration in New Caledonia. Other important U.S. interests involved in relations with Australia included the key role played by joint U.S.-Australian military facilities in monitoring Soviet nuclear ballistic missiles.

Both the United States and Australia, however, saw the farm trade policy as their most divisive issue. According to official estimates, about 40 percent of Australian foreign exchange earnings came from agricultural exports. The farm issue became a major source of friction in the 1980s, when the United States repeatedly took steps authorized by the Export Enhancement Program to promote sales of U.S. wheat and other farm products to the Soviet Union, China, and other markets. Australian officials repeatedly and vehemently criticized these moves on the grounds that they endangered Australian export markets in these countries, lowered world prices for agricultural commodities, and thus had a major negative effect on Australian farmers and foreign exchange earnings. Australians found the U.S. practice particularly galling because Australia did not use subsidies to promote agricultural exports. Government officials claimed that these U.S. actions reduced popular support for the alliance relationship.

As for defense issues, the future of the ANZUS alliance without New Zealand became a concern in the mid-1980s in bilateral U.S.-Australian relations, although both countries were generally comfortable with their respective, and differing, policies toward New Zealand. In 1984 New Zealand elected a Labor party government that strongly opposed the presence of U.S. or other nations' nuclear weapons in the Pacific. It initiated a policy, confirmed by parliament in 1987, of denying access to New Zealand's ports for warships that were nuclear powered or carried nuclear weapons. Because 40 percent of the U.S. warships were nuclear powered and it remained U.S. policy neither to confirm nor deny the presence of nuclear weapons aboard navy ships, the new policy effectively halted visits to New Zealand by U.S. naval vessels. The United States responded by cutting back on military, intelligence, and other bilateral exchanges. As a result, the U.S.–New Zealand leg of the thirty-five-year-old ANZUS alliance, an important strategic framework for allied interests in the South Pacific, became moribund, although bilateral defense ties among the three countries continued. Australia, for its part, supported the U.S. decision to halt its alliance relations with New Zealand, but it was not prepared to provide logistics, training, and intelligence support to New Zealand to fill the gap caused by the loss of those ties.

In the 1980s Australia and the United States placed somewhat different emphases on perceived threats to stability in the South Pacific and appropriate responses to them. The Australian government joined the United States in criticizing Soviet and Libyan efforts to gain a foothold among the poor South Pacific island states. Australian officials, however, also criticized U.S. tuna fishing practices in the region, the small size of the U.S. foreign aid effort there, and the U.S. refusal to sign protocols of the South Pacific Nuclear Free Zone (SPNFZ) treaty or to criticize French nuclear testing and colonial administration in the South Pacific.

The end of the Cold War, the collapse of the Soviet Union, and other developments in the 1990s reduced many U.S. security concerns that had been major elements in relations with, and overall policy attention to,

Australia and other countries of the region. On one hand, the United States instituted a nuclear-testing moratorium that had the effect of encouraging France to suspend nuclear tests in the region; modified past policy and resumed high-level official contacts (although not alliance relationships) with New Zealand; and worked closely with Australia in promoting region-wide groupings for economic and other cooperation. On the other hand, the United States cut back its diplomatic posts in the region, reduced foreign aid there, and continued to take an assertive position on farm and other trade disputes with Australia.

ROBERT G. SUTTER

See also Anzus Treaty; Korean War; New Zealand; Nixon Doctrine; Pacific Island Nations and U.S. Territories; Vietnam War

FURTHER READING

Albinski, Henry S. *ANZUS, The United States and Pacific Security.* New York, 1987.
American University. *Area Handbook for Australia.* Washington, D.C., 1974.
Australian Consulate-General New York. *Australia and the U.S.A.: Partners in the Asia-Pacific Future.* New York, 1992.
Embassy of Australia. *Australia and the United States of America: Issues for the Clinton Administration.* Washington, 1993.

AUSTRIA

A Central European republic bordered by Germany, Slovenia, Italy, Switzerland, the Czech Republic, Slovakia, and Hungary. Today, Austria represents but one small segment of the predominantly German-speaking lands of the former Austro-Hungarian (Habsburg) empire, which reached its height between the end of the seventeenth century and the outbreak of World War I. More than half of the population lives in the lowlands north of the Carnic Alps. There is a Slovene minority in Carinthia and, in Burgenland, minority groups of Croatian, Hungarian, and Roma (Gypsy) descent. The large majority of the population (85 percent) is Roman Catholic.

Official U.S. relations with Austria proper began only after the defeat of the Central Powers in late 1918, the subsequent proclamation of the Austrian Republic (along with the abolition of the monarchy), and the signing of the Treaty of Saint-Germain (1919), which fixed Austria's new borders while forbidding (as did the Versailles Treaty with Germany) any sort of German-Austrian union (or *Anschluss*). Unresolved at the time were certain Italian territorial claims to the South Tyrol. In any event, U.S.-Austrian contacts during the early interwar years were unremarkable; but beginning with Hitler's rise to power, Washington watched with growing concern the Nazi's

expansionist aims, leading to Germany's annexation of Austria in March 1938—an early harbinger of the coming of World War II in Europe.

Economic hardship and constant political tension made the interwar period quite unstable within Austria itself. In 1934 Chancellor Engelbert Dollfuss was murdered in a coup attempt engineered by Austrian Nazis. In 1938, following the Anschluss, the official reactions of the European powers and the United States were quite subdued—in line with the general policy of appeasement toward Hitler being pursued at the time by both Great Britain and France; indeed only Mexico formally protested against the occupation. Ironically, during World War II, the United States, Great Britain, and the Soviet Union, through the 1943 Moscow Declaration, chose to recognize Austria as the first country to fall victim to Nazi aggression—disregarding, in the process, the enthusiasm with which most Austrians had welcomed the Nazi occupation and annexation—and called for its reestablishment as an independent state after the defeat of the Axis.

True enough, once Austria was subjected to political and economic integration in the Third Reich and later to forced participation in the German war effort, some of the original enthusiasm for the Anschluss vanished among the Austrian population. Yet it was only in late 1944 that the Provisional Austrian National Committee was formed and its military units began effective resistance activities. At the end of World War II, Austria was in a state of economic chaos, with its population literally starving. The Allies occupied Austria in the spring of 1945, dividing it into four zones of occupation, although under a single coalition government. The Socialist Karl Renner won Soviet and U.S. approval, and elections to the national parliament were held in November 1945. The Socialists and Christian Democrats won the vast majority of the seats, while the Soviet-supported Austrian communists won almost no popular support. The successor coalition government under Chancellor Leopold Figl signed a bilateral agreement with the United States, and joined the Marshall Plan, which helped stabilize the Austrian food supply and rebuild former heavy industries. While negotiations were also begun with the Allied forces over putting an end to the occupation regime, initial hopes for the prompt signing of a peace treaty were shattered by the onset of the Cold War, and the corresponding increase in Austria's geopolitical salience.

For years the leaders of both major Austrian political parties had advocated a policy of neutrality and non-alliance with either the Western or Eastern military blocs, if the occupation were to end; but the Soviets showed little interest. Then, following Stalin's death in 1953, the Soviet attitude vis-à-vis Austria suddenly became more flexible. This reflected both the Kremlin's interest in relaxing tensions in Central Europe and a gambit apparently aimed at trying to dissuade West Germany from joining NATO, and then—when that failed—from Bonn's planned rearmament program. As signed in May 1955, the Austrian State Treaty declared Austria a neutral country, bringing about the disengagement of the United States and the Soviet Union in one of the more effective early examples of Cold War conflict management. The Austrian parliament then enacted a constitutional law establishing the permanent neutrality of Austria. In December of the same year Austria became a member of the United Nations (UN).

Despite its neutrality, Austria always saw its economic and political future tied to the Free World. It was a founding member of EFTA (European Free Trade Association) in 1959, and in the 1970s Austria signed free trade agreements with the European Community (EC), abolishing industrial tariffs. In addition to its trade orientation, in the 1960s the Austrian Army introduced NATO-compatible military standards. Increasingly, Austria pursued a policy of active neutrality and sought to play an intermediary role in the East-West conflict, as it did in hosting in Vienna the Strategic Arms Limitation Talks (SALT). Since 1979 Vienna has been one of the permanent seats of the UN.

Austria formed its first Socialist government in 1971 under Chancellor Bruno Kreisky. Kreisky, who was Jewish and had been forced into exile during the Nazi-German occupation, was highly critical of Israel's occupation policies in the Palestinian territories, and recognized, de facto, the Palestine Liberation Organization (PLO). These positions strained Austria's relations with the United States.

Another major thorn in U.S.-Austrian relations involved Kurt Waldheim. Waldheim had served as UN Secretary-General in the 1970s, and was then elected president of Austria in 1986. While this was largely an honorary position, it took on much greater significance when records surfaced of Waldheim's apparent involvement in Nazi war crimes while serving in the Balkans during World War II. Waldheim denied the charges and remained in office; but the Reagan administration refused to grant him a visa to visit the United States.

As the communist bloc began to break up in 1989, Austria played a crucial role in providing it with a bridge to the West. It was through Austria that the first groups of East Germans traveled on their route from Hungary to West Germany. Throughout the early 1990s Austria developed closer political and economic relations with all the former Soviet bloc countries. At the same time, it pushed for its own deeper integration into Western Europe, in particular by seeking full membership in the European Union (EU). Austria formally applied for EU membership in 1989, and after a period of delay—until

after the signing of the Maastricht Treaty and the completion of successful negotiations—the government got the popular support it needed in a 1994 referendum (66.6 percent voted in favor). Austrian membership in the EU commenced officially on 1 January 1995.

A month later, Austria joined NATO's Partnership for Peace program. The earlier constraints of neutrality no longer pertained with the Cold War now over, all the more so with the Partnership for Peace gradually including former Warsaw Pact countries as well.

MARTIN ROSSMANN

See also Cold War; European Union; Hungary; World War I; World War II

FURTHER READING

Bader, William B. *Austria Between East and West.* Stanford, Calif., 1966.
Kohl, Andreas, ed. *Österreichisches Jahrbuch füer Politik.* Annual. Wein, Germany.
Larson, Deborah Welch. "Crisis Prevention and the Austrian State Treaty." *International Organization* 41 (Winter 1987):27–60.
Sully, Mellany A. *Contemporary History of Austria.* London, 1990.
U.S. Department of State. *Austria: Economic Policy and Trade Practices.* U.S. Department of Commerce, Bureau of Economic Analysis, 1994.

AUTOMOTIVE COMPANIES

Almost from its inception, the U.S. automobile industry was international in scope, with the Ford Motor Company opening a plant in Canada in 1904. During the early twentieth century, hundreds of small producers arose in the United States and Europe, but only with the Model T (1908) did motor vehicles become a major industry. The mass production methods pioneered by Henry Ford and the divisional management structure implemented by Alfred Sloan gave U.S. producers a large advantage by the 1920s. Ford lost no time in extending his reach into other markets, setting up wholly owned "greenfield" (built from scratch) operations throughout the world. In contrast, General Motors (GM) was founded through a series of mergers and acquisitions, and its preferred route of entry continued to be through the purchase of existing producers, such as Vauxhall in England (1928), Adam Opel in Germany (1929), and Holden Motors in Australia (1931). Meanwhile, Ford's plant at Dagenham in England (1928) was the largest automotive complex outside of the United States. Both firms had operations in various smaller markets, such as Argentina (Ford from 1916) and Japan (Ford from 1925, GM from 1927). They dominated virtually every market—in Japan they were the only producers, while in Germany Opel was the largest firm and Ford the second largest.

Direct investment was chosen largely because of the cost of transporting finished vehicles, and assembly plants were likewise scattered across the United States and Canada. After World War I, however, tariffs strengthened the incentive to establish local operations. (In Great Britain the 1915 McKenna Tariffs raised the rate on autos from zero to 33.33 percent.) The major foreign ventures of both GM and Ford rapidly localized their operations, purchasing parts locally and even designing and engineering their own cars, rather than merely assembling kits imported from the United States. In turn it was these overseas plants that became the production base for exports to nearby markets. They sought to be good citizens—GM's subsidiaries maintained their previous names, as with Opel in Germany, which even turned to the Department of State in 1933 for help in gaining certification as a "German" firm.

Access to Growing Markets: 1945–1970

Even before World War II, the auto industry's prominence in the public and political eye made it a symbol of industrial success, and led to protection of the home market in an effort to foster a domestic industry. The manufacture of a car, however, calls upon the full range of metalworking and materials industries, and most countries lacked this foundation. Economies of scale are also significant, making a large market essential. Efforts at promotion thus bred inefficiency, leading inevitably to trade conflicts, as seen in examples from Canada, Japan, and Mexico.

The Big Three auto manufacturers—GM, Ford, and Chrysler Corporation—all had operations in Canada, turning out multiple models. Before World War II, Canadian vehicles were sold throughout the British Empire and exports surpassed those of the United States. After 1945, however, this export market disappeared, and despite wages 30 percent below U.S. levels and a 17.5 percent tariff, the small Canadian industry found it hard to compete against imports from the United States. In the face of a large trade deficit, the 1962 Bladen Report thus urged renewed attention to exports to obtain scale economies. The key policy was a duty remission scheme, in which exports would earn credits that could be used to reduce import duties. This was in effect an export subsidy, and a U.S. firm filed a countervailing duty suit in 1964, threatening to set off a full-fledged trade war. The frantic negotiations that followed ended with the U.S.-Canada Automotive Parts Trade Agreement of 1965 (the Auto Pact), which provided for the removal of all trade barriers between the United States and Canada for qualified firms. Canada, however, feared that the Big Three would simply close their Canadian operations, and so imposed temporary safeguards. Thus, to qualify as importers under the Auto Pact, Canada required that firms match total sales in Canada with total production and maintain an average domestic content of 60 percent.

Production in Canada increased as the Big Three cut the number of product lines and thereby achieved efficient volumes, which helped ease overall Canadian fears of domination by the United States. Thus, the Auto Pact proved a crucial first step toward the Free Trade Agreement (FTA) of 1988 and the North American Free Trade Agreement (NAFTA) of 1992, but neither the Auto Pact nor the FTA brought an end to trade disputes, because the so-called temporary safeguards were never dropped. In 1971 a U.S. withdrawal was averted at the last minute (the press release had already been printed), and in 1978 Canada reinstituted duty remission, under which exports to the United States could potentially facilitate imports from Japan. The rules were quickly amended, and the program ended under the FTA, but it was not until NAFTA that all the "temporary" Canadian safeguards were finally phased out.

The Mexican case is typical of Latin America and Asia, where the auto industry served first as a target of import substitution policies, and then, with the success of Japan and Korea, of export promotion measures. Initially, high tariffs on vehicles coupled with low tariffs on parts encouraged "screwdriver" production from imported kits. The Big Three established such operations by 1937, while Volkswagen of Germany entered in 1954 and Nissan of Japan in 1960. There were also thirteen smaller European operations building at most a few hundred vehicles a year. Auto parts soon accounted for 10 percent of total imports.

In 1962 Mexico thus sought to force these firms to localize production, requiring them to submit plans to attain 60 percent "local content" via a combination of domestic parts purchases and exports and to manufacture engines and power trains locally. To the government's surprise, eighteen firms submitted plans, and the U.S. ambassador was soon personally lobbying the government on behalf of the Big Three. (Nissan used similar leverage, because Mexico's single largest export was cotton to Japan.) While most of these firms eventually left the market, the requirement to use expensive local parts made the industry even less efficient, setting off a cycle under which higher auto trade deficits led to yet more stringent localization policies, as in 1969 and again in 1972. The Mexican government tried, with moderate success, to play firms off against each other. Thus, Nissan decided to use Mexico as its base for exports to Latin America, while Chrysler built an engine plant to make engines for export to the United States. The response of others—the United Auto Workers (UAW), Ford, and GM—was to lobby. In 1977, for example, Henry Ford II met with President Lopez Portillo of Mexico and personally contacted U.S. Ambassador Patrick Lucey and Secretary of State Cyrus Vance. In this case, however, GM decided that it could live with the new policy and broke ranks; others then fell in line. The underlying tensions remained, however, and despite piecemeal localization, automotive imports still accounted for half of Mexico's trade deficit at the time of the 1981 balance of payments crisis. While the resulting 1982 decree finally had enough teeth to force full localization, that did not leave Mexico with an efficient industry.

Japan resembled France and Italy, in that World War II left all three countries with indigenous firms that their governments tried to protect from foreign competition. In Japan imports and "screwdriver" assembly flourished briefly under the U.S. Occupation, but after the mid-1950s foreign exchange controls were used to eliminate imports and licensed production and to block foreign direct investment. On paper the market was gradually liberalized in the 1960s, but differential taxes and other non-tariff barriers remained. In the late 1960s, however, the Big Three began exploring joint ventures, both for access to the growing domestic market and as a potential source of captive imports of small cars to counter the success of the Volkswagen Beetle in the United States. Despite the General Agreement on Tariffs and Trade (GATT) and Organization for Economic Cooperation and Development (OECD) obligations to liberalize inward investment, the Japanese government resisted, leading in the fall of 1967 to the first major U.S.-Japan confrontation over autos. The United States, however, proved reluctant to pressure a loyal Cold War ally, and autos also took a backseat to wrangles over textiles and televisions. While the Japanese government caved in eventually, it was only because domestic firms opposed government policy. Mitsubishi broke ranks in 1969, announcing an agreement to sell 35 percent of its shares to Chrysler. The government, whose bluff had been called, proved unable to enforce the investment prohibition, but by that time Chrysler faced a financial crisis, and ultimately bought only a 15 percent share. GM likewise became a minority shareholder in Isuzu and Suzuki, and Ford later purchased 25 percent of Mazda (then Toyo Kogyo).

As these examples illustrate, U.S. firms invested in local production wherever they could. Trade appeared not to be an option; while the GATT Kennedy and Tokyo Rounds lowered automotive tariffs in many markets, other barriers remained high. Even within Europe trade faced many restrictions, and the Big Three never broke into the Italian and French markets, where a sense of xenophobia prevailed. During this era the Big Three did on occasion seek to use U.S. government influence overseas, but within the United States the auto industry remained an advocate of free trade.

Import Competition: 1970–1990

Under the Big Three's tight oligopoly, management faced few challenges and rapidly became complacent. By 1957 the United States was a net importer of passenger vehicles. European subcompacts captured 9 percent of the domestic market in 1959, but their share fell when the Big Three launched small cars of their own. They were unsuccessful in exporting these cars, while Ford and GM had also lost their dominant shares of the principal European markets.

Despite the Big Three's high costs and poor products, foreign firms were slow to enter the U.S. market. A national dealership network required massive investment, while Americans favored cars much larger than those driven by Japanese or Europeans. Even though the major European and Japanese firms established a beachhead in the 1960s, sales were never more than 10 percent of the market, and typically much less. The oil crises of 1973 and 1979 changed this, shifting demand toward subcompacts. The Big Three made none in North America and imports soon flooded the market. The Big Three explored filing an antidumping suit in 1975, but oil prices fell in 1976 and the effort was dropped. With the second oil crisis imports from Japan and Europe rose again, from 2 million units in 1978 to 2.5 million units in 1980, but this coincided with the onset of a sharp recession, and the import share thus jumped from 18 percent to 27 percent. Chrysler teetered near bankruptcy, Ford was kept afloat only because of high profits in Europe, and layoffs were severe at GM. Limiting imports offered a quick fix. President Jimmy Carter refused to call for higher tariffs or quotas but did offer trade adjustment assistance as a sop to the unions. Ford and the UAW then filed a Section 201 "escape clause" suit, but the International Trade Commission blamed the recession instead of imports in its November 1980 negative finding. Carter left office rejecting all calls for protection.

In 1981 legislation to restrict imports was immediately introduced into Congress, and by April, Republican Senator John Danforth of Missouri claimed to have the votes for passage. The administration of President Ronald Reagan acted quickly, and by May 1981 a three-year voluntary export restraint agreement (VER) with Japan was hammered out. Under the VER the Japanese initially agreed to limit exports to 1.68 million units, or about 20 percent of the market, with the Ministry of International Trade and Industry (MITI) allocating shares on a firm-by-firm basis. An era of U.S. protectionism in the industry had begun. As hoped, the VER led to an immediate hike in car prices, both imported and domestic, and by 1983 the Big Three returned to profitability. The Japanese, however, reaped tremendous profits from the start. The United States in effect had asked them to form a cartel, and they gladly obliged. The Japanese government may have viewed the VER as a crisis, but for the Japanese car companies the VER meant some $4 billion a year in excess profits during 1981–1985, from what amounted to a tax on American consumers of $1,500 per new car. These profits in turn helped the Japanese to finance the development of upscale vehicles. The VER thus enabled them to maintain their presence in the market when Americans began moving to the purchase of larger cars. As it turned out, imports fell continuously from 1986 due to the strengthening yen, rising "transplant" production in the United States and stronger competition from the Big Three. With periodic modifications, the VERs continued for a dozen years, until April 1994. Even though for most of the period the quotas were not binding, the Japanese and U.S. governments apparently judged them to be useful in forestalling further automotive trade friction.

The UAW voiced hopes that the Japanese would invest in U.S. facilities, providing jobs; the Big Three were convinced they had little to fear, expecting that (as at Volkswagen's short-lived Pennsylvania plant) foreign firms would lose their cost and quality advantages once forced to produce with American workers. But Honda, which opened the initial Japanese transplant operation in Ohio in 1982, achieved high quality and productivity from the start. By 1995 eight Japanese and two German carmakers had built 2.9 million units in new assembly capacity, over 20 percent of normal U.S. sales. The VERs thus stimulated new entry, spread across nine different states and Ontario, and generally avoided the UAW's home turf. These new, more efficient plants ended the Big Three's comfortable oligopoly, displacing production at older facilities; UAW rolls fell by a half million members. In the end, neither consumers, producers, nor labor benefited from the VER.

The transplants planned their factories in the mid-1980s, when the dollar was strong. But the dollar plummeted in 1985, going from 240 yen per dollar to under 80 yen per dollar by 1995. Imports of finished vehicles fell, but the strong yen also hit the transplants, because virtually all parts and components were imported. The wave of assembly transplants was thus followed by a tide of suppliers. Europeans joined in, accounting for about 150 ventures, while Japanese firms added nearly 300 plants. Again, much of this production displaced existing, less efficient producers. Politically, this resulted in pressure to change the terms on which direct investment took place. In auto parts, this began with the 1986–1987 market-oriented sector-specific (MOSS) talks with Japan. The real aim was to exert political pressure to get the Japanese transplants to purchase parts from U.S. firms rather than import them from Japan. Formally, however, the talks sought to open up the Japanese domestic market, focusing on regulations and certification that effectively excluded imported original equipment manufacturer (OEM) and replacement parts. One precedent- setting element was that private Japanese

business practices were an explicit negotiating topic. Japanese firms did officially open up their traditional *keiretsu* supplier systems, began regular seminars for U.S. parts firms, and started submitting data on purchases from American firms, but "American" was defined in terms of location rather than ownership, and "purchases" included not only exports to Japan but also procurement for assembly plants in the United States. So while the Japanese could demonstrate an increase in their purchases, most of this was from transplant Japanese parts firms in the United States for cars assembled in the United States. While this may have been good for local economies in the United States, it brought scant benefits to traditional U.S. suppliers.

Nevertheless, increasing Japanese parts purchases continued as a formal element of U.S. policy. This was most visible at the January 1992 meeting in Tokyo between George Bush and Kiichi Miyazawa, where along with agreeing to sell a token number of cars for the Big Three—how was not made clear—the Japanese auto firms agreed to increase their U.S. parts purchases from the existing level of $9 billion annually in fiscal year (FY) 1990 to $19 billion in FY 1994. The Japanese government lacked leverage, however, and the firm-by-firm goals were merely a public version of internal projections. The increase, then, reflected objective economic factors: the doubling of the yen after 1985 and the rapid increase in volume of cars built at the automakers' U.S. plants.

Auto parts continue to be at the center of bilateral disputes. They were one of the sectors in the July 1993 U.S.-Japan Framework Agreement. Formally the United States pursued three areas: dealer access, parts purchases, and the replacement parts market. In addition, the United States insisted on negotiating "objective criteria" to gauge progress, and changes in antitrust and domestic regulatory policy. After months of stalemate, the dispute boiled over in May 1995, when the United States announced it would place 100% tariffs on 13 imported Japanese luxury cars. Both the United States and Japan filed cases with the yet-untested World Trade Organization. An agreement was reached just before the sanctions were to take effect. But the bottom line was that the United States accepted what effectively was a compilation of business plans, many of which had been made public before the dispute escalated. One element was greater dealer access within Japan, but Chrysler had just announced an investment of $100 million, long in the works, to obtain control of 103 dealers. Similarly, the agreement promised greater parts purchases by Japanese firms, but under the impact of the strong yen both local content and output at the United States "transplant" factories—and hence parts purchases—were already increasing. Reforms were also promised in the Japanese domestic replacement market. It is not clear that the

United States obtained any "objective criteria," while the Japanese government itself issued no numbers. Helping push the United States to drop its threat of sanctions was a vigorous protest by the EU, and general worries about the impact on the WTO. In addition, the Japanese "transplants" and dealers mobilized employees in their operations, accompanied by a vigorous advertising campaign in California, utilizing for the first time the leverage gained by their sizable direct investments in the U.S. auto industry. In these aspects the agreement was novel, as was the visibility of the dispute to the general public, but the agreement itself will have little impact.

In contrast, NAFTA will have a major impact on the domestic industry, by integrating Mexico into the North American automotive market, paralleling the integration of the U.S. and Canadian industries achieved under the 1965 Auto Pact. Subject to phase-in provisions over ten years, all intraregional tariffs will be eliminated, as will ownership, export, and national content restrictions (including the "temporary" restrictions Canada imposed in 1965, which were largely untouched under the 1988 FTA). In the short run, this will not lead to major new investment in Mexico. At 2.5 to 3.1 percent, U.S. tariffs on parts are not a major barrier to imports, and many labor-intensive items are already made in Mexico. Assembly operations are also unlikely to shift to Mexico except for Chrysler's. Potential foreign entrants would need to achieve 62.5 percent domestic content rather than the 50 percent level mandated by the U.S.-Canada FTA. NAFTA will, however, lead to a rationalization of production in Mexico, given the current inefficiency of the local industry, as occurred in Canada after the 1965 Auto Pact. This, in turn, will lead to an initial surge of imports, one element in the 1994–1995 Mexican peso crisis, followed by a gradual growth in exports. There are also tariff and regulatory issues. The 1962–1964 "chicken war" with Europe led to a "temporary" 25 percent retaliatory tariff on light trucks, with Volkswagen as the intended target. They remained in place more than thirty years later. Unlike cars, which face a 2.5 percent tariff, pickup truck imports have remained minimal, even though they comprise the most profitable segment of the North American industry. Attempts to circumvent the tariff led to Customs Court suits over product classification of chassis and (in 1992–1994) over sports utility vehicles. The Big Three lobbied (as of 1995 unsuccessfully) to have minivans reclassified as light trucks and filed an antidumping suit against Japanese minivans in 1991. (While the Department of Commerce found them "guilty" of dumping, the International Trade Commission declined to impose sanctions, citing lack of damage to the domestic industry.)

Other U.S. policies also differentiate among foreign and domestic vehicles. The corporate average fuel economy (CAFE) regulations are calculated separately for domestic and imported vehicles. Ironically, CAFE regulations encouraged the Big Three to turn large cars into imports, whose low gas mileage could then be averaged and offset by the import of fuel-efficient small cars from Asia, as with the Ford Crown Victoria, which began in 1992 as a domestic car, became an import in 1993 with the inclusion of components from Mexico and England, and in 1995 again became a domestic vehicle. It also effectively discriminates against European producers: German firms pay the majority of penalties under CAFE and similarly pay 80 percent of the separate "gas guzzler" tax and the luxury tax on cars selling for more than $30,000. Safety and emissions standards have historically been stricter than those imposed in Europe and Japan. These all resemble policies that, when employed in Japan or Europe, have been characterized by the United States as unfair trade practices.

The most blatant protectionist actions, however, were the 1992 Labeling Act and the formation of the American Automobile Manufacturers Association (AAMA). For decades the Motor Vehicle Manufacturers Association (MVMA), whose members included Honda and Volkswagen, compiled sales and other data for the industry and coordinated lobbying efforts. This proved awkward for the Big Three as they strengthened their protectionist stance, and in 1992 the MVMA kicked out Honda and the others, moved its headquarters from Detroit to Washington, and changed its name to the AAMA. Its first success was the Motor Vehicle Labeling Act, requiring that domestic parts content be posted on all new cars, but under the act domestic content excludes value added by assembly in the United States, and a 70 percent "rollup" threshold must be exceeded for a part count as domestic. Furthermore, these criteria differ from those used by CAFE, and both differ from those used by NAFTA. These various content criteria are inevitably vague. There has already been one tiff with Canada, when U.S. Customs attempted to label Hondas assembled in Ontario as "foreign" and so subject to a 2.5 percent tariff.

In sum, during this era the United States engaged in protectionist behavior that proved very costly in the short run. These policies also changed the face of the industry, as the VER stimulated foreign entry, permanently ending the Big Three's oligopoly. Since 1980 total industry employment has changed little, but the geographic locus of the industry shifted, uprooting at least a half million lives. European-style protection, which permits investment in existing plants but discourages new plants, might have been preferable.

Export Competitiveness: 1990 and Beyond

The collapse of the Big Three's oligopoly brought an end to complacent management. Meanwhile, the weakening dollar rendered production costs in North America lower than in Japan and Europe. The market also shifted away from subcompacts toward pickup trucks and minivans, the Big Three's forte. The issues in the 1990s were access to foreign markets, through both investment and exports. Not all disputes over access were genuine; the Big Three pushed bilateral issues that were designed to fail, in the hope of generating political capital for use at home. Disputes have also diverted attention from domestic protection, illustrating the commercial policy maxim that a good offense is often the best defense. The Big Six—Toyota, Honda, and Nissan should now be counted as U.S. car companies—became more serious about selling abroad. In the mid-1990s Honda was exporting 100,000 units a year, about 20 percent of its output, while Chrysler began producing right-hand drive vehicles in North America in 1993, all destined for export. Through the acquisition of a dealership chain from the troubled Mazda, Ford gained a credible distribution channel in Japan for the first time since the 1930s; its sales started to increase at triple-digit rates. Exports of cars from the United States to non-NAFTA countries exploded, from $400 million in 1985 to $8.1 billion in 1993. Similarly, by 1994 parts exports were more than $1 billion a year to Japan and $2 billion to Europe, both more than double the 1989 level. These levels were still modest when compared to 1993 imports from outside of NAFTA of $34 billion in vehicles and $31 billion in parts, but to even suggest that exports of this magnitude were possible was considered ludicrous as recently as 1990. In light of this, it became important for the United States to push for access to emerging markets, such as Korea, China, and Southeast Asia. The United States signed an "Accord Accord" with France under which Hondas assembled in Ohio will be counted as American and thus will not be subject to France's auto VER with Japan. Formal barriers are not affected under the GATT Uruguay Round, which ended in 1994. Tariffs in the European Union were to remain at 9.1 percent and were far higher in many emerging markets. A host of tax and regulatory issues remained as the twenty-first century approached, while exclusionary business practices were prevalent in distribution and the repairs market in Europe and elsewhere, all of which remained contentious issues.

MICHAEL SMITKA

See also Canada; General Agreement on Tariffs and Trade; Japan; Most-Favored-Nation Principle; North American Free Trade Agreement; Organization for Economic Cooperation and Development; Tariffs

FURTHER READING

Bennett, Douglas C., and Kenneth E. Sharpe. *Transnational Corporations Versus the State: The Political Economy of the Mexican Auto Industry.* Princeton, N.J., 1985.
Bergsten, C. Fred, and Marcus Noland. *Reconcilable Differences? United States–Japan Economic Conflict.* Washington, D.C., 1993.
Conybeare, John A. C. *Trade Wars: The Theory and Practice of International Commercial Rivalry.* New York, 1987.
Crandall, Robert W. "The Effects of U.S. Trade Protection for Autos and Steel." *Brookings Papers on Economic Activity.* Washington, D.C., 1987.
Duncan, William Chandler. *U.S.–Japan Automobile Diplomacy: A Study in Economic Confrontation.* New York, 1973.
Nelson, Douglas R. "The Political Economy of U.S. Automobile Protection." In *The Political Economy of Trade Policy.* Edited by Anne O. Krueger. Chicago, 1996.
Samuels, Barbara C., II. *Managing Risk in Developing Countries: National Demands and Multinational Response.* Princeton, N.J., 1990.
Wilkins, Mira. *The Maturing of Multinational Enterprise: American Business Abroad from 1914 to 1970.* Cambridge, Mass., 1974.
Wonnacott, Paul. *The United States and Canada: The Quest for Free Trade. An Examination of Selected Issues.* Washington, D.C., 1987.

AVIATION

See Civil Aviation

AZERBAIJAN

Soviet successor state located in southwestern Asia between Armenia and Turkmenistan, bordering the Caspian Sea. When Azerbaijan emerged out of the USSR as an independent state in 1991, it was literally on the margins of the U.S. diplomatic global map. After the collapse of the Soviet Union, Washington had to draft a policy de novo with respect to Azerbaijan. Because of the sudden end of the Cold War, the administration of President George Bush was initially caught unprepared conceptually and institutionally to deal with this oil-rich new nation. The initial U.S. concern centered on which direction Azerbaijan would take in its search for national identity and security. Would the Turkic, secular side of its Muslim identity draw it closer to Turkey or would its Shi'ite Muslim side lead it toward Iran? Prior to the onset of Russian power in the early nineteenth century, Iran and Turkey had for centuries competed for control of the Transcaucasia region of which Azerbaijan is a part. As the Cold War receded, the United States took a greater interest in Azerbaijan because Washington feared the spread of radical Muslim fundamentalism. The United States would have had no concrete interest in Azerbaijan were it not for the large offshore oil deposits. Oil companies eager to obtain the rights to pump out the oil formed an combined international consortium of U.S. and West European corporations to strengthen their bids.

Although the U.S. government opened an embassy in Baku, between 1991 and 1993 it otherwise showed little direct interest in Azerbaijan and its volatile presidential politics. Because thousands of Armenian Americans aroused overt sympathy for Armenia in its undeclared war with Azerbaijan over Nagorno-Karabakh, an Armenian-populated enclave in eastern Azerbaijan, U.S. relations with Baku were strained. In late 1993, however, U.S. interest in Azerbaijan was heightened because of the lobbying of the AMOCO oil company, which made Congress and the White House aware of the strategic value of the offshore oil in the Caspian Sea in general and of that under Azerbaijani waters specifically. (As of 1995 Azerbaijan's offshore borders had not been internationally drawn or recognized.) Controversy with Russia arose because of Moscow's growing interest in diverting Caspian oil through its pipelines and, thereby, exporting it out of its own Black Sea ports rather than out of Turkish ports on the southern shore of the Black Sea. This tug-of-war between Russia and the United States became the major determinant of U.S. policy toward Azerbaijan in the 1990s. In the summer of 1994 an agreement was signed by the consortium and the government of Azerbaijan which included considerable sums upfront. In response, the Russian government declared that Caspian Sea oil could not be extracted without its participation, including transportation via Russian pipelines. Russia intended to bring the region and its natural resources within its sphere of influence.

In contrast to its policies toward Armenia, by the mid-1990s the United States had extended neither humanitarian aid to Azerbaijan, even though it had a severe refugee problem, nor any economic assistance to jump-start the process of privatization. Several privatization programs and land laws were still languishing in parliament in 1995. Instead of marketing its oil for hard currency, Azerbaijan was using it for barter trade with other former Soviet republics in the Commonwealth of Independent States, particularly with Uzbekistan. Another problem was the basic instability of the government, which, in signing the lucrative deal with the international oil consortium, made itself vulnerable to coups by domestic clan rivals, which, it was suspected, were engineered by Russia.

HENRY R. HUTTENBACH

See also Armenia; Oil and Foreign Policy; Oil and World Politics; Russia and the Soviet Union; Turkey

FURTHER READING
Altstadt, Audrey L. *The Azerbaijani Turks*, Stanford, Calif., 1992.
Bremmer, Ian, and Ray Taras, eds. *Nations and Politics in the Soviet Successor States.* New York, 1993.
Goldenberg, Suzanne. *Pride of Small Nations: The Caucasus and Post-Soviet Disorder.* London, 1994.
Mesbahi, Mohiaddin, ed. *Central Asia and the Caucasus After the Soviet Union.* Tampa, Fla., 1994.

AZORES

A group of nine small Portuguese islands, located in the Atlantic Ocean 800 miles from Lisbon and 1,200 miles from the Strait of Gibraltar, that have housed a key U.S. air installation at Lajes do Pico and have been a prime North Atlantic Treaty Organization (NATO) site for launching antisubmarine warfare. The United States first became strategically interested in the Azores just before World War II, when it was feared that Germany might seize the islands. Although Portugal was reluctant to give the United States rights on the Azores for fear of compromising its neutrality, Washington was able for a time to operate there informally in cooperation with Great Britain, which for centuries had guaranteed Portugal's security. During the war refueling stops in the Azores allowed U.S. pilots to reach North Africa from Newfoundland or Bermuda. Washington formally received basing rights in the Azores in November 1944, rights that were extended by treaty in 1948. In 1949 Secretary of State Dean Acheson justified Portugal's inclusion in NATO on the grounds that the Azores had enabled the United States to increase its strategic reach. The importance of the islands was demonstrated again when the ability of pilots to refuel in the Azores made possible the 1948–1949 Berlin airlift. Under the 1951 bilateral U.S. defense agreement with Portugal, U.S. rights to bases in the Azores were further formalized.

Use of NATO bases in the Azores by foreign military aircraft peaked in the early 1960s, but the islands again proved valuable to the United States during the 1973 Yom Kippur War in the Middle East, when the islands were used as a refueling station by pilots airlifting supplies to Israel. By the late 1980s the island were still servicing planes sent to Africa and the Middle East as well as to Europe. Over the years there have been several squabbles over renewal of the basing agreement, with Portugal often asking for more money than Washington was prepared to give and expressing resentment of U.S. pressure to abandon its colonies. U.S. officials continue to value the Azores base, however, because Portugal has usually been more willing than other U.S. allies to allow military bases to be used for non-NATO purposes.

JOSEPH LEPGOLD

See also Acheson, Dean Gooderham; North Atlantic Treaty Organization; Portugal

FURTHER READING
Acheson, Dean. *Present at the Creation: My Years at the State Department.* New York, 1969.

B

BAGHDAD PACT

See Central Treaty Organization

BAHAMAS

A chain of more than 700 islands located in the western North Atlantic Ocean southeast of Florida and north of Cuba. Although Christopher Columbus made landfall in the Bahamas in 1492, there was no permanent European presence there until British settlers arrived in 1649. The Bahamas became a British crown colony in 1717. They achieved full independence on 10 July 1973, becoming officially the Commonwealth of the Bahamas, and are governed under a parliamentary system, with the British monarch as the titular head of state. The two major political parties are the Free National Movement and the Progressive Liberal Party. Since independence the country has maintained full diplomatic relations with the United States. It is a member of the United Nations and an active participant in the Commonwealth of Nations, has membership in the Non-Aligned Movement, and entered the Caribbean Community and Common Market (CARICOM) in 1983. Concerned by the undue influence it perceived the United States was exerting within the Organization of American States (OAS), the Bahamas deferred joining that body until 1982.

Geographical proximity forged close links between the Bahamas and the United States. British loyalists fled the United States for the Bahamas with their slaves after the American Revolution and established a cotton plantation economy. The Bahamas profited from blockade-running during the U.S. Civil War (1861–1865) and from rum-running during Prohibition (1919–1933). Later in the twentieth century, the Bahamian tourist industry began to target U.S. vacationers, and the country's offshore banking facilities attracted U.S. investors, while drug traffickers used the islands as transshipment bases to smuggle illegal drugs, especially cocaine and marijuana from Colombia, into the United States.

Since Bahamian independence, relations between the Bahamas and the United States have generally been cordial. The Bahamas did, however, unequivocally condemn the U.S. role in the 1983 invasion of Grenada, while throughout the 1980s the United States periodically expressed dissatisfaction with Bahamian efforts in their joint drug interdiction program. Bahamian claims to territorial rights over its surrounding waters that conflicted with U.S. interests were included in the 1982 convention of the third United Nations Commission on the Law of the Sea, which the United States refused to sign. The Caribbean Basin Initiative, a foreign policy program begun during the administration of Ronald Reagan and aimed at spurring economic development and improving political stability among Caribbean countries, accorded the Bahamas favorable trading terms through the Caribbean Basin Economic Recovery Act. As a CARICOM member, and motivated by growing Haitian refugee problem, the Bahamas participated in the 1994 U.S.-led, UN-sanctioned military intervention in Haiti that ousted the military dictatorship and reinstalled the democratically elected president, Jean-Bertrand Aristide.

RODERICK A. MCDONALD

See also Caribbean Basin Initiative; Grenada Invasion; Haiti; Nonaligned Movement; Organization of American States

FURTHER READING

Craton, Michael. *A History of the Bahamas*, 3rd ed. Waterloo, Ont., 1986.

Craton, Michael, and Gail Saunders. *Islanders in the Stream: A History of the Bahamian People*, 2 vols. Athens, Ga., 1992–1995.

Meditz, Sandra W., and Dennis M. Hanratty, eds. *Islands of the Commonwealth Caribbean: A Regional Study*. Washington, D.C., 1989.

BAHRAIN

A sheikdom consisting of a group of islands located in the western coast of the Central Persian Gulf, near the coasts of Saudi Arabia and Qatar. A hereditary monarchy, ruled by the Al-Khalifa family since the end of the eighteenth century, Bahrain—ruled by Portugal and Persia before becoming a British protectorate in 1861—has maintained a moderate, pro-West foreign policy orientation since its independence from Great Britain in August 1971. Economic relations between the United States and Bahrain began with the development of the Bahraini oil industry by U.S. oil companies in the 1930s. Military relations began after World War II, when the U.S. Navy sought to establish communication and logistical facilities in the gulf region. The United States acquired a strategic stake in August 1947, when the U.S. Middle East Force (MEF) was created and headquartered in Bahrain. Washington's strategic interest in Bahrain increased after Great Britain withdrew from the gulf. Formal diplomatic relations between Washington and Manama, Bahrain's capital, began in September 1971, but it was not until May 1974 that the first full-time U.S. ambassador was appointed. In 1972 Washington signed a base-leasing agreement with Bahrain, with an annual rent of $600,000 (raised to $4 million in 1975), providing access rights to Bahraini military facilities.

Despite Manama's pro-West orientation, U.S. relations with Bahrain have not always been smooth. During the Six Day Arab-Israeli War, in 1967, anti-U.S. demonstrations broke out in Bahrain. Bahrain participated in the 1973–1974 Arab oil embargo against the United States and threatened to terminate the lease agreement with Washington and ban U.S. warships from its ports because of U.S. support for Israel during the October 1973 Yom Kippur war. Manama also condemned and broke relations with Egypt for signing the Camp David Peace Accords with Israel in March 1979. Despite these differences, the MEF continued to operate from Bahrain. Manama's fear of Iran, which had controlled Bahrain at various times during the seventeenth and eighteenth centuries and was allegedly behind a December 1981 plot to overthrow the Bahraini government, prompted Manama to tilt toward Iraq during the Iran-Iraq War. Bahrain also provided logistical support for the U.S. reflagging of Kuwaiti oil tankers and Western minesweeping operations in the gulf during 1987–1988. In the mid-1980s Washington began selling sophisticated military hardware to Bahrain, and these sales increased after the Iraqi invasion of Kuwait in August 1990. During the Gulf War of 1990–1991, Manama provided the United States with base facilities and contributed combat forces for the Gulf Cooperation Council's frontline military contingent. After the liberation of Kuwait, Washington considered locating an advance headquarters of the Central Command (CENTCOM) in Bahrain. While CENTCOM headquarters remain in Tampa, Florida, U.S. Navy forces assigned to CENTCOM maintain a forward base in Bahrain. By the mid-1990s Manama's fear of Iraq and Iran had led to an even closer and more open military relationship with the United States.

JEFFREY A. LEFEBVRE

See also Camp David Accords; Gulf War of 1990–1991; Iran-Iraq War; Middle East; Oil and U.S. Foreign Policy

FURTHER READING

Cordesman, Anthony. *The Gulf and the West: Strategic Relations and Military Realities.* Boulder, Colo., 1988.
Gause, F. Gregory. *Oil Monarchies: Domestic and Security Challenges in the Arab Gulf States.* New York, 1994.
Graz, Liesl. *The Turbulent Gulf.* London, 1990.
Kelly, J. B. *Arabia, the Gulf, and the West.* New York, 1980.
Twinam, Joseph Wright. *The Gulf, Cooperation, and the Council: An American Perspective.* Washington, D.C., 1992.

BAKER, JAMES ADDISON III

(*b.* 28 April 1930)

Secretary of state (1989–1992). A graduate of Princeton University and the University of Texas, Baker managed the presidential campaigns of Gerald R. Ford (1976) and George Bush (1979–1980, 1988), served as White House chief of staff (1981–1985), and was secretary of the Treasury (1985–1988) during Ronald Reagan's administration. After serving as chairman of the successful Bush campaign in 1988, Baker was appointed secretary of state the following year; during the last five months of Bush's presidency in 1992, he was appointed chief of staff and senior counselor to the president. Baker's close friendship with Bush gave him unrivaled access to power and made their individual policy contributions difficult to separate. His political skills served him well in his relationships with Congress, the press, and foreign leaders such as Soviet Foreign Minister Eduard Shevardnadze. Baker's pragmatic, nonideological approach to international affairs helped guide East-West relations peacefully through momentous developments—the dissolution of the Soviet empire, the collapse of communism and liberation of Eastern Europe, and the unification of Germany within the North Atlantic Treaty Organization (NATO)—that brought an end to the Cold War. Baker ran the Department of State with a small circle of advisers, enabling him (according to supporters) to control the bureaucracy but limiting his capacity (according to critics) to manage effectively a multitude of complex issues.

Critics fault him for contributing to the military buildup in Iraq prior to the Gulf War of 1991 and misreading the intentions of that country's leader, Saddam Hussein; for being inattentive to the deterioration in U.S.-Japanese relations; for being slow to react to the democratization needs of Eastern Europe and to political changes in the Soviet Union; for not doing more to manage the ethnic-regional conflicts that emerged with the end of the Cold War; for being more reactive than constructive; and, by lacking an overarching vision, for doing little to implement a "new world order." Nevertheless, his major accomplishments were of historic importance and far outweigh such criticisms, which ignore the complexity of the post–Cold War era and the capacity of the United States to control events. In addition to his stewardship of a peaceful end to the Cold War and the reduction of nuclear and conventional weapons through the Strategic Arms Reduction Talks and the Conventional Forces in Europe Agreement, he was instrumental in mobilizing and maintaining the coalition that opposed Iraqi aggression against Kuwait and defeated Iraq in the Gulf War. Subsequently, he engineered the first face-to-face negotiations between Palestinians and Israelis and, with significant support from the president, set in motion a process that led to the first Palestinian-Israeli peace agreement (1993).

BRUCE R. KUNIHOLM

See also Bush, George Herbert Walker; Cold War; Gulf War of 1990–1991; Israel; Middle East; Reagan, Ronald Wilson; State, U.S. Department of; Treasury, U.S. Department of

FURTHER READING

Baker, James Addison III, and Thomas M. Frank. *The Politics of Diplomacy: Revolution, War, and Peace 1989–1992*. New York, 1995.
Woodward, Robert. *The Commanders*. New York, 1991.

BALANCE OF PAYMENTS AND BALANCE OF TRADE

Two of the principal measures of a nation-state's international economic position. The balance of payments is a set of accounts prepared for a nation that presents estimates of total transactions between residents of that nation and the rest of the world during a period of time, normally a calendar year. Summaries of these accounts can be found in the country pages of the *International Financial Statistics of the International Monetary Fund* (IMF). More detail for each country can be found in the IMF *Balance of Payments Yearbook*. In these accounts any transaction that causes a payment to be made into a country from abroad is a credit and gets a plus sign; any transaction that causes a payment to be made by a domestic resident to the rest of the world is a debit and gets a minus sign. Exports sales and inflows of investment from abroad are credits; purchases of imported goods and foreign securities by domestic residents from residents of the rest of the world are debits. The sum of current transactions (trade and services) and capital transactions (purchases and sales of capital assets in transactions with nonresidents) represents the country's balance of payments surplus or deficit, which is normally offset by movements of foreign exchange reserves.

Balance of payments deficits are typically seen as a far more serious problem than surpluses. If a payments deficit is sufficient to deplete a country's preexisting stock of foreign exchange reserves, that country becomes unable to purchase imports, which implies a serious domestic economic crisis. Such countries, or even those whose foreign exchange reserves are approaching exhaustion, frequently must borrow from the IMF, which can impose rather demanding requirements for policy reform. Until such borrowings are repaid, the debtor country can lose partial control over major aspects of its economy, including fiscal, monetary, and exchange rate policy. Large balance of payments surpluses are far less of a problem, except that by definition they necessitate that other countries run deficits, because the balance of payments of the world must be zero. After World War II, for example, large U.S. payments surpluses were a problem because they made it very difficult for the European countries to adjust their payments deficits and return to equilibrium. In the 1960s the problem was reversed because large German surpluses made it difficult for the United States and the United Kingdom to adjust their payments deficits.

U.S. MERCHANDISE TRADE BALANCE HISTORICAL PATTERN
1800–1990
(millions of dollars)

	Exports	Imports	Balance
1800	71	91	- 20
1850	144	174	- 30
1900	1,394	850	545
1920	8,228	5,278	2,950
1940	4,021	2,625	1,396
1960	19,650	14,758	4,892
1980	224,269	249,750	- 25,481
1990	389,303	498,336	- 109,033
1995	574,879	749,348	- 174,469

Source: U.S. Department of Commerce

The balance of trade is a measure of a country's total export revenues minus import expenditures during a period of time, normally a calendar year. The trade balance appears as part of a country's balance of payments accounts and may be expressed in local currency or in terms of foreign exchange. The balance of trade is of considerable importance to national governments because it reflects a country's competitive position in world markets and because a large deficit may be associated with a loss of foreign exchange reserves, which becomes threatening to the nation's international solvency. A large balance of trade deficit, which means that import expenditures exceed export revenues by a large amount, implies that a country's products are not competitive in price or quality, or both, in world markets.

During the nineteenth century the U.S. balance of trade fluctuated repeatedly in response to factors such as wars in Europe and changes in protectionist sentiment that led to shifts in tariff levels. From 1937 to 1971 the United States consistently ran a favorable balance of trade. Since 1971, however, trade deficits have been much more common, occurring in twenty-three of twenty-five years through 1995. The peak trade deficit was $159.6 billion in 1987, before declining to $74.1 billion per year in the 1994–1995 period.

ROBERT M. DUNN, JR.

See also International Monetary Fund; International Trade and Commerce; Tariffs

FURTHER READING

Dunn, Robert M., Jr., and James C. Ingram. *International Economics*, 4th ed. New York, 1996.
International Monetary Fund. *Balance of Payments Manual*. Washington, D.C., 1993.

BALANCE OF POWER

A theory based on the assumption that nations will rally around a potential victim state, providing arms, military guarantees, and general support, thereby helping it to fend off a potential aggressor. Many statesmen and international affairs theorists have asserted that it takes such a balance of power to preserve peace when aggression threatens. The theory originated in the eighteenth century with the initial work of David Hume but found its most profound expression at the Congress of Vienna in 1814–1815, where Friedrich von Gentz of Prussia, Klemens von Metternich of Austria, and Viscount Castlereagh of Great Britain sought to create a system in which French aggression would no longer disrupt the peace of Europe. They did so by creating a balance of power (enshrined in the Quadruple Alliance of 1814 including England, Russia, Austria, and Prussia) against renewed French militarism. The theory also had (largely neglect-

ed) implications for containing Germany following World War I. In U.S. foreign policy, balance of power theory was most apparent in the U.S. creation of a bipolar balance against the Soviet bloc after World War II. Since the end of the Cold War, balance of power proponents have been at a loss to decide against whom to direct balance mechanisms.

Despite their many adherents, balance of power theories have not won general acceptance by the international relations community. Some critics argue that if the balance of power uniformly obtains, there should be little if any war in the international system. The first hint of aggression should bring forth a balancing coalition, which in turn should force the potential aggressor to postpone or abandon aggressive intentions. That war has been endemic in the past continues to cast doubt on the universal operation of balancing mechanisms. A second criticism, stemming from the public goods perspective, takes the opposite view, suggesting that balancing occurs less often than claimed by its theorists. Nations as well as individuals have a rational tendency to wait for others to create any public good, such as security, preferring to ride for free on the contributions made by others. Hence, aggressors will not always have to face a united international community. Many nations refuse to balance and will in fact opt out of the balancing coalition; others will hop on the bandwagon in favor of the aggressor. It thus appears that the balance may not always form. If the balance does form, it may be created too late to restrain an aggressor and may therefore precipitate rather than prevent a war. Informal or tentative alliance arrangements may not be powerful enough to face down an aggressor, but they may be sufficiently strong to drag their participants into war. This seems to have been the case in 1914, at the start of World War I, and in 1939, at the beginning of World War II. In both cases British policy was uncertain until the final moment and did not have sufficient deterrent weight, absent U.S. participation, to derail an onrushing Germany.

In salient cases the ultimate creation of a balance of power may await the aggressor's own intemperate behavior, leading it to attack a state it should have left alone. In both world wars, Germany acted to place itself at war with the United States, thereby committing two of the most egregious blunders in military history. Other examples abound. In 1812 Napoleon blundered in attacking Russia, and in 1941 Adolf Hitler opted as well to attack the Soviet Union. Thus, the actions of aggressors have frequently sounded their own death knell, creating an overbalance against them that would not otherwise have arisen. Failing overreaching actions by the aggressor, however, nations can by no means rely on the automatic creation of a reliable balance against aggression. In addition, some theorists argue that only an overbalance of power will be sufficient to deter aggression, whereas it may well be stimulated by an approximate balance. From this point of view, World Wars I and II were brought on not only by delayed balancing but also by an insufficient amount of balancing power in both cases. Nations also use many techniques to prevent aggression, including that of coopting the aggressor to pursue peaceful purposes. Nations may hide in the interstices of the system, divert attention to others, or seek to transcend the rivalry through a change in systemic procedures.

It follows from balance of power theory that in the post-Cold War period the United States faced the need to prevent the emergence of two blocs contending against each other, as was the basic structure of international relations from 1945 to 1989. This suggests the formation of an overbalance, or a concert, among the great powers, including the United States, Europe, Japan, Russia, and China. Such action would follow the precedents set by the Concert of Europe (1815–1848). If this unity were to be achieved, action against such an overwhelming accord by other states would be unlikely, and war would practically be obviated, at least among the great powers. Just as its precursor neglected challenges in Eastern Europe, such agreement would not prevent all war in the periphery of the system. In the end, it thus appears that, even in the best-case version, the balance of power is a one-sided and insufficient international strategy. It may apply at the great-power level but less so at other levels of conflict in the post–Cold War world. Moreover, even among the great powers, unless the threat of punishment is accompanied by the judicious use of reinforcement as well as reward techniques, the balance of power is unlikely to achieve the objective of producing a stable international system.

RICHARD N. ROSECRANCE

See also Cold War; Quadruple Alliance

FURTHER READING

Gulick, Edward Vose. *Europe's Classical Balance of Power*. Ithaca, N.Y., 1955.
Schroeder, Paul W. "Historical Reality Versus Neo-Realist Theory." *International Security* 19 (Summer 1994):108–148.
Rosecrance, Richard. "A New Concert of Powers." *Foreign Affairs* 71 (Spring 1992):64–82.

BALDWIN, STANLEY,
1st Earl Baldwin of Bewdley

(*b.* 3 August 1867; *d.* 13 December 1947)

Three-time British prime minister (May 1923–January 1924, November 1924–May 1929, and June 1935–May 1937) and chancellor of the exchequer (November 1922–May 1923) who negotiated the 1923 settlement providing for Great Britain's payment to the United States of debts incurred during World War I. He had previously been elected (1908) a Conservative member of Parliament, served as financial secretary of the treasury (1917–1921), and was president of the Board of Trade (1921–1922). During World War I the United States had financed through loans the purchase of U.S. products by Great Britain, France, and Italy. Great Britain's former allies owed debts to the government in London and claimed that they could not meet their obligations unless Germany paid its reparations on schedule. Great Britain preferred either to cancel all debts or to demand all payments. The United States, however, refused to consider war debts and reparations as related and called for payment of British loans as soon as possible. In 1923, as chancellor of the exchequer, Baldwin went to Washington to resolve this crisis. The Anglo-American agreement provided for a sixty-two-year amortization period with a 3 percent interest rate for the first ten years and 3.5 percent for the remainder. The British government, however, rejected the proposal. Upon his return to London, Baldwin persuaded the cabinet to accept the settlement as essential to improving Anglo-American relations. He then became prime minister for the first time. Economic crises stemming from a protective tariff policy and high unemployment plagued his first two ministries. As prime minister from 1935 to 1937, Baldwin's overriding dedication to preventing a new European war led him to tolerate Italy's conquest of Ethiopia and Germany's military reoccupation of the Rhineland. During the Spanish civil war, he also opposed providing arms to the republican government in its struggle against General Francisco Franco. Baldwin retired in 1937, having previously presided over the abdication of King Edward VIII.

CAROL A. JACKSON

See also Great Britain; Reparations; War Debt of World War I; World War I

FURTHER READING

Jenkins, Roy. *Baldwin*. London, 1987.
Middlemas, Keith, and John Barnes. *Baldwin: A Biography*. London, 1969.
Young, Kenneth. *Stanley Baldwin*. London, 1976.

BALFOUR, ARTHUR JAMES, 1st Earl

(*b.* 25 July 1848; *d.* 19 March 1930)

British conservative statesman who influenced Anglo-American relations during World War I and its aftermath. As prime minister from 1902 to 1905, Balfour approved the Entente Cordiale with France in 1904 and renewed the Anglo-Japanese alliance a year later in anticipation of deteriorating relations with Germany. As foreign secretary from 1916 to 1919, Balfour visited Washington in

April 1917, after the United States had declared war. He addressed Congress, an unprecedented privilege for a British minister, appealed for financial credits, and discussed with President Woodrow Wilson Allied war aims while apparently also revealing the existence of Allied secret treaties. Balfour later issued a statement, in November 1917, declaring that the British government favored a Jewish national home in Palestine. Great Britain selected Balfour, a supporter of arms limitations, to lead its delegation at the Washington Naval Conference (1921–1922). His proposal to preserve the status quo in the Pacific Ocean, thus guaranteeing each nation's possessions in the region while abrogating Great Britain's alliance with Japan, became the Four Power Naval Limitation Treaty, signed by Great Britain, the United States, Japan, and France. After the United States refused to cancel the debts incurred by Great Britain during World War I, Balfour, as acting foreign secretary, drafted the official position on the crisis. The Balfour Note of 1922 suggested the liquidation of all debts and claimed that U.S. failure to do so would force the London government to collect payments owed by its former allies. Great Britain, however, would demand only a sufficient amount to meet its financial obligations to the United States. Although the United States considered the Balfour Note an attempt to avoid payment, it negotiated a settlement with Great Britain in 1923.

CAROL A. JACKSON

See also Baldwin, Stanley; Balfour Declaration; Israel; Palestine (to 1948); Washington Conference on the Limitation of Armaments; Wilson, Thomas Woodrow; World War I

FURTHER READING

Buckley, Thomas H. *The United States and the Washington Conference, 1921–1922.* Knoxville, Tenn., 1970.
Mackay, Ruddock F. *Balfour: Intellectual Statesman.* New York, 1985.
Zebel, Sydney H. *Balfour: A Political Biography.* Cambridge, 1973.

BALFOUR DECLARATION

(2 November 1917)

Statement issued during World War I by the British Foreign Secretary, Arthur James Balfour, that his government favored a national home for the Jewish people in Palestine. The statement also said that nothing should be done to prejudice the civil and religious rights of non-Jews living in Palestine. The main motivation, as Balfour argued to the British War Cabinet, was to gain the support of Jewish leaders in Great Britain, the United States, and other countries for Great Britain's efforts to take over control of Palestine from the Ottoman Empire. Russian and American Jews supported Zionism, the movement

for a Jewish homeland. When the Lloyd George government initially sought President Woodrow Wilson's opinion on 3 September 1917, he answered that the time was not right for a pro-Zionist declaration because of the uncertainty of the war's outcome. Balfour cabled Washington inaccurately that the German government was making efforts to enlist Zionist sympathies. President Wilson then approved the declaration but insisted that his answer remain confidential. Great Britain received a mandate over Palestine in 1922 from the League of Nations to prepare the region for independence, and the United States officially endorsed the declaration the same year. The British government claimed that the Balfour Declaration had not entitled Jews to a Jewish state, only that it guaranteed them a home. In 1939 the British, fearing Arab support for Adolf Hitler's Germany, virtually repudiated the Balfour Declaration by promising to restrict Jewish immigration into Palestine to a trickle, with the likelihood of banning it altogether after 1944. For thirty years the incompatibility of the goals outlined by Balfour created problems for the mandatory power with both Jews and Palestinian Arabs and became a point of contention in Anglo-American relations. The United Nations voted in 1947 to partition Palestine into a state for the Jews and one for the Palestinian Arabs. Jewish inhabitants created Israel in May 1948, despite the efforts of local Palestinian Arabs.

CAROL A. JACKSON

See also Balfour, Arthur James; Israel; Middle East; Palestine (to 1948); World War I

FURTHER READING

Friedman, Isaiah. *The Question of Palestine: British-Jewish-Arab Relations: 1914–1918,* 2nd ed. New Brunswick, N.J., 1992.
Lebow, Richard Ned. "Woodrow Wilson and the Balfour Declaration." *Journal of Modern History* 40 (December): 501– 523.
Stein, Leonard. *The Balfour Declaration.* New York, 1961.

BALL, GEORGE WILDMAN

(*b.* 21 December 1909; *d.* 26 May 1994)

Undersecretary of state (1961–1966) and policymaker distinguished by a breadth of experience in government, politics, and international law that was rivaled by few in the post–World War II era. Hailing from Des Moines, Iowa, in the isolationist heartland of the United States, Ball became an Atlanticist and, in time, personified the most ambitious internationalist schemes of his generation. A graduate of Northwestern University, Ball served as counsel to the Farm Credit Administration from 1933 to 1934, worked in the Lend-Lease Administration in 1940, and gained valuable experience as a director of the U.S. Strategic Bombing Survey, which studied the effects of the Allied bombing of Germany. He sought but failed to prevent the escalation of the war in Vietnam and was a critic of Israel's uncompromising stance toward the Palestinians. Ball also served briefly as United Nations ambassador from June to August 1968, when he resigned to become a political adviser to Hubert Humphrey during his unsuccessful presidential campaign against Richard Nixon. Ball's experience in international law, representing foreign clients for the Washington firm of Cleary, Gottlieb, Steen, and Ball from 1945 to 1961, allowed him to cultivate professional relationships and close personal friendships on both sides of the Atlantic. A Europeanist, Ball embraced Secretary of State Dean Acheson's advocacy of strong U.S.-European ties in the 1950s, worked closely with French economist Jean Monnet in his efforts to gain support in the United States for the European Coal and Steel Community, advised Democratic presidential candidate Adlai Stevenson in 1952 and 1956, and, as undersecretary of state, was the primary spokesperson on European policy and trade matters in the administrations of Presidents John F. Kennedy and Lyndon B. Johnson. Following his retirement from government service in 1968, Ball continued to makes his views known on a variety of issues. His several books and innumerable articles all challenged conventional wisdom. Although regarded as a member of the postwar foreign policy establishment, Ball regularly took positions on issues that put him at odds with the establishment's prevailing orthodoxy. His opposition to the Vietnam War, beginning in 1961, was notable for its singularity in the top echelons of the Kennedy and Johnson administrations. He argued that Vietnam was not a vital U.S. interest and that the bloody, expensive involvement was injuring the truly important relationship with Europe. His advocacy of liberal trade policies and the opening of world markets subjected him to criticism from congressional conservatives. In the 1980s and early 1990s, Ball's criticism of what he considered the lavish U.S. support of Israel's security and territorial policies revived his reputation as a maverick among the nation's foreign policy elite.

DAVID L. DiLEO

See also Humphrey, Hubert Horatio; Israel; Johnson, Lyndon Baines; Kennedy, John Fitzgerald; Monnet, Jean; Vietnam War

FURTHER READING

Ball, George W. *The Past Has Another Pattern: Memoirs*. New York, 1982.

Ball, George W., and Douglas B. Ball. *The Passionate Attachment: America's Involvement with Israel, 1947 to the Present*. New York, 1992.

DiLeo, David L., *George Ball, Vietnam, and the Rethinking of Containment*. Chapel Hill, N.C., 1991.

BANGLADESH

Located in Southern Asia, at the head of the Bay of Bengal and almost completely surrounded by India; a deeply impoverished country, formerly known as East Pakistan. Bangladesh—which occupies territory that in the days of the British Raj belonged to the province of East Bengal—was born when the two halves of Pakistan, separated by 1,000 miles of Indian territory, split up in 1971. The break was fueled by resentment over the political domination of the Pakistani government by the distant, less populous West Pakistan. Bengali demands for autonomy were led by the Awami League, headed by Sheik Mujibir Rehman. The Pakistani government responded with force.

The Nixon administration considered the matter an internal Pakistani problem, despite international condemnation of the suppression of the Bengalis and the flight of hundreds of thousands of refugees to India. Ignoring widespread criticism from Congress and the media, Nixon continued military assistance to Pakistan. He urged the Bengalis to compromise with the Pakistan government and sided with Pakistan in December 1971 when warfare erupted between Pakistan and India over the crisis. When an independent Bangladesh emerged after months of bloodshed, its leaders and people regarded the United States with understandable hostility. However, they recognized that U.S. involvement in the war had been limited largely to diplomatic posturing.

Despite India's assistance in gaining independence, Bangladesh was determined to avoid becoming a colony of its benefactor. To balance Indian influence, the new nation pursued a policy of accommodation with Pakistan, China, and the United States. It also stressed the Islamic basis of Bangladesh to forge closer ties with other Muslim states. In 1980 President Ziaur Rehman proposed a multilateral system of regional economic cooperation modeled on the Association of Southeast Asian Nations, resulting in the establishment of the South Asian Association for Regional Cooperation.

The U.S.-Bangladesh relationship has remained distant. Bangladesh has not been of critical importance to the United States, especially in an era of decreasing congressional and popular support for foreign assistance program. At the same time, concern for regional stability has led the United States to use its influence in international organizations to promote multilateral assistance projects. For its part, Bangladesh has supported a number of U.S. policy initiatives in the United Nations.

GARY R. HESS

See also India; Pakistan; Nixon, Richard Milhous

FURTHER READING

Buzen, Barry and Gowher Rizvi. *South Asian Insecurity and the Great Powers*. New York, 1986.

Choudberry, G.W. *The Last Days of United Pakistan*. Bloomington, Ind., 1974.

Cohen, Stephen Philip. *The Security of South Asia: American and Asian Perspectives*. Urbana, Ill., 1987.

BARBADOS

An island nation located in the extreme eastern Caribbean Sea about 375 km northeast of Venezuela. Portuguese and Spanish vessels visited the island throughout the sixteenth century, during which time Spanish slaving expeditions eradicated the indigenous Carib population. Great Britain established the first permanent European settlement there in 1627, and Barbados remained its colony until it achieved full independence on 30 November 1966. Barbados is governed under a parliamentary system with the British monarch recognized as titular head of state. The two major political parties are the Democratic Labour Party (DLP) and the Barbados Labour Party (BLP). Full diplomatic relations have been maintained with the United States since independence, as has membership in the United Nations and the British Commonwealth of Nations. Barbados joined the Organization of American States (OAS) in 1967, holds membership in the Nonaligned Movement, and helped found the Caribbean Community and Common Market (CARICOM) in 1973.

Changing economic circumstances in Barbados after World War II, especially the development of tourism and manufacturing, helped produce increasingly close ties with the United States. The generally friendly relations between the two nations have accommodated Barbados's preference for nonalignment, as well as its commitment to ideological pluralism in the Caribbean region. This was reflected in the 1973 decision, over U.S. and OAS objections, to extend diplomatic recognition to Cuba. In the early 1980s, regional security concerns, especially following the 1979 success of Maurice Bishop's New Jewel Movement in neighboring Grenada, led the administration of Barbadian premier J. M. G. M. ("Tom") Adams to espouse closer alignment with the United States, as was most clearly evinced during the 1983 U.S.-led invasion of Grenada. To the chagrin of some of its Caribbean neighbors, especially Trinidad and Tobago, Barbados played an important role, providing the bases from which the U.S. expedition was mounted. Participation in President Ronald Reagan's Caribbean Basin Initiative (CBI), which accorded favorable trade terms through the Caribbean Basin Economic Recovery Act (CBERA), continued Barbados's gravitation toward the United States, a course generally followed by Adams's successors.

RODERICK A. McDONALD

See also Caribbean Basin Initiative; Cuba; Grenada Invasion; Haiti; Nonaligned Movement; Organization of American States; Reagan, Ronald Wilson

FURTHER READING

Beckles, Hilary McD. *A History of Barbados: From Amerindian Settlement to Nation-State*. New York, 1990.

Meditz, Sandra W., and Dennis M. Hanratty, eds. *Islands of the Commonwealth Caribbean: A Regional Study*. Washington, D.C., 1989.

BARBARY STATES

Four states—Algiers, Tripoli, Morocco, and Tunis (present-day Algeria, Libya, Morocco, and Tunisia)—bordering the Mediterranean Sea along the northern and northwestern coast of Africa. The area was dominated by the Ottoman Turks until the early eighteenth century; thereafter, Ottoman power weakened, but the four states still rendered annual tribute to Constantinople, and their populations shared a common devotion to Islam with the Ottomans. For almost three centuries the Barbary powers practiced piracy, and wealthy nations such as Great Britain protected their shipping by paying tribute to them. Smaller and poorer nations such as Denmark could not afford such an expense, and their commerce suffered accordingly. Punitive expeditions against the Barbary States, such as the one undertaken by Spain in the summer of 1775, proved ineffective.

Flying the flag of an independent nation, U.S. merchant ships first encountered marauding Barbary corsairs in 1785 when two U.S. vessels were seized and their captured crews detained in Algiers. The hapless crew languished in captivity for years because its government lacked the resources to ransom them. In the mid-1790s, a more prosperous United States began tribute payments (including a thirty-six-gun frigate) through a treaty with the strongest of the Barbary States, Algiers. These presents and the skillful diplomacy of the remarkable man of letters Joel Barlow won the freedom of the captive sailors and secured peace and protection for Americans in the Mediterranean. Critics, however, thought it inconsistent for the United States to bribe the Barbary pirates while simultaneously rejecting French requests for payoffs in the XYZ affair, and they noted how expensive the tribute was. One critic was Thomas Jefferson; after becoming president in 1801, he dispatched a small naval force to patrol the Mediterranean. Operating far from home and hobbled by internal dissension, the tiny squadron nevertheless won praise for such exploits as Captain Stephen Decatur's audacious raid on Tripoli in February 1804. It was only after the War of 1812, however, that the new republic acted decisively against the corsair plague; Con-

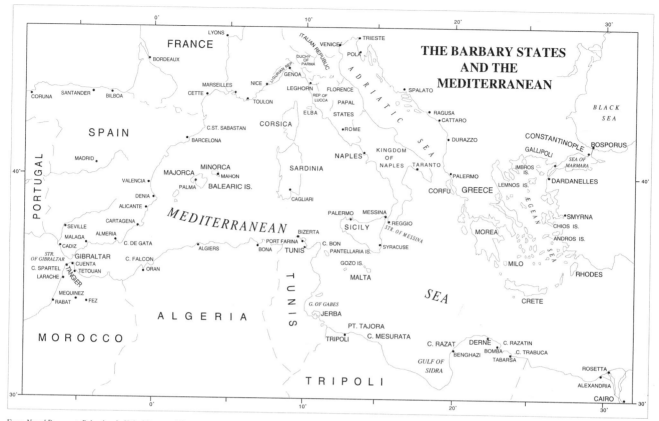

The map labels include: FRANCE, LYONS, ITALIAN REPUBLIC, VENICE, TRIESTE, POLA, DUCHY OF PARMA, LIGURIAN REP., GENOA, LEGHORN, FLORENCE, REP. OF LUCCA, PAPAL STATES, ELBA, ROME, SPALATO, RAGUSA, CATTARO, DURAZZO, BORDEAUX, MARSEILLES, NICE, TOULON, CETTE, CORUNA, SANTANDER, BILBOA, C.ST. SABASTAN, BARCELONA, CORSICA, ADRIATIC SEA, THE BARBARY STATES AND THE MEDITERRANEAN, BLACK SEA, CONSTANTINOPLE, BOSPORUS, GALLIPOLI, SEA OF MARMARA, DARDANELLES, SPAIN, MADRID, VALENCIA, DENIA, ALICANTE, MAJORCA, MINORCA, MAHON, PALMA, BALEARIC IS., SARDINIA, KINGDOM OF NAPLES, NAPLES, TARANTO, PALERMO, CORFU, GREECE, LEMNOS IS., IMBROS IS., SMYRNA, CHIOS IS., ANDROS IS., MOREA, AEGEAN SEA, MILO, RHODES, PORTUGAL, SEVILLE, MALAGA, ALMERIA, CADIZ, CARTAGENA, C. DE GATA, MEDITERRANEAN, PALERMO, MESSINA, REGGIO, STR. OF MESSINA, SICILY, BIZERTA, SYRACUSE, CAGLIARI, STR. OF GIBRALTAR, GIBRALTAR, CUENTA, C. SPARTEL, TETOUAN, LARACHE, TANGIER, C. FALCON, ORAN, ALGIERS, BONA, PORT FARINA, TUNIS, C. BON, PANTELLARIA IS., GOZO IS., MALTA, SEA, CRETE, MEQUINEZ, RABAT, FEZ, ALGERIA, TUNIS, MOROCCO, G. OF GABES, JERBA, PT. TAJORA, TRIPOLI, C. MESURATA, C. RAZAT, DERNE, C. RAZATIN, BENGHAZI, BOMBA, C. TRABUCA, TABARSA, GULF OF SIDRA, TRIPOLI, ROSETTA, ALEXANDRIA, CAIRO

From *Naval Documents Related to the United States and Wars with the Barbary Powers.* Washington, D.C., 1939. Prepared by the U.S. Office of Naval Records and Library, Navy Department.

gress declared war on Algiers on 2 March 1815, and two powerful U.S. navy squadrons brought an end to the Barbary States's reign of terror.

CLIFFORD L. EGAN

See also Jefferson, Thomas; Piracy; XYZ Affair

FURTHER READING

Barnby, H. G. *The Prisoners of Algiers: An Account of the Forgotten American Algerian War, 1785–1797.* London, 1966.

Irwin, Ray W. *The Diplomatic Relations of the United States with the Barbary Powers, 1776–1816.* Chapel Hill, N.C., 1931.

Wright, Louis B., and Julia H. Macleod. *The First Americans in North Africa: William Eaton's Struggle for a Vigorous Policy Against the Barbary Pirates, 1799–1805.* Princeton, N.J., 1945.

BARUCH, BERNARD MANNES

(*b.* 19 August 1870; *d.* 20 June 1965)

Financier, economic pundit, Democratic party supporter, and irrepressible adviser to presidents. Born in Camden, South Carolina, the second of four sons, Baruch came of age in comfortable circumstances in the post-Reconstruction South. He attended private school in South Carolina and graduated from the City College of New York (1889),

where he had moderate success as a student but exceptional success as an athlete and campus personality. In 1891 he became a bond salesman but soon reached his financial stride as a speculator. By 1900 his speculations in sugar, tobacco, and railroads had made him a millionaire. Having achieved financial security, he turned his prodigious energies to gaining influence, renown, and power through political associations and activities.

Baruch's political career began when he met Woodrow Wilson in 1912. An informal adviser during President Wilson's first term, Baruch was appointed to head the newly formed War Industries Board (WIB) when the United States entered World War I in 1917. In this capacity Baruch oversaw the production and allocation of resources for the war; the WIB was the beginning of the military-industrial complex. World War II brought Baruch back into government. In 1942 President Franklin D. Roosevelt appointed him "rubber czar," chairman of a presidential committee dealing with the critical rubber shortage. A year later he became assistant to fellow South Carolinian James F. Byrnes, then director of the Office of War Mobilization.

In 1946 Byrnes, now secretary of state, encouraged President Harry S. Truman to appoint Baruch head of the

U.S. delegation to the United Nations Atomic Energy Commission (UNAEC). Baruch's assignment was to present the U.S. proposal for the international control of atomic energy, the so-called Acheson-Lilienthal Plan, but Baruch altered the plan in ways that made its rejection by the Soviet Union predictable. He eliminated the veto power of the five powers on the UN Security Council (the United States, Great Britain, France, China, and the Soviet Union), added automatic "swift and condine punishment" for violators, and insisted that the United States be permitted to maintain its monopoly of atomic bombs until it decided that all other nations had complied fully with the plan's requirements. Announcing the Baruch Plan in June 1946 to the UNAEC as "a choice between the quick and the dead," he presented it as a nonnegotiable proposal. On 31 December he forced a vote, fully aware that it would result in the plan's rejection by the Soviet Union and Poland. Baruch's heavy-handed diplomacy was criticized by most of the nuclear physicists who had worked on the atomic bomb project and by such journalists as Walter Lippmann. In 1948 Baruch fell out of favor with Truman after criticizing his recognition of the new state of Israel and recommending that the Democratic party seek an alternative presidential candidate. He spent most of the remainder of his life polishing his public image, especially through philanthropy, from his estate in South Carolina.

Martin J. Sherwin

See also Acheson-Lilienthal Report; Military-Industrial Complex; Nuclear Weapons and Strategy; Truman, Harry S.; Wilson, Thomas Woodrow

FURTHER READING

Baruch, Bernard M. *My Own Story*, repr. Cutchogue, N.Y., 1993.
———. *The Public Years*, repr. Cutchogue, N.Y.,1960.
Coit, Margaret. *Mr. Baruch*. Boston, 1957.
Schwartz, Jordan. *The Speculator: Bernard M. Baruch in Washington*. Chapel Hill, N.C., 1981.

BATISTA Y ZALDÍVAR, FULGENCIO

(*b.* 16 January 1901; *d.* 6 August 1973)

Cuban strongman at two junctures in the mid-twentieth century. In the 1930s he served U.S. policies by preventing the triumph of a full-scale social revolution in Cuba, permitting a subsequent U.S. disengagement from its protectorate over Cuba. In the 1950s U.S. policies were undermined when he became the target of an eventually triumphant social revolution that aligned Cuba with the Soviet Union and expropriated all U.S. property in Cuba.

Born to poor rural folk in eastern Cuba, the light-skinned mulatto Batista joined the Cuban army as a private in 1921 and was promoted to sergeant-stenographer in 1928. In the wake of the collapse of Cuba's sugar industry, violent protests helped to force dictator President Gerardo Machado to resign on 12 August 1933; on 4 September, Batista led the army's sergeants and corporals, joined by the university students' Revolutionary Student Directorate, to overthrow the provisional government. After a few days the revolutionaries appointed Ramón Grau San Martín president, and Batista became colonel and army chief. The United States refused to recognize the Grau government, judging it too radical and actively lobbied for its demise. On 14 January 1934 Batista forced Grau to resign. On 16 January, Batista appointed Carlos Mendieta as Cuba's president; five days later the U.S. government recognized the Mendieta government. For the next six years Batista ruled Cuba through Mendieta and three other puppet presidents. In 1934 and 1935 Batista's army crushed the political left and repressed communist-led militant labor unions. Batista later launched programs in health and education, protected many of Cuba's tenant farmers from eviction, and profited from corruption. Batista's regime lobbied the U.S. government to change its policies toward Cuba. In 1934 the United States abrogated its protectorate over Cuba established in 1901 (the Platt Amendment to Cuba's constitution), and the United States enacted the Jones-Costigan Sugar Act and renegotiated its trade treaty with Cuba to establish a system of sugar import quotas to protect U.S. domestic producers and to reactivate Cuba's sugar economy.

In 1940, backed by a coalition of conservatives and communists, Batista was elected president of Cuba. After Cuba declared war on Japan, Germany, and Italy in December 1941, Batista allowed for the establishment of various U.S. military facilities on Cuban territory, and Cuba sold its increased wartime sugar output to the United States at below-market prices. The opposition won free elections in 1944, after which Batista stepped down and went to live in the United States, where he owned property. Seeking to reclaim power, on 10 March 1952 Batista and the military overthrew President Carlos Prío Socarrás's constitutional government. Having banned the Communist Party, Batista won an uncontested presidential election in 1954 and thereafter enjoyed friendly relations with the U.S. government and its ambassadors. U.S. direct investment in Cuba boomed, and Cuba's tourism industry (including gambling casinos) became highly developed. As the Cuban economy flourished, Batista and his close associates became immensely rich through corruption.

In December 1956 Fidel Castro launched a guerrilla insurgency in the Sierra Maestra. The United States had been supplying military assistance, advice, and training to Cuba under four treaties (signed in 1951) designed to defend the hemisphere but suspended a shipment of rifles to the Cuban government in March 1958 because the Cuban army was using U.S.-supplied weapons to combat the insurgency, in violation of its treaty obligations; further weapons shipments were embargoed. The U.S. government simultaneously sought to enforce the Neutrality Act (which prohibited the use of U.S. territory to provide support for rivals in a war that the United States had not entered) against Cubans who gathered weapons for the insurgency in the United States; U.S. military advisers also remained in Cuba. In November 1958 Batista rigged the elections so that his handpicked candidate would win the presidency, thereby eliminating all prospects that his successor could govern legitimately. The Batista regime's repression of the opposition had become quite bloody, and the level of corruption in the armed forces had demoralized the officer corps and weakened the army's capacity for combat.

The key issue that had bedeviled U.S. policy toward Cuba had long been how to disengage from a corrupt and repressive dictator without opening the door to a rebel whose views were at best uncertain and perhaps radical. On 9 December 1958 William Pawley, President Dwight D. Eisenhower's personal emissary, asked Batista to resign in favor of a military junta that would be both anti-Batista and anti-Castro. By this time, however, such a middle option (or "third force") no longer existed, and Castro was able to seize and retain power. Batista fled to the Dominican Republic on 31 December and subsequently went to Portugal. In his memoirs, he blamed U.S. policy for Castro's victory.

JORGE I. DOMÍNGUEZ

See also Castro, Fidel; Cuba; Platt Amendment

FURTHER READING

Batista y Zaldívar, Fulgencio. *The Growth and Decline of the Cuban Republic*, translated by Blas M. Rocafort. New York, 1964.
Gellman, Irwin F. *Roosevelt and Batista: Good Neighbor Diplomacy in Cuba, 1933–1945*. Albuquerque, N. Mex., 1973.
Paterson, Thomas G. *Contesting Castro: The United States and the Triumph of the Cuban Revolution*. New York, 1994.
Thomas, Hugh. *Cuba: The Pursuit of Freedom*. New York, 1971.

BAYARD, THOMAS FRANCIS

(*b.* 29 October 1828; *d.* 28 September 1898)

U.S. senator (1869–1885) and secretary of state (1885–1889). Born in Wilmington, Delaware, to a prominent family, Bayard was educated in private schools, studied law in Washington, D.C., joined the bar in 1851, and established a highly successful practice. In 1869 he was elected to the U.S. Senate and quickly emerged as a leader among the Democratic minority, opposing the Reconstruction policies of the radicals. In 1885 he resigned from the Senate to accept President Grover Cleveland's appointment as secretary of state. Although Bayard believed in civil service reform, he was besieged

with demands for patronage appointments. He endeavored to protect, through international agreement, the Bering Sea fur seal herds, despite protests by Canadians and the British over the U.S. seizure of Canadian sealing vessels. Bayard labored to bring about compromise among Great Britain, Germany, and the United States over conflicts in Samoa, but his offer of the good offices of the United States in 1886 failed to resolve a boundary dispute between Great Britain and Venezuela. He also sought to resolve a dispute with Great Britain and Canada over fisheries in the North Atlantic through negotiation, thereby resisting jingoist pressures, but the resulting Bayard-Chamberlain Treaty of 1888 failed to win Senate approval. In 1890 he insisted on the recall of Lord Lionel Sackville-West because of the publication during the presidential campaign of 1888 of a letter in which the British minister intimated that Cleveland would be more friendly toward Great Britain than Republican candidate Benjamin Harrison. In 1893 Bayard was appointed ambassador to Great Britain, the first chief of mission to London to hold ambassadorial rather than ministerial rank. He remained in London until 1897, working to maintain good relations despite continuing problems related to North Atlantic fisheries, Bering Sea fur seals, and the Venezuelan boundary dispute of 1895–1896.

MICHAEL J. DEVINE

See also Canada; Cleveland, Stephen Grover; Fisheries; Great Britain; Sealing; Venezuelan Boundary Dispute

FURTHER READING

Tansill, Charles Callan. *The Foreign Policy of Thomas F. Bayard, 1885–1897*. New York, 1940.

BAY OF PIGS INVASION

(1961)

A failed Central Intelligence Agency (CIA) operation against Cuba designed to topple the government of Fidel Castro. On 17 April 1961, 1,453 anti-Castro Cuban exiles, armed and trained by the CIA, invaded Cuba's beaches at the Bay of Pigs. Premier Castro's forces routed the invaders in three days and took hundreds of them prisoner.

U.S. planning to remove Castro and blunt the Cuban revolution began under the administration of President Dwight D. Eisenhower, which viewed Castro as excessively nationalistic, procommunist, and threatening the Western Hemisphere because he advocated revolution. Eisenhower ordered the CIA in March 1960 to train Cuban exiles who could be sent back to Cuba to conduct armed struggle against Castro. The CIA developed a plan to invade Cuba with a brigade of Cuban exiles, whose early military successes, the CIA expected, would trigger popular uprisings that would topple Castro.

When President John F. Kennedy took office in January 1961, CIA operatives were training the brigade covertly in Guatemala, where the CIA had successfully overthrown a leftist government in 1954—a success CIA officials expected to repeat in Cuba. The Kennedy administration shared Eisenhower's Cold War assumptions and fears that revolutionary Cuba might become a model for other Latin American nations. Canceling the expedition preparations, moreover, would have exposed Kennedy to domestic criticism that he was not serious about fighting communism. The CIA pushed for the invasion, describing the chances of success as good. Kennedy asked the Joint Chiefs of Staff to review the plan. It found serious weaknesses but voiced only mild criticism because the plan had been prepared by another agency. Kennedy worried, however, about having the United States appear as an aggressor, especially as he was in the process of launching the Alliance for Progress. He approved the operation on the assumption that U.S. support would remain covert, and he made it clear that he would not commit U.S. forces if the invasion ran into trouble or failed.

Because of poor planning, the brigade encountered logistical problems upon landing in Cuba from Nicaragua. The CIA also miscalculated the strength of Castro's regime, which rallied most Cubans and imprisoned thousands of opponents within hours of the landing. Hundreds of Cubans were killed or wounded defending against the invasion. Castro's superior forces eventually crushed the brigade, which lost 114 dead and more than 1,100 captured. The CIA pressed for the use of U.S. forces, especially air strikes, to salvage the operation, but Kennedy refused. His confidence in the CIA and the military shaken, Kennedy then took a more critical view of so-called expert opinion. A post-invasion study by General Maxwell Taylor detailed how the CIA and other agencies botched the operation. The invasion pushed Cuba closer to the Soviet Union, which began to send military supplies. Worried that the United States might strike again, next with U.S. troops, Castro brought in Soviet nuclear weapons—setting the stage for the Cuban missile crisis of October 1962. The brigade prisoners were freed in December 1962, when the United States sent medical supplies to Cuba in exchange for them.

LUCIEN S. VANDENBROUCKE

See also Alliance for Progress; Castro, Fidel; Central Intelligence Agency; Cuba; Cuban Missile Crisis; Kennedy, John Fitzgerald

FURTHER READING

Higgins, Trumbull. *The Perfect Failure: Kennedy, Eisenhower, and the CIA at the Bay of Pigs.* New York, 1987.
Pérez, Louis A., Jr. *Cuba and the United States: Ties of Singular Intimacy.* Athens, Ga., 1990.
Vandenbroucke, Lucien S. *Perilous Options: Special Operations as an Instrument of U.S. Foreign Policy.* New York, 1993.

BEARD, CHARLES AUSTIN

(*b.* 27 November 1874; *d.* 1 September 1948)

Historian noted for his controversial interpretations of U.S. history, beginning with *An Economic Interpretation of the Constitution of the United States* (1913), in which he argued that the framers of the Constitution were motivated primarily by a desire to safeguard their property interests. Born in Indiana, Beard earned a Ph.D. from Columbia University, where he taught until his resignation in 1917 to protest the dismissal of colleagues who opposed U.S. entry into the war. He endorsed U.S. intervention in World War I but criticized the administration of President Woodrow Wilson for violations of civil liberties. In the 1920s he questioned U.S. economic ventures overseas that could lead the nation into war and jeopardize domestic reform. In the 1930s, as the Great Depression continued and wars raged in Asia and Europe, Beard joined other so-called isolationists in voicing suspicions of President Franklin D. Roosevelt; he believed the president's diplomatic and military policies, including Lend-Lease and peacetime conscription, would plunge the country into an unnecessary war. After World War II, Beard renewed his pre-1941 suspicions in two books critical of Roosevelt's record. The conspiratorial overtones and methodology of these volumes evoked widespread criticism. Some of Beard's writings nevertheless continued to elicit scholarly respect, including two 1934 studies on national interest that argued for the priority of domestic reform over foreign policy activism.

THOMAS C. KENNEDY

See also Isolationism; Lend-Lease; Roosevelt, Franklin Delano; World War I

FURTHER READING

Beard, Charles A. *The Idea of National Interest: An Analytical Study in American Foreign Policy.* New York, 1934.
———. *President Roosevelt and the Coming of the War, 1941: A Study in Appearances and Realities.* New Haven, Conn., 1948.
Borning, Bernard C. *The Political and Social Thought of Charles A. Beard.* Seattle, Wash., 1962.
Hofstadter, Richard. *The Progressive Historians: Turner, Beard, Parrington.* New York, 1968.
Kennedy, Thomas C. *Charles A. Beard and American Foreign Policy.* Gainesville, Fla., 1975.
Nore, Ellen. *Charles A. Beard: An Intellectual Biography.* Carbondale, Ill., 1983.

BEAUMARCHAIS, PIERRE AUGUSTIN CARON DE

(*b.* 24 January 1732; *d.* 18 May 1799)

French dramatist who promoted and then administered covert official French aid to the rebellious North American colonies during the early years of the American Revolution. The son of a jeweler and watchmaker, Beaumarchais became an inventor, musician, playwright (*Le Barbier de Séville*, 1775), and publisher who participated in the politics of the French court. While in England as a French government agent (April 1775–May 1776), he became an ardent advocate of French aid to Great Britain's North American colonies in their conflict with the mother country. In the fall of 1775 he wrote to the French foreign minister, Charles Gravier, Comte de Vergennes, pleading for French support of the rebels. Vergennes presented Beaumarchais's proposal to King Louis XVI to act as the agent in providing aid to the colonies. Beaumarchais requested 1 million livres (about $200,000), one-half of which would go to the American revolutionaries in return for tobacco and the other half to purchase gunpowder. The king endorsed the project in April 1776. A royal decree made military supplies available, and Beaumarchais set up the fictitious firm Rodrigue Hortalez and Company to channel French and some Spanish aid to the North Americans. The large operation could not be kept secret. Although the British monitored the supplies (muskets, cannon, shells, gunpowder, tents, and clothing) leaving French ports for America, their protests were ignored. Most ships arrived in North America via the West Indies. These military supplies made a crucial difference, providing 90 percent of American arms during the first two years of the conflict. Beaumarchais personally invested about 3.6 million livres in the project, but because the colonies considered the supplies a free gift, no tobacco was ever sent to France. Beaumarchais never recovered his investment and ultimately faced bankruptcy. It was not until thirty-six years after his death that the U.S. government paid his descendants the relatively small sum of $160,000. Beaumarchais was arrested in 1792 as an enemy of the French Revolution but soon gained release. Facing financial ruin, he fled to Hamburg in 1795.

REBECCA G. GOODMAN

See also American Revolution; Vergennes, Charles Gravier

FURTHER READING

Bemis, Samuel Flagg. *The Diplomacy of the American Revolution*, 4th ed. New York, 1955.
Lemaître, Georges Édouard. *Beaumarchais*. New York, 1949.
Schama, Simon. *Citizens: A Chronicle of the French Revolution*. New York, 1989.

BEGIN, MENACHEM

(*b.* 16 August 1913; *d.* 9 March 1992)

Prime minister of Israel (1977–1983) who negotiated the first peace treaty between Israel and an Arab state, leader of the terrorist underground group Irgun Zvai Leumi (IZL) during Israel's struggle for independence against Great Britain, and a longtime leader of the major rightist political coalition, Likud. Begin was born in Brest-Litovsk, Russia (now Brest, Belarus), and received a degree in law from the University of Warsaw. After taking on a leadership role in Betar, the revisionist Zionist youth movement, escaping from the Nazis, and being imprisoned by the Soviet government, he made his way to Palestine in 1942. Within a year Begin was head of the IZL, the militant underground paramilitary movement that fought both the British and the Arabs. The IZL carried on a guerrilla war against the British Mandatory Government of Palestine and the British army. IZL tactics reflected the desperation of the Palestinian Jews at the British policy of sharply restricting Jewish immigration at a time when European Jewry was being slaughtered by the Nazis. The IZL attacked British troops, installations, and police stations, blew up British military and governmental headquarters in Jerusalem's King David Hotel in 1946, bombed the British embassy in Rome in 1946, and in general strove to make the British presence in Palestine untenable. In retaliation for the execution of three IZL members, two British soldiers were kidnapped and hanged in 1947. After the end of World War II, the Irgun began to fight the Arabs, separate from the Haganah, the main Jewish force. IZL was responsible for the massacre at the village of Deir Yassin in 1948, which deepened the rift with the mainstream Jewish movements. After Israel achieved statehood in 1948, Begin brought his followers into open political activity, forming and leading the Herut (Freedom) party. In 1973 the Likud (Unity) coalition was created with Begin as its leader. The Likud, which had absorbed the Herut party, was Israel's main opposition party for most of the period until 1977, when Begin became prime minister.

Begin's six years as the head of Israel's government proved to be momentous for the nation's history, primarily because of the successful negotiation of the 1979 peace treaty with Egypt after Egyptian President Anwar as-Sadat's landmark visit to Israel in 1977 and the 1978 Camp David meetings between Begin, Sadat, and U.S. President Jimmy Carter. Despite Begin's tough position on territorial issues and his refusal to accept the creation of an independent Palestinian homeland, he proved willing to return the Sinai Peninsula to Egypt in exchange for peace, normal relations, and security guarantees. Begin and Sadat shared the 1978 Nobel Peace Prize in recognition of their courageous efforts. At Camp David, Begin's plan providing for autonomy and self-government for the Palestinians in the West Bank and the Gaza Strip was adopted. The idea of Begin's autonomy plan was to give the Palestinian residents of Judea, Samaria, and Gaza control over most aspects of their daily lives while retaining military and security control for Israel. It was an attempt to balance the Palestinian desire to be independent of Israel with Israel's security needs and explicitly did not provide for an independent Palestinian state. Subsequent attempts to negotiate the details of the plan under the auspices of the Camp David Accords proved unsuccessfully (although some elements later were incorporated in the 1993 Israel-Palestine Liberation Organization Declaration of Principles). Begin's strong views on maintaining Israel's borders, building settlements in the occupied territories, and resisting Palestinian nationalism often brought him into sharp conflict with the U.S. government during the administrations of both Carter and his successor, Ronald Reagan. When Israel destroyed Iraq's nuclear reactor in a bombing raid in 1981, the Reagan administration was openly critical of the action.

The 1982 Israeli invasion of Lebanon, an effort to destroy the Palestine Liberation Organization's "state within a state" in the southern part of the country and to bolster the Christian Maronites in the internal struggle between the Lebanese factions, proved to be Begin's political undoing, despite its initial success. The combination of intense international opposition and effective guerrilla tactics by Lebanese groups created a morass for Begin's government. Mounting Israeli casualties encouraged a level of public opposition unprecedented in Israeli politics. Moreover, President Reagan was outraged over the Israeli bombardment during the siege of Beirut in August 1982. Reagan expressed dismay at the scope of the operation, which by then had extended far beyond the original target in the south, and at the extent of civilian casualties and destruction. The international and national reaction to the war prompted Begin's decision to resign as prime minister in 1983. He retired to a life of seclusion.

HAROLD M. WALLER

See also Camp David Accords; Israel; Lebanon; Palestine (to 1948); Palestine Liberation Organization; Sadat, Anwar El-

FURTHER READING

Peleg, Ilan. *Begin's Foreign Policy, 1977–1983: Israel's Move to the Right.* New York, 1987.
Quandt, William B. *Camp David: Peacemaking and Politics.* Washington, D.C., 1986.
Sofer, Sasson. *Begin: An Anatomy of Leadership.* Oxford, 1988.

BELARUS

Located in Eastern Europe bordering Russia, Ukraine, Poland, Lithuania, and Latvia. Formerly the Byelorussian Soviet Socialist Republic of the Soviet Union (also known as White Russia), Belarus became an independent republic on 25 August 1991, and was recognized by the United States on 25 December 1991. Belarus's intention to remain neutral in terms of military alliances, especially its readiness to give up the nuclear weapons inherited from the Soviet Union, provided the basis for establishing friendly relations with Washington.

There are indications that immigrants from Belarus came to the United States as early as the eighteenth century. A massive influx arrived at the beginning of the twentieth century and in the wake of World War II (during which Belarus was devastated by the German occupation forces), for a total of some 650,000. Whereas pre–World War II arrivals included mostly laborers, several thousand nationally conscious Belarusans, committed to the cause of Belarusan independence and democracy, came after 1945. A number of them testified at congressional hearings on crimes allegedly committed by the communist regime in Belarus. The Belarusan American Association and the Byelorussian Congress Committee of America lobbied since the early 1950s for support of Belarusan independence. In 1974 President Richard M. Nixon, during his Moscow summit, made a trip to Belarus to mark the thirtieth anniversary of the liberation of Belarus in World War II and to acknowledge the republic's contribution to the defeat of Nazi Germany. Since the establishment of the U.S. embassy in Minsk (January 1993) and the Belarusan embassy in Washington (April 1993), U.S.-Belarusan relations have gradually widened to include cooperation in military matters (disarmament), parliamentary contacts, and scholarly exchanges. In July 1993 the chairman of the Belarusan parliament, Stanislau Shushkievich, visited Washington and met with President Bill Clinton. Clinton in turn was a guest in Minsk in January 1994, where he met not only with government officials, but also visited Kurapaty near Minsk, a ground of massive killings of civilians by Communists. In December 1994 the United States, the United Kingdom, and Russia signed at the Budapest summit a memorandum guaranteeing Belarus's sovereignty. In September 1995, the shooting down of two American sport balloons in the Belarusan airspace and the death of two American pilots marred American-Belarusan relations. Another strain was added in July 1996 when two leaders of the Belarusan Popular Front, Zianon Pazniak and Siarhei Navumchyk, fled Belarus in fear for their freedom and lives; they applied in Washington for political asylum, which was granted.

Belarus, a nation of 10 million people, has a strong industrial sector and enjoys an enviable geographical location, between Western Europe and Russia, especially advantageous for trade purposes. Foreign investments, however, have been meager so far because of the slowness of market reforms. The United States ranks high on the list of Belarus's foreign trade partners. In 1994 the U.S. Commerce Department designated $1 million for establishing a U.S. Business Center in Minsk.

JAN ZAPRUDNIK

See also Russia and the Soviet Union

FURTHER READING

Helen Fodor, ed. *Belarus and Moldova: Country Studies.* Washington, D.C., 1995.

Jan Zaprudnik. *Belarus at a Crossroads in History.* Boulder, Colo., 1993.

BELGIUM

Located in Western Europe, bordering the North Sea, France, the Netherlands, Germany, and Luxembourg, a kingdom with which the United States has had long and largely friendly relations. A part of the Spanish and Austrian Netherlands during the early modern period, occupied by France in 1794, and given to the new Kingdom of the Netherlands by the Congress of Vienna (1815), the Belgians—highly resentful of Dutch predominance—revolted successfully fifteen years later and (with British support) achieved full independence at the London Conference of 1830–31.

During the American War of Independence, American revolutionaries were supplied with weapons manufactured in the Belgian cities of Liège and Verviers. Otherwise, there was no discernible Belgian factor in U.S. foreign relations for over forty years—except indirectly, the Treaty of Ghent negotiated in 1814 by the United States and Great Britain that brought an end to the War of 1812. At the time of the Belgian Revolution in 1830, diplomatic correspondence reveals U.S. officials to have been sympathetic to the cause of the rebels. Belgian leaders were in turn significantly influenced by the example of the United States in its formative period, particularly the constitutional imperative of the separation of church and state. The United States, along with France and Great Britain, was one of the first nations to grant diplomatic recognition to Belgium in 1832.

For nearly fifteen years after that the United States and Belgium thrice negotiated, signed, and attempted to ratify a Treaty of Commerce, Navigation and Amity. As the name suggests, the treaty concerned agreement on maritime laws protecting trade, property rights granted by each government to citizens of the other while residing in the first country, and the rights of neutrals in time of war. Both nations were anxious to reassert Belgian and American neutrality in any future European wars. First negotiated and signed in 1830, the treaty was ratified by the U.S. Senate but rejected by Belgium for fear of incurring Great Britain's displeasure by exacerbating commercial rivalries. By 1842, however, Belgian interests depended more on the United States than Great Britain, and in early 1846 the final treaty was signed and put into effect.

Amicable relations between Belgium and the United States continued undisturbed until the U.S. Civil War.

Belgian involvement began in the final two years of the war when the Union Army purchased Belgian weapons and recruited Belgian soldiers and sailors without difficulty. Belgians living in New York and Louisiana also served in military units. However, near the end of the Civil War, King Leopold of Belgium supported the ill-fated attempt by his son-in-law, Archduke Maximilian of Austria, to establish himself, with substantial French assistance, as emperor of Mexico in clear violation of the strictures of the Monroe Doctrine. Also during the reign of Leopold I, the Belgians attempted to establish footholds in Guatemala, Brazil, and Haiti. Leopold I's successor, Leopold II, briefly contemplated intervention in the Philippines in 1898. With respect to the colonization of Africa, relations were more cordial as the United States rendered signal diplomatic assistance to Belgium in the Congo in 1884, recognizing the *Association Internationale du Congo* established by King Leopold II. While the Berlin Conference of the same year confirmed the *Association* to be a free state, the United States was not a signatory of the Berlin Accord; yet it recognized the Belgian presence in the Congo before and after its absorption by Belgium in 1908.

Ties of amity between the United States and Belgium grew warmest during World War I. Germany invaded Belgium at the outbreak of hostilities, violating its neutrality, massacring civilians, and deporting Belgian workers. U.S. citizens spontaneously formed relief committees to provide humanitarian aid to more than seven million civilians inside German lines, transporting food through the naval blockade for distribution by U.S. and other neutral agents. The U.S. ambassador to Belgium remained in Brussels after the German invasion to aid individuals, protest the deportations, and facilitate relief efforts. Even more significant, in Belgian eyes, were the herculean efforts of future U.S. president Herbert Hoover in his capacity as chairman of the commission for Relief in Belgium during the years 1915–1919.

With the United States failing to ratify the Treaty of Versailles and in retreat from international responsibilities after 1919, Belgian-U.S. relations were less intensive until the outbreak of World War II. Following the German invasion of Belgium in May 1940, the United States became a haven for Belgian intellectuals and one Belgian businessman living in New York purveyed Congolese uranium ore, far richer than either Canadian or domestic sources, to serve Allied military purposes.

In 1944, U.S. forces liberated Luxembourg and Belgium. Marshall Plan aid was supplied to Belgium by the United States during the postwar years. The failure of Belgian policies of neutrality prior to World War II led to Belgium's signing of the Treaty of Brussels in 1948, a collective defense agreement and forerunner to the NATO alliance. It was the first time Belgium had belonged to a peacetime military alliance and, until the mid-1970s, Belgian defense policies were consistent with the wishes of the United States, its most powerful ally. There was little Belgian resistance, in 1950, to the idea of German rearmament and virtually no opposition to its entrance into NATO in 1955. Practically no debate occurred in Belgium over the 1957 NATO decision to equip the European Allies with tactical nuclear weapons; and they were installed in Belgium in 1963. In 1962, however, Belgium did not approve President John F. Kennedy's Multilateral Nuclear Force (MLF) plan, which called for the storage of strategic nuclear weapons on Belgian territory. Nevertheless, ever a staunch NATO member, in 1966, the Belgian parliament approved the transfer of NATO headquarters from Paris to Brussels; later, ground-launched cruise missiles were deployed in Belgium during the 1980s. The United States and Belgium also overcame strains that had developed over UN-sponsored intervention in the former Belgian Congo at the time of its independence.

During most of the postwar period Belgium has been active in both military and economic spheres of European cooperation. In 1957 Belgium helped in the signing of the Treaty of Rome which established the European Economic Community (EEC), or Common Market. The European Commission and Council offices were established in Brussels in 1958. During the early 1970s, while remaining unquestionably loyal to the Atlantic Alliance, Belgium also supported initiatives by the GATT, the Council of Europe, and the OECD to open trade relations with Eastern Europe. Belgian representatives also participated in disarmament forums sponsored by the Conference on Security and Cooperation in Europe (CSCE). During the 1980s, NATO was still viewed by most Belgians as the best possible framework for their country's security. In the post–Cold War era, fundamental bases of cooperation between the United States and Belgium persist on all fronts.

REBECCA BRITTON

See also Hoover, Herbert; Marshall Plan; North Atlantic Treaty Organization; World War I; World War II; Zaire

FURTHER READING

Flynn, Gregory, ed. *NATO's Northern Allies: The National Security Policies of Belgium, Denmark, the Netherlands and Norway.* Totowa, N.J., 1985.
Rooney, John W., Jr. *Belgian-American Diplomatic and Consular Relations, 1830–1850.* Louvain, Belg., 1969.
Skemer, Don C. *American History in Belgium and Luxembourg: A Bibliography.* Brussels, 1975.

BELIZE

See Appendix 2

BEMIS, SAMUEL FLAGG

(*b.* 20 October 1891; *d.* 26 September 1973)

American historian, considered by many to have been the greatest of his generation in chronicling U.S. diplomatic history. Bemis was born in Worcester, Massachusetts. He received his bachelor of arts and masters degrees from Clark College in 1912 and 1913 and his doctorate from Harvard University in 1916. While doing research for his dissertation in Europe during World War I, he was aboard the ship *Sussex* in the English Channel when a German submarine torpedoed it. He survived the incident and went on to do his early teaching in the western part of the United States. Following several additional moves, Bemis spent the final twenty-five years of his distinguished career at Yale University. He was elected president of the American Historical Association in 1961.

Among historians of U.S. foreign relations, Bemis was the leading advocate and exemplar of multi-archival research. He applied his high standards of scholarship to his works on Jay's and Pinckney's treaties, the diplomacy of the American Revolution, the Latin American policy of the United States, a widely respected college textbook on U.S. diplomatic history that went through four editions, and numerous articles and reviews. The culmination of his publishing career was his two-volume biography of John Quincy Adams for which he won the second of his Pulitzer Prizes. Bemis wrote so well of Adams because he obviously identified strongly with him, sharing Adams's intelligence, broad education, rectitude, and aggressive patriotism along with his stiff formality and a degree of personal prickliness.

All of Bemis's work was suffused with his patriotic fervor. Until World War II, this patriotism took the form of a conservative hemispheric isolationism. He thoroughly approved of his nation's westward expansion and assertive policy toward Latin America, but he considered the U.S. acquisition of colonies in Asia after the Spanish-American-Cuban-Filipino War to be a "great aberration" and called Europe an "*abattoir.*" As demonstrated by the subtitle of his book on Pinckney's treaty, he rejoiced that the United States in its early years derived "advantage from Europe's distress." As late as 1941 he was a prominent opponent of U.S. intervention into either the European or Pacific theaters of World War II. After the war, however, Bemis publicly recanted his former isolationism and became an ardent Cold Warrior.

Bemis's influence on policymakers was not great. His highly nationalistic views on the history of U.S. foreign relations were considered somewhat idiosyncratic even in his own time and have met with considerable criticism in recent years. But his scholarly contributions to the study of early U.S. foreign relations remain seminal.

JERALD A. COMBS

See also Adams, John Quincy; Isolationism

FURTHER READING

Allen, H. C. "Samuel Flagg Bemis." In *Pastmasters*, edited by Marcus Cunliffe and Robin W. Winks. New York, 1969.

Bemis, Samuel Flagg. *Jay's Treaty: A Study of Commerce and Diplomacy.* New York, 1923. Rev. ed., New Haven, Conn., 1962.

———. *Pinckney's Treaty: A Study of America's Advantage from Europe's Distress, 1783–1800.* Baltimore, Md., 1926 (rev. ed., New Haven, Conn., 1960).

———, ed. *The American Secretaries of State and Their Diplomacy,* 10 vols. New York, 1927–1929.

———. *The Diplomacy of the American Revolution.* New York, 1935. 3d ed. Indianapolis, Ind., 1957.

———. *A Diplomatic History of the United States.* New York, 1936. 4th ed. New York, 1955.

———. *The Latin American Policy of the United States.* New York, 1943.

———. *John Quincy Adams and the Foundations of American Foreign Policy.* New York, 1949.

———. *John Quincy Adams and the Union.* New York, 1956.

———. *American Foreign Policy and the Blessings of Liberty.* New Haven, Conn., 1962.

Bostart, Russell H., and John De Novo. "Samuel Flagg Bemis." *Massachusetts Historical Society Proceedings* 85 (1973): 117–129.

Smith, Gaddis. "The Two Worlds of Samuel Flagg Bemis." *Diplomatic History* 9 (Fall 1985): 295–302.

BENEŠ, EDUARD

(*b.* 8 May 1884; *d.* 3 September 1948)

President of Czechoslovakia, 1938–1938; 1945–1948. Born in Kožlany to a farming family, Beneš studied at Charles University in Prague and at the École des Sciences Politiques and the Sorbonne in Paris. He completed a doctorate of law at the University of Dijon in 1908 and became a lecturer at the Commercial Academy of Prague and a professor of sociology at the Czech University in Prague.

A protege of Tomáš Masaryk, the first president of Czechoslovakia, Beneš worked hard to gain international support for an independent Czechoslovak state. He was one of the founders, while in exile in Paris during World War I, of the organization that became the Czechoslovak National Council and served as its secretary. When this organization became the provisional government of the newly independent Czechoslovakia in October 1918, Beneš became its first foreign minister (a post he held until 1935). He also served as prime minister of Czechoslovakia from 1921 to 1922.

As foreign minister, Beneš helped to establish the Little Entente between Czechoslovakia, Romania, and Yugoslavia. He looked to France as Czechoslovakia's primary ally and was an active supporter of the League of Nations.

Beneš's actions as president are the subject of continued historical controversy. Abandoned by Great Britain

and France in the Munich Agreement of September 1938, Beneš submitted to German demands to cede the Sudetenland on 30 September. On 5 October he resigned and left the country. In July 1940 he founded a government in exile in London, which was recognized later by both Great Britain and the United States.

After 1943, Beneš made efforts to act as an intermediary between the United States and Great Britain on one side and the Soviet Union on the other. These attempts caused him to be viewed with suspicion by both sides.

Beneš returned to Czechoslovakia in May 1945 and was reelected president in June 1946. Prior to his return, he visited Moscow in recognition of the Soviet Union's new role in Central Europe. In February 1948 Czechoslovak communist leaders, in preparation for a coup, provoked a crisis over control of the police forces. Faced with an armed militia and the threat of widespread civil disturbances, Beneš yielded to communist demands that he accept the resignation of the democratic ministers and allow a communist dominated government to be formed. Beneš resigned as president on 7 June 1948 and died three weeks later.

SHARON L. WOLCHIK

See also Czech Republic; Munich Conference

FURTHER READING

Beneš, Eduard. *Memoir of Dr. Eduard Beneš: From Munich to New War and New Victory.* New York, 1972.

———. *Eduard Beneš in His Own Words: Threescore Years of a Statesman.* New York, 1944.

Tàborsky, Edward. *President Beneš: Between East and West, 1918–1948.* Stanford, Calif., 1981.

Ullmann, Walter. "Beneš Between East and West." In *Czechoslovakia, 1918–88: Seventy Years from Independence,* edited by H. Gordon Skilling. New York, 1991.

BEN-GURION, DAVID

(*b.* 10 October 1886; *d.* 1 December 1973)

Leader of the Jewish community during the latter part of the British mandate over Palestine (1935–1948), who headed the struggle to achieve independence for Israel and served as its first prime minister (1948–1953, 1955–1963). Born David Gruen in Plonsk, Poland, he became an ardent Zionist as a teenager and emigrated to Palestine in 1906. From Palestine, he went to study law in Salonika and Constantinople. In 1921 he became general secretary of the Histadrut, a confederation of Jewish workers in Palestine, and in 1930 formed Mapai, the Zionist Labor party. In 1935 he was made chairman of the executive committee of the Jewish Agency for Palestine, the top post in the Jewish government-in-the-making.

Soon after World War II began, Ben-Gurion outlined his goals: "The world war of 1914–1918 brought us the

Balfour Declaration. This time, we have to bring about a Jewish state." By the eve of Israel's independence in 1948, he had become the dominant Jewish political figure in Palestine. After the Partition Plan—meant to create two states, Jewish and Arab, in Palestine—was adopted by the United Nations General Assembly on 29 November 1947, Ben-Gurion led the effort to organize the Jewish community, to prepare for statehood, and to defend the nascent state against Arab attempts to eradicate it. On 14 May 1948, as the British mandate ended, Ben-Gurion proclaimed the independence of the new State of Israel, citing the historical connection of the Jewish people with the land of Israel. In a decisive response that is remembered as a landmark in U.S.-Israel relations, President Harry S. Truman immediately extended de facto recognition to Israel, the first head of government to do so. In subsequent dealings with Israel, Truman was inconsistent, reflecting conflicting pressures within his administration. A number of issues, such as Israel's boundaries and Arab refugees, introduced elements of dispute into the U.S.-Israeli relationship, although the policy differences between Ben-Gurion and Truman were never personalized. The two leaders met in 1951 when Ben-Gurion made an official visit to the United States, and again in 1960. The Israeli also met President John F. Kennedy during a visit in 1961.

As Israel's first prime minister and defense minister, as well as leader of Mapai, Ben-Gurion shaped the character of Israel's institutions, political processes, and public policies. After consolidating the state and unifying the army, he resigned in 1953 but was recalled to his two posts in 1955 after a government scandal. During the 1956 Suez Crisis, he directed the Sinai Campaign, launched against Egypt in cooperation with Great Britain and France, after Egypt had seized and nationalized the Suez Canal. The Israel Defense Forces gained control of the Sinai Peninsula in a few days, but President Dwight D. Eisenhower strenuously opposed the operation and Israeli control over the Sinai. The confrontation between Eisenhower and Ben-Gurion became intense, and U.S. economic and political pressure compelled Israel to withdraw from the Sinai. Israel had nevertheless succeeded in ending terrorist attacks from Gaza, placing a UN buffer between the Egyptian and Israeli armies, and opening the vital Strait of Tiran to Israeli shipping.

During the Kennedy administration, Washington's increasingly supportive orientation led to a markedly warmer relationship. Prime Minister Ben-Gurion was particularly pleased by the 1962 deal for Hawk missiles, Israel's first arms agreement with the United States, as well as by general U.S. backing for Israeli positions on international and Middle East issues. Ben-Gurion resigned his ministerial posts in 1963 but remained active in politics until 1969, when he retired to his kibbutz at Sde Boker in the Negev desert.

HAROLD M. WALLER

See also Balfour Declaration; Eden, Robert Anthony; Egypt; Israel; Middle East; Palestine (to 1948); Suez Crisis

FURTHER READING

Bar-Zohar, Michael. *Ben-Gurion: A Biography*, translated by Peretz Kidron. New York, 1986.
Ben-Gurion, David. *Israel: Years of Challenge*. New York, 1963.
———. *Israel: A Personal History*. New York, 1971.
Brecher, Michael. *Decisions in Israel's Foreign Policy*. New Haven, Conn., 1974.
Gal, Allon. *David Ben-Gurion and the American Alignment for a Jewish State*. Bloomington, Ind., 1991.
Safran, Nadav. *Israel: The Embattled Ally*. Cambridge, Mass., 1981.
Snetsinger, John. *Truman, the Jewish Vote, and the Creation of Israel*. Stanford, Calif., 1974.

BENIN

See Appendix 2

BENJAMIN, JUDAH PHILIP
(*b.* 6 August 1811; *d.* 6 May 1884)

Lawyer, railroad promoter, senator from Louisiana (1853–1861), and secretary of state of the Confederate States of America (1862–1865). Born on the island of Saint Croix in the Danish West Indies and raised in South Carolina, Benjamin became a prominent New Orleans attorney and an active member of the Louisiana Whig party. Always a partisan of the South, he vigorously advocated Southern commercial expansion and lobbied for a group that sought to construct a railroad across the Isthmus of Tehuantepec in Mexico, which he insisted would allow the South and New Orleans to capture the trade with East Asia and so protect the South from Northern domination. Elected to the U.S. Senate in 1852, he joined the Democratic party in 1856 following the collapse of the Whigs. He emerged as an eloquent champion of Southern independence and developed a close friendship with Jefferson Davis, who later became president of the Confederacy. After Benjamin resigned from the Senate in February 1861 during the secession crisis, he served as Confederate attorney general and secretary of war. On 17 March 1862 Benjamin replaced Robert M. T. Hunter as secretary of state. After losing several months trying to establish secure lines of communication with Confederate agents in Europe, Benjamin vainly attempted to secure British and French intervention through offers of free access to Southern markets, cotton subsidies, diplomatic support for Great Britain in

Canada and for France in Mexico, and then, in final desperation, an offer in January 1865 to emancipate the slaves (albeit after conscripting them into military service). The lack of decisive Southern military victories in the early part of the war, and the subsequent defeat of Confederate armies at Gettysburg and Vicksburg (in 1863) had convinced Great Britain and France that the Southern cause was lost. Following the defeat of the Confederacy in 1865, Benjamin escaped to England, where he became a distinguished barrister and queen's counsel.

KINLEY J. BRAUER

See also American Civil War; Confederate States of America; Davis, Jefferson

FURTHER READING

Evans, Eli N. *Judah P. Benjamin: The Jewish Confederate.* New York, 1988.
Meade, Robert D. *Judah P. Benjamin: Confederate Statesman.* New York, 1943.
Osterweis, Rollin G. *Judah P. Benjamin: Statesman of the Lost Cause.* New York, 1933.

BERLE, ADOLF AUGUSTUS, JR.

(*b.* 29 January 1895; *d.* 17 February 1971)

Assistant secretary of state for Latin American affairs (1938–1944) and ambassador to Brazil (1945–1946). A member of President Franklin D. Roosevelt's brain trust, Berle was widely known for his 1932 work, *The Modern Corporation and Private Property*, which warned of a dramatic and growing concentration of economic power in the hands of the managers of a few great corporations and urged that this power be held socially accountable. As assistant secretary of state for Latin America, Berle championed the Good Neighbor Policy as a model for mutually beneficial relations between a great power and its weaker neighbors. He advocated hemispheric solidarity as a partial response to Nazi Germany before World War II and to the Soviet Union during the Cold War. His public support of democracy as ambassador to Brazil led to charges of intervention from the supporters of the ousted dictator, Getúlio Vargas. Out of public office until President-elect John F. Kennedy asked him to head a task force on Latin America in 1960, Berle maintained a network of contacts among prominent democrats in the hemisphere, including José Figueres, Rómulo Betancourt, and Luis Muñoz-Marín. Although much of the program recommended by Berle's task force was incorporated into the Alliance for Progress, its advocacy of a "democratic international," which would help finance democratic movements in other countries, was not.

STEVEN SCHWARTZBERG

See also Alliance for Progress; Brazil; Cold War; Good Neighbor Policy; Latin America

FURTHER READING

Berle, Adolf A. Papers. Franklin D. Roosevelt Library, Hyde Park, N.Y.
Berle, Beatrice Bishop, and Travis Beal Jacobs, eds. *Navigating the Rapids, 1918–1971.* New York, 1973.
Schwarz, Jordan A. *Liberal: Adolf A. Berle and the Vision of an American Era.* New York, 1987.

BERLIN

The capital of Germany and a major focus of East-West tensions in the four decades after World War II. Berlin in many respects was the keystone of U.S. foreign policy toward Europe over the entire course of the Cold War. As early as 1943, in discussions concerning a postwar settlement and the occupation of Germany, President Franklin D. Roosevelt conceded that there would be "a race for Berlin" and expressed an interest in planning for U.S. control of the city. Berlin then became the symbolic focal point and the constant physical manifestation of the larger East-West political and ideological struggle that would rage for almost forty years.

Postwar Settlement and Occupation

Although the Cold War confrontation between the United States and the Soviet Union was generally fought indirectly, fueled by the arms race, regional wars, or tit-for-tat trade restrictions, if a military engagement had erupted, it most likely would have been over Berlin. In order to understand why Berlin became the battleground of the Cold War, it is necessary to examine the origins of the Cold War and the agreements that led to the four-party occupation of Germany and Berlin.

Even before World War II ended, relations between the Soviet Union and the Western Allies had soured. The Soviets were resentful of the United States for its late entry into the war and of the West's failure to provide more military aid to the Soviet Union in its effort to defeat the Nazis on its front. As the end of the war approached, some in the United States feared that unless that nation acted decisively and promptly, Germany could turn into an anarchic power vacuum, a state soon ripe for a Nazi revival or, perhaps worse, a communist regime. U.S. policymakers, especially those in the Department of State, therefore pursued an occupation policy that had been carefully coordinated with Great Britain in hopes of winning the best possible terms from the Soviets. President Roosevelt was eager to control Berlin in the war's closing months, but General Dwight D. Eisenhower made the final decision that Allied troops would not be diverted prematurely in order to meet that end. Eisenhower ruled that a rush to Berlin would not serve the primary military objectives, a decision contrary to the views of General George S. Patton and the civilian leadership. Eisenhower maintained that Berlin was militarily insignificant compared to other concerns facing the Allies and that, in any case, the political formalities of joint occupation had already been worked out on paper.

Consequently, there was a window of several months when the Soviets alone occupied all of Berlin, a period in which they took full advantage of their unlimited access to Berlin's population and its resources, rich even in defeat. They immediately took direct revenge on the city, creating an image that would last for decades. Ignoring wartime Allied agreements on joint control of the city and its resources, they proceeded to loot and rob Berlin of everything from industrial equipment to boxcars for the reconstruction of Soviet society. More important, the Soviets tried to establish an all-entry legal and political order that would be favorable to Soviet interests. There was a broad effort to kill or punish members of the surviving political apparatus of the Nazi regime and to place in power Germans who were returning from Moscow or who were émigrés sympathetic to the cause of Joseph Stalin. All other political activities were brutally suppressed, and even traces of the anti-Nazi resistance were systematically eradicated.

Although the Soviets did agree to the broad outlines of temporary cooperative arrangements for the occupation of Berlin and Germany that were formulated during the war, the tripartite European Advisory Commission (EAC), established in London in October 1943 to recommend terms of surrender and methods of enforcing Allied policy in Germany, was plagued by fundamental disagreement, broadly economic in nature, over the role of Germany in the postwar period. These disagreements foreshadowed the later conflicts that would eventually divide Germany into two separate nations. The EAC eventually agreed on the Attlee Plan, a three-way occupation scheme that called for Germany as it existed in 1937 to be divided into three zones, to be occupied respectively by the United States, Great Britain, and the Soviet Union. As outlined in the plan, the Soviet sector contained 40 percent of Germany's territory, 36 percent of its population, and 33 percent of its vital resources. In addition, the plan stipulated that the three powers should establish a separate control for Berlin and occupy Berlin jointly, although the city was 110 miles inside what would become the Soviet zone. Roosevelt, citing poor U.S. access to sea routes from its zone in Germany's southwest region and the lack of direct access to Berlin, initially rejected the plan, but he failed to win the support of the other Western Allies and eventually accepted the zones as drawn. After the Yalta Conference in February 1945, the plans were renegotiated to include France in the Western Allies' occupation scheme without altering the basic settlement between the Soviet Union and the West.

On 28 March 1945 General Eisenhower cabled Stalin to inform him that the Allied forces would begin driving south to Berlin. By 4 July, U.S. and British occupation forces had reached Berlin, and later that month the Big Three—the United States, Great Britain, and the Soviet Union—met in Potsdam to discuss further occupation plans for Germany. On 12 August, French forces joined Allied forces in the former capital and the occupation of Berlin was complete. Agreements were signed by all, guaranteeing the Western allies fuel access by air, sea, and land through specified corridors for military and civilian traffic.

By this time Berlin's own local governing authority had also been established. In September 1944 the Big Three had created a special Berlin governing authority, the Kommandatura, which controlled all four sectors of the city and consisted of one appointed delegate from each of the four Allied powers. This governing authority could act only if all members were in complete unanimity. In contrast to the broader Allied Control Council that coordinated the all-powerful zonal governments for Germany as a whole, the Kommandatura was to act as a central unit, responsible for all decisions affecting control and governance of and access to Berlin. Within months after U.S. and British troops joined the Soviet forces in Berlin, this arrangement proved unworkable. By 1946 the predominant pattern was one of deadlocks and an overall escalation of tensions. The tensions in the Kommandatura reflected concretely the ideological conflicts acted out elsewhere in the world. Disputes in Berlin were rarely truly about streetcars or water (although such mundane problems certainly did exist) and were actually about global East-West confrontation. In a very real sense, Berlin became the battlefield of a war in which the combatants were careful to avoid armed conflict except where escalation could be scrupulously controlled. In Berlin, therefore, the war was mostly one of words, while proxy wars raged around the globe.

The Blockade: 1948–1949

When World War II ended, the United States was prepared to encourage Europe's economic renewal and independent defense and was inclined to withdraw its own military forces from the Continent at the earliest possible date. Roosevelt had believed he could negotiate with the Soviets to this end. Despite their stern warnings about malevolent Soviet intentions, the hawks in the administration of Harry S. Truman, who succeeded to the presidency upon Roosevelt's death in April 1945, were outnumbered by the optimists. Prime Minister Winston Churchill's "iron curtain" speech at Fulton, Missouri, describing the emergence of an insuperable East-West divide, was criticized by many observers in the United States as being ill-informed and unnecessarily cynical.

By 1948, however, Western-Soviet relations had deteriorated substantially, postwar conditions throughout Europe were dismal, and the mood in Washington had darkened. There was still no final agreement with the Soviets on the governance or the role of postwar Germany, and U.S. negotiators worried that Soviet demands were indeed unlimited. On 30 March 1948 the Soviets began tightening their grip on Berlin with the closing of freight lines between Munich and Hamburg, thereafter allowing only limited freight traffic to Berlin from Helmstedt. Such tightening continued on into June, step by step, until 18 June 1948, when the West announced a currency reform that would affect Western-occupied Germany but not Berlin.

It was at this moment that Berlin achieved special significance in Western and particularly in U.S. foreign policy. Berlin's value as a bastion of liberty was greatly enhanced because of its role as a conduit for those wishing to escape Soviet-style communism. Crossing out of the Soviet zone was difficult almost everywhere, but in Berlin one needed only to walk or take a train or taxi to move from East to West. One hundred fifty thousand East Berliners went to West Berlin to work each day and 2 million others left permanently between 1945 and 1952. The continuing exodus made Walter Ulbricht's East German regime politically vulnerable and imposed heavy economic costs in terms of lost labor (about one-half of those leaving were under twenty-five years of age).

On 24 June 1948 the Soviets imposed a blockade and began suspending all telephone, postal, and transport services to Berlin. In addition, the East Berlin regime claimed the right to check baggage and passengers on military trains running through the eastern zone, citing the need to hinder black market activity. On 25 June, in response to escalating Soviet pressure, a Western airlift began to provide survival supplies to the western sectors of the city. With the blockade firmly in place and the Western airlift operating like clockwork, the ensuing confrontation centered largely around trying to increase control over the city in small steps. In February 1949, for example, the West tightened the counterblockade, impeding all truck traffic to the Soviet zone; in March it announced that the West German mark would be considered the only legal tender in West Berlin. In the meantime, East Germany enforced its political system by expropriating all houses, land, insurance companies, and banks from East Berlin residents who were deemed bourgeois or who were thought to have capitalist ties. Having failed to force the West to yield control over West Berlin, the Soviets and the East Germans lifted the blockade on 12 May 1949, ten months and eighteen days after it had been imposed. During this period the West had delivered 2.3 million tons of food, coal, and other supplies in more than 275,000 flights. Berlin had indeed become "a symbol of resistance to the imposition of communist rule."

By the time communist leaders in the Soviet Union and in East Germany imposed the blockade, relations between the opposing blocs had become so acrimonious and so rife with suspicion that Western commanders believed the loss of Berlin might mean the loss of Germany and eventually all of Europe. For the United States, West Berlin had become a vital democratic stronghold buried 110 miles inside the Soviet empire. It represented the bulwark from which the West might exert its economic, social, and political influence in the years to come. It was the "lighted show window," the beacon of liberty and democracy. Most important, the Berlin blockade set the tone for the Cold War that would be waged within Berlin for the next forty years. Despite great pressure and political maneuvering, the Soviets failed to force the West to yield control over West Berlin. In comparison to the Soviets, the Western powers assumed the role of fundamentally decent allies, no longer occupiers but protectors of West Berliners and Germans alike. This was to be a crucial factor in later German debates about rearmament and about membership in the North Atlantic Treaty Organization (NATO).

The Cold War in Europe was largely characterized by restrained aggression; neither the Soviets nor the Americans wanted to provoke direct confrontation. That Berlin was indefensible with conventional forces made it the likely site of the first shots fired in any exchange and therefore a trip wire to eventual nuclear escalation. In 1948–1949 both sides appeared to recognize this, choosing to proceed with caution when the blockade went into effect. The Soviets clearly blinked. They did not yet have nuclear capabilities, so, despite their powerful conventional forces, any war that escalated would have been strategically one-sided. They did not dare shoot down U.S. and British aircraft and risk the loss not only of Berlin but of the rest of their Eastern European security zone and perhaps the Russian homeland as well. The risk limits, however, were almost as clear on the Western side. In 1948, given the weakness of their conventional capabilities, the United States and its British and French allies were not prepared to challenge Soviet control over either the eastern zone of Germany or East Berlin. Nor were they willing to demand real cooperation or demilitarization in Berlin, even in administrative terms.

East Berlin Uprising: 1953

If the Soviets blinked during the blockade, they reasserted their position on 17 June 1953, when they brutally suppressed an uprising, primarily in East Berlin, among East German workers. The West did not take any action, military or political, to support the East Germans but instead signaled their intentions not to intervene. This decision had far-reaching implications for the future of Western, particularly West German, policy. On the one hand, the West expressed, at least rhetorically, its strong desire to destabilize the Soviet stranglehold over Eastern Europe and to encourage East Berliners to resist the increasingly restrictive East German government. The 1953 uprising, however, was a grim reminder that the Soviets would protect with bullets what they perceived as their vital interests within their sphere. The West Germans thereafter celebrated the Berlin revolt annually on the "day of German unity," even while acknowledging that, given the bellicose nature of the Soviet regime, reform would have to await a top-down process and would not be precipitated by popular uprisings. This realization led to a West German policy that was rhetorically committed to improving the lives of the "brothers and sisters" trapped behind the iron curtain but that left fundamental improvements to an eventual reunification that would result from West Germany's policy of strength and its membership in the Western alliance.

Berlin, however, posed a somewhat different challenge. Berlin still represented a porous, if not totally open, boundary between East and West. West Germany provided increasing subsidies to West Berlin, and nonvoting representatives of Berlin sat in the Bundestag, but the fundamental basis of Berlin's legal identity, and therefore its security, rested on Allied rights and controls. These promised not only a refusal to extend formal recognition to the East German state but, more important, the hope of a Germany reunified through free elections and with a free and integrated Berlin as its capital.

The Rise of the Wall: 1958–1962

The Soviet desire to promote the sovereignty of the German Democratic Republic (GDR), as East Germany was formally known, and their growing dissatisfaction with the entanglements of the four powers in Germany led to the deadline crisis in 1958. This protracted crisis once again placed Berlin and its future not only at the center of the debate over the future of Germany but at the heart of East-West tensions. Berlin's significance in the crisis was far from purely symbolic; the conflict represented a serious test of the political commitments of both the East and the West. The confrontation began when the Soviets condemned the Western members of the alliance for violating the Potsdam Agreement by rearming West Germany and incorporating it into NATO in 1955. More significant, Soviet leader Nikita Khrushchev announced in November 1958 through a series of notes to the Western allies and in public statements that the "Berlin question" had to be solved within the next six months. To back up his demand Khrushchev threatened to take unilateral action in Berlin by disrupting transportation across the occupation zones and suggested the possibility that the

Soviets would attempt to conclude a separate peace with the East Germans. Such a threat posed serious problems for the West. By refusing to agree to the peace settlement or acknowledge the de facto partition of both Germany and Berlin, the West appeared to be unnecessarily prolonging the occupation. The Soviets argued that East Germany no longer required Soviet occupation and that the West, through its continued presence in Germany, was deliberately trying to provoke the Soviets and harm the socialist cause, as well as to maintain a forward military base to increase pressure on the East-West frontier.

The Soviets broadened the scope of their initiative in January 1959, when Khrushchev released a draft outline of a comprehensive German peace treaty. The treaty carefully avoided any provision for German reunification, but, like earlier Soviet proposals, it did provide for an independent, neutral, and demilitarized Germany. The treaty proposed that the four powers withdraw their forces and establish Berlin as a model for the future solution to the German question. The Western alliance took the Soviet initiative as an opportunity to conduct broader negotiations on the disposition of Germany and the continued rights of the four powers. The Soviets were interested primarily in securing a peace that protected their interests in East Germany and ended the formal occupation of Germany by the Allies. The Western position linked the future of Berlin to the future of Germany as a whole, a position the Soviets rejected out of hand. This linkage laid the foundation for a policy that would keep the United States and the Western Alliance in Berlin for the remainder of the Cold War.

Above all else, it was West German Chancellor Konrad Adenauer's insistence on reunification from strength that precluded recognition of the GDR and a positive response to the Soviet proposal. The Western Allies could not negotiate a peace treaty that recognized any significant East German rights without undermining Adenauer both at home and internationally. The United States was committed to supporting West Germany, already a critical NATO partner, on reunification and (somewhat more reluctantly) on the Hallstein Doctrine, which stated that the West German government had the sole right to speak internationally for all of Germany until a freely elected all-German government took office. In replying to both the Soviet ultimatum and the draft of the proposed peace treaty, the West accepted the concept of all-German negotiations but reasserted its right to stay in Berlin until a final peace treaty was signed.

Broad negotiations between the four powers and representatives from the two Germanies began in Geneva on 11 May 1959, but negotiators met with little success in their talks on the future of Germany. Limited compromises over Berlin that allowed the Soviets to hand over access controls and transportation regulation duties to

East German "agents" in Berlin were agreed upon in July. The West retained agreements on free access to West Berlin for military personnel and civilian traffic. After the failure at Geneva, the Camp David Summit in September marked a turning point in the crisis. Khrushchev backed down on Soviet demands for an immediate solution to the Berlin crisis. He also lessened the Soviet emphasis on the demilitarization of Berlin but continued to promote the notion of Berlin as a free city. The Soviets rejected the notion of any connection or political link between West Berlin and West Germany and attacked Adenauer and Willy Brandt, then mayor of West Berlin, as being responsible for much of the East-West tension over Berlin and the future of Germany. To many, including U.S. observers, Khrushchev appeared to have become more conciliatory, dropping the demand for a quick solution to the Berlin problem and reaffirming the right of the Western Allies to be in Berlin. At the same time, by renewing the attack on Adenauer and Brandt, the Soviets attempted to undermine the connection between West Berlin and West Germany and also to weaken the notion that West Germany could or should speak for all of Germany.

In the wake of the downing of a U.S. spy plane deep inside the Soviet Union, planned discussions on Germany's future at the 1960 Paris summit between Khrushchev and Eisenhower never occurred. Khrushchev maintained the right to seek a separate peace with East Germany but refused to act on this right. In Berlin the situation was made worse by selective blockades, imposed by the East German government, of West German access routes, thereby demonstrating the range of the GDR's power.

After criticizing Eisenhower's action in the 1960 presidential campaign, President John F. Kennedy inherited the Berlin crisis from his predecessor and immediately informed the Soviets that the new administration would need more time to formulate a position on Berlin. Impatient and perhaps unnerved by Kennedy's plans to restructure and bolster U.S. conventional and nuclear forces, Khrushchev started a second deadline crisis by issuing an ultimatum on the settlement of the free city of West Berlin from the East. In response to increasing Soviet hostility and demands regarding settlement in Berlin, Kennedy endorsed a plan to build up U.S. conventional forces and to expand U.S. nuclear missile and bomber programs. The U.S. emphasis on military readiness led to heightened pressure and a more hostile posture from Khrushchev.

The escalating tensions in Berlin had set both sides of the divided city on edge. East Berliners and not a few East Germans poured across the sector boundary into West Berlin seeking refuge. Economic difficulties, including food shortages, were partly responsible for pro-voking people to move West; the announcement by the GDR of a renewed push to nationalize farms and industries provided additional impetus. The greatest stimulus was the widespread sense of impending crisis and the increasing likelihood of war.

On 13 August 1961 the East German government closed the border between East and West Berlin. In the following weeks the East Germans erected a wall between the sectors, closing all but seven crossing points. As the wall grew, the division of Berlin became a physical fact. Allied officials condemned the wall as a violation of the four-power agreement, and U.S. Vice President Lyndon Johnson drove down the autobahn to Berlin to demonstrate the United States's commitment to preserving West Berlin's freedom. The United States also announced that it would reinforce the Berlin garrison and return General Lucius Clay, the hero of the 1948 airlift, to a Berlin command. More fundamentally, the United States was relieved that the East German actions had not affected the Western sectors. As long as the East did not interfere or intervene inside West Berlin, Kennedy was not prepared to go to war, nor were Adenauer or his British or French counterparts; in addition, despite his wish for forceful action, neither was Mayor Brandt.

Ostpolitik

In the 1960s Berlin suffered the fate of an aging symbol, still praised but somewhat neglected. There were still spurts of confrontation and dramatic flare-ups but little of the day-to-day drama of 1961. The symbolism was still strong, as Kennedy's "Ich bin ein Berliner" ("I am a Berliner") speech proved, but symbolism neither mitigated the harsh reality of division nor served to keep the younger generations in the fortress city. Subsidies, clever city planning, and cultural attractions could not ease the sense of growing isolation, if not abandonment. War might still come at any hour.

By the late 1960s West Germany's failure to acknowledge or reconcile the political division of Germany had become an embarrassment to Washington and its European allies, all of which established outreach programs to the East. While unification was the declared policy of Adenauer's government, its policy of strength and the Hallstein Doctrine isolated West German foreign policy and limited Western flexibility in negotiations. There was virtually no one in Eastern Europe with whom to negotiate. The West German policy of strict nonrecognition both constrained the increasingly détente-minded Allies and failed to address the political realities of a divided Europe.

The West German policy of strength began to soften during the Grand Coalition government, comprising representatives of the Christian Democratic Union (CDU), the Social Democratic Party (SDP), and the Free Democratic Party (FDP), which ruled from 1966 until 1969. The Hallstein Doctrine came to a formal end when West Berlin's Mayor Brandt became foreign minister in 1966, but West Germany was slow to overcome the paralysis that characterized its relations with the East, largely because it was unwilling to address the question of recognizing the GDR. Real progress began when Brandt ascended to the chancellorship. The coalition government made up of members of the SPD and the FDP adopted the line advanced since the 1950s by the Berlin SPD—that policies dedicated to preserving the formal and technical distinctions of the early postwar period were inhibiting the development of productive and fuller relations.

Much to the discomfort of President Richard Nixon and his national security adviser and, later, secretary of state, Henry Kissinger, Brandt's policy of Ostpolitik breathed new life into the petrified West German foreign relations. Brandt was an émigré, a wartime exile, and a new-style politician who modeled himself after Kennedy but who ultimately rejected Kennedy's willingness to accept a divided Europe for the foreseeable future. Although he was unwilling to recognize the GDR as an independent and legitimate state, Brandt was willing to acknowledge its existence and the reality of a divided Europe as political facts of the post–World War II era. Acknowledgment, however, was not a rejection or a renunciation of reunification or solidarity within Germany, nor was it a surrender to the communists. Brandt's policy shifted the focus of West German relations with the East away from the question of Germany's future and suggested that improved relations with Eastern Europe and with the Soviet Union would lead to progress on other issues.

Brandt's initial policy statement, issued on 28 October 1969 signaled the new government's desire to improve relations with the East. Brandt was willing to build on the "peace note" of 1966 and to issue mutual renunciation-of-force declarations with the Soviet Union, Poland, and Czechoslovakia. While not specifically mentioning the GDR, Brandt's statement clearly implied that East Germany was not excluded from this new policy and that West Germany was willing to make the same declaration with any other interested countries in the East.

Progress on the difficult issues surrounding Berlin was slow at first, but the early success of Brandt's outreach to the East was exemplified by West Germany's improved relations in Eastern Europe. In 1967 West Germany established formal diplomatic relations with Romania and in 1968 with Yugoslavia. Improved relations with Moscow led to the signing on 12 August 1970 of the Treaty of Moscow, in which both parties renounced the use or the threat of force and agreed to respect the territorial integrity of all the European states. Again, formal recognition of the GDR was left out, but West German acceptance of the prevailing political realities had provided a detour around the roadblock in intra-German relations. Disagreement and concern over Berlin and its future did not disappear, but the opening of new channels of communication and the discussion of new issues placed the tensions over Berlin in the context of the overall aims of West German foreign policy and relations between the West and the East.

The success of Ostpolitik meant that Berlin was no longer the flashpoint or the crucible for East-West conflict. With considerable U.S. support, the Quadripartite Agreement, signed on 3 September 1971, marked another major turning point. The agreement did not change the status of Berlin or the role of the Western powers within it, but it did formally acknowledge the ties between the Federal Republic of Germany (FRG), or West Germany, and the city. In Brandt's words, it marked "an important step on the road to détente in Europe." Traffic restrictions between East and West were eased considerably. West Berliners could travel to both East Berlin and the GDR. External consular representation of West Berlin within the Soviet Union and the East was included in the agreement, although action on this point remained a source of friction for some time.

The next major step was the 1972 signing of the Basic Treaty between the two Germanys. In this document the concept of "two states in one nation" was recognized, and West Germany gave de facto recognition to East Germany for the first time. The signatories renounced the use of force and agreed to similar provisions intended to alleviate still further the tensions that persisted between West Germany and the Eastern bloc. The treaty did not explicitly address Berlin's future, but it did reaffirm the rights and responsibilities of the four powers in Germany. No previous treaty or agreement between East and West was altered by this agreement. Following the Basic Treaty, the last major achievement of Ostpolitik came in 1973 when the FRG and the GDR were both admitted to the United Nations. This and the implementing Berlin Protocol helped to end the atmosphere of crisis and fear that had existed in Berlin for much of the first half of the Cold War, but East Berlin still remained behind the wall, and unification of Berlin or Germany seemed to recede further in the expectations of all.

The Fall of the Wall
and the Road to Reunification

The end of détente and Ronald Reagan's election to the presidency led to a more confrontational U.S. policy toward the East. The hard line taken by the conservative president placed Berlin at the focal point of East-West tensions. In a speech in West Berlin in 1987, Reagan called on the Soviets in the era of perestroika (restructuring) to tear down the wall that divided the German city. Chancellor Helmut Kohl took up the theme as well, asking the Soviet president, Mikhail Gorbachev, in their first Moscow meeting, to dismantle the divide.

Berlin's role in Reagan's foreign policy was primarily symbolic. The atmosphere of crisis and fear that had characterized the postwar occupation did not return. The Basic Agreement and the Quadripartite Agreement continued to ensure peaceful and relatively stable relations between the halves of the city, but the overall change in the tone of East-West relations under Reagan placed renewed significance on the city and its most prominent landmark. In the decades since the wall's construction, it had become a powerful metaphor in Western rhetoric. For many the wall had become the physical embodiment of Churchill's "iron curtain," the primary example of the incompatibility of individual freedom and communism. The spread of Gorbachev's reforms throughout Eastern Europe and the success of perestroika generally posed a basic challenge in Berlin. On the one hand, relations between the two Germanys had remained cordial even as rivalry between the superpowers increased in the early 1980s. Berlin was more and more an international backwater, despite its importance as the access point for German-German contacts and deals. There were even efforts to establish a new mutually acceptable cultural history, as in the coordinated all-Berlin celebration of Prussia and Frederick the Great.

An aging East German leadership, however, rejected Gorbachev's reforms and his willingness to accommodate the West with respect to the FRG. East Berlin and East Germany represented a unique model and a clear success; in the minds of the East German leaders, there was no reason to change anything. Moreover, East Germany wanted to maintain an enduring bulwark against a return of fascism or the triumph of confiscatory capitalism. Liberalized travel policies in the GDR had resulted in a sharp increase in applications from East Germans wishing to visit the West. East Germany's experimentation with more open borders, in Berlin and along the rest of the intra-German border, had failed, leading to serious concerns within the East German government about the country's long-term domestic stability.

The end of the Berlin wall began in the spring of 1989, when the Hungarian government decided to remove the fortifications and barriers along its Austrian border, part of Hungary's overall policy of liberal reform and openness with the West. In doing so, the Hungarian government created a way for East Germans wishing to flee to the West to detour around the Berlin wall. A trickle soon became a flood, with dramatic repercussions for East German society. At first, the reaction in East Berlin was to bid good riddance to those traitors who chose to leave for the West. Despite massive emigration to the

West and growing unrest among those who remained behind, East German party chief Erich Honecker kept plans to celebrate East Germany's fortieth birthday. The highlight of the celebration was a visit by Gorbachev, who made it clear that the Soviets would not interfere in the exodus of East Germans to the West, nor would Soviet troops in East Germany support the Honecker government in the event of domestic unrest. This message only bolstered the confidence of the increasingly defiant political dissentients. Protestors took to the streets to demand reforms but were initially arrested and beaten by the police. Organized efforts were banned as subversive and antistate. The protests continued.

It was not in Berlin but in Leipzig on 9 October that 70,000 East Germans assembled to press for democratic reform. In a surprise move, the police did not interfere, and the protestors demonstrated peacefully. This success provided the spark necessary to encourage demonstrations in East Berlin. On 4 November 1989 a crowd estimated between 500,000 and 1 million East Germans marched peacefully for democracy with little interference from police. The government attempt to catch up and gain control of the growing people's movement was too little too late. After the resignation of key members of the government and the party, the remaining leaders announced a policy of active reform with liberal travel rights and a host of other civic and political reforms.

On 9 November, one day after the resignation of the entire Politburo, the East German government announced, somewhat confusingly, that East Germans would no longer be prohibited from crossing over the border to West Germany. While the official announcement made no specific mention of the wall or of Berlin, the citizens of East Berlin and East Germany headed for the wall, and in a few hours they breached the structure that had divided East and West for almost thirty years. The Cold War ended much as it had begun, with the eyes of the world focused on Berlin.

The sight of East and West Berliners chipping away at the wall stands out as one of the most provocative pictures in a Cold War replete with powerful images. Few in West or East Germany ever imagined that the wall would come down in such a dramatic fashion. Gradual reform and democratization of East Germany was eclipsed by the symbolic and emotional power of the wall being torn down by the ordinary Berliners who had lived in its shadow for so many years. The symbolism of the wall's destruction, however, is once again only a beginning. A generation of Berliners had grown up with the wall and all the political dissonance that it represented; two generations of West and East Germans had very different images of the "normal" status of Berlin and of a divided German nation. The difficulties that had frustrated and divided Berlin and the rest of Germany could not be overcome with the removal of the physical barrier that separated East and West Berlin. Berlin thus once again stood on the edge of complex, interrelated issues. It is the capital of Germany, a state that in the mid-1990s was only slowly adjusting to its new legitimate power and exploring its far greater room for international maneuver.

CATHERINE KELLEHER

See also Adenauer, Konrad; Brandt, Willy; Cold War; Germany; Khrushchev, Nikita Sergeyevich; Kohl, Helmut; Russia and the Soviet Union

FURTHER READING

Adenauer, Konrad. *Memoirs*, 2 vols., London, 1966, 1968.
Catudel, Honoré. *Kennedy and the Berlin Wall Crisis: A Case Study in U.S. Decision Making*. Berlin, 1980.
Clay, Lucius D. *Decision in Germany*. Garden City, N.Y., 1950.
Davison, W. Phillips. *The Berlin Blockade*. Princeton, N.J., 1958.
Gelb, Norman. *The Berlin Wall: Kennedy, Khrushchev, and a Showdown in the Heart of Europe*. New York, 1987.
Gimbel, John. *The American Occupation of Germany: Politics and the Military, 1945–1949*. Stanford, Calif., 1968.
Hanrieder, Wolfram F. *West German Foreign Policy, 1945–1953*, Stanford, Calif., 1967.
———. *Germany, America, Europe: Forty Years of German Foreign Policy*. New Haven, Conn., 1989.
Kaiser, Karl. *German Foreign Policy in Transition*. New York, 1968.
Kelleher, Catherine McArdle. *Germany and the Politics of Nuclear Weapons*. New York, 1975.
Schick, Jack M. *The Berlin Crisis, 1958–1962*. Philadelphia, Pa., 1971.
Shlaim, Avi. *The United States and the Berlin Blockade, 1948–1949: A Study in Crisis Decision-making*. Berkeley, Calif., 1983
Slusser, Robert. *The Berlin Crisis of 1961: Soviet-American Relations and the Struggle for Power in the Kremlin, June–March 1961*. Baltimore, Md., 1973.
Smith, Jean Edward. *The Defense of Berlin*. Baltimore, Md., 1963.
Strauss, Franz Joseph. *The Grand Design*. New York, 1965
Sutterlin, James S., and David Klein. *Berlin: From Symbol of Confrontation to Keystone to Stability*. New York, 1989.
Wyden, Peter. *Wall: The Inside Story of a Divided Berlin*. New York, 1989.

BERNSTORFF, JOHANN HEINRICH

(*b.* 14 November 1862; *d.* 6 October 1939)

German career diplomat and ambassador to the United States during World War I. Born in London, the son of Prussia's ambassador to Great Britain, he spent his first decade in England, finished his education in Germany, served in the army in Berlin, and began his diplomatic career. His foreign assignments included Belgrade, St. Petersburg, London, and Cairo. His most important diplomatic post was as ambassador to the United States from 1908 to 1917. He advised his superiors that U.S. intervention on the side of the Anglo-French Entente in World War I would ensure Germany's defeat. Ignoring this reality, however, the imperial government in Berlin,

in defiance of the United States, resorted to unrestricted submarine warfare early in 1917. Bernstorff had failed to convince both Chancellor Theobald von Bethmann Hollweg and Kaiser Wilhelm II, who yielded to pressure from Germany's military leadership, to avoid this suicidal decision. The ambassador had also failed to persuade President Woodrow Wilson to disregard this German threat to American lives and property. The United States declared war on Germany on 6 April. During the period of U.S. neutrality before the war, Bernstorff had established a network of agents to foster pro-German sentiment among German Americans and Irish Americans. He also sanctioned attempts to entangle the United States in the Mexican Revolution and to sabotage munitions shipments for the Allies in New York Harbor and at a New Jersey assembly plant. Bernstorff's methods poisoned Wilson's attitude toward Germany, making the president even less tolerant of its submarine warfare.

After serving as ambassador in Constantinople until the war's end, Bernstorff returned home to oversee Germany's preparation for the Paris Peace Conference of 1919. He denounced the Treaty of Versailles as a gross violation of Wilson's Fourteen Points and called for its extensive revision, although he recognized that the new Weimar Republic had no realistic option but to sign. While serving in the Reichstag in the 1920s, he advocated German membership in the League of Nations. When his friend German Foreign Minister Gustav Stresemann achieved this goal in 1926, Bernstorff represented Germany at meetings of the League Assembly and headed the German delegation to the Preparatory Disarmament Conference (1929) in Geneva. Poor health forced his retirement before Adolf Hitler's seizure of power in 1933, and he lived in exile in Geneva until his death.

LLOYD E. AMBROSIUS

See also Germany; League of Nations; Submarine Warfare; Versailles Treaty of 1919; World War I

FURTHER READING

Bernstorff, Johann Heinrich, Graf von. *Memoirs of Count Bernstorff*. New York, 1936.
Doerries, Reinhard R. *Imperial Challenge: Ambassador Count Bernstorff and German-American Relations, 1908–1917*. Chapel Hill, N.C., 1989.

BETANCOURT, RÓMULO

(*b.* 2 February 1908; *d.* 28 September 1981)

Head of the revolutionary junta that controlled Venezuela from 1945 to 1948, and the elected president from 1959 to 1964. Forced into political exile in 1948, he returned in 1958, when he was elected president. He dedicated his political career to bringing democracy and social justice to Venezuela. As an official, he conducted warm relations with the United States and considered himself a "New Dealer," admiring the socioeconomic reforms of Franklin D. Roosevelt. He applauded the Alliance for Progress, John F. Kennedy's economic aid program for Latin America, and during his presidency welcomed $2.5 billion of U.S. investments in Venezuela, insisting only that the oil companies return a fair share of their profits in taxes. He also favored a high price for oil and supported the formation of the Organization of Petroleum Exporting Countries. At the same time, Betancourt was a foe of right-wing dictatorships in Latin America and a vigorous anticommunist. He supported U.S. efforts to isolate Fidel Castro's Cuba, and, in turn, the Kennedy administration embraced Betancourt, providing the Venezuelan president with economic aid to underwrite change and military aid to help him defeat political radicals.

STEPHEN G. RABE

See also Alliance for Progress; Cuba; Organization of Petroleum Exporting Countries; Roosevelt, Franklin Delano; Venezuela

FURTHER READING

Alexander, Robert J. *Venezuela's Voice for Democracy: Conversations and Correspondence with Rómolo Betancourt*. New York, 1990.
Betancourt, Rómulo. *Venezuela: Oil and Politics*. Boston, 1979.
Rabe, Stephen G. *The Road to OPEC: United States Relations with Venezuela, 1919–1976*. Austin, Tex., 1982.

BEVERIDGE, ALBERT JEREMIAH
(*b.* 6 October 1862; *d.* 27 April 1927)

Senator, author, and advocate of imperial expansion. Admitted to the bar in 1887, he practiced in Indianapolis, Indiana, until elected to the U.S. Senate as a Republican in 1899. Beveridge was defeated in 1911 following his break with the administration of William Howard Taft and devoted much of his time thereafter to writing history, including a four-volume biography of Chief Justice John Marshall (1916–1919). Beveridge championed U.S. acquisition of Cuba and the Philippines, U.S. hegemony over the Caribbean, and an aggressive search for overseas markets. He justified such actions on grounds of racial superiority, disposal of surplus domestic production, and national defense. Nationalistic and anglophobic, he advocated a strict neutrality prior to U.S. entry into World War I and rigidly opposed U.S. membership in the League of Nations. His colorful, hyperbolic speeches are often quoted by historians of U.S. imperialism.

JOSEPH A. FRY

See also Imperialism; League of Nations; Philippines; Race and Racism

FURTHER READING

Bowers, Claude. *Beveridge and the Progressive Era*. Boston, 1932.
Braeman, John. *Albert J. Beveridge: American Nationalist*. Chicago, 1971.
Thompson, J. A. "An Imperialist and the First World War: The Case of Albert J. Beveridge." *Journal of American Studies* 5 (1971): 133–150.

BEVIN, ERNEST
(*b.* 9 March 1881; *d.* 14 April 1951)

British foreign secretary (1945–1951) and staunch supporter of the United States in early Cold War confrontations with the Soviet Union. One of Great Britain's most prominent trade union leaders in the 1920s and 1930s, Bevin was a member of Winston Churchill's War Cabinet during World War II. Following the Labour party's electoral triumph under Clement Attlee in July 1945, he was named foreign secretary, a post he held until ill health forced his resignation. A grade-school dropout who came to office without diplomatic experience, Bevin nonetheless proved to be one of Great Britain's most successful postwar foreign secretaries. He and U.S. Secretary of State Dean Acheson established a particularly close and fruitful partnership. Bevin played a decisive role in the establishment of the Marshall Plan and was perhaps the single most influential figure behind the creation of the North Atlantic Treaty Organization. His most bitter policy failure was in the Middle East, where his pro-Arab views created considerable antipathy among supporters of Israel in the United States. On the other hand, some U.S. officials believed his hard-line approach to an Anglo-Iranian oil dispute threatened to push Iran closer to the Soviet Union. The dismantling of the British empire began during Bevin's years at the Foreign Office.

ROBERT M. HATHAWAY

See also Attlee, Clement Richard; Great Britain; Marshall Plan; North Atlantic Treaty Organization

FURTHER READING

Barker, Elisabeth. *The British Between the Superpowers, 1945–1950*. Toronto, 1983.
Bullock, Alan. *The Life and Times of Ernest Bevin*, 3 vols. London, 1960–1983.
Williams, Francis. *Ernest Bevin*. London, 1952.

BHUTAN
See Appendix 2

BIG FOUR
See Paris Peace Conference of 1919

BIODIVERSITY TREATY

Formally known as the Convention on Biological Diversity, a 1992 international agreement stemming from long-standing concerns about the scale and scope of species loss, and signed at the Earth Summit in Rio de Janeiro. The treaty went into force on 29 December 1993 after thirteen nations, including the United States, ratified it. Biological diversity is a term referring to the variability among living systems, including terrestrial and marine and other aquatic ecosystems. Evidence indicating that human activities lead to the progressive loss of the earth's biological diversity has raised this issue to a high level of political salience. The convention was negotiated by an intergovernmental negotiating committee (INC) under the auspices of the United Nations Environmental Programme (UNEP). The primary goal of the convention is to preserve biological diversity and to reduce the rates of loss in species. Major provisions include conservation of species, undertaking surveys and information-gathering activities on biological diversity, and promoting scientific research and international collaboration. Special attention is given to benefits from traditional and local knowledge and the distribution of biotechnology. The first Convention of the Parties (1995) gave considerable attention to financing for implementation of the convention, including specification of "incremental costs" for meeting obligations. With UNEP being accorded the role of the secretariat for the convention, this issue is placed squarely within the purview of the international community's leading environmental agency. Further, the convention reinforces an evolving notion of humanity as being intimately connected with, and dependent on, the earth's life-supporting properties. This notion undermines any sense of society's being isolated from natural environments and provides additional support for strengthening evolving conceptions of sustainability of social and environmental systems. The conservation focus of the convention is explicitly connected to the goal of preserving for present and future generations access to the benefits of biological diversity. As such, it is an explicit manifestation of the international community's growing acknowledgment of the imperatives of sustainable development.

NAZLI CHOUCRI

See also Earth Summit, Rio de Janeiro; Environment; United Nations Environment Program

FURTHER READING

Wilson, Edward O., ed. *Biodiversity.* Washington, D.C., 1988.
World Resources Institute. *Biodiversity Prospecting: Using Genetic Resources for Sustainable Development.* Baltimore, 1993.

BIOLOGICAL WEAPONS

Weapons of war that use microorganisms or toxins to cause disease in people, livestock, or crops. Use of biological weapons was banned by the 1925 Geneva Protocol that also first prohibited use of chemical weapons. Despite many allegations, there is only one generally accepted example of military employment of biological weapons. Japan is known to have used biological agents against China during the 1940s, but despite a massive research program the biological weapons had little real impact. Other reports, including allegations in the early 1980s by the United States that the Soviet Union had employed biological agents in Southeast Asia, have not been generally accepted.

Thousands of potential agents have been researched, but only a few have proven well suited for use in biological weapons. Among the organisms identified as biological agents are anthrax, brucellosis, Q fever, and tularemia. In addition, botulism toxin is known to have been adopted for use in biological weapons. The most important innovation in biological warfare was the development of aerosolization techniques in the 1950s, which made it possible to disseminate biological agents through the air. When spread as an aerosol, biological agents can pose a threat comparable in scope to that posed by thermonuclear weapons, if conducted effectively. Biological weapons can be used in assassinations aimed at single individuals. The widespread commercial availability of the relatively inexpensive technology needed to support biological warfare programs makes it difficult to constrain the proliferation of biological weapons.

The United States unilaterally ended its biological weapons program in 1969. Possession of biological weapons is prohibited by the Convention on Biological and Toxin Weapons of 1972. Despite the agreement, proliferation of biological weapons continued. By 1990, U.S. government officials claimed that at least ten countries had biological weapons programs. The list of alleged proliferators has never been made public, but is believed to include China, Egypt, Iran, Iraq, Israel, North Korea, Libya, Syria, and Taiwan.

Two countries—the former Soviet Union and Iraq—have admitted to violations of the convention. In the early 1970s the Soviet Union initiated a massive effort to develop biological warfare capabilities, and U.S. government officials believe that these efforts have been continued by the successor government of Russia. Iraq's program was ostensibly terminated in 1991 under United Nations's auspices. Extensive disclosures during 1995 of previously secret biological research have further fueled suspicions by U.S. and UN officials that Iraq maintains a covert biological warfare capability.

W. SETH CARUS

See also Chemical Weapons

FURTHER READING

Carus, W. Seth. *"The Poor Man's Atomic Bomb?": Biological Weapons in the Middle East*. Washington Institute for Near East Policy Paper, 23. Washington, D.C., 1991.

Stockholm International Peace Research Institute. *The Problem of Chemical and Biological Warfare*, 6 vols. New York, 1971–1976.

World Health Organization. *Health Aspects of Chemical and Biological Weapons*. Geneva, 1970.

BIPARTISANSHIP

The assumed tradition that in U.S. foreign policy "politics stops at the water's edge," and that the two major political parties will adopt a unified position on the most important foreign policy issues. This tradition is usually dated from shortly after the end of World War II, when Arthur Vandenberg, a Republican senator from Michigan and chairman of the Senate Foreign Relations Committee, cooperated with Democratic President Harry S. Truman to put into place an internationalist, Cold War-oriented foreign policy agenda.

Bipartisanship refers to the assumed cooperation both between the legislative and executive branches and between the Republican and Democratic parties. This cooperation entails two components. First, cooperation should occur in the development of foreign policy options, that is, the executive and legislative branches and members of the two major political parties consult with one another during the process of policy formulation. Second, cooperation should continue once an action or policy is chosen. A majority of both political parties within Congress would be expected to support such initiatives along with the president.

The basis for this bipartisan tradition has been attributed to the pragmatic nature of both the Democratic and Republican parties; their attempt to adopt policy positions with broad national appeal; and the perception of a threatening global environment that emerged immediately after World War II. Both major political parties came to stand for many of the same general principles during the height of the Cold War: an active role for the United States in global affairs, a vigorous national defense, and staunch anticommunism. Narrow partisan interests were seemingly replaced by common national security concerns.

Some critics, however, have questioned whether bipartisanship was ever particularly strong, especially in the post-Vietnam period. To the extent bipartisanship really existed in the post World War II years, it did so perhaps more over European than Asian issues. Analyses of congressional foreign policy-related voting in the four decades after World War II show that partisan and ideological divisions across the parties, and between Congress and the White House, were more often the norm.

JAMES M. MCCORMICK

See also Cold War; Congress; Democratic Party; Presidency; Republican Party; Vandenberg, Arthur Hendrick

FURTHER READING

Collier, Ellen C., ed. *Bipartisanship and the Making of Foreign Policy: A Hisotircal Survey*. Boulder, Colo, 1991.

Carroll, Holbert N. *The House of Representatives and Foreign Affairs*. Pittsburgh, Pa., 1958

Crabb, Cecil Jr. *Bipartisan Foreign Policy*. Evanston, Ill., 1957.

Destler, I. M., Leslie H. Gelb, and Anthony Lake. *Our Own Worst Enemy: The Unmaking of American Foreign Policy*. New York, 1984.

McCormick, James M., and Eugene R. Wittkopf. "Bipartisanship, Partisanship, and Ideology in Congressional-Executive Foreign Policy Relations, 1947–1988." *Journal of Politics* 52 (November 1990): 1077–1100.

Meernik, James. "Presidential Support in Congress: Conflict and Consensus on Foreign and Defense Policy." *The Journal of Politics* 55 (August 1993): 569-587.

BIPOLARITY

An international system with two principal powers. As a term, bipolarity came into vogue during the Cold War because of the pivotal struggle between the United States and the Soviet Union, and their respective allies, which formed two poles of global power.

Bipolarity contended with *multipolarity* in an academic debate within the realist school of international relations. As opposed to idealism or liberalism, realism focused on simple national interests, measured in terms of power, as the key to behavior in international relations as contrasted to the principles of universal morality or the progressive goals of idealists. Realists, then, were prepared to settle for the goal of stability, rather than peace, but they disagreed among themselves over how stability was best achieved. Classical realists, led by Hans Morgenthau, contended that the historical record of conflict between Athens and Sparta, Rome and Carthage, and England and Spain proved that bipolarity was a prescription for convulsive warfare. Multipolarity, on the other hand, dissipated conflict among four or five roughly equal powers through the stability produced by a balancing power, such as England in Europe's "century of peace" from 1815 to 1914.

Neorealists, led by Kenneth Waltz, argued that the "peace" of the Cold War demonstrated the superior stability of bipolarity. Two factors accounted for this stability. First, because of their capacity to wreak absolute destruction, the presence of nuclear weapons in the arsenals of the two super powers made the avoidance of war the central goal of their foreign policies. A key point of the argument by Waltz (and others) is that bipolarity reduces uncertainty—and that uncertainty is highly dangerous. Second, the two dominant powers could regulate their relationship through the internal balancing of taking corrective action within their societies, such as by the raising or lowering of defense budgets, rather than through the more unpredictable external diplomatic balancing required by multipolarity. By bringing international relations more under the control of the two powers themselves, internal balancing produced a more stable system by permitting a learning process of confidence-building that led to trust between the two poles. This was reflected in the numerous arms control agreements of the Cold War.

TIMOTHY J. LOMPERIS

See also Cold War; Morgenthau, Hans; Realism

FURTHER READING

Morgenthau, Hans J. *Politics Among Nations*, 6th ed. Revised by Kenneth W. Thompson. New York, 1985.
Waltz, Kenneth N. *Theory of International Politics*. Reading, Mass., 1979.

BISMARCK, OTTO EDWARD LEOPOLD VON

(*b.* 1 April 1815; *d.* 30 July 1898)

Minister-president to King Wilhelm I of Prussia (September 1862–December 1872), the principal architect of the unification of Germany, and the German Empire's first chancellor (January 1871–March 1890). Although his mastery of realpolitik was often seen as mere opportunism, Bismarck held throughout his career to a deeply rooted conservatism that combined a passionate loyalty to the Hohenzollern monarchy with an antipathy to parliamentary government. Bismarck's significance in the history of U.S. foreign relations developed only after his death, when the powerful united Germany of his creation, first under Kaiser William (Wilhelm) II, and later under Adolf Hitler, challenged the European balance of power and led to U.S. intervention in two world wars.

The son of an East Elbian landowner, Bismarck was a relatively obscure civil servant and spokesman for the Junker aristocracy until he became Prussia's representative to the Diet of the loosely structured German Confederation in 1852. A decade later William I chose Bismarck as minister-president when liberals in the Prussian assembly were refusing to approve funding for military reform, a deadlock Bismarck resolved by openly flouting the constitution and authorizing expenditures without parliamentary approval. Instigating and manipulating three wars, against Denmark (1864), Austria (1866), and France (1870–1871), Bismarck was able by 1871 to transform thirty-eight separate states into a unified—and Prussianized—German Empire under William I. After 1871 Bismarck sought to ensure Germany's security through a network of alliances, including the Triple Alliance (1881) with Austria and Italy and the Reinsurance Treaty (1887) with Russia. The deaths in 1888 of William I and his son, the "ninety-day kaiser," Frederick III, brought to the throne William II who, within eighteen months, forced Bismarck into retirement and set German foreign policy onto a more expansionist and increasingly provocative new course.

German-American opinion, noting Bismarck's pro-Union sympathies during the Civil War, generally applauded the creation of the German Empire, despite the illiberal means by which it was achieved. George Bancroft, the U.S. minister to Berlin and an ardent Germanophile, extolled the new empire as "the United States of Germany." U.S.-German relations remained cordial through the 1870s until Germany's move to a protectionist trade policy after 1879, including a total ban on the importation of salt pork in 1883, produced considerable resentment among U.S. producers. Given Bismarck's largely Eurocentric focus, the United States was peripheral to his diplomacy, even when, under pressure at home, he acquiesced in the 1880s to the acquisition of the first German overseas colonies. Bismarck went out of his way to avoid any entanglements in the Western Hemisphere, where he openly acknowledged "the paramount influence of the United States."

Early in 1889, shortly before Bismarck left office, a crisis developed in the South Pacific over Samoa. The United States, Germany, and Great Britain had signed treaties with various native chiefs. Civil war among the latter led to calls in Congress and the American press for the creation of a U.S. protectorate and even talk of possible military action against German naval forces in Samoa. Bismarck, although irritated, saw no reason for a rupture in relations with the United States over what in his view were "remote and unimportant islands" and agreed, in a treaty signed in Berlin on 14 June 1889, to the creation of a tripartite administration over Samoa on terms favorable to U.S. interests.

F. X. J. HOMER

See also Germany; Realism; Samoa, American

FURTHER READING

Gall, Lothar. *Bismarck: The White Revolutionary*, 2 vols. London, 1986.
Palmer, Alan. *Bismarck*. New York, 1976.
Pflanze, Otto. *Bismarck and the Development of Germany*, 3 vols. Princeton, N.J., 1990.

BLAINE, JAMES GILLESPIE

(*b.* 31 January 1830; *d.* 27 January 1893)

Secretary of state (1881, 1889–1892). Born in West Brownsville, Pennsylvania, Blaine graduated from Washington and Jefferson College in 1847, then taught school and read law in Philadelphia. A Whig and admirer of Henry Clay, Blaine was a founder of the Republican party in Maine, where he had moved in 1854, and won election to the State House of Representatives in 1858, serving as speaker from 1861 to 1862. He was elected to the U.S. House of Representatives in 1862 and enthusiastically supported Abraham Lincoln and the Union but later opposed the radical Reconstruction measures and allied himself with moderate western leaders of his party. Elected speaker of the House in 1869, Blaine appeared to be the leading contender for his party's presidential nomination in 1876, but opposition from party stalwarts and unproved charges of corruption destroyed his chances. He was, however, appointed to a U.S. Senate seat that year and later elected in his own right. Denied his party's nomination again in 1880, Blaine was named secretary of state by his party's successful candidate, James A. Garfield. Blaine, a nationalist who believed that the United States deserved a place among the world's great powers, worked closely with the president to develop a more ambitious foreign policy to advance U.S. interests in Latin America and the Pacific. Blaine initiated planning for a Pan-American conference to be held in Washington, D.C., a move that many in the United States and abroad viewed as an effort to preserve the status quo in the Western Hemisphere under U.S. leadership. The assassination of Garfield in July 1881 and the succession of Chester A. Arthur to the presidency effectively ended Blaine's influence in the cabinet, and he left office on 18 December.

Blaine's brief and unhappy tenure did mark an effort to move U.S. foreign policy in new directions. Besides the Pan-American initiative, he sought to void, unilaterally if necessary, the Clayton-Bulwer Treaty of 1850 and thereby open the way for construction of a canal across the Isthmus of Panama under sole U.S. control. He also intervened to prevent the French from seizing Venezuelan customhouses over unpaid debts and offered the services of the United States in arbitrating disputes among various Latin American nations. Blaine secured his party's presidential nomination in 1884, only to lose to Grover Cleveland in a bitter election campaign. Called the "Plumed Knight" by his loyalists, or "the Continental Liar from the State of Maine" by his detractors, Blaine remained the most prominent figure in his party.

Following the election of Republican Benjamin Harrison in 1888, Blaine was asked by the president-elect to serve as secretary of state. Blaine accepted, but he and Harrison were never close. In addition, Blaine's failing health and the deaths of several family members kept him from exerting the influence he had enjoyed in the Garfield administration. Nevertheless, Blaine sought to direct an assertive foreign policy in the Pacific and Latin America. He presided over the Pan-American Conference

of 1889, initiated reciprocal trade agreements with Brazil and with Spain for its colonies of Puerto Rico and Cuba, secured a joint protectorate over Samoa with Great Britain and Germany, and tried unsuccessfully to acquire the Danish West Indies, a lease for Samaná Bay in the Dominican Republic, and the concession of Môle Saint Nicolas in Haiti. He took a strong stand against Great Britain over the harvesting of Alaskan fur seals by Canadian vessels, but he urged restraint in dealing with Chile following attacks on sailors of the USS *Baltimore* in 1891. Blaine resigned abruptly in June 1892, but a rumored challenge to wrest the Republican nomination from Harrison that year never materialized.

MICHAEL J. DEVINE

See also Canada; Chile; Clay, Henry; Danish West Indies, Acquisition of; Dominican Republic; Garfield, James Abram; Harrison, Benjamin; Pan-Americanism; Samoa, American; Sealing; Venezuela

FURTHER READING

Langley, Lester D. "James G. Blaine: The Ideologue as Diplomatist." In *Makers of American Diplomacy: From Benjamin Franklin to Henry Kissinger*, edited by Frank J. Merli and Theodore A. Wilson. New York, 1974.
Muzzey, David S. *James G. Blaine: A Political Idol of Other Days.* New York, 1934.
Tyler, Alice Felt. *The Foreign Policy of James G. Blaine.* Minneapolis, Minn., 1927.

BLISS, TASKER HOWARD

(*b.* 31 December 1853; *d.* 9 November 1930)

U.S. Army general and chief of staff (1917–1918) and U.S. representative on the Allied Supreme War Council (1918). Bliss graduated from the U.S. Military Academy in 1875 and throughout his long career he showed outstanding ability as an administrator, educator, linguist, and, toward the end of his life, diplomat. He helped found and was the first president of the Army War College in 1903 and became military governor of the Philippines in 1906. When the United States entered World War I in April 1917, he was in charge of mobilization. By fall, however, he was promoted to chief of staff and spent much of his time abroad until the war ended in November 1918. President Woodrow Wilson, who admired Bliss's encyclopedic mind and modesty, appointed him the U.S. representative on the Supreme War Council, which coordinated Allied war efforts. Bliss, as did Wilson and General John J. Pershing, favored a separate U.S. force in Europe, although he pushed successfully for a unified command under French marshal Ferdinand Foch. At war's end, Bliss strongly favored, as did Pershing, unconditional German surrender, which was rejected by the Allies and Wilson. Nonetheless, he fervently supported President Wilson's Fourteen Points and Wilson's plan for a postwar League of Nations. As a member of the U.S. peace commission to the Paris Peace Conference in 1919, Bliss advised the Council of Four on the arms reduction aspects of the proposed treaty with the Germans and pushed successfully for a small-scale (as opposed to massive) Allied military intervention in Bolshevik Russia. Bliss also shared Wilson's disappointment at the harshness of the Versailles Treaty and Germany's exclusion from membership in the League of Nations. Upon his return to the United States from Paris in late spring 1919, Bliss retired from the army. He helped found the Council on Foreign Relations in New York City, and became a popular speaker on behalf of international disarmament and U.S. membership in the League of Nations and the World Court. From 1920 until 1927, he also served as governor of the Soldiers Home in Washington, D.C.

SINA DUBOVOY

See also Council on Foreign Relations; Paris Peace Conference of 1919; Pershing, John; Versailles Treaty of 1919; Wilson, Thomas Woodrow; World War I

FURTHER READING

Palmer, Frederick. *Bliss, Peacemaker: The Life and Letters of General Tasker Howard Bliss.* New York, 1934.
Trask, David F. *The United States in the Supreme War Council: American War Aims and Inter-Allied Strategy, 1917–1918.* Middletown, Conn., 1961.
Walworth, Arthur. *Wilson and His Peacemakers: American Diplomacy at the Paris Peace Conference, 1919.* Westport, Conn., 1981.

BLOCKADE

A method of maritime warfare that originated as the naval counterpart of the land siege. In its more modern adaptation, it is a measure of economic warfare designed to cut off all seaborne commerce to designated enemy ports or shores. Under generally accepted rules of international law, a blockade is lawful if it meets four requirements: (1) it must be officially proclaimed and notified; (2) it must be effective, in the sense that it must subject vessels attempting to enter or exit the blockaded area to substantial risk of capture; (3) it must be enforced impartially; and (4) it must not deny access to neutral coasts or ports.

Prior to World War I the traditional method of enforcing a blockade was by stationing a cordon of naval units off the blockaded coast. A neutral ship breaching or attempting to breach a blockade was subject to capture and, upon adjudication by a prize court of the blockading nation, to condemnation and confiscation of ship and cargo. Under British and later U.S. interpretations of the concept, a ship was guilty of breach of or attempt to breach blockade the moment it left a neutral port with an intended destination within a blockaded area; if the breach was successful, the ship remained liable to capture until the return voyage ended. The Continental states interpreted the right of capture more narrowly, asserting that it existed only in the vicinity of the blockading force.

Since its infancy as a nation, the United States has been a major contributor to the formation of the international law of blockade—first as a neutral mercantile nation but weak naval power in the European and Latin American wars of the late eighteenth and early nineteenth centuries, then as a blockading belligerent nation in the Civil War and the Spanish-American War, as a neutral in the early stages of World Wars I and II, again as a belligerent in the blockade of Germany later in those wars, and finally as a superpower in the Cold War and its aftermath. While consistently expressing adherence to the requirements of a legal blockade, the United States, like other nations, has on occasion advanced interpretations of these requirements that accommodate its status at the time as either neutral or belligerent.

Soon after obtaining independence, the United States faced the challenge of maintaining its maritime commerce with Europe despite Great Britain's attempt to use its dominant naval power to blockade almost all the coast and ports of Europe during the wars of the French Revolution and the Napoleonic wars. As a neutral in these European wars, the infant republic insisted on the right to carry on commerce with those European ports that were not invested by a naval force sufficient to constitute a bona fide blockade, asserting that ports not so cordoned off were subject only to a "paper blockade." Great Britain, on the other hand, insisted on the right of its naval forces to enforce its proclaimed blockade against all neutral ships destined for or returning from "blockaded" ports, whether or not those ports were effectively invested by British warships. The United States repeatedly protested these paper blockades, stating that the law of nations required the "presence and position of a force rendering access to the prohibited place manifestly difficult and dangerous." The refusal of Great Britain to refrain from its practices, together with its practice of impressment of U.S. seamen, led the United States into the War of 1812.

After the conclusion of that war, the British ceased to claim that blockades were effective unless supported by a naval force adequate substantially to seal the port, but the United States was again thrust into a defense of its neutral rights in the Latin American wars of independence in the first half of the nineteenth century. In those wars the Spanish government proclaimed that all ports of territories that were in a state of insurrection were closed to foreign commerce. The United States, joined by Great Britain and some European states, asserted that while a nation had the right to close its ports in time of peace, when there was an insurrection, such a right did not exist for ports not under the control of the blockade-declaring power.

The American Civil War

During the Civil War, for the first time in its history, the United States established a blockade rather than being subjected to another nation's blockade. At the outbreak of hostilities in 1861, Congress passed legislation authorizing the president to close the entire coast of the states in rebellion, but on protest of the British government, Secretary of State William H. Seward advised that the legislation was permissive only and that President Abraham Lincoln had no intention of implementing it except upon compliance with the requirements for a blockade. The ingenuity of blockade-runners, however, forced the United States to make a major innovation in its interpretation and implementation of the law of blockade. Because of the proximity of Bermuda, the Bahamas, and the Caribbean islands to the shores of the Confederacy, ports in these islands provided convenient locations for transshipment of cargo from Europe to the Confederacy. These ports, and Nassau in the Bahamas in particular, became bases for the construction and operation of small, fast, shallow-draft vessels that could quickly reach isolated creeks and rivers of the rebellious states.

To combat this swarm of blockade-runners, the United States adopted what came to be known as the continuous-voyage doctrine, a doctrine that, although approved by the U.S. Supreme Court and upheld by the post–Civil War U.S.-British claims commission, was universally criticized at the time by neutral governments and jurists and remains controversial today. This doctrine, which was based on a reinterpretation of an earlier British practice used to control the commerce of neutral nations with British colonies in time of war, held that a voyage to an intermediate neutral port with cargo that was to be transshipped from there to a blockaded port was a continuous voyage to a blockaded port, thereby subjecting the ship to capture in any segment of the voyage and also to the condemnation of its cargo by a prize court.

The Spanish-American-Cuban-Filipino and Russo-Japanese wars appear not to have had significant impact on the law of blockade. As a result of its previously inexperienced status as a neutral in the U.S. Civil War and the Russo-Japanese War, however, Great Britain proposed at the Hague Peace Conference of 1907 that an international prize court be established to avoid allegedly partisan decisions by national courts. Hague Convention XII brought such a tribunal into effect, at least on paper. As a follow-on, the British government sponsored a diplomatic conference in London in 1909 to agree on a set of substantive rules to be applied by the prize court. The results of that conference, embodied in the London Declaration of 1909, codified the law of blockade. In most respects the London Declaration reflected the customary law of blockade as it had existed in state practice for a century. In several important respects it adopted positions that purported to resolve unsettled issues. Article 17 stated that "neutral vessels may not be captured for breach of blockade except within the area of operations of the warships detailed to render the blockade effective," resolving the controversy on this issue essentially in favor of the Continental position, although allowing some flexibility by leaving undefined the somewhat ambiguous term "area of operation." Article 19 explicitly repudiated the continuous-voyage doctrine: "Whatever may be the ulterior destination of a vessel or of her cargo, she cannot be captured for breach of blockade, if, at the moment, she is on her way to a non-blockaded port." Neither of these modifications survived in the practices of World Wars I and II.

The Two World Wars

World War I ushered in an entirely new era in the traditional law of blockade and, according to some, its demise. The advent of the submarine, naval mine, and airplane made the maintenance of a closed-in cordon of warships impossible. The concept of total war, with its massive requirements for material support, made the enemy's economy a principal target, and strangulation of ocean-borne commerce became a major objective of both sides in the war. Germany resorted to unrestricted submarine warfare. Great Britain instituted a long-distance or strategic blockade. Neither side attempted to justify its actions on the traditional rules of blockade but rather resorted to the doctrine of reprisal, which allows a belligerent that is the subject of illegal acts by an opponent to adopt "in reprisal" means or methods of warfare that would otherwise be illegal, thus freeing it from having to comply with the traditional rules. Protests by neutrals that the doctrine of reprisal could apply only to the enemy that had acted illegally—and not to nonbelligerents—were rejected by both Great Britain and Germany. Nevertheless, because the British characterized their actions as "methods of blockade" and proclaimed them as such, neutral states, and particularly the United States, protested their impact on neutral commerce, basing their protests on the violation of the London Declaration of 1909 (although unratified) and the customary law of blockade. The blockade was enforced by warships stationed as far as several hundred miles away and a massive minefield, which eventually covered a large part of the North Sea. It overlapped and blocked access to a number of neutral neighboring countries. In 1916 the British government announced that it would no longer follow Article 19 of the London Declaration but would apply the doctrine of continuous voyage; the Order in Council stated that a vessel would not be "immune from capture for breach of blockade upon the sole ground that she is at the moment on her way to a non-blockaded port." In response to protests by the United States, the British Foreign Office cited U.S. practice during the Civil War as well as the upholding of that practice by the U.S. Supreme Court and the U.S.-British claims commission. When the United States joined the war on the side of the Allies in 1917, however, it shed any doubts it might have had about the British practices and in fact joined in their implementation.

Woodrow Wilson, in his declaration of U.S. war aims known as the Fourteen Points, introduced in 1918 the concept of international blockade as an instrument of collective security. He gave lip service to the traditional U.S. devotion to "absolute freedom of navigation upon the seas…alike in peace and in war" but added this sweeping qualification: "except as the seas may be closed in whole or in part by international action for the enforcement of international covenants." This concept was formalized in Article 16 of the League of Nations Covenant. The idea was that an aggressor nation would be punished by a blockade of all against the one. In such a situation there would be no neutrals.

World War II was essentially a reprise of World War I insofar as the practice of blockade in the Atlantic was concerned. Both Great Britain and Germany again based their maritime commerce-control measures on the right of reprisal. Germany's "total blockade" of the British Isles, declared in 1940, was implemented by unrestricted submarine and air attacks and the laying of mines. Great Britain again resorted to a massive minefield and ships patrolling as far as a thousand miles away. All governments and the public, however, continued to speak of these measures as blockade. In the Pacific none of the belligerents formally proclaimed or implemented a blockade in the traditional sense, although the United States carried out unrestricted warfare against Japanese merchant-marine shipping from its entrance into the war with Japan.

The Cold War and Beyond

Publicists are divided as to whether the long-distance blockades practiced by Allied forces in World Wars I and II were true blockades or were in fact long-term transformations of the traditional law of blockade. The resort to the justification of reprisal by all parties has complicated the analysis of this question. Several developments of great significance have further clouded the issue of whether blockade in its traditional sense remains a viable principle of maritime warfare. The most important development is contained in the United Nations Charter, which makes unlawful the resort to force against the territorial integrity or political independence of another

state except in self-defense or in implementation of enforcement measures adopted by the UN Security Council. Blockade is one of the enforcement measures listed in Chapter VII that may be adopted by the Security Council. Whether blockade taken by decision of the Security Council would be subject to the conditions governing traditional maritime blockades had not been tested as of the mid-1990s.

A second post–World War II development is the tendency of states to engage in coercive measures, including maritime interdiction measures, against other states without a formal declaration of war or assumption of a state of belligerency. Some of these coercive measures have borne a strong resemblance to blockade even though the state proclaiming them has carefully refrained from giving them that label. Only in the police action against North Korea (1950–1953) and the brief Indo-Pakistani War of 1971 have formal blockades been proclaimed, and the former had the imprimatur of the United Nations. The U.S. "quarantine" of Cuba during the missile crisis of 1962 had many of the earmarks of a blockade, although U.S. officials were careful to avoid that term. The mining of North Vietnamese ports and internal waters in 1972 is denominated as a blockade by the official U.S. Navy operational law manual, although some commentators assert that a blockade cannot be maintained by mines alone, because they are unable to discriminate between blockade-runners and legitimate users of the waterways. The British exclusion zone around the Falkland Islands during the British-Argentine conflict in 1982 also had the appearance of a blockade. The practices of Iraq and Iran during the so-called "tanker war" in the 1980s went beyond blockade, in that the penalty for violation of the exclusion zones was the attack and sinking of the violators rather than capture and adjudication. In the Gulf War following Iraq's invasion of Kuwait in 1990, the interdiction measures taken by coalition forces in the Persian-Arabian Gulf and Red Sea had many of the characteristics of a blockade, although the enforcement ships and aircraft merely diverted the offending ships to an alternate destination rather than capturing them. In 1994 U.S. warships off Haiti, acting under a UN Security Council resolution and carrying out economic sanctions against the Haitian military regime, also diverted cargo vessels.

Despite the practices of World Wars I and II and the postwar practices that have rendered dubious the survival of the rules for blockade developed in the nineteenth century, the 1995 official U.S. Navy operational law manual appears to accept them as valid, at least in some situations. It states that while strict conformity with the traditional rules of blockades does not further the objective of isolating the enemy from outside assistance and resources during general war, blockade is a useful method of regulating the competing interests of neutrals and belligerents in more limited conflicts.

HORACE B. ROBERTSON

See also Economic Sanctions; Hague Peace Conferences; International Law; Neutral Rights; Shipping Companies

FURTHER READING

Browning, Robert M. *From Cape Charles to Cape Fear: The North Atlantic Blockading Squadron During the Civil War.* Tuscaloosa, Ala., 1993.

Matson, Robert W. *Neutrality and Navicerts: Britain, the United States, and Economic Warfare, 1939–1940.* New York, 1994.

Savage, Carlton. *Policy of the United States Toward Maritime Commerce in War,* 2 vols. Washington, D.C., 1934, 1936.

Tucker, Robert W. *The Law of War and Neutrality at Sea.* Newport, R.I., 1957.

Vincent, C. Paul. *The Politics of Hunger: The Allied Blockade of Germany, 1915–1919.* Athens, Ohio, 1985.

BOGOTÁ CONFERENCE AND ACT
(1948)

See Organization of American States

BOHLEN, CHARLES EUSTIS
(*b.* 30 August 1904; *d.* 1 January 1974)

A highly respected Department of State official who specialized in Soviet affairs and consistently advocated a firm but flexible policy toward Russia. Born in Clayton, New York, Bohlen was graduated from Harvard in 1927. Trained by the Foreign Service as a Soviet expert, he served with the first mission to Moscow after U.S. recognition of Soviet Russia in 1933 and as adviser and interpreter for Presidents Franklin D. Roosevelt and Harry S. Truman at all of the wartime summit conferences. In the postwar Department of State, as counselor under Secretaries George C. Marshall and Dean Acheson, Bohlen helped formulate the containment policy and drafted Marshall's June 1947 Harvard address calling for U.S. aid to assist European economic reconstruction. President Dwight D. Eisenhower nominated Bohlen to be ambassador to the Soviet Union in 1953, but before his confirmation by the Senate, Bohlen had to endure McCarthyite attacks because of his participation in the Yalta Conference of 1945 and his role as foreign policy adviser to Democratic administrations. After four years in Moscow, he became ambassador to the Philippines (1957–1959), where his main task was negotiating naval and air base leases for the United States. In 1962, as a member of President John F. Kennedy's Executive Committee during the Cuban missile crisis, he was in the minority in advising quiet diplomacy over confrontation.

He served as ambassador to France from 1962 to 1968, a critical period when President Charles de Gaulle took steps to withdraw France from the North Atlantic Treaty Organization. Bohlen retired in 1969 and wrote his memoirs, *Witness to History, 1929–1969* (1973).

T. MICHAEL RUDDY

See also Cold War; Containment; Cuban Missile Crisis; de Gaulle, Charles André Joseph Marie; France; Marshall Plan; Philippines; Russia and the Soviet Union; Yalta Conference

FURTHER READING

Isaacson, Walter, and Evan Thomas. *The Wise Men: Six Friends and the World They Made.* New York, 1986.

Mayers, David. *The Ambassadors and America's Soviet Policy.* New York, 1995.

Ruddy, T. Michael. *The Cautious Diplomat: Charles E. Bohlen and the Soviet Union, 1929–1969.* Kent, Ohio, 1986.

BOLÍVAR, SIMÓN
(*b.* 24 July 1783; *d.* 17 December 1830)

Native-born Venezuelan who led the South American struggle for independence from Spanish rule in the early nineteenth century. Born into the Creole nobility, he studied under private tutors who introduced him to the ideals of the Enlightenment. While visiting Europe at the turn of the century, he became disillusioned with the Spanish monarchy and with the reactionary turn of the French Revolution. Napoleon's invasion of Spain in 1808 created enough turmoil and instability within the Spanish empire in South America to permit the liberation movement in the colonies to flourish. Venezuela declared independence on 5 July 1811, but royalist supporters of King Ferdinand VII wrested control of the country from proindependence forces. Bolívar's command of the soldiers who entered Caracas in August 1813 earned him the epithet "the Liberator." When the patriots failed to hold power, Bolívar fled to Jamaica in May 1815.

In his 1815 "Letter from Jamaica," Bolívar defined his political philosophy. He predicted that South American citizens would be unable to live under radical democracy, suggesting instead a strong, conservative republic run by an intellectual elite. Bolívar pointed to the British government as an appropriate model for Venezuela. Military victories finally drove the Spanish out of South America by 1824 and won political power for Bolívar. New Granada (present-day Colombia), Venezuela, and Quito (present-day Ecuador) had united as the Republic of Gran Colombia, with Bolívar as president, in 1822. His aid to Peruvian patriots led to his election as president of that country in 1825 even as internal fighting threatened Gran Colombia.

To achieve his goal of cooperation among the American nations, Bolívar organized the 1826 Pan-American or

Panama Congress. He originally wanted to exclude countries of non-Spanish heritage, but, despite his objections, Brazil and the United States were invited. Although Bolívar admired the government of the United States, he perceived the success and power of North America as a threat to the emerging nations in the Southern Hemisphere. Distrusting the United States and suspecting that self-interest had motivated the declaration of the Monroe Doctrine, he had imposed increasingly high tariffs on products of the United States sold in Gran Colombia during the 1820s. The United States delayed sending two delegates to the Panama Congress after a request by President John Quincy Adams for congressional funding for the trip led to four months of debate over foreign entanglements and economic interests in Latin America. The delegates finally departed, but one, Richard C. Anderson, died en route and the other, John Sergeant, arrived after the congress had adjourned. Representatives from Mexico, Central America, New Granada, and Peru attended, but only New Granada under Bolívar's influence ratified any of the points discussed, including creating a permanent army and navy supported by members of a federation, denouncing the slave trade, extending rights to citizens of other American nations, arbitrating disputes, and guaranteeing territorial integrity. The congress also failed to create a South American League. Disappointed with the results, Bolívar lost interest in creating an American confederation. Bolívar's popularity declined by the end of the 1820s, after he resorted to using dictatorial powers to the detriment of the economy of Gran Colombia. He struggled for power with Francisco de Paula Santander, and in 1830 Venezuela and Quito seceded from Gran Colombia. Bolívar resigned the presidency and died later that year of tuberculosis.

CAROL A. JACKSON

See also Latin America; Monroe Doctrine; Pan-Americanism; Spain; Venezuela

FURTHER READING

Bushnell, David, ed. *The Liberator, Simon Bolívar.* New York, 1970.
Bushnell, David, and Neill Macaulay. *The Emergence of Latin America in the Nineteenth Century,* 2nd ed. New York, 1994.
Masur, Gerhard. *Simon Bolívar.* Albuquerque, N. Mex., 1969.
Shurbutt, T. Ray, ed. *United States–Latin American Relations, 1800–1850: The Formative Generations.* Tuscaloosa, Ala., 1991.
Worcester, Donald E. *Bolívar.* Boston, 1977.

BOLIVIA

A landlocked South American republic, bordered by Chile, Peru, Brazil, Paraguay, and Argentina. Bolivia began friendly relations with the United States soon after its independence in 1825. The main initial aspects of relations involved U.S. investment in Bolivian mining enterprises after 1860. Between 1900 and 1930 the United States exerted growing diplomatic influence in Bolivia in conjunction with the strength of U.S. financial houses. The United States successfully pressed Bolivian governments to pass regulations conducive to U.S. investment and trade. In addition, after 1906 several private U.S. bank loans and bond issues financed the spread of rail lines and other infrastructure improvements. Anti-American sentiment in Bolivia influenced relations for much of the twentieth century; many Bolivians blamed Standard Oil Company of New Jersey for precipitating the Chaco War with Paraguay (1928–1935), and in 1937 the Bolivian government nationalized the oil company's holdings.

The Bolivian revolution of 1952 threatened to disrupt the friendly bilateral relations that had been founded on economic cooperation during World War II, but U.S.-Bolivian relations improved during the 1950s. The administration of President Dwight D. Eisenhower considered Bolivian nationalism a potential bulwark against communism and approved an increase in economic assistance to Bolivia from $11 million in 1953 to $20 million in each of the next two years. Between 1952 and 1964 Bolivia received $200 million in U.S. military and economic assistance. In the 1960s and 1970s, the U.S. government cooperated closely with military governments in La Paz, receiving consistent support from Bolivia in the United Nations and the Organization of American States (OAS). In return, the Central Intelligence Agency and the U.S. Army cooperated with the Bolivian military in its 1967 campaign to capture the Cuban revolutionary Ernesto ("Che") Guevara.

Although bilateral relations generally have been amicable between the United States and Bolivia's democratically elected governments, the latter have been less supportive of specific U.S. policy objectives. It was not until 1964, for example, after the United States suspended an economic agreement with the government of Víctor Paz Estenssoro, that the elected president bowed to U.S. pressures and broke ties with the revolutionary government in Cuba. After 1980 tensions developed over Bolivian cocaine production. In the early 1990s relations improved again as Bolivia embarked on a program of debt reduction, privatization, and the liberalization of foreign-investment laws.

DAVID SHEININ

See also Latin America; Narcotics, International; Organization of American States

FURTHER READING

Abecia Baldivieso, Valentín. *Las relaciones internacionales en la historia de Bolivia,* 2 vols. La Paz, Bolivia, 1979.
Blasier, Cole. *The Hovering Giant: U.S. Responses to Revolutionary Change in Latin America.* Pittsburgh, 1976.
Wilkie, James W. *The Bolivian Revolution and U.S. Aid Since 1952.* Los Angeles, 1969.

BOLSHEVIK REVOLUTION

See Russia and the Soviet Union

BORAH, WILLIAM EDGAR

(*b.* 29 June 1865; *d.* 19 January 1940)

Republican senator from Idaho from 1907 until his death. He was appointed to the Foreign Relations Committee in 1913, served as chair from 1924 to 1932, and remained on the committee until 1940. Although he was a maverick who frequently opposed Republican party policies, he became one of the most powerful members of the Senate largely because of his persuasive speeches and his excellent relationship with the press. As an antiwar progressive, anti-imperialist, and isolationist, Borah opposed U.S. military interventions in Latin America, entry into World War I (until 1917), and the presence of U.S. forces in Russia between 1918 and 1920. Borah believed that neutrality best served U.S. interests in 1914 because he attributed the war to European decadence and imperialist politics, but he reluctantly voted for war in 1917 to defend U.S. neutral rights. Known as one of the "irreconcilables," a group of U.S. senators opposed to the Treaty of Versailles and U.S. membership in the League of Nations, Borah also later blocked U.S. membership on the World Court, which he saw as a "back door" to the league. He became the catalyst for the 1921–1922 Washington Naval Conference on arms reduction and the 1928 Kellogg-Briand Pact to outlaw war when he introduced Senate resolutions for an arms limitations conference in 1920 and for an international agreement to outlaw war in 1927. In the last months of his life, he fought against President Franklin D. Roosevelt's policy of securing adjustments in neutrality laws that would allow arms shipments to France and Great Britain. Borah feared that such policy would bring the United States into World War II on the Allied side. He was convinced that the punitive terms of the Treaty of Versailles and great-power politics had caused the war and that Great Britain and France could defeat the Axis Powers without U.S. assistance. Borah also thought that, given the opportunity, Great Britain would manipulate the United States and its resources to further the British selfish great-power agenda.

JANET M. MANSON

See also Isolationsim; Kellogg-Briand Pact; Neutrality Acts of the 1930s; Versailles Treaty of 1919; Washington Conference on the Limitation of Armaments

FURTHER READING

Johnson, Claudius O. *Borah of Idaho*. New York, 1936.
McKenna, Marian C. *Borah*. Ann Arbor, Mich., 1961.
Maddox, Robert James. *William E. Borah and American Foreign Policy*. Baton Rouge, 1969.

BOSNIA-HERZEGOVINA

The former Yugoslav constituent republic, bordered on the one side by Serbia and Montenegro and on the other by Croatia, having no coastline of its own. It declared independence in late 1991, and became the scene of Europe's most devastating conflict since World War II. Bosnia was particularly vulnerable, even in the historical context of the deep-seated rivalries and tensions of the Balkans, given its geography and its highly heterogeneous ethnic-religious composition—forty-three percent Muslim, thirty-one percent Serb, and seventeen percent Croat—before the killings and population dislocations of the recent war. And while there was acrimonious debate over precisely what might or should have been done by the United States and others in the international community, there was little disagreement that what was done was woefully inadequate, and had tragic consequences.

Bosnia's modern history may be said to begin in the fourteenth century when the Ottomans destroyed the Serb nobility at the battle of Kosovo Polje, and later (in the second half of the fifteenth century) occupied most of modern-day Yugoslavia, except for Croatia and Slovenia, but including Bosnia-Herzegovina. In the following three centuries almost two-thirds of the Slav population converted to Islam. As a result of the Russo-Turkish War of 1877–1878, at the Congress of Berlin, Austria-Hungary gained administrative rights in Bosnia-Herzegovina (while leaving the province under nominal Ottoman suzerainty), fostered economic growth and financed some modernization of its public infrastructure. In 1908, Bosnia-Herzegovina was formally annexed to the Habsburg Empire, a development that further fanned the flames of South Slav nationalism. It was a Bosnian Serb who assassinated Archduke Francis Ferdinand, heir to the Habsburg throne, in Sarajevo in June 1914, the precipitating event of World War I.

With the collapse of Austria-Hungary in October 1918, Bosnia-Herzegovina became part of the new Kingdom of Serbs, Croats, and Slovenes, which was later renamed Yugoslavia in 1929. At the Paris Peace Conference the kingdom was recognized by the Allies as well as by the United States. In the interwar period the Bosnian Muslims, the most politically united among Bosnia's ethnic groups, attempted to balance Serb centralist ambitions in the kingdom. The single most important question was agrarian reform, where a compromise was reached in the early 1930s. However, most Bosnians continued to feel aggrieved as King Alexander transformed the kingdom into a unitary, centralized state dominated by Serbia.

When Yugoslavia was occupied in early 1941 by Nazi Germany, Bosnia-Herzegovina was incorporated into the Croatian Ustaša puppet state. During World War II, some

Bosnians (mostly Croats) supported the Axis powers, but the majority fought with the communist-led partisans under Josip Broz Tito, or the royalist Četnik resistance led by Draza Mihailović. At the Teheran Conference in December 1943, President Franklin D. Roosevelt, Winston Churchill, and Joseph Stalin together decided to give their full support to Tito's partisans, after Tito won control over large territories in Bosnia and the coastal areas. The United States kept a military mission accredited to Mihailović, however, until the end of the war.

After World War II, Bosnia-Herzegovina became a constituent republic of the Yugoslav Socialist Federation, but the Bosnian Muslims were not recognized officially as a "national" group. Constitutional changes made in 1971 and 1974, granting wider autonomy to the republics, gave greater—albeit still limited—legal and political status to the Bosnian Muslims as a distinct ethnic group. Following Tito's death in 1980, and with the creation of the collective and rotating federal presidency, Bosnians became particularly concerned about their interests and rights as first Serbia and then Croatia maneuvered to achieve dominance within the federation.

When the winter Olympics were held in Sarajevo in 1984, the world hailed the city as a symbol of multicultural accommodation and cooperation, as a model of how people of different religions and ethnicities could learn to live together. Yet less than a decade later Sarajevo would become the symbol of quite the opposite: of barbarous sieges, ethnic cleansing, war crimes, and relearning how to hate passionately.

Ominous ethnic divisions were already apparent in the 1990 legislative elections, in which the main parties organized along ethnic lines. Alija Izetbegović, head of the Muslim Party of Democratic Action (PDA), became president of the republic. After Slovenia and Croatia declared their independence, his fears of Serbian domination heightened, and Izetbegović supported a looser Yugoslav federation. The Bush administration, although pressing for a peaceful resolution, favored continuation of the federative arrangement. In mid-1991, following the onset of the Croatian-Serbian war, and amidst some outbreaks of ethnic violence in Bosnia, the United States and the European Community (EC) banned arms sales to all Yugoslav republics. Although all six Yugoslav republics accepted an EC-brokered ceasefire plan in September, and the Izetbegović government declared Bosnia-Herzegovina's neutrality in the Croat-Serb conflict, Serb-populated areas in Bosnia-Herzegovina began to form Serb autonomous regions around Banja Luka, Sarajevo, and elsewhere.

As brutal as the war in Croatia was, given Bosnia's even more complex ethnic divisions and its greater territorial proximity to the heart of Serbia, the potential for ethnic warfare there was even more foreboding. In early 1992 the EC tried to broker a "cantonization" agreement, but it did not hold. When a referendum was held (February 29–March 1) on the issue of full independence as a unitary state, the vast majority of Bosnian Muslims and Croats voted for it, but Bosnian Serbs boycotted it. On March 3, Izetbegović declared the independence of Bosnia-Herzegovina. The United States and Europe waited over a month to grant recognition, seeking first (but again without success) to work out a compromise arrangement through the mediation efforts of former U.S. secretary of state, Cyrus R. Vance, and former British foreign minister, Lord Carrington.

By late spring 1992, Bosnia-Herzegovina had been accepted as a member state of the United Nations, and international mediation efforts continued, but one truce after another was broken as Bosnian Serbs, with the support of Serbian President Slobodan Milošević and the Serbian-dominated Yugoslav People's Army, began attacks on Muslim and Croat areas. At the beginning of May, in protest against Serbia's role, the United States and the EC member states recalled their ambassadors from Belgrade. On May 30, the UN Security Council imposed economic sanctions against the Federal Republic of Yugoslavia (Serbia and Montenegro). But it was not until August that the UN authorized a military force to help insure the delivery of humanitarian aid within Bosnia. By then Bosnian Serbs had laid siege to cities, shelled civilian centers, interrupted food deliveries, and cut off utilities. Reports were widespread of executions of noncombatants, herding of prisoners into concentration camps, rape as a tool of war, and other aspects of ethnic cleansing that were perpetrated principally, albeit not exclusively, by Bosnian Serbs against Muslims.

The UN took other steps, including expelling Yugoslavia from the General Assembly, establishing a war crimes tribunal, declaring a no-fly zone over Bosnia from which Serb military aircraft were banned, and authorizing a naval blockade to enforce the sanctions against Serbia. Diplomatic efforts also continued, most notably with negotiations by Vance and former British foreign minister David Owen that combined UN and EC efforts. Their peace plan foresaw the partition of Bosnia-Herzegovina into ethnic cantons, but was rejected (as was later the modified Owen-Stoltenberg plan). Further mediation was also unsuccessful and even the so-called safe havens, protected by UN forces, were besieged and virtually stripped of any such meaning. By the end of 1992 the Bosnian government controlled little more than ten percent of its own territory. The Serbs controlled about seventy percent, and the Croats, who also had launched their own attacks on the Bosnian government, about twenty percent.

The Clinton administration came into office having made numerous campaign statements criticizing the

Bush policy and pledging to take tougher measures. "[We will bring] the full weight of American policy to bear," Secretary of State Warren Christopher stated. But while some new steps were taken, such as high-altitude air-drops of humanitarian supplies, and pushing tougher sanctions through the UN, the campaign promises of lifting the arms embargo against the Bosnian Muslims and launching air strikes against Serbian forces were not fulfilled. The Clinton administration did, however, tolerate if not encourage clandestine Iranian arms shipments via Croatia to the Bosnian government forces.

In August 1993 the North Atlantic Treaty Organization (NATO) threatened air strikes if the Bosnian Serbs did not stop the strangulation of Sarajevo and start being more forthcoming in the Geneva peace talks. But whatever deterrent value the threat could have had was weakened by discord within NATO even over its issuance, and then by NATO's reluctance to deliver on it despite continuing Bosnian Serb aggression. This defiance of NATO came to a head when in February 1994 the gruesome scene of sixty-eight civilians killed and over 200 wounded in a Bosnian Serb mortar attack on an open-air market in Sarajevo were picked up by the Cable News Network (CNN). The dramatic effect of this episode led to a NATO ultimatum for the Bosnian Serbs to withdraw their heavy weapons within ten days. This and a cease-fire agreement were complied with, at least for a while; yet one challenge after another again was mounted by the Bosnian Serbs to the United States, the UN, and NATO in succeeding months.

In February 1994, prodded by strong U.S. pressure, Bosnia and Croatia signed a cease-fire. This was followed the next month by an agreement signed in Washington to form a Muslim-Croat federation in Bosnia, with a degree of joint governance and the goal of achieving eventual links with Croatia proper. Actual implementation of the agreement was slow, and there was concern as to the seriousness of the commitments being made by Croatian leader Franco Tudjman, who continued to give signs of still holding on to his previous "Greater Croatia" aspirations.

In May 1994, the Clinton administration tried another diplomatic stratagem for achieving a general settlement of the Bosnian war, by joining with France, Great Britain, Germany, and Russia in what was called the "Contact Group." The intent was to better manage differences among the major powers, both those between the United States and its European allies and those between the United States and Russia. Citing its historical allegiance to Serbia, and spurred on further by rising (anti-Western) nationalistic fervor within its own domestic political scene, Moscow had largely supported the Serbian side throughout the war. When the Contact Group did manage to forge agreement on a plan for a fifty-one/forty-nine

percent division between the Bosnian-Croat federation and the Bosnian Serbs, it still was rejected by the Serbs. And the war continued.

In April, NATO had launched its first air strike against the Serbs in response to their heavy attacks around the safe-haven and heavy weapon-exclusion zone of Goražde. The Serb forces eventually halted but retained large gains already made. Later in the summer, NATO also launched air strikes against Serb targets in the exclusion zone around Sarajevo. In November 1994, NATO aircraft attacked the Udbina airfield in Serb-held Croatia in response to attacks launched from that airfield against targets in the Bihać area, sparking a dispute between the United States and its European allies over how extensive the use of air strikes should be.

In January 1995 the Bosnian Serbs and the Muslim-led government signed a four-month truce, which was mediated by former U.S. President Jimmy Carter. This too did not hold. And in May 1995 another and even more severe crisis erupted as the Bosnian Serbs stepped up attacks on Sarajevo and took the provocative step of seizing UN peacekeepers as hostages as protection against NATO's threat of further air strikes. Serbian President Milošević, feeling the pinch of economic sanctions and with his own political position beginning to be threatened by the challenge from Bosnian Serb leaders such as Radovan Karadžić, intervened to help get the release of the hostages. But NATO finally stepped up its air strikes to a more substantial level. In one of these operations a U.S. pilot, Scott O'Grady, was shot down, and then rescued in dramatic fashion.

In July the Bosnian Serbs overran the UN safe havens in Srebrenica and Zepa, murdering thousands of Muslim civilians. In response, NATO threatened further major air strikes if any of the four remaining "safe areas" were attacked. At the same time Croatian and Bosnian government leaders, with quiet U.S. support, agreed on a common military strategy, and two weeks later the Croats launched a lightning military offensive overrunning Serb-held parts in the Krajina. Although this successful Croatian offensive faced criticism by several European states, the United States and Germany tacitly supported Croatia to counterbalance Serbia, stabilize the situation in Bosnia, and force the Serb rebels to the peace table.

At the same time, U.S. diplomatic efforts intensified, led by Assistant Secretary of State Richard Holbrooke. The Clinton administration was feeling increasing political pressure at home, as the Republican Congress voted to unilaterally lift the Bosnian arms embargo, and polls showed high levels of public disapproval of the president's handling of the Bosnian crisis. The tragic deaths of the leading U.S. diplomatic team, killed when their jeep ran over a land mine on a mountain road in Bosnia, gave Washington a further impetus to move the talks ahead, and marked the point at which Holbrooke increased his personal and direct involvement. This more assertive diplomacy was coupled with continued and more forceful NATO action. The combination of force and diplomacy along with the military setbacks inflicted on the Serbs by the Croatian offensive, made the Dayton peace conference possible.

After weeks of intense negotiations and a near breakdown as the deadline set by the United States approached, an agreement finally was reached. The November 1995 Dayton peace accord provided for an end to hostilities, a mandate to NATO to impose and oversee the prescribed cease-fire and demobilization, and terms for a political settlement that provided a good deal of autonomy for Bosnian Serbs but within a Muslim-Croat dominated unitary Bosnian state. The NATO Implementation Force (IFOR) was deployed in December 1995, with American troops accounting for about 20,000 of the total force of 60,000. The U.S. Congress stopped short of fully supporting the president's decision to deploy U.S. troops, but it did not block it. President Clinton stressed that the deployment was to be for not more than a year, and that IFOR's mission was to help create conditions conducive to a political settlement but not to bear "state-building"-type responsibilities per se. The Organization for Security and Cooperation in Europe (OSCE) was given principal international responsibility for establishing a process for free and fair elections, as well as other confidence-building initiatives.

One of the most controversial issues dealt with at Dayton concerned the relationship between IFOR and the international war crimes tribunal. Among those indicted by the tribunal set up by the United Nations were Bosnian Serb leader Karadžić and General Ratko Mladić. While the War Crimes Tribunal moved ahead in 1996 in prosecuting a few cases, IFOR stuck to a narrow interpretation of its mandate according to which it did not have to make much of an effort to arrest either Karadžić or Mladić. International pressure did eventually get Karadžić to agree not to be a candidate in the scheduled September 1996 Bosnian elections; but he remained very much a power behind the scenes, and in the eyes of many his continued freedom—despite the serious war crimes charged against him—called into question the very credibility and viability of the Dayton accords peace settlement.

MARTIN ROSSMANN

See also Clinton, William Jefferson; Croatia; Humanitarian Intervention and Relief; North Atlantic Treaty Organization; Serbia; United Nations; Yugoslavia

FURTHER READING

Donna, Robert, J., and Fine, V.A. John, Jr. *Bosnia and Hercegovina: A Tradition Betrayed.* New York, 1984.
Hopner, Jacob B. *Yugoslavia in Crisis.* New York, 1962.
Malcolm, Noel. *Bosnia: A Short History.* New York, 1994.
Rieff, David. *Slaughterhouse: Bosnia and the Failure of the West.* New York, 1995.

Singleton, Fred. *A Short History of the Yugoslav Peoples.* Cambridge, Mass., 1985.
Woodward, Susan L. *Balkan Tragedy: Chaos and Dissolution after the Cold War.* Washington D.C., 1995.

BOTSWANA

A South African republic bordered by Namibia, Zambia, Zimbabwe, and South Africa. In the late nineteenth century Botswana became a British protectorate (known as Bechuanaland) and was administered indirectly by the British High Commissioner for South Africa. Botswana gained its independence in 1966 but remains a member of the Commonwealth. Botswana's primary foreign policy goal is to promote economic growth while maintaining sufficient autonomy from South Africa, its much larger southern neighbor. Under Seretse Khama's leadership (1966–1980), Botswana's capital of Gaborone emerged as a major diplomatic center in the region. Most important, the Southern Africa Development Council, the major regional economic organization, is based in Gaborone.

The United States recognized Botswana at independence. The subsequent relationship has been cordial but punctuated with occasional disputes. The United States values Botswana as a model democratic government in the Third World. For this reason, the U.S. Agency for International Development (USAID) provided more development aid to Botswana in per capita terms than all but one or two other sub-Saharan countries during the 1970s and 1980s. The Peace Corps also has consistently maintained one if its largest African contingents in Botswana. Botswana has reciprocated by working with the United States to promote peace and establish stable political systems in Rhodesia (Zimbabwe), Namibia, Mozambique, and Angola. Botswana has hosted critical meetings between contending political factions in these countries, and supported other African states—and the Western democracies—in promoting racial equality and democratic change in apartheid South Africa. However, because of its small population (1.4 million in 1994) and its development orientation, Botswana did nothing which might seriously harm its membership in the South African Customs Union.

In the 1990s, Botswana concentrated on promoting foreign investment to generate new growth sectors as diamond production began to level off. The United States provided more than $115 million in direct investment. Botswana imports from the United States are largely capital goods, averaging some $26 million per year. But Washington closed its aid program on the grounds that Botswana had become sufficiently developed (per capita GDP in 1994 was $2,118).

In recent years, U.S. relations with Botswana have become more contentious. Washington's decision to terminate aid angered Gaborone. Another source of dis-agreement has been the U.S. insistence that the Kalahari bushmen receive equal treatment with respect to educa-tion, jobs, and criminal justice. Botswana views this request as misinformed interference in its domestic affairs. Finally, environmental groups have pressed Wash-ington to promote conservation of Botswana's wildlife areas against local development interests. Gaborone has resisted, especially in view of rising domestic demand for opening up more ranch land and water sources.

JOHN D. HOLM

See also Africa; Agency for International Development; Peace Corps; South Africa

FURTHER READING

Duignan, Peter and Lewis H. Gann. *The United States and Africa: A History*. New York, 1984.
Hickey, Dennis. *An Enchanted Darkness: The American Vision of Africa in the Twentieth Century*. East Lansing, Mich., 1993.
Jackson, Henry F. *From Congo to Soweto: U.S. Foreign Policy Toward Africa Since 1960*. New York, 1982.
Noer, Thomas J. *Cold War and Black Liberation: The United States and White Rule in Africa, 1948-1968*. Columbia, Mo., 1985.
Rothchild, Donald, and John Ravenhill. "Retreat from Globalism: U.S. Policy Toward Africa in the 1990s." In *Eagle in a New World*, edited by Kenneth A. Oye, Robert J. Lieber, and Donald Rothchild. New York, 1992.
Schraeder, Peter J. *United States Foreign Policy Toward Africa*. New York, 1994.
Ungar, Sanford J. *Africa: The People and Politics of an Emerging Continent*. New York, 1985.
Whitaker, Jennifer Seymour. *Africa and the United States: Vital Interests*. New York, 1978.

BOURNE, RANDOLPH SILLIMAN
(*b*. 30 May 1886; *d*. 22 December 1918)

Literary and cultural critic best known for his vehement denunciation of U.S. participation in World War I. Born in Bloomfield, New Jersey, he graduated from Columbia Uni-versity in 1913. His writings celebrated youth, individual-ism, and cultural pluralism. Fearing that U.S. entry into the war would destroy any chance of the United States's becom-ing truly pluralistic, Bourne challenged the view of prowar Progressive intellectuals, including educator John Dewey. In his celebrated essay "The War and the Intellectuals" (1917), Bourne labeled as "childish" the prevailing desire of Woodrow Wilson and like-minded reformers to reshape the world in the image of the United States. He wrote that "the real enemy is War." Bourne's pacifist stance alienated many friends and associates. Shortly after the armistice, he died in the great influenza epidemic of 1918. His writing was much admired in the 1960s by opponents of the Vietnam War.

JOHN M. CRAIG

See also Vietnam War; World War I

FURTHER READING

Abrahams, Edward. *The Lyrical Left: Randolph Bourne, Alfred Stieglitz, and the Origins of Cultural Radicalism in America*. Char-lottesville, Va., 1986.
Resek, Carl, ed. *War and the Intellectuals: Essays by Randolph S. Bourne, 1915–1919*. New York, 1964.
Vitelli, James R. *Randolph Bourne*. Boston, 1981.

BOUTROS-GHALI, BOUTROS
(*b*. 14 November 1922)

The sixth secretary-general of the United Nations, appointed in January 1992. Boutros-Ghali received a law degree in 1946 from Cairo University in Egypt and a doctorate in international law from the University of Paris in 1949. He was a professor of political science for many years at Cairo University before his appointment as Egypt's minister of state for foreign affairs in 1977. He served in that position until 1991, when the UN Security Council chose him to replace Secretary-Gener-al Javier Pérez de Cuéllar, a choice that generated little controversy. Developing nations, particularly from the Arab and African groups, welcomed one of their own in the position, and Israel trusted Boutros-Ghali because of his role in support of Egyptian President Anwar el-Sadat at the Camp David meetings seeking Arab-Israeli peace. The Western nations wanted a younger, more dynamic leader, but they tolerated Boutros-Ghali because of his educational background in France and his reputation for moderation. As secretary-general, Boutros-Ghali set three goals. First, he called on the UN to be more active in promoting democracy. Second, he sought to use the UN to conduct preventive diplo-macy to anticipate and avert crises. Third, he expressed a desire to see the UN expand its role as a peacekeeper. On paper, his activist agenda fit well with President George Bush's call for a cooperative new world order to replace the Cold War. Boutros-Ghali nonetheless often clashed with the United States. His efforts to involve the UN more deeply in the catastrophic civil wars in Somalia in 1992 and Rwanda in 1994 failed to win sup-port from U.S. leaders, who refused to tie their policies or commit U.S. military forces to UN leadership. In May 1993 the United States turned over its humanitari-an functions in Somalia to UN troops, but those forces withdrew on 1 March 1995 under U.S. and Italian pro-tection. Boutros-Ghali also struggled to find a strategy to stop the civil war in Bosnia. The ineffectiveness of the UN peacekeeping force led to intervention by NATO in December 1995. In Haiti peace operations went much better, first with the U.S. force that inter-vened in September 1994 and then with the UN-led force that took over in March 1995. Even so, Boutros-Ghali's relations with the United States deteriorated further. Republicans in the U.S. Congress frequently attacked him personally, and in June 1996 the Clinton administration announced that it would not support him for a second term as UN secretary-general.

KURK DORSEY

See also Bosnia-Herzegovina; Bush, George Herbert Walker; Camp David Accords; Egypt; Haiti; Rwanda; Somalia; United Nations

FURTHER READING

Boutros-Ghali, Boutros. "Empowering the UN." *Foreign Affairs* 71 (Winter 1992–1993):89–102.
———. "Global Leadership After the Cold War," *Foreign Affairs* 75 (March/April 1996):86–98.

BOWERS, CLAUDE GERNADE

(*b.* 20 November 1878; *d.* 21 January 1958)

U.S. ambassador to Spain (1933–1939) and Chile (1939–1953). A self-proclaimed Jeffersonian Democrat, Bowers gained national prominence during the 1920s as an editorial writer for the *New York World*, as the author of several best-selling books on American history, and as a keynote speaker at the 1928 Democratic National Convention. After President Franklin D. Roosevelt sent him to Madrid in 1933, Bowers became a staunch supporter of the Spanish Republic, which enacted reforms curbing the power of the clergy, the landowning elite, and the business community. In his reports to Washington, Bowers likened twentieth-century Spanish peasants and workers to the artisans and yeomen farmers idealized by Thomas Jefferson. Regarded as a rank amateur by Department of State professionals, Bowers often found himself at odds with his bureaucratic superiors during the mid-1930s. When General Francisco Franco and other conservative officers instigated a military coup that plunged Spain into civil war in July 1936, Bowers openly sided with the Loyalists, as those backing the Spanish Republic came to be called. Convinced that Franco's rebellion would collapse without outside help, Bowers at first recommended that the United States join the other great powers in a policy of nonintervention in the Spanish Civil War. Once German and Italian assistance for Franco's forces began to tilt the balance against republican Spain in 1937, however, Bowers unsuccessfully pressed the Roosevelt administration to aid the Loyalists and prophesied that U.S. failure to help Spanish democracy would invite fascist aggression elsewhere in Europe. Shortly before Franco's victory in March 1939, Bowers was recalled to Washington and was soon reassigned to Chile. His reporting from Santiago reflected the fear of German and, after 1945, Soviet, influence.

After an uneventful fourteen-year stint in Chile, Bowers retired in 1953 and returned to New York City, where he drafted three volumes of memoirs.

DOUGLAS LITTLE

See also Franco, Francisco; Spain

FURTHER READING

Bowers, Claude G. *Chile Through Embassy Windows, 1939–1953.* New York, 1958.
———. *My Life: The Memoirs of Claude Bowers.* New York, 1962.
———. *My Mission to Spain: Watching the Dress Rehearsal for World War II.* New York, 1954.
Little, Douglas. "Claude Bowers and His Mission to Spain: The Diplomacy of a Jeffersonian Democrat." In *U.S. Diplomats in Europe, 1919–1941*, edited by Kenneth Paul Jones. Santa Barbara, Calif., 1981.

BOWLES, CHESTER BLISS

(*b.* 5 April 1901; *d.* 25 May 1986)

Twice ambassador to India (1951–1953 [also to Nepal]), (1963–1969), briefly undersecretary of state (1961), and Democratic member of Congress from Connecticut (1959–1961). Bowles consistently argued for U.S. economic assistance to Third World nations for the "betterment of life in all corners of the world" and as the best means to counter communism during the Cold War.

Born in Springfield, Massachusetts, the grandson of the noted abolitionist newspaper editor Samuel Bowles, Chester Bowles graduated from Yale University (1924) and five years later cofounded the highly successful advertising firm of Benton and Bowles. A self-described Wilsonian who believed that the United States could promote democracy abroad, and a strong supporter of President Franklin D. Roosevelt's New Deal in its efforts to address the social and economic crises generated by the Great Depression, Bowles was an outspoken "noninterventionist" after the outbreak of World War II in Europe. He feared that U.S. involvement would shift national resources away from a necessary priority on domestic reform and that the United States would be drawn into support for European colonialism. Although a critic of rigid isolationism, he served on the national board of the America First Committee and opposed passage of the Lend-Lease Act to assist Great Britain and other nations battling Germany.

After the Japanese attack on Pearl Harbor in December 1941, however, Bowles entered public service to become eventually (1943) Roosevelt's wartime director of the Office of Price Administration and, at war's end, President Harry S. Truman's chief of the Office of Economic Stabilization. In 1948 Bowles served as a delegate to the first session of the United Nations Educational, Scientific, and Cultural Organization (UNESCO). The following year he worked on UN projects, becoming international chairman of the Appeal for Children. After one turbulent term as governor of Connecticut (1949–1951), during which he launched liberal programs in housing and education but met considerable conservative reaction, he narrowly lost his bid for reelection.

In 1951 Truman appointed Bowles ambassador to India and Nepal. He established a warm relationship with Indian Prime Minister Jawaharlal Nehru. India had only recently gained its independence from Great Britain (1947) and its government was struggling to feed its people. Because it endorsed democracy and bordered the People's Republic of China, the populous, highly nationalistic India held strategic importance and represented a democratic alternative in Asia. Bowles argued, moreover, that nationalism served as the most effective means to counter and transform communism. India's leadership of the nonaligned movement, he added, better served the United States in its Cold War competition with the Soviet Union than military alliances. Ambassador Bowles, who often spoke in the language of the New Deal and envisioned Tennessee Valley Authority-type projects for the Tigris, Euphrates, and Jordan river basins, pressed Washington to offer generous dollar aid and technical assistance to India. U.S. officials and Congress, resentful of India's criticism of U.S. intervention in the Korean War and of India's neutralism in the Cold War, seldom satisfied his calls for substantial funds. U.S. agriculture, literacy, and health projects nonetheless reached hundreds of thousands of Indians, and by the late 1950s Indo-American relations had markedly improved.

During the administration of President Dwight D. Eisenhower (1953–1961), Bowles emerged as a prolific writer, lecturer, and liberal Democratic activist. He published several books, including *Ambassador's Report* (1954), *The New Dimensions of Peace* (1955), and *Africa's Challenge to America* (1956). His home became a meeting place for diplomats, Democratic party leaders, and professors. During the presidential campaigns of 1956 and 1960, Bowles served as a foreign policy adviser to Adlai E. Stevenson and then John F. Kennedy, and in the latter case, as a conduit to party liberals. With Kennedy's victory, speculation circulated that Bowles would be named secretary of state. Dean Rusk received the appointment, but Bowles became his undersecretary of state, a post he used to staff U.S. embassies with a new breed of high caliber "outsiders" from universities, foundations, and journalism, and he became a mentor to many young people who entered public service.

Bowles's early opposition to the invasion of Cuba at the Bay of Pigs; his advice that negotiations, land reform, and regional neutralization, not military escalation, should be tried in Vietnam; his appeal for a two-China policy to open a dialogue with the People's Republic of China; and his penchant for writing long memoranda and letters to impatient policymakers, all prompted Kennedy to demote him in late 1961 to a new, ineffective position as roving ambassador to Africa, Asia, and Latin America. By late 1962, Bowles could not tolerate the "cursory attention" his reports received and submitted his resignation to Kennedy.

Rather than letting Bowles go, Kennedy persuaded him to undertake a second tour of duty as ambassador to India, where Bowles worked to improve agricultural production and to increase U.S. shipments of food grain after a drought spread hunger in India in 1965–1966. Washington officials, such as national security adviser Walt W. Rostow, thought that Bowles suffered from a "bad case of localitis," tending to see foreign policy through New Delhi's eyes. India's criticism of the U.S. war in Vietnam and Washington's growing alliance with India's nemesis, Pakistan, dampened Indo-American relations.

Bowles retired from public service in 1969 to his home in Essex, Connecticut. Although he wrote his memoirs and visited India again in 1972, Parkinson's disease gradually muted his public voice. Criticized by some as a verbose, liberal do-gooder, Bowles remains notable for the idealism and personal visibility he brought to U.S. policy toward the nations of the Third World. He consistently argued that foreign aid should be extended, not because of the communist threat, but because such assistance would help create a peaceable world order.

JAMES C. THOMSON, JR.
THOMAS G. PATERSON

See also America First Committee; Bay of Pigs Invasion; China; Cold War; Foreign Aid; India; Isolationism; Kennedy, John Fitzgerald; Korean War; Nehru, Jawaharlal; Nonaligned Movement; Third World; Vietnam War

FURTHER READING

Bowles, Chester, *View from New Delhi: Selected Speeches and Writings.* New Haven, 1969.

———. *Promises to Keep: My Years in Public Life, 1941–1969.* New York, 1971.

———. *The Conscience of a Liberal: Selected Writings and Speeches.* New York, 1962.

Merrill, Dennis. *Bread and the Ballot: The United States and India's Economic Development, 1947–1963.* Chapel Hill, N.C., 1990.

Schaffer, Howard B. *Chester Bowles: New Dealer in the Cold War.* Cambridge, Mass., 1993.

BOXER REBELLION

(1900)

An uprising of xenophobic Chinese elements who opposed the adoption of European ways and hoped to eliminate external influences by driving all foreigners out

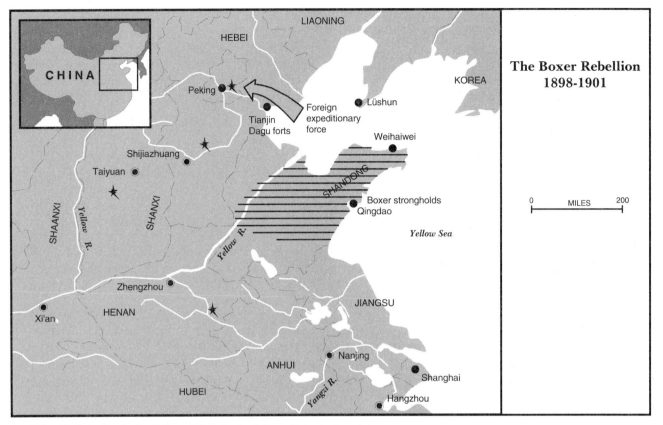

The Boxer Rebellion
1898-1901

From *The Search for Modern China*, Jonathan D. Spence. ©1990 by Jonathan D. Spence. Reprinted with permission of W. W. Norton & Company, Inc.

of China. The extension after 1897 of foreign influence in China in the form of spheres of influence helped stimulate the efforts of various secret societies in that country, collectively known as the Righteous and Harmonious Band. Opponents of the movement deliberately mistranslated the word "band" into "fist," causing non-Chinese to refer to the group as "Boxers." Tacitly encouraged by China's imperial government, the Boxer Rebellion spread through northeastern China and into the capital of Beijing itself in the summer of 1900. The rebels directed their hatred against all foreigners, including missionaries and merchants. Edwin Conger, the U.S. minister, led a retreat of the U.S. resident community into the British Legation, where nationals from many countries found sanctuary. While U.S. marines and military personnel from other nations inside the legation managed to prevent the besieging forces from penetrating the compound's walls, the beleaguered foreign enclave was cut off from external communication for fifty-five days.

The U.S. government responded both diplomatically and militarily. Not wanting to abandon the "open door" policy he had recently announced, Secretary of State John Hay sent his second Open Door Note on 3 July 1900. Refusing to acknowledge the imperial government's

complicity in the rebellion, Hay called for continued international respect for the "territorial integrity" of China and urged other nations to avoid using the Boxer Rebellion as an excuse for the partition of China. Meanwhile, the United States transferred 2,500 (later 5,000) troops under the command of General Adna Chaffee from the Philippines to join contingents from Russia, Japan, Great Britain, and France. These forces invaded the port city of Tianjin (Tientsin) on 14 July 1900. The international force left for Beijing on 4 August and fought several skirmishes before reaching the British Legation on 14 August. Conger could then report that seven marine guards had been killed and another fourteen Americans wounded during the siege.

It was the weight of the international balance of power, not U.S. arms or diplomacy alone, that squashed the Boxer Rebellion and helped preserve the principle of territorial integrity that Hay had championed, although the political situation within China remained unsettled. An international tribunal later called on China to pay an indemnity of $333 million to compensate foreign governments for losses to their citizens and the expenses of the military relief mission. The U.S. claim of $25 million was more than sufficient to pay these expenses. The

United States accordingly returned nearly $17 million, most of which the Chinese government used to establish a fund for the education of Chinese students in the United States.

JOHN DOBSON

See also China; Jay, John; Open Door Policy

FURTHER READING

Esherick, Joseph W. *The Origins of the Boxer Uprising.* Berkeley, Calif., 1987.
Fleming, Peter. *The Siege at Peking.* New York, 1959.
Hunt, Michael H. "The Forgotten Occupation: Peking, 1900–1901." *Pacific Historical Review* 48 (November 1979): 501–529.

BOYCOTTS

Refusals to do business with or have contact with a person, corporation, or state. The word comes from Captain Charles Boycott, an English land agent in the 1880s, who was so harsh in collecting rents that his Irish tenants completely ostracized him and his family. The practice, however, antedates the word and was first used by American colonists against British products, especially tea, during the period preceding the American Revolution. Modern boycotts are viewed as forms of transnational economic coercion by a state or international organization and are intended to deny economic intercourse with some targeted state. Boycotts are used as weapons against the foreign trade of one state in order to secure governmental redress for what the boycotter deems to be legitimate grievances. As coercive sanctions, national boycotts generally enjoy official government support, are foreign-directed, and tend to curtail both demand and supply aspects of a target state's economy. Boycotts can also be employed by nongovernment organizations or individuals against states or specific commodities. Consumer groups, for example, might organize a boycott against coffee grown in a country whose regime offends them.

The Chinese imposed no fewer than nine national boycotts against Japan between 1905 and 1931. The best-known contemporary boycott is that imposed by the League of Arab States against Israel, beginning in 1947. The Arab boycott is multitiered: a primary boycott compels Arab states to refuse to purchase Israeli products; a secondary boycott targets and blacklists international corporations suspected of trading with Israel; a tertiary boycott aims to reject trade with businesses that continue to trade with companies doing business with Israel; and a personal boycott blacklists individuals and institutions believed to be overly sympathetic to Israel. A Central Boycott Office, headquartered in Damascus, Syria, coordinates the Arab League effort, and regional offices operate as governmental agencies in each of the Arab League's boycotting states. The U.S. government in 1977 passed stringent antiboycott legislation aimed at dissuading U.S. corporations from complying with the Arab boycott's discriminatory restraint of trade against some U.S. firms. The United States has also tried to persuade other Western nations to oppose the boycott and to convince the Arab League to lift it. Following the signing of the Arab-Israeli Declaration of Principles on Interim Self-Government Arrangements on 13 September 1993, some Arab countries took initial steps toward lifting the boycott.

Other noteworthy transnational boycotts include the sanctions imposed by the United Nations on South Africa because of its discriminatory apartheid policy, the refusal by Western states in 1980 to attend the Olympics in the Soviet Union in protest against the latter's invasion of Afghanistan, and the no-trade policy instituted by the UN Security Council against Iraq as punishment for its invasion of Kuwait in 1990.

CHRISTOPHER C. JOYNER

See also Blockade; Economic Sanctions; Export Controls; Extraterritoriality; International Law

FURTHER READING

Joyner, Christopher C. "The Transnational Boycott as Economic Coercion in International Law: Policy, Place and Practice." *Vanderbilt Journal of Transnational Law* 17 (Spring 1984): 205–286.
Sarna, Aaron J. *Boycott and Blacklist: A History of Arab Economic Warfare Against Israel.* Totowa, N.J., 1986.

BRACERO PROGRAM

See Mexico

BRADEN, SPRUILLE

(*b.* 13 March 1894; *d.* 10 January 1978)

U.S. businessman and outspoken diplomat active in Latin American affairs. Born in Montana, Braden graduated from Yale University (1914) and became active in several businesses in Chile and the United States. In 1933 he was named a U.S. delegate to the Seventh Pan-American Conference in Montevideo. From 1935 to 1938 he led the U.S. delegation at the Chaco Peace Conference in Buenos Aires. As ambassador to Colombia (1939–1942), Braden alerted Colombian officials to the threat of Nazi influences in South America. In the early 1940s Braden's abrasive diplomatic style contributed to an aggressive and controversial antiauthoritarian U.S. policy in Latin America. As ambassador to Cuba (1942–1945), Braden's public criticism of President Fulgencio Batista y Zaldívar angered many Cubans and caused concern in the State Department. During a brief period as ambassador to Argentina in 1945, Braden publicly challenged Juan Domingo Perón's nationalistic campaign for the presidency. In an effort to discredit the Argentine leader, Braden circulated the "Blue Book on Argentina," a State Department manuscript that denounced Argentine links to the Nazis during World War II. Braden's highly publicized attacks not only failed to undermine Perón but also contributed to the heightened anti-American sentiment in Buenos Aires that helped Perón's election. Alarmed by Braden's blatant interference in Argentine affairs, the Department of State recalled him in September 1945. Braden next served as assistant secretary of state for American republic affairs until 1947, after which he retired from public life to private business.

DAVID SHEININ

See also Argentina; Batista y Zaldívar, Fulgencio; Colombia; Cuba; Perón, Juan Domingo

FURTHER READING

Braden, Spruille. *Diplomats and Demagogues*. New Rochelle, N.Y., 1971.
Frank, Gary. *Juan Perón Versus Spruille Braden: The Story Behind the Blue Book*. Lanham, Md., 1980.
Tulchin, Joseph S. *Argentina and the United States: A Conflicted Relationship*. Boston, 1990.

BRADY PLAN
(1989)

Proposal for easing or ultimately ending the Latin American debt crisis, presented by Secretary of the Treasury Nicholas F. Brady of President George Bush's administration. It was designed to replace the Baker Plan, named for former Secretary of the Treasury James A. Baker, which had provided for rescheduling but not reducing the debts of Latin American countries. The Brady Plan represented a shift in the emphasis of U.S. policy away from the interests of U.S. commercial banks, which were owed large sums of money, and toward the interests of Latin American debtor countries. It also symbolized a focus on the problems of Latin America on its own terms in place of the previous administration's emphasis on the threat of Soviet influence in Central America and the Caribbean. The plan called for U.S. banks to accept reductions (write-downs) of the debt in exchange for guaranteed payment of the balance. By the mid-1990s U.S. banks and many Latin American countries were in better financial condition, interest in the debt crisis had largely faded, and less was heard of the Brady Plan.

ROBERT M. DUNN, JR.

See also Foreign Aid; International Debt; Latin America; Third World Debt

FURTHER READING

Sachs, Jeffrey. "Making the Brady Plan Work." *Foreign Affairs* 68 (Summer 1989): 87–104.

BRANDT, WILLY
(Herbert Ernst Karl Frahm)
(*b.* 18 December 1913; *d.* 8 October 1992)

Foreign Minister of the Federal Republic of Germany (1966–1969), and chancellor (1969–1974), who orchestrated the West German détente policy known as *ostpolitik*. A member of the Social Democratic party (SPD), Brandt emigrated to Scandinavia in 1933 after Adolf Hitler came to power. He returned to Berlin in 1945 and sat as an SPD member of the Bundestag from 1949 to 1957. As mayor of West Berlin (1957–1966), Brandt governed the city during the building of the Berlin Wall in August 1961 and President John F. Kennedy's visit in June 1963. As SPD chairman beginning in 1964, Brandt oriented the party toward détente with the communist states. As foreign minister Brandt broke with previous West German policy by opening diplomatic relations in 1967 with Romania, a close Soviet ally. As chancellor he signed the Nuclear Nonproliferation Treaty of 1968 in November 1969, thereby renouncing any future West German claim to nuclear weapons, and treaties with the Soviet Union and Poland in 1970, in which West Germany recognized for the first time German territorial losses from World War II. In exchange, Brandt obtained the 1971 Quadripartite Agreement on Berlin, signed by the United States, Great Britain, France, and the Soviet Union. The agreement guaranteed Western access to and ties with West Berlin and contained a pledge that no power would attempt to alter the situation in Berlin unilaterally, thereby precluding future Berlin crises.

Ostpolitik culminated in the "Basic Treaty" (December 1972) with the German Democratic Republic (GDR), which normalized relations between the two German states, but the Federal Republic still refused to recognize the GDR as a foreign country. Instead of ambassadors the two Germanys exchanged standing representatives. Brandt hoped that an easing of tensions might induce the Soviets to allow genuine reform of Stalinist programs in Eastern Europe, perhaps even with some softening of the East-West division. Because Brandt's pursuit of détente dovetailed with the simultaneous U.S. pursuit of European stability through détente, the administration of President Richard M. Nixon generally supported Brandt's eastern policies even as it remained ambivalent about West German actions. Although national security adviser Henry Kissinger trusted Brandt personally and noted that Brandt's détente goals were "historically correct," he worried about the "latent incompatibility" between German national goals and the cohesion of the western alliance (*The White House Years*, 1979). Brandt was forced to resign as chancellor in 1974 when an espionage scandal implicated one of his personal secretaries. After the fall of the Berlin Wall in

1989, Brandt reemerged briefly from retirement and helped bring the SPD to a position favoring early unification of the two Germanys. ROBERT MARK SPAULDING, JR.

See also Berlin; Détente; Germany

FURTHER READING

Brandt, Willy. *A Peace Policy for Europe.* New York, 1969.
———. *My Life in Politics.* New York, 1992.
Griffith, William E. *The Ostpolitik of the Federal Republic of Germany.* Cambridge, Mass., 1978.

BRAZIL

Occupying almost half of the South American continent, bordering the Atlantic Ocean on its east, it is the largest country in South America and one with which the United States has competed for influence in the Western Hemisphere. U.S.-Brazilian relations have exhibited a remarkable continuity from the early nineteenth century to the end of the Cold War. The two territorial giants of the Western Hemisphere have maintained an outwardly friendly, but often distant and strained, relationship since the United States welcomed the transfer to Brazil of the Portuguese court fleeing Napoleon's armies in 1808. Even in 1824, when the United States became the first country to recognize Brazil's independence from Portugal, there were few contacts between the two nations and little understanding of each other's political system or culture. Stereotypical images of each other prevailed as each pursued its own self interests in the relationship. For example, Brazilian officials have consistently attempted to establish a privileged, special relationship with the United States in order to maintain and promote close links with the large U.S. market, counterbalance the Argentine threat, and increase Brazil's worldwide power and prestige.

Although U.S. policymakers have often proclaimed their special affection for Brazil, they have always stopped short of creating a special relationship involving any major change in basic policies. For much of the nineteenth century, U.S. officials dealt with a Brazilian monarchy and a Brazil firmly attached to the institution of slavery. Relations were outwardly friendly but distant. Even after Brazil became a republic in 1889 and abolished slavery, U.S. attitudes remained essentially unchanged. It was only at the onset of World War I, World War II, and the Cold War that Washington actively pursued Brazilian cooperation. Whatever the Brazilian government of the moment—a democratic civilian government, a dictatorship, or a military regime—during each crisis the United States wooed Brazil, only to neglect it again once the crisis had passed. The United States also consistently sought Brazilian military cooperation even

when that military intervened in internal politics, as it did repeatedly between 1889 and 1968. U.S. officials saw the Brazilian military as defenders of stability, allies against Germany and the Axis powers, and, during the Cold War, as staunch supporters of anticommunism. In economic relations, U.S. policymakers faithfully pursued the Brazilian market for U.S. goods and attempted to incorporate Brazil into the capitalist, market-oriented world economy. In the twentieth century Brazil was seen as the source of raw materials for U.S. industry and as a market for manufactured goods. U.S. officials constantly and continually advocated a free enterprise system, in part to facilitate U.S. investments. According to U.S. leaders, Brazil would develop as a noncompetitive partner in a U.S.-led world trading system. Even when Brazil emerged in the late 1970s as a competitive industrial power, it remained firmly in the capitalist, free enterprise camp and strongly anticommunist.

General Attitudes and Mutual Images

In both Brazil and the United States, stereotyped attitudes and images have remained constant through nearly two centuries. Despite the myth of geographical proximity and a shared sense of separateness from Spanish America, the two nations have had relatively little contact and few common interests. Few U.S. citizens have visited Brazil or settled there. The U.S. public knows little about Brazil and has generally been indifferent to it, seeing it as a backward and exotic country. Even U.S. policymakers have displayed only a vague, distorted awareness of Brazil. In the 1990s there remained a huge cultural gap between the two societies, despite rhetoric about sister republics and New World hemispheric solidarity. Brazil's rapid industrialization and urbanization have not produced any greater understanding.

From the popular press, in both the nineteenth and twentieth centuries, the U.S. public saw Brazil as a raw primitive society with a teeming Amazon jungle and primitive tribes. At the same time, the U.S. press has also pictured Brazil as a "sleeping giant" and land of unlimited opportunity. Americans thought Brazil was much like the early United States. Optimistic about Brazil's future, U.S. writers have consistently stressed the myth of the fabulous wealth and potential of Brazil, which merely needed to be developed in the "American way." Nineteenth-century news accounts and articles also harbored racial and cultural feelings of U.S. superiority. Brazil was a mixed-race society, a country of stark contrasts between the very rich and the very poor, and these representations changed little in the twentieth century. The stereotypical image of Brazil as the land of coffee, the Rio Carnival, and the great Amazon rain forest remained. Brazil remained underreported in the media, a nation much like its Latin American neighbors, a one commodity country—coffee, with great wealth for a few and huge slums reflecting the plight of most of the population.

For their part, the Brazilian elites tended to view U.S. culture and manners as vulgar, alien, and repellent: Brazil's historic and cultural ties were to Europe, where they looked for fashion and culture, especially in France; and Great Britain was the foreign power most admired in the nineteenth century. At the same time Brazilians markedly refrained from adopting the anti-American attitudes that were common in the rest of Latin America. Following World War II, however, U.S. popular culture suddenly inundated Brazilian society, and Brazilians thirsted after things American. The United States became an adjective for anything new or modern. After participating actively in both world wars, Brazilians acquired a new sense of their own importance. They wanted to be thought of as the leader of South America and a rising international power. Despite these attitudes they retained a distinct sense of cultural inferiority toward their powerful neighbor to the north. Nevertheless, for most Brazilians, close relations with the United States remained a cardinal principle of Brazilian diplomacy. Brazil's economic boom in the 1970s and 1980s reinforced traditional Brazilian views of the world and of the United States. Experiencing a type of "manifest destiny," Brazilians expected that Brazil would now be taken seriously on the international stage. They resented their perceived third world class treatment by the United States and felt, despite their giant economic gains, they were still taken for granted by U.S. leaders. Nevertheless, Brazilians continued to respect and admire many things American. U.S. officials, however, even in the twentieth century, clearly assigned Brazil to the category of minor nations, and during the Cold War, Brazil was not a major area of concern.

Political Affairs

Until 1889 Brazil was a monarchy, first as part of the Portuguese empire and later as an independent empire under rulers of the Portuguese royal house. For more than a century after the British ferried the Portuguese court to Brazil in 1808, Great Britain exhibited the most influence of any foreign nation in Brazil. The United States remained preoccupied with developments in Mexico, Central America, and the Caribbean until the early twentieth century. President James Monroe, for example, was slow to grant recognition to Brazil when it declared its independence in 1822 as a monarchical empire. Monroe's distaste for monarchy was eventually overcome in 1824 by political reality and the belief that Brazil as a New World nation would naturally and inevitably move toward republicanism and the desire for commercial benefits. Brazil's continued support for the institution of slavery and a continuing monarchy contributed to a U.S. sense

that Brazil and its institutions were somehow out of place in the Americas.

When the Brazilian military overthrew the monarchy in 1889 and established a republic, U.S.-Brazilian relations grew more cordial. Although Brazilian leaders were inspired more by the French than the North American model, they rejected the European parliamentary system in favor of a federal government openly modeled on that of the United States and declared Brazil the Republic of the United States of Brazil. It was, however, a republic in name only. Despite a democratic facade, the masses were excluded from the new government and political affairs, and the old rural and urban elites continued to control the oligarchic government. Nevertheless, U.S. officials and the press saw the 1889 coup as a victory for republicanism in the hemisphere. As the drama of the coup subsided and talk of U.S. intervention to protect U.S. business interests decreased in the U.S. press, interest in Brazil waned again.

With the new republic and the ascendancy of Foreign Minister Baron de Rio Branco (1902–1912), Brazilian officials now considered the friendship and support of the United States crucial to Brazil's national interests. Rio Branco regarded the United States as a benevolent guardian that would restrain European aggression. He looked to Washington rather than London and sought to align Brazilian foreign policy with that of the United States. He wanted to establish a special status for Brazil and form a partnership that would guide the destiny of the Western Hemisphere. Brazil was the only Latin American country to sympathize publicly with the United States during the Spanish-American Cuban-Filipino War in 1898 and supported U.S. gunboat diplomacy in the Caribbean, the Roosevelt Corollary to the Monroe Doctrine, the independence of Panama, and the U.S. position with regard to Mexico and its revolutionary government in 1914. In 1906 Brazil became the first (and for a long time the only) South American country to exchange envoys with the rank of ambassador with the United States, rather than the ministers Washington usually exchanged with less important countries. Brazilians thought this extremely important, but it had little effect on U.S. attitudes or policies.

The declared closeness of the two countries and the Brazilian assumption that a special relationship existed created unrealized expectations and disillusionment among the Brazilians as they looked for preferential treatment from the United States that was not forthcoming. Although U.S. officials appreciated the cooperation and cordial response of the Brazilians to U.S. initiatives and supported Brazil in its territorial and boundary disputes with Bolivia and Argentina, they did not wish to see any major South American power become dominant and attempted to treat all South American countries equally.

As the World War I crisis in Europe deepened, U.S. efforts turned to promoting an improved image of the United States in the hemisphere by reaffirming Pan-American solidarity and the Monroe Doctrine but remained primarily concerned with events in Europe, despite military interventions in Cuba, Haiti, and the Dominican Republic. When the United States declared war on Germany, however, Washington made a strenuous and successful effort to get Brazil to join the Allies and thereby set a precedent for the other Latin American states. Although no other Latin American country followed suit, Brazil's entry into the war and its pro-U.S. position at the Paris Peace Conference delighted U.S. officials. President Woodrow Wilson took little account of Brazilian views at the peace conference, however, and the United States refused to recognize Brazil's claim that its wartime cooperation entitled it to a special-status relationship. After the war, the U.S. objective shifted to hemispheric solidarity, and Washington focused on winning Argentine diplomatic cooperation, despite Argentina's neutrality during the war, and Brazil remained a third-rate, underdeveloped, unimportant country for U.S. policymakers.

The perceived threat of Germany and Japan to the security of the United States and its position of dominance in the Western Hemisphere during the 1930s produced a reaction toward Latin America similar to that during World War I. The administration of President Franklin D. Roosevelt (1933–1945) promoted the Good Neighbor Policy, the Monroe Doctrine, and continental solidarity as a basis for the protection of the American system and U.S. interests in Latin America and to reaffirm the almost mystic "Western Hemisphere Idea" of hemispheric unity. U.S. officials again sought Brazil's solid support for U.S. actions against the Axis menace. Administration officials, much like their earlier counterparts, pressed Brazilian leaders to enter the war as an example to the rest of Latin America. Stability and order, however, became far more important for U.S. officials than promoting democracy in Brazil. The United States strongly supported the authoritarian government of President Getúlio Vargas (1930–1945, 1951–1954) and collaborated closely with it during the war. Although the Brazilian government was a dictatorship, according to U.S. officials, it had considerable roots in popular support and, on the whole, was benevolent. Vargas, cut off from Europe and with little choice, responded by actively cooperating with the United States against Germany and the Axis powers. Brazil declared war on Germany and sent a small expeditionary force to Europe. Despite Brazil's participation on the side of the Allies and pro-German Argentine neutrality, at the end of the war U.S. policymakers once again stressed a unified hemisphere and eventually courted Argentine cooperation. U.S. offi-cials strove for a balanced hemispheric policy. Brazil's advocacy of a special relationship with the United States was not a priority for U.S. officials.

The onset of the Cold War brought few changes. Perceiving the Soviet threat as a danger not only to the United States but to the entire hemisphere, U.S. officials committed themselves to an increasingly vigorous anti-communist line with regard to Brazil and the rest of Latin America. It was strikingly similar to Wilson's World War I hemispheric rhetoric and Roosevelt's antifascist hemisphere defense and solidarity policies. With the outbreak of the Korean War in 1950, U.S. officials once again pressed the Brazilians for a military commitment to set a precedent for the rest of Latin America in the all-out struggle against communism. This time, however, the Brazilians did not send troops, although they remained sympathetic to the U.S. position.

Although the United States supported the democratically elected president Juscelino Kubitschek (1956–1960), it saw João Goulart (who succeeded Janio Quadros in 1961), it saw Brazilian President João Goulart as a communist sympathizer and was not adverse to the military coup that deposed him and established military rule in Brazil in 1964. U.S. officials viewed Goulart as weak, left-leaning, and a danger to the hemisphere. By the 1960s what mattered most to U.S. policymakers was a stable, anticommunist Brazil, strongly supportive of the United States, and not the development of democracy. Brazil was seen as the key to U.S. anticommunist policies in Latin America. President John F. Kennedy's Alliance for Progress, created in part to promote economic prosperity in underdeveloped countries, was also part of the U.S. effort to promote Brazil as a bastion against communism and the spread of Castroism in Latin America.

For its part, Brazil continued to support U.S. objectives, primarily to ensure U.S. support for Brazil's dominance in South America and to promote its own economic development. After World War II the United States was the only country with the available capital to finance Brazilian development. During much of the Cold War era, despite receiving little more than rhetorical assurances about Washington's continued concern and friendship for Brazil, the Brazilian government continued to follow a constructive, cooperative policy toward the United States and its foreign policy objectives in the inter-American system and in the United Nations. Under the military rule of Castelo Branco in the early 1960s, Brazil became closely aligned with the United States, sharing U.S. concepts for hemispheric security and development. Brazilian leaders also felt strongly, however, that the United States owed Brazil assistance because it had "thrown-out" the communists. With the restoration of democratic government in 1985, after twenty years of military rule, Brazil began to pursue a more independent policy both internally and externally. It pushed a continuation of import substitution policies domestically and instituted a more assertive foreign policy resisting efforts led by the United States in population control, environmental protection, and nuclear nonproliferation.

Military Relations

One of the most consistent and important features of U.S. policy toward Brazil was Washington's cultivation of the Brazilian military as a valuable ally. According to most U.S. officials in the Cold War era, the Brazilian military was the most important force in Brazil and formed the core of stability in the country. It was the upholder of the democratic order and, although somewhat too nationalistic, the promoter of free enterprise. The Brazilian military had overthrown the monarchy in 1889, a military junta had installed Vargas in the presidency in November 1937, deposed him in 1945, forced him to resign in 1954, engineered the countercoup of 1955 that allowed Kubitschek to assume office, and overthrew Goulart in 1964. In general, however, U.S. officials saw the Brazilian military as performing a moderating and modernizing role in Brazilian life. It seemed to be much like the U.S. military, at least until the 1964 coup, when the Brazilian military assumed direct control of the government. Even then, U.S. officials saw it as being strongly anticommunist and pro-American.

During the First Republic (1889–1930), Brazil sought to modernize its military and increase its armed strength by imitating European military establishments. In 1906 Brazil signed a military mission agreement with France, and during the early stages of World War I Brazilian leaders were awed by the success of the German military machine; Europeans, chiefly French and German, therefore guided the professionalization of Brazilian forces before World War II. This European tutelage stimulated rather than lessened Brazilian military interest in politics and motivated the elite professional officers to assume responsibility for the conduct of national affairs. The Brazilian military, although not monolithic in its thinking, generally viewed itself as the technocratic nation-builder in a backward and divided land where domestic order and internal security were prerequisites to progress and stability.

These attitudes fit well with most U.S. objectives for Brazil and Latin America. What U.S. policy planners wanted was a stable Brazil, supportive of U.S. positions. Unlike most military groups in Latin America after World War I, the Brazilian armed forces maintained close contacts and relations with the United States military establishment. In the late 1930s the Roosevelt administration courted the favor of the Brazilian military, hoping to eliminate the influence of the Berlin-Rome Axis from the hemisphere. In 1938 and 1939 Washington made tactful inquiries as to the termination date of Brazil's existing contracts with Germany and Italy and the chances of replacing the Axis missions with ones from the United States. U.S. officials impressed on their Brazilian counterparts that the presence of non-American military missions in the hemisphere was incompatible with the perfect realization of continental solidarity. Cut off from German and French influence by the war, the Brazilian military relied more and more on U.S. training techniques and equipment. During World War II, Brazil was the only Latin American nation to send troops abroad to aid the Allies. The Joint Brazilian-U.S. Defense Commission (JBUSDC) coordinated defense policy in Washington and Rio de Janeiro. A variety of U.S. training missions replaced the German and French missions and exposed the Brazilians to U.S. military doctrines. By the end of the war the United States had acquired a near-monopoly over the training and equipping of the Brazilian armed forces.

The U.S. attitudes and policies with regard to the Brazilian military during the world wars also fit the perceived hemispheric threat of the Soviet Union during the Cold War. U.S. military advisers believed that the Soviets could, by establishing strong military ties and supplying arms, instill their communist doctrine on the continent. Accordingly, U.S. officials moved to strengthen U.S.-Brazilian military ties and goodwill and pushed steadily for a continuation of a united, U.S.-led effort in planning hemispheric defense. Proceeding on the assumption that the United States wanted Brazil to play a strong and cooperative role in hemispheric defense, U.S. armed forces officials proposed a vast program of aid that would make the Brazilian military the strongest force in Latin America and give it great international prestige. Brazilian officials expected this type of treatment, given the alliances during the world wars, and thought they deserved substantial economic and military benefits. Although U.S. officials continually expressed their desire for close cooperation and the hope of providing the Brazilian military with modern equipment, U.S. officials refused to grant Brazil any special favors and generally ignored Brazilian requests for modern military equipment. Europe and Asia again took precedence in U.S. policy considerations.

Despite the lofty goals of the U.S. military, the administrations of Harry S. Truman and Dwight D. Eisenhower provided little military aid to Brazil. Events in Greece, Turkey, China, and Korea relegated arms programs for Brazil to the background. Unable to supply Brazil with large amounts of equipment, U.S. planners searched for other ways to maintain and strengthen Brazilian military support and cooperation. General Dwight D. Eisenhower enthusiastically supported, for example, the establishment of a Brazilian war college modeled on the National

War College in the United States, and in 1949 the Escola Superior de Guerra (ESG) was founded with a U.S. advisory mission. The ESG promoted the idea of interdependence with the United States, saw Brazil firmly aligned with the West, accepted the U.S. concept of communist world aggression, and projected a firm anticommunist policy with strong support for the leadership of the United States in the Cold War. Although the influence of the ESG doctrine was not pervasive within the Brazilian military in the early 1950s, it had a profound effect on later military governments, when it became increasingly anticommunist and committed to rapid economic development. In Marshall Humberto Castelo Branco's government in the 1960s, for example, 80 percent of the core group of Brazilian policymakers had attended either the ESG or U.S. military schools. Despite little actual military aid, under U.S. supervision the Brazilian military became the most modern and developed sector of Brazilian society and a major component of the overall Brazilian modernization and industrialization effort. Blaming the communists for the chaos, corruption, and subversion in Brazil, the Brazilian military became dominated by anticommunist hard-liners, who viewed the international scene in much the same way as U.S. leaders. Accordingly, Brazil broke relations with Fidel Castro's Cuba, voted against seating Communist China in the United Nations, supported the early United States' efforts in Vietnam, and participated in the U.S. intervention in the Dominican Republic in 1965. The Brazilian military also guaranteed U.S. investors major opportunities in Brazilian economic development programs. This close working relationship began to unravel in the late 1960s and early 1970s with growing Brazilian opposition to the U.S. role in Vietnam and, despite U.S. pressure, a Brazilian vote in the UN to condemn Zionism. Clearly, Brazil and the Brazilian military were developing a more independent, nationalistic policy. Nevertheless, Washington continued to view Brazil as a stable, conservative, pro-United States, anti-communist, pro-private enterprise bastion, and U.S. officials actively cultivated its support.

Economic Relations

U.S. economic relations with Brazil also showed considerable continuity from the nineteenth century through the Cold War era. Presidents from James Monroe to Ronald Reagan sought to aid U.S. business in grasping commercial opportunities in Brazil. Washington has consistently tried to increase U.S. exports, secure basic raw materials for U.S. industry, oust European competitors, and secure U.S. commercial ascendancy not only in Brazil but in all Latin America. Before World War I trade with Brazil was dominated by Great Britain, and London was the major source of new capital investment. Throughout most of the nineteenth century, Brazil

accounted for only 3 to 4 percent of total U.S. trade, although Washington encouraged the efforts of U.S. business to increase trade with Brazil. When Brazilian coffee was introduced into the United States in the late 1800s, a profitable commercial relationship emerged, ranking Brazil alongside Cuba and Mexico as one of the largest trading partners in Latin America.

At the beginning of the twentieth century, the rising international economic preeminence of the United States and a booming domestic economy made U.S. businessmen eager to take advantage of increased markets abroad. Rediscovering Latin America, U.S. leaders acclaimed Brazil as a particularly enticing market, because of its large population and proximity to the United States. With the outbreak of war in Europe in 1914, U.S. traders sought to take full advantage of Europe's commercial disarray and challenge Great Britain's economic dominance and to expand their economic influence throughout Latin America. U.S. officials eagerly sought to secure Brazilian raw materials, especially manganese and rubber for U.S. steel mills and industry, and to eliminate all foreign competition. U.S.-manufactured goods literally flooded the Brazilian market. By the end of the war the United States controlled 40 percent of Brazil's overseas trade, and U.S. business had become preeminent. Wall Street replaced London as the world's leading money market and financial center, and U.S. loans, both private and governmental, financed improvements in the Brazilian infrastructure. Despite the large increase of U.S. trade with Brazil, the United States refused to give Brazil preferential economic treatment or establish a special trading partnership.

For their part, the Brazilians, from the early nineteenth century on, hoped to protect and promote their growing share of the vast U.S. market for such exports as sugar, coffee, and rubber and to avoid economic dependence on Great Britain. By the 1920s Brazil was also looking to the United States to supply much of its growing demand for the new products of the modern age. Impressed by the dynamic economic growth of the United States and its technological achievements, Brazilians attempted to play off the United States against their traditional European suppliers. In the 1920s the United States was also seen as the only country with the necessary investment capital to finance long-term Brazilian development programs.

The economic policies put forward by Franklin D. Roosevelt's administration in an effort to guide and protect U.S. business interests during the 1930s and World War II, and the economic policies subsequently proclaimed by U.S. policymakers during the Cold War, resembled the policies of earlier administrations. Using the Good Neighbor Policy and New Deal principles of government-business cooperation, the Roosevelt administration sought to tie the Brazilian economy more closely than ever to the United States and its corporate capitalist system, in the belief that prosperity and security depended upon a constructive interaction between the two countries. During World War II, U.S. officials sought and obtained commodity and purchasing agreements with Brazil to ensure Brazilian sources of manganese, iron ore, rubber, diamonds, and quartz crystal for U.S. industry. Threats of closure from traditional sources, such as Russia and India, enhanced the importance of Brazilian sources. This remained true for much of the Cold War era. The need to establish secure sources of strategic raw materials for any future war effort played a major role in U.S. policy decisions during the 1950s and 1960s. The U.S. strategy was to create a closed hemisphere in an "open world" both for economic and hemispheric security reasons. Moreover, after 1945 U.S. policymakers once again advocated free trade and open competition because they knew that U.S. business would benefit most.

The emergence of the Soviet Union and the Soviet bloc as a perceived economic threat to the U.S. position in Brazil and in Latin America during the Cold War era produced similar reactions by U.S. policymakers. Once again U.S. officials strove to secure the strategic materials of Brazil and to limit or deny Brazilian trade with the Soviet Union and its satellites. The Cold War also saw the reemergence in most U.S. decision-makers of an unqualified belief that private entrepreneurs, unrestrained and encouraged by government, could duplicate the American success story. U.S. decision-makers defined Brazilian economic development in terms of traditional liberal economic terms. In general, they opposed Brazilian economic nationalism, statism, and excessive industrial development and condemned the Brazilian government for intervening in the economy. They suggested that the Brazilian government needed only to make the country more attractive to private North American investors rather than developing competitive industries, which meant adhering to U.S. advice regarding sound financial practices and the promotion of the private sector and private investment in noncompetitive products.

These policies were not that much different from those put forth earlier by U.S. leaders designed to protect and promote U.S. economic interests in the hemisphere through a mercantile-like system in which the United States would provide the manufactured goods and Brazil the raw materials, making their economies complementary and not competitive. Brazilian leaders did not seriously challenge this relationship until Brazil developed its own manufacturing base. The Brazilian economic boom of the late 1970s and 1980s, triggered by its export diversification programs, altered dramatically the economic interests of Brazil's leaders and established a competitive rather than complementary economic status with the United States. For example, coffee, sugar, and cocoa decreased from nearly 50 percent of Brazil's exports in the early 1970s to around 15 percent in 1985. At the same time, Brazilian exports of industrial goods increased from under 20 percent to over 58 percent. Although the United States remained Brazil's single largest market (the United States took 25 percent and of all Brazilian exports in 1982), biggest supplier of goods and services (the U.S. share of Brazil's non-oil imports was 33 percent in 1983), and its primary source of investment and finance (more U.S. investment is concentrated in Brazil than in any other Latin American country), Brazil's trading interests broadened, bringing tensions and frequent conflicts with U.S. trade policies. Brazilian manufacturers became strong competitors in the U.S. market in shoes, textiles, steel, and transportation equipment. Brazil began competing with the United States in world markets to sell agricultural products such as soybeans, orange juice, and poultry. Moreover, Brazil became the fifth largest exporter of arms and military hardware. In addition, Brazil enjoyed a growing surplus in its trade with the United States. Subsidiaries of U.S. corporations contributed significantly to Brazil's exports to the United States, primarily in parts and components for the automatize and electronic industries. U.S. officials objected to Brazil's subsidized export programs and protectionist policies for its domestic markets. They also clashed with the Brazilians on profit remittances by U.S. firms, technology transfer issues, trade competition in the third world, banking procedures, and debt issues.

No longer simply an exporter of primary products, Brazil has emerged as a modern, industrialized, urbanized nation, with a more sophisticated vision of its role in the world. Brazil's determination to expand as an independent industrial power has also radically altered its economic positions and interests. It has become a serious trade competitor of the United States.

Despite the changing nature of the relationship, the United States remains central to the Brazilian worldview, and Brazil's single most important trading partner; U.S. corporations continue to have a major presence in Brazil and a significant impact on Brazilian development. Brazilians also continue to maintain an extraordinary admiration for and interest in the United States—its political system, its life style, its ideals, and its consumer production.

Brazil, however, remains of only passing interest to U.S. policymakers. Although U.S. officials continue to pay rhetorical deference to Brazil and its development, Brazil remains of interest only to Brazilian specialists. The classical U.S. approach to Brazil and Brazilian affairs continues to dominate U.S. thinking.

GERALD K. HAINES

See also Alliance for Progress; Argentina; Berle, Adolf Augustus, Jr.; Bolivia; Cold War; Cuba; Good Neighbor Policy; Inter-American Development Bank; Latin America; Monroe, James; Monroe Doctrine; Organization of American States; Pan-Americanism; Paraguay; Portugal; Roosevelt Corollary; Slave Trade and Slavery; Uruguay

FURTHER READING

Black, Jan Knippers. *United States Penetration of Brazil*. Philadelphia, Pa., 1977.

Burns, Bradford E. "Tradition and Variation in Brazilian Foreign Policy," *Journal of Inter-American Studies* 9 (1967): 195–212.

Cobbs, Elizabeth A. *The Rich Neighbor Policy, Rockefeller and Kaiser in Brazil*. New Haven, Conn., 1992.

Freye, Gilberto. *The Mansions and the Shanties*. New York, 1966.

Green, David, *The Containment of Latin America: A History of the Myth and Realities of the Good Neighbor Policy*. Chicago, 1971.

Haines, Gerald K. *The Americanization of Brazil: A Study of U.S. Cold War Diplomacy in the Third World, 1945–1954*. Wilmington, Del., 1989.

Hilton, Stanley E. *Brazil and the Great Powers 1930–1939: The Politics of Trade Rivalry*. Austin, Tex., 1975.

Leacock, Ruth. *Requiem for Revolution, The United States and Brazil, 1961–1969*. Kent, Ohio, 1990.

McCann, Frank D. *The Brazilian-American Alliance 1937–1945*. Princeton, N.J., 1973.

Rodriques, José Honório. "The Foundations of Brazil's Foreign Policy," *International Affairs* 38 (1962): 324–328.

Skidmore, Thomas E. "Brazil's American Illusion: From Dom Pedro II to the Coup of 1964," *Luso-Brazilian Review* 23 (1986): 71–84.

Smith, Joseph. *Unequal Giants: Diplomatic Relations Between the United States and Brazil, 1889–1930*. Pittsburgh, Pa., 1991.

Weiss, W. Michael. *Cold Warriors and Coups d'Etat: Brazilian-American Relations, 1945–1964*. Albuquerque, N. M., 1993.

BRAZZAVILLE

See Congo

BRETTON WOODS SYSTEM

The postwar international economic order established in July 1944 at a conference held over a three-week period at Bretton Woods, New Hampshire. Although forty-four participants failed to meet expectations in several respects, they did put into place an economic system under U.S. leadership that allowed unprecedented economic growth and enshrined liberalism as the premier international economic theory. The Bretton Woods system was based on the belief that prosperity and peace could be best assured with a free flow of goods on the one hand and monetary stability based on fixed exchange rates on the other. These principles were to be enshrined in three new institutions: the International Bank for Reconstruction and Development (World Bank), the International Monetary Fund (IMF), and the stillborn International Trade Organization (ITO). During the conference, the participants, among them Harry Dexter White of the United States and John Maynard Keynes of Great Britain, debated the details of the agreement, ultimately settling on a system of relatively weak organizations with modest resources, in keeping with U.S. preferences. The voting power of the institutions was based on a weighted system that gave the United States a de facto veto over key policy decisions—a source of resentment for many developing nations.

Early on, the weaknesses of the IMF and the World Bank created a need for dramatic unilateral U.S. intervention in the form of the Marshall Plan to prevent economic and financial collapse in Europe. The ITO never even came into existence; in a bitter disappointment for the Bretton Woods planners, the United States rejected the plan for the organization in 1950, largely because it proposed to interfere too much in the liberal marketplace. The only part of the ITO to survive was the provisional arrangement under the General Agreement on Tariffs and Trade (GATT) to liberalize trade. From this modest beginning, GATT went on to liberalize trade domestically, utilizing the principles of reciprocal concessions made available to all nations under the most-favored-nation principle. GATT has resulted in almost immeasurable increases in global trade and prosperity.

In August 1971 the administration of President Richard M. Nixon took the United States off the gold standard, devalued the dollar, and imposed a 10 percent tariff on imports to deal with a growing balance of payments and trade deficit. The result ended the formal rules of the Bretton Woods system while preserving its institutions. The system has since gone through a series of redefinitions and adjustments with the result that the World Bank, the IMF, and GATT have adopted new and often significant roles that both differ from and transcend their founders' expectations. With the end of fixed exchange rates and a move toward a regulated floating exchange rate system, the IMF's role in currency stabilization waned while it took on a new, expanded role as "lender of last resort" and "master rescheduler" during the Third World debt crisis. Beginning with Mexico in 1982, the IMF interceded on behalf of developing nations with private and public creditors. The World Bank moved away from a focus on European reconstruction and, with the establishment of the International Development Association (IDA) in 1960, began to take the lead in concessionary lending to Third World nations. The IDA and the consortia for agricultural development have been credited with organizing the Green Revolution, a dramatically successful application of hybrid seed technology to Third World agriculture in the 1960s and 1970s, and numerous large-scale infrastructure projects. Meanwhile, GATT grew to include the overwhelming majority of the world's nations. A new section was added to the GATT treaty in 1979 to give special preference to developing countries. Some have argued that the Uruguay Round of GATT-sponsored trade talks, by incorporating free trade in agriculture and services, could make the institution as comprehensive as the ITO was originally envisioned. All in all, despite the disappointment of their founders, the Bretton Woods system and institutions have proven flexible, useful, and resilient. The reliance on the IMF in the rehabilitation of Eastern Europe and the 1995 transformation of GATT into the World Trade Organization are further testament to the continued relevance of the Bretton Woods system.

KENDALL W. STILES

See also General Agreement on Tariffs and Trade; International Bank for Reconstruction and Development; International Monetary Fund; International Trade Organization; World Trade Organization; World War II

FURTHER READING

Gardner, Richard. *Sterling-Dollar Diplomacy: The Origins and the Prospects of Our International Economic Order.* New York, 1969.

BREZHNEV, LEONID ILYICH

(*b.* 6 December 1906; *d.* 10 November 1982)

First secretary (later general secretary) of the Communist party of the Soviet Union (1964–1982), simultaneously serving from 1977 as president of the Soviet Union (actually chairman of the Presidium of the Supreme Soviet of the USSR) until his death. He provided stolid, unimaginative, but consistent leadership for the Soviet Union and negotiated with five U.S. presidents—Lyndon B. Johnson, Richard M. Nixon, Gerald R. Ford, Jimmy Carter, and Ronald Reagan. Brezhnev's life and career were typical for the generation that came to maturity in the early years of Joseph Stalin's rule. He joined the Communist party in 1931 and in 1935 graduated from the Dneprodzerzhinsk Metallurgical Institute. After a brief period as a worker and conscription service in the Red Army, he entered a lifelong career in the Communist party bureaucracy. In addition to serving in various party positions in the Ukraine, Moldavia, and Kazakhstan, Brezhnev served intermittently in the party secretariat in Moscow from 1952 to 1964. During World War II, and again briefly in 1953–1954, he served in the main political administration of the Soviet armed forces. In 1964, he succeeded Nikita S. Khrushchev as party leader, and consolidated his position as primus inter pares in the Soviet collective leadership from 1964 to 1971. Thereafter, until his death, Brezhnev presided over a relatively uneventful period in the country, but one marked by growing corruption and the onset of gradual economic decline, later described as the "period of stag-

nation." A gradual stagnation also developed in the Soviet-led socialist bloc in Eastern Europe. There were, however, intermittent outbreaks of popular discontent, notably in Czechoslovakia. Brezhnev and his colleagues in the Soviet leadership quelled that unrest with military intervention in Czechoslovakia in August 1968 and by articulating a doctrine of collective maintenance of socialism within the Soviet bloc, known as the Brezhnev Doctrine.

Under Brezhnev, the Soviet Union attained strategic nuclear parity with the United States, which contributed to Soviet confidence and led in the 1970s to agreements on strategic arms control and, more broadly, to a détente with the United States and Western Europe. After 1975 Brezhnev's health seriously deteriorated, adversely affecting foreign and domestic policy decision-making. Soviet support of radical Third World regimes in Africa, the Middle East, and South Asia undercut détente; Soviet military intervention in Afghanistan in 1979 proved to be his worst mistake—a Soviet Vietnam. By the last years of Brezhnev's life, despite his wishes but partly because of his foreign policies, the détente of the 1970s had been replaced by a renewal of Cold War confrontation.

RAYMOND L. GARTHOFF

See also Afghanistan; Brezhnev Doctrine; Cold War; Détente; Russia and the Soviet Union

FURTHER READING

Institute of Marxian-Leninism, CPSU Central Committee. *Leonid Ilyich Brezhnev: A Short Biography.* New York, 1977.
Murphy, Paul J. *Brezhnev, Soviet Politician.* Jefferson, N.C., 1981.

BREZHNEV DOCTRINE

The term that came to be applied in the West to the Soviet justification for the Soviet-led occupation of Czechoslovakia in August 1968. While Soviet authorities denied the existence of a Brezhnev Doctrine, also known as the doctrine of limited sovereignty, Soviet leader Leonid Brezhnev himself, in a speech on 12 November 1968, said that a threat to socialist rule in any state of the Eastern European bloc constituted a threat to all and therefore "must engage the attention of all the socialist states." Under the Brezhnev Doctrine, the Soviet Union arrogated to itself the right to prevent the overthrow of communist rule or defection from the bloc of any member. The last Soviet leader, Mikhail Gorbachev, in effect repudiated the Brezhnev Doctrine during the late 1980s. Soviet acceptance of the remarkably peaceful overthrow of communist rule in the countries of Eastern Europe (except for some internal violence in Romania) in late 1989 and the dismantling of the socialist bloc in 1990–1991 bore witness to the demise of the doctrine.

RAYMOND L. GARTHOFF

See also Brezhnev, Leonid Ilyich; Czech Republic; Russia and the Soviet Union

FURTHER READING

Jones, Robert A. *The Soviet Concept of "Limited Sovereignty" from Lenin to Gorbachev: The Brezhnev Doctrine.* New York, 1990.

BRICKER AMENDMENT

A series of constitutional amendments, proposed mainly by Republican Senator John Bricker of Ohio in the early to mid-1950s, that sought to control the treaty-making and executive agreement–making powers of the executive branch of the federal government and to preserve states' rights. On a procedural level, these amendments sought to ensure greater congressional involvement in the approval of treaty and executive agreements and to provide a mechanism for keeping any self-executing agreements from coming into effect by granting Congress the right to enact appropriate legislation for putting treaties and executive agreements into operation. On a substantive level, the amendments sought to ensure that no treaties or executive agreements would obligate the United States to domestic actions that would infringe on the rights of the states or on congressional prerogatives under the U.S. Constitution.

Substantive targets of the Bricker proposals demonstrate why these procedural concerns were important. The amendments, for example, sought to alter the Supreme Court's ruling in *Missouri* v. *Holland* (1920), a decision that found constitutional congressional legislation protecting migratory birds because a treaty calling for the protection of the birds in the United States and Canada had been signed between the United States and Great Britain. In an earlier decision, the Court had ruled that similar legislation passed prior to the signing of the treaty was unconstitutional because there was no delegated constitutional power to protect migratory birds. In effect, the later court decision weakened the powers reserved to the states under the Constitution and allowed the executive branch (and the federal government as a whole) to expand its powers through the use of the treaty powers.

The legal standing given the executive agreement in such cases as *United States* v. *Belmont* (1937) and *United States* v. *Pink* (1942) was also a source of discontent because these decisions overruled the rights of states, following much the same reasoning as that used in *Missouri* v. *Holland.* The Brickerites also feared the impact of human rights treaties and executive agreements passed or under consideration by the United Nations at the time, arguing that such treaties and agreements might cost Americans their basic constitutional rights or make them subject to rights and responsibilities imposed by the United Nations or other international organizations. They also suggested that the rights of states under the Constitution were similarly threatened.

The Bricker movement paralleled congressional efforts, such as the Case-Zablocki Act (1972), during the 1970s to limit the president's right to assume commitments, in that both movements sought to rein in the foreign policy powers of the executive. The movements, however, were dissimilar in at least three key ways: the Bricker movement sought to enact a constitutional amendment to restrict treaties and executive agreements by the president, whereas the 1970s effort sought only to require the president to report to Congress on executive agreements after the commitments were already made; the Bricker movement was largely a conservative-led effort, whereas the 1970s movement was led by liberals; and the congressional efforts of the 1970s achieved some limited success, while the Bricker effort ultimately failed. Although various forms of the Bricker amendment were voted on in the U.S. Senate, none ever obtained the necessary two-thirds majority required for constitutional amendments. President Dwight D. Eisenhower actively sought to thwart the Bricker Amendment and continued to do so until its defeat in 1954, when the amendment came closest to winning approval; it failed by one vote to obtain the necessary two-thirds majority. While similar amendments were introduced in subsequent years, they never came as close to winning Senate approval as did the 1954 amendment.

JAMES M. McCORMICK

See also Case-Zablocki Act; Congress; Constitution; Executive Agreements; Presidency

FURTHER READING

Garrett, Stephen A. "Foreign Policy and the American Constitution: The Bricker Amendment in Contemporary Perspective," *International Studies Quarterly* 16 (June 1972): 187–220.

Kaufman, Natalie Hevener. *Human Rights Treaties and the Senate.* Chapel Hill, N.C., 1990.

Tananbaum, Duane. *The Bricker Amendment Controversy: A Test of Eisenhower's Political Leadership.* Ithaca, N.Y., 1988.

BRINKMANSHIP

A facet of U.S. diplomacy—a willingness to go to war—specifically associated with John Foster Dulles, secretary of state (1953–1959). As part of a promised "new look" at containment, Dulles sought to deter aggressive Soviet foreign policy ventures by making the costs to such ventures clear, severe, and unacceptable. Towards this end, he explicitly incorporated nuclear weapons into the arsenal of U.S. diplomacy and embraced a declaratory military strategy of "massive retaliation" against Soviet expansion. Diplomatic leverage was increased, according to the logic of this strategy, by convincing the Soviets that the United States was willing to go to war if necessary. The goal of course was to avoid war, but "if you are scared to go to the brink," as Dulles put it in an interview, "you are lost." To the American public, it was this rhetoric—and episodic crises of the period, such as the American threats to bomb China in 1953 in order to bring an end to the Korean War, the support of Nationalist China against the shelling of the offshore islands of Quemoy (Jinmen) and Matsu (Mazu) by mainland China in 1958, and the dangerous posturing over Berlin with the Soviet Union in the next year—that identified brinkmanship as the hallmark of the Republican new look. The academic Thomas C. Schelling called this deliberate use of the threat of nuclear weapons for political influence the "diplomacy of violence."

The Soviet Union had its own version of brinkmanship, labeled "adventurism," which led to the Cuban Missile Crisis of October 1962. The clear danger of nuclear war in this episode forced a reevaluation of brinkmanship. The Kennedy administration developed an alternative military strategy of "flexible response," which placed less reliance on nuclear weapons in foreign policy and more emphasis on a buildup of conventional forces.

Timothy J. Lomperis

See also Berlin; Cuban Missile Crisis; Dulles, John Foster; Jinmen-Mazu Crises; Korean War; Massive Retaliation; Nuclear Weapons and Strategy

FURTHER READING

Gaddis, John Lewis. *Strategies of Containment.* New York, 1982.
Schelling, Thomas C. *Arms and Influence.* New Haven, Conn., 1966.

BRITISH LOAN OF 1946

Loan provided by the United States to fund Great Britain's post–World War II reconstruction. The British loan of 1946 had its origins in two powerful historical factors. The first was the U.S. government's desire, enshrined in wartime policy and various proposals that became the basis for the Bretton Woods System, to create a multilateral economic postwar order that required British participation and the end of imperial preference in international trade. The second was Great Britain's desperate need for financial assistance in the first years of postwar reconstruction. In early 1944 President Franklin D. Roosevelt's emissary told the British that congressional approval of an interest-free loan was expected that summer. In fact, formal negotiation, led by Assistant Secretary of State William L. Clayton, began only in late 1945. By that time the prospect of the loan, which had always been problematic, was further complicated by

congressional reluctance and by the appearance of a partially socialist, Labour party government in Great Britain.

The aim of President Harry S. Truman's administration was a small (around $3 billion) interest-bearing loan that could be justified to a suspicious Congress by a British commitment to the full convertibility of sterling, which was seen as the key to opening up the worldwide British economic system. The British delegation, led by economist John Maynard Keynes, hoped for up to $6 billion, free of interest and conditions. The British successfully deflected efforts by different sectors of Washington officialdom to secure extensive civil aviation privileges and numerous military bases, and the delegation stressed that without a satisfactory credit, Great Britain would necessarily revert to imperial preference. The United States, however, predominated in the negotiations, and the final agreement, signed on 6 December 1945, contemplated a $3.75 billion credit at 2 percent over fifty years, plus $650 million to cover promised full convertibility of sterling within a year of congressional approval.

This was by no means assured. The negotiations had been characterized by bureaucratic infighting (mainly between the State and Treasury departments) and public hostility or indifference. In Congress a mixture of nationalism, anglophobia, and tightfistedness threatened passage of the loan. Eventual approval, on 15 July 1946, was due only to the rapid deterioration of political relations with the Soviet Union in the intervening period. Anticommunism saved the loan; Great Britain was needed. The loan proved insufficient to shore up the British economy. Convertibility, carried through in July 1947, proved a disaster: capital fled abroad, and bankruptcy loomed ahead. A long period of austerity followed in Great Britain, offset in part by a second, more comprehensive U.S. aid commitment through the Marshall Plan.

Fraser J. Harbutt

See also Clayton, William Lockhart; Marshall Plan

FURTHER READING

Gardner, Richard N. *Sterling-Dollar Diplomacy,* rev. ed. New York, 1969.
Paterson, Thomas G. *Soviet-American Confrontation: Postwar Reconstruction and the Origins of the Cold War.* Baltimore, Md., 1973.

BROADCAST AND FILM COMPANIES

An industry that is small compared to the automobile or electronics sectors, but critical because these companies produce the television shows and movies that people around the world spend a fair amount of their time watching. Predictably, the global success of these quintessential twentieth-century industries raises important foreign-policy issues as companies try to protect their intellectual property and countries or ethnic groups strive to defend their local cultures against what they perceive as the onslaught coming from the United States and Hollywood. These industries are currently in transition. The boundaries separating the big-seven communications industries—telephone, cable, computer, film studios, television broadcasting, publishing, and consumer electronics—are eroding. Large companies are making huge bets on new technologies, acquisitions, and mergers to position themselves so as to be part of the new world information economy. Telephone, cellular, cable, and satellite providers each want to provide the network of choice to bring images, data, and voice to the residence or office. But they need content to send over their sophisticated networks. This provides broadcast and film industries with leverage. At the end of the 1980s many believed that the three major broadcast networks—ABC, CBS, and NBC—would continue to lose market share to cable offerings. Some predicted that offerings such as movies from Home Box Office and Showtime, news from CNN and C-SPAN, music from MTV, sports from ESPN, and home shopping from the Home Shopping Network and QVC would further squeeze the networks. Others worried that when viewers routinely taped shows and watched them later or could call up any show on demand, the networks would lose viewers. Instead, the network audience stabilized after 1991. General Electric maintained its ownership of NBC. In 1995, Disney bought Capitol Cities/ABC and Westinghouse purchased CBS. In addition, Fox Broadcasting and Viacom (through Paramount) invested large sums of money in an effort to launch new networks. As communications, computer, and entertainment technologies merged, recognition grew that the film and broadcast companies mattered because they already own huge amounts of programming with which to fill the proposed 500 channels of the future. New domestic and international investment entered the film industry during the 1980s. Sony bought Columbia. Matsushita bought and then sold MCA to Seagrams. Credit Lyonnais took control of MGM. Rupert Murdoch acquired Fox. So far, foreign control has left the content produced by Hollywood unchanged. In 1994 Viacom, whose properties included Nickelodeon and MTV, won control of the much larger Paramount Studios, and with it Simon & Schuster with its huge educational and trade publishing empire. Time Warner owns Time Magazine and Home Box Office as well as the profitable Warner Bros. Studio and is seeking to acquire control of Turner Broadcasting and CNN. Disney, now combined with Capitol Cities/ABC, has added a network to augment its brand name recognition, resurgent animated film business, and large theme park franchise. Others, including Microsoft, the regional Bell operating companies, and DreamWorks SKG also want to provide content to flow over the networks of tomorrow. The globalization of content is proceeding. BBC and CNN provide instant global news coverage. Television series and films are presold, filmed, and broadcast around the world. U.S. movies and television shows are seen worldwide but at the same time local language programming is proliferating. Direct TV satellite services are spreading globally. Foreign policy issues related to the film and broadcast industries have climbed the policy agenda. Mundane but important details are being negotiated. For example, firms from different countries and sectors are working to collaborate in setting international standards so that global consumers can plug into the global network. In addition, companies and countries that export copyrighted materials are trying to agree on how to price voice, data, and video services on the information superhighway. French and U.S. trade negotiators were so divided over the terms for access of U.S. film and broadcast product to the French market that the Uruguay Round of multilateral trade negotiations almost foundered in December 1993. Large-scale piracy of films, music, and software—in China, Mexico, and elsewhere—led firms dependent on copyrighted materials to press for better guarantees that their intellectual property would be protected. Indeed, U.S. unhappiness about Chinese intellectual property piracy erupted into a major trade dispute between the United States and China in the mid-1990s and continues to bedevil Sino-American relations.

JONATHAN D. ARONSON

See also Cable News Network; Telecommunication Companies; Television and Foreign Policy

FURTHER READING

Auletta, Ken. *Three Blind Mice: How the TV Networks Lost Their Way.* New York, 1991.
Wildman, Steven S., and Stephen E. Siwek. *International Trade in Films and Television Programs.* Cambridge, Mass., 1988.

BROOKINGS INSTITUTION
See Think Tanks

BROWN, HAROLD
(*b.* 19 September 1927)

First scientist to serve as secretary of defense (1977–1981). A graduate of Columbia University, Brown held positions as director of the Lawrence Radiation Laboratory at Livermore, California; director of research at the Pentagon under Secretary of Defense Robert S. McNamara; secretary of the air force (1965–1969) under President Lyndon B. Johnson; and president of the California Institute of Technology (1969–1977). As secretary of defense in the administration of President Jimmy Carter, Brown reorganized the Defense Department and supported the improvement of weapons systems that undergirded the strategic triad of land-based, sea-based, and air-breathing weapons systems. He reluctantly favored B-52s with air-launched cruise missiles over the B-1 bomber and backed development of the MX missile and Trident submarine. An advocate of a strong North Atlantic Treaty Organization (NATO), he pushed for increased defense spending by NATO countries and backed the deployment of Pershing II missiles and ground-launched cruise missiles in Western Europe. At the same time, he supported the notion of essential equivalence (a term that contested the unjustified perception that Soviet systems were superior to those of the United States and, instead, stressed the rough equality of dissimilar systems that conferred no unilateral advantage to either side); developed the countervailing strategy (which, if deterrence failed, anticipated a flexible response to Soviet aggression at various levels, including a counterforce strategy for fighting a nuclear war that would deny the Soviets a range of limited nuclear options) articulated in Presidential Directive 59; and, building on a long-time commitment to arms control, was a strong proponent of the Second Strategic Arms Limitation (SALT II) treaty (June 1979), whose failure to win ratification was his biggest disappointment in office. Never an enthusiast of ballistic missile defenses while secretary of defense, Brown was also skeptical about the prospects of the Strategic Defense Initiative, which he saw as incapable of population defense.

BRUCE R. KUNIHOLM

See also Defense, U.S. Department of; Carter, James Earl; North Atlantic Treaty Organization; Nuclear Weapons and Strategy; Strategic Arms Limitation Talks and Agreements; Strategic Defense Initiative

BRUCE, DAVID KIRKPATRICK ESTE

(*b*. 12 February 1898; *d*. 5 December 1977)

U.S. diplomat, cofounder of the Office of Strategic Services (OSS), administrator of the Marshall Plan in France (1948), and ambassador to France (1949–1952), West Germany (1957–1959), and Great Britain (1961–1969). Bruce attended Princeton University (1915–1917), served in the army during World War I, and studied law at the Universities of Virginia and Maryland (1919–1921). He became a full-time public servant in 1941 when he helped William "Wild Bill" Donovan organize the OSS. Bruce served as its European chief from 1943 to 1945, then in 1947 was named assistant secretary of commerce.

President Harry S. Truman next appointed Bruce to administer the Marshall Plan in France while serving as U.S. ambassador to that country. Bruce's work helped repair the war-torn French economy and earned him praise in both France and the United States. He subsequently became undersecretary of state, while simultaneously acting as both alternate U.S. governor to the International Monetary Fund (IMF) and governor of the International Bank for Reconstruction and Development (World Bank). During the administration of President Dwight D. Eisenhower, Bruce became critical of Central Intelligence Agency (CIA) interventionism throughout the Third World. He supported western European economic and military integration and from 1953 through 1955 acted as an American observer to the European Defense Community interim committee and a U.S. representative to the European Coal and Steel Community. As U.S. ambassador to West Germany and Great Britain, he continued to advocate European integration. In 1970 he headed the U.S. delegation to the Vietnam peace talks in Paris, then became the first U.S. liaison officer to the People's Republic of China (1972). He left Beijing in 1974 to accept his final appointment, as ambassador to NATO (1974–1975).

DEBORAH KISATSKY

See also China; France; Marshall Plan; Monnet, Jean; North Atlantic Treaty Organization; Office of Strategic Services

FURTHER READING

Bruce, David K. E. *OSS Against the Reich: The World War II Diaries of Colonel David K. E. Bruce*, edited by Nelson Douglas Lankford. Kent, Ohio, 1991.
Duchêne, François. *Jean Monnet: The First Statesman of Interdependence*. New York, 1994.
Winard, Pascaline. *Eisenhower, Kennedy, and the United States of Europe*. New York, 1993.

BRUNEI DARUSSALAM

See Appendix 2

BRYAN, WILLIAM JENNINGS

(*b*. 19 March 1860; *d*. 26 July 1925)

Democratic member of Congress from Nebraska (1891–1895), presidential candidate (1896, 1900, 1908), and secretary of state (1913–1915). In the 1896 presidential campaign, Bryan adopted a proposal advanced by Populists and other agrarian radicals that silver as well as gold be used by the government as backing for the currency. Bimetallism, as this policy was called, would increase the amount of money in circulation, thus promoting inflation and raising the prices farmers received for their products while reducing their debts. Narrowly defeated for the presidency by William McKinley, Bryan ran again unsuccessfully against McKinley in 1900, this time as an opponent of U.S. imperialism after the Spanish-American-Cuban-Filipino War. He especially opposed U.S. annexation of the Philippines, which he believed would benefit only big business. Known as the "Great Commoner," he remained a leader of the Democratic party and received the party's presidential nomination for the third time in 1908, losing to William Howard Taft. After helping to secure the adoption of a reformist platform and the nomination and election of Woodrow Wilson in 1912, Bryan became Wilson's first secretary of state. He was frequently ridiculed by the press for refusing to serve alcohol at State Department functions, for appointing unqualified party loyalists to diplomatic posts, and for continuing to lecture on religious and moral topics at Chautauqua Movement meetings. Like others on the Chautauqua circuit, Bryan offered his audiences a mixture of moral uplift, entertainment, and populist culture. He valued the speech-making opportunities because they kept him in contact with his rural supporters.

More a peace advocate than a pacifist, Bryan's principal goal as secretary of state was the negotiation of a series of bilateral "cooling off" treaties requiring that before going to war, signatories would submit disputes to arbitration or to investigation by an international commission of inquiry. He believed that publicizing the facts in a dispute would make war unlikely, and he secured ratification of thirty such treaties, but none has ever been used to settle a dispute. Bryan also tried to improve relations with Latin American nations, applauding the president's October 1913 renunciation of imperialism and urging U.S. businessmen to treat Latin Americans honorably and fairly. During a revolution in Mexico he agreed with President Wilson that threats to U.S. economic interests did not justify military intervention but reluctantly supported the landing of U.S. troops at Veracruz in April 1914 to pressure a Mexican dictator into resignation. In dealing with smaller Caribbean nations, such as Haiti and the Dominican Republic, Bryan was even more willing to use U.S. marines to overthrow dictators and to attempt to impose democracy. Elsewhere, he persuaded Wilson to promise independence to the Philippines, loyally supported the president's recognition of the new Chinese Republic, discouraged U.S. bankers from participating in an international loan to China that Bryan believed jeopardized the new government's autonomy, and struggled to resolve a conflict with Japan over California's restrictions on land ownership by Asian aliens.

When war broke out in Europe in August 1914 Bryan strongly favored U.S. neutrality, urging the president to discourage private loans to the belligerents. He coun-

seled patience and drafted protests to both sides when the British and the Germans interfered with trade and travel by U.S. citizens. After German submarines attacked Allied ships in early 1915, the president insisted upon U.S. rights to trade and travel in the war zone. Bryan, in contrast, advised keeping U.S. ships and passengers out of the area. The sinking of the British passenger liner *Lusitania* by a German submarine on 7 May 1915, with the loss of 128 American lives, made the split between Bryan and Wilson irreconcilable, and Bryan resigned on 8 June 1915, protesting that Wilson's harsh note to the Germans about the *Lusitania* sinking, and the president's refusal to reprimand Great Britain for its own wartime obstruction of U.S. shipping, would lead to war with Germany. Bryan saw neutrality as a means of keeping the United States out of the war, not as a status conferring rights to be defended at the risk of war.

After his resignation Bryan campaigned against U.S. belligerency, but he supported the government once war was declared in April 1917. He subsequently became a strong advocate of the League of Nations and of ratification of the Treaty of Versailles. He devoted his last years largely to supporting religious fundamentalism and the prohibition of alcohol. In July 1925 Bryan joined the prosecution in the celebrated "monkey trial" of John T. Scopes for teaching the theory of evolution in violation of Tennessee law. Bryan played only a small role in the trial until defense counsel Clarence Darrow called him to the stand as an expert on the Bible. During lengthy testimony Bryan defended the literal truth of the Bible but undermined his case by saying that each of the six days of the Creation might have been longer than twenty-four hours. Ridiculed by Darrow and exhausted by his ordeal, he died five days after the end of the trial.

KENDRICK A. CLEMENTS

See also Arbitration; Lusitania; Latin America; Wilson, Thomas Woodrow; World War I

FURTHER READING
Clements, Kendrick A. *William Jennings Bryan, Missionary Isolationist.* Knoxville, Tenn., 1982.
Coletta, Paolo E. *William Jennings Bryan*, 3 vols. Lincoln, Nebr., 1964–1969.
Curti, Merle E. *Bryan and World Peace.* Northampton, Mass., 1931.

BRZEZINSKI, ZBIGNIEW KAZIMIERZ
(*b.* 28 March 1928)

National security adviser to President Jimmy Carter (1977–1981). Born in Warsaw, Poland, Brzezinski and his family moved to Canada in 1938, and he came to the United States in 1953 to pursue a Ph.D. at Harvard. He taught political science at Harvard (1955–1960) and then at

Columbia until 1977, when he joined the Carter administration. Among his publications during his teaching career were *The Permanent Purge* (1956), *Political Power USA/USSR* (1964, with Samuel P. Huntington), and *Between Two Ages* (1970). As National Security Council (NSC) head, Brzezinski was particularly skeptical about détente with the Soviet Union. He believed that President Gerald Ford and Henry Kissinger's approach to dealing with the Soviet Union had been flawed, because it allowed the Soviets to expand and build military forces while perpetuating an anachronistic status quo in Europe. Differences in philosophical approach toward the use of force, the Soviet Union, and the functional focus of U.S. foreign policy led to a schism between the Brzezinski-led NSC and the State Department under Secretary of State Cyrus Vance. A virtual break occurred when the NSC informed Vance that a planned military mission to rescue U.S. diplomatic personnel from the besieged U.S. embassy in Tehran, Iran, in the spring of 1980 had become an imminent military undertaking. Secretary Vance had just reassured European allies that the United States would not use force to free the hostages, in return for which he was promised cooperation regarding the imposition of more stringent economic sanctions against Iran. Put in an untenable position by the rescue mission, Vance resigned.

Brzezinski's tendency to support policies that called for the United States to confront the Soviet Union was in conflict with the institutional tendency of the Department of State to seek accommodation with the USSR and was the primary source of the discord between the NSC and the Department of State. Another point of conflict was Brzezinski's belief that the NSC should be the leading institution in managing foreign affairs, leaving the Department of State to an ancillary support role. At the NSC Brzezinski argued the case for Soviet vulnerability. He suggested five strategies, all of which were eventually adopted: enhancing the Sino-American relationship in order to enlist the Chinese as a quasi-ally against Moscow; confronting the Soviets in the Third World from Somalia to Afghanistan, mostly by covert means; tightening export controls on materials that might be used in Soviet defense efforts (he attempted to dissuade the Europeans from becoming dependent on Soviet natural gas); promoting human rights groups and dissidents, especially in the Soviet Union and Eastern Europe; and expanding military spending and investments in new defense technologies, promoting counterforce missile systems, antiballistic defense systems, and civil defense programs in order to appear ready to match and dominate the Soviets at all levels of force.

In the 1980s Brzezinski remained a staunch advocate of firm and forceful policies toward the Soviet Union. His 1987 book *Game Plan* argued the need for a revitalized U.S. domestic consensus around a strategy of confronting

a militarized Soviet Union—a country "rotten" at the core and lacking all ideological moorings save those that urged it toward geopolitical hegemony. In 1989 Brzezinski argued, in *The Grand Failure: The Birth and Death of Communism in the Twentieth Century*, that communism was doomed as an ideology and as a methodology of governance. The next century, he asserted, would belong to democracy. Even after the dissolution of the Soviet Union, Brzezinski held to the view that Russian power would continue its historic propensity for reaction and repression. He thus was among those who argued for the expansion of the North Atlantic Treaty Organization (NATO) to include some countries of Eastern Europe. In the late 1980s Brzezinski was a member of the Private Advisory Panel on foreign policy for President George Bush. In the 1990s he served as counselor at the Center for Strategic and International Studies and was a professor of U.S. foreign policy at the School of Advanced International Studies of Johns Hopkins University. He also served on the boards of the National Endowment of Democracy, the Polish-American Enterprise Fund, and the American-Ukrainian Advisory Committee, as well as the President's Advisory Board on U.S. Intelligence. In 1981 he was awarded the Medal of Freedom for his role in normalizing U.S.-Chinese relations and for his contribution to fostering human rights in the Soviet bloc.

JAMES NATHAN

See also Carter, James Earl; China; Cold War; Détente; Iran; Russia and the Soviet Union; Vance, Cyrus Roberts

FURTHER READING

Brzezinski, Zbigniew. *Out of Control: Global Turmoil on the Eve of the Twenty-First Century*. New York, 1993.
———. *Power and Principle: The Memoirs of the National Security Advisor*. New York, 1983.
———. *The Fragile Blossom: Crisis and Change in Japan*. New York, 1972.
———. *The Soviet Bloc: Unity and Conflict*. New York, 1961.

BUCARELI AGREEMENTS
(1923)

Several accords negotiated between Mexico and the United States that sought to resolve issues arising from Mexico's constitutional provision that subsoil mineral rights belonged to the nation, thus imperiling U.S. oil company holdings. The agreements emerged from a series of meetings between personal representatives of President Warren G. Harding and Mexican President General Alvaro Obregón held in Mexico City from 14 May to 15 August 1923. Tension between the two nations were high because of the prolonged impact of the Mexican Revolution of 1910. The sessions were named after the site of the conference.

The Mexican Constitution of 1917, written by the victorious revolutionaries, reasserted traditional Hispanic legal principles, declaring in Article 27 that all subsoil mineral rights belonged to the nation, and consequently that oil concessions to U.S. oil companies by the previous regime were illegal. The United States upheld the Anglo-Saxon legal principle that surface ownership granted subsoil rights and defended the legality of concessions granted prior to the adoption of the constitution. Confidential and personal exchanges between Harding and Obregón made the negotiations possible and established the basis for the settlement. Although closely allied to oil and business interests, Harding proved more flexible in dealing with Mexico than his predecessor, Woodrow Wilson.

In the absence of formal diplomatic relations with the revolutionary Mexican government, the agreements comprised the signed minutes of the formal sessions rather than formal treaties. They provided for the establishment of two joint U.S.-Mexican claims commissions to adjudicate government and individual claims. The accords also established a settlement of agrarian land ownership claims with U.S. citizens owning land in Mexico. The United States accepted the Mexican insistence on payment in bonds rather than cash, while Mexico agreed to limits on land holdings seized and guaranteed that all rightful owners would receive compensation. Most important, the Bucareli Agreements first established the doctrine of positive acts to modify the effects of Article 27. Under this interpretation, Mexico recognized the legitimacy of oil concessions made prior to the constitution in instances in which the owners had taken positive acts to initiate production on their oil holdings. This arrangement made a settlement possible. Even though the dispute resurfaced when subsequent Mexican governments contended that the accords were binding only on the Obregón regime, the Bucareli Agreements began a long-term improvement in U.S.-Mexican relations. By muting the oil controversy, they cleared the way for U.S. recognition of the Obregón government. When the Mexican government faced another revolt, the United States backed the government. This development enabled transfer of governmental power to the Obregón backed election winner, a step that began the stabilization of Mexico after the prolonged turmoil of the revolution.

KENNETH J. GRIEB

See also Harding, Warren; Mexico; Oil and Foreign Policy; Oil Companies

FURTHER READING

Grieb, Kenneth J. *The Latin American Policy of Warren G. Harding.* Fort Worth, Texas, 1977.
Pani, Alberto J. *Las Conferencias de Bucareli.* Mexico City, 1953.
Vázquez, Josefina Zoraida, and Lorenzo Meyer. *The United States and Mexico.* Chicago, 1987.

BUCHANAN, JAMES
(*b.* 23 April 1791; *d.* 1 June 1868)

Diplomat, U.S. congressman (1821–1831), senator (1834–1845), secretary of state (1845–1849), and fifteenth president of the United States (1857–1861). Born near Mercersburg, Pennsylvania, he graduated from Dickinson College in 1809, gained admittance to the Pennsylvania bar in 1812, joined a volunteer company of dragoons in the War of 1812, and served in the Pennsylvania House of Representatives (1815–1816) before being elected to the House of Representatives and then the Senate.

Buchanan brought to the presidency considerable experience in the conduct of foreign affairs. As minister to Russia (1832–1833) he negotiated a commercial treaty between that country and the United States, and for part of his tenure in the Senate he chaired the Committee on Foreign Relations. While James Knox Polk's secretary of state, Buchanan helped settle the Oregon controversy with Great Britain in 1846, engaged in diplomacy with Mexico before and during the War with Mexico (1846–1848), and sought to annex Cuba. Buchanan tried to restrain Polk from claiming the entire Oregon Territory and attempted, at the beginning of the War with Mexico, to commit Polk to a public circular disavowing U.S. territorial interests south of the Rio Grande. Later, Buchanan espoused different positions on both matters. He served as minister to Great Britain (1853–1856) during Franklin Pierce's administration, when the United States challenged British influence in Central America. In 1854 Buchanan helped draft the Ostend Manifesto, which suggested U.S. seizure of Cuba in the event that Spain refused to sell Cuba to the United States. Buchanan capitalized on his role in the attempted acquisition of the slave island to boost his popularity in the South during the 1856 presidential election.

Despite President Buchanan's expertise in diplomacy, he and Lewis Cass, secretary of state for most of Buchanan's administration, achieved limited success in their foreign policy. Buchanan's plan to purchase Cuba from Spain encountered insurmountable resistance from Congress. The administration's Cass-Yrissari Treaty with Nicaragua (1857), which would have given the United States a virtual protectorate over that country's isthmian transit route by allowing the United States to deploy forces to guarantee the security and protection of the route as well as to protect U.S. citizens in the area, failed to win ratification by Nicaragua. Overtures to Russia, seeking the cession of Alaska, and to Mexico, regarding additional land cessions, proved unsuccessful. Moreover, the Senate refused Buchanan's requests for the establishment of a U.S. protectorate over the Mexican states of Chihuahua and Sonora, ratification of the McLane-Ocampo Treaty with Mexico, and the deployment of U.S.

military forces to guarantee U.S. transit across the isthmuses of Mexico, Nicaragua, and Panama, as well as to protect U.S. lives and property in the region.

Widespread perception in the United States that Buchanan's foreign policies were being manipulated by southern expansionists intending the further spread of slavery hampered the president's effectiveness. Buchanan, however, alienated many southern expansionists by refusing to return filibusterer William Walker to Nicaragua after U.S. Commodore Hiram Paulding in December 1857 interfered with Walker's second invasion of that country and compelled Walker and his followers to surrender and return to the United States.

Buchanan's most significant foreign policy triumphs occurred in the area of Anglo-American relations. His threat to abrogate the Clayton-Bulwer Treaty (1850), which provided for joint construction of a canal through the Central American isthmus, helped convince British leaders to give up their colony in the Bay Islands (off the coast of Honduras) and the British protectorate over Central America's Mosquito Coast. By sending a naval squadron to the West Indies in 1858, Buchanan pressured Great Britain into accepting the U.S. position that British warships had no right to enforce the Webster-Ashburton Treaty's (1842) provisions for suppression of the African slave trade by visiting U.S. merchant vessels and searching them for slaves. The administration also weathered the Pig War crisis (1859) with Great Britain regarding competing national claims over San Juan Island, near Vancouver Island in the Straits of Juan de Fuca, and triggered by the occupation of the island by U.S. troops. The administration worked out an agreement for joint occupation of the island pending final resolution of the two nations' competing claims.

Buchanan's achievements also included the Treaty of Tientsin (Tianjin) with China (1858), which extended the privileges of foreigners, including missionaries and traders, in China; trade agreements with France and Brazil; a disavowal by France of jurisdiction over (and the right to conscript) naturalized U.S. citizens who had been born in France and were traveling in that country; and settlement of U.S. claims against New Granada regarding the Panama riot of 15 April 1856 and against Paraguay for the *Water Witch* incident in 1855, when Paraguayan soldiers fired on a U.S. steamer engaged in a river survey. In the latter case, Buchanan dispatched nineteen warships to enforce U.S. demands for an indemnity and apology by Paraguay. Had Buchanan's diplomatic efforts not become entangled in the issues of slavery and sectionalism, his administration most likely would have achieved many more of its diplomatic goals. The Civil War erupted shortly after Buchanan had left office and retired to his home in Pennsylvania.

ROBERT E. MAY

See also Cass, Lewis; China; Clayton, John Middleton; Cuba; Great Britain; Mexico, War with; Oregon Question; Ostend Manifesto; Paraguay; Pierce, Franklin; Polk, James Knox; Slave Trade and Slavery; Walker, William; Webster-Ashburton Treaty

FURTHER READING

Jones, Wilbur Devereux. *The American Problem in British Diplomacy, 1841–1861*. Athens, Ga., 1974.

Klein, Philip Shriver. *President James Buchanan: A Biography*. University Park, Pa., 1962.

Smith, Elbert B. *The Presidency of James Buchanan*. Lawrence, Kans., 1975.

BULGARIA

Located in the Balkan peninsula, bordering the Black Sea, Turkey, Greece, the former Yugoslavia, and Romania, a nation that was under communist domination from 1946 until 1991. After more than five centuries of Turkish occupation, and quasi-autonomous status (still under the Ottoman Empire) achieved following the Congress of Berlin (1878), modern Bulgaria emerged as a fully independent nation only in 1908, in the wake of the Young Turk revolt in Constantinople. Normal diplomatic relations between the United States and Bulgaria were maintained during World War I despite the fact that Bulgaria entered the war on the side of the Central Powers. After the war ended, the United States supported Bulgaria's claims to a larger share of the perenially contested region of greater Macedonia (claims were also being made by Serbia and Greece), but economic and cultural relations between the two countries were poor during the interwar years, when Bulgaria experienced many of the same problems that were confronting other states in the region.

The efforts of Bulgarian leaders to industrialize their country failed, in part because of the worldwide economic dislocation brought on by the Great Depression. Social and economic problems, coupled with continuing dissatisfaction over the Macedonian issue, fed extremist movements on the right and on the left. In 1935 King Boris dissolved the parliament, taking advantage of a constitutional clause that allowed the king to rule by decree in cases of internal or external threat. The authority of the government deteriorated so badly that the Internal Macedonian Revolutionary Organization, a group dedicated to regaining all of Macedonia for Bulgaria, ruled parts of the country.

Bulgaria thus became easy prey for Germany's efforts to penetrate the region, and it joined the Axis Pact in 1941, seduced in part by Nazi offers to acquire additional territory at the expense of Yugoslavia and Greece. Under German pressure Bulgaria declared war on the United

States and Great Britain in December 1941. The United States in turn declared war on Bulgaria in June 1942.

Soviet troops entered Bulgaria in the fall of 1944, and by 1946 the communist regime of Georgi Dimitrov was in complete control of the country. The United States and its wartime allies finally signed a peace treaty with Bulgaria in 1947. Subsequently, the Sofia government sided with Moscow following the Stalin-Tito break, having in the meantime actively supported the ongoing communist insurgency in Greece.

Relations between the United States and Bulgaria deteriorated as Bulgaria's leaders copied the Soviet model for political organization and economic development and as relations between the Soviet Union and the United States worsened during the Cold War years. The tight political control exerted by Bulgaria's communist leaders and the fact that Bulgaria was a member of the Warsaw Pact and the Council for Mutual Economic Assistance, and, more generally the fact that Bulgaria continued to be one of the Soviet Union's most loyal allies—for example, aiding the Soviets in the invasion of Czechoslovakia in 1968—left little room for improved U.S.-Bulgarian relations until the breakup of the Soviet Union in 1991. Following the end of communist domination in Bulgaria itself, a bilateral investment treaty was approved by Washington in 1992. The United States also provided economic assistance to support Bulgaria's move to a market economy, and was granted most-favored-nation status by the United States in November 1992. In 1994 Bulgaria became a signatory to the Partnership for Peace, an organization established to facilitate military cooperation between the West and the former communist countries.

SHARON L. WOLCHIK

See also Cold War; Eastern Europe; Russia and the Soviet Union; Warsaw Pact

FURTHER READING

Bell, John. *The Bulgarian Communist Party from Blagoev to Zhivkov.* Stanford, Calif., 1986.
Oren, Nissan. *Revolution Administered: Agrarianism and Communism in Bulgaria.* Baltimore, 1973.

BULLITT, WILLIAM CHRISTIAN

(*b.* 25 January 1891; *d.* 15 February 1967)

U.S. diplomat often credited with the establishment of diplomatic relations with the Union of Soviet Socialist Republics (USSR). Born in Philadelphia, Bullitt graduated from Yale University (B.A. 1913). After dropping out of Harvard Law School, he served briefly as a newspaper correspondent for the *Philadelphia Public Ledger.* Following several months in Europe reporting on World War I,

the newspaper named Bullitt its Washington bureau chief. This assignment allowed Bullitt to establish important government contacts, most notably with President Woodrow Wilson's advisor Edward M. House. The two developed a close working relationship, and as a result Bullitt was appointed an assistant secretary of state within the Department of State's Division of Western European Affairs in December 1917.

In late 1918, Bullitt, now the Department of State's new chief of the Division of Current Intelligence, joined the U.S. delegation at the Paris Peace Conference. In early spring 1919 President Wilson allowed the twenty-eight-year-old Bullitt to go on a fact-finding mission to Russia. After meeting with top Bolshevik officials, including Vladimir Ilyich Lenin, Bullitt returned to Paris with a plan that he believed offered an opportunity for a peaceful settlement between the Bolsheviks and the Allies. The Western leaders, however, rejected Bullitt's efforts, partly as a result of strong British pressure. Critical of the harsh terms of the Treaty of Versailles and of U.S. intervention in the Russian civil war, Bullitt resigned in protest. Disappointed with his failure at Paris and roundly condemned for his advocacy of recognizing the Bolshevik government, Bullitt left the United States and spent the 1920s as an expatriate in Europe—but not before harshly criticizing Wilson and the Versailles Treaty at open Senate hearings.

In 1932 Bullitt returned to the United States and immediately began working on Franklin D. Roosevelt's ultimately successful presidential campaign. Prior to Roosevelt's inauguration, Bullitt served as his advisor on European affairs and twice traveled to Europe to gather information about the unstable political environment there. Roosevelt then appointed Bullitt as a special assistant to Secretary of State Cordell Hull to work on improving relations with the Soviets. Although negotiations proved laborious, Bullitt secured a treaty between the two nations and, for his success, received appointment as the first U.S. ambassador to the Soviet Union in 1933.

From the beginning, Bullitt's relations with the government of Joseph Stalin were troubled. Most of the problems that plagued U.S.-Soviet relations, he believed, resulted from the obstinate attitude of the Soviet foreign ministry and particularly its head, Maxim Litvinov. To counter Litvinov's influence, Bullitt unsuccessfully attempted to gain the support of Soviet military leaders. Yet the military could not help, since both they and the civilian government were suffering from the brutality of Stalin's ongoing purges. By 1935, Bullitt had assumed an ardently anti-Soviet perspective. He returned to the United States in June 1936 and soon accepted a position on Roosevelt's reelection campaign. Two months later, however, Bullitt became the new ambassador to France.

For more than four years Bullitt wielded great influence not only within the European diplomatic community but also in the Roosevelt administration. He was also quite influential in forming U.S. policy toward Nazi Germany. Bullitt was at first not overly concerned with the Nazis. Instead, the possibilities of a general European war, one which would exhaust the European continent and permit Soviet aggression, worried him more. His attitude changed with the failure of appeasement. Fear of a Nazi-dominated Europe soon displaced his contempt for the Soviets. He believed it was important to keep the Franco-Polish alliance alive and also to arrange for an Anglo-French agreement with the Soviets. Bullitt left Paris in June 1940, after the fall of France.

After his resignation became effective in January of the following year, Bullitt participated in the Congressional debates over Lend-Lease. He then toured the country, urging the nation to assume a tougher stance against Germany.

In November 1941 Roosevelt asked Bullitt to report on the war effort in North Africa and the Middle East. Although an important tour, it lasted only two months. Bullitt then returned to Washington but was not immediately reassigned. From June 1942 until July 1943, he served in minor posts in the administration, including as a special assistant to Secretary of the Navy Frank Knox. After an unsuccessful attempt to become the mayor of Philadelphia, he applied for a commission in the U.S. Army. Rejected because of his age, Bullitt soon accepted an offer from General Charles de Gaulle to join the Free French Army, where he served until the end of the war.

After World War II, Bullitt offered his diplomatic services to the new administration of Harry S. Truman. The president declined, and Bullitt vented his frustrations in a book, *The Great Globe Itself* (1946), which attacked Roosevelt and his foreign policy—especially the former president's alleged acquiescence to Soviet demands at Yalta. Out of favor in the United States because of his outspoken views, the now bitterly anticommunist Bullitt once again left the United States, living first in Taiwan and then in France until his death.

Scott D. Keller

See also Appeasement; France; House, Edward Mandell; Lenin, Vladimir Ilyich; Litvinov, Maxsim Maksimovich; Paris Peace Conference of 1919; Roosevelt, Franklin Delano; Russia and the Soviet Union; Stalin, Joseph; Wilson, Thomas Woodrow; Versailles Treaty of 1919; Yalta Conference

FURTHER READING

Billings, Richard N., and Will Brownell. *So Close to Greatness: A Biography of William C. Bullitt.* New York, 1987.

Browder, Robert Paul. *The Origins of Soviet-American Diplomacy.* Princeton, N.J., 1953.

Bullitt, Orville H., ed. *For the President: Correspondence Between Franklin D. Roosevelt and William C. Bullitt.* Boston, 1972.

Bullitt, William C. *Report to the American People.* Boston, 1940.

———. *The Great Globe Itself, A Preface to World Affairs.* New York, 1946.

———. *The Bullitt Mission to Russia: Testimony Before the Committee on Foreign Relations United States Senate of William C. Bullitt.* New York, 1920. Reprint, Westport, Conn., 1977.

Farnsworth, Beatrice. *William C. Bullitt and the Soviet Union.* Bloomington, Ill., 1967.

Kaufmann, William W. "Two American Ambassadors: Bullitt and Kennedy." In *The Diplomats*, edited by Craig and Gilbert. Princeton, N.J., 1953.

Thompson, John M. *Russia, Bolshevism, and the Versailles Peace.* Princeton, N.J., 1966.

BUNAU-VARILLA, PHILIPPE

(*b.* 26 July 1859; *d.* 20 May 1940)

French engineer who was a central figure in arranging U.S. recognition of an independent Panama and thus of the Panama Canal treaty in 1903. Educated at the École Polytechnique in Paris, in 1880 Bunau-Varilla was inspired by a convocation address given by Ferdinand de Lesseps, the builder of the Suez Canal, who was then involved in plans for a canal across Panama. During Bunau-Varilla's required five-year state service as a colonial civil engineer in North Africa, he volunteered to work in yellow fever–riddled Panama, then part of Colombia. By 1886, when the French Compagnie Universelle du Canal Interocéanic went bankrupt and stopped work, he was the company's chief engineer. Implicated in the scandals following de Lesseps's failure, Bunau-Varilla bought the Paris newspaper *Le Matin* and worked to salvage French pride and recoup French investments by persuading the United States to give up its own plan for a canal across Nicaragua and instead buy the French option on the Panama site. In 1901 he visited the United States and convinced Congress that Nicaraguan earthquakes might imperil a canal there and helped win congressional approval for Panama as the canal site in the Spooner Act (1902). He had also persuaded the French receiver to accept the U.S. offer of $40 million for the French excavation, buildings, and equipment.

The Hay-Herrán Treaty of 1903 between the United States and Colombia would have implemented the conditions of the Spooner Act but Colombia refused to ratify the treaty. Bunau-Varilla then helped finance and organize Panama's revolt, and Panama declared its independence on 3 November 1903. Nine days later he became the controversial first minister of the new Republic of Panama to the United States. He negotiated the one-sided Hay-Bunau-Varilla Treaty, regarded in Panama as the "Bunau-Varilla sellout," which gave the United States full sovereignty in perpetuity over a ten-mile-wide canal zone and ownership of the existing canal and railroad properties. These terms were designed to overcome the considerable support for a Nicaraguan canal route championed by Alabama Senator John T. Morgan.

Bunau-Varilla still remains a figure shrouded in controversy. He was a patriot who in middle age lost a leg at the Battle of Verdun (1916) and a brilliant engineer whose innovations proved helpful to the Panama Canal's final design, but he was also a *panamiste*, which became a French synonym for "thief." President Theodore Roosevelt, relying on Bunau-Varilla's information that an indigenous Panamanian insurrection was imminent even without outside help (confirmed by U.S. Army intelligence), had agreed to support Panamanian independence but only if it was won without U.S. help. Bunau-Varilla, however, misled the Panamanians into thinking the United States would be a willing participant in the revolution. Bunau-Varilla's motives remain ambiguous. Many newspaper accounts accused him of profiting financially from Panama's independence, but there is no evidence for this charge. Vindicating the original French canal concept and recovering some of the losses of the original investors may better explain his motives. Both Roosevelt and Bunau-Varilla wanted to see the United States finish the canal that the French had begun, but the evidence does not support the charges of collusion made by their critics. Bunau-Varilla remained active as an engineer, a financial writer, and an acclaimed specialist in water chlorination technology, for which he received the Grand Medal of the city of Paris (1936). In 1938 France awarded him the Grand Cross of the Legion of Honor, citing his actions at Panama and Verdun.

RICHARD H. COLLIN

See also Colombia; Panama and Panama Canal; Roosevelt, Theodore

FURTHER READING

Anguizola, Gustave. *Philippe Bunau-Varilla: The Man Behind the Panama Canal.* Chicago, 1980.
Collin, Richard H. *Theodore Roosevelt's Caribbean: The Panama Canal, the Monroe Doctrine, and the Latin American Context.* Baton Rouge, La., 1990.
LaFeber, Walter, *The Panama Canal.* New York, 1989.
Major, John. "Who Wrote the Hay-Bunau-Varilla Convention?" *Diplomatic History* 8 (Spring 1984): 115–123.

BUNCHE, RALPH JOHNSON

(*b.* 7 August 1904; *d.* 9 December 1971)

African-American diplomat with a variegated, twenty-four-year career in the highest echelons of the United Nations. Born in Detroit, Michigan, Bunche graduated first in his class at the University of California at Los Angeles in 1927 and received a Ph.D. in government and international relations from Harvard University in 1934. He taught political science at Howard University from 1928 to 1950. In 1941 he entered government service as an analyst in the African and Far Eastern Section of the Office of the Coordinator of Information, later the Office of Strategic Services. He joined the Department of State's postwar planning agency in 1944 and served as an adviser on colonial matters to the U.S. delegations to both the Dumbarton Oaks and San Francisco conferences that drafted the UN charter. Bunche was a member of the U.S. delegation to the First Session of the UN General Assembly in 1946, then joined the UN Secretariat as head of the Trusteeship Department. His scholarly focus on the relationship between race and international relations made him a logical choice to serve on the UN Special Committee on Palestine at the time of partition. In 1948 he became acting mediator for the Middle East and succeeded the chief mediator, Count Folke Bernadotte, after the latter's assassination. Bunche succeeded in negotiating an armistice agreement between Egypt and Israel that set the pattern for Israel's agreements with Lebanon, Syria, and Jordan. For these efforts, he was awarded the Nobel Peace Prize in 1950. During the next twenty years Bunche served as the key UN representative during the crises in the Sinai (1956), the Congo (1960), Yemen (1963), Cyprus (1964), and Bahrain (1970), working closely with the first three UN secretaries-general, Trygve Lie, Dag Hammerskjöld, and U Thant. He also chaired a committee that examined the development of water resources in the Middle East, particularly the allocation of the waters of the Jordan River. In 1957 he was appointed undersecretary for special political affairs, with prime responsibility for peacekeeping activities, and in 1965 he supervised the cease-fire following the India-Pakistan War. Bunche retired from the UN in 1971 because of poor health.

ROBERT C. HILDERBRAND

See also Hammarskjöld, Dag Hjalmar Agne Carl; Lie, Trygve; Middle East; Palestine (to 1948); Race and Racism; Thant, U; United Nations

FURTHER READING

Mann, Peggy. *Ralph Bunche: UN Peacemaker.* New York, 1975.
Rivlin, Benjamin, ed. *Ralph Bunche: The Man and His Times.* New York, 1990.
Urquhart, Brian. *Ralph Bunche: An American Life.* New York, 1993.

BUNDY, MCGEORGE

(*b.* 30 March 1919; *d.* 16 September 1996)

One of the principal architects of U.S. foreign policy during the Kennedy and Johnson administrations, serving as national security affairs adviser from 1961 to 1966. Bundy was born in Boston to a distinguished Massachusetts family. His father, Harvey H. Bundy, served as assistant secretary of state under Henry L. Stimson during the Hoover administration. Bundy graduated from Yale in 1940 and became a junior fellow at Harvard in 1941, compiling an outstanding academic record. A World War II intelligence officer, Bundy helped plan the invasions of Sicily and Normandy and was an aide to Admiral Alan G. Kirk. After his discharge, Bundy worked as a research assistant to Henry L. Stimson and co-authored Stimson's memoirs, *On Active Service in Peace and War* (1948).

In April 1948 Bundy served as a government consultant on the Marshall Plan for European reconstruction. In the fall of that year he accepted a position as foreign policy adviser for the Republican presidential candidate, Thomas E. Dewey. After Dewey's defeat, Bundy worked as a foreign policy analyst for the Council on Foreign Relations before returning to Harvard in 1949 as a popular lecturer in the government department. In 1951 he was promoted to the rank of professor of government. The next year Bundy edited *Patterns of Responsibility* (1952), a collection of Secretary of State Dean Acheson's public papers. That year, too, Bundy served on the Oppenheimer Panel of Consultants, of which Dr. J. Robert Oppenheimer was chairman and Dr. Vannevar Bush, John Sloan Dickey, president of Dartmouth College, and Allen W. Dulles of the Central Intelligence Agency, were prominent members. The panel took a fresh look at the problems of nuclear disarmament and atomic energy control in light of the growing Soviet-American arms race. The chief concern of the classified panel report delivered in January 1953 was to reduce the danger of a "surprise knockout blow" through U.S.-Soviet arms control negotiations as soon as such talks became feasible. The Oppenheimer panel report stressed the limited utility of arms accords and the need to maintain a powerful defense even with an agreement. In 1953 Harvard appointed the thirty-four-year-old Bundy dean of the faculty of arts and sciences, the youngest man ever to hold this post.

President John F. Kennedy named Bundy special assistant to the president for national security affairs in December 1960. Under Bundy the office of the national security adviser gained new prominence and importance as JFK sought a reorganization of this position in the White House, partly to circumvent what the president regarded as the inertia and "softness" of the Department of State under Secretary of State Dean Rusk. Bundy emerged as one of a small coterie of advisers and special assistants, along with Theodore C. Sorensen and Jerome B. Wiesner, who held a good deal of influence and formed JFK's unofficial "kitchen cabinet." Critics of JFK's new executive arrangement pointed to a dangerous narrowing in the range of options and opinions on vital security matters within this "inner club" chaired by

Bundy. Bundy proved an activist adviser who moved meetings along, summarized key points, and offered incisive personal recommendations. Bundy became the White House's self-styled "traffic cop" and a prototype for future influential national security advisers such as Henry A. Kissinger. Bundy, along with Secretary of Defense Robert McNamara, emerged as the chief supporter of U.S. escalation in Vietnam. During the 1962 Cuban Missile Crisis, Bundy helped form the special Executive Committee (EXCOM) made up of past and present government officials that advised President Kennedy on U.S. options during the crisis. Bundy initially sided with the so-called "hawks" who favored an air strike against the missile sites, but he eventually moved to support the more moderate course of blockade, which ultimately resolved the crisis. In 1965, Bundy strongly advocated U.S. armed intervention in the Dominican Republic to prevent Dominican rebels from installing a "leftist pro-Cuban" regime hostile to the United States. In February 1965 Bundy witnessed the Vietcong raid on U.S. air installations at Pleiku and strongly recommended a major bombing campaign against North Vietnam in retaliation.

Disillusioned with the emerging Vietnam quagmire in 1966, Bundy resigned from the administration to head the Ford Foundation. During Bundy's presidency (1966-1979), the Ford Foundation markedly increased its support for civil rights organizations, minority scholarships for higher education, public television, and arms control; and the foundation also addressed the problems of global hunger, population, and the environment. In 1979 he left the foundation to become professor of history at New York University. Bundy spent his later years writing and speaking on global environmental issues and on the dangers of nuclear weapons proliferation.

MICHAEL E. DONOGHUE

See also Cuban Missile Crisis; Dominican Republic; Johnson, Lyndon Baines; Kennedy, John Fitzgerald; Marshall Plan; Nuclear Weapons and Strategy; Rusk, David Dean; Stimson, Henry Lewis; Vietnam War

FURTHER READING

Bundy, McGeorge. *The Dimensions of Diplomacy.* New York, 1964.
———. *The Strength of Government.* New York, 1968.
———. *Presidential Promise and Performance.* New York, 1980.
———. *Danger and Survival: Choices About the Bomb in the First Fifty Years.* New York, 1988.
———. *Reducing Nuclear Danger: The Road Away from the Brink.* New York, 1993.
Gardner, Lloyd. "Harry Hopkins with Hand Grenades? McGeorge Bundy in the Kennedy and Johnson Years." In *Behind the Throne: Servants of Power to Imperial Presidents: 1898–1968.* McCormick, Thomas J., and LaFeber, Walter, eds. Madison, Wisc., 1993.
Giglio, James N. *The Presidency of John F. Kennedy.* Lawrence, Kansas, 1991.
Halberstam, David. *The Best and the Brightest.* New York, 1972.

BUNDY, WILLIAM PUTNAM

(*b.* September 24, 1917)

Assistant secretary of state for Far Eastern affairs (1964–1969) during the period of U.S. escalation of the Vietnam War. Born in Washington, D.C., Bundy, the brother of McGeorge Bundy, national security adviser to Presidents John F. Kennedy and Lyndon B. Johnson, was educated at Yale College and Harvard Law School. After serving in the U.S. Army in Europe during World War II, he joined a prominent Washington law firm and from 1951 until 1960 worked for the Board of National Estimates of the Central Intelligence Agency (CIA). In 1960 he served as staff director for the Commission on National Goals. From 1961 to 1963 he held the positions of assistant secretary and undersecretary (October 1963) of defense for international security affairs. In February 1964 he transferred to the Department of State as assistant secretary for Far Eastern Affairs. He served in that office until 1969, where he reinforced Secretary of State Dean Rusk's perception of the People's Republic of China as a major threat to Southeast Asia and resisted the improvement of relations with Beijing. In 1964 and 1965 he advocated continuing the war in South Vietnam, even if that required initiating U.S. bombing campaigns against North Vietnam and deploying increasing numbers of U.S. ground troops in South Vietnam. He hoped that these limited military actions would demonstrate the credibility of U.S. commitments around the world. Once the United States had shown its resolve, he argued, it might then withdraw with honor even if the Saigon government continued to suffer setbacks. Bundy remained a staunch defender of the domino theory in his public statements. From 1972 to 1984 he served as editor of *Foreign Affairs*, the journal of the Council on Foreign Relations. Bundy subsequently retired to Princeton, New Jersey, taught occasionally at the Woodrow Wilson School of International Affairs and Public Policy, and worked on an analysis of the foreign policies of President Richard Nixon's administration.

STEPHEN E. PELZ

See also Bundy, McGeorge; Central Intelligence Agency; China; Rusk, David Dean; Vietnam War

FURTHER READING

Cohen, Warren I. *Dean Rusk.* New York, 1980.

BUNKER, ELLSWORTH

(*b.* 11 May 1894; *d.* 27 September 1984)

Ambassador to South Vietnam (1967–1973) during the climax of the Vietnam War. Born in Yonkers, New York, and educated at Yale University, Bunker was the owner and manager of a sugar company that had holdings in Cuba and Mexico. Bunker began his career as an ambassador in 1951 by improving relations with Argentina during the time of Juan Perón, and in 1952 he served as ambassador to Italy. The next year he became president of the American Red Cross, a post he held until 1956, when he was named ambassador to India and Nepal, where he oversaw the expansion of the U.S. aid program. He remained ambassador to Nepal until 1959 and ambassador to India until 1961. In 1962 he negotiated the end of Dutch rule in West New Guinea, which became the West Irian province of Indonesia. In 1963 he helped to mediate a dispute between Egypt and Saudi Arabia over the Republic of Yemen. By this time he was known as the "Refrigerator" for his patience and inscrutability. In 1965, after U.S. troops intervened in the Dominican Republic against the leftist revolt led by Juan Bosch, Bunker headed a three-person team from the Organization of American States (OAS) that established a government friendly to the United States. From 1967 to 1973, as ambassador to South Vietnam, he presided over the Vietnamization program and attempted to induce the Vietnamese generals to create a representative government in Saigon. In 1970 he reluctantly backed the uncontested reelection of General Nguyen Thieu as president of South Vietnam. In his reports to Washington during these years, Bunker remained stubbornly optimistic about the prospects of winning the war, despite such setbacks as the Tet Offensive in early 1968. He served as ambassador-at-large from 1973 to 1978 and was the principal negotiator of the 1977 Panama Canal treaties, which gave the United States the right to defend the waterway but also agreed to pass on sovereignty over the canal to the Panamanians in the year 2000.

STEPHEN E. PELZ

See also Argentina; Dominican Republic; India; Indonesia; Panama and Panama Canal; Vietnam War; Yemen

FURTHER READING

Bunker, Ellsworth. *The Bunker Papers: Reports to the President from Vietnam, 1967–1973*, edited by Douglas Pike. Berkeley, Calif., 1990.

Burke, Lee H. *Ambassador at Large: Diplomat Extraordinary.* The Hague, 1972.

BUREAUCRACY

Organizations characterized by hierarchy of authority; definition of positions based on task requirements, rules, and regulations; and personnel recruitment and advancement based on technical expertise. During World War II numerous agencies conducting U.S. foreign policy were established or expanded; the proliferation of agencies continued after the war as the United States assumed a greater role in international affairs. The result has been one of the most immediately apparent characteristics of U.S. foreign policy as conducted in the 1990s—a very large number of governmental organizations actively engaged in issues relating to foreign affairs. Foreign policy, therefore, often reflects the interplay and competition of these bureaucracies—each with distinctive missions and preferences.

The cast of organizational players includes some of the most familiar ones, such as the Department of State, the Department of Defense, the individual military services and Joint Chiefs of Staff, the Central Intelligence Agency (CIA), and the National Security Council. One must then quickly add the Agency for International Development, the U.S. Information Agency, the Arms Control and Disarmament Agency, the Peace Corps, the National Security Agency, the Export-Import Bank, the National Aeronautical and Space Administration, and a number of cabinet-level departments that have major divisions dealing with international affairs, including the Departments of the Treasury, Agriculture, Energy, Commerce, Labor, Justice, and Transportation. The multiplicity and centrality of government agencies in the conduct of foreign policy invites a number of questions from a bureaucratic perspective. How do they differ from one another? What drives and controls these agencies? What explains the so-called bureaucratic behavior of these organizations? When is change achieved?

Definitions

Although there is a tendency to regard modern governmental bureaucracy as a product of the nineteenth century, antecedents can be found throughout history, for example, in ancient Egypt or China. In Mesopotamia, Hammurabi (circa 1700 B.C.) delegated his authority to subordinates for the administration of his code when he was physically absent from a region, thus extending his control but also creating a differentiated administrative class. The pioneering scholarship of Max Weber (1864–1920), who viewed bureaucracies as agents for furthering rationality in Western societies, has exercised a lasting influence on those who examine such organizations. Features of Weber's ideal type definition of bureaucracy characterize agencies charged with conducting U.S. foreign policies. Hierarchy of authority is most evident in the structure of the military, with its command structures and officer ranks. It is also characteristic of civilian agencies such as the Department of State (as of 1994 the structure included the secretary of state, a deputy secretary, five undersecretaries, eighteen assistant secretaries, and so on). Specialization characterizes the CIA and other intelligence agencies, which are staffed by mathematicians (who make and break codes), computer specialists, economists, historians, photographic analysts, and other highly specialized professionals beyond the

popular image of "secret agents." Rules and regulations as a defining characteristic of bureaucratic organizations is obvious to anyone who has applied for a passport. Personnel selection and advancement as determined by technical qualifications can be seen in the rigorous entrance examinations to the foreign service and the armed forces, along with highly specified criteria for advancement.

These four characteristics distinguish contemporary foreign and domestic bureaucracies from those forms of government administration based on political patronage, hereditary office, kinship, or tribal relations. In governments lacking bureaucratic structures, operations are routinely conducted using bribes, force of personality, or tradition. Weber's attributes differentiate modern organizational characteristics from other types of authority structures, but they do not clearly distinguish government bureaucracies from private corporations and other formal organizations, which often have some of the same features.

The sociologist James Q. Wilson suggests that the administrators of government bureaucracies operate under three constraints that distinguish them from their counterparts in the private sector. First, bureaucratic administrators typically cannot—at their own discretion—legally divert earnings of their organizations for the private benefit of their own employees or managers, as might be done elsewhere for incentives or bonuses. Second, for the most part, managers or executives of bureaucracies cannot allocate the resources as they might believe appropriate. Third, the leadership of such agencies normally must pursue organizational goals set by others. In the United States, foreign and domestic policy objectives are made by the president and his representatives or by Congress, not by the agencies charged with carrying them out.

The U.S. Congress can insist on (or deny) a pay raise for uniformed military personnel or members of the civil service, regardless of the judgment of the agency director or cabinet secretary. Private corporations raise capital by going to banks or investors and demonstrating that they can obtain a significant return on their investment. Along with all the other federal bureaucracies, agencies charged with the conduct of foreign affairs must seek appropriations annually from the Office of Management and Budget, representing the president, and then from the Congress, whose decisions seldom are based mainly on expected financial return. The leadership of a corporation may close an unprofitable plant, but the secretary of defense and the Joint Chiefs of Staff must go to Congress to close a military base. Because of perceived consequences for their constituencies, members of Congress may insist on keeping the base open regardless of costs. It is, however, often the bureaucracy that is held responsible for such inefficiencies.

What is most notable about these external controls or constraints over bureaucratic operation is that they are made by political actors drawing upon political considerations that differ from the economic ones in for-profit organizations. An episode from the Cold War in the history of the Department of State dramatizes the problems of political constraints. In the early 1950s Senator Joseph R. McCarthy corroded the effectiveness of many foreign service officers by charging in extensive public hearings and speeches that the department was infiltrated with communist sympathizers, security risks, and alien influences. Although most of his allegations were without evidence, he was successful in forcing the department to appoint his candidate as director of an internal security office. Investigations undertaken by the new director created a climate of caution among foreign service officers, who minimized initiatives and suppressed any proposals for dealing with international problems that might have caused them to be regarded with suspicion. Secretary of State John Foster Dulles decided that to conduct efficiently U.S. foreign policy during this period he would distance himself from the very department he was appointed to lead—a phenomenon that has repeated itself with other secretaries of state, who have discovered that their personal success can be disconnected from the effective administration of the department. Such a pattern may be understandable from the perspective of the individual secretary concerned with personal reputation and bent on addressing immediate foreign policy issues, but it undermines the more permanent bureaucratic structure, which, if properly used and led, should bring vastly greater resources than any one person can provide to the conduct of foreign policy.

When compared to other types of organizations, the existence of external political constraints on the leadership of foreign policy bureaucracies can generate anomalies. This structure, however, can ensure values important to a democratic society, such as accountability and equality of treatment.

Types of Bureaucracies

An agency's mode of operation and its power to influence its external political control depends upon its type. Wilson differentiates agencies whose activities can be observed from those whose operations are obscure, and agencies whose results are observable from those whose results are not. Based on the observability of activities and outcomes, Wilson identifies four kinds of bureaucracies: production (observable activities and outputs); procedural (observable activities, obscure outcomes); craft (obscure activities, observable outputs); and coping (both activities and outcomes are obscure). Although few agencies fit one category completely, most approximate one of them enough to provide revealing insights.

Production bureaucracies, with both observable activities and outcomes, are rare in the conduct of U.S. foreign policy. Some international assistance agencies, such as the Export-Import Bank, approximate the type. The bank promotes international trade and development through loans to U.S. and foreign private companies. Outsiders can observe the bank's activities, learning who gets loans and for what amounts and purposes. The outcomes also are visible: Was the pipeline or processing plant constructed? Was the loan repaid or did the borrower default? Did the company's foreign trade increase? Executives of production bureaucracies are likely to be careerists with technical expertise. This is a type of agency that wants to emphasize efficiency, for example, in showing what kind of return can be achieved on an investment. Such agencies are likely to shun activities and objectives that cannot be measured, preferring to concentrate on those for which they can demonstrate quality performance to outside authorities.

Procedural bureaucracies have observable activities but obscure outputs, as illustrated by the peacetime military. The task is to prepare for an outcome—victory in a war—that does not currently exist and obviously cannot be observed, but the peacetime preparations are observable: the acquisition of sophisticated equipment, training and practice, and the presentation of evidence of foreign threats. Unfortunately, the connection between the peacetime activities and the desired outcome remains uncertain. Observable procedures become emphasized and evaluated. The means (preparations) can end up being substituted for the ends. Standards for activities are of critical importance, and to maintain adherence to correct practice, professionalism and the development of standard operating procedures are encouraged.

If war occurs, military organizations shift abruptly into craft bureaucracies, in which victory or defeat (the outcome) may be clear, but the actions leading to it are obscured by the fog of war. In many other craft agencies, such as those engaged in intelligence gathering, observation of what workers do is difficult because of their isolation or independence rather than confusion and physical danger. The reputation of craft bureaucracies depends on the results they achieve. Precisely because the actions of individual agents remain hidden there is a worry about corruption or dishonorable practices. To guard against the difficulties, craft organizations seek to develop among their members not only professionalism but a personal commitment and loyalty to the organization and its mission. In the face of great personal risk, the crews of tanks, submarines, and bombers all need a dedication to each other and their mission.

Many foreign policy agencies can best be categorized as coping bureaucracies, those whose activities and outcomes lack observability. The Department of State frequently approximates this condition. Diplomatic activity, representing the United States to others and reporting and assessing their response, is often conducted in secret or in the relative obscurity of distant places. With infrequent exceptions, negotiations are complex and involve compromises that make outcomes ambiguous. External appraisal is difficult in a tough negotiation. Did the ambassador really get the best deal possible? Did the other side really understand the message the secretary conveyed even though it professed publicly that it did not? For coping bureaucracies, the political support by which all government organizations operate tends to be based on a specific occasion where something appears to have gone wrong. Under such circumstances it is hard to sustain effective political constituencies, with the result that the reputation of such bureaucracies is often in question.

In summary, all bureaucracies operate under external political constraints, but they can be distinguished in ways that reveal something about their practices based on how well those that head the agency and those outside of it can observe what it does. When something can be observed, it can more readily be evaluated, leading either to support or opposition. Those in a position to engage in assessment must have an interest in exercising influence. For example, the political scientist Samuel P. Huntington distinguished between strategic and structural defense issues. Structural issues—such as the number of combat personnel or the location of military bases—are of intense interest to Congress because they can have immediate implications for their constituents. Congressional pressure and constraints on the Defense Department thus become very strong on structural issues. Strategic questions, such as the type of war to prepare for or the nature of a military alliance, may be very important to a few members of Congress who are either ideologically oriented or have made this one of their areas of substantive expertise, but for the most part, members of Congress are willing to let the president exercise primary control over such matters. Thus, there is an interaction between what is observable in a bureaucracy's work and what has political consequences for those able to regulate it.

Mission

The actions of bureaucracies can be understood not only by differentiating them by type, but also by their sense of mission. Some bureaucracies have a strong sense of the primary tasks that are the core purpose of the organization. To have a powerful effect on the behavior of the agency a sense of mission or organizational essence must be broadly shared among members of the bureaucracy. In some instances, a mission may center around an organizational technology and a belief about cause and effect. If a certain problem arises, members of the bureaucracy

may share a belief about how their specific capabilities or technology can treat that problem. A sense of mission can have an important impact on what participants in the agency do and do not do.

Various military services or components of services in the U.S. armed forces have been characterized by a strong sense of mission. The Strategic Air Command (SAC), for example, developed a very strong sense of mission built around the development of the long-range bomber and the ability to deliver a retaliatory strike against the heartland of an enemy. The strong and widely held commitment to that mission enabled SAC to develop a loyalty among its people that resulted in an impressive dedication to their task, even under very difficult working conditions and despite tempting offers from civilian aviation. A sense of mission also provides the foundation for intense opposition, as when one bureaucracy acquires a task that is perceived to intrude on what those in another agency regard as their essential purpose. Its clear mission initially led the SAC to resist the development and acquisition of the intercontinental ballistic missile (ICBM), even though it could have meant greater budget allocations, more personnel, and expansion of other resources. Similarly, the air force vigorously opposed the development of submarine-launched ballistic missile capability after they had accepted ICBMs as part of their own core function.

A bureaucracy may have not just a single sense of mission, but several different missions. The navy, for example, has competing missions between the surface navy (which for a while was further divided between battleships and carriers) and submarines. The CIA has two competing missions: operatives engaged in the collection of information and other activities (often by clandestine means) and analysts engaged in the assessment of information. Competing missions within a bureaucracy can lead to major internal struggles and to efforts to get outside constituencies to ally with internal advocates of a preferred mission.

The Theory of Bureaucratic Politics

The pervasiveness of bureaucracies in the conduct of foreign policy has fostered the development of theory seeking to explain foreign policy in terms of bureaucratic politics. Rather than explaining foreign policy in terms of the international system or the actions or relative capabilities of foreign nations, the theory of bureaucratic politics seeks to explain foreign policy as it centers on the competition among bureaucracies within any one government. Many have contributed to the development of bureaucratic theories of foreign policy, but the political scientist Graham Allison unquestionably has had a dramatic influence on the popularity of such explanations. In his seminal work *Essence of Decision* (1971) he interpreted the 1962 Cuban Missile Crisis in terms of three different frameworks, one of them bureaucratic politics. Although Allison's work has attracted numerous critics, it continues to generate considerable interest.

The tenets of a theory of bureaucratic politics can be summarized in a series of statements. Many governments have multiple, permanent agencies, ministries, or departments (i.e., bureaucracies) that deal with selected aspects of foreign and defense policy. Each of the bureaucracies has one or several basic missions and associated sets of interests that it strives to maintain and advance. Foreign policy problems are interpreted by those in each bureaucracy in terms of the mission and interests of that organization, and its leaders tend to believe that the resulting specification of the foreign policy problem in terms of their bureaucracy's interests closely parallels that of the entire government. The interests of various bureaucracies and their interpretations of problems often differ from one another. Most decision-makers and others influential in the policy process tend to be affiliated with one of the bureaucracies as career employees, political appointees assigned to the agency, or as consultants. Most of these decision-makers internalize the missions and interests of the bureaucracy with which they are associated or they receive substantial side payments to support those interests and therefore tend to see no conflict between their personal interests and those of their bureaucracy. Usually the power to establish a government policy and implement it are shared (not necessarily equally) among decision-makers representing different bureaucracies. With respect to most foreign policy problems the involvement and support (or nonopposition) of multiple bureaucracies is necessary; those representing the involved bureaucracies, however, are likely to interpret the problem differently and will prefer differing policies. In the absence of a powerful individual who can choose from among the competing interests and the varying approaches to a given foreign policy problem, the representatives of the bureaucracies must negotiate an acceptable compromise or face deadlock. Any resulting agreement is likely to entail a bargaining process involving mutual concessions, circumvention of differences, or trade-offs of one issue for another.

Bureaucratic politics theory stresses the conflict among dedicated representatives of multiple agencies pursuing different and sometimes directly competing interests. In the absence of a powerful leader who insists on a single approach, the multiple agencies remain in stalemate or resolve their differences by compromises. Compromises may fail to resolve differences or could lead to an unsatisfactory patchwork solution that may be unworkable.

Advocates of bureaucratic politics theory identify a variety of historical foreign policy cases that appear to conform to their explanations. For example, bureaucratic politics theory can be applied to the U.S. government to interpret the conflict between the Agency for International Development (AID) and the Departments of State and Defense. During the 1970s Congress directed AID to allocate more of its foreign assistance in developing countries to address the direct causes and effects of poverty—called the basic human needs approach. The intent was to assign more aid to specific village-level efforts to help people in dire need rather than award cash grants to friendly governments or to fund large-scale, splashy infrastructure projects such as harbors and airports. Other U.S. foreign policy bureaucracies favored the older practice of payments to governments whose support was needed to pursue diplomatic and strategic policies. Providing aid to reduce poverty and winning the cooperation of Third World governments for U.S. diplomatic initiatives were elements of U.S. foreign policy, but primary responsibility for each was assigned to different agencies. With respect to southern Africa, Caleb Rossiter documents the resulting series of unbalanced compromises triggered by this bureaucratic struggle that resulted in minimal commitments to fighting poverty. Bureaucratic explanations have been used to explain government actions in other countries as well. The emigré scholar Jiri Valenta interprets the Soviet Union's invasion of Czechoslovakia in 1968 as the eventual outcome of a long struggle between competing forces on the ruling Politburo of the Communist party of the USSR.

Critics of bureaucratic theory make various points, including the possibility of consensus rather than conflict among bureaucratic policymakers. By placing emphasis on consensus rather than conflict, Irving Janis advanced the alternative theory of groupthink, which occurs when group members such as representatives from different bureaucracies put agreement and group solidarity ahead of constructive debate about their differences. Other critiques of explanations grounded in bureaucratic politics contend that the theory too frequently neglects the impact of an authoritative leader (i.e., the president) or that it overstates the commitment that key players may have to a bureaucracy's perspective. Such criticisms may suggest the need for specifying the limiting conditions under which bureaucratic politics may operate.

Coping with Change

The theory of bureaucratic politics treats each episode of foreign policy as a distinctive occasion over which the agencies of government battle. It is precisely the struggles involving the task of reaching intragovernment agreements (characterized by the theory) that provide one of the reasons why bureaucracies are often seen as resisting change. Having forged the bruising compromises and the difficult coalitions necessary to adopt a policy, participants are reluctant to change an agreement and start the process anew. If the agency has a strong sense of mission and the change challenges that mission's dominance, it will be opposed. If a strong performance of observable activities or outcomes by a procedural or production bureaucracy has resulted in the support of external constituencies, then a change that diverts attention to other tasks will be resisted. If the bureaucracy has an organizational "technology" captured in a set of well-established standard operating procedures, changes that disrupt that technology will lack support.

Nevertheless, the unqualified contention that bureaucracies always are an impediment to change certainly is incorrect. Government agencies can aggressively pursue change when it enhances a valued mission or makes more efficient or effective the realization of an observable procedure or outcome cherished by external constituencies and those political entities that control the agency. More fundamental change, concerning basic mission or new tasks and goals, poses greater difficulties for any organization, but under some conditions that are not well understood, profound change and innovation can transpire. The U.S. Marine Corps, for example, underwent a transformation into an assault amphibious warfare organization some time between the two world wars. Further study may reveal the importance of leadership, having a combination of vision and organizational skill, together with an environment that provides clear signals of the need for change without posing immediate crushing demands that absorb any organizational slack needed for freeing some talent to think and experiment.

The ability to cope with change in an inventive manner poses a particular problem to foreign policy bureaucracies in the post–Cold War world. The U.S. government, and many of its allies, developed a set of foreign and defense bureaucracies designed to meet the challenges of the international environment of the Cold War. The major bureaucracies of U.S. foreign and defense policy developed ways of handling the bipolar international system that featured one dominant military-political adversary. Various intelligence systems evolved to monitor and access the threat from the Soviet Union and its allies. Diplomats gradually became skilled at managing the repeated crises between East and West. The military developed an increasingly integrated military alliance with its North Atlantic Treaty Organization (NATO) allies; they shaped technologies and strategies in conformity to the varying requirements of strategic deterrence.

In the post–Cold War world, the nature of threats and international problems will come from different sources, not necessarily military in nature. Issues as diverse as energy, drug trafficking, environmental degradation, proliferation of weapons of mass destruction, inadequately regulated international financial transfers, the massive movement of refugees, the terms of international trade, or the control of global communications may demand considerable, continuing attention from the government in the conduct of foreign policy. The United States must redefine its role in world affairs as it confronts a changing international environment. Such shifts are likely to create substantial strain on the present configuration of foreign policy and defense bureaucracies. Missions will be modified. New organizational technologies will be developed and adopted. Systems for detecting and monitoring new kinds of threats will be required. As a consequence some bureaucracies will undergo substantial change, others will shrink or disappear, and new bureaucratic agencies will emerge.

CHARLES F. HERMANN

See also Agency for International Development; Arms Control and Disarmament Agency; Central Intelligence Agency; Defense, U.S. Department of; Export-Import Bank; Joint Chiefs of Staff; National Security Agency; National Security Council; Peace Corps; State, U.S. Department of

FURTHER READING

Bendor, Jonathan, and Thomas H. Hammond. "Rethinking Allison's Models." *American Political Science Review* 86 (June 1992).

Destler, I. M. *Presidents, Bureaucrats, and Foreign Policy.* Princeton, N.J., 1972.

George, Alexander L. *Presidential Decisionmaking in Foreign Policy.* Boulder, Colo., 1980.

Halperin, Morton H. *Bureaucratic Politics and Foreign Policy.* Washington, D.C., 1974.

Huntington, Samuel P. *The Common Defense.* New York, 1961.

Janis, Irving L. *Groupthink*, 2nd ed. Boston, 1982.

Rossiter, Caleb. *The Bureaucratic Struggle for Control of U.S. Foreign Aid.* Boulder, Colo., 1985.

Simon, Herbert A. *Administrative Behavior.* New York, 1947.

Valenta, Jiri. *Soviet Intervention in Czechoslovakia.* Baltimore, 1968.

Warwick, Donald P., et al. *A Theory of Public Bureaucracy.* Cambridge, Mass., 1975.

Weber, Max. "Bureaucracy." In *From Max Weber: Essays in Sociology,* translated and edited by Hans H. Gerth and C. Wright Mills. New York, 1946.

Wilson, James Q. *Bureaucracy: What Government Agencies Do and Why They Do It.* New York, 1989.

BURKINA FASO

See Appendix 2

BURLINGAME, ANSON

(*b.* 14 November 1820; *d.* 23 February 1870)

Lawyer, member of Congress (1855–1861), and U.S. minister to China (1861–1867). Born in New Berlin, New York, Burlingame received a bachelor's degree from the University of Michigan and a law degree from Harvard University. As a Free Soiler and later a Republican congressman from

Massachusetts, he supported Abraham Lincoln's presidential campaign in 1860. Appointed minister to China the following year, Burlingame developed a close friendship with Chinese officials and an appreciation for Chinese culture and soon became the leading diplomat in Beijing. At the time foreign governments were forcing Chinese officials to make trading concessions that they were unable to fulfill because of the chaotic political situation in China. When these failures brought even more radical demands upon the Chinese from foreign merchants, Burlingame acted as mediator. His actions probably forestalled a partitioning of China and won him the gratitude of the Chinese government. To show Burlingame and the United States their appreciation, the Chinese refused to assist the Confederate raider *Alabama* when it operated in Asia during the American Civil War. After Burlingame's resignation as minister in 1867, he led a delegation of Chinese officials to meet the leaders of the principal world powers. The Chinese hoped that with Burlingame's help, they could prevent the major powers from making unreasonable demands on their nation. With his assistance, China secured pledges from Great Britain, France, and Russia not to seek special privileges in times of Chinese unrest. In 1868 Burlingame escorted this delegation to the United States, and, with Secretary of State William H. Seward, he negotiated the Burlingame Treaty of 1868. The treaty provided for the stationing of Chinese consuls in the United States and gave China unrestricted immigration privileges to the United States. The latter provision opened the door for numerous Chinese laborers to emigrate to the United States as railroad construction workers, but Sinophobia, especially in the American West, eventually undermined the treaty. A new treaty in 1880 permitted Congress to suspend Chinese immigration, which it did in 1882.

LOUIS R. SMITH, JR.

See also Alabama Claims; American Civil War; China; Immigration; Seward, William Henry

FURTHER READING

Anderson, David L. *Imperialism and Idealism: American Diplomacy in China, 1861–1898.* Bloomington, Ind., 1985.
Hunt, Michael H. *The Making of a Special Relationship: The United States and China to 1914.* New York, 1983.

BURMA

See Myanmar

BURR, AARON

(*b.* 6 February 1756; *d.* 14 September 1836)

Military officer in the American Revolution, lawyer, U.S. senator from New York (1791–1797), vice president of the United States (1801–1805), and killer of Alexander Hamilton in a duel in July 1804. Also linked to shadowy schemes involving foreign governments, Aaron Burr's reputation has suffered accordingly through the years. A graduate of the College of New Jersey (now Princeton University), Burr served on General George Washington's staff in the Revolutionary War. He became a prominent New York politician and received thirty electoral votes in a losing bid for president in the 1796 election. Elected to the New York Assembly, he maneuvered to gain the national vice-presidency as a Republican in the election of 1800. When Jefferson (the Republican candidate for president) and Burr received the same number of votes in the electoral college, however, Burr's ambition came to the forefront as he saw an opportunity to achieve the presidency for himself. This ill-advised effort failed. After thirty-six ballots in the House of Representatives, the electoral tie was finally broken and Jefferson was elected president, leaving Burr as vice president.

Because of his duplicity, Burr was dropped as the Republican vice-presidential candidate in the 1804 election. He unsuccessfully sought the governorship of New York. His fellow New Yorker and political foe, Alexander Hamilton, the former Federalist secretary of the treasury in the George Washington administration, worked to defeat Burr. Hamilton also had helped deny Burr the presidency in 1800 by lobbying the House of Representatives against his rival. Angered by Hamilton's activities, the outgoing vice president demanded satisfaction and challenged Hamilton to a duel. Fought at Weehawken, New Jersey, on 11 July 1804, the duel left Hamilton mortally wounded.

Out of a job in March 1805, the disgruntled and bitter Burr became linked, to an extent still unknown, with British and Spanish agents who, it seemed, would assist him in separating western lands from the United States. One rumor held that he contemplated the capture of Washington, D.C., with the help of naval officers, either with or without Spanish aid, and the establishment of a Cromwellian-style dictatorship. Whatever Burr's intentions, his name is inextricably tied to the unscrupulous U.S. Army General James Wilkinson, governor of Upper Louisiana, who was on the Spanish payroll.

After leaving office, Burr, in the summer of 1806, established headquarters in Lexington, Kentucky, ostensibly for organizing with Wilkinson an expedition to the Southwest. In August his force of perhaps eighty men in ten flatboats floated down the Ohio River to the Mississippi. While the president's cabinet deliberated, Wilkinson decided to desert Burr, writing to Jefferson in the autumn of 1806 about an alleged conspiracy involving the former vice president.

As Burr entered Orleans Territory, he learned of the president's proclamation calling for the arrest of the alleged conspirators on 10 January 1807. Surrendering to U.S. authorities at Natchez, Burr then jumped bail and fled south toward Spanish Florida. On 10 February 1807 he was arrested on U.S. territory in what is now Alabama for the misdemeanor of forming and leading an expedition against Spanish territory. On 24 June, Burr was indicted for treason in federal court in Richmond, Virginia. On 1 September he was acquitted due to a lack of evidence that he was present when an overt act of treason was committed. Burr still had to stand trial on other charges, including the murder of Hamilton. Before the trial began, Burr escaped to Europe, where he plotted to overthrow Jefferson. Returning to the United States in 1812, Burr reestablished his law practice, but never overcame his reputation as a scandalous traitor.

THOM M. ARMSTRONG

See also Continental Expansion; Hamilton, Alexander; Jefferson, Thomas; Spain

FURTHER READING

Abernathy, Thomas P. *The Burr Conspiracy*. New York, 1954.
Lomask, Milton. *Aaron Burr: The Conspiracy and Years of Exile, 1805–1836*. New York, 1982.
———. *Aaron Burr: The Years from Princeton to Vice President, 1765–1805*. New York, 1979.
Malone, Dumas. "Jefferson the President: Second Term, 1805–1809." In *Jefferson and His Time*, vol. 5. Boston, 1974.
Schachner, Nathan. *Aaron Burr*. New York, 1937.

BURUNDI

See Appendix 2

BUSH, GEORGE HERBERT WALKER

(*b*. 12 June 1924)

The 41st president of the United States (1989–1993) and widely regarded as being one of the most experienced in foreign affairs. Bush was born to a wealthy and politically-minded Connecticut family. His father, Prescott S. Bush, was a managing partner in the prominent New York investment banking firm of Brown Brothers, Harriman and Company, and also served as U.S. senator (Republican, Connecticut) from 1952 to 1963. George Bush was educated in private preparatory schools (Greenwich Country Day School and Phillips Exeter Academy) and had been accepted to Yale University when World War II broke out. He enlisted in the Naval Reserve and after flight training was commissioned as an ensign in 1943, becoming at the time the navy's youngest pilot. He served valiantly in the Pacific theater, and received the Distinguished Flying Cross for heroism after his plane was shot down by the Japanese. Upon his return from the war, he married Barbara Pierce and enrolled at Yale.

After graduating from Yale with a degree in economics he moved to Texas and entered the oil industry, becoming quite successful financially. He became politically active, named chairman of the Harris County (Houston) Republican party in 1962 and running as the Republican Senate candidate in 1964. He lost the 1964 election to incumbent liberal Democrat Ralph Yarborough. In 1966 Bush ran for the House of Representatives, and this time he won.

After a relatively brief tenure in the U.S. House of Representatives, Bush lost another bid for a U.S. Senate seat from Texas in 1970, this time to Democrat Lloyd Bentsen. From that point, except for one brief interregnum as chair of the Republican National Committee (1973–1974), Bush was appointed to a number of diplomatic and national security positions: ambassador to the United Nations (1971–1973) for President Richard Nixon; the first head of mission to China when pre-ambassadorial relations were established, for President Gerald Ford (1974–1975); Director of the Central Intelligence Agency (CIA); and Director of Central Intelligence (D.C.I.), also for President Ford (1976–1977).

In 1980 Bush campaigned for the Republican presidential nomination as an experienced moderate but lost to the hero of the party conservatives, Ronald Reagan. In order to consolidate support across the party spectrum, Reagan selected Bush to be his vice-presidential nominee; Bush served two terms as vice president. His role in some of the more controversial foreign policy ventures of the Reagan administration, such as the Iran-Contra episode, remain clouded. Whereas Bush in other circumstances touted his foreign policy expertise and involvement, during the Iran-Contra Affair Bush claimed to have been outside of the decision-making circle. The extent to which he was or was not "in the loop" remains controversial. As one of his last official acts as president, Bush closed off the possibility of further criminal investigation by pardoning one of the other officials accused of being involved in the affair, former Secretary of Defense Caspar Weinberger.

Bush and the End of the Cold War

Bush's interest in foreign policy issues far outweighed any concern he displayed for domestic affairs. In the end, after being in office during a long lasting recession, Bush's perceived disinterest in domestic policy severely damaged his prospects for being reelected. However, Bush presided over a world that was changing dramatically, and so long as events on the world stage dominated the news, these played to Bush's comparative advantage. Not since the Truman administration's response to the upheavals following World War II had a U.S. president been so starkly challenged to generate new policies for what was a new era in world affairs.

Bush assembled a foreign policy team that had two principal characteristics. Its members were professionals with foreign policy and other relevant governmental experience. And many were long-time friends and associates of the president. James Baker, Bush's oldest friend and political confidante who had been White House Chief of Staff and secretary of the Treasury, became secretary of state. Brent Scowcroft became national security adviser, a position he also held in the Ford administration and to which he abrought such other credentials as being a retired Air Force General, a Columbia University Ph.D., chairman of the 1983 Scowcroft Commission on the MX missile and arms control, and member of the 1987 Tower Commission investigating the Iran-Contra Affair. Following the major political blunder of nominating John Tower as Secretary of Defense, Bush recouped with the appointment of Dick Cheney, congressman from Wyoming since 1978, member of the House Intelligence Committee and newly elected House Whip, a position into which Newt Gingerich then moved. The fourth key team member was the chairman of the Joint Chiefs of Staff, Colin Powell, who had emerged in the Reagan years as a top aide and then, following the Iran-Contra Affair, as national security adviser.

Although changes in the policies of the Soviet Union became apparent with the ascendancy of Mikhail Gorbachev in 1985 these changes moved with stunning speed during the first year of the Bush administration. Free parliamentary elections were held in Poland and in Hungary, the two least oppressive regimes of the Warsaw Pact. The clear indications of Soviet reluctance to intervene in the Warsaw Pact states gave rise to mass expression of public discontent with the communist regimes of those states. The most pivotal of these regimes was the German Democratic Republic (GDR), then known as East Germany. When its leadership was toppled, a reform communist element came to power. With unexpected rapidity it brought down the classic symbol of the Cold War, the Berlin Wall, in November 1989. Within a year a referendum on reunification of the two German states took place and passed overwhelmingly, a process that was nurtured by the Bush administration. Prodded more by necessity than desire, the Bush administration managed to bring along the other three major postwar occupying powers—Great Britain, France, and the Soviet Union— none of whom were brimming with enthusiasm about the prospect of German reunification.

After the Berlin Wall fell, Czechoslovakia peacefully turned out its communist regime in the so-called "velvet revolution" led by former dissident Vaclav Havel followed later by Bulgaria. At the end of the year, the Romanian dictatorship was ousted through violent means. Eventu-

ally, even isolated Albania's communist dictatorship was brought down. In turn, these events accelerated change in Poland and Hungary and whetted the appetites of nationalists in many of the Soviet Republics, most immediately and critically the Baltic states of Lithuania, Estonia, and Latvia, which had been incorporated into the Soviet Union in 1940. They also stimulated nationalist movements within the former Yugoslavia, leading to its break up and subsequent civil wars beginning in 1991.

The political reforms within the Soviet Union and the stirring of political change in some of the Eastern European communist states had, by the spring of 1989, encouraged demonstrations for greater political openness and democracy in China as well. These actions led eventually to the violent repression of the demonstrators in Tiananmen Square in June of 1989, handing the Bush administration its first major foreign policy crisis. Its response to this crisis was in the main a reflection of George Bush's past experience in China and his unarticulated philosophy of realism in international politics. In regard to China, Bush believed that he was his own best expert: he concluded that U.S. interests were so inextricably linked with China's role in Asia that placing human rights pressures on the Chinese government would be counterproductive to U.S. economic, diplomatic, and security interests. While under pressure to react to the Tiananmen crisis, Bush overtly did the minimum required for his public relations needs. A more significant indication of his views and his reluctance to provoke the Chinese regime was that he opposed legislation to extend the visas of Chinese students studying in the United States. An especially powerful signal was that, not long after the Tiananmen events, Bush secretly sent his national security adviser to China to reassure its leadership of his administration's willingness to do business more or less as usual.

As events unfolded in Eastern Europe and liberalization pressures proceeded apace there and in the Soviet Union, the Bush administration remained skeptical of their consequences for U.S. security. The administration's limited support for changes in NATO doctrine and strategy, advocated by some of the European Allies (no more than "containment-plus"), and its commitment to a military posture still premised on the Soviet Union as its chief adversary, reflected this skeptical world view. Superficial change that might prove to be temporal must not be allowed to obscure the need to protect permanent interests. This too was a part of Bush's so-called realist conception of international affairs.

The collapse of the Soviet Union itself at the end of 1991 hastened a change of focus from nuclear arms agreements to nuclear arms security. The tight grip of a centralized Soviet governing authority in control of nuclear weaponry could no longer be taken for granted.

Who had control of what now became the operative question, as the Soviet Union splintered into its constituent republics. This splintering instantly proliferated the possession of warheads and of delivery systems. In addition, the departure of former Soviet troops from outposts to the west and the Baltic republics opened up a black market for arms, nuclear and otherwise. Hence, a fundamental problem for the Bush administration was to ensure the existence of predictable political order in the former Soviet republics, especially those that carried nuclear weapons. In practical terms, Russia and Ukraine, the two largest republics, became the principal focal points of the Bush administration's concerns for political stability.

The end of the Cold War worked to Bush's immediate political advantage, as it enabled him to lay claim to having been responsible for it having been "won" on his watch. Ultimately, however, it worked to his political disadvantage as a "foreign policy president." One of the consequences of the end of the Cold War, which actually predated the collapse of the Soviet Union, was to lessen the popularly perceived dangers in the world and increase the salience of domestic problems and policies. While in actual fact, the world had become more confusing, less orderly, and subject to many more lower-level conflagrations even if these conflicts no longer carried with them the specter of catastrophic nuclear war, the perception was of a less-threatening world. There was decreasing public support for expending resources, or even paying much attention to foreign policy ventures.

Bush's Military Operations

Despite the growing risks attached to putting troops at risk abroad, there were two clear instances in which Bush committed military forces. On each occasion Bush came away a winner. The first occurred near the end of 1989, when U.S. military forces invaded Panama for the purpose of bringing down the regime of Manuel Noriega and capturing him. The second instance, which seemed a much larger gamble at the time, was the unleashing of Operation Desert Storm in January of 1991 to drive the Iraqi forces of Saddam Hussein out of Kuwait, the oil-rich country that Iraq had invaded in early August of 1990, and defend Saudi Arabia, an even more oil-rich and more important strategic ally.

A one-time CIA intelligence source and anticommunist ally of the Cold War, Noriega was declared an enemy of the United States. This was in part a foreign policy consequence of changing domestic priorities, namely the escalation of the war against drugs in the United States. During the Cold War, Noriega's involvement in the drug trade had been a secondary concern of the CIA's in comparison to his value as a Cold War intelligence operative. But as the domestic policy of waging war on drug smuggling heated

up, Noriega had become an embarrassment and, indeed, had been indicted in a U.S. court. The fact that Noriega was ruthless in his dealings with the opposition in Panama did nothing to enhance his image. Further, after Noriega smashed a coup attempt in October of 1989, Bush was embarrassed, because while the United States had supported the coup attempt, it did so without sufficient commitment to allow it to succeed. While of much less magnitude, the incident did evoke memories of the Bay of Pigs. Unlike Kennedy, who lacked the necessary degree of freedom to atone for his earlier failure, Bush had the discretion to invade Panama and quickly overwhelm Noriega's forces and subsequently capture him. The invasion occurred so suddenly that U.S. public opinion had yet to form around it until it succeeded, after which public support for Bush's action was extremely strong.

The Persian Gulf crisis was a more diplomatically complex and militarily massive affair. In contrast to the unilateral actions taken by U.S. forces in Panama, which were disapproved of by the Organization of American States (OAS), those taken in defense of Saudi Arabia and offensively against Iraq in the Gulf were multilateral and based on a succession of United Nations (UN) Security Council mandates. Although Bush made an early commitment to reversing the Iraqi invasion of Kuwait, which had precipitated the crisis, the obvious first step was protection of the Saudi oil fields and the Saudi regime against possible Iraqi incursion. This buildup of defensive forces became known as Operation Desert Shield.

Bush and his team skillfully handled the military and diplomatic aspects of Desert Shield. This rapid, massive deployment of U.S. forces proceeded with limited logistical difficulties. Assembling the twenty-seven nations was far from a given: European countries (such as France and Germany) had been active trading partners with Iraq; Arab states had to overcome fears of nationalist and fundamentalist-fed backlash to allying with Western powers against any other Arab state; and Iraq had been a long-time Soviet ally. Yet the Bush administration succeeded in getting resolutions through the UN Security Council, in working the issues bilaterally through the Baker-Schevardnadze channel (the product of Secretary of State James Baker and Soviet Foreign Minister Edvard Schevardnadze), and in organizing and mobilizing the joint command structure for the multilateral military forces.

The shift from Desert Shield to Desert Storm began right after the November 1990 midterm congressional elections. There were a number of reasons for this shift, including the practical difficulties of maintaining such a large force for an extended period of time in a desert climate and somewhat inhospitable culture. However, while Congress and U.S. public opinion had been supportive of the initial defensive deployments, a change to a more offensive strategy and the concomitant greater imminence of going to war was met with greater congressional opposition and more divided public opinion.

In early January 1991 the Senate, by the narrow margin of 52 to 47, and the House of Representatives, by a somewhat more generous 250 to 183, passed resolutions allowing the use of force to remove the Iraqi invaders from Kuwait. About a week later, intense U.S. and British aerial bombardments of Iraqi military and command targets commenced, followed a month later by the ground war. Within a matter of days, and with minimal U.S. casualties, the Iraqi forces were devastated. Bush was celebrated as a leader who helped form a consensus for decisive action. His popularity, which had been relatively high, reached astronomical levels (89% according to the Gallup survey) in the immediate aftermath of the Gulf War. The Democrats were sent reeling and, despite the fact that the election was almost two years away, Bush was virtually inaugurated by pundits for a second term.

The Persian Gulf crisis, although more protracted than the Cuban missile crisis, resembled it nonetheless in that it helped enhance the foreign policy reputation of the sitting president. In each case, at the time the events occurred, the president was perceived to be a skilled decision maker. In Bush's case, he clearly hoped that the success of the operation would have long-lasting effects and allow him, therefore, to be reelected. Unfortunately for Bush, the euphoria produced by the U.S. military success did not last nearly so long as he had hoped.

Part of the reason was that the Gulf War victory itself was tarnished by controversies: first, over whether Bush had ended the war too soon, should have further decimated the Iraqi forces, and even tried to occupy Baghdad; then over whether enough support was being given to the Iraqi Kurds, who had rebelled with some expectation of U.S. support. A more compelling reason, however, was that domestic issues now dominated the agenda, and the public evinced a mood of sour discontent, fed by concerns over economic insecurity.

The "New World Order"

When Bush first addressed the Congress following the Iraqi invasion of Kuwait, he sought to look beyond the immediate crisis and spoke of "a new world order... stronger in the pursuit of justice and more secure in the quest for peace...[in which all nations] can prosper and live in harmony." Later, as disintegration and conflict became a more apparent condition than order, this phrase was sardonically referred to as "the new world disorder." Bush was never very clear as to the precise shape of the new world order, but a reasonable inference as to what he had in mind was the world envisioned by the UN Charter, namely, a syndicate of significant powers that could serve a collective enforcing role for world stability. Such a col-

lective entity could be imagined only in the absence of the Cold War—and also probably required the presence of an integrated Soviet Union. It also required that the need for enforcement would be low, a condition that has hardly existed since Bush enunciated the doctrine.

Indeed, not long after the victory in the Persian Gulf, both positive and negative developments occurred. On the positive side, the loss of the Soviet Union as an ally and the devastating defeat suffered by the Iraqi regime provided incentives for front-line Arab states and Palestinians to enter peace negotiations with the Israelis. The Israeli government remained a reluctant partner in the talks until elections brought a change of leadership. The Bush administration, and particularly Secretary Baker, deserve substantial credit for establishing both the bilateral and multilateral tracks of Arab-Israeli peace talks, and then playing the role of interlocutor in the talks, seeking to sustain them rather than to define their course.

On the negative side, numerous civil and intercommunal conflagrations around the globe either began or worsened. The one that became most central to the Bush administration was the dissolution of the former Yugoslavia, and the brutal wars that accompanied the creation of independent Croatian and Bosnian states. Following German recognition of these two states, the United States also recognized their breakaway status on the grounds that international recognition of their legitimacy as independent states would protect them from the Serb-dominated government in Belgrade. This hopeful result did not come to pass, partly because in 1991 the Bush administration appeared to give mixed signals to the various parties, an action which at a minimum failed to dissuade or deter the Serbs from aggression. Thus, the new Croatian republic and then the new Bosnian republic were embroiled in intercommunal war. Serbian forces gained the upper hand in both locations, with the most intense and durable conflict shifting to Bosnia, the most ethnically pluralized of all the former Yugoslav republics. Civilian populations became direct targets of military fire. "Ethnic cleansing" of the Muslims by Serbs struck parallels with the Nazi brutalities of half a century earlier.

The Bush administration faced questions that in some respects were more complex than those in the Gulf War. What, if any, were the U.S. or NATO interests or obligations? What were the limits of U.S. military power as a lever in influencing a situation that was as equally complicated politically as it was militarily? Would the U.S. public support yet another major military commitment? The conclusion drawn by the Bush administration was that these limits were quite severe. In a mix of analysis and wishful thinking there was some effort to cast the problem as fundamentally a European one to resolve, rather than one for the United States. As well, the success in the Persian Gulf actually reinforced the lessons of the failed venture in Vietnam. Military intervention in Bosnia would have had to take place over mountainous and forested terrain unsuitable to the *blitzkrieg* tactics used in the desert warfare of the Persian Gulf. In sum, the Bush administration was willing to broker a bad deal on the grounds that a worse deal was more likely. It was certainly unwilling to commit forces on the ground and remained skeptical as to what could be done through air power. The administration projected a detachment from a situation in which a civilian population in Europe was being terrorized and one in which numerous interest groups tried to engage the Bush administration to intervene by raising the specter of another European holocaust. During the 1992 campaign, the Democratic challenger, Bill Clinton, repeatedly criticized the Bush administration for its impotent policies in the Balkans.

Yet political charges and countercharges aside, the Bush administration's policy on Yugoslavia also could be seen to be rooted in Bush's own conception of realism: for those matters deemed to be central to U.S. interests, commit U.S. resources fully; for those deemed to be peripheral to U.S. interests, avoid engagements that could be costly. The major (but not only) rub in this formula is that what is and is not central to U.S. interests is always a matter of considerable debate.

The Balkans were not the only scene of intercommunal strife. Ethnic conflicts were also raging in Nagorno-Karabakh and other republics of the former Soviet Union, and civil strife led to the collapse of African states such as Somalia and Liberia. Clearly, the United States could not intervene everywhere, despite the compelling circumstances of mass famine and slaughter engendered by the increasingly anarchic nature of these societies. By the end of the Bush administration, however, it had bequeathed to its successor a military contingent meant to operate under UN auspices in Somalia in order to provide sufficient order to ensure that food supplies reached targeted populations. Because the U.S. public responds emotionally to pictures of children dying of malnutrition, there is generally overwhelming support for providing military assistance to create order and save lives—that is, in cases where the U.S. military appears to face little resistance. Later, however, under the Clinton administration, when the mission had changed to undertake a more aggressive policy against the warlords in Somalia and casualties were incurred, resistance to putting U.S. soldiers actively in harm's way resurfaced.

Another dramatic change during the Bush administration was the evolution toward a multiracial government in South Africa. The fall of apartheid, of course, was fundamentally a consequence of internal dynamics, but it also was influenced by the economic sanctions that had been imposed on the white-ruled South African regime by Congress (over President Reagan's veto). Whatever impact these external pressures may have had on the evolution toward full political incorporation in South Africa, the Bush administration did nothing to reverse the sanctions visited upon the white rulers of South Africa by a reluctant Reagan administration. The continuation of sanctions against the white South African government led to the perception among its more moderate leadership, which included President de Klerk, that liberalization was essential to getting the sanctions lifted. The long-imprisoned black leader Nelson Mandela was released from prison in 1990, setting in motion a process of political power-sharing and Mandela's own ascendancy to the presidency of South Africa.

In sum, George Bush served as president in times of immense change in the nature of the world order. Bush's assets as a foreign policy maker lay in his ability to concentrate on the problem at hand and in his conservative temperament, which helped engender skepticism toward overcommitting U.S. resources. In this sense, Bush was more a decision maker than a policy maker, except as decisions beget policies by default. Ironically, however, among his chief liabilities was that his passion for foreign affairs so outdistanced his domestic concerns that ultimately he lost the popular support needed to stay in office. If his conservative temperament was in some ways an asset in deterring rash action, it also inhibited him from generating a rationale for U.S. foreign policy in a world that had so rapidly and dramatically changed.

BERT A. ROCKMAN

See also Baker, James Addison III; Bosnia-Herzegovina; Central Intelligence Agency; Clinton, William Jefferson; Cold War; Croatia; Cuban Missile Crisis; Germany; Gulf War of 1990–1991; Iran-Contra Affair; Panama and Panama Canal; Reagan, Ronald Wilson; Russia and the Soviet Union; Somalia; South Africa; Yugoslavia

FURTHER READING

Berman, Larry, and Bruce W. Jentleson. "Bush and the Post-Cold War World: New Challenges for American Leadership." In *The Bush Presidency: First Appraisals*, edited by Colin Campbell and Bert A. Rockman. Chatham, N.J., 1991.

Duffy, Michael, and Dan Goodgame. *Marching in Place: The Status Quo Presidency of George Bush*. New York, 1992.

Hybel, Alex Roberto. *Power over Rationality: The Bush Administration and the Gulf Crisis*. Albany, N.Y., 1993.

LeoGrande, William M. "From Reagan to Bush: The Transition in U.S. Policy Toward Central America." *Journal of Latin American Studies* 22 (1990): 595–621.

Maynes, Charles William. "America Without the Cold War." *Foreign Policy* 78(1990): 3–25.

Waas, Murray, and Craig Unger. "In the Loop: Bush's Secret Mission." *The New Yorker* 68 (1992): 64–83.

Wayne, Stephen J. "President Bush Goes to War: A Psychological Interpretation From a Distance." In *The Political Psychology of the Gulf War: Leaders, Publics and the Process of Conflict*, edited by Stanley A. Renshon. Pittsburgh, Pa., 1993.

Woodward, Bob. *The Commanders*. New York, 1991.

BYRNES, JAMES FRANCIS

(b. 2 May 1879; d. 24 January 1972)

U.S. congressman (1911–1925), U.S. Senator (1931–1941), Supreme Court justice (1941–1942), wartime "assistant president" to Franklin Delano Roosevelt (1942–1945), secretary of state (1945–1947), and governor of South Carolina (1951–1955). Born in Charleston, Byrnes studied law while working as a court reporter and began his politcal career by election to the House of Representatives in 1911 and went on to serve ten years in the Senate. He resigned from the Supreme Court to head up the Office of Economic Stabilization (1942–1945).

Byrnes's influence upon U.S. foreign relations during the immediate postwar period belies his brief tenure. He played a key role in the transition from the conciliatory diplomacy of Roosevelt to the Cold War policy of containment espoused by Roosevelt's successor, Harry S. Truman. *Time* magazine's "Man of the Year" for 1946, Byrnes's high-profile, independent style set the pattern for modern globe-trotting secretaries of state. Relying upon his talents as a former senatorial "fixer," Byrnes favored face-to-face summit diplomacy, confiding in only a few trusted advisers chosen from outside the Department of State's bureaucracy.

Truman chose Byrnes as his first and highest appointment, replacing the innocuous Edward R. Stettinius, in part because Byrnes had served as Roosevelt's "Yalta salesman," lobbying the Senate and the press with an insider's account of what happened at the Big Three meeting in 1945. This incomplete, sanitized version of Yalta raised hopes of U.S.-Soviet cooperation that proved illusory. As secretary of state, Byrnes, who believed that he rather than Truman should have been Roosevelt's choice as vice president, was, under the rules then in effect, next in the line of succession to the presidency. Before publicly taking over as secretary, Byrnes served behind the scenes as Truman's representative on a top-secret committee charged with recommending how to best use the newly developed atomic bomb. Byrnes became history's first atomic diplomat. Even before the bomb was tested, he realized that possession of such a powerful weapon by the United States could be useful in making the Soviets more "manageable" in Eastern Europe. Anxious that the bomb be kept secret even from U.S. allies until it had been used in combat, Byrnes vetoed a suggestion that Soviet observers be invited to the first test detonation in New Mexico.

Byrnes's public debut as Truman's chief foreign policy adviser came at the Potsdam Conference in July 1945, where he advised Truman how to use the atomic bomb to end the war with Japan while containing Soviet influence in Asia. As Byrnes put it, he hoped to use the bomb to end the war quickly before the Soviets could "get in so much on the kill." Having found it difficult to deal with the Soviets in Europe, Byrnes wanted to avoid sharing the victory in Asia and the Pacific with the Soviets. At Potsdam, Byrnes also helped draw up a compromise formula for German reparations. Upon his return to the United States, he helped craft Japan's conditional unconditional surrender by implicitly giving assurances regarding the status of Emperor Hirohito.

Much of Byrnes's postwar diplomacy was conducted in a series of Council of Foreign Ministers meetings in London, Moscow, and Paris. His initial attempt to use the bomb as a threat or stick in these negotiations failed to impress his Soviet counterpart, Vyacheslav Molotov. His frequent absence from Washington, independent style, and shift to a more conciliatory approach to sensitive issues, such as U.S. recognition of Soviet-dominated regimes in Eastern Europe and the possibility of the international control of atomic weapons, caused critics at home to brand Byrnes an "appeaser." By early 1946 Truman himself was tired, as he privately put it to Byrnes, of "babying" the Soviets. Truman also was tired of Byrnes presuming that he alone decided what U.S. foreign policy was at any moment. Although Truman's private tough talk was largely cathartic, Byrnes got the message and joined the growing Cold War consensus. During his remaining months in office Byrnes rid himself of the "appeaser" label with tough public rhetoric about standing up to the Soviets "from Korea to Timbuktu." He delivered his single most important speech at Stuttgart, West Germany, in September 1946, where he announced U.S. support for a restored German economy and signaled acceptance of a divided Germany and a divided Europe.

Returning to private life in 1947, Byrnes wrote a best-selling memoir, *Speaking Frankly,* in which he defended his "firm but fair" approach to postwar foreign affairs. A Southern Democrat, he publicly broke with Truman in 1948 over the issue of civil rights and went on to serve as a segregationist governor of South Carolina.

ROBERT L. MESSER

See also Cold War; Containment; Germany; Hiroshima and Nagaski Bombings of 1945; Molotov, Vyacheslav Mikhailovich; Nuclear Weapons and Strategy; Stimson, Henry Lewis; Truman, Harry S.; World War II; Yalta Conference

FURTHER READING

Byrnes, James F. *Speaking Frankly.* New York, 1947.

Curry, George. "James F. Byrnes." In *The American Secretaries of State and Their Diplomacy* edited by Samuel Flagg Bemis and Robert H. Ferrell. New York, 14 (1965): 87–396.

Messer, Robert L. *The End of an Alliance: James F. Byrnes, Roosevelt, Truman, and the Origins of the Cold War.* Chapel Hill, N.C., 1982.

Robertson, David. *Sly and Able: A Political Biography of James F. Byrnes.* New York, 1994.

C

CABLE NEWS NETWORK

A set of broadcast news services produced by Turner Broadcasting System in Atlanta, Georgia, and founded by the peripatetic entrepreneur Ted Turner, who turned a local television station into a global empire; *Time* magazine called him "prince of the global village." CNN began in 1980 as a pair of domestic cable channels. The main channel offered expanded traditional news and information programming, while *CNN Headline News* offered a thirty-minute mix of headlines, sports, and weather, available around the clock. Extended live coverage became a CNN specialty. An extensive network of foreign bureaus—the largest of any U.S. network—and a sophisticated satellite system for news gathering and distribution allowed CNN to capitalize on dramatic international events in the late 1980s and early 1990s. By the time of the Gulf War in 1991, CNN had become an essential presence in foreign ministries, newsrooms, and major hotels around the world. Many national broadcasters relied on CNN for their own newscasts or simply retransmitted CNN's live coverage. World leaders used the network to address the world and each other; scholars speculated on how the network had altered international politics and even war itself.

Under Turner's direction, CNN became aggressively international. The word "foreign" was banned, and the separate CNN International (CNNI) service distributed outside the United States increased the proportion of programming that it produced itself. A group of ethnically diverse anchorpersons and global weather and sports reports strengthened the effort to give CNNI a global look and perspective. Turner responded to Third World complaints about Western dominance of the news by inviting broadcast organizations around the world to submit short weekly reports that he promised to transmit without editing or censorship. The *CNN World Report* became a showcase of global journalism styles and ran several hours a week on both CNNI and the domestic U.S. service. Despite competition from Sky News in Europe and the British Broadcasting Corporation's World Service Television, which attracted a growing audience in Asia, CNN retained the unique ability to provide unlimited live coverage of major events anywhere in the world to viewers anywhere in the world.

ROBERT L. STEVENSON

See also Communications Policy; Telecommunication Companies; Television and Foreign Policy; Third World

FURTHER READING

Flournoy, Don M. *CNN World Report: Ted Turner's International New Coup.* London, 1992.
Hank, Whittemore. *CNN: The Inside Story.* Boston, 1990.

CABOT, JOHN MOORS
(*b.* 11 December 1901; *d.* 23 February 1981)

U.S. career diplomat who specialized in Latin American affairs. Cabot grew up in a wealthy Massachusetts family and attended Harvard and Oxford Universities. He entered the Foreign Service in 1924 and served in posts in Peru (1927–1928), the Dominican Republic (1929–1931), Mexico (1931–1932), Brazil (1932–1935), Guatemala (1939–1941), and Argentina (1945–1946). During the early Cold War, Cabot believed that international communism emanating from the Soviet Union represented a serious threat to U.S. security in Latin America. In 1953 President Dwight D. Eisenhower appointed him assistant secretary of state for inter-American affairs. After fiscal conservatives in the administration defeated Cabot's proposal for a development assistance program for Latin America, he was appointed ambassador to Sweden in 1954. He then served as ambassador to Colombia (1957–1959) and Brazil (1959–1961). Toward the end of his career, Cabot found himself in conflict not only with Washington, but also with Latin American nationalists. In Brazil, for example, his pro-U.S. speeches and public relations campaigns on behalf of U.S. corporations aroused the wrath of nationalist politicians, students, and military officers. After President Jânio Quadros of Brazil publicly rebuked Cabot for criticizing Brazil's independent foreign policy and its tolerance of the Cuban Revolution, President John F. Kennedy recalled Cabot early in 1961. Cabot retired from the Foreign Service in 1966.

STEPHEN M. STREETER

See also Argentina; Brazil; Cold War; Cuba; Guatemala; Latin America; Mexico; Peru

FURTHER READING

Cabot, John Moors. *First Line of Defense: Forty Years' Experiences of a*

Career Diplomat. Washington, D.C., 1979.

————. *Toward Our Common Destiny: Speeches and Interviews on Latin American Problems.* Medford, Mass., 1955.

Streeter, Stephen M. "Campaigning Against Latin American Nationalism: U.S. Ambassador John Moors Cabot in Brazil, 1959–1961." *The Americas* 51 (October 1994): 193–218.

CAIRO CONFERENCE

World War II meeting of President Franklin D. Roosevelt, British Prime Minister Winston Churchill, and Generalissimo Jiang Jieshi (Chiang Kai-shek) in Cairo, Egypt, between 22 and 26 November 1943. This was Roosevelt's only meeting with Generalissimo Jiang. Roosevelt's immediate purpose was to bolster Chinese confidence and provide political encouragement when the capacity to send significant military aid for China's war against Japan was lacking. The long-term purpose was to announce agreement among "the Three Great Allies" on the peace terms to be imposed on Japan. The Cairo Declaration signed by the three leaders and issued 1 December 1943 declared that "Japan shall be stripped of all the islands in the Pacific which she has seized or occupied since…1914, and that all the territories Japan has stolen from the Chinese, such as Manchuria, Formosa [Taiwan], and the Pescadores, shall be restored to the Republic of China. Japan will also be expelled from all other territories she has taken by violence and greed." Furthermore, "in due course Korea shall become free and independent." Korea had been annexed to the Japanese Empire, without U.S. objection, following the Russo-Japanese War of 1904–1905. The "other territories" referred to the Philippines, Indochina, Malaya, and the Netherlands East Indies (Indonesia). The Cairo Declaration was a step toward adding some specificity to the principle of "unconditional surrender" as applied toward Japan.

GADDIS SMITH

See also China; Korea; Japan; Jiang Jieshi; Unconditional Surrender; Roosevelt, Franklin Delano; World War II

CALHOUN, JOHN CALDWELL
(*b.* 18 March 1782; *d.* 31 March 1850)

U.S. congressman (1811–1817), secretary of war (1817–1825), vice president of the United States (1825–1832), secretary of state (1844–1845), and U.S. senator (1833–1843; 1845–1850). A theoretician and champion of states' rights, Calhoun was born near Abbeville in South Carolina, nurtured on plantation life, and educated at Yale College. Calhoun practiced law and became active briefly in state politics before being elected to the U.S. House of Representatives in 1810. As acting chairman of the House Committee on Foreign Affairs, the nationalistic Calhoun pressed for U.S. territorial expansion and, as a leader of the southern War Hawks, called for war with Great Britain over that country's impressment of U.S. sailors, its incitement of western Indian tribes to acts of harassment against American settlers, and its challenge to America's national honor. Although he supported the peace efforts reflected in the Treaty of Ghent, which ended the War of 1812, Calhoun's cautious nature led him to promote a strong U.S. military; as James Monroe's secretary of war from 1817 to 1825, he helped reorganize the U.S. Army.

From 1825 to 1832 he served as vice president, first under President John Quincy Adams and then under President Andrew Jackson. An irreparable breach with Jackson provoked by the revelation of Calhoun's censure of the general's Florida adventure of 1818, the so-called Peggy Eaton affair, and incompatible opinions on federal policy—opinions that climaxed with the nullification controversy over tariff policy—prompted Calhoun's resignation in 1832. He did not, however, leave Washington but rather moved to the Senate—where he wielded considerable influence almost without interruption until his death. During one of those rare interruptions, Calhoun unwittingly delayed the annexation of Texas, for which he had worked diligently throughout the 1830s and early 1840s. While serving as secretary of state under John Tyler, he responded to a rumored British plan to abolish slavery in Texas by publishing a reply to the British minister in Washington, Richard Pakenham, in which he contended that such a move by Great Britain would threaten the security of the South. His association of slavery with Texas doomed the annexation treaty to failure.

Calhoun took a different tack with Pakenham over British and U.S. claims to the Oregon Territory. As author of the concept of "masterly inactivity," which argued that the territory would over time become part of the United States, Calhoun, to the frustration of the British minister, consistently postponed and stalled negotiations. Back in the Senate during the Oregon crisis of early 1846, when the possibility of war with Great Britain arose, Calhoun played a major role in smoothing the way for a compromise settlement. He spent the remainder of his life vigorously arguing over the disposition of western territorial acquisitions and slavery. His political philosophy later provided justification for the secession of the states that formed the Confederacy.

DONALD A. RAKESTRAW

See also Florida; Impressment; Jackson, Andrew; Oregon Question; Slave Trade and Slavery; Texas; War Hawks; War of 1812

FURTHER READING

Bartlett, Irving H. *John C. Calhoun: A Biography.* New York, 1993.

Lander, Ernest M., Jr. *Reluctant Imperialists: Calhoun, The South Carolinians, and the Mexican War.* Baton Rouge, La., 1980.
Niven, John. *John C. Calhoun and the Price of Union: A Biography.* Baton Rouge, La., 1988.
Wilson, Clyde N., ed. *The Papers of John C. Calhoun.* Columbia, S.C., 1993.
Wiltse, Charles M. *John C. Calhoun: Nationalist, 1782–1828.* Indianapolis, Ind., 1944.
———. *John C. Calhoun: Sectionalist, 1840–1850.* Indianapolis, Ind., 1951.

CALIFORNIA

Part of the territory acquired by the United States from Mexico under the 1848 Treaty of Guadalupe-Hidalgo ending the War with Mexico. U.S. ambitions to acquire the 158,000 square miles that became the state of California in 1850 derived from U.S. interest in the Pacific trade, accessible through the excellent ports of San Francisco and San Diego. Brief diplomatic efforts during the presidencies of Andrew Jackson and John Tyler to purchase or negotiate California away from Mexican control came to nothing. When the expansionist James K. Polk reached the White House in 1845, he gave high priority to the acquisition of California. The U.S. consul in the Mexican province, Thomas O. Larkin, soon reported the presence of nearly a thousand American settlers, many of them drawn there by his own accounts of the fortunes to be made in the region. Polk sent Senator John Slidell to Mexico in 1845 to deal with the bad relations produced by the recent U.S. annexation of Texas. Slidell's instructions included an offer to purchase California and New Mexico. The Mexican government, politically unable to entertain such a proposal and still remain in power, refused to receive the mission, further embittering relations with the United States. When the two nations declared war in 1846, U.S. agents and military officers on the scene in California—Larkin, Captain John C. Frémont, Commodore Robert F. Stockton, and Commodore John D. Sloat—assisted in the creation of the independent Bear Flag Republic and encouraged its annexation to the United States. Frémont had actually intruded into California and challenged Mexican authority before the war began. As part of the Treaty of Guadalupe-Hidalgo, Mexico officially relinquished California, which achieved statehood in one of the series of congressional bills known collectively as the Compromise of 1850. The territory's rapid progress to statehood was largely due to the discovery of gold at John A. Sutter's sawmill less than two weeks before the treaty was signed. Within a year the gold rush had raised California's population beyond the 60,000 necessary to apply for admission as a state.

PAUL R. GRASS

See also Frémont, John Charles; Larkin, Thomas Oliver; Mexico; Mexico, War with; Polk, James Knox; Slidell, John

FURTHER READING
Bean, Walton. *California: An Interpretive History*, 3rd ed. New York, 1982.
Graebner, Norman A. *Empire on the Pacific: A Study in American Continental Expansion.* New York, 1955.
Harlow, Neal. *California Conquered: War and Peace on the Pacific, 1846–1850.* Berkeley, Calif., 1982.
Pletcher, David M. *The Diplomacy of Annexation: Texas, Oregon, and the Mexican War.* Columbia, Mo., 1973.

CALVO CLAUSE

Derived from a treatise published in 1868 by Argentine diplomat and jurist Carlos Calvo, which advanced the concept of sovereign immunity. Under this principle a sovereign nation should be immune from external intervention in its internal affairs, whether or not there is political stability in that nation or a reliable national court system in operation. Calvo's main concern was that foreign governments not seek to use Latin American political instability and court decisions hostile to foreign nationals as justification for direct intervention to protect their nationals. Between 1899 and 1934 the U.S. government intervened repeatedly to take over the fiscal management of debtor states in the Caribbean and Central America, something quite unacceptable under the Calvo philosophy. Expanded investment and the negotiation of contracts between Latin American states and foreign nationals heightened concern that such foreign contracts would result in external political, legal, or military intervention to protect foreign interests. In the 1860s Europe appeared to pose the main danger to Latin American sovereignty; by the early twentieth century, the United States was the main source of concern. "Calvo Clauses" were included in the contracts that many Latin American governments negotiated with foreign nationals, prohibiting the latter from appealing beyond the courts of the nations in the event of disputes arising from those contracts, even in instances of alleged denial of justice. In the first half of the twentieth century, when debate over the principle of nonintervention was especially heated in inter-American relations, some Latin American states, specifically Venezuela and Peru, enshrined Calvo's principles in their constitutions. For its part, the U.S. Congress passed a number of measures intended to counter with protection for U.S. companies against expropriation and other threats to their overseas investments. One such measure, the Hickenlooper Amendment of 1962 cut off foreign aid to any country that expropriated or nationalized private U.S. holdings without appropriate compensation or due process.

STEPHEN J. RANDALL

See also Drago Doctrine; Foreign Aid; Latin America

FURTHER READING

Bemis, Samuel Flagg. *The Latin American Policy of the United States: An Historical Interpretation.* New York, 1943.

Eagleton, Clyde. *The Responsibility of States in International Law.* New York, 1928.

Finan, John J. "Argentina." In *Latin American Foreign Policies: An Analysis,* edited by Harold E. Davis and Larman C. Wilson. Baltimore, Md., 1975

Shea, Donald Richard. *The Calvo Clause.* Minneapolis, Minn., 1955.

CAMBODIA

A republic located in Southeastern Asia, bordered by Laos, Vietnam, the Gulf of Siam, and Thailand. Cambodia was officially known as the Khmer Republic from 1970 to 1975 and as Kampuchea from 1975 to 1989. U.S.-Cambodia relations from the 1950s to the 1990s were primarily defined by the Cold War struggle against communism. In 1953–1954, under the leadership of King Norodom Sihanouk, Cambodia gained independence from France, under whose control it had been since 1863, when France first established a formal protectorate. The United States established full diplomatic relations with Cambodia following the 1954 Geneva Conference, which ended the French Indochina War and granted independence to a Vietnam divided into a communist North and an anticommunist South. The administration of President Dwight D. Eisenhower sought to have Cambodia join the U.S.-sponsored Southeast Asia Treaty Organization (SEATO). Prince Sihanouk (he had stepped down from the throne to become prime minister) refused to join SEATO, proclaiming a neutral foreign policy, but in 1955 he signed a military aid agreement with the United States. The next year he also signed an aid agreement with the People's Republic of China (PRC), making Cambodia the first noncommunist state to receive aid from the PRC.

At the same time that the United States was officially providing Sihanouk with aid, it was also providing covert assistance through the Central Intelligence Agency (CIA) to Sihanouk's exiled opponent, Son Ngoc Thanh, as did Washington allies in Thailand and South Vietnam. A 1959 Pentagon study lamented that Cambodians "cannot be counted on to act in any positive way for the benefit of the United States." The study recommended that the United States not only encourage "the preoccupation of the individual with his personal rather that his social situation," but also foster "discouragement, defeatism and apathy." The study saw the elite, increasingly humiliated by Sihanouk, as susceptible to exploitation by the United States. Thai and South Vietnamese incursions, coup plots, and assassination attempts aggravated U.S.-Cambodian relations, as did the massive U.S. buildup in South Vietnam. In 1963 Cambodia canceled the U.S. military aid program, and in 1965 expelled the U.S. diplomatic mission. "We even kicked out the Asia Foundation," Sihanouk boasted to communist Khmer Rouge rebels, who nevertheless labeled him a secret agent of the United States. In July 1966 a Cambodian border village was twice attacked by U.S. aircraft from South Vietnam. The next year the United States rejected Sihanouk's call to recognize Cambodia's frontiers, claiming that Vietnamese communists were using Cambodian territory for sanctuary from U.S. attacks.

In 1969 the U.S. Air Force began secret B-52 bombardments of these sanctuaries. A year later Sihanouk was overthrown in a coup by General Lon Nol. Some evidence suggests U.S. personnel played a role in the overthrow. The Vietnam War now more fully spilled across the border, with both sides committing troops. The U.S. troops destroyed Vietnamese communist bases, but others were rebuilt deeper in Cambodia. The U.S. bombing escalated. In 1973 the United States withdrew its troops from Vietnam but switched its air arm to Cambodia. Half of the 540,000 tons of bombs dropped on Cambodia fell in 1973, before the August bombing halt imposed by Congress. Warfare continued, however, with the Khmer Rouge fighting and then toppling the pro-U.S. government. Paradoxically, the U.S. bombing and its huge damage and death toll—with an estimated 100,000 civilians killed—proved to be one of the key factors contributing to the Khmer Rouge victory. A U.S. Army report stated that "the civilian population fears U.S. air attacks far more than they do communist rocket attacks or scorched-earth tactics."

The rule of the Khmer Rouge was among the most brutal and vicious in history. An additional 1.7 million Cambodians perished at the hands of the Pol Pot regime by the time Vietnam forces invaded Kampuchea in 1979, forced Pol Pot into exile, and installed a new communist regime in his place. The United States did not recognize either regime and continued a policy of diplomatic isolation and opposition, including a trade embargo. In 1989 Vietnam withdrew its forces but civil war ensued again. A peace treaty was signed in 1991 under the auspices of the United Nations, a UN peacekeeping force was deployed in 1992, and UN-supervised elections were held in 1993. The elections created a coalition government and restored the monarchy under King Sihanouk, but the elections were boycotted by the Khmer Rouge, which also violated the cease-fire agreement. The United States was supportive of the UN efforts but played a limited role in them. In its direct bilateral relations the United States lifted the trade embargo and reestablished full diplomatic relations with the restored monarchy and coalition government under Sihanouk. Future stability remained very much in doubt, however, in particular because of the continued opposition and insurgency of the Khmer Rouge. Since 1975 approximately 200,000 Cambodian refugees have settled in the United States, mostly in California and along the eastern seaboard.

BEN KIERNAN

See also Southeast Asia Treaty Organization; Vietnam War

FURTHER READING

Chandler, David P. *The Tragedy of Cambodian History: Politics, War and Revolution Since 1945.* New Haven, Conn., 1991.

Kiernan, Ben. *How Pol Pot Came to Power: A History of Communism in Kampuchea, 1930–1975.* London, 1985.

———. *The Pol Pot Regime: Rice, Power, and Genocide in Cambodia under the Khmer Rouge, 1975–1979.* New Haven, Conn., 1996.

Kiernan, Ben, ed. *Genocide and Democracy in Cambodia: The Khmer Rouge, the United Nations and the International Community.* New Haven, Conn., 1993.

Ross, Russell R., ed. *Cambodia: A Country Study,* 3rd ed. Washington, D.C., 1990.

Shawcross, William. *Sideshow: Kissinger, Nixon and the Destruction of Cambodia.* New York, 1979.

CAMEROON

See Appendix 2

CAMP DAVID ACCORDS

Two agreements on the Middle East reached by Israeli prime minister Menachem Begin and Egyptian President Anwar Sadat at Camp David, the presidential retreat, on 17 September 1978 after thirteen days of negotiations mediated and personally directed by President Jimmy Carter. The first of the agreements concerned the future status of the West Bank of the Jordan River and Gaza Strip, which the Israelis had occupied since the Six Day War of June 1967. The accord provided for a transitional period of no more than five years during which Egypt, Israel, Jordan, and "representatives of the Palestinian people" would determine the final status of the territories based on the "full autonomy" and a "self–governing authority" for the inhabitants of the two areas. The second agreement provided for a peace treaty between Egypt and Israel within three months after the signing of the accords and for the phased withdrawal within three years of Israeli forces from the Sinai Peninsula and the dismantling of Israeli settlements and air bases in the Sinai. In return, Egypt agreed to establish normal diplomatic and commercial relations with Israel. Although the accords did not meet the specified time tables, they moved the peace process forward and are widely acknowledged as one of Carter's major diplomatic achievements as president.

BURTON I. KAUFMAN

See also Begin, Menachem; Carter, James Earl; Egypt; Israel; Middle East; Palestine (to 1948)

FURTHER READING

Quandt, William B. *Peace Process: American Diplomacy and the Arab-Israeli Conflict Since 1967.* Washington, D.C., 1993.

CANADA

The North American parliamentary state of ten provinces and two territories, lying directly north of the United States. "The Americans," a Canadian politician remarked in the House of Commons in Ottawa early in the 1960s, "are our best friends whether we like it or not." That splendid witticism sums up the relationship between Canada and the United States almost perfectly. The two nations have had their historic difficulties, but for almost two centuries since the War of 1812 they have maintained cordial relations out of sheer necessity. Whether the people of Canada and the United States like it or not, ties of self-interest, military defense, kinship, trade, finance, language, and culture have bound them inextricably together.

Early Relations

Before the fall of Quebec to Great Britain in 1759, relations between the French settlers of Canada and the British colonists in America were punctuated with frequent armed conflict. The British victory in the Seven Years' War (1756–1763) brought only a brief peace, and the American Revolution two decades later left a legacy of bitterness. Feelings of hatred and mistrust toward the new United States characterized the attitudes of some 40,000 loyalists (supporters of Great Britain during the American Revolution) who had migrated to the Canadian wilderness after the war. Many U.S. citizens, in turn, looked to complete their revolutionary victory by seizing what remained of British North America. Such attitudes guaranteed that the War of 1812, a by-product of the Napoleonic Wars in Europe, would be viciously fought in North America. The Treaty of Ghent ended the fighting in 1815, which from the Canadian point of view counted as a victory if only because Canada remained British. Exhausted by the struggle, Canada and the United States in 1817 made their first real gesture toward amity along their border by signing the Rush-Bagot Agreement, which regulated the presence of naval vessels on the Great Lakes; this accord was followed by the Convention of 1818, which resolved most of the outstanding border disputes.

The spread of U.S. democratic ideas into the Canadas helped provoke the Rebellions of 1837, which were crushed by forces loyal to the Crown; the United States proved unwilling to assist the Canadian rebels. The same reluc-

U.S. DIPLOMATIC REPRESENTATIVES TO CANADA

AMBASSADOR	PERIOD OF APPOINTMENT	ADMINISTRATION
William Phillips	1927–1929	Coolidge
Hanford MacNider	1930–1932	Hoover
Nathan William MacChesney[1]		
Warren Delano Robbins	1933–1935	Roosevelt
Norman Armour	1935–1938	Roosevelt
Daniel C. Roper	1939	Roosevelt
James H. R. Cromwell	1940	Roosevelt
Jay Pierrepont Moffat[2]	1940–1943	Roosevelt
Ray Atherton[3]	1943–1948	Roosevelt
		Truman
Laurence A. Steinhardt	1948–1950	Truman
Stanley Woodward	1950–1953	Truman
R. Douglas Stuart	1953–1956	Eisenhower
Livingston T. Merchant	1956–1958	Eisenhower
Richard B. Wigglesworth	1958–1960	Eisenhower
Livingston T. Merchant	1961–1962	Eisenhower
		Kennedy
W. Walton Butterworth	1962–1968	Kennedy
		Johnson
Harold Francis Linder	1968–1969	Johnson
Adolph W. Schmidt	1969–1974	Nixon
William J. Porter	1974–1975	Ford
Thomas O. Enders	1975–1979	Ford
		Carter
Kenneth M. Curtis	1979–1981	Carter
Paul Heron Robinson, Jr.	1981–1985	Reagan
Thomas Michael Tolliver Niles	1985–1989	Reagan
Edward N. Ney	1989	Bush
Peter Teeley	1989–1993	Bush
James J. Blanchard	1993–	Clinton

[1]Not commissioned; nomination not confirmed by the Senate.
[2] Accredited also to Luxembourg; resident at Ottawa.
[3]Accredited also to Denamrk and Luxembourg; resident at Ottawa.

Sources: *Principal Officers of the Department of State and United States Chiefs of Missions*. ©1991 by Office of the Historian, Bureau of Public Affairs, Washington, D.C.; *The U.S. Government Manual*, Annual. Washington, D.C.

tance to intervene militarily was apparent after the American Civil War, when Irish-American veterans, calling themselves Fenians, repeatedly launched minor attacks across the Canadian border. This threat from the south helped push the colonies of Nova Scotia, New Brunswick, Ontario, and Quebec to unite in 1867 as the Dominion of Canada. The movement for confederation was also hastened by the U.S. abrogation of the Elgin-Marcy Reciprocity Treaty of 1854, a tariff package that had brought substantial prosperity to Canada. Angered by British support for the Confederacy and pressed by protectionist elements, the U.S. Congress had allowed the treaty to lapse after a decade.

The new dominion was still an integral part of the British empire, with London retaining power over Canada's foreign relations. During the next sixty years, Canadian governments gradually sought and won increasing control over external relations. There were notable milestones in this evolution. When Great Britain and the United States settled their differences (stemming from the American Civil War) in the Treaty of Washington (1871), the Canadian prime minister, Sir John A. Macdonald, participated as a member of the British delegation. To his chagrin, Canadian aims were brushed aside in the rush to settle the two main parties' concerns, although as a result of the negotiations the United States did at last formally recognize the existence of Canada. Many Canadians nonetheless drew the appropriate lessons about the dangers of relying on British diplomacy. This skepticism was reinforced when a tribunal set up by Great Britain and the United States to resolve the disputes over Canada's boundary with Alaska decided in 1903 in favor of the United States, the sole British judge siding with the United States and against Canada. The Canadian response, in part, was to press for the creation of the first of what would eventually become a web of international agencies with Washington. The establishment of the International Joint Commission in 1909 was a way of amicably resolving boundary-water disputes. Also that year the Department of External Affairs, Canada's first tentative move onto the world stage, took form in Ottawa. Great Britain did not participate when the Liberal government of Sir Wilfrid Laurier in 1911 negotiated a new reciprocal trade agreement with Washington; the Canadian electorate, however, stirred by anti-U.S. rhetoric, imperial patriotism, and a massive scare campaign mounted by Canadian industrialists, rejected the Liberals and reciprocity. Robert L. Borden's Conservatives, elected under the banner "No Truck or Trade with the Yankees," tried to turn their back on the United States.

The Impact of World War

Events confounded the Conservatives when the coming of world war in 1914 forced Canada's burgeoning industries to import more from the south. British investment dried up, and Canadian governments and businesses turned for the first time to the New York market for funding. Then the U.S. entry into the war in April 1917 accelerated the movement toward direct relations. The necessity to coordinate the supply of scarce commodities and the need to ration shortages equitably obliged a direct Canadian presence in Washington. Imperial unity still forbade setting up an embassy, but a Canadian war mission took up residence to deal directly with departments of the U.S. government, striving to win Canada consideration as the equivalent of a U.S. region when supplies such as iron and coal were allocated. There was substantial U.S.-Canadian naval cooperation in Atlantic waters, and the United States also drew on Canadian air training facilities. Although after the war military planners in each country drew up contingency plans for action against the other, the unlikelihood of resorting to those plans was apparent to all.

Unlike the United States, Canada in 1919 eagerly joined the League of Nations, seeing membership in its own right as a milestone on the road to diplomatic independence. Four years later, Canada and the United States signed a treaty regulating the Pacific halibut fishery, the first such agreement negotiated and signed independently by Canada. Then, in 1927, the two countries put the cap on their relations by exchanging diplomatic representatives and for the first time dealt with each other without any intermediation of Great Britain. The British government was not pleased but could do nothing; in any case, in 1931 the Statute of Westminster confirmed that Canada, while still a member of the British Commonwealth and still owing allegiance to the British monarchy, was nonetheless wholly responsible for its own foreign policy.

With intermittent hiccups, relations between Canada and the United States continued to grow closer. One such interruption was the Ottawa Agreements of 1932, which bound Canada into a web of imperial trade preferences that threatened U.S. markets in Canada (and elsewhere), already hard hit by the Great Depression. This case was an aberration, however, and the return to power of the Liberals under William Lyon Mackenzie King in October 1935 led to major trade agreements in 1935 and 1938, the first since 1854, which began the process of chipping away at the preferential structure erected just a few years earlier. Then, faced with the rise of fascism in Europe and Asia, President Franklin D. Roosevelt in 1938 pledged to come to Canada's aid in the event of an attack on Canadian territory, a pledge that Canada promptly reciprocated. The outbreak of World War II forced further cooperation in defense and economic policy. In August 1940, just after the fall of France, Prime Minister King and President Roosevelt met at Ogdensburg, New York, and created the Permanent Joint Board on Defense and set defense talks in motion. Canada had been forced by Great Britain's military weakness to seek protection under the wing of the United States, a historic switch. Joint war plans soon followed for both the Atlantic and Pacific coasts. The next year, when Canada's reserves of U.S. dollars were running dry and when Roosevelt's Lend-Lease bill, offering to loan Great Britain military supplies, posed a threat to British purchases in Canada, the two leaders met at the president's home in Hyde Park, New York, and effectively integrated their economies for war purposes. Industrial components intended for inclusion in war matériel made in Canada for British use were to be charged to the United Kingdom's Lend-Lease account, thus bolstering Canada's dollar holdings. Roosevelt agreed, moreover, that the United States would increases defense purchases in Canada. The two measures spared Canada a foreign exchange crisis and obviated any necessity to accept Lend-Lease.

After the attack on Pearl Harbor in December 1941 and the resultant U.S. entry into World War II, the United States, fearful of Japanese power, won quick Canadian consent to build the Alaska Highway through the Northwest Territories, as well as pipelines, air bases, and weather stations in the north. Ottawa seemed oblivious to any threats to its sovereignty until a British diplomat pointed out that there was literally no official Canadian presence in the far north. An alarmed Canadian government appointed a military proconsul to show the flag in 1943 and at last began to pay close attention. At war's end Canada bought back every U.S. installation at full price to ensure that there was no potential threat to its sovereignty.

The Cold War Era and Beyond

The coming of the Cold War renewed Canadian reliance on the United States for defense and economic help. A shortage of U.S. dollar reserves in late 1947 led to an abortive free-trade agreement, but a defense agreement in 1947 and Canadian adhesion to the North Atlantic Treaty in 1949 were indications that the two countries saw eye to eye on the important issues posed by the potential for aggression from the Soviet Union. Canada participated in the Korean War with a brigade of infantry, a number of ships, and substantial air transport support. Fear of direct Soviet attack led to the joint construction of the Distant Early Warning (DEW) line across the Canadian north in the late 1950s. By 1957 it seemed natural to combine the air defenses of the two countries in the North American Air Defense Agreement with a joint command based in Colorado Springs and to establish the Defense Production Sharing Agreement that increased Canadian access to the lucrative U.S. defense market. Difficulties soon arose, however, over nuclear weapons installations in Canada, as Prime Minister John G. Diefenbaker, who opposed them, and President John F. Kennedy clashed. The resulting Canadian election of 1963, the first since 1911 that was primarily fought over U.S.-Canadian relations, saw the Liberals—and nuclear weapons—win.

By this time, however, U.S. foreign investment had become another flash point. Until just after World War I, Great Britain had been the largest investor in Canada, but a war-weakened Great Britain was unable to maintain the pace, and by the early 1920s U.S. investment in Canada exceeded that of Great Britain. By 1939 fully 60 percent of foreign investment in Canada was from the United States, a percentage that continued to rise. By the mid-1950s this had begun to alarm Canadians, and Diefenbaker capitalized on the concerns. Liberals also expressed concern, however, and Lester Pearson's Liberal government in the mid-1960s introduced several measures to curtail the flow of funds, actions that stirred sharp responses in Washington and on Wall Street. The measures were duly watered down, but the disputes demonstrated that Canadian nationalism could be testy. The Vietnam War exacerbated matters further as Canada, claiming that its membership on the International Control Commission futilely monitoring the 1954 Geneva Agreements obviated participation in the conflict, occasionally criticized U.S. policy. In the years after 1945 Ottawa almost always placed greater value on the United Nations than did Washington. Canadian defense forces became highly experienced specialists in UN peacekeeping operations, serving throughout the world in crises where Canada's role as a middle power, not one of the heavy-footed giants, made its presence useful.

Further signs of the growing differences appeared under Pierre Trudeau, the Liberal prime minister from 1968 to 1984. Trudeau had little use for the Cold War rhetoric that emanated from the administration of President Richard Nixon. He cut Canadian troop strength in the North Atlantic Treaty Organization (NATO) by half, recognized the People's Republic of China, and signed a treaty of consultation with Moscow. Although he later did agree to allow the testing of U.S. cruise missiles over Canada, he set out on a major peace initiative in late 1983 with the intention of halting the drift toward war that, in his view, had been produced by the accession to the presidency of Ronald Reagan and the shooting down of a Korean airliner (KAL-007) by Soviet interceptors in 1983. Trudeau's initiative became wildly popular in Canada but much less so in Washington. Relations at the highest levels became cool.

Elected in 1984, the Progressive Conservative prime minister Brian Mulroney set out to rectify matters. His object was "super" relations with the United States, and he and Presidents Reagan and George Bush brought the two nations closer together. Canadian efforts in defense were increased, troop strength in NATO briefly was enhanced, and Mulroney and Reagan began a push for a major free trade agreement in 1985. This effort culminated in success in 1988, and the agreement, a major one with genuine implications for tariffs, investment, and U.S. access to Canadian energy resources, won the Canadian public's support in the general election of 1988. This agreement was followed up four years later with the North American Free Trade Agreement (NAFTA), which added Mexico to the arrangement. In 1991 Mulroney also cautiously aligned Canada with the United States in the Gulf War, dispatching ships and fighter aircraft to serve alongside his friends, but Mulroney's close relationship with the United States and the failure of the free trade agreement to produce the promised prosperity in Canada stirred bitter resentment. When he left office in 1993, Mulroney was as unpopular as any Canadian leader had ever been. What seemed clear, however, was that his trade agreement has become irreversible; for better or for worse Canada and the United States moved in economic lockstep.

Certainly this seemed to be so when the Liberal party regained power in 1993 under the leadership of Jean

Chrétien. Although the Liberals had campaigned on a pledge to renegotiate the continental free trade agreement, they quickly settled for cosmetic changes that altered nothing. Where Chrétien was different, however, was in the manner in which he conducted relations with the United States. Instead of actively seeking meetings with President Bill Clinton and playing up the closeness of the link, Chrétien hung back, ensuring that Canadian interests, not American, remained paramount in his and the public's mind. The differences were ones of atmosphere, but they were important, and Chrétien's standing in the polls remained high. Still, the effects of the free trade agreements, ever more profound in enhanced trading and in creating a continental market, remained a monument to Mulroney's achievement in forging the agreements.

J. L. GRANATSTEIN

See also Alaska Boundary Dispute; American Revolution; Distant Early Warning (DEW) Line; Fenians; Ghent, Treaty of; Great Britain; International Joint Commission; King, William Lyon Mackenzie; Lend-Lease; Loyalists; Macdonald, John Alexander; North American Free Trade Agreement; Rush-Bagot Agreement; Trudeau, Pierre Elliott; United Nations; War of 1812

FURTHER READING

Bothwell, Robert. *Canada and the United States: The Politics of Partnership.* Toronto, 1992.
Doran, Charles F. *Forgotten Partnership: U.S.-Canada Relations Today.* Baltimore, 1984.
Doran, Charles F., and John H. Sigler, eds. *Canada and the United States: Enduring Friendship, Persistent Stress.* Englewood Cliffs, N.J., 1985.
Granatstein, J. L. "When Push Came to Shove." In *Kennedy's Quest for Victory: American Foreign Policy, 1961–1963,* edited by Thomas G. Paterson. New York, 1989.
Granatstein, J. L., and Norman Hillmer. *For Better or for Worse: Canada and the United States to the 1990s.* Toronto, 1991.
Lamont, Lansing, and J. Duncan Edmonds, eds. *Friends So Different: Essays on Canada and the United States in the 1980s.* Ottawa, 1989.
Lipset, Seymour Martin. *Continental Divide: The Values and Institutions of the United States and Canada.* New York, 1990.
Muirhead, B. W. *The Development of Postwar Canadian Trade Policy: The Failure of the Anglo-American Option.* Buffalo, N.Y., 1992.
Smith, Denis. *Diplomacy of Fear: Canada and the Cold War 1941–1948.* Toronto, 1988.
Stairs, Denis. *The Diplomacy of Constraint: Canada, the Korean War, and the United States.* Buffalo, N.Y., 1974.
Stuart, Reginald C. *United States Expansionism and British North America, 1775–1871.* Chapel Hill, N.C., 1988.

CANNING, GEORGE

(*b.* 11 April 1770; *d.* 8 August 1827)

Eminent British statesman and twice foreign secretary (1807–1809; 1822–1827): first, during a period of Anglo-American tensions before the War of 1812; and again, more prominently, during the years of James Monroe's presidency. Canning was elected to the House of Commons in 1793 after aligning himself with William Pitt and other opponents of the French Revolution. As foreign secretary in 1809 he instructed David Erskine, British minister in Washington, to negotiate U.S. claims against Great Britain resulting from the *Chesapeake-Leopard* Affair. Canning also offered to repeal the Orders in Council, which restricted shipping during the Napoleonic Wars by establishing a blockade of the French coast and by forcing ships to stop in Great Britain to pay taxes on cargo before entering French ports. In return, Canning demanded that U.S. ports admit British, but not French, ships during the duration of the Anglo-French conflict. Further, the Royal Navy would be free to seize American vessels that violated the U.S. Nonintercourse Act of 1809 by trading with France. Recognizing the futility of such stipulations, Erskine abandoned them and promised that the Orders in Council would be canceled on 10 June 1809. Although Congress then reopened trade with Great Britain, Canning denounced Erskine's agreement, recalled him, and named an unpopular replacement, Francis James Jackson. U.S. officials thereafter distrusted Canning. He left office later in 1809 after quarreling with the War Minister, Viscount Castlereagh. Canning subsequently served as president of the Board of Control for India (1816–1820).

Although George IV opposed Canning's return to the cabinet, advisers convinced the monarch to reconsider. Canning succeeded Castlereagh as foreign secretary in 1822, following the latter's suicide, and he sought to maintain improved relations with the United States and to prevent European intervention in rebellious Spanish America. He also disapproved of Great Britain's continued membership in the Quadruple Alliance, fearing that England would be drawn into continental entanglements growing out of the French invasion of Spain and the restoration of Ferdinand VII. In March 1823 Canning warned France against intervening in the former Spanish colonies in America in an effort to restore them to Spain. As independent Latin American republics opened their ports to British trade, Canning judged that a policy of nonintervention would bring Great Britain vast commercial benefits. The widening breach between England and the conservative European powers encouraged Canning to find a new ally; he chose the United States.

In August 1823 Canning suggested a joint Anglo-American declaration against European interference in Latin America and any attempts to acquire new territory. Secretary of State John Quincy Adams, downplaying the European threat, advised President James Monroe against accepting the offer. Meanwhile, Canning secured a pledge on 9 October 1823 from Prince Auguste-Jules de Polignac, the French minister in London, not to intervene in the Spanish colonies. The government in Washington, however, did not learn of the Polignac Memorandum. The Monroe administration rejected Canning's proposal, and the president announced in his message to Congress of 2 December 1823 his own warning against European intervention in Latin America and against future attempts to colonize in the New World. Canning rebounded from this diplomatic failure by informing the Latin American nations of the Polignac Memorandum and of his role in preventing French meddling in the region. In 1826, in justifying his American policy in the House of Commons, Canning famously claimed that he had "called the New World into existence to redress the balance of the Old." He remained in office as foreign secretary until 1827, when, upon Lord Liverpool's death, he became prime minister for a mere one hundred days until his own death in August.

CAROL A. JACKSON

See also Castlereagh, Second Viscount; Chesapeake-Leopard Affair; Great Britain; Monroe Doctrine; Napoleonic Wars; Orders in Council; Quadruple Alliance; War of 1812

FURTHER READING

Dixon, Peter. *Canning: Politician and Statesman.* London, 1976.
Hinde, Wendy. *George Canning.* New York, 1973.
Kaufmann, William W. *British Policy and the Independence of Latin America, 1804–1828.* New Haven, Conn., 1951.
Perkins, Bradford. *Prologue to War: England and the United States, 1805–1812.* Berkeley, Calif., 1961.
———. *Castlereagh and Adams: England and the United States, 1812–1823.* Berkeley, Calif., 1964.

CAPE VERDE

See Appendix 2

CARIBBEAN BASIN INITIATIVE

Authorized by amendments to the Caribbean Basin Economic Recovery Act of 1983, the Caribbean Basin Initiative (CBI) provided permanent tariff-free and reduced-tariff entry into the United States for most products shipped by the twenty-four Caribbean Basin countries certified in 1992 as being eligible for participation in the program. In 1982, amidst political turmoil in some Central American states and stagnant growth in most countries in the Caribbean, President Ronald Reagan launched the CBI to strengthen the economies of the region against further emergence of insurgencies, civil wars, and Marxist governments. As later approved by Congress, the initiative consisted of increased U.S. foreign assistance and preferential trade access to the U.S. market. Preferential market access

was extended by the CBI on a unilateral basis (no reciprocal action was required). The initiative was designed specifically to increase the foreign exchange-earning capacities of these countries, mainly by encouraging the growth of nontraditional export industries. During 1993 goods worth about $1.9 billion, about 19 percent of total U.S. imports from participating countries, entered duty free under the CBI. The precise impact of the CBI in generating exports from the Caribbean countries is impossible to assess because many of these goods would be eligible for duty-free status under other U.S. preferential market access programs. One of the principal criticisms of the CBI was its exclusion from duty-free status of several labor-intensive products that could be efficiently manufactured in the Caribbean basin, but which had strong U.S. domestic lobbies, such as textiles, apparel, and certain footwear products. Critics also argued that, at best, the CBI only offset the economic damage of continuing restrictions (quotas) on U.S. imports of sugar from these countries. Furthermore, the long-term net value of the market access provisions of the CBI were called into question by the implementation of the North American Free Trade Agreement (NAFTA), which aroused concern among Caribbean countries that U.S. trade and foreign investment would be diverted from their region to Mexico by the latter's free-trade status with the United States.

STEPHEN D. COHEN

See also Generalized System of Preferences; International Trade and Commerce North American Free Trade Agreement

FURTHER READING

Bakan, Abigail B., David Cox, and Colin Cox. *Imperial Power and Regional Trade: The Caribbean Basin Initiative.* Waterloo, Ontario, 1993.
U.S. Congress, House Ways and Means Committee. *Review of the Impact and Effectiveness of the Caribbean Basin Initiative.* Washington, D.C., 1986.
U.S. International Trade Commission. *Impact of the Caribbean Basin Economic Recovery Act on U.S. Industries and Consumers.* Report No. 2675. Washington, D.C. 1993.

CARIBBEAN LEGION

A loosely organized series of military operations and plots aimed against Caribbean dictators, particularly during the period from 1947 to 1950. After World War II, figures such as President Juan José Arévalo of Guatemala (1944–1950) and President Carlos Prío Socarrás of Cuba (1948–1952), and heads of revolutionary juntas such as Rómulo Betancourt of Venezuela (1945–1948) and José Figueres of Costa Rica (1948–1949) argued that the liberal principles enunciated in the Atlantic Charter and the Four Freedoms should be established everywhere in Latin America.

These leaders gave military support to exiles and expatriates dedicated to overthrowing the dictatorships of Rafael Trujillo in the Dominican Republic and the Somoza family in Nicaragua. The dictators, however, handily routed these feckless attacks. By the early 1950s leaders such as Betancourt and Prío Socarrás had themselves been overthrown. The United States opposed this attempted interventionism: in the early Cold War years, it favored security and stability in the Caribbean, fearing that revolutionary turmoil might provide openings for communists.

STEPHEN G. RABE

See also Atlantic Charter; Betancourt, Rómulo; Cold War; Cuba; Dominican Republic; Latin America; Nicaragua

FURTHER READING

Ameringer, Charles D. *The Caribbean Legion: Patriots, Politicians, Soldiers of Fortune, 1946–1950*. University Park, Pa., 1974.

Langley, Lester D. *The United States and the Caribbean in the Twentieth Century*, rev. ed. Athens, Ga., 1985.

Mecham, J. Lloyd. *The United States and Inter-American Security, 1889–1960*. Austin, Tex., 1961.

CARLUCCI, FRANK CHARLES III
(*b.* 18 October 1930)

Government official and secretary of defense (1988–1989). Carlucci was born in Scranton, Pennsylvania, and educated at Princeton and Harvard universities. He joined the Foreign Service in 1956 and was stationed in Africa from 1957 to 1965. His most challenging assignment took place in the former Belgian Congo during its turbulent transition, from 1960 to 1962, to becoming the independent nation of Zaire. Able and unflappable in the face of crisis, Carlucci established himself among his fellow Foreign Service professionals. He next served as deputy and, from 1969 to 1970, as director of the Office of Economic Opportunity, where he exhibited his management skills, political acumen, and ability to accommodate differing policy goals. In 1971 he moved to the Office of Management and Budget, where he formed a close relationship with its director, Caspar Weinberger. Carlucci moderated another political crisis when he was appointed ambassador to Portugal (1975–1978). He maintained friendly relations with the left-of-center Lisbon government despite Secretary of State Henry Kissinger's anger over its electoral victory. He next served as deputy director of the Central Intelligence Agency from 1978 to 1981; and when Weinberger was appointed secretary of defense in 1981, Carlucci became deputy secretary to help manage the massive arms buildup of President Ronald Reagan's administration. He returned to the private sector in 1982. In January 1987, responding to the revelations of the Iran-Contra scandal, President Reagan appointed Carlucci national security adviser to restore the reputation of the National Security Council and to redirect the disorderly policy that had resulted. Carlucci became secretary of defense the following year, following Weinberger's resignation. Despite his support of the earlier arms buildup, Carlucci found himself faced with congressional concern over the size of the budget. His brief term of office was marked by the cancellation of some defense programs and a reduction in manpower. Throughout his career Carlucci was a supporter and advocate of a strong defense posture and large national security budget. In 1989 he resigned and became vice chairman of the Carlyle Group, an international investment house.

ANNA K. NELSON

See also Africa; Iran-Contra Affair; Portugal; Reagan, Ronald Wilson; Weinberger, Caspar Willard; Zaire

FURTHER READING

Cannon, Lou. *President Reagan: The Role of a Lifetime*. New York, 1991.

Kalb, Madeleine G. *The Congo Cables: The Cold War in Africa from Eisenhower to Kennedy*. New York, 1982.

Wirls, Daniel. *Build Up: The Politics of Defense in the Reagan Era*. Ithaca, N.Y., 1992.

CARNEGIE, ANDREW
(*b.* 25 November 1835; *d.* 11 August 1919)

Industrialist and wealthy philanthropist whose interests included creating institutions to promote world peace. Born in Dunfermline, Scotland, Carnegie was the son of an impoverished handloom weaver who emigrated to the United States with his family in 1848 and settled near Pittsburgh. Carnegie labored in a cotton mill and worked as a telegraph operator and messenger until 1853, when he became the personal secretary of Thomas A. Scott, a superintendent of the Pennsylvania Railroad Company. Six years later Carnegie rose to the position of superintendent of the railroad's western division. After serving in the Department of War during the Civil War, Carnegie made shrewd investments and turned his attention to the steel industry, building what became the Carnegie Steel Company in 1889. In the aftermath of the Spanish-American-Cuban-Filipino War, he emerged as an ardent anti-imperialist. Carnegie sold his highly prosperous but labor-troubled company to the U.S. Steel Corporation in 1901 for $250 million and devoted his remaining years to extensive philanthropic endeavors, in accordance with his "gospel of wealth" and sense of obligation to human betterment.

Among his varied charitable works were the construction of numerous public libraries in the United States, Great Britain, and other English-speaking countries, and the creation of the Carnegie Institute for the Advancement of Teaching (1905) and the Carnegie Corporation for the

Advancement of Civilization (1911). Carnegie maintained an extensive correspondence with educators, diplomats, and political leaders in the United States and abroad. In sometimes naive efforts to further world peace, he established the Simplified Spelling Board (1903) to enhance international communication, the Hero Fund (1904) to reward valiant deeds by people other than uniformed soldiers, the Church Peace Foundation (1914) to involve religious leaders in peace efforts, and the Carnegie Endowment for International Peace (1910) to examine world affairs and advance the notion of peace through international law arbitration. Carnegie also provided the funding for three "temples of peace": the Palace of Peace (1913) at The Hague in the Netherlands; the Pan American Union Building in Washington, D.C.; and the Central American Court of Justice (1910) in Cartago, Costa Rica. Carnegie was horrified by the outbreak of World War I in 1914 and, with the approval of Secretary of State William Jennings Bryan, wrote a personal letter to German Emperor William (Wilhelm) II urging peace. Carnegie opposed those leaders such as Theodore Roosevelt who advocated preparations for war and a buildup of the U.S. military; but he eventually supported the U.S. entry into the war, writing to President Woodrow Wilson in 1917 that "Germany is beyond reason." During the war years Carnegie suffered from poor health, which ended his active participation in public affairs.

MICHAEL J. DEVINE

See also Carnegie Endowment for International Peace; Pan-Americanism; Peace Movements and Societies to 1914

FURTHER READING

Patterson, David S. "Andrew Carnegie's Quest for World Peace," *Proceedings of the American Philosophical Society* 114 (1970): 5, 371–383.

Wall, Joseph F. *Andrew Carnegie*. Pittsburgh, Pa., 1989.

CARNEGIE ENDOWMENT FOR INTERNATIONAL PEACE

A tax-exempt nongovernmental institution that seeks to inform debate on central international issues. Founded by Andrew Carnegie in 1910, the endowment was the first major U.S. foundation devoted to world affairs. Through the years, it has served as a financially and ideologically independent forum for foreign policy analysis and debate, adjusting its focus and methods to reflect the changing world. Andrew Carnegie believed that war could be eliminated by strengthening international laws and organizations, and the endowment's initial efforts were devoted to that end, though expectations were shattered by World War I. In the interwar period, the endowment promoted international conciliation, financed

reconstruction projects, founded the Academy of International Law at The Hague, and published the unprecedented twenty-two volume series *Classics of International Law* (1911–1950) and the seminal *Economic and Social History of the World War* (1924). Following World War II, endowment programs highlighted the new United Nations and the future of the international legal system; the endowment also published the journal *International Conciliation*. Throughout the 1970s and 1980s the endowment focused on contributing to the public debate on foreign policy, covering numerous subjects from arms control and regional conflicts to the impact of global interdependence. In the post–Cold War period, the endowment has concentrated on such subjects as worldwide migration; adapting European security structures; U.S. relations with Russia, Ukraine, and Japan; conflict in the Balkans; the building of a Pacific Community; democracy assistance; economic policy challenges in Latin America; and the use of military force.

The endowment conducts all activities from its headquarters in Washington and its pioneering Center for Russian and Eurasian Programs, which opened in Moscow in 1993. The Moscow center promotes intellectual collaboration among scholars and specialists in the United States, Russia, and other successor states of the Soviet Union; together with Carnegie's Russian and Eurasian Program in Washington, the center explores and encourages debate on issues ranging from the politics of transition to nuclear nonproliferation. Other recent endowment contributions to international institution-building include Carnegie's catalytic role in developing a new nongovernmental organization, the International Crisis Group, established in 1995 to strengthen and speed international response to manmade crises.

Carnegie senior associates have diverse professional backgrounds and are selected purely on the substance of their intellectual contributions. Carnegie personnel are encouraged to express their views to expert and general audiences through writing, public and media appearances, congressional testimony, and participation in conferences. The endowment publishes the quarterly journal *Foreign Policy*. It also publishes books and policy studies written by its associates and issues reports of commissions or study groups convened under its auspices. Recent publications include *The Other Balkan Wars: A 1913 Carnegie Endowment Inquiry in Retrospect*, with a new introduction and reflections on the conflict by George F. Kennan (1993); *Intervention: The Use of American Military Force in the Post-Cold War World,* by Richard Haass (1994); and *The New Tug-of-War: Congress, the Executive, and National Security After the Cold War*, by Jeremy D. Rosner (1995).

MORTON I. ABRAMOWITZ

See also Carnegie, Andrew; International Law; Think Tanks

CAROLINE AFFAIR

(29 December 1837)

An incident that could have led to war between the United States and Great Britain. Canadian and British volunteers, provoked by the participation of some U.S. citizens in the Lower Canadian rebellion, crossed the Niagara River and attacked the U.S.-owned rebel supply steamboat *Caroline* at Fort Schlosser, New York, near Buffalo. The passengers and crew were driven ashore and the steamer towed into the Niagara River, set afire, and released to the current. It sank above the falls. After the raid one U.S. citizen, Amos Durfee, was found dead on the Fort Schlosser wharf.

The result was a diplomatic crisis between the United States and Great Britain, further aggravated when New York State authorities arrested a Canadian, Alexander McLeod, for the murder of Durfee. Despite a threat of war from Britain if McLeod were executed and the strenuous efforts of Secretary of State Daniel Webster to obtain his release, New York tried McLeod in 1841. He was acquitted.

During the Webster-Ashburton negotiations of 1842, which aimed at a settlement of outstanding Anglo-American differences, Webster formulated the *Caroline* doctrine, holding that to justify a preemptive attack on another nation, the aggressor had to prove "a necessity of self-defense, instant, overwhelming, leaving no choice of means, and no moment of deliberation." Also in 1842, Congress passed the Remedial Justice Act, which empowered the federal government to order the release of a defendant held by a state when the case involved the foreign relations of the United States.

KENNETH R. STEVENS

See also Canada; Webster-Ashburton Treaty

FURTHER READING

Stevens, Kenneth R. *Border Diplomacy: The Caroline and McLeod Affairs in Anglo-American-Canadian Relations, 1837–1842.* Tuscaloosa, Ala., 1989.
Stuart, Reginald C. *United States Expansionism and British North America, 1775–1871.* Chapel Hill, N.C., 1988.

CARR, WILBUR JOHN

(*b.* 31 October 1870; *d.* 26 June 1942)

Department of State official who played the decisive role in developing a professional U.S. diplomatic corps, hence removing it from the influence of domestic politics. Carr graduated from the Commercial College of the University of Kentucky (1889), Georgetown University (LL.B., 1894), and Columbian University (later George Washington University; LL.M., 1899). In 1892 he began a forty-seven-year career in the Department of State as a clerk.

He was successively chief of the department's Consular Bureau, in which capacity he directed 300 consular posts (1902–1907); chief clerk of the department, with the additional responsibility of directing the Consular Service (1909–1924); assistant secretary of state, with responsibility for the general administration of the department, including budget and personnel (1927–1937); and minister to Czechoslovakia (1937–1939) during the crises that led to World War II.

In his efforts to bring professionalism to the foreign services Carr was instrumental in achieving passage of the Lodge Act of 5 April 1906, which placed Consular Service officers on regular salaries and thereby ended the system by which consuls kept fees for services rendered; President Theodore Roosevelt's executive order of 27 June 1906, which removed presidential patronage rights by introducing consular appointments based on departmental expansion, promotions by merit, and competitive examinations; the Reclassification Act of 5 February 1915, which provided for payment of officers by rank not post; and the Moses-Linthicum Act of 23 February 1931, which created the Division of Foreign Service Personnel, first chaired by Carr himself. Most important, Carr personally drafted the Rogers Act of 24 May 1924, which united the Consular and Diplomatic services into the Foreign Service. Carr also helped frame the final provisions of the quota system incorporated in the Immigration Act of 1924, and he gave consular officials overseas authority over the issuance of all visas. Carr strongly defended consular interests within the department, seeing their role as promoters of commerce as essential to U.S. prosperity. He nonetheless often found himself stymied by the superior influence of old-line diplomatic personnel, even after the passage of the Rogers Act.

JUSTUS D. DOENECKE

See also Czech Republic; Foreign Service; Immigration; Rogers Act; State, U.S. Department of

FURTHER READING

Crane, Catherine. *Mr. Carr of State: Forty-Seven Years in the Department of State.* New York, 1960.
Heinrichs, Waldo H., Jr. "Bureaucracy and Professionalism in the Development of American Career Diplomacy." In *Twentieth Century American Foreign Policy*, edited by John Braeman, Robert H. Bremner, and David Brody. Columbus, Ohio, 1971.
Schulzinger, Robert D. *The Making of the Diplomatic Mind: The Training, Outlook, and Style of United States Foreign Service Officers, 1908-1931.* Middletown, Conn., 1975.

CARTER, JAMES EARL

(*b.* 1 October 1924)

President of the United States (1977–1981) who emphasized human rights, advanced the Middle East peace process, and endured the Iranian hostage crisis. Born in Plains, Georgia, Jimmy Carter graduated from high school in 1941. He spent the next two years at Georgia Southwestern College and the Georgia Institute of Technology before being admitted to the U.S. Naval Academy at Annapolis in 1943. In 1946, he graduated from the Academy and married Rosalyn Smith, also from Plains. He resigned from the Navy and returned to Plains in 1953 following the death of his father. A successful businessman and community leader, he was elected in 1962 to the Georgia Senate as a Democrat. After an unsuccessful bid for governor in 1966, he ran a second time in 1970 and won overwhelmingly.

Carter decided to run for president in 1976 after establishing a reputation in Georgia as a reform leader and a moderate on racial issues. Virtually unknown outside Georgia, he was able to win the Democratic nomination and then to defeat his Republican opponent, President Gerald Ford, by running as a centrist candidate. Although the election focused on domestic matters rather than on foreign policy, the deeply religious Carter made support for human rights abroad an important issue in his campaign. He was able to take advantage of a major mistake by Ford when, during a televised debate, the president said that Eastern Europe was not dominated by the Soviet Union. Although Ford later tried to amend that statement, polls showed that it hurt him badly with the electorate. In November 1976, Carter won a narrow victory over Ford and Congressman John Anderson of Illinois, who ran as an Independent.

As president, Carter intended to take charge of his own foreign policy. His secretary of state, former Deputy Secretary of Defense Cyrus Vance, would be largely responsible for administering the Department of State and conducting the nation's business abroad. But the president, assisted by his national security adviser, former Columbia University professor Zbigniew Brzezinski, would be responsible for formulating foreign policy. Diplomacy would be conducted more openly than during the administrations of Richard Nixon and Gerald Ford. More attention also would be paid to Western Europe than under previous administrations, and there would be less emphasis on the Cold War struggle with the Soviet Union and more emphasis on Third World issues. Carter's appointment of the African American civil rights leader, Georgia Member of Congress Andrew Young, as ambassador to the United Nations signaled this intention. Although the administration would seek to continue a policy of détente with Moscow, it would not do so at the expense of its strong commitment to promoting human rights.

Almost immediately, Carter's conduct of foreign policy ran into trouble. In March 1977, Soviet President Leonid Brezhnev abruptly canceled negotiations with Secretary of State Vance for a comprehensive strategic arms limitations agreement (SALT II to replace the 1972 SALT I agreement). The Soviet leader was angered by the White House's public support for Soviet dissidents and by its proposals for a SALT II agreement, which would have forced the Soviets to make far greater cuts in their strategic weapons than the United States. Although talks were resumed in Geneva two months later, the two sides remained far apart on the specifics of an agreement. Carter's human rights campaign continued as a major sore point in Soviet-American relations.

In contrast to his problems with the Soviet Union, the president won a major victory in March 1978 when the Senate ratified the Panama Canal treaties ceding the canal to Panama at the end of 1999 but giving the United States the right to use military force if necessary to keep the waterway open and to guarantee its neutrality. Carter was persuaded that relinquishing the Canal was both morally right and necessary to avoid violence in Panama, where nationalistic sentiments ran high. But the treaties were unpopular with the American public and political conservatives who believed they amounted to giving away one of the nation's great treasures. Without an intense grass-roots effort from the White House and the president's successful courting of senate minority leader Howard Baker of Tennessee, the agreements would never have gained the two-thirds vote in the Senate necessary for ratification. In the end, they passed with only one vote over the two-thirds requirement. Unfortunately for Carter, his achievement gained him little favor with American voters.

Another matter to which the new administration devoted a great deal of effort was the long-festering Arab-Israeli dispute in the Middle East. In November 1977, Egyptian leader Anwar Sadat went to Israel where he called for new negotiations to end the dispute. Other Arab leaders, however, refused to join in the talks. In the negotiations between Israel and Egypt that followed Sadat's dramatic trip to Israel, moreover, Israeli leader Menachem Begin continued to pursue a hard line on the return of Arab lands seized during the 1967 Six Day War and on Palestinian autonomy, the two major issues preventing a peace settlement.

In September 1978, Carter decided to end the stalemate that had developed in the peace process by personally directing negotiations. Worried about renewed conflict in the Mideast, he invited Begin and Sadat to a summit meeting at Camp David, the presidential retreat in Maryland. After thirteen days of negotiations, during which he acted as intermediary between the two leaders, the president announced that an agreement had been reached providing for a peace treaty between Egypt and Israel and setting forth a framework for settling the problem of the occupied territory. The signing of the Camp

David Accords at a White House ceremony was carried by all the major television networks, and Carter was singled out for praise.

The agreements reached at Camp David remain the most important foreign policy achievement of the Carter administration and helped to reverse the president's downward spiral in public opinion polls. The political capital he gained from Camp David, however, was short-lived. Although this was due largely to the American people's worries over a troubled economy, developments in Iran and Afghanistan also added to the president's problems.

The Iranian Crisis

In January 1979 the shah of Iran was overthrown in a revolution led by the Ayatollah Ruhollah Khomeini, spiritual head of Iran's 32 million Shiite Muslims, who was committed to establishing an Islamic Republic. In February, Khomeini's followers briefly occupied the U.S. embassy in Teheran. Iranian militants again seized the embassy on 4 November, taking sixty Americans hostages after learning that the shah had been allowed into the United States to receive medical treatment. They vowed to hold onto the hostages until the United States returned the shah to Iran and paid financial damages for the crimes the U.S. had allegedly committed against the Iranian people. The next month, the Soviet Union sent 85,000 troops into Afghanistan to prop the Marxist regime of Abarbrak Kamal.

President Carter responded to the seizure of the hostages by trying to gain their release through diplomatic channels and economic restrictions. He hoped that the pressure from the international community and Iran's middle class would persuade the Ayatollah Khomeini to give up the hostage. The president responded to the invasion of Afghanistan by imposing a grain embargo on the Soviet Union, asking the Senate to delay consideration of the SALT II agreement, and barring the sale of high technology to the Soviets. He also indicated that the United States might boycott the 1980 Summer Olympics scheduled for Moscow. The American public gave Carter high marks for his handling of these two crises.

Yet the hostage crisis helped defeat Carter's bid for reelection in November. In the early morning of 25 April 1980, the president went on television to announce that a military effort to rescue the hostages, to which he had agreed reluctantly after resisting for five months, had failed. Eight members of the rescue mission died in a collision between a helicopter and a C-130 transport aircraft. Although initial reaction to the hapless mission supported the president, as details of the botched plan were revealed, it became another entry in a long list of failures that many Americans attributed to Carter.

Indeed, by mid-1980, the president's whole foreign policy seemed in disarray. The Soviets remained in

Afghanistan despite the president's issuance of the Carter Doctrine. Efforts to build on the Egyptian-Israeli peace treaty in the Middle East went nowhere. The country's growing dependence on oil imports and a decline in the value of the dollar left it increasingly exposed to the whiplashes of the international economy. Sharp differences arose between Carter and European leaders, especially German Chancellor Helmut Schmidt, on a variety of issues including international economic policy, the president's handling of the Iranian crisis, and the invasion of Afghanistan. When Vance, who had opposed the Iranian rescue mission and favored continued diplomatic efforts, announced that he was resigning as secretary of state, the news media seized on the announcement as evidence that the president's foreign policy had entered a quagmire.

To replace Vance, President Carter named former Maine Senator Edmund Muskie. Muskie was initially one of the president's most outspoken critics, but Carter had developed a warm personal relationship with him. The president intended Muskie to serve as the administration's spokesman on foreign policy, leaving other matters, including the day-to-day administration of the Department of State, to his deputy secretary of state, Warren Christopher.

In 1980 Carter was defeated in his bid for re-election by his Republican opponent, former Governor Ronald Reagan of California. More than any other factor, public frustration with a seemingly ineffectual administration was responsible for Reagan's decisive victory. Although much of the public's despair with Carter stemmed from the economic issues of high inflation and unemployment, the president's conduct of foreign policy, particularly his inability to resolve the hostage crisis, added to the widespread perception of presidential incompetence.

Throughout much of the 1980 campaign, Carter was actually able to put his opponent on the defensive by raising doubts about Reagan's own competence to be president and by pounding the theme that a Reagan presidency would be more likely to lead the nation into war than his own. Reagan was able to snatch victory from defeat, however, by dispelling doubts about his presidential caliber and then refocusing the campaign on Carter's record as president. In a masterful stroke during a debate with Carter in October, he asked the American people whether they felt better off economically or thought the United States was safer and more respected in the world than when Carter took office. In this way he made the election a referendum on Carter's conduct of domestic and foreign policy.

On the Sunday before the election, the president also turned the voters against him by indicating in a televised address that a breakthrough in the hostage crisis might be near. Although the president made his announcement on the basis of an optimistic communication he had received from the Teheran government, many voters suspected the motivations behind his announcement, especially because the Republicans had been warning for some time against such an "October surprise." Furthermore, the hostages were not released, so that the president's message served only to highlight his inability to secure the hostage's freedom.

Although Carter was defeated on 4 November, he worked to gain the release of the hostages before he left office. The Iranians denied him even this consolation prize, however. Following long and complex negotiations, the Iranians agreed to a deal involving the transfer to Iran of $9 billion in frozen assets in return for the hostages. But they waited purposely until after Reagan had taken the oath of office on 20 January 1981 before announcing that an agreement had been reached. At Reagan's invitation, though, Carter flew to Germany to welcome back the American hostages held in Iran for 444 days.

Since leaving office Carter has devoted much of his time to foreign affairs. He established the Carter Presidential Center in Atlanta, Georgia, and made it a locus of social and political activism, with programs on such diverse problems as human rights, preventive health care, the world environment, and conflict resolution in the Middle East, Latin America, and Africa. The former president has traveled throughout the world, promoting improved agricultural methods and better health care in the world's most poverty-stricken countries, especially in Africa.

Since the mid-1980s Carter also has been publicly and politically more visible. He began to speak out more frequently on national issues and to criticize the Reagan administration's policies and programs, such as its Strategic Defense Initiative (SDI) and its policy of "constructive engagement" with South Africa. He also has played an increasingly important role as an elder statesman, attempting to mediate the long-running war in Ethiopia between its Marxist government and Eritrean rebels (1989), monitoring elections in Panama (1989) and Nicaragua (1990), and negotiating with Haiti's military leader to remove themselves in favor of a duly elected civilian government (1994).

The Middle East has remained, however, the region of most concern to Carter. As he watched the promise of the Camp David Accords of 1978 go largely unfulfilled, he became publicly critical of Israel for its refusal to stop building settlements on the West Bank and to grant Palestinians greater autonomy. He also spoke out in support of an international peace conference to mediate the Arab-Israeli dispute. He was highly gratified, therefore, when Prime Minister Yitzhak Rabin of Israel and Chairman of the Palestinian Liberation Organization (PLO) Yasir Arafat met at the White House in September 1993 and signed an agreement by which they exchanged mutual recognition and Israel promised Palestinian autonomy in the Gaza Strip and in the city of Jericho on the West Bank. It appeared to Carter that the promise of the Camp David Accords of 1978 might finally be realized.

BURTON I. KAUFMAN

See also Brzezinski, Zbigniew Kasimierz; Camp David Accords; Carter Doctrine; Cold War; Détente; Egypt; Haiti; Human Rights; Iran; Israel; Middle East; Muskie, Edmund Sixtus; Panama and Panama Canal; Strategic Arms Limitation Talks and Agreements; Strategic Defense Initiative; Vance, Cyrus Roberts

FURTHER READING

Brzezinski, Zbigniew. *Power and Principle: Memoirs of the National Security Adviser, 1977-1981*. New York, 1985.
Carter, Jimmy, *Keeping Faith*. New York, 1982.
Garthoff, Raymond. *Détente and Confrontation: American Foreign Relations from Nixon to Reagan*. Washington, 1985.
Kaufman, Burton I. *The Presidency of James Earl Carter, Jr.* Lawrence, Kans., 1993.
Smith, Gaddis. *Morality, Reason, and Power: American Diplomacy in the Carter Years*. New York, 1986.
Thornton, Richard C. *The Carter Years: Toward a New Global Order*. New York, 1991.
Vance, Cyrus. *Hard Choices: Critical Years in American Foreign Policy*. New York, 1983.

CARTER DOCTRINE

A policy for the Persian Gulf that President Jimmy Carter enunciated in his State of the Union address before a joint session of Congress on 23 January 1980. Carter delivered his speech a month after the Soviet Union had invaded Afghanistan and at a time when much of the Islamic world, including the vital Persian Gulf region, was in turmoil. Carter feared that unless he took a firm stand against the Afghan invasion, the entire region might be vulnerable to Soviet attack. Thus he warned in his address that an "attempt by any outside force to gain control of the Persian Gulf region will be regarded as an assault on the vital interests of the United States of America, and such force will be repelled by any means necessary, including military force." To show that he meant business, he took a number of steps directed against Moscow, including asking for five annual increases of 5 percent in real military spending rather than the 3 percent that had been his goal since 1977. Furthermore, the administration negotiated for the use of naval and air facilities near the Persian Gulf and expanded the American military presence in the Indian Ocean. Critics such as George F. Kennan and Senator Edward Kennedy charged that Carter had overreacted, exaggerating the Soviet threat and abandoning diplomacy. The Soviet Union occupied Afghanistan until 1989.

BURTON I. KAUFMAN

See also Afghanistan; Carter, James Earl; Iran; Kennan, George Frost; Middle East; Russia and the Soviet Union

FURTHER READING

Smith, Gaddis. *Morality, Reason, and Power: American Diplomacy in the Carter Years*. New York, 1986.

CASABLANCA CONFERENCE

See World War II

CASEY, WILLIAM JOSEPH

(*b.* 13 March 1913; *d.* 6 May 1987)

Office of Strategic Services (OSS) official during World War II, businessman, attorney, and director of the Central Intelligence Agency (1981–1987). Born in New York City, Casey received a law degree from St. John's University in New York (1937). After Casey served as chairman of the Securities and Exchange Commission and head of the Export-Import Bank during 1973–1975, President Ronald Reagan, whose 1980 campaign Casey had managed, gave him a mandate to "restore" the Central Intelligence Agency (CIA) from the allegedly low estate into which it had fallen during Jimmy Carter's presidency; to help achieve this end, Reagan accorded him "cabinet rank," which critics said blurred what should be the director's nonpolitical role. Casey urged that national intelligence estimates (NIEs), one of the CIA's main analytic products, be made more responsive to political objectives. He secured increased intelligence funding and developed more aggressive covert paramilitary capabilities to counter Soviet expansion in the Third World, in line with the dicta of the Reagan Doctrine. Support of the Afghan resistance to the Soviet invasion proved successful and (at the time) largely noncontroversial. The arming of the Contras against the Sandinistas in Nicaragua, however, was not and repeatedly embroiled Casey in conflict with Congress, especially given his resistance to that body's greatly strengthened oversight rules. One result was the Iran-Contra covert operation, in which Casey bypassed legal restrictions, working through the National Security Council staff (particularly Colonel Oliver North) and using external funding sources. Casey died just as this scandal broke.

MARK M. LOWENTHAL

See also Central Intelligence Agency; Intelligence; Iran-Contra Affair; Nicaragua; North, Oliver Lawrence; Reagan Doctrine; Reagan, Ronald Wilson

FURTHER READING

Lowenthal, Mark M. *U.S. Intelligence: Evolution and Anatomy*, 2nd ed. Westport, Conn., 1992.

Persico, Joseph E. *Casey: From the OSS to the CIA*. New York, 1990.

Woodward, Bob. *Veil: The Secret Wars of the CIA, 1981–1987*. New York, 1987.

CASE-ZABLOCKI ACT

(1972)

Named after its two principal sponsors, Democratic Representative Clement Zablocki of Wisconsin and Republican Senator Clifford Case of New Jersey, the first significant piece of legislation passed to regulate commitment-making by the president in the post-Vietnam era. The act was signed into law 22 August 1972. Its aim was to ensure that Congress be informed about the international commitments made by executive agreements in a prompt manner. The legislation was a reaction both to the Vietnam War, a conflict largely conducted through executive initiative, and to the congressional investigations that revealed a large number of secret international commitments made by the executive branch during the 1950s and 1960s. The legislation required that all executive agreements be reported to Congress within sixty days of their entering into force. All classified executive agreements would be transmitted to the House Foreign Affairs Committee and the Senate Foreign Relations Committee under an injunction of secrecy. The act was amended and strengthened in 1977 by requiring that all executive agreements be reported to the Department of State within twenty days of their signing and that these agreements in turn be transmitted to Congress under the original provisions of the act.

In 1978 two additional legislative actions were taken to strengthen the procedures concerning the reporting of executive agreements in conjunction with this act. The first legislative action sought to spell out the reporting requirements in more detail. The president was now directed to report annually on those agreements that were transmitted to Congress after the sixty-day period. The secretary of state was also now required to establish guidelines on what constituted an executive agreement and thus was subject to the reporting requirements. Oral agreements would now be "reduced to writing" for transmittal to the Congress under the Case-Zablocki Act. The second legislative action was a nonbinding resolution called the International Agreements Consultation Resolution. Its aim was to establish a coordination mechanism between the Congress and the executive branch for determining the form of future U.S. commitments. Under this resolution periodic consultations would occur between the Department of State and the Senate Foreign Relations Committee to determine which international agreements would take the form of executive agreements and which would take the form of treaties. While these two additional efforts were refinements in the Case-Zablocki process, they did not go much beyond the initial reporting requirements in the legislation. Nevertheless, these accommodations between the Congress and the executive branch undoubtedly contributed to easing congressional efforts to enact stronger restrictions on executive agreements, including a congressional veto over such agreements that was being discussed at the time.

On balance, compliance with the Case-Zablocki Act has not been wholly timely or complete, and its impact on the policy process has been limited. Analyses from 1978 to 1992 show that roughly 19 percent of the agreements, on average, were still reported after the sixty-day requirement. Furthermore, the explanations for the late reporting were incomplete. The reporting of some non-controversial executive agreements, such as water access agreements for a U.S. base abroad, may not be critical for congressional involvement in the policy process. Other, more controversial agreements, however, such as intelligence commitments or access to military bases, may be very important to that process. Both types of agreements were among those reported late. Although Congress gained some more timely knowledge about foreign policy commitments made by the executive through this act, its involvement in this area remained limited.

JAMES M. MCCORMICK

See also Bricker Amendment; Congress; Executive Agreements; Presidency

FURTHER READING

Franck, Thomas M., and Edward Weisband. *Foreign Policy by Congress.* New York, 1979.

McCormick, James M. *American Foreign Policy and Process,* 2nd ed. Itasca, Ill., 1992.

U.S. Congress, Senate Committee on Foreign Relations. *Treaties and Other International Agreements: The Role of the United States Senate.* Washington, D.C., 1992.

CASH-AND-CARRY

See Neutrality Acts of the 1930s

CASS, LEWIS

(*b.* 9 October 1782; *d.* 17 June 1866)

Secretary of state (1857–1860) at a time of serious sectional division in the United States. A native of Exeter, New Hampshire, he served as governor of Michigan Territory (1813–1831), secretary of war under President Andrew Jackson (1831–1836), minister to France (1836–1842), and U.S. senator from Michigan (1845–1848, 1851–1857), and was the presidential nominee of the Democratic party in

1848. Cass was a prominent northwestern politician and an intense Anglophobe. He resigned his post in France in protest over a provision in the Webster-Ashburton Treaty that U.S. and British warships would cooperate in intercepting slave ships. He also engaged in an acrimonious public correspondence with Secretary of State Daniel Webster over that treaty commitment. President James Buchanan, who disliked Cass, reluctantly appointed him secretary of state in 1857 for political reasons. Cass's only apparent accomplishment was pressuring the British government in 1858 to formally abandon any pretension of a right to search U.S. vessels during peacetime in order to suppress the African slave trade. Otherwise, with Buchanan acting as his own secretary of state and his friend John Appleton running the Department of State, Cass had little influence. When Cass resigned on 12 December 1860, because of the president's refusal to take a strong stand against South Carolina's secessionist steps, Buchanan ungraciously characterized him as incompetent and indecisive. Cass pursued literary and scholarly interests in his retirement.

KENNETH E. SHEWMAKER

See also Buchanan, James; Slave Trade and Slavery; Webster, Daniel

FURTHER READING

Moore, John Bassett, ed. *The Works of James Buchanan,* 12 vols. Philadelphia, 1908–1911.

Shewmaker, Kenneth E. "The War of Words: The Cass-Webster Debate of 1842–1843." *Diplomatic History* 5 (1981): 151–163.

Smith, Elbert. *The Presidency of James Buchanan.* Lawrence, Kans., 1975.

Soulsby, Hugh G. *The Right of Search and the Slave Trade in Anglo-American Relations, 1814–1862.* Baltimore, Md., 1933.

CASTLE, WILLIAM RICHARDS, JR.

(*b.* 19 June 1878; *d.* 13 October 1963)

U.S. diplomat who served as ambassador to Japan (1929–1931). Born in Honolulu, Hawaii, and educated at Harvard College (A.B. 1900), Castle first served as the assistant dean (1906–1913) and dean (1913–1915) of his alma mater. Following two years as the editor of the *Harvard Graduates' Magazine,* Castle was appointed the director of the American Red Cross's Bureau of Communications in 1917. In 1919 he began his tenure at the Department of State; within two years he became chief of the Western European Division. By 1927 he was an assistant secretary of state, and emphasized "isolationist" views towards Europe. Castle helped shape the Kellogg-Briand Pact (1928). The French government's desire to conclude a bilateral treaty of friendship with the United States that would not only renounce war as a legitimate policy option but also make it illegal, caused the Department of State unwanted difficulties. The United States responded by suggesting a multinational agreement along the same lines. France at first rejected the idea because it would have nullified French desires to extend France's alliance system and improve its national prestige. Castle initiated discussions with French ambassador Paul Claudel and explained that a bilateral agreement would be perceived more as a Franco-American alliance than as a step toward world peace. Secretary of State Frank B. Kellogg and Castle persuaded the French government that the only possibility of success lay in the multilateral proposal.

In December 1929 the Department of State named Castle ambassador to Japan. This appointment was made specifically to give the United States a diplomatic presence in Japan while the 1930 London Naval Conference convened. Castle developed an extremely sympathetic view toward the Japanese while at this post. Promoted to undersecretary of state in 1931, Castle contributed to the Hoover Moratorium (1932) on debts and reparations stemming from the Great War and to the formulation of the Stimson Doctrine (1932). The doctrine, a response to the Japanese invasion of Manchuria, drew originally on a speech Castle made in May and consisted of only a formal declaration of nonrecognition.

A Republican and friend of President Herbert Hoover, Castle surrendered his position when Franklin D. Roosevelt became president. Until 1941 Castle spent the majority of his time espousing, both orally and in numerous magazine articles, his political beliefs, particularly his support for Japan. In an October 1940 article for *Atlantic Monthly*, Castle encouraged the development of a Monroe Doctrine for Japan, which, in his opinion, would solidify U.S.-Japanese friendship and combat German military aggression. From 1945 to 1952, Castle completed his public career as the president of Garfield Memorial Hospital in Washington, D.C.

SCOTT D. KELLER

See also France; Hoover, Herbert; Isolationism; Japan; Kellogg-Briand Pact; Kellogg, Frank Billings; War Debt of World War I

FURTHER READING

Castle, Alfred L. "William R. Castle and Opposition to U.S. Involvement in an Asian War, 1939–1941." *Pacific Historical Review* 54 (August 1985): 337–356.

Ellis, L. Ethan. *Frank B. Kellogg and American Foreign Relations, 1925–1929.* New Brunswick, N.J., 1961.

Ferrell, Robert H. *Peace in Their Time: The Origins of the Kellogg-Briand Pact.* New Haven, Conn., 1952.

———. *American Diplomacy in the Great Depression: Hoover-Stimson Foreign Policy, 1929–1933.* New Haven, Conn., 1957

Ferrell, Robert H., ed. *The American Secretaries of State and Their Diplomacy.* vol. 11 of *Frank B. Kellogg-Henry L. Stimson.* New York, 1963.

Morrison, Elting E. *Turmoil and Tradition: A Study of the Life and Times of Henry L. Stimson.* Boston, 1960.

CASTLEREAGH, SECOND VISCOUNT
Robert Stewart

(*b.* 18 June 1769; *d.* 22 August 1822)

Conservative British statesman and foreign secretary (1812–1822), famously vilified by Shelley and Byron but respected in Washington for seeking to improve Anglo-American relations. Born in Ireland, he became highly unpopular there, when as chief secretary for Ireland he supported the Act of Union and the dissolution of the separate Irish Parliament in 1800. Castlereagh then served in the House of Commons and in the cabinet as Irish secretary and secretary of state for war (1805–1806, 1807–1809) under William Pitt and William Henry Portland. As foreign secretary (1812–1822), in June 1812 Castlereagh, realizing the immense value of American goodwill during the latter phase of the Napoleonic Wars, repealed the infamous Orders in Council—British maritime restrictions on trade with the neutral United States. Before news of the repeal could reach Washington, however, Congress had declared war on Great Britain. Despite Castlereagh's desire to avoid war with the United States, he rejected an offer by Czar Alexander I to mediate Anglo-American hostilities. Peace talks did not begin until August 1814, in Ghent, Belgium.

After the War of 1812, Americans continued to look upon the British with suspicion. Castlereagh sought a reconciliation with the United States, particularly in order to aid British commercial interests in the Western Hemisphere. One result was the Rush-Bagot Treaty of 1817, which required disarmament by both nations on the Great Lakes. To settle the disputed Canadian-U.S. border, Castlereagh suggested the formation of a binational commission to study the various claims. Secretary of State John Quincy Adams countered that negotiations should also include the dispute over fishing rights off the North American coast. The resulting Anglo-American Convention of 1818 defined the boundary from the Lake of the Woods along the 49th parallel to the Oregon Territory, which Great Britain and the United States would occupy jointly. The agreement also provided for U.S. fishing and curing privileges off Labrador and Newfoundland.

Castlereagh had represented Great Britain at the Congress of Vienna (1814–1815), where he resisted Russian and Prussian territorial demands against Poland and drafted Article VI of the Quadruple Alliance between Great Britain, Austria, Prussia, and Russia, which created the Congress System of periodic consultations meant to enforce peace and prevent future French aggression. Although deeply conservative by nature and sympathetic to Prince Klemens Metternich's views on dynastic legitimacy, Castlereagh resisted the use of British force to squelch popular uprisings on the Continent or to restore monarchical rule. Furthermore, he toyed with the idea of recognizing the independence of Spain's Latin American colonies, preferably in conjunction with other major European powers. Before he could implement his new thinking, Castlereagh, who had long suffered from a serious nervous condition and bouts of extreme despondency, committed suicide. (A year earlier, he had become the 2nd marquess of Londonderry upon his father's death.) Ironically, his former rival, George Canning (with whom he had fought a duel in 1809), succeeded him as foreign secretary and further refined Great Britain's policy of (selective) nonintervention in the internal affairs of other nations while cautiously promoting constitutionalism in Europe and Latin America.

CAROL A. JACKSON

See also Canada; Canning, George; Ghent, Treaty of; Great Britain; Monroe Doctrine; Quadruple Alliance; Rush-Bagot Agreement; War of 1812

FURTHER READING

Derry, John W. *Castlereagh.* London, 1976.
Hinde, Wendy. *Castlereagh.* London, 1981.
Perkins, Bradford. *Castlereagh and Adams: England and the United States, 1812–1823.* Berkeley, Calif., 1964.
Webster, Charles. *The Foreign Policy of Castlereagh, 1815–1822: Britain and the European Alliance.* London, 1947.
——— . *The Foreign Policy of Castlereagh, 1812–1815: Britain and the Reconstruction of Europe.* London, 1963.

CASTRO, FIDEL

(*b.* 13 August 1926)

Cuba's principal leader beginning in 1959, whose revolution and government put Cuba at odds with the United States over a great many issues. Born in 1926 to a prosperous family in rural eastern Cuba and educated in the country's best Jesuit schools, Fidel Castro obtained a law degree from the University of Havana. On 10 March 1952, Fulgencio Batista y Zaldívar and the military overthrew Cuba's constitutional government. On 26 July 1953 Castro led an unsuccessful assault on the Cuban army's Moncada barracks and soon founded the 26th of July Movement. He served two years in prison and then went into exile in the United States and Mexico to gather funds and weapons to stage a rebellion against Batista's government.

In December 1956 Castro's expedition landed in eastern Cuba and launched a guerrilla insurgency in the Sierra Maestra mountains. Castro gave assurances against the expropriation of most foreign property, emphasized his noncommunist nationalism (he had not belonged to the Communist party), highlighted issues of land reform and employment, worked with U.S. journalists to project a friendly image, and pressured the U.S. government to cut

off military support for the Batista government. In mid-1958 he commanded about 400 guerrillas; by year's end, that number had increased tenfold. During the final months of 1958, Batista's ineptly led forces retreated, refused to fight, surrendered, and eventually disintegrated. The only pitched battle of the insurgency, for control of the city of Santa Clara, was fought between 29 December 1958 and 1 January 1959, and was won by the rebels. On 31 December 1958 Batista fled to the Dominican Republic.

A man of extraordinary energy, Castro emerged from the guerrilla war a hero to many Cubans, who were grateful for deliverance from a despised regime. Tall by Cuban standards, Castro was a gifted public speaker; he could challenge and soothe, exhort and mobilize, charm and educate. In the early years of his rule, Castro's speeches typically lasted several hours, and he delivered a couple of speeches every week, which were covered live on radio and television and reached the entire country. He also roamed the country, meeting ordinary Cubans face to face. His government promoted extensive participation to support its policies, which fostered economic and social equality under centralized and politically repressive control.

Remaining as commander in chief of the revolutionary armed forces, Castro first appointed a caretaker government but in February 1959 he became prime minister. In April he visited the United States, professing friendship despite his postponement of elections; he instructed his ministers not to ask for economic assistance. In May a far-reaching land reform law was enacted, but in June the United States objected to the arbitrary implementation of the agrarian reform, albeit agreeing to Cuba's right to carry out land reform. From June through November, Castro ousted most moderate ministers from his government; threatened international action against hostile dictatorships in neighboring countries; and began a courtship of the Communist party and the Soviet Union.

Castro also accused the United States government of collaboration with terrorists. In October 1959 he claimed that Havana was bombed, and in March 1960, a ship loaded with weapons blew up in Havana harbor. He had no proof of U.S. participation in either incident. Along with other events under way in Cuba, the first accusation shifted President Dwight D. Eisenhower's administration toward hostility; in response to the second accusation, and to a Soviet-Cuban economic treaty signed in February 1960, Eisenhower authorized the Central Intelligence Agency (CIA) to train Cuban exiles to overthrow Castro's government.

In June 1960 the Castro government seized all foreign-owned oil refineries that had refused to refine crude petroleum purchased by the Cuban government from the Soviet Union. Days later, Eisenhower cut off all sugar imports from Cuba. The Soviet Union promised to replace U.S. sugar purchases and to defend Cuba against external attack. Later in 1960 Castro's government expropriated all foreign-owned property, and the United States imposed a trade embargo on Cuba. From 1960 to at least 1966, U.S. operatives working for the CIA sought to assassinate Castro. In January 1961 diplomatic relations were broken. In April a U.S.-sponsored brigade of Cuban exiles landed at Cuba's Bay of Pigs but was defeated within three days. In December 1961 Castro announced that he was a communist and in 1962 secretly requested the deployment of Soviet missiles and nuclear warheads as a deterrent to an expected U.S. invasion. In October he obstructed the missile crisis settlement that the United States and the Soviet Union had negotiated by his refusal to accept any international inspection of Cuba's territory.

In the 1960s Castro sought to transform Cuba into a model revolutionary state. He launched a vast literacy campaign and years later successfully increased median schooling levels. His government launched efforts to improve public health care for all Cubans free of charge, and although the record in the 1960s was uneven, the health policies were successful by the 1970s and 1980s. In the late 1960s and, to a lesser extent, in the late 1980s, Castro sought to reduce the role of the market in the operation of Cuba's economy as much as possible. Peasants were prohibited from selling their products to anyone but the state. Citizens were importuned to work for the sake of the nation, future generations, and the revolution, not for the rewards of "vile money." The economy was owned and operated by state enterprises to an extent greater than in other communist countries. When these economic policies failed in the early 1970s, Castro turned to Soviet-style orthodox central planning to reactivate his economy.

Castro saw himself as a leader for a worldwide revolution. In the 1960s Cuba supported insurgencies in several dozen Latin American and African countries, and the United States countered those efforts by providing assistance to the governments threatened by those rebels. In 1965 Castro became secretary-general of a refounded Communist party. In 1966 Cuba and China fought bitterly over various ideological and political issues, and although diplomatic and trade links continued, their relations would become warm again only after the collapse of the Soviet Union in the early 1990s. In 1967 and 1968 Cuba publicly opposed Soviet policies toward Latin America and protested Soviet meddling in Cuba's domestic affairs. In 1968 the Soviets slowed down the rate of petroleum deliveries. Cuba backed down and Castro signalled his acknowledgment of Soviet primacy in their relations by endorsing the Soviet invasion of Czechoslovakia in 1968. (In 1980, he also would endorse the Soviet invasion of Afghanistan.)

In 1975 Castro dispatched 36,000 troops to Angola to fight off a South African invasion. With the enactment of a new constitution in 1976, Castro became Cuba's president. In 1977 he dispatched over 10,000 troops to defend Ethiopia against a Somali invasion—a decision that prevented further progress on efforts begun by President Jimmy Carter's administration to improve relations with Cuba. The United States opposed Cuba's decisions to go to war in both instances, while the Soviet Union supported Cuba in these actions. The USSR armed the Cuban military to a high level of proficiency and transferred vast sums of money to subsidize the Cuban economy. In 1987 Castro raised the number of Cuban troops in Angola to about 50,000 to combat a new South African invasion. Cuban troops won all three wars thanks to Castro's leadership skill, the skills and loyalty of his commanders and soldiers, and the backing of the Soviet Union. With the end of the Cold War in much of the world except the Caribbean, all Cuban troops overseas had returned home by the early 1990s.

With the collapse of the Soviet Union in 1991, subsidies to Cuba dropped off, accelerating a steep economic decline. Castro changed course in his economic policies, welcoming direct foreign investment, permitting freer markets in agriculture and industry, and fostering tourism. His government sought to improve relations with Canada and with Latin American and European governments and ceased its policy of supporting insurgencies in other countries. In the 1990s, U.S.-Cuban relations remained hostile and tense, however, because the United States condition for improved bilateral relations was, in effect, Castro's resignation. The two governments had negotiated some successful agreements, such as one in 1988 to bring about an end to warfare in Angola and on bilateral migration in the 1980s and early 1990s. Nevertheless, U.S. and Cuban forces fought each other in Grenada in 1983, when the United States invaded the island of Grenada to overthrow a government supported by Cuba. In 1980 more than 100,000 Cubans left the country through Mariel Harbor and entered the United States illegally, many in effect expelled by the Cuban government; a smaller but similar crisis of exiles occurred in 1994. By then, more than one million Cubans (out of a Cuban population of eleven million) had emigrated to the United States since 1959. In the 1990s, Castro was confident that his regime could survive, thanks to some economic reforms and the Cuban government's ongoing ability to maintain control. The United States, on the contrary, continued to pursue increasingly coercive policies in an attempt to force the Castro regime's termination, imposing economic penalties even on foreign firms trading with or investing in Cuba.

JORGE I. DOMÍNGUEZ

See also Angola; Batista y Zaldívar, Fulgencio; Bay of Pigs Invasion; Cold War; Cuba; Cuban Missile Crisis; Economic Sanctions; Eisenhower, Dwight David; Ethiopia; Export Controls; Grenada Invasion; Kennedy, John Fitzgerald; Latin America; Russia and the Soviet Union

FURTHER READING

Domínguez, Jorge. *To Make a World Safe for Revolution: Cuba's Foreign Policy.* Cambridge, Mass., 1989.

Harnecker, Marta. *Fidel Castro's Political Strategy: From Moncada to Victory.* New York, 1987.

Paterson, Thomas G. *Contesting Castro.* New York, 1994.

Quirk, Robert E. *Fidel Castro.* New York, 1993.

CENTO

See Central Treaty Organization

CENTRAL AFRICAN REPUBLIC

See Appendix 2

CENTRAL AMERICA

See Latin America

CENTRAL INTELLIGENCE AGENCY

The most prominent intelligence service of the United States established by the National Security Act of 1947. Through the creation of a modern intelligence service after World War II, U.S. government officials hoped, in part, to avoid another military debacle like the surprise attack by the Japanese at Pearl Harbor on 7 December 1941.

The attack on Pearl Harbor, during which the Japanese sank five battleships and two destroyers, destroyed a large number of aircraft, and killed 2,330 military personnel, represented the most disastrous intelligence failure in the history of the United States, whose leaders had failed to appreciate fully either the capabilities or the intentions of the enemy. Until that "day of infamy," as President Franklin D. Roosevelt would call it, the U.S. military remained unaware that the Japanese possessed a new type of aerial torpedo that could navigate the relatively shallow waters of Pearl Harbor. Nor did government officials have reliable information about the likely targets of a Japanese air attack; conventional wisdom at the time pointed to the Philippines as the probable site. Moreover, the fragments of information obtained by U.S. military intelligence that did point to Hawai'i were never adequately analyzed and coordinated within the government; the president and other high officials were never given access, for example, to decoded intercepts of Japanese military communications that indicated Pearl Harbor could be in jeopardy.

Appalled by the findings of an inquiry into this intelligence failure, Harry S. Truman, who succeeded President Roosevelt, vowed to create an intelligence service that would provide the White House with much better analysis and coordination of information about foreign threats and opportunities. Soon after the defeat of the Axis powers, Truman signed an executive order on 22 January 1946 establishing a Central Intelligence Group patterned after the Office of Strategic Services (OSS), one of the more productive and successful intelligence agencies formed by the government during the war years. With the passage of the National Security Act, signed by Truman on 26 July 1947, the Central Intelligence Group evolved into the Central Intelligence Agency (CIA).

Although the creation of the CIA proceeded with little interference, largely because of strong White House support, its survival as a new agency in a government that already had several other secret intelligence agencies was a more contentious matter. The CIA's early leaders, many of whom had served together in the OSS, immediately found themselves in a bureaucratic struggle over funding and turf with U.S. Army intelligence staff (G-2), the Federal Bureau of Investigation (FBI), and the Atomic Energy Commission. Each of these organizations already had information-gathering duties abroad and resisted CIA encroachment. Moreover, the Department of State insisted that CIA personnel abroad had to serve under the jurisdiction of the U.S. ambassador—an arrangement the new agency often resisted.

Under the skillful administrative and political leadership of its early directors—notably General Walter Bedell Smith (1950–1953), Allen Dulles (1953–1961), and John A. McCone (1961–1965)—the CIA successfully negotiated the rough shoals of Washington politics and emerged as the chief coordinating intelligence agency that President Truman had envisioned. Yet, despite its bureaucratic successes, the CIA has never been able to achieve undisputed dominance over intelligence policy. In addition to the CIA, the government has twelve other major intelligence entities, including the National Security Agency (NSA) and the Defense Intelligence Agency (DIA). Rather than a strongly centralized structure for intelligence with the CIA clearly in charge, the relationship among these agencies has continued to resemble more of a tribal federation. Powerful centrifugal forces, especially the competing authority of the secretary of defense over military intelligence, continue to retard attempts by reformers to create a centralized management control over government-wide intelligence programs and budgets.

In 1995, however, President Bill Clinton's second intelligence chief, John M. Deutch, vowed to improve

DIRECTORS OF THE CENTRAL INTELLIGENCE AGENCY

ADMINISTRATION	DIRECTOR	PERIOD OF APPOINTMENT
Truman	Sidney W. Souers	1946
	Hoyt S. Vandenberg	1946–1947
	Roscoe H. Hillenkoetter	1947–1950
	Walter Bedell Smith	1950–1953
Eisenhower		
	Allen W. Dulles	1953–1961
Kennedy		
	John A. McCone	1961–1965
L. Johnson		
	William F. Raborn, Jr.	1965–1966
	Richard M. Helms	1966–1973
Nixon		
	James R. Schlesinger	1973
	William E. Colby	1973–1976
Ford	George Bush	1976–1977
Carter	Stansfield Turner	1977–1981
Reagan	William J. Casey	1981–1987
	William H. Webster	1987–1991
Bush		
	Robert M. Gates	1991–1993
Clinton		
	R. James Woolsey, Jr.	1993–1995
	John M. Deutch	1995–Present

Source: U.S. Central Intelligence Agency

the cohesion of the intelligence agencies through a series of reforms. Deutch envisioned the establishment of more uniform personnel policies across the agencies; the creation of a National Imagery Agency to consolidate photographic intelligence collected by satellites and reconnaissance aircraft; a joint space-management board to provide better coordination for satellite procurement and supervision; and the strengthening of his own authority as director of all U.S. intelligence agencies, not just the CIA. Above all, Deutch sought greater control over the intelligence budget—some 85 percent of which supported military intelligence activities and was, therefore, of considerable interest to the secretary of defense as well.

The Director of the CIA

The CIA (often referred to as "the Agency" or "the Company" by insiders) is organized into five directorates, led by an Office of the Director. The director wears two organizational hats: he—there have been only male directors so far—is simultaneously director of the CIA (with the acronym DCIA) as well as director of Central Intelligence (DCI). In his capacity as DCIA, he is the chief officer at the CIA itself, which is located in Lang-

ley, Virginia, along the banks of the Potomac River in the suburbs of Washington, D.C. In guiding the CIA, the DCIA relies heavily on his second in command, the deputy director of CIA (DDCIA), who runs the agency's routine daily affairs. In his capacity as DCI, the CIA director has much broader responsibilities: the coordination of all the secret intelligence agencies, which are collectively known by the euphemism "intelligence community." As DCI, he is also in charge of the National Foreign Intelligence Program (NFIP).

The DCI's duties with respect to the National Foreign Intelligence Program are extensive. Within this program fall not only the CIA and its operations, but all satellite and airplane reconnaissance programs, code-making and codebreaking activities, and other intelligence operations pursued by the government's secret agencies. The DCI is further responsible for reporting on intelligence activities to Congress and to the president. Within the executive branch, he presents for approval important intelligence policy initiatives to the National Security Council (NSC), whose full statutory members include the president, the vice president, and the secretaries of state and defense.

Those proposals that gain the president's approval take the form of National Security Council Intelligence Directives (NSCIDs). Here are the vital instructions from the highest levels of government to guide the DCI. The operational details are then filled by intelligence officers at Langley and the other secret agencies, before being carried out by "station" officers located in virtually every country around the globe.

Within the CIA are a number of units designed to assist the DCIA/DCI in supervising the agency itself and the wider intelligence community. The Office of the Director has a Center for Weapons Nonproliferation and an Arms Control Intelligence Staff to provide advice on how to halt the flow of dangerous weapons worldwide and monitor the adherence of other nations to arms-control agreements. The Director's Office also houses an Executive Director, who serves as an important gatekeeper between the DCI and the CIA and is third in command at the agency; an Office of Congressional Affairs to work with legislative overseers; an Office of Public Affairs to handle public and media relations; an Office of General Counsel, workplace of the agency's lawyers (who have increased more than tenfold in the past decade); an Office of the Comptroller, for budgetary control; and an Office of Inspector General (IG), who is expected to investigate allegations of wrongdoing by CIA officials.

Further, a National Intelligence Council (NIC) reports directly to the DCI. The NIC is composed of sixteen or so (the number has varied from time to time) National Intelligence Officers (NIOs), who are respected intelligence analysts from throughout the community and sometimes from academe. The NIC works closely with senior intelligence officers in each of the secret agencies to prepare analytic papers on foreign political and military leaders, as well as about important unfolding events around the world. These papers are meant to assist policy makers in formulating their decisions about how the United States should carry out its foreign relations.

A Community Management Staff (CMS) further assists the DCI in his responsibilities for coordinating intelligence policy. For this purpose, the CMS has established several interagency working groups (IWGs) and various panels for coordinating espionage (human intelligence or HUMINT); for intelligence collection by satellites and other technical means (technical intelligence or TECHINT); for signals intelligence (SIGINT), a generic term that encompasses the interception and analysis of communications intelligence (COMINT) and electronic intelligence (ELINT); and measurement and signature intelligence (MASINT), which exploits the physical properties of targets through the use of special technical sensors, such as in-flight missile emissions (a technique known as "telemetry"). Interagency coordination takes place as well for photographic or imagery intelligence (IMINT), guided by a Committee on Imagery Requirements and Exploitation or COMIREX; counterintelligence; annual budget deliberations; and long-range community planning.

The CIA Directorates

Donning his other hat, the DCIA and his deputy administer the CIA chiefly through its four directorates. The largest is the Directorate of Operations (DO), where the agency's spy handlers and covert action officers reside. The DO's covert action duties have been particularly controversial, because they involve the secret manipulation of political and economic events in other nations, including covert warfare (paramilitary action). The CIA successfully removed unfriendly governments in Iran (1953) and in Guatemala (1954). The failed Bay of Pigs operations in Cuba during 1961 remains a large black mark on the agency's record. So does another form of covert action: the assassination plots against Fidel Castro of Cuba and Patrice Lumumba of the Congo during the early 1960s. Ever since they came to light in 1975, assassination plots have been prohibited by executive order (except in time of war).

The DO is divided into geographic units (the former Soviet republics, East Europe, West Europe, the Near East, Africa, and the Western Hemisphere) and several specialized staffs, including a Center for Counterterrorism, a Center for Counterintelligence, and a "Special Activities" branch for the planning and conduct of covert action. In each foreign nation, the CIA's top official is called the chief-of-station (COS), who serves as the DO's country spymaster. Beneath the COS in the field chain-of-command are "case officers"—U.S. CIA officers in charge of indigenous spies (agents or "assets").

The Directorate of Administration (DA) is responsible for charge of the day-to-day housekeeping chores of the CIA, but it also administers the controversial polygraphy tests to new and, periodically, to seasoned intelligence officers in search of potential or existing double agents. This directorate also houses the Office of Security (OS), which at the request of the White House violated the CIA's legislative charter by spying on U.S. citizens during the Vietnamese War protests of the 1960s (an illegal activity known by the codename Operation CHAOS that was investigated by Congress in 1975).

The Directorate of Science and Technology (DS&T) is devoted to TECHINT, notably improving satellite and other spying "platforms." This directorate works closely with the National Reconnaissance Office (NRO), an agency that coordinates U.S. high-altitude spying and reports to both the DCI and secretary of the Air Force.

Finally, the Directorate of Intelligence (DI) is where the agency's research and analysis is conducted—the primary purpose of the U.S. intelligence apparatus. The CIA's mission is to understand the world and convey that knowledge in a timely fashion to the president and other decisionmakers. The DI, in conjunction with the National Intelligence Council, is where this vital task is chiefly lodged.

Supervision of the CIA

Scandals such as Operation CHAOS have led the president and Congress to tighten their supervision of the CIA. President Gerald R. Ford established an Intelligence Oversight Board within the executive branch in 1975 and reinvigorated the President's Foreign Intelligence Advisory Board (PFIAD); Congress created an Intelligence Committee in both the Senate and the House during 1976–1977. Both branches issued a fresh set of rules designed to keep the CIA within the bounds of U.S. law.

Despite these rules, the CIA managed to violate its statutory bounds once again in 1986 in what came to be known as the Iran-Contra Affair. Ignoring requirements to report all covert actions to Congress, the administration of Ronald Reagan chose to bypass legislative overseers altogether. The Reagan administration sold weapons secretly to Iran and used the proceeds (augmented by private funding) to support additional covert actions on behalf of the anti-Marxist Contra faction in Nicaragua—completely sidestepping the appropriations process in Congress.

In the aftermath of the Iran-Contra Affair, Congress passed another oversight statute designed to further tighten its reins over the CIA. The Intelligence Authorization Act of 1991 stiffened the approval and reporting requirements for covert actions, and legislators also enacted a separate law to strengthen the power of the CIA's inspector general and make this office more directly accountable to the Congress.

With the end of the Cold War in 1991, the CIA turned its attention toward redefining its role after the sudden dissolution of its chief nemesis, the USSR. The agency had no lack of outside observers joining in the discussion of its future. Some commentators believed the nation no longer needed a CIA—especially since it had failed to anticipate the fall of the Soviet Union. (In fact, the CIA had traced the decline of the USSR fairly closely but—like everyone else—misgauged the swiftness of its final disintegration.) Others thought the world had become an even more dangerous place, requiring additional funding for intelligence.

In 1994 the debate heated up when CIA officer Aldrich H. Ames was exposed as a traitor who had sold intelligence secrets to the USSR for several years and compromised over two dozen U.S. assets in Moscow (at least ten of whom were executed by the Soviet govern-

ment). Presidents Clinton and legislators created a special joint Presidential-Congressional Commission on Intelligence in 1994 to examine the roles and missions of all the U.S. secret agencies. While it was unlikely the CIA would be abolished, it clearly faced a turbulent future, buffeted by reform proposals from every direction.

In 1995 the CIA suffered another setback when it became known that one of its assets in Guatemala may have been involved in the murder of a U.S. citizen living there and a second murder of the Guatemalan husband of another U.S. citizen. The IG's investigation into these charges made it clear that the CIA had been aware of these allegations but had never reported them to Congress as required by law. Once again the CIA appeared to have dismissed the relevance of its legislative overseers; and once again, the agency was in trouble.

The stains on the ledger brought about by the Bay of Pigs, Operation CHAOS, the assassination plots, Iran-Contra, Ames, and then the rogue asset in Guatemala were unfortunate. For these misdirections tended to overshadow the substantial achievements of the CIA during the Cold War, particularly its ability to monitor the military developments in the USSR and its compliance to arms-control treaties. The fact that leaders in the United States had a fairly reliable understanding of the Soviet Union's strengths and weaknesses, and were able to watch closely its military activities—the fruits of a sophisticated TECHINT and some HUMINT capability—were integral parts of U.S. Cold War strategy.

LOCH K. JOHNSON

See also Bay of Pigs Invasion; Covert Action; Deutch, John M.; Dulles, Allen Welsh; Guatemala; Helms, Richard McGarrah; Intelligence; Iran; Iran-Contra Affair; McCone, John Alex; National Security Act; Office of Strategic Services

FURTHER READING

Colby, William, and Peter Forbath. *Honorable Men: My Life in the CIA.* New York, 1978.
Jeffreys-Jones, Rhodri. *The CIA and American Democracy.* New Haven, Conn., 1989.
Johnson, Loch K. *America's Secret Power: The CIA in a Democratic Society.* New York, 1989.
Ranelagh, John. *The Agency: The Rise and Decline of the CIA: From Wild Bill Donovan to William Casey.* New York, 1986.
Turner, Stansfield. *Secrecy and Democracy: The CIA in Transition.* Boston, 1985.

CENTRAL INTELLIGENCE AGENCY ACT

An enabling addendum to the 1947 National Security Act creating the Central Intelligence Agency (CIA), the act permitted the CIA to receive funds secretly under budgetary cover of other federal agencies. In practical terms, this law allowed the director of the CIA to serve as his own accountant, thus preventing hostile foreign governments from learning the scope of U.S. intelligence operations. Other provisions of the law provided for the official seal of the CIA, personnel training, relocation arrangements, and the director's authority to fire personnel for national security reasons without challenge. Passed in an era of intense and broadly held anticommunist sentiment, congressional debate occurred behind closed doors; only mild dissent was heard from one member of the House of Representatives. President Harry S. Truman signed the CIA Act without public comment on 20 June 1949.

The "black budget" provision of the law permits the CIA director to transfer and receive money with greater discretion and subject to less congressional oversight than other executive branch agencies. The CIA can receive funds from other agencies "without regard to limitations of appropriations from which transferred," and funds can be exchanged without regard to ordinary transfer regulations. In addition, the CIA director can reimburse other agencies for personnel services; authorize couriers and guards to carry firearms when classified documents and materials affecting the national security are transported; authorize admission to the United States of certain aliens; and alter, improve, repair, and rent agency facilities without regard to procurement regulations. Neither the Office of Management and Budget nor the General Accounting Office, an arm of Congress, are permitted to examine CIA accounting records, an issue of substantial congressional and public debate in the 1970s. Unchecked secret funding of CIA operations, especially covert actions, continued in the 1980s under the administrations of Presidents Ronald Reagan and George Bush, including funds for rebels in Afghanistan and Contra guerrillas in Nicaragua. Despite evidence of CIA-sponsored and White House-backed Middle East gunrunning operations in the 1980s, the CIA's total budget and the whereabouts of agency funds remain secret. Political pressure to declassify millions of pages of CIA documents increased in the 1990s but CIA Director R. James Woolsey, appointed in 1993, did not support any congressional initiative to reveal the secret budget. The 1996 report of the Commission on the Roles and Capabilities of the United States Intelligence Community addresses the issue of budgetary authority of the Director of Central Intelligence, but it avoids asserting a position on secret funding for CIA operations. The report reveals, however, that 96 percent of national intelligence funding is contained in the budget of the Department of Defense.

JAMES D. CALDER

See also Central Intelligence Agency; Iran-Contra Affair

Darling, Arthur B. *The Central Intelligence Agency: An Instrument of Government, to 1950*. University Park, Pa., 1990.
Johnson, Loch K. *America's Secret Power: The CIA in a Democratic Society*. New York, 1989.
Ranelagh, John. *The Agency: The Rise and Decline of the CIA from Wild Bill Donovan to William Casey*. New York, 1986.

CENTRAL TREATY ORGANIZATION

A regional defense organization, the Central Treaty Organization (CENTO) in 1959 replaced the Baghdad Pact (1955–1959). CENTO's members were Turkey, Iraq, Great Britain, Pakistan, and Iran. Although the Baghdad Pact reflected U.S. interest in a regional defense organization, the United States did not join because of Arab reaction to Iraq's adherence (and Iraq's alliance with Great Britain, whose imperial interests in the region were strongly opposed by Nasser). The pact was extremely unpopular with nationalists in Iraq, and after the overthrow of pro-Western King Faisal II's monarchy in 1958, Iraq withdrew from the pact (24 March 1959). The remaining countries—Great Britain and the three "northern tier" countries, with which the United States concluded three executive agreements in 1959—moved the headquarters from Baghdad to Ankara and renamed the alliance the Central Treaty Organization (21 August 1959), with the intention of linking it with the North Atlantic Treaty Organization. Although CENTO was designed to contain Soviet expansion to the south, the organization lacked a permanent command structure and regularly assigned forces; more important symbolically than in fact, it served primarily as a mechanism for channeling development and infrastructural assistance. While the United States participated in CENTO meetings, it did so as an observer and associate member. After the Islamic revolution in Iran in 1979, the new regime announced (March 1979) that it would withdraw from the organization. Pakistan also withdrew (March 1979) because it felt that CENTO was no longer relevant to Pakistan's security concerns. CENTO was officially dissolved in September 1979.

BRUCE R. KUNIHOLM

See also Middle East

CEYLON
See Sri Lanka

CFE TREATY
See Conventional Armed Forces in Europe, Treaty on

CHAD

A north central African republic bordered by Cameroon, Niger, Nigeria, Libya, Sudan, and the Central African Republic. Before gaining independence in 1960, Chad was the largest and perhaps poorest of France's African possessions. The northernmost part of French Equatorial Africa, Chad shared a contested Saharan border with Libya and stretched south to the more fertile cotton-growing region (known to the French as "useful Chad"). In 1965 tensions between Muslim northerners and Christian/Animist southerners erupted in violence and soon led to factionally complex and widespread conflict.

During the administration of President Ronald Reagan, Chad became a focus of U.S. foreign policy when Secretary of State Alexander Haig charged his department with finding a new way to undermine Libya's Moammar al-Qaddafi. The plan was to attack from Qaddafi's southern flank through Chad, where Libyan troops—in the guise of supporting a factional government under Goukouni Weddeye—occupied and administered much of the northern half of the country. William Casey's first covert action as director of the Central Intelligence Agency (CIA) was arms support for the anti-Qaddafi faction leader, Hissene Habre. When Qaddafi, in quest of the chairmanship of the Organization of African Unity, withdrew most of his troops from Chad, leaving Weddeye's government to its internal squabbles, Habre chased the governmental forces from the capital. Skillfully mixing force and political inducements, Habre brought the southern two-thirds of Chad under governmental control. The United States and France, which provided air cover to prevent Libyan planes from attacking south of the Saharan north, gave useful support.

Between December 1986 and May 1987, Habre's forces conducted a brilliant desert campaign that ousted the Libyans and their Chadian clients from most of their positions in the north, while seizing vast quantities of heavy arms and a large number of Libyan prisoners. The CIA persuaded several hundred of the Libyans to change sides, and set up a secret training camp for these Libyan "Contras." Habre was invited to Washington for a triumphant state visit in June 1987.

Factional strife soon broke out in Habre's government, abetted by quarrels over the disposition of the Libyan arms and the profits from their sale. Habre's rule became more harsh, and a number of opponents were arrested and tortured or simply disappeared. The U.S.-equipped Presidential Security Regiment was used to discipline villages and other army units. By 1991 a significant opposition was being outfitted in Sudan with Libyan support. With French air power remaining studiedly neutral, the opposition, under the leadership of Idriss Deby, in turn chased Habre out of the capital in December 1991. Over

Qaddafi's objections, Deby allowed the CIA to evacuate its Libyan "Contras."

The administration of President George Bush, less obsessed by the Libyan leader than the Reagan administration, quietly liquidated the operation. Neither it, nor its successor, has shown more than routine interest in Chad. Even the prospective billion dollar investment in producing oil in southern Chad by an Exxon-led consortium was not enough to keep Chad off the list of countries whose Agency for International Development (AID) missions were closed in 1994.

WILLIAM J. FOLTZ

See also Africa; Libya

FURTHER READING

Buijtenhuijs, Robert. *Le Frolinat et les Guerres Civiles du Tchad (1977–1984)*. Paris, 1987.
Foltz, William J. "Reconstructing the State of Chad." In *Collapsed States: The Disintegration and Restoration of Legitimate Authority*, edited by I. William Zartman. Boulder, Colo., 1995.

CHADHA DECISION

(*Immigration and Naturalization Service* v. *Chadha*, 462 U.S. 919 [1983])

A case in which the Supreme Court declared a legislative veto, authorized by the Immigration and Nationality Act of 1952, to be unconstitutional. The act had delegated to the executive branch the power to decide that a particular deportable alien should not be deported on grounds such as hardship but empowered either the House of Representatives or the Senate, acting alone, to invalidate such a decision. In an opinion written by Chief Justice Warren Burger, the Court found this one-house legislative veto clearly contrary to the plain words of the Constitution, both the bicamerality requirement that legislation must be passed by both houses of Congress and the presentment clauses requiring that legislation be presented to the president for signature. *Chadha* interpreted the system of separation of powers as preventing delegation of legislative powers (defined as powers to alter the legal rights, duties, and relations of persons outside the legislative branch) both to Congress alone and to subsets of the legislature.

The legislative veto was a response to the problems of reconciling the separation of powers system with the complexities of the burgeoning administrative state. Unable itself to give serious legislative consideration to the vast array of general regulations and specific decisions necessitated by the modern regulatory system, Congress increasingly had delegated such authority to the executive branch. Legislative vetoes were a means to maintain some congressional oversight and control, and their availability encouraged more extensive delegations than might otherwise have been willingly contemplated by Congress. In their various forms they enabled both houses together, or one house alone, or even a congressional committee, to exercise power over executive action much more freely than if the full legislative process were required in each case.

Legislative veto provisions were first enacted as practical accommodations between Congress and the executive branch in the Reorganization Act of 1932, some successor statutes, and in such wartime legislation as the Lend-Lease Act of 1941, although Presidents Herbert Hoover and Franklin D. Roosevelt doubted the constitutionality of such provisions. They became steadily more common, leading in the late 1970s to proposals in Congress to subject all federal regulations to such vetoes. Reacting against what they saw as congressional overreaching, the administrations of President Jimmy Carter and Ronald Reagan proposed treating such veto provisions as legally ineffective and moved to challenge them in court.

Chadha and related cases cast doubt on a wide range of legislative veto provisions contained in some 120 laws then in force, including provisions requiring approval as well as disapproval of executive action and provisions for prospective as well as retrospective congressional action. Several major statutes dealing with foreign relations were potentially affected. Legislative veto powers had not been formally exercised to block executive action on significant foreign relations questions. The inclusion, however, of veto provisions in statutes dealing with such matters as arms sales, supply of nuclear materials, and foreign aid, gave considerable political influence to Congress and lobby groups and had an impact on executive branch behavior. The political importance of veto provisions in the relationship between Congress and the executive branch in international affairs led to mixed responses to *Chadha*. Some statutes, including those dealing with national emergencies and export administration, were amended to replace provisions for concurrent resolutions (not requiring presentment) with requirements for joint resolutions (requiring presentment). In other statutes legislative veto provisions remained but have not been exercised. Further legislative veto provisions have been enacted since *Chadha*, and they have often been politically efficacious despite executive branch denials of their legal effectiveness.

Judicial review of legislative veto provisions in foreign relations statutes is likely to be rare. If such review occurred particular problems could arise if a court were to find that an unconstitutional legislative veto provision could not be severed, rendering the entire statute unconstitutional. One such controversial clause (which is probably severable) is section 5(c) of the War Powers Resolu-

tion of 1973, which provides that, if there is no declaration of war or statutory authorization, U.S. forces engaged in hostilities outside the United States must be removed by the president if Congress so directs by concurrent resolution. While this clause does not on its face delegate power to the executive branch, it does contemplate the exercise of congressional power without presentment and thus without the possibility of presidential veto. Post-*Chadha* proposals to amend this to require a joint resolution or bill did not pass, with some arguing that the clause related to constitutional war powers is not subject to the presentment rules applicable to legislation.

Within its areas of constitutional competence, Congress may enhance its oversight and control of executive action by such generally lawful methods as writing laws narrowly or with time limits, imposing report-and-wait or consultation requirements, toughening its own rules of procedure, creating such tightly controlled systems as the fast track for international trade agreements, issuing guidelines, striking informal deals between agencies and congressional committees controlling future appropriations, negotiating political agreements with the president, holding hearings, and passing Sense of Congress resolutions.

The felt necessities of political practice have also resulted in continued post-legislative involvement of Congress and its members in ways inconsistent with the Court's reasoning in *Chadha*, often with the practical acquiescence of the executive branch. This long-standing political practice has been one basis for criticism of the *Chadha* opinion. Despite the reluctance of the other branches to give full effect to the decision in practice, the courts have shown no inclination to back away from the broad principles of *Chadha*, preferring on the contrary to emphasize the checks on the legislature contained in the constitutional framework, and in this respect to adhere to Chief Justice Burger's observation in *Chadha* that "convenience and efficiency are not the primary objectives—or the hallmarks—of democratic government."

BENEDICT W. KINGSBURY

See also Congress; Immigration; Immigration and Naturalization Service; Legislative Veto; Presidency; War Powers Resolution

FURTHER READING

Craig, Barbara Hinkson. *Chadha: The Story of an Epic Constitutional Struggle*. New York, 1988.

Fisher, Louis. "The Legislative Veto: Invalidated, It Survives," *Law and Contemporary Problems* 56 (1993): 273.

Franck, Thomas M., and Clifford A. Bob. "The Return of Humpty-Dumpty: Foreign Relations Law After the *Chadha* Case." *American Journal of International Law* 79 (1985): 912–960.

Tribe, Laurence H. *American Constitutional Law*, 2nd ed. Mineola, N.Y., 1988.

CHAMBERLAIN, ARTHUR NEVILLE
(*b.* 18 March 1869; *d.* 9 November 1940)

Conservative British statesman, son of Joseph Chamberlain, and prime minister of Great Britain (1937–1940) who advocated a policy of appeasement toward Adolf Hitler and Benito Mussolini. Born in Edgbaston, England, Chamberlain was educated at Rugby and Mason College, Birmingham; managed a plantation in the Bahamas from 1890 to 1897; entered local politics in Birmingham; and was elected to Parliament in 1918. Beginning in 1922 he held several cabinet positions. As chancellor of the exchequer (1931–1937), he pushed for the adoption of a system of protective tariffs and the abandonment of the gold standard. These changes helped create the imperial customs union adopted at the Imperial Economic Conference in Ottawa, Canada, in August 1932. Many U.S. citizens perceived the imperial preference system as retaliation against the high Smoot-Hawley Tariff of 1930.

When he became prime minister in 1937, Chamberlain, troubled by German and Italian aggressiveness, decided to protect British interests in the Mediterranean by signing an agreement with Italy recognizing the conquest of Ethiopia on condition that Benito Mussolini discontinue Italian involvement in the Spanish civil war. Chamberlain's major test came when Germany annexed Austria in 1938 and threatened to annex the Sudeten area of Czechoslovakia. Firm in his belief that Adolf Hitler could be trusted to keep his word, Chamberlain met with French, German, and Italian leaders at Munich in September 1938 and agreed that Germany could annex the Sudetenland— ostensibly to prevent a German invasion of the territory and avoid a general European war. He returned to London proclaiming that he had brought "peace for our time." Unenthusiastic about closer U.S.-British relations, he considered the U.S. government and President Franklin D. Roosevelt unreliable. Chamberlain believed that Hitler was basically reasonable, could be appeased, and that war would be averted. In his view central and eastern Europe were destined to be dominated by either Germany or the Soviet Union. He also thought, at the time of the Munich conference, that Hitler was largely satisfying principles of self-determination desired by the German people. When Hitler annexed the rest of Czechoslovakia in 1939, Chamberlain lost his illusions. Belatedly recognizing that Hitler's intent was expansion by conquest, Chamberlain did his best to hasten British military preparations and joined France in a commitment to defend Poland. Germany's invasion of Poland, therefore, brought Great Britain into the war in September 1939. Under criticism for ineffective conduct of the war, Chamberlain resigned as prime minister in May 1940 and was replaced by Winston Churchill, much to the delight of President Roosevelt.

BERNARD V. BURKE

See also Appeasement; Czech Republic; Germany; Gold Standard; Great Britain; Hitler, Adolf; Munich Conference; Mussolini, Benito; Self-Determination; World War II

FURTHER READING

Dilks, David. *Pioneering and Reform, 1869–1929*, vol. 1 of *Neville Chamberlain*. New York, 1984.
Macleod, Iain. *Neville Chamberlain*. London, 1961.
Parker, R. A. C. *Chamberlain and Appeasement: British Policy and the Coming of the Second World War*. New York, 1993.
Rock, William R. *Chamberlain and Roosevelt: British Foreign Policy and the United States, 1937–1940*. Columbus, Ohio, 1988.

CHAPULTEPEC CONFERENCE
(21 February–8 March 1945)

Known formally as the Inter-American Conference on Problems of War and Peace, it took place in Mexico City, and established the principle of regional self-defense, pending United Nations action. Latin American nations insisted on a conference with the United States, because they sought to resolve the U.S. confrontation with Argentina over that country's alleged pro fascist wartime policies. The Latin Americans also wanted to discuss U.S. postwar economic assistance and the role of the inter-American system in the emerging United Nations. Although the conferees, which included the United States and all Latin American nations except Argentina, decided to postpone economic discussions for another conference, they agreed that Argentina could rejoin the inter-American community if it declared war against Nazi Germany. In the Act of Chapultepec, the conferees resolved to support the principle of collective self-defense through regional security pacts. This act served as a basis for Article 51 of the UN Charter, authorizing regional security arrangements, and for the Rio Treaty of 1947, an inter-American collective security pact.

STEPHEN G. RABE

See also Argentina; Latin America; Rio Treaty; United Nations

FURTHER READING

Connell-Smith, Gordon. *The Inter-American System*. London, 1966.
Green, David. *The Containment of Latin America*. Chicago, 1971.
Smith, Gaddis. *The Last Years of the Monroe Doctrine*. New York, 1994.

CHEMICAL WEAPONS

Weapons that disable, injure, or kill by disrupting the normal biological processes of their victims. They include lethal nerve, blister, blood, and choking agents; nonlethal disabling agents that induce temporary paralysis in their victims; and tear gas. Means of delivery include missiles, tube and rocket artillery, aerial bombs, spray dispensers, and mines. Although chemical weapons are usually classified as weapons of mass destruction, their destructive potential is significantly less than that of nuclear and biological weapons. Chemical agents must be used in massive quantities in order to attain lethal concentrations over broad areas. Their effectiveness depends on favorable conditions of employment, including appropriate delivery means and atmospheric conditions (such as wind speed and direction and air temperature). The impact of chemical-agent use can be significantly reduced through countermeasures such as protective masks and overgarments. Consequently, chemical weapons are most effective against armies or civilian populations that lack such protection.

Chemical weapons were first used on a widespread basis by both sides during World War I and have subsequently been used by the Japanese in Manchuria in the 1930s; Egypt in Yemen in the 1960s; and, in the 1980s, by both sides during the Iran-Iraq War, by Libya in Chad, and by the Iraqi government against Kurdish insurgents and civilians. They may also have been used by Soviet forces in Afghanistan. In the mid-1990s, the United States and Russia retained the largest inventories of chemical-warfare agents and weapons in the world, although both countries were dramatically reducing their stocks. At the same time, more than two dozen countries were engaged in chemical-warfare research and development efforts. Of these, nearly twenty possessed an offensive chemical warfare capability, including China, Egypt, India, Indonesia, Iran, Israel, Libya, Myanmar, North Korea, Pakistan, Saudi Arabia, South Africa, South Korea, Syria, Taiwan, Thailand, and Vietnam. Many of these countries were also developing ballistic or cruise missiles to deliver these agents. Until the early 1990s, Iraq had one of the largest chemical-warfare programs in the developing world; as a result of the Gulf War of 1991 and subsequent action by United Nations inspectors, however, all of Iraq's known chemical-warfare capabilities had been destroyed by mid-1994.

The international community has taken a number of steps to stem the spread of chemical weapons: the Geneva Protocol for the Prohibition of the Use in War of Asphyxiating, Poisonous or Other Gases, and of Bacteriological Methods of Warfare (1925); the creation of the Australia Group (1984); the U.S.-Soviet Chemical Weapon Destruction Accord of 1990; and the Chemical Weapons Convention of 1992. By 1995 more than 130 states had become party to the Geneva Protocol (the United States in 1975), which banned the use of chemical and biological weapons in war. While the protocol bans the use of chemical weapons, it does not prohibit their development, production, possession, or transfer.

Thus, in effect, the protocol only bans first use of chemical weapons. In addition, the protocol lacks provisions for verification or enforcement. Because of these shortcomings, the violation of the protocol by Iraq and others, and the failure to address the problem of proliferation, efforts since the 1970s have focused on establishing a multilateral convention banning chemical weapons.

The Australia Group was established in 1984 by several major industrial states in order to regulate the supply of equipment and precursor chemicals used to produce chemical agents. The group conducts informal consultations to exchange intelligence and coordinate export controls. It has likewise adopted informal guidelines on the transfer of chemical-weapon-related equipment and a warning list of fifty chemical-weapon precursors, although the group has no formal monitoring or enforcement authority. By 1994 the Australia Group had twenty-two members and eleven other states had agreed to adhere to group guidelines. While the group had achieved some success in stemming the spread of chemical weapons, the lack of an enforcement mechanism and the growth of chemical industries around the world have, in part, undercut this effort.

The U.S.-Soviet Chemical Weapon Destruction Accord was concluded in June 1990. This bilateral agreement required the United States and the Soviet Union to slash their existing chemical weapons stocks, estimated at 30,000 and 40,000 tons, respectively, to 5,000 agent-tons each by the year 2002, with provisions for additional cuts at a later date. Implementation of this agreement has been slow, however, because of the considerable cost of the destruction effort (which is expected to run as high as $10 billion), technical and safety problems, and environmental concerns. Reports that Russia was continuing work on a new generation of highly lethal binary nerve agents, in violation of this agreement, raised questions about Russia's commitment to chemical disarmament.

By 1995, the Chemical Weapons Convention, unveiled in January 1993, had been signed by more than 150 states (although less than 20 had ratified it). The convention was scheduled to go into force once it has been ratified by sixty-five countries. It bans the development, production, stockpiling, transfer, or use of chemical weapons and requires that all existing chemical weapons and stocks be destroyed within ten years of the treaty's entry into force. (The convention does, however, permit the use of riot-control agents by internal security and police forces.) This treaty is considered unique among arms control agreements of all kinds, for several reasons. It is universal in scope; it provides for sanctions against violators or holdouts who refuse to join (namely, denial of access to chemical industrial equipment and products); and it establishes the most intrusive on-site inspection regime mandated by any existing arms control treaty,

---

CHEMICAL WEAPONS GLOSSARY

Australia Group: an organization of 20 Western states that meets biannually to share intelligence on and coordinate export control regulations of chemicals and technology necessary to develop a CW-production capability, in an effort to stem the proliferation of chemical weapons. The group is so called since the meetings originated in 1985 at the Australian embassy in Paris.

binary weapons: chemical munitions in which the relatively nontoxic components of the lethal chemical agent are stored in two separate canisters. Upon launch or firing, the membrane separating the canisters ruptures and the chemical react, creating a nerve agent.

Chemical Weapons Convention (CWC): the multilateral treaty that bans development production, stockpiling, and transfer of chemical weapons.

Geneva Protocol: the treaty negotiated in 1925, in response to the massive use of chemicals in World War I, which prohibits the use of chemical weapons. The treaty makes no prohibitions on the production or stockpiling of CW agents or munitions. (The full name of the treaty is the "Protocol for the Prohibition of the Use in War of Asphyxiating, Poisonous or Other gases, and of Bacteriological Methods of Warfare.")

From *International Handbook on Chemical Weapons Proliferation*, Gordon M. Burck and Chrales C. Flowerree. ©1991 by Greenwood Press, Westport, CT. Reprinted with permission of Greenwood Publishing Group, Inc.

---

including provisions for routine and no-refusal challenge inspections. As of late 1996, the United States had not yet ratified the treaty because of concerns about congressional opposition to the treaty, doubts about the verifiability of the treaty, and reports of Russian noncompliance with the U.S.-Soviet Chemical Weapons Destruction Accord. Several holdout states have also refused to sign the treaty, raising questions about the treaty's universality and hence its ultimate utility. These states include Egypt, Libya, Iraq, and Syria—countries that have linked their participation to the dismantling of Israel's nuclear capability—as well as North Korea and Vietnam. However, the magnitude of the verification challenge will make it difficult, if not impossible, to detect all proscribed facilities or activities and undeclared stocks of agents or weapons.

MICHAEL EISENSTADT

See also Biological Weapons; Iraq; Russia and the Soviet Union

FURTHER READING

Burck, Gordon M., and Charles C. Flowerree. *International Handbook on Chemical Weapons Proliferation.* Westport, Conn., 1991.

Smithson, Amy E., ed. *The Chemical Weapons Convention Handbook.* Washington, D.C., 1993.

U.S. Congress, Office of Technology Assessment. *Proliferation of Weapons of Mass Destruction: Assessing the Risks.* Washington, D.C., 1993.

———. *Technologies Underlying Weapons of Mass Destruction.* Washington, D.C., 1993.

CHENEY, RICHARD BRUCE
(b. 30 January 1941)

Secretary of defense (1989–1993). A graduate of the University of Wyoming, Cheney served on the staff of Donald Rumsfeld at the Office of Economic Opportunity (OEO) (1969), and as deputy (1970–1971) to Rumsfeld when the latter became President Richard Nixon's White House counselor. He also served as President Gerald R. Ford's chief of staff (1975–1977), then was elected to the House of Representatives (1979–1989) and became House minority whip, supporting President Ronald Reagan's efforts to increase defense spending. As secretary of defense during the administration of President George Bush, he asserted control over the Pentagon bureaucracy and advocated reforms in the procurement process (e.g., canceling the navy's A-12 attack plane). With Chairman of the Joint Chiefs of Staff General Colin Powell, whom he was instrumental in appointing, Cheney supported the invasion of Panama in December 1989. He also played a major role in many of the decisions following the Iraqi invasion of Kuwait in August 1990 that led to U.S. successes in the Gulf War of 1991—persuading Saudi Arabia to permit a defensive military buildup in the Persian Gulf, subsequently supporting development of an offensive military capability in the region, and being one of the first to raise the idea of an attack on Iraqi forces in Kuwait from the west (the so-called "left hook"). Skeptical of reform in the Soviet Union, he nevertheless initiated efforts to downsize the military, developing a plan to reduce U.S. forces by 25 percent through the creation of cadre forces.

Bruce R. Kuniholm

See also Bush, George Herbert Walker; Gulf War of 1990–1991; Panama and Panama Canal

FURTHER READING

Gordon, Michael R. and Bernard E. Trainor. *The General's War.* New York, 1995.

CHENNAULT, CLAIRE LEE AND ANNA CHAN

(*b.* 6 September 1893; *d.* 27 July 1958)

(*b.* 23 June 1925)

Claire Chennault was a U.S. Army officer and pioneer in the development of U.S. and Chinese aviation; Anna Chan was a Chinese-American entrepreneur and supporter of the Chinese Nationalist (Taiwanese) government. Claire Chennault volunteered for flight training when the United States entered World War I and served in the Army Air Corps until he retired as a captain in 1937. On the eve of Japan's attack on China in 1937, he accepted a job as aviation adviser to Jiang Jieshi's (Chiang Kai-shek) Nationalist government. Chennault assisted China's tiny air force and developed a close friendship with Generalissimo and Madame Jiang. China became a beneficiary of U.S. Lend-Lease aid in 1941, and Chennault organized the American Volunteer Group, or Flying Tigers, with U.S. pilots flying P-40 fighter planes in operations against the Japanese just before and after the Pearl Harbor attack in December 1941.

Chennault reentered U.S. military service in 1942 as a brigadier general and the next year assumed command of the Fourteenth Air Force. He became a bitter rival of General Joseph W. Stilwell, commander of the China-Burma-India theater. Stilwell, who had little respect for Jiang, wanted to use the scarce supplies to retrain Chinese armies. Chennault, who opposed disrupting Jiang's chain of command, advocated an expanded air war against the Japanese. During 1943 and 1944 Washington backed Chennault. Then, as Stilwell had predicted, air attacks provoked a Japanese offensive that nearly drove China out of the war. His strategy discredited, Chennault retired from military service shortly before Japan surrendered. In 1946 he created Civil Air Transport (CAT), a cargo service that flew for the Nationalists in China's civil war (1945–1949). In 1950 the Central Intelligence Agency purchased control of CAT, renamed Air America, and used it as a cover for covert operations in Asia, especially in Vietnam. Chennault retired from CAT in 1955.

In 1947 Chennault married Anna Chan, a Chinese national who later became a U.S. citizen. Chan became a successful business executive, influential supporter of Taiwan, and a prominent member of the conservative wing of the Republican party. She served as an intermediary in 1968 between presidential candidate Richard Nixon and the South Vietnamese government and conveyed Nixon's advice that Saigon block any progress at the Paris peace talks on the Vietnam War lest an early settlement help the candidacy of Democrat Hubert Humphrey. After Nixon restored U.S. contact with the People's Republic of China, Chan actively promoted U.S.-Chinese trade. In the mid-1970s, her name was linked to an influence-peddling scheme involving South Korean lobbyists and members of Congress.

Michael Schaller

See also Central Intelligence Agency; China; China Lobby; Jiang Jieshi

FURTHER READING

Chennault, Claire. *Way of a Fighter.* New York, 1949.
Schaller, Michael. *The U.S. Crusade in China, 1938–1945.* New York, 1979.
Tuchman, Barbara. *Stilwell and the American Experience in China.* New York, 1972.

CHESAPEAKE-LEOPARD AFFAIR

(1807)

An engagement between British and U.S. frigates off Chesapeake Bay, touching upon the important question of national sovereignty arising from the practice of impressment of seamen. On 22 June 1807 the forty-gun British frigate *Leopard* demanded to search the thirty-six-gun U.S. frigate *Chesapeake*, off the coast of Norfolk, Virginia, for British deserters from the British navy believed to be on board. Because a warship was considered an extension of a nation's territory and thus not subject to search or seizure in time of peace, the *Chesapeake*'s commanding officer, Commodore James Barron, refused to allow the search. The *Leopard* responded by firing on the U.S. ship, killing three men and wounding eighteen. Unready for action, the *Chesapeake* struck its colors and four men, including one British deserter and three U.S. citizens, were removed. The *Chesapeake*, its masts damaged and its hull pummeled, made it back to Hampton Roads, Virginia. President Thomas Jefferson ordered British warships from U.S. waters. Although the British government disavowed the incident and offered reparations, a settlement was delayed until 1811 because the United States insisted on a British abandonment of the practice of impressment. In the meantime, the *Chesapeake* affair continued to fester, underscoring Anglo-American differences and contributing to the rising tide of anti-British feeling in the United States that led to the War of 1812.

Donald R. Hickey

See also Impressment; War of 1812

FURTHER READING

Perkins, Bradford. *Prologue to War: England and the United States, 1805–1812*. Berkeley, Calif., 1961.

———. *The Creation of a Republican Empire, 1776–1865*, vol. 1 of *The Cambridge History of American Foreign Relations*, edited by Warren I. Cohen. New York, 1993.

Zimmerman, James Fulton. *Impressment of American Seamen*. New York, 1925.

CHIANG KAI-SHEK

See Jiang Jieshi

CHILE

A South American republic, bordering the South Pacific Ocean, Argentina, Bolivia, and Peru. Chile did not establish formal diplomatic relations with the United States until 1832, but the U.S. consul in the port of Valparaíso, Joel Roberts Poinsett, was active throughout the period during which Chile struggled for its independence from Spain (1810–1818). A trade treaty was signed in 1834, and U.S. relations with Chile during the nineteenth century were mainly concerned with trade and commerce. U.S. entrepreneurs such as William Wheelwright promoted steamship travel and built railroads and bridges in Chile. In mid-century, commercial relations expanded as a result of the opening of California during the gold rush, which made Valparaíso an important fueling and trading port. As the Latin American country with the largest navy and as the victor in the War of the Pacific against Bolivia and Peru (1879–1883), Chile was regarded by the United States as a potential rival in the South Pacific section of the hemisphere. Both Washington and Santiago felt that Chile was closer to Great Britain, a major investor in its nitrate mines, than to the United States. U.S. diplomatic pressure in connection with the *Baltimore* incident in 1891, in which two American sailors were killed in a brawl in Valparaíso, led to the payment by Chile of an indemnity but also to growing resentment of U.S. strong-arm tactics.

In the early twentieth century, U.S. investors developed large and efficient copper mines at El Teniente and Chuquicamata, and U.S. ownership of Chile's principal source of foreign exchange became a continuing source of nationalist resentment. Chile resisted U.S. pressure to declare war against Germany in World War I, in part because of the large German population in the agricultural areas of southern Chile. In the 1920s the United States acted to assist in the settlement of the Tacna-Arica border controversy between Chile and Peru, although the final settlement in 1929 was the result of direct negotiations between the two countries. During World War II Chile again resisted U.S. pressure to break relations with the Axis, finally doing so in January 1943, when the U.S. government revealed instances of German subversive activity in Chile. During the war U.S. copper companies cooperated in keeping the price of copper down—an action that Chileans resented, because it not only resulted in lost tax revenues but, when the accumulated wartime revenues were spent after the war, their value was diminished by the postwar inflation.

After World War II the United States set up the Inter-American Defense Board, based in Washington, D.C., with Chile and most other Latin American states as members. This led in 1947 to the signing of the Inter-American Treaty of Mutual Assistance, which provided for the collective defense of the Americas against external attack. In 1948 Chile participated in the establishment of the Organization of American States (OAS) at the Bogotá (Colombia) Conference in 1948. In the same year, partly as a result of U.S. pressure, Chile outlawed its Communist party, a ban that lasted until 1956. During the Korean War (1950–1953) the United States again attempted to impose a price ceiling on copper, although it allowed some sales at higher prices on the London metals market. In 1953, Chile signed a Mutual Defense Assistance Pact with the United States, and the Chilean military began to participate in U.S. training programs and to receive grants and low-interest loans. During the 1950s U.S. policy concentrated mainly on fostering Chile's integration into the inter-American system—especially its military aspects—and on smoothing over its differences with U.S.-owned copper companies.

In 1958, when Salvador Allende Gossens, the candidate of a socialist-communist coalition, nearly won the presidency, Washington became interested in combating the influence of the Chilean Communist party, especially through the covert activities of the Central Intelligence Agency (CIA). In 1961 President John F. Kennedy announced the Alliance for Progress, a ten-year program of aid to Latin America aimed at demonstrating that democratic reforms could be more effective than the communist revolution preached by Fidel Castro, who had come to power in Cuba in 1959, and Chile became a showcase of the alliance. The conservative government of President Jorge Alessandri passed a mild agrarian reform bill and received significant loans for housing, education, and health. The presidential election of 1964 pitted Allende against reformist Christian Democrat Eduardo Frei Montalva. The CIA spent $2.6 million in support of Frei's successful candidacy, although his election probably did not need outside support; the right, fearing an Allende victory, had thrown its reluctant support to Frei, who promised a "revolution in liberty." With U.S. backing, he pushed through a more sweeping agrarian reform, as well as "Chileanization"—Chile's purchase of majority ownership of the U.S.-owned copper mines with the purchase price invested in the expansion of Chile's refining capacity. U.S. advisers also assisted in improving tax collections, expanding housing, and improving education. During the 1960s the Chilean military received a total of $125 million in military aid, most of it in the form of grants.

After Richard M. Nixon became president in January 1969, relations between the United States and Chile became notably cooler. Nixon announced a low-profile policy in Chile and reduced U.S. aid. President Frei withdrew an invitation to Nelson A. Rockefeller when he toured Latin America as Nixon's representative, and the Chileans presented Nixon with the all-Latin American Consensus of Viña del Mar, which was critical of U.S. aid policies. In addition, Chile's claim to 200 nautical miles of territorial waters was resisted by the United States in the third United Nations conference on the law of the seas. Despite the low-profile policy, the Nixon administration became deeply involved in Chile when it became apparent that the left had a serious chance of winning the 1970 presidential elections. Once again Allende was their candidate. Policy disputes in Washington about whether to support Alessandri, the candidate of right, or Radomiro Tomic from the left wing of the Christian Democratic party, were resolved by authorizing the CIA to spend $300,000 for an anti-Allende spoiling campaign of propaganda without giving direct aid to any candidate. Alessandri received as much as $600,000 from U.S. businesses, and later investigations revealed that the International Telephone and Telegraph Company (ITT) had attempted unsuccessfully to use the CIA to fund candidates. After Allende won the popular election by only 1.2 percent of the vote, necessitating a congressional runoff with second-place finisher Alessandri, President Nixon ordered the CIA to do everything possible to prevent Allende's election by the Chilean congress. The CIA program included propaganda, economic destabilization, and a top-secret (even the ambassador was kept uninformed), ultimately unsuccessful, effort to promote a military coup. After Allende was elected the CIA carried out a program of covert support for opposition newspapers, radio, and electoral candidates. It was also in touch with the Chilean military and provided a small amount of support to an extreme rightist group. There is no evidence that the CIA had any direct role in the 11 September 1973 coup that overthrew Allende.

While Allende was in office the United States cut back its economic assistance, pressured both the World Bank and the Inter-American Development Bank to deny multilateral loans, and discouraged private loans, especially after Allende nationalized the remaining U.S. copper shares in the mines, deducting "excess profits," which meant that except for recent investments, the copper companies received nothing. Allende also took over most

of the other U.S.-owned companies in Chile, often using measures of dubious legality. Allende received credits from Europe and Latin America, as well as from the Soviet Union, so the U.S. pressures were not a major factor in his economic difficulties, which were principally due to heavy deficit financing, a drop in farm and factory production due to government and worker takeovers, and shortages of spare parts for the copper industry that the former owners refused to supply. It is, however, possible that CIA aid went indirectly to support a crippling truckers strike that began in July 1973 and lasted until the September coup. Meanwhile, U.S. military aid continued.

Pinochet and After

The 11 September 1973 coup led by a military junta headed by General Augusto Pinochet Ugarte, against what was, despite its flaws, a democratically elected government, and, in particular, the harsh repression and killings that followed the coup, including the deaths of two U.S. citizens, provoked outrage in the United States. In 1974 details about the CIA role in Chile were leaked, leading to a full-scale investigation by the Senate Select Committee on Intelligence Activities, which recommended tightened controls on covert action that were later enacted into law. Liberal senators moved to cut aid to Chile, and in June 1976 the Kennedy Amendment ended all U.S. military aid and sales, pending improvements in human rights. Tension was further heightened by the September 1976 murder in Washington, D.C., by the Chilean intelligence agents of Orlando Letelier, Allende's former ambassador to the United States.

The administration of President Jimmy Carter gave greater emphasis to the promotion of human rights as an important element in U.S. foreign policy, leading to a further worsening in relations with Chile. Under pressure from Washington, Pinochet's government extradited a U.S. citizen living in Chile who had organized the Letelier assassination and, along with several Cuban-Americans who had actually carried out the bombing, he was sentenced to prison. The United States, however, played an important role in securing the mediation of the Vatican in late 1978 to head off an impending war between Chile and Argentina over the ownership of four islands in the Beagle Channel at the southern tip of the continent. In 1979 a threatened boycott of Chilean exports by the American Federation of Labor–Congress of Industrial Organizations (AFL-CIO) led to the reestablishment of limited trade union activity in Chile.

Ronald Reagan came to the White House in 1981 promising a change in U.S. human rights policy that would emphasize quiet diplomacy and limited pressure on authoritarian governments that were friendly to the United States. Efforts were made to lift the sanctions on Chile, but Congress insisted that Chile must first try to bring to justice the Chileans who were responsible for the Letelier assassination. Human rights violations had diminished in Chile but the Pinochet government still imposed a state of siege, and there were occasional spectacular murders of opposition leaders. Between 1983 and 1985 the Reagan policy began to shift toward greater support for a return to democracy in Chile. This was in part a reaction to Pinochet's intransigence about a political opening. It was also intended by the Reagan administration to match U.S. demands for democratization by the Marxist government in Nicaragua, and was part of a broader effort to give greater global emphasis to democracy. The arrival as ambassador to Chile of Harry Barnes, a professional diplomat strongly committed to democracy, signaled that shift, and public statements by the Department of State stressed the need for a return to democracy. The policy change was facilitated by the formation in Chile of a broad-based opposition movement that excluded the Communist party because it had adopted a policy of armed struggle against the Pinochet regime.

The first major and tangible demonstration of the impact of the shift of U.S. policy took place in June 1985, when Pinochet lifted the state of siege, the basis for press censorship and indefinite detentions, in response to a U.S. threat to oppose international loans and guarantees unless such steps were taken. The United States also introduced a resolution at the March 1986 meeting of the UN Human Rights Commission, expressing "profound concern" over the human rights situation in Chile. It was adopted unanimously. The Chilean constitution, ratified in a snap plebiscite back in 1980, provided for a vote in 1988 on the renewal of President Pinochet's eight-year term as president. In 1987 the U.S. Congress voted to appropriate $1 million to promote democracy in Chile through the National Endowment for Democracy, and the U.S. Agency for International Development allocated $1.2 million to support a voter registration drive. These U.S. funds were spent for polling, vote monitoring, FAX and telephone networks to report election results, and media support. While it was a contributory rather than a decisive factor, the U.S. aid helped to bring about the 55-to-43 percent vote against Pinochet in the October 1988 plebiscite.

Democracy returned to Chile with the victory of the *Concertación* for Democracy, a sixteen-party coalition headed by Christian Democrat Patricio Aylwin Azócar, in December 1989 elections. Aylwin was inaugurated as president in March 1990. Pinochet remained as army chief, but the former head of DINA, the intelligence agency that murdered Letelier, was put on trial, and a full report was made on the deaths and disappearances since 1973. The U.S. arms ban was lifted and Chile pushed for a free trade agreement with the United States. The new government continued the free market

policies of its predecessor but supplemented them with programs of health, education, and job training. The cabinet was made up principally of Christian Democrats and Socialists, many of whom had received advanced degrees from U.S. universities. Foreign investment, especially but not only from the United States, soared, and the past tension and mutual distrust between Chile and the United States was replaced by cooperation and support.

PAUL E. SIGMUND

See also Allende (Gossens), Salvador; Alliance for Progress; Central Intelligence Agency; Human Rights; National Endowment for Democracy; Pinochet (Ugarte), Augusto

FURTHER READING

Bowers, Claude G. *Chile Through Embassy Windows, 1939–1953.* New York, 1958.
Davis, Nathaniel. *The Last Two Years of Salvador Allende.* Ithaca, N.Y., 1986.
Francis, Michael. *The Limits of Hegemony: United States Relations with Argentina and Chile During World War II.* Notre Dame, Ind., 1977.
Munoz, Heraldo, and Carlos Portales. *Elusive Friendship: A Survey of U.S.–Chilean Relations.* Boulder, Colo., 1991.
Pike, Fredrick B. *Chile and the United States, 1880–1962.* Notre Dame, Ind., 1963.
Sigmund, Paul E. *The United States and Democracy in Chile.* Baltimore, 1993.

CHINA

A "people's republic" with an estimated population of 1.2 billion, located in East Asia, and bordered by a 4,000-mile coastline in the east and south, and by the former Soviet Union, Mongolia, Pakistan, India, Nepal, Burma, Laos, and Vietnam. The history of U.S. relations with China has been a painful saga, beset by confrontation, cultural misperception, and indifference. Ignorance often led the United States to anticipate decisions and actions from the Chinese incompatible with their history, national priorities, and traditions, while pride encouraged the Chinese to disparage U.S. power, wealth, and values, leading to acrimony and, on occasion, a sense of betrayal. Whether in strategic, economic, or political contexts, U.S. foreign policy often has sought to use China to resolve problems with other countries while paying relatively little direct attention to Chinese needs and interests. Similarly, the Chinese believed they could maneuver U.S. "barbarians" into deflecting pressures on them that came initially from Europeans and later from the Japanese and Russians.

The Eighteenth and Nineteenth Centuries

Colonial America saw China as exotic and curious, a civilization and a people to be wondered at but too distant to be taken seriously as a threat or an ally. Wealthy colonists appreciated Chinese porcelains and silk and copied the contemporary European fondness for chinoiserie (Chinese-style furniture and artifacts). More influential was the taste for tea, which swept the colonies as it did England. When protests against London's efforts to tax the colonists began in 1773, it was tea shipped from southern China that Bostonians threw into the harbor.

U.S. citizens arrived in China under their own flag for the first time in 1784, after their newly won independence freed them from the British East India Company's trade monopoly. That first voyage of the *Empress of China* returned a handsome profit for its New York investors, and soon every port in the new United States dispatched ships to join in opening the China market. The commercial lure prevailed despite social customs and legal practices that U.S. merchants, along with Europeans, found alien and dangerous. Anxious to preserve their commercial access, they went so far as to abandon their own legal procedures in 1821 and surrender to local authorities, and certain death, a seaman named Terranova, whose killing of a Chinese woman had prompted a boycott of U.S. goods. Willing to jettison the due process of Western law, they had few moral qualms about disregarding Chinese government opposition to, and social dislocation caused by, their lucrative sales of opium.

The alacrity with which individual Americans responded to such early opportunities was not matched or accompanied by comparable U.S. government interest in China. Preoccupied with domestic issues, such as continental expansion and slavery, Washington proved content to follow in the wake of the leading imperialist power of the day, Great Britain. When London's determination to continue selling opium brought about the Opium War (1839–1842) and the imposition of the Nanjing (Nanking) Treaty of 1842, the first of a series of unequal treaties, the United States opportunistically pressured the Chinese to grant it a similar agreement. In the 1844 Treaty of Wangxia, Washington, like London, radically changed its power relationship with China. Suddenly U.S. citizens also had the right to most-favored-nation treatment (guaranteeing privileges granted to all other foreigners), extraterritoriality (the right to be tried under U.S. rather than Chinese law), access to five new ports, and the enjoyment of a fixed and modest tariff rate (to substitute for arbitrary and capricious exactions previously derived from trade).

Despite such one-sided agreements, some Chinese believed that the United States, whose gunboats were less in evidence, might not be as rapacious as Great Britain and could be used against other Western "barbarians" to protect Chinese interests. On several occasions throughout the remainder of the nineteenth century Chinese diplomats tried to enlist the help of U.S. officials to intercede in sensitive diplomatic encounters. Former

President Ulysses S. Grant attempted to save the Liuchiu (Ryukyu) Islands from Japan in 1879. Naval officer and diplomat Robert Shufeldt negotiated a treaty with Korea, which China hoped to use as a model for limiting foreign activity to preserve Chinese predominance there despite growing Japanese power. But in both of these cases, as in most others, U.S. goals and interests were sufficiently divergent to leave Chinese statesmen frustrated and angry.

Missionaries and merchants became those most involved in China during the nineteenth and the early twentieth centuries. The first American missionary arrived in 1830, but the U.S. missionary effort never won large numbers of conversions (the first of which did not appear until 1837). Its greatest success came rather in its humanitarian enterprises, particularly education and medical services. Missionaries established thirteen Christian colleges and the influential Peking Union Medical College, which trained a generation of Chinese physicians.

Businessmen similarly persevered but found the China market less profitable than expected. Despite the large population, few Chinese had the money to purchase U.S. goods or the desire for what Americans had to offer. Nevertheless, the United States continued to see China as a major potential market. American merchants also brought Chinese laborers to the United States, where they lived in primitive conditions, earning a pittance, while building the transcontinental railroad and opening mines across the western territories. In 1868 Secretary of State William Seward, who believed it vital to ensure a predictable supply of cheap labor, authorized negotiation of the Burlingame Treaty, which guaranteed the right of free immigration for Chinese to the United States. Chinese immigrants, nevertheless, began to encounter violence shortly after the end of railway expansion contracted the supply of jobs. Suddenly it became unacceptable that they intended only to be sojourners who sent their wages home, refused to learn English, rejected Christianity, and lived in isolated enclaves as though they were still in China. Californians, in particular, passed discriminatory legislation that barred Chinese from local schools, law courts, and government jobs. Eventually the objective widened to keep Chinese out of the United States entirely.

The movement for exclusion began slowly as a regional question but gathered momentum as Chinese workers arrived on the East Coast in 1870 and both national political parties saw it as a winning campaign issue. By 1881 Washington had negotiated the Angell Treaty, which allowed the United States to "regulate, limit or suspend" Chinese immigration, and the following year Congress legislated a ten-year moratorium on the entry of laborers and a system of identification certificates that resident Chinese had to carry at all times. That the victimization

China, Asia, and The Great Powers at the Turn of the Century

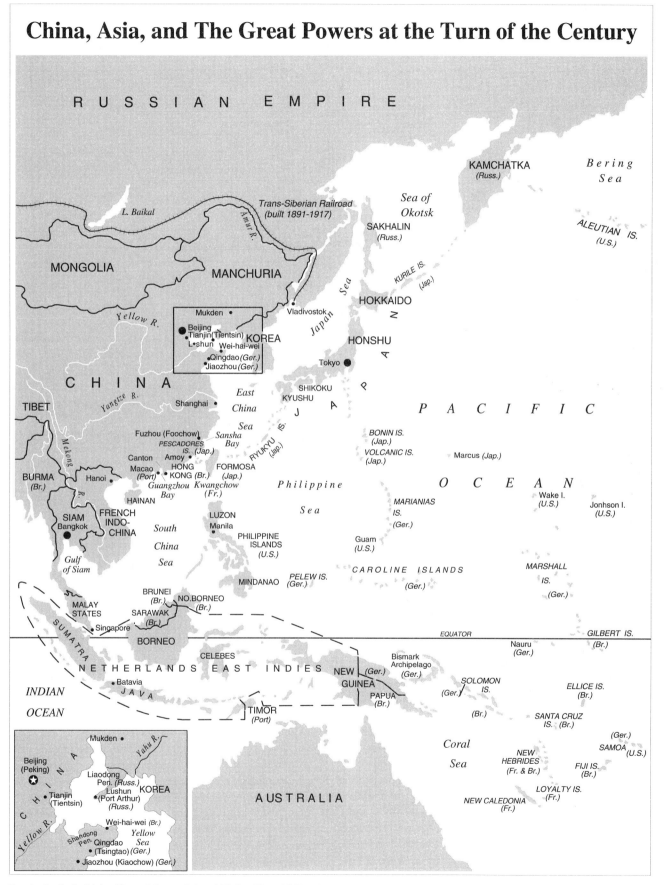

From *American Foreign Relations*, Thomas G. Paterson, J. Garry Clifford, and Kenneth J. Hagan, Volume I. ©1995 by D.C. Heath and Company.
Reprinted with permission of Houghton Mifflin Company

China

National Capital
Province Capital
City
Province Border
Road
Railroad
International Border

0   500 km
0   500 mi

©1993 Magellan Geographix℠Santa Barbara, CA

of Chinese in the United States did not have more serious repercussions on Sino-American relations attested to the weakness of China's government. Americans failed to appreciate the irony of blatant discrimination against Chinese in the United States when Americans in China backed up their demands for privileged treatment with gunboats. The Geary Act renewed the suspension in 1892 and in 1904 exclusion followed, which provoked a boycott of U.S. trade in southern China in 1905. President Theodore Roosevelt demanded that the central government take action to suppress it, determined that the Chinese not be allowed to do to Americans what they did not dare do to the British or French. In the end, the boycott died of its own lack of momentum, and U.S. prestige did not suffer seriously.

From the "Open Door" to World War II

At the turn of the century, growing power gave the United States greater weight in world affairs. Americans had come to believe that given equal commercial opportunity they would prosper. Victory in the Spanish-American Cuban-Filipino War of 1898, with the subsequent acquisition of the Philippines, provided the United States with a long-sought Asian base of operations, augmented by the almost simultaneous annexation of Hawaii. But in the aftermath of China's defeat in the 1894–1895 Sino-Japanese War a scramble for concessions threatened to partition China into a series of colonies whose markets could be closed to U.S. trade. In reaction, and in full recognition that the American people would not support the use of military force to defend U.S. commercial interests, Washington sent diplomatic notes to the European powers and Japan, calling upon them to respect the Open Door policy in China—that is, not discriminate against the trade of other countries in their spheres of influence. They reluctantly agreed. At no point did Washington consult Chinese officials regarding such an approach; this was a policy of self-interest that only coincidentally bestowed economic viability and a paternalistic security upon China.

Americans were not, however, alone in fearing the consequences of heightened foreign intervention, and from 1899 to 1900 a nativist movement put foreigners in jeopardy across the north China plain. The Boxer uprising, although initially opposed to the Manchu dynasty as well as foreigners, was quickly seduced by the imperial court, and together the court and the Boxers declared war on the foreign powers in China. Alarmed by the possible impetus toward colonization, Secretary of State John Hay sent a second Open Door note to the powers, declaring respect for China's "territorial and administrative entity." Once again, the Europeans and Japan grudgingly agreed. The subsequent interpretation of the Open Door policy by the United States would endow it with mythic force in saving China from dismemberment as well as assuming a profound gratitude among the Chinese people for U.S. actions. The belief in American altruism ignored U.S. commercial ambitions and Washington's (unsuccessful) plans to acquire a naval base on the south China coast.

The years following the Open Door initiative witnessed war between Russia and Japan (1904–1905), revolution in China (1911), and World War I, as well as a U.S. policy that uncomfortably alternated between dollar diplomacy and moralism. The desire of some Americans to remain involved in China increasingly clashed with Japan's determination to join the club of great powers by establishing an empire, a desire that could only fulfill itself on the mainland of Asia. President Roosevelt, who admired the modernizing Japanese and felt contempt for the benighted Chinese, dismissed any U.S. involvement in China that might conflict with maintaining good relations with Japan. His successor, William Howard Taft, attempted to change that policy by promoting investments and financial consortiums with other foreign states in China. His plans, however, foundered on a deadly combination of Japanese resistance and American disinterest. Taft's successor, Woodrow Wilson, worsened a deteriorating situation by withdrawing the United States from cooperative financial ventures he deemed immoral, only to return to them when it proved impossible to circumvent Japanese dominance.

President Wilson was similarly erratic on political issues. In 1913, when Sun Zhongshan (Sun Yat-sen), a Hawai'ian-educated Chinese who had been central to the ouster of the Qing (Ch'ing Manchu) dynasty, was hailed in the United States as the father of a modernizing China eager to emulate the U.S. system, Wilson moved precipitously to offer diplomatic recognition to the new Chinese republican government. By then, however, Sun had been pushed aside by a militarist leader, Yuan Shikai (Yuan Shih-k'ai), and Wilson's action ignored evidence that Yuan had engineered the assassination of a leading political rival, that the country was on the brink of a civil war, and that other governments, believing Yuan to be an incipient autocrat, would not establish relations. Wilson also took issue with Japan's 21 Demands, which sought to impose a protectorate over China in 1915 and helped to ward off the most onerous concessions. On the other hand, Wilson refused to deal vigorously with anti-Chinese legislation in California and adhered to the Lansing-Ishii Agreement (1917), in which Japan's special, if not preeminent, interests in China were accepted on the grounds of geographic propinquity.

In 1919 at the Paris Peace Conference, called to make peace after World War I, Wilson's idealistic wartime declarations about open diplomacy, self-determination, and democracy, which many Chinese welcomed enthusiastically, succumbed to European and Japanese demands for confirmation of secret deals made during the war. Wilson rationalized his stance by emphasizing the importance of having Japan remain at the peace conference and join the new League of Nations. For the Chinese, however, the priority Wilson gave to cooperation with Japan as opposed to observing Chinese rights proved profoundly disillusioning. Beginning on 4 May 1919 (the May Fourth Incident) hundreds of thousands of students demonstrated in the streets of China's cities, forcing the Chinese government to refuse to sign a peace treaty that permitted Japan to retain control over former German holdings in Shantung province.

In reality, U.S. efforts to cope with the growing challenge from Japan captured American attention far more than the travails of Chinese nationalists. Many U.S. officials continued to disparage China's weakness and blamed efforts to recover economic and political rights for the aggressive foreign behavior that followed. Repeatedly they insisted that revision of the unequal treaties under which China labored could not begin until the Chinese actually lived up to their obligations, however onerous, under those same treaties.

For Washington, a much more important issue was the costly and potentially dangerous naval arms race that was developing between the United States, Europe, and Japan in the wake of World War I. In 1921 the naval powers met in Washington, D.C., and negotiated the Four

U.S. MINISTERS AND AMBASSADORS TO CHINA[1]

MINISTER	PERIOD OF APPOINTMENT	ADMINISTRATION
Edward Everett[2]	1843	
Caleb Cushing	1843[3]–1844	Tyler
Alexander H. Everett[4]	1845–1847	Polk
John W. Davis	1848–1850[5]	Polk
		Taylor
Thomas A. R. Nelson[6]	1851	Taylor
Joseph Blunt[7]	1851	
Humphrey Marshall	1852–1854	Pierce
Robert J. Walker[8]	1853	Pierce
Robert M. McLane	1853–1854	Pierce
Peter Parker	1855–1857	Pierce
		Buchanan
William B. Reed	1857–1858	Buchanan
John E. Ward	1858–1860	Buchanan
Anson Burlingame	1861–1867	Lincoln
		A. Johnson
J. Ross Browne	1868–1869	A. Johnson
William A. Howard[9]		
Frederick F. Low	1869–1873	Grant
Benjamin P. Avery	1874–1875	Grant
George F. Seward	1876–1880	Grant
		Hayes
James B. Angell	1880–1881	Hayes
		Garfield
John Russell Young	1882–1885	Arthur
Charles Denby	1885–1898	Cleveland
		B. Harrison
		Cleveland
		McKinley
Henry W. Blair[10]	1891	McKinley
Charles Page Bryan[11]	1897	McKinley
Edwin H. Conger	1898–1905	McKinley
		T. Roosevlet
William Woodville Rockhill	1905–1909	T. Roosevelt
		Taft
Charles R. Crane[12]	1909	Taft
William James Calhoun	1909–1913	Taft
Paul S. Reinsch	1913–1919	Wilson
Charles R. Crane	1920–1921	Wilson
Jacob Van A. MacMurray	1925–1929	Coolidge
		Hoover
AMBASSADOR		
Nelson T. Johnson	1929–1941	Hoover
		F. D. Roosevelt
Clarence E. Gauss	1941–1944	F. D. Roosevelt
Patrick J. Hurley	1944–1945	F. D. Roosevelt
		Truman
J. Leighton Stuart	1946–1949[13]	Truman

(table continues on next page)

AMBASSADOR	PERIOD OF APPOINTMENT	ADMINISTRATION
Karl L. Rankin[14]	1953–1957	Eisenhower
Everett F. Drumright	1958–1962	Eisenhower
		Kennedy
Alan G. Kirk	1962–1963	Kennedy
Jerauld Wright	1963–1965	Kennedy
		L.B. Johnson
Walter P. McConaughy	1966–1974	L.B. Johnson
		Nixon
Leonard Unger	1974–1979[15]	Nixon
		Ford
		Carter
Leonard F. Woodcock	1979–1981	Carter
Arthur W. Hummel, Jr.	1981–1985	Reagan
Winston Lord	1985–1989	Reagan
		Bush
James Roderick Lilley	1989–1991	Bush
J. Stapleton Roy	1991–1994	Bush
Jim Sasser	1994–Present	Clinton

[1] Representatives from Everett to McConaughy were commissioned to China; Unger to the Republic of China; Woodcock to the present, to the People's Republic of China.
[2] Declined appointment.
[3] Issued two separate commissions during a recess of the Senate, one as Commissioner and one as EE/MP; after confirmation recommissioned as Commissioner only.
[4] Nominated 26 Feb. 1845 to be EE/MP; the Senate did not confirm this nomination.
[5] Peter Parker served as Chargé d' Affaires ad interim, May 1850–July 1853.
[6] Did not proceed to post.
[7] Declined appointment.
[8] Declined appointment.
[9] Took oath of office, but did not proceed to post.
[10] Took oath of office, but did not proceed to post, the government of China having objected to his appointment.
[11] Took oath of office under recess appointment, but did not proceed to post; nomination of 5 Jan. 1898 was withdrawn before the Senate acted upon it.
[12] Took oath of office, but did not proceed to post.
[13] Karl L. Rankin served as Chargé d' Affaires ad interim at Taipei, Aug. 1950–Apr. 1953.
[14] Ambassadors Ranking through Unger were resident at Taipei.
[15] The United States established diplomatic relations with the People's Republic of China and terminated them with the Republic of China, 1 Jan. 1979. Embassy Taipei closed 28 February 1979.

Sources: *Principal Officers of the Department of State and United States Chiefs of Missions.* ©1991 by Office of the Historian, Bureau of Public Affairs, Washington, D.C.; *The U.S. Government Manual,* Annual. Washington, D.C.

Power and Five Power Treaties, which extricated the British from an increasingly uncomfortable alliance negotiated with Japan in 1902 and slowed naval building. At the same time, the United States recognized the degree to which peace hinged on resolving problems in and around China. Thus, they also reconfirmed, in a typically paternalistic approach, Chinese sovereignty in the Nine Power Treaty, which pledged respect for China's territorial integrity and nonintervention in its internal affairs, but did not, despite Chinese hopes, grant tariff autonomy, end extraterritoriality, or prompt the withdrawal of foreign troops from Chinese soil.

Nevertheless, during the 1920s the idea began to catch hold that Chinese nationalism must be noticed and demanded a response. The fury of the 30 May 1925 movement protesting the shooting of strikers at a Japanese-controlled textile mill in Shanghai convinced Secretary of State Frank Kellogg and his China adviser Nelson T. Johnson to relinquish power over Chinese tariffs as soon as China had a government stable enough to take over the responsibility. By 1928 Generalissimo Jiang Jieshi (Chiang Kai-shek), the leader of the Guomindang (Kuomintang/Nationalist) party had completed a military expedition centralizing power. U.S. representatives, although skeptical about his capacity to govern, applauded his success in achieving unity and sympathized with his determination to suppress the fledgling communist movement. In 1928, uncertainly, the United States opened diplomatic relations with Jiang's regime and signed a treaty recognizing Chinese tariff autonomy.

Solicitude for Jiang and Chinese nationalism did not extend so far as to occasion any strong U.S. action when in September 1931 the Japanese army, which had been stationed in Manchuria (China's three northeastern provinces) to protect the South Manchurian Railroad since Japan's victory in the Russo-Japanese War of 1904–1905, staged an incident to serve as an excuse to take over the area. Instead, Washington contented itself with the Stimson Nonrecognition Doctrine (1932), denying the validity of any agreements between China and another power, which contravened U.S. rights in China. Caught in the economic crisis of the Great Depression, Washington had no energy to invest in righting wrongs in Asia, particularly if efforts to uphold the Kellogg-Briand Pact of 1928, which ostensibly outlawed war as an instrument of national policy, or the Nine Power Treaty threatened to plunge the United States into war with Japan. Not surprisingly, the Stimson Doctrine did nothing to stop Japanese aggression. Japan had become increasingly worried about Chinese nationalism. Whereas Washington considered it a hopeful trend toward a stronger, more stable China, the Japanese saw it as a barrier to securing great-power status as an imperial state. Tokyo also was disturbed by the possibility of communist influence spreading on the Asian mainland. It promptly secured its hold on China's three northeastern provinces by declaring establishment of the nation of Manchukuo in February 1932. Condemnation by the League of Nations Lytton Commission, to which a U.S. observer was a silent partner, even when ameliorated by a parallel denunciation of Chinese provocation, led Japan to quit the League.

Throughout the 1930s Washington watched the chaotic events in China, sympathizing with the travails of the Chinese people but lacking any willingness to become involved. If not pro-Japanese like the British and French, the United States had no national interests in China that merited opposition to Japanese policies. Washington thus stood aside as Japanese expansion continued, engulfing territories along the northern border of China proper until in 1937 full-scale war erupted. U.S. passivity was encouraged by Jiang's decision to focus his attention not on stopping foreign aggression but rather on first ridding China of the domestic communist menace.

Indeed, disillusioned U.S. diplomats in the 1930s and 1940s frequently articulated a view of China that shaped policymaking both before and after World War II. To them it seemed fruitless for the United States to risk its security when the Chinese themselves would not abandon factional feuding to unify and stand up for their own national sovereignty. Jiang was becoming increasingly dictatorial, allying himself with urban gangsters and the most conservative landlord class, as well as demonstrating contempt for Western values and democratic reforms. If not thoroughly opposed to industrialization and modernization, he nevertheless judged such measures by the degree to which they would strengthen his power and ruled out all other innovations.

It is not clear, however, that a more united and energetic China could have motivated the United States to act. U.S. decisionmakers consciously avoided strategies in the 1930s that might alienate Japan. President Franklin D. Roosevelt did not take any strong measures to aid China. At best, he declined to invoke neutrality provisions after full-scale war erupted in 1937 because such laws would have made it impossible for the U.S. to supply China with war material. Given that China lacked the ships to transport guns and the money to buy them, the gesture proved empty. United States financial support for China remained modest, and appropriations were loans not grants. Further than this neither Roosevelt nor the Congress would go. No economic sanctions were applied against Japan, and the United States remained a primary supplier of oil and scrap steel to the Japanese war machine. Not until Japan joined the Axis alliance with Germany and Italy in September 1940 did the United States begin to consider taking action in Asia.

World War II and Communist Victory

The descent into war thereafter was certain, if not swift, and China did have its role to play. Washington feared Japanese aggression would cut supplies of raw materials and manpower from Asian colonies to Europe and distract Moscow from its struggle against Germany. China must, therefore, remain in the war, tying down Japan's army. Compromise with Tokyo, however tempting, could not be accepted. The Chinese responded to Japan's attack on Pearl Harbor on 7 December 1941 with the joyful expectation that the United States would now mount an energetic campaign to destroy their common enemy. Instead, Jiang found that talk of joint purpose did not yield much equipment or money. The Roosevelt administration committed its resources to defeat Germany first.

Friction characterized the wartime Chinese-American relationship. When the United States sought to supplement minimal concrete assistance with military advice, Jiang bridled, developing a thoroughgoing hatred for Roosevelt's emissary, General Joseph Stilwell, who argued that Chinese military capabilities could be much improved by the removal of officers who had gained their positions for reasons of loyalty to Jiang rather than ability. Jiang rebuffed U.S. pressures to fight in Burma to keep open overland supply lines, preferring to have U.S. pilots (the Flying Tigers) take the risks and fly goods in over the Himalaya mountains. In fact, Jiang favored support for an air war more generally, opting to side with General Claire Chennault against Stilwell to minimize demands on his own ground forces. When the air campaign began to take a serious toll on Japanese forces, however, Jiang refused to protect vulnerable air bases because commanders were not politically reliable. Nationalist Chinese troops often fought the Japanese badly or not at all.

Repeated evidence that aid from the United States was squandered or misappropriated alienated U.S. diplomats in China and eventually Washington.

The Chinese communists provided the only viable alternative to cooperation with Nationalist forces. Their ideological identification with Marxism-Leninism probably would have precluded all collaboration had it not been for the fact that, with guerrilla units scattered behind Japanese lines, they could offer assistance to downed U.S. pilots and, more critically, to U.S. expeditionary force landings on the China coast in preparation for a proposed final assault on Japan in 1945 or 1946. Early reports on the communist enclave in the northwest had come from Edgar Snow, a young American journalist, who visited Yenan, communist headquarters, in 1936. In contrast to the corruption and inefficiency that Americans found among the Nationalists, Snow declared the communists to be dynamic, selfless, dedicated, determined and honest. In 1944 communist leaders Mao Zedong (Mao Tse-tung) and Zhou Enlai (Chou En-lai) treated a delegation of military analysts, technicians, and diplomats to a celebration of U.S. independence on the Fourth of July and offered to go to Washington to coordinate war operations with Roosevelt.

Initially, Washington hoped they could help to negotiate a coalition that, by providing the communists with a subordinate role in governing, would prevent a return to civil war. For this purpose, Roosevelt dispatched a personal emissary, General Patrick J. Hurley, who arrived in Yenan in November and quickly reached agreement on a five-point proposal. Hurley knew little about China, understood nothing of the dynamics of the internal conflict, and seemed easily misled by whomever he talked to last. With the agreement in his pocket and Zhou Enlai at his side, he flew on to Chongqing (Chungking) only to be berated by Jiang, who tore up the proposal and persuaded Hurley to take an entirely new, draconian line. The talks with the communists promptly broke down, and Hurley, embarrassed and angered, insisted on driving out of China those Foreign Service officers who had dared to contradict his disastrous approach to diplomacy.

The Rise of the People's Republic of China

When the United States resumed its attempt to build a coalition some months later, its efforts were under the far more judicious leadership of war hero General George C. Marshall. The Marshall Mission (December 1945–January 1947), although more carefully conducted than Hurley's bungled mediation, also failed. There simply could be no compromise over communist demands for a social revolution that struck at the very fabric of the Nationalists' political and economic structure. Moreover, it became clear to the communists that even Marshall was not unbiased and that the United States would support Jiang regardless of his attitudes or policies.

Similarly, the effort to disengage Joseph Stalin and the Soviet Union from the Chinese communists proved misguided. The United States persuaded Stalin to sign a friendship treaty with Jiang in 14 August 1945, fundamentally undermining the expectations and security of the Chinese Communist Party (CCP). However much this left Mao and Zhou feeling betrayed and disillusioned, it had no impact on the CCP's revolutionary commitment.

By the time Japan surrendered in August 1945, sporadic civil war between the Nationalists and communists in China had in fact been under way for four years. The United States transported Nationalist troops to try to control territory, but communist forces rapidly demonstrated their more effective military tactics and political skills. The Marshall mission of 1946–1947 sought to negotiate a settlement. Efforts by the U.S. to coerce Jiang into reforming his political, economic, and military policies foundered on his intransigent conviction that Washington had no option but to support him. By October 1949, much sooner than even the communists had imagined, Nationalist forces had been largely defeated on the mainland, Jiang and his loyalists had fled to the offshore island of Taiwan (Formosa) reconstituting the Republic of China (ROC) there, and Mao proclaimed the establishment of the People's Republic of China (PRC).

As the Nationalist regime disintegrated, U.S. decision makers faced the dilemma of whether to go into exile with Jiang or open diplomatic relations with the new communist government. The question had long since become a domestic as well as a foreign policy issue, as result of the activities of the pro-Nationalist China Lobby in Congress, the media, the business community, and among church groups. Attacks on President Harry S. Truman's administration for supposed softness on communism intensified after Truman's unexpected election victory over Thomas Dewey in 1948. Republicans blamed the Nationalist Chinese defeat on the White House, in the hope of improving their chances to capture the presidency in 1952. Publication of a China White Paper in August 1949, although intended to make the administration's case that nothing more could have been done to rescue Jiang, actually provided critics with more ammunition. Senator Joseph R. McCarthy in particular made the so-called loss of China and the presence of communism in the U.S. government the central elements of his ruthless campaign for power that began in February 1950. The Truman administration, however, continued to have some flexibility regarding China for several months. On 5 January 1950 President Truman had announced at a press conference that the United States would not intervene again in the Chinese civil war to prevent a communist assault on Taiwan. On 12 January Secretary of State Dean Acheson reiterated the policy, putting Taiwan as well as Korea outside the U.S. defense perimeter in a speech at the National Press Club.

Many historians have argued that there was in fact no possibility of better relations between the United States and the PRC, that communism was an insurmountable barrier. Others contend that Truman and Acheson were dedicated "cold warriors" who lacked the imagination to understand that communism was not monolithic. Such judgments seem, in fact, too simplistic. They overlook the important element of apathy toward Asia that rendered the stakes there lower, disregard the contempt for Jiang that made abandonment of the Nationalists easier, and ignore the existence of a nuanced policy toward Yugoslavia after Moscow broke with it in 1948, which provided a precedent for dealing with a communist regime. In any case, the Korean War erupted on 25 June 1950, effectively ending the possibility of resolving the China issue rapidly.

The Korean War

Simultaneously with the decision to oppose the North Korean invasion of South Korea, the U.S. government placed the Seventh Fleet in the Formosa Strait to prevent expansion of the war either through a PRC attack on Taiwan or a Nationalist assault on the mainland. Acheson in particular feared that the Nationalists could not carry out a successful operation and would have to be rescued on the beaches by the United States. Truman intended the commitment of the Seventh Fleet to be temporary, but the United States quickly became entangled in providing economic as well as military aid to the government in Taiwan and discovered that such ties could not be painlessly severed. At the same time the renewed collaboration between the Nationalists and Washington infuriated the Chinese communists, who had taken the Truman and Acheson statements as a firm policy commitment and thought they could settle the Taiwan issue promptly and without U.S. interference.

Once Beijing entered the Korean conflict in the autumn of 1950, U.S. perceptions of the regime on the mainland of China worsened precipitously. To U.S. policymakers, there appeared to be no logical reasons for Chinese intervention. Truman and Acheson explicitly reassured them that U.S. forces in Korea posed no threat to the PRC. Having just survived a prolonged civil war and the anti-Japanese conflict before that, the Chinese seemed, in Washington's view, to have enough reconstruction and development work to keep them occupied at home. Truman and Acheson, seduced by the opportunity to reunify Korea and roll back communism, dismissed public and private warnings given by Zhou Enlai and others that the PRC could not stand by and watch U.S. forces cross the 38th parallel and approach the Yalu River boundary with China. Thus, the United States was stunned when Chinese troops poured into Korea, inflicting heavy casualties and leading to a stalemate that was settled only through an armistice agreement in 1953.

Chinese intervention seemed to Truman, Acheson, and most Americans to confirm earlier assumptions that both the North Koreans and the Chinese were acting as puppets of the Soviet Union. The Chinese communists were widely portrayed as bloodthirsty and vicious, an image that would dissipate only slowly over the years ahead. In fact, most historians contend, Mao acted for national security reasons when he decided to send in Chinese soldiers, protecting his border rather than international communism. Stalin had promised the Chinese support but proved loath to deliver it. Whereas Mao anticipated that the United States would probably attack China eventually from either Korea, Vietnam, or Taiwan, and that there were some logistical benefits to be gained from fighting in Korea, Stalin sought to avoid war with the United States entirely.

The "Two Chinas" Issue

President Dwight D. Eisenhower and Secretary of State John Foster Dulles came into office in 1953 more comfortable with close relations to the Nationalist Chinese than the previous administration. Having campaigned on a platform that disparaged containment and talked about the liberation of captive peoples around the world, Eisenhower saw it natural, as one of his early foreign policy actions in 1953, to "unleash" Jiang. The Seventh Fleet would remain in the Formosa Strait and continue to protect Taiwan, but, the president suggested, the United States would no longer shield the PRC from Jiang. In reality, however, Eisenhower and Dulles had no intention of permitting the Nationalists to create a crisis that would plunge the United States into a new war. Instead, they repeatedly extracted secret pledges from Jiang that any large-scale military action against the mainland would be cleared with the United States, never intending to give such approval.

Eventually, a long-running crisis developed over a series of tiny islands off the coast of the China mainland that had remained in Nationalist hands after 1949. Two island groups in particular, Jinmen (Quemoy) and Mazu (Matsu), occasioned confrontations in 1954–1955, 1958, and 1962. The United States approached each of these situations hesitantly, believing it had to support Jiang to sustain morale in Taiwan but recognizing that the islands were worthless and virtually indefensible. The 1954–1955 episode began with Beijing's determination to convince the United States that a rumored alliance with Taiwan would be too dangerous to negotiate and that a regional association aimed against the PRC was similarly unwise. In fact, the shelling of the islands had precisely the opposite impact than that intended by Beijing. It failed to disrupt the already scheduled inauguration of the Southeast Asia Treaty Organization (SEATO) and actually drove the United States into the Mutual Defense Treaty with Taipei, a treaty that Dulles had been trying to avoid despite Jiang's orchestration of political pressures inside and outside the administration.

In 1958 the Chinese again sought to shape U.S. policy by resuming their shelling of the offshore islands. Disturbed by what seemed to be increasing determination on Washington's part to follow a "two Chinas" policy, which meant dealing with both the PRC and Taiwan as separate states, Beijing sought to deter the United States and the world from viewing Taiwan as independent. Mao may also have been motivated by the need to distract his people from domestic problems made public by the Hundred Flowers Movement in 1957 or to galvanize them into adopting the difficult economic policies of the Great Leap Forward, announced in 1958. After the earlier conflict Dulles and Eisenhower had tried in vain to persuade Jiang to evacuate or at least sharply reduce garrison forces lest the loss of the islands strike a serious blow to Nationalist power and survival. When the new attack began, Eisenhower invoked the Formosa Resolution passed by Congress in 1955, which gave him the power to protect territories vital to the defense of Taiwan, and once again assisted the Nationalists to provision the islands. In the end, Jiang did not evacuate and Mao did not attempt to seize the islands, because both realized that severing the island links between Taiwan and the mainland would validate the "two Chinas" approach that the United States sought to impose.

The final Straits crisis in 1962 began with Nationalist threats to use the islands as a base from which to attack the mainland. Encouraged by deteriorating conditions in the PRC following the disastrous agricultural policies of the Great Leap Forward, Jiang believed that he could finally launch a successful return to the mainland. President John F. Kennedy had, however, made it clear during the 1960 presidential campaign that he would not risk war over such inconsequential territory; he refused to support Jiang and assured Beijing there would be no attack. He did this initially through the Sino-American ambassadorial talks held sporadically since 1955, first in Geneva and later in Warsaw. The talks had quickly secured the release of U.S. war prisoners and spies in China, and Chinese, mostly scientists, trapped in the United States as a result of the Korean conflict. Thereafter the conversations yielded little, particularly after Dulles insisted that Beijing agree to renounce the use of force in the Taiwan Strait. Ambassadorial exchanges, nevertheless, provided for regular contact between Washington and Beijing, sometimes with more frequency than enjoyed by diplomats from countries with embassies in Beijing. Eventually, the talks would facilitate rapprochement during the presidency of Richard M. Nixon.

Ironically, although engaging in periodic direct contacts with the PRC, Washington continued to keep Beijing out of the multinational diplomatic forum provided by the United Nations. The UN issue dated back to 1949 when, upon establishment of the People's Republic of China, the Chinese communists expected to inherit the Chinese seat in both the UN General Assembly and the Security Council. Initially the U.S. government accepted the likelihood that representation would change and declined to make it a critical issue. But, when the UN's bureaucratic wheels turned slowly, the Soviet Union created a confrontation by walking out of the Security Council in protest in mid-January 1950. Ostensibly a gesture of solidarity, it also may have been a way to ensure that Beijing would not be admitted to the UN, keeping China isolated and dependent on the Soviet Union.

Once the PRC intervened in the Korean War, adoption of a UN resolution in February 1951 branding China an aggressor foreclosed admission. Thereafter the Eisenhower administration had little trouble rallying opposition to China's inclusion year after year. Although Eisenhower himself believed that the PRC ought to be in the UN and that the United States should recognize its government, he was unable to take action in the face of pressure from the China Lobby and the Committee of One Million Against Admission of Communist China to the United Nations. Still, Eisenhower and Dulles refused to promise Jiang that they would use the U.S. veto in the Security Council to prevent the PRC's entry.

In 1961 President John F. Kennedy, despite the conviction of his admirers that he was flexible on China, made such a pledge secretly. President Lyndon B. Johnson subsequently renewed the Kennedy guarantee, although the votes supporting the U.S. position diminished year by year. As the PRC grew stronger and more belligerent, the feeling spread that the world would be safer if Beijing's representatives participated in UN dialogues.

The widening Sino-Soviet split encouraged the view that the PRC should have its own voice in world forums. The United States, however, proved slow even to acknowledge the existence of a breach. Kennedy insisted that Beijing and Moscow disagreed over nothing more than how best to bury the United States. When policymakers finally conceded that a split had developed, they declared the rupture temporary. Kennedy and Secretary of State Dean Rusk accepted the Soviet portrayal of a fanatic and irresponsible China that was trying to radicalize communist bloc policies as a whole. During the 1962 Cuban missile crisis, for example, Soviet ambassador Anatoly Dobrynin convinced the president and Rusk that Soviet leader Nikita Khrushchev had been forced to be more confrontational than he initially intended by Chinese zealots.

Kennedy's concerns about China would not have been allayed even if he had believed in the Sino-Soviet rift. He remained deeply troubled about the imminent production of a Chinese atomic bomb (actually detonated in 1964) and fearful of the power of China's ideological and racial attraction in the underdeveloped world. China competed for influence in Africa and throughout Asia, granting foreign aid, providing technological assistance, and bringing young people to Beijing for a higher education. Mao extolled antiimperialistic struggle, and Zhou Enlai, on a tour of Africa in 1963–1964, encouraged revolution. At the same time, Beijing's stature rose as a result of its thoughtful diplomacy at the Geneva Conferences of 1954 and 1962 and the Bandung Conference of 1955. Only China's descent into the abyss of the Great Proletariat Cultural Revolution, during which its foreign policy consisted of violence against foreigners at home and abroad, temporarily arrested the growing advocacy for UN admission.

The "Opening" of China and Normalization of Relations

Despite Beijing's extremism, by the mid-1960s the atmosphere in the United States had changed considerably and a consensus slowly began to form around the proposition that the United States ought to consider better relations with the PRC. Congressional hearings in 1966 broadcast the formula "containment without isolation," international affairs organizations such as the Council on Foreign Relations explored alternative scenarios, and a new group, the National Committee on U.S.-China Relations, devoted all its energies to better understanding and informal contacts.

The moment, however, could hardly have been less auspicious, given China's descent into anarchy in the mid-1960s. Mao Zedong launched the Cultural Revolution to imbue a new generation with revolutionary principles, to wage a power struggle within the communist leadership, and to prevent the resurgence of capitalist ideas. Although largely focused on domestic issues, the fury of the decade-long upheaval did occasionally spill into foreign affairs and rendered better relations with the United States anathema. This remained true until 1969, when Sino-American frictions were overshadowed by clashes between China and the Soviet Union. The Sino-Soviet split became public and escalated during the 1960s until border harassment erupted in 1969 into exchanges of gunfire. To the Chinese the situation seemed especially precarious given the 1968 Soviet invasion of Czechoslovakia. When combined with growing deployments of Soviet troops along the Chinese border, denunciations of Beijing for having undermined socialism with its Cultural Revolution policies, and declaration of the Brezhnev Doctrine, which claimed the Soviet right

to intervene in socialist states to protect them from world imperialism, the threat to Chinese security appeared imminent. Beijing turned to the United States to act as a deterrent.

For U.S. policymakers the opening provided an extraordinary opportunity to use China to curb Soviet power. Having Beijing on its side would free Washington from fears of fighting a two-front war while allowing it to intimidate the Soviets and leverage them into increased defense expenditures in Asia. In addition, the creation of a strategic triangle would allow Washington to negotiate better relations with Moscow as well as Beijing.

U.S.-China rapprochement also gained impetus from involvement by both countries in Vietnam. Although the United States had committed itself in Indochina initially in the 1940s out of concern for French cooperation in fighting the Soviet menace, it quickly identified China as a central threat in Southeast Asia. During the 1960s it became apparent not only that the Chinese provided advice and sanctuary to the North Vietnamese but also that Chinese soldiers manned antiaircraft guns and built roads for the North Vietnamese government. At the same time, the danger that the PRC would, as in Korea, feel compelled to enter the war formally if the United States either violated the Chinese border or jeopardized the continued existence of North Vietnam through a ground force operation set strict limits on U.S. strategy in Vietnam. Beijing, however, was no more eager to risk war than Washington, so both sides sent signals to clarify their intentions and relieve some of the pressure and peril. After taking office in 1969, President Nixon considered the possibility that he might be able to use China to persuade Hanoi to negotiate a peace agreement.

Apart from strategic triangles, Chinese security, and U.S. Vietnam policy, other concerns helped to bring Washington and Beijing together. For Nixon these included severe domestic economic problems that added to the lustre of the China market, political benefits in the next presidential election, and hopes that China could be induced to sign a nuclear nonproliferation agreement. Chinese leaders sought not only a counterweight to the Soviet Union but also a seat in the United Nations and access to technology from and trade with the United States and Japan. The irony of undertaking rapprochement with Nixon, who had built much of his career as a hardline cold warrior and who had aimed much of his venom specifically at China, did not appear to trouble Beijing.

The major barrier to reconciliation remained Taiwan, but Washington proved ready to make significant concessions on this central issue. At a meeting in Warsaw in 1970 the United States indicated its willingness to recognize that the Taiwan controversy would have to be solved by the Chinese themselves. Beijing abandoned its demand that resolution of the status of Taiwan would have to precede any other agreements. In 1971 the Chinese advanced rapprochement with the dramatic gesture of inviting a U.S. table tennis team to Beijing, which led to the sobriquet "ping pong diplomacy" for the whole China opening. Henry A. Kissinger, Nixon's national security adviser, made a secret trip to Beijing that July, and shortly thereafter the White House announced that President Nixon would visit China. In October 1971 the PRC was admitted into the United Nations with U.S. approval and the Republic of China was expelled, despite U.S. efforts to keep it in the UN by securing dual representation.

President Nixon's visit to China in February 1972 culminated in the landmark Shanghai Communiqué, in which the United States acknowledged the Chinese position that only one China existed and that Taiwan was a part of it. On the other hand, the Chinese conceded that one China could not be achieved immediately and accepted the U.S. promise to withdraw its troops from Taiwan once tensions in the area decreased. Both pledged to oppose efforts by any power, meaning the Soviet Union, to extend hegemony in East Asia.

Although Beijing and Washington exchanged liaison offices in 1973 and trade burgeoned, unanticipated problems slowed progress toward full diplomatic relations. President Nixon became caught up in the Watergate scandal, which not only distracted him from foreign policy issues but also made conservative Republicans in Congress, who opposed the China initiative, crucial to his future. Following Nixon's resignation in 1974, his successor, Gerald R. Ford, proved even more dependent on conservative goodwill. In China, the prime movers behind the opening to the United States, Mao Zedong and Zhou Enlai, died, and Zhou's protégé Deng Xiaoping (Teng Hsiao-p'ing) lost power. Moreover, Beijing was unhappy with U.S. policies toward the Soviet Union, including the Strategic Arms Limitation Talks (SALT) and confirmation of Soviet dominance in Eastern Europe in the 1975 Helsinki Accords. Beijing wanted a staunch partner in opposition to Moscow; nothing less could justify association with the United States.

In the late 1970s President Jimmy Carter and Deng Xiaoping, now restored to power, finally undertook to normalize relations. Carter gave the China issue high priority, placing it just behind efforts to negotiate and pass a Panama Canal treaty and secure ratification of the SALT II treaties. His advisers, nevertheless, proved divided. Secretary of State Cyrus R. Vance, sympathized with the objective but opposed a precipitous pursuit of reconciliation with the Chinese that risked alienating Soviet leaders and jeopardizing SALT. Zbigniew Brzezinski, the national security adviser, on the other hand, believed that détente had been highly overrated as a policy, that

Soviet sensibilities could be disregarded, and recommended "playing the China card"—exploiting the relationship with Beijing to manipulate Moscow.

Carter accepted the Brzezinski approach just at the moment when Deng, anxious to obtain U.S. help regarding Beijing's mounting problems with the Vietnamese, also decided to improve relations. Although Deng inaugurated a series of fundamental economic reforms at the end of 1978, and commercial and technological benefits therefore weighed heavily in his decision, the PRC's looming military confrontation with Hanoi comprised his most immediate concern. Determined to punish Vietnam for its invasion of Cambodia, Deng wanted a relationship with Washington that would neutralize Moscow, preventing Soviet retaliation under its treaty of friendship and mutual support with Vietnam.

Thus, on 15 December 1978, to the surprise of Congress and the American people, President Carter announced that, following months of secret talks, full diplomatic relations would be opened with the PRC on 1 January 1979. Washington agreed to end formal relations with Taiwan, abrogate the U.S.-ROC Mutual Defense Treaty, and withdraw U.S. forces from the island. In Taipei, the event had not been unanticipated but came as a shock nonetheless. Carter pledged that arms sales to the ROC would continue after a one-year moratorium and that informal contacts would be maintained in economic and cultural affairs, but, abandoned by their major supporter, the Nationalists faced intensification of the international isolation that had engulfed them since 1972.

Angered by the administration's secret diplomacy, members of Congress from both parties rallied to provide Taipei more reliable guarantees than offered by the Carter administration. The Taiwan Relations Act (TRA) of 1979 created a framework that gave Taiwan many of the rights and privileges normally reserved for nation-states fully recognized by Washington. Most critically, the TRA mandated arms sales based on Taiwan's defense requirements and not subject to veto by the PRC. To many longtime proponents of the Nationalist cause, however, the TRA did not seem sufficient. Senator Barry Goldwater, along with six other senators and eight representatives, filed suit in federal court in an attempt to invalidate Carter's abrogation of the Mutual Defense Treaty. Although the suit was dismissed by the courts on the grounds that the president possessed "well-established authority to recognize, and withdraw recognition from, foreign governments," during the 1980 presidential campaign Ronald Reagan said that if elected he would restore relations with Taiwan.

Reagan never carried through on his promise, having been convinced that the relationship with Beijing mattered too much in the more consequential struggle against the Soviet Union. His continued rhetorical slips, however, soured the atmosphere and the PRC shifted from its tilt toward Washington into a more equidistant position between the United States and the USSR. Central to Beijing's disenchantment was the Reagan administration posture on arms sales to Taiwan. Although in January 1982 the White House finally abandoned plans to sell advanced fighter aircraft to Taipei, PRC leaders exerted heavy pressure to resolve the broader issue permanently. Arduous negotiations ensued, finally eventuating in a 17 August 1982 communiqué that disavowed any intention by the United States to implement a "two Chinas" or "one China, one Taiwan" policy. The United States agreed that thereafter arms sales would not exceed in quantity or quality the level of sales since 1978 and would gradually be reduced. The 1978 ceilings, however, were recalculated immediately to raise them substantially, the Nationalists received confidential assurances that the TRA would continue to govern their relations, and an enormous loophole regarding transfer of technology began to be exploited to make up for even modest decreases in direct weapons sales.

Despite this rocky beginning, the Reagan years proved to be positive ones for the U.S.-China relationship. Reagan visited China and was captivated by the people and the sights. Economic and cultural ties multiplied. By the middle of the 1980s diplomats on both sides talked of the maturity of contacts as they facilitated U.S. investment in the PRC and negotiated scientific and educational exchanges.

Tiananmen Square

Beneath the surface calm, however, problems remained. Chinese leaders found the intimacy of their links with the United States disturbing as foreigners spread the "spiritual pollution" of Western values and practices among the populace. As early as the 1979–1980 Democracy Wall Movement, efforts to suppress dissent and curb Western ideas led to arrests of the politically outspoken. These purges occurred several times in the 1980s even as Coca-Cola, blue jeans, and Kentucky Fried Chicken made their inroads on Chinese culture. The Reagan administration attempted to apply pressure on human rights issues, particularly regarding the future of Tibet, and focused considerable attention on birth control policies, cutting U.S. financial contributions to the United Nations Fund for Population Activities on the basis of claims that China practiced coercive abortion.

Little noticed by Americans, who were enthralled with the enormous changes occurring in the PRC, dissatisfaction had also increased in China. A broad cross-section of the population was dismayed when the immediate impact of economic reforms included not just greater prosperity but corruption, nepotism, inflation, and unemployment. Since political reform did not keep pace with economic change, people also found themselves unable to draw attention to inequities or to secure relief. As a result, in the spring of 1989 a massive political protest movement began, utilizing the occasion of the death of Hu Yaobang, a former general secretary of the Chinese Communist Party who had been stripped of his office in 1987. Students chose to mourn him as a fallen champion of freedom in China. Their demonstrations on Tiananmen Square, in the heart of Beijing, encouraged communist party members and factory workers to speak out and received extraordinary international attention. The latter followed from the coincidental visit to China of Soviet leader Mikhail Gorbachev, who had come to normalize relations between the PRC and the Soviet Union. Television cameras broadcast not only the historic meeting between Gorbachev and Deng but also the crowds in the streets and their demands for relief from corruption and political liberalization.

American journalists, observing the massive encampment on the square, reached the unwarranted conclusion that China was on the verge of a democratic revolution. Calls for greater press freedom and more opportunity to express political opinions were interpreted to U.S. television audiences as demands for American-style multiparty elections. The inaccurate portrayal produced an uncommon degree of interest in the developments in China on the part of Americans and engendered international disillusionment when the end came. China's gerontocracy, who had watched the crowds grow and endured the embarrassment of world attention during Gorbachev's stay, struck on the early morning of 4 June 1989. Sending in troops and tanks, they crushed the movement in a bloodbath and then imposed a reign of political terror throughout the country, arresting dissidents and purging high officials seen as sympathetic with or too weak to curb the dissidents.

The repercussions proved serious for China and for the United States. China passed through a period of economic sanctions and political ostracism. The PRC's willingness to fulfill its guarantees to give Hong Kong fifty years of autonomy after reversion of the colony to China in 1997, as provided for in the Sino-British Joint Declaration of 1984, was called into question. For Nationalist Chinese authorities in Taiwan, these events vindicated their rejection of unification talks. The ROC also benefited from the worldwide disillusionment with the PRC, which served to highlight the enormous progress Taiwan had been making in democratizing and liberalizing its system.

For the United States the China issue once again became a domestic economic and political matter, as the administration of President George Bush wrestled with policy options. Immediately following the Tiananmen

Square massacre, President Bush suspended high level visits, but in July 1989 he secretly dispatched emissaries to Beijing, in part to urge an improvement in human rights conditions but also to ensure that relations were not disrupted. When word of these secret contacts came out months later, the Bush administration was strongly criticized.

The events of Tiananmen Square and its aftermath would have undermined Sino-American understanding in any case, but when reinforced by the collapse of communism in Eastern Europe and the end of the Cold War, which eliminated the strategic justification for the relationship, a crisis materialized. The United States had come to think of the Chinese as being at the forefront of reform in the communist world—daring, innovative, and increasingly capitalist. Abruptly that image was shattered and a disillusioned American public turned away from China.

During the 1990s the U.S.-China relationship suffered from suspicion on the part of the Chinese and tougher, more demanding attitudes of the Americans. Central disputes involved trade imbalances, nuclear proliferation, and human rights. Huge U.S. trade deficits reflected the impenetrability of the China market and Chinese commercial practices that condoned such things as the use of prison labor, copyright infringement, and deceptive foreign labeling. U.S. policymakers objected as vehemently to sales by China of ballistic missiles and components to such governments as those of Syria, Pakistan, and Iran. To the Chinese, on the other hand, the United States seemed hypocritical given the fact that it continued to be the world's foremost arms merchant. Beijing adamantly declared human rights to be a purely domestic matter while the United States asserted that the treatment of China's people should be subject to universal norms. Frictions multiplied, encompassing not only old disputes regarding religious tolerance and Tibet, but also the fate of political prisoners incarcerated after Tiananmen and the future of Hong Kong. In the absence of the strategic imperative that the Cold War had supplied, such disagreements loomed larger and could not be resolved with the ambiguous compromises of earlier years.

In fact, dissatisfied with the Bush administration policy toward China, Congress targeted renewal of China's most-favored-nation (MFN) trade status (which remained subject to annual review under the 1973 Jackson-Vanik Amendment mandating free emigration from communist countries) as the vehicle for eliciting change in the PRC's human rights practices. Moreover, during the presidential campaign of 1992, candidate Bill Clinton took a forceful stand for human rights in China, insisting that he would place sanctions on China's trade to force greater compliance. Once in office, however, the pressures of U.S. business interests compelled Clinton to break the link between MFN and human rights. In 1994 he opted instead for a policy of "comprehensive engagement," through which the administration hoped to negotiate understandings on a variety of sensitive trade, human rights, and proliferation questions. The principal accomplishment of the new approach proved to be agreement on intellectual property rights protection. The two sides remained far apart on China's accession to the World Trade Organization (WTO), formerly the General Agreement on Tariffs and Trade (GATT), as well as on missile sales to Pakistan and imprisonment of dissidents. Washington also worried about Chinese naval activity in the South China Sea and its approaching takeover of Hong Kong in 1997.

The most divisive issue, however, became Taiwan. President Bush's sale of F-16 fighter aircraft to the Republic of China in an attempt to capture votes in Texas and to counter the PRC's acquisition of weapons from Russia undermined the carefully crafted August 1982 communiqué. Beijing also protested U.S. actions boosting Taiwan's international prestige even though relations between Beijing and Taipei had improved significantly and a high volume of trade, investment, and tourism encouraged observers to speak of an evolving Greater China. At the same time, democratization and economic prosperity led Taiwan to seek admission to the UN, to encourage semidiplomatic ties with many nations through aid and trade, and to revive discussion of independence. Further, in 1995 Taipei used its formidable lobbying apparatus to obtain a congressional resolution calling for an "unofficial visit" by Taiwan's President Lee Teng-hui to his alma mater, Cornell University, in New York State. When Clinton bowed to congressional pressure, Beijing denounced the visit as interference in China's internal affairs, recalled its ambassador from Washington, and refused to approve the nomination of a new U.S. ambassador to China. Having previously seen Clinton as soft and pliable, Beijing now concluded that the United States sought to follow a containment policy, keeping China weak and divided. In addition, because China faced a succession struggle with the imminent death of Deng Xiaoping, none of the contenders for power could appear willing to compromise.

The situation only worsened with the approach of elections in Taiwan. Balloting for the national legislature in 1995 and for the first popularly elected president in Chinese history during 1996 challenged Beijing's leaders. Jiang Zemin, Deng Xiaoping's heir presumptive, lacked his own power base, and, therefore, found it necessary to placate military hardliners by taking forceful action to deter the people of Taiwan from voting for pro-independence candidates. China staged a series of intermediating military exercises in the Taiwan Straits, including the firing of missiles and the use of live ammunition. In response, the United States deployed two aircraft carrier groups to the immediate vicinity of Taiwan to demonstrate Washington's grave concern and to try to ensure a peaceful resolution of the crisis.

Thus, as the end of the twentieth century approached, Sino-American relations once again only could be characterized as troubled and uncertain, weaker than at any time since rapprochement began. As in the early days of U.S.-China contact, misunderstanding and misperception brought on by cultural differences and disparate goals played a major role in defining interaction. In contrast to times past, however, neither the United States nor China could afford any longer the luxury of ignorance or apathy, given the enormous impact each would have on the other's economy and security in the twenty-first century.

NANCY BERNKOPF TUCKER

See also Boxer Rebellion; Chennault, Claire Lee and Anna Chan; China Hands; China Lobby; Gunboat Diplomacy; Hurley, Patrick Jay; Immigration; Jiang Jieshi; Jinmen-Mazu Crises; Kissinger, Henry Alfred; Korean War; Lansing-Ishii Agreement; Manchurian Crisis; Mao Zedong; Marshall, George Catlett, Jr.; McCarthyism; Nixon, Richard Milhous; Open Door Policy; Russia and the Soviet Union; Sino-Japanese War; Stilwell, Joseph; Sun Zhongshan; Taiwan; Zhou Enlai

FURTHER READING

Borg, Dorothy, and Waldo Heinrichs, eds. *Uncertain Years: Chinese-American Relations, 1947–1950.* New York, 1980.

Chang, Gordon H. *Friends and Enemies: The United States, China, and the Soviet Union, 1948–1972.* Stanford, Calif., 1990.

Cohen, Warren I. *America's Response to China,* 3rd ed. New York, 1990.

———. *East Asian Art and American Culture.* New York, 1992.

Cohen, Warren I., and Akira Iriye, eds. *The Great Powers in East Asia, 1953–1960.* New York, 1990.

Foot, Rosemary. *The Practice of Power: U.S. Relations with China Since 1949.* London, 1995.

Harding, Harry. *A Fragile Relationship: The United States and China Since 1972.* Washington, D.C., 1992.

Harding, Harry, and Yuan Ming, eds. *Sino-American Relations, 1945–1955: A Joint Reassessment of a Critical Decade.* Wilmington, Del., 1989.

Hunt, Michael H. *The Making of a Special Relationship: The United States and China to 1914.* New York, 1983.

Isaacs, Harold. *Images of Asia.* New York, 1962.

Kuznitz, Leonard A. *Public Opinion and Foreign Policy: America's China Policy, 1949–1979.* Westport, Conn., 1984.

Mayers, David Allan. *Cracking the Monolith: U.S. Policy Against the Sino-Soviet Alliance, 1949–1955.* Baton Rouge, La., 1986.

Saxton, Alexander. *The Indispensable Enemy: Labor and the Anti-Chinese Movement in California.* Berkeley, Calif., 1971.

Schaller, Michael. *The U.S. Crusade in China, 1938–1945.* New York, 1979.

Shambaugh, David. *Beautiful Imperialist: China Perceives America, 1972–1990.* Princeton, N.J., 1991.

Tucker, Nancy Bernkopf. *Patterns in the Dust: Chinese-American Relations and the Recognition Controversy, 1949–1950.* New York, 1983.

———. *Taiwan, Hong Kong, and the United States, 1945–1992: Uncertain Friendships.* New York, 1994.

Westad, Odd Arne. *Cold War and Revolution: Soviet-American Rivalry and the Origins of the Chinese Civil War, 1944–1946.* New York, 1993.

Young, Marilyn. *The Rhetoric of Empire: American China Policy, 1895–1901.* Cambridge, Mass., 1968.

Zhang Shu Guang. *Deterrence and Strategic Culture: Chinese-American Confrontation, 1949–1958.* Ithaca, N.Y., 1992.

CHINA HANDS

A small but important group of largely unofficial American experts on China, a country that for a long time was a mystery to most Americans. Ever since the first regular contact between China and the United States, a number of missionaries, educators, journalists, travelers, and businessmen with personal experience of that country have been called China hands. They have had a variety of views and interests, having in common only a familiarity with China. The phrase has also been used to refer to diplomats with deep experience in China and usually facility in the Chinese language in the years before the Cold War. Prominent China hands in the twentieth century included the diplomats Stanley K. Hornbeck, John Paton Davies, and John S. Service; the scholars John Leighton Stuart, John K. Fairbank, and Owen Lattimore; and the writers Theodore H. White and Pearl Buck. In 1950 Senator Joseph R. McCarthy charged that some of the China hands of the 1930s and 1940s had communist sympathies and were responsible for undermining U.S. support for the defeated Nationalist government of Jiang Jieshi (Chiang Kai-shek). Following the rapprochement between the People's Republic of China and the United States in the 1970s, a distinction was made between the old China hands, who had experience with precommunist China, and the new China hands, such as writers Edgar Snow and Anna Louise Strong, diplomat Winston Lord, and scholar Harry Harding, who were familiar with Communist China.

GORDON H. CHANG

See also China; China Lobby; Davies, John Paton, Jr., Fairbank, John King; Hornbeck, Stanley Kuhl; Jiang Jieshi; McCarthyism; Stuart, John Leighton

FURTHER READING

Cohen, Warren I. *America's Response to China,* 3rd ed. New York, 1990.

Kahn, E. J. *The China Hands: America's Foreign Service Officers and What Befell Them.* New York, 1972.

CHINA LOBBY

A network of fervent anticommunist U.S. supporters of Chinese leader Jiang Jieshi (Chiang Kai-shek) and his

Nationalist government that was the most prominent voice on the China issue from the 1940s to the 1960s. Not a formal group of paid lobbyists, the China Lobby included such powerful figures as publisher Henry R. Luce, Congressman Walter C. Judd, Senators William F. Knowland and H. Alexander Smith, and Generals Claire L. Chennault and Albert C. Wedemeyer. Members of the China Lobby blamed several leaders, including President Harry S. Truman and Secretaries of State Dean Acheson and George C. Marshall, academic specialist John K. Fairbank, and Foreign Service officers Edmund O. Clubb and John S. Service for what they called the "loss of China" to the communists in 1949 and for being "soft on Chinese communism." They attacked U.S. contact with the People's Republic of China (PRC) or any hint of weakened U.S. support for Jiang on Taiwan. By keeping U.S. China policy a highly sensitive domestic political issue, the lobby helped freeze a policy of nonrecognition of the PRC for more than twenty years. In the early 1950s many China lobbyists supported Senator Joseph R. McCarthy's demagogic anticommunist campaign, which was built in part on their charges against such prominent China specialists as Owen Lattimore. By the early 1960s the China Lobby had lost much of its influence as the result of a changing political climate and the simple passage of time.

GORDON H. CHANG

See also Chennault, Claire Lee and Anna Chan; China; China Hands; Fairbank, John King; Jiang Jieshi; Luce, Henry Robinson; McCarthyism

FURTHER READING

Koen, Ross Y. *The China Lobby in American Politics.* New York, 1974.
Tucker, Dorothy Bernkopf. *Patterns in the Dust: Chinese-American Relations and the Recognition Controversy, 1949–1950.* New York, 1983.

CHOU EN-LAI

See Zhou Enlai

CHRISTOPHER, WARREN MINOR

(*b.* 27 October 1925)

Deputy secretary of state (1977–1981) and secretary of state (1993–). Christopher's quiet, unruffled, almost self-effacing manner served him well in a distinguished legal career in Los Angeles after his 1949 graduation from Stanford University Law School. These qualities, however, diminished his effectiveness as a foreign policy leader and public spokesman. As deputy secretary under Secretary of State Cyrus Vance, Christopher was respected for his careful judgment, attention to detail, concern for human rights, and negotiating skills. He was widely praised for his role in negotiating the 1981 release of U.S. hostages in Iran.

After serving as the head of President-elect Bill Clinton's transition team, Christopher was appointed secretary of state. He focused on supporting the transition to democracy in the former Soviet Union, containing the proliferation of dangerous weapons, changing the role of the North Atlantic Treaty Organization (NATO) in the post–Cold War era, advancing the Middle East peace process, and recasting the U.S. trade relationship with Japan. Foreign policy problems that he inherited from his predecessor were compounded by serious constraints on the conduct of foreign policy in the post–Cold War era: the lack of a defining focus for U.S. foreign policy in the absence of the old rivalry with the Soviet Union; a national and presidential priority given to domestic concerns; the difficulty of constructing a visionary foreign policy on the basis of a desirable but vague notion of expanding democracy and markets; and a national reluctance (because of the lack of a defining vision that would justify it) to use military force in addressing difficult situations (in Bosnia, Somalia, and Haiti). He devoted a great deal of time and effort to the Middle East peace process, shuttling frequently within the region. He also was quite involved in relations with Russia and in efforts to adapt NATO to the post–Cold War world.

The extent to which Christopher was responsible for the problems facing U.S. foreign policy in the post–Cold War world, and the extent to which he or anyone else could manage them, was the subject of extended discussion in the press, as were the rumors that Clinton would select a new secretary of state before the end of his first term. Christopher's public criticism of the human rights record of the People's Republic of China (PRC) during a February 1994 trip to Beijing put him at cross-purposes with those in the Clinton administration who believed that U.S.-China trade should not be jeopardized by a squabble over human rights. While his resignation was rumored in early 1995, and it was reported that he had offered to stay on only until a successor had been chosen, he continued in office. By the end of that year, moreover, he was able to cite a peace agreement in Bosnia, democracy in Haiti, multiparty elections in Russia, some progress toward reconciliation in Northern Ireland, an economic rescue package for Mexico, and the avoidance of confrontation with North Korea as evidence for describing 1995 as "the best year for American foreign policy since the end of the Cold War." While these achievements remain tentative, as critics pointed out, and responsibility for them must be shared with others in the administration, the exercise of increased leadership by the Clinton administration in the much more complicated post–Cold War world was broadly welcomed by America's allies.

BRUCE R. KUNIHOLM

See also Bosnia-Herzegovina; China; Clinton, William Jefferson; Iran; Mexico; Middle East; Northern Ireland; Russia and the Soviet Union

FURTHER READING

Christopher, Warren M. "America's Leadership, America's Opportunity, *Foreign Policy* 98(Spring 1995).

CHURCH, FRANK FORRESTER III

(*b.* 25 July 1924; *d.* 7 April 1984)

Democratic senator from Idaho (1957–1981) who strongly opposed U.S. interventionism abroad. Born and raised in Boise and educated at Stanford University (B.A., 1947, LL.B., 1950), he included among his boyhood heroes Idaho's famed Senator William E. Borah. Like Borah, Church became a powerful orator who distrusted the meddling of large corporations and the U.S. government in the affairs of other nations. Church's aversion to colonialism intensified during World War II, when he served in Asia as a military intelligence officer. Although he entered the Senate with orthodox Cold War views, he soon criticized U.S. foreign policy for mirroring that of the Soviets and for underestimating the power of modern nationalism and anti-imperialism. By mid-1964, openly skeptical of deepening U.S. intervention in Vietnam, he became a leader in the Senate's emerging antiwar coalition, thereby damaging his previously good relationship with President Lyndon B. Johnson. Church ultimately cosponsored the Cooper-Church amendment and other legislation to halt an expansion of the U.S. role in the war and to ultimately stop the war. He urged Congress to reclaim prerogatives in foreign policy that it had conceded to the executive branch, and he questioned an indiscriminate application of the containment doctrine. He warned against his country's dominant role in the burgeoning arms trade and its "colonialist economics" in Latin America. Initially a supporter of foreign aid, he bade it farewell in October 1971, saying that it benefited mainly U.S. corporations and repressive military governments.

In the mid-1970s Church chaired landmark Senate investigations that revealed how the private needs of U.S.-based multinational corporations too often conflicted with the national interest. The Church Committee documented the misconduct of intelligence-gathering agencies, such as the Central Intelligence Agency (CIA); exposed U.S. assassination plots against Cuba's Fidel Castro; and revealed U.S. complicity in toppling the government of President Salvador Allende Gossens in Chile in 1973. Church tried to improve U.S.-Cuban relations by meeting in 1977 with Castro. In 1978 Church guided the Panama Canal treaties through the Senate. During his last two years in office, he chaired the Foreign Relations Committee. He was defeated in 1980 when right-wing organizations campaigned against him, claiming that he had weakened the United States. In 1984, just before he died of cancer, he asked in his last published statement why the United States found "it so difficult to live in a world of revolutionary change."

LeRoy Ashby

See also Central Intelligence Agency; Chile; Cold War; Congress; Cuba; Multinational Corporations

FURTHER READING

Ashby, LeRoy, and Rod Gramer. *Fighting the Odds: The Life of Senator Frank Church.* Pullman, Wash., 1994.
Church, F. Forrester. *Father and Son: A Personal Biography of Senator Frank Church of Idaho.* New York, 1985.

CHURCH COMMITTEE

See Church, Frank Forrester III

CHURCHILL, WINSTON LEONARD SPENCER

(*b.* 30 November 1874; *d.* 24 January 1965)

British political leader who forged an Anglo-American partnership during World War II to defeat the Axis Powers and who, early in the Cold War, famously described an "Iron Curtain" drawn by the Soviets across Europe. Prime minister of Great Britain (1940–1945 and 1951–1955) and holder at various times of nearly all other high cabinet offices except that of foreign secretary, Churchill occupies a unique place in the history of U.S. foreign relations. In each of the nation's comprehensive twentieth-century struggles—World Wars I and II and the Cold War—Churchill stood at the center both of efforts to bring the United States to the point of political or military commitment, and of the politics that shaped the U.S. experience in each conflict. He was the principal architect of the Anglo-American partnership ("special relationship") in the twentieth century. He also influenced public opinion as orator, journalist, historian, and symbol of resistance to modern totalitarianism.

Churchill's mother, who was from the United States, did little to encourage any early curiosity about that country. His interest quickened, however, upon a brief visit in 1895 and an extensive lecture tour in 1900 exploiting his celebrity as a war correspondent in the Boer War. He became a member of parliament in 1900 and later held a succession of high posts in the pre–World War I Liberal government, viewing the United States variously as a reform model, a commercial threat, and as an increasingly powerful factor in world affairs. As First Lord of the Admiralty until his forced resignation in 1915 over the failure of the Dardanelles operation, Churchill confronted the vexing problems created for Great Britain by U.S. neutrality. He later became the leading British protagonist of a permanent Anglo-American bond, but he lamented President Woodrow Wilson's failure to support effectively the armed intervention against the Bolsheviks in Russia in 1919. He also helped lay the foundation of what became a classic European grievance by criticizing Wilson's enthusiasm for self-determination in postwar Europe at the expense of more traditional power structures.

As the Conservative government's chancellor of the exchequer (1924–1929), Churchill resented the persistent Washington pressure upon Great Britain to repay her war debt, to restore the gold standard (which he nevertheless did), and to reduce British naval power. Between the wars his sporadic interest in a closer European association was prompted largely by fear of U.S. economic competition. But in 1929, after the Conservative electoral defeat, Churchill made a long tour of North America that produced a more positive outlook. He became captivated by the vitality of U.S. capitalism and its corporate leadership. The ensuing economic depression did not shake his growing conviction that, despite the rising German and Japanese threats, the potential power of the United States would become a decisive factor in world affairs.

World War II

This insight, soon vindicated by events, contributed to Churchill's self-confidence upon his succeeding Neville Chamberlain as prime minister in May 1940. Many in the United States were already familiar with his robust approach to international politics through American publication of his various writings between the wars. Now his inspirational leadership in the face of German aggression gave him a high standing in U.S. public opinion that he never lost. Periodic suggestions that he somehow propelled the United States towards war by withholding detailed foreknowledge of the Japanese attack upon Pearl Harbor remain unsubstantiated. He did, to be sure, cultivate President Franklin D. Roosevelt assiduously. Together they arranged in 1940 for the United States to transfer fifty U.S. destroyers to Great Britain in exchange for long leases of various British bases. The Lend-Lease program followed early in 1941, and at their first meeting off Newfoundland in August 1941, the two leaders produced the Atlantic Charter.

Churchill gave the highest priority during World War II to association with the United States. His remarkable partnership with Roosevelt functioned successfully at the top of a highly centralized Anglo-American directorate. At the personal level, Churchill's gratitude to Roosevelt remained constant. In 1944–1945, however, strains appeared. Churchill's affection and respect for Roosevelt were now qualified by the latters' personal elusiveness, his determination to assert U.S. strategic and postwar

economic policies that cut across British purposes, and his apparent inability to discern what Churchill increasingly saw as a looming Soviet menace. Churchill did not focus his energy upon Roosevelt alone. He built useful relationships with other influential U.S. figures, such as FDR's confidant Harry Hopkins, W. Averell Harriman, General Dwight D. Eisenhower, and the Republican leader Wendell Willkie.

Until 1943 Churchill was instrumental in guiding Anglo-American strategy towards a Mediterranean campaign rather than the landings in France favored by both the U.S. military chiefs and the Soviets. Stalin blamed Churchill for the repeated delays in forming a substantial second front. In fact, Roosevelt supported Churchill on the issue until late 1943. Nevertheless Churchill was charged at the time, and afterwards by U.S. historians, with excessive concern for British imperial interests and, less persuasively, with an overriding desire to thwart Soviet expansionism in Eastern Europe and the Balkans. This last motive is probably best viewed as an impulse that surfaced at opportune moments rather than as an expression of consistent policy. In essence, deeply conscious of limited British resources, Churchill was determined to put off the hazardous invasion of France until the optimum moment. Only Roosevelt's insistence forced the action in 1944.

As far as the second front was concerned, the decisive moment came at the Teheran concurrence in late 1943. Roosevelt sided ostentatiously with Stalin on the preeminent importance of the cross-channel operation and also showed, in Churchill's view, an alarming indifference toward postwar European security. Then, in early 1944, a series of U.S. economic pressures seemed to threaten Great Britain's hopes of postwar economic independence. Anglo-American political relations declined, therefore, even as their military collaboration intensified and flourished. Against this background and confronted with the rapid Soviet advance into Eastern and Southern Europe, Churchill felt obliged to make his celebrated "spheres" agreement with Stalin at Moscow in October 1944. This involved the recognition of certain percentages as registers of each power's supposed interest in a given country. The Soviets received high percentages in Romania, Bulgaria, and Hungary; the British in Greece; and in Yugoslavia an equal share was agreed upon. Implicit in this was the division of Europe into British and Soviet spheres of influence.

Roosevelt, who had promised Churchill in September 1944 that the United States would continue to collaborate with Great Britain on the new atomic military technology, appears to have recognized and accepted the Anglo-Soviet agreement at first. By the end of 1944, however, he came to believe that the increasingly obvious revival of traditional European politics was beginning to chill public support for postwar U.S. internationalism. Consequently, and much to Churchill's chagrin, Roosevelt allowed some public criticism by the U.S. Department of State of British conduct in Greece, Italy, and Yugoslavia. Then, at the Yalta Conference in February 1945, Roosevelt, with Churchill's support, tried to persuade Stalin to pursue acceptable policies in Eastern Europe. The ensuing diplomatic confusion led to a serious crisis in which Churchill, with some success, pressed first Roosevelt, then President Harry S. Truman, to resist provocative Soviet actions in Poland and elsewhere. These events marked both the end of the short-lived Anglo-Soviet collaboration and the tentative beginnings of an Anglo-American front against the Soviet Union. After a brief U.S. return to a policy of collaboration with the Soviet Union in the second half of 1945 foundered in the aftermath of the Foreign Ministers Conference that December, an Anglo-American common line began to emerge more clearly.

The Cold War

That denouement owed something to Churchill, too. Though out of office after July 1945 (his Conservative party having been defeated on mostly domestic issues) he then returned to his prewar Cassandra role, striving now to bring U.S power to bear against Soviet expansionism. In early 1946 he visited the United States, reinforced Truman's rising suspicion of Stalin's intentions, and helped mobilize public support for firmer policies through his "Iron Curtain" speech of 5 March at Fulton, Missouri. Churchill warned of a Soviet threat to peace and asserted the necessity of an Anglo-American "fraternal association" to resist it. Truman had approved Churchill's message beforehand and his administration was already acting in accordance with it. The Fulton speech was effective as well in defining the issue at stake in the concurrent U.S.-Soviet confrontation over Iran. It seems likely also that it influenced Stalin's diplomacy in that crisis, which, some historians argue, brought on the Cold War.

In his last term as prime minister (1951–1955), Churchill continued to view the Anglo-American association as fundamental to the preservation of a wholesome peace. He maintained cordial personal relations with President Dwight D. Eisenhower, but regretted the U.S. disinclination to pursue the possibility of a summit conference with the Soviets after Stalin's death in 1953. Differences between the United States and Great Britain also developed over the Middle East and Southeast Asia. By Churchill's retirement the two countries seemed to be drifting apart. This was partly a matter of personalities, as Churchill and his ministers considered Secretary of State John Foster Dulles a difficult partner. More substantively, there was now a clash of perspectives. The

Eisenhower administration, consistent with its election mandate, was intent upon a zealous prosecution of the Cold War. The British were increasingly preoccupied, as the Suez Crisis of 1956 soon showed, with the preservation of their prestige as they tried to extricate themselves from the coils of empire without losing their status as a Great Power.

Churchill was quite often controversial in his policy views; some in the United States thought him a reactionary. But his influence upon U.S. leaders and public opinion was immense, especially in the period 1940–1946. Churchill thought his influence derived from a mutually shared pride of ancestry, the heritage of "the English-speaking peoples." In fact, it derived more substantially from admiration for his courage and vitality, and from respect for his leadership ability and his geopolitical insight. Millions read approvingly his best-selling postwar publications, especially his uniquely authoritative (though sometimes inaccurate) memoirs of World War II. His presentation of the great events through which his generation passed cast the United States in a generally favorable light and thus served as a kind of heroic overture to this country's postwar emergence as a truly global power.

FRASER J. HARBUTT

See also Cold War; Destroyers-for-Bases Deal; Great Britain; Roosevelt, Franklin Delano; Stalin, Joseph; Suez Crisis; War Debt of World War I; World War II; Yalta Conference

FURTHER READING
Churchill, Winston S. *The Second World War,* 6 vols. Boston, 1948–1953.
Gilbert, Martin. *Winston S. Churchill,* 8 vols. Boston, 1966–1988.
Harbutt, Fraser J. *The Iron Curtain: Churchill, America and the Origins of the Cold War.* New York, 1986.
Kimball, Warren F., ed. *Churchill and Roosevelt: The Complete Correspondence,* 3 vols. Princeton, N.J., 1984.
James, Robert Rhodes, ed. *Winston S. Churchill: His Complete Speeches, 1897–1963,* 8 vols. New York, 1974.

CIA

See Central Intelligence Agency

CIVIL AVIATION

The business of nonmilitary or commercial airlines, for which the Department of State has to negotiate a bilateral air services agreement with each country to which U.S. airlines fly. Such agreements typically determine the routes and airports used, define the type and volume of the market, and establish fare structures. U.S. negotiators have often had to deal with governments that want to protect their flag carrier (national airline) from competition and, as a result, negotiations can be very political. There have been three phases in U.S. aviation policy. In the first, 1919–1944, there was a laissez-faire attitude that allowed Pan American World Airways (Pan Am) to achieve a near monopoly over foreign routes. The second phase, 1944–1977, had more regulated competition. The third began in 1977, when the U.S. government began a process of deregulation.

Until 1944, in the absence of established international rules, governments and airlines used cut-throat political and commercial tactics to gain operating rights. In this free-for-all system, Pan Am became in effect the U.S. flag carrier and a powerful force in diplomatic negotiations. Concern gradually developed, however, about the unregulated infant airline industry. President Franklin D. Roosevelt decided to intervene and nurture the airlines through regulation. In 1938 the Congress passed the landmark Civil Aeronautics Act, which led to the creation of a regulatory agency, the Civil Aeronautics Board (CAB), in 1939.

During World War II domestic operators, such as Eastern Airlines, performed military transport duties and gained valuable experience in foreign operations. Roosevelt, and later President Harry S. Truman, wanted to take advantage of this to break Pan Am's dominance of overseas airline routes and create more competition after the war. The second phase of U.S. policy, which reflected those wishes, began at the Chicago International Conference on Civil Aviation, 1 November–4 December 1944, convened by the United States and attended by over fifty nations. The United States proposed a multilateral exchange of five freedoms to allow airlines to fly over and stop in another country and to disembark and pick up passengers for both an airline's country of origin and third party destinations. Great Britain blocked this open-skies policy because it feared U.S. hegemony in aviation. In 1946, however, Great Britain agreed to do bilaterally what it had refused to do multilaterally. The Anglo-American Civil Air Services (Bermuda) Agreement of that year embodied the five freedoms and was hailed by the United States as a liberal model that other countries should follow. The previous year two other important components of the new system had been born—the International Civil Aviation Organization, which deals with technical and safety matters, and the International Air Transport Association (IATA), which compiles market data and until the 1980s played a major role in the setting of fares.

Although these steps created a more general structure after 1945, the heart of the system was still bilateralism. Nevertheless, the Bermuda Model provided for fair and equal opportunity to operate routes, and the five freedoms allowed a relatively liberal system to develop. The Department of State negotiated many bilateral agreements that gave competitive scope to U.S. airlines. In the 1970s, how-

ever, U.S. companies encountered difficulties because of increased fuel and equipment costs and foreign competition. Under Presidents Richard M. Nixon in 1970 and Gerald R. Ford in 1976, U.S. policy statements reaffirmed commitment to the Bermuda Model and competition. Nevertheless, policy remained ambivalent as the United States strove to protect its private airlines against what it saw as unfair foreign subsidized competition and discrimination.

Phase three began in 1977, when equivocation between protection and competition ended. President Jimmy Carter and CAB Chairman Alfred Kahn began to dismantle the domestic regulatory framework and sought to make the international market more competitive. Notably, Kahn challenged IATA fare setting. Dynamics released by Carter's reforms drove domestic U.S. carriers into the international marketplace as they developed hub-and-spoke systems that fanned out ever further in search of global economies of scale. The Department of State sought to renegotiate as many bilateral agreements as possible and to obtain rights for U.S. carriers to fly to various countries without regulations that would restrict competition. Foreign governments, however, such as Great Britain and Japan, largely thwarted larger U.S. ambitions. In the 1990s recession and domestic and foreign competition hit U.S. airlines hard. President Bill Clinton addressed this problem by establishing the National Commission to Ensure a Strong Competitive Airline Industry. In August 1993 it recommended multilateralism to create a fairer competitive international market. No effective action had been taken by 1996, but a number of bilateral "open skies" agreements have been negotiated.

ALAN P. DOBSON

See also Airline Companies

FURTHER READING

Dobson, Alan P. *Peaceful Air Warfare: The United States, Britain, and the Politics of International Aviation.* Oxford, 1991.
———. *Flying in the Face of Competition: The Policies and Diplomacy of Airline Regulatory Reform in Britain, the U.S.A., and the European Community, 1968–1994.* Aldershot, Eng., 1995.
Gidwitz, B. *The Politics of International Air Transport.* Boston, 1980.
U.S. National Commission to Ensure a Strong Competitive Airline Industry. *Change, Challenge and Competition.* Washington, D.C., 1993.

CIVIL WAR

See American Civil War

CLARK AMENDMENT
(1976)

Measure barring additional financial support for covert Central Intelligence Agency operations in Angola, the

Portuguese colony in southwest Africa which became independent in 1975. The amendment was one manifestation of Vietnam War-era presidential-congressional conflict in foreign policy. Sponsored by Democratic Senator Dick Clark of Iowa, it gained congressional approval by veto-proof margins and was therefore signed by President Gerald Ford despite his objections to its provisions regarding intelligence operations. In the complicated civil war in Angola, involving three rebel contingents with different tribal and ideological orientations, the United States, South Africa, and China, each for reasons of its own, opposed the Popular Movement for the Liberation of Angola (MPLA), the Angolese faction supported by the Soviet Union and Cuba, and the ultimate victor. Although the MPLA won an election deemed free and fair by international observers, the National Union for the Total Independence of Angola (UNITA) continued its resistance and guerrilla warfare. In 1986, as part of the Reagan Doctrine, the Clark Amendment was repealed, and U.S. aid and other assistance was again provided to UNITA. After the repeal of the Clark Amendment, aid (arms, communications gear, mercenaries, and payments to anti-MPLA political figures) resumed until various international agreements brought about international disengagement in Angola in the late 1980s.

MARK T. GLIDERHUS

See also Africa; Angola; Congress; Presidency; Reagan Doctrine

FURTHER READING

Garthoff, Raymond L. *Détente and Confrontation: American Soviet-Relations, From Nixon to Reagan.* Washington, D.C., 1985.
———. *The Great Transition: American-Soviet Relations and the End of the Cold War.* Washington, D.C., 1994.

CLARK MEMORANDUM

Also known as the "Memorandum on the Monroe Doctrine," written in autumn 1928, an official Department of State renunciation of the previously claimed right of the United States, as stated in the Theodore Roosevelt Corollary to the Monroe Doctrine, to intervene in the internal affairs of Latin American countries. Prepared by Undersecretary of State J. Reuben Clark at the request of Secretary of State Frank B. Kellogg and published by the Department of State in 1930, the memorandum described the Monroe Doctrine as solely a statement of the U.S. position toward European intervention. U.S. intervention, therefore, was "not justified by the terms of the Monroe Doctrine, however much it may be justified by the application of the doctrine of self-preservation."

The Clark Memorandum appeared when there was no apparent threat from outside the hemisphere to the independence of Latin American states and the security of the United States. Latin American governments, however, greatly resented past U.S. interventions and pressed the United States to bind itself to absolute non-intervention. The memorandum represented a partial move toward non-intervention, served as an antecedent to the Good Neighbor Policy of President Franklin D. Roosevelt, and helped make the case for the withdrawal of U.S. military forces from Nicaragua, Haiti, and the Dominican Republic.

GADDIS SMITH

See also Good Neighbor Policy; Kellogg, Frank Billings; Latin America; Monroe Doctrine; Roosevelt Corollary

FURTHER READING

Munro, Dana. *The United States and the Caribbean Republics, 1921–1933.* Princeton, N.J., 1974.
Wood, Bryce. *The Making of the Good Neighbor Policy.* New York, 1961.

CLAY, HENRY

(*b.* 12 April 1777; *d.* 29 June 1852)

Lawyer, U.S. senator (1806–1807, 1810–1811, 1831–1842, 1849–1852) and member of Congress from Kentucky (1811–1814, 1815–1821, 1823–1825), diplomat, secretary of state (1825–1829), famed orator, and presidential aspirant. As a member of the U.S. House of Representatives in 1811, he emerged as a leader of the War Hawks, who were ready to press grievances against Great Britain to the point of war. Chosen Speaker of the House during his first term in Congress, he placed War Hawks in key committee appointments. In 1814 President Madison named Clay—along with John Quincy Adams, James A. Bayard, Albert Gallatin, and Jonathan Russell—to the U.S. Peace Commission that met at Ghent, Belgium, to negotiate an end to the War of 1812. At the conference, Clay supported the interests of the Western states, resisting the efforts of another member of the negotiating team, John Quincy Adams, to grant Great Britain navigation rights on the Mississippi River.

Returning to the House and the Speaker's chair in 1815, Clay used his office to attack the administration of President James Monroe and to further his own ambition for the presidency. In 1819 he denounced Andrew Jackson's invasion of Spanish Florida and the execution of two British subjects there as the dangerous deeds of a military chieftain. He opposed the Monroe administration's neutrality toward Latin American revolutions against Spain and advocated recognition of the new republics. He favored the Greek Revolution against the Turks and argued that the United States should encourage the cause of liberty over despotism.

Clay became John Quincy Adams's secretary of state in the so-called "corrupt bargain" following the election of 1824, in which Clay allegedly threw his support to Adams in return for the office that was the stepping-stone to the presidency. During his tenure as secretary of state, Clay concluded twelve commercial treaties, a larger number than any earlier administration and a reflection of the growth of U.S. trade during this period. He failed, however, to obtain a treaty reestablishing U.S. trade with the British West Indies. He supported U.S. participation in the Panama Congress of 1826, a meeting of Western Hemisphere nations intended to encourage discourse and cooperation. The issue was debated heatedly in the U.S. Congress before winning approval, but in the end Commissioner Richard Anderson died en route and John Sergeant arrived too late to participate.

Clay was reelected to the Senate in 1831, where he remained until 1842 and served as chair of the Foreign Relations Committee. During James Polk's administration, he opposed the War with Mexico even before his son Henry Jr., was killed at the Battle of Buena Vista in February 1847. In a speech at Lexington, Kentucky, in November 1847, Clay denounced the war and called on Congress to disclaim any intention of annexing Mexico or of acquiring any territory from Mexico for the purpose of introducing slavery.

Sectional strife over slavery concerned Clay throughout his political career. In the crisis that followed the acquisition of territory from Mexico, Clay proposed and helped win passage of the Compromise of 1850—a series of measures that called for admission of California without slavery, territorial government in New Mexico without restriction on slavery, settlement of the Texas boundary and assumption of Texas debts by the U.S. government, abolishment of slave trading in the District of Columbia, a new federal fugitive slave law, and limitations on the power of Congress to interfere with slave trading in the states. Although he remained a part of the political scene, the compromise was his last great political effort.

KENNETH R. STEVENS

See also Adams, John Quincy; Ghent, Treaty of; Mexico, War with; War Hawks; War of 1812

FURTHER READING

Burton, Theodore E. "Henry Clay, Secretary of State, March 7, 1825, to March 3, 1829." In *The American Secretaries of State and their Diplomacy*, vol. 4, edited by Samuel Flagg Bemis et al. New York (1958): 112–158.
Remini, Robert V. *Henry Clay: Statesman for the Union*. New York, 1991.

CLAY, LUCIUS DUBIGNON
(*b.* 23 April 1897; *d.* 17 April 1978)

A member of a generation of soldiers who also won distinction as diplomatists after World War II, Clay was born in Marietta, Georgia, and the early years of his military career after graduating from the U.S. Military Academy in 1918 were uneventful. He began to gain international experience through assignments to represent the United States at the Permanent International Naval Conference in Brussels in 1934 and to the staff of General Douglas MacArthur in the Philippines in 1937. World War II brought rapid advancement and varied responsibilities, notably as deputy director for war programs in 1944. In 1945 he became deputy to General Dwight D. Eisenhower, and then deputy military governor of the U.S. zone in Germany in 1946. As commander of U.S. forces in Europe and military governor in Germany (1947–1949), he won international attention during the Berlin airlift of 1948–1949, carried out in response to the Soviet blockade of the city. For West Germans, Clay symbolized the steadfastness of U.S. support for Berlin. He often spoke bluntly about the dangers of Soviet expansionism in the Cold War. He retired from military service in 1949 to enter business. President John F. Kennedy recalled Clay to active duty as his personal representative during the Berlin Wall crisis of the summer and fall of 1961. Once again, Clay symbolized U.S. commitment to containment to those Germans worried about Soviet pressures on the city. On 25 October, with President Kennedy's permission to take a tough stance, Clay ordered ten M-48 tanks to move to Checkpoint Charlie, the wall's entry point. The Soviets soon lined up a similar force on the East Berlin side, while Kennedy made a special, secret appeal to Soviet Premier Nikita Khrushchev to defuse the crisis. All tanks withdrew. From Clay's perspective, he had called the Soviet bluff; from the Soviet perspective, the decision to counter U.S. tanks with Soviet tanks deterred a U.S. provocation. After the crisis Clay went back to Continental Can Company, where he served as chairman of the board from 1950 to 1962.

LAWRENCE S. KAPLAN

See also Berlin; Germany; Kennedy, John Fitzgerald

FURTHER READING

Backer, John H. *Winds of History: The German Years of Lucius DuBignon Clay*. New York, 1983.
Clay, Lucius D. *Decision in Germany*. Garden City, N.Y.,1950.
———. *The Papers of General Lucius D. Clay: Germany 1945–1949*, 2 vols., edited by Jean Edward Smith. Bloomington, Ind., 1974.
Krieger, Wolfgang. *General Lucius D. Clay und Die Amerikanische Deutschlandpolitik, 1945–1949*. Stuttgart, 1987.

CLAYTON, JOHN MIDDLETON
(*b.* 24 July 1796; *d.* 9 November 1856)

Secretary of state (7 March 1849–22 July 1850) under Presidents Zachary Taylor and Millard Fillmore. Born in

Delaware, Clayton graduated from Yale College in 1815, studied law at the Litchfield Law School in Connecticut, and was admitted to the bar in 1819. During the next three decades, he emerged as a leader of the Whig party. In his home state, he served in the legislature (1824–1826), as secretary of state (1826–1828), and as chief justice (1837–1839). In 1829–1836, 1845–1849, and 1853–1856, Clayton represented Delaware in the U.S. Senate. As secretary of state, Clayton's lack of experience in foreign affairs contributed to crises with France (his disregard for diplomatic protocol in treating with William Tell Poussin, the French minister in Washington, concerning the *Eugénie* claims), Portugal (the *General Armstrong* claims from the War of 1812), and Spain (Narciso López's filibustering expeditions against Cuba). His advocacy of commercial expansion advanced plans for opening relations with Japan, resulting in Matthew C. Perry's expeditions of 1853–1854 and the 1854 treaty of peace, amity, and commerce with Japan. In accordance with the Whig party's policy of compromise and peace with Great Britain, Clayton negotiated the Clayton-Bulwer Treaty of 1850 (with British plenipotentiary Sir Henry Bulwer) which sought to settle Anglo-American difficulties in Central America. The treaty provided for joint control of a future transisthmian canal...and specifically stated that "neither [power]...will ever obtain or maintain for itself any exclusive control over the said ship canal...[or] ever erect or maintain any fortifications commanding the same...or occupy, or fortify, or colonize, or assume, or exercise any dominion over Nicaragua, Costa Rica, the Mosquito Coast, or any part of Central America." Clayton returned to the Senate in 1853, where he defended himself against charges from the Young America faction of the Democratic Party that the Clayton-Bulwer Treaty violated the Monroe Doctrine because it permitted Great Britain to maintain its presence in Central America. The treaty remained one of the most controversial in U.S. history until it was abrogated by the second Hay-Pauncefote Treaty in 1901.

DEAN FAFOUTIS

See also Filibusters; Fillmore, Millard; Japan; Hay, John Milton; Monroe Doctrine; Perry, Matthew Calbraith; Taylor, Zachary; Young America

FURTHER READING

Smith, Elbert B. *The Presidencies of Zachary Taylor and Millard Fillmore.* Lawrence, Kans., 1988.

Williams, Mary Wilhelmine. "John Middleton Clayton." In *The American Secretaries of State and Their Diplomacy,* 10 vols., edited by Samuel Flagg Bemis. New York, 1928.

CLAYTON, WILLIAM LOCKHART

(*b.* 7 February 1880; *d.* 8 February 1966)

One of the chief architects of U.S. foreign economic policy in the post–World War II period. A courtly southern gentleman of humble origins (the son of a Mississippi cotton farmer), Clayton was a self-made millionaire who left school after the seventh grade. He rose from clerk-stenographer to chairman of the board of Anderson-Clayton, the world's largest cotton trading company. A self-described "liberal capitalist," Clayton was an advocate of international free trade. Although he had doubts about the New Deal's agricultural policies, Clayton publicly endorsed President Franklin D. Roosevelt's reelection in 1936, primarily because of the free trade Reciprocal Trade Agreements Act (1934) program advocated by Secretary of State Cordell Hull. At Roosevelt's personal request, Clayton joined the administration in 1940, serving first as deputy loan administrator in the Reconstruction Finance Corporation and vice president of the Export-Import Bank and later as assistant secretary of commerce. His wartime work in securing access to strategic raw materials overseas involved considerable international intrigue. It also deepened his appreciation for the importance of global economic policies. In late 1944 Clayton moved to the Department of State as assistant secretary of state for economic affairs. Two years later he became undersecretary for economic affairs. When he resigned in October 1947, one newspaper described him as "the driving force in a score of efforts to bring order out of chaos." Clayton, in fact, helped launch major programs to support the U.S. Cold War doctrine of containment.

Clayton served as principal U.S. economic adviser at the 1945 Chapultepec and Potsdam conferences. He successfully lobbied Congress for United Nations Relief and Rehabilitation Administration aid and for a $3.75 billion postwar loan to Great Britain. He also played a key role in the Bretton Woods conference that established the International Monetary Fund (IMF) and the World Bank, and he negotiated the first General Agreement on Tariffs and Trade (GATT). As early as August 1946, Clayton began laying the economic groundwork for aid to Greece and Turkey later implemented by way of the Truman Doctrine. Drawing upon his research on the economic implications of President Harry S. Truman's public commitment to contain communism, Clayton fashioned what Secretary of State Dean G. Acheson called the "concrete outline" of the recovery plan for postwar Europe, the Marshall Plan. Clayton and his more celebrated colleagues Acheson and George Kennan saw the integration of the U.S. and European economies as key to the containment of communist, and therefore Soviet, influence. That integration also helped to assure full employment and postwar prosperity for the United States. As special envoy to the 1948 Havana Conference, Clayton helped draw up the charter of the International Trade Organization (ITO), signed by fifty-four nations. Congressional protectionists who did not share Clayton's free-trade philosophy blocked Senate ratification. A disappointed Clayton returned to private life. Over the years, however, many of the goals of the ITO have been met under the GATT treaties. As a semiretired businessman, Clayton continued to proselytize for the gospel of free trade and the necessity to wage the Cold War by economic rather than military means.

ROBERT L. MESSER

See also Bretton Woods System; Cold War; Foreign Aid; Free Trade; General Agreement on Tariffs and Trade; International Trade Organization; Marshall Plan; Truman Doctrine; United Nations Relief and Rehabilitation Administration

FURTHER READING

Clayton, William L. *Selected Papers of Will Clayton*, edited by Frederick J. Dobney. Baltimore, 1971.
Fossedal, Gregory A. *Our Finest Hour: Will Clayton, the Marshall Plan, and the Triumph of Democracy*. Stanford, Calif., 1993.
Garwood, Ellen Clayton. *Will Clayton: A Short Biography*. Austin, Tex., 1958.

CLAYTON-BULWER TREATY

See Clayton, John Middleton

CLEMENCEAU, GEORGES

(*b.* 28 September 1841; *d.* 24 November 1929)

Premier of France (1906–1909, 1917–1920) and one of the principal architects of the Treaty of Versailles that ended World War I. Born in the Vendée, Clemenceau was trained as a medical doctor. He spent the years 1865–1869 in the United States, teaching at a female academy in Connecticut (where he fell in love with and married one of his pupils). On his return to France he turned to journalism and began his political career with his election as mayor of the Montmartre district of Paris in 1871. He was elected in 1876 a member of the Chamber of Deputies, where he gained a reputation for biting criticism, a harsh wit, and a certain ruthlessness (hence his nickname, the "Tiger"). When he lost his reelection bid to the National Assembly in 1893, he returned to journalism and the writing of books. He also staunchly defended the innocence of French army officer Alfred Dreyfus, falsely accused of treason. Clemenceau made a political comeback in 1902, when he won election to the National Assembly. In 1906 he assumed the cabinet post of minister of the interior and became premier later that year. Although he fell from power in 1909, he devoted his energies as a deputy in the National Assembly to raising public awareness of the need for military preparedness. After the outbreak of World War I, Clemenceau served on important legislative committees concerned with the war effort, and in the fall of 1917 he again became premier. The militant Clemenceau turned out to be the ideal wartime leader, supporting French generals (later marshals) Ferdinand Foch and Philippe Pétain without subordinating himself to them and by cracking down on lukewarm patriots, pacifists, and war profiteers.

Clemenceau's chauvinism and Germanophobism nevertheless made him a poor choice to lead the French delegation at the Paris Peace Conference. He also regarded President Woodrow Wilson, who led the U.S. delegation, "as a strange and unwelcome dog" because of Wilson's opposition to the imposition of harsh peace terms on Germany. Clemenceau, in turn, found little support in obtaining French security guarantees, and his deep fears of another German invasion were taken lightly. His effort to achieve an Anglo-American defense agreement that would assist France in case of a German attack proved unsuccessful. He also failed to obtain the annexation of German territory (except for the provinces of Alsace-Lorraine, which the Germans had seized from France in 1871), and his plea for a League of Nations peacekeeping force also faltered. He was, however, able to satisfy the French electorate by winning Allied approval for German reparation payments equaling the cost of the war and getting approval for territorial changes that strengthened France's allies in eastern Europe (Czechoslovakia, Poland, Romania). Clemenceau resigned as premier in 1920 and later toured the United States. He returned home, deeply disappointed with what he identified as growing evidence of American isolationism.

SINA DUBOVOY

See also France; Germany; Paris Peace Conference of 1919; Versailles Treaty of 1919; Wilson, Thomas Woodrow; World War I

FURTHER READING

Clemenceau, Georges. *In the Evening of My Thoughts*, 2 vols. Boston, 1929.
Dallas, Gregor. *At the Heart of a Tiger: Clemenceau and His World, 1841–1929*. New York, 1993.
Newhall, David S. *Clemenceau: A Life at War*. Lewiston, N.Y., 1991.
Watson, David Robin. *Georges Clemenceau: A Political Biography*. London, 1974.

CLEVELAND, STEPHEN GROVER

(*b.* 18 March 1837; *d.* 24 June 1908)

President of the United States (1885–1889, 1893–1897). Born in Caldwell, New Jersey, in 1853 Grover Cleveland moved to Buffalo, New York, where he practiced law, served as Democratic mayor (1881–1882), and was elected governor of New York State (1883–1885). Like most Gilded Age presidents, he gave only limited time to foreign relations, leaving much of the diplomacy in the hands of Secretaries of State Thomas F. Bayard (1885–1889), Walter Q. Gresham (1893–1895), and Richard Olney (1895–1897). Upon entering the White House, he based his foreign policy on the settlement of disputes by arbitration and the avoidance of European power politics. Although an economic expansionist, Cleveland opposed the acquisition of foreign territories and the establishment of U.S. protectorates abroad.

During his first term Cleveland withdrew the Frelinghuysen-Zavala Treaty, which would have made Nicaragua a U.S. protectorate. He also ended the possibility of U.S. participation in the Berlin agreements of 1884, designed to end international competition over the Congo. At the same time, he endorsed commercial reciprocity with Hawai'i, seeing the islands as "virtually an outpost of American commerce and a stepping-stone to the growing trade of the Pacific." In 1887 the Senate approved a reciprocity treaty with Hawai'i. On the other hand, Cleveland opposed commercial reciprocity in Central America and the Caribbean, and he withdrew treaties with the Dominican Republic and Spain for reciprocity with Cuba and Puerto Rico and blocked a similar agreement with Mexico. Sponsorship by the previous Republican administration, possible negative effects on Cleveland's efforts at tariff reduction, and fear of establishing economic protectorates in the Caribbean played a role in his decision.

Problems arose over Canadian fisheries after Congress in July 1885 abrogated provisions in the Treaty of Washington (1871), which permitted Canada to export its fish to the United States without duty ("free fish") in return for allowing U.S. fishing within its three-mile limit ("free fishing"). In the spring of 1886 infuriated Canadians began to seize U.S. fishing craft, prompting Congress on 2 March 1887 to pass retaliatory legislation that empowered the president to bar Canadian goods and ships from U.S. ports if U.S. fishing interests received unjust treatment. Cleveland did not enforce the law but used it as a bargaining chip for a new agreement—the Bayard-Chamberlain Treaty of 15 February 1888. This treaty defined fishing boundaries and promised the United States additional privileges if it ever agreed to continue the "free fish" practice. Meanwhile, a temporary arrangement pending a final settlement would be in effect. On 21 August a Republican majority in the Senate turned down the treaty. Furious at the overt partisanship of the move, Cleveland sought to embarrass the Senate by fostering a bill giving the president power to "prohibit the transit of goods, wares, and merchandise" across the Canadian border. The Democratic House of Representatives passed the legislation, but because the bill would have severely injured U.S. commerce, an embarrassed Senate balked.

In the Bering Sea, Canadian seal hunters were indis-criminately slaughtering Alaskan seals, threatening the survival of the herds. To stop this practice, Cleveland in 1886 ordered revenue-cutters to arrest the Canadians. Two years later Bayard, dubious of such unilateral action in violation of international law and contrary to traditional U.S. advocacy of freedom of the seas, convinced the president to halt the arrests. On the day before he left office, however, Cleveland signed a law enabling the U.S. Navy to arrest all poachers.

Tensions with Germany over Samoa in May 1886 caused the U.S. consul at Apia to fly the U.S. flag over Samoan public buildings and announce a temporary protectorate over the Pacific islands. Although the consul was acting at the invitation of the Samoan king, the government in Washington immediately disavowed the move and recalled the consul. In August 1887 Germany took over the islands, and when in December 1888 it suppressed a native rebellion, Cleveland ordered three warships to Samoa. On 15 January, in a special message to Congress, he warned against the preponderance of German power in Samoa. The United States, he said, insisted upon the preservation of Samoan independence and autonomy. On 14 June, three months after Cleveland left office, the United States signed a treaty with Germany and Great Britain establishing a tripartite protectorate over Samoa, which at the same time recognized limited independence for that nation.

In 1893, when Cleveland again entered the White House, he immediately withdrew a pending treaty that would have annexed Hawai'i to the United States. He appointed James H. Blount, a retired representative from Georgia and former chairman of the House Foreign Affairs Committee, to investigate the recent revolution. In his July 1893 report to Cleveland, Blount declared that the new U.S.-led Hawai'ian regime resulted from a "great wrong," the immoral overthrow of Queen Liliuokalani. On 18 October, Cleveland's minister to Hawai'i, Albert S. Willis, received instructions to convince Hawai'ian President Sanford B. Dole to abdicate in favor of the queen and to persuade her to grant clemency to the provisional government. Cleveland's bid proved abortive when Queen Liliuokalani at first spoke of beheading all enemies (although she later relented), and Dole denied the right of the United States to intervene in Hawai'i's internal affairs. In a special message on 18 December 1893, Cleveland told Congress that the new insurrectionist Hawai'ian government lacked popular support and annexation would violate "a high standard of honor and morality." He left the issue "to the extended powers and wide discretion of Congress," which he undoubtedly knew would quarrel incessantly. On 31 May 1894 the Senate passed a resolution asserting the right of the islands "to establish and maintain their own form of government and domestic policy" without U.S. interference. The insurrectionists proclaimed the Republic of Hawai'i on 4 July 1894, and Cleveland reluctantly recognized it three days later. In August he ordered the U.S. cruiser Philadelphia out of Honolulu, thus ending U.S. military pressure.

The greatest crisis of Cleveland's presidency centered around the Venezuelan boundary dispute with Great Britain. Cleveland encouraged Secretary of State Olney's blunt hegemonic language, which admonished the British to respect the Monroe Doctrine and declared U.S. predominance in the Western Hemisphere. (The crisis was eventually resolved in 1899, with terms generally favorable to Great Britain.) The Cuban insurrection, which broke out on 24 February 1895, also drew U.S. attention. On 12 June 1895, Cleveland proclaimed neutrality, thereby refusing to recognize the belligerency of the Cubans in their revolt against Spain and forbidding Americans to underwrite military enterprises for the rebels. He then detailed U.S. naval units to patrol the Florida coast, but such policing was difficult to enforce. The Senate on 28 February 1896 and the House on 6 April passed concurrent resolutions calling for extending belligerent rights to the rebels and use of the president's good offices to secure Cuban independence. Cleveland balked. He feared that a sovereign Cuba would fall prey to anarchy and European intervention, which would endanger U.S. security. He consequently favored Spanish pacification. For Spain to triumph, he believed, it had to make real concessions to the Cubans. In Cleveland's annual message to Congress on 7 December 1896, he openly advised Spain to grant "genuine autonomy," while preserving its own sovereignty over the island. He warned that the continued upheaval might eventually force U.S. intervention. "The United States," he declared, "is not a country to which peace is necessary." When the Spanish foreign minister promised extensive reforms, Cleveland remained hopeful.

During Cleveland's second term the United States arbitrated boundary disputes between Columbia and Costa Rica and between Brazil and Argentina (the Misiones arbitration), reinforced a U.S. squadron in Rio de Janeiro harbor to help suppress a Brazilian naval revolt, and landed sailors at Bluefields, Nicaragua, thereby inducing the British to recognize Nicaraguan sovereignty over the Mosquito Islands. In the summer of 1895 the United States maneuvered warships in Turkish waters to protect U.S. missionaries and sent a three-man commission to Ch'eng-tu, China, to investigate offenses against U.S. citizens. In January 1895 the Senate passed a bill, endorsed by Cleveland, to guarantee the construction of an isthmian canal across Nicaragua, but the House failed to act on the measure. Repudiated in the Democratic party's 1896 convention by Silverites who disputed

Cleveland's hard-money views, Cleveland retired from politics but remained active as a writer for periodicals and as a trustee of Princeton University.

JUSTUS D. DOENECKE

See also Arbitration; Bayard, Thomas Francis; Brazil; Canada; Fisheries; Gresham, Walter Quintin; Hawai'i; Nicaragua; Olney, Richard; Samoa, American; Sealing; Spanish-American-Cuban-Filipino War, 1898; Venezuelan Boundary Dispute

FURTHER READING

Campbell, Charles C. *The Transformation of American Foreign Relations, 1865–1900.* New York, 1976.

Eggert, Gerald G. *Richard Olney: Evolution of a Statesman.* University Park, Pa., 1974.

Grenville, John A. S., and George Berkeley Young. *Politics, Strategy, and American Diplomacy: Studies in Foreign Policy, 1873–1917.* New Haven, Conn., 1966.

May, Ernest R. *Imperial Democracy: The Emergence of America as a Great Power.* New York, 1961.

Nevins, Allan. *Grover Cleveland,* rev. ed. New York, 1966.

Welch, Richard E. *The Presidencies of Grover Cleveland.* Lawrence, Kans., 1988.

CLIFFORD, CLARK MCADAMS

(*b.* 25 December 1906)

An influential lawyer and foreign policy adviser in the post–World War II era, first as the equivalent of a national security adviser to President Harry S. Truman (1946–1950), then as foreign policy adviser to President John F. Kennedy (1961–1963), and briefly as secretary of defense (1968) under President Lyndon B. Johnson. Clifford was a highly connected lawyer and political confidant for people of power who generally respected him for his wise counsel, smooth manners, and political savvy. Born in Fort Scott, Kansas, and educated at Washington University in St. Louis, Missouri, where he received his LL.B. (1922) degree, Clifford was a comfortable but atypical member of the foreign policy establishment. His law firms wrote legislation for the Democrats, lobbied Congress, and established him as the highest paid attorney in Washington.

From 1946 to 1950, as special counsel to President Truman, he helped orchestrate the adoption of the policy of containment. In 1946, with the help of his aide George Elsey, Clifford prepared a report for Truman that paralleled the better-known 1946 "Long Telegram" by Foreign Service officer George F. Kennan. The Clifford-Elsey report added a militaristic twist to Kennan's recommendations, however, when it concluded that "the language of military power is the only language that disciples of power politics understand." When the White House prepared the Truman Doctrine speech in March

1947, Clifford helped shape the dramatic rhetoric about the fundamental conflict between totalitarianism and freedom that Truman employed to persuade Congress to pass enabling legislation. In 1948 Clifford urged Truman to recognize Israel despite the objections of major foreign policy advisers, including James Forrestal, Robert Lovett, and George C. Marshall. In 1949 Clifford suggested that Truman make his inaugural address more positive by adding Point Four, which called for aid to underdeveloped countries.

Having served President Kennedy as a foreign policy adviser and political troubleshooter, Clifford returned to the center of policymaking in 1968, when President Lyndon Johnson asked him to replace Robert McNamara as secretary of defense. Johnson wanted Clifford to review Vietnam policy, especially General William C. Westmoreland's request for 200,000 additional troops. Clifford's own views on the war were never fixed. In 1965 he warned that escalation would lead to disaster, not victory; once the United States was more fully committed to the war, he recommended more troops and heavier bombing; then, as secretary of defense, he opposed the war, because in his opinion the war was unwinnable. Although many foreign policy establishment figures, such as W. Averell Harriman and Paul Nitze, author of NSC-68, advised him that the war was lost, Clifford could find no generals or admirals in the Pentagon with a plan to end the war. To orchestrate a shift, Clifford reconvened the "wise men," a group that included major architects of the containment policy, who concluded not only that the war could not be won but also that it endangered containment in Europe, a policy that they had designed. Clifford's maneuvering contributed to Johnson's decision on 31 March 1968 to announce a unilateral bombing halt in Vietnam and his withdrawal as a candidate for reelection to the presidency.

With the Republicans in power under President Richard M. Nixon, Clifford returned to his lucrative law practice and in 1982 became chairman of First American Bank Shares. In 1991 investigators determined that First American was illegally owned by the Bank of Credit and Commerce International (BCCI), a bank controlled by the sheik of Abu Dhabi. BCCI, whose bankruptcy cost investors as much as $12 billion, had engaged in fraudulent international finance activities, Central Intelligence Agency (CIA) operations, and drug deals involving Manuel Noriega of Panama and the Medellín cartel in Colombia. Both federal and New York State prosecutors indicted Clifford for his role in covertly tying First Bank Shares to BCCI but dropped the indictment in 1993 after his partner, Robert Altman, was acquitted. This episode seriously tarnished the reputation of one of Washington's ultimate insiders.

MARK H. LYTLE

See also Cold War; Containment; Democratic Party; Harriman, William Averell; Israel; Johnson, Lyndon Baines; Kennan, George Frost; Marshall, George Catlett, Jr.; Nitze, Paul Henry; NSC-68; Point Four; Truman Doctrine; Truman, Harry S.; Vietnam War

FURTHER READING

Clifford, Clark. *Counsel to the President: A Memoir*. New York, 1991.
Isaacson, Walter, and Evan Thomas. *The Wise Men: Six Friends and the World They Made—Acheson, Bohlen, Harriman, Kennan, Lovett, McCloy*. New York, 1986.

CLINTON, WILLIAM JEFFERSON

(*b.* 19 August 1946)

The forty-second president of the United States, sworn in on 20 January 1993. A fifth generation Arkansan, Bill Clinton (as he prefers to be called) was born in Hope. He graduated from Georgetown University in 1968 and from the Yale Law School in 1973. He studied at Oxford University on a Rhodes Scholarship from 1968 to 1970. After law school, Clinton returned to Arkansas to involve himself in state politics, and was elected attorney general in 1976 and then governor in 1978.

A five-term governor of Arkansas, Clinton campaigned for the presidency in 1992 largely on domestic themes, criticizing the incumbent, George Bush, for his obsession with foreign policy. In this respect, Clinton's presidency was consistent with his campaign. There were successes and failures, advances and setbacks, but in his first three years, Clinton devoted less time, energy, and political capital to the conduct of U.S. foreign relations than has any president in half a century. Part of this shift in focus at the Oval Office was related to Clinton's own interests and agenda. Part of it, however, was a reflection of the end of the Cold War, the more relaxed security environment, and the movement of American public attention toward domestic economic and social issues. In this matter, separating those attitudes specific to the Clinton administration from those stemming from the end of the Cold War will be an important task for future scholars.

The composition of Clinton's foreign policy team was unsurprising: mostly old Democratic hands who had served in the Johnson and Carter administrations. Prominent among them was Warren Christopher, a lawyer-diplomat who was Jimmy Carter's deputy secretary of state; Anthony Lake, a career foreign service officer and then academic, who served as director of policy planning in the Carter State Department; and Strobe Talbott, formerly a columnist for *Time* magazine, who first took charge of relations with Russia and later became deputy secretary of state. If this group had any ideological orientation toward foreign policy it was surely set by Lake, a neo-Wilsonian who argued forthrightly in the first year of

Clinton's presidency that U.S. foreign policy should be concerned with the promotion of ideals, not simply interests, and that the "enlargement" of the world of democracy and free markets should be the next great project of U.S. foreign policy.

The foreign policy themes that Clinton sounded most consistently through his campaign did not deal primarily with traditional items of national security, but with matters economic—the restoration of U.S. strength and competitiveness abroad through a more aggressive trade policy. His foreign economic policy team contained many of his key political advisers, like Commerce Secretary Ron Brown, and U.S. Trade Representative Mickey Kantor, who had immense political clout within the government.

Trade Policy

The administration contended that ever since the end of the Cold War the United States had made unilateral concessions in trade, opening its own markets to foreign goods, regardless of other countries' policies. As Undersecretary of the Treasury Lawrence Summers wrote: "That was the way it should have been in 1954; that was reasonable in 1964; that was becoming inappropriate in 1974; and that makes no sense in 1994." The administration promised to change this "turn-the-other-check approach" to trade policy and to make reciprocity and aggressive "export activism" the hallmarks of its approach. In office, the administration maintained certain established trade policies. It signed two important free trade agreements in 1993—the North American Free Trade Agreement (NAFTA) with Mexico and the latest round (the so called "Uruguay Round") of the General Agreement of Tariffs and Trade (GATT)—although both were initiated by Republican administrations. President Clinton's own trade initiatives have been more consistent with his campaign rhetoric. He refused to sign the largest expansion of the free trading system in decades, the lowering of barriers in the area of services in July 1995, arguing that the agreement opened the U.S. market unduly without sufficient reciprocal concessions—the first time in fifty years that the United States was not a signatory of a general agreement to lower tariffs.

"Export activism" marked the administration's approach to trade and international economic policy in general and Japan was the country to which it paid the greatest attention. The administration pointed out that, fueled by a high savings rate, an undervalued yen, and an abnormally low reliance on imports, Japan had for years been running large trade surpluses with the rest of the world in general and the United States in particular. It was thus occupying an anomalous and unstable position in the world economy and had to be made to converge to international norms. On the basis of this analysis the United States pursued a highly aggressive campaign,

marked by high-profile public diplomacy, aimed at getting Japan to agree to reduce its trade surplus, increase its imports and, in particular, to open its markets to U.S. products.

Clinton's trade policy has been praised by members of both political parties who could be described as "neo-mercantilists." Most Republicans and academic economists, however, have been more critical. They have pointed out that Tokyo has made only token concessions to Washington. More than the failure of specific negotiating goals, critics made two more general arguments. First, was that the Clinton administration was fighting the last war. It misconstrued the nature of the Japan of the 1990s, seeing it as the relentless and predatory economic dynamo of the past. In fact, Japanese growth rates had tapered off, its economic system was showing signs of real trouble, and its closed political system was cracking. U.S. policy, far from pushing Japan along this path, was retarding it. Moreover, if Japan violated its commitments to free trade, the United States should have worked to open its markets through the existing procedures of the GATT, rather than itself becoming the prosecutor, judge, jury, and hangman. Second, the main reasons for the U.S. trade deficit with Japan had to do with its own low savings and investment rates and high consumption rate. Rather than adopt the difficult measures at home that would change this situation, Washington chose the easier path of Japan-bashing. In any event, by 1996 the administration seemed to recognize that its policy toward Japan was focusing too strongly—and negatively—on trade. Joseph Nye, until late 1995 a senior Defense Department official, articulated the case for U.S.-Japan security relations to remain primary, and President Clinton visited Japan to reaffirm the security relationship between the two countries.

Haiti, Bosnia, Somalia, and China

In the area of national security, defined in political and military terms, the first two years of the Clinton administration were dominated by crises in small countries not central to vital U.S. interests. Because the president had not set out his own conception of U.S. interests, he was forced to react to the crisis of the moment. Over time a pattern developed in the Clinton administration's foreign policy. The president and his advisers would define U.S. objectives in a strikingly expansive manner—the transformation of Russia into a democratic and capitalist state; the preservation of Bosnia as a multiethnic state within its original borders; the restoration of democracy to Haiti; the building of a new nation-state in Somalia; the simultaneous expansion of trade and human rights in China.

All these goals were praiseworthy; but most required a significant expenditure of energy, resources, and political capital over a long period of time. Given the stakes involved, were they all worth that kind of effort? The administration did not seem to have made its priorities clear to the public, or even to itself. As a crisis in each of these areas unfolded, when confronted with the reality that its goals would require significant economic assistance (as in the case of Russia) or hardline diplomacy coupled with sanctions (as with China) or a vigorous assertion of U.S. military power (as in Bosnia or Somalia) the administration would back off, scaling down its objectives. The only exception to this rule was in Haiti, where the costs of adhering to its original goals were not substantial. The threat of U.S. force proved enough to help usher out the junta ruling Haiti and to usher in Jean-Bertrand Aristide's regime in late 1994. The extent to which the U.S. intervention brought democracy to Haiti, however, remains unclear.

With regard to Bosnia, the pattern was more complicated. Clinton had criticized George Bush during the election season for declaring the Balkan conflict outside the U.S.'s vital interests; instead Clinton likened it to the Holocaust. Once in office and confronted with this rhetoric, the administration chose to move back to something suspiciously similar to the Bush policy. Secretary of State Christopher explained to the Congress that Bosnia did not engage U.S. vital interests. Though it would not involve itself militarily in the conflict, the administration made clear that it would not support any plan that "ratified" Serbian ethnic cleansing or aggression. By September 1995, the United States had intervened in the conflict through a NATO air campaign and had put forth a peace plan that accepted the Serbian demand for a quasi-independent state. In other words, it reversed both its positions. The Dayton Peace Accords, skillfully brokered by Richard Holbrooke, assistant secretary of state for European affairs, appear to have stopped the war by mid-1996, but at a price—Bosnia was weakened, Croatia strengthened, ethnic cleansing ratified, and Serbian self-determination accommodated. This may have been the only viable formula for peace, but it is worth asking whether the United States could have accepted this very formula—indeed with terms even more advantageous to the Bosnians—three years before it finally did.

In Somalia the Clinton administration expanded, in March 1993, the goals of the U.S. military mission set by George Bush in December 1992 as a food aid mission to what the ambassador to the United Nations, Madeleine K. Albright, described as, "an unprecedented enterprise, aimed at nothing less than the restoration of an entire country as a proud, functioning and viable member of the community of nations."

When criticized about their responses to these crises the Clinton administration offered a spirited defense, arguing that the problems they inherited were difficult, that they effectively limited U.S. exposure in these areas, and that most importantly, on the "big" issues, they had done well. There is certainly some truth to this claim, particularly in the Middle East where the administration helped broker a tenuous but real peace process between Israel, the Palestinian Liberation Organization, and Jordan and Egypt, although this policy seemed to be exhausted with the assassination of Yitzak Rabin in November 1995 and the election of a Likud government in 1996. It maintains a staunch and consistent policy of sanctions against both Iraq and Iran, though with regard to the latter it is increasingly isolated in its refusal to trade with the regime.

Yet the process of policy reversal described above repeated itself toward China. After raising the profile of human rights throughout early 1994 and threatening to deny China Most Favored Nation (MFN) status as a trading partner, the administration then renewed the MFN status, upsetting both the Chinese and the human rights community. On the range of difficult issues relating to China—its defense buildup, Taiwan, its enforcement of intellectual copyright laws—the administration seemed torn between a model of deterrence and one of constructive engagement. Again, in the end the administration moved back to a sensible middle path. In March 1996, as relations between China and Taiwan deteriorated during the runup to Taiwan's first presidential elections, Washington sent a sober mix of signals to both capitals designed to stop Taiwan from declaring independence and Beijing from acting militarily across the Taiwan Straits.

Russia and the Post–Cold War World

Toward Russia, the administration was more consistently supportive and in general managed this crucial relationship with care and skill, albeit with too much concern for Russian President Boris Yeltsin's political career. But having promised Moscow major assistance, it proved unable to garner Congressional support for a large aid package. The relations between the North Atlantic Treaty Organization (NATO) and Russia remain tense. Having constructed a complicated mechanism called "Partnership for Peace," which included Russia and did not include NATO membership or security guarantees for the countries of East-Central Europe, the administration changed course in early 1995 and embraced an expansion of NATO, extended to an indefinite number of countries in the indefinite future. It then explained that while full-fledged NATO members—with concomitant security guarantees—these countries would not have NATO troops stationed in their countries so as not to provoke Moscow. Whether or not this policy is wise, the method of getting to it, surely left something to be desired. With both Russia and China the administration's inconsistency may have encouraged the two powers to move somewhat closer to each other, symbolized by a meeting between Yeltsin and Jiang Zemin in Shanghai in April 1996.

It could be argued that the goals articulated by the Clinton administration were correct but that it should have employed the means to achieve them. But perhaps the administration should have scaled back its goals so that the means it was prepared to use would have been adequate to attain them. In any event, to do neither was the worst of all possible worlds because it exposed the nation internationally to the image of hypocrisy and the reality of a "Lippmann Gap" with its commitments exceeding its power. Some argue that the United States loses credibility when it chooses not to intervene in foreign crises. In fact credibility does not require that the United States respond to every act of aggression anywhere in the world at any price. It does requires that the United States choose carefully its interests, that protect those interests vigilantly, and most importantly that in all matters it make only those threats and promises that it intends to fulfill. Thomas Schelling has remarked that in international relations it is always important to remember how expensive are threats when they fail and promises when they succeed. It is the casual use of threats and promises that has damaged U.S. credibility.

By late 1994 Clinton's foreign policy had begun to change substantially, moving closer to a policy that weighed traditional questions of national interest first in its dealings with other nations. The president and his advisers moved from spending almost all their time, energy, resources, and political capital on the three televised hot spots—Haiti, Somalia, and Bosnia—to deal with larger, longer-term matters like Russia, relations with Japan, the rise of China, GATT, and NAFTA—though the tragedy of Bosnia continued to command attention in 1996, in part because of the degeneration of the Dayton Accords into de facto partition. Clinton would run for reelection in 1996 on a foreign policy record that involved no major setbacks, but no major triumphs.

The overwhelming reality of post–Cold War U.S. foreign policy is that the United States has the luxury to make mistakes. None of President Clinton's initial flip-flops cost the country much. In the end his foreign policy mostly returned to a normal path. But in terms of opportunities missed, one might have wished for more. In the early 1990s, the United States stood astride the globe like a colossus, with the power and reputation to sustain and widen the extraordinary world it has helped bring into being since 1945—a world of open markets and liberal politics. Preserving and strengthening that world, and bringing into the system the two great powers that remain outside of it, Russia and China, are ambitious goals that would require ambitious efforts. It is these larger issues that require major U.S. involvement and, intervention, for in the long run what happens in the hot

spot of the moment will not matter, but these larger, vital issues, trends, and relationships will determine the fate of the post–Cold war world.

FAREED ZAKARIA

See also Bosnia-Herzegovina; China; General Agreement on Tariffs and Trade; Haiti; International Trade and Commerce; Japan; Middle East; North American Free Trade Agreement; North Atlantic Treaty Organization; Presidency; Russia and the Soviet Union; Somalia

FURTHER READING

Hendrickson, David. "The Recovery of Internationalism." *Foreign Affairs* 73(September/October 1994): 26–43.
Hyland, William G. "Mediocre Record." *Foreign Policy* 101(Winter 1995–1996): 69–74.
Kagan, Robert. "American Power: A Guide for the Perplexed." *Commentary* 101(April 1996): 21–31.
Krauthammer, Charles. "The Unipolar Moment." *Foreign Affairs* 70(America and the World, 1990/1991): 23–33.
Mandelbaum, Michael. "Foreign Policy as Social Work." *Foreign Affairs* 75(January/February 1996): 16–32.
Maraniss, David. *First in His Class: A Biography of Bill Clinton.* New York, 1995.
Steel, Ronald. *Temptations of a Superpower.* Cambridge, Mass., 1995.
Ullman, Richard H. "Late Recovery." *Foreign Policy* 101(Winter 1995–1996): 75–79.
Zakaria, Fareed. "A Framework for Interventionism in the Post–Cold War Era." In *U.S. Intervention Policy for the Post–Cold War World,* edited by Arnold Kanter and Linton F. Brooks. New York, 1994.

CNN

See Cable News Network

COCOM

See Coordinating Committee on Multilateral Export Controls

COERCIVE DIPLOMACY

A defensive strategy designed to influence an aggressor government to either halt or reverse actions it has already taken, in which the coercing power may or may not use, or threaten to use, military force. Although the concept of coercive diplomacy incorporates elements of "carrot and stick" employed by state governments for centuries, its formulation as a coherent strategy occurred in the aftermath of the Cuban Missile Crisis of 1962 and reflected some of the policy judgments applied successfully by the administration of President John F. Kennedy in that crisis. Variations of the strategy have been tried by subsequent U.S. administration in Third World crises. The strategy usually consists of four elements: a demand that the adversary take specific steps or meet specified conditions; a time-limit for the adversary's compliance; a threat of punitive action by the coercing power if the adversary does not comply; and a set of positive inducements, or side-payments, that may tend to lower the adversary's resistance to the particular demands being made. Its strongest variant is the classic ultimatum; the weaker variants may contain implied threats of harsher actions to come and/or suggestions of urgency regarding compliance, which are signaled through the actions of the coercing power.

WILLIAM E. SIMONS

See also Cuban Missile Crisis

FURTHER READING

George, Alexander L., and William E. Simons, eds. *The Limits of Coercive Diplomacy*, 2nd ed. Boulder, Colo., 1993.

George, Alexander L., David K. Hall, and William E. Simons. *The Limits of Coercive Diplomacy: Laos, Cuba, Vietnam*. Boston: 1971.

U.S. Department of Defense. "Military Pressures Against North Vietnam, February 1964–January 1965." In *The Pentagon Papers: The Defense Department History of U.S. Decisionmaking on Vietnam*, vol. 3. Boston, 1971.

COLBY, BAINBRIDGE

(*b.* 22 December 1869; *d.* 11 April 1950)

Woodrow Wilson's last secretary of state (1920–1921). Colby was born in St. Louis, Missouri, and attended Williams College (A.B. 1890) and the New York Law School (L.L.B. 1892). While practicing law in New York City—he represented such prominent figures as Samuel L. Clemens—Colby became active in New York politics as a Republican. In 1912 Colby helped found the Progressive party, but he broke with it four years later when Theodore Roosevelt failed to win the party's nomination. He then supported President Woodrow Wilson's reelection campaign and soon became a Democrat. After the United States entered World War I, Colby was appointed to the U.S. Shipping Board. After a year and a half of successfully administering not only U.S. merchant shipping but other industrial enterprises, Colby resigned his post in 1919 with the intention of resuming his law practice. But President Wilson appointed him secretary of state in March 1920.

As secretary of state, Colby worked unsuccessfully to win Senate approval of the Treaty of Versailles and of U.S. membership into the League of Nations. In addition to settling Anglo-American differences regarding the transfer of the former territories of the Central Powers, Colby, an ardent anticommunist, helped shape the administration's nonrecognition policy toward Bolshevik Russia. Colby explained in August 1920 that the United States did not reject Soviet Russia's new political or economic systems. Instead, the United States disapproved of the Bolsheviks' disregard for international law, particularly Russia's invasion of Poland, and their support of communist activities within the United States.

Colby's most significant contribution to U.S. foreign policy was his assistance in the formation of a new Latin American policy. Not only did Colby promise to withdraw U.S. troops from the Dominican Republic and Haiti, he also announced the establishment of a nonintervention policy for the region. Colby also made a goodwill tour of Latin America, where he attempted to improve both diplomatic relations and the image of his country. Finally, Colby initiated negotiations with the Obregó and announced the establishment of a non-intervention policy for the region. These talks led directly to a diplomatic rapprochement between Mexico and the United States in 1923.

In 1921 Colby established a law practice with former President Wilson, which ended in 1923 when Wilson's deteriorating health forced the firm to dissolve. Colby continued to practice law and initially supported Franklin D. Roosevelt's presidency. Yet he soon became critical of the president's New Deal program. Colby wrote articles criticizing Roosevelt and his agenda and resigned as the special assistant to the U.S. Attorney General in order to help form an opposition group to the New Deal, the American Liberty League. In 1936 Colby retired from his law practice and returned to the Republican party.

SCOTT D. KELLER

See also Bucareli Agreements; Mexico; Roosevelt, Theodore; Russia and the Soviet Union; Versailles Treaty of 1919; Wilson, Thomas Woodrow

FURTHER READING

Bemis, Samuel Flagg, ed. *The American Secretaries of State and Their Diplomacy*, vol. 10 of *William Jennings Bryan–Robert Lansing–Bainbridge Colby–Charles Evans Hughes*. New York, 1929.

Daniels, Josephus. *The Wilson Era: Years of War and After, 1917-1923*. Chapel Hill, N.C., 1946.

Link, Arthur S., ed. *The Papers of Woodrow Wilson*. Princeton, N.J., 1966.

Smith, Daniel M. *Aftermath of War: Bainbridge Colby and Wilsonian Diplomacy, 1920–1921*. Philadelphia, Pa., 1970.

Smith, Gene. *When the Cheering Stopped: The Last Years of Woodrow Wilson*. New York, 1964.

COLBY, WILLIAM EGAN

(*b.* 4 January 1920; *d.* 27 April 1996)

Director of the Central Intelligence Agency (CIA) (1973–1976). Born in St. Paul, Minnesota, Colby traveled to foreign lands early in his life. His father, Elbridge Colby, was a career military officer whose assignments included China and Panama. Colby graduated from Princeton University in 1940 and became an army officer. He began his intelligence career in 1943 in the Office of Strategic Services (OSS), serving in France and Norway in the special operations unit known as the Jedburghs. Distinguished service brought him the Silver Star, Bronze Star, Croix de Guerre, and St. Olaf's Medal. After the war, he completed law school at Columbia University in 1947, hiring on as a labor lawyer with his former OSS boss, William J. Donovan. In 1950 Colby joined the CIA, serving as a clandestine intelligence officer in Sweden, Italy, and Vietnam. Colby's CIA work in Vietnam from 1959 to 1962 put him in an ideal position for a headquarters job in Washington to advise on policy matters and to organize intelligence operations in China, Laos, and Vietnam. As chief of the Far East Division he returned to the secret war in Vietnam in 1968, taking control of the Civilian Operations Revolutionary Development Staff, which included the Phoenix program for finding and neutralizing North Vietnam army personnel and Vietcong spies. Colby returned from Vietnam in 1971 to serve as executive director under Richard Helms and was later promoted to deputy director of plans under James Schlesinger. Named head of the CIA in 1973 amid congressional inquiries into the Watergate affair, Colby initiated a comprehensive review and disclosure of certain agency activities (the so-called "family jewels"). Fired by President Gerald Ford for cooperating too comprehensively with congressional investigating committees, Colby received the National Security Medal in January 1976. He returned to the practice of law and to lecturing and consulting in various capacities in Washington, D.C. He wrote two books, *Honorable Men: My Life in the CIA* (with Peter Forbath) and *Lost Victory: A Firsthand Account of America's Sixteen-Year Involvement in Vietnam* (with James McCargar). His sudden death from a heart attack or stroke while boating alone on 27 April 1996, on the Wicomico River in Maryland brought forth tributes to his government service from many former OSS and CIA associates and friends.

JAMES D. CALDER

See also Central Intelligence Agency; Covert Action

FURTHER READING
Colby, William E. "The CIA's Covert Actions." *Center Magazine* (March–April, 1975).
———. "Why I Was Fired from the CIA." *Esquire* (May 1978).

COLD WAR

The global contest that dominated international relations for forty-five years (1945–1990). The Cold War began almost immediately after World War II. Changes in the global distribution of power, advances in weapons technology, shifts in the balance of social and political forces within and among nations, problems in the world economy, and the onset of decolonization created a high degree of tension between the United States and the Soviet Union. The tension had several important consequences: an arms race, the polarization of domestic and international politics, and the division of the world into economic, military, and political spheres. The Cold War shaped the foreign policies of the United States and the Soviet Union and deeply affected their societies and their government institutions. By providing a justification for the projection of U.S. power and influence all over the world, the Cold War became the means by which the United States assumed and asserted global leadership. By providing Soviet dictator Joseph Stalin and his successors with an external enemy to justify their repressive internal regime, the Cold War helped perpetuate the grip of the communist party on the Soviet Union. The Third World especially felt the effects of the Cold War; indeed, hardly any part of the world escaped its influence.

The World in 1945: Sources of Tension

World War II accelerated fundamental changes in the global distribution of power set in motion by World War I, ending centuries of European dominance. As National Security Council Paper No. 68 (NSC-68), the seminal statement of U.S. Cold War policies, pointed out in April 1950: "Within the past thirty-five years the world has experienced two global wars of tremendous violence…two revolutions—the Russian and the Chinese—of extreme scope and intensity…the collapse of five empires—the Ottoman, the Austro-Hungarian, German, Italian, and Japanese—and the drastic decline of two major imperial systems, the British and the French."

Before World War II there were six great powers: Great Britain, France, Germany, the Soviet Union, Japan, and the United States. By the end of the war, the United States stood alone, easily the most powerful nation in the world, its power greatly increased by its mobilization and war effort, its rivals defeated, and its allies exhausted. The Soviet Union suffered devastating damage during the war and ranked a distant second, its power largely concentrated along its borders in Eastern Europe and northeast Asia. Great Britain—drained by six years of fighting, which had cost a quarter of its prewar wealth and resulted in a massive external debt—was in danger of slipping from the ranks of the great powers. France, humiliated by its collapse in 1940, severely damaged by war and the Nazi occupation, and deeply divided over the issue of Nazi collaboration, no longer counted as a great power. In important parts of their empires Great Britain and France faced rising unrest that threatened to turn their once valuable colonies into liabilities. Germany, its second bid for European hegemony thwarted, lay in ruins, occupied by its enemies and anticipating partition. Japan, shorn of its colonial empire and occupied by U.S. forces, was devastated by massive manpower losses and the relentless U.S. strategic bombing campaign, which had culminated in the August 1945 atomic attacks on Hiroshima and Nagasaki.

The United States thus entered the postwar era in a uniquely powerful position. Four hundred thousand U.S. citizens died in World War II, but American factories, farms, mines, and transportation networks remained unscathed. During the war, the United States almost doubled its gross national product, and by 1945 the country accounted for about half of the world's manufacturing capacity, most of its food surpluses, and almost all of its financial reserves. The United States held the lead in a wide range of technologies essential to modern warfare and economic prosperity. Possession of extensive domestic oil supplies and control over access to the vast oil reserves of Latin America and the Middle East contributed to the U.S. position of global dominance. The United States, despite a rapid demobilization that dropped the level of its armed forces from 12.1 million in 1945 to 1.7 million by mid-1947, still possessed the world's mightiest military machine: the U.S. Navy controlled the seas, U.S. air power dominated the skies, and the United States alone possessed atomic weapons and the means to deliver them. Finally, the U.S. role in the defeat of fascism and its espousal of such principles as the four freedoms (freedom of speech, freedom of worship, freedom from want, freedom from fear) had earned tremendous international prestige for the United States.

World War II had brutalized the Soviet Union. Late twentieth-century estimates of Soviet losses during World War II have reached 27 million. Extensive destruction of its factories, farms, mines, transportation networks, and housing stock left the Soviet Union with an economy one-quarter the size of the U.S. economy. Soviet military capacity lagged behind that of the United States: Soviet air defenses were meager, they lacked a long-range strategic air force, and (aside from a large submarine force) had an ineffective navy. The Soviets also lacked atomic weapons. Nevertheless, although the Soviets demobilized rapidly, from approximately 11.3 million troops in 1945 to some 2.9 million by early 1948, the advantageous positioning of the bulk of Soviet military power in Eastern Europe posed a potential threat to Western European security. Owing to the devastation and defeat of Germany and Japan, powers that historically had checked Russian power in Central Europe and northeast Asia, the Soviets' relative position had improved, at least in the short term. On the other hand, the measure of security arising from divisions among its

capitalist rivals was now lost. The defeat of Germany and Japan and the weakening of Great Britain and France could serve to unite the capitalist powers.

Great Britain, the third major power in 1945, occupied a key position in the postwar international system. The British maintained a large military (827,000 men in 1951), possessed a global network of bases, and in 1952 were to become the world's third atomic power. Great Britain had the leading economy in Europe, and through the pound sterling currency area played an important role in international economic affairs. On the other hand, maintaining its military might severely strained Great Britain's financial position. The British also were vulnerable to nationalist upheaval in their far-flung empire.

During World War II conventional weapons reached new heights of destructiveness. Power-projection capabilities, in particular, took a quantum leap forward, as the aircraft carrier and long-range bombers extended the reach of weapons. The atomic bomb magnified the destructive capability of warfare to a previously unimagined scale—a destruction that held the prospect of worldwide annihilation—and became a key focus of international relations. The realization that the atomic bomb could be used as a diplomatic tool in peacetime as well as a winning weapon in wartime preceded the U.S. decision to use the bomb against Japan. While some analysts believed that the mere existence of atomic weapons would discourage aggression, others, driven by fears of an "atomic Pearl Harbor," were convinced that heightened military preparedness and possibly even preemptive strikes were the best means to safeguard national security. The advent of weapons capable of such massive destruction started an arms race as Great Britain, the Soviet Union, and subsequently other nations sought to develop their own atomic weapons and the United States sought to maintain its lead in atomic capability.

Changes in the balance of political forces both within and among nations took place after World War II. The potential impact of internal political alignments on the global balance of power invested domestic political struggles with international political and strategic significance.

In the 1930s, a regime's internal ideological underpinnings often determined its international alignment. Nations internally dominated by fascist forces—Germany, Italy, and Japan—collaborated. The liberal democratic powers—Great Britain, France, and the United States—tended to share similar interests, however difficult it was for them to work together. The Soviet Union, as the only Communist power, stood alone until August 1939, when Stalin and Hitler signed a nonaggression pact clearing the way for the Nazi invasion of Poland on 1 September 1939.

After the German invasion of the Soviet Union in June 1941 broke up the Nazi-Soviet alliance, World War II,

United States Aggression as Perceived by the Soviet Union

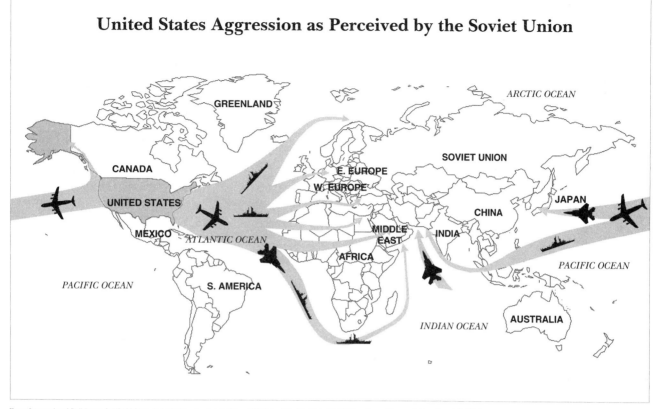

both internationally and within nations, pitted the right—Germany, Italy, and Japan—against an uneasy alliance of the center—Great Britain and the United States (France had surrendered to Germany in June 1940)—and the left—the Soviet Union. With the defeat of the right in the war, the major fault line in international relations and within most industrial nations shifted to the left, reflecting and underpinning the emerging superpower tension.

By the end of World War II, the future of capitalism as an organizing principle for society was anything but secure. Already on the defensive owing to the depth and duration of the Great Depression, capitalism and conservative parties also suffered from association with fascism. The defeat of fascism in the international arena discredited the right in most nations. Moreover, the socioeconomic climate after World War II tended to favor the political left; the experiences of depression and global war accentuated existing social and political divisions and generated popular demands for widespread land, welfare, and economic reform. Many people believed that economic planning was necessary to ensure economic growth and equity. British politics, for example, moved to the left with the victory of the Labour Party in

July 1945, demonstrating that deep-seated desires for widespread social and economic reform outweighed gratitude to Prime Minister Winston S. Churchill for his wartime leadership. Among the major powers, only the United States underwent a political shift to the right. Conservative opposition to the New Deal had gained strength during the war, and in the 1946 midterm elections the Republicans captured control of both houses of Congress.

The Soviet Union entered the postwar era with enormous prestige because of the key role it played in defeating Nazi Germany. Within the Soviet Union the war seemed to solidify popular respect for the communist regime. Unlike the Czarist regime a generation earlier, it had emerged victorious from its conflict with Germany rather than collapsing. Throughout Europe and in important parts of the Third World communist parties had gained ground as a result of their participation in resistance movements during the war and as a consequence of chaotic economic, social, and political conditions. In some countries, such as France, Italy, Greece, and Vietnam, communists and their allies appeared poised to take power. In addition, for many people in the Third World, the Soviet Union served as a model for a rapid

Soviet Aggression as Perceived by the United States

transition from a backward and weak agrarian society to a modern industrial power.

The chaotic state of the world economy threatened to rekindle conflict within and among nations. In the 1930s the world had, in effect, split into economic blocs. The United States had turned inward and, to a lesser extent, south toward Latin America; Great Britain and other colonial powers had closed off their empires behind financial and trade barriers; Germany had built up an informal economic empire in central and southeastern Europe; the Soviet Union had focused on building "socialism in one country" through collectivization of agriculture and forced industrialization; and Japan had sought to extend its economic sway beyond its colonial holdings and organize East Asia in a "co-prosperity sphere." A downward spiral of international trade and national production had ensued as attempts to gain unilateral advantages at the expense of others elicited countermeasures that further restricted trade and production, deepened and prolonged the depression, and exacerbated international tensions.

Wartime mobilization had intensified the autarchic economic policies of the 1930s as nations sought to harness economic processes to political and military purpos-

es. Trade and financial controls had proliferated as part of the war effort. Faced with massive reconstruction requirements and constrained by their shortages of dollars and limited financial resources, many governments in Europe and elsewhere extended economic controls into the postwar period. Despite the multilateral monetary arrangements and financial institutions fashioned at the 1944 Bretton Woods Conference, these developments, coupled with the destruction and disruption caused by the war, seemed to foreshadow a repeat of the experiences of the 1930s—economic stagnation, followed by political extremism and interstate conflict—not reform and reconstruction and a world economy free from restrictive trade and financial barriers.

Movements toward independence in the Third World created much tension in the postwar international system. United States, European, and Japanese leaders feared that decolonization would lead to the loss of access to raw materials, oil, food sources, and markets needed to rebuild the economies of Western Europe and Japan and to ensure continued U.S. prosperity.

Independence movements blossomed in the postwar world, especially throughout postwar Asia, where the Japanese empire had spread in the early part of the century and supplanted Western colonial regimes during World War II. With their World War II defeat, the Japanese lost control of Taiwan, Korea, and Manchuria. Japanese expansion into China in the 1930s had affected the ongoing internal struggle for power between the Nationalists and the Communists and had intensified Chinese efforts to regain control over their nation's destiny. After the defeat of Japan the Communists, who had grown in strength as a result of their resistance to the Japanese, fought with the Nationalists for control over the Japanese-occupied areas. In Southeast Asia, the British, French, and Dutch faced nationalist challenges to their control of Malaya (Malaysia), Indochina (Vietnam, Laos, and Cambodia), and Indonesia respectively.

Challenges to French control—in Lebanon, Syria, Algeria, Tunisia, and Morocco—and to British influence—in Palestine, Egypt, and Iran—threatened the Western position in the Middle East by fueling internal power struggles and providing potential openings for the expansion of Soviet influence.

The Cold War Begins: 1945–1950

In the five years following World War II the foreign policies of the United States and the Soviet Union, guided by their respective interests concerning the points of international tension, evolved to divide the world into two opposing spheres—the Communist and the "free world."

Despite the lingering presence of isolationist sentiment in parts of the United States, the experience of World War II facilitated a global conception of U.S. national security interests and requirements. Drawing on what they believed to be the lessons of the 1930s, U.S. leaders sought to create and maintain a favorable balance of power in Europe and Asia, to fashion an international economic environment that would promote peace as well as prosperity, and to maintain the integration of the Third World in the world economy in an era of decolonization and national liberation. U.S. Cold War policies were designed to protect the physical security of the United States and its main allies and to preserve a broadly defined "American way of life" by constructing an international order that would be open to and compatible with U.S. interests and ideals.

President Franklin D. Roosevelt (1933–1945) had hoped to achieve these goals in cooperation with the Soviet Union, albeit with the Soviets playing a subordinate, regional role. The agreements reached by the United States, Great Britain, and the Soviet Union at the February 1945 Yalta Conference reflected this vision. Roosevelt died in April 1945, and his hopes for peaceful coexistence died with him. By the time the leaders of the United States, Great Britain, and the Soviet Union met at the Potsdam Conference in July 1945, postwar rivalry was replacing wartime cooperation. Nevertheless, the three allies reached final agreement on Soviet participation in the war against Japan and on dividing Germany into four occupation zones (U.S., British, French, and Soviet).

Harry S. Truman (1945–1953) faced a postwar international environment that seemed to offer the Soviet Union and its ideological allies myriad opportunities to expand their power and influence. By the end of the war the Soviets had reabsorbed Estonia, Latvia, and Lithuania, and installed subservient regimes in Poland, Romania, Bulgaria, and their occupation zone in Germany. In early 1946, the Soviets delayed withdrawing their occupation forces from Iran while supporting separatist movements there and demanding an oil concession. The Soviets also put pressure on Turkey in the summer of 1946 to revise the terms controlling access to the Black Sea through the Turkish-controlled Bosporus, Sea of Marmara, and Dardanelles, and to grant base rights along the straits to the USSR. In addition, the civil war in Greece resumed in the spring of 1946 when communist-led guerrillas took up arms against the government after disputed elections. The Soviets also rejected the U.S. plan for the international control of atomic energy, presented to the United Nations in the summer of 1946 by Bernard Baruch. The Soviets charged that the plan's provisions, which allowed the United States to retain its atomic arsenal until an international control system was fully functioning, perpetuated the U.S. atomic monopoly while preventing other nations from developing atomic weapons. These actions seemed to many observers to indicate that the Soviets were intent on expanding.

Drawing on an influential February 1946 analysis—the "long telegram," by George Kennan, a relatively young State Department Soviet expert then serving in Moscow—U.S. leaders began to view the Soviet Union as an intractable foe and to fashion a foreign policy that focused on containing the spread of Soviet power and communist influence. The Soviets, in turn, believed that the United States was bent on "world supremacy," as the Soviet ambassador in Washington put it.

Aware that the Soviet Union was too weak to risk a war and confident in the military power of the United States, U.S. leaders did not expect the Soviets to attack Western Europe or other vital areas. Rather, U.S. leaders feared that communists and other groups sympathetic to the Soviet Union and hostile to capitalism and the West could exploit postwar vacuums of power in Germany and Japan, socio-economic dislocation in Europe, civil wars in China and Greece, and decolonization in the Third World to take power. U.S. policy makers assumed that regardless of where and how communist groups gained control, they would pursue policies that would serve Soviet interests. Such gains could turn the global balance of power against the United States, deny U.S. companies and the U.S. economy access to important markets, raw materials, and investment opportunities, and eventually jeopardize economic and political freedom in the United States. To avoid such outcomes, U.S. policy makers believed they had to find a way to rebuild the world economy, beginning with the reconstruction of Western Europe and Japan. Economic growth would forestall another depression and help mitigate class conflict, thus weakening the appeal of leftist groups.

The Truman Doctrine of March 1947 called for the global containment of communism and elicited the political support that enabled U.S. leaders to act on their beliefs about the relationship between politics, economics, and U.S. security. Anticommunism provided a framework for understanding a complicated world and resonated with traditions that ran deep in U.S. society and political culture. U.S leaders regarded communism as a strategic threat because of its connection with Soviet power, and as an ideological and economic threat because of its hostility to private property and free markets, concepts that U.S. political beliefs linked directly to political freedom. Anticommunism became a guiding principle of U.S. foreign policy and a significant force in U.S. domestic politics, as politicians such as Republican Senator Joseph McCarthy used it as a weapon against their opponents and as a means of gaining national attention.

New government institutions reinforced the shift to a more activist foreign policy. The National Security Act of 1947 established the National Security Council to advise the president on international affairs; created the Central Intelligence Agency to gather and analyze foreign intelligence and conduct covert operations; and united the previously separate branches of the armed services in the Department of Defense. Following Secretary of State George Marshall's June 1947 call for a European recovery program (better known as the Marshall Plan), President Truman established the Economic Cooperation Administration to manage U.S. foreign assistance programs. In Europe, representatives from sixteen Western European governments, joined by the three military governors of the western zones in Germany, set up the Organization for European Economic Cooperation to coordinate European aid requests.

Through the Marshall Plan (1948–1952), the Mutual Security Agency (1951–1954), and other aid programs (West Germany and Japan, for example, received large amounts of aid through the U.S. occupation authorities), the United States channeled over $41 billion in economic and military assistance to Western Europe, the western zones of Germany, and Japan in the eight years following World War II. At least $31 billion of this total was in the form of grants. This assistance paid for vital imports allowing those regions to obtain the raw materials, fuel, and foodstuffs they desperately needed for reconstruction. U.S assistance allowed moderate governments to devote massive resources to reconstruction and to expand their countries' exports without imposing politically unacceptable and socially divisive austerity programs that would have been necessary without U.S. aid. U.S. assistance also helped counteract what U.S. leaders saw as a dangerous drift away from free enterprise and toward collectivism. By favoring some policies and opposing others the United States not only influenced how European and Japanese elites defined their own interests but also altered the internal balance of power among the decision-making groups. Thus U.S. aid policies facilitated the ascendancy of centrist parties, such as the Christian Democrats in West Germany and Italy and the more conservative Liberal Democratic Party in Japan.

U.S. leaders, in the belief that rebuilding German economic strength was central to the recovery of the European economy, led the way in uniting the three Western occupation zones and moving them toward self-government. To assuage Western European anxieties over the revival of German power and the danger of preemptive moves by the Soviet Union, the United States, Great Britain, and ten other nations forged the North Atlantic Treaty Organization (NATO) in April 1949. NATO pledged its members to the common defense of Western Europe and through its unified command structure provided a vehicle for the denationalization of Western Europe's military forces. Japan, however, remained more directly dependent on the United States for its security: It had no neighbors strong enough to balance its strength; it did not face a security threat comparable to that facing Western Europe; and its citizens responded favorably to the demilitarization forced on them by the U.S.-imposed 1947 constitution. Control of atomic weapons and over access to oil supplies enabled the United States to oversee economic reconstruction in Germany and Japan while at the same time preventing a resurgence of German and Japanese aggression.

U.S. policymakers believed that controlling access to the resources, markets, and labor of the Third World was crucial to containing the Soviet Union, to maintaining U.S. leadership of the Western alliance, and to the economic health of the United States, Western Europe, and Japan. In this view, the best way to overcome shortages of dollars in Western Europe and Japan was to expand trade and investment in the Third World. U.S. investment and imports of raw materials would increase the flow of dollars to the Third World. Western Europe and Japan, in turn, could obtain the dollars they needed from the Third World through trade, taxation, and other means. Efforts to promote European and Japanese reconstruction influenced Western policies toward the Third World, at times pitting the United States and its allies against the rising tide of decolonization and revolutionary nationalism. Indonesia, Indochina, and Malaya, for example, were important potential sources of Third World dollars for the Netherlands, France, and Great Britain, respectively. All three experienced anticolonial revolts in the late 1940s, and U.S. policymakers saw resolution of these conflicts as essential to achieving their economic, political, and military goals in Europe as well as in Asia.

World War II also profoundly affected Soviet security policies and perceptions. The very limited availability of archival records on Soviet foreign policy has made it difficult to discern Soviet motives with certainty. As a result, the influence of the Stalinist system on the objectives, as distinct from the means, of Soviet foreign policy has remained a contested issue. Many scholars still see Stalin as an incorrigible expansionist. In contrast, others have questioned the long-assumed links between Stalin's repressive internal regime and Soviet foreign policy and have downplayed the impact of Marxism-Leninism and totalitarianism on Soviet foreign policy while highlighting Russian history and geography, bureaucratic differences within the Soviet decision-making elite, and the security requirements arising from the Soviet Union's unique geopolitical position.

Most scholars agree that Soviet objectives at the end of the war were to create strong safeguards against future German aggression, secure borders, and a buffer zone in Eastern Europe; to reconstruct the Soviet Union's war-damaged industrial base; and to maintain a powerful military. That the Soviets initially sought cooperation with the United States to achieve these goals is apparent to some scholars who have cited the following examples of Soviet caution in postwar foreign policy: The Soviets allowed relatively free elections in Hungary and Czechoslovakia in 1945; they cooperated in the creation of representative governments in Austria and Finland; they discouraged communist parties from taking revolutionary action in France, Italy, Greece, and Spain; they urged the new communist government in Yugoslavia under Marshal Josip Broz Tito to limit its demands for territory and to stop supporting Greek communists; they offered only limited aid to the Chinese communists; and, under pressure from the United States, the Soviets withdrew their troops from Iran in May 1946.

Regardless of possible hopes for post-World War II U.S.-Soviet cooperation, the Soviet Union's key objectives—circumscribing German power and maintaining a secure sphere of influence in Eastern Europe—were incompatible with Western ideals, economic objectives, and security requirements. The Soviets desperately desired extensive reparations from Germany to rebuild their economy and to reduce Germany's military potential. But their goal of limiting German power clashed with U.S. efforts to promote German and European recovery. Attempts to force the West to take Soviet interests into account backfired and reinforced Western resolve to rebuild and defend Western Germany and Western Europe. The Soviet imposition of a blockade on all land routes to Berlin (June 1948–May 1949) helped pave the way for the creation of the Federal Republic of Germany in September 1949. The Soviets responded by establishing the German Democratic Republic in their occupation zone the following month.

The Soviets' desire to create more secure borders by means of friendly relations with neighboring governments ran up against Soviet reconstruction requirements; hostile local populations that the Soviets often harshly repressed; and Western fears that Soviet domination of Eastern Europe could limit access to needed markets, foodstuffs, and raw materials, as well as pose a threat to Western Europe. In addition, Soviet use of such means as fraudulent elections, a controlled press, and suppression of dissent to maintain their influence in Eastern Europe exacerbated tensions with the West, which tended to view Soviet actions in Eastern Europe as an indicator of overall Soviet intentions.

To many Western observers Stalin seemed to believe that only countries controlled by communist parties could be trusted to respect the Soviet Union's security needs. More recent scholarship has shown that the establishment of Communist regimes in Eastern Europe was not solely the consequence of a conscious effort by the Soviet Union to dominate the region. World War II created revolutionary conditions in Eastern Europe by disrupting social, political, and economic structures. Under German pressure, the prewar governments had collaborated with the Nazis or collapsed and gone into exile, leaving a vacuum of authority at war's end into which Communists and other groups moved. In addition to the annihilation of European Jews, the mass exodus of ethnic Germans before the advancing Red Army disrupted the region's economic organization. Germans had made up an important part of the region's property-owning classes and had expanded their holdings during the war by taking over property owned by Jews and other "enemies" of the Third Reich. These properties passed into the hands of the newly formed postwar governments, thus facilitating land reform and the nationalization of industry.

The Soviets pursued a relatively cautious and differentiated policy in Eastern Europe until the fall of 1947 when the West offered to include Eastern Europe in the Marshall Plan. The Soviets feared Western aid would undermine their influence in the region and prohibited Eastern European countries from participating in the Marshall Plan. The Soviets also created a new international communist organization, the Communist Information Bureau, better known as Cominform, and pushed local communists to end the "democratic interludes" in Hungary (1945–1947) and Czechoslovakia (1945–1948). The 1948 Tito-Stalin split further intensified Soviet efforts to control the internal affairs of the region and led to a series of purge trials (1948–1949) that cut Eastern European communist parties off from their mass base and undermined whatever legitimacy they had earned during the war and in the immediate postwar years. While the short-term result was greater Soviet control over Eastern Europe, the long-term effect was counterproductive. Lacking indigenous sources of support, the Communist regimes of Eastern Europe became a permanent source of tension and instability, and eventually a drain on Soviet resources.

Finally, in a classic example of what scholars call the "security dilemma"—the tendency for a country's quest for increased security to raise the anxieties of its prospective adversaries and to provoke countermeasures—Soviet efforts beginning in 1948 to strengthen and modernize their armed forces and their successful test of an atomic bomb in August 1949 raised Western suspicions and galvanized public support for Western rearmament. Likewise, Soviet efforts to use Western European communist parties to disrupt the Marshall Plan failed miserably, increased Western suspicions of Soviet intentions, and undermined popular support for those parties.

In Asia, the British were forced to grant independence to India-Pakistan (1947), Ceylon, (1947), and Burma (1948). The United States redeemed its wartime pledge by granting the Philippines independence in 1946, even though it retained extensive military and economic privileges. In China, the Communists, led by Mao Zedong and Zhou Enlai, triumphed and established the People's Republic of China (PRC) in 1949. Taiwan, with U.S. assistance, remained under Nationalist control. Communist and other radical groups were active throughout Korea, as the peninsula was racked by widespread violence following the collapse of Japanese rule. In the area north of the 38th parallel, Soviet occupation forces helped Kim Il Sung eliminate his rivals and inaugurate a personal rule that lasted until his death in 1994. In the southern part of the country, U.S. occupation forces helped conservative Koreans defeat their moderate and leftist opponents and establish, under United Nations auspices, the Republic of Korea in May 1948. The Soviets responded by sponsoring the establishment of the Democratic People's Republic of Korea in September 1948. Both regimes claimed jurisdiction over all of Korea. Soviet occupation forces withdrew from North Korea in December 1948; U.S. occupation forces left South Korea in June 1949. In Vietnam, the communists, led by Ho Chi Minh, dominated the nationalist revolt against French rule. In contrast, noncommunist nationalists led Indonesia to independence from the Netherlands in

1949. These conflicts were largely indigenous in origin, and their eventual success or failure was as much due to their internal histories and characteristics as to U.S. and Soviet policies toward them. Nevertheless, the conflicts intensified the Soviet-American rivalry.

In the Middle East, France was forced to grant independence to Lebanon and Syria (1946) and faced ultimately successful challenges to its control in Morocco (1956), Tunisia (1956), and Algeria (1962). Weakened by the loss of the Indian Army, its main power projection force east of Suez, Great Britain encountered strong resistance to its position in the region. The British withdrew from Palestine in 1948, leaving the United Nations to deal with the fighting that immediately broke out between Arabs and Jews. Great Britain also faced increasingly powerful challenges to its privileged position in Egypt, where it controlled a huge military base at Suez as well as the Suez Canal Company. In Iran, nationalists sought to gain control of the British-owned Anglo-Iranian Oil Company, which monopolized oil reserves and production and operated the largest oil refinery in the world. These developments came at a time when Middle East oil supplies were increasingly important to Western security and prosperity. World War II had demonstrated the crucial importance of oil to modern warfare, and after the war the United States looked to Middle Eastern oil to fuel European and Japanese economic recovery.

The Soviet acquisition of atomic weapons and the Communist victory in China came at a time when economic recovery seemed to falter in Western Europe and Japan. Faced with the loss of their atomic monopoly and continued instability in the Third World when its resources were increasingly needed for European and Japanese recovery, U.S. leaders feared that without corrective measures the global distribution of power would turn against the "free world." NSC-68, drafted in early 1950 by State Department official Paul Nitze in close consultation with Secretary of State Dean Acheson, painted the Soviet Union as a relentlessly expansionist adversary and called for the United States to undertake a "rapid build up of the political, economic, and military strength" of the "free world."

On 25 June 1950 North Korean forces invaded South Korea. Recent research has revealed that in early April 1950, Stalin, after rejecting previous pleas by North Korean leader Kim Il Sung for Soviet approval and assistance in taking over South Korea, acquiesced and agreed to provide the necessary military assistance. U.S. leaders interpreted the North Korean invasion as a test of U.S. resolve to resist communist aggression. Determined to stand firm, the Truman administration secured a mandate from the United Nations to send U.S. forces to aid the beleaguered South Koreans. Although the Soviets stayed out of the war, the PRC, which had signed a treaty of friendship and alliance with the Soviet Union in February 1950, intervened in late fall 1950 when U.S. troops approached its border. After heavy fighting, battle lines soon stabilized, and the July 1953 armistice that ended the war left Korea divided along the thirty-eighth parallel. The Korean War led to over three million deaths (including over 50,000 U.S. servicemen and -women). It also provided political support for a massive and costly expansion of U.S. military forces and covert-action capabilities; and sharply escalated international tensions, especially when the United States considered using atomic weapons to end the war.

Competition and Coexistence: 1950–1962

By 1950, Europe was divided into Eastern and Western political, military, and economic spheres. The arms race and competition in the Third World emerged as the most active and fluid aspects of the Cold War. The dual sources of tension combined in 1962 to bring about the Cuban missile crisis.

The Cold War in Europe had largely stabilized by late 1949 following the end of the Berlin Blockade, the establishment of separate German states, and the victory of the anticommunist forces in the Greek Civil War. Marshall Plan aid and covert assistance to anticommunist groups helped ensure the dominance of pro-U.S. governments in Western Europe. Soviet power kept the lid on much more unsettled conditions in Eastern Europe. Soviet troops and tanks quelled widespread riots in East Germany in 1953 and a major nationwide revolt in Hungary in 1956. The division of the continent became sealed in 1955 when a rearmed and fully sovereign West Germany joined NATO and the Soviet Union drew its East European satellites together in the Warsaw Pact. Although the two camps maintained massive forces along the East-West divide in Central Europe for the rest of the Cold War, only the anomalous situation of West Berlin as a Western outpost deep within East Germany remained as a major source of superpower tension in Europe. There was a protracted crisis over Berlin between 1958 and 1962 when the Soviets, concerned over the stability of the East German regime and under pressure from East German leaders to resolve the Berlin "problem," tried to pressure the West into negotiations by threatening to turn over control of East Berlin and the access routes to West Berlin to the East German government.

When the United States retained its atomic monopoly, U.S. leaders helped rebuild Germany and Japan without fear of war with the Soviet Union. Following the Soviet Union's acquisition of atomic weapons in 1949, the United States sought to maintain nuclear superiority through increased production of atomic bombs and the development of the hydrogen bomb (1952). Between 1950 and 1953, the United States expanded its armed forces by over a million troops and massively increased production of aircraft, ships, combat vehicles, and other conventional weapons. Only a small part of the increases was related directly to the Korean conflict. Most was devoted to countering Soviet conventional superiority in Europe. U.S. leaders believed that nuclear superiority coupled with a rough balance of power in Europe would extend deterrence and preserve the U.S. freedom of action all over the world. Although President Dwight D. Eisenhower and his "new look" cut back conventional forces somewhat, the U.S. nuclear arsenal grew during his administration (1953–1961) from around 1,000 warheads to approximately 18,000 warheads.

The Soviets responded in kind, locking themselves into a competitive strategic relationship with the United States. Accepting a definition of deterrence that viewed nuclear parity as necessary to discourage attack on the USSR, the Soviets developed their own hydrogen bomb, expanded their fleet of long-range bombers, and worked to develop medium-range and intercontinental ballistic missiles. The 1957 launching of the Soviet satellite *Sputnik* revealed Soviet technological advances. To offset the U.S. advantage in productive capacity, the Soviets also sought to maintain sufficient conventional forces to overrun Western Europe quickly in a conflict with the United States. The resulting arms race led to ever higher levels of military spending, destabilizing technological competition, and constantly growing nuclear arsenals. Established early in the Cold War, this pattern of action and counteraction continued to its end.

Instability in the Third World became an increasingly important source of international tension and conflict during the 1950s. Many independence movements, made more radical by years of colonial control and repression, sought more than political sovereignty. They also wanted to free their economies from foreign control and to eliminate all vestiges of colonial rule within their societies by means of thoroughgoing social and cultural revolutions. Indeed, because they were fighting against Western capitalist control, many independence movements assumed an anticapitalist tinge, and communists were active in many movements. Decolonization thus could bring about changes in government that would be hostile to Western capitalism and sympathetic to state-controlled methods for rapidly modernizing their economies. Although some leading Third World nations such as Egypt, Indonesia, and India declared their neutrality in the Cold War at the Afro-Asian Conference (1955) in Bandung, Indonesia, many Third World movements and regimes seemed to be aligned with the Soviet Union and against the United States and its allies. Indeed, there seemed to be at least a symbiotic relationship between revolutionary nationalism in the Third World and the interests of the Soviet state.

The Soviet Union moved relatively slowly to seize the opportunities offered by the "revolt against the West" in the Third World. Vladimir Lenin, the Soviet Union's founder and first leader (1917–1924), had put great emphasis on the value of the colonial world in the global struggle against imperialism. Stalin, preoccupied with problems closer to home, paid less attention to the Third World. After Stalin's death in 1953, the Soviets sought again to turn turmoil in the Third World to their global advantage. Beginning in 1955 the Soviets launched an economic offensive in the Third World, extending aid to several non-Communist countries, most notably Egypt and India.

The Soviets gained no lasting advantages from these efforts, but their actions, coupled with continued conflict in the Third World, led to the creation of Western alliances and numerous clashes between the superpowers. In August 1953, the United States and Great Britain, concerned that the dispute between Great Britain and Iran over nationalization of the Anglo-Iranian Oil Company was creating conditions that could lead to a communist takeover, covertly organized and financed the overthrow of the nationalist prime minister of Iran Mohammed Mosaddeq. After Egyptian leader Gamal Abdal Nasser nationalized the Suez Canal Company in 1956, Great Britain, joined by France and Israel attacked Egypt. The ensuing crisis delivered the final blow to European colonialism in the Middle East as the United States, fearing that the attack could undermine its position in the region, forced its allies to withdraw. Both the Soviet Union and the United States expanded their influence in the region. The Arab-Israeli dispute also provided a continuing source of regional instability that threatened to draw the two superpowers into conflict. In July 1958, the United States sent over 14,000 troops to Lebanon after a coup by army officers in Iraq—which overthrew the pro-Western monarchy, intensified fears that tensions within Lebanon could similarly erupt. The Iraqi coup also removed the only Arab state from the Baghdad Pact (Turkey, Iraq, Iran, Pakistan, and Great Britain), which had been organized with U.S. support in 1955 to solidify the "northern tier" of states separating the Soviet Union from the Eastern Mediterranean and the Persian Gulf. After Iraq's withdrawal, the remaining members reorganized as the Central Treaty Organization.

A temporary end to warfare—though not tension—in East Asia came with the end of the Korean War in 1953 and the first Indochina War in 1954, as well as the defeat of the radical Hukbalahap (Huk) movement in the Philippines and the communist-led insurgents in Malaysia in the mid-1950s. To contain communism in Southeast Asia, the United States in September 1954 sponsored the formation of the Southeast Asia Treaty Organization composed of the United States, Great Britain, France, Australia, New Zealand, the Philippines, Thailand, and Pakistan. Confrontations between the United States and the PRC in 1954 and 1958 over the status of some small islands (Jinmen and Mazu) in the Taiwan Strait threatened at times to escalate into open warfare. At the end of the decade the breakdown of the 1954 Geneva settlement led to renewed conflict in Vietnam between communist-led insurgents and the anticommunist government of South Vietnam.

In postwar Latin America the dynamics of social and political change intertwined with the Cold War. Narrow openings for democratization arose in several countries as World War II spurred economic growth and political mobilization. Emboldened by the democratic discourse and ideological fervor that accompanied the fight against fascism, miners, factory workers, and some rural laborers organized and became politically active. The region's middle sectors, as well as entrenched traditional and military elites, became worried. These groups successfully exploited U.S. concerns about securing U.S. economic interests amid instability and communist penetration and gained U.S. support for the repression of democratic and popular movements. In the most dramatic case, the United States engineered the removal of the Guatemalan government in 1954 because of concerns that Communist influence had played a role in Guatemala's revolution and threatened U.S. economic interests and political influence. On 1 January 1959, guerrillas led by Fidel Castro overthrew the pro-U.S. regime of Cuban President Fulgencio Batista. Castro soon clashed with the United States, but U.S. efforts in the early 1960s to oust his increasingly radical and Soviet-supported government failed completely.

U.S. hostility to the Cuban Revolution intersected with the arms race to produce the single most dangerous crisis of the Cold War. In the wake of the Soviet Union's successful development of intercontinental ballistic missile technology, the United States feared that the Soviet Union was poised to take the lead in the arms race. In fact, the ongoing development and deployment of U.S. ballistic missiles and other strategic weapons systems coupled with Soviet technical and economic problems produced a massive U.S. lead in the arms race by the early 1960s. In an effort to offset the political impact of U.S. nuclear superiority, Soviet leader Nikita Khrushchev decided to augment the Soviet strategic arsenal by secretly installing medium- and intermediate-range ballistic missiles in Cuba. Khrushchev also assumed that Soviet missiles in Cuba would help deter an expected U.S. invasion of Cuba. Khrushchev's gamble almost led to disaster in October 1962 when the United States discovered the deception. President John F. Kennedy interpreted the Soviet move as an intolerable challenge to the political as well as strategic balance, and forced the Soviets to remove the missiles in exchange for a U.S. pledge not to invade Cuba. Recent research has revealed that the United States also secretly agreed to remove nuclear-armed missiles from Turkey as part of the understanding that ended the crisis.

From Cold War to Détente: 1963–1972

The aftermath of the Cuban Missile Crisis ushered in a new stage in the Cold War, though the main areas of action continued to be the arms race and the Third World. Determined never to be humiliated again, the Soviets, following Khrushchev's ouster in October 1964, renewed with heightened intensity their costly nuclear arms buildup. As the Soviet nuclear arsenal grew, U.S. Secretary of Defense Robert S. McNamara gradually lost faith in the importance of U.S. nuclear superiority and moved toward acceptance of the doctrine of mutually assured destruction, which sought to convince the Soviet Union that an attack on the United States would result in nuclear retaliation and the assured destruction of both sides. In addition, the United States and the Soviet Union signed a Limited Test Ban Treaty in 1963, the Non-Proliferation Treaty in 1968, and began the Strategic Arms Limitation Talks (SALT) in 1969. Under Presidents John F. Kennedy (1961–1963) and Lyndon B. Johnson (1963–1969), the United States expanded its conventional forces to allow a more "flexible response" to possible communist aggression. The United States also intensified its support of anticommunist groups and governments in the Third World, combining calls for economic development and social and political reform with greatly increased military assistance, extensive covert activities, and, in the cases of Vietnam and the Dominican Republic, military intervention.

The U.S. intervention in the Dominican Republic was relatively small (around 28,000 troops) and relatively brief (April 1965–September 1966) compared to far higher costs of containment in Vietnam. U.S. involvement in Vietnam began in the late 1940s as an attempt to shore up a beleaguered France and to ensure markets and raw materials for a rebuilding Japan. In the 1950s, the United States committed itself to ensuring the survival of a noncommunist state in Vietnam south of the seventeenth parallel. U.S. leaders feared that the loss of another area to communism would initiate, in President Eisenhower's memorable phrase, a "falling domino" effect that would lead to communist control of all of Southeast Asia and threaten Japan. Viewing efforts by Vietnamese communists to overthrow U.S.-backed governments in South Vietnam as a case of communist aggression, U.S. policy makers argued that what was at stake was not merely Vietnam but the credibility of U.S. commitments all over the world. During the 1960s, the United States reacted to growing threats to noncommunist South Vietnam by

sending increasing numbers of troops to Vietnam. When Kennedy took office there were some 600 U.S. military advisers in Vietnam; by the time he died in November 1963, the U.S. troop total exceeded 16,000. Under Johnson, the number of U.S. troops in Vietnam reached 535,000.

The strategic, economic, and political costs of treating Vietnam as a vital country in the global containment of Communism proved too great. By the end of the decade, many U.S. defense planners were becoming alarmed at the war's drain on U.S. resources at a time when the Soviets were expanding their nuclear forces. The Vietnam War also had begun to damage the American economy by the end of the 1960s, feeding inflation and further undermining the U.S. balance-of-payments position. Rather than reassuring U.S. allies, the intervention in Vietnam fed doubts about U.S. foreign policy priorities. The war's growing unpopularity at home convinced President Johnson not to run for reelection in 1968 and helped Richard Nixon, who promised to end U.S. intervention "with honor," win the election. Nevertheless, it took Nixon and his National Security Adviser, Henry Kissinger, four years to negotiate U.S. withdrawal from the war, years during which the killing continued and the economic costs mounted. By the time the last U.S. combat forces left in 1973, almost 59,000 U.S. servicemen and servicewomen had died. Estimates of Vietnamese deaths have reached three million.

The Cold War in Europe, in contrast, remained relatively stable. The East German construction of the Berlin Wall in August 1961 helped stabilize East Germany by stemming the outflow of refugees and allowed Khrushchev a way out of the crisis he had begun. In Western Europe, members of the newly created European Economic Community, or Common Market, submerged old animosities and focused on economic integration and growth. France developed nuclear capability (1960) and withdrew its forces from NATO military command in 1966. Willy Brandt, as West German Foreign Minister (1966–1969) and later as Chancellor (1969–1974), attempted to improve relations with the Soviet Union and Eastern Europe. The Federal Republic of Germany negotiated treaties with the Soviet Union (1970), Poland (1970), and Czechoslovakia (1971) that recognized post–World War II boundary changes. In 1971, the United States, Great Britain, France, and the Soviet Union signed a Quadripartite Agreement regulating the status of Berlin. The following year, the Federal Republic and the German Democratic Republic concluded a series of agreements governing relations between them.

In Eastern Europe, Romania pursued an increasingly independent foreign policy in the 1960s, expanding its trade with the West and at times refusing to participate in Warsaw Pact military maneuvers. Because the Romanians never threatened to leave the Warsaw Pact and the communist party kept a very tight rein on internal dissent, the Soviets tolerated Romania's deviation. In contrast, when the communist party's monopoly of political power seemed threatened in Czechoslovakia in 1968, Soviet leader Leonid Brezhnev (1964–1982) sent in Soviet military forces to remove the reformist communist government and restore hardline communist control.

The greatest shift in the global balance of power came with the Sino-Soviet split. Already evident by the late 1950s, the split opened to a chasm in the mid-1960s with the escalation of ideological and territorial disputes. Chinese hostility greatly complicated the Soviet strategic position, forcing the Soviets to deploy large numbers of troops along their long land border with the PRC and, after 1964, to devise defenses against Chinese nuclear weapons. For the United States, however, the Sino-Soviet split offered an opportunity to regain its dominant position in world politics, which had been severely shaken by the Vietnam War. President Nixon opened relations with the People's Republic of China in 1972.

Détente and Confrontation: 1972–1979

The opening of China constituted part of an overall shift in U.S. grand strategy that also included arms control, relaxation of tensions with the Soviets, and reduction of direct U.S. military intervention in the Third World. Nixon and Kissinger believed a new strategy was needed because the Vietnam War had strained, or perhaps shattered, public support for an interventionist foreign policy and weakened the solidarity of NATO. In addition, the war had exacerbated long-standing economic difficulties. In August 1971, Nixon took steps to allow foreign exchange rates to float and devalued the dollar, setting in motion the end of the Bretton Woods system that had governed the world financial order since World War II.

Owing to their increased military power and the negative effect of the Vietnam War on U.S. global power and influence, the Soviets believed that the global correlation of forces had turned in their favor. They wanted, nevertheless, to improve relations with the United States. The Soviets sought to stabilize the arms race at a rough parity before a new U.S. technological surge left them behind once more. Fearful of a U.S.-Chinese alliance, the Soviets hoped to neutralize the threat of collusion by giving the West a greater stake in good relations with the USSR. In addition, the Soviets faced mounting economic problems and set out to increase trade with the West, especially in grain and advanced technology. Finally, the Soviets wanted to gain international recognition of the status quo in Central and Eastern Europe.

The signing of the SALT I agreements in May 1972 marked the beginning of a short-lived period of limited détente, or relaxation of superpower tensions. The agreements curbed the destabilizing development of antiballistic missile (ABM) systems and set interim limits on offensive strategic nuclear weapons systems. Arms control analysts had argued that ABMs were destabilizing because they might reduce one or both sides' confidence in their ability to retaliate if attacked. This loss of confidence could increase incentives to strike first in a crisis. Analysts also feared that ABMs could stimulate the arms race as each side sought to overwhelm the other's defenses by building more missiles. SALT I did not, however, limit the number of multiple independently targetable reentry vehicles (MIRVs), multiple missile warheads capable of being aimed at separate targets. The United States had begun deploying MIRVs in the early 1970s, and the Soviets followed suit later in the decade. MIRVs permitted the superpowers to increase the number of warheads and thus, the destructive power they could launch per missile, thereby reducing the cost of expanding nuclear forces. Analysts feared that MIRVs could also weaken mutual deterrence. The large number of warheads relative to launch vehicles rewarded offensive action by allowing an attacker to overwhelm its opponent's forces while putting the defender at a disadvantage.

Another outcome of the period of détente was the thirty-five nation Conference on Security and Cooperation in Europe (CSCE), which convened in Helsinki, Finland, in July 1973. These negotiations culminated in the summer of 1975 with a Final Act containing agreements on security, economic, and human rights issues. While recognizing existing borders in Europe, the CSCE process also provided in its economic and human rights provisions means for eventually breaking down the political barriers that divided Europe.

Détente soon foundered as continued instability in the Third World intensified Soviet-American mistrust and undercut political support for relaxed tensions between the two superpowers. The September 1973 overthrow of the socialist government of President Salvador Allende Gossens in Chile amid allegations of U.S. involvement in the coup raised questions about the pledges of mutual restraint made in the Basic Principles Agreement that had accompanied the SALT I accords. The October 1973 Middle East War further strained relations between the United States and the Soviet Union and almost led to a nuclear confrontation when the United States went on a nuclear alert in response to a Soviet threat to intervene in the conflict. After the war U.S. diplomacy focused on excluding the Soviets from the peace settlement, which reinforced Egypt's earlier decision to expel Soviet military advisers and to rely in the future on U.S. military and economic assistance.

Détente coincided with a remarkable period of turbulence in the Third World, marked by several radical revolutions. Left-wing elements of the Ethiopian military overthrew Emperor Haile Selassie in 1974; the Vietnam War ended in April 1975 with the victory of the communists; the triumph of national liberation movements in Portugal's African colonies in 1975 brought left-leaning regimes to power in Angola, Mozambique, and Guinea-Bissau; fundamentalist Muslims led by the Ayatollah Ruhollah Khomeini spearheaded a nationwide revolt that ended the reign of the shah of Iran in January 1979; and in Nicaragua the Frente Sandinista de Liberación Nacional, better known as the Sandinistas, organized and led a national uprising that ended the rule of the Somoza family in July 1979. Although these revolutions stemmed predominantly from indigenous sources, the Soviets sought to use the resulting turmoil to advance their interests in the Third World. The 1975 intervention of Cuban forces in Angola (in response to South African incursions) and again in Ethiopia in 1977 (in response to Somalia's attempt to seize the Ogaden region of Ethiopia), and Vietnam's 1978 invasion of Cambodia, seemed to some observers to indicate a Soviet attempt to take unilateral advantage of détente.

Some U.S. analysts viewed Soviet activism in the Third World as confirming their fears that the growth and development of the Soviet nuclear arsenal had put the Soviets ahead in the arms race and thus eroded extended deterrence and possibly put the United States itself at risk of a Soviet preemptive strike. These analysts viewed arms control efforts such as the SALT II agreements, signed in June 1979 but not ratified, as part of the problem rather than a solution. In addition, the human rights focus of U.S. foreign policy under President Jimmy Carter (1977–1981) restored a degree of public confidence in the basic morality of U.S. foreign policy, provided a popular rationale for renewed U.S. foreign policy initiatives in the Third World, and complicated relations with the Soviet Union. The United States had already begun an extensive military buildup when the Soviet invasion of Afghanistan in December 1979 sealed the fate of détente.

The "Second Cold War": 1980–1990

President Ronald Reagan (1981–1989) denounced the Soviet Union as an immoral "evil empire" and fought the last phase of the Cold War vigorously on many fronts. Charging that the Soviets were the source of most of the world's problems, Reagan called on Congress to approve a massive buildup of U.S. military power and pursued an aggressive policy to rollback Soviet influence in the Third World. The Reagan administration spent over $2 trillion between 1981 and 1989 to build up U.S. conventional and nuclear forces. Reagan also expanded U.S. covert action capabilities and increased U.S. support of anticommunist insurgents in Afghanistan, Angola, and Nicaragua. In March 1983, Reagan committed the

United States to the development of the Strategic Defense Initiative (popularly known as Star Wars), an expensive and technically ambitious antiballistic missile system that would deploy weapons based in outer space to destroy enemy missiles in flight. Reagan's policies created a mushrooming budget deficit; a powerful, and at times anti-U.S., peace movement in Europe; strains within the NATO alliance; and a heightening of Cold War tensions. The "second Cold War" proved short-lived, however.

After Mikhail Gorbachev came to power in March 1985, the Soviets began to pursue policies aimed at improving relations with the United States. The reasons for the shift in Soviet policies are still in dispute. Some scholars have claimed that the Soviets shifted to less confrontational policies in response to the U.S. military buildup and political offensive. In this view, U.S. actions raised the costs of confrontation and forced the Soviets into a corner from which there was no escape save surrender. Other scholars have argued that the new generation of Soviet leaders that emerged in the 1980s had already concluded that the policies of Gorbachev's predecessors had been counterproductive and that continued conflict threatened their goal of overcoming the disastrous legacy of Stalinism, reforming their economy, democratizing their politics, and revitalizing their society. According to these analysts, U.S. policies did not cause the changes in Soviet domestic and foreign policies and may have delayed them by providing opponents of reform with arguments against better relations with the West and relaxation of internal controls.

The initial thawing of relations occurred in the arms race. Soviet leaders and defense planners, recognizing that military expenditures were crippling the Soviet economy, came to the conclusion that a limited number of nuclear weapons provided sufficient security against both a U.S. nuclear attack and against any possible invasion by conventional forces. At the same time, President Reagan and his advisers abandoned their earlier emphasis on winning the arms race and decided to test the Soviets' willingness to curtail competition in nuclear weapons. After a series of summit meetings between Reagan and Gorbachev beginning in November 1983 in Geneva, Switzerland, the United States and the Soviet Union in December 1987 signed the Intermediate-Range Nuclear Forces Treaty pledging removal of U.S. and Soviet intermediate-range nuclear missiles from Europe. Strategic Arms Reduction Talks followed and led to a July 1991 treaty in which each country agreed to reduce stockpiles of long-range nuclear weapons.

The relaxation of the arms race helped to reduce tensions in other areas. Faced with chronic unrest in Eastern Europe and economic decline at home, Gorbachev and his reformist colleagues became convinced that maintaining a sphere of influence in Eastern Europe was no longer necessary for national security and was detrimental to their domestic as well as their foreign policy goals. In the fall of 1989, the Soviets allowed communist regimes in Eastern Europe to collapse. The following year the USSR reluctantly agreed to German reunification on Western terms—the absorption of the German Democratic Republic into the Federal Republic of Germany. Improved East-West relations and the Soviet Union's retreat from a world role also led to the withdrawal of Soviet troops from Afghanistan in early 1989 and facilitated negotiated settlements to local and regional conflicts in southern Africa, Southeast Asia, and Central America. In December 1989, President George Bush (1989–1993) and Gorbachev met on Malta and jointly declared the end of the Cold War.

The End of the Cold War

The Cold War ended when the structure and dynamics of international relations no longer supported it. Changes in the global distribution of power, weapons technology, the balance of political forces within and among nations, the world economy, and relations between the industrialized nations and the underdeveloped periphery led to the Cold War. Changes in these areas brought about its end.

Despite the upsurge in Soviet power in the 1970s and a relative decline in U.S. economic strength, the global distribution of power remained tilted against the Soviet Union throughout the Cold War. If popular support, industrial infrastructure, skilled manpower, and technological prowess are factored into the definition of power, the postwar era was bipolar only in a narrow military sense. By any broad definition of power, the Soviet Union remained until its demise an incomplete superpower.

This imbalance emerges even more starkly when the strength of the Western alliance is measured against that of the Soviet bloc. Even in military terms the Soviet position had as many elements of weakness as of strength. Throughout the Cold War, the Soviet Union and its Warsaw Pact allies possessed numerical superiority in ground forces along the central front in the heart of Europe. In addition, Soviet and Chinese communist ground forces outnumbered any possible opponent in Northeast Asia during the 1950s. In the mid-1970s, the Soviet Union also achieved rough parity with the United States in strategic nuclear weapons. The Soviets were never able to count on the loyalty of their Warsaw Pact partners. After the Sino-Soviet split in the late 1950s almost a third of their ground forces had to be deployed along their border with the PRC. In assessing the nuclear balance, the Soviets had to take into account the arsenals of the other nuclear powers—Great Britain, France, and the PRC—as well as that of the United States.

The Soviet strategic position worsened over time relatively as well as absolutely. Although the weakening of German and Japanese power initially improved the Soviets' relative position, the defeat of these two powers along with the decline of Great Britain and France left undisputed leadership of the noncommunist world to the United States. The successful reconstruction of West Germany and Japan, the economic recovery of the countries of Western Europe, and their incorporation into a U.S.-led alliance meant that the great bulk of the world's industrial might stayed outside Soviet control. Moreover, the PRC's break with the USSR in the late 1950s and the growing hostility between the two communist giants put enormous demands on the Soviet military, strains that the Soviet economy eventually could not bear.

The arms race was the most dynamic focus of the Cold War. At various times, technological advances threatened to give one superpower or the other a dangerous edge over its rival, thereby triggering vigorous countermeasures and threatening nuclear disaster. Although some analysts have argued that atomic weapons and the near certainty of retaliation may have helped prevent a war between the superpowers, they did not prevent numerous non-nuclear conflicts in the Third World. Eventually, leaders in the United States and the Soviet Union began coming to terms with the implications of the nuclear revolution. Nuclear wars, they finally realized, might be fought but could not be won. While possession of nuclear weapons might help expand influence abroad and deter encroachments on their truly vital interests, marginal increments in nuclear weaponry did not provide commensurate additional leverage in the struggle for international influence, and more and better weapons often decreased rather than increased security.

The collapse of communism as an ideology preceded the decline in the Soviet strategic position. Highly regarded at the end of World War II, the appeal of communism and the Soviet model of development declined sharply in most of the world. Repression in the Soviet Union, Eastern Europe, and the PRC tarnished communism's image. Attempts by European communist parties in the 1960s and 1970s to reform themselves and to divorce communism from the harsh reality of Soviet practice failed to have a lasting impact. Growing international awareness of human rights and environmental abuses inside the Soviet Union further discredited communism's appeal as did the faltering Soviet economy.

The inability of the Soviet Union's economy to compete with the West undermined its citizens' standard of living, its national security, and the legitimacy of the communist system. Although the roots of Soviet economic problems go back at least to the emergence of the Stalinist system in the late 1920s, military competition with the United States forced the Soviets to devote a much larger share of their smaller gross national product to defense. The diversion of investment away from productive sectors and consumer goods ultimately undermined the Soviet Union's willingness and ability to compete with the United States and to maintain its empire. Economic growth in the Soviet bloc, which had soared in the late 1940s and the 1950s, began to slow in the 1960s and never recovered.

The failure of communism to deliver the goods contrasted sharply with Western consumer culture. The new generation of Soviet citizens measured their economic status against that of their counterparts in the West rather than that of their parents, who had witnessed significant improvements in living standards in their lifetimes. The 1986 Chernobyl nuclear disaster and subsequent cover-up attempts delivered the final blow to communist rule by demoralizing the few who still believed the system could be transformed from within. By the end of the 1980s, the Soviet Union inspired and attracted almost no one, least of all those who knew it best.

The reconstruction, reform, and relative resilience of the world capitalist system contrasted sharply with the failure of communism. Despite periods of stagnation and continuing inequalities in the distribution of income and wealth, the Western economies experienced unprecedented economic growth in the 1950s and 1960s, and functioned sufficiently well to sustain their military might and to legitimize Western political and economic institutions. The United States supported the reconstruction of Western Europe and Japan, promoted economic integration, helped forge a stable global financial order, and encouraged international trade and investment through the lowering of tariffs and the removal of other impediments to the free flow of goods and capital. While the oil crises of the 1970s caused economic difficulties and financial disorder in the West, they did not redound to the advantage of the Soviet Union (although as oil exporters the Soviets benefited briefly from higher oil prices). The vitality of the West German and Japanese economies and the emergence of Western-oriented "newly industrializing countries" such as Taiwan and South Korea ensured the West's economic dominance over the Soviet Union and its allies, even as U.S technological and financial leadership declined and the U.S. share of world production decreased.

The prosperity associated with the long boom stretching from the late 1940s to the early 1970s undercut the appeal of leftist and communist parties, perpetuated the ascendancy of moderate elites who associated their own well-being with that of the United States, and sustained the cohesion of the Western alliance. The defeat of the far right in World War II helped reduce divisions among noncommunist elements facilitating, at least in Western Europe, the emergence of a consensus supporting some form of capitalist welfare state and alignment with the United States. In addition, the Cold War justified the repression and marginalization of indigenous communist and other radical groups in the name of national security.

Struggles in the Third World for political independence, economic justice, racial equality, and cultural respect often threatened Western interests and led to conflicts between Western and Third World countries as well as among and within Third World countries. All but 200,000 of the 20 million people who died in wars between 1945 and 1990 were casualties in the more than 100 wars that took place in the Third World in this period. In addition, most of the crises that threatened to escalate into nuclear war occurred in the Third World.

The Soviets proved unable to turn turmoil in the Third World to their advantage, however. The era of decolonization (1945–1975) represented a window of opportunity for the Soviet Union and a window of vulnerability for the United States and its allies. Although communist parties eventually came to power in several Third World countries, these gains were either marginal or ephemeral as most national liberation movements proved to be beyond the control of any outside power. Soviet involvement in the Third World also galvanized Western counteractions. The declining competitiveness of the Soviet economy and unpromising experience with Soviet-style planning in the Third World left Third World countries with little choice but to abide by the economic rules set by the Western-dominated International Monetary Fund and World Bank, and to look to the United States and its allies for capital, technology, and markets. By the end of the 1980s, the threat that Third World radicalism would weaken the West and add to Soviet power had dissipated.

Although the Soviet-American rivalry that was at the core of the Cold War ended with the collapse of Soviet power and the disintegration of the Soviet Union and its empire, controversies over the meaning of the Cold War have continued. In contrast to those who celebrate U.S. victory in the Cold War, others have emphasized that the costs of waging the Cold War were high, perhaps higher than necessary. The United States, the Soviet Union, and many other countries suffered great harm from waging the Cold War. With its insatiable demand on resources, its exacerbation of ideological and political intolerance, its emphasis on external threats, and its consequent neglect of internal problems, the Cold War deformed U.S., Soviet, and other societies, distorted their priorities, and dissipated their wealth. The Cold War also exacerbated such problems as chronic poverty, environmental degradation, ethnic conflict, and the proliferation of weapons of mass destruction. Any assessment of the legacy of the Cold War must take these costs into account.

DAVID S. PAINTER

See also Berlin; Bretton Woods System; Carter, James Earl; Communism; Containment; Cuban Missile Crisis; Détente; Eastern Europe; Eisenhower, Dwight David; Foreign Aid; Germany; Gorbachev, Mikhail Sergeevich; Greece; Intermediate-Range Nuclear Forces Treaty; Iran; Johnson, Lyndon Baines; Kennan, George Frost; Kennedy, John Fitzgerald; Khrushchev, Nikita Sergeyevich; Kissinger, Henry Alfred; Korean War; Limited Nuclear Test Ban Treaty; Marshall Plan; Nixon, Richard Milhous; Nonaligned Movement; North Atlantic Treaty Organization; NSC-68; Nuclear Nonproliferation; Nuclear Weapons and Strategy; Oil and Foreign Policy; Reagan, Ronald Wilson; Russia and the Soviet Union; Stalin, Joseph; Strategic Arms Limitation Talks and Agreements; Strategic Arms Reduction Treaties; Strategic Defense Initiative; Third World; Tito; Truman Doctrine; Truman, Harry S; Vietnam War; Warsaw Pact; World War II; Yalta Conference

FURTHER READING

Betts, Richard K. *Nuclear Blackmail and Nuclear Balance*. Washington, D.C., 1987.

Bowker, Mike, and Phil Williams. *Superpower Détente: A Reappraisal*. London, 1988.

Cox, Michael. "From the Truman Doctrine to the Second Superpower Détente: The Rise and Fall of the Cold War." *Journal of Peace Research* 27 (February 1990): 25-41.

Daniels, Robert V. *The End of the Communist Revolution*. London, 1993.

DePorte, A. W. *Europe Between the Superpowers: The Enduring Balance*, 2d ed. New Haven, Conn., 1986.

Gaddis, John Lewis. *Strategies of Containment: A Critical Appraisal of Postwar American National Security Policy*. New York, 1982.

———. *The Long Peace: Inquiries into the History of the Cold War*. New York, 1987.

Garthoff, Raymond L. *Détente and Confrontation: American-Soviet Relations from Nixon to Reagan*, rev. ed. Washington, D.C., 1994.

———. *The Great Transition: American-Soviet Relations and the End of the Cold War*. Washington, D.C., 1994.

Hogan, Michael J., ed. *The End of the Cold War: Its Meaning and Implications*. New York, 1992.

Holloway, David. *Stalin and the Bomb: The Soviet Union and Atomic Energy, 1939-56*. New Haven, Conn., 1994.

Kennedy, Paul. *The Rise and Fall of the Great Powers: Economic Change and Military Conflict from 1500 to 2000*. New York, 1987.

Kolko, Gabriel. *Century of War: Politics, Conflict, and Society Since 1914*. New York, 1994.

LaFeber, Walter. *America, Russia, and the Cold War, 1945-1992*, 7th ed. New York, 1993.

Lebow, Richard Ned, and Janice Gross Stein. *We All Lost the Cold War*. Princeton, N.J., 1994.

Leffler, Melvyn P. *A Preponderance of Power: National Security, the Truman Administration, and the Cold War*. Stanford, Calif., 1992.

———. *The Specter of Communism: The United States and the Origins of the Cold War, 1917-1953*. New York, 1994.

Leffler, Melvyn P., and David S. Painter, eds. *Origins of the Cold War: An International History*. London, 1994.

Maier, Charles S. *In Search of Stability: Explorations in Historical Political Economy*. New York, 1987.

McGwire, Michael. *Perestroika and Soviet National Security*. Washington, D.C., 1991.

McCormick, Thomas J. *America's Half-Century: United States Foreign Policy in the Cold War*, 2d ed. Baltimore, Md., 1995.

Nation, R. Craig. *Black Earth, Red Star: A History of Soviet Security Policy, 1917-1991*. Ithaca, N.Y., 1992.

Paterson, Thomas G. *Meeting the Communist Threat: Truman to Reagan*. New York, 1988.

———. *On Every Front: The Making and Unmaking of the Cold War*. rev. ed. New York, 1992.

Smoke, Richard. *National Security and the Nuclear Dilemma: An Introduction to the American Dilemma*, 3d ed. New York, 1992.

Vadney, T. E. *The World Since 1945*, 2d ed. London, 1992.

Woodrow Wilson International Center for Scholars. *Cold War International History Project Bulletin*. Washington, D.C., 1992–1996.

Zubok, Vladislav and Constantine Pleshakov. *Inside the Kremlin's Cold War: From Stalin to Khrushchev*. Cambridge, Mass., 1996.

COLLECTIVE SECURITY

Multilateral action taken by cooperating nations to ensure international peace and security. The goal is to transcend national arms buildups and balance-of-power mechanisms in an international community lacking supranational political authority. Responsibility for the security of cooperating members is vested in an international body. Members assume two major obligations: to refrain from employing military force against any other member as a way of settling disputes among themselves, and to take retaliatory action against those who violate the first objective. The second obligation implies a willingness to pool resources for the purpose of deterring aggression, or to punish it if deterrence fails. While retaliatory action of a nonmilitary nature, such as economic sanctions, is usually an option, collective security assumes an ultimate readiness to use armed force if necessary. Because such obligations are automatically triggered by aggression, the system significantly limits the sovereignty of its members and is, therefore, usually established by a formal treaty. Although the most noteworthy examples of collective security have aimed for global coverage, nothing in the concept's definition precludes a purely regional application of collective security.

Despite the manner in which the concept of collective security is often used in casual and journalistic reference, it does not in fact apply to all collective systems of security. It does not, for example, apply to the mutual defense arrangements of military alliances, which are designed to pool military resources to deter aggression from a nation or nations located outside the alliance system. Collective security directs its force against any aggressor, typically from within the membership of the collective security system. As the scholar Inis Claude explains the difference in a collective security system, "The world is conceived not as a we-group and a they-group, but as an integral we-group in which danger may be posed by 'one of us' and must be met by 'all of us.'" Viewed in this light, for example, the North

Atlantic Treaty Organization (NATO), directed primarily at external threats, has long been conceived as a military alliance, not as a system of collective security. Although its development in the post-Cold War era portends such a possibility, especially if it should expand to include a number of former Soviet-bloc nations, it was established at U.S. initiative with the primary purpose of confronting the Soviet bloc by pooling its members' resources and coordinating their military and political strategies.

Visions of collective security have been advocated at least since the seventeenth century, but the concept has had its greatest resonance in the twentieth century, with the League of Nations and United Nations. Although the United States ultimately did not sign the Covenant of the League of Nations, the initiative for the League was contained in President Woodrow Wilson's Fourteen Points, his proposal for the basis of post–World War I peace. Article 10 of the covenant stated, "Should any Member of the League resort to war in disregard of its covenants…it shall, ipso facto, be deemed to have committed an act of war against other members of the League." Although the same article went on to specify the means of confronting aggression, the League never succeeded in transforming its covenant into a working collective security system, as was demonstrated by its failure to deal with Japan's de facto occupation of Manchuria in 1931 or with Italy's invasion of Abyssinia (Ethiopia) in 1935.

In the Atlantic Charter, promulgated by President Franklin D. Roosevelt and British Prime Minister Winston Churchill in August 1941, the United States once again endorsed the concept of collective security as a basis for a postwar world order. Detailed discussions were held in Dumbarton Oaks, near Washington, D.C., in 1944 and in San Francisco in 1945. In July 1945 the U.S. Senate approved the United Nations Charter and the United States became a permanent member of the UN Security Council, as well as host to the UN headquarters, in New York City. The Charter of the United Nations declares (Article 1) that one of the organization's leading purposes is to "take effective collective measures for the prevention and removal of threats to the peace, and for the suppression of acts of aggression or other breaches of the peace," and the Charter's Chapter 7 discusses the mechanisms by which this is to be achieved. Nevertheless, during the first decades of its existence, with the possible exception of UN intervention in Korea, the UN's collective security performance was hardly more impressive than that of the League of Nations. Under Chapter 7 of the UN Charter, responsibility for collective security was vested with the Security Council, wherein decisions were subject to the veto of the Council's permanent members—a veto used frequently during the Cold War.

A successful system of collective security requires that three basic conditions be met. First, the participants must be willing to subordinate their individual interests for the common good, as defined by the collective security agreement. Second, the collective security system should be able to muster power sufficient to overwhelm that of a potential aggressor or coalition of aggressors. Third, the system's members must share a relatively unambiguous and generally accepted definition of aggression. None of the conditions were met during the Cold War decades. Definitions of aggressions depended on which side of the East-West divide it might occur. Moreover, the first and second conditions were rarely satisfied because competitive Cold War interests often superseded those of truly collective international security. Thus, although the absence of the Soviet representative enabled the Security Council to endorse resistance to North Korea's invasion of South Korea, it was essentially a U.S.-led military operation conducted as part of its strategy of containing communist expansion. The first authentic instance of collective security in the context of the United Nations occurred after the Cold War ended— the Gulf War of 1991 (again, largely at U.S. initiative), to free Kuwait from Iraqi military occupation.

Although collective security is generally held to be a desirable objective, critics point out that it may not be the best way of containing conflict, because it presupposes the massive application of force against an aggressor. Furthermore, it tends to be biased in favor of the international status quo. Nevertheless, despite its practical problems, collective security remains an objective to which most world leaders declare their fealty and a standard that, under the most favorable international conditions, seems achievable.

MIROSLAV NINCIC

See also Atlantic Charter; Ethiopia; Fourteen Points; Gulf War of 1990-1991; Japan; Korean War; League of Nations; Manchurian Crisis; North Atlantic Treaty Organization; United Nations

FURTHER READING

Claude, Inis L., Jr. *Power and International Relations*. New York, 1962.
Russett, Bruce M., and James S. Sutterlin. "The UN in a New World Order," *Foreign Affairs* 70 (1995): 69–83.
Weiss, Thomas G., ed. *Collective Security in a Changing World*. Boulder, Colo., 1993.

COLOMBIA

A republic located in northwestern South America, bordered by Panama, Venezuela, Ecuador, Peru, and Brazil. Since its independence from Spain in the 1820s, Colombia has played an important, though secondary, role in U.S.–Latin American relations. With coastlines on both the Pacific Ocean and the Caribbean Sea, Colombia was strategically important to the United States throughout the nineteenth century, especially the years prior to 1903 when Panama was still part of Colombian national territory and a Panama Canal was already under consideration. In 1848, Colombia (then New Granada) and the United States concluded the Mallarino-Bidlack Treaty, in which the United States guaranteed to protect New Grandad's rights of sovereignty and property on the isthmus. The 1850 Clayton-Bulwer Treaty committed Great Britain and the United States not to build or fortify a canal in the area without mutual consent. That provision remained in force until the end of the century. In 1901 it was superseded by two Hay-Paunceforte Treaties negotiated between Secretary of State John Hay and the British ambassador to the United States. In the first of these treaties the British granted the United States sole right to construct an interoceanic canal; the second treaty, signed later that year, gave the United States the right to build, control, and fortify a future canal.

A canal route through Nicaragua was also under consideration by the United States at this time, and in fact had been recommended by the Walker Commission. However, Philippe Bunau-Varilla, the French representative of the canal company, convinced President Theodore Roosevelt that the Panamanian route was superior. In June of 1902 the U.S. Senate authorized President Roosevelt to negotiate with the Colombian government for a right of way to build a canal in the province of Panama. The Hay-Herrán Treaty, negotiated by John Hay with the Colombian representative Tomas Herrán, ceded a canal zone six miles wide on both sides of the canal in return for $10 million and an annual payment of $250,000 to begin in ten years. Colombia rejected the treaty, believing that the price agreed to by Herrán was inadequate. While the Colombians waited for a better offer, Bunau-Varilla, with the apparent knowledge of Roosevelt, organized a Panamanian liberation army that was to stage a revolt, and declared the province's independence from Colombia. On 2 November 1903, the USS *Nashville* docked in Panama. Intimidated by the presence of the U.S. Navy and weakened by a three-year Civil War, the Colombians chose not to suppress the revolt by the rebels on 3 November. On the next day Panama declared its independence, and on 6 November, President Roosevelt recognized the new state of Panama. Less than two weeks later the Hay-Bunau-Varilla Treaty was signed, granting U.S. sovereign rights in the canal "in perpetuity."

The resultant anti-Americanism and bitterness in Colombia over the U.S. role in Panama's secession from Colombia hampered relations for the subsequent generation; yet Colombia in general retained through the twentieth century a largely positive, though at times ambivalent, friendship with the United States, pursuing a policy based on pragmatism and realpolitik. Foreign investment in the development of Colombian natural resource and growing economic nationalism characterized the 1920s; yet Colombia did not follow the Mexican model of nationalization. Colombian officials cooperated with U.S. agencies during World War II; the country sent troops to Korea to fight as part of the United Nations forces; in the 1960s, after ending more than a decade of civil war and reestablishing formal democratic institutions, Colombia became a "showplace" for the Alliance for Progress; and in the 1980s the country, as a participant in the Contadora process, was one of the leading voices in favor of a negotiated settlement and the withdrawal of all foreign influence in Central America.

One defining element in U.S.-Colombian relations during the 1980s and 1990s has been the flow of illegal drugs to the United States from Colombia, as well as the latter's counternarcotics performance. Throughout the 1980s, Colombian governments cooperated with the United States in an effort to resolve the international drug trade. One such form of cooperation was the extradition to the United States of Colombian nationals wanted for drug trafficking. The primary U.S. contribution to the effort to fight the drug trade has been in the form of military aid; by the early 1990s, Colombia had become the largest recipient of U.S. foreign military aid in Latin America. In the 1990s, the drug trade issue has led to tense relations between the United States and Colombia. The United States became upset at the inclusion in Colombia's new (1991) constitution of an article prohibiting the extradition of Colombian nationals; arguing that Colombia's legal institutions are weak, the United States feared that narcotraffickers would escape prosecution or receive light sentences. In March 1996, based on strong evidence that Colombian president Ernesto Samper had accepted $6 million in campaign contributions from the Cali cocaine cartel, the Clinton administration imposed a series of economic sanctions on Columbia, including a freeze on trade and investment financing through the Overseas Private Investment Corporation and the Export-Import Bank, a refusal to approve multilateral economic assistance for Colombia, and a ban on travel to the United States by President Samper.

In general, the foreign policies of Colombia toward the United States in the past century have adhered to the concept of the Suarez Doctrine, named after President Marco Fidel Suarez (1918–1921). Suarez viewed the proximity and power of the United States as a given and argued that the only rational foreign policy for Colombia was one of cautious cooperation. This foreign policy stance is one to which Colombia continued to adhere to in the late 1990s.

STEPHEN J. RANDALL

See also Alliance for Progress; Bunau-Varilla, Phillippe; Contadora Group; Hay, John Milton; Narcotics International; Panama and Panama Canal; Roosevelt, Theodore

FURTHER READING

Bushnell, David. *Eduardo Santos and the Good Neighbor.* Gainesville, Fla., 1987.

Lael, Richard. *Arrogant Diplomacy.* Wilimington, Del., 1988.

Randall, Stephen J. *Colombia and the United States: Hegemony and Interdependence.* Athens, Ga., 1992.

Parks, E. Taylor. *Colombia and the United States, 1765–1934.* Chapel Hill, N.C., 1935.

COLONIALISM

An imperial nation's practice or policy of acquiring or controlling foreign countries, territories, or peoples, as dependent colonies for the purpose of exploiting them. In the nineteenth and twentieth centuries imperial powers established colonies primarily for strategic and economic reasons. Military colonies controlled other important dependent territories and secured strategically vital sea routes, while economic colonies provided raw materials for colonial powers and markets for overseas investment and manufactured goods. Imperial powers often asserted racial and cultural superiority over the peoples they colonized.

Americans have historically maintained an ambivalent attitude towards colonialism. The United States, after all, was created through armed resistance against the colonial policies of the British Empire. Americans, chastened by their own colonial experience, deplored the very idea of colonial empires as a European or alien concept, beyond the pale of their own liberal ideology. Americans applauded the Latin American wars of independence (1810–1824), which cast off the yoke of Spanish colonialism. The Monroe Doctrine of 1823 proscribed any European attempt to reimpose colonialism in the Western Hemisphere.

Throughout the early nineteenth century, the United States progressively expanded its own frontiers west and southward. The Louisiana Purchase (1803), acquisition of Florida (1819), annexation of the Republic of Texas (1845), and war with Mexico, which gained California and New Mexico (1848), vastly increased the U.S. domain. At the same time, Americans did not regard their "Manifest Destiny" to rule the continent as a colonial venture, since their newly acquired territories were contiguous, sparsely populated, and later admitted into the Union as states. Still, the original inhabitants of these newly annexed territories—Native Americans and Mexicans—were certainly victims of racism and discrimination and experienced an American rule basically colonial in nature and reality.

Beginning with President Andrew Jackson's Indian Removal Policy of the 1830s, the U.S. government, often through its armed forces, systematically defeated and confined Native American tribes to reservations. By the 1880s all American Indians were restricted to these settlements, wholly dependent upon the government and ruled from Washington. The United States' Indian reservation system constituted an early example of what scholars call "internal colonialism," a practice seen later in the twentieth century in the white South African government's "black homelands" policy.

After the Civil War, Secretary of State William Seward advocated an openly expansionistic program and the acquisition of colonies. He negotiated the purchase of Alaska from Russia in 1867 and formally annexed Midway Island in the same year. Both of these acquisitions broke the mold of earlier U.S. expansionism because they were noncontiguous territories, located hundreds of miles from the U.S. mainland. While Alaska would later be admitted as a state (1959), Midway represented a purely strategic colony, a coaling station for naval patrols and merchant ships trading in Asia. Besides spreading westward, the U.S. colonial gaze also turned southward to the Caribbean. During the Grant Administration (1869–1877) the United States came close to annexing the Dominican Republic, though Congress temporarily blocked the president and Seward's expansionist designs in this region.

In the period 1880–1914, the nations of Europe launched an era of intensive expansionism. The scramble for Africa, large areas of Asia, and the Pacific created vast colonial empires for France, Great Britain, Holland, Belgium, and Germany. National greatness, according to expansionist ideology, demanded colonies; economic prosperity could not be maintained without them. The United States emerged in this period as a new industrial colossus. In the 1890s advocates for U.S. expansionism, including the naval theorist Alfred Thayer Mahan, politicians such as Theodore Roosevelt and Henry Cabot Lodge, as well as secretaries of state such as James G. Blaine, Elihu Root, and John Hay, all called for the United States to join the imperial race or else fall behind as a "second class" nation in the realm of world politics.

A bloody rebellion in Cuba against repressive Spanish rule in the mid-1890s propelled the United States to major colonial-power status. In 1898, the United States declared war on Spain and quickly invaded and occupied Cuba, Puerto Rico, Guam, and the Philippines. In the same year Washington annexed the Hawai'ian Islands, completing its "island stepping stones" to the fabled Asian Pacific trade. The United States maintained a formal colonialism in Puerto Rico, Guam, and the Philippines, directly controlling all internal and external affairs. In Cuba, through the highly restrictive Platt Amendment (1901–1934) and substantial economic investment, Washington exercised a more "informal" colonialism that would presage the "neo-colonialism" of the post–World War II era.

Since the mid-nineteenth century, the United States had coveted the construction and control of a transoceanic canal through Central America that would enhance trade and naval predominance. In 1903, President Theodore Roosevelt supported a nationalist revolt in Panama against the Colombian government, well aware that the rebels would cede land for an American canal across their isthmus. Construction began the following year. Through control of the fifty-mile long, ten-mile wide canal "zone"—a virtual colonial possession—the United States dominated Panama throughout most of the twentieth century. With the announcement of the Roosevelt Corollary to the Monroe Doctrine in 1904, the president affirmed the U.S. role as "policeman" of the Western Hemisphere, establishing—particularly in the Caribbean and Central American nations—an informal system of U.S. colonies or protectorates. The United States reserved the right to intervene militarily to restore order, collect debts, or protect investments. Latin American nations typically sold the vast majority of their largely agricultural and mineral exports to the United States, and in turn purchased most of their imported manufactured goods from America. U.S. investment dominated many Latin American economies. By 1910 in Mexico, for example, U.S. businesses owned 40 percent of all property, including 80 percent of mines, oil, and railroads. A pattern of economic and political dependency and neocolonial control, if not actual military occupation, emerged.

In January 1918, in the midst of World War I, President Woodrow Wilson denounced colonialism in his famous Fourteen Points. Yet in the postwar peace settlement, the United States acquiesced in the "mandate system" which ceded former German and Ottoman territories in the Middle East, Africa, and the Pacific to its wartime allies, Great Britain, France, and Japan as "trusts" until the mandates' peoples merited self-governance. In the 1941 Atlantic Charter, President Franklin D. Roosevelt likewise championed self-determination and espoused the traditional U.S. aversion to European colonialism, especially in France's Indochina. Still, the exigencies of the Cold War for the most part pushed his successor, Harry S. Truman, to aid his weakened allies' efforts to hold onto their tottering colonial empires. In 1945 the United States itself acquired mandates over numerous Japanese controlled Pacific islands. The other major protagonist in the Cold War, the Soviet Union, developed its own brand of imperialism, with some "colonial" elements, in Eastern Europe, where Soviet trade pacts, fixed elections, and military occupations made the region subservient to Soviet power. All the while, the Soviets expressed an anticolonial ideology that carried some appeal in colonial areas, but less so after the Soviet Union invaded Hungary in 1956 to quell a revolution against Soviet rule.

Both the Truman and Eisenhower administrations supported France in its Indo-China War (1946–1954) against Vietnamese nationalists, citing the need to prop up an ally and contain the spread of communism in the Third World. In 1950 Washington recognized the French-backed Bao Dai government in Vietnam and substantially increased U.S. aid to the French war effort, eventually shouldering 80 percent of the war's cost. The U.S. alliance with French colonialism in Indochina and Washington's establishment of a noncommunist South Vietnamese government after the 1954 Geneva Conference helped lead the United States into the Vietnam War of the 1960s and 1970s.

The accelerating Third World decolonialization movement of the postwar era placed the United States in a political and economical quandary. On occasions, such as the Dutch-Indonesian War (1945–1949) and the Suez Crisis (1956), Washington backed Third World nations against U.S. allies. In the case of Suez, the Eisenhower administration used economic and diplomatic pressure to force British, French, and Israeli troops from Egypt after Egypt nationalized an example of colonialism—the Suez Canal. But in other instances, such as the Indo-China War, the French-Algerian War (1954–1962), the British-Malaysian War (1948–1960), and the Portuguese-Angolan War (1961–1974), the United States either favored the colonial powers or maintained a sympathetic neutrality. Successive U.S. administrations cited the need of preventing Third World nationalist movements, vital raw materials, or geostrategic areas from falling under the control of the Soviets (and their allies) as reasons for supporting colonial powers. The 1959 Cuban Revolution presented a formidable challenge to U.S. hegemony in Latin America, inflaming nationalist movements throughout the region, including Puerto Rico and Panama. In 1977, the United States agreed to give up its key "colonial" possession in the area—the Panama Canal Zone—by 2000.

After 1945 formal colonialism increasingly lost its political, moral, and economic appeal in the United States as Third World peoples demanded more self-governance and the United States found that it could still maintain influence. In 1946 the United States, fulfilling a promise made in 1934, granted the Philippines its independence, although it maintained vast influence over Filipino internal affairs through the use of foreign aid, military bases, and economic leverage. In 1952 Washington awarded Puerto Rico "commonwealth" status. Third World critics of colonialism protested, however, the rise of a new form of dependency—"neocolonialism," in which powers like the United States dominate Third-World countries through powerful military, economic, political, and cultural institutions and relationships. According to dependency theory, large industrial states' control of the world trading system severely hindered the economic development of smaller formerly colonized nations and kept the countries in continued economic and political bondage. The World Bank, International Monetary Fund (IMF), American motion pictures, and Coca-Cola thus replaced gunboats, missionaries, and U.S. marines as agents of U.S. power. In the post–Cold War era of shrinking U.S. military and economic power, increased global competition, the fracturing of "Free World" alliances, and a resurgence of radical nationalism, the future of neocolonialism remains uncertain. Still, most Third World nations remain mired in debt and dependency to the West.

MICHAEL E. DONOGHUE

See also Alaska Purchase; Atlantic Charter; Continental Expansion; Cuba; Dependency; Fourteen Points; French Indonesia; Hawai'i; Imperialism; Indonesia; Mahan, Alfred Thayer; Mandates and Trusteeships; Native Americans; Pacific Island Nations and U.S. Territories; Panama and Panama Canal; Philippines; Platt Amendment; Puerto Rico; Roosevelt, Theodore; South Africa; Spanish-American-Cuban-Filipino War, 1898; Suez Crisis; Vietnam

FURTHER READING

Dirks, Nicholas B., ed. *Colonialism and Culture.* Ann Arbor, Mich., 1992.
Drake, Paul W. *Money Doctors, Foreign Debts and Economic Reforms in Latin America from the 1890s to the Present.* Wilmington, Del., 1994.
Jones, Dorothy V. *License for Empire: Colonialism by Treaty in Early America.* Chicago, 1982.
Kolko, Gabriel. *Confronting the Third World: U.S. Foreign Policy 1945–1980.* New York, 1988.
LaFeber, Walter. *The Panama Canal: The Crisis in Historical Perspective.* New York, 1989.
Meléndez, Edwin, and Edgardo Meléndez. *Colonial Dilemma: Critical Perspectives on Contemporary Puerto Rico.* Boston, 1993.
Pomeroy, William J. *The Philippines: Colonialism, Collaboration, and Resistance.* New York, 1992.

COMMERCE, U.S. DEPARTMENT OF

Cabinet-level department created in 1913 by legislation splitting the Department of Commerce and Labor, formed in 1903, into two separate units. The Department of Commerce (DOC) has subsequently sought to promote U.S. economic growth in general and growth in the manufacturing sector in particular by advocating domestic economic and international commercial policies supportive of American industry, providing a variety of advisory and informational services, and administering a number of technical and statistical programs. The DOC's organization has been fluid over the years, and its policy impact has been limited because its exact mission

has never been clearly defined. The ambiguity that characterizes the DOC's responsibilities is rooted in the long-standing unwritten consensus between the private sector and the federal government that the U.S. industrial sector (and its foreign trade) should be guided more by the free market and less by an all-powerful commercial ministry that would engage in economic planning, as is done in many other governments. With 31,000 employees and a budget that exceeded $3 billion in the mid-1990s, the DOC is an agglomeration of more than 100 separate programs; its responsibilities include conducting the census, issuing patents and trademarks, and forecasting the weather.

The DOC administers many U.S. laws affecting international trade. Although the department lacks the international economic policy clout of the Departments of Treasury and State or the U.S. Trade Representative, it has played an increasingly important role as a result of three trends that surfaced in the late 1980s: the growing appreciation in the United States of the degree to which foreign trade and investment flows affect domestic economic performance, escalating U.S. concerns about international competitiveness, and diminished U.S. patience with unfair foreign trade practices. The DOC's expanding role in technology enhancement and trade relations has put it in a strategic position to affect governmental trade policy priorities. Under the administration of President Bill Clinton (1993–1997) the DOC's National Institute of Standards and Technology became a key player in financing the growing federal effort to stimulate the competitiveness of the commercial high-technology sector through such programs as the Advanced Technology Program. That program provides matching funds (on a grant basis) to U.S. industry initiatives seeking to develop new generic technologies in the high-tech and advanced manufacturing sectors.

The DOC's role in U.S. foreign economic policy is played out primarily through the International Trade Administration (ITA) and the Bureau of Export Administration. The ITA participates in interagency trade and international direct investment policymaking in a number of ways. It provides technical expertise on individual manufacturing and service sectors to domestic and international economic policymakers; it promotes exports by dispensing guidance and marketing data to U.S. businesses interested in selling or investing abroad; it staffs and, since 1980, manages the U.S. and Foreign Commercial Service, which maintains forty-seven district offices within the United States and has operations in sixty-eight countries; and it operates most of the major programs affecting the flow of U.S. imports and exports.

In addition to managing a broad array of trade promotion programs, the DOC is active on the other side of export policy. It administers export controls, which may

SECRETARIES OF COMMERCE

ADMINISTRATION	SECRETARY	PERIOD OF APPOINTMENT
T. Roosevelt	George B. Cortelyou*	1903–1904
	Victor H. Metcalf*	1904–1906
	Oscar S. Straus*	1906–1909
Taft	Charles Nagel*	1909–1913
Wilson	William C. Redfield	1913–1919
	Joshua W. Alexander	1919–1921
Harding	Herbert C. Hoover	1921–1928
Coolidge		
	William F. Whiting	1928–1929
Hoover	Robert P. Lamont	1929–1932
	Roy D. Chapin	1932–1933
F. Roosevelt	Daniel C. Roper	1933–1939
	Harry L. Hopkins	1939–1940
	Jesse H. Jones	1940–1945
	Henry A. Wallace	1945–1946
Truman		
	W. Averell Harriman	1946–1948
	Charles Sawyer	1948–1953
Eisenhower	Sinclair Weeks	1953–1958
	Lewis L. Strauss	1958–1959
	Frederick H. Mueller	1959–1961
Kennedy	Luther H. Hodges	1961–1965
L. Johnson	John T. Connor	1965–1967
	Alexander B. Trowbridge	1967–1968
	C. R. Smith	1968–1969
Nixon	Maurice H. Stans	1969–1972
	Peter G. Peterson	1972–1973
	Frederick B. Dent	1973–1975
Ford		
	Rogers C. B. Morton	1975–1976
	Elliott Richardson	1976–1977
Carter	Juanita M. Kreps	1977–1980
	Philip M. Klutznick	1980–1981
Reagan	Malcolm Baldrige	1981–1987
	C. William Verity, Jr.	1987–1989
Bush	Robert A. Mosbacher	1989–1992
	Barbara H. Franklin	1992–1993
Clinton	Ronald H. Brown	1993–1996
	Mickey Kantor	1996–Present

*Secretary of Commerce and Labor, prior to the division into separate departments in 1913.

Source: U.S. Department of Commerce

be imposed for a variety of reasons, among them national security considerations, foreign policy goals, U.S. efforts to limit the spread of nuclear technology, and inadequate domestic supply. In addition to issuing (or refusing to issue) licenses for the export or reexport of dual-use commodities and technical data, the DOC participates in the development of U.S. policy within the context of multilateral export control agreements, such as the now-defunct seventeen-nation Coordinating Committee on Multilateral Export Controls, which from 1949 to 1994 coordinated controls on exports from Western nations to the Soviet Union and other communist countries. The

DOC also enforces U.S. legislation barring domestic companies from complying with unsanctioned foreign boycotts against friendly countries.

The most controversial aspect of the DOC's foreign affairs activities is its administration of several import control programs, which foreign exporters charge discriminate against them. The DOC administers laws (administered by the Treasury Department prior to 1980) that seek to neutralize, by the imposition of special import duties, two major unfair foreign trade practices: dumping (the exporting of goods at prices less than fair value) and the subsidization of overseas industrial production by foreign governments (the countervailing duty statute). Foreign governments have become increasingly vociferous in criticizing what they believe to be the DOC's arbitrary rulings upholding the accusations by domestic industries of dumping by foreign companies. The DOC also monitors import control programs, whether unilaterally imposed by the U.S. government or negotiated in the form of a "voluntary" export restraint agreement by a foreign government.

STEPHEN D. COHEN

See also International Trade and Commerce

FURTHER READING

Cohen, Stephen D. *The Making of U.S. International Economic Policy*, 4th ed. New York, 1994.

U.S. Department of Commerce. *Annual Report*. Issued every U.S. government fiscal year.

COMMITTEE ON PUBLIC INFORMATION

The first sustained effort by the U.S. government to make the deliberate shaping of public opinion an instrument of foreign policy. It was established in April 1917, during World War I, by executive order of President Woodrow Wilson and later abolished by Congress at the end of the war in June 1919. Unlike the United States Information Agency of the late twentieth century, the Committee on Public Information (Creel Committee) functioned both at home and overseas. The committee technically comprised the secretaries of war, state, and the navy, but it became familiarly known by the name of its head, George E. Creel, a personal friend of Wilson and a partisan journalist who had worked for his election in 1916. Some members of Congress, especially Republicans, believed Creel was more a propagandist for the Wilson administration than for the United States or its war efforts. In his final report to the president, Creel noted, "There was no part of the great war machinery that we did not touch, no medium of appeal that we did not employ. The printed word, the spoken word, the motion picture, the poster, the signboard—all these were used in our campaign to make

our own people and all other peoples understand the causes that compelled America to take arms in defense of its liberties and free institutions." This statement was at most only a slight exaggeration. Among other activities at home, the committee mobilized 75,000 volunteers, known as Four Minute Men, to give short speeches in support of the war, and published a daily newspaper for government offices with a circulation of 100,000. Abroad, an international news agency was established, and the committee itself carried out a wide range of activities to disseminate information and propaganda from South America to Scandinavia to Russia.

ROBERT L. STEVENSON

See also Communications Policy; Wilson, Thomas Woodrow; United States Information Agency; World War I

FURTHER READING

Creel, George. *The War, the World, and Wilson*. New York, 1920.

Mock, James R., and Cedrick Larson. *Words that Won the War: The Story of the Committee on Public Information*. Princeton, N.J., 1939.

COMMITTEE ON THE PRESENT DANGER

An organization originally formed in 1950 by a group of prominent U.S. citizens from business, academe, and government to alert the nation to the threat of communism and to promote a state of strong military preparedness. It was reconstituted during the administration of President Jimmy Carter (1977–1981) in response to similar concerns. Throughout the 1950s the committee was an active supporter of Presidents Harry S. Truman and Dwight D. Eisenhower's containment policies and then became inactive until the late 1970s, when it largely opposed the Carter administration's foreign and defense policies as being not "tough enough" against the Soviet Union. The committee's major criticism was that the efforts of the Carter administration were inadequate to contain Soviet military and political involvement in the Third World (for example, Angola, Horn of Africa, Central America) and that the Soviet Union had gained advantages because of declining U.S. defense spending and the terms of the Strategic Arms Limitation Treaties (SALT I and SALT II). The titles of some of its publications were indicative of the committee's thinking— "Common Sense and the Common Danger," "What Is the Soviet Union Up To?" and "Is America Becoming Number 2?" Paul Nitze was the key individual in the organization, both in the 1950s and the 1970s. Nitze and other prominent members of the committee became top-level appointees in the administration of President Ronald Reagan, Nitze as a principal arms control negotiator, Richard Allen as a national security adviser, William

Casey as director of the Central Intelligence Agency (CIA), Eugene Rostow as director of the Arms Control and Disarmament Agency, and Jeane Kirkpatrick as ambassador to the United Nations (UN). The influence wielded by the Committee on the Present Danger coincided with the rise of anticommunism during the 1950s and again from the late 1970s though the 1980s, until the disappearance of the Soviet threat.

JEREL A. ROSATI

See also Casey, William Joseph; Cold War; Kirkpatrick, Jeane Duane; Nitze, Paul Henry; Public Opinion; Reagan, Ronald Wilson; Rostow, Walt Whitman

FURTHER READING

Dalby, Simon. *Creating the Second Cold War.* New York, 1990.
Sanders, Jerry W. *Peddlers of Crisis: The Committee on the Present Danger and the Politics of Containment.* Boston, 1983.

COMMON MARKET

See European Union

COMMUNICATIONS POLICY

Electronic communications have transformed the practice of diplomacy in modern times. They have also made telecommunications and information issues an important part of foreign policy agendas throughout the world. The United States has played a leading role in the evolution of international communications policy and use of global communications resources, particularly since World War II. In the United States and other countries, communications policy affects a broad range of diplomatic concerns, including trade, national security, finance, human rights, transportation, technology, media, and the amorphous area of cultural relations.

Communications resources were slow to develop, both as a diplomatic tool and as a policy issue. It was not until 1869, twenty-five years after the first telegram was sent by Samuel F. Morse's telegraph in 1844, that the Department of State assigned a clerk to deal with the new technology. His job was to walk over to the Western Union office in Washington, D.C., every day and pick up telegrams addressed to the department. It took longer for communications to become even a minor policy concern for U.S. diplomacy. Because the American focus was on development of domestic telegraph and telephone networks, policymakers saw no compelling reason to encourage further international links, even after the first successful transatlantic telegraph cable was opened in 1866. In contrast, Great Britain, France, and other European countries recognized that telegraph networks could be a strategic resource in controlling their overseas colonies.

As a result, the British and French dominated international communications resources for a century after the invention of the telegraph.

The expansion of global networks by the European powers led to the creation of the first international organization dealing with the cross-border regulation of a technology. The International Telegraph Union was founded in 1865, primarily to establish common technical standards for international telegraph traffic. The United States chose not to join the new organization, a decision reflecting fears of possible foreign interference in U.S. domestic telecommunications networks. U.S. policymakers did not respond to the international expansion of electronic communications resources until the British attempted, early in the twentieth century, to establish a worldwide monopoly for the new wireless radio technology through the London-based Marconi Wireless Telegraph Company. This threat led the United States to join the International Telegraph Union, where it actively worked to thwart the British monopoly and, in the process, helped establish a policy precedent for unimpeded access by all nations to global communications facilities.

The strategic value of these facilities became clear during World War I. Cable and wireless resources occupied an important place in the strategies of all the major combatants, and the future of international telecommunications became an issue at the Paris Peace Conference in 1919. Both the victors and the losers sought to preserve and expand their advantages in exploiting the new technologies. The U.S. delegation proposed an open international communications regime that had, in addition to its idealistic overtones, the pragmatic purpose of positioning the United States to compete more effectively with the Europeans, who then dominated global telecommunications resources. The U.S. proposal was sidetracked at Paris, but the subject was reopened in a series of Washington conferences from 1920 to 1922, again without result. Nevertheless, these initiatives, emphasizing open access, have influenced U.S. policy ever since.

During the interwar years U.S. communications companies made their first significant efforts to expand facilities abroad, often with diplomatic support from the Department of State. The U.S. government also resisted European cable-communications incursions into Latin America and encouraged U.S. firms, particularly American Telephone and Telegraph (AT&T), International Telephone and Telegraph (ITT), and Western Union, to establish links with countries in the region. The U.S. military establishment was especially anxious to exploit technological breakthroughs in telegraphy and voice broadcasting for national security purposes. The navy played a significant role in establishing a commercial firm, the Radio Corporation of America (RCA), to advance this goal. The military services led the development and implementation of international communications policies until the 1950s. During World War II the Army Signal Corps and the navy built a vast global network to support land and naval operations. As a result, the United States displaced the British and the French as the most influential communications power in the world. Defense-related issues dominated U.S. global communications strategy until the early 1960s. The military's emerging dominance in communications relegated the Department of State largely to a secondary coordinating function. For example, when a small communications policy group was set up in the White House during the administration of President Harry S. Truman, it was staffed mainly by Department of Defense officers.

The Communications Satellite Era

A major technological breakthrough—communications satellites capable of providing instant telecommunications connections with any place on the earth—changed the balance between military and civilian interests. The successful 1962 launch of the first Telstar satellite, developed by AT&T, established communications policy as a significant civilian concern under the Department of State control for the first time. Major policy decisions were involved because the United States had an effective monopoly on the new satellite technology and the economic resources and the political will to exploit the technology. No diplomatic precedents existed, however, for creating a complex global communications facility, creating a unique problem. The U.S. response was both bold and successful.

The Communications Satellite Act of 1962 established the foreign policy mandate for the technology. The legislation called for the United States to take the lead in setting up a worldwide satellite network. It also authorized a congressionally chartered corporation, the Communications Satellite Corporation (COMSAT), to represent U.S. interests in the global system. In a compromise designed to involve the U.S. private sector, half of COMSAT's stock was to be owned by the major U.S. international telecommunications companies. The remaining stock was sold to the general public. Although the legislation gave COMSAT substantial independence from government controls, the company was required to consult the Department of State on issues and actions that affected overall foreign policy concerns.

Although the Communications Satellite Act set out a broad mandate for a global network, it did not provide specific guidelines on the construction and management of the network. The pressure for a decision on these issues was fueled by U.S. fears that the Soviet Union would soon have a comparable communications satellite capability. These fears eventually proved to be unwar-

ranted. It took the Soviets almost a decade to catch up technologically in this area. Meanwhile, the United States pressed for negotiations to create an interim global satellite consortium that would begin to build and operate a network while details were worked out for a more permanent organization. The negotiations, primarily involving the United States and its European allies, began in February 1964 and were concluded in August. The agreement provided for the establishment of the International Telecommunications Satellite Consortium (Intelsat), along with procedures for making the transition to a permanent organization. Invitations were sent to all member countries of the International Telecommunications Union (ITU), successor in 1934 to the International Telegraph Union. Countries joining the interim arrangement bought shares in proportion to their use of the new system. They also shared proportionally in the system's profits. Under this formula, COMSAT, the U.S. representative in the consortium, became the major investor, with more than half of the shares, and was designated manager of the new network.

The U.S. decision to move decisively in implementing global satellite communications was a policy success. The network worked well from the start, growing many times beyond original projections of its deployment and use. This rapid expansion encouraged developing countries to join the system. Their initial skepticism about the network and the dominant role of the United States in the system was largely overcome by the pragmatic benefits of efficient access for the first time to the world beyond their borders.

The Intelsat System

Despite the early success of the new satellite network, U.S. foreign policy planners encountered opposition in implementing their plans for a more permanent organization. Domestic opponents objected to what they regarded as proposals to surrender U.S. control over a strategic new global resource. The Europeans and Japanese were concerned that the proposed permanent arrangements would confirm U.S. technical and economic dominance over Intelsat, effectively reducing them to second-level status in the space communications field. Negotiations on a treaty establishing Intelsat's permanent organization took place in a series of Washington conferences between 1969 and 1972. The critical compromise in the negotiations was U.S. agreement to transfer COMSAT's management of the network to Intelsat. At the same time, the Europeans and Japanese were given assurances that their space industries would be able to compete fairly with U.S. industry for Intelsat's satellite-equipment business.

The final treaty approved a permanent Intelsat facility known as the International Telecommunications Satellite

Organization. Under the treaty provisions, Intelsat was essentially a commercial cartel of the world's post–telephone and telegraph (PTT) organizations, plus COMSAT. The treaty guaranteed each governmental PTT an operating voice in the system, as well as a proportionate share of its profits based on usage. By the late 1970s more than 100 countries had signed the Intelsat treaty. The Soviet Union and the People's Republic of China were notable exceptions. Each had separately attacked the new organization as a U.S. conspiracy to control world communications. The Soviets refusal to participate stemmed from the fact that under Intelsat rules governing share ownership, they would have had less than a 1 percent ownership stake in the system. The Soviet government chose instead to set up its own global network, Intersputnik, with less than a dozen of its client states as members and only a minuscule share of international satellite traffic. China eventually joined Intelsat in an arrangement that required the Republic of China (Taiwan) to give up its shares in the system. After the breakup of the Soviet Union in 1991, Russia and most of the other former Soviet republics became Intelsat members.

Since Intelsat became a permanent organization, it has been a major factor in the expansion of international communications traffic. Its network links more than 160 countries and other political entities. Intelsat services have been supplemented by many smaller regional and domestic satellite networks. Since the 1980s these satellite services have had to compete with a new generation of advanced cable systems using fiber optics technology. Another factor driving competition in international communications is the swift pace of privatization and deregulation of formerly government-controlled telecommunications agencies in Europe, Asia, and Latin America. These developments were eroding Intelsat's original role as a virtual monopoly supplier of international communications. Faced with new competition, the organization was under pressure in the mid-1990s to transform itself from an international entity, controlled by governments, to one that would have more of the characteristics, and the flexibility, of a commercial enterprise.

Reshaping Communications Policy

Rapid economic and technological changes have given communications policy an increasingly high profile in U.S. foreign affairs. Policy decisions about telecommunications and the global flow of information affect other areas, such as trade, finance, national security, technology transfer, and cultural affairs. More and more international agreements negotiated between the United States and other countries or international organizations have at least some communications or information component.

Foreign ministries around the world have been generally slow to adjust their operational styles to these changes. In most countries the development and implementation of international communications policy is still largely the responsibility of a ministry of communications or other national telecommunications agency, with some policy oversight by the foreign ministry. The U.S. experience is different. Lacking a national authority, U.S. policymaking in communications emphasizes a collegial approach between major federal agencies, mainly the Departments of State, Defense, and Commerce, as well as the independent Federal Communications Commission (FCC). The private sector, particularly telecommunications service providers and manufacturers, is also consulted on policy issues.

Although given primacy in determining policy, the Department of State has often had difficulty defining and implementing global communications policy. The department was slow to set up adequate organizational procedures to deal with communications issues after the introduction of satellites and other advanced technologies in the 1960s. Twenty years passed before the department moved communications policy operations out of a third-level office in its economic bureau and made it an independent bureau. The Bureau of International Communications and Information Policy was authorized in 1982, primarily as the result of pressures from Congress. The delay was caused largely by bureaucratic considerations. A half-dozen other units within the Department of State had some communications-policy responsibilities, which they were reluctant to surrender. Other government agencies with similar responsibilities were also not happy about the creation of the new bureau. Significantly, the first head of the bureau, Diana Lady Dougan, was given the dual titles of assistant secretary of state and U.S. coordinator for international communications and information policy, in a move designed to strengthen the State Department's overall role in this area. A senior interagency group was set up under the department's direction to coordinate global communications policy planning and implementation within the executive branch.

Despite these formal arrangements, communications policy management is often contentious. The FCC tends to champion the interests of an expanding and politically powerful domestic communications sector. The Department of Defense focuses on protecting its global networks, as do the Central Intelligence Agency and the National Security Agency. The Department of Commerce views international communications issues primarily from its perspective on trade. For example, the National Telecommunications and Information Administration, a commerce agency that promotes domestic business interests, often voices its concern for international policy issues. The State Department's management of communications policy issues underwent a major change in 1994 as part of President Bill Clinton's reorganization of departmental functions. The communications policy bureau was phased out and its functions shifted to a second-level role in the department's economic and business bureau.

Negotiating International Agreements

Despite this apparent downgrading, communications issues remain an important part of the Department of State's policy agenda. Although most diplomatic activity in communications policy involves bilateral agreements with other countries, multilateral negotiations have sharply increased. A highly publicized example involved the United Nations Educational, Social, and Cultural Organization (UNESCO). In the 1970s UNESCO championed controls over international media flows, in response to a call by many Third World nations for a "new world information order." The initiative's purpose was to curb the alleged cultural imperialism represented by television, film, and other media exports from Western countries, particularly the United States. The issue was a primary reason for the U.S. decision to withdraw from UNESCO in 1984. One result of the American decision was changes in UNESCO policies, particularly those that proposed restrictions on global media trade. In November 1995, the American government informed UNESCO that, as a result of these changes, it was prepared to take steps toward rejoining the organization.

Most multilateral negotiations on communications issues have been sponsored by the Geneva-based ITU. Originally dominated by the industrialized powers, the ITU's mission and operational style changed in the 1960s. It tripled its membership to include more than 100 newly independent countries. In addition, it was forced to reorganize its primary activities—coordinating technical and administrative standards for global telecommunications—to fit the new age of communications satellites and other advanced technologies. These changes were negotiated in a series of conferences over a twenty-year period beginning in the late 1960s. Known as World Administrative Radio Conferences (WARCs), the meetings were generally successful in adjusting global telecommunications policy to new political and technological realities. A 1979 WARC on the global allocation of the radio spectrum was probably the most complex international conference held until that time. It involved a ten-year preparation period for a meeting attended by delegations from more than 150 ITU member nations and dealt with more than 15,000 proposals in a continuous three-month session.

In the early 1990s the ITU underwent further restructuring of its functions, reacting to changes in the global telecommunications environment. An important change was a new emphasis on trade in negotiating telecommunications issues. It was estimated that by the year 2000 electronics would replace automobiles as the world's largest industry. Communications and information products and services are the most important components in the electronics sector. As a result, global trade considerations have risen to the top of the communications policy agenda. The issue is particularly important to the United States and other advanced industrial countries, but it also concerns economies such as those emerging in Mexico, China, Malaysia, Brazil, and Singapore, all of which have significant electronics sectors.

Communications trade issues came to a head in the Uruguay Round of the General Agreement on Tariffs and Trade (GATT) negotiations, which concluded in 1993. In meetings stretching over seven years, GATT members agreed to expand the organization's charter to include rules on trade in services as well as on manufactured goods. Setting the rules for telecommunications services turned out to be one of the most difficult issues in the Uruguay Round, primarily because many countries rejected American proposals which would open their monopoly telecommunications systems to greater foreign competition. The issue was so contentious that it was not resolved in the 1993 Uruguay Round agreement setting up the World Trade Organization (WTO), successor to the GATT. In 1995–1996, the WTO sponsored a special round of negotiations to deal with the unresolved telecommunications-services issues, which resulted in some progress towards establishing more liberal trade rules in this sector.

American leadership in global communications was underscored in 1993 by the Clinton administration's sponsorship of a national information infrastructure ("information highway") initiative. The initiative proposed a dramatic upgrading of domestic and international information resources, based on advanced computer and telecommunications technologies. In announcing the plan, President Clinton stressed the information highway's role in strengthening U.S. export competitiveness. Vice President Al Gore added an international dimension to this theme at a 1994 conference in Buenos Aires, where he outlined an American proposal for a "global information infrastructure," stressing the need for cooperative actions to make advanced communications resources available in all countries.

This theme was the focus of a February 1995 ministerial conference of representatives from the Group of Seven, the world's largest industrialized countries, in Brussels. This meeting, convened at the suggestion of the United States, proposed a series of steps to promote an effective transition to a global information society. Common ground was found on such issues as the interconnectivity of the world's communications networks, opening up government-controlled networks to competition, protection of intellectual property, and data security. The conferees also agreed on the particular need to strengthen communications and information resources in the emerging countries of Asia, Africa, and Latin America. A Group of Seven conference to develop specific plans to implement these proposals was held in Midrand, South Africa, in 1996.

WILSON DIZARD, JR.

See also General Agreement on Tariffs and Trade; Telecommunication Companies

FURTHER READING

Codding, George A., and Anthony M. Rutkowski. *The International Telecommunications Union in a Changing World.* Dedham, Mass., 1982.

Frederick, Howard H. *Global Communications and International Relations.* Belmont, Calif., 1992.

Headrick, Daniel R. *The Invisible Weapon: Telecommunications and International Politics, 1851–1945.* New York, 1991.

Malone, Gifford D. *American Diplomacy in the Information Age.* Lanham, Md., 1991.

National Telecommunications and Information Administration, U.S. Department of Commerce. *Telecommunications in the Age of Information*, NTIA Special Publication 91–26. Washington, D.C., 1991.

Office of Technology Assessment, U.S. Congress. *Global Communications: Opportunities for Trade and Aid.* Washington, D.C., 1995.

Savage, James G. *The Politics of International Telecommunications Regulation.* Boulder, Colo., 1989.

COMMUNISM

The single most central "ism" of the twentieth century in terms of impact on and shaping of U.S. foreign policy.

The term derives from the Latin *communis*, meaning common or belonging to all, as in communal forms of ownership of property. As such it has a long lineage in political and social philosophy, including in Plato's *Republic* (third century B.C.E.), with its design for an enlightened ruling class that owned everything in common and used its position to govern in the interest of all citizens, and in Sir Thomas More's *Utopia* (1516), with its vision of the equal sharing of wealth among all and consequent societal harmony.

Communism as a doctrine was first and fundamentally defined by the German social philosopher Karl Marx and the economist Friedrich Engels in the *Communist Manifesto* (1848) and *Das Kapital* (1867). Marx and Engels took a class-based view of society, focusing on the fundamental and highly unequal division between the wealthy bourgeoisie and the working class proletariat. The communist economic system they envisioned and advocated would be characterized by common public ownership of the means of production, economic production and organization decisions made more through planning than through market mechanisms, and an equal sharing of wealth in a classless society marked by "the dictatorship of the prole-

tariat." Not only did Marx and Engels argue that communism should replace capitalism, but they also viewed this change as historically inevitable, especially in the leading industrial countries of their day such as Great Britain, given what they considered the inherent and ultimately self-undermining contradictions of capitalism.

The first successful communist revolution, though, came in Russia in 1917, ultimately creating the Union of Soviet Socialist Republics (USSR). Vladimir Ilyich Lenin was both leader of the Russian Revolution and modifier-developer of communist doctrine. In societies such as Russia which were not yet ready for the full Marxian socioeconomic transformation, Lenin argued, there needed to be a vanguard that would lead the people toward that stage and that vanguard needed to be endowed with full political power—in other words, a dictatorship of the Communist Party in the name of the proletariat. Lenin also stressed the need for an international movement to provide the organization and direction for communist revolutions elsewhere; in 1919 he established the Comintern, or Communist International, to bring together communist parties everywhere, albeit under tight Soviet control.

The Russian Revolution made communism a major concern for U.S. foreign policy for three principal reasons. First was the immediate issue of the effect on the World War I alliance of the loss of the Eastern Front against Germany when Lenin's government, seeing it as a necessary peace for a ruined nation, signed the Brest-Litovsk treaty with Germany in 1918. Second was the broader concern about Soviet and Leninist influence, both directly and as a model, on the shaping of the postwar order and the challenges they posed to U.S. interests and ideology. Third was the reverberation within the United States and the feared further strengthening of anticapitalist forces such as the Socialist Party. The antiradical U.S. response came in the form of the "Red Scare" and its infamous Palmer Raids and other repressive measures. In the 1950s McCarthyism targeted communists as a dire threat at home.

During the interwar period, a greater degree of uncertainty as to how to deal with communism and the Soviet Union became evident in U.S. foreign policy. Prominent capitalists such as Henry Ford, W. Averell Harriman, and Armand Hammer set out to do business in the Soviet Union, although with mixed experiences and returns. President Franklin D. Roosevelt decided in 1933 to grant diplomatic recognition to the Soviet Union, although relations were kept quite limited until World War II when, as FDR put it, "I can't take communism, but to cross this bridge [the defeat of Nazi Germany] I would hold hands with the Devil."

One of the defining aspects of the Cold War that followed World War II was that while in some aspects it could be seen just as yet another struggle for dominance in the long historical tradition of great power realpolitik, it also had a powerful ideological dimension. Even taking into account intentionally manipulative rhetoric and propaganda, American leaders and the American public were driven by a strong sense of communism as antithetical to their basic views of the organization of society based on private property ownership and the rights of the individual. Whether it had to be this way—whether relations with the Soviet Union had to be so antagonistic for so long, whether all Third World countries and movements labeled as communist fit that label and that characterization, and whether U.S. interests were served by opposing them—are important but separate questions. The analytic fact is that fear of and resistance to communism provided the basis for the central organizing concept of U.S. foreign policy for almost a half century—from the Truman Doctrine, the Marshall Plan and the formation of the North Atlantic Treaty Organization (NATO), through the Korean War and the Vietnam War, into numerous interventions in the Third World, in pursuit of "containment" everywhere.

With the collapse of the Soviet Union and the demise of communism in Eastern Europe and many of the Third World countries where it had prevailed, an era unquestionably came to a close. Ex-communist candidates and parties remain active in some ex-communist countries, including Russia, but with as much emphasis on the "ex-" as on the "communist." The demise of communism did not necessarily mean, however, the triumph of capitalism, as some trumpeted. Indeed other ideologies and political movements already began to emerge, and more, inevitably, will. Which one or ones become the new central organizing concept or concepts for U.S. foreign policy remains to be seen.

BRUCE W. JENTLESON

See also China; Cold War; Containment; Cuba; Korean War; Lenin, Vladimir Ilyich; Marshall Plan; McCarthyism; North Atlantic Treaty Organization; Russia and the Soviet Union; Third World; Truman Doctrine; Vietnam War

FURTHER READING

Avineri, Shlomo. *The Social and Political Thought of Karl Marx.* New York, 1970.
Feuer, Lewis, ed. *Marx and Engels: Basic Writings on Politics and Philosophy.* New York, 1959.
Lenin, V.I. *Imperialism: The Highest Stage of Capitalism.* New York, 1937
Mao Zedong. *Quotations from Chairman Mao.* Beijing, 1972.
Marx, Karl, and Friedrich Engels. *Manifesto of the Communist Party 1848*
———. *Das Kapital.* 1867.
Popper, Karl R. *The Open Society and Its Enemies, Volume II: Hegel and Marx.* 1945.

COMOROS
See Appendix 2

COMPREHENSIVE TEST BAN TREATY

Public calls for an end to nuclear testing date back to the use of "atomic" weapons against Japan to end World War II. Disaffected U.S. nuclear scientists who participated in the Manhattan Project's crash effort to build the bomb took the initial lead in calling for an end to testing, but President Harry S. Truman found their arguments less persuasive than the need to build far more destructive "hydrogen" bombs, like those he presumed would be built by Joseph Stalin. Those who wished to stop testing found a powerful leader in Indian Prime Minister Jawaharlal Nehru. In 1954, Nehru publicly challenged the United States, the Soviet Union, and Great Britain to suspend and ultimately ban nuclear testing as a prelude to disarmament. The nonaligned states quickly followed Nehru's lead, but with little appreciable affect on the test programs of nuclear weapon states. Fallout from atmospheric nuclear tests galvanized public opposition to testing during the 1950s. The National Committee for a Sane Nuclear Policy (SANE) was formed in 1957. Its newspaper advertisements ("No contamination without representation") and political campaigns struck a chord with citizens worried about published reports of the possibility of increased birth defects due to above-ground tests. As U.S. and international protests mounted, President Dwight D. Eisenhower proposed a conference of experts to examine test ban verification issues. The 1958 Conference of Experts from North Atlantic Treaty Organization (NATO) and Warsaw Pact countries made progress in defining the extent of a global array of seismic stations needed to monitor testing. President Eisenhower then proposed U.S., Soviet, and British negotiations in Geneva on a comprehensive test ban treaty (CTBT). At these negotiations, which began in October 1958, Western negotiators proposed that twenty inspections annually be carried out to help verify compliance with a CTBT. Meanwhile, some in the U.S. nuclear laboratories were reassessing the technical feasibility of cheating under a CTBT by muffling or "decoupling" blasts in large underground cavities. Soviet officials viewed these concerns with deep suspicion, questioning the United States' true interest in a CTBT and the significant intrusiveness that would be required to address uneasiness over decoupled explosions. Negotiations foundered in Geneva.

In 1962, the Cuban missile crisis placed the world on the brink of nuclear confrontation. After the crisis, President John F. Kennedy and Soviet leader Nikita Khrushchev exchanged letters discussing, among other topics, the desirability of a CTBT. Khrushchev altered the Kremlin's longstanding opposition to on-site inspections, advising Kennedy of the Politburo's acceptance of two to three inspections annually on Soviet territory. Kennedy responded by proposing eight to ten inspections annually. Kennedy's commencement speech at American University in June 1963, generally advocating more cooperative U.S.-Soviet relations as well as announcing a moratorium on atmospheric testing if the Soviet Union reciprocated, spurred a new round of negotiations. Khrushchev agreed, and tripartite negotiations resumed in Moscow in July.

Verification concerns became the focus of opposition for powerful constituencies in the United States against restraints on nuclear testing. Other arguments against a CTBT were raised by key Pentagon and nuclear laboratory officials, such as the need to test either very high-yield weapons or "clean" weapons, and the desirability of additional atmospheric tests to perfect missile defenses. These arguments resonated with a significant block of Republican and Democratic senators who were opposed to treaties with the "Red" Russians. Kennedy privately indicated his willingness to accept slightly less than eight inspections annually, but Khrushchev had little room for maneuver. Facing severe domestic constraints of his own, and with little likelihood that the details of monitoring and inspection could be satisfactorily resolved, Kennedy opted for a Limited (or Partial) Test Ban Treaty (LTBT). In less than two weeks of intensive negotiations in Moscow, the LTBT was completed on 5 August 1963. The LTBT prohibited nuclear testing in the atmosphere, under water, and in space. No inspections were permitted; the United States, the Soviet Union, and Great Britain agreed to monitor compliance solely by their own national means, such as by seismic stations. To monitor testing in space, the United States launched a new generation of satellites shortly after the treaty was concluded. After requiring a series of "safeguards" to maintain a strong U.S. test program, including the requirement to carry out underground testing, the Senate consented to ratification of the LTBT by a vote of eighty to nineteen. One year after the LTBT entered into force, China joined the nuclear club. France, too, carried out atmospheric tests in Algeria and in the South Pacific. The U.S.-Soviet test competition continued unabated, albeit underground. Meanwhile, test ban negotiations continued in desultory fashion in Geneva, deadlocked over arcane issues of verifying a ban or other limits on underground tests. The ability to distinguish between nuclear tests and earthquakes became a central concern for treaty opponents.

Rather than pursue a comprehensive ban, President Richard M. Nixon and Soviet General Secretary Leonid Brezhnev decided to negotiate the intermediate step of a threshold nuclear test ban treaty (TTBT). The TTBT, banning tests underground with yields in excess of 150 kilotons, was signed on 3 July 1974. Two months earlier, India carried out a "peaceful" nuclear explosion;

two months after the signing of the TTBT, France carried out its last atmospheric nuclear explosion at its Mururoa test site in the South Pacific. On 28 May 1976, President Gerald Ford and Brezhnev signed a companion treaty to the TTBT outlawing individual peaceful nuclear explosions (PNEs) with yields above 150 kilotons. Incoming President Jimmy Carter decided not to ratify the TTBT and the PNET. Instead, he made a renewed effort to complete a comprehensive treaty. Tripartite negotiations made considerable progress, but foundered amid the deterioration of U.S.-Soviet relations and the political weakness of the Carter presidency. Incoming President Ronald Reagan called a halt to CTBT negotiations, while Reagan administration officials compiled long lists of perceived Soviet treaty violations. Some items on these lists had a strong basis in fact; others were highly contentious, including citations of Soviet underground tests in excess of the 150 kiloton threshold signed in 1974. Amid increased clamor for a resumption of test ban negotiations, President Reagan instead authorized negotiations for new verification measures for the TTBT and PNET. In 1987, Soviet leader Mikhail Gorbachev agreed to draft verification protocols for both treaties. The conduct of joint verification experiments at U.S. and Soviet test sites in 1988 symbolized the marked improvement in bilateral relations. On 1 June 1990, both countries signed the verification protocols, to which the Senate and Supreme Soviet subsequently consented without a single dissenting vote. President George Bush continued to oppose negotiations for a CTBT, but his successor, President Bill Clinton, renewed this quest, four decades and over 2,025 global and 1,054 U.S. tests after the first nuclear explosion. Negotiations resumed on the impetus of moratoria authorized by Clinton, Russian President Boris Yeltsin, and French President Francois Mitterrand. The resumption of French testing by Mitterrand's successor, President Jacques Chirac, as well as continued underground testing by the People's Republic of China, provided further impetus to the negotiations. The Conference on Disarmament (CD) completed draft treaty text in August 1996, including a provision requiring all CD states with nuclear facilities to deposit ratifications before the accord's entry into force. The Government of India blocked consensus support for the CTBT, declaring it could not ratify without comments from all nuclear weapon states to accept time-bound nuclear disarmament. The Government of Australia then led an effort to circumvent India's veto, taking the CTBT directly to the UN General Assembly, where it was approved in September 1996 by a vote of 158 to three, with five abstentions. India's opposition leaves the CTBT's formal entry into force in doubt.

MICHAEL KREPON

See also Limited Nuclear Test Ban Treaty; Nuclear Weapons and Strategy; Peace Movements and Societies, 1914–Present

FURTHER READING

Fetter, Steve. *Toward a Comprehensive Test Ban.* Cambridge, Mass., 1988.
Loeb, Benjamin S. "The Limited Test Ban Treaty." In *The Politics of Arms Control Treaty Ratification,* edited by Michael Krepon and Dan Caldwell. New York, 1991.
McBride, James H. *The Test Ban Treaty: Military, Technological, and Political Implications.* Chicago, 1967.
Seaborg, Glenn T. *Kennedy, Khrushchev, and the Test Ban.* Berkeley, Calif., 1981.

COMPUTER COMPANIES

To be competitive in a post-industrial era, countries need strong computer, semiconductor, and software industries. The United States was the early leader in all three areas, but its edge in the computer and semiconductor sectors has slipped, particularly vis-à-vis Japan. The United States remains dominant in software, although Europe is now also strong. As countries work to promote their own computer, semiconductor, and software industries, important foreign policy issues arise.

During the 1980s the focus of the computer industry was on hardware. Three U.S. companies were at the forefront of their market segments. Cray was the innovator for supercomputers. IBM held an overwhelming lead in the mainframe market and entered the new personal computer (PC) business in 1981. Apple developed the personal computer market and introduced the Macintosh, its most stunning success, in 1984. Just over a decade later, Cray succumbed to competition from two Japanese firms, NEC and Fujitsu. IBM was struggling back from the brink of collapse, having lost $70 billion in stock valuation and cut 200,000 jobs after betting unwisely on the future dominance of large mainframe computers. Apple limped along, unable to expand its share of the PC business or to reestablish its earlier luster.

By the 1990s it was clear that the drivers of the computer industry were semiconductors, the guts of the computer, and the software that run computers. Thus, one winner of the computer wars was Intel, which provides the chips that run most personal computers. Although Intel briefly lost its lead to Japanese companies in the late 1980s, it rebounded in the early 1990s to become once again the world's largest manufacturer of microprocessing chips.

Microsoft emerged as the other main winner of the global computer wars between IBM and Apple. Microsoft started with a contract to provide the operating system for IBM PCs, developed Windows to make IBM PCs easier to use, and leveraged its control of this software to become the most powerful company in the computer sector, not just the dominant software firm. Microsoft's market power attracted antitrust probes from the U.S. Department of Justice. Under pressure, Microsoft agreed to modify certain of its competitive practices and withdrew its bid to buy Intuit, but emerged largely unscathed. The government did not want to penalize Microsoft just because it was successful and did not want to undermine its international competitive position.

Foreign policy issues involving computers echo the shift from hardware to software dominance in the sector. In the 1960s and 1970s IBM routed Europe's computer hardware industry and raised alarms that unless the "American challenge" was met, Europe also would lose its high-technology capability in areas such as telecommunications equipment. Japanese firms, because of the difficulty of programming in Japanese, trailed the United States and Europe in software development, but the Japanese share of the world market share in mainframes, microcomputers, and peripherals more than doubled between 1984 and 1990. In addition, the United States was justifiably worried that NEC and Fujitsu, two vertically integrated Japanese makers of supercomputers, would crush the small, independent U.S. entry, Cray, and dominate the field.

The computer industry was a primary preoccupation of America's on-and-off flirtation with industrial policy. The Defense Advanced Research Projects Agency (DARPA, now ARPA after "Defense" was dropped) helped fund and facilitate a wide range of innovation from the creation of the Internet to parallel supercomputing. When Intel and the rest of the U.S. industry seemed to fade in the 1980s, the U.S. foreign policy and defense establishment worried that the United States might grow dependent on imported semiconductors. To resist the Japanese challenge, U.S. government and industry collaborated in a series of projects, SEMATECH, a $500 million joint government-industry effort to restore U.S. leadership in manufacturing technology. The United States also pushed Japan to sign the U.S.-Japan Semiconductor Agreement in 1986 to help open the Japanese semiconductor market.

Since the mid-1980s, greater standardization of equipment and components, the increasing prevalence of "open" systems relative to proprietary systems, and industry downsizing made possible by the increasing power of smaller machines shuffled relative power and increased the importance of international alliances within the computer sector. In addition, the computer and software industry and U.S. foreign policy officials focused more on international intellectual property issues such as software piracy, counterfeiting, and trademark violations. More attention also is being paid to patent and copyright protection of computer software. With the rise of the Internet, the emergence of multimedia, and expectations that information superhighways will girdle the globe, computer executives and government officials are reassessing how to guarantee the security of the data stored within and passed among computers, how to protect their competitiveness and how to promote continuing innovation in an information age.

JONATHAN D. ARONSON

See also International Trade and Commerce; Science and Technology

FURTHER READING

Ferguson, Charles, and Charles Morris. *Computer Wars: How the West Can Win in a Post-IBM World.* New York 1993.

Flamm, Kenneth. *Targeting the Computer: Government Support and International Competition.* Washington, D.C., 1987.

Negroponte, Nicholas. *Being Digital.* New York, N.Y., 1995.

CONANT, JAMES BRYANT

(*b.* 26 March 1893; *d.* 11 February 1978)

Scientist and government official who helped develop the atomic bomb during World War II and promoted close U.S.-German relations after the war. Born in Dorchester, Massachusetts, Conant earned his Ph.D degree from Harvard University (1916). During World War I, he joined the Chemical Warfare Service, where he led the Organic Research Unit, earning a commendation for overseeing the production of mustard gas and devising an arsenic-based gas. After the war Conant taught chemistry at Harvard until becoming its president in 1933. His major task during the 1930s was dodging the conflicts between right- and left-wing groups both on campus and in national politics. A registered Republican, he frequently disagreed with President Franklin D. Roosevelt's domestic program but opposed Republicans whose isolationist perspectives led to criticism of Roosevelt's favoritism toward Great Britain and France. After Germany invaded Poland in September 1939, Conant joined such Republicans as Henry L. Stimson in advocating aid to the democracies against the Nazis. Conant joined interventionist groups, advocated U.S. preparedness, and worked with the scientist Vannevar Bush to enlist scientists in war preparations through the National Defense Research Committee. Following Japan's attack on Pearl Harbor, Bush became head of the Office of Scientific Research and Development and appointed Conant as his deputy in charge of the atomic bomb project.

During World War II Conant believed that the "battlefield is no place to question the doctrine that the end justifies the means" for winning the war. Thus, in June 1945, based on information from Secretary of War Stimson that from 500,000 to one million U.S. soldiers would die in an invasion of Japan, Conant proposed targeting the atomic bomb against a Japanese war plant employing many workers with nearby homes as the best means to both save American lives and shock Japanese leaders into an immediate surrender. Stimson's Interim Committee approved, and President Harry S. Truman based his targeting of Hiroshima on this suggestion.

Following World War II Conant returned to Harvard as president and served on the General Advisory Council of the Atomic Energy Commission. With Cold War tensions growing, Conant became a prominent educator and advocate of moderate ways to counteract communism without denying the nation's heritage of civil liberties and democracy. His 1948 book, *Education in a Divided World*, emphasized the public education system's role in strengthening the nation's political, social, and economic structure, thereby nurturing democratic values and demonstrating democracy's superiority over communism. Conant opposed preventive war, agreed with physicist Robert Oppenheimer that the hydrogen bomb was unnecessary because fission weapons were sufficient to defend America, and favored developing tactical nuclear weapons to limit nuclear destruction.

In 1950 the Korean War significantly altered Conant's views because, like others, he perceived North Korea's attack on South Korea as Soviet aggression. Fearing a Soviet attack on Western Europe, Conant joined Tracy S. Voorhees in organizing the Committee on the Present Danger to promote the stationing of up to one million U.S. troops in Europe under the North Atlantic Treaty Organization (NATO). The proposal suited Truman's plans to augment NATO and name Dwight D. Eisenhower as NATO commander. Conant chaired this citizens' lobby from 1950 to 1952. Having been consulted about the classified National Security Council Paper Number 68 (NSC-68), which called for a massive U.S. military buildup to counteract communist expansion around the world, Conant followed its prescription for committee action. During the Great Debate of 1951, when "isolationist" Republicans tried to prevent Truman from "permanently" stationing U.S. troops in Europe under NATO, Conant's group opposed the isolationist and "Asia first" proposals of Senator Robert A. Taft and many Senate Republicans who backed General Douglas MacArthur's program to roll back communists by liberating North Korea and mainland China. Conant's work also took him to Europe in 1951, where he informed prominent scientific, educational, and political leaders that the Taft-MacArthur group did not represent U.S. policy.

Because of his committee activities and eminence as a national figure—*Newsweek* magazine dubbed him "U.S. Education's No. 1 Man"—few were surprised when President Dwight D. Eisenhower named Conant to replace John J. McCloy as U.S. high commissioner to Germany

(1953–1955). When the Federal Republic of Germany became sovereign in 1955, Conant became ambassador and served until February 1957. These four years were critical in U.S.-German relations because U.S. policy wanted the "new Germany" to become a democratic, reliable, and rearmed NATO partner against communism. Despite problems with Chancellor Konrad Adenauer and Germany's slowness in adopting U.S. rearmament timetables, Conant engaged in extensive public relations activity in Germany and the United States to establish trust between the two nations.

Conant's final years of public service principally focused on fostering close U.S.-German relations and on improving public schooling for all American children. Funded by the Carnegie Foundation, he conducted surveys of U.S. high schools and recommended instructional improvement to encourage a well-rounded education for students of all backgrounds.

LESTER H. BRUNE

See also Atomic Energy Commission; Cold War; Committee on the Present Danger; Germany; Hiroshima and Nagaski Bombings of 1945; MacArthur, Douglas; North Atlantic Treaty Organization; NSC-68; Nuclear Weapons and Strategy; Stimson, Henry Lewis; Taft, Robert A.; Truman, Harry S.; World War II

FURTHER READING
Conant, James B. *My Several Lives: Memoirs of a Social Inventor.* New York, 1970.
Hershberg, James. *James B. Conant: Harvard to Hiroshima and the Making of the Nuclear Age.* New York, 1993.

CONFEDERATE STATES OF AMERICA

The eleven slaveholding states that seceded from the United States of America between December 1860 and May 1861. The ensuing civil war between the Confederacy and the Union was a diplomatic as well as military struggle. The Confederacy, through diplomatic missions and propaganda, sought recognition from the European powers as well as aid in sustaining the trade necessary for a war economy, and diplomatic assistance in bringing pressure on the North. The Union tried, with considerable success, to thwart Confederate objectives.

King Cotton Diplomacy

In February 1861 the first states that seceded framed a constitution, established a provisional government, elected Jefferson Davis of Mississippi president, and approved the appointment of Robert Toombs of Georgia as secretary of state. Toombs served only until 24 July, when Robert M. T. Hunter of Virginia replaced him. Hunter served until 17 March 1862, and was replaced by Judah P.

Benjamin of Louisiana, who remained in office until the Confederacy collapsed in April 1865.

Confederate foreign policy rested on the notion that cotton was "king," that is, that the demand in industrial Great Britain and France for southern cotton guaranteed the support and recognition of the independence of the Confederacy by those nations. Believing that their cause was just, that Europe would welcome the independence of the southern states for economic and strategic reasons (to balance the power of the North), and that the European economy would collapse without southern cotton, the Confederate government was optimistic at first. Confederate officials merely explained to European officials the rationale and legitimacy of secession, argued that the Confederacy was a de facto government, and affirmed a determination to preserve its independence.

The Confederate diplomatic program began in February 1861, when the Confederate Congress sent diplomatic missions to Washington and to Europe. On 25 February, Davis appointed A. B. Roman, Martin J. Crawford, and John Forsyth to negotiate the evacuation of southern forts and arsenals and generally to secure a peaceful and friendly separation from the U.S. government. Two days later Davis chose William Lowndes Yancey, Pierre A. Rost, and Ambrose Dudley Mann to travel to Europe to secure de jure recognition of the Confederacy and to conclude treaties of amity and commerce.

The Confederate mission to Washington failed. President Abraham Lincoln's secretary of state, William H. Seward, refused to meet with Roman, Crawford, and Forsyth, and Lincoln refused to acknowledge the legitimacy of the Confederacy. Seward ultimately communicated with the Confederate commissioners through a third party, and although Seward assured them that the Union would not initiate hostilities, the commissioners remained unconvinced. On 8 April Crawford warned Davis that despite Seward's pledges, the Lincoln cabinet was committed to war, and within a few days the commissioners ended their mission and returned home. War began with the South's attack on Fort Sumter on 12 April 1861.

The European mission did somewhat better. Secretary of State Toombs instructed Yancey, Rost, and Mann to explain to the British government that Southern secession was caused by Northern exploitation and was not an act of rebellion but the exercise of a right protected by the U.S. Constitution. He advised the commissioners to avoid the slave question and to emphasize the economic benefits to Great Britain of an independent Confederacy. Toombs authorized the commissioners to negotiate a treaty of amity and commerce with Great Britain and then repeat the process in France, Russia, and Belgium. Davis and Toombs had no plans to establish permanent missions in any of these nations.

The Confederate commissioners arrived in London in April and met with British Foreign Secretary Lord John Russell. Russell was not unsympathetic toward the Southern cause and, believing Southern independence a foregone conclusion, doubted that any attempt by the North to coerce the South to return to the Union would fail. Well before the commissioners had arrived, however, Russell committed Great Britain to strict neutrality in the American crisis. Following advice from the British attorney general, Russell advised Queen Victoria to issue a proclamation of neutrality and to grant the Confederacy belligerent rights, which she did on 14 May. The British foreign secretary was prepared to go no further and rejected the commissioners' request for immediate recognition of Confederate independence.

The Southern commissioners moved on to Paris, where they soon learned that even though Napoleon III was sympathetic to the Confederacy, he would not move beyond recognition of Southern belligerency without British concurrence. Following an informal interview with Foreign Minister Edouard Thouvenel, the commissioners concluded that neither Great Britain nor France would grant recognition until they required new supplies of southern cotton and the Confederacy had scored significant military victories. Neither country would act until it was clearly to its advantage. Yancey also suspected that Napoleon was far more interested in European affairs and plans for an Anglo–Spanish–French intervention in Mexico. Failure to secure recognition from either Great Britain or France led the commissioners to decide not to open discussions in Russia and Belgium. They returned to England to wait for a propitious moment for a second appeal and to maintain support from Confederate sympathizers in Parliament.

Confederate Propaganda

With diplomacy at a standstill, Davis and Hunter, Toombs's successor, and the Confederate commissioners turned their attention to winning the support of the middle class and liberal community in Great Britain and France. The Confederates were initially optimistic that British partiality toward the South would win them full support with little effort on their part. They believed that the landed aristocracy already identified with southern planters and that the wealthy commercial and industrial classes depended on southern cotton for their prosperity, profited from the southern market, and detested their rivals in the North. They dismissed the British working class as having little political power.

Confederate officials instituted an official propaganda campaign in November 1861, when Hunter sent Henry Hotze, a Swiss-born journalist, to London with modest funds (later generously increased by Hunter's successor) and instructions to publicize the Confederate cause.

Hotze initially contributed articles to sympathetic British journals, but in May 1862 he began publishing a weekly journal, *The Index*, which quickly became the standard source of information about the Confederacy in Europe. To attract liberal support, he emphasized Lincoln's despotism and Confederate determination to preserve its independence. Edwin de Leon, a highly regarded journalist, was far less successful in France, where the people were largely uninterested in U.S. affairs and the government was already sympathetic to the southern cause. Following de Leon's failure, Hotze established a close connection with a major telegraphic agency that provided American news to French journals.

The Confederate commissioners badly misjudged British opinion. There is no question that the Confederacy drew support from all classes. Even some liberals sympathized with Southerners who sought to free themselves from control of a government they believed had exploited them. More important, however, were British perceptions of the role of slavery in the U.S. conflict. Great Britain had long led an international crusade against the slave trade and slavery, and, despite Confederate attempts to dismiss the protection of slavery as central to the southern cause and Lincoln's clear statement that he had no intention of abolishing slavery in the South, the British never lost sight of the issue. British abolitionists and partisans of the North succeeded in keeping the question alive and dominant in the British press.

The same sentiments that shaped public attitudes existed in the British cabinet, although there never were vigorous supporters of Southern independence. Lord Palmerston, the prime minister, was inclined against compromising British antislavery activities and had no interest in intensifying cabinet divisions. Before he would actively support the Confederacy, he needed clear and compelling economic or strategic reasons along with assurance that the Union would not take exception. Lord Palmerston, Russell, and the rest of the cabinet pointedly snubbed the Confederate commissioners, whose sole political influence rested with a few conservative spokesmen in Parliament and a few journalists who were generally more critical of the North than supportive of the South. In addition, the belief that the Union could never subdue the Confederacy implied that Great Britain would need to deal with two American nations when the war ended. It made no sense to antagonize the North by hastening the inevitable.

The *Trent* Affair

The failure of Confederate diplomatic agents in London and Paris to make progress during the summer of 1861 caused President Davis to revise his European strategy. Russell appeared unimpressed by the Confederate success at the Battle of Bull Run in mid-July 1861 and notified the commissioners that he would no longer meet with them—a decision made partly in response to the demands of Seward and the Union minister to Great Britain, Charles Francis Adams. Mann and Rost prepared to wait until pressure for cotton forced Great Britain to change its policy. Yancey grew disheartened and submitted his resignation, which Davis accepted in September. Davis, however, had already decided that it was necessary for the Confederacy to establish permanent missions in Great Britain, France, Belgium, and Spain. He chose James Murray Mason of Virginia for Great Britain and John Slidell of Louisiana for France. Secretary of State Hunter ordered Mann to take up residence in Brussels and Rost to go to Madrid.

The departure of Mason and Slidell for Europe led to the first major crisis in Anglo-American relations. The two Confederate agents ran the blockade from Charleston, South Carolina, to Nassau in the Bahamas on 12 October and continued on to Cuba. On 7 November, they boarded the *Trent*, a British mail packet bound for Saint Thomas. On the following day, Captain Charles Wilkes, aboard the USS *San Jacinto*, stopped and boarded the *Trent* and seized Mason and Slidell. Wilkes carried the prisoners to Fort Monroe, Virginia, and then to Boston, where they were placed under arrest. Wilkes's seizure was irregular and smacked of impressment. The British claimed that he had violated international law, demanded an apology from the United States, and insisted upon the immediate release of the two Confederate diplomats. Confederates were certain that Lincoln would never acquiesce to British demands. Northerners regarded Wilkes as a hero and still smarted from the "premature" British recognition of Confederate belligerency, Russell's early meeting with the Confederate commissioners, and the British refusal to accept secession as rebellion. Much to the surprise and dismay of the Confederates, on 25 December, Seward informed the British that Wilkes had acted without orders, expressed gratitude that Great Britain had finally adopted the U.S. position on impressment, and thanked Great Britain for its neutrality. Seward also announced that Mason and Slidell would be released and allowed to proceed to Europe. Southern hopes for British support now rested solely upon British need for southern cotton.

Cotton Famine and Intervention Crisis

In the spring and summer of 1862, the long-awaited "cotton famine" finally arrived. British stockpiles of cotton had dwindled because of the Union blockade and especially the voluntary decision by southerners to withhold cotton shipments to Europe. Without fresh supplies of cotton fiber, the massive British cotton textile industry, which employed approximately 900,000 workers and provided the British with its most important single export,

appeared to be in jeopardy. As distress in the cotton districts increased, so too did calls for British intervention in the Civil War among Confederate sympathizers and propagandists. The British cabinet wavered but refused to change its policy.

Although the cotton famine grew serious, it did not endanger the British economy or cause Great Britain to alter its policy toward the United States. At the beginning of the Civil War, British warehouses were glutted with American cotton, the result of two bumper crops in 1859 and 1860. When the war began British importers thus had an oversupply of cotton on hand. The blockade and embargo caused the value of that raw cotton and both old and newly manufactured cotton to rise dramatically. Although workers suffered reduced hours and massive layoffs, which severely strained the British philanthropic and welfare system, many powerful merchants and manufacturers enriched themselves. Soaring world prices for raw cotton, in fact, led British merchants to export cotton to Europe during the crisis at home. Planters and exporters of cotton in Egypt, India, and elsewhere prospered as never before, and some welcomed the possibility of breaking the American monopoly. Further, the soaring price of cotton goods proved a boon to woolen textile manufacturing, and the American conflict increased demand for war materials exported principally to the North. Except for the county of Lancashire and its environs, where distress hit the hardest, the British economy continued to prosper. In addition, beginning in 1862, British shipowners began to benefit when Confederate commerce raiders drove U.S. flag merchant ships from the seas.

By the fall of 1862, however, the distress in Lancashire, combined with the perception of a military stalemate in America, led the British cabinet to consider intervening in the war through a formal proposal of mediation. Working closely with France, Russell won the support of William E. Gladstone, chancellor of the exchequer, and the agreement of Palmerston to bring the issue formally to the cabinet. After weeks of private debate and considerable press speculation, Palmerston retreated. Following receipt of news of the apparently indecisive Battle of Antietam and hearing the effective arguments of Secretary of War George Cornwall Lewis, Palmerston decided, over the strenuous objections of Russell and Gladstone, that Great Britain should continue its policy of watchful waiting. Napoleon III, less constrained by his advisers and eager to demonstrate his support for beleaguered cotton manufacturers, decided to propose a six-month armistice to the Union and Confederacy if Great Britain and Russia would agree. Russia declined the French invitation immediately. On 13 November, the British cabinet also declined to intervene, and the French effort collapsed. The mediation crisis of 1862 marked the closest the Confederacy came to securing effective official European support.

Commerce Raiders and Ironclads

Whereas Confederate diplomacy in Europe ended in utter failure, the Confederate naval effort in Europe had limited but significant success. British and French recognition of Southern belligerent rights allowed Confederate agents to purchase war materials, contract for commerce raiders, and obtain loans in these nations. Accordingly, in May 1861, Confederate Secretary of the Navy Stephen Mallory sent James Dunwoody Bulloch, a retired naval officer, and Lieutenant James H. North to Great Britain with orders to purchase or build six steam-driven commerce raiders and two ironclads. British neutrality laws allowed belligerents to build or purchase, but not arm or equip, naval vessels in Great Britain. By August Bulloch had contracted for the construction of two commerce raiders, the *Oreto* (later renamed the *Florida*), which left Great Britain in March 1862 and received armaments in Nassau, and *No. 290*, which departed on 29 July. The latter, renamed the *Alabama*, was outfitted off the Azores and received a British crew. Under the command of Raphael Semmes, the *Alabama* became the most successful Confederate commerce raider. These ships threatened to destroy the Northern blockade of southern ports.

Confederate satisfaction with its triumphs was short-lived. Union efforts to prevent the departures of the *Florida* and *Alabama* had been unsuccessful, but by amassing evidence that these and other vessels were Confederate ships intended for military action against U.S. merchants and protesting British policy, Russell agreed to prevent the construction and departure of any other Confederate commerce raiders. On 5 April 1863, Russell ordered the Confederate-owned *Alexandria* seized, solely on the basis that it was apparently intended for Confederate service. Perhaps more important, in the following September, Russell ordered the seizure of two ironclad rams that Bulloch was having built by Laird Brothers. A third ironclad contracted by Lieutenant North was never completed.

By 1863 Slidell and Confederate sympathizers in Europe had convinced themselves that the best hope of the Confederacy lay with France rather than with Great Britain. Following the collapse of the Anglo-French mediation effort in 1862, Napoleon unilaterally proposed mediation to the Americans in the following January. That same month, Slidell negotiated a loan of $14.5 million with the French firm of Émile Erlanger and Company, based on the sale of cotton bonds. Although the Confederacy realized only $8.5 million from the sale of the bonds, the proceeds allowed Confederate agents to scour Europe for war supplies. At Bulloch's request, Mallory transferred him to France, and in April and June 1863, he

and Slidell contracted for four commerce raiders and two ironclad rams. Although Napoleon III was sympathetic and friendly to the Confederates and their cause, he also retreated when Union officials presented him with extensive evidence of the character and purposes of the ships. One French-built ironclad did eventually reach the United States, but only after the war ended.

The year 1863 was clearly the turning point in Confederate diplomacy. Lincoln's Emancipation Proclamation of 1 January 1863 made clear that a Union victory would mean the end of slavery in the United States. Although Europeans initially regarded the Emancipation Proclamation as an act of desperation meant to incite servile insurrection and race war, they quickly realized that any support for the Confederacy would mean support for American slavery. In addition, while southerners had argued with some effectiveness that the Union could not defeat the Confederacy militarily, the great Union victories at Gettysburg and Vicksburg in July 1863 began to make conquest of the Confederacy considerably more plausible. As Generals Ulysses S. Grant and William T. Sherman applied relentless pressure on southern forces, Europeans came to regard a total Union victory as inevitable. It thus became increasingly important not to antagonize the Union needlessly through acts sympathetic to the South.

A final desperate measure of the Confederate government in its search for European recognition and aid occurred in November and December 1864. On 7 November, Jefferson Davis proposed that the Confederate government purchase 40,000 slaves for military service as noncombatants and emancipate them at the end of their service. While debate raged at home over the proposal, Davis and Benjamin sent Duncan F. Kenner of Louisiana on a secret mission to Europe at the end of December to offer emancipation in exchange for recognition. Kenner first went to Paris, where Napoleon rejected the offer. He would not act without concurrent British assent. Kenner then traveled to London, where Palmerston informed him through an intermediary that Great Britain had no intention of recognizing the Confederacy under any circumstances. Thus ended Confederate diplomacy in Europe.

Mexico

The only nation outside Europe with which the Confederate government attempted to open relations was Mexico. On 17 May 1861 Davis appointed John T. Pickett, a former Cuban filibusterer and U.S. consul at Veracruz, as commissioner to Mexico. Toombs instructed Pickett to propose recognition and negotiation of a treaty of amity and commerce only if Mexican agreement seemed likely. Unlike the instructions Toombs drew up for the commissioners in Europe, these instructions explicitly commented on the similarity of the Confederate and Mexican agrarian economies and the similarity of slavery and peonage in the two nations.

Pickett won little sympathy from the government of Benito Juárez in Mexico City and bungled his mission badly. Mexican hostility toward slavery and misgivings about future southern expansionism were deeply ingrained and fostered by the U.S. minister, Thomas Corwin, who had opened negotiations with Juárez for an $11 million loan from the United States. Pickett's conduct in Mexico City was blustering, threatening, and insulting. Contemptuous of Mexicans, he filled his private correspondence with demeaning and racist comments. In August 1861 Pickett attempted to entice Mexican officials into supporting the Confederacy with a transparent scheme that offered to return some of the territories lost after the Mexican War. In November, after provoking a fight with a Union sympathizer, for which Mexican authorities imprisoned him as a common criminal, Pickett left Mexico in disgrace. When Davis and his cabinet learned of Pickett's diplomacy, they became outraged and repudiated him.

Other Confederate agents sent to Mexico fared considerably better. A number of them secured valuable commercial agreements with independent-minded Mexican governors across the border. The most important of these agents was Juan A. Quintero, a Confederate of Cuban birth, who developed an especially friendly relationship with Santiago Vidaurri, the governor of Nuevo León and Coahuila. Secretary of State Hunter instructed Quintero not only to cultivate Vidaurri and block attempts by union troops to cross Mexican territory, but also to resist any offers of alliance or annexation from the Mexican leader. The Confederate Congress would likely reject annexation, and other Mexican governors and Juárez would deeply resent the intrigue. Despite Pickett's blundering and Confederate relations with Mexican authorities in the border states, Juárez maintained a neutral policy, even after the collapse of the loan negotiations with Corwin. In 1861 Juárez endured intervention by Great Britain, France, and Spain to force payments of debts owed their citizens, and after Great Britain and Spain withdrew in April 1862, Juárez faced an aggressive, imperialistic French army that had the support of Juárez's enemies in Mexico City. In 1863 the French army occupied Mexico City and Juárez fled with his government to San Luis Potosí, from which he led guerrilla resistance against the French, their Conservative party allies, and the French-installed Emperor Maximilian. Juárez had no reason to antagonize the Confederates.

Albert Pike completed another Confederate diplomatic initiative that had some success. On 12 August 1861 Pike completed several treaties with Indian nations living in the Indian territory of present-day Oklahoma. When the Confederacy promised the Indians that it would pro-tect them from encroachment by the United States, the Indians allied with Confederate forces. They fought with the Confederates in Missouri in March 1862 and in several other battles early in the war but withdrew their support with the waning of Confederate military fortunes. The final Confederate diplomatic effort at home occurred in February 1865. At Davis's request, Francis P. Blair, Sr., arranged a peace conference on 3 February to be held aboard a steamboat at Hampton Roads, Virginia. Lincoln and Seward met with Confederate Vice President Alexander H. Stephens, former Confederate Secretary of State Hunter, and former U.S. Supreme Court Justice and Confederate Assistant Secretary of War John A. Campbell. Davis instructed the Confederate negotiators to demand only independence; Lincoln's sole demand was reunion. Because neither side would retreat, the conference failed. Within months virtually all elements of the Confederate army had surrendered to Union forces and Jefferson Davis had been captured and imprisoned.

Confederate diplomacy was marked by a number of inconsistencies and misjudgments. Confederate officials at first expected that sentiment and economic necessities would overcome ideology and international realities. They calculated that time was on the side of the agrarian South rather than the industrial North, and they expected that a defensive military strategy would convince Europe of the Confederacy's invincibility. The failure of the government of Jefferson Davis to marshall a clear, realistic, and determined foreign program at the very beginning of the struggle robbed the Confederacy of any effective support from abroad. Even had the Confederacy constructed a more effective diplomacy, however superb Union diplomacy, international rivalries, and the world economy still would have worked against southern success. The Confederate cause was lost from the beginning.

KINLEY J. BRAUER

See also Adams, Charles Francis; Alabama Claims; American Civil War; Benjamin, Judah Philip; Davis, Jefferson; France; Great Britain; Impressment; Juárez, Benito Pablo; Lincoln, Abraham; Mexico; Propaganda; Slave Trade and Slavery; Slidell, John; Trent Affair; Wilkes, Charles

FURTHER READING

Blumenthal, Henry. "Confederate Diplomacy: Popular Notions and International Realities." *Journal of Southern History* 32 (1966): 151–171.

Brauer, Kinley J. "British Mediation and the American Civil War: A Reconsideration." *Journal of Southern History* 38 (February 1972): 49-64

Crook, D. P. *The North, the South, and the Powers, 1861–1865.* New York, 1974.

Graebner, Norman A. "Northern Diplomacy and European Neutrality." In David Donald, ed. *Why the North Won the Civil War.* Baton Rouge, La., 1960.

Ferris, Norman B. *The Trent Affair: A Diplomatic Crisis.* Knoxville, Tenn., 1977.

Jones, Howard. *Union in Peril: The Crisis over British Intervention in the Civil War.* Chapel Hill, N.C., 1992.

Meade, Robert D. *Jonah P. Benjamin, Confederate Statesman.* New York, 1943.

Merli, Frank. *Great Britain and the Confederate Navy, 1861-1865.* Bloomington, Ind., 1970.

Owsley, Frank Lawrence. *King Cotton Diplomacy: Foreign Relations of the Confederate States of America,* 2nd ed. Chicago, 1959.

Spencer, Warren F. *The Confederate Navy in Europe.* Birmingham, Ala., 1983.

Warren, Gordon H. *Fountain of Discontent: The Trent Affair and Freedom of the Seas.* Boston, 1981.

CONGO

For many years the hub of French Equatorial Africa, the Congo—a west central African republic bordered by Gabon, Cameroon, the Central African Republic, Zaire, and the Atlantic Ocean—gained its independence from France in August 1960. Its first President, Abbe Fulbert Youlou, a defrocked Catholic priest who had served as Prime Minister under a French governor, soon found that the limitations of parliamentary government were too restrictive for his taste.

In 1961, constitutional revisions strengthened Youlou's hand, but when he proposed a one-party state in 1963, mass demonstrations took place and he was replaced by Alphonse Massamba-Debat, who had the support of labor leaders. Massamba's regime moved quickly to the left, becoming by 1964 a one-party Marxist state. This leftward movement coincided with a drastic economic slump, as French merchants were scared off. The Congo then turned to the Soviet Union, proclaiming the People's Republic of the Congo. Farms and businesses were nationalized and Bulgarian pig farmers replaced the French colonialists. Photos of Karl Marx, Vladimir Lenin, and Cuban President Fidel Castro adorned the walls of the People's Palace, and emissaries from communist-bloc countries arrived in droves.

After several abortive coups and struggles between the army and labor groups, Marion N'Gouabi, an army major and physics professor, abruptly ended Massamba's term of office with a coup in August 1968. N'Gouabi quickly consolidated his power, becoming President on 31 December 1968. Congo moved even further to the left, as N'Gouabi changed the name of the National Revolutionary Movement to the PCT (Congolese Labor Party). N'Gouabi nursed the "father of his country" image, while depending almost wholly on the Soviets for economic support. On 16 March 1977, President N'Gouabi was assassinated in a bloody coup. Several suspects were executed, but conventional wisdom at the time was that army officers, led by Colonel Denis Sassou-Nguesso, were involved.

An interim government under Colonel, later General, Joachim Yhomby-Opango held power for two years until he was accused of corruption and replaced by Colonel Sassou. As Sassou began to face the problems of economic disruption and diminishing Soviet aid, he slowly turned toward the West. With the Congo's oil resources being the sole backing of the economy and in the hands of Western producers, Sassou began to see the need for a market economy. With support and encouragement from Western diplomats and businessmen, he swallowed the Marxist idealogy and asked the World Bank and the International Monetary Fund for help. The Congolese were then obliged to tighten their belts in a structural adjustment program and to begin the sensitive process of privatization and dismantlement of their swollen bureaucracy and state enterprises.

Sassou was Chairman of the Organization of African Unity (OAU) in 1986 and consequently made the ritual trip to the UN. He was received by Vice President George Bush and Secretary of State George Schultz, but at the last minute White House officials denied his access to President Ronald Reagan. This removed some of the gloss from the trip and briefly set back the Congolese turn to the West. Sassou, not unlike the Chinese, thought he could modernize the economy without political liberalization. In 1991, Sassou called a national conference to review the process of democratization and free elections. At a crucial moment when he thought he could manipulate this conference, the Army withdrew its support for him and the opposition gained the day. Presidential elections finally took place in August 1992, when Sassou had to concede defeat to Pascal Lissouba, who was inaugurated on 31 August 1992.

The Congo's advance toward democracy continued on a bumpy road. Whole series of elections for different levels of offices took place, many leading to factional and ethnic violence. Lissouba's first administration was toppled by a motion of censure in the newly created parliament, which caused Lissouba to dissolve the National Assembly. Finally a peace accord was signed between the government and the opposition on 30 January 1994, restoring calm to the capital. Two prominent opposition leaders, Bernard Kolelas and Jean-Pierre Thystere-Tchicaya, were installed as Mayors of Brazzaville, the capital, and Pointe Noire, thus creating a tenuous balance between them and the Lissouba regime.

During the riots of 1993–1994, private militias fought each other, with the army and security police losing control. There were many human rights abuses, as police continued to use brutal measures against detainees and the courts were snowed under by a tremendous backlog. Nevertheless, by mid-1995 the situation seemed improved, as the government set up a Special Interpellation Group (GSIP) to dampen ethnic-inspired violence.

The United States greeted Congo's accession to independence in 1960 with enthusiasm, setting up a full embassy, United States Information Service (USIS), and Agency for International Development (AID) programs. In 1963, after several American diplomats had been jailed and the leftist propaganda against the United States became too loud to ignore, Washington decided to close the embassy to avoid further incidents. During the next fifteen years the Congolese occasionally made friendly gestures, but it was not until 1977 that the United States decided the time had come to reopen relations. A new ambassador, William Swing, arrived in 1980, after which relations began to warm slowly, although antipathy toward the U.S. government by the Soviets and their Congolese followers continued for some time. The warming trend continued under Ambassadors Brown, Lukens, Shurtleff, Phillips and Ramsey.

The Congolese economy depends in very large part on the petroleum sector. Large offshore oil fields have been exploited by the French company Elf, which works closely with its junior partner from Italy, Agip. Over the past dozen years Amoco, Conoco, Chevron and other companies have tried to break into the French monopoly but without great success. In 1995, the only U.S. company present was Occidental with about 10 percent of the market. Using these petroleum assets, the Congo has mortgaged itself into the future, as oil revenues are needed to repay the heavy debts.

The Congo also has large timber resources and diamonds, but these are mostly in the hands of French monopolies. On the rare occasions when U.S. investors have shown interest in the country, bureaucratic snags have inevitably appeared, many caused by French commercial interests. In the days of the Cold War, the French were happy to have U.S. support vis-à-vis the heavy Soviet presence. Since then and with the total withdrawal of Soviet bloc aid, the French have reverted to a *"chasse gardée"* approach, where when Paris did not oppose U.S. investment, it was invariably sabotaged on the local level. Furthermore, U.S. investors also have been discouraged by an expensive and strike-prone labor force.

Ever since the independence of the Congo and neighboring Zaire in 1960, there has been a seesaw effect between the two. U.S. interests in Zaire have far overshadowed those in the Congo, but as the situation in Zaire grew more untenable in the 1990s, it became all the more important to use the U.S. Embassy in Brazzaville as eyes and ears to follow what was happening across the Congo River. Except for the 1963-1977 period when the Brazzaville embassy was closed and for a few years in the 1980s, the Congo has been more stable than Zaire. For that reason alone the Congo has continued to play a vital role in the preservation of U.S. strategic interests.

ALAN W. LUKENS

See also Africa; Zaire

FURTHER READING

Badien, Seydu. *Congo*. Paris, France, 1983.

CONGO CRISIS
(1960–1962)

Period of instability, civil war, and foreign and United Nations intervention that occurred during the precipitous termination of the colonial status of the Belgian Congo (now Zaire). The United States initially hoped that Belgium would continue as a stabilizing force but that hope faded fast. The administrations of Presidents Dwight D. Eisenhower and John F. Kennedy moved, through open diplomacy and covertly through the Central Intelligence Agency (CIA), to shape events in the vast central African country in order to block the Soviet Union and to maintain access to copper, cobalt, and other strategic minerals. Independence came to the Congo in June 1960. The United States, after some indecision, encouraged covert operations to overthrow the regime of Patrice Lumumba's Mouvement National Congolais (MNC), believing that it had come under Soviet control. The CIA plotted to kill Lumumba, but he was assassinated in January 1961 by political rivals. The United States also opposed a secessionist attempt by Belgium-backed rebels and mercenaries in mineral-rich Katanga (now Shaba) province, led by Moise Tshombe and supported by the powerful Belgian mining concern Union Minière du Haut Katanga. Later, in July 1960 the United States supported UN military intervention (the United Nations Operation in the Congo, or ONUC) to prevent secession and maintain the Congo's territorial integrity. ONUC was strongly endorsed by UN Secretary-General Dag Hammarskjöld and backed by the Kennedy administration but was criticized by the Soviet Union. Hammarskjöld died in a still-mysterious plane crash in the Congo in 1961.

Throughout 1961 the conflict intensified as the UN peacekeeping force battled the secessionists. With Belgian influence diminished, the United States became the primary external power engaged in the conflict. Beginning in February 1961, the Kennedy administration helped vest sufficient military capability in the UN mission to defeat the secessionists; the insurrection collapsed in early 1963. The influence of the United States was central in the Congo crisis. By backing the UN's military intervention, the United States achieved its objectives: preventing Soviet influence in Africa, ensuring the territorial integrity of the country, and eventually earning a reliable client nation, albeit under the autocratic and corrupt President Mobutu Sese Seko, throughout the Cold War, thereby also preserving access to the country's strategic mineral wealth.

Timothy D. Sisk

See also Belgium; Hammarskjöld, Dag Hjalmar Agne Carl; Kennedy, John Fitzgerald; Zaire

FURTHER READING

Gibbs, Richard David N. *The Political Economy of Third World Intervention: Mines, Money, and U.S. Policy in the Congo Crisis.* Chicago, 1991.

Kalb, Madeleine G. *The Congo Cables: The Cold War in Africa from Eisenhower to Kennedy.* New York, 1982.

Weissman, Stephen R. *American Foreign Policy in the Congo, 1960–1964.* Ithaca, N.Y., 1974.

CONGRESS

The role Congress plays in the shaping of U.S. foreign policy results from the constitutional structure among the three branches of the American system established at the founding of the nation and from the evolution of the relationship among those branches over the history of the Republic. Its role also emanates from institutional mechanisms available to the Congress, ranging from passing legislation to establishing reporting requirements for the executive branch, and from the actions of individual members of Congress, ranging from writing to the executive on policy issues to filing lawsuits against particular executive actions. Finally, the role is increasingly shaped by the anticipated reaction between the executive and legislative branches and by the partisan or ideological makeup of key congressional and White House players.

Under the Articles of Confederation, Congress was primarily responsible for the conduct of foreign policy through its Committee for Foreign Affairs, originally established by the Continental Congress in 1777. During these initial years of the nation, however, the Congress did not fare very well in conducting foreign affairs. Its inability to conduct effective foreign trade policy, maintain clear boundaries, and secure U.S. rights with Great Britain and Spain contributed to the call for a revision of the Articles of Confederation and for different arrangements to manage foreign policy in the young Republic.

The writing of the Constitution in 1787 did not resolve this problem, and controversy remained over the appropriate division of foreign policy powers between the two principal branches of the new constitutional structure, the Congress and the president. On one side in this debate was Alexander Hamilton, who called for a strong executive who would dominate foreign policy. In his view, the responsibility for foreign affairs rested with the president, except for those powers explicitly delegated to the Congress. On the other side of the debate was James

Madison, who saw executive power as only those powers expressly provided to the president, with the rest of the foreign policy powers left to the Congress. The Constitution ultimately divided foreign policy responsibility in a "check and balance system" that its authors thought would balance power between the two branches.

The powers delegated to each branch of government in the U.S. Constitution appear straightforward. Under Article 1, section 8, the Congress is given an array of specific and implied foreign policy powers in the areas of national defense and warfare, international commerce, and in the spending of funds to implement any law, including foreign policy actions:

a. "To provide for the common Defence...; To declare War...; To raise and support Armies...; To provide and maintain a Navy…"

b. "To regulate commerce with foreign nations...."

c. "No money shall be drawn from the Treasury, but in Consequence of Appropriations made by Law...."

d. The Congress shall "make all Laws which shall be necessary and proper ...."

Under all three sections of Article 2, the president is given foreign policymaking powers as the chief executive, commander of the armed forces, and chief negotiator and diplomat:

a. "The Executive Power shall be vested in a President," and "he shall take Care that the Laws be faithfully executed."

b. "The President shall be Commander in Chief of the Army and Navy of the United States."

c. "He shall have Power, by and with the Advice and Consent of the Senate, to make Treaties,...shall appoint Ambassadors,...and he shall receive Ambassadors and other public Ministers...."

In addition to the powers delegated to each branch, some powers are shared between the branches, especially in the areas of treaties and diplomatic appointments. While the president may negotiate a treaty, the Congress (the Senate) must give its advice and consent. While the president may appoint ambassadors, these appointments shall only be made "by and with the Advice and Consent of the Senate."

Problems arise between the branches because the power granted to one branch sometimes clashes with the power granted to the other. For example, while the Congress has the responsibility to write laws on international commerce (such as establishing trade policy or tariffs), the president, as the chief executive, can determine how they will be put into force. While the Congress has the right to declare war, presidents—as commanders in chief—have often used their power to initiate war. While the president may declare a policy toward another country or call for the building of a new weapons system, the Congress has the responsibility to provide or reject the funding for such actions. Although this constitutional approach was consciously chosen by the founders in an attempt to balance power between branches of government, it has created considerable uncertainty and gaps in delineating the foreign policy powers of the Congress and the president. Former Supreme Court Justice Robert Jackson has characterized the gaps in authority between the two branches as "a zone of twilight in which [the president] and Congress may have concurrent authority, or in which its distribution is uncertain." The result of this ambiguity has been a historic conflict between Congress and the president over the process of foreign policymaking.

A Cyclical Interpretation of Foreign Policy Control

Commentators have identified a cyclical pattern of foreign policy control in which one branch rises to dominance over the other during certain historical periods. Although analysts do not always agree on the duration of particular historical cycles, some trends are discernible. During the country's first several decades presidential control of foreign policy was on the ascendancy, and congressional foreign policy efforts were often rebuffed or ignored. President George Washington, for example, unilaterally declared U.S. neutrality toward France and Great Britain in 1793, and the Congress endorsed his wishes. When President Washington later refused to share information about his request for appropriations to implement the Jay Treaty with the House of Representatives, the House eventually provided funding. Other early presidents similarly gained the upper hand in foreign policy. President John Adams, for instance, recognized other states and rejected congressional efforts to interfere in the process. President Thomas Jefferson, seemingly a strong advocate of legislative governance, took strong executive initiative in completing the Louisiana Purchase. While President Madison was somewhat more deferential to Congress on the question of recognizing Latin America, he ultimately held sway. The Monroe Doctrine, which would shape U.S. relations with Latin America henceforth, was the product of a speech by President James Monroe, and did not involve any congressional action or approval.

Congress was not entirely left out of the foreign policy process in this early period, however. Some presidents, most notably Jefferson, were particularly cautious in using U.S. military force without congressional action. When Jefferson, for example, had to decide on a response to attacks on U.S. shipping in the Mediterranean, he was seemingly careful to limit the response to defensive actions. (Yet recent evidence suggests that Jefferson apparently ordered a naval squadron to the region to initiate offensive actions and then was not candid with the

Congress about his directive.) More significant, perhaps, was the congressional involvement in precipitating the War of 1812. By congressional action to pass various embargo acts, political scientist Holbert Carroll argues, a "congressional war" was the result. Others have labeled the War of 1812 "Henry Clay's War," after the speaker of the House who forcefully led a group of War Hawks in that chamber.

Beginning with the administration of President Andrew Jackson and continuing until the presidency of Abraham Lincoln, Congress and the president sparred more equally for foreign policy control. Jackson deferred to Congress when actions were necessary over attacks upon U.S. shipping in South America, and when France refused to pay a U.S. claim. More importantly, when Texas sought U.S. recognition after the revolution against Mexican control, Jackson asked Congress to consider the national response.

Executive dominance reemerged a decade later, however, during the presidency of James K. Polk, who moved U.S. forces into land disputed by Texas and Mexico, without congressional authorization. The result was a retaliatory attack by Mexican forces and the opportunity for Polk to force the Congress's hand. He quickly sought and obtained a resolution of war against Mexico, which eventually led to the annexation of Mexican territory extending to the Pacific coast. With the election of Lincoln, executive dominance in the foreign policy arena perhaps reached its zenith in the nineteenth century. During the Civil War, Lincoln exercised substantial unilateral control over foreign policy in an effort to hold the Republic together. He ordered the blockade of Southern ports, enlarged the army forces, made huge unauthorized expenditures of $2 million and incurred credits of $250 million, suspended some civil liberties—all without congressional authorization. Moreover, in separate actions, both the Congress and the Supreme Court upheld Lincoln's actions.

Such presidential preeminence was short-lived, however. After the Civil War, Congress began to reassert control that lasted until about the turn of the century. In 1869, for example, the Senate refused to give its advice and consent to a treaty involving the virtual annexation of Santo Domingo in the Caribbean. Constitutional scholar Harold Koh reports that congressional-executive relations became so strained that no treaties except those dealing with immigration were recommended for ratification for roughly the next thirty years.

Beginning with the actions of Presidents William McKinley and Theodore Roosevelt and lasting through most of President Woodrow Wilson's administration—with the administration of President William Howard Taft as an exception—the pendulum began to swing back to executive control. Roosevelt's assertive foreign policy

CHAIRS OF THE HOUSE FOREIGN AFFAIRS COMMITTEE

ADMINISTRATION	CHAIRMAN	PERIOD OF APPOINTMENT
Monroe	Jonathan Russell	1822–1823
	John Forsyth	1823–1827
J. Q. Adams		
	Edward Everett	1827–1829
Jackson	William S. Archer	1829–1834
	James M. Wayne	1835
	Edward Everett	1835
	Churchill C. Cambreleng	1835
	John Y. Mason	1835–1837
	Benjamin C. Howard	1837–1839
Van Buren		
	Francis W. Pickens	1839–1841
W. H. Harrison	Caleb Cushing	1841
Tyler		
	John Quincy Adams	1842–1843
	Samuel W. Inge	1843–1847
Polk		
	Truman Smith	1847–1849
Taylor	John A. McClernand	1849–1851
Fillmore		
	Thomas H. Bayly	1851–1855
Pierce		
	Alexander C. M. Pennington	1855–1857
Buchanan	Thomas L. Clingman	1857–1858
	George W. Hopkins	1858–1859
	Thomas Corwin	1859–1861
Lincoln	John J. Crittenden	1861–1863
	Henry Winter Davis	1863–1865
	Nathaniel P. Banks	1865–1873
A. Johnson		
Grant		
	Leonard Myers	1873
	Godlove S. Orth	1873–1875
	Thomas Swann	1875–1879
Hayes		
	Samuel S. Cox	1879–1881
Garfield	Charles G. Williams	1881–1883
Arthur		
	Andrew G. Curtin	1883–1885
Cleveland	Perry Belmont	1885–1888
	James B. McCreary	1888–1889
B. Harrison	Robert R. Hitt	1889–1891
	James H. Blount	1891–1893
Cleveland	James B. McCreary	1893–1895
McKinley	Robert R. Hitt	1895–1907
T. Roosevelt		
	Robert G. Cousins	1907–1909
Taft	James B. Perkins	1909–1910

(table continues on next page)

ADMINISTRATION	CHAIRMAN	PERIOD OF APPOINTMENT
	David J. Foster	1910–1911
	William Sulzer	1911–1912
	Charles B. Smith	1912–1913
	Henry D. Flood	1913–1919
Wilson		
	Stephen G. Porter	1919–1931
Harding		
Coolidge		
Hoover		
	J. Charles Linthicum	1931–1932
	Samuel D. McReynolds	1932–1939
F. Roosevelt		
	Sol Bloom	1939–1947
Truman		
	Charles A. Eaton	1947–1949
	Sol Bloom	1949
	John Kee	1949–1951
	James P. Richards	1951–1953
Eisenhower	Robert B. Chiperfield	1953–1955
	James P. Richards	1955–1957
	Thomas S. Gordon	1957–1959
	Thomas E. Morgan	1959–1977
Kennedy		
L. Johnson		
Nixon		
Ford		
Carter	Clement J. Zablocki	1977–1983
Reagan		
	Dante B. Fascell	1983–1993
Bush		
Clinton	Lee H. Hamilton	1993–1995
	Benjamin A. Gilman	1995–Present

Source: U.S. House of Representatives

actions in the Western Hemisphere and his incipient efforts to project U.S. power on a global scale reflect this trend, as did Wilson's proposal for a collective global security system centered in the League of Nations. This dominance also proved to be short-lived, however, with the defeat of the Versailles Treaty and the rejection of U.S. membership in the League of Nations. During the interwar years, the Congress asserted its control again through such actions as the passing of the neutrality acts of the 1930s and with the enactment of restrictive trade and immigration policies.

In roughly the first century and a half of the Republic, then, congressional involvement in foreign policy might best be described, to borrow Carroll's phrase, as "episodic and fitful." While the Congress did from time to time shape foreign affairs, it was continuously challenged by assertive executives. Prior to the United States' entry into World War II in December 1941, President Franklin Delano Roosevelt took actions to aid Great Britain that usually are identified with the beginning of the "imperial presidency" in foreign affairs—an executive dominance that continued into the Cold War in the late 1940s and early 1950s. As a result, the congressional role changed dramatically.

During the ensuing three decades, the president resolved foreign policy questions with limited congressional involvement until the Vietnam War. As U.S. involvement in that conflict deepened and domestic unrest increased, the Congress slowly began to reassert its role in foreign policy. A series of congressional foreign policy reforms—establishing procedures for the executive to follow in carrying out foreign policy and systemat-

CHAIRS OF THE SENATE FOREIGN RELATIONS COMMITTEE

ADMINISTRATION	CHAIRMAN	PERIOD OF APPOINTMENT
Madison	James Barbour	1816–1818
Monroe	Nathaniel Macon	1818–1819
	James Brown	1819–1820
	James Barbour	1820–1821
	Rufus King	1821–1822
	James Barbour	1822–1825
Adams	Nathaniel Macon	1825–1826
J. Q. Adams	Nathan Sanford	1826–1827
	Nathaniel Macon	1827–1828
	Littleton W. Tazewell	1828–1832
Jackson		
	John Forsyth	1832–1833
	William Wilkins	1833–1834
	Henry Clay	1834–1836
	James Buchanan	1836–1841
Van Buren		
W. H. Harrison	William C. Rives	1841–1842
Tyler		
	William S. Archer	1842–1845
Polk	William Allen	1845–1846
	Ambrose H. Sevier	1846–1848
	Edward A. Hannegan	1848–1849
Taylor	William R. King	1849–1850
Fillmore	Henry S. Foote	1850–1851
	James M. Mason	1851–1861
Pierce		
Buchanan		
Lincoln	Charles Sumner	1861–1871
A. Johnson		
Grant		
	Simon Cameron	1871–1877
Hayes	Hannibal Hamlin	1877–1879
	William W. Eaton	1879–1881
Arthur	William Windon	1881–1883
	John F. Miller	1883–1887
Cleveland		
	John Sherman	1887–1893
B. Harrison		
Cleveland	John T. Morgan	1893–1895
	John Sherman	1895–1897
McKinley	Cushman K. Davis	1897–1901
T. Roosevelt	Shelby M. Cullom	1901–1913
Taft		
Wilson	Augustus O. Bacon	1913–1914
	William J. Stone	1914–1918
	Gilbert M. Hitchcock	1918–1919
	Henry Cabot Lodge, Sr.	1919–1924
Harding		
Coolidge		

(table continues on next page)

ADMINISTRATION	CHAIRMAN	PERIOD OF APPOINTMENT
	William E. Borah	1924–1933
Hoover		
F. Roosevelt	Key Pittman	1933–1941
	Walter F. George	1941–1942
	Tom Connally	1942–1947
Truman		
	Arthur H. Vandenberg	1947–1949
	Tom Connally	1949–1953
Eisenhower	Alexander Wiley	1953–1955
	Walter F. George	1955–1957
	Theodore F. Green	1957–1959
	J. William Fulbright	1959–1975
Kennedy		
L. Johnson		
Nixon		
Ford		
	John Sparkman	1975–1979
Carter		
	Frank Church	1979–1981
	Jacob Javits	4 December 1980
Reagan	Charles H. Percy	1981–1985
	Richard G. Lugar	1985–1987
	Claiborne Pell	1987–1995
Bush		
Clinton		
	Jesse Helms	1995–Present

Source: U.S. Senate

ically scrutinizing presidential actions in foreign affairs—sought to more firmly balance foreign policy powers between the two branches. Conflict between the Congress and the president over foreign policy has continued. Congressional-executive relations since the end of World War II, in particular, provide greater insight both into presidential dominance in the 1950s and 1960s and into congressional resurgence in the 1970s and 1980s, and helps assess the relationship between the two branches in the late twentieth century.

Sources of the "Imperial Presidency"

The growth of the "imperial presidency" arguably provided the greatest challenge to the congressional role in the foreign policy process. Several factors accounted for this growth in executive dominance (and the concomitant decline in the congressional role) beginning in the late 1940s, although some of the factors actually had their origins prior to that time. Some factors relate to the changes made by individual presidents in the interpretation of presidential powers (executive precedent); others relate to the support of presidential dominance provided

by the courts; a third set of factors focuses on congressional behavior; and a fourth can be seen as the threatening international context in which foreign policy is made.

Beginning with Washington, presidents have used the necessity to act and respond to international events as a means of dominating the foreign policy process. Whether in recognizing other governments, sending emissaries abroad, issuing executive policy proclamations, initiating wars with other nations, or signing executive agreements—powers not explicitly granted to the executive in the Constitution—early presidents set precedents by taking unilateral foreign policy actions, often leaving Congress in the wake of their initiatives.

The use of precedent by presidents enhanced and expanded the constitutional powers of the president. When Franklin Roosevelt, for example, signed executive agreements without congressional approval for the "destroyer-bases" deal with Great Britain in 1940 and at the Yalta conference regarding the future of Europe, he was following in the footsteps of earlier presidents. Similarly, when President Harry S. Truman claimed that he did not need congressional approval to engage the United

States in the Korean "police action," or when Presidents John F. Kennedy and Lyndon B. Johnson initiated intervention in Cuba and the Dominican Republic, they were largely following earlier presidential precedent in the use of the commander in chief clause to justify these activities. Similarly, when Truman declared in a speech to a joint session of Congress in March 1947 that the United States would "assist free peoples to work out their own destinies in their own way," he was simultaneously announcing the beginning of the Doctrine of Global Containment and asking Congress to approve $400 million in aid to Greece and Turkey. He was thus following such precedents as Washington's 1793 neutrality declaration and the Monroe Doctrine of 1823.

Overall, actions by executive precedent had the effect of strengthening and expanding the delegated constitutional powers of the president at the expense of the Congress. The use of executive agreements, for example, weakened the Senate's treaty powers in the agreement-making process; the use of the commander in chief clause to initiate war weakened Congress's power to declare war; and the initiation of presidential foreign policy weakened Congress's ability to set policy. As the years of the imperial presidency set in, more and more commitments abroad took the form of executive agreements; about 95 percent of all U.S. foreign commitments after 1950 have taken this form. U.S. military interventions in the post-World War II years, too, have been increasingly justified under the inherent executive powers of the commander in chief from Presidents Johnson to Clinton, using historical precedents from the earlier days of the Republic. Foreign policy initiatives have generally taken the form of presidential initiatives, with virtually each administration declaring a presidential doctrine to summarize and thus control its foreign policy. Though summary statements such as the Truman Doctrine, the Eisenhower Doctrine, the Nixon Doctrine and the Reagan Doctrine—all resting on presidential precedent—were not new in a historical sense, the frequency with which presidents have issued them has greatly increased.

Supreme Court decisions, especially several in the early twentieth century, strengthened the president's role in foreign policymaking by supporting the use of precedents and thus further contributed to the erosion of congressional power in foreign policy after World War II. Four cases prior to the end of World War II set the stage for the Court's deference to the executive on foreign policy matters. Perhaps the such best-known case was the decision in *U.S.* v. *Curtiss-Wright Export Corporation et al.* in 1936. In that case, the Court stated that "the President alone has the power to speak or listen as a representative of the nation." Greater discretion, the Court held, must be afforded to the president in foreign policy than in domestic policy: "If ... embarrassment—perhaps serious embarrassment—is to be avoided and success for our aims achieved, congressional legislation which is to be made effective through negotiation and inquiry within the international field must often accord to the President a degree of discretion and freedom from statutory restriction which would not be admissible were domestic affairs alone involved." In an earlier landmark case, *Missouri* v. *Holland* (1920), the Court strengthened executive power by allowing the president to use the treaty process to expand the federal government's power under the Constitution. In effect, the decision eroded the implied powers granted to the Congress by the Constitution and further enabled the president to dominate the process. Finally, two other decisions made prior to the onset of the Cold War allowed even greater executive control of foreign policy. In *U.S.* v. *Belmont* (1937) and *U.S.* v. *Pink* (1942), the Supreme Court gave legal standing to executive agreements. According to the legal scholar Louis Henkin, moreover, the latter two cases were sufficiently expansive that any executive agreement made by a president would be covered by these rulings.

Several cases of the 1970s and 1980s, too, have strengthened the executive treaty powers, the commander in chief powers, and executive prerogatives in foreign affairs. In the treaty power area, the *Edward* v. *Carter* case upheld President Jimmy Carter's decision to return the Panama Canal to Panama, largely without congressional approval, and the *Goldwater et al.* v. *Carter* case let stand Carter's administration decision to abrogate a defense treaty with the Republic of China, without the approval of the Senate. Challenges issued by members of Congress to the commander in chief clause to send military advisers or even to intervene abroad during the administrations of Presidents Ronald Reagan and George Bush (for example, *Crockett* v. *Reagan* [1984]; *Conyers* v. *Reagan* [1985]; and *Dellums* v. *Bush* [1990]) were dismissed or rejected by the courts. Finally, one important case, *INS* v. *Chadha* (1983), ruled that the "legislative veto" was unconstitutional, weakening one important mechanism that the Congress had developed to regulate or even challenge executive actions in foreign affairs.

The Congress itself is in part responsible for the growth of executive dominance in foreign affairs. Despite immediate post-World War II calls for "bipartisanship" in foreign policymaking, the Congress was often deferential to the president's foreign policy initiatives during the early decades after World War II. According to one prominent analyst, there were "two presidencies" during this time—one for domestic policy, another for foreign policy. In the former arena, the president gained support for his initiatives from the Congress only about 40 percent of the time; for the latter arena, the president gained support up to 70 percent of the time. While congressional foreign policy support has declined in the post-Vietnam era, presidents since have more easily gained support for their foreign policy actions than for their domestic agendas.

Further, congressional deference has led even to some delegation of its foreign policy powers to the executive. A variety of resolutions passed by the Congress (such as the Formosa Resolution [1955], the Eisenhower Doctrine Resolution [1957], and the Berlin Resolution [1962]) endorsed presidential foreign policy and afforded the executive wide discretion in his actions, including, on occasion, the use of U.S. forces abroad. Perhaps the best-known example of this delegation of power was the Gulf of Tonkin Resolution, passed by the Congress at the beginning of U.S. involvement in the Vietnam War. This resolution authorized the president "to take all necessary steps, including the use of armed forces, to assist any member or protocol state of the Southeast Asia Collective Defense Treaty requesting assistance." The broad mandate was subsequently used by the Johnson administration as the "functional equivalent" of war to justify continued U.S. involvement in Vietnam. This delegation of authority extended to other areas as well. The Congress enacted foreign aid and trade legislation that allowed the executive considerable latitude. The delegation of trade powers predated the Cold War years and extends back at least to the Reciprocal Trade Agreements Act of 1934, which granted the executive wide freedom in negotiating tariff reductions. The executive thus gained more and more control over foreign policy at the expense of the Congress.

Structural changes in the executive branch enacted by Congress have also accounted in part for congressional deference and delegation of foreign policy powers to the president. With the passage of the National Security Act in 1947, the president began to establish a comprehensive foreign policy bureaucracy that allowed him greater control over foreign policy, as well as the ability to gather and process information and respond more quickly to the changing global political climate. Under the 1947 act, the Central Intelligence Agency (CIA), the National Security Council, the Joint Chiefs of Staff, and the National Military Establishment (shortly thereafter called the Department of Defense) were created, as well as a number of high-level presidential foreign policy advisory positions, including the director of the Central Intelligence Agency, the Joint Chiefs of Staff (military), and the Secretary of Defense (national security). Later, the Congress added other agencies to assist the president with foreign policy activities: the Arms Control and Disarmament Agency (ACDA) and the Agency for International Development, both in 1961, and the Office of the United States Trade Representative (USTR) in 1963.

By contrast, the Congress had few sources of independent information and limited staff expertise in the area of foreign affairs. Further, with its large size, elaborate committee system, and members seemingly more concerned with domestic and local issues than foreign policy matters, Congress was ill-equipped to act quickly or in an informed way on foreign policy. It was not until the 1970s, when congressional reforms were undertaken and more staff were added for members of Congress, that this situation changed. At that time, the Congressional Research Service and the General Accounting Office provided more staff to monitor foreign policy, and the Office of Technology Assessment was established (although subsequently disbanded in 1995) to lend scientific and technical expertise to the legislative branch. Nonetheless, the executive branch still possessed a distinct advantage in gathering and processing foreign policy information and acting quickly upon it.

A final factor that contributed to greater presidential discretion in foreign policy was the perceived dangerous global political environment that began in the late 1930s, continued through World War II, and accelerated with the emergence of the Cold War in the late 1940s and early 1950s. Franklin Roosevelt's use of precedent to provide assistance to the British in 1941 helped set executive discretion in foreign affairs on the ascendancy. While the expansion of executive discretion continued through World War II, it gained even greater support in the immediate years after the end of the war. Facing the perceived ideological and geopolitical threat from the Soviet Union, the Congress and the American public were willing to afford the president considerable latitude. Only the president, it was believed, could promptly receive and process information about the changing and dangerous world; only the president could act quickly and decisively in such situations; and only the centralized control of foreign policy, as represented by the president, could guarantee the United States a means of decisive action in a nuclear-armed world. The underlying Cold War consensus—a set of values and beliefs about the world and the United States' role in it held by the public and elites, including Congress—further strengthened the executive role in foreign policy matters.

Congressional Response and Resurgence

The Vietnam War and the Watergate episode were instrumental in weakening the imperial presidency and in prompting Congress to regain some of its foreign policy powers. As the Vietnam War dragged on in the face of declining public support, Congress and the public began to question underlying assumptions about the conduct of foreign policy. In addition, revelations about the abuse of presidential power that emerged from the Watergate crisis, followed by the resignation of Richard M. Nixon in August 1974, weakened the presidential office. Several members of the House and the Senate began initiatives to restore what they perceived as the imbalance of power between the Congress and the president in shaping foreign policy. A number of these initiatives were enacted into law, and several new procedures were developed to provide an opportunity for Congress to play a larger role in foreign affairs.

Several key areas were targets of these reform actions. Major efforts, for example, were undertaken to restore a greater congressional role in the war-making arena, in the making of U.S. commitments abroad, in the monitoring and conduct of intelligence activities (covert operations) in the world, and in using the funding powers of the Congress to direct foreign policy. A final area in which the Congress sought to restore its role was in the oversight of executive actions in the foreign policy field.

Presidents had long used the commander in chief and the executive power clauses of the Constitution to initiate wars, but in light of the Vietnam experience, the Congress was determined to limit the president's war-making power. By November 1973, the Congress had succeeded in passing the War Powers Resolution over the veto of President Nixon. The aim of this resolution was to allow Congress to fulfill its constitutional responsibilities in the commitment of forces abroad, even as it allowed the president some discretion in the use of those forces. The War Powers Resolution limited the president's sending of U.S. forces abroad for more than sixty days without explicit authorization from the Congress. It also required the president to consult with Congress "in all possible instances" prior to the dispatching of U.S. forces, report within forty-eight hours to the Congress the justification of sending these troops abroad, and keep the Congress informed on a regular basis while the troops are deployed. The resolution also contained a legislative veto provision allowing the Congress to withdraw the deployed troops prior to the sixty-day limit through the passage of a concurrent resolution in both houses. The *INS* v. *Chadha* decision, however, declaring the legislative veto unconstitutional has cast doubt on the legality of this aspect of the resolution.

Presidential compliance with the War Powers Resolution has been weak. While presidents have sent to the Congress more than fifty reports (through early 1996) on such subjects as the evacuation of U.S. forces from Vietnam and the use of troops in Saudi Arabia and Kuwait against Iraq in 1990, chief executives have rather uniformly rejected the constitutionality of the resolution and have reported to the Congress "consistent with," but not in compliance with the resolution. That is, presidents report to the Congress to keep that branch informed on the use of armed forces, but they almost universally have refused to acknowledge that they are complying with the specific sections of the War Power Resolution in making the reports. The prior consultation provision, too, has

been little honored by presidents, Democrats or Republicans, since the enactment of the resolution. Even when the president and the Congress were of the same party, as in the case of President Clinton's decision in September 1994 to restore Haitian President Jean Bertrand Aristide to power in Haiti with the aid of U.S. military forces, compliance and genuine consultation between the executive and Congress failed to occur.

Although the War Powers Resolution has come under attack (including a narrowly defeated House vote to repeal the Resolution in 1995), no successful action has been taken either to alter or to repeal it. Instead, debate remains over the resolution's future direction. Some believe that the resolution, despite its shortcomings, has served as a psychological and political restraint on presidential action. The president must consider possible congressional and public reaction to his intended use of force, and if Congress is determined, that body has a mechanism to stop military actions. Others view the resolution as an ineffective and counterproductive obstruction of presidential prerogatives that should be repealed. Still a third view sees a need to change the resolution and to address some of the loopholes used by presidents to avoid full compliance and consultations. This could be accomplished by clarifying and strengthening the reporting and consultation requirements, specifying which congressional officials need to be consulted and when, and by more clearly identifying the situations that require presidential reporting.

The Congress also sought to regain foreign policy power in the area of foreign commitments. Executive agreements had become the preferred instrument of making commitments abroad by post-World War II presidents, and a Senate committee inquiry in the late 1960s revealed that a large number of commitments (written, oral, and informal) had been made by the executive branch without ever informing the Congress. In 1972 in an effort to forestall, or at least to be aware of, these kinds of commitments, the Congress passed the Case-Zablocki Act, bearing the names of its sponsors, Senator Clifford Case (R-New Jersey) and Congressman Clement Zablocki (D-Wisconsin). This measure was not the first congressional effort to control and shape executive agreements made by the president. Nearly two decades earlier a series of unsuccessful amendments introduced primarily by Republican Senator John Bricker from Ohio sought to curb the treaty and executive agreement activities of the president and to preserve the rights of states under the Constitution. These amendments sought to prevent the making of treaties and executive agreements that would obligate the United States to undertake domestic actions that might infringe upon the constitutional rights of states or that might undermine congressional prerogatives in these areas. Further, the amendments sought to prevent self-executing agreements (agreements not requiring legislation) from coming into effect and thus to ensure congressional involvement in the process. While numerous votes were taken on these amendments, none succeeded in obtaining the necessary two-thirds support of the Senate, although an amendment vote in 1954 came within one vote of that requirement.

By contrast, the Case-Zablocki Act succeeded, although its provisions were less demanding of the executive than had been the earlier Bricker amendment proposals. Case-Zablocki specified that the secretary of state must report all international agreements to the Congress within sixty days of their taking effect. Five years later, this act was strengthened through an amendment that required the executive branch (not just the Department of State) to report all agreements to the secretary of state for transmittal to Congress. Other efforts also were made to expand the congressional role in international agreements. These included legislation allowing congressional disapproval through a legislative veto provision and enabling the Senate Foreign Relations Committee to decide if some significant agreements should take the form of a treaty requiring Senate approval. Although neither of these two approaches became law, the Congress was subsequently able to achieve a series of understandings on greater consultation between the Department of State and the Senate Foreign Relations Committee over the commitment-making process and the transforming of oral agreements into written form.

Much as with the War Powers Resolution, the compliance by presidential administrations with the Case-Zablocki Act and its various additions since their enactment has been spotty. It is estimated that about 20 percent of all presidential agreements are not reported to Congress within the required time period. Nonetheless, at the very least, these reporting requirements allow the Congress to gain greater knowledge of presidential foreign policy commitments and to react to them.

Monitoring Covert Operations

A third area in which the Congress sought to strengthen its foreign policy involvement was the monitoring of covert operations, sometimes euphemistically called "intelligence operations" or "special activities." As a congressional investigation by the Church Committee, also known more formally as the Senate Select Committee to Study Governmental Operations with Respect to Intelligence Activities, noted, covert operations were not "exceptional measures used only in rare instances" by the United States but had become "a routine program with a bureaucratic momentum." Monitoring covert operations was an especially difficult task for the Congress because it had rarely required much accountability for these activities from the executive branch, but the

Congress eventually passed the first piece of legislation to monitor covert operations in the form of an amendment to the 1974 Foreign Assistance Act. Known as the Hughes-Ryan Amendment after its sponsors, Senator Harold Hughes (D–Iowa) and Congressman Leo Ryan (D–California), the legislation required that the president be informed about all covert operations, that he certify or "find" these actions to be "important to the national security interest of the United States," and that these operations be reported to the appropriate committees in Congress "in a timely fashion." In this way the Congress would have some way of learning about the foreign policy covert actions undertaken by the executive branch.

In 1975 congressional interest in covert intelligence activities deepened when both the House and the Senate initiated select committees to investigate possible CIA abuses. The Church Committee conducted a wide-ranging investigation and made a number of recommendations for reform, including the creation of a joint congressional oversight committee. The House Select Committee on Intelligence (the Pike Committee, named after its chair, Representative Otis Pike of New York) conducted a similar investigation and made numerous recommendations as well. The result of these investigations (and an executive investigation) was the establishment of two new congressional committees to monitor intelligence community activities: the Select Committee on Intelligence in the Senate and the Permanent Select Committee on Intelligence in the House.

By 1981 further legislative actions were made to monitor intelligence activities. The Hughes-Ryan legislation was changed somewhat both to meet some objections raised by the executive branch and to provide the Congress with prior knowledge of covert operations. The Intelligence Oversight Act of 1980, as it was popularly known, maintained the requirement of the Hughes-Ryan Amendment that the president must issue a "finding" for a covert operation, but it required that congressional notification be done prior to the initiation of a covert operation and that only two committees, the Select Committee on Intelligence in the Senate and the Permanent Select Committee on Intelligence in the House, be informed. At the same time, the new legislation provided the president with some discretion on reporting by allowing the executive branch to report only to the leaders of the Congress and the two intelligence committees on what he deemed particularly sensitive covert operations.

As such episodes as the CIA mining of Nicaraguan harbors in 1984 and the Iran-Contra Affair of 1984–1986 indicated, these new accountability measures were not always followed by the executive branch. In the former covert operation in 1984, Nicaraguan harbors had been mined by the CIA in an effort to disrupt the Sandinista government in power at that time. Some members of congress, however, contended that it had not been properly informed of this operation as required by the Hughes-Ryan Amendment. While a subsequent investigation revealed that the CIA had provided some information to the Congress, the report to the Senate committee was not found to be wholly complete. In the latter case, the Reagan administration had kept the Congress in the dark from mid-1985 until mid-November 1986 about its clandestine operation of selling arms as a means to assist in freeing the funds obtained in sales to the Nicaraguan Contras (the rebel force opposing the Sandinista government). This episode, too, had not complied with the requirements of the Hughes-Ryan Amendment in the view of the Congress.

Especially in light of the latter event, both the executive branch and Congress sought to increase the monitoring of covert operations. Some of the measures undertaken by executive order under the Reagan administration (the outlawing of oral and retroactive findings on covert operations, and the provision of findings to members of the National Security Council) tightened accountability, but other measures (the commitment to notify Congress within two days after the initiation of an action except in exceptional circumstances) did not. By 1991, Congress succeeded in placing some of the elements of President Reagan's executive order into law, but congressional ability to enforce prior notification of all covert operations remained doubtful. While the Congress succeeded in increasing awareness of the executive of its foreign policy responsibility and in placing some new requirements upon the executive branch, it did not curb executive dominance of these activities. Congress has had only modest success in gaining a larger role in foreign policy through involvement in monitoring the covert operations controlled by the executive branch.

Beginning in the early 1970s, the Congress attempted to shape U.S. foreign policy actions through funding levels and restrictions. Sometimes funding was used as a blunt instrument. In the waning years of the Vietnam War, for example, the Congress passed a broad measure that halted all funding for U.S. military activities "in or over or from off the shores of North Vietnam, South Vietnam, Laos, or Cambodia." When Turkey invaded Cyprus in the summer of 1974 and used U.S.-supplied weapons to do so, the Congress subsequently cut off all military and economic assistance to Turkey for three years, over the objection first of President Gerald Ford and later of President Jimmy Carter. In the 1980s, the Congress, much to the opposition of President Reagan's administration, passed a series of amendments (known as the Boland Amendments) that limited military aid and later cut off all such aid to the Nicaraguan Contras. Use of the funding power was hardly new in U.S. politics. The denial—or more accurately, the threat of denial—of funding dates from the House of Representatives' attempt in 1796 to withhold funding to implement the Jay Treaty. While the House ultimately relented by a narrow margin, the prospects of the Congress's using this funding power became a reality.

A more subtle funding approach taken by Congress has been to make funding "conditional" on executive actions. In the 1980s, for example, U.S. military aid to El Salvador was conditioned on a human rights reporting requirement. Every six months, the Reagan administration had to certify that progress was being made in El Salvador in the areas of human rights compliance, social and economic reform, and the development of democratic institutions. Later, during the administrations of Presidents Reagan and Bush, aid to El Salvador was conditioned on the progress of reporting on the status of investigations into the murders of several clergy in that country. Another example of conditioned funding by Congress is in the granting of most favored nation (MFN) trading status to other countries in the Trade Act of 1974. Congress specified that the president could not grant MFN status to a nation unless it had demonstrated a free emigration policy for its citizens. Popularly known as the Jackson-Vanik amendment, the law was directed at the Soviet Union, which did not have such a policy and in fact placed restrictions on the emigration of its Jewish population. More generally, foreign aid legislation prohibited the provision of military or economic aid to countries that engaged in "gross violations of internationally recognized human rights" of its citizens. Similarly, the transfer of nuclear fuel was limited to those countries with adequate safeguards against the use of the fuel for nuclear weapons and which had not exploded a nuclear device.

Another variant of this conditional approach for the use of foreign policy funds is the implementation of direct "earmarks" by the Congress. Earmarking is Congress's way of directing the executive branch to use funds for particular purposes and prohibiting their use for others. Foreign assistance funding has been most often identified with earmarking. Congress has specified through the appropriations process that specific levels of funding must be provided to particular countries (Egypt and Israel). In fiscal year 1990, about 88 percent of Economic Support Fund assistance and more than 95 percent of military aid was earmarked. Sometimes earmarking can involve the specific rejection of aid or trade with a country for some political reason. Congress cut off military aid to the authoritarian regimes in Argentina and Chile, for example, and placed a trade embargo on Iran in the 1980s over its holding of American hostages and its involvement in international terrorism.

Two other kinds of congressional restrictions focus more directly on the ability of Congress to carry out its responsibility to regulate and condition foreign commerce. One piece of legislation deals with the arms sales area, the other with general U.S. trade policy. In the mid-1970s, the Congress enacted legislation (initially, the Nelson-Bingham Amendment to the Foreign Assistance Act of 1974) that not only established procedures for the regulation of arms sales, but also allowed Congress the right to disapprove such arms sales. Under the legislation and its subsequent revisions, all arms sales offers of more than $50 million in defense articles or services as well as any major piece of defense equipment totaling $14 million or more would be subject to congressional review. In all, a total of fifty days' notification (thirty days' formal notification and twenty days' informal notification) must be given the Congress to review and, if desired, to enact a concurrent resolution of disapproval. While the *Chadha* decision probably has invalidated this legislative veto provision, the review procedure set up by the act continues to operate.

In the late 1980s the Congress passed the Omnibus Trade and Competitiveness Act. In a unique feature, it incorporated a provision known as "Super 301," which required the executive branch (through the U.S. Trade Representative) to identify countries that had discriminatory or unfavorable trade policies toward the United States. If such countries failed to alter their practices over an eighteen-month period of negotiations, sanctions would be imposed. The congressional aim was not only to eliminate trade imbalances that developed with Japan, but also to signal that Congress would not grant the executive branch as much discretion in the area of trade relations as in the past. Both of these pieces of legislation on trade policy have met with limited success. No arms sales have been directly disapproved by the entire Congress, although some arms sales offers have been withdrawn or altered before their consummation, and the Super 301 provision, which expired in 1990, was only mildly effective. Although in the first year of its implementation, Japan, India, and Brazil were cited for being in violation of this provision and discussions were undertaken with these countries, progress in trade relations has been arguably slow.

Another congressional response to the legacy of executive dominance since the Cold War has been greater scrutiny and oversight of presidential actions in foreign affairs. Although in a historical sense congressional oversight is not new (it dates at least from the House of Representatives' call for presidential documents on the Jay Treaty in 1796), the extent of this oversight since the 1970s has been more far-ranging. It has been estimated that the legislative branch imposed more than 600 foreign policy reporting requirements on the executive branch from the early 1970s to the late 1980s—a 300 percent increase. As policy analyst Ellen Collier notes, three

types of reports were imposed upon the executive branch. One type is the periodic reports, which the executive branch is required to submit to the Congress at regular intervals. Annual reports are now required from various foreign policy agencies within the executive branch (such as ACDA and USTR) and from the executive branch concerning specific foreign policy programs (the annual assessment of global human rights conditions to comply with the foreign aid bill requirement, or an evaluation of the voting records of UN member countries to comply with the Department of State authorization bill). A second kind of report is the notification. While exemplified by the well-known War Powers Resolution and the foreign arms sales amendment, the notification requirements placed upon the executive branch may number in the hundreds in any given year. Any "reprogramming" of foreign assistance from one country to another or upheaval of funding for a specific program (military or economic assistance) above specified limits ($5 million for the former, and $1 million for the latter) requires a notification to the Congress. The third type of report is the one-time report required from the executive branch to the Congress. This requirement was specified in the 1986 Anti-Apartheid Act and compelled a whole series of reports on the operation of this legislation. The various one-time reporting requirements in this legislation were to ensure executive action to implement the economic sanctions against South Africa and to encourage the executive branch to work with other countries to end apartheid. In addition, however, the president, upon reporting to Congress, was allowed to end the sanctions if particular conditions were met in South Africa or if the U.S. economy became dependent on communist countries for strategic materials as a result of the sanctions.

While executive branch reporting increases congressional oversight capacity, the actions of various committees and individual members of Congress are ultimately more crucial. The House Committee on Foreign Affairs, (now, International Relations) for example, under such chairs as Dante Fascell and Lee Hamilton, was a model for broad, rather comprehensive, and quite steady oversight. The Senate Foreign Relations Committee, in contrast, during the same period was less rigorous about the oversight process. In addition to the two principal foreign policy committees in the Congress, the armed services committees, the intelligence committees, and a variety of select committees have sought to enlarge their own domains of congressional monitoring of the presidency in foreign affairs. The House Armed Services (now, National Security) and Senate Armed Services Committees developed from committees that simply accepted administration or Pentagon proposals on foreign and defense policy matters into more independent evaluators of foreign and defense policy actions. The intelligence committees played a more prominent role as the use of covert operations increased, and as the Congress sought (albeit not always successfully) to increase executive branch accountability. The various Boland Amendments on Nicaraguan aid initiated in the House Intelligence Committee in the early 1980s represent perhaps the most intense effort of that committee to oversee and ultimately shape foreign policy. The most dramatic illustration of the use of the select committees were those established in the Congress—one by the House, the other by the Senate—to investigate the events and actions surrounding what came to be called the Iran-Contra Affair.

Increased congressional scrutiny of executive branch activities in foreign policy has drawn complaints about congressional "micromanagement." The continuous string of oversight hearings, the foreign policy reporting requirements imposed upon the president, the numerous conditions and limits placed upon executive branch behavior, and the constant threat of congressional retaliation at various turns have frustrated the executive branch to the point where some believe that Congress is trying to direct and fine-tune virtually all foreign policy actions. Instead of speaking of the imperial presidency in U.S. foreign policymaking, some have come to speak of the "imperial Congress." To these critics, Congress is equipped neither structurally nor procedurally for micromanagement; to them the real loser from this process is U.S. foreign policy, which they see as no longer clear or coherent in its actions toward the rest of the world.

Mechanisms of Foreign Policy Influence by Congress

A variety of legislative and nonlegislative activities are used by the Congress to influence foreign policy. These mechanisms have been summarized under two major headings: legislative and nonlegislative mechanisms.

Legislative mechanisms refer to the Congress's constitutional prerogatives to pass laws to both direct and alter U.S. foreign policy. James M. Lindsay notes that the legislative mechanism can be further subdivided into substantive and procedural legislation. Substantive legislation directly and immediately affects foreign policy. Procedural legislation affects the process of policymaking and may allow Congress to indirectly shape U.S. foreign policy. The Congress's record in using substantive legislation to direct U.S. foreign policy has been unimpressive even during decades of presumed Congressional resurgence. Relatively few foreign policy bills that sought to direct U.S. foreign policy have been initiated and passed by the Congress. The most often cited instance in the 1980s was the Anti-Apartheid Act of 1986. This legislation had its origins in the Congress in the early 1980s, and was opposed and vetoed by President Reagan. While the executive branch sought to divert attention away from this legislation by signing an executive order with some sanctions a year earlier, the Congress revisited the issue in 1986 and passed new legislation over Reagan's veto. A second well-known instance in which Congress used its substantive legislative power involved the funding of the Nicaraguan Contras. By a series of actions—most notably the Boland Amendments that first restricted and then ended military aid to the Nicaraguan rebels and imposed human rights restrictions on aid to El Salvador—the Congress has been credited with putting its own stamp on U.S. foreign policy action in this region. A third such instance occurred in the Congress in the summer of 1995. Frustrated over the deteriorating situation in the civil war in Bosnia, first the Senate voted, by a wide margin, to lift the Clinton administration's policy of supporting the United Nations (UN) arms embargo against that country, and a week later the House followed suit. While the legislation offered several loopholes for the eventual continuation of the embargo and would need to withstand an expected presidential veto, it was, once again, a dramatic example of congressional efforts to legislate American foreign policy in the current era.

A typical response to Congress's effort to employ substantive legislation in the foreign policy area is the executive branch's attempts to forestall the passage of such legislation or to sustain a veto of unfavorable legislation. During the first year of the Bush administration, for example, the president successfully vetoed four pieces of foreign policy legislation. Moreover, even on a controversial issue, such as legislation extending the visas of Chinese students in the United States in light of the Tiananmen Square actions in June 1989, the Congress was not successful in challenging the president. President Clinton was able to win more than 80 percent of the foreign policy votes in the Congress on which he took a position during his first two years in office. Clinton's initial success should be viewed cautiously for at least three reasons. The success rate is based upon a limited number of votes. It masks the significant degree of trouble that the president had across party lines prior to the final votes. And it is likely to be short-lived with a Republican-controlled One Hundred Fourth Congress. Still, the success rate strongly conveys the uphill battle that Congress faces in challenging the executive branch in foreign policy, even after several decades of attempted reform.

The use of procedural legislation has become the preferred way for the Congress to seek to influence the foreign policy process. By changing the process of how policy will be made and implemented, the Congress attempts to shape the direction of the United States' actions in the world. Major congressional reforms undertaken in the 1970s—attempting to recapture the war powers, changing the procedures on covert operations, and seeking to monitor and regulate arms sales and trade policy—took the form of procedural changes to affect the formulation of policy. The increased reporting required of the executive branch also reflects this procedural approach.

Procedural measures include creating new bureaucracies and assigning new responsibilities to key officials within an agency. One of the newest foreign policy bureaucracies, the USTR, was created by the Congress to ensure greater attention to trade policy within the U.S. government. The individual appointed as the U.S. Trade Representative (USTR) has been given increasingly more power over policy by several pieces of congressional trade legislation over the past two decades to ensure that the executive official is attentive to congressional concerns. In addition, five House members are now required by law to be appointed as congressional advisers on trade matters.

The most significant procedural legislative mechanism developed by the Congress to influence foreign policy was the legislative veto (sometimes called the "congressional veto"). While the legislative veto originated in the early 1930s, its use in the foreign policy arena dates from the 1950s and 1960s, but especially the 1970s. This device allows Congress to incorporate within a piece of legislation a provision that enables it to halt or change the president's implementation of the law by declaring its objection through a subsequent legislative resolution. Depending upon the particular statute, the resolution could be either a single chamber resolution (passed by a majority in either the Senate or the House), a concurrent resolution (a resolution passed by a majority in both houses), or a committee (passed by a majority). The Congress, for example, incorporated such a provision into the War Powers Resolution allowing Congress to withdraw U.S. armed forces prior to the sixty days granted to the president through a concurrent resolution passed by the House and the Senate. Numerous statutes also contained a legislative veto provision to allow Congress to change or stop executive action that it opposed. In addition to controlling the war powers, the legislative veto sought to monitor the sale of weapons abroad, the issuance of presidential declarations of national emergencies, the granting of foreign assistance to countries with records of gross violations of human rights, and the detailing of Americans to serve in the Sinai Peninsula as part of the Middle East peace efforts, among others.

The *Chadha* decision declaring the legislative veto provision as unconstitutional, however, weakened this mechanism considerably and left Congress with the joint resolution as the only device for changing a presidential action. Since a joint resolution, unlike a concurrent resolution, requires the president's approval, in effect a two-thirds majority is required to overturn an executive branch action in the foreign policy arena. An

exception, however, remained in effect for actions affecting congressional procedure. The president's request for approval of trade legislation under so-called "fast track" procedures within Congress, for example, can be overturned by a resolution of disapproval within sixty days of the request. Furthermore, the *Chadha* decision has not completely altered the procedures created by the initial legislative provision. For instance, arms sales abroad continued to be reviewed by the Congress in the required time period, and human rights monitoring of foreign aid recipients were maintained as well. Despite the exceptions, though, the result of the *Chadha* decision has been that it is more difficult for the Congress to control executive branch behavior.

Nonlegislative mechanisms, as Eileen Burgin notes, refer to a wide array of activities that Congress and its individual members undertake to communicate their views on foreign policy to the executive branch. These can perhaps be summarized under two general headings: actions by the Congress as an institution and actions by individual members of Congress. All of these actions—whether institutional or individual—set out likely congressional reactions to executive action and arguably comprise perhaps the most powerful congressional weapon in the nonlegislative arena: the "anticipated reaction" by the Congress over potential presidential foreign policy actions.

Nonlegislative actions that convey Congress's foreign policy position include some of the oversight activities already noted. Hearings by standing or select committees are important venues for informing the president about the Congress's views on subjects ranging from trade and aid policy toward the new states of the former Soviet Union, to the appropriateness of lifting the arms embargo against the Muslims in Bosnia-Herzegovina. Although hearings have been used since the beginning of the Republic, the advent of televised hearings by cable and network television since the 1960s has increased their impact dramatically. Forums such as Senator J. William Fulbright's televised hearings on U.S.-Vietnam policy in the 1960s, the Iran-Contra hearings of the mid-1980s, and various committee hearings on the Persian Gulf War in the 1990s have become an increasingly important means for Congress to affect the foreign policy process.

In addition to the formal consultation requirements on arms sales or sending troops abroad, and informal consultation between the congressional leadership and the president, a third collective kind of activity by the Congress to demonstrate its position is the passing of concurrent resolutions, "sense of the House," or "sense of the Senate" resolutions. While these kinds of resolutions do not have the force of law (and are often used when substantive foreign policy legislation is likely to fail), they do indicate the level of congressional interest in, and attention to, an issue. Sometimes, too, such resolutions can be part of the political maneuverings between the two branches to affect the direction of foreign policy. In July 1994, for example, the Clinton administration, in order to defeat a binding amendment for lifting the arms embargo on the Bosnian Muslims, was forced to support a nonbinding resolution seeking a multilateral end to the arms embargo. Another illustration of nonbinding institutional actions by the Congress is the use of the report accompanying any bill. The "report language" is a weaker mechanism than would be a binding law for indicating the Congress's position on a policy and how it should be implemented, but the reports accompanying foreign aid or Department of State authorization bills are important instruments for informing the executive branch of how the Congress wants the legislation implemented, the legislative intent of particular sections of the bills, and how much discretion the Congress is willing to allow the executive branch in carrying out the policy.

Individual actions by members of Congress are another nonlegislative way to convey the sentiments of that body on foreign affairs. At one extreme, individual members of Congress may initiate lawsuits against the executive branch over foreign policy actions. Since the 1970s, a flurry of such lawsuits has been filed, often claiming that congressional foreign policy prerogatives are being violated by the president. At the other extreme, some members may write letters to executive branch officials over the policies that they are pursuing. One longtime member of Congress, for example, puts out a monthly newsletter on a foreign policy issue for widespread distribution. While the publication may be intended primarily for the member's constituency, it also conveys to other members of Congress and, ultimately, to the executive branch a congressional view on foreign policy matters.

In between these two extremes, Burgin identifies several other kinds of individual member activities on foreign policy. These range from individual members dealing with other governments as a mechanism to break policy deadlocks, to the use of the floor of the Congress and the media to convey their foreign policy views. Perhaps the best-known illustration of a member's working with other governments was the concerted activities by former House Speaker Jim Wright in the spring of 1987 to seek peace in Central America. He first formulated a peace plan for dealing with the stalemate between the Contras and the Sandinista government in Nicaragua and then shared his plans with representatives within the region and with the U.S. Department of State. Although his plan did not proceed very far, it did revive regional efforts to complete a peace plan, which was signed in August 1987. Such diplomatic actions by members of Congress are not without risks. Speaker Wright, for

instance, drew sharp criticism for "meddling" in executive branch matters. While his actions had a constructive outcome, U.S. diplomatic efforts may send mixed messages when different congressional and executive tracks are pursued.

With House and Senate sessions regularly broadcast on cable television, members of Congress increasingly use the opportunity to speak on the floor of the Congress to convey their foreign policy views. Two congressional operating procedures are particularly useful venues for conveying individual views. "Special Orders" in the House and "Morning Business" in the Senate are forums for members to comment on recent foreign (and domestic) policy actions. Perhaps the most important recent development in the way Congress conveys its foreign policy views has been in its efforts to appeal directly to the public on particular issues. Members of Congress make frequent appearances on such weekly or nightly interview shows as *Face the Nation*, *Meet the Press*, *This Week with David Brinkley*, and *The MacNeil/Lehrer News Hour*, as well as the morning shows on the major networks and a host of cable interview and discussion programs. The Congress itself also has television and radio facilities available for weekly "conference calls" with local radio stations and satellite links for local TV news programs.

From a congressional perspective, nonlegislative mechanisms create the conditions for the operation of the "law of anticipated reaction," especially in a system where the executive branch still largely shapes the process. When Congress and its members communicate their foreign policy views and seek to shape or redefine the policy agenda, the president can anticipate how the Congress will react to his foreign policy initiatives and actions and will usually modify his behavior and expectations accordingly, lending credence to the notion of anticipated reaction.

As Lindsay indicates, the impact of anticipated reaction is much easier to describe than to demonstrate conclusively, since it is impossible to know what would have occurred without the presence and implicit pressure of the other branch in the development of policy. In a real sense, reciprocal interaction between the Congress and the presidency increasingly reflects the routine, continuous bargaining between the two branches. Still, Congress's ability to influence foreign policy indirectly is much greater than the substantive legislation that the institution might or might not pass in the foreign affairs realm. Executive effort to gain congressional passage of the 1993 North American Free Trade Agreement (NAFTA), a pact to eliminate tariff and non-tariff barriers among Canada, Mexico, and the United States, for example, illustrates the anticipated reaction phenomenon. President Clinton's administration quickly became aware of opposition to this agreement by members of

Congress representing several different interests and made various commitments to several groups such as orange growers, beef producers, and wheat farmers in the hope of gaining congressional support. The administration negotiated "side agreements" with Mexico, particularly on environmental standards, as a further incentive to reduce congressional opposition, and NAFTA passed relatively narrowly in the House and more comfortably in the Senate.

Congress, the President, and the Future

Recently, the Congressional resurgence in influencing foreign policymaking has been both attacked and questioned. It has been decried by some, such as Gordon S. Jones and John A. Marini, as portending the rise of an "imperial Congress," while it has been largely dismissed by others, such as Harold Hongji Koh, as "much ado about nothing." Others, such as Barbara Hinckley, have joined the latter group by raising serious doubts that any congressional resurgence had actually occurred. Among the former critics, the Congress is viewed as having imperiled the presidency by regularly engaging in the "micromanagement" of foreign policy. The inevitable result of such actions, they claim, is a disjointed, incoherent, and possibly dangerous, approach to foreign policy. The latter set of critics sees a continued congressional deferral to the executive branch in the foreign policy realm, and thus little change in congressional-executive relations. Hinckley, in fact, sees relatively little significant change in congressional activity over the past three decades and suggests that even a decrease in congressional foreign policy influence may have occurred.

In point of fact, only on a few occasions has substantive legislation been passed by the Congress that directly challenged the wishes of the executive branch, and the vast array of procedural legislation has been used sparsely by the Congress to stop presidential actions. In addition, many of the procedural legislation initiatives by the Congress also contain "escape clauses" for the executive branch. Under such provisions, if the president certifies that an action such as an arms sales or an aid package is necessary for U.S. national security, it may proceed despite a congressional objection. Third, the unconstitutionality of the legislative veto as decided in the *Chadha* case further weakens congressional limits on presidential foreign policy action. While the Court's decision does not preclude congressional response to a presidential action that the Congress does not support, the decision does mean that Congress must muster a two-thirds majority in both the House and the Senate, assuming an expected presidential veto. Finally, yet another, more intangible factor militates against the Congress's expanding its foreign policy role significantly: Most members of Congress recognize that their function largely remains a secondary one in monitoring foreign policy, and they are prepared to give the initiation and execution of policy largely to the president. Congressman Hamilton, former Chair of the House Foreign Affairs Committee, perhaps put this view best in an address at the Department of State in late 1993: "I do not fool myself about the role of Congress on foreign policy. It is an important actor, but presidential leadership is by far the most important ingredient in a successful foreign policy. Only the president can lead…We in the Congress…can help and support him."

Yet neither the initiatives passed by the Congress in recent years, nor its possible role in the future should be overlooked. First, because the Congress has put in place numerous procedural legislative measures, it has the ability to reshape or redirect a presidentially inspired foreign policy. Second, the Congress as an institution has become much more vocal on foreign policy issues through nonlegislative techniques that are likely to expand in the future.

With the end of the Cold War—and the end of the unified congressional-executive stance against communism as a major determinant of foreign policy—the congressional role in shaping and legitimizing a new American foreign policy is not likely to be lessened. Indeed, the struggle between the Congress and the president over foreign affairs will continue much as the founders of the Republic had intended. As Arthur Schlesinger judged more than two decades ago, and as Hamilton and Madison implied more than two centuries ago, the give-and-take between Congress and the presidency over foreign policy will remain "primarily political." It has been so for more than 200 years and will persist for the foreseeable future.

James M. McCormick

See also Case-Zablocki Act; Chadha Decision; Constitution; Covert Action; Executive Agreements; Foreign Aid; Iran-Contra Affair; Legislative Veto; Most-Favored-Nation Principle; Presidency; Supreme Court and the Judiciary; Television and Foreign Policy; War of 1812; War Powers Resolution

FURTHER READING

Burgin, Eileen. "Congress, the War Powers Resolution, and the Invasion of Panama." *Polity* 25 (Winter 1992): 217–242.

———. "Congress and Foreign Policy: The Misperceptions." In *Congress Reconsidered*, 5th ed., edited by Lawrence C. Dodd and Bruce I. Oppenheimer. Washington, D.C., 1993.

Collier, Ellen. "Foreign Policy by Reporting Requirement." *The Washington Quarterly* 11 (Winter 1988): 75–84.

———. *The War Powers Resolution: Twenty Years of Experience.* Washington, D.C., January, 1994.

Congressional Quarterly Almanac 1986. Washington, D.C., 1987.

Congressional Quarterly's Guide to the Supreme Court. Washington, D.C., 1979.

Corwin, Edward S. *The President: Office and Powers, 1878–1957.* New York, 1957.

Crabb, Cecil V., Jr. *Bipartisan Foreign Policy*. Evanston, Ill., 1957.

Crabb, Cecil, V., Jr., and Pat M. Holt. *Invitation to Struggle: Congress, the President, and Foreign Policy*, 4th ed. Washington, D.C., 1992.

Dahl, Robert A. *Congress and Foreign Policy*. New York, 1950.

The Federalist Papers. Introduction by Clinton Rossiter. New York, 1961.

Fisher, Louis. *Presidential War Power*. Lawrence, Kans., 1995.

Franck, Thomas M., and Edward Weisband. *Foreign Policy by Congress*. New York, 1979.

Gibson, Martha Liebler. *Weapons of Influence: The Legislative Veto in American Foreign Policy, and the Irony of Reform*. Boulder, Colo., 1992.

———. "Managing Conflict: The Role of the Legislative Veto in American Foreign Policy." *Polity* 26 (Spring 1994): 441–472.

Hamilton, Lee H. "American Foreign Policy: A Congressional Perspective," speech at the Department of State. Washington, D.C., December 14, 1993.

Henkin, Louis. *Foreign Affairs and the Constitution*. Mineola, N.Y., 1972.

———. "Foreign Affairs and the Constitution." *Foreign Affairs* 66 (Winter 1987/1988): 284–310.

Hinckley, Barbara. *Less Than Meets the Eye: Foreign Policy Making and the Myth of the Assertive Congress*. Chicago, Ill., 1994.

Jentleson, Bruce W. "American Diplomacy: Around the World and Along Pennsylvania Avenue." In *A Question of Balance: The President, the Congress, and Foreign Policy*, edited by Thomas E. Mann. Washington, D.C., 1990.

Jones, Gordon S., and John A. Marini, eds. *The Imperial Congress: Crisis in the Separation of Powers*. New York, 1988.

Koh, Harold Hongju. *The National Security Constitution: Sharing Power after the Iran-Contra Affair*. New Haven, Conn., 1990.

Lindsay, James M. "Congress and Foreign Policy: Why the Hill Matters." *Political Science Quarterly* 107 (Winter 1992/1993): 607–628.

———. "Congress and Foreign Policy: Avenues of Influence." In *The Domestic Sources of American Foreign Policy*, edited by Eugene R. Wittkopf. New York, 1994.

———. *Congress and the Politics of U.S. Foreign Policy*. Baltimore, 1994.

———. "Congress, Foreign Policy, and the New Institutionalism." *International Studies Quarterly* 38 (June 1994): 281–304.

McCormick, James M. *American Foreign Policy and Process*. Itasca, Ill., 1992.

———. "Decision Making in the Foreign Affairs and Foreign Relations Committees." In *Congress Resurgent: Foreign and Defense Policy on Capitol Hill*, edited by Randall B. Ripley and James M. Lindsay. Ann Arbor, Mich., 1993.

McCormick, James M., and Eugene R. Wittkopf. "Bipartisanship, Partisanship, and Ideology in Congressional-Executive Foreign Policy Relations, 1947–1988." *Journal of Politics* 52 (November 1990): 1077–1100.

McCubbins, Mathew D., and Thomas Schwartz. "Congressional Oversight Overlooked: Police Patrols Versus Fire Alarms." *American Journal of Political Science* 28 (February 1984): 165–179.

O'Halloran, Sharyn. "Congress and Foreign Trade Policy." In *Congress Resurgent: Foreign and Defense Policy on Capitol Hill*, edited by Randall B. Ripley and James M. Lindsay. Ann Arbor, Mich., 1993.

Peterson Paul E., ed. *The President, the Congress, and the Making of Foreign Policy*. Norman, Okla., 1994.

Ripley, Randall B., and James M. Lindsay, eds. *Congress Resurgent: Foreign and Defense Policy on Capitol Hill*. Ann Arbor, Mich., 1993.

Schlesinger, Arthur, Jr. "Congress and the Making of American Foreign Policy." *Foreign Affairs* 51 (October 1972): 78–113.

———. *The Imperial Presidency*. Boston, 1989.

Sundquist, James L. *The Decline and Resurgence of Congress*. Washington, D.C., 1981.

Varg, Paul A. *Foreign Policies of the Founding Fathers*. East Lansing, Mich., 1963.

Warburg, Gerald Felix. *Conflict and Consensus: The Struggle Between Congress and the President over Foreign Policymaking*. New York, 1989.

Weissman, Stephen R. *A Culture of Deference: Congress's Failure of Leadership in Foreign Policy*. New York, 1995.

Yankelovich, Daniel. "Farewell to 'President Knows Best.'" In *Foreign Affairs: America and the World 1978*, edited by William P. Bundy. New York, 1979.

CONNALLY, THOMAS TERRY

(*b*. 19 August 1877; *d*. 28 October 1963)

Member of the U.S. House of Representatives (1917–1929) and U.S. Senate (1929–1953) who advocated U.S. participation in post–World War I international organizations. Born in McLennan County, Texas, Connally graduated from Baylor University in 1896 and began studies at the University of Texas Law School before serving in the army during the Spanish-American-Cuban-Filipino War. He was awarded an LL.B. in absentia in 1898 and began practicing law. As a congressman, he was a staunch Wilsonian Democrat and campaigned for U.S. involvement in the League of Nations and cooperation with the World Court, attended numerous international conferences, and served on the foreign relations committees in both chambers. As chair of the Senate Committee on Foreign Relations in 1941, he supported President Franklin D. Roosevelt's anti-Axis policies. He also helped to ensure U.S. ratification of the United Nations Charter in 1945 with his impassioned oratory: "They know that the League of Nations was slaughtered here….Can't you see the blood? There it is on the wall." Working closely with Republican Senator Arthur H. Vandenberg, Connally made the Committee on Foreign Relations an effective bipartisan instrument in support of the Truman Doctrine, the Marshall Plan, and the North Atlantic Treaty. When Connally retired in 1953, he was perhaps best known for authoring the Connally Amendment of 1946, which restricts the jurisdiction of the World Court in U.S. cases.

J. GARRY CLIFFORD

See also Bipartisanship; League of Nations; Marshall Plan; North Atlantic Treaty Organization; Permanent Court of International Justice; Truman Doctrine; United Nations; Wilson, Thomas Woodrow

FURTHER READING

Connally, Thomas T., and Alfred Steinberg. *My Name is Tom Connally*. New York, 1954.

Porter, David L., *The Seventy-Sixth Congress and World War II, 1939–1940*. Columbia, Mo., 1979.

CONSTITUTION

The organic written law of the United States, adopted at the Philadelphia Convention in 1787, ratified by the necessary number of states in 1788, put into effect in 1789, and amended twenty-seven times by 1992. On its face, the Constitution of the United States of America says almost nothing about how authority for conducting foreign relations is allocated among the branches of government. The words "foreign affairs," "foreign relations," and "national security" appear nowhere in the document. The first three articles simply create a Congress, President, and Supreme Court and vest in them powers, some of which affect foreign relations.

In some cases, the text of the Constitution conditions one branch's exercise of a foreign affairs power upon another's—for example, the president's powers to make treaties and appoint ambassadors requires the Senate's advice and consent (Art. II, § 2, cl. 2). More frequently, the text grants related powers to separate institutions without specifying their precise relationship: for example, Congress's power to declare war (Art. I, § 8, cl. 11) and the president's power as commander in chief (Art. II, § 2). In still other areas—for example, treaty making, and declarations of war—the Constitution does not clarify whether the textually specified method is intended to be exclusive. Finally, the text says nothing about who has constitutional prerogative in many modern issue areas—for example, international emergency powers, covert action, or the launching of nuclear weapons.

This textual brevity forces us to look to the Constitution's structure, history, judicial precedents, and customary practice. From these sources, interpreters have derived a subset of U.S. constitutional law, called "U.S. foreign relations law" or "Foreign Affairs Constitution." This doctrine derives, first, from textual exegesis of particular constitutional clauses; second, from inferences drawn from the broader constitutional structure and relationships; and third, from those few Supreme Court decisions that have authoritatively construed the Constitution on these matters. A fourth, clearly subordinate source of constitutional law is historical practice, particularly executive actions of which Congress has approved. Justice Felix Frankfurter, concurring in *Youngstown Sheet & Tube Co.* v. *Sawyer*, 343 U.S. 579, 610–11 (1952), wrote that such "a systematic, unbroken, executive practice, long pursued to the knowledge of the Congress and never before questioned,...may be treated as a gloss on 'executive power' vested in the president by § 1 of Art. II." Although such customary practice represents an informal interbranch accommodation regarding who decides on particular issues, such compromises lack full constitutional stature, because an authoritative court decision might override them at any time.

The core concept underlying this doctrine, embodied in the original intent of the framers and elaborated over time in the practice of the political branches, is straightforward: the foreign affairs powers of the United States are shared among the three branches of the national government. The Constitution as a whole rests upon a system of institutional checks and balances, which are not suspended simply because foreign affairs are at stake. In foreign as well as domestic affairs, the Constitution mandates a system of separated institutions sharing foreign-policy powers.

As this constitutional power-sharing scheme has evolved, the president has come to play the leading role. In some limited areas, the president wields exclusive powers; for example, in negotiation, diplomacy, and the recognition of nations and governments. Outside this realm, however, the branches share concurrent decision-making authority, with the president leading, but subject to congressional consultation and judicial review.

The constitutional historian Edwin S. Corwin has called the Constitution "an invitation to struggle" between the executive and legislative branches. Five discrete eras mark the evolution of constitutional rules: (1) from the Founding to the American Civil War; (2) from the American Civil War to 1900; (3) from 1900 to World War II; (4) from World War II to the Vietnam era; and (5) from Vietnam to the present.

From the Nation's Founding to the American Civil War

Under the Articles of Confederation, the young United States suffered a string of foreign policy failures, attributable, argued many, to the national government's impotence. To avoid creating an American king, the Articles' framers vested both executive and legislative powers in a one-house Congress. Congress was to appoint and supervise ambassadors, to approve treaties, and to exercise "the sole and exclusive right and power of determining on peace and war." Yet the Continental Congress lacked the crucial power to enforce treaty commitments upon the states through federal supremacy. Individual states thus remained free to violate the 1783 Treaty of Paris, which had secured the independence of the United States, thereby jeopardizing stronger treaty relations with other nations.

By the late eighteenth century, this constitutional weakness had reached crisis proportions. No fewer than twenty-five of the first thirty-six "Federalist Papers," written by James Madison and others in support of ratification, addressed foreign affairs, particularly the need to strengthen national government to cure the Republic's external weakness. The framers accordingly wrote the foreign affairs provisions of the Constitution with three goals in mind: first, to fashion a stronger national government, particularly in the areas of taxation, military establishment, regulation of foreign commerce, and treaty enforcement; second, to ensure that each branch remained accountable to the others through a strong system of checks and balances; and third, to avoid creating a new American monarch. Thus, the first three Articles divided foreign affairs powers among the three national branches, giving Congress, not the president, the dominant foreign relations role.

Article I bestowed upon Congress legislative powers to lay and collect Duties, Imposts and Excises, and "provide for the common Defence;" to regulate commerce with foreign nations and Indian tribes; to establish a uniform rule of Naturalization; to define and punish Piracies, Felonies committed on the high Seas, and "Offences against the Law of Nations;" to declare War, grant Letters of Marque and Reprisal, and make Rules concerning Captures on Land and Water; plus numerous powers regarding raising, supporting, maintaining, or regulating the army, navy, and militia. An early draft of the Constitution significantly gave Congress the exclusive power to "make war," but James Madison and Elbridge Gerry jointly moved to substitute "declare" for "make," to recognize the president's freedom to repel sudden attacks.

Even as Article I conferred foreign affairs authority on the federal government, it denied such authorities to the states. Thus, Article I, § 10 decreed that "No State shall enter into any Treaty, Alliance, or Confederation; grant Letters of Marque and Reprisal...without the Consent of the Congress, [or] lay any Imposts or Duties on Imports or Exports, except what may be absolutely necessary for executing its inspection Laws." The same provision further specified that "No State shall, without the Consent of Congress, lay any duty of Tonnage, keep Troops, or Ships of War in time of Peace, enter into any Agreement or Compact with another State, or with a foreign Power, or engage in War, unless actually invaded, or in such imminent Danger as will not admit of delay." Article I finally granted Congress broad power "[t]o make all Laws which shall be necessary and proper for carrying into Execution the foregoing Powers, and all other Powers vested by this Constitution in the Government of the United States...."

Article II vested in the president an "Executive Power," but did not incorporate within that grant any general foreign affairs or warmaking power, or unenumerated inherent authority. Instead, the framers granted specific authorities: the commander in chief power, the power to receive ambassadors, and the power to appoint ambassadors and to make treaties with the advice and consent of the Senate. By naming the president, a political leader, as commander in chief, the framers sought to entrench the principle of civilian control over the military. They pointedly denied the president powers that

the king had abused, such as the power to declare war and the exclusive right to make treaties. Recognizing that "[e]nergy in the executive is a leading character in the definition of good government" (*The Federalist* No. 70, by Alexander Hamilton), the framers spoke of "executive Departments" (Art. II, § 2, cl. 1), thereby anticipating the creation of cabinet government. Finally, Article II declared that the president shall have the duty to "take Care that the Laws be faithfully executed."

Article III addressed judicial authority, creating a federal judiciary and extending the judicial power of the United States to cases and controversies arising under treaties, affecting ambassadors and consuls, and involving foreign states, citizens, and subjects. As implemented by the first Judiciary Act of 1789, these authorizations gave the Supreme Court (and such lower courts as Congress might create) an important checking function against the political branches with regard to most foreign matters.

In the first years of the Republic, it became clear that Congress was ill-suited to exercise its assigned dominance over foreign affairs. The tasks of nation-building—recognition of and by foreign states, establishment of diplomatic relations, and conclusion of treaties—all demanded a branch of government that could react quickly and coherently to foreign initiatives. The office of the president was structured ideally for such responsive action, and was filled during these years by men of unusual personal force. The presidencies of George Washington, Thomas Jefferson, Andrew Jackson, and James K. Polk thus marked high points in the transfer of foreign affairs powers from Congress to the president. Particularly where powers were textually enumerated—recognition, treatymaking, and appointment and reception of ambassadors—the president's constitutional authority grew rapidly during this first era. Significantly, however, little claim was heard in these early years that the Constitution created an "inherent" unenumerated constitutional authority that empowered the president to act externally.

The first president, George Washington, consciously avoided major tests of presidential power, but still took several unilateral foreign affairs actions. Virtually all of these acts were driven by Washington's determination to assert sole constitutional responsibility for communicating with foreign nations and to protect his foreign-policy priorities: avoiding errors in America's relationship with Great Britain and preserving the young nation's neutrality from foreign struggles. Thus, Washington rejected the French diplomat Citizen Genet as a foreign emissary, conducted diplomacy with special envoys instead of with congressionally approved ambassadors, negotiated treaties without prior consultation, withheld documents regarding Jay's Treaty from the House, and issued the

Neutrality Proclamation of 1793 without consulting Congress. Washington remained both mindful and respectful of Congress's constitutional prerogatives. He based his decision to withhold information about the Jay Treaty from the House (but not the Senate) not on general claims of executive privilege, but on the constitutional exclusion of the House from the treatymaking process. He took military action only once without express congressional authorization, against the Wabash Indians, and even then Congress arguably endorsed his decision by subsequent acts. After the Neutrality Proclamation of 1793 received overwhelming congressional support, Washington conceded that it "rested with the wisdom of Congress to correct, improve, or enforce" that policy.

The Neutrality Proclamation provoked a heated exchange between Alexander Hamilton (using the pen name "Pacificus") and James Madison (writing under the name "Helvidius"). Hamilton recited for the first time the broad argument that the president's "executive power" and duty to "take Care that the laws be faithfully executed" in Article II carried within them unilateral power to proclaim neutrality and prosecute private citizens who violate that proclamation. Madison responded by defending the framers' original power-sharing principle, characterizing Hamilton's claim as "no less vicious in theory than it would be dangerous in practice" and nowhere "countenanced…by any general arrangements…to be found in the Constitution."

The ensuing presidencies of John Adams, Thomas Jefferson, James Madison, and James Monroe did not fundamentally alter these basic patterns. Congress maintained strict control upon the president's military powers, but in areas such as recognition, use of special envoys, and diplomatic relations, Congress largely acquiesced in executive prerogatives. In 1800, then-member of Congress John Marshall supported the president's right to surrender a U.S. citizen to Great Britain under an existing extradition treaty by calling the president "the sole organ of the nation in its external relations," apparently recognizing his role as the country's prime organ of diplomatic communication.

Several presidents took external measures that Congress had not authorized. John Adams led the country into its first undeclared war, with France, but otherwise regularly sought legislative approval for his external actions. The Supreme Court repeatedly upheld the constitutionality of Adams' undeclared war. In *Bas* v. *Tingy*, 4 U.S. (4 Dall.) 37 (1800), the Court found that Congress had intended to authorize limited hostilities by means other than formally declared war. In *Talbot* v. *Seeman*, 5 U.S. (1 Cranch) 1, 28 (1801), a unanimous Court headed by the new Chief Justice John Marshall similarly reasoned that: "The whole powers of war being, by the Constitution of the United States, vested in Congress, the

acts of that body can alone be resorted to as our guides in this inquiry." In *Little* v. *Barreme*, 6 U.S. (2 Cranch) 170, 177–78 (1804), Marshall held that a navy officer who had executed a presidential order during the undeclared war was liable for his acts, because he had acted in violation of a statute enacted by Congress.

President Jefferson conducted diplomacy with vigor and secrecy, effecting the Louisiana Purchase and retaliating against the Barbary States. In military matters, however, he proceeded cautiously, declaring in 1805 that because "Congress alone is constitutionally invested with the power of changing our condition from peace to war, I have thought it my duty to await their authority for using force in any degree which could be avoided." Presidents Madison and Monroe worked aggressively to seize West Florida, but neither claimed inherent constitutional powers as chief executive or commander in chief. Nor did the Supreme Court suggest that executive actions in foreign affairs were not amenable to judicial review or that a legislative regulation would unconstitutionally intrude upon an exclusive, inherent presidential prerogative. In *Brown* v. *United States*, 12 U.S. (8 Cranch) 110 (1814), for example, the Court invalidated an executive seizure of British property, holding the executive powerless to confiscate enemy property before Congress had authorized the seizure by declaring the War of 1812.

The early nineteenth century maintained the basic scheme of checks and balances. Although Congress neither authorized nor ratified President Monroe's unilateral declaration of the Monroe Doctrine in 1823, even Monroe did not assert that the doctrine authorized him unilaterally to commit military forces to protect the hemisphere. Only one year later, John Quincy Adams rejected Colombia's invocation of the Monroe Doctrine to enlist the United States in a defensive alliance, stating that "by the Constitution of the United States, the ultimate decision of this question belongs to the Legislative Department of the Government." Similarly, although Andrew Jackson's populist presidency greatly expanded the president's domestic authorities, in foreign affairs Jackson regularly shared information with Congress and frequently requested legislative authorization for particular acts.

In the mid-nineteenth century, the U.S. foreign policy agenda became consumed by relations with neighboring Cuba and Central America. The courts were sympathetic to the expansionist U.S. agenda, led by the executive branch. *Fleming* v. *Page*, 50 U.S. (9 How.) 603 (1850), reaffirmed the president's military powers as commander in chief "to invade [Mexico] the hostile country, and subject it to the sovereignty and authority of the United States."

As the first era closed, the fledgling United States moved beyond the defensive task of protecting itself from the outside world toward affirmative efforts to consolidate its control over its continent. After Madison and Monroe annexed Florida, Presidents John Tyler and James K. Polk authored an aggressive period of territorial conquest. In 1845, Polk dispatched troops to Mexico and misrepresented evidence to Congress to provoke a declaration of war. The House disapproved Polk's actions by resolving that the war had been "unnecessarily and unconstitutionally begun by the President of the United States." By mid-century, the executive branch was increasingly provoking external conflict, claiming an independent warmaking capacity, and restricting the information flow to Congress. The courts made fewer rulings, which were increasingly deferential to executive prerogative. In *Martin* v. *Mott*, 25 U.S. (12 Wheat.) 19 (1827), the Supreme Court sustained the president's authority to call forth the militia to repel an invasion, holding that president's decision as to whether an exigency has arisen "is conclusive upon all other persons." Similarly, Congress began retroactively to ratify executive actions—even those undertaken unilaterally, without its knowledge or consent—so long as the actions themselves were viewed as politically successful.

In sum, the first era saw a substantial de facto amendment of the Foreign Affairs Constitution. Although the Constitution intended Congress to have the dominant role in foreign affairs, the president's functional superiority in responding to external events enabled him to seize the preeminent foreign-policy role, while Congress accepted a reactive, consultative role. This switch placed the president in a position to propose, leaving Congress to dispose. Still, the dominant constitutional notion remained one of separated institutions sharing foreign policy powers. Although Congress acquiesced in the president's leadership, the president took pains to keep Congress informed and to secure its approval, and the courts regularly delimited the scope of his authority.

From the American Civil War to 1900

Before assuming the presidency in 1861, Abraham Lincoln had criticized executive adventurism in foreign affairs, having opined that Polk's military actions toward Mexico rivaled "the most oppressive of all Kingly oppressions" that the framers had sought to suppress. Yet Lincoln's own presidency was marked by usurpations of constitutional authority: suspension of the writ of habeas corpus, refusal to convene Congress, enlargement of the armed forces beyond congressionally authorized limits, large expenditures without congressional appropriation or authorization, and blockading of Southern ports without a congressional declaration of war. To deal with the ongoing domestic rebellion, Lincoln invoked not only the commander-in-chief power, but also his duty to "Take Care that the Laws be faithfully Executed," a clause previously seen as imposing a duty, not a license. In *The*

Prize Cases, 67 U.S. (2 Black) 635 (1862), the Supreme Court narrowly sustained the Union's seizures of ships trading with the Confederacy after Lincoln's blockade of Southern ports, evincing growing receptivity toward expansive claims of executive power. The Court held that Lincoln had inherent authority to suppress armed insurrection and that Congress had ratified his blockade by subsequent acts. It ruled moreover, that the president's decision in suppressing the insurrection was a "question to be decided by him, and this Court must be governed by the decisions and acts of the political department of the Government to which this power was entrusted."

Lincoln's Civil War actions did not expand presidential foreign affairs powers, as much as they expanded executive use of statutory and constitutional powers against a domestic insurrection. Later presidents also employed their commander in chief powers liberally against rebels, Native Americans, pirates, brigands, and slave traders, but generally did not invoke those powers to initiate warmaking against sovereign states without congressional approval. Beset by impeachment proceedings and incompetence, respectively, Lincoln's weak successors, Andrew Johnson and Ulysses Grant, did not continue Lincoln's aggressive exercise of expanded presidential powers. The Reconstruction Congress reacted against Lincoln's activism by asserting itself against these relatively passive presidents, battling over such issues as removal, nominations, use of appropriations riders, and the use of the veto.

The president generally refused to acquiesce in the new congressional assertiveness. In 1867, hostility toward Secretary of State William Seward's acquisition of Alaska triggered a House resolution opposing future territorial purchases, dampening expansionist presidential plans. Nevertheless, presidents continued to make efforts to obtain land and bases in the Pacific, the Caribbean, Central America, and Greenland. In 1869, the Senate rebuffed President Grant by refusing to advise and consent to his treaty permitting de facto annexation of Santo Domingo. But even then, Grant refused to withdraw the naval force he had ordered to implement the "inchoate treaty," and Senate resolutions condemning his military resolutions failed.

Thereafter, interbranch struggle shifted to the area of treatymaking, as the Senate refused to ratify any important treaty outside of the immigration context for nearly thirty years. As century's end approached, the institutional balance of power in foreign affairs had shifted heavily in Congress's favor. But a confluence of domestic and international pressures forced a pendulum back the other way. In time, the twin trends of outward expansion and internal consolidation replenished the president's store of power vis-à-vis Congress.

Low-wage immigrant labor, the new intercontinental rail system, and large inflows of foreign capital all enabled the United States to utilize its vast natural resources for economic growth. As U.S. economic production grew, domestic markets became glutted, creating domestic demand for markets in East Asia, Latin America, and Africa and modern naval power to protect global trading routes. So spurred, in the 1890s executive officials adopted interventionist measures in Brazil and Chile and clashed with Great Britain over Venezuela's boundaries.

Another consequence of the American Civil War was a dramatic expansion of U.S. military might. Between 1870 and 1890, the United States fought a string of internal wars against Native Americans, consolidating the territorial United States. By the early 1890s, the United States had established itself as the dominant hemispheric military power. Administration supporters in Congress began to reassert Hamilton's vision of unchecked executive discretion as a means of reviving diminished presidential power. To defeat statutory attempts to limit presidential executive authority over the armed forces, they contended that the president's constitutional duty to execute the laws carried with it an inherent authority to use physical power to protect the "peace of the United States."

The Supreme Court soon threw support to this view with expansively worded dicta. In *Ex Parte Siebold*, 100 U.S. 371 (1880), the Supreme Court declared that the U.S. government and its agents may exercise on U.S. soil "the power to command obedience to its laws, and hence the power to keep the peace to that extent." Ten years later, in *In re Neagle*, 135 U.S. 1 (1890), the Court further announced that the president's inherent constitutional authority to execute the laws encompassed not only enforcement of acts of Congress or of treaties of the United States, but also "rights, duties and obligations growing out of…our international relations, and all the protection implied by the nature of the government under the Constitution." Within five years, in *In re Debs*, 158 U.S. 564 (1895), the Supreme Court had invoked this inherent power rationale to uphold President Grover Cleveland's decision to enjoin the Pullman strike for the public good, even without congressional authorization.

Starting with the Spanish-American-Cuban-Filipino War in 1898, a generation of strong presidents triggered a resurgence of executive power. Quick victory in the Spanish-American-Cuban-Filipino War transformed the United States into an overseas imperial power, as it acquired control over Cuba, Puerto Rico, and the Philippines. In the Philippines, President William McKinley initiated military action and the United States fought a three-year war without congressional approval. After the Senate blocked McKinley's effort to annex Hawai'i by treaty, he accomplished it anyway by joint resolution.

Without consulting Congress, McKinley implemented the Open Door Policy and dispatched troops to China to put down the Boxer Rebellion, setting the stage for a new era of U.S. overseas power.

From 1900 to World War II

As in the post-Civil War years, the first decades of the twentieth century marked modulation, not fundamental transformation, of the basic pattern described above. By executive practice, the president increasingly dominated foreign affairs decision-making, but Congress did not acquiesce in that trend unequivocally. Toward the end of the era, Congress fully exercised its power-sharing role, particularly regarding treaty ratification.

Following Hamilton's views in the Pacificus letters, Theodore Roosevelt aggressively argued that, as a "a steward of the people…," the president's power was "limited only by specific restrictions and prohibitions appearing in the Constitution or imposed by the Congress under its Constitutional powers." During Roosevelt's presidency, a compliant Congress and Court did little to test the limits of this "stewardship" theory. Roosevelt intervened in Cuba and the Dominican Republic, built the Panama Canal, and sent the U.S. Fleet around the world despite Congress's express threat to withhold funds. Casting himself in the role of international peacemaker, Roosevelt put the executive agreement to unprecedented new uses. He concluded a 1904 accord with the Dominican Republic, asserting U.S. control over its customshouses, after the Senate had declined to ratify a similar treaty. Without congressional authorization, he also concluded the secret Taft-Katsura Agreement of 1905, which approved Japan's military protectorate of Korea, and the 1908 Root-Takahira accord, which entrenched the status quo in East Asia.

The Supreme Court broadly deferred to the foreign affairs judgment of the political branches regarding the new U.S. conquests. In *The Insular Cases*, the Court effectively ratified McKinley's conquests by holding that the newly acquired territories belonged to the United States, but were not "incorporated" into it. In *Neely* v. *Henkel*, 180 U.S. 109 (1901), the Court declared that "it is not competent for the judiciary to make any declaration upon the question of the length of time during which Cuba may be rightfully occupied and controlled by the United States in order to effect its pacification—it being the function of the political branch of the Government to determine…."

Roosevelt's successor, William Howard Taft, took a far narrower view of presidential power. In words reminiscent of Madison's in the Pacificus-Helvidius debate, Taft called Roosevelt's willingness to "ascrib[e] an undefined residuum of power to the President…an unsafe doctrine [which]…might lead under emergencies to results of an arbitrary character." Following this narrower view, Taft substantially contracted unilateral foreign policy initiatives, largely confining his "dollar diplomacy" to modest moves toward China and Latin America.

Long before becoming president, Woodrow Wilson had argued that "When foreign affairs play a prominent part in the politics and policy of a nation, its Executive must...take every first step of action." Inspired by his desire to "make the world safe for democracy," Wilson ordered troops into Russia and numerous Latin American countries, including Mexico, Haiti, Santo Domingo, and Cuba. Because Wilson conceived of his presidency as a form of prime ministership, he generally sought congressional approval for his acts. But he did not hesitate to commit troops first and obtain approval later, as he did in 1914 during the Vera Cruz Affair. After Congress declared war against Germany in 1918, Wilson dispatched two expeditions to Russia under his commander in chief power, without consulting Congress.

Predictably, World War I fueled rapid growth of presidential power. But at war's end, a period of forceful congressional reaction set in, culminating in Wilson's repeated failure to win two-thirds Senate approval for the Treaty of Versailles, which established the League of Nations. Unlike McKinley, who named three senators to help negotiate the end of the Spanish-American-Cuban-Filipino War, Wilson took no senators with him to the Paris Peace Conference that negotiated the Versailles Treaty, impairing later efforts to rally congressional support for it. Senate procedures not only allowed the Senate Foreign Relations Committee to adopt restrictive reservations to the treaty by majority votes, but also gave its chairman, Henry Cabot Lodge, unusual power to undercut the treaty, which was never ratified. Much the same fate befell the president's attempt to win advice and consent to ratification of the charter of Permanent Court of International Justice.

Like Taft, Wilson's successors did not accept his expansive view of presidential power as constitutional orthodoxy. During the interwar years, which straddled the Great Depression and the presidencies of Warren Harding, Calvin Coolidge, and Herbert Hoover, congressional government once again reasserted itself. Wary of reliving Wilson's fate, the new Republican presidents accentuated an international economic diplomacy that focused less on negotiating treaties that would be subject to Senate approval than upon securing arrangements with private banks to rebuild a war-torn Europe. Congress took the lead in freeing the Philippines, passing one bill to do so over Hoover's veto, and began to reexpress strong isolationist sentiments through a series of neutrality statutes in the 1930s. Although the president resorted with increasing frequency to executive agreements over treaties, the vast majority were "congressional-executive" agreements that Congress approved by legislation, not agreements concluded upon the president's "sole" constitutional authority.

Franklin D. Roosevelt's four terms in office redefined the constitutional politics of U.S. foreign affairs. As much as any other event, the Supreme Court's 1936 decision in *United States* v. *Curtiss-Wright Export Corp.*, 299 U.S. 304 (1936), helped Roosevelt consolidate his transformation of the president's foreign affairs authority. In *Curtiss-Wright*, private parties challenged the president's right, pursuant to a joint resolution of Congress, to prohibit arms sales to belligerents in Latin America. Writing for the Court, Justice George Sutherland not only upheld the executive act, but articulated a sweeping theory to support the president's unenumerated foreign affairs authority.

Echoing Theodore Roosevelt, Justice Sutherland suggested that the "investment of the federal government with the powers of external sovereignty did not depend upon the affirmative grants of the Constitution." Quoting from John Marshall's 1800 speech to the House of Representatives, Sutherland further declared that this "extraconstitutional power" was vested entirely in the president:

> In this vast external realm with its important, complicated, delicate and manifold problems, the president alone has the power to speak or listen as a representative of the nation....
>
> [W]e are here dealing not alone with an authority vested in the President by an exertion of legislative power, but with such an authority plus the very delicate, plenary and exclusive power of the President as "the sole organ of the federal government in the field of international relations"

—a power which does not require as a basis for its exercise an act of Congress, but which, of course, like every other governmental power, must be exercised in subordination to the applicable provisions of the Constitution.

As *Curtiss-Wright*'s numerous critics have recognized, Sutherland's key language was dicta, for Congress had passed a joint resolution in the case that expressly authorized the president to take the challenged action. There appears to be little historical basis for Justice Sutherland's "extraconstitutional theory" of paramount unenumerated presidential power in foreign affairs. The opinion also contains important words of limitation. By saying that "the president alone has the power to speak or listen as a representative of the nation," Justice Sutherland only acknowledged the well-established presidential power to negotiate, not a novel executive power to conclude, agreements on behalf of the United States. Similarly, his conclusion that the president's "sole organ power must be exercised in subordination to the applicable provisions of the Constitution" plainly suggests that it does not override congressional powers granted by the Constitution—for example, the power of the purse or the right to advise and consent—or individual liberties recognized in the Bill of Rights.

Despite these defects, later presidents have sought to treat *Curtiss-Wright* as an effective judicial amendment of Article II to add to the powers enumerated there an indeterminate reservoir of executive foreign affairs authority. Exclusive presidential power in foreign affairs had been traditionally construed as limited: embracing the president's textually enumerated powers and control of diplomatic communications. Outside that realm, most foreign affairs decisions transpire in a sphere of concurrent authority: under presidential management, but subject to congressional oversight and judicial review.

Curtiss-Wright posited a dramatically different constitutional vision, which viewed the entire field of foreign affairs as falling under the president's inherent authority. While accepting the notion that the president should manage foreign policy, the opinion effectively rejected the attendant condition of congressional consultation and participation.

In the years immediately after *Curtiss-Wright*, the Court remained strongly supportive of presidential power in foreign affairs. In *United States* v. *Belmont*, 301 U.S. 324 (1937), Justice Sutherland upheld the validity of the Litvinov Assignment, an executive agreement made by President Roosevelt in 1933, as part of a transaction connected to recognition of the Soviet Union. In *United States* v. *Pink*, 315 U.S. 203 (1942), the Court confirmed that holding, declaring that "[p]ower to remove such obstacles to full recognition…is a modest implied power of the President who is the sole organ of the federal government in the field of international relations."

Taken together, these decisions provided the constitutional rationale for a dramatic expansion of presidential power. In 1940, President Roosevelt concluded the destroyers-for-bases deal with Great Britain, relying on his commander in chief power, his *Curtiss-Wright* authority, and two statutes of dubious relevance. In early 1941, Roosevelt employed executive agreements to send U.S. troops to Greenland and Iceland, declared a state of "unlimited national emergency," and ordered the navy to convoy U.S. ships and shoot Nazi U-boats on sight, all without express congressional consent. After Pearl Harbor, Congress's declaration of war authorized Roosevelt to lead the nation into an all-out war. That war did not conclude until after President Harry S. Truman had ordered the dropping of the atomic bombs on Japan, a decision made without congressional consultation and based exclusively on the commander in chief power.

From World War II to Vietnam

Franklin Roosevelt's presidency triggered an activist phase in U.S. foreign policy. Beginning with Pearl Harbor and ending with Vietnam, the United States stood as a world superpower. The president simultaneously personalized his role as world leader and institutionalized it within a White House bureaucracy that came to include the Council of Economic Advisers, the National Security Council, and the Special Trade Representative.

As the United States emerged from World War II, the courts bowed to the president's broad assertions of foreign affairs authority. Although nothing in the *Curtiss-Wright* case had suggested that executive actions in foreign affairs should be immune from judicial review, in *Chicago & S. Air Lines, Inc.* v. *Waterman Steamship Co.*, 333 U.S. 103 (1948), the Court refused to examine the basis for presidential orders under the Civil Aeronautics Act, declaring that "the very nature of executive decisions as to foreign policy is political, not judicial….They are decisions of a kind for which the Judiciary has neither aptitude, facilities nor responsibility and which ha[ve] long been held to belong in the domain of political power not subject to judicial intrusion or inquiry."

In the years following the war, Congress reasserted itself, as the Senate refused to ratify the Charter of the International Trade Organization, the Genocide Convention, and other human-rights conventions. In 1946 the Senate also imposed the notorious Connally Resolution on the United States' acceptance of the compulsory jurisdiction of the International Court of Justice, stipulating that the United States would not subject itself to the World Court's compulsory jurisdiction with respect to "[d]isputes with regard to matters which are essentially within the domestic jurisdiction of the United States of America as determined by the United States." Despite initial protests, the president ultimately abided by all of these congressional actions.

But in other foreign policy areas, Congress soon demonstrated that it could work together with the president to promote multilateral cooperation. In the late 1940s, the Senate advised and consented to the Charter of the United Nations, the Marshall Plan, Truman Doctrine aid to Greece and Turkey, the North Atlantic Treaty Organization (NATO), and U.S. entry into a host of other global arrangements. Congress and the president also cooperated to enact a series of framework statutes to govern U.S. participation in the international trading system. Beginning with the Reciprocal Trade Agreements Act of 1934, Congress delegated broad advance authority to the president to negotiate and conclude reciprocal tariff-cutting agreements with foreign nations without further congressional reference. Successive Congresses extended the president's authority under the act nine times between 1937 and 1958, each time extracting concessions from the president as the price of renewed negotiating authority. The broad advance delegation permitted the president to negotiate and accept thirty-two bilateral agreements between 1935 and 1945, and to consummate the postwar entry of the United States into the General Agreement on Tariffs and Trade (GATT).

U.S. foreign policy began increasingly to focus on rising Soviet expansionism. The Truman Doctrine, the Marshall Plan, military alliances such as NATO, ANZUS, the Inter-American Defense System, and the Mutual Defense Assistance Program all formed interrelated planks of U.S. containment strategy. At the same time, however, World War II revealed the need for greater centralized management of both military and intelligence services.

The National Security Act of 1947 answered that need by placing U.S. governmental decisions regarding warmaking, intelligence, covert operations, military sales, and military aid under the executive branch's unified and coordinated control. The act served as a subconstitutional "framework statute," which effectively embedded the constitutional power-sharing scheme in national security legislation. Much as the Administrative Procedure Act of 1946 imposed due process of administration upon the domestic actions of executive officials, the National Security Act of 1947 formalized the principle of accountable, centralized presidential management of those officials' external acts. The system envisioned that overt wars would be managed by military officials subject to civilians under presidential control and that covert intelligence-gathering would be conducted by agencies directed by the president, advised by the National Security Council.

The 1947 act said nothing about the role of courts in national security matters, a question that was not resolved until five years later, in *Youngstown Sheet & Tube Co.* v. *Sawyer* (The Steel Seizure Case), 343 U.S. 579 (1952). By the time that case reached the Supreme Court, the Cold War had markedly intensified. President Truman had implemented the "containment" policy in Greece and Turkey, and after the communist takeover of Czechoslovakia in 1948, had authorized the Central Intelligence Agency to conduct covert operations in Italy. When North Korea invaded South Korea in June 1950, Truman responded by committing U.S. troops to combat without consulting Congress, relying not on a declaration of war but on his constitutional powers as president and commander in chief. Although Senator Robert Taft declared that Truman "had no authority whatever to commit troops to Korea without consulting Congress," Congress could generate no binding resolution to challenge the president's act. In April 1952, fearing that a nationwide steel strike would stop the flow of war

matériel, Truman ordered his secretary of commerce to seize the steel mills, again citing his inherent powers as president and commander in chief. When the steel companies' challenge to that action arrived at the Supreme Court, the Court rejected the president's constitutional claims by a 6-3 vote. Chief Justice Fred Vinson's dissent invoked Theodore Roosevelt's "Stewardship Theory" of presidential power and "the 'Take Care' clause…[as] adopted by this Court in Re Neagle, [and] In Re Debs" as authority for Truman's acts. Justice Black's opinion for the Court rejected that view, holding that Congress had the exclusive constitutional prerogative to make law and that the president's acts, which were not authorized by any statute, transgressed that prerogative.

The most famous and enduring opinion to emerge from *The Steel Seizure Case* was neither the majority nor the dissent, but Justice Robert Jackson's famous concurrence, which articulated a powerful constitutional vision of how Congress, the courts, and the executive should interact in foreign affairs. In at least five subsequent decisions, Supreme Court majorities have now embraced Jackson's concurring opinion as the lodestar of modern separation-of-powers jurisprudence. Justice Jackson's opinion espoused a flexible theory of decision-making premised on separated institutions sharing powers. "Presidential powers," he wrote, "are not fixed but fluctuate, depending upon their disjunction or conjunction with those of Congress." Using congressional action as a guide, he went on to establish a famous three-tiered hierarchy of presidential actions: "1. When the president acts pursuant to an express or implied authorization of Congress, his authority is at its maximum, for it includes all that he possesses in his own right plus all that Congress can delegate….2. When the President acts in absence of either a congressional grant or denial of authority, he can only rely upon his own independent powers, but there is a zone of twilight in which he and Congress may have concurrent authority, or in which its distribution is uncertain….3. When the President takes measures incompatible with the express or implied will of Congress, his power is at its lowest ebb, for then he can rely only upon his own constitutional powers minus any constitutional powers of Congress over the matter."

Jackson's concurrence squarely rejected the vision of unrestrained executive power endorsed by *Curtiss-Wright* and reaffirmed the concept of institutional power-sharing. Justice Jackson's opinion recognized that the Constitution grants the president "conclusive and preclusive" power only in certain limited areas, for example, the president's textually enumerated powers. Outside those narrow pockets of exclusive authority, he suggested, Congress may approve, be silent, or disapprove presidential initiatives. Legislative approval would bring the president's act into Category One, "supported by the strongest of presumptions;" congressional silence would bring it into Category Two, where "congressional inertia, indifference or quiescence may sometimes...enable, if not invite, measures on independent presidential responsibility;" and congressional objection would bring it into Category Three, where the president would be obliged to abstain from acting, unless he possessed exclusive constitutional power to complete the act without congressional approval (recognition).

Jackson's opinion filled the gap left in the 1947 Act by defining a pivotal role for courts within this foreign policy process. When others challenge the president, Jackson suggested, the courts should not abstain, but "must...scrutiniz[e those claims] with caution, for what is at stake is the equilibrium established by our constitutional system." Furthermore, Jackson read *Curtiss-Wright* not as a constitutional decision, raising the "question of the president's power to act without congressional authorization," but as raising the narrower "question of his right to act under and in accord with an Act of Congress." While recognizing the dramatic postwar accretion of presidential power, Jackson nevertheless rejected the president's "[l]oose and irresponsible use of adjectives" such as "'[i]nherent' powers, 'implied' powers, 'incidental' powers, 'plenary' powers, 'war' powers, and 'emergency' powers..." Far from excluding the judiciary, as the *Curtiss-Wright* vision would have done, Jackson reaffirmed the federal courts' vital role as the balance wheel of the national security system.

In retrospect, *Curtiss-Wright* and *Youngstown* sketched diametrically opposite visions of the Foreign Affairs Constitution. *Curtiss-Wright* was decided during the rise of both the imperial presidency and the American empire. By giving constitutional legitimacy to presidential conduct of foreign affairs, it contributed forcefully to the activist presidency fostered by Franklin Roosevelt. *Curtiss-Wright's* vision carried the nation through World War II, when the nation of necessity drew together and Congress and the president shared a consensus about national ends. The president and Congress then designed the National Security Act of 1947 to extend that national consensus into the Cold War wars through a model of management by an institutional and plebiscitary presidency. But when President Truman used that system to extend the national security state and to lead the nation into a war which was both undeclared and increasingly unpopular, the *Youngstown* Court reaffirmed the constitutional limits upon his authority. Justice Jackson's *Youngstown* opinion rejected *Curtiss-Wright's* vision of unrestrained executive discretion in favor of a normative vision of the policymaking process in which all three branches of government participate in maintaining "the equilibrium established by our constitutional system."

During the Warren Court years, the mid-1950s through late 1960s, the *Youngstown* theory took hold. The administrations of Dwight D. Eisenhower and John F. Kennedy provoked few conflicts with Congress in foreign affairs. Eisenhower followed his stated view "that the Constitution assumes that our two branches of government should get along together," illustrated by his decision to seek joint resolutions before dispatching troops to the Formosa Straits in 1955 and the Middle East in 1957. Although Kennedy clashed with Congress over international trade, he kept key members of Congress closely informed regarding the implementation of his blockade during the Cuban Missile Crisis.

Most of the foreign affairs disputes that came before the Supreme Court during this era involved not interbranch conflicts, but claims that government conduct had infringed individual rights. In such cases, the Warren Court applied the so-called "clear statement" principle: judges must find a clear statutory statement that Congress has authorized the executive act in question before condoning an executive infringement upon an individual's constitutional rights. As articulated in *Kent* v. *Dulles*, 357 U.S. 116 (1958), and *Greene* v. *McElroy*, 360 U.S. 474, 507-08 (1959), this canon of statutory construction reaffirmed *Youngstown* by underscoring the importance of specific legislative consent to executive acts in foreign affairs, when individual rights are at stake.

From Vietnam to the 1990s

In 1964, in response to an alleged attack on U.S. ships, President Lyndon Johnson asked Congress for the Tonkin Gulf Resolution, a joint resolution that he subsequently construed as broad congressional authorization to escalate the Vietnam War. The Tonkin Gulf Resolution authorized the president to "take all necessary measures to repel any armed attack against the forces of the United States and to prevent further aggression" and "to assist any member or protocol state of the Southeast Asia Collective Defense Treaty requesting assistance in defences of its freedom." President Richard Nixon relied on that act as a blank check to extend the war secretly into Cambodia and Laos without congressional knowledge, much less approval. The Indochina war and its aftermath marked a watershed in nearly every area of the constitutional law of U.S. foreign relations. The war disrupted both the dialogue and the foreign policy consensus between Congress and the president that the *Youngstown* decision had sought to foster.

After Nixon's re-election in 1972, the Watergate scandal broke, severely hobbling the president and eventually forcing his resignation. It emerged that the White House had covered up its involvement in a break-in at the Democratic National Headquarters, executed by a White House unit staffed by former Central Intelligence

Agency (CIA) agents formed to plug leaks by government officials suspected of having exposed the secret bombing of Cambodia. Congress responded aggressively to the president's Vietnam-era overreaching and subsequent weakening by embedding the *Youngstown* vision in a series of subconstitutional framework statutes. The most prominent was the War Powers Resolution of 1973, passed over the crippled President Nixon's veto. The joint "resolution," passed by a majority of both houses (an interchangeable term for "War Powers Act" or "Statute"), imposed consultation and reporting requirements and a sixty-day time limit upon the president's commitment of troops overseas without express congressional authorization. In addition, Congress enacted the Case-Zablocki Act of 1972 to govern international agreements; the 1977 International Emergency Economic Powers Act and the National Emergencies Act to govern exercises of emergency economic power; the Arms Export Control Act of 1976 to regulate arms sales; the International Development and Food Assistance Act of 1975 and the 1974 Hughes-Ryan Amendment to the Foreign Assistance Act to regulate foreign and military aid; the Trade Act of 1974 and the Export Administration Act of 1979 to manage import and export trade; and the Foreign Intelligence Surveillance Act of 1978 and the Intelligence Oversight Act of 1980 to oversee intelligence activities. These framework statutes typically conditioned presidential exercises of delegated authority upon adherence to elaborate statutory procedures, including factual findings, public declarations, committee oversight, prior reporting and subsequent consultation requirements, and legislative vetoes. Yet surprisingly, in each of these areas—warmaking, covert operations, international agreements, emergency economic powers, restrictions on military aid, and conflicts between foreign policy and free expression—the executive branch has continued to circumvent the relevant statute, largely supported by the federal courts.

This pattern emerges most clearly in the war-powers area. In 1973 Congress had passed the War Powers Resolution to prevent undeclared creeping wars by requiring that Congress approve, or the president withdraw, any foreign commitment of U.S. "armed forces" within sixty days. But by its terms, that statute did not address either covert wars by intelligence operatives or short-term military strikes, that could be completed within the Resolution's sixty-day time limit. In the two decades after the Resolution's passage, the executive branch treated the Resolution as de facto legislative permission to commit troops abroad for up to sixty days. In 1975 President Gerald Ford sent troops briefly to Vietnam to evacuate U.S. citizens and to Cambodia to free the *Mayaguez*, a U.S. merchant ship. President Jimmy Carter attempted an abortive military rescue of U.S. hostages in Iran in April

1980. President Ronald Reagan engaged in the most aggressive unilateral use of presidential warmaking in decades. He sent aid to the Contra rebels in Nicaragua and mined Nicaraguan harbors, sent U.S. troops to Lebanon in August 1982 without prior congressional consultation, dispatched forces to Grenada in October 1983, authorized a "surgical" strike against Libya in April 1986, and ordered attacks upon Iranian oil platforms in October 1987 and April 1988, each time avoiding full compliance with the Resolution's consultation and reporting requirements.

Although President George Bush sent small numbers of troops to El Salvador, the Philippines, and Panama without prior congressional approval, in January 1991, he requested and Congress voted a joint resolution authorizing the use of more than 500,000 troops to drive Iraq out of Kuwait. The president's hand was forced by a district court decision, *Dellums* v. *Bush*, 752 F. Supp. 1141 (D.D.C. 1990), which held that "in principle, an injunction may issue at the request of Members of Congress to prevent the conduct of a war which is about to be carried on without congressional authorization...." But in the waning days of 1992, shortly before leaving office, Bush reverted to form, committing U.S. troops without congressional approval, under UN auspices, to provide humanitarian relief in Somalia. U.S. casualties soon turned public opinion sharply against the Somalian operation, and Congress and the president eventually negotiated the removal of U.S. troops under Bush's successor, Bill Clinton. During his presidential campaign, Clinton had promised to abide by constitutional principles of meaningful consultation and prior congressional approval, but in his first year in office Clinton used force unilaterally against Iraq, in retaliation for a planned plot to assassinate former President Bush. In September 1994 Clinton committed thousands of troops to Haiti to depose a military junta and restore the ousted President Jean-Bertrand Aristide. Although a presidential mission headed by former President Jimmy Carter averted a full-scale invasion of Haiti by brokering a deal whereby the junta leaders consented to the commitment of U.S. troops in exchange for a legislative amnesty, President Clinton's lawyers nevertheless argued that the planned invasion would have been lawful even without specific congressional approval, citing as legal authority the War Powers Resolution, a defense appropriations bill, and an invitation from the deposed government.

Neither the Supreme Court nor any of the lower courts has yet to decide the constitutionality of the War Powers Resolution. In most cases where private parties have attempted to challenge presidential warmaking, the courts have refused to decide the issue, leaving the action intact.

Thus, at this writing, institutional custom appears to permit the president to act without congressional approval in repelling sudden attacks, attacking entities other than sovereign states, or committing small numbers of troops abroad for less than sixty days. In cases of large-scale premeditated combat, however, the president has now come to Congress for prior approval in four of the five most relevant instances—the two World Wars, Vietnam, and Iraq—with the Korean War being the only modern exception. Since the Tonkin Gulf Resolution, however, formal declarations of war have fallen into desuetude, now supplanted by more detailed congressional statutes that approve the troop commitment, but set certain conditions and restrictions on the duration and scope of the commitment.

Covert Operations

Although covert operations began with Nathan Hale during the Revolutionary War, and flourished during World War II, the Central Intelligence Agency, created in 1947, did not become a major actor until the 1950s and 1960s, with operations in Iran, Indonesia, Guatemala, and Cuba. During the Vietnam War, the agency conducted secret illegal domestic break-ins, mail intercepts, wiretaps, and domestic surveillance and designed secret military and paramilitary activities in Chile, Cuba, and the Congo, all contrary to stated U.S. policy objectives and without accountability to Congress. By the early 1970s, the Central Intelligence Agency was running secret wars in Vietnam, Laos, and Cambodia.

In late 1974, as revelations of CIA misconduct multiplied, Congress enacted the Hughes-Ryan Amendment to the Foreign Assistance Act, which sought to ensure future accountability for covert operations through stiffer certification and reporting requirements. In the Intelligence Oversight Act of 1980, Congress stiffened the reporting requirement to mandate that the executive give two intelligence committees prior notice of any "significant anticipated intelligence activity."

During the Reagan administration, however, covert CIA activities in Nicaragua multiplied. In 1986 it came to light that the staff of the National Security Council had secretly sold arms to Iran to secure the release of U.S. hostages in Lebanon and diverted profits from those sales to the Contras—Nicaraguan military forces seeking to overthrow the communist Sandinista government. Investigations revealed that the arms sales had violated procedural and substantive statutes regulating arms transfers to nations supporting international terrorism, principally the Arms Export Control Act. This four-part chain of events—the covert sale of arms to Iran, the diversion of funds to the Contras in violation of congressional funding restrictions, the "operationalization" of the NSC staff, and the circumvention of the intelligence laws—came to be known as the "Iran-Contra Affair." Although the Iran-Contra Affair was exhaustively investi-

gated by an executive branch commission, several congressional committees, and an independent prosecutor, no key participant was severely punished, no meaningful legislation was enacted to prevent its recurrence, and congressional oversight of covert activities remains weak.

International Agreements

In the years before Vietnam, the president asserted increasing control over the making of international agreements. In the 1950s, Congress sought repeatedly to enact the so-called "Bricker Amendment," which would have restricted the president's ability to achieve legislative effects by entering treaties, but by the mid-1960s Congress had largely acquiesced in the president's freedom to make international agreements by non-treaty "executive agreements." During the nineteenth century, the United States entered approximately one executive agreement and three treaties per year; by the mid-1980s, treaties stood at twelve a year, while executive agreements had risen to nearly 183 annually. In the *Belmont* and *Pink* cases, the Supreme Court largely validated the executive agreement, enabling postwar presidents to use such agreements to lead the United States into postwar multilateral commitments.

During the Vietnam War, however, Congress began to fear that the president would employ secret executive agreements to make binding commitments about overseas bases and troop deployment. After several false starts, Congress enacted the Case-Zablocki Act of 1972, a relatively toothless provision which required the president to notify Congress of any recently concluded international agreement. The Nixon, Ford, Carter, and Reagan administrations responded by developing a host of subtle, innovative methods to create or amend international obligations without congressional review. Presidents Nixon and Reagan employed the technique of "nonagreement agreements"—characterizing some executive agreements, particularly with Japan, as "voluntary export restraints"—in the process, avoiding notifying Congress of trade accords on steel, automobiles, machine tools, and semiconductors. To accept some, but not all, provisions of unratified arms control treaties, Carter and Reagan selectively complied with those treaties by issuing "parallel unilateral policy declarations." Reagan also refused to sign several treaties, such as the United Nations Convention on the Law of the Sea and the Protocol II Addition to the 1949 Geneva Conventions, while simultaneously announcing that the United States would comply with many of their provisions as a matter of customary international law. Similarly, Reagan used a "selective nullification" technique with regard to the Genocide and Torture Conventions (later applied by President Bush in ratifying the International Covenant on Civil and Political Rights), whereby the president ratified those treaties with so many conditions that the exceptions nearly swallowed the U.S. acceptance.

The post-Vietnam years also witnessed executive patterns of treaty-breaking and bending. In its 1979 decision in *Goldwater* v. *Carter*, 444 U.S. 996 (1979), the Supreme Court summarily dismissed Senator Barry Goldwater's challenge to President Carter's decision unilaterally to terminate the U.S. Mutual Defense Treaty with Taiwan in accordance with its terms. After *Goldwater*, President Reagan unilaterally terminated without congressional consent the U.S. acceptance of the compulsory jurisdiction of the International Court of Justice, the Bilateral Friendship, Commerce, and Navigation Treaty with Nicaragua, and U.S. membership in the United Nations Education, Scientific, and Cultural Organization (UNESCO). Reagan also purported to "modify" treaties without congressional consent, for example, when he "modified" for two years the U.S. acceptance of the World Court's compulsory jurisdiction.

With judicial support, the executive branch also circumvented congressional efforts to enforce existing multilateral treaties, by entering new executive agreements. In *Japan Whaling Ass'n* v. *American Cetacean Soc'y*, 478 U.S. 221 (1986), for example, the Supreme Court upheld the Secretary of Commerce's authority to conclude a side agreement authorizing Japanese fishermen to evade the "zero quota" imposed by the International Whaling Commission against the killing of whales.

Finally, the executive branch adopted a novel technique of unilaterally "reinterpreting" treaties to alter pre-existing treaty commitments. The best-known case transpired in the mid-1980s, when the Reagan administration sought unilaterally to "reinterpret" the 1972 Anti-Ballistic Missile (ABM) Treaty to accommodate executive planning for a Strategic Defense Initiative (SDI). President Clinton ultimately restored the original interpretation after Congress issued a threefold response to the president's actions: barring use of appropriated funds for new SDI tests; reporting a Senate resolution reaffirming the narrow understanding of the treaty; and attaching a restrictive condition on the Senate's ratification of the Intermediate Nuclear Forces (INF) Treaty.

In recent years, however, the Supreme Court has sustained two other dramatic treaty reinterpretations. In *United States* v. *Alvarez-Machain*, 112 S.Ct. 2188 (1992), the Court upheld the Bush administration's reinterpretation of a bilateral extradition treaty with Mexico to permit extraterritorial governmental kidnapping of criminal suspects. In *Sale* v. *Haitian Centers Council*, 113 S. Ct. 2549 (1993), the Court sustained the Bush and Clinton administration's reinterpretation of a multilateral refugee treaty to permit extraterritorial interception and repatriation of fleeing Haitian refugees.

In short, the years after Vietnam witnessed increased presidential domination of agreement-making, breaking and bending, largely ratified by the courts and by Congress. At this writing, that trend continues. In 1994, over the objection of some constitutional scholars, but with the approval of Congress, the Clinton administration submitted both the North American Free Trade Agreement (NAFTA) and the Uruguay Round accords of the General Agreement on Tariffs and Trade (GATT) for approval by statutes approved by a majority of both houses, rather than as "treaties" consented to by two-thirds of the Senate as specified in Article II of the Constitution.

Emergency Economic Powers

A similar post-Vietnam pattern of executive ascendancy appears in the realm of emergency economic powers, best illustrated by the International Emergency Economic Powers Act of 1977 (IEEPA). Congress enacted IEEPA specifically to limit executive abuses of national emergency powers under the 1916 Trading with the Enemy Act, which had authorized the president to wield enormous delegated power, simply by declaring a national emergency. Congress drafted IEEPA to narrow the president's authority in non-wartime situations, and conditioned his exercise of emergency powers upon prior congressional consultation, subsequent review, and legislative veto termination provisions.

Yet three successive Supreme Court decisions quickly emasculated IEEPA's congressional control devices, while preserving the president's access to the delegated foreign affairs authority. In *Dames & Moore* v. *Regan*, 453 U.S. 654 (1981), the Supreme Court upheld President Carter's authority to nullify judicial attachments, transfer frozen Iranian assets, and suspend private commercial claims against Iran as part of a sole executive agreement to free the Iranian hostages. Notwithstanding *Kent* v. *Dulles*, the Court demanded no "clear statement" that Congress had authorized the president to suspend individual claims, despite the suspension's impact on individual rights. Rather than construing IEEPA's silence regarding the acts in question as impliedly disapproving the president's claims of inherent power, the Court concluded that Congress had impliedly authorized the act, thereby converting legislative silence into legislative consent.

Two years later, in *INS* v. *Chadha*, 462 U.S. 919 (1983), the Court invalidated the legislative veto provision, which had authorized Congress to terminate presidentially declared IEEPA emergencies by a majority of two Houses. In the process, the Court invalidated similar legislative veto provisions in the War Powers Resolution, the Arms Export Control Act, the Nuclear Non-Proliferation Act, and the National Emergencies Act. After *Chadha*, Congress now could disapprove an executive act in those areas only by passing a joint resolution by a majority of both Houses and presenting it to the president, who would in turn be entitled to veto it. Consequently, the president has gained new freedom to make major foreign policy decisions with "congressional approval," when in fact he possesses support from only the thirty-four senators needed to defeat a veto override.

Finally, in *Reagan* v. *Wald*, 468 U.S. 222 (1984), the Court upheld President Reagan's power to regulate travel to Cuba under IEEPA's "grandfather clause." Despite unambiguous statutory language and legislative history to the contrary, the Court cited *Curtiss-Wright* as mandating "traditional deference to executive judgment '[i]n this vast external realm.'" These rulings have jointly freed the president to use tenuous statutory authority to conduct widescale economic warfare merely by declaring a national emergency with respect to a particular country, as Presidents Carter, Reagan, Bush, and Clinton have subsequently done against Iran, Libya, Nicaragua, South Africa, Panama, Iraq, and Haiti. In 1983 and 1984, Reagan triggered IEEPA for even more tenuous reasons: to sustain the existing export control laws after Congress had failed to reauthorize the Export Administration Act and to punish Nicaragua in 1985 after the House had rejected covert aid for the Nicaraguan Contras.

Nevertheless, the courts have regularly rebuffed challenges to the president's declarations of emergency under IEEPA on the ground that such determinations constitute nonjusticiable political questions. At this writing, President Clinton has declared several national emergencies under IEEPA, and used ambiguous statutory authority to bail out the failing Mexican peso in 1995. Thus, in only a few decades, the executive branch has largely succeeded in extracting from emergency economic statutes the very authorities that Congress expressly sought to remove from it in the years after Vietnam.

Restrictions on Military Aid

Since Vietnam, successive Congresses have sought to use their exclusive power of the purse to rein in executive adventurism. In 1971, Congress debated the famous Cooper-Church Amendment to the Foreign Military Sales Act, which would have cut off funds for U.S. actions in Cambodia. The Hatfield-McGovern Bill would similarly have terminated the use of any appropriated funds in Vietnam for purposes of military conflict after December 1970. In 1973 and 1974, Congress finally enacted seven separate provisions denying the use of funds authorized or appropriated pursuant to various laws to support U.S. military or paramilitary forces in Vietnam, Cambodia, or Laos.

Yet even these funding limitations proved unable to curtail the executive's foreign military and paramilitary campaigns. Notwithstanding express statutory funding prohibitions barring use of U.S. forces to carry out "military operations" in or near Cambodia or South Vietnam, within a year President Ford had sent U.S. armed forces to rescue the *Mayaguez* and to evacuate personnel from Viet-

nam and Cambodia. Even after the Hughes-Ryan Amendment became law, secret U.S. paramilitary aid to Angola persisted; Congress then passed the Clark Amendment to the Arms Export Control Act of 1976, which only partially succeeded in barring aid to private groups aiding military or paramilitary operations in Angola.

The Iran-Contra Affair marked the most blatant circumvention of funding restrictions. Officials of the Reagan administration spent funds in Nicaragua in apparent disregard for the Boland Amendments, which were attached to successive appropriations bills between 1982 and 1986 and barred any "agency or entity of the United States involved in intelligence activities" from spending funds available to it "to support military or paramilitary operations in Nicaragua."

In *United States* v. *Lovett*, 328 U.S. 303 (1946), the Court had held that Congress could not use its appropriations power to effect a bill of attainder under Article I, § 9, cl. 3 of the Constitution. During the Iran-Contra Affair, presidential supporters argued by analogy that the Boland Amendments placed overly strict conditions upon presidential expenditure of authorized funds, thereby encroaching unconstitutionally upon the executive branch's "inherent" authority to conduct foreign affairs. Subsequent court rulings have not clarified precisely how far Congress may go in exercising or enforcing its appropriations power to constrain the president's foreign affairs authorities. In *American Foreign Service Association* v. *Garfinkel*, 109 S. Ct. 1693 (1989), the Court voided on procedural grounds a lower federal court decision invalidating an appropriations statute on the ground that it unconstitutionally impinged upon the president's unenumerated foreign affairs authority.

That ruling left the underlying issue unresolved, and the president free to challenge future appropriations limitations on executive actions as unconstitutional exercises of Congress's power of the purse. Moreover, as the Iran-Contra Affair revealed, the executive branch may also seek to escape Congress's power of the purse altogether by soliciting private entities to support U.S. foreign policy initiatives with wholly private monies.

Foreign Affairs and Free Expression

Finally, the courts have increasingly accepted claims of foreign policy necessity over individual claims of free expression. This pattern first surfaced in the Pentagon Papers Case, *New York Times Co.* v. *United States*, 403 U.S. 713 (1971). Although a majority of the Court rejected the Nixon administration's efforts to enjoin publication of the Pentagon Papers without statutory authorization, three dissenters would have upheld the president's power under *Curtiss-Wright* and two others openly contemplated situations where they would approve a prior restraint against publication based on national security claims. Less than a decade later, in a suit the government later dropped, a lower federal court relied on this reasoning to enjoin publication by the *Progressive* magazine of an article explaining how to build a nuclear bomb.

In the Burger and Rehnquist Courts, national-security concerns have regularly overridden private interests in free expression. Late in the Carter administration, and with scarcely a mention of First Amendment concerns, the Court permanently enjoined Frank Snepp, a former CIA agent, from writing a book without preclearance, under a nondisclosure agreement, and imposed a constructive trust to recover profits from the book. Similarly, in *Haig* v. *Agee*, 453 U.S. 280 (1981), the Burger Court cited *Curtiss-Wright* to uphold the secretary of state's revocation of an author's passport based upon a dubious reading of the Passport Act, giving short shrift to the individual rights infringed by the executive action.

The Rehnquist Court has strongly supported the executive branch's expansive claims of foreign affairs power. In addition to the treaty interpretation cases cited above, the Court broadly deferred to executive discretion in *Department of Navy* v. *Egan*, 108 S. Ct. 818 (1988), in which the U.S. Navy discharged an employee after revoking his security clearance without a hearing. In *Goldman* v. *Weinberger*, 475 U.S. 503, 507-08 (1986), the Court deferred to executive discretion in military affairs to uphold a ban on the wearing of yarmulkes in the military, and the Clinton administration has invoked similar arguments in support of its restrictive policies on homosexuals in the military.

As important as these rulings on the merits have been numerous cases in which the Court has effectively condoned executive initiatives in foreign affairs by refusing to hear challenges to the president's authority. In *Burke* v. *Barnes*, 479 U.S. 361 (1987), the Court dismissed as moot a congressional challenge to President Reagan's pocket veto of a foreign aid bill that would have required him to certify El Salvador's progress in protecting human rights. Similarly, a large number of lower federal court cases refused to hear challenges to various aspects of the Reagan administration's support for the Nicaraguan Contras. Recent decisions have also invoked the procedural doctrines of standing governmental immunity, and "equitable discretion" as bars to foreign affairs suits.

In short, far from maintaining a rough balance in the congressional-executive tug-of-war, judicial decisions in foreign affairs cases have encouraged a steady flow of policymaking power from Congress to the executive branch. Through deferential techniques of statutory construction, since Vietnam the courts have read *Curtiss-Wright* and its progeny virtually to supplant *Youngstown*'s constitutional vision of shared power in foreign affairs.

Conclusion

The U.S. Constitution was designed to require institutional power-sharing in foreign affairs. During the Republic's early years, the president seized the leadership role in foreign affairs from an acquiescent Congress. With a few modulations, since the American Civil War, U.S. history has witnessed a steady accretion of executive power. The New Deal and the *Curtiss-Wright* decision sought to legitimize that trend as a constitutional corollary of the president's role as "sole organ" of our nation in foreign affairs, but the Court's 1952 decision in the Steel Seizure case restored the original vision of balanced institutional participation. Since the Vietnam War and the Iran-Contra Affair, however, the trend toward executive unilateralism has continued. The current national security system encourages the president to act secretly and with the advice of only a few close advisers, allows Congress to acquiesce in and avoid accountability for important foreign policy decisions, and permits the courts to abstain and defer to the political branches. The constitutional flaw of this system is that the structure of checks and balances is dramatically weakened when foreign affairs are at stake.

HAROLD HONGJU KOH

See also American Revolution; Articles of Confederation; Case-Zablocki Act; Central Intelligence Agency; Congress; Curtiss-Wright Case; Federalist Papers; Iran-Contra Affair; National Security Act; Presidency; Supreme Court and the Judiciary; Trading with the Enemy Act; War Powers Resolution

FURTHER READING

Corwin, Edwin S. *The President: Office and Powers*. New York, 1940.
Cox, Henry B. *War, Foreign Affairs, and Constitutional Power: 1829–1901*. New York, 1984.
Ely, John Hart. *War and Responsibility: Constitutional Lessons of Vietnam and Its Aftermath*. Princeton, N.J., 1993.
Fisher, Louis. *Presidential War Power*. Lawrence, Kans., 1995
Franck, Thomas M., and Michael J. Glennon. *Foreign Relations and National Security Law*, 2nd. ed. St. Paul, Minn., 1993.
Glennon, Michael J. *Constitutional Diplomacy*. Princeton, N.J., 1990.
Henkin, Louis. *Foreign Affairs and the Constitution*. New York, 1972.
———. *Constitutionalism, Democracy, and Foreign Affairs*. New York, 1990.
Johnson, Loch. *A Season of Inquiry: Congress and Intelligence*. Chicago, 1988.
Koh, Harold Hongju. *The National Security Constitution: Sharing Power After the Iran-Contra Affair*. New Haven, Conn., 1990.
LaFeber, Walter. "The Constitution and United States Foreign Policy: An Interpretation." *Journal of American History* 74 (1987): 695–717.
Schlesinger, Arthur. *The Imperial Presidency*. New York, 1973.
Sofaer, Abraham. *War, Foreign Affairs, and Constitutional Power: The Origins*. New York, 1976.
Stern, Gary M., and Morton H. Halperin, eds. *The U.S. Constitution and the Power to Go to War: Historical and Current Perspectives*. Westport, Conn., 1994.
Wormuth, Francis P., and Edwin G. Firmage. *To Chain the Dog of War: The War Powers of Congress in History and Law*, 2nd ed. Urbana, Ill., 1989.

CONSTRUCTIVE ENGAGEMENT

See Crocker, Chester Arthur; South Africa

CONSUL

See Foreign Service

CONTADORA GROUP

Four Latin American nations—Colombia, Mexico, Panama, and Venezuela—that pushed for negotiated settlements of the armed conflicts in Central America from 1983 to 1987. In the early 1980s armed conflicts were escalating between the Contras and the Sandinista-led government of Nicaragua and between rebel forces and the conservative governments in Guatemala and El Salvador. Convinced that the Sandinistas in Nicaragua (a rebel military and political coalition that took power in 1979) and the rebel forces in Guatemala and El Salvador were Soviet-oriented communists, the administration of President Ronald Reagan appeared bent on military victory for its allies, the Contras and the governments of El Salvador and Guatemala. While it did bow to domestic and international opinion by appearing to endorse the idea of a negotiated peace, Washington, in fact, was firmly opposed to such a solution, which would have accepted the existence of the revolutionary government in Nicaragua and legitimized at least some of the demands of rebel forces in El Salvador and Guatemala.

Alarmed by foreign interference and the escalating conflict that was destroying the economies of the region and threatening to spill over into neighboring countries, the foreign ministers of Colombia, Mexico, Panama, and Venezuela met on the Panamanian island of Contadora on 8–9 January 1983 and issued a statement urging a negotiated peace. On 9 September the Contadora Group and representatives of all five Central American governments published the Contadora Document of Objectives, which called for self-determination of peoples, nonintervention, prohibition of terrorism and subversion, peaceful settlement of disputes, promotion of social justice and democracy, political pluralism, and respect for human rights. The Contadora Group then worked in consultation with representatives of the United States and the Central American countries to produce a document to effect those objectives.

On 7 September 1984 the Contadora Act for Peace and Cooperation was formally presented in Panama City. U.S. Secretary of State George P. Shultz immediately called it "an important step forward." While noting the conditional acceptance of Costa Rica, El Salvador, Guatemala, and Honduras, he lamented that "Nicaragua, on the other hand, has rejected key elements...including those dealing with binding obligations to internal democratization and to reductions in arms and troop levels." Two weeks later, however, when Nicaraguan President Daniel Ortega informed the Contadora Group that his government would accept the act "in its totality, immediately and without modifications," U.S. spokespersons revised their opinion, calling the provisions one-sided and unsatisfactory. Soon the three Central American countries most closely tied to the United States—El Salvador, Honduras, and Costa Rica—presented a long list of objections to the very document that, only weeks before, their representatives had indicated they would sign.

Nevertheless, the Contadora process continued. The original group enlisted the help of Argentina, Brazil, Peru, and Uruguay—dubbed the Contadora Support Group. The two groups, representing more than 80 percent of all Latin Americans, produced another draft in June 1986, which addressed many of the objections raised since the 1984 act. After some delay the government of Nicaragua again agreed to sign. The United States, the major promoter of the Contras, continued to oppose the agreement; Costa Rica, El Salvador, and Honduras once again demurred, and the Contadora process stagnated. Although doomed by the opposition of the United States, the Contadora initiatives provided an experience in negotiations that laid the foundation for Esquipulas II, the Central American–generated peace agreement of 7 August 1987.

THOMAS W. WALKER

See also Contras; El Salvador; Esquipulas II; Guatemala; Latin America; Nicaragua

FURTHER READING

Bagley, Bruce M., Roberto Alvarez, and Katherine J. Hagedorn, eds. *Contadora and the Central American Peace Process.* Boulder, Colo., 1985.
Goodfellow, William. "The Diplomatic Front." In *Reagan Versus the Sandinistas: The Undeclared War on Nicaragua*, edited by Thomas W. Walker. Boulder, Colo., 1987.

CONTAINMENT

The U.S. doctrine encapsulating a comprehensive, complex, and shifting strategy for confronting perceived Soviet expansionism after World War II. In the lexicon of U.S. diplomatic history few terms have acquired the prominence of "containment." Since its inception in 1946, containment's precise goals, practical implications, and efficacy have been the subject of debate among policymakers, scholars, and commentators. Nevertheless, it stands as a useful summation of the logic and activity through which the United States sought to counter the power of the Soviet Union and its ideological allies. In the process, containment also defined U.S. security and foreign policy objectives from the mid-1940s to the late 1980s—the Cold War. Containment's implements ranged from military and economic support and development programs for siding with the United States, to widespread espionage, covert operations, psychological warfare, assassination plots, and more. Originally centered in Europe, where U.S. interests were reasonably clear and Soviet threats quite real, it expanded into a global policy of resistance to an ever-widening range of forces thought to serve the power and prospects of Soviet communism. Adapted by succeeding administrations to the changing character and demands of the East-West conflict, containment lost all concrete meaning with the collapse of the Soviet Union and came to refer to balance-of-power policies for resisting whatever forces and developments threatened vital U.S. interests.

George F. Kennan and Early Formulations of Containment

The grand alliance that won World War II disintegrated very soon after Japan's surrender in August 1945. By year's end, while the new international order remained largely undefined, the United States became frustrated and alarmed by the Soviet Union's uncooperative behavior. Taking advantage of its enormous military strength, Joseph Stalin's government appeared bent on imposing a stranglehold on east-central Europe and Germany; it also began to exert influence in the eastern Mediterranean (Turkey) and the Persian Gulf (Iran) despite the protests of the Western powers. Moreover, Moscow's increasingly bellicose rhetoric—including Stalin's speech of 9 February 1946 blaming World War II on capitalist policies and predicting similar "crises and military catastrophes" in the future—rejected accommodation. Influential Americans received Stalin's speech as a declaration of ideological war.

Diplomatic solutions still seemed possible: The Foreign Ministers Conference continued to hold sessions, the United Nations Organization was inaugurated, and peace treaties were signed with Italy, Bulgaria, Hungary, and Finland. Nevertheless, President Harry S. Truman and his principal foreign policy advisers, many of whom had been suspicious of Stalin's intentions from the outset, began to search for ways to block further Soviet postwar gains. They succeeded in defeating Moscow's moves against Turkey and Iran and in holding the line over German issues. On the other hand, in March 1946, when Winston Churchill, Great Britain's wartime leader, proposed an Anglo-American alliance to confront Stalin in his "Iron Curtain" speech at Fulton, Missouri, most U.S. officials and commentators were not yet ready to contemplate such a bold move. In a matter of weeks, however, they would have their own anti-Soviet strategy.

In February 1946 the Department of State, headed by George C. Marshall and his deputy, Dean Acheson, invited its chargé d'affaires in Moscow and expert on Stalin's regime, George F. Kennan, to explain the deeper reasons for Soviet hostility toward the West. Kennan's "Long Telegram" of 22 February 1946 offered a comprehensive and penetrating analysis of Soviet behavior, which he attributed to a combination of historical, ideological, and opportunistic power-politics considerations. Kennan concluded that Moscow's hostility to the West and aggressive tendencies were the unalterable mainstay of the Soviet regime. He also recommended that the United States establish a barrier of stable states that would eventually frustrate Moscow's expansionist designs and force it to seek accommodation with the capitalist-democratic West. Kennan's secret telegram was greeted by President Truman's administration, and especially James Forrestal, the staunchly anticommunist secretary of the navy, as a brilliant dissection of the central issues in U.S.-Soviet relations and as a sound blueprint for policy. Accordingly, Forrestal encouraged Kennan to make his ideas available to foreign policy elites. In a *Foreign Affairs* article in July 1947 (which he signed as "X"), Kennan presented his thesis in a more elaborate and eloquent form. Arguing that the Soviet Union's intention was "to make sure that it has filled every nook and cranny available to it in the basin of world power," he concluded that henceforth the basic goal of U.S. policy should be the "patient but firm and vigilant containment of Russian expansive tendencies." In reality, Kennan had articulated a grand strategy his superiors had already adopted in principle, but whose specific dictates and tactics remained to be defined.

The Truman Doctrine, Marshall Plan, and NATO

On 21 February 1947 Great Britain's Labour government informed the Truman administration that, for reasons of economy, British support of Greece and Turkey was about to end. Fearing that the communist-led insurrection in Greece and Moscow's pressures on Turkey, regarding control of the Straits (Bosporus and Dardanelles) and territorial disputes, would open the eastern Mediterranean to Soviet power, the United States unveiled its new policy of containment. Without specifically accusing the Soviet Union of aggression, President Truman solemnly pledged U.S. support to "free peoples who are resisting attempted subjugation by armed minorities or by outside pressure" in an address to a joint session of Congress on 12 March 1947. Although the recipients of the proposed economic and military assistance were Greece and Turkey, the president's speech committed his government to indiscriminate opposition to Soviet power, communism, and attempts to overthrow anticommunist regimes anywhere—a pledge that came to be known as the Truman Doctrine. Thus, from its inception containment took on the form of a crusade not only against Moscow's power but also against the disciples of an ideology. As commentator Walter Lippmann argued in a series of articles eventually published in *The Cold War* (1947), the Truman administration committed the United States to oppose all manner of political developments in unspecified regions, a policy likely to drain U.S. resources and military power; moreover, it bypassed the consideration of the United Nations.

A more ambitious if less ideologically defined application of containment followed in quick succession. Alarmed by the war's devastating effects on Europe's economic and social conditions, which the Soviet Union might exploit for its expansionist designs, the Truman administration offered both the funds and blueprint for European recovery. The Marshall Plan (5 June 1947) offered assistance to all European countries, regardless of ideological considerations, but it required participating states to achieve recovery through regional cooperation and economic integration, on the basis of private ownership of the means of production and free and open markets. As the plan's principal architects anticipated, the Soviet government denounced the offer as a capitalist plot to undermine the sovereignty of European states.

The Marshall Plan revived the nations of Western Europe and enabled them to serve as the barrier envisioned in Kennan's notion of containment; it also provided the impetus for the establishment of the European Economic Community in the late 1950s. On the other hand, U.S. policy also accentuated Europe's East-West divisions, especially since the three western occupation zones of Germany, now reunited in a political entity, were included in the recovery program. The Soviet government responded by imposing tighter controls across east-central Europe and in East Germany. Thus, from the outset containment was a response to Soviet initiatives as well as a self-fulfilling prophecy. By consistently assuming the worst in Soviet intentions, it served as justification for the strongest countermeasures, which in turn very probably elicited even harder Soviet positions.

Moscow's hostile reaction to the Marshall Plan caused President Truman's administration to shift its attention from economic recovery to security. In February 1948 a communist coup turned Czechoslovakia into a Soviet satellite, and in June, Soviet military authorities cut off the West's surface access to Berlin. Given the Red Army's decisive numerical superiority, a showdown in central Europe would have been disastrous for the Western powers. Although the U.S. airlift of supplies to Berlin induced the Soviets to end the blockade, the lesson appeared to be clear: economic power alone was no match for military force. To succeed, containment's barrier needed arms. In April 1949, responding to such European initiatives as the Treaty of Dunkirk and the Brussels Pact, the United States invited Canada and ten European states to join the North Atlantic Treaty Organization (NATO). In effect, President Truman's administration declared that the defense of Western Europe was vital to U.S. security, a concept that had enormous implications for U.S. planners given the Soviet superiority in conventional forces and their strategic advantage in Europe. Despite massive U.S. military assistance and prodding, NATO's European partners showed little inclination to produce the forces needed for their defense. Accordingly, the United States could preserve the existing balance of power and deter a Soviet attack by stationing large numbers of its own troops in Europe and, ultimately, through the threat of nuclear retaliation against the Soviet Union itself. When the Soviets developed their own nuclear capability, containment would be credible only as long as the United States retained a clear advantage in strategic and tactical nuclear weapons. By the mid-1950s Greece, Turkey, and West Germany had joined NATO; the Soviets responded with their own alliance system, the Warsaw Pact Treaty Organization. A race for more arms and more allies was on.

NSC-68, the Korean War, and the Cold War

For all its sweeping rhetoric, the Truman administration had been careful to distinguish between conflicts where U.S. power could be successfully employed and where it could not. Thus, the policy of containment was not applied to China, where, as in Greece, communists were fighting to overthrow an incompetent and unpopular regime. Claiming to have done all they reasonably could to support the Chinese nationalists, the president's advisers professed to see no major threat to U.S. security interests in the communists' victory in 1949. They prepared to recognize the Peoples' Republic of China under Mao Zedong, but the "loss" of China precipitated a review of containment's requirements. Domestic critics took advantage of disturbing international developments to charge that the Truman administration was soft on communism. In the early months of 1950, responding to the Soviet Union's development of atomic weapons and to the establishment of the communist regime in China, President Truman's administration commissioned a new comprehensive analysis of U.S. security. The resulting document, National Security Council Paper Number 68 (NSC-68), issued in April 1950, called for an all-out effort to mobilize the economic, political, and military resources of the Western world to confront Soviet power anywhere and by all available means. Written under the guidance of Paul Nitze, Kennan's replacement as director of the Policy Planning Staff, NSC-68 assumed that the Soviet regime was "animated by a new fanatic faith, antithetical to our own, and seeks to impose its absolute authority over the rest of the world," by armed force if necessary. While Kennan's containment had called for the Western alliance to deny the Soviets control of the principal centers of industrial and military power, NSC-68 strategy sought to encircle the Soviet Union and contain it within a continuous perimeter of the United States' allies and clients. Expecting the worst and focusing on the Soviets' enormous potential for military action, President Truman's administration prepared to respond in kind virtually around the globe and with more powerful weapons, including the hydrogen bomb.

In June 1950, the communist regime of North Korea invaded anticommunist South Korea. The president and his advisers decided to oppose the invasion, viewing it as a Soviet threat to U.S. security interests in the Far East, including Japan. The geographic scope of containment was suddenly extended to the Asian mainland, and the United States committed itself to fighting a major war, especially after China entered the conflict in November 1950. The United States appeared to be battling at once both twins of the communist behemoth. To make matters worse, activities of Republican Senator Joseph McCarthy, who suggested that communists had infiltrated the U.S. government and other institutions, generated anticommunist hysteria that threatened to undermine the very democratic principles U.S. foreign policy claimed to be defending around the world.

Following Stalin's death on 5 March 1953, the Soviet government adopted a more pragmatic and conciliatory outlook, leading to pressures on both sides for the resumption of dialogue across the ideological divide. Starting in 1954 a series of summit meetings became periodic events in the East-West confrontation, but, except for agreement to end the occupation of Austria (which was neutralized), no compromise could be reached on the central issues of dispute: the future of Germany, Europe's division, mutually threatening postures, and the nuclear arms race. In Asia the East-West confrontation continued to deepen and expand. After three years of ferocious fighting, an armistice in July 1953 returned Korea to its division into a communist North and an anticommunist South. A similar fate soon befell Vietnam, as Southeast Asia became the focus of tension. Although the United States and Great Britain encouraged France to suppress the communist-supported insurgent Vietminh, the French were left to fight alone and were defeated at the decisive battle of Dien Bien Phu in May 1954. The Geneva conference on Korea and Indochina, convened at the request of the Soviet Union and China in July 1954, produced agreements on the independence and neutralization of Laos and Cambodia, and on the "temporary" division of Vietnam near the 17th parallel, pending national elections in 1956. U.S. efforts to fill the vacuum created by the end of French

rule, and to bolster Vietnam's anticommunist southern half, paved the way for direct U.S. involvement in the region a few years later. In another manifestation of containment directed at China, the United States signed a defense treaty, which was vaguely enhanced by formal congressional support—the Formosa Resolution of 29 January 1955—with the Nationalist Chinese.

A serious blow to U.S. attempts to confront the Soviet Union with a solid Western alliance followed the nationalization of the Suez Canal Company by Egyptian President Gamal Abdel Nasser in July 1956. When Great Britain and France joined Israel in attacking Egypt, the Soviets threatened to expel the invaders by force and to subject London and Paris to nuclear strikes. President Dwight D. Eisenhower castigated his two allies and compelled them to withdraw and both governments soon fell. The Suez crisis weakened NATO and revealed that Washington's view of containment was not always shared by its partners on whose cooperation the strategy depended. France, for example, withdrew from NATO's unified command structure in 1966. Conversely, the crisis enhanced Moscow's image as the patron of Arab nationalism and added the Middle East to the battlefronts of the Cold War. Anxious to reduce the damage, improve its own image among Arab rulers, and block further Soviet penetration of the area, the United States promised military assistance to Middle East states that might become victims of communist aggression (later known as the Eisenhower Doctrine). The Suez crisis also overshadowed the anti-Soviet uprising in Hungary in October-November 1956, which Soviet troops crushed while Hungarian appeals for U.S. assistance went unanswered, although since the late 1940s U.S. broadcasts had encouraged the nations of Eastern Europe to oppose their Soviet-imposed regimes.

For a brief period in the late 1950s, the death of the staunchly anticommunist Secretary of State John Foster Dulles, Nikita Khrushchev's successful visit to the United States in September 1959, a scheduled summit in Paris, and President Eisenhower's proposed trip to Moscow appeared to herald a period of détente and the possibility of major breakthroughs in the East-West stalemate. On 1 May 1960, however, the shooting down of a U.S. spy plane over Soviet territory in the U-2 incident and the subsequent diplomatic crisis dashed hopes for a lasting U.S.-Soviet accommodation. In his farewell address President Eisenhower warned the nation that efforts to confront the Soviet threat, especially the heavy emphasis on military power, were depleting the United States' resources and undermining its democratic institutions.

Containment and Détente

Under Presidents John F. Kennedy and Lyndon B. Johnson preoccupation with a perceived Soviet challenge intensified, and the strategy of containment was given new and broader interpretations. The race to remain ahead of the Soviets escalated in virtually every field of human endeavor, including space exploration. It also became more risky as the superpowers came perilously close to open war over Berlin and, much more ominously, in the Cuban missile crisis of October 1962, which briefly brought Soviet nuclear weapons to the doorstep of the United States. Efforts to bolster tottering regimes in the Third World as a counterforce to suspected communist subversion increased U.S. covert operations and counterinsurgency activities and led to containment's costliest climax—the Vietnam War. Unable to defeat the communist North Vietnamese, successive administrations fought less to save the regime of South Vietnam than to uphold the United States' reputation as a superpower. In 1967 an embattled President Johnson cited containment as the basis for his policy in Vietnam, where he still believed victory was possible; two years earlier he had succeeded in imposing a pro-U.S. regime in the Dominican Republic by the use of force. After attempting to combine massive air power with negotiations in 1971, President Richard M. Nixon and his principal foreign policy adviser, Henry Kissinger, finally abandoned the administration's clients in Saigon, and by mid-1975 the United States' influence in Southeast Asia had collapsed. If the settlement in Korea had been a painful stalemate, the outcome in Vietnam was total defeat whose impact on both the policy and the national psyche of the United States was devastating and lasting.

While still seeking to extricate itself from the debilitating morass of Vietnam, the Nixon administration adjusted its brand of containment. The post-Vietnam realities were reflected in President Nixon's "new strategy for peace," or Nixon Doctrine, which pledged U.S. support for regimes battling local communist opponents but without direct U.S. military involvement. In essence, containment was restored to its original and more selective preoccupation with the strategically vital areas of Europe and Asia, to be pursued less by military confrontation than by diplomatic and economic power, in which the United States continued to hold the advantage. Avoiding the risks of military action in the Third World, the United States sought to engage the Soviet Union in a direct and vigorous dialogue designed to produce security through balance-of-power arrangements and arms-control agreements. Although substantive progress proved elusive and tensions remained, U.S.-Soviet relations acquired a level of stability, self-restraint, and mutual acceptance of each other's security perimeter. The Nixon-Kissinger strategy benefited greatly from the Sino-Soviet split, which had, since the late 1960s, turned the once monolithic Soviet bloc into a battleground between the two communist giants. The United

States' bold opening to China precipitated by President Nixon's historic 1972 visit to the country produced an intricate triangular power relationship that rendered the original concept of containment problematic at best.

Despite President Nixon's claim in 1969 that the Cold War had ended, and even as U.S.-Soviet relations no longer seemed the defining element in global politics, containing Soviet power remained the goal of U.S. foreign policy. In the late 1970s President Jimmy Carter's national security adviser, Zbigniew Brzezinski, spoke eloquently of interdependence, of the wish to accommodate reformist pressures in the Third World, and of the need for the United States to escape a "siege mentality." Nevertheless, in the end the Soviet Union continued to hold the key to most international issues of concern to U.S. officials. This was obviously true of the prospects for arms control, instability, and violent conflict across much of southern Africa (where Cuban dictator Fidel Castro appeared to act as Moscow's agent), and in the new theme in U.S. foreign policy—defense of human rights. If the 1975 Helsinki Accords committed the communist regimes to respect such rights, they also solidified Moscow's position by declaring the inviolability of European borders. President Carter succeeded in brokering a spectacular settlement, the Camp David Accords, between Israel and Egypt by launching a promising but painfully slow process toward eventual accommodation between Arabs and Jews. The agreement highlighted Moscow's relatively marginal role in the Middle East, where containment through peacemaking appeared to be gaining ground. At the same time, other developments nearby indicated that Soviet communism was not the only ideological foe. The collapse in 1979 of Shah Mohammad Reza Pahlavi's regime in Iran, Washington's vaunted friend and ally, and the emergence in that strategic region of a fanatically anti-American Islamic state, underscored the fact that the position of the United States in the Middle East as well as in the entire non-Western world remained precarious. When the Soviets invaded Afghanistan in December 1979 to prop up a Moscow client, President Carter's administration invoked containment policy by talking of dangerous confrontation between the superpowers, increasing defense spending, strengthening the strategic presence of the United States in the Persian Gulf, announcing military sales to China, and supporting the anti-Moscow Afghan rebels. Reaffirming similar pronouncements dating back to the Truman Doctrine, the Carter Doctrine affirmed that the United States would view any Soviet aggression in the direction of the Persian Gulf as a threat to vital security interests of the United States.

Reagan and Gorbachev

At first the presidency of Ronald Reagan (1981–1989) appeared to restore containment to its original urgency and to signal U.S. resolve to win a clear victory over the main ideological enemy. The Soviet Union was publicly and persistently portrayed as the "evil empire" suspected of preparing for war. It was accused of acquiring new strategic weapons and defense systems in violation of treaty obligations and of committing atrocities that included mass murder by the use of internationally banned biological weapons in Afghanistan and by shooting down a South Korean commercial airliner on 1 September 1983, the KAL-007 incident. Charging previous administrations with defeatism, President Reagan's administration declared its resolve to regain military superiority over the Soviets by upgrading the U.S. nuclear arsenal, expanding the navy's offensive capabilities, and authorizing the air force to purchase the strategic B-1 bomber. Secretary of State Alexander Haig spoke of tactical nuclear "shots across the bow" to deter Soviet forces in Europe, while the president's pet project, the Strategic Defense Initiative (Star Wars) system, appeared at first to undo any progress toward limiting intercontinental ballistic missiles. President Reagan and his advisers, especially Central Intelligence Agency Director William Casey, saw a Moscow-inspired communist campaign in Central America and South America and intervened to undermine Nicaragua's Sandinista government. They also sent U.S. troops in 1983 to overthrow a Marxist faction in Grenada. Echoing the Republican Party's rhetoric of the late 1940s, which had criticized containment as defeatist and had advocated instead the "liberation" of nations enslaved by communist rule, Washington appeared eager to take the offensive. In Asia the desire to maintain normal relations with Taiwan threatened to destroy Washington's "China card." The confrontational posture and activism of the Reagan administration more than matched the aggressive policies of Leonid Brezhnev's regime, and the Cold War had entered a new and ominous phase.

The heightened sense of conflict was short-lived. In 1985 a new Soviet leader, Mikhail Gorbachev, set out to modernize the Soviet system and, in the process, to seek accommodation with the West, whose goodwill he needed if his domestic "restructuring" was to succeed. Self-confident and unafraid to make concessions, he soon dazzled his adversaries with his diplomatic dexterity and willingness to concede what to his predecessors had been unthinkable, that the Soviet Union could not continue to compete against the West along a broad economic and military front. Seizing the initiative in a series of spectacular summits in Geneva (1985), Reykjavík (1986), and Washington (1987), Gorbachev proposed far-reaching agreements on arms limitations while gradually easing Moscow's control over east-central Europe. The Intermediate Range Nuclear Forces Treaty of 8 December 1987, which eliminated such weapons from Europe and Asia,

was a dramatic step toward genuine reductions in nuclear weapons. It was followed by significant agreements on strategic weapons reached in the spring of 1988 at the Moscow summit. At the same time the Soviet Union withdrew its forces from Afghanistan, allowing the eventual collapse of Kabul's puppet regime. The following year, one after another, the communist governments of east-central Europe were swept aside by popular uprisings whose success was assured by Moscow's nonintervention. Gorbachev also permitted free elections in East Germany, dooming the communist dictatorship there and paving the way for the country's reunification under the West German government.

The End of the Cold War

Some observers have argued that Gorbachev's domestic reforms and nonaggressive policies were forced upon him by the Soviet Union's inability to keep pace with the United States in the race for superpower status, especially in view of the Reagan administration's increased military spending. It has been claimed that the more spirited brand of containment of the 1980s finally drove the Soviets to bankruptcy and ended the Cold War with a decisive victory for the United States. Others have posited, however, that for all its many weaknesses and limitations, the Soviet Union retained sufficient military power, institutional stability, and economic resources to maintain its control over communist Europe and challenge the United States around the globe virtually indefinitely. In hindsight, Gorbachev's radical reforms, which proved catastrophic to Soviet power, were hardly inevitable. This alternative view portrays Gorbachev more as the initiator of change that escalated beyond his control than the hapless leader reacting to circumstances created by U.S. superiority. Still others have argued that the accommodationist policies of Western Europe and the courage of the peoples of Eastern Europe, more than U.S. containment policies, helped end the Cold War.

During the presidency of George Bush (1989–1993), the collapse of Soviet military power across east-central Europe, the disappearance of Moscow's client regimes, the discrediting of communism as a system of government, and the conciliatory tactics of Gorbachev—who was soon battling domestic forces he could not control—changed Europe's political landscape and ended the East-West confrontation. At least in Europe, the United States no longer had an adversary to contain. As the uncertainties of the new international order became apparent, U.S. foreign and security policy required sweeping review and the nation's capabilities and goals needed to be redefined.

Stripped of its theoretical superstructure, containment encompasses the complex and shifting assortment of policies through which the United States sought to respond to the Soviet challenge. Accordingly, no definitive assessment of the concept is possible as long as the perceptions, objectives, and strategies of the Soviet Union remain a matter of subjective interpretation. Those who attribute the Cold War to the aggressive character of Soviet communism are likely to see in the containment policies of succeeding administrations the necessary and ultimately successful response to Moscow's global threat. Those who hold the United States principally responsible for the postwar East-West divisions regard containment as a U.S. strategy to deny the Soviet Union its rightful place in the international order and preserve the supremacy of the capitalist West over the underdeveloped regions of the world. Containment is certain to remain a much-debated concept in contemporary U.S. diplomatic history.

JOHN O. IATRIDES

See also Carter Doctrine; Cold War; Cuban Missile Crisis; Eisenhower Doctrine; Gorbachev, Mikhail Sergeevich; Helsinki Accords; KAL-007 Incident; Kennan, George Frost; Korean War; Marshall Plan; Nitze, Paul Henry; Nixon, Richard Milhous; North Atlantic Treaty Organization; NSC-68; Nuclear Weapons and Strategy; Reagan, Ronald Wilson; Russia and the Soviet Union; Suez Crisis; Truman Doctrine; Vietnam War

FURTHER READING

Dougherty, James E., and Robert L. Pfaltzgraff, Jr. *American Foreign Policy: FDR to Reagan.* New York, 1986.
Etzold, Thomas H., and John Lewis Gaddis, eds. *Containment: Documents on American Policy and Strategy, 1945–1950.* New York, 1978.
Gaddis, John Lewis. *Strategies of Containment: A Critical Appraisal of Postwar American National Security Policy.* New York, 1982.
———. *The Long Peace: Inquiries into the History of the Cold War.* New York, 1987.
———. *The United States and the End of the Cold War: Implications, Reconsiderations, Provocations.* New York, 1992.
Herring, George C. *America's Longest War: The United States and Vietnam, 1950–1975.* 3rd ed. New York, 1996.
Kegley, Charles W., ed. *The Long Postwar Peace: Contending Explanations and Projections.* New York, 1991.
Kennan, George F. *Memoirs: 1925–1950.* Boston, 1967.
———. *Memoirs: 1950–1963.* Boston, 1972.
———. *The United States and the End of the Cold War: Implications, Reconsiderations, Provocations.* New York, 1992.
Lippmann, Walter. *The Cold War: A Study in U.S. Foreign Policy.* New York, 1947.
Leffler, Melvyn P. *A Preponderance of Power: National Security, the Truman Administration, and the Cold War.* Stanford, Calif., 1992.
May, Ernest R., ed. *American Cold War Strategy: Interpreting NSC 68.* Boston, 1993.
Paterson, Thomas G. *Meeting the Communist Threat: Truman to Reagan.* New York, 1988.
Stoessinger, John G. *Crusaders and Pragmatists: Movers of Modern American Foreign Policy.* New York, 1979.
Ulam, Adam B. *The Rivals: America and Russia Since World War II.* New York, 1971.
Wohlforth, William C. *The Elusive Balance: Power and Perceptions During the Cold War.* Ithaca, N.Y., 1993.

CONTINENTAL EXPANSION

The acquisition of territory in North America, first by the British colonies and then by the United States, from the early colonial period to about 1867. Continental expansion was driven by a rapidly expanding population, an aggressive foreign policy, and an ideology that combined belief in divine inspiration with perceived natural law. From the earliest days of European colonization of the east coast of North America in the seventeenth century, settlers viewed the vast continent as an area to tame and the Native American tribes as an impediment to remove or destroy. A high birth rate and massive immigration produced a booming U.S. population and, subsequently, an inexorable drive to claim new land. Political leaders, both in the colonies and in the young United States, responded by making landed expansion a high priority. Religious and intellectual leaders played important roles by justifying the spread of Western institutions throughout the continent. Although continental expansion dominated U.S. foreign policy for decades, it lost its appeal in the middle of the nineteenth century, as the country descended into the Civil War—in part over the issue of expansion. The United States then shifted its attention largely to commercial expansion after the war.

Several factors influenced continental expansion. In the part of North America that would become the United States, continental expansion served primarily as an antidote to perceived overcrowding. For most of history, the eastern seaboard has been less densely populated than Western Europe, but colonists and their forebears, pondering the seemingly endless wilderness before them, felt crowded and sought more land. Pockets of unproductive land, combined with high birth rates, caused many family crises that prompted westward migration. Much of the land in the original thirteen colonies was too sandy or too rocky for efficient agriculture. High birth and survival rates meant that a farmer might have multiple adult sons in need of farm land, but because the arable land was limited, the farms usually could not be divided; younger sons then either moved to the cities or left the farm in search of open land elsewhere.

Especially in the South, the choice of crops could reduce the land's ability to support agriculture. The two most important crops in the region were cotton and tobacco, both of which were notorious for stripping nutrients from the soil. The seventeenth-century settlers at Jamestown found that land could support tobacco for only three years, and plantation owners in later years had similar results with cotton. Soil exhaustion forced small farmers to look for more fertile land.

The final force pushing people into the frontier was immigration. Although immigrants came to North America for many reasons, the leading motivator was economic opportunity, and in the seventeenth and eighteenth centuries that meant land. Immigrants found that most of the good land in the coastal regions had been taken, and the vast expanse of land with at best a sparse population lured newcomers. Thus, immigrants joined displaced farmers and landless sons of farmers in the move to the frontier.

The settlers' concept of the frontier was crucial to spurring westward expansion. Over the years the colonists developed the belief that free access to land was necessary to ensure freedom. President Thomas Jefferson later popularized this idea, linking the widespread existence of yeoman farmers with political independence, which in turn guaranteed the stability of the Republic. This ideology intensified the common belief that the American colonies were, in John Winthrop's famous words, "a city upon a hill," visible to the entire world. Throughout their history, many Americans saw their experiments in political freedom in North America as evidence of divine intervention. God, they believed, had set aside the large, rich continent to be the crucible of a new political system; their job was to fill the continent and carry out God's plan.

The widespread presence of Native Americans presented a challenge to the settlers' reasoning. Military, social, and economic interaction with Indians proved to the settlers that North America was not empty, but because the tribes did little to improve the land in the Western economic sense, they were fundamentally in conflict with white settlers who equated clearing the land with advancing Christian civilization. Americans wavered between two basic visions of the Indians. Many saw the tribes as a part of the wilderness that had to make way for the advance of civilization. Adherents of this approach described Indians as "savages" not far removed from wild beasts; to some, they even represented the devil and his evil ways. Alternatively, many perceived the Indian as someone to be brought into civilization. Beginning with William Penn in the 1680s, a few American leaders tried to deal with the Native Americans equitably. After U.S. independence, these people came to believe that only converting the Indians from their semi-nomadic lifestyle to yeoman farming could provide a peaceful solution. Whatever the differences among settlers about Native American policy, they all agreed that tribal land-use patterns should not be allowed to continue.

Although powerful forces propelled expansion, three influences sought to impede them. First, the British Empire generally worked to limit colonial and U.S. landed expansion, especially northward. In the colonial era, British officials tried to restrict colonists to the eastern seaboard. After U.S. independence, the powerful British thwarted U.S. ambition more successfully than did the Spanish, French, Russians, Mexicans, or the Indian tribes. Second, throughout the period, U.S. citizens hesitated to assimilate nonwhite and Roman Catholic residents of conquered areas, fearing that these people would not be able to live under the Constitution. Third, between 1815 and the Civil War, the domestic debate over the expansion of slavery changed continental expansion from an unquestionable right to a point of contention. Thus, the United States, which President Jefferson had speculated might one day control the entire New World, ended its quest for more land after acquiring about one-third of North America, unable to absorb Mexico to the south or Canada to the north.

The Colonial Period

From the earliest days of colonization, whites anticipated that their progeny would some day move west into the mountainous regions of the interior. Many of the British colonies, such as New York and Virginia, received charters that extended their borders into the unknown spaces of the continent, even to the Pacific Ocean. British, French, and Spanish colonial officials struggled to lay claim to as much land as possible and win the cooperation of various Indian tribes. Enjoying relative peace, freedom, and prosperity, the thirteen British colonies between Spanish Florida and disputed Canada grew in population in the seventeenth and eighteenth centuries. By 1750 Great Britain's North American colonies had 1.25 million people, compared to fewer than 75,000 in French Canada and Louisiana. Gradually, people began to move inland towards the Appalachians, seeking fertile land and freedom from overcrowding.

This first westward movement had international repercussions. Skirmishes with Native Americans became more common, forcing the British government to balance its support for colonists with its desire to maintain good relations with Indian allies and trading partners. The French, who competed with the British for influence with the Indians, were concerned that such migration would sever their communication lines between Canada and New Orleans. In the French and Indian War (1756–1763), early French victories brought the Indians to their side in an effort to push the colonists back to the coastal plateau, but the British army, with some help from the colonials, eventually conquered Canada and defeated Pontiac and his Indian followers. The peace settlement gave Florida and Canada to Great Britain, while transferring Louisiana to Spain. At least a few colonial leaders saw in the British victory the opportunity for rapid expansion throughout the area east of the Mississippi River.

In Great Britain, however, concern grew over the management of such a large and unruly populace. British officials decided that their American colonies needed a standing army for protection from both other colonial

Continental Expansion

From *American Foreign Relations*, Thomas G. Paterson, J. Garry Clifford, and Kenneth J. Hagan, Volume I. ©1995 by D.C. Heath and Company.
Reprinted with permission of Houghton Mifflin Company.

powers and Native Americans. To pay for such an army, they had to be sure of more central control of the colonies. At the same time, they struggled to find a fair policy for dealing with the many Indian tribes—most of whom had been allied with the French—inhabiting the area between the Mississippi River and the Appalachians. Fearing that settlers who crossed the mountains would be beyond their control and spark conflict with the Indians, British officials issued the Proclamation of 7 October 1763, declaring the land west of the crest of the

Appalachians closed to settlement. If Americans wanted to move into unsettled land, the government had decreed, they could go to Florida or the Canadian coastal regions.

The Proclamation of 1763 helped cause the American Revolution, as colonists added its restrictions to their list of grievances. In 1774 Great Britain infuriated leaders of the northern colonies by extending Canada's borders south to the Ohio River, thus further blocking the route west. In order to plot a unified course, twelve of the colonies formed the Continental Congress in the fall of 1774. By emphasizing "continental," the delegates suggested that they were forming the embryo of a government that would some day rule all of North America. Thus, when fighting broke out in 1775, the Continental Congress wanted to bring Canada into the cause, figuring that the French Catholics would rebel against the British and that other Canadians would have aspirations similar to those in the thirteen colonies. When the Canadians refused to join, the colonials decided to conquer Canada. The Canadians and British easily repulsed the ill-prepared colonial forces.

The decision to invade Canada revealed three important themes at the heart of U.S. foreign policy. First, U.S. citizens believed that controlling Canada was part of their destiny. Even before declaring independence, colonial leaders determined that Canada had to be drawn into an alliance. Second, by appealing to Canadians as "fellow sufferers," U.S. leaders displayed a fundamental belief in their own righteousness. They were not just representing national interests, but rather executing God's will. Last, by placing such a high priority on conquering Canada, the colonials emphasized that they would not be content to remain a coastal nation. If need be, they would fight to absorb the continent.

Early Republic

The Declaration of Independence in July 1776 established an important ideological basis for westward expansion. Supporters of the Revolution agreed with Thomas Paine's idea that the British colonies in North America should be a haven for political liberty. As the self-appointed protectors of liberty, U.S. citizens felt an obligation to spread their institutions as far as possible, and the idea that the new nation would govern the entire continent gained favor. Closely tied with this expectation was what might be called the "science" of empire, the notion that natural law predetermined the fate of the United States. Many citizens believed, as Anglican Bishop George Berkeley wrote in 1752, that "Westward the course of empire takes its way." In other words, the United States was destined to replace the supposedly fading and corrupt British Empire. Science also told U.S. citizens that a sort of gravity would pull smaller political units, such as Cuba, into the U.S. empire. A combination of theology and natural law seemed to demand an aggressive policy of continental expansion.

The eventual success of the American Revolution forced another adjustment of the map of North America in 1783. In return for their half-hearted efforts to fight the British, the Spanish reclaimed Florida. Colonial diplomats, led by Benjamin Franklin, failed to win Canada at the conference table but settled for independence and a large piece of land between the Great Lakes, the 31st parallel, and the Mississippi River. With this acquisition, the fledgling United States almost doubled its size. The nation now seemed to have all of the land it could use for the foreseeable future.

Two problems hindered the settlement of this new land. First, the government under the Articles of Confederation proved weak. The new states often had overlapping claims to the western land, and the national government did not have strength enough to force a resolution. The area south of the Ohio River was vulnerable to Spanish interference, while that north of the river had more British than American soldiers. Individual states could not effectively deal with such threats or establish local governments. People poured into the region and chaos ensued. Second, the tens of thousands of Native Americans who already inhabited these territories opposed white expansion. Some had been driven back from their ancestral lands in earlier decades; others saw that the British defeat opened the way for U.S. citizens to flood the region. Although wars and plagues had weakened them, the tribes in the region remained a formidable military force. The British took advantage of their position in Canada and encouraged Indian raids in order to drive out settlers and maintain influence in the area. The threat of such raids made a move to the west too risky for some people.

Recognizing that the United States needed a new system of government to address these challenges, in 1787 the leaders of the nation gathered in Philadelphia. After the original thirteen states agreed to surrender their western land claims, the Confederation Congress passed the Northwest Ordinance of 1787, which created a system through which the western territories could become states. This law gave Congress almost unlimited power to control the territories. The Republic's leaders simultaneously created a constitution for a federal government that could, among other things, deal with threats from Indians and foreign powers. The ratification of the Constitution in 1789 finally gave the United States the structure around which to organize expansion on a truly continental scale.

U.S. citizens were justifiably proud of their Constitution and its emphasis on freedom and the rule of law, but that pride was sometimes tempered with xenophobia, a fear of foreigners. White Protestant men, many of whom shared the belief that they were fulfilling Winthrop's desire to found a divinely inspired society, formed the vast majority of the voting public, and many of them did not believe that other ethnic or religious groups were capable of living in such a society. They often held the racist opinion that Native Americans, African Americans, and Hispanics could not be trusted with democratic responsibilities. They had a similar view of Spanish and French Catholics in North America, whose loyalty to the pope, they reasoned, made them incapable of participating in a democracy. The persistence of these opinions presented problems throughout the period of continental expansion. U.S. citizens wanted land but not necessarily the people already on it. They could either drive out nonconformists, through force or diplomacy, or overwhelm them numerically and hope to assimilate them. The United States pursued both courses at various times.

After the legislative reforms of the late 1780s, U.S. leaders opened a debate on how to deal with the Indians in the western territories. The nation's leaders thought that the tribes had a straightforward choice—join civilization or continue a primitive life-style outside of the boundaries of the United States. Most agreed that the tribes would have to yield their land; westerners wanted the quick use of force, while easterners were more willing to explore opportunities for assimilation. Many Native Americans, however, preferred a third option, that they could continue to live in their traditional manner on ancestral lands. At the center of the conflict was a different approach to the land. U.S. citizens believed that individuals owned land and worked hard to improve it, usually for agriculture. Native Americans generally held land communally and took what it produced. The two systems could not coexist.

U.S. representatives sought to resolve conflicts between settlers and Indians through negotiations leading to the cession of tribal lands to the government. In 1784 the Iroquois agreed to cede land along the southeastern shore of Lake Erie in the Treaty of Fort Stanwix. The next year, Cherokee chiefs ceded a huge tract of land south of the Ohio River through the Treaty of Hopewell, and in 1790 the Creek did the same in Georgia. Because of the cultural differences, Indians and U.S. citizens had very different concepts of the meaning of the agreements. Many tribes, such as the Shawnee, became disillusioned with government treaties and took up arms to stop white encroachments.

With a stronger central government, the United States was able to muster the necessary military force to challenge the Indians in the trans-Appalachian west. Showing too little respect for the military prowess of the tribes, U.S. troops suffered defeat in Ohio in 1790 and 1791, leaving white settlers at risk. Three years later, General Anthony Wayne defeated the Shawnee at the Battle of Fallen Timbers and opened the way for relatively safe settlement of the Old Northwest. Seeing no chance for assimilation and reflecting a frontier suspicion that all Indians were taking orders from Canada, Wayne destroyed every Native American village in his path. In 1795, through the Treaty of Greenville, Wayne removed the tribes from most of the current state of Ohio.

Not all American leaders agreed with Wayne's dealings with the Indians. President Jefferson, in particular, advo-

cated the peaceful assimilation of Native Americans into white society. He argued that an Indian could be like any other yeoman farmer who owned a tract of land and participated in democracy. Assimilation seemed to be the perfect solution: Indians could enter a new era of prosperity, and land disputes could be resolved. The desire to assimilate Native Americans into U.S. society was usually well intentioned, but it reflected a lack of understanding of people who had little desire to change their lifestyle. In addition, behind assimilation policy was a thinly veiled threat to use force if necessary. President Jefferson himself made it clear that the United States was prepared to drive the trans-Appalachian tribes across the Plains to the Rocky Mountains.

In the long run, the Indians were simply too few to prevent the United States from expanding westward. Diseases and intertribal conflicts weakened Native American resistance, while the population of the United States grew at an astounding rate. Between 1750 and 1775 the population of the eastern colonies doubled to 2.5 million; by 1800 it had more than doubled again. An immigration wave and a sustained baby boom overwhelmed the Indians with a flood of settlers. By 1803 enough citizens had moved west to carve out the states of Kentucky, Tennessee, and Ohio, and the other parts of the western territory were filling rapidly. By 1820 six more states (Louisiana, Indiana, Mississippi, Illinois, Alabama, and Maine) had entered the Union. Meanwhile, Indian populations declined steadily.

The Native Americans were not the only ones feeling the power of "the American multiplication table," as one congressman characterized the country's fecundity. In the 1790s, hoping to strengthen their position in Florida, the Spanish began to encourage U.S. citizens to move south. Spain quickly lost control of both white settlers and angry Indians. In an attempt to halt the momentum that threatened to make Florida and Louisiana part of the United States, Spain accepted Pinckney's Treaty in 1795. Spain agreed to cooperate with the United States in stopping Indian attacks in the south, relinquished claims to some disputed land north of the 31st parallel, and granted U.S. citizens tax-free use of New Orleans for three years.

The Louisiana Purchase

Despite Pinckney's Treaty, stability did not come to the region. Napoleon believed that France needed the Louisiana Territory to supply its lucrative sugar-producing colony in Haiti. Under pressure, the Spanish government ceded Louisiana to France in 1801, placing a much stronger power on the western border of the United States. Free passage of the Mississippi River, which was crucial to the development of the western half of the United States, was now in jeopardy. In 1802 authorities in New Orleans closed the river to trade from the United States. U.S. leaders feared that, without an outlet, the trans-Appalachian region might sink into economic depression and, perhaps, become ripe for foreign intrigue.

President Jefferson and Secretary of State James Madison resolved to take New Orleans. They sent diplomats to Europe with authority to buy New Orleans and Florida, shipped aid to rebels in Haiti, ordered the removal of Indians across the Mississippi, and made a public show of building up the military. The French initially refused to sell any portion of their empire, but the success of the revolution in Haiti changed their perspective. Napoleon, who was organizing for a new war with Great Britain, decided that money was more valuable than an untenable empire in North America. In 1803 he offered to sell the entire Louisiana Territory for $15 million and President Jefferson accepted. Referring both to the territory's vague borders and the growing U.S. reputation for aggressive expansion, French Foreign Minister Charles-Maurice de Talleyrand-Périgord told one U.S. diplomat, "I suppose you will make the most of it."

The Louisiana Purchase was quite popular, although no one knew exactly how much land the United States had bought (later calculations put the area at 827,000 square miles). U.S. citizens understood that they no longer had to worry about control of the Mississippi and that the country had nearly doubled in size. President Jefferson believed that the territory would provide space for settlers for centuries and would be a good place to relocate Native Americans. At the same time, however, the borders to the Louisiana Territory were not entirely clear. The western and northern sections ran into empty and ill-defined Spanish and British holdings, opening the way for future border disputes. Few whites had seen the interior of the territory, leading to speculation that it might contain fertile land, great mineral deposits, abundant fur-bearing animals, and a river route to the Pacific Ocean.

President Jefferson then sent out exploration parties, most notably one led by Meriwether Lewis and William Clark, to learn more about the trans-Mississippi west and prepare the way for settlement. Leaving St. Louis in the spring of 1804, Lewis and Clark ascended the Missouri River in the hope of finding a transcontinental transportation route. After crossing the Rocky Mountains, the expedition descended the Columbia River to the Pacific Ocean in 1805. Upon their return to St. Louis in 1806, they thrilled President Jefferson and the public with accounts of abundant natural resources and river routes that reinforced enthusiasm for the Louisiana Purchase.

For the first time since the Revolution, the United States had acquired land, and with it came a constitutional crisis. The Constitution did not provide a means for adding new land, and many wondered how the country would govern such a large dominion. President Jefferson, a strict constructionist, argued that the checks and balances of the Constitution allowed for the spread of democracy. To safeguard the territory against the influence of the Spaniards, French, Indians, Creoles, convicts, and others who inhabited Louisiana, however, the federal government appointed a governor and marshals who held complete power.

The presidential election of 1804 seemed to vindicate President Jefferson's decisions regarding the Louisiana Purchase, but it also suggested that continental expansion could spark sectional differences. Many Federalists in New England worried that the creation of new states in the West would destroy the balance of power between the various regions, leaving them at a disadvantage. Although few New Englanders seriously considered leaving the Union over this issue, their concern was a precursor for future disputes between that region and the West, as well as a harbinger of North-South animosity that would dominate the United States from 1815 to 1865.

As more people pushed into the reaches of the Old Northwest and the Mississippi Territory, the western and southern states gained political power. Led by the War Hawks John Calhoun of South Carolina and Henry Clay of Kentucky, citizens of these regions demanded an aggressive approach toward the Native Americans and a firm line against Great Britain and Spain. When fighting broke out in Indiana in 1811 between Governor William Henry Harrison and the Shawnee Chief Tecumseh over ownership of the land, Clay led westerners in blaming the British for inciting Indian raids. Citing a string of British outrages, western and southern politicians pushed the nation toward war with the world's leading power. As many New Englanders had feared, expansion had brought a change in the national balance of power.

President James Madison saw in the international tension an opportunity to extend the country's borders. Late in 1811 the administration engineered a covert operation to relieve Spain of West Florida—the area that now forms the panhandles of Alabama and Mississippi—ostensibly to keep it out of British hands. A similar attempt failed to capture East Florida. At the same time, Madison and the War Hawks in Congress believed that if war came, invading Canada presented the best method for striking a military blow at Great Britain. Success would remove British power from the continent and weaken Indian resistance.

In the initial months of the War of 1812, it looked more likely that the British would reclaim the Northwest Territory. After the U.S. invasion of Canada failed miserably, Tecumseh's warriors joined with British forces to capture Detroit and drive into Ohio. Eventually, Harrison and naval forces on Lake Erie regained control of the region, and Tecumseh was killed in battle in southern Ontario. Sensing that Canada was not as vulnerable as hoped, U.S. forces withdrew rather than try to exploit their victories. In the Southwest, General Andrew Jackson and his Cherokee allies defeated the powerful Creek tribe in Alabama and then defended New Orleans from the British. Thus, Jackson and Harrison emerged from a futile war as heroes who had defeated dangerous enemies and assisted continental expansion. They also became the first westerners to serve as president.

The failure of the U.S. effort to capture Canada drove home the lesson that military strength would not produce northward expansion. U.S. citizens continued to see Canada as a natural part of a continental empire, but British naval supremacy and the Canadians' ability to defend their territory made conquest unlikely. U.S. leaders concluded that it was better to wait for the inevitable decision of Canadians to join the Union than to challenge Great Britain again. With northern expansion checked, the United States was forced to look south and west in its quest to fulfill its perceived destiny.

John Quincy Adams

Shortly after the War of 1812 focused the United States' view westward, President James Monroe appointed John Quincy Adams as secretary of state (1817–1825). Adams epitomized the national attitude that the United States and North America should be coterminous. He believed that continental expansion had God's blessing, that Canada would eventually move to join the United States, that Native Americans could not maintain their position, and that the United States could grow at Spain's expense. Adams began his career as an aggressive expansionist, but eventually his abolitionist beliefs led him to oppose further expansion as a threat to the stability of the United States.

Adams also understood that the transportation and market revolutions were changing U.S. society. The expansion of road and canal networks in the 1810s and 1820s as well as improved river transportation facilitated travel and communication throughout the country. Those developments in turn made it easier to transport crops and raw materials to markets. Adams advocated a national program of infrastructure improvements as a means to better unify the country and pave the way for further continental expansion. Although he hoped to strengthen the bonds among the regions, southern suspicion of centralized power destroyed his plans.

One of Adams's first acts was to conclude the Convention of 1818 with Great Britain, which defined some of the limits of the Louisiana Purchase. The treaty established the 49th parallel as the Canadian border with the United States between Lake of the Woods, Minnesota, and the Rocky Mountains. Adams also persuaded the British to agree to joint occupation of the Oregon Territory on the basis of a loose interpretation of the Louisiana

Purchase and Lewis and Clark's exploration. Remarkably, with little to back him up, he thus obtained a claim to the Pacific coast. Adams had no doubt that the booming population of the United States could fill Oregon and bring the land into the Union. At the time, however, travel to Oregon by wagon or ship was arduous and slow. Adams's impressive foresight and willingness to compromise with the British brought an important victory.

In stark contrast to their evolving attitude toward the British empire, statesmen in Washington challenged Spain's dominion on the continent. Spain simply could not exert power on the borders of the United States. Spanish North America held few people loyal to Spain, Native Americans were fighting Spanish authorities, and Spain itself had begun an extended period of decline. In addition, U.S. citizens believed that the Catholic monarchy was flawed by its very nature. They justified westward expansion as a moral cause with God's blessing. Adams, therefore, turned his sights toward Spain's holdings. He and the Spanish minister to Washington, Luis de Onís y Gonzalez, clashed over the future of Spain's rapidly crumbling New World empire. Revolutions in South America threatened the most valuable parts of that empire, and Onís demanded assurances that the United States would not assist the rebels. Adams wanted East Florida's 72,000 square miles, which, it seemed, the Spanish had no intention of using.

In 1817 President Monroe ordered General Jackson to subdue Seminole Indians who were wreaking havoc among the settlers in southern Georgia. The flamboyant Tennessean pursued the tribe into East Florida, burned their villages, executed two British subjects, and captured two Spanish forts. This gross violation of British sensibilities and Spanish sovereignty mortified President Monroe's cabinet, but Secretary of State Adams successfully defended General Jackson's actions. He understood that the British would not start another war over the incident, and he observed that the Spanish were incapable of controlling their frontier.

Adams realized that he held the upper hand and gave Onís an ultimatum—negotiate or lose East Florida. Adams confidently looked for further concessions in the west. President Monroe rejected his plan to extort Texas from Spain, forcing Adams to settle for lesser goals. In 1819 Onís signed the Transcontinental Treaty (also known as the Adams-Onís Treaty), through which Spain relinquished its claims to Oregon, agreed to a generous interpretation of the borders of the Louisiana Territory, and turned over East Florida in exchange for less than $5 million and U.S. recognition of Spain's claim to Texas.

One result of the Convention of 1818 and the Adams-Onís Treaty was a sudden increase in U.S. power in the Pacific Northwest, where Russia had staked a claim to coastal regions. Dismayed at the effectiveness of Yankee traders in his American realm, Czar Alexander I declared in 1821 that Russia held exclusive rights to the coast and offshore waters north of the 51st parallel. The U.S. government balked at this fresh assertion of Russian power, and Adams began to craft a statement that the United States would oppose any further colonization of the New World. This principle became the first part of President Monroe's 2 December 1823 address to Congress on foreign policy that later became known as the Monroe Doctrine.

The genesis of President Monroe's message came at least partially from Adams's insight that the British were trying to prevent the United States from further expansion. In August 1823 British Foreign Secretary George Canning proposed that the United States and Great Britain should make a joint declaration that they would not tolerate European interference in the New World, specifically any attempts by the Holy Alliance (Russia, Prussia, and Austria) to shore up the Spanish empire. To show good faith, Canning suggested that both countries should also vow not to take any more territory themselves. While Monroe, Madison, and Jefferson were stunned by their country's good fortune to ally with the world's greatest power, Adams saw the trap. The British were not adjusting their policies to accommodate the United States; rather they were asking the United States to surrender any hope of absorbing Cuba or Texas into the Union. Adams thought it better to maintain independence of action than "to come in as a cockboat in the wake of the British man-of-war." Adams believed that the rest of the continent would eventually side with the United States as long as its leaders remained patient and careful. Persuaded, President Monroe proceeded in December 1823 with an independent announcement of opposition to European interference in the Western Hemisphere.

Thus, by the 1820s the United States contained almost 1.8 million square miles with a rapidly growing population of about 10 million. The urge to settle the West remained an important force in American society, and the acquisition of land had tentatively preserved the balance between the eastern cities, western agriculture, and unsettled frontier. After the 1820s, however, further continental expansion was jeopardized. The North's expanding advantages in economic strength, population, and political power generated a growing imbalance between the northern free-labor states and the southern slave states that threatened to turn expansion into a sectional dispute.

Southerners feared that they might become vulnerable to northern political pressure and saw a need to expand slavery to maintain their power as well as to accommodate the growing slave population. Other than Florida, the only land open to statehood was to the northwest in the Louisiana Territory. In 1819 residents of Missouri petitioned Congress for admission as a slave state. Northerners in Congress, many of whom were beginning to see slavery as immoral, regarded Missouri's petition as an attempt by southerners to control landed expansion. The normally routine matter of admitting a new state had now become a source of bitter sectional conflict.

The speaker of the House, the nationalist Henry Clay, engineered a compromise that established the dividing line between free and slave territories at 36°30′. In addition, all parties agreed that incoming states would be paired, free and slave, in order to maintain a balance of power in the Senate. The Missouri Compromise of 1820 temporarily solved the crisis, but it opened up new possibilities for turmoil. Those who favored slavery could see that the land available below 36°30′ was considerably less than that above the line. Thus, southern politicians became the most aggressive expansionists, as they looked for land that was both below the compromise line and capable of supporting slave-based agriculture. Northerners generally accepted existing U.S. boundaries and gradually came to see continued expansion as a risky southern adventure. In later years, these sentiments hardened into deep sectional animosity.

Indian Removal

While political leaders battled over slavery and expansion, people continued to look for new opportunities and better land in the West. Native Americans still held large tracts throughout the area east of the Mississippi, but they faced severe pressure to yield to white settlers. The debate over policies of assimilation and expulsion resurfaced, and once again assimilation was unacceptable to either side. Most Indians were not interested in taking up American-style agriculture, and most white settlers were too impatient to wait for assimilation to take hold. Through Adams's presidency (1825–1829), most leaders recognized that assimilation was not feasible, but they generally agreed that expulsion was immoral. They saw no easy option.

In 1824 President Monroe proposed a solution to the growing conflicts between settlers and Indians. Prodded by southerners, he offered the tribes the opportunity to live west of the Mississippi in perpetuity, free from harassment. Whereas most of the northern tribes had been broken in the War of 1812, the so-called Five Civilized Tribes in the South—the Cherokee, Creek, Seminole, Choctaw, and Chickasaw—had developed stronger political organizations than their northern counterparts. They refused to leave the last remnants of their tribal lands, having regretted similar deals in the past. State authorities, especially in Georgia, increased the pressure on the Indians while the federal government wavered.

The deadlock in federal policy ended with the election of Andrew Jackson to the presidency in 1828. The general had fought with many of the southwestern tribes against the British and felt an emotional bond with them. He believed that they could not withstand the onslaught of white settlers, but he also believed that he could not interfere with states' rights to make Indian policy. Removal of the tribes to beyond the Mississippi, it seemed to Jackson, was the only humane alternative. White settlers could have valuable and improvable land; Native Americans would get federal assurances that they would never be bothered again on their remote western lands. Although Jackson claimed that he was presenting the tribes with a choice, he also made it clear that refusal to move would bring reprisal.

The Cherokee put up the most resistance. They had organized a constitutional government in 1827 and declared themselves an independent nation. When Georgia moved to annul their actions, the Cherokee retained a former attorney general, William Wirt, who filed a suit that reached the Supreme Court. Chief Justice John Marshall ruled that Indian tribes had peculiar rights that made them subject only to federal laws. Despite the decision, President Jackson used the Indian Removal Act of 1830 to relocate the tribes to undesirable lands in present-day Oklahoma. The Choctaw and Chickasaw left peacefully by 1832, but the government had to remove the Creek forcibly. Most Seminole also left peacefully, but some remained behind to fight for years in the swamps and forests of Florida. Finally, in 1835, the army arrested 18,000 Cherokee and took them on a forced march westward. During this "Trail of Tears" thousands died. Similar removal efforts in Wisconsin and Illinois eliminated the remaining barriers to settling the land east of the Mississippi River.

Manifest Destiny and Mexico

Westward expansion had been a national priority since independence, but in the 1840s it became something of a national obsession. The advent of inexpensive newspapers, a strong religious revival movement, improved transportation, continued population growth, and the dearth of expansion in the 1830s all helped to promote the growing opinion that God had destined the United States to bring freedom to the rest of the continent. The term "Manifest Destiny" summed up the common belief that the laws of nature preordained peaceful U.S. dominance of the entire continent. Most citizens believed the process was both unstoppable and beneficial.

Newspaper editor John L. O'Sullivan stood as the spokesman for continental expansion in the 1840s. Writing eloquently in the *Democratic Review*, O'Sullivan coined the phrase "Manifest Destiny" in 1845 and explained its principles. With a strong belief in God's role

in these developments, he argued that U.S. citizens would bring the blessings of civilization with them in their westward movement. Like Adams, he predicted that the United States would eventually occupy all of North America. Whereas Adams foresaw that the expansion of slavery was incompatible with the good of the Union and eventually turned against further landed expansion, O'Sullivan became an ardent defender of slavery and the southern desire to claim islands in the Caribbean.

The rise of Manifest Destiny coincided with the culmination of long-simmering crises in Texas and Oregon. Beginning in the 1830s U.S. citizens had begun to move into those regions in large numbers, setting the stage for a decade of aggressive foreign policy toward Mexico and Great Britain. The growing U.S. population—increasing by one-third each decade and nearing 13 million—pushed ahead of the country's borders. The land east of the Mississippi was hardly filled, but the promise of western lands seemed to captivate the national imagination. The opportunity for freedom, commercial opportunity, and abundant fertile land tantalized many U.S. citizens. Many moved west, believing that U.S. institutions would eventually catch up to them.

This attitude was most evident in Texas. Beginning in 1821 the newly independent Mexican government had encouraged settlers to move to Texas. Led by Moses and Stephen Austin, 300 U.S. citizens had accepted Mexico's terms: 4,400 acres of land per person in exchange for a few hundred dollars, conversion to Catholicism, abolition of slavery, and a pledge of allegiance to Mexico. By 1834, 20,000 people had moved to Texas, including some of the most notorious ruffians of the day. Texans displayed no loyalty to the Mexican government, continued to hold slaves, and ignored the Catholic church.

In Mexico City, President Antonio López de Santa Anna concluded that the central government had to regain control of Texas. In 1835 he led 3,000 soldiers into the rebellious state to restore Mexican sovereignty. Citing the precedent of 1776, the Texans declared their independence and sought U.S. volunteers for military service. Recovering from defeat at the Alamo in March 1836, the Texans routed the Mexicans in April near present-day Houston. General Sam Houston captured Santa Anna and gave him a choice between hanging from the nearest tree or recognizing Texas as an independent republic bounded by the Rio Grande River. Upon his return to Mexico, Santa Anna renounced the treaty, but he was in no position to reassert Mexican authority. In the eyes of many U.S. citizens, the outcome represented the inevitable triumph of their Protestant democratic society over Catholic autocracy.

Texans did not anticipate being independent for long, as most of them wanted to join the United States. President Jackson, who had tried to purchase Texas from Mexico, was prepared to annex the new republic. He recognized, however, that such action would spark a domestic political crisis. Northerners feared that the inclusion of a slave area the size of nine northern states could destroy the political balance of power. Southerners complained that the Missouri Compromise left them at a distinct disadvantage unless the Union expanded below the compromise line. On his last day in office, President Jackson conferred upon Texas full diplomatic recognition, but he did not urge annexation.

Texan leaders were unwilling to wait for a settlement, and they embarked on their own foreign policy in an effort to force some action from the United States. By 1840 they had secured diplomatic recognition from the British, who wanted to use the Lone Star State as a foil against the United States. Rumors spread that Great Britain would support Texas's claim to a swath of land to the Pacific if Texas would agree to outlaw slavery. Although such an agreement would not have been especially beneficial for either side, some southerners imagined Texas as a haven for runaway slaves. Others, in both the North and South, feared that Great Britain was pulling Texas too tightly into its empire.

Perhaps seeking to leave his mark on history, ineffectual President John Tyler pressed to annex Texas. In April 1844 he sent to the Senate a treaty of annexation that ignited heated debate. After some injudicious remarks about slavery by Secretary of State Calhoun, the Senate voted 35-16 against the treaty; Tyler had not even won the votes of all the southern senators. For the first time, the United States had refused to absorb a substantial portion of land.

The 1844 election proved to be a referendum on Texas. The leading candidates, Whig Henry Clay and Democrat Martin Van Buren, agreed not to make annexation an issue in the campaign. Both men believed that Texas would make a fine addition to the Union, but they were not willing to risk war with Mexico over the matter. A rebellion by southern Democrats led the party to nominate Speaker of the House James K. Polk of Tennessee, an ardent expansionist, instead of Van Buren. Polk made it clear that he intended to annex Texas and expel the British from Oregon. Clay held his ground and called for caution, especially when dealing with Great Britain. By a thin margin of the popular vote, Polk won the election and proclaimed annexation of Texas a mandate for his foreign policy. In Washington, Tyler asked Congress to approve a joint resolution to annex Texas. Over strident objections from Adams, the House agreed. The Senate hesitated until President Polk assured senators that he would move quickly to negotiate a peaceful solution with Mexico.

Upon receiving news of the annexation, the Mexican government promptly severed relations with the United States. Instead of carrying through on his pledge to soothe Mexico, President Polk fanned the flames of Mexican indignation. Casting his gaze farther than had even the most ardent expansionist, the president decided that the United States must also have California with its excellent harbors at San Francisco and San Diego. He believed, correctly, that the British were maneuvering to use their control over Mexican debt to gain rights to the region. British success might allow them to squeeze the United States out of Oregon. President Polk consequently made a series of offers to buy the land west of Texas for as much as $25 million. The Mexican government refused them all.

At the same time that he proposed negotiations, President Polk pressured Mexico militarily. In July 1845 he further provoked the Mexican government by sending General Zachary Taylor and several thousand men into the region between the Nueces River and the Rio Grande. The questionable U.S. claim to this land was based on the 1836 treaty that the Texans had extracted from Santa Anna after his capture. Mexico protested General Taylor's movements but did not want war. After several months of frustrating inaction, in January 1846 President Polk ordered Taylor to set up camp on the north bank of the Rio Grande. Taylor took it upon himself to blockade the Mexican town of Matamoros. On 24 April 1846 Mexican soldiers attempting to break the blockade attacked Taylor's forces. President Polk had succeeded in starting a war with Mexico.

The president sent his war message to Congress on 11 May and received wide but not deep support. Many northerners suspected that President Polk wanted war in order to increase the amount of land below the Missouri Compromise line for the expansion of slavery. Some members of Congress, from both North and South, believed that the president had been dishonest about his actions in provoking the fighting. Basically, however, they were not willing to withhold support from troops in the field, and most still endorsed continental expansion.

President Polk's effort to pay for the war presented suspicious northerners with an opportunity to test his intentions. When the president asked for $2 million to buy California from Mexico, northern representatives tacked on the Wilmot Proviso, named for Pennsylvania Democrat David Wilmot. This document stipulated that any land purchased would not become slave territory. After fierce debate in both houses, the more evenly balanced Senate killed the proviso in February 1847. All southern Democrats voted against the measure, while most northern Democrats voted for it. Landed expansion had now split the nation's leading political party.

U.S. forces won a series of impressive victories, and in September 1847 General Winfield Scott entered Mexico City. While the main forces of the U.S. Army took the

Mexican capital, President Polk had ensured that naval and ground forces captured California. U.S. leaders expected that, with California and their capital in foreign hands, the Mexicans might surrender. The diplomat accompanying Scott, Nicholas Trist, searched in vain for a government in Mexico that might negotiate a peace treaty. As word of his difficulty reached Washington, the All-Mexico movement gained strength, led by citizens who wanted simply to annex the whole country. President Polk encouraged the idea by expressing a willingness to broaden the war if Mexico did not make immediate concessions. Like many U.S. citizens, Trist believed that Mexico would join the United States one day of its own free will, but the time was not right.

Trist finalized the Treaty of Guadalupe Hidalgo in February 1848, thereby killing the All-Mexico movement. The Mexicans surrendered almost 500,000 square miles of territory, including California and the province of New Mexico. In addition, the Mexican government accepted the Rio Grande as the border between Texas and Mexico. In exchange, the United States paid Mexico $15 million and assumed claims against the Mexican government that totaled more than $3 million. The United States was now a major power on the Pacific Ocean and the dominant power in the Western Hemisphere. The war, however, had further driven the wedge between North and South, intensifying the suspicion and animosity that would lead to the Civil War.

Manifest Destiny and Oregon

The champions of Manifest Destiny continued to cast their gaze toward Canada, even as the crisis with Mexico was beginning. Because the Treaty of Paris of 1783 had left the northern boundaries of present-day Maine and Minnesota undefined, Great Britain and the United States reached no agreement for many years about the border between Canadian and U.S. territories. In the 1830s, however, explorers discovered fertile land in the disputed Aroostook Valley. Citizens of Maine and New Brunswick prepared to resolve the disagreement with force. In Washington, cooler heads prevailed, and the two sides ultimately decided to negotiate.

Neither side moved until 1842, when Secretary of State Daniel Webster and his old business associate, Lord Ashburton (Alexander Baring), resolved to set the border. Each side held maps that supported the other's claim in the east, which only encouraged the atmosphere of cooperation. In effect, the Webster-Ashburton Treaty split the difference in both Maine and Minnesota. Because of the number of conflicting maps, it is difficult to determine what the negotiators had intended in 1783, but it seems likely that the United States ended up with less land than it was entitled to. The U.S. government was willing to pressure Mexico, but, for reasons of power

and cultural affinity, it was not interested in provoking the British Empire or Canadians into yet another war. This basic concern for power diplomacy became more evident as President Polk handled the Oregon crisis that he incited later in the decade.

During President Tyler's administration, Webster and his successor, John Calhoun, sought a peaceful end to the joint occupation of Oregon that had been in place since 1818. Webster offered to relinquish all land north of the Columbia River—basically, the current state of Washington and most of British Columbia—if the British would persuade Mexico to sell California to the United States. In 1844 Calhoun proposed dividing the territory along the 49th parallel. While the British considered both offers unfair, expansionists in the United States believed both to be far too generous. Led by the Democratic platform of 1844, expansionists demanded the entire Oregon territory, up to latitude 54°40′.

By 1845, after three years of "Oregon fever," about 5,000 U.S. citizens lived in the territory, especially in the lush valleys south of the Columbia River. The 700 British subjects—most of whom were affiliated with the Hudson's Bay Company—all lived north of the river. Still, many midwesterners rallied to the popular cry "Fifty-four forty or fight," suggesting that they were willing to look beyond reason in their nationalism. The United States not only had a weak claim to the land that far north, but also irrationally expected the British to yield all access to the Pacific between the United States and Russian America. While proponents of these claims did not speak for the majority, they did represent a logical extension of Manifest Destiny fervor: any disputed land was, by divine right, destined to be part of the United States.

As president, Polk was indecisive on the question. In his inaugural address in March 1845, he soothed the expansionists by demanding all of the Oregon Territory. Just months later, however, he authorized Secretary of State James Buchanan to offer division of the region at the 49th parallel. After the British minister rejected the idea with dispatch, an annoyed President Polk again asserted the U.S. claim to the entire territory. By December the president invoked the Monroe Doctrine as justification for claiming all of Oregon, and he urged Congress to notify Great Britain that the United States would withdraw from the joint occupation agreement. Twice the British offered to settle the matter through arbitration, but President Polk maintained a hard line.

Eventually President Polk accommodated the widespread opinion that the United States was in no position to fight a war for Oregon. With war looming in the Southwest, the United States could spare no troops to fight in the Northwest. When Foreign Secretary Lord Aberdeen (George Hamilton-Gordon) mentioned in February 1846 that he was prepared to dispatch thirty warships to resolve the dispute, President Polk took the British seriously. He privately expressed willingness to accept the 49th parallel if the British offered, and Aberdeen obliged. In June 1846 the Senate approved a deal that set the current boundary of the United States in the Pacific Northwest. President Polk had pushed the United States to the brink of war on two fronts in his effort to facilitate expansion, but he had chosen not engage the country in a war with Great Britain.

Sectional Deadlock

By 1848 the United States had basically established its current boundaries between Canada and Mexico, but the relative stability of the borders did not mean an end to debates over issues regarding landed expansion. Parts of the newly acquired land filled up rapidly, especially California. A U.S. citizen had discovered gold near Sacramento in January 1848, and the news had sparked a gold rush of thousands of people. Congress, however, could not agree on a system of government for the territory. On both sides of the Mason-Dixon line, political leaders had become more intransigent. Southerners wanted to extend the Missouri Compromise line to the Pacific, but more and more northerners had concluded that the expansion of slavery must end.

Deadlock turned to crisis in 1850, when the people of California organized their own government and applied for admission as a free state. President Zachary Taylor, a slaveholder himself, supported the Californians, but his Whig party was weak. In Congress, the fading leaders of the past, Calhoun, Clay, and Webster, battled over the status of slavery in the Mexican Cession. With no solution in sight and southerners considering secession, young Democrat Stephen Douglas stepped into the fray and engineered the Compromise of 1850. California became a free state, Utah and New Mexico territories were allowed to decide the fate of slavery within their own boundaries, and the federal government was enjoined to hunt fugitive slaves. The compromise allowed for organized settlement of the new western lands, but it also demonstrated that the debate over slavery had the ability to paralyze foreign policy.

Despite repeated efforts to expand into areas that could support slavery, southern leaders had limited success after the Mexican War. In 1853 James Gadsden negotiated a deal in which the United States would pay Mexico $15 million for about 45,000 square miles northeast of the Gulf of California. Southerners saw the land as vital for a transcontinental railroad that would connect cotton lands with the great western port at Los Angeles. Northerners saw it as another example of national funds paying for southern expansion. After heated debate, the Senate settled on paying Mexico $10 million for about

30,000 square miles that now make up the southern end of Arizona and New Mexico.

Throughout the 1850s expansionists continued to push southward, hoping to acquire Caribbean regions that could support slavery and trade. At the time many U.S. citizens recognized Central America and the Caribbean as parts of North America and considered foreign control thereof a threat to U.S. interests. A major focus of attention was Cuba, one of the last remnants of the Spanish empire. With slavery still intact, geographical proximity, fine ports, and a strong commercial link to northern cities, Cuba seemed destined to become part of the United States. U.S. diplomats had worked to acquire the island for decades, but most had agreed with John Quincy Adams that patience would eventually yield possession. In 1854, however, expansionist U.S. diplomats in Europe, led by future president James Buchanan and frustrated by Spain's unwillingness to sell Cuba, produced the Ostend Manifesto, which secretly urged President Franklin Pierce to conquer Cuba.

When news of the manifesto leaked, a searing debate broke out over the value of further southern adventures. Manifest Destiny still had many supporters, but more and more people could think of reasons to oppose annexation of any Caribbean territory. In addition to the standard concerns of abolitionists and northern politicians, many other citizens began to see expansion as a question of race. In stark contrast to the Louisiana Territory or the Mexican Cession, Cuba supported a substantial population. U.S. citizens could not drive the 750,000 inhabitants—many of them people of color—off the island, as they had the Native Americans. Annexation would mean a state dominated by a darker-skinned and substantially Roman Catholic population. Many U.S. citizens believed that such people were not capable of living in a democracy.

With official efforts checked, private citizens known as filibusters undertook their own expansionist foreign policy. The first to gain prominence was Narciso López, who tried three times to conquer Cuba. In 1851 Spanish authorities captured him and his supporters and executed them. The king of the filibusters, however, was William Walker, who attempted to conquer Baja California in 1853 and Nicaragua four times between 1855 and 1860. The United States actually recognized Walker's government of Nicaragua in 1856, revealing a level of official tolerance for such illegal acts. In 1860 the Honduran government captured Walker and executed him, putting an end to the filibuster movement.

The halt to southward expansion marked an important turning point in U.S. foreign policy. In the short term, it provided the South with a major grievance against northern politicians, one that would help to justify secession. Even after the Civil War ended the slavery question, however, continental expansion had only sporadic support. By and large, Americans became hesitant to add any inhabited territory to their realm, and by the end of the Civil War in 1865 most of the uninhabited land was gone.

Alaska

The three years immediately after the end of the Civil War demonstrated that continental expansion had lost support. In 1865 the United States had a strong position from which to conquer Canada. The Grand Army of the Republic was large and battle-tested, and the U.S. government had a grievance against Great Britain for providing some support to the Confederates. Senator Charles Sumner suggested that the deed to Canada would be fair compensation for the U.S. claims against Great Britain, and British officials worried about U.S. willingness to invade Canada one last time. Instead, the United States demobilized, accepted Canada's move to confederation, and pursued a diplomatic solution. From that point on, the United States was content to maintain a position as Canada's dominant trading partner—what some historians have called commercial expansion. Likewise, the U.S. government could have invaded Mexico, which was reeling from its own civil war and three years of French occupation. War weariness and a lack of desire to assimilate Mexicans into U.S. society prevented any serious discussion of Manifest Destiny south of the Rio Grande. After a U.S. show of force convinced the French to leave in 1865, the U.S. government left Mexico to its own devices.

Two years later, Secretary of State William H. Seward saw an opportunity to purchase Alaska from the czar of Russia. For 586,000 square miles of territory that they could no longer control, the Russians wanted only $7.2 million. To Seward, Alaska represented not Manifest Destiny but rather an important part of U.S. efforts to dominate trade in the Pacific basin. The vast land held untold wealth in minerals, fisheries, and wildlife and, Seward recognized, offered an excellent bridge for trade with Asia. In addition, few people lived there. Last, the purchase of Alaska would prevent the land from falling into British hands and might help hasten the eventual annexation of Canada. Despite these strong arguments, the Alaska purchase aroused much criticism, with dissenters calling the land "Walrussia" and "Seward's Ice Box." The United States needed no more land, they argued, and could not afford to spend the money in the midst of Reconstruction. In the end, only Seward's decision to hoist the flag over Sitka and generous bribes from Russian diplomats persuaded Congress to approve the measure. Continental expansion had run its course.

Final Indian Wars

Although the United States acquired no more land in North America after 1867, one final chapter remained in the conquest of the land: the destruction of the Native American tribes west of the Mississippi River. Despite promises that Andrew Jackson had made in the 1830s, the government did not allow the Indians to remain unmolested. By 1870 the U.S. population had grown to 40 million, and the demand for arable farmland kept pace. To compound land hunger, the government supported the construction of multiple transcontinental railroads, each of which required huge tracts of land. Prospectors were also scouring the West, searching for evidence of rich mineral deposits. Almost every tribe held land that either the settlers or the government wanted.

In 1871 the government stopped negotiating treaties with the various tribes and turned instead to congressional legislation. With wide popular support, the United States initiated a policy that would either destroy the Native Americans or drive them onto what seemed to be the most worthless land. With nowhere to go and numerous broken promises behind them, many of the tribes fought back. Numbering about 350,000, they were hopelessly outnumbered and lacked the technology or resources to defeat the U.S. Army. In addition, many of the tribes harbored grudges against each other and failed to unite against the whites. Perhaps the most important element in the eventual government victory was the destruction of the bison, upon which so many tribes depended. The Indians fought hard until 1890, when the massacre at Wounded Knee, South Dakota, destroyed Sioux power.

Continental expansion dominated the first seventy-five years of U.S. foreign policy. For decades, continental expansion was not just popular, it represented fundamental tenets of U.S. ideology. As long as the country had abundant arable land, the founders believed, yeoman agriculture would sustain political liberty. At a relatively low cost to U.S. citizens, both in lives and money, the United States had grown from a struggling collection of seaboard states to a continental colossus with unprecedented human and natural resources, a country powerful enough to dominate the entire Western Hemisphere. The nation overcame obstacles and challenges from Great Britain, Canada, Spain, France, Mexico, and dozens of Indian tribes. Still, the common expansionist desire to rule all of North America was never fulfilled. The existence of two other large nations on the North American continent, Mexico and Canada, reveals the forces that finally brought continental expansion to a halt: British strength, sectional crisis, the nationalism of other peoples, and U.S. dislike for foreigners.

KURK DORSEY

See also Adams, John Quincy; Adams-Onís Treaty; Alaska Purchase; Canada; Filibusters; French and Indian War; Great Britain; Lewis and Clark Expedition; Louisiana Purchase; Manifest Destiny; Mexico, War with; Monroe

Doctrine; Native Americans; Northwest Ordinance; Oregon Question; Ostend Manifesto; Pinckney's Treaty; Polk, James Knox; Seward, William Henry; War of 1812

FURTHER READING

Bemis, Samuel Flagg. *John Quincy Adams and the Foundations of American Foreign Policy*. New York, 1956.

DeConde, Alexander. *This Affair of Louisiana*. New York, 1976.

Horsman, Reginald. *Race and Manifest Destiny: The Origins of Racial Anglo-Saxonism*. Cambridge, Mass., 1981.

Hunt, Michael. *Ideology and U.S. Foreign Policy*. New Haven, Conn., 1987.

Jensen, Ronald J. *The Alaska Purchase and Russian-American Relations*. Seattle, Wash., 1975.

Nash, Roderick. *Wilderness and the American Mind*, 3rd ed. New Haven, Conn., 1982.

Pletcher, David M. *The Diplomacy of Annexation: Texas, Oregon, and the Mexican War*. Columbia, Mo., 1973.

Remini, Robert. *Andrew Jackson and the Course of American Freedom, 1822–1832*. New York, 1981.

Stagg, J. C. A. *Mr. Madison's War: Politics, Diplomacy, and Warfare in the Early American Republic, 1783–1830*. Princeton, N.J., 1983.

Stuart, Reginald C. *United States Expansionism and British North America, 1775–1871*. Chapel Hill, N.C., 1988.

Utley, Robert M. *The Indian Frontier of the American West, 1846–1890*. Albuquerque, N.Mex., 1984.

Weinberg, Albert K. *Manifest Destiny: A Study of Nationalist Expansionism in American History*. Baltimore, 1935.

CONTRAS

Contra-revolucionarios or counterrevolutionaries who fought the Sandinista government of Nicaragua from 1979 to 1990. The Contras were composed of, or supported by, former adherents of the deposed regime of President Anastasio Somoza Debayle, especially national guardsmen; defectors from the Sandinista revolution; peasants dragooned during raids or aggrieved by specific Sandinista acts they thought intrusive in their lives; businesspeople opposed to heavy government involvement in the economy; and soldiers of fortune. The long argument between the administration of President Ronald Reagan and Congress over the nature and purpose of U.S. military and economic support to the Contras was a central issue in U.S. foreign policy debates in the 1980s.

Viewing the human rights–oriented administration of President Jimmy Carter as dangerously soft on communism, Argentine Army Intelligence Battalion 601 (then coordinating that country's "Dirty War") sent advisers to Central America in 1978 to fight on the "ideological frontier." In Nicaragua the Argentine advisers worked with Somoza's National Guard and, after his overthrow by the Sandinista Front for National Liberation, began organizing and training former guardsmen—the first Contras—to combat the new government. On the day of the Sandinistas's victory, 19 July 1979, the Central Intelligence Agency (CIA) also played a role in the development of the Contras by evacuating guard commanders from Managua to Miami aboard a cargo plane disguised with Red Cross insignia. Throughout the next year, moreover, an unidentified source fed, clothed, and housed hundreds of former guardsmen in organized camps in Honduras. Many of these officers and men were soon transformed into Contras.

The Reagan administration used the Contras to destabilize the Sandinistas, whom it viewed as Soviet-backed communists. In November 1981 the president signed National Security Decision Directive 17, authorizing $19.95 million in CIA support for 500 Contras to "interdict" an alleged flow of arms from Nicaragua to rebels fighting the U.S.-backed government in El Salvador. This force would merge with 1,000 Contras already under Argentine command. After the 1982 Falklands War and Argentina's return to democracy in 1983, that country's support for the Contras dwindled and U.S. backing became central. The Reagan administration hired and fired their leaders and coordinated their public relations and military tactics. The administration met congressional opposition to the use of U.S. resources to overthrow the government of Nicaragua with the disingenuous argument that U.S. support for the Contras was designed only to stop alleged Nicaraguan support for the insurgents in El Salvador; the Contras actually aimed to overthrow the Nicaraguan government, and so did the United States.

Through the mid-1980s Congress passed a series of amendments—named for Congressman Edward Boland, a Democrat from Massachusetts—restricting the purpose, scope, and nature of aid for the Contras. The administration responded with secret fund-raising from foreign governments and private groups, support for Contra military operations in violation of congressional authority, and diversion of "profits" from the clandestine sale of arms to Iran. The public revelation in 1986 of the connection with arms sales to Iran, soon known as the Iran-Contra Affair or Iran-Contragate, embarrassed the Reagan administration.

By implementing conscription, using such weaponry as Soviet-built helicopters, and employing techniques borrowed from U.S. Army counterinsurgency manuals and practices, the Sandinistas contained and largely demoralized the Contras by 1987. Although it failed militarily, the Contra war against Nicaragua inflicted pain. The sabotage of bridges and utilities wracked the nation's infrastructure, nearly 31,000 died, and the Nicaraguan economy slumped because the government had to divert massive but increasingly scarce resources toward defense. This economic catastrophe stimulated much of the discontent that led to the Sandinista defeat in the February 1990 elections. The Contras formally disbanded in June of that year.

THOMAS W. WALKER

See also Argentina; El Salvador; Iran-Contra Affair; Nicaragua; Reagan, Ronald Wilson; Somoza Debayle, Anastasio

FURTHER READING

Armony, Ariel C. "Argentina and the Origins of Nicaragua's Contras." *Low Intensity Conflict and Law Enforcement* 2 (Winter 1993): 434–459.

Dickey, Christopher. *With the Contras: A Reporter in the Wilds of Nicaragua.* New York, 1985.

Walker, Thomas W., ed. *Reagan Versus the Sandinistas.* Boulder, Colo., 1987.

CONVENTIONAL ARMED FORCES IN EUROPE, TREATY ON

(1990)

A treaty among the sixteen North Atlantic Treaty Organization (NATO) and seven Warsaw Treaty Organization (WTO) members that reduced conventional firepower in Europe. The negotiations occurred at a time of profound political change in Europe and in the waning of the Cold War. When the talks commenced in March 1989, Germany was divided, two united alliances remained stuck in military confrontation, and the Cold War still marked East-West relations. By the time the treaty was signed in November 1990, Germany was united, the WTO had virtually collapsed, and the Soviet Union was withdrawing its military forces from Eastern Europe. When the treaty was ratified in November 1992, the Soviet Union had ceased to exist and the treaty had gained eight new parties. Despite these earth-shattering political changes, the Conventional Forces in Europe (CFE) Treaty ranks as a historic achievement. When fully implemented in November 1995, the treaty reduced major conventional firepower in Europe by one-third from the number of forces deployed at the beginning of the negotiations. Although initially designed to stabilize the East-West military confrontation, the treaty remained relevant to the increasingly volatile post–Cold War European security environment.

The CFE negotiations succeeded the talks on Mutual and Balanced Force Reductions (MBFR) that began in 1973 and had intermittently sought to reduce NATO and WTO troop levels in central Europe to equal levels. The new negotiations proved more productive because of changes in Soviet military thinking in the late 1980s, which, on the urging of Soviet President Mikhail Gorbachev, had moved from an emphasis on superiority to a preference for defensive sufficiency. For the NATO countries the desire to achieve a conventional balance of forces through negotiations was made more urgent by the 1987 Intermediate-Range Nuclear Forces Treaty, which eliminated a substantial portion of U.S. and Soviet nuclear forces deployed in Europe.

The mandate for the CFE negotiations, adopted by the parties on 10 January 1989, was to create a conventional arms balance at lower levels and to eliminate the capability for launching a surprise attack and for initiating large-scale offensive actions. The focus of the negotiations were major conventional weapon systems (so-called treaty-limited equipment, or TLE), which included battle tanks, armored combat vehicles (ACVs), artillery, combat aircraft, and attack helicopters. Both the actual negotiations and the final treaty closely reflected NATO's initial proposals, which were based on four interrelated "rules": equal force levels for each alliance or group of states within overall ceilings on TLE deployed within the Atlantic-to-the-Urals (ATTU) region; a limit on the maximum number of TLE any one country could deploy within the ATTU (the so-called sufficiency rule); constraints on the number of forces that could be deployed outside national territory; and sublimits on forces within each alliance or group of states that could be deployed in different geographical zones. These rules served four objectives. Reflecting the existing imbalance of forces, the first rule forced drastic reductions in WTO force levels while imposing only a modest reduction in NATO levels. The second rule ensured that the bulk of the reductions would fall on Soviet forces, while the third would limit the USSR's military presence in Eastern Europe. The fourth rule would compel the redeployment of Soviet forces to its strategic rear and away from NATO territory in the central region.

The CFE Treaty was signed on 19 November 1990 by the twenty-two NATO and Warsaw Pact states. It limited the total number of TLE within the ATTU to 40,000 tanks, 40,000 artillery, 60,000 ACVs, 13,600 aircraft, and 4,000 helicopters. No one country could deploy more than approximately 34 percent of this overall total. In addition, the treaty established sublimits on the amount of ground equipment in active units that could be deployed in four geographical zones, with the greatest constraints placed on equipment in the flank and central regions. Although the CFE Treaty set de jure TLE limits for each group of states, it placed de facto limits on TLE holdings of individual states that, when combined, cannot exceed the TLE totals for each group. Each country's maximum level of holdings could be revised upward only if another country in the same group of states agreed to reduce its forces by an equal amount and, as a practical matter, only if all other members of the group agreed to the revision. The effect of this provision was to establish national ceilings for each party to the treaty that can be changed upward only with the consent of others.

Ratification and implementation of the treaty was delayed for two years by momentous political changes in Europe. Initial concern was directed at various activities by the Soviet Union that appeared to undermine the spirit if not the letter of the treaty, including the redeployment of some 60,000 TLE east of the Urals just prior to the treaty's signing. These difficulties were resolved in June 1991, and the U.S. Senate voted 90-4 on 25 November 1991 to give its advice and consent to ratification. By late 1991, however, the political disintegration of the Soviet Union once again called the treaty's future into question. Legal and political questions arose concerning how to ensure that the eight former Soviet republics with territory in the ATTU would adhere to a treaty premised on a single Soviet Union. (The three Baltic states, which gained independence in September 1991, did not possess any TLE and were not treaty parties.) Furthermore, the treaty's zonal limits did not conform to the political boundaries of the new states. There were also differences among the eight states on how the force levels allocated to the Soviet Union should be divided among them. These issues were resolved in May 1992, when the former Soviet republics agreed on how to divide the Soviet allocation, and the treaty was accordingly amended in June 1992 to reflect its expanded membership to twenty-nine parties. In January 1993 membership was again expanded, to thirty, when Slovakia and the Czech Republic formally separated.

Although the impetus for the CFE Treaty derived from the military stalemate that characterized Europe through four decades of Cold War confrontation, its primary legacy was to help stabilize the potential military competition between the newly independent states in Eastern Europe and the former Soviet Union. The inclusion of de facto national TLE ceilings; the requirement to exchange detailed data on the strength, location, and capabilities of military formations to all treaty parties; and the provision granting states belonging to the same group to conduct on-site inspections on each other's territory provided all parties with a degree of predictability regarding the military capabilities of their potential or actual adversaries. Thus, although a product of the Cold War, the CFE Treaty was transformed into a valuable instrument of security cooperation in very different political circumstances.

IVO H. DAALDER

See also Cold War; Intermediate-Range Nuclear Forces Treaty; North Atlantic Treaty Organization; Russia and the Soviet Union; Warsaw Pact

FURTHER READING

Daalder, Ivo H. *The CFE Treaty: An Overview and An Assessment.* Washington, D.C., 1991.
Dunay, Pál. *The CFE Treaty: History, Achievements, and Shortcomings,* Peace Research Institute of Frankfurt Report No. 24. Frankfurt am Main, 1991.
Sharpe, Jane M. O. "Conventional Arms Control in Europe." In *SIPRI Yearbook: World Armaments and Disarmament.* Oxford, 1989.

CONVENTION OF 1800

An agreement, also known as the Convention of Mortefontaine, between the United States and France ending the Quasi-War that had started in 1797. In mid-1798, at the height of U.S. war fever, evidence materialized indicating that France wished a peaceful settlement of outstanding disputes between the two countries. To conduct negotiations, in February 1799 President John Adams nominated William Vans Murray, a youthful Maryland-born Federalist diplomat, to be minister to France. Adams's action touched off a storm of protest among staunch Federalists, some of whom thought a war with France would be politically beneficial in upcoming elections. Hoping to minimize dissent, Adams named two prominent Federalists—Chief Justice Oliver Ellsworth and North Carolina Governor William R. Davie—to Murray's peace mission. A year elapsed before Napoleon Bonaparte received Davie, Ellsworth, and Murray. The long delay was caused by political wrangling in the United States, Davie's and Ellsworth's torturously long transit to Paris, and Napoleon's ouster of the ruling French government in November 1799. Almost another month passed before negotiations started on 2 April 1800. While the proceedings were painfully slow and sometimes seemed hopelessly deadlocked, both sides desired an agreement. The Convention of 1800 was finally agreed upon in the early hours of 1 October. The definitive text of the convention, effectively exchanged more than a year later, ended the Quasi-War, effectively scrapped the treaties of 1778, and restored peaceful relations between two nations. France also accepted a liberal interpretation of neutral rights. Although none of the participants knew it, they had prepared the way for France's sale of Louisiana to the United States.

CLIFFORD L. EGAN

See also Adams, John; American Revolution; France; French Revolution; Louisiana Purchase; Napoleon Bonaparte; XYZ Affair

FURTHER READING

DeConde, Alexander. *The Quasi-War: The Politics and Diplomacy of the Undeclared War with France, 1797–1801.* New York, 1966.
Hill, Peter P. William Vans Murray, *Federalist Diplomat: The Shaping of Peace with France, 1797–1801.* Syracuse, N.Y., 1971.

CONVENTION OF 1818

See Great Britain

CONVENTION ON INTERNATIONAL TRADE IN ENDANGERED SPECIES

See Wildlife

COOLIDGE, CALVIN

(*b.* 4 July 1872; *d.* 5 January 1933)

President of the United States (1923–1929). Born in Plymouth Notch, Vermont, John Calvin Coolidge was educated in the local one-room school and at Black River Academy in nearby Ludlow. He graduated from Amherst College in 1895. He read law in Northampton, Massachusetts, passed the bar in 1897, and began a slow ascent through town and state offices that led to the governorship in 1919–1920. His stand against the striking Boston police in 1919 made him a national figure and brought his nomination and election in 1920 as vice president under President Warren G. Harding. Succeeding to the presidency upon Harding's death in 1923, Coolidge won election in his own right the following year.

Coolidge was expert in the ways of U.S. politics. His quiet, even dour demeanor, his occasional witticisms (he believed that humor, in the Vermont way, required a purpose), and his thoughtful, carefully calculated approach to public matters—all these talents he devoted mostly to domestic political concerns. In his autobiography he wrote nothing at all about foreign affairs. Yet he could not ignore the world, nor did he simply delegate international matters to his two secretaries of state, Charles Evans Hughes and Frank B. Kellogg. Despite a relaxed style exemplified by long afternoon naps, he expected his subordinates to report their problems and in turn he often suggested solutions. He relied on special envoys, for example, appointing his Amherst classmate, Dwight W. Morrow, to settle tense relations with Mexico, especially the dispute over the rights of U.S. oil companies. To Nicaragua, after sending the U.S. Marines to suppress a revolutionary insurgency in early 1927, he dispatched Henry L. Stimson to provide U.S. supervision for peaceful elections in 1928. To emphasize his own concern for Latin American problems and Pan-Americanism, Coolidge himself in 1928 attended a session of the Sixth International Conference of American States in Havana. As for Asia, President Coolidge stood for U.S. rights—that is, the protection of U.S. citizens and property. He backed up Secretary Kellogg in demanding "profound regret" and compensation from China for nationalist disorders in Nanjing in 1927.

An exemplar of self-reliance, the president grew irritated with Europeans—who, he believed, always looked to the United States to bail them out. He rejected U.S. membership in the World Court. Regarding debts owed by the former allies of World War I, Coolidge reportedly snapped: "They hired the money, didn't they?" During his presidency, however, government officials worked with private bankers and business executives to stabilize European finances, restore trade, and encourage private loans to Germany on the assumption that an economically revitalized Germany would mean peace and security for Europe. Under the Dawes Plan of 1924, U.S. investors such as the J.P. Morgan Company loaned millions of dollars to Germany and, in return, Berlin accepted a systematic schedule of reparations payments. Even though the Young Plan of 1929 scaled down Germany's reparations from $32 billion to $8 billion, the economic burden became too heavy for Europe once the Great Depression cut off the flow of U.S. capital. Coolidge did support the Kellogg-Briand Pact of 1928, but with a modest enthusiasm that forbade Kellogg from visiting England after signing the antiwar treaty in Paris; the British had irritated Coolidge by urging the limitation of heavy cruisers in a future naval conference, a proposal the U.S. Navy regarded as anathema. After leaving the presidency, Coolidge published his *Autobiography* (1929) and wrote a much-read newspaper column that dealt almost entirely with domestic issues.

J. GARRY CLIFFORD

See also China; Dawes Plan; Hughes, Charles Evans; Kellogg, Frank Billings; Kellogg-Briand Pact; Mexico; Morrow, Dwight Whitney; Nicaragua; Pan-Americanism; Permanent Court of International Justice; Reparations; Stimson, Henry Lewis; War Debt of World War I

FURTHER READING

Cohen, Warren I. *Empire Without Tears.* New York, 1987.
Coolidge, Calvin. *The Autobiography of Calvin Coolidge.* New York, 1929.
Kamman, William. *A Search for Stability.* South Bend, Ind., 1968.
Leffler, Melvyn P. *The Elusive Quest: America's Pursuit of European Stability and French Security, 1919–1933.* Chapel Hill, N.C., 1979.
McCoy, Donald R. *Coolidge: The Quiet President.* New York, 1967.
Quint, Howard H., and Robert H. Ferrell, eds. *The Talkative President: The Off-the-Record Press Conferences of Calvin Coolidge.* Amherst, Mass., 1964.

COOPER-CHURCH AMENDMENT

See Church, Frank Forrester III

COORDINATING COMMITTEE FOR MULTILATERAL EXPORT CONTROLS

An agreement between the members of the North Atlantic Treaty Organization (NATO)—with the exception of Iceland—and Japan and later Australia, created in 1949 primarily to deny the Soviet Union and its Warsaw Pact allies any technology and equipment, such as computers and machine tools, that could serve military purposes. Coordinating Committee for Multilateral Export Controls (COCOM) members devised confidential lists of items to be restricted in trade with Warsaw Pact nations and coordinated the implementation and enforcement of these restrictions. COCOM is credited with some success during the Cold War in helping the Western allies maintain a lead over the Warsaw Pact countries in access to militarily relevant technologies. The coordination of controls often proved contentious because the United States routinely pushed for tougher restrictions than preferred by its more trade-dependent Western allies. When the Cold War ended, members disbanded COCOM in 1994 and in 1995 developed a successor export control organization, called the Wassenaar Arrangement. With Russia and other ex-communist states among its 28 members, the Wassanaar Arrangement seeks to restrict the export of dual-use technologies and conventional weapons to pariah states such as Libya, North Korea, Iran, and Iraq.

MICHAEL MASTANDUNO

See also Australia; Cold War; Export Controls; Japan; North Atlantic Treaty Organization; Russia and the Soviet Union; Technology Transfer; Warsaw Pact

FURTHER READING

Adler-Karlsson, Gunnar. *Western Economic Warfare, 1947–1967.* Stockholm, 1968.
Mastanduno, Michael. *Economic Containment: COCOM and the Politics of East-West Trade.* Ithaca, N.Y., 1992.

COPYRIGHT AND INTELLECTUAL PROPERTY

Proprietary information of economic value, including patents, trademarks, brand names, and the works of authors and artists. According to international conventions, countries are expected to protect the intellectual property of foreign firms, that is, not allow their nationals to use patented information, copyrighted material, or foreign trademarks or brand names without the owners' permission. Intellectual property has become an important focus of U.S. international trade policy because many foreign countries do not abide by these conventions, and piracy of U.S. intellectual property is quite common, particularly in Asia. Because the United States typically has a strong comparative advantage in product areas heavily dependent on research and development, this piracy threatens U.S. export performance. More broadly, the theft of intellectual property reduces the profitability of research and development efforts that are both expensive and risky, which reduces the willingness of firms to spend money on such efforts and slows the progress of science and technology.

The U.S. government has undertaken vigorous efforts to encourage foreign governments to increase protection for U.S. intellectual property. Threats of retaliation against the exports of countries allowing such piracy have had some positive effects in getting China and some other Asian countries to promise better behavior. The protection of intellectual property was also a major item in the Uruguay Round of the General Agreement on Tariffs and Trade (1986–1994). The final agreement did include even greater protection for intellectual property, with particular emphasis on pharmaceutical patents.

ROBERT M. DUNN, JR.

See also Foreign Direct Investment; General Agreement on Tariffs and Trade; International Trade Commission

FURTHER READING

Besen, Stanley M., and Leo J. Raskind. "An Introduction to the Law and Economics of Intellectual Property." *Journal of Economic Perspectives* 5 (Winter 1991): 3–28.
Mossinghoff, G. J. "The Importance of Intellectual Property Protection in International Trade." *Boston College International and Comparative Law Review* 7 (1984): 235–249.

CORPORATIONS

See Multinational Corporations

COSTA RICA

Historically the leading democratic republic in Central America, a small mountainous country located between Panama and Nicaragua and with coasts along the Caribbean Sea and the Pacific Ocean. Full diplomatic relations between the United States and Costa Rica got off to a slow start, only becoming established in 1858 when the first U.S. minister commissioned to Costa Rica and Nicaragua presented his credentials, five years after his appointment and thirty-seven years after Costa Rican independence from Spain. The year before, Costa Rica had joined a British-backed regional armed force to overthrow William Walker's U.S.-backed regime in Nicaragua. U.S. diplomats, hoping to defeat British rivalry in the region and resolve Mosquito Coast territorial disputes, soon found themselves faced with Costa Rica's proposal for a reverse Monroe Doctrine in the form of an 1859 manifesto signed by Costa Rica and Nicaragua requesting England and France to protect them from U.S. intervention.

Since its first free elections in 1889, Costa Rica has shared a long, although occasionally disrupted, history of democratic institutions with the United States. In 1917, amidst the economic crisis brought on by the disruption of trade during World War I, General Federico Tinoco led a military coup against the democratic Costa Rican government. Although the Woodrow Wilson administration helped to oust Tinoco, the U.S. intervention offended both the growing urban middle and working classes in Costa Rica and led to a break in relations that lasted until 1922. The annulment of the 1948 elections led to a short but violent civil war in Costa Rica, followed by the restoration of democracy and a constitutional prohibition against a standing national army.

During the Cold War, disagreements between Costa Rica and the United States frequently occurred. Costa Rica's lack of hostility toward Fidel Castro's Cuba in the 1960s and its establishment of diplomatic and economic relations with the Soviet Union and Eastern Europe in the 1970s directly opposed the U.S. Cold War policy. During the 1980s, President Oscar Arias challenged U.S. President Ronald Reagan's covert and anticommunist policy in the region, brokering the 1987 Esquipulas Peace Accord to end civil wars in Nicaragua, El Salvador, and Guatemala, for which he won the Nobel Peace Prize.

Foreign debt, primarily to U.S. banks, began to burden Costa Rica's foreign economic relations in the late 1970s when prices for the country's agricultural exports slumped while imported oil prices rose. The U.S. government conditioned foreign aid and lending policies by the World Bank and International Monetary Fund during the 1980s and 1990s to promote reforms in Costa Rica that included privatizations, trade liberalization, and reduced government spending. Costa Rica has been the world's leading participant in innovative swaps of foreign debt for environmental conservation, which U.S. officials sanctioned by modifying creditor banks' tax regulations.

CHRISTOPHER WELNA

See also Esquipilas II; International Monetary Fund; Latin America; Monroe Doctrine; Nicaragua

FURTHER READING

Edelman, Mark, and Joanne Kenan, eds. *Costa Rica Reader*. New York, 1989.

Winson, Anthony. *Coffee and Democracy in Modern Costa Rica*. New York, 1989.

CÔTE D'IVOIRE

See Appendix 2

COUGHLIN, CHARLES EDWARD

(*b.* 25 October 1891; *d.* 27 October 1979)

Canadian-born, Roman Catholic "radio priest," who became one of the first widely popular broadcasters. In 1926, his program—beamed from his pastorate, the Shrine of the Little Flower in Royal Oak, Michigan— began broadcasting in Detroit. His sermons won a national audience in 1930 when the Columbia Broadcast-

ing System (CBS) began to transmit them. By 1934 he claimed the largest steady radio audience in the world. Although Coughlin was orthodox in his religious views, his goals were political, not evangelical. A populist, he was among the first to use the radio to attack poverty and injustice in American society. He assailed both capitalism and communism and denounced their internationalist component. A severe critic of bankers and Wall Street financiers, he nonetheless strongly supported the right to private property. Although Coughlin was an early advocate of the New Deal, by the end of 1934, when he formed the National Union for Social Justice, he distanced himself from President Franklin D. Roosevelt's recovery program, labeling it just another alliance with cartels. Coughlin lost considerable public support when he opposed Roosevelt in the 1936 election. Coughlin supported neutrality legislation, opposed U.S. involvement in European affairs, and emerged as a vociferous isolationist. By 1938 he had become a highly embittered man, an open admirer of Adolf Hitler and Benito Mussolini, and a strident anti-Semite. In 1942, shortly after the United States entered World War II, Attorney General Francis Biddle took steps to silence what the government now considered to be Coughlin's seditious activity. His publication *Social Justice* was banned from the mails, and Biddle interceded with Coughlin's bishop to put a stop to his political activity. The National Union for Social Justice disbanded in 1944, and little was heard from Coughlin thereafter.

BERNARD V. BURKE

See also Hitler, Adolf; Isolationism; Mussolini, Benito; Neutrality Acts of the 1930s

FURTHER READING

Brinkley, Alan. *Voices of Protest, Huey Long, Father Coughlin, and the Great Depression*. New York, 1982.

Marcus, Sheldon. *Father Coughlin: The Tumultuous Life of the Priest of the Little Flower*. Boston, 1973.

Tull, Charles J. *Father Coughlin and the New Deal*. Syracuse, N.Y., 1965.

COUNCIL ON FOREIGN RELATIONS

A privately funded, nonprofit and nonpartisan membership organization founded in 1921, headquartered in New York City and dedicated to an improved understanding of American foreign policy and international affairs. The first seventy-five members of the Council on Foreign Relations (CFR) came from two separate groups. Some were leading academics and foreign policy experts whose participation in the Paris Peace Conference of 1919 had convinced them of the need to educate Americans about the increasing international responsibilities of the United

States. Typical of this group was Archibald Cary Coolidge of Harvard University, who in 1922 became the first editor of the council's flagship publication, *Foreign Affairs* magazine. The other group of founding members was made up of public-spirited businessmen, bankers, and lawyers with international knowledge and exposure, mostly from New York City. It included lawyers like John W. Davis and Paul D. Cravath, and businessmen like the publisher of the New York *Evening Post*, Edwin F. Gay. During the 1920s, the Council concentrated on disarmament and the work of the League of Nations. An array of distinguished American and foreign leaders addressed the organization and/or published articles in *Foreign Affairs*, among them former Secretary of State Elihu Root and the former French premier Georges Clemenceau. In the early 1930s, the Council's focus shifted to the threat to peace posed by the rise of Adolf Hitler and his consolidation of power in Germany. As the decade progressed, leading CFR members began to speak out publicly in favor of intervention in European affairs as the only way to preserve the vital interests of the United States.

After war broke out in Europe in 1939, the Council organized what came to be known as its War and Peace Project. Four study and discussion groups of members and government officials met regularly to assess likely outcomes of the war; how these might affect the shape of the post-war world, including the United States; and what could be done to influence that future. This project, which lasted until 1945, had from the outset the full cooperation and participation of the Department of State. After the United States entered the war in December 1941, the department recruited several project participants to build a planning and research program of its own. The study-discussion group process that proved its worth in the War and Peace Project has remained central to the Council's studies program to this day. Through that program, the CFR explores questions of foreign policy, utilizing individual research by the Council's professional staff, its visiting fellows and others. Study groups and conferences continue to involve both members and outside experts, American and foreign. The Council publishes books and papers that draw on its deliberations and makes them available to the public. *Foreign Affairs*, widely recognized as the leading journal in the field, now appears bi-monthly and has more than 100,000 subscribers. The organization holds meetings (primarily in New York, Washington, D.C., and with its affiliated Pacific Council on International Policy in Los Angeles) at which foreign policy officials and experts from the United States and abroad present their views to members on a not-for-attribution basis, and sponsors a variety of visiting fellowships (for academics, journalists, diplomats, and military officers on leave) and independent task forces that address current policy.

CFR membership, restricted to U.S. citizens, has grown to more than 3,000 nationwide. New members are nominated by other members and directors and elected by the board of directors. The Council is funded by members' dues, sale of publications, corporate subscriptions, endowment funds, foundation grants, and voluntary gifts. The CFR has no affiliation with the U.S. government. Host to many views, it takes no institutional positions on issues of foreign policy and advocates none. It is, however, often a target of critics on the right, who believe it is too international in outlook, and those on the left, who see it as an elitist club of the foreign policy establishment. The men and women who make up its membership have standing as individual leaders in their respective communities—business, academia, or government. Books and articles written under Council auspices, have traditionally commanded attention and respect. For example, in 1947 George F. Kennan published an article in *Foreign Affairs* outlining a rationale for a policy of containment of the Soviet Union which became the basis of Washington's Soviet policy for the next forty years. The ideas were Mr. Kennan's, but they owed their wide dissemination to the Council's journal. Another influential work, Henry A. Kissinger's *Nuclear Weapons and Foreign Policy*, which framed the nuclear debate for decades, was published under CFR auspices in 1957. Again, the views were Mr. Kissinger's, but the institution that chose him as an author and organized the study group he worked with lent added weight to his findings. To this day, the institutional prestige of the CFR, the professional eminence of its members, and the weight of their policy views contribute to its continuing influence in the world of international affairs.

JOHN TEMPLE SWING

See also Kennan, George Frost; Kissinger, Henry Alfred; Think Tanks

FURTHER READING

Armstrong, Hamilton Fish. *Peace and Counterpeace from Wilson to Hitler: Memoirs of Hamilton Fish Armstrong*. New York, 1971.
Bundy, William P. *The Council on Foreign Relations & Foreign Affairs: Notes for a History*. New York, 1994.
Santoro, Carlo Maria. *Diffidence and Ambition: The Intellectual Sources of United States Foreign Policy*. Boulder, Colo., 1991.
Schulzinger, Robert D. *The Wise Men of Foreign Affairs: The History of the Council on Foreign Relations*. New York, 1984.
Shephardson, Whitney H. *Early History of the Council on Foreign Relations*. Stamford, Conn., 1960.
Wala, Michael. *The Council on Foreign Relations and American Foreign Policy in the Early Cold War*. Providence, R.I., 1994.

COVERT ACTION

The purpose of covert action is to influence events abroad, secretly, in the best interests of U.S. foreign policy. Covert action has been viewed by practitioners as a "third option," one between diplomacy and open warfare; or as "the quiet option," apt to be less noisy and obtrusive than other foreign policy instruments, such as the landing of a marine brigade. This supposition has been incorrect on occasion, as underscored by the "covert" wars that soon made their way into the newspapers, most conspicuously the anti-Cuban Bay of Pigs operation in May 1961.

Covert action, or "special activities" (in a more euphemistic nomenclature sometimes used in government documents), embraces a set of clandestine policy options that have generated considerable controversy over the years, for reasons of substance (policy) and procedure (democratic norms and customs). Substantively, this secret approach to U.S. foreign policy objectives has frequently involved methods fraught with ethical implications, including the global dissemination of false propaganda, the bribing of politicians in other countries, the disruption of foreign economic systems, the sponsorship of clandestine warfare, and the use of assassination plots ("executive action") directed against foreign leaders. Procedurally, serious questions arise as well about whether covert action—relying as it does on secret decision-making and the use of hidden intelligence agencies—can be squared with avowed U.S. principles that favor democracy and an open society.

Despite these reservations, U.S. policymakers have often turned to covert action in hopes of finding a quick and discreet solution to their foreign policy woes. The temptation is great to bypass, on the one hand, the seemingly endless wrangling of diplomatic negotiations with other nations and, on the other hand, the unpredictability of public debate at home (and the foreign response) that attends the use of overt military force.

The Evolution of Covert Action

In the United States, covert action preceded the establishment of the nation itself. In one of several examples from the Revolutionary War, Benjamin Franklin urged the government of France to join with the colonists in the creation of a secret conduit for the supply of military aid in support of the rebellion against Great Britain. General George Washington resorted to false propaganda techniques as a means for fooling British commanders, including exaggerated claims about his military troop strength in Continental Army documents that intentionally found their way into the hands of Redcoat spies.

After the new nation was created, President Thomas Jefferson approved a covert action to supply arms for a coup aimed at placing on the throne of Tripoli a man friendlier toward the United States than the incumbent ruler. President James Madison authorized a military attack in Florida to wrest this territory away from the Spanish—the first failed U.S. covert action; skillful diplomacy would subsequently win Florida away from Spain. Among other instances of covert action employed during the nation's first century, at the time of the Civil War the North planted propaganda in European newspapers to help counteract pro-Confederate sympathies, while the South secretly financed a group of plotters in Toronto to rally antiwar Northerners (Copperheads) against the Union.

Not until World War II, though, did the United States carry out covert action in a concerted manner. During the administration of Franklin D. Roosevelt, the Office of Strategic Services (OSS) launched not only espionage and counterespionage operations against the Axis powers, but also covert actions that included the sabotage of bridges and railroad tracks, the dissemination of propaganda, and the support of resistance groups, secretly battling the Nazi war machine throughout Europe and North Africa. Several of the intelligence officers who would head up covert action for the United States during the ensuing Cold War era gained their initial training with the OSS.

Comparable to the massive demobilization of U.S. forces immediately following World War II, U.S. intelligence organizations were scaled back dramatically as well—including the dismantlement of the OSS. Yet the memory of the Japanese attack on Pearl Harbor in 1941 remained vivid in the minds of top U.S. officials. While still vice president, Harry S. Truman vowed to help create a modern intelligence service designed to shield the nation against surprise military attacks in the future. In 1947, President Truman signed the National Security Act, reorganizing the military services and establishing a Central Intelligence Agency (CIA). The legislation made no explicit mention of covert action, but contained an ambiguous catchall phrase that permitted the new agency to "perform such other functions and duties related to intelligence affecting the national security as the National Security Council may from time-to-time direct."

The driving force behind the use of covert action during the Cold War was the challenge of global communism, which, Washington policymakers decided, had to be resisted whenever and wherever it threatened U.S. international objectives. As the Cold War began to heat up in 1948, the executive branch interpreted the language of the 1947 act as an invitation to unleash the CIA on a wide range of covert actions around the world in opposition to Soviet expansion and communist movements generally. In the late 1940s secret funding and other support to pro-West labor unions, political parties, and publishers in Europe helped shore up their resistance to communist infiltration; covert arms supplies and other forms of assistance to pro-Western factions in Greece, Guatemala, Iran, Laos, Afghanistan, and elsewhere aided the defeat of Soviet-supported communist factions in the 1940s and 1950s. Many covert actions failed and controversy persistently stalked this approach to foreign policy; nevertheless, the occasional successes—with the CIA-sponsored coups in Iran in 1953 and Guatemala in 1954 the most spectacular—coupled with the relative ease of using this hidden instrument, assured its ongoing appeal to presidents and their advisers.

By the late 1960s the CIA had hundreds of operations underway. By 1968, over half of its budget was dedicated to covert action, particularly in Vietnam. As the Vietnam War began to sour (1970), and as the CIA found itself caught up in scandals over Watergate (1973), Operation CHAOS (a CIA domestic spying operation disclosed in 1974), and controversial covert actions in Chile (also revealed in 1974), the budget for covert action started to shrink. By the beginning of the Carter Administration in 1977, less than 5 percent of the CIA's budget dealt with covert action. This figure subsequently rose again, to just below 30 percent, in the wake of the Islamic revolution in Iran and the seizing of American hostages in Tehran (1979) and the Soviet invasion of Afghanistan in December of that year.

This restoration of covert action accelerated during the Reagan administration. President Ronald Reagan and his foreign policy team strongly believed in the need to defeat Marxist-Leninist and other pro-Soviet forces wherever they were. Covert action was a principal instrument for doing so. Covert operations were mounted in Nicaragua (the Contras), El Salvador, Afghanistan, Angola, Kampuchea (Cambodia), Eastern Europe, within the Soviet Union, and elsewhere. However, in the wake of the Iran-Contra Affair over the improper use of covert action (1984–1986), the budget fell to its lowest levels since the first days of the Cold War—to less than one percent of the CIA's annual appropriation of approximately $30 billion. This low level of spending for special activities continued through the Bush administration and into the Clinton administration.

Methods of Covert Action

Covert actions may be grouped into four general categories: propaganda, political operations, economic operations, and paramilitary (PM) operations. Respectively, these activities are estimated to have made up 40, 30, 10, and 20 percent of the total number of covert actions during the Cold War. In terms of expense and risk, though, PM operations have been by far the most costly and controversial.

The most extensive form of covert action has been various uses of propaganda. As a supplement to the overt information released worldwide by the United States Information Agency, the CIA has pumped through its vast network of secret media agents a torrent of covert propaganda. These foreign agents have included correspondents, magazine and newspaper editors, television producers, talk show hosts, and anyone else in a position to disseminate without attribution the United States' views as if they were their own.

One of the major examples of such activities was the financing of Radio Free Europe (RFE) and Radio Liberty (RL) during the Cold War. RFE and RL broadcast into the Soviet Union and the Soviet bloc with programming geared to break the communist government's totalitarian control of the news, entertainment, and culture, as well as to propagandize for a highly favorable view of the United States and the West. While there was some criticism of the danger of "blow back" or "replay," that is, the drifting of CIA propaganda back into the United States where it might deceive U.S. citizens, RFE and RL generally are credited with having helped sustain dissident movements and to have contributed to the eventual fall of Soviet communism and control of Eastern Europe.

Of greater controversy were the CIA's propaganda efforts in Chile during the 1960s. In 1964, the CIA spent $3 million to blacken the name of Salvador Allende, the socialist presidential candidate with suspected ties to the Soviet Union. An expenditure of $3 million in Chilean presidential elections was roughly equivalent, on a per capita basis, to $60 million in a U.S. presidential election during this period—a staggering sum. Allende was democratically elected, nonetheless, in 1970. The CIA continued its propaganda operations designed to destroy his regime, spending an additional $3 million between 1970 and 1973. According to U.S. Senate investigators, the forms of propaganda included press releases, radio commentary, films, pamphlets, posters, leaflets, direct mailings, paper streamers, and wall paintings. The CIA relied heavily on images of communist tanks and firing squads, and paid for the distribution of hundreds of thousands of copies, in this very Catholic country, of an anti-communist pastoral letter written many years earlier by Pope Pius XI.

The "quiet assistance" advocated by proponents of covert action sometimes takes the form of financial aid to pro-Western politicians and bureaucrats in other nations, money used to assist groups in their electoral campaigns or for party recruitment. Anticommunist labor unions in Europe received extensive CIA funding during the Cold War, as did many politicians throughout the world; one well-publicized case involved the Christian Democratic Party in Italy during the 1960s, when its principal opponent was the Italian Communist Party. Another case involved support for the Christian Democrats in El Salvador in the early 1980s against the electoral challenge of ARENA, a more right-wing party closely linked to the "death squads."

The CIA also has resorted to disrupting the economies of adversaries. In one instance during the

Kennedy administration (though evidently without the president's knowledge), the CIA tried to spoil Cuban-Soviet relations by lacing sugar bound from Havana to Moscow with an unpalatable, though harmless, chemical substance. A White House aide discovered the scheme and had the 14,125 bags of sugar confiscated before they were shipped to the USSR. Other methods have reportedly included the incitement of labor unrest, counterfeiting foreign currencies, depressing the world price of agricultural products grown by adversaries, contaminating oil supplies, and—raising the ante—dynamiting electrical power lines and oil-storage tanks, as well as mining harbors to discourage the adversary's commercial shipping ventures.

Paramilitary, or secret warlike activities, have stirred the most criticism of covert action. This category includes small- and large-scale "covert" wars, which fail to stay covert for long; training activities for foreign military and police officials; providing military advisers, a wide array of weaponry, and battlefield transportation; and the planning and implementation of assassination plots.

This last endeavor has been particularly controversial and was prohibited by executive order in 1975. That year congressional investigators uncovered CIA files on assassination plots against foreign leaders, referred to euphemistically in secret documents as "termination with extreme prejudice" or simply "neutralization." At one time, the CIA created a special panel—the "Health Alteration Committee"—to screen assassination proposals. The agency's numerous attempts to murder Fidel Castro of Cuba all failed; and its plot against Congolese leader Patrice Lumumba, requiring a lethal injection of poison into his food or toothpaste, became a moot point when he was murdered by a rival faction in the Congo.

In 1984, a plan of systematic assassinations by pro-U.S. Contras against village representatives of the ruling Sandinista regime in Nicaragua came to light. An assassination manual, distributed by CIA officers in northern Nicaragua, outlined the arts of "neutralizing" local civil officials. The CIA director, William J. Casey, dismissed the incident as nothing more than the overzealousness of junior officers, operating without authority from headquarters. President Reagan called the matter "much ado about nothing."

Supervision of Covert Action

Given the extreme form that U.S. secret interventions sometimes took during the Cold War, beginning in 1975 some presidents and legislators attempted to put in place tighter controls over the nation's "special activities."

Amending the 1947 National Security Act, the Hughes-Ryan statute of 1974 defined covert action succinctly as "operations in foreign countries, other than activities intended solely for obtaining necessary intelligence." The law also required presidents to authorize formally all important covert action approvals in the executive branch, and to report their approvals "in a timely manner" to the appropriate committees of Congress. Covert action was no longer the exclusive preserve of the CIA and the National Security Council (NSC); Congress would now play an important supervisory role.

Following the Hughes-Ryan Act, Congress passed the the Clark Amendment (1976), which halted a covert action for the first time (in Angola). Then, four years later, it passed the Intelligence Oversight Act of 1980—the boldest of the intelligence reform bills—which mandated *prior* notification to the Congress of all covert actions before they were implemented. Subsequently, a series of seven Boland amendments (1984–1986) placed sharp limitations on aggressive covert actions in Nicaragua. Most recently, as a result of the Iran-Contra affair, in which the Reagan administration violated the 1980 Oversight Act and the Boland amendments, the Congress enacted the Intelligence Authorization Act of 1991. This law requires written presidential approval for covert actions, along with prior notification to Congress (except in the most extreme emergencies). The Intelligence Authorization Act of 1991 also defined covert action more elaborately than ever before. According to this law, covert action is…an activity or activities of the United States Government to influence political, economic, or military conditions abroad where it is intended that the role of the United States Government will not be apparent or acknowledged publicly, but does not include: (1) activities the primary purpose of which are to acquire intelligence, traditional counterintelligence activities, traditional activities to improve or maintain the operational security of United States Government programs, or administrative activities; (2) traditional diplomatic or military activities or routine support to such activities; (3) traditional law enforcement activities conducted by United States Government law enforcement agencies or routine support to such activities; or (4) activities to provide routine support to the overt activities (other than activities described above) of other United States Government agencies abroad. With this law, Congress provided the policy of covert action a much firmer legal footing than did the Hughes-Ryan Amendment.

From 1947 to 1974, the CIA decided upon and conducted covert actions with only limited supervision by the Congress and the White House. With the new oversight statutes in place, covert action has become substantially more accountable. Unlike the pre-1975 era, judgments about America's secret intervention abroad are now more likely to be made with the participation of elected representatives in Congress—not by the president and the clandestine services alone.

Not only will covert action continue to be closely supervised in the post–Cold War era—doubly so in light of the attempt by Reagan Administration officials to bypass the new oversight laws during the Iran-Contra affair—but it is likely to be resorted to far less than during the days of bitter rivalry between the United States and the Soviet Union that marked the Cold War. The slice of the intelligence budget allocated to this mission is apt to remain below the 5 percent level for the foreseeable future. In place of support for large-scale secret wars and massive propaganda campaigns, the CIA will probably focus on precisely targeted covert action operations designed to thwart weapons proliferation and disrupt terrorist activities. Relatively small sums of money also will be channeled covertly to individuals and groups with a pro-Western agenda in the developing world. Much of this kind of financial support for friends abroad—once the warp and woof of covert action during the Cold War—is now being carried out overtly, through various government foreign assistance programs and by the National Endowment for Democracy, a federal agency established by the Reagan administration to fund openly various democratic movements abroad.

LOCH K. JOHNSON

See also Central Intelligence Agency; Cold War; Congress; Cryptology; Cuban Missile Crisis; Iran-Contra Affair; National Security Agency

FURTHER READING

Godson, Roy, ed. *Intelligence Requirements for the 1980s: Covert Action.* Washington, D.C., 1991.

Goodman, Allan E., and Bruce D. Berkowitz. *"Background Paper," The Need to Know.* New York, 1992.

Johnson, Loch K. "On Drawing a Bright Line for Covert Operations." *American Journal of International Law* 86 (April 1992): 284–309.

Prados, John. *President's Secret Wars: CIA and Pentagon Covert Operations Since World War II.* New York, 1986.

Reisman, E. Michael, and James E. Baker. *Regulating Covert Action.* New Haven, Conn., 1992.

Rositzke, Harry. *The CIA's Secret Operations: Espionage, Counterespionage, and Covert Action.* Pleasantville, N.Y., 1977.

Shackley, Theodore. *The Third Option: An American View of Counterinsurgency.* Pleasantville, N.Y., 1981.

Treverton, Gregory F. *The Limits of Intervention in the Postwar World.* New York, 1987.

U.S. Senate. Select Committee to Study Governmental Operations with Respect to Intelligence Activities (the Church Committee). "Alleged Assassination Plots Involving Foreign Leaders," *Interim Report.* S. Rept. Nos. 94–465. Washington, D.C. (November 20, 1975).

CREEL COMMITTEE

See Committee on Public Information

CREOLE AFFAIR

(October 1841)

An incident that led to a dispute between the United States and Great Britain over fugitive slaves from the United States. The brig *Creole* had sailed from Hampton Roads, Virginia, for New Orleans with 135 slaves aboard. At sea, nineteen slaves led by Madison Washington mutinied and forced the crew to sail to Nassau, in the Bahamas, where the British had abolished slavery. The United States had no extradition treaty with Great Britain, but requested return of the slaves on the basis of comity, the principle that a nation has a duty to assist foreign vessels that involuntarily enter its ports. British officials, committed to antislavery, instead released the slaves, including the mutineers.

For many in the United States—especially Southerners—the *Creole* became a matter of national honor. During the 1842 Treaty of Washington negotiations, the *Creole* case temporarily hindered the general settlement of Anglo-American differences that Secretary of State Daniel Webster and the British emissary, Lord Ashburton, desired. Disposing of the matter in an exchange of notes, Ashburton stated that henceforth British officials would avoid "officious interference" with vessels forced into British ports. In 1853 an Anglo-American claims commission awarded the U.S. slaveholders compensation for their losses.

KENNETH R. STEVENS

See also Great Britain; Slave Trade and Slavery; Webster-Ashburton Treaty

FURTHER READING

Jones, Howard. *To the Webster-Ashburton Treaty: A Study in Anglo-American Relations, 1783–1843.* Chapel Hill, N.C., 1977.

Jones, Wilbur Devereux. *The American Problem in British Diplomacy, 1841-1861.* Athens, Ga., 1974.

CROATIA

Formerly a constituent republic within the (old) Yugoslav federation and an independent nation since 1991, Croatia is bordered by Slovenia, Hungary, the (new) Federal Republic of Yugoslavia (Serbia), and Bosnia-Herzegovina. It also has a long, but in parts very narrow, coastline along the Adriatic Sea. Historically, the ethnic composition of its population has been predominantly Croatian (and Catholic), but with a significant Serbian (and Orthodox) minority—to wit seventy-five percent Croatian, twelve percent Serbian at the time of independence in 1991.

A prosperous Roman province, then (during the Middle Ages) an independent kingdom, it was conquered by the Turks in the sixteenth century but later emerged as a Habsburg outpost and was eventually absorbed by the Austro-Hungarian empire—becoming formally a semi-autonomous province of the Kingdom of Hungary after the "Compromise" of 1867. Croats chafed under their enforced Magyarization and, while also mistrusting their Serb "cousins," joined forces with Belgrade leaders in preparing to shed their Vienna-Budapest "yoke."

Following the break-up of the Austro-Hungarian empire at the end of World War I, Croatia became part of the newly independent Kingdom of Serbs, Croats, and Slovenes (also including Montenegro and Bosnia-Herzegovina) which was renamed Yugoslavia in 1929. The United States was the first great power to grant recognition to the newly independent state. And while the new state's creation was partially consistent with the Wilsonian principle of self-determination, it was not entirely so: the Southern Slav people were being given freedom from Habsburg rule, but not to the extent of establishing entirely separate states, as many Croatian nationalists desired. This reflected (among other factors) pressure from Italy against the emergence of a single, homogenous, and too powerful Balkan state able to challenge Italy's dominance in the Adriatic.

The conflicting historical, administrative, and cultural aspirations between Croats and Serbs during the interwar period, when the Serbian monarchy autocratically imposed its will over the entire country, led many Croats to welcome Nazi German support for an "independent Croatian state" during the early stages of World War II under the puppet fascist Ustaša regime, led by Ante Pavelić. This now included most sections of Bosnia-Herzegovina, as well as parts of Serbia. The Ustaša state, which was notorious for its political repression and brutal treatment (and extermination in concentration camps) of its Serb and Jewish minorities, eventually lost control over its territories and collapsed in 1944. In the meantime, several partisan movements had united in the antifascist council for the liberation of Yugoslavia (AVNOJ), which was militarily supported by the United States and its allies following the invasion of Italy. The communist-dominated partisans were under the leadership of Josip Broz Tito, who was of Slovene-Croatian descent, and became the most influential group in the liberation of Yugoslavia; by 1945 they had emerged as the sole rulers. With Western approval, Croatia was thereupon restored to a Yugoslavia again ruled from Belgrade by a strong central government and a Soviet-style constitution.

Although Tito maintained the unity of the Yugoslav federation during his lifetime, the old inter-republic and inter-ethnic tensions never disappeared. For example, as part of the 1960s debate over economic reform leading toward "market socialism" at a time of deep recession throughout Yugoslavia, conflicting regional economic interests rekindled ethnic rivalries, and nationalist claims and complaints reemerged between Slovenia and Croatia in the north and the underdeveloped southern republics. Croatia in particular saw a sharp rise in nationalist agitation, as communist party leaders began calling for radical constitutional changes that would give the republic virtual independence. Tito purged the party, and several prominent Croatians were arrested. In 1974, however, a new constitution—with an almost confederal character—was adopted to placate nationalist sentiments, while still restraining them in a collective Yugoslav framework. Throughout the 1980s, following Tito's death, Serbia was the foremost exponent of a stronger federal government while Slovenia and Croatia were the principal exponents of regional autonomy.

Communist Party power began to decline in Croatia in 1989, and the then prime minister Ante Marković promised multiparty elections to the republican legislature. Franjo Tudjman—a self-styled historian, partisan leader during World War II, and sometime communist dissident—won the elections in 1990. His newly founded Croatian Democratic Union party conducted a ferocious anti-Yugoslav/anti-Serbian campaign further stirring up Croatian nationalist sentiments. The new government changed the constitution, dismantled the old communist power structure, and proclaimed Croatia's full sovereignty as well as the right to secede from Yugoslavia. Less emphasis was laid on the further liberalization of the Croatian political landscape; and indeed Tudjman started to fill government and other positions with relatives and loyal friends. In response to the increasing anti-Serbian mood kindled by the Tudjman regime, and under the influence of the Serbian leader Slobodan Milošević, the leaders of the Croatian Serb minority formed the Serb National Council and pushed for Serb autonomy within Croatia. The Croatian Serbs then held a referendum in support of joining Serbia while staying within the Yugoslav federation. At the same time, inter-republic relations were breaking down at the whole federal level as Milošević opposed the scheduled rotation of the chairmanship of the collective presidency to the Croatian member, Stipe Mesić. A few days later the Tudjman government held its own referendum on the question of independence, in which the vote was overwhelmingly in its favor—but, ominously, with most Croatian Serbs boycotting. Secretary of State James Baker came to Belgrade to meet with all of the federation leaders in a last minute effort to hold Yugoslavia together. But on 25 June, the same day that Slovenia took parallel action, Croatia declared its independence.

The Serb-dominated Yugoslav National Army (JNA) moved first against Slovenia, but quickly switched its focus to Croatia, both because of their shared border and because of the large Serbian minority there. Following the outbreak of hostilities, the European Community (EC) mediated a cease-fire on the condition of Mesić being appointed federal president and of a moratorium on the implementation of Slovene and Croatian independence for three months. The George Bush administration signalled its preference for a European resolution to the conflict, and gave precedence to the European Community and later to the UN, respectively. In August 1991, the Serbs in Western Slavonia, nominally a province of Croatia, proclaimed an independent Serb enclave.

When the EC moratorium expired, Croatia declared all federal laws null and void, and the Serb autonomous areas in Croatia reunified. The JNA, together with paramilitary forces from Serbia and from Serb-inhabited areas of Croatia, then attacked Eastern Slavonia, put Dubrovnik under siege, committed "ethnic cleansing" and other atrocities, and ultimately established control over a quarter of Croatia's territory. Some in the West, including U.S. Ambassador to Yugoslavia Warren Zimmermann, pushed for North Atlantic Treaty Organization (NATO) air strikes against the Serbs, but the political will was not there. The West was fragmented even on simple strategic diplomatic decisions, as demonstrated when, despite both U.S. and general European Union (EU) opposition, Germany unilaterally recognized Croatia and Slovenia in December 1991. The rest of the EU followed suit soon thereafter, although the United States did not do so until April 1992, when it also recognized Bosnian independence.

While international attention focused principally on Serb-committed atrocities during the early phase of the Yugoslav civil war, Helsinki Watch and other groups also pointed to the Tudjman government's own violence against ethnic Serbs. In March 1992, as part of a peace plan approved by the UN Security Council and negotiated by former U.S. Secretary of State Cyrus R. Vance, a UN Protection Force (UNPROFOR) was deployed in Croatia with its mission defined largely in humanitarian terms, including safeguarding areas designated as "safe havens." UNPROFOR included contingents of Canadian, Dutch, British, and French troops, but no American ones. While UNPROFOR did have some ameliorative effects on the fighting in the safe havens, and a truce held fairly well for about a year, little progress was made toward a resolution of the overall conflict. And in January 1993 Croatian-Serbian fighting was reignited, although by then the worst fighting was taking place on Bosnian territory.

Croatian forces also had entered the war in Bosnia, supporting Bosnian Croat territorial claims against the Sarajevo government and perpetrating their own ethnic cleansing against the Muslim population. The EU and the United States threatened sanctions against Croatia, with only limited impact. In early 1994 U.S.-led diplomatic efforts did succeed in forging a Bosnian-Croatian agreement to form a federation. The idea was to make this the core of a future Bosnian state, while bringing the Serbs into the peace process later. Tudjman, who feared domestic troubles in the case of sanctions and international condemnation of Croatia's activities in Bosnia, made the necessary changes in the Bosnian Croat leadership and thus gained support for multilateral assistance. Among the effects of the agreement was the opening of a weapons smuggling route from Croatia to Bosnian government-held territory, as a way of getting around the Bosnian arms embargo. Closer U.S.-Croatian military cooperation also ensued as the Pentagon signed a military cooperation accord with Croatia's defense ministry in November 1994.

In May 1995, coinciding with major new NATO air strikes against the Serbs, Croatia recaptured Western Slavonia. In July, Croatian and Bosnian government leaders agreed on a common anti-Serbian military strategy at a meeting with U.S. Ambassador Peter Galbraith, and two weeks later, in August, the Knin area was taken in a lightning military offensive. Although this elicited harsh criticism from several European allies, both the United States and Germany tacitly supported Croatia in order to counterbalance Serbia, help stabilize the military situation in Bosnia, and force the Bosnian Serbs to the peace table. (Similarly, the Bill Clinton administration had earlier on tolerated clandestine Iranian arms shipments to Zagreb and to the Bosnian government forces.)

The combined effects of the NATO air strikes, the Croatian offensive, the continuing economic sanctions implemented against Serbia, and more assertive U.S. diplomatic efforts, now orchestrated by Assistant Secretary of State Richard Holbrooke, led to the major breakthroughs of the Dayton agreements of the fall of 1995. For Croatia, the main points of concern in the Dayton plan were assuring the return of Eastern Slavonia in a two-year period under international supervision, possible war crimes charges against Croatian leaders, the return of the Bosnian refugees in Croatia, and the status of areas such as Brčko (along the Serbian supply corridor) and a small but strategically important peninsula near Dubrovnik.

As implementation of the Dayton agreements slowly proceeded through 1996, U.S. policy toward Croatia continued to exhibit a degree of ambivalence, reflecting both Washington's concerns about Tudjman's commitments to political pluralism at home as well as doubts about Zagreb's ostensibly nonaggressive intentions toward its neighbors.

MARTIN ROSSMANN

See also Bosnia-Herzegovina; Serbia; Yugoslavia

FURTHER READING

Hopner, Jacob B. *Yugoslavia in Crisis.* New York, 1962.
McAdams, C. Michael. *Croatia: Myth and Reality.* New York, 1992.

Rieff, David. *Slaughterhouse: Bosnia and the Failure of the West.* New York, 1995.

Singleton, Fred. *A Short History of the Yugoslav Peoples.* Cambridge, Mass., 1985.

Woodward, Susan L. *Balkan Tragedy: Chaos and Dissolution After the Cold War.* Washington D.C., 1995.

CROCKER, CHESTER ARTHUR

(*b.* 29 October 1941)

Assistant secretary of state for African affairs from 1981 to 1989 and architect of the policy of constructive engagement. He earned degrees at Ohio State University (1963), Johns Hopkins University (1965), and the Johns Hopkins School of Advanced International Studies (1969). Between teaching stints at American University (1969–1970) and Georgetown University (1972–1981, 1989–), he served as the African affairs expert on President Richard Nixon's National Security Council staff (1970–1972). In 1981 Crocker joined President Ronald Reagan's administration and implemented the policy of constructive engagement toward the Republic of South Africa. He argued that the United States should continue to condemn apartheid but should encourage gradual reform rather than applying overt pressure to end racial separatism in the all-white South African government. Crocker claimed that this policy had a better chance of success and would preserve U.S. strategic and economic interests. Critics argued that the policy amounted to "all carrot and no stick." The Reagan administration loosened its adherence to constructive engagement and implemented tougher sanctions against the separatist government when black South African protests intensified in the 1980s. In 1988 Crocker succeeded in linking independence for Namibia with the withdrawal of Cuban troops from Angola and the end of border clashes between Angolan and South African troops. Since leaving government, Crocker has served as chairman of the board of directors of the U.S. Institute of Peace, and among other works, is co-editor of *Managing Global Chaos.*

SHANE J. MADDOCK

See also Africa; Angola; Namibia; Nixon, Richard Milhous; Reagan, Ronald Wilson; Somalia; South Africa

FURTHER READING

Crocker, Chester A. *South Africa's Defense Posture: Coping with Vulnerability.* Beverly Hills, Calif., 1981.

———. *High Noon in Southern Africa: Making Peace in a Rough Neighborhood.* New York, 1992.

CROLY, HERBERT DAVID

(*b.* 23 January 1869; *d.* 17 May 1930)

Author, editor, and political philosopher who was the founding editor of *The New Republic* magazine. Born in New York City, he studied philosophy at Harvard under George Santayana, Josiah Royce, and William James. Croly's most celebrated book, *The Promise of American Life* (1909), stands as a seminal work of progressive ideology. In this book he called on the national government to take the lead in domestic reform and to adopt a policy of aggressive market expansionism. Criticizing isolationist sentiment, he argued that U.S. policymakers should pursue a vigorous defense of peace and democracy throughout the world. Consistent with this view, Croly's *The New Republic* in 1914 celebrated the "new opportunities" to promote democratic institutions abroad offered by the war. When hostilities ended, a disillusioned Croly condemned the Treaty of Versailles as too harsh. He supported Robert La Follette's failed candidacy for president in 1924 but then shifted his interest from political to religious affairs.

JOHN M. CRAIG

See also La Follette, Robert Marion; Versailles Treaty of 1919; World War I

FURTHER READING

Forcey, Charles. *The Crossroads of Liberalism: Croly, Weyl, Lippmann, and the Progressive Era, 1900–1925.* New York, 1961.

Levy, David W. *Herbert Croly of The New Republic: The Life and Thought of an American Progressive.* Princeton, N.J., 1985.

CRUISE MISSILES

See Nuclear Weapons and Strategy

CRYPTOLOGY

The two opposing technologies of signal security (ways of keeping messages secret) and signal intelligence (ways of getting information from communications). These technologies range from whispering and eavesdropping to formulating mathematical ciphers and breaking codes by computer. In its more important function, preserving secrets, U.S. cryptology has by and large succeeded since World War II, while in its more glamorous role, stealing the secrets of others, it has been extremely useful but not critical.

For much of its existence the United States was deficient in cryptography, the branch of signal security that deals with making and using codes and ciphers. The Deciphering Branch of Great Britain solved dispatches of U.S. ministers from 1798 to 1800, and France cracked U.S. messages in 1812. During the 1920s and 1930s, Germany, Japan, Italy, and Great Britain broke Department of State codes. The Department of State's "gray code"—named for the color of the codebook's binding—was so old and so notorious for its transparency that President

Franklin D. Roosevelt minuted to Secretary of State Cordell Hull on 6 December 1941, about his appeal for peace to the emperor of Japan, "Dear Cordell: Shoot this Grew [the U.S. ambassador to Japan]—I think can go in gray code—saves time—I don't mind if it gets picked up. FDR." Justifiably concerned about the Department of State's weak codes, Roosevelt used U.S. Navy cryptosystems for his cable correspondence with British prime minister Winston Churchill. Later in World War II, Germany cracked a major Department of State code and learned about diplomat Robert Murphy's negotiations to win control of French North Africa.

To improve the security of its messages, the Department of State, whose cryptography section had been under the control of its archivist, established the Division of Cryptography in 1944 under an experienced naval cryptologist. He introduced modern cipher machines whose cryptograms were practically unbreakable with the technology of the time; these machines were replaced with newer ones after the Cuban missile crisis of 1962 because diplomatic communications had seemed too slow. No evidence has come to light that Department of State messages have been cryptanalyzed, and only one case of betrayal of a Department of State cipher machine (the KW-26, also used by other governmental departments) has been reported, so the vast majority of American diplomatic messages have probably been transmitted securely. On the other hand, the Soviet Union repeatedly bugged the U.S. embassy in Moscow with microphones in the walls and decorations, tiny transmitters on typewriter keys, and taps on cipher machines to read messages before they were encrypted.

The Department of State first obtained information from solved foreign intercepts in World War I, when the army serviced it. It began paying for cryptanalysis (popularly called codebreaking), a part of signal intelligence, in 1919. That year it contributed $40,000 to help establish the Cipher Bureau, a joint U.S. Army–Department of State cryptanalytic organization led by Herbert O. Yardley, who had run a similar unit for the army during World War I. In the next ten years the Department of State contributed $230,404 to the bureau, which solved the codes of nineteen nations. The bureau first significantly served the Department of State during the Washington Naval Conference of 1921–1922, at which the United States, Great Britain, Japan, France, and Italy negotiated capital-ship tonnage limits and ratios. Intercepted Japanese messages disclosed that the empire would take a weaker position on the size of its navy than it was publicly stating. With this knowledge, the U.S. delegates pressed Japan, which fell back from a tonnage ratio of 7:10 with the United States to 6:10, losing in effect a battleship and a half.

In 1929 the new secretary of state, Henry L. Stimson, who believed that surreptitiously reading another government's mail undermined the principle of mutual trust on which he conducted foreign relations, withdrew the Department of State's support from the Cipher Bureau. It closed on 31 October 1929. The army and, to a lesser degree, the navy took over diplomatic cryptanalysis, continuing through World War II. Cryptanalyzed messages, chiefly those of Japan, were first forwarded to the White House in 1937. Although they provided insight into Japanese negotiations, they did not warn the United States of the attack on Pearl Harbor because none of the intercepts ever mentioned anything about the attack. Near the end of World War II codebreaking provided intelligence that helped the United States shape the United Nations organization the way it wanted.

Since its formation on 4 November 1952, the Defense Department's National Security Agency has overseen the Department of State's cryptography operations and has furnished the department with the results of interception and cryptanalysis. During the Cold War, intelligence taken from Soviet telemetry provided details of Soviet missile capability, which proved useful in arms limitation negotiations. Henry Cabot Lodge, the U.S. ambassador to the United Nations, is said to have thanked the codebreakers for their information. In 1986 the solution of Libyan diplomatic telegrams revealed that Libya had been responsible for the bombing of the La Belle discotheque in Berlin in which a U.S. soldier was killed; this led to President Ronald Reagan's reprisal raid against Libyan President Muammar al-Qaddafi on 15 April 1986. Since the end of the Cold War, the National Security Agency has focused more and more on terrorist and international drug and crime communications. But the increasing availability of strong voice and data cryptosystems is making its work more difficult.

DAVID KAHN

See also Intelligence; National Security Agency; Pearl Harbor, Attack on; Washington Conference on the Limitation of Armaments

FURTHER READING

Bamford, James. *The Puzzle Palace.* Boston, 1982.
Kahn, David. *The Codebreakers.* New York, 1967.
Kruh, Louis. "Stimson, the Black Chamber, and the 'Gentlemen's Mail' Quote." *Cryptologia* 12 (April 1988): 65–89.
Weber, Ralph E. *Masked Dispatches: Cryptograms and Cryptology in American History, 1775–1900.* United States Cryptologic History, Series 1, vol. 1. Fort Meade, Md., 1993.
Yardley, Herbert O. *The American Black Chamber.* Indianapolis, 1931.

CUBA

An island republic located in the northern Caribbean Sea, 145 km south of the coast of Florida. Following the 1959 revolution, Cuba became a firm foe of U.S. policies in the Western Hemisphere, suffered a U.S.-sponsored invasion, and, after it had allied itself with the Soviet Union, became a Cold War contestant. Something of an inexorable reciprocity linked the fate of the United States and Cuba. Both Cuba and the United States very early developed a sense of history that included cognizance of the other, central to which was the recognition that differences in culture and nationality notwithstanding, mutual interests formed the bonds that linked both people indissolubly. Each country intruded on the other at formative moments of national development, and henceforth the character of each would retain permanent traces of this convergence.

Americans and Cubans came to know each other well at an early stage. Indeed, there was no nation in Latin America with which the United States was as closely involved as early, and with which it perceived its commercial and strategic interests to be more directly intertwined. Some of this was a function more of chance than of choice, the result of the peculiarities in the historical experiences of each nation. It is no less clear, however, that once the connections were made, relations between Americans and Cubans assumed a logic of their own, out of which developed a duality in which a pervasive ambivalence served to define the character of the interaction, between trust and suspicion, esteem and scorn, a desire to emulate and a need to repudiate. These were tensions that were evident early in the nineteenth century and persisted through the end of the twentieth and appeared to have acquired something of a permanence in the cosmology of Cuba-U.S. relations.

Geography and proximity explain much. Nearness facilitated trade and commerce, encouraged travel, and promoted a familiarity that was almost without parallel. Timing was also a factor, and circumstances unique to the historical development of each country served to promote linkages that assumed institutional and structural forms. Products and markets vital to each could be provided by the other. The well-being of both became intertwined in ways that were real and imagined, and that some of the ways were only imagined did not make them any less potent of a factor in policy formulation. Before either Cuba or the United States became sovereign nations, each had participated in the other's internal development in ways that were decisive and permanent.

The United States more than adequately replaced the loss of trade with the British West Indies after 1776 through new and expanded commercial ties made with the Spanish colony of Cuba. Increasingly, strategic considerations combined with trade, after the U.S. acquisition of Louisiana and Florida, to give Cuba a new and heightened importance, as it lies across the principal sea lanes of the Caribbean and guards the entrance to the Gulf of Mexico, could not omit Cuba from the contemplation of the regional defense of U.S. southern boundaries and the well-being of maritime interests in the Gulf of Mexico. The early nineteenth century was also a period when the Cuban economy assumed structural forms around the U.S. connection. Cuba found new markets in the United States at a time of expanding sugar production and soon relied on these markets to sustain its economic growth. Commercial ties with the United States loomed large over Cuban production strategies, consumption patterns, and, inevitably, political alignments. The logic of this relationship seemed at once self-evident and incontrovertible, and central to almost everything else happening in Cuban society. By the late nineteenth century, the United States had emerged as the principal market for Cuba's exports and the major source of the island's imports.

Annexationist Stirrings

So fully did both countries seem to meet each other's needs that it was perhaps natural if not inevitable that some Americans and Cubans would contemplate annexation as the consummation of a relationship that in almost every other regard seemed complete. The proposition that Cuba would one day be joined to the United States established a powerful grip on the U.S. imagination through much of the nineteenth century. Cuba was "almost in sight of our shores," as President John Quincy Adams (1825–1829) exaggerated to make the point.

For many Americans the withering of Spanish sovereignty in Cuba represented the last act of a historic drama, one predestined to culminate with U.S. annexation. Still, throughout the nineteenth century the United States defended the status quo, and the Spanish claim to rule, against both internal challenge and outside threat. In 1823 Thomas Jefferson counseled President James Monroe to "oppose, with all our means, the forcible interposition of any power, either as auxiliary, stipendiary, or under any other form or pretext, and most especially [Cuba's] transfer to any power, by conquest, cession or in any other way." Twenty years later Secretary of State John Forsyth authorized the U.S. minister in Madrid to reassure Spanish authorities "that in case of any attempt, from whatever quarter, to wrest from her this portion of her territory, she may securely depend upon the military and naval resources of the United States to aid her in preserving or recovering it." Secretary of State John M. Clayton restated this policy succinctly in 1849: "The news of the cession of Cuba to any foreign power would, in the United States, be the instant signal for war."

Annexationist stirrings peaked and subsided during the 1840s and 1850s. In the United States expansionist elements were in political ascendancy and pursued the acquisition of Cuba with new vigor. The South in partic-

Cuba and the Caribbean 1950s-Present

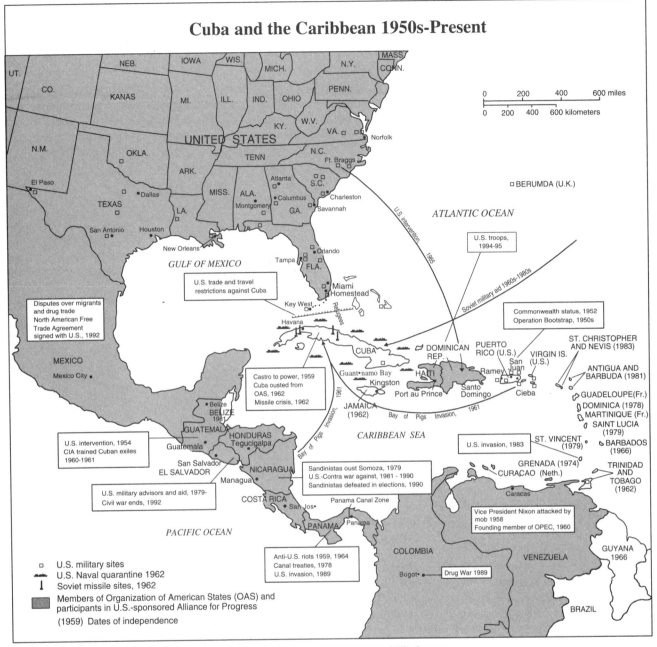

From *A People and A Nation: A History of the United States,* Mary Beth Norton et al., 4th Edition. ©1994 by Houghton Mifflin Company.
Reprinted with permission

ular looked covetously upon Cuba as an addition to the the political strength of slaveholding states. Presidents James K. Polk and Franklin Pierce attempted to buy the island but without success. In 1854 U.S. ministers to Spain, France, and Great Britain met in Ostend, Belgium, and publicly urged the United States to renew its offer to purchase Cuba. The Ostend Manifesto warned that if Spain refused to sell, "then, by every law, human and divine, we shall be justified in wresting it from Spain if we possess the power." Increasingly, however, the

United States became absorbed with its own domestic issues as the country edged closer to civil war. The debate over slavery in the United States all but foreclosed any possibility that new slave territories would be admitted into the Union.

Economic Connections and Insurrection

The U.S. presence in Cuba expanded throughout the nineteenth century in all sectors of property and production. Americans took up residence in Cuba, and as their numbers increased and their roles expanded, so did their importance. Americans organized trading companies and established boardinghouses. They were moneylenders and shippers, buyers and sellers, engineers and machinists. They arrived in growing numbers to operate and service the industrial equipment imported from the United States, especially steam-powered mill machinery, steamships, and railroads. U.S. capital was invested in Cuba's economy, including sugar plantations, mines, commerce, cattle ranches, and coffee estates. For nearly a century, the Cuban economy was organized around its commercial relations with the United States, depending increasingly on U.S. markets and imports. By the 1890s U.S. investments in Cuba reached at least $50 million, and Cuba was functioning almost entirely within U.S. economic structures. Nearly 94 percent of Cuban sugar exports flowed to U.S. markets. By 1893 Cuban imports from the United States accounted for almost half of the total U.S. exports to Central and South America. Cuban exports to the United States increased from $54 million in 1890 to $79 million in 1893.

The reorientation of Cuban trade away from Spain and toward the United States exposed the contradictions of Spanish rule and set in relief the many and varied ways that continued Cuban development could no longer be contained within existing colonial structures. Discontent deepened and in February 1895 erupted into armed conflict. Economic crisis and separatist pressures converged to produce conditions for insurrection. Under the leadership of José Martí, Máximo Gómez, and Antonio Maceo, Cubans of all classes joined the expanding rebellion. The war for independence began modestly enough, in eastern Cuba, but before the year ended insurgent armies had blazed westward across the island. In the course of ten months, the insurrection had dramatically expanded from its provincial dimensions and reached regions never before disturbed by nationalist stirrings. By late 1897 the United States understood that Spain's days in Cuba were numbered. "Spain will lose Cuba," Secretary of State John Sherman predicted bluntly in August 1897. "That seems to me to be certain. She cannot continue the struggle." Assistant Secretary of State William R. Day concurred in a confidential memorandum written in March 1898: "Spain's struggle in Cuba has become absolutely hopeless....Spain is exhausted financially and physically, while the Cubans are stronger."

The Cuban insurrection threatened more than Spanish colonial rule. It also threatened the U.S. pretension of becoming the successor to Spain. Against the landscape created by the receding tide of Spanish sovereignty, the United States now confronted what had been the anathema to policymakers ever since the days of President Thomas Jefferson—the prospect of Cuban independence. Acquisition of Cuba was always envisaged as an act of colonial continuity, formally transferred and legitimately ceded by Spain to the United States. The success of the Cuban rebellion changed all this. If the United States could not permit Spain to transfer sovereignty over Cuba to another power, it also could not permit Spain to cede sovereignty to Cubans. The United States prepared for intervention, as alarmed at the prospect of a Cuban victory as it was exasperated at Spain's inability to end the war. The publication on 9 February 1898 of a letter written by Enrique Dupuy de Lôme, the Spanish minister in the United States, which criticized President William McKinley, and the explosion of the U.S. battleship *Maine* in Havana harbor six days later were two incidents that certainly contributed to a climate increasingly favorable to war. The prospects of a Cuban victory over Spain, however, was the real impetus that propelled the United States into war. If Washington did not act, Cuba would be lost and its strategic and economic interests permanently endangered.

Thus, in April 1898 President McKinley asked Congress for authority to intervene militarily in Cuba, ostensibly in a war against Spain, but in fact also against the Cubans. No mention was made of Cuban independence, recognition of the Cuban provisional government, or even an allusion to the renunciation of territorial aggrandizement. The U.S. purpose in Cuba, McKinley emphasized in his war message, consisted of a "forcible intervention...as a neutral to stop the war." McKinley explained: "The forcible intervention of the United States...involves...hostile constraint upon both the parties to the contest." War was directed against both Spaniards and Cubans; it was the means to neutralize the two competing claims of sovereignty. The Teller Amendment to the congressional resolution authorizing U.S. intervention guaranteed Cuban independence as a part of U.S. pacification. It was only a matter of time before pacification came to mean the neutralization of all opposition to U.S. hegemony.

Aftermath of Intervention

The intervention changed everything. A Cuban war of liberation was transformed into a U.S. war of expansion, better known as the Spanish-American-Cuban-Filipino War. The very name given to the war at the time—Spanish American—served to legitimize the U.S. claim over the island as a spoil of victory. The Americans had not arrived as allies of the Cubans or as agents of Cuban independence. They had gone to war, as they always said they would, to prevent the transfer of Cuban sovereignty to a third party. Sovereignty formally passed to the United States in the Treaty of Paris (1898), and the U.S. military occupation began in January 1899. For three and a half years, Cuba was administered as an occupied territory by military governors appointed by

Washington. These were years of reconstruction and revival that set in place the essential elements from which U.S. hegemony would subsequently flow. During the military occupation Cuba was obliged to cede territory to the United States for a naval station, acquiesce to limitations on its national sovereignty, and authorize the United States to intervene in the defense of its life, liberty, and property. These were the conditions Cubans were obliged to accept before obtaining independence, formulated in 1901 in the Platt Amendment, appended to the Cuban constitution of 1901, and ratified in the Permanent Treaty of 1903.

Through the early decades of the twentieth century, U.S. armed intervention and political interference were accompanied by an expansion of U.S. capital. Armed interventions occurred in 1906, 1912, and 1917, all in response to insurrection and destruction of U.S. property. Political meddling was unrelenting and U.S. ambassadors exercised authority equivalent to that possessed by a proconsul. In 1960 former Ambassador Earl E. T. Smith acknowledged that "the United States was so overwhelmingly influential in Cuba that…the American ambassador was the second most important man in Cuba, sometimes even more important than the president." By the 1930s U.S. control over the Cuban economy was virtually unchecked in almost every sphere. U.S. capital had expanded into sugar, mining, and tobacco and had established a preponderant presence in banking, transportation, utilities, and ranching. The United States dominated Cuban trade and provided Cubans with most of their capital goods and consumer durables. By the late 1950s the total U.S. investment in Cuba approached the $1 billion mark. The expansion of the U.S. presence was almost overwhelming and was highly visible through social clubs, civic and professional organizations, newspapers and magazines, the endless stream of tourists, diplomats, missionaries, and sailors. In addition to controlling every major sector of the Cuban economy, U.S. citizens owned vast portions of land, operated the better schools, presided over the most prestigious social clubs, and lived in privileged circumstances in Havana and on the great sugar estates. They were the moneylenders, the landowners, and power brokers. They bought and sold Cuban politicians and policemen the way they bought farms and factories.

Because the U.S. presence in Cuba was so visible, and so visibly privileged, it naturally aroused hostility and resentment. It offended national self-esteem, from radicals who denounced the demise of *patria* to conservatives who lamented the debasement of *cultura*. Cuban efforts at collective mobility and self-determination increasingly included anti-U.S. sentiment. Much of the surge of Cuban nationalism after the 1920s derived directly from an abiding abhorrence of the Platt Amend-

ment. A source of enduring injury to Cuban national sensibilities, the amendment became the focal point of growing nationalist sentiment. The Platt Amendment so offended Cuban national pride that in the end it served to contribute to the development of the very forces it sought to contain—nationalism and revolution. During the 1930s economic collapse and political repression contributed to a popular revolution against the government of Gerardo Machado y Morales (1925–1933), whose ouster provided the opportunity to give expression to mounting anti-U.S. sentiment and a surge of nationalism that challenged the premises that had driven U.S. policy. The government of Ramón Grau San Martín (1933–1934) gave political form to these sentiments. Grau enacted a series of decrees that impinged on the privileged U.S. position, but his government lasted only four months.

By the end of the 1930s many Cuban grievances had been remedied. Between 1934 and 1940 a series of puppet presidents ruled under the authority of Colonel Fulgencio Batista y Zaldívar, after which he assumed the presidency (1940–1944). U.S. policymakers found in Batista an ambitious defender of order and property, and connections made in the early 1930s would last until the late 1950s. The formal terms of Cuba-U.S. relations changed with the abrogation of the Platt Amendment in 1934. The United States retained use of the Guantánamo Naval Base but agreed to abolish the other clauses of the 1903 Permanent Treaty. Gradually, Cuban sugar production recovered from the effects of the Great Depression. By the terms of the Jones-Costigan Act (1934), the United States lowered protectionist tariffs on sugar imports. Cuban participation in the U.S. market increased gradually through the 1930s, from 25.4 percent in 1933 to 31.4 percent in 1937.

U.S. investments in Cuba continued to expand during the 1940s and 1950s, and U.S. interests controlled more than 90 percent of telephone and electrical services, 83 percent of the public service railways, and 42 percent of sugar production. Nearly 70 percent of petroleum imported, refined, and distributed in Cuba was controlled by two corporations, Standard Oil of New Jersey and Texaco. Commerce with the United States continued to account for the larger share of Cuban foreign trade, averaging almost 73 percent of the total in the late 1940s and declining slightly to about 68 percent through the mid-1950s. Imports from the United States remained fairly constant, varying from 80.5 percent of the total during 1946–1950 to 75.9 percent for 1951–1953. By the terms of the Jones-Costigan Act, the U.S. Department of Agriculture determined annually domestic sugar needs and allocated quotas for domestic and foreign producers. Cuba was thus guaranteed the sale of approximately 2 million tons to the U.S. market. Sugar remained the principal export, almost 90 percent during the late 1940s and early 1950s, and the United States continued as the most important single market, consuming approximately 41 percent of Cuban sugar exports. Import-export patterns for the 1940s and 1950s, however, only partially suggest the degree to which Cuba intersected with the U.S. economy. Cubans were depending on imports of consumer goods, both durables and nondurables. Between 1948 and 1954 Cuban spending on imports of consumer goods, primarily from the United States, increased from $189 million to $226 million, and those figures do not include the vast amounts of consumer goods purchased by Cubans during weekend shopping trips to Florida. "Cuban buying habits," noted the U.S. Department of Commerce in 1956, "ease of communication, prompt deliveries, and excellent transportation facilities give United States merchandise a competitive edge in the Cuban market…and assure the United States a high percentage of the Cuban export trade."

The Eclipse of the Old Order

Between 1944 and 1952 Cuba was governed by the Auténtico Party under the administrations of Grau San Martín and Carlos Prío Socarrás (1948–1952). Graft and corruption became pervasive and mismanagement and miscalculation made difficult conditions impossible ones. Under the Auténticos the government was all but discredited, creating a pervasive crisis of confidence. The final blow came in March 1952, when Batista used violence in an illegal military seizure of power against the constitutional government of Prío Socarrás. The end of the old regime had arrived. Political conflict deepened and expanded across the island. Resistance increased, as did repression. Shootouts in the cities, ambushes in the countryside, strikes and demonstrations, and abductions and assassinations became the more visible expressions of a nation at war with itself. In the mountains of eastern Cuba a full-scale guerrilla war was expanding and gaining support; in the cities to the west, the urban underground was engaged in a ferocious campaign of violence and sabotage.

Of the several revolutionary groups opposed to Batista, the 26th of July Movement led by Fidel Castro soon gained the ascendancy. Almost from the outset, the movement came to represent powerful nationalist sentiments, steeped in patriotic traditions and embodying the principles of José Martí. The Fidelistas called themselves the "generation of the centenary," commemorating the one hundredth anniversary of Martí's birth. Castro appealed to workers and peasants, to the middle class and property owners, to all who would respond to the defense of the nation against political repression from within and foreign exploitation. Support for the movement was widespread across Cuba. The failure of the

economy to sustain expansion and accommodate the growing expectations of the upwardly mobile middle class disillusioned Batista's supporters. By 1958 he had acquired another adversary—the United States. Impatience increased in Washington over Batista's inability to restore political order. In March 1958 the United States imposed an arms embargo on Cuba, designed to force Batista into making reforms. Politically the embargo was tantamount to a withdrawal of U.S. support and further undermined the government's internal position. The embargo was followed by the return of U.S. Ambassador Smith to Washington for consultation. There was no mistaking the portents. Smith's departure confirmed the suspicion raised by the arms embargo, and Batista's opposition and his supporters were not slow to conclude that Batista no longer enjoyed U.S. confidence.

Revolution and Reaction

The triumph of the armed insurrection in January 1959, and indeed the early success of the Cuban revolution, were related to more than simply grievances against the Batista government. Cubans of all classes had grievances, and much of that was a result of Batista's ties with the United States. For one critical moment in 1959, all Cubans participated in a joyful nationalist celebration. It was perhaps inevitable that after the triumph of the revolution Cuban determination to adjust relations with the United States, particularly attempts to assert the primacy of national interests, placed Cuba and the United States on a collision course. Relations deteriorated quickly. U.S. efforts to force the revolutionary government into moderation had the opposite effect and served only to sharpen confrontation. By 1960 Cuban policy acquired an internal logic of its own.

Cubans were unable to resolve the contradictions created by traditional relations with the United States. In fact, these contradictions could not be resolved without challenging existing social and economic relationships within Cuba, which in turn required challenging relationships between Cuba and the United States. The revolution's demand for the primacy of Cuban interests as the principal consideration of national policy struck a responsive chord from all classes, but it implied more than a simple adjustment of domestic programs. In fact, the sources of U.S. hegemony were so profoundly institutional and intrinsically structural that Cuban determination to advance national interests over foreign ones could not fail to produce an international crisis. The revolution's commitment to social change required more than changing the internal structures that had sanctioned privilege. It also required redefining the terms of relations with the Americans, the most privileged participants of the old order. Confrontation with the United States could only accelerate a radicalization of the revolution and the centralization in government while also resulting in the mobilization of vast numbers of Cubans. It aroused powerful nationalist sentiments, revived historic grievances, and in the end promoted a national unanimity of purpose previously unimaginable and perhaps unattainable by other means.

The Cuban revolution challenged U.S. hegemony on the island. Never before had the U.S. presence anywhere in Latin America been challenged as directly or as completely as it was in Cuba between 1959 and 1960. Much in U.S. policy during the preceding decades was directed toward guaranteeing the privileged place of the United States in the Cuban economy and its role as a political power broker. Many of the early Cuban reform measures in 1959 were designed to reduce the U.S. capacity to continue in these roles as well as to improve Cuban living conditions. Egalitarian politics, however much justified by historic conditions of vast inequality and injustice, served as a source of social integration and national mobilization. The net effect of the early strategies of the revolution was to fuse social justice and national identity and to provide an explicit ideological content to the meaning of *patria*.

The triumph of the revolution released powerful forces for change, and perhaps with no greater effect than on the U.S. economic presence on the island. Reform decrees in 1959 provided immediate material relief to vast numbers of people, but at the expense of property owners, many of whom were American. In March 1959 the revolutionary government enacted the first Urban Reform Law, obliging a reduction of rents by as much as 50 percent. The government reduced telephone rates and drastically cut the electricity rate—services provided by U.S. corporations. Virtually all labor contracts were renegotiated and wages raised. The Agrarian Reform Law of May 1959 restricted land titles to 1,000 acres, with the exception of property engaged in the production of sugar, rice, and livestock, for which the maximum limit was fixed at 3,333 acres.

Far-reaching changes were transforming the island, in large part the result of Cuban attempts to readjust on its own terms the nature of relations with the United States. This readjustment served to shape the internal dynamics of transformation. Confrontation with the United States necessitated realignment, and the realignment further deepened the confrontation, and Cuba's alignment with the Soviet Union was a response to this confrontation. As the Cuban leadership moved implacably to eliminate U.S. influence in Cuba, the United States moved with equal determination to remove the Cuban leadership.

Relations with the United States continued to deteriorate. In February 1960 a Soviet trade delegation headed by Deputy Premier Anastas Mikoyan arrived in Havana, followed in the spring by a resumption of Soviet-Cuban

diplomatic relations. Events moved rapidly thereafter. According to the terms of a 1960 economic pact, the Soviets agreed to purchase 425,000 tons of sugar immediately, and 1 million tons in each of the following four years. The Soviet Union also pledged $100 million in the form of credits, technical assistance, and crude and refined petroleum. In April 1960 the Soviet Union agreed to sell Cuba crude oil at prices considerably lower than those charged by U.S. oil companies to their Cuban refineries, thereby providing immediate foreign exchange savings for the island. In the same month President Dwight D. Eisenhower authorized the Central Intelligence Agency (CIA) to proceed with the arming and training of Cuban exiles.

Tensions between the United States and Cuba mounted through 1960, as Cubans began to expropriate U.S. property. In July, Eisenhower cut the Cuban sugar quota by 700,000 tons. In August, Cuba nationalized most remaining U.S. properties on the island. In October, the United States responded with an economic embargo on Cuba, a ban of all U.S. exports except medicines and some foodstuffs. The same day Cuba seized almost all remaining U.S. properties and in one last strike eliminated nearly all U.S. investments in Cuba. In January 1961 the United States severed diplomatic relations with Cuba. When the U.S.-backed invasion of Cuba by exiles took place in April 1961 at the Bay of Pigs, the only surprise was the ease and speed with which it was crushed. The survival of the revolution was all but guaranteed the following year, when in October the United States, as part of the negotiations to remove Soviet missiles from Cuba, agreed not to invade the island.

The U.S. Policy of Isolation

The United States was unprepared to accept and unwilling to acknowledge the depth and breadth of Cuban grievances. The failure to take Cuba seriously had far-reaching policy implications. The remarkable triumph of arms and spirit over the U.S.-backed Batista government served to confer on Cuban demands a heightened sense of confidence and expectation. The affirmation by Cubans of national sovereignty and self-determination and the demand for control over their resources, lives, and future were not accepted at face value by Americans. The demand for parity, the insistence on equal opportunity, and an appeal to fair play, very much formulated in U.S. terms, was incomprehensible in the United States, coming from Cubans. "You Americans will never understand us," a character in the John Sayles novel *Los Gusanos* (1991) concludes ruefully. At a February 1959 National Security Council meeting on Cuba, CIA director Allen Dulles expressed the view that the Cuban leaders "had to be treated more or less like children," precisely the treatment Cubans set out to change.

The revolution had jolting effects on the island throughout the early 1960s and precipitated a vast Cuban emigration to the United States. This emigration represented nothing less than the exportation of counterrevolution and all but foreclosed any possibility of a sustained and extensive internal challenge to the revolution. The flight of the opposition served also to strengthen the revolutionary consensus within the island, thereby contributing to the consolidation of the government. Thus, organized opposition to the revolution developed principally outside of Cuba, largely in the United States, but the possibilities of Cubans organizing independent and autonomous opposition capabilities were severely impaired by the circumstances of their expatriation. Dependent upon funding and support from the CIA, Cuban exiles became instruments of U.S. policy, without the means of organizing into a genuine opposition force, unable to articulate autonomous strategies, and incapable of developing objectives independent of U.S. policy needs. Once the source of political opposition was transferred outside the island, the defense of the revolution became synonymous with the defense of national sovereignty. Once the question of sovereignty was evoked, a deep wellspring of national sentiment was tapped on behalf of the revolution.

The emphasis of U.S. policy after 1960 and through the early 1990s was based on political and economic isolation, designed to create difficulties and sustain hardships, principally in the form of internal shortages and scarcities, the denial of markets, the rupture of trade and international relations, and the withholding of needed imports. These conditions were meant to limit the Cuban capacity to support armed insurgency abroad as well as to promote discontent to produce from within the changes that U.S. policy had failed to obtain. Policy conceived initially in a context of bilateral conflict quickly assumed global dimensions. Both sides expanded the dispute into a larger international arena. Cuba obtained relief from the first round of U.S. sanctions by securing aid from the Soviet Union. The United States responded to the Soviet presence by expanding the isolation of Cuba. As early as January 1962, the United States obtained the expulsion of Cuba from the Organization of American States (OAS). Economic isolation was increased further by denying Cuba access to economic assistance and developmental loans from the Inter-American Development Bank and other hemispheric credit and financial institutions.

After 1962 the United States faced an anomalous situation in Cuba. The initial application of sanctions as a way to arrest and reverse Cuban reforms had failed. The attempt to remove the Cuban regime by armed intervention at the Bay of Pigs had also failed. At the same time, as part of the settlement of the October 1962 missile crisis, the United States formally renounced the use of direct military force against Cuba. Having thus agreed to accept de facto the presence of a government in Cuba allied to the Soviet Union, the United States was reduced fundamentally to limited policy means to obtain desired political ends. Efforts to remove Castro focused on covert activities and wider sanctions. Covert operations were directed against the Cuban economy, principally in the form of sabotage operations against industry, agriculture, and livestock. Clandestine operations were organized by the CIA to disrupt sugar production and destroy tobacco plantations, farm machinery, and oil refineries. Communication facilities were attacked and transportation systems were disrupted.

At the same time the United States obtained wider support for sanctions. In 1964 Washington secured OAS endorsement of a resolution calling for the mandatory termination of all trade and diplomatic relations with Cuba. Japan and Western Europe also imposed an embargo against Cuba. By the late 1960s two-thirds of Cuban trade with Western Europe had ended. Nations receiving U.S. Mutual Security Act economic assistance were notified that continued foreign aid depended on ending purchases of Cuban sugar. Between 1962 and 1963 the number of ships from capitalist countries entering Cuban ports declined from 352 to 59. Virtually all financial transactions between Cuba and Western Europe and international lending institutions were suspended.

U.S. policy through the 1960s and early 1970s pursued several objectives. The ultimate goal was the elimination of the Castro government, which involved sustained pressure and denial in combination with subversion and isolation, all designed to produce disruption and disarray of sufficient magnitude to force political change inside Cuba. Sanctions were designed to create instability and uncertainty, without relief, as a way to keep Cuban leaders on the defensive and impair their ability to govern. The embargo sought to reduce the capacity of the Cuban government to expand its authority, principally by demonstrating its failure to deliver vital services. The goal was to promote economic havoc, increase domestic distress, and encourage internal discontent—short-term conditions designed to weaken the government from within and eventually hasten its fall. Assistant Secretary of State Edwin M. Martin predicted in 1963 that "Isolation will keep the [Cuban] economy descending until it is clear to all that the glowing promises of a better life for all Cubans which proved so alluring at the outset of the July 26th movement can never be fulfilled by Castro and his cohorts but must be sought from new leaders."

Concern was also expressed that Cuban programs backed by Soviet support might actually succeed, thereby providing an appealing alternative model for economic development and social change in Latin America.

Sanctions were thus developed as a means to obtain Cuban failure and thereby reduce the appeal of the Cuban revolution. Overall, the embargo sought to demonstrate the high political and economic cost of socialism in the Western Hemisphere. Cuba was to serve as an object lesson to other Latin American countries that might otherwise be tempted to emulate the Cuban model and adopt a socialist path of development. U.S. policy was unambiguous—sanctions so complete and isolation so sustained to suggest the imposition of a blockade.

While ultimate U.S. objectives remained more or less constant, the character of the dispute changed and with it the nature of sanctions, from defense of traditional interests to preoccupation with national security and from regional to international sanctions, all within the larger context of Cold War calculations. As the scope of the conflict widened, so did the meaning and purpose of sanctions. After 1962 sanctions were designed to increase the cost of revolution for the Cubans and especially for the Soviets. Sanctions had thus acquired an important secondary purpose. If indeed Moscow was prepared to assume the role of protector and provider of Cuban socialism, it would be obliged to pay dearly for the part, at costs so high and so open-ended as to be a drain on Soviet resources and, in the long run, encourage the Soviets to pause before assuming another socialist dependency in Latin America. "In its essentials," Assistant Secretary Martin affirmed in 1963, "the isolation policy is designed to deny to the Castro regime the wherewithal and the plaudits of success that it requires to consolidate itself. And by increasing the costs to the Soviets in Latin America, we are determined to convince Moscow that it is backing a sure loser, and an expensive one at that." Undersecretary of State George W. Ball spoke in similar terms of a policy of "economic denial," as "a way to demonstrate to the peoples of the American republics that communism has no future in the Western Hemisphere" and "to increase the cost to the Soviet Union of maintaining a communist outpost in the Western Hemisphere."

Challenge to U.S. Security Interests

The Cuban challenge to U.S. property interests and political influence on the island during 1959 and 1960 was soon eclipsed by Cuban challenges to larger U.S. strategic and security interests in the Western Hemisphere. Cuban leaders had provided the Soviets with entry into the Caribbean—long considered the *mare clausum* of the United States—and, through the Caribbean, access to all of Latin America. The installation of Soviet missiles in 1962, the deployment of Soviet combat troops, the establishment of intelligence-gathering facilities and of the Soviet naval base in Cienfuegos heightened U.S. security concerns. The worst night-

mares of Thomas Jefferson and John Quincy Adams— that a potentially hostile European power would insert itself in Cuba and menace U.S. interests—seemed to have come to pass. In a security culture shaped by notions of balance of power and spheres of influence, the sudden presence of the Soviet Union at a distance of ninety miles from the United States wrought havoc on some of the most influential premises of U.S. strategic planning. The Monroe Doctrine appeared to have passed into desuetude, and the security offered by the buffer of continents and oceans seemed to have vanished and with far-reaching implications. "Castro took over in Cuba," Ball recalled years later, "slowly strengthening his dependence on Moscow and thus confronting America with a patent violation of a revered item of our national credo—the Monroe Doctrine. That doctrine forbade European powers from intrusion into the Western Hemisphere, which we regarded… as our own exclusive sphere of interest and influence." A Cuba "fully oriented to Moscow," CIA Director John McCone warned in mid-1962, would "serve on one hand as a model for similar activities in Central and South America." Director McCone's conclusion was slightly apocalyptic: "Cuba [is] the key to all of Latin America; if Cuba succeeds, we can expect most of Latin America to fall."

That the Soviets established themselves in the Caribbean was cause enough for U.S. apprehension, but that the Cubans seemed determined to project themselves beyond the Caribbean served to add one more dimension to U.S. security concerns. Moral and material aid to guerrilla movements in Latin America was one expression of Cuba's expanding global presence. Another was the deployment of Cuban physicians, teachers, engineers, and construction workers in Africa, the Middle East, and Latin America. The presence of Cuban combat troops in Africa and the Middle East—in Angola, Somalia, Ethiopia, and South Yemen—was the most troublesome, suggesting to many in Washington that the Cubans had assumed the role of surrogate for Soviet expansion. Sanctions designed initially as a response to a regional dispute found a larger purpose within the context of the Cold War. Henceforth, strategic considerations dominated U.S. policy calculations to involve itself outside the island and increase the cost of Soviet involvement inside the island.

By the 1970s, however, the U.S. embargo policy had stalled and seemed no longer capable of achieving its objectives. The Cuban government had consolidated itself and was unchallenged inside the island. Cuban integration into the socialist bloc was virtually complete, and Soviet aid, technical assistance, and subsidies began to insulate Cuba from the embargo and even underwrote modest economic growth. Support for sanctions in Latin America and Western Europe, moreover, began to wane.

Countries formerly supporting the embargo broke with the United States and reestablished diplomatic ties with Cuba and resumed trade. By the mid-1970s even the United States had taken tentative steps toward normalizing relations. In 1975 Washington voted with the majority in the OAS to end the political and economic sanctions imposed eleven years earlier. The ban against economic aid to countries trading with Cuba was lifted. Two years later Cuba and the United States established limited diplomatic relations and established interests sections in each capital, even as one embargo remained in place. In 1977 U.S. tourists began to return to the island.

New Confrontations, 1980s–1990s

Rapprochement was limited and brief, and by the early 1980s Cuba-U.S. relations had taken a turn for the worse. The triumph of the Sandinistas in Nicaragua, the deepening insurgency in El Salvador, political developments in Grenada, and the election of President Ronald Reagan set the stage for a new round of confrontation. The U.S. policy of choice was the resumption of full sanctions and renewed efforts to isolate Cuba. President Reagan moved quickly to restrict and eventually eliminate U.S. tourism to Cuba as a way to deny Havana foreign exchange. At the time of the new travel ban, an estimated 40,000 people from the United States were traveling to Cuba annually. Other measures soon followed. Washington inaugurated Radio Martí to broadcast news and antigovernment propaganda to Cuba. New pressure was applied to U.S. allies. Washington maneuvered to make Cuban foreign debt negotiation with Western creditors as difficult as possible. Cuban access to Western capital was blocked. The United States also sought to expand the global trade sanctions, raising the specter of a secondary boycott of products and services against trading or investing in Cuba.

Through the 1980s and early 1990s sanctions against Cuba increased and commando raids resumed. By the 1980s a new factor had been added to the domestic politics of U.S. foreign policy in the form of Jorge Mas Canosa and the Cuban-American National Foundation (CANF). Organized as a lobby group with a political action committee, the CANF became an important political force in the shaping of Cuba policy. The passage of the Torricelli Bill in 1992 further tightened the trade embargo, prohibiting subsidiaries of U.S. corporations in third countries from trading with Cuba. Other features of the bill authorized the president to withhold U.S. assistance, debt relief, and free trade agreements with countries that provided assistance to Cuba. All ships trading with Cuba were denied access to U.S. port facilities for a period of 180 days after having visited Cuba.

The U.S. policy of sanctions and embargo took a new toll after the late 1980s, as the socialist bloc collapsed and Cuba lost its principal trading partners and source of subsidies. All through the early 1990s, conditions deteriorated. Pressure for Cubans to emigrate increased, less for political reasons than economic ones. The Cuban leadership expressed repeatedly an interest in resolving outstanding differences with the United States, but three successive administrations—those of Reagan, George Bush, and Bill Clinton—seemed determined only to remove the Cuban leadership.

The U.S. policy of sanctions, moreover, was flawed and in fundamental contradiction with itself. The embargo had created pressure that was at times real and substantial, but Washington itself played a willing role in assisting the Cuban government to relieve some of the very pressures created by U.S. policy. The use of economic hardship as a means of political change could not have reasonably succeeded as long as Cuban discontent was able to find alternative expression, and this was made possible through the readily available immigration option. Sanctions did indeed contribute to economic distress and added to daily hardships for countless tens of thousands of Cubans, many of whom sought relief through migration abroad rather than reform at home. The relative ease with which disaffected Cubans were able to emigrate was no small factor in accounting for the weakness of internal political opposition in the face of mounting hardships. No less important, the Cuban government continued to use emigration as a relatively cost-effective and convenient way to dispose of discontented people. Mounting hardships were no doubt factors that persuaded Cuban authorities to lower the travel age and relax restrictions to permit Cubans to visit families abroad.

The results were predictable: many did not return to Cuba. An estimated 13,000 Cubans per year gained permanent U.S. residency by entering on visitor visas and remaining. Thousands of others entered through third countries. Hijacking, mutinies, and the steady flow of émigrés fleeing the island in small boats and rafts (*balseros*) were among other desperate ways that Cubans sought to escape economic hardship and an uncertain future. The increase in the numbers of *balseros* that arrived to the United States—from 467 in 1990 to 2,203 in 1991, 2,548 in 1992, and 3,656 in 1993—was as much a result of the apparent decision of Cuban authorities to refrain from interception as of deteriorating economic conditions.

All through 1993 and early 1994, as conditions on the island deteriorated, illegal seizures and hijackings increased. In early August 1994 a series of ferry hijackings resulted in the death of Cuban officials and a riot on the Havana waterfront. Official Cuban protests notwithstanding, few persons implicated in these acts were prosecuted or returned to the island to face charges. The

Cuban government alleged that the United States was engaged in deliberate provocation by denying most Cubans legal entry but welcoming them from *balseros* or aboard hijacked planes and ships. In mid-August 1994 Castro announced that the Cuban government would no longer interdict or otherwise hinder the departure of Cubans wishing to leave for the United States.

The effects were immediate. Hundreds of Cubans boarded boats, constructed rafts, and used almost anything capable of floating to leave for the United States. President Bill Clinton rescinded the thirty-five-year-old policy of automatic asylum—a measure designed to "demagnetize the United States," one U.S. official commented. Henceforth, Cubans could enter the United States only through visas formally issued by the U.S. Interests Section in Havana. To this end, Washington established a naval cordon outside Cuban territorial waters to interdict and transfer Cubans to the Guantánamo Naval Base. In fact, the U.S. naval presence served to make a bad situation worse. In an effort to demagnetize the United States, Washington actually "magnetized" the Florida Straits. It became necessary for Cubans to journey only twelve miles—and not ninety—to reach U.S. authorities. In the days that followed, the number of Cubans increased, often reaching more than 1,000 a day. By the end of September more than 21,000 Cubans had been interned at the U.S. naval station. The crisis ended in mid-September 1994 when both countries negotiated an immigration pact. Cuban authorities pledged to prevent illegal departures in exchange for which Washington agreed to allow 20,000 Cubans per year to emigrate to the United States.

Relations between Cuba and the United States took a decided turn for the worse in February 1996, when two civilian airplanes operated by the exile organization Hermanos al Rescate (Brothers to the Rescue) were shot down by the Cuban air force. The incident had been preceded by year-long violations of Cuban air space by Brothers to the Rescue and official Cuban protests to Washington, with no effect.

The plane incident provided new impetus for the passage of the Helms-Burton bill. The proposed legislation had previously languished in Congress, without prospects for passages. Everything changed after February. Once again, as in 1992 and the Torricelli law, election-year politics in 1996 proved to be decisive. The Clinton administration, which had previously announced its opposition to the bill, reversed itself and yielded to congressional pressure.

Within a month of the shot-down incident, Helms-Burton had become law. The measure sought to internationalize the U.S. embargo by coercing other countries into suspending trade relations with Cuba and halting investments on the island. The law threatened foreign companies that "trafficked" in property previously owned by U.S. citizens with lawsuits. The foreign executives of those companies, and members of their immediate family, were also to be denied visas to enter the United States. Another provision of the law required the United States to reduce aid to Russia by the same amount that Moscow paid to Cuba for the use of intelligence facilities on the island, estimated at approximately $200 million annually. Lastly, and perhaps most important, Helms-Burton codified all existing executive orders relating to Cuba in effect as of 1 March 1996 into law. The Cuba policy of the United States was thus transferred to the control of Congress. Not perhaps since the early 1960s had relations between both countries been as strained as they were after March 1996.

Much in the Cuban-U.S. relationship has had to do with both countries learning to coexist as neighbors on vastly unequal terms. From the Cuban perspective, to be at the subordinate end of this equation created a host of obvious and objective difficulties, many of which served to shape national identity. From the U.S. view, Cuban sensibilities seemed to matter little, if at all. Together these countervailing forces acted to influence in decisive ways the character of relations between both countries.

Louis A. Pérez, Jr.

See also Batista y Zaldívar, Fulgencio; Bay of Pigs Invasion; Castro, Fidel; Cold War; Containment; Covert Action; Cuban Missile Crisis; Immigration; Maine, USS; Monroe Doctrine; Ostend Manifesto; Platt Amendment; Radio Martí; Spanish-American-Cuban-Filipino War, 1898; Teller Amendment

FURTHER READING

Benjamin, Jules R. *The United States and Cuba: Hegemony and Dependent Development, 1880–1934.* Pittsburgh, 1977.
———. *The United States and the Origins of the Cuban Revolution.* Princeton, N.J., 1990.
Bonsal, Philip W. *Cuba, Castro, and the United States.* Pittsburgh, 1971.
Domínguez, Jorge. *To Make a World Safe for Revolution: Cuba's Foreign Policy.* Cambridge, Mass., 1989.
Fitzgibbon, Russell H. *Cuba and the United States, 1900–1935.* Menasha, Wisc., 1935.
Foner, Philip S. *A History of Cuba and Its Relations with the United States,* 2 vols. New York, 1962–1965.
Guggenheim, Harry F. *The United States and Cuba.* New York, 1934.
Jenks, Leland H. *Our Cuban Colony.* New York, 1928.
Langley, Lester P. *The Cuban Policy of the United States.* New York, 1968.
Morley, Morris H. *Imperial State and Revolution: The United States and Cuba, 1952–1986.* New York, 1987.
Paterson, Thomas G. *Contesting Castro: The United States and the Triumph of the Cuban Revolution.* New York, 1994.
Pérez, Louis A., Jr. *Cuba and the United States: Ties of Singular Intimacy.* Athens, Ga., 1991.
Plank, John. *Cuba and the United States: Long Range Perspectives.* Washington, D.C., 1967.

Smith, Robert F. *The United States and Cuba: Business and Diplomacy, 1917–1960.* New Haven, Conn., 1960.
Welch, Richard E., Jr. *Response to Revolution: The United States and the Cuban Revolution, 1951–1961.* Chapel Hill, N.C., 1985.
Williams, William Appleman. *The United States, Cuba and Castro.* New York, 1962.

CUBAN MISSILE CRISIS

A confrontation between the United States and the Soviet Union over the Soviet placement of nuclear-capable missiles in Cuba that brought the two superpowers, in October 1962, closer to nuclear war than at any other time during the Cold War. To the Soviets, the crisis has long been called "the Caribbean Crisis," as a way of minimizing their emplacement of missiles; and to the Cubans it has often been termed "the October Crisis" as a way of emphasizing that it was one among a number of U.S.-Cuban crises.

On 22 October 1962, on nationwide radio and television, President John F. Kennedy announced that U.S. intelligence had discovered Soviet medium-range ballistic missiles (MRBMs) in Cuba and uncompleted sites for intermediate-range ballistic missiles (IRBMs) there. Labeling these missiles "offensive weapons," Kennedy implied that they endangered the United States. He asserted that they must be withdrawn speedily and that their use against any nation in the hemisphere would be defined by the United States as a Soviet attack on the United States. The president declared that he would institute a "strict quarantine," basically a modified naval blockade around Cuba, to halt the shipment of all military equipment to that island, only ninety miles from U.S. shores.

In the United States, with comparatively little dissent, Americans rallied around the president and the flag. Few challenged Kennedy's analysis of the danger and of the need and right to take action. On the U.S. left, some little noticed groups assailed the U.S. action as self-righteous and dangerous. From the political center and right, some grumbled that the "quarantine" would not deal with the real menace: Soviet MRBMs, with a range of about 1,000 nautical miles, that soon would become operational. Generally, however, it was period of near-unanimity and of substantial bipartisanship in time of crisis, despite forthcoming congressional elections in early November 1962.

On Sunday morning, 28 October, to the relief of U.S. and Soviet leaders, as well as the citizens in much of the world and certainly of North Atlantic Treaty Organization (NATO) nations, the crisis seemed to be over. Premier Nikita Khrushchev agreed to remove the weapons, accepted United Nations (UN) on-site inspection, urged Cuban leader Fidel Castro to concur, and believed that a promised U.S. no-invasion pledge for Cuba would soon be forthcoming. The Sunday deal was strained, and badly undercut, by Castro's refusal to grant on-site inspection and by the U.S. demand, moving beyond earlier statements, that the Soviets also would have to withdraw their forty-two IL-28 (light jet) bombers from Cuba.

On 20 November, after tense negotiations, the Soviets reluctantly yielded on the bombers, removing them in December. But Castro had refused to allow on-site inspection of the missiles, so the superpowers instead arranged for inspection on the high seas when the dismantled missiles were transported back to the USSR. Citing Castro's unwillingness to allow any inspection in Cuba, Kennedy refused to grant the no-invasion pledge, but Khrushchev nevertheless implied to Castro that the final terms of the settlement protected Cuba from a U.S.-instigated assault. Khrushchev also had to labor to assuage Castro, who believed that the Soviets had "sold out" Cuba's interest. The Soviets, in fact, had not consulted Cuba in settling the October crisis and then had removed the bombers, which Castro insisted the Soviets actually had given to Cuba.

The resolution of the October missile crisis won wide support in the United States, and it probably helped the Democrats in the November election. Most important, the president's apparent triumph—soon hailed as his "finest hour"—undoubtedly helped him and his party by reducing Republican attacks over Cuba, by establishing that he was not pursuing a spineless Cuba policy, and by portraying Kennedy as a courageous hero. His action, as generally interpreted then and soon after, seemed a wonderful blend of toughness, shrewdness, and reasonableness: a willingness to go near the brink on the missiles, the ability to push Khrushchev and the Soviets to accede, and a capacity to end the crisis without pressing for excessive Soviet concessions or the overthrow of Castro.

For scholars and memoirists the missile crisis fpresented a rich opportunity: to explore and establish theories of decision-making, to study "coercive diplomacy," to understand "crisis management," and to assess Kennedy. For a time the near-consensus was that "toughness" was the best strategy, short of actually going to war, for dealing with the Soviets and that U.S. Cold War victories could be achieved safely and skillfully through such toughness.

By the late 1980s and early 1990s, however, under the impact of new evidence and new claims by missile-crisis participants, the understanding and interpretation of the crisis had shifted substantially from earlier views: the Soviet placement of missiles in Cuba has been reinterpreted as defensive, not aggressive; events during the crisis came closer to going out of control than many realized in 1962 and soon thereafter; the Soviets had larger forced, more military weapons and more nuclear warheads in

Cuba than detected in 1962; and the 28 October settlement included an important but concealed Kennedy concession—a secret deal for the withdrawal of U.S. nuclear missiles in Turkey.

Origins of the Crisis

Dating the origins of the Cuban missile crisis is tricky. It could start with the United States photographing the missiles on 14 October, the interpretation of the film the next day, and the president's appointment of a special advisory group, the Executive Committee of the National Security Council (ExComm), on 16 October. Most of the U.S. memoirists, and many of the early studies, dated the crisis basically from this period, leading, for example, to Attorney General Robert Kennedy entitling his recollections *Thirteen Days* (1969), to focus on the thirteen-day period, 16–28 October 1962.

Or, the origins can be traced back to U.S.-Cuba antagonism starting at least with the ill-fated U.S.-instigated Bay of Pigs invasion of April 1961 and including subsequent clandestine efforts: CIA assassination attempts on Castro; the establishment in November 1961 of Operation Mongoose, with Robert Kennedy's strong endorsement, to overthrow the Castro regime; and the plan to involve U.S. forces in a Mongoose operation targeted for mid-October 1962 against Cuba. Focusing on anti-Cuban actions, such an analysis also would stress the U.S.-directed decision by the Organization of American States in January 1962 to exclude Cuba from that body and to prohibit OAS members from selling military equipment to Cuba; the Joint Chiefs of Staff (JCS) decision in February 1962 to establish on a "first priority basis" contingency plans for a military attack on Cuba; the April 1962 well-publicized and threatening U.S. military exercise of practicing an amphibious invasion of a Caribbean island; and the August 1962 announcement of another U.S. military exercise, this one scheduled for October, against a Caribbean island and fictional leader, named Ortsac, which is Castro spelled backward.

Or, focusing on U.S.-Soviet relations, such an analysis might well date events from the October 1961 U.S. announcement that the United States was considerably ahead and the Soviets greatly behind both in the number of intercontinental ballistic missiles (ICBMs) and in total numbers of strategic weapons; the U.S. emplacement of Jupiter (IRBMs) nuclear missiles in eastern Turkey, near the Soviet border, in 1961–1962; and Khrushchev's repeatedly expressed outrage in 1961–1962 about this extension of the U.S. nuclear arsenal.

Certainly, all such events—producing Soviet and Cuban fears of another U.S.-sponsored attack on Cuba, resentment about the fifteen Jupiter missiles in Turkey, and Khrushchev's and Soviet fears of being far behind in strategic-vehicle numbers—helped define the context, and the motivation, for the Soviet emplacement in 1962 of twenty-four MRBM launchers and forty-two MRBM missiles, which were to be followed by the thirty-two IRBMs for the sixteen IRBM launchers that also had been shipped before 16 October.

It is now known that in 1962, before the discovery of Soviet missiles in Cuba, the United States had developed serious military plans for conducting an attack on Cuba. On 1 October, Secretary of Defense Robert McNamara ordered military preparations for a blockade, an air strike, an invasion, with "maximum readiness" for the last two actions to be achieved by 20 October. On 2 October, he informed the JCS that military action against Cuba might by called for if any one of six conditions occurred, including a Soviet move against Berlin, the presence of Soviet offensive weapons in Cuba, a presidential decision of the need to maintain "U.S. national security," or a Mongoose scenario of a "substantial popular uprising in Cuba, the leaders of which request assistance...." The available evidence, because many documents remain classified, is still too skimpy to determine whether these contingency plans might have gone into effect if the Soviet missiles had not been discovered in mid-October. McNamara, when queried about this evidence of military planning, has consistently denied that there was any U.S. intention, before the 16 October discovery of the Soviet missiles, to attack Cuba. The earlier planning, he asserted, was not meaningful.

Whatever the ultimate factual resolution, there is ample evidence that Khrushchev and Castro feared an imminent U.S. attack, that there were alarming U.S. preparations, that some of the evidence of earlier U.S. thinking and planning had reached them by early spring, and that these two leaders were reasonable—even if incorrect—in fearing such an attack. In part, then, the Soviet emplacement of missiles can be defined as defensive—to defend Cuba. Khrushchev privately advanced that argument before the October crisis, and it became his primary explanation after the October events.

To Khrushchev and the Soviet Union, charged by the Chinese with being "paper tigers" for not advancing communist revolutions around the world, Cuba was also a test case of Soviet credibility and will at a time of fierce Sino-Soviet polemics. The Cuban state, despite early communist opposition to Castro's revolution, had become part, symbolically and substantively, of the Soviet network of cliency and dependency. The "loss" of Cuba could be a powerful blow to the Soviets as Khrushchev acknowledged.

Perhaps even more important was the fact of substantial Soviet strategic inferiority, as exacerbated by the 1961–1962 emplacement of fifteen U.S. Jupiter missiles in Turkey. Turkey was a Soviet neighbor, as Khrushchev stressed, and this action added to Soviet fears about nuclear encirclement. President Dwight D. Eisenhower had made the original arrangements to put Jupiters in Turkey, but he dallied on delivering them, probably because he feared that they would be provocative. After the unsettling Khrushchev-Kennedy 1961 summit in Vienna, where Kennedy resented Khrushchev's "bullying," the young president apparently decided to send these missiles to Turkey. They would be under a "dual-key" arrangement, with each nation having to approve use and each possessing a veto, but to the Soviets, quite reasonably, this represented the extension of the U.S. nuclear arsenal to their very borders.

Those fifteen Jupiters, even when added to thirty Jupiters recently sent to Italy, did not greatly increase the United States's strategic superiority of missiles and bombers able to hit the USSR. According to Secretary McNamara's later calculations, the United States had a better than twelve-to-one strategic margin. By the late summer of 1962, Khrushchev knew that the Soviets had only about twenty ICBMs and that the United States had roughly eight-to-one superiority in ICBMs, and overall even greater superiority if bombers and submarine-based missiles were included. To Khrushchev and the Soviets, who had built far fewer ICBMs than U.S. intelligence had earlier forecast, this one-to-eight inferiority was undoubtedly threatening. It could even possibly suggest that the United States was developing a first-strike capability, bolstered by the Jupiters and other nuclear weapons in Europe, to initiate an attack on the USSR. There is no evidence that Kennedy in 1962 ever seriously considered such action, and undoubtedly he did not realize that U.S. superiority was so great. In October 1962, for example, U.S. intelligence estimates placed the Soviet ICBM arsenal at about sixty to seventy-five weapons, when the U.S. arsenal actually exceeded 170, so U.S. intelligence calculated slightly under three-to-one U.S. superiority, when in fact it was much greater.

Over the years, Castro has given two different reasons for agreeing in the summer of 1962 to the Soviet-conceived plan for emplacing missiles in Cuba—solidarity with the Soviet Union and world communism, and the defense of Cuba. Since 1974, he has primarily emphasized his desire to contribute to "socialist solidarity," to "reinforce socialism on an international scale," and secondarily to deter a U.S. attack. He has asserted that Cuba "had an absolute right [to take] the measure that would fortify its defense." What he had not foreseen in 1962 was that Soviet missiles might draw, not deter, a U.S. attack. In 1962, he did regret that the Soviets never actually signed the summer missile agreement, and that they insisted upon keeping the agreement and the missiles secret. Castro, in contrast, desired to publicize the arrangement and the missiles in order to indicate that Cuba was under the Soviet nuclear umbrella. Well after the crisis, he admitted that he had not known of the United States's great nuclear superiority over the Soviets in 1962, implying that he might have been more cautious if he had understood the strategic imbalance.

While many analysts, including Kennedy's national security adviser, McGeorge Bundy, came to accept by the late 1980s that the Soviet missile emplacement had been defensive, in 1962, Kennedy, Bundy, and most advisers saw the Soviet action as "aggressive." Thus, those men focused generally in the early missile-crisis days, on and after 16 October, not on the reasons for Soviet actions, but, rather, on how to get the missiles speedily out of Cuba.

The Executive Committee (ExComm)

Upon learning from Bundy early on the morning of Tuesday, 16 October, of the presence of the missiles in Cuba, a shocked president decided to set up a special advisory committee. He appointed to the body Secretary of State Dean Rusk, Secretary of Defense McNamara, National Security Affairs Adviser Bundy, Chairman of the Joint Chiefs of Staff General Maxwell Taylor, CIA Director John McCone (a Republican), Undersecretary of State George Ball, Deputy Undersecretary of State U. Alexis Johnson, Assistant Secretary of State for Latin America Edward Martin, Assistant Secretary of Defense Paul Nitze, Deputy Secretary of Defense Roswell Gilpatric, former Ambassador to the USSR and Soviet specialist Llewellyn Thompson, Vice President Lyndon B. Johnson, and the president's special counsel and major speech writer, Theodore Sorensen. The president also appointed a few men who may, but should not, be regarded as surprises: his brother, Attorney General Robert Kennedy, possibly the president's most trusted adviser; Secretary of the Treasury C. Douglas Dillon, who was useful both as a Republican and as a shrewd adviser; Dean Acheson, Harry Truman's former secretary of state who was then a private citizen but valued for his experience in dealing with the Soviets; and Robert Lovett, Truman's former secretary of defense and a private citizen who also was valued for his experience in national security affairs.

Meeting twice as a committee on 16 October, the newly created ExComm only briefly discussed likely Soviet motives: a test of the United States' and Kennedy's will; the possibility of trying to stimulate a Berlin-Cuba deal; the desire to place Soviet missiles nearer to the United States (Rusk explained possible Soviet thinking: "we don't really live under fear of his [Soviet] nuclear weapons to the extent he [Khrushchev] has to live under fear of ours"); or possibly some response to Soviet uneasiness about U.S. nuclear superiority. In the discussions, as Kennedy and others mentioned the president's recent public and private warnings against the Soviets putting such missiles in Cuba, Bundy shrewdly noted that Khrushchev's decision and the operation had undoubtedly been set in motion before the U.S. warnings of late August and September 1962. In the discussions, some ExComm members expressed a sense of betrayal—that Khrushchev, both publicly and through trusted intermediaries, had stated or implied that he would not put missiles in Cuba, and now he had done exactly that.

Not until the Tuesday evening session did the group explicitly focus on the military significance of these Soviet missiles, which were estimated as adding about fifty percent to the Soviet ICBM capacity, because these short-range missiles in Cuba, by being able to reach the United States, were the functional equivalents of Soviet ICBMs. The Joint Chiefs thought that the MRBMs imperiled the United States, but that was decidedly a minority view, shared on the ExComm by only one or two members. McNamara, who was generally considered the ExComm's major strategic expert, asserted that these additional Soviet missiles did not alter the strategic balance or significantly add to the danger for the United States.

President Kennedy accepted McNamara's analysis, and stated, "Last month, I should have said...that we don't care [about the Soviets putting such missiles in Cuba.] But when we said we're not going to [accept it] and then they go ahead and do it, and then we do nothing...." For him, the issue was not essentially military, but rather that he had drawn a line, mostly because of Republican attacks, and now he was being tested and embarrassed. He easily linked challenges to self and to nation, and most members of the ExComm similarly saw this as a challenge to the president, the government, and the nation. NATO might even be weakened, and U.S. hegemony in Latin America might be threatened. In the ExComm's general conception, credibility, prestige, power, alliance relations, and domestic politics were easily merged into one conclusion: Doing nothing was unacceptable, and the question was what action to take to achieve speedy withdrawal of the missiles. That was the ExComm's mandate.

At one point in the Tuesday discussions, Attorney General Robert Kennedy, contrary to claims in his posthumously published memoir, *Thirteen Days*, suggested looking for a pretext—"sink the *Maine* or something"—and go to war with the Soviets. Better then than later, he concluded. In contrast, McNamara, perhaps the most frightened of war and of a nuclear exchange, counseled that an attack on Cuba could easily escalate into a Soviet-U.S. nuclear war. "I don't quite know what kind of world we will be living in," he said in fear and despair. On at least two occasions that evening, McNamara offered his dissenting view of the crisis. He said, "this is a domestic, political [U.S.] problem....It's primarily a...domestic political problem." In so assessing matters, he seemed to imply that not acting militarily was the right answer; that, contrary to the president and others, maybe doing nothing, or virtually nothing, was the best response. That was not a position that McNamara stuck with, perhaps largely because the president's own expressed desires, and the nearly unanimous wishes of the ExComm, strongly favored doing something.

The Quarantine Chosen Over Other Options

Between Tuesday, 16 October, and Saturday, 20 October, the ExComm members met in formal sessions, but usually without the president, and in various smaller groups, aided by other advisers, to try to work out what was to be done. The possibilities, allowing for some "mixes," included the following: an approach to Khrushchev or Castro privately or through the United Nations; an air attack on Cuba; an invasion and bombing of Cuba; some kind of private tradeoff (most often, the Jupiters in Turkey for Soviet withdrawal of its missiles in Cuba, and possibly some deal on the U.S. base at Guantánamo in Cuba); or some form of blockade, including a limited one, called a "quarantine" largely to avoid the fact that in international law a blockade was an act of war. During this period, many of the ExComm members apparently shifted from position to position, thus seriously undercutting later contentions that, in this crisis, bureaucratic politics ("you stand where you sit," meaning that leaders represented organizational constituencies) substantially operated. The evidence points strongly to the opposite; organizational loyalties were easily transcended for a number of ExComm members, and especially for Secretary of Defense McNamara.

At one of the secret ExComm sessions, Adlai Stevenson, the United States's ambassador to the United Nations, suggested some kind of a Turkey-Cuba missile tradeoff, and maybe something on Guantánamo, too. At the time, probably because of the Kennedy brothers' dislike for Stevenson, whom they regarded as "soft" and resented as a result of earlier political differences, Stevenson's ideas were brushed aside. Well after the crisis, the president would leak to trusted journalists Charles Bartlett and Stewart Alsop, and then deny to Stevenson Kennedy's own responsibility for the published accusation "Adlai [had] wanted a Munich" sellout. Similar thinking during the secret deliberations by McNamara and others was not disclosed in the immediate aftermath of the crisis, amid the celebrations of Kennedy's triumph. The evidence on McNamara and others did not surface for well over a decade because of the classification of key records, and had no effect on domestic politics or general public assessments in the late 1970s or in the 1980s.

On 18 October, longtime Soviet expert Charles Bohlen wrote a special memorandum to the president, unsuccessfully urging a secret diplomatic approach to Khrushchev before the United States moved to take any bellicose action. A diplomatic approach might succeed, Bohlen suggested, and if it did not the process might well indicate Khrushchev's depth of commitment to the missiles and his willingness to press on. A diplomatic approach, Bohlen implied, could always be followed by military action, if the diplomacy failed; but the reverse course of military action first and hoped-for diplomacy later was less likely and far more dangerous in the nuclear world. Bohlen's counsel lost out.

According to Sorensen and others, during the week of secret deliberations they had found it impossible to frame a private approach to Khrushchev without the great likelihood of his outflanking the United States, even first announcing the presence of the missiles, and stealing the initiative. Other explanations of why such a private approach was not tried include the contention that there was inadequate time, that the missiles would become operational in about a week after 22 October, and that then the problem would be even more difficult for the United States.

These explanations, taken individually or together, seem wanting. It is doubtful, critics contend, that the fear of a "lost initiative" did, or should, shape policy: a lost initiative could be regained, if needed and desired. The "operational missile" argument also has a serious weakness: During the days of ExComm deliberations, the CIA repeatedly reported that a number of the Soviet missiles would be operational by about 22 October (the date of Kennedy's public address), and most ExComm members assumed—correctly, as it turned out—that the warheads for the MRBMs were already in Cuba.

Some analysts have contended that President Kennedy chose not to move first to private negotiations because he really did not want them, and because he desired a victory in this confrontation, which he believed the Soviets had willfully conceived to test him. In addition, some analysts argue that the proximity of the forthcoming congressional elections in early November, and the likelihood that the secret of the Soviet missiles would leak out during the week of 22 October, required Kennedy to seize the initiative, avoid private diplomacy, and move to a public confrontation, partly because of domestic politics. Not doing so, and risking an overwhelming Republican and right-wing triumph, would have destroyed him politically, imperiling any likelihood of defining new, less bellicose courses in Soviet-U.S. relations. Both of these interpretations—Kennedy's desire for victory, and his fear of leaks and domestic political damage—have some supportive evidence, but critics of these analyses argue that the evidence is thin

and sometimes strained. Thus, the important question of why the choice of a public confrontation, rather than a secret diplomatic approach, remains deeply contested among scholars.

Defenders of Kennedy point out that the public confrontation route succeeded, and they argue that Khrushchev very probably would not have removed the missiles without the quarantine and the added implicit, if not explicit, U.S. threats. In turn, critics sometimes challenge this assessment of Khrushchev, contending that the private approach would have been safer, and (like Bohlen) that it still would have allowed a public confrontation if private negotiations did not succeed. They argue that the reverse—a confrontation ideally to be followed by private negotiations—was terribly dangerous because war might have erupted and there would not have been any negotiations. Thus, Kennedy's critics regret that the president, when meeting with Soviet Foreign Minister Andrei Gromyko on 17 October, five days before the president's public address, purposely avoided both informing the Soviets that the U.S. leadership knew of the missiles and seeking to open private negotiations.

Before Kennedy's Monday night speech, and after the ExComm and the president had substantially committed themselves to the quarantine route as the least dangerous strategy likely to be successful, the president did canvas once more, on Sunday, 21 October, the prospect of an air strike on Cuba. The commander of the Tactical Air Command, General Walter Sweeney, outlined the need for about 500 sorties to attack the MRBM and IRBM sites, the surface-to-air missiles, and the air fields. He predicted that the best the Air Force could accomplish was destruction of "ninety percent of the known" MRBMs, and the known missiles were regarded as only about sixty percent of the total. Put bluntly, in retrospect, of the forty-two MRBMs, at least four would survive and possibly about ten. Undoubtedly chastened by that frightening prediction, Robert Kennedy stated at this Sunday meeting that he opposed a U.S. attack on the missiles because "it would be a Pearl Harbor in reverse," and he thought that the United States should start with the quarantine and "play for the breaks."

The Crisis: 22–26 October

On 22 October, in his alarming public address, President Kennedy focused on, among other themes, that the Soviets had lied to him and to the United States, disregarded his clear public and private warnings (they were not really all that clear), and "clandestinely" placed "offensive" missiles in Cuba. That was unacceptable, he declared, and stressed that the United States', and his own, "courage and commitments" were at stake. He referred to the 1930s and the Munich analogy, asserting that "the 1930s taught us a clear lesson: aggressive conduct, if allowed to go unchecked and unchallenged, leads to war." Adding to the united administration's public claims, McNamara denied, contrary to his own and others' private ExComm deliberations, that there was any reasonable analogy between the United States' Jupiters in Turkey (they were there for "defensive" purposes, he asserted) and Soviet missiles in Cuba (labeled "offensive").

Quickly rejecting such distinctions, though not admitting that the Soviets had placed long-range missiles in Cuba, Khrushchev on 23 October informed Kennedy, "the armaments which are in Cuba, regardless of the classification to which they belong, are intended solely for defensive purposes in order to secure the Republic of Cuba against the attack of an aggressor." In short, his missiles, like the Jupiters, were "defensive."

On Tuesday, 23 October, the Organization of American States, acting at a meeting just before the United States was scheduled to deal with economic assistance to member states, approved the quarantine. The next day, on Wednesday, it went into effect. There were informal warnings that the Soviets would challenge it, and there were warranted fears of war at sea with the possibility of escalation. Fortunately, for all, the quarantine went untested, and Soviet ships carrying IRBMs even turned around at sea.

In Cuba, according to journalist Herbert Matthews, the response to Kennedy's speech was "a curious mixture of exhilaration and calm." There was a full-scale mobilization, 270,000 people were placed under arms within a few days, and preparations were made for the expected U.S. bombing and invasion. The party newspaper, *Hoy*, on 24 October showed Castro with his rifle, declaring, "To the struggle, victory will be complete."

During the week, in private sessions, Attorney General Kennedy and Soviet Ambassador Anatoly Dobrynin met to discuss the events, to help facilitate communications between the White House and the Kremlin, and to feel one another out about what was likely to happen. In a cable on 24 or 25 October, Dobrynin, as he later summarized in his memoir, warned the Kremlin "that the president himself, like a gambler, actually was staking his reputation as a statesman and his chances for reelection in 1964, on the outcome of this crisis. That was why we could not rule out—especially given the more reckless members of his entourage—the possibility of a reckless reaction such as a bombing raid on the Cuban missile bases or even an invasion, although the latter was clearly less likely."

By Friday night, 26 October, the sense of bleak crisis and great danger lifted—at least temporarily. The combination of a Khrushchev letter that day and two informal Friday meetings between a high-ranking KGB person, Aleksandr Fomin (actually, Feklisov) and a U.S. reporter, John Scali, seemed to suggest the terms of a deal: Soviet withdrawal of the missiles, UN on-site inspection, and a U.S. no-invasion pledge for Cuba. That night, the exhausted ExComm members, after eleven days of meetings and fears, planned to return on Saturday to work out the details to end the perilous crisis.

The 27–28 October Secret Deal: Missiles in Turkey for Missiles in Cuba

But on Saturday, described often as "the blackest day of the crisis," the earlier optimism soon turned sour. A new Kremlin letter, one issued publicly, increased the terms of the deal to require a public United States agreement to withdraw the fifteen Jupiters from Turkey, a demand that many ExComm members saw as weakening both NATO and U.S. relations with Turkey. In addition, word came through that in Washington the Soviets were burning embassy codes, thus possibly betokening that war was near. And, to add to the sense of peril, reports arrived that the Soviets were firing on U.S. U-2 "surveillance" planes, and that one had been downed and the pilot presumably killed. He did die in the crash. Also, at one point in the morning of the 27th, the ExComm learned that a U-2 had accidentally entered Soviet air space, broken radio silence and asked for U.S. help, and that Soviet fighters took off to intercept the U.S. plane. According to one account, McNamara "turned absolutely white and yelled hysterically, 'This means war with the Soviet Union.'" Fortunately the U-2 scurried back without any shooting.

That morning and afternoon, in the first two ExComm meetings of the day, the president seemed the most inclined to move toward some kind of a deal on the Jupiters, while many of his advisers urged remaining firm on the grounds that the NATO alliance would otherwise be imperiled and U.S. credibility undermined. At one point, the president became testy, contending incorrectly that he had ordered that some kind of deal with the Turks should have been initiated during the week—though, actually, he had given no such orders. It was going to be hard to turn down this public demand by the Soviets, he stated. "Most...people think," Kennedy said at the meeting, "if you're allowed an even trade you ought to take advantage of it. Therefore [not doing so] makes it more difficult to move with world support." Maybe, the president suggested, the Turks could be induced to offer such a deal, and that would settle the crisis while protecting NATO and U.S. credibility. Worrying that war might otherwise result, Kennedy said, "We all know how quickly everybody's courage goes when the blood starts to flow, and that's what's going to happen in NATO."

That Saturday, the administration publicly issued at the time what seemed a rebuff to the Soviets. The U.S. statement actually was more subtle, sidestepping the

Soviet demand, calling for negotiations after Soviet work on the missile sites ceased (the CIA reported that many of the missiles were operational), and suggesting post-crisis discussions on arms control. In addition, upon the initial suggestions of Sorensen and Bundy, then taken up by Robert Kennedy, the president agreed to send a private letter—the so-called "Trollope ploy" of accepting the arrangement not formally offered—which went back to the loose Friday terms and entirely omitted the new Soviet demand on the Jupiters.

The ExComm discussion that day, leading to the "Trollope ploy" letter, is very revealing. The president had kept worrying about the likelihood of war, and kept saying that the deal on the Jupiters, while painful, was far better than war. "I'm just thinking about [U.S. attacks on Cuba] and possibly an invasion, all because we wouldn't take missiles out of Turkey." He added fearfully, "Today it sounds great to reject it, but it's not going to after we do something." He acceded to the Trollope tactic with limited hope, and probably not great conviction, upon the persuasive advice of Soviet expert Llewellyn Thompson, who concluded that, the Soviets "are beginning to give way. Let's push harder."

At the same meeting, despite the bellicose counsel by General Maxwell Taylor, representing himself and the Joint Chiefs, for military action against Cuba in reprisal for the shoot-down of the U-2, the president and others backed away from a military response. They could see, and greatly feared, the likely chain of reprisal, Soviet retaliation and more U.S. action. Partly defusing the sense of great urgency, McNamara at a propitious juncture in the discussions stressed that a U.S. military attack could safely be delayed until the next Wednesday or Thursday, if surveillance and the quarantine were both continued in the interim.

When the meeting ended near early evening, basic matters seemed dangerously unresolved. The wishes expressed initially by President Kennedy, and later in the session by Lyndon B. Johnson, who seldom spoke at these sessions, by Undersecretary Ball, and by CIA Director McCone for a public deal on the Jupiters had seemingly collapsed. McCone, a conservative Republican, had unsuccessfully advised, "I'd trade those Turkish things out right now. I wouldn't even talk to anybody [meaning specifically Turkey and NATO] about it." It was unclear how the Soviets might respond to the "Trollope ploy" and whether more U.S. planes might be shot down.

Between the second and third ExComm meetings that Saturday, some important events occurred: a small group—McNamara, Rusk, Bundy, Sorensen, Ball, Thompson, and Gilpatric—met with the Kennedy brothers, and they agreed that Attorney General Kennedy would confer with Soviet Ambassador Dobrynin to make an explicit private, secret deal. The fifteen Jupiters definitely would be removed from Turkey, he was to promise the ambassador. That evening, at a 7:45 session, the attorney general offered this trade of missiles for missiles to end the crisis. In that meeting, Kennedy warned of the military pressures on the president from U.S. hard-liners, of the dangers if more U-2s were shot down, and of the need for a speedy settlement before the crisis hurtled out of control with shoot-downs, U.S. attacks, and Soviet reprisals. In his summary telegram to the Kremlin that night, Dobrynin quoted Kennedy as having said, "A real war will begin, in which millions of Americans and Russians will die. We want to avoid that any way we can." There was no explicit U.S. ultimatum, according to Dobrynin's cable to the Kremlin and contrary to *Thirteen Days*, but the frightening scenario sketched at the meeting did seem to entail the need for a speedy settlement. There was great danger—to be averted only by a prompt agreement. "I should say," Dobrynin added, "that at our meeting R. Kennedy was very upset."

At the third ExComm session that Saturday, 27 October, held after the top secret session between Dobrynin and the attorney general, none of the nine men who knew about this secret offer of a deal disclosed it to the other ExComm members. That third ExComm meeting was conducted as if there had been no U.S. secret offer and as if the president was unsure about what to do in the next few days. If another U-2 was fired upon, he did say that he would issue a warning and then order destruction of "all those SAM-sites," referring to Soviet surface-to-air missile sites. Nobody directly asked how many Soviets would be killed in such an attack, or whether there would be a Soviet reprisal—against Berlin or even the United States.

That night, with the president still unsure whether his offer of a secret missile trade would be acceptable to the Soviets, Rusk suggested, and the president agreed, to a possible backup strategy: that Rusk would ask Andrew Cordier, then at Columbia University and formerly a UN official, to agree to pass on, if necessary, to UN Secretary General U Thant a proposal that U Thant would then publicly make for a trade of the Jupiters for the Soviet missiles in Cuba. Rusk called Cordier and gave him the message, but this backup strategy proved unnecessary.

Though the Kremlin and Khrushchev had demanded a public swap involving the Jupiters, the Soviet premier speedily accepted the private terms that Robert Kennedy had presented to Dobrynin, with the clear mutual understanding that this part of the deal must be kept secret. Thus, Khrushchev did not gain the public concession that he desired, and yet he did quickly agree. Probably he feared that the crisis was going out of control, and that any Soviet tactics of hard bargaining—by dallying and dickering—were too dangerous. Apparently,

Khrushchev believed, contrary to fact but encouraged by Castro, that the Cubans, not the Soviets, had shot down the U-2. Khrushchev did know that Castro's forces were trying to shoot down more U-2s, and Dobrynin's Saturday evening cable stated that the United States would then retaliate against Cuba and the Soviets on the island. Khrushchev understood that Castro could not be halted in his attacks on U-2s, and the Cuban leader had stressed his nation's right to defend its air space from U.S. "surveillance" planes. That meant, Khrushchev well understood, that Castro was extremely likely to create the very situation, a U-2 shootdown, that would unleash a U.S. reprisal, one that could kill thousands of Soviet soldiers in Cuba and possibly have even worse consequences.

Khrushchev also knew what Kennedy and the ExComm did not: There were at least nine Soviet short-range tactical warheads in Cuba, and there was reason to fear, despite formal orders, that the Soviet commander might use them against a U.S. attack. "Use them or lose them" might well dictate the commander's action. In addition, the Soviets had about 42,000 troops in Cuba, and not just the 10,000 that U.S. intelligence had reported, so the Soviets might find it very difficult to avoid military retaliation if the United States launched the feared attack on Cuba.

For all these reasons, undoubtedly, Khrushchev chose to settle speedily—and for less than he desired. He did believe that he would receive the promised U.S. no-invasion pledge, and Khrushchev undoubtedly did not foresee that Castro would refuse to permit on-site inspection in Cuba. For Khrushchev, the world on 27–28 October was too close to the brink for further negotiations, demands, and hopes. The Soviet leader would take what he could get, and thereby avoid the worst. And Kennedy, predictably, was delighted, for he had ended the crisis, gained the glory of a great victory, and concealed his important symbolic concession—the secret deal on the Jupiters. Probably Kennedy would have agreed to a public deal on the Jupiters, despite the political cost, if that had seemed essential to ending the crisis, but he did not have to face that choice. Kennedy did not want war—as he repeatedly told the ExComm on "black" Saturday, 27 October.

The Crisis in Retrospect

The uneasy settlement, lacking any public victory for Khrushchev and concealing one of the key terms, probably helped to bring the Soviet leader down in 1964, when he was deposed. In contrast, Kennedy, while allegedly advising his aides not to gloat publicly, basked in the accolades for what seemed a great triumph. And only in the late 1980s would the details of the secret Jupiter deal become public, ironically at a time when the standards for presidential greatness had shifted and the willingness to make concessions became one of the criteria for

"greatness." In the 1960s and 1970s, the members of the surviving "Camelot court," through memoirs and interviews, withheld the evidence of the secret deal. But in the late 1980s, with new emerging standards for assessment of presidents, Sorensen and others provided this new evidence, which raised John Kennedy's reputation.

To those who had once viewed the Cuban missile crisis as a good example of a well-managed crisis, a model of how to manage crises, the emergence of new evidence undercut that view. During the crisis, serious operational mistakes were made, including the dangerous test launch of a U.S. missile into the Pacific, which could have betokened to the USSR a U.S. first-strike, and a mistaken attack alert at a SAC base in the United States which almost launched nuclear-armed bombers against the USSR. U.S. intelligence also failed to learn of the presence in Cuba of tactical nuclear weapons or of the large size of the Soviet force there. All this unsettling evidence meant to some that, as McNamara pungently phrased it in the late 1980s, "you *can't* manage crises," and therefore they had to be avoided. That was one of the "lessons" drawn, rather belatedly and at odds with 1960s conclusions, from the missile crisis.

Beyond that, by the late 1980s, analysts began to place Cuba itself near the core of the missile crisis, whereas earlier Cuba usually had been treated as a near-pawn, or simply as the place where Soviet missiles had been based. In the reinterpretation of the crisis, analysts began to accept, as did ExComm members, that the Soviet missiles had been sent to Cuba, at least in part, to defend Cuba. McNamara later acknowledged that the Cubans and Soviets in 1962 were not unreasonable, in view of the evidence available to them then, to fear a U.S. attack on Cuba, though he has steadfastly insisted that no such attack had been seriously considered before the crisis erupted. The evidence of Mongoose planning and of McNamara's own military orders in early October 1962 has left others less sure about U.S. intentions if the Soviet missiles had not been discovered.

Of course, nuclear weapons, the fact of substantial U.S. nuclear superiority, and the belief in the advantage of such superiority were near the heart of the crisis. Had the United States not built what it knew was a much larger nuclear arsenal than the Soviets possessed, Khrushchev would not have felt strategically inferior and quite possibly would have felt no need to move Soviet missiles near the United States' shores. The enlarged system of deterrence, operating differently for the two superpowers, may well have helped inspire the very actions that helped produce the crisis. To some analysts, the Cuban missile crisis underscored the dangers of nuclear deterrence itself; to others, the crisis suggested that strategic parity, rather than superiority for one power, was safer.

Well after the crisis, many analysts came to reject the Kennedy administration's October 1962 public distinction between "offensive" and "defensive" long-range nuclear missiles. Archival evidence disclosed that some ExComm members during the crisis had actually likened the Jupiters in Turkey to the Soviet missiles in Cuba, concluding that each deployment could be defined plausibly by the other superpower as "offensive." During the crisis, however, U.S. leaders were not able to understand that the Soviet emplacement in Cuba was "defensive." Over the years, analysts have continued to dispute whether U.S. nuclear superiority, or regional superiority in conventional weapons, or some mixture produced the October settlement of the crisis. Surprisingly, perhaps, two decades after the crisis a few ExComm members argued that conventional superiority, and not nuclear superiority, had helped force Khrushchev and the Kremlin to back down.

In the 1960s, most analysts mistakenly concluded that the United States had given a no-invasion pledge for Cuba. They did not know that U.S. clandestine efforts under Kennedy, and then under Johnson, continued in the quest to harass the Castro regime, sabotage Cuba's economy, and even topple Castro. The actual no-invasion pledge was not forthcoming until 1970, in the Nixon administration.

When Bundy and McNamara, among others, accepted by the late 1980s that the Soviet 1962 missile emplacement in Cuba had been defensive and not aggressive, they implicitly but not explicitly raised questions for assessing Kennedy's October 1962 response to that Soviet deployment. Analysts could not agree on whether the U.S. response was just, why it occurred, nor whether Kennedy would have acted differently, in October 1962, if he had defined the Soviet missile deployment as defensive—to help defend the Soviet Union and protect Cuba. And some analysts also speculate, as has Sorensen, about what would have happened in 1962 if Khrushchev, as Castro had desired, had publicly announced Soviet intentions to place missiles in Cuba and not acted secretly instead.

But most would agree that the Cuban missile crisis was the closest the two major powers came to the brink of nuclear war, though many disagree on whether either superpower leader, or government, had the right to imperil most of the people in the world. Most analysts do agree, however, that the fear of having been near the brink in the crisis led both Kennedy and Khrushchev, in their remaining time in power, to act more cautiously in dealing with the other superpower. The 1962 peril of nuclear war in the crisis undoubtedly helped propel the 1963 U.S.-Soviet agreement on the Limited Nuclear Test Ban Treaty and on the Kremlin-White House "hot line." But analysts disagree on whether Kennedy's apparent success in the missile crisis helped pave the way for the United States' expanding intervention in Vietnam and led President Lyndon B. Johnson, who never learned of the secret Jupiter deal, to seek his own victory there, while rank-and-file Americans, also believing that the missile crisis had been an unalloyed U.S. triumph, expected—well into the mid-1960s—that their nation could achieve a similar victory over communism in Indochina. At times in the 1960s, but more often thereafter, the "lessons" of the missile crisis were highly contested issues in understanding the past and in shaping U.S. policy for the future.

BARTON J. BERNSTEIN

See also Bundy, McGeorge; Castro, Fidel; Central Intelligence Agency; Cold War; Cuba; Kennedy, John Fitzgerald; Kennedy, Robert Francis; Khrushchev, Nikita Sergeyevich; Limited Nuclear Test Ban Treaty; McNamara, Robert Strange; Nuclear Weapons and Strategy; Russia and the Soviet Union; Turkey; Vietnam War

FURTHER READING

Allison, Graham. *Essence of Decision: Explaining the Cuban Missile Crisis.* Boston, 1971.

Blight, James, Bruce Allyn, David Welch, with David Lewis. *Cuba on the Brink: Fidel Castro, the Missile Crisis, and the Collapse of Communism.* New York, 1993.

Blight, James, and David Welch. *On the Brink: Americans and Soviets Reexamine the Cuban Missile Crisis.* New York, 1989.

Bundy, McGeorge. *Danger and Survival: Choices About the Bomb in the First Fifty Years.* New York, 1988.

Chang, Laurence, and Peter Kornbluh, eds. *The Cuban Missile Crisis, 1962.* New York, 1992.

Divine, Robert, ed. *The Cuban Missile Crisis.* New York, 1988.

Dobrynin, Anatoly. *In Confidence: Moscow's Ambassador to America's Six Cold War Presidents.* New York, 1995.

Garthoff, Raymond. *Reflections on the Cuban Missile Crisis,* 2nd ed. Washington, D.C., 1989.

George, Alexander. *Avoiding War: Problems of Crisis Management.* Boulder, Colo., 1991.

Gribkov, Anatoli, and William Y. Smith. *Operation Anadyr: U.S. and Soviet Generals Recount the Cuban Missile Crisi.* Chicago, 1994.

Hilsman, Roger. *To Move a Nation.* Garden City, N.J., 1967.

Kennedy, Robert F. *Thirteen Days: A Memoir of the Cuban Missile Crisis.* New York, 1969.

Khrushchev, Nikita. *Khrushchev Remembers.* Trans. and ed. by Strobe Talbott. Boston, 1970.

———. *Khrushchev Remembers: The Last Testament.* Trans. and ed. by Strobe Talbott. Boston, 1974.

———. *Khrushchev Remembers: The Glasnost Tapes.* Trans. and ed. by Jerold Schechter with Vyacheslav Luchkov. Boston, 1990.

Larson, David, ed. *The Cuban Crisis of 1962: Selected Documents, Chronology, and Bibliography.* Lanham, Md., 1986.

Nathan, James, ed. *The Cuban Missile Crisis Revisited.* New York, 1992.

Paterson, Thomas G. *Contesting Castro: The United States and the Triumph of the Cuban Revolution.* New York, 1994.

Pope, Ronald, ed. *Soviet Views on the Cuban Missile Crisis: Myth and Reality in Foreign Policy Analysis.* Lanham, Md., 1982.

Schlesinger, Arthur, Jr. *A Thousand Days: John F. Kennedy in the White House.* Boston, 1965.

————. *Robert F. Kennedy and His Times.* Boston, 1978.

Scott, Len, and Steve Smith. "Lessons of October: Historians, Political Scientists, Policymakers, and the Cuban Missile Crisis." *International Affairs,* 70 (1994): 659–684.

Sorensen, Theodore. *Kennedy.* New York, 1965.

CULTURAL DIPLOMACY

The pursuit through governmental initiatives of cultural objectives, as distinct from more traditional goals such as security, territorial expansion, or economic advantage. Although in practice it is not always possible to differentiate between cultural and other objectives, cultural diplomacy involves the effort of a government to promote better knowledge about and understanding of its culture in other lands. Cultural diplomacy usually consists of little more than such matters as negotiating agreements for the exchange of students, scholars, athletes, and entertainers or arranging for an exhibition of art works, a musical or ballet performance, or a lecture tour by a literary figure. There are many other ways, however, in which governments engage in cultural relations as part of their foreign policy objectives. Facilitating the arrival of foreign students is one example and the encouragement of religious missionary endeavors abroad is another. Nations undertake such activities because they believe stable international relations must be built on better understanding across national boundaries. Because it is individuals, not nations, that do the understanding, cultural diplomacy cannot be left to diplomats alone; rather, it has to be promoted by individual citizens. One task of governments is to facilitate exchange among individuals of different countries.

Increasing Role of U.S. Government

Traditionally, Americans jealously safeguarded their cultural pursuits as private activities, to be protected from governmental interference. Diplomacy belonged to the public sphere and culture to the private sphere. In a sense, cultural diplomacy was a contradiction in terms. Nevertheless, the state could facilitate private cultural endeavors, as best exemplified by the support given religious missionaries, educators, and explorers abroad as they engaged in evangelical, educational, and scientific missions. In the nineteenth century, the U.S. government negotiated treaties with Turkey (the Ottoman empire), China, Japan, and others to enable Protestant missionaries to proselytize in these countries. When Admiral Matthew C. Perry presented model locomotives to Japanese officials in 1854, he was initiating a process of Japan's cultural transformation, an objective that Washington welcomed, as it did the introduction of Western civilization to the rest of Asia and to the Middle East through U.S. diplomats, merchants, and educators. In the meantime, through its participation in (and hosting of) various world's fairs, the United States sought actively to acquaint itself with the artifacts and products of other countries.

In the first decades of the twentieth century the U.S. government consciously added a cultural dimension to its foreign policy. A good example is the decision in 1908 to return unused portions of the indemnity funds received as a result of the Boxer Rebellion (1900) to China so that country could use the money to send hundreds of students to the United States. This is perhaps one of the first specific instances of U.S. cultural diplomacy. When the United States entered World War I, President Woodrow Wilson established the Committee on Public Information (CPI) under the directorship of George Creel, a Colorado journalist, to educate the U.S. public on the significance of the war. Wilson and Creel decided to use the new agency to engage in propaganda activities in Europe, thus considerably broadening the scope of U.S. foreign relations. CPI representatives were sent to Spain, Switzerland, Italy, Russia, and other countries to try to influence public opinion in support of the war and to disseminate the idea that the United States was promoting such goals as open diplomacy, democratization, and self-determination.

CPI activities in Russia became bound up with the momentous developments taking place in that country during 1917–1919, in the wake of the Bolshevik seizure of power. The Bolsheviks had their own propaganda organs—the Communist parties in Russia and elsewhere and, after 1919, the Communist International, which coordinated radical ideological and political movements in various parts of the world. U.S. cultural diplomacy was thus confronted with a new challenge. In addition to spreading messages about the democratizing aims of the war, it had to show that U.S. visions responded more effectively than Bolshevik propaganda to the aspirations of the masses everywhere. After the war the CPI was dismantled, and whatever anti-Bolshevik propaganda the nation engaged in abroad originated in private sources, such as the press, the churches, overseas Young Men's Christian Association (YMCA) branches, and the like. Nevertheless, the wartime experience left an important legacy; the government had shown itself keenly interested in spreading U.S. ideas abroad; it had been willing to establish institutions for carrying out such a task; and it had made use of new communications technologies, which continued to be an important development in the postwar years. The Department of State and the Department of Commerce were aware of the tremendous impact radio and motion pictures were making on popular consciousness at home and abroad, and they helped U.S. broadcasting companies and Hollywood studios obtain access to foreign markets. Although these were primarily private business activities, Washington's promotion of them was a manifestation of postwar cultural diplomacy.

Despite such beginnings, the United States did not have a comprehensive strategy for engaging in cultural diplomacy, which was in sharp contrast to many other countries that were active in the pursuit of cultural foreign relations. The postwar years, in fact, generated new forces in international relations, which can be termed "cultural internationalism," or the movement for cultural contact, communication, and cooperation as the best way to build international understanding, which in turn was believed to be a necessary foundation of a more stable world order. The United States had its share of cultural internationalists, but they were private individuals and organizations carrying out their work without official endorsement or financial support. In other countries, governments took the initiative in establishing institutions for engaging in cultural exchange programs. When the League of Nations created the International Committee on Intellectual Cooperation, more than thirty countries established their own national committees on intellectual cooperation. A group from the United States likewise founded such a committee but had no formal connection with official Washington.

For U.S. cultural diplomacy to become a central part of foreign policy, the U.S. government would once again have to assume a role in promoting cultural objectives, which came about during the 1930s. Cultural issues, if anything, increased in importance as the worldwide depression destabilized social and political conditions everywhere and as totalitarian and militaristic states threatened the international order. Cultural foreign policy, an attempt at influencing domestic and foreign opinion, gained unprecedented urgency. At the 1936 Buenos Aires Conference of Western Hemisphere states, an agreement was signed for an exchange of university students. Whereas earlier exchanges (except for the Boxer program with China) had been undertaken through private initiatives, the U.S. government became involved for the first time, officially inviting scores of students annually from Latin American countries. Other agreements on cultural exchange were signed at Buenos Aires and again at the Lima Conference of 1938, signaling the coming of the age of cultural diplomacy within the Western Hemisphere. Hemispheric solidarity appeared to be one of the keys to national security in a period of global instability and perceived Nazi threat.

In 1938 the Department of State established an office of cultural relations and appointed as its first director Ben M. Cherrington, a scholar at the University of Denver who had long been active in grass-roots exchange activities through the YMCA and adult education classes. He was one of the many individuals who made up the cultural exchange community in the United States after World War II and who sensed that by the late 1930s they were finally gaining official endorsement for their missions. In 1940 the Office of Coordinator of Inter-American Affairs was established under the direction of Nelson A. Rockefeller, an office that was more powerful than the Department of State's Cultural Relations Division, because it stood outside the framework of the department. Rockefeller was a strong believer in cultural exchanges, and his office sponsored various programs for bringing Latin American scholars to the United States and for sending North American artists to South America.

At this time President Franklin D. Roosevelt began establishing contact with Hollywood studios to encourage them to produce films that described the danger posed by totalitarianism abroad and emphasized the need for national preparedness. Such governmental initiatives, however, contained inherent risks for a country that had prided itself on the separation of private and public spheres. Official endorsement, indeed initiation, of cultural programs as an instrument of foreign policy would mean setting up a structure of priorities and desiderata that might not coincide with those in the private sector—individual artists, universities, foundations, and others. Activities in the private sphere that did not fit into official agendas might not be funded, and thus this sphere might become bifurcated between the officially sanctioned segment and the rest. In such a situation, there was the danger that in a democratic society, which thrived on unrestricted cultural expression, the state might impinge itself on private activities.

World War II and Cold War

Such concerns were temporarily put aside as the United States was drawn into war. With Japan's attack on Pearl Harbor in 1941, wartime propaganda once again became a matter of top priority. The Office of War Information (OWI), established in 1942, was much larger and more ambitious than the Committee on Public Information, although the two shared the same goals. The fact that the OWI often found it difficult to distinguish its work from that of the Office of Strategic Services (OSS), also founded in 1942, is illuminating. The OWI was to focus on psychological warfare and the OSS on intelligence, but both were government agencies concerned with information and education, that is, with the cultural dimensions of the war effort. Professional scholars, bright young students, journalists, lawyers, and many others were recruited into OWI and OSS service, and they engaged in such activities as the gathering and analysis of data on enemy production and morale, the reeducation of prisoners of war, and the evacuation of art treasures from occupied areas. The line between military action and cultural work was tenuous.

An important aspect of wartime cultural diplomacy, however, was to prepare for the postwar world order.

More than ever before, it was considered imperative to promote better understanding among nations as a foundation of a durable peace. During the war, education ministers of the Allied nations, including the Soviet Union, met regularly in London. U.S. delegates to these meetings included Archibald MacLeish, librarian of Congress and (after 1944) assistant secretary of state for public and cultural affairs, and J. William Fulbright, former Rhodes scholar and president of the University of Arkansas. The deliberations in London laid the groundwork for the founding of the United Nations Educational, Scientific, and Cultural Organization (UNESCO), the successor to the League of Nations' Committee on Intellectual Cooperation.

Although the activities of the OWI and the OSS were curtailed when the war ended, that did not end the government sponsorship of cultural relations. As President Harry S. Truman said shortly after Japan's surrender, "The nature of present-day foreign relations makes it essential for the United States to maintain informational activities abroad as an integral part of the conduct of our foreign affairs." At that time, the dissemination of information was considered an educational undertaking and an important part of U.S. cultural relations after the war. In the former enemy countries, the U.S. occupation authorities vigorously promoted policies designed to bring about the cultural transformation of those peoples. The 1948 United Nations Declaration on Human Rights asserted that wars arose in the "hearts and minds" of people. To eradicate war, therefore, it was necessary to remove prejudice, deepen mutual understanding, and promote contact across national boundaries. The United States did its share in carrying out such objectives, participating in UNESCO's work, launching an ambitious student exchange program with other countries (the Fulbright Program), and establishing U.S. libraries in selected countries.

Cultural diplomacy became part of U.S. Cold War strategy. U.S. officials defined the increasingly serious confrontation with the Soviet Union as ideological warfare to be waged on all fronts, which called for propaganda, intelligence, and educational work of a magnitude that surpassed the wartime undertaking. The Cold War was perceived as a perpetual test of will with communist adversaries and thus would require long-range and sustained efforts at cultural diplomacy. The creation in 1953 of the United States Information Agency (USIA) reflected the awareness that a powerful agency was needed even in peacetime, because the Cold War was seen as a peacetime struggle to be won through constant vigilance at the cultural and military levels. The USIA opened libraries in many cities of the world, published magazines, and through the Voice of America beamed radio programs in many languages to every part of the globe. It also subsidized art exhibits and musical and theatrical performances that went abroad and foreign productions in the United States.

It would be difficult to say whether these cultural initiatives paid off—whether they had anything to do with the ultimate "victory" in the Cold War. Certainly, the United States "won" the battle over the "hearts and minds" of many people, best exemplified by the tearing down of the Berlin Wall and the fall of communism in Eastern Europe and the Soviet Union. In any event, the United States did not abandon cultural diplomacy after the end of the Cold War, but it emphasized programs to assist the former communist countries with educational, economic, and political reform. For example, the USIA established the Benjamin Franklin fellowships to pay for the training of Russian economists in the United States. Naming the program after Franklin suggests the awareness of the long tradition of cultural diplomacy, dating back to the eighteenth century when Franklin established close connections with Europe's intellectuals as well as statesmen, thereby indicating that culture and diplomacy are often inseparable.

AKIRA IRIYE

See also China; Cold War; Committee on Public Information; Fulbright Program; Human Rights; Missionaries; Perry, Matthew Calbraith; Propaganda; Rockefeller, Nelson Aldrich; Russia and the Soviet Union; United Nations; United States Information Agency; Voice of America; World War II

FURTHER READING

Coombs, Philip M. *The Fourth Dimension of Foreign Policy: Educational and Cultural Affairs.* New York, 1964.

Costigliola, Frank. *Awkward Dominion: American Political, Economic, and Cultural Relations with Europe, 1919–1933.* Ithaca, N.Y., 1984.

Fejes, Fred. *Imperialism, Media, and the Good Neighbor: New Deal Foreign Policy and United States Shortwaving Broadcasting to Latin America.* Norwood, N.J., 1986.

Iriye, Akira. *The Globalizing of America, 1913–1945.* New York, 1993.

Koppes, Clayton R., and Gregory D. Black. *Hollywood Goes to War: How Politics, Profits and Propaganda Shaped World War II Movies.* New York, 1989.

Ninkovich, Frank. *The Diplomacy of Silence: United States Foreign Policy and Cultural Relations, 1938–1950.* Cambridge, Mass., 1981.

Rosenberg, Emily S. *Spreading the American Dream: American Economic and Cultural Expansion, 1890–1945.* New York, 1982.

Thomson, Charles A., and Walter H. C. Laves. *Cultural Relations and U.S. Foreign Policy.* Bloomington, Ind., 1963.

CURTISS-WRIGHT CASE

(United States v. *Curtiss-Wright Export Corporation,* 299 U.S. 304) [1936])

A Supreme Court case that arose when the defendants sold arms to Bolivia during the Chaco War (1932–1935), a conflict between Paraguay and Bolivia over disputed territory. The case set a major precedent for determining presidential authority in foreign affairs. A congressional joint resolution had authorized President Franklin D. Roosevelt to prohibit by proclamation some or all arms sales to these countries if he believed it would help to restore peace. Roosevelt thereupon issued such a proclamation. The principal issue before the Supreme Court was whether the joint resolution had impermissibly delegated legislative power to the president. The Court addressed this issue only with regard to foreign affairs and chose not to discuss whether such a delegation of power to address a purely domestic matter would have been constitutional. Although the delegation doctrine was subsequently relaxed to a large extent, this was a contentious issue during this period of legal confrontations about New Deal legislation. In an opinion joined by six other justices, Justice George Sutherland held that in the field of foreign affairs Congress may lawfully confer on the president broader discretion and freedom from statutory restriction than in domestic affairs. He held that this particular delegation was subject to the standards applicable to foreign affairs matters and was lawful.

The lasting importance of the case lies not so much in the result as in Justice Sutherland's reasoning, which has been cited in many subsequent constitutional arguments. Three elements of this reasoning are particularly noteworthy. First, Sutherland asserted that when the Constitution was ratified, the states were given no powers to address foreign affairs individually because sovereignty had passed from the British Crown to the colonies collectively. The historical record is not as uniform and tidy as this assertion suggests, but there is a reasonable body of material to support the juridical outcome of this evaluation, which also has implications for such diverse matters as rights to seabed areas and the powers of states to regulate extraterritorially. Second, Sutherland argued that although the powers to address domestic affairs were transferred from the individual states to the federal government by the Constitution, with regard to foreign affairs the federal government has whatever powers international law and practice confer upon all sovereign entities. One interpretation of this is that the source of the U.S. government's foreign affairs powers lies outside the Constitution, deriving perhaps from international law. Most commentators prefer to associate these powers in some way with the Constitution, despite the fact that the Constitution's text does not comprehensively address foreign affairs powers. Third, Sutherland shifted from propositions about the powers of the federal government to sweeping commentary on presidential foreign affairs powers. The most often cited passages of his opinion (particularly popular with lawyers for the executive branch) concern "the very delicate, plenary and exclusive power of the President as the sole organ of the federal government in the field of international relations." The opinion contains a number of important qualifications to these sweeping dicta. For example, it concentrates primarily on powers "to speak or listen" and suggests that these powers are subordinate to applicable provisions of the written Constitution. In addition, it is important to note that the case itself involved a presidential action that was explicitly authorized by legislation.

Nevertheless, the *Curtiss-Wright* case has been used as a basis to advocate both wide executive power in foreign affairs and judicial circumspection in reviewing executive branch action involving foreign affairs. In these matters, the case is often set up against such cases as *Youngstown Sheet and Tube Company* v. *Sawyer*, 343 U.S. 579 (1952), in which the nonstatutory executive seizure of strike-threatened steel mills during the Korean War was held unconstitutional, and *Little* v. *Barreme*, 6 U.S. (2 Cranch) 170 (1804), in which the executive-ordered seizure of a neutral merchant ship was held unlawful as breach of a statute within the power of Congress to enact.

Much of the *Curtiss-Wright* reasoning was based on the possibility of sharp distinctions between foreign and domestic affairs, but such distinctions are becoming increasingly difficult to draw in many areas. Problems regarding presidential powers, institutional participation, and judicial self-restraint continue to have special legal features in some important areas where foreign affairs remains a recognizably distinct realm, but in many other areas the foreign affairs element is just one part of much wider constitutional and international debates.

BENEDICT W. KINGSBURY

See also Bolivia; Congress; Constitution; Presidency

FURTHER READING

Henkin, Louis. *Foreign Affairs and the Constitution.* Mineola, N.Y., 1972.

Koh, Harold. *The National Security Constitution: Sharing Power After the Iran-Contra Affair.* New Haven, Conn., 1990.

Lofgren, Charles. *Government from Reflection and Choice: Constitutional Essays on War, Foreign Relations, and Federalism.* New York, 1986.

CUSHING, CALEB

(*b.* 17 January 1800; *d.* 2 January 1879)

Diplomat and ardent territorial and commercial expansionist. An opportunistic politician, who switched party allegiances several times during his long career, including four congressional terms representing Massachusetts (1835–1843), Cushing promoted the acquisition of Texas, Oregon, and Cuba and believed that extending the American empire would fulfill "the great destiny reserved for this exemplar American Republic." In 1844, as U.S. commissioner to China and under the direction of President John Tyler and Secretary of State Daniel Webster, Cushing secured the nation's first treaty with China, the Treaty of Wangxia, which gave U.S. merchants access to five Chinese ports. As attorney general under President Franklin D. Pierce (1853–1857), he was an apostle of "Young America" and Caribbean expansion. After the Civil War, Cushing negotiated a treaty with Colombia for a right of way for a canal across the Isthmus of Panama, helped to attain the favorable settlement of the *Alabama* Claims at Geneva, and as minister to Spain in the 1870s crowned his diplomatic career by helping to defuse the troublesome *Virginius* Affair.

EDWARD P. CRAPOL

See also Alabama Claims; Colombia; Manifest Destiny; Mexico; Panama and Panama Canal; Pierce, Franklin; Spain; Wangxia, Treaty of; Webster, Daniel; Young America

FURTHER READING

Donahue, William J. "The Caleb Cushing Mission." *Modern Asian Studies* 16 (1982): 193–216.

Fuess, Claude M. *The Life of Caleb Cushing*, 2 vols. New York, 1923.

Hietala, Thomas R. *Manifest Design: Anxious Aggrandizement in Late Jacksonian America*. Ithaca, N.Y., 1985.

CYPRUS

A mountainous island in the eastern Mediterranean off the southern coast of Turkey that has had a long and troubled history dating back to the thirteenth century B.C. Originally inhabited by a Greek-speaking people, it was ruled by a succession of foreign invaders until 1571, when it was conquered by the Ottoman Turks. Leased to Great Britain in 1878, it became a crown colony in 1925. After World War II its population of approximately 650,000 comprised 80 percent Greek Orthodox Christians and 18 percent Turkish Moslems. Greek Cypriot demands for union with Greece were rejected by Great Britain, resulting in violence in the island and tension between Athens and London. Cyprus achieved independence in 1960, following agreement between Great Britain, Greece, and Turkey (the Zurich and London Accords of 1959), which formally prohibited Cypriot union with another state, granted Great Britain sovereign rights over two military bases, and authorized Greece and Turkey to station small military contingents in Cyprus. As guarantors of the new republic, the three signatories reserved the right to intervene, unilaterally if necessary, to safeguard the provisions of their agreement. Government authority in Cyprus was to be determined on the basis of a rigid power ratio between the Greek majority and the Turkish minority.

Predictably, the arrangement proved unworkable. Violence between the two ethnic communities erupted in 1963, following attempts by the republic's first president, Archbishop Makarios III, to abolish the Turkish Cypriots' veto power over government activity. In 1964 and 1967 Turkey appeared poised to intervene militarily but desisted under heavy pressure from the United States. In July 1974, however, the military junta that had been in power in Athens since 1967 engineered a coup that toppled Makarios and replaced him with Nicos Sampson, a disreputable ultranationalist. Within days a large Turkish invasion force swept across the island's northern region, causing many casualties and uprooting nearly 200,000 Greek Cypriots. By the end of August 1974, Turkish forces occupied about 40 percent of the island and established an autonomous administration under Ankara's tutelage. De facto division was achieved in 1983, when Turkish Cypriot leader Rauf Denktash announced the establishment of the Turkish Republic of Northern Cyprus, which was promptly recognized by Turkey but ignored by all other states and international organizations. A large Turkish army remained in place while thousands of Turks from the Anatolian mainland were brought to Cyprus and settled in areas once inhabited by Greeks. International mediation efforts continued to be unsuccessful into the 1990s and, although both Greece and Turkey were allied as members of the North Atlantic Treaty Organization (NATO), relations between Greece and Turkey remained near the flash point.

As long as Cyprus was under British rule the United States took no particular interest in the island, although in the 1950s the administration of President Dwight D. Eisenhower used its influence to prevent Greek Cypriot demands for union with Greece from receiving support at the United Nations, where the issue was certain to be exploited by the Soviets. U.S. officials were motivated by fear that escalating friction between Greece and Turkey was paralyzing NATO's southeastern arm. The United States welcomed the 1959 accords, and the Republic of Cyprus received Washington's prompt recognition and modest aid.

U.S. officials were irritated by Makarios's neutralist orientation and occasional flirting with the Soviet Union, whose naval forces in the eastern Mediterranean were a matter of serious concern for NATO. Nevertheless, in January 1964 President Lyndon B. Johnson sternly warned Turkey not to invade Cyprus. Subsequently, Johnson held separate meetings with Greek and Turkish leaders in an effort to broker an agreement on Cyprus. These talks led to the Acheson Plan, under which most of Cyprus was to be united with Greece. For its part, Turkey was to receive the remainder of the island and also acquire Kastellorizon, a small Greek island off Turkey's Aegean shore. The plan, however, was opposed by Makarios and was rejected by the Greek side. A new crisis on the island in 1967 was similarly contained through concerted U.S. efforts.

Turkey was again prevailed upon not to invade, and the Greek junta was forced to withdraw about 9,000 troops. When the 1974 crisis erupted, however, the United States did little beyond appealing for moderation. The administration of President Richard M. Nixon failed to adequately warn the Greek junta against toppling Makarios or, once that occurred, again to dissuade Turkey from launching an invasion.

In 1975, in the wake of the invasion, Congress imposed an arms embargo on Turkey, but it was generally considered ineffective and was lifted in 1978. Succeeding U.S. administrations have declared their resolve actively to seek a fair and peaceful solution that would preserve Cyprus as an independent state. In January 1996 Assistant Secretary of State Richard Holbrooke, the chief architect of the accords on the Bosnian crisis the previous fall, declared that the United States intended to make a "big push" on the Cyprus problem soon, adding: "if you let the [Cyprus] issue fester…it could explode." But a new crisis in Greek-Turkish relations, this time over an uninhabited islet in the Aegean, appeared to derail the new initiative even before it was launched. U.S. and UN mediation efforts appeared to favor a modest reduction of the area under Turkish control and the establishment of a confederation under which the two communities would govern themselves in separate zones. To be effective, however, any solution must be accepted by the two Cypriot communities, as well as by Greece and Turkey. Despite international efforts such a solution remains elusive. As a result, in the mid-1990s Cyprus continued to be divided into two rigidly separate enclaves. In the south the Greek Cypriots managed to build a flourishing economy and an internationally active polity, but in the northeast the Turkish Cypriots still found themselves isolated and dependent upon Turkey for all but the most basic of their needs.

JOHN O. IATRIDES

See also Greece; North Atlantic Treaty Organization; Turkey

FURTHER READING

Bahcheli, Tozun. *Greek-Turkish Relations Since 1955*. London, 1990.

Coufoudakis, Van, ed. *Essays on the Cyprus Conflict*. New York, 1976.

Couloumbis, Theodore A. *The United States, Greece, and Turkey: The Troubled Triangle*. New York, 1983.

Markides, Kyriacos C. *The Rise and Fall of the Cyprus Republic*. New Haven, Conn., 1977.

Stearns, Monteagle. *Entangled Allies: U.S. Policy Toward Greece, Turkey, and Cyprus*. New York, 1992.

CZECH REPUBLIC

Located in central Europe and bordered by Slovakia, Germany, Austria, and Poland, it was one of two successor states to the former Czechoslovakia. The latter was established in 1918, dismembered in 1939, recreated after World War II, and replaced in 1993 by the separate states of the Czech Republic and Slovakia after the collapse of the Soviet Union and the Soviet bloc. This is a history that profoundly reflects the country's location at the heart of Europe and its consequent vulnerability to the forces that have swept the region, including war, communism, and post–Cold War neonationalism.

The independent state of Czechoslovakia was first created in the wake of the dissolution of the Austro-Hungarian Empire following World War I. It included Bohemia, Moravia and Slovakia, and a year later Subcarpathian Ruthenia. In addition to Czechs and Slovaks the populace was comprised of Germans, Hungarians, Ukrainians, Jews, and a number of other smaller minorities. U.S. President Woodrow Wilson, while originally reluctant to see independent states created in the region, by the end of the war had made the principle of self-determination central to his thinking and, correspondingly, at the core of the Versailles peace settlement. Indeed it was in Washington that Tomás G. Masaryk declared Czechoslovakia's independence. Masaryk became the country's first president; other early leaders included Milan Štefanik and Edvard Beneš.

U.S. relations with the new state remained cordial throughout the interwar period, but they reflected the low priority Washington gave to this region at the time. Czechoslovakia's relationship with France was far more significant, because Prague relied on its treaty with France as well as on good relations with Great Britain to guarantee its security. Relations with the Soviet Union reflected the tensions that existed within the country between traditional pro-Russian sentiments and anti-Soviet feelings. The Soviet-Czechoslovak treaty signed in 1935 obligated the Soviet Union to come to the aid of Czechoslovakia only if France honored its own treaty commitments. Czechoslovakia also was a member of the Little Entente, which linked it to Yugoslavia and Romania against the threat of Hungarian irredentism, and played an active role in the League of Nations.

In contrast to many of the other states in the region, Czechoslovakia's democratic government persisted until it was ended by outside powers in 1938–1939. The fact that internal conditions were more favorable was in part responsible for maintaining democracy. The country, and particularly the Czech areas, had a level of economic development that was higher than that of the other new states in the region; a social structure that resembled that of developed Western countries, including a large middle class; and near universal literacy. Political stability also stemmed from the fact that Czechoslovakia's leaders formed stable coalitions and adopted progressive social policies designed to defuse discontent. They were not as successful, however, in dealing with ethnic issues. Members of the sizable German minority, often referred to as the Sudeten Germans for the region in which most of them lived, resented the loss of the privileges they had enjoyed as part of the ruling German group under the Austro-Hungarian Empire. The negative impact of a number of economic policies adopted by the Czechoslovak government also increased the ability of radical nationalists to mobilize the German population, whose dissatisfaction in turn provided the pretext for Adolf Hitler to annex part of the country in 1938. Slovak dissatisfaction with the interwar republic also festered. Efforts to industrialize Slovakia failed, in part because of the impact of the Great Depression. Economic hardship, coupled with Slovak perceptions of domination from Prague, fed support for extremist nationalist movements, including the Slovak People's Party led by Father Andrej Hlinka and Josef Tiso. Many of the supporters of this movement welcomed the creation of the pseudo-independent Slovak state in March 1939 as the satisfaction of Slovak national aspirations.

Abandoned by Great Britain and France as the result of the Munich Agreement of 29 September 1938, Czechoslovakia's leaders submitted to German demands the very next day that they cede the Sudetenland to Germany. The creation of a truncated Czecho-Slovak state in October 1938 was followed by the creation of the Slovak Republic and the German Protectorate of Bohemia and Moravia, and the German occupation of the entire country in March 1939. Subcarpathian Ruthenia, which became autonomous in October 1938, soon came under Hungarian control. The United States did not recognize the results of the Munich Agreement or the subsequent territorial dismemberment of Czechoslovakia; but initially U.S. policymakers also were reluctant to recognize the government in exile, headed by Beneš in London. It was not until July 1941 that the United States recognized the Czechoslovaki National Council as a provisional government and not until October 1942 that U.S. diplomats dropped the term "provisional" in their references to this government.

Liberation and the Establishment of Communism

U.S. policies toward Czechoslovakia after World War II were largely influenced by developments in U.S.-Soviet relations and by the onset of the Cold War. In 1945 U.S. troops helped to liberate from the Nazis some of the western part of the country around Plzen (Pilsen), but most of Czechoslovakia's territory was liberated by Soviet troops, whose then continued occupation, along with the results of U.S.-Soviet agreements reached during the war, greatly shaped domestic political life. The government in exile, headed by Beneš, had returned to Prague at the end of the war. From 1945 to February 1948 the country enjoyed a period of modified pluralism. As the result of the Košice government program adopted in 1945 as the basis of the postwar government, the political spectrum was narrowed. Most parties to the right of center were banned from politics, and those that remained became part of a government coalition that also included the Social Democrats and the Communists. There was thus no true democratic opposition. The Communist party's leaders enjoyed a number of advantages in the new situation. Communists held many of the key ministerial posts in the new government, and the party, which had won 38 percent of the vote in the 1946 elections, also derived additional advantages from its close association with the victorious Soviet troops.

Czechoslovakia's foreign policy during this period reflected the divisions within the government coalition, as well as the country's experiences during World War I. The unwillingness of its Western allies to come to Czechoslovakia's aid during the Munich crisis in 1938 had led to a fair degree of disillusionment with the West. The country's leaders, including Beneš, also emerged from the war years convinced of the need for Czechoslovakia to work out a special relationship with the Soviet Union. Still, most Czechs and Slovaks continued to look to the West culturally, and the country's leaders participated in the creation of new international organizations in the aftermath of the war. The country's representatives also indicated interest in participating in the Marshall Plan. They accepted the invitation to the preliminary conference in Paris on 7 July 1948; as a result of Soviet pressure, however, they reversed themselves the next day and declined the invitation.

In February 1948, Czechoslovakia's communist leaders provoked a government crisis that led to the resignation of the country's democratic ministers and the formation of a government clearly dominated by the Communists. President Beneš's resignation on 7 June 1948, followed by his death on 6 September, was a clear sign of the end of democracy in postwar Czechoslovakia. The country's new leaders moved very quickly to eliminate political pluralism and install a Soviet-type political and economic system. They took steps to neutralize their political opponents and ensure the complete dominance of the Communist party. They also subordinated government bodies to party organizations at all levels, outlawed all mass organizations except those controlled by the party, and set up censorship to control public information. In the economic area, they instituted a system of centralized planning, completed the process of nationalization begun after 1945, and collectivized agriculture. Emulating Soviet practice, they adopted measures to change the country's stratification system and tried to subordinate all areas of life, including education and culture, to communist political ends.

As relations soured between the Soviet Union and the Western allies, Czechoslovakia's foreign policy shifted accordingly. The country withdrew from Western institutions. Its foreign trade, previously heavily concentrated with West European countries, was redirected toward the east. Citizens were forbidden to travel to the West, and efforts were made to limit all contact with Western ideas. Czechoslovakia became a founding member of the Soviet-bloc Council for Mutual Economic Assistance (CMEA) and the Warsaw Treaty Organization. Czechoslovak foreign policy came to be determined largely by Soviet objectives, and Prague became one of Moscow's most loyal allies.

U.S. policy toward Czechoslovakia during this period reflected the overall deterioration of U.S.-Soviet relations as well as the intent of Czechoslovakia's leaders to isolate their country from contact with the West. Bilateral relations were further complicated by the unwillingness of the Czechoslovak government to compensate U.S. citizens whose assets were confiscated in the course of nationalization and collectivization, and by the refusal of the U.S. government to return the 18.4 tons of gold reserves held at Fort Knox, Kentucky, to the Czechoslovak government in advance of such compensation.

The Prague Spring and its Aftermath

The communist system weathered the death of Joseph Stalin and subsequent Soviet moves at de-Stalinization quite easily. In contrast to Poland and Hungary, where partial de-Stalinization led to political upheavals and, in the Hungarian case, invasion by Soviet troops to restore orthodoxy, the conservative communist leadership in Czechoslovakia did little more than give lip service to the need for change in the 1950s. By the early 1960s, however, many of the factors that allowed the regime to persist had changed. Czechoslovakia's economy, which had been buffered from the negative impact of the Stalinist model of economic organization and development in the 1950s, slowed down dramatically. Coupled with the impact of a slight loosening of orthodoxy after the twenty-second Communist Party Congress in the Soviet Union, a realization of the need to improve economic performance led party leaders to initiate a process of reform. Originally, this process remained at the elite level, that is, economists, sociologists, and other intellectuals engaged in a far-reaching reformulation of the theoretical bases of socialist society, while creative intellectuals tested the limits on freedom of expression and called for less ideological interference in cultural affairs. At the same time, Slovak dissatisfaction with Slovakia's second-class status also grew, as did the nonconformist activities of students and young people.

In January 1968 the reformers within the party succeeded in ousting Antonín Novotny as party leader and replacing him with Alexander Dubček, former head of the Slovak Communist party. With this step the movement for change came into the open. The effective end of censorship in early 1968 allowed the development of mass support for reform. Freed from the constraints of party control on public debate, citizens began to discuss political issues openly once again and to push the leadership toward more fundamental changes than those outlined in the action program of the party adopted in April 1968. The Dubček leadership proved unable to satisfy the demands of its citizens for continued reform and at the same time reassure its conservative allies that socialism per se was not being threatened. The invasion of Czechoslovakia by Warsaw Pact troops on 21 August 1968 ended the effort to create "socialism with a human face." Resistance continued at all levels of society throughout the early months of 1969. The ouster of Dubček and his replacement by Gustáv Husák as leader of the party signaled the end of reform. Reformists were soon removed from positions in intellectual as well as political life, censorship was restored, and the dominance of the Communist party was reestablished. By relying on selective repression, primarily against nonconformist intellectuals, and improvements in the standard of living, the Husák leadership was able to preserve a surface stability that lasted for much of the rest of the communist period. Citizens once again retreated to the private sphere, and orthodoxy prevailed in political, cultural, and intellectual life.

Czechoslovakia's foreign policy also reverted to its pre-1968 pattern. Although many of the 1968 reforms centered on the domestic political system, Dubček and the reformers also sought to make certain changes in the country's foreign relations. Thus, while reaffirming their loyalty to the Warsaw Pact, they also sought to improve relations with the country's Western neighbors, particularly Germany. For a few years, Czech and Slovak citizens also had greater freedom to travel to the West. However, with the forcible end of the reforms, the country's new leaders once again followed the Soviet Union's lead in foreign policy. Czechoslovakia's foreign relations with noncommunist European and other Western countries continued to be cool. In contrast to Hungary and Poland, Czechoslovak leaders did not turn to the West for credits, technology, or trade to boost their ailing economy in the 1970s and 1980s. Czechoslovakia borrowed very little from the West and continued to look eastward for imports and markets. The country's trade continued to be very heavily concentrated in the socialist world until the collapse of CMEA in 1991.

U.S. relations with Czechoslovakia improved slightly in 1982, when the gold claims issue was finally resolved. The agreement stipulated that the 18.4 tons of gold would be returned to Prague in exchange for $81.5 million to be paid to American claimants whose property had been seized and nationalized when the communists came to power. Although the agreement resolved outstanding financial issues between the two governments, it did little to change the basic nature of relations between the two countries. U.S. plans to open a consulate in Bratislava were not realized until after the collapse of the communist system. The United States, however, continued to quietly support dissidents in Prague, a policy that had numerous benefits after November 1989.

The End of Communism and the Restoration of Democracy

In the late 1980s Mikhail Gorbachev's policies of *glasnost* and *perestroika* in the Soviet Union seemed at first to have little impact in Czechoslovakia. Fearful that any reform would lead to a repetition of the events of 1968, the country's leaders did little but give lip service to the need to follow the Soviet example. Czechoslovakia, however, experienced many of the same problems as other communist regimes at this time. Although it did not suffer the acute economic crises that threatened political stability in neighboring Poland, economic performance declined. This decline in turn threatened the leadership's strategy of survival, because it undermined its ability to use material benefits to obtain citizens' continued acquiescence if not real support.

Despite the surface stability of the Czechoslovak regime, there were important changes in the last two years of communist rule. These occurred at the leadership level, where almost half of the top leaders of the party were replaced between 1987 and November 1989. The party's new leaders did not differ significantly from those they replaced, nor were they reformers. They were, however, younger, less experienced, and less committed than their predecessors to the policies of so-called "normalization." As a result, they vacillated in their responses to the increasing challenges they now faced. Although their numbers remained small, an increasing number of citizens came to support openly the activities of dissidents. The number of independent groups increased significantly, as did the number of people, including those in official positions, who were willing to participate in activities that openly criticized or challenged the regime. The importance of these developments became apparent in November 1989, when a brutal police beating of peaceful student demonstrators sparked massive popular demonstrations that very quickly brought down the communist regime. Unable to count on Soviet support, the Czechoslovak communist leadership relinquished power to the leaders of two of the major dissident organizations, the Civic Forum in the Czech areas, led by internationally known playwright Václav Havel, and Public Against Violence in Slovakia. Havel's election as president of Czechoslovakia in December 1989 capped the victory of what came to be known as the "Velvet Revolution."

The end of communist rule was followed by an abrupt and thorough reorientation of Czechoslovakia's foreign as well as domestic policies. Led by Havel and Foreign Minister Jiří Dienstbier, the country's new leaders took energetic steps to assert Czechoslovakia's independence from the Soviet Union, to normalize relations with Western governments, including the United States, and to reclaim their country's place on the European stage. Soviet troops were withdrawn from Czechoslovak territory by 30 June 1991 in accordance with an agreement reached in early 1990. The formal demise of the CMEA in September 1991 and of the Warsaw Treaty Organization in July 1991 reflected the dramatic change in Czechoslovakia's foreign policy commitments. The country's new leaders continued to look to trade with the Soviet Union—and later with its successors—for certain critical imports, including energy products and raw materials, but the country's trade was very quickly reoriented toward Western Europe, especially Germany, which by 1992 accounted for 26.2 percent of Czechoslovakia's imports and 33.3 percent of its exports.

Czechoslovakia's new leaders also moved quickly to reestablish the country's traditionally warm relationship with the United States. A series of high level visits, including two by President Havel to the United States, and official visits by Presidents George Bush and Bill Clinton to Czechoslovakia, symbolized the restored friendship. The United States also played an important role in providing assistance to support the recreation of democratic institutions and the move to a market economy. The central focus of Czechoslovakia's foreign policy after 1989, however, was Europe, an orientation evident in campaign slogans in the 1990 parliamentary elections, which promised "a return to Europe." It was also reflected in the emphasis Havel and Dienstbier gave to normalizing Czechoslovakia's relations with its immediate neighbors and gaining entry to European institutions. The success of their efforts was evident in Czechoslovakia's admission to the Council of Europe and its association agreement with the European Community, as well as in the aid and assistance Prague received from Western European countries and institutions. In 1990 and 1991, before the collapse of the Soviet Union, Havel and Dienstbier argued for the elimination of both Cold War security blocs and the creation of a European security system centered in the Conference on Security and Cooperation in Europe process. As political instability increased in the Soviet Union, however, Prague came to view membership in the North Atlantic Treaty Organization (NATO) as a necessary guarantee of Czechoslovakia's longer-term security.

In January 1993 the Czechoslovak federation was replaced by two independent states, the Czech Republic and the Slovak Republic. A reflection of historical differences, differences in the impact of the move to a market economy in both regions, and elite politics, the breakup of the federation also reflected the different orientations of Czech and Slovak citizens to many of the central issues of the day. The westward orientation that characterized Czechoslovakia's foreign policy was especially evident in the policies of the Czech Republic. Prime Minister Vacláv Klaus in particular argued for recognition of the Czech Republic's status as a Western European, rather than a Central European, country and called for it to be admitted as rapidly as possible to the European Union (EU) and NATO. In Slovakia, disagreements between Prime Minister Vladimir Mečiar and Foreign Minister Milan Kňažko over the extent to which Slovakia should look west or east led to Kňažko's resignation in March 1993. That same year Slovakia signed a military agreement with Russia. Still, both countries joined the Partnership for Peace program in 1994. The interim coalition government formed in Slovakia after Mečiar was removed as prime minister after a no-confidence vote in March 1994 assertively affirmed Slovakia's interest in joining the EU and other European institutions. It also took steps to reduce tensions between Hungary and Slovakia over the issues of the Gabčikovo-Nagymaros hydroelectric dam on the Danube and the treatment of Slovakia's Hungarian minority. Slovakia's leaders also adopted measures to encourage higher levels of foreign investment. Both countries also continued to participate in the activities of regional groupings.

The Mečiar government formed in December 1994 reaffirmed Slovakia's interest in joining NATO and the EU. It also continued to pursue good relations with Ukraine and Russia. In March 1995, Slovak leaders signed a state treaty with Hungary, but the Slovak parliament did not ratify it in 1995 as planned.

SHARON L. WOLCHIK

See also Beneš, Eduard; Cold War; Fourteen Points; Havel, Václav; Munich Conference; National Endowment for Democracy; Russia and the Soviet Union; Slovakia; Versailles Treaty of 1919; Warsaw Pact; Wilson, Thomas Woodrow; World War II

FURTHER READING
Johnson, Owen. *Slovakia, 1918–1938: Education and the Making of a Nation.* Boulder, 1985.
Korbel, Josef. *Twentieth-Century Czechoslovakia: The Meanings of its History.* New York, 1977.
Korbel, Josef, Hans Brisch, and Ivan Volges, eds. *Czechoslovakia, the Heritage of Ages Past: Essays in the Memory of Josef Korbel.* Boulder, N.Y., 1977.
Leff, Carol. *National Conflict in Czechoslovakia: The Making and Remaking of a State, 1918–1987.* Princeton, N.J., 1988.
Mamatey, Victor S., and Radomir Luza. *A History of the Czechoslovak Republic, 1918–1948.* Princeton, N.J., 1973.
Skilling, Gordon. *Samizdat and an Independent Society in Central and Eastern Europe.* Columbus, Ohio, 1988.
———. *Czechoslovakia, 1918–1988: Seventy Years from Independence.* New York, 1991.
Suda, Zdenek. *The Czechoslovak Socialist Republic.* Baltimore, 1969.
Wolchik, Sharon. *Czechoslovakia in Transition: Politics, Economics and Society.* London, New York, 1991.

D

DANIELS, JOSEPHUS, JR.
(b. 18 May 1862; d. 15 January 1948)

Progressive Democratic newspaper editor, secretary of the navy (1913–1921), and ambassador to Mexico (1933–1941), where he worked to implement the Good Neighbor Policy of President Franklin D. Roosevelt. Born in Washington, North Carolina, Daniels became the editor of a small-town paper at the age of eighteen and its publisher two years later. He edited and published a succession of newspapers in his home state, principally the *Raleigh News and Observer*. Daniels expressed his political views in favor of the progressive wings of the Democratic party and the reforms it advocated through his editorial columns, drawing him into state and national politics. He was noted for his strident opposition to the U.S. acquisition of the Philippines after the Spanish-American-Cuban-Filipino War of 1898. Daniels fervently supported William Jennings Bryan's several attempts to gain the presidency from 1896 onward, sharing Bryan's idealism and penchant for moralistic stands. In 1912 Daniels supported the candidacy of Woodrow Wilson.

Daniels served as secretary of the navy throughout Wilson's tenure, administering the navy effectively during World War I. He initiated numerous administrative reforms, such as instituting educational programs for enlisted men. Daniels issued the orders that led to the U.S. seizure of Veracruz, Mexico, on 21 April 1914. This misguided effort reflected the Wilson administration's opposition to the regime of General Victoriano Huerta and Wilson's sympathy with the Mexican revolutionaries. The landing took place in response to the seizure of a few U.S. sailors in Tampico and in an effort to prevent the landing of a German shipment of arms destined for the Huerta regime. Daniels, Wilson, and Secretary of State Bryan all mistakenly assumed that the Mexican population would welcome Yankee troops as saviors from an oppressive regime and that the landing would cause the fall of the Huerta regime. Instead, the local garrison resisted the landing as a violation of Mexican sovereignty, and even the revolutionaries distanced themselves from the landing, citing national sovereignty. Although U.S. forces easily took control of the port, Huerta remained in control of the capital and the government for several more months, and the civil war continued uninterrupted. The revolutionaries continued to dispute control of Vera-cruz with the United States after the fall of Huerta, and eventually the United States simply withdrew.

After resuming his newspaper career during the Republican administrations that succeeded Wilson, Daniels returned to politics in 1932, in support of Roosevelt's candidacy. Daniels had selected Roosevelt as his assistant secretary of the navy during the Wilson administration, and Roosevelt appointed Daniels ambassador to Mexico. Daniels embarked on his mission to Mexico at the age of seventy and in the face of considerable skepticism because of his role in the Veracruz incident. Daniels worked vigorously to develop personal friendships with Mexican leaders, actively courting the leaders of the revolutionary regimes and seeking to become a personal link between the presidents of Mexico and the United States. He developed a genuine fondness for the country, its culture, and people and later described his eight years in Mexico as the happiest days of his life.

Daniels's tenure in Mexico coincided with an era of difficult relations between the two nations, reflecting the numerous disputes resulting from the turmoil, atrocities, and property seizures of the revolutionary era and the tumultuous conditions that prevailed during the extended period of civil war from 1910 to 1920. Striving to bridge the resulting disputes and sensitivities and overcome the mistrust between the peoples of Mexico and the United States, Daniels used his personal friendship with Roosevelt to advocate compromise settlements in terms acceptable to the Mexicans. Daniels was particularly active during the tense period following the 18 March 1938 decision of Mexican president Lázaro Cárdenas to expropriate foreign oil holdings, which resulted in the seizure of U.S. and British firms. Daniels strongly resisted the calls for a hard-line stance from jingoistic nationalists, rigid legalists, and aggrieved oil company owners, in one instance averting a confrontation by refusing to deliver a formal protest note from Secretary of State Cordell Hull and relying on his close ties with Roosevelt. Daniels's cautious advice to Roosevelt and his insistence on compromise allowed time for tempers to cool. The question was ultimately settled through negotiations during 1940 and 1941, although Daniels was not directly involved in the talks, which were conducted by special envoys and arbitration panels. Ultimately, the United States rejected calls for intervention, accepting Mexican expropriation of the oil companies and focusing negotiations on the question of compensation. Basing its position on the larger national interest, the Roosevelt administration adopted a stand between the claims of the Mexican government and the U.S. oil companies, brokering a compromise on the amount and type of compensation. The resulting settlement cemented U.S.-Mexican friendship on the eve of U.S. intervention in World War II, launching an extended period of close cooperation between the two nations. After his service in Mexico, Daniels returned to his home and resumed his editorship of the *Raleigh News and Observer* in 1941, at the age of eighty, and completed his autobiography.

KENNETH J. GRIEB

See also Bryan, William Jennings; Good Neighbor Policy; Mexico; Navy, U.S. Department of; Roosevelt, Franklin Delano; Wilson, Thomas Woodrow

FURTHER READING

Cronin, E. David. *Josephus Daniels in Mexico*. Madison, Wisc., 1960.
Daniels, Josephus. *Editor in Politics*. Chapel Hill, N.C., 1940.
———. *The Wilson Era: Years of Peace*. Chapel Hill, N.C., 1944.
———. *The Wilson Era: Years of War and After*. Chapel Hill, N.C., 1946.
———. *Shirt-Sleeve Diplomat*. Chapel Hill, N.C., 1966.
Morrison, Joseph L. *Josephus Daniels: The Small-d Democrat*. Chapel Hill, N.C., 1966.

DANISH WEST INDIES, ACQUISITION OF

(1917)

U.S. purchase of the Danish West Indies—comprising the islands of Saint Thomas, Saint John, and Saint Croix—located east of Puerto Rico in the Caribbean Sea. The islands were purchased on 31 March 1917 by the United States from Denmark for $25 million and renamed the U.S. Virgin Islands. Negotiations commenced during the American Civil War (1861–1865) and continued intermittently for more than half a century. The United States sought a naval base and did not want a hostile European power to take possession of the islands. Denmark increasingly considered the islands an economic liability. The islanders, mired in increasing poverty, looked toward transfer to the United States with some enthusiasm. In 1867, however, the U.S. Senate failed to ratify a treaty providing for such a transfer. Denmark's upper house of parliament fell short of approving a similar treaty in 1902. After the Panama Canal opened in 1914 and the United States was on the verge of entering World War I, the fear of a possible takeover of the islands by Germany propelled the United States and Denmark to conclude the sale.

The United States had threatened to occupy the islands by force should Denmark balk at selling them.

Although no plebiscite was held, the islanders appeared to support transfer because they mistakenly expected to be accorded the constitutional rights of U.S. citizens. Article 6 of the 1917 treaty provided that those islanders who did not within one year make a declaration to retain their Danish citizenship "shall be held…to have accepted citizenship in the United States." Nevertheless, by a ruling of the Department of State, Virgin Islanders were denied U.S. citizenship for ten years after the transfer. The islands were governed under carried-over Danish colonial laws by the U.S. Navy for fourteen years. In the last decade of the twentieth century, the Virgin Islands, with a population of some 100,000 and economically dependent on the United States, remained an unincorporated territory of the United States. Although local democracy prevailed, islanders could not vote in U.S. presidential or congressional elections. A nonvoting delegate was assigned to the U.S. House of Representatives. The United Nations still considered the islands a non-self-governing territory.

WILLIAM W. BOYER, JR.

See also Virgin Islands

FURTHER READING

Boyer, William W. *America's Virgin Islands*. Durham, N.C., 1983.
Tansill, Charles C. *The Purchase of the Danish West Indies*. Baltimore, 1932.

DARWINISM

The scientific theory developed by British naturalist Charles R. Darwin in *The Origin of the Species* (1859) and *Descent of Man* (1871). Darwin viewed the evolutionary process of plants and animals as a series of genetic adaptations whereby those hereditary variants that best equip an organism to cope with its environment are preserved in a "struggle for existence" and become the prevailing type. Darwin used the term "natural selection" for this process. Concerning human evolution, Darwin suggested that those races considered less advanced might disappear as civilization advanced. Early twentieth-century science found fault with the simplicity of Darwin's ideas, and neo-Darwinism had to be reformulated in the complex language of Mendelian genetics (a process whereby a shuffling and reshuffling of genes provides variants upon which natural selection works, and new genetic information, or genetic code, can arise through the random and unpredictable process called mutation). The notion of scientific proof of racial superiority, however, had great appeal in Western Europe and the United States. Nineteenth-century social philosophers—in particular followers of Herbert Spencer, a British sociologist who coined the term "survival of the fittest"—used Darwinian science to advance theories of racial superiority and to justify conservative, laissez-faire individualism in claiming that both nature and society evolved from natural law. Spencer and his followers seized upon the authority of Darwin's scientific work to the extent that social Darwinism influenced all aspects of intellectual life, including the writings of prominent Protestant theologians. Whereas nineteenth-century concepts of Anglo-Saxon racial superiority had roots in the rise of modern nationalism and the Romantic Movement, Darwin's ideas were employed by social theorists and politicians to justify society's inequities and the subordination of those they viewed as belonging to "less fit" races.

In the United States, where centuries of experience with Native American warfare and slavery had shaped racial prejudices, social Darwinism found a receptive audience. Social Darwinists such as historian John Fiske, clergyman Josiah Strong, social philosopher William Graham Sumner, and U.S. senator Albert J. Beveridge advocated an imperialist foreign policy and a new manifest destiny that included the acquisition of insular possessions. The exclusion of foreigners through immigration laws was also justified by the gospel of Social Darwinism, as it was argued that an influx of lesser races into the United States might lower the nation's intellectual level. In addition, the concept of Anglo-Saxon racial superiority suggested closer ties between the United States and Great Britain, and Darwinian ideas assisted in bringing about a rapprochement between the two nations that developed into an alliance in the twentieth century.

MICHAEL J. DEVINE

See also Beveridge, Albert Jeremiah; Great Britain; Race and Racism; Strong, Josiah

FURTHER READING

DeConde, Alexander. *Ethnicity, Race and American Foreign Policy.* Boston, 1992.

Hofstadter, Richard. *Social Darwinism and American Thought*, rev. ed. Boston, 1992.

DAVIES, JOHN PATON, JR.

(*b.* 6 April 1908)

Foreign Service officer (1931–1954) dismissed during the period of McCarthyism. The son of missionaries, Davies was born and raised in China. After receiving a college education in the United States and at Yenching University, Davies joined the Foreign Service and spent most of the 1930s in China. Following the 1941 Japanese attack on Pearl Harbor, Davies served in China as a political adviser to General Joseph W. Stilwell. The reports Davies and other Foreign Service officers wrote from China during World War II later became the basis for

charges of disloyalty and incompetence. Davies's wartime reports from China emphasized the growing strength of the Chinese communists. He became particularly concerned about the possibility that U.S. policy might neglect the growing Chinese communist movement and offer unqualified support to the increasingly ineffective Nationalist government of Jiang Jieshi (Chiang Kaishek). If this happened, Davies reasoned, Jiang would be encouraged by U.S. backing to wage a civil war he could not win, and the Chinese communists would become more dependent upon the Soviet Union. An early advocate of containment, Davies thought it important to diminish the chances for increased Soviet influence in China.

After World War II, Davies's reports were interpreted against the background of growing Cold War tensions and, in particular, the victory of the communists in China in 1949. Some critics from the U.S. right and the China Lobby charged that Davies's assessments during the war contributed to the communist victory. His assessments were, in fact, sometimes inaccurate, but often sound and hardly responsible for what happened in China. Beginning in 1951 Davies was subjected to a three-year series of suspensions and investigations. In 1954 Secretary of State John Foster Dulles fired Davies for "lack of judgment, discretion, and reliability." Davies joined the list of several China hands (experts on China, several of them Foreign Service officers), who were fired or forced into early retirement in the era of McCarthyism. Following his dismissal, Davies moved to South America and pursued business interests. In 1969 his security clearance was restored, but he did not reenter government service.

JAMES A. FETZER

See also China; China Hands; China Lobby; McCarthyism

FURTHER READING

Davies, John Paton. *Dragon by the Tail.* New York, 1972.

Fetzer, James. "The Case of John Paton Davies, Jr." *Foreign Service Journal* 54 (November 1977): 15–22, 31–32.

DAVIES, JOSEPH EDWARD

(*b.* 29 November 1876; *d.* 9 May 1958)

U.S. ambassador to the Soviet Union (1937–1938) and a specialist on U.S.-Soviet relations during World War II. Born in Watertown, Wisconsin, and educated at the University of Wisconsin (A.B. 1898, L.L.B. 1901), Davies became a successful Washington, D.C., attorney. He remained politically inactive until the presidential nomination of his friend Franklin D. Roosevelt in 1932 induced him to support the Democratic party. While a defender of Roosevelt's New Deal policies, Davies did not receive his first governmental appointment until January 1937. As the ambassador to the Soviet Union, Davies sought to improve relations between the two nations and solve the problems of debts owed to the United States by Soviet Russia. He personally disagreed with the Soviet system of government, but unlike his predecessor William C. Bullitt, Davies advocated the establishment of a more cooperative policy toward the Soviet Union. Although he failed to resolve the debt problem, Davies succeeded in establishing a cordial relationship with the Soviet government and Premier Joseph Stalin. Davies's tenure in Moscow ended in June 1938 when he became ambassador to Belgium and minister to Luxembourg. After fifteen months in Belgium reporting on the volatile political scene, and an additional year as special envoy for Secretary of State Cordell Hull, Davies resigned from the Department of State and returned to his private law practice.

Germany's invasion of the Soviet Union in June 1941 brought Davies back to government service as Roosevelt's liaison to the Soviet embassy in Washington. Davies once again worked to improve U.S.-Soviet relations. The publication of his *Mission to Moscow* (1941) assisted this endeavor by giving the Soviet government an extremely favorable image, and by providing the administration with an effective means for gaining public support for the Soviet war effort. Davies's most important contribution to U.S.-Soviet cooperation was his assistance in arranging the November 1943 Teheran Conference—the tripartite meeting that cemented war aims and initiated discussions of the postwar world order. His missions to Moscow and Mexico City—where he met with Soviet ambassador Konstatin Umanskii—convinced Stalin of the necessity to convene a conference. Yet the success of the Teheran Conference reduced Davies's role within the Roosevelt administration, as the president no longer needed him to communicate with Stalin. Having lost his influence with the president, Davies became, for most of 1944, the Department of State's mediator in a dispute over the defection of an official from the Soviet Purchasing Commission. With Roosevelt's death in April 1945, Davies served again as an adviser on U.S.-Soviet relations. After a mission to London, where he informed Prime Minister Winston Churchill of President Harry S. Truman's decision to conduct a separate meeting with Stalin prior to the upcoming tripartite discussions, Davies accompanied Truman to the Potsdam Conference (July–August 1945). As Truman's personal adviser, Davies greatly influenced the president's decision to emphasize U.S.-Soviet collaboration during the conference. The subsequent failure of this conciliatory approach, however, damaged his professional ties with top officials. Davies continued to support conciliation and became a critic of U.S. foreign policy toward the Soviet Union—particularly the containment doctrine. Although isolated from the administration, Davies's personal relationship with Truman remained cordial.

In early 1950 Davies and his wife traveled to Latin America with Truman's approval to garner support for the president's plan to supply aid to the developing areas of the world. With the inauguration of President Dwight D. Eisenhower in January 1953, Davies found himself excluded from the Republican administration.

SCOTT D. KELLER

See also Belgium; Bullitt, William Christian; Cold War; Containment; Roosevelt, Franklin Delano; Russia and the Soviet Union; Truman, Harry S.; World War II

FURTHER READING

Beloff, Max. *The Foreign Policy of Soviet Russia.* London, 1947.
Davies, Joseph E. *Mission to Moscow.* New York, 1941.
Eagles, Keith David. *Ambassador Joseph E. Davies and American-Soviet Relations, 1937–1941.* New York, 1985.
MacLean, Elizabeth Kimball. *Joseph E. Davies: Envoy to the Soviets.* Westport, Conn., 1992.
Ullman, Richard H. "The Davis Mission and United States-Soviet Relations, 1937-41." *World Politics* 9 (January 1957):220–239.

DAVIS, ELMER HOLMES

(*b.* 13 January 1891; *d.* 18 May 1958)

Director of the Office of War Information (1942–1945). An Indiana-born journalist and Rhodes scholar who joined the *New York Times* in 1914, Davis gained fame between the world wars as a radio commentator for CBS News. His commonsense broadcasts after the August 1939 outbreak of World War II seemed to reflect U.S. public opinion as it evolved from isolationism to interventionism. Wartime service as head of the Office of War Information (OWI) capped his career. Trying to balance the public's right to know against the demands of national security, and caught between zealous colleagues wanting to promote a liberal postwar world and Presi-dent Franklin D. Roosevelt's pragmatic approach to official propaganda, Davis avoided the excesses of the World War I Committee on Public Information. Against the advice of Admiral Ernest J. King, Roosevelt supported Davis in reporting full naval losses. For Davis the basic message of OWI was that "we are coming, that we are going to win, and that in the long run everybody will be better off because we won." After the war he worked as an analyst for ABC News until his retirement in 1956.

J. GARRY CLIFFORD

See also Committee on Public Information; Journalism and Foreign Policy; World War II

FURTHER READING

Culbert, David. *News for Everyman: Radio and Foreign Affairs in Thirties America.* Westport, Conn., 1976.

Winkler, Allan M. *The Politics of Propaganda: The Office of War Information, 1942–1945.* New Haven, Conn., 1978.

DAVIS, JEFFERSON

(*b.* 3 June 1808; *d.* 6 December 1889)

U.S. congressman (1845–1846), senator (1847–1851, 1857–1861), secretary of war (1853–1857), and president of the Confederate States of America (1861–1865). Born in Fairview, Kentucky, Davis was raised in Mississippi. He received a commission from the U.S. Military Academy in 1828 and served in the army until 1835. After serving as a Democrat in the House of Representatives, he reentered the army in 1846 to fight in the Mexican War and distinguished himself at the Battle of Buena Vista. He returned to Mississippi a popular hero in 1847 and that year was elected to the Senate, where he opposed the movement to annex all of Mexico, although he ultimately supported the Treaty of Guadalupe Hidalgo of 1848. Concerned about the decline of the South's power in the federal government, Davis became a prominent Southern partisan and expansionist, participating in the movement to acquire both the Yucatán Peninsula and Cuba in 1848.

Davis entered the expansionist cabinet of President Franklin Pierce as secretary of war in 1852, following an unsuccessful campaign for governor of Mississippi. He opposed the filibustering schemes of his rival, Mississippi governor John A. Quitman, and of William Walker, but he actively supported the Ostend Manifesto of 1854, which called for Spain either to sell Cuba or face its military seizure by the United States. Davis led the movement to acquire from Mexico the territory needed for construction of a southern transcontinental railroad and was chiefly responsible for convincing Pierce to negotiate the Gadsden Purchase of 1853. Davis returned to the Senate in 1857, and during the secession crisis of 1860–1861 he worked for a mutually acceptable compromise. When these efforts failed in January 1861, he resigned and joined the secessionists.

Davis coveted a military commission in the new Confederate States of America, and it was with reluctance that he accepted the presidency. His inauguration took place in February 1861. Davis did not have a strong foreign policy program in mind when he became president and expected that European attraction to the Confederate promise of free trade and dependence on "King Cotton" would guarantee European recognition of the Confederacy and support for its survival. When Great Britain and France held back their support, Davis dispatched James M. Mason and John Slidell to London and Paris to establish permanent missions. He also selected two journalists, Henry Hotze and Edwin De Leon, to inaugurate extensive propaganda campaigns in those nations to win popular and governmental support for the Southern cause.

Davis's program failed. Great Britain and France both survived their cotton famines, and Great Britain refused to intervene in support of the Confederacy until Confederate military successes could clearly convince the North of the futility of continuing the war. That moment never arrived. By December 1864, in desperation, Davis sent Duncan F. Kenner on a secret mission to Great Britain and France to offer emancipation of slaves in exchange for recognition, but neither country showed interest. Davis's last diplomatic effort was the dispatch of a mission to meet with President Abraham Lincoln and Union secretary of state William H. Seward at Hampton Roads, Virginia, in February 1865, but because Lincoln insisted upon reunion and Davis remained firm on independence, that effort failed as well. One month after the surrender of General Robert E. Lee in April 1865, federal troops captured Davis in Georgia. He was imprisoned until 1867; although he was indicted for treason, he was never brought to trial. Between that time and his death in 1889, Davis went to Canada and England and lived quietly and away from public affairs. His *Rise and Fall of the Confederate States* appeared in 1881.

KINLEY J. BRAUER

See also American Civil War; Confederate States of America; Filibusters; Gadsden Purchase; Mexico, War with; Ostend Manifesto; Slidell, John; Walker, William

FURTHER READING

Crist, Lynda L., and May S. Dix, eds. *The Papers of Jefferson Davis,* 8 vols. Baton Rouge, La., 1971–1994.

Davis, William C. *Jefferson Davis.* New York, 1992.

Eaton, Clement. *Jefferson Davis.* New York, 1977.

Owsley, Frank Lawrence. *King Cotton Diplomacy: Foreign Relations of the Confederate States of America,* 2nd ed. Chicago, 1959.

Patrick, Rembert Wallace. *Jefferson Davis and His Cabinet.* Baton Rouge, La., 1944.

Strode, Hudson. *Jefferson Davis,* 3 vols. New York, 1955–1959.

Thomas, Emory M. *The Confederate Nation, 1861–1865.* New York, 1979.

Vandiver, Frank E. *Jefferson Davis and the Confederate State.* Oxford, England, 1964.

DAVIS, NORMAN HEZEKIAH

(*b.* 9 August 1878; *d.* 2 July 1944)

Businessman and public servant who represented the United States at numerous disarmament and economic conferences between 1919 and 1944. Born in Bedford County, Tennessee, Davis spent the years 1902 through

1917 in Cuba, where he amassed a considerable fortune as president of the Trust Company of Cuba and as an investor in several other island businesses. Having become independently wealthy, Davis volunteered his services to and became influential among the makers of foreign policy, particularly in Democratic administrations, even though he only occasionally held official positions. He was known as a patient, persuasive idealist and a fervent internationalist.

Davis served briefly in the Treasury Department before becoming an adviser to the U.S. delegation at the Paris Peace Conference of 1919, where he achieved prominence as U.S. representative to the Reparations Commission. Davis then served as undersecretary of state in the waning days of Woodrow Wilson's administration, from June 1920 through March 1921. Throughout the 1920s and 1930s Davis represented the United States at virtually every economic, reparations, and disarmament conference. An opponent of the harsh reparations terms imposed on Germany in the wake of World War I, he argued for a practical assessment of Germany's capacity to pay. Convinced that the Kellogg-Briand Pact outlawing war was too broad to achieve peace, he promoted disarmament while representing the United States at both the London Naval and Geneva Disarmament conferences. He was often dispatched to such sessions with no specific instructions, an arrangement that allowed him to use his own judgment in negotiations. A frequent visitor at the Department of State, he enjoyed access to top officials, including the right to walk into meetings in the office of Secretary of State Cordell Hull, even though he held no formal post.

Davis also served as head of the League of Nations Commission, which met in 1924 to determine the status of the port of Memel, known in Lithuania as Klaipéda. With the reestablishment of an independent Lithuania after World War I, the Paris Peace Conference placed the territory around this important port, disputed since the thirteenth-century conquests by Teutonic knights and claimed by Germany, Lithuania, and Poland, under a French high commissioner on behalf of the Allies. When the inhabitants of the city and its hinterland sought independent status, the Lithuanian military occupied the area, resulting in the establishment of a League of Nations Commission, headed by Davis, which ultimately recognized Lithuanian control of the area. In 1921 Davis helped establish the Council on Foreign Relations and its publication *Foreign Affairs*, to which he was a frequent contributor. He also served as president of the American Red Cross and president of the board of the International Red Cross from 1938 until his death.

Kenneth J. Grieb

See also Council on Foreign Relations; Cuba; Germany; Hull, Cordell; International Red Cross and Red Crescent Movement; Kellogg-Briand Pact; League of Nations; Lithuania; London Naval Conferences of 1930 and 1935–1936; Paris Peace Conference of 1919; Reparations

FURTHER READING

Pratt, Julius W. *Cordell Hull.* Vol. 1 of *The American Secretaries of State and Their Diplomacy,* edited by Samuel Flagg Bemis. New York, 1964.
Smith, Daniel M. *Aftermath of War: Bainbridge Colby and Wilsonian Diplomacy: 1920–1921.* Philadelphia, 1970.

DAWES PLAN

(1924)

The arrangement devised by Chicago banker Charles G. Dawes to settle the World War I European reparations problem. In 1921 the Allied Reparations Commission established by the Treaty of Versailles fixed Germany's obligations at 132 billion gold marks (approximately $33 billion). If Germany met its annual payment, then France, Great Britain, Italy, and other Allied nations could begin paying their war debts to the United States. In late 1922, however, and again in January 1923, Germany defaulted in its payment because of inflation and a ruined economy. The Reparations Commission then authorized France and Belgium to occupy Germany's Ruhr Valley. Germany passively resisted this occupation, while the economies of both Germany and France continued to decline.

In 1923 all German reparations payments stopped, and Secretary of State Charles Evans Hughes proposed that a committee of experts draft a plan to solve the problem. The Reparations Commission actually appointed two committees. Dawes headed one committee that also included banker Henry M. Robinson and the chairman of the board of General Electric, Owen D. Young. They produced the Dawes Plan. Implemented in 1924, the plan reorganized the Reichsbank under Allied supervision in order to stabilize the German currency, and it provided for a graduated reparations payment schedule over an indefinite period of time to help Germany's economy and monetary system recover. Under the Dawes Plan, Germany had to pay $250 million in reparations in 1925; as the German economy improved, the reparations payments were to increase. As part of the plan Germany received a loan of $200 million from U.S. and Allied investors, which helped Germany to restore its industries and back a new currency issue.

During the prosperous years from 1924 to 1928 the Dawes Plan worked well. German prosperity returned and the currency stabilized, but Germany continued to borrow to finance increasingly shaky economic expansion from eager U.S. bankers who sold German bonds in the U.S. market. A cyclical pattern developed: U.S.

banks loaned Germany money; Germany paid its reparations payments; and the European nations then paid their war debts to the United States. In 1928, when Germany's reparations payments became larger, Berlin asked for further reductions in reparations. At that point the Dawes Plan was replaced by the Young Plan (1929), which drastically reduced the amount owed by Germany. With the crash of the U.S. stock market in 1929 and a drastic decline in U.S. private investment abroad, the system disintegrated and German reparations payments came to an end.

LOUIS R. SMITH, JR.

See also Germany; Hughes, Charles Evans; Reparations; Versailles Treaty of 1919; War Debt of World War I

FURTHER READING

Cohen, Warren I. *Empire Without Tears: America's Foreign Relations 1921–1933.* Philadelphia, 1987.
Kent, Bruce. *The Spoils of War: The Politics, Economics, and Diplomacy of Reparations, 1918–1928.* Columbia, Mo., 1989.
Schuker, Stephen A. *American "Reparations" to Germany, 1919–1933: Implications for Third World Debt Crises.* Princeton, N.J., 1988.
———. *The End of French Predominance in Europe: The Financial Crisis of 1924 and the Adoption of the Dawes Plan.* Chapel Hill, N.C., 1988.

DAY, WILLIAM RUFUS

(*b.* 17 April 1849; *d.* 9 July 1923)

Secretary of state during the Spanish-American-Cuban-Filipino War of 1898 and head of the U.S. delegation to the 1898 Paris Peace Conference, where the treaty ending the war was negotiated. Born in Ravenna, Ohio, Day graduated from the University of Michigan and practiced law in Canton, Ohio. In May 1897, finding aging Secretary of State John Sherman to be unreliable, President William McKinley selected Day, his hometown friend, to be assistant secretary of state. When Sherman resigned in April 1898, McKinley named Day to succeed him. Day had no diplomatic experience and relied on Assistant Secretary of State John Bassett Moore for advice. Completely loyal to McKinley, self-effacing, and discreet in public, Day carefully handled the difficult U.S. involvement in Cuba's revolt against Spain and its eruption into war on 21 April 1898. He came to favor intervention in Cuba to stop the suffering of starving Cubans and to end Spanish misrule on the island. At war's end Day favored keeping a port in the Philippine Islands but cautioned McKinley against acquiring all of the islands. In 1903 President Theodore Roosevelt appointed him to the U.S. Supreme Court, where he remained until 1922.

JOHN L. OFFNER

See also Cuba; McKinley, William; Spanish-American-Cuban-Filipino War, 1898

FURTHER READING

Offner, John L. *An Unwanted War: The Diplomacy of the United States and Spain over Cuba, 1895–1898.* Chapel Hill, N.C., 1992.
Shippee, Lester B., and Royal B. Way. *William Rufus Day.* Vol. 9 of *The American Secretaries of State and Their Diplomacy,* edited by Samuel Flagg Bemis. New York, 1928.

DEANE, SILAS

(*b.* 24 December 1737; *d.* 23 September 1789)

A leader in the American Revolution who helped gain and organize French support for the colonies' independence from Great Britain. Born in Groton, Connecticut, Yale graduate Silas Deane, assisted by two advantageous marriages, rose rapidly as a lawyer, merchant, politician, and revolutionary leader in Connecticut. Elected to the first and second Continental Congresses (1774–1775), he served on the important Naval and Marine Committees, the Committee of Secret Correspondence, and the Secret Committee of Trade. Like other committee members, Deane shared in Secret Committee contracts, notably the so-called Indian Contract, which imported gifts that were used to secure the friendship or neutrality of local tribes. Failing to win reelection, he withdrew from Congress early in 1776 and was immediately recruited by his partners in Secret Committee contracts to implement their overseas ventures. In March 1776 the Committee of Secret Correspondence appointed him its agent to procure supplies and to sound out the French on questions of U.S. independence, official reception of a U.S. minister, and treaties of commerce and alliance. Deane recruited engineers and other foreign officers, including not only the excellent officers Marquis de Lafayette, Johann Kalb, Friedrich von Steuben, and Casimir Pulaski, but also a number of well-connected but useless adventurers who antagonized Congress.

In September 1776 Congress appointed as its official diplomatic mission to Europe a three-person commission consisting of Deane, Benjamin Franklin, and Arthur Lee. On arrival in France, Franklin assumed most high-level diplomatic functions, and Deane specialized in acquiring ships and supplies, arming privateers, and sponsoring controversial raids on British ships. Deane's goals were to raise British insurance rates, arouse opposition to the American Revolution in England, divert the British Navy from its blockade of the U.S. coastline, and precipitate European involvement in the war. Arthur Lee was often not informed of the work of Franklin and Deane, and forwarded his suspicions of their chicanery and that of their contacts to the United States. Lax practices of court-connected merchants and agents, stock speculations and private investments of Deane and his associates, and their acquisition of British goods through neutral channels for supply ventures provided Lee with ample fuel for his charges.

In February 1778, Franklin, Lee, and Deane signed treaties of commerce and alliance with France. Eight cargoes of munitions had been forwarded with Caron de Beaumarchais's assistance, but controversy arose as to whether they were entirely a French subsidy, as Lee believed, or were to be paid for, as Deane and Beaumarchais contended. Deane was recalled, purportedly to brief Congress, but really to answer to Lee's allegations. Having left most of his documents in Europe, Deane failed to refute charges and to settle his accounts with Congress. The resulting controversies, known as the Deane-Lee affair (1778–1779), embarrassed France by exposing details of early French assistance to the United States. They also intensified personal and partisan divisions between Deane's backers—who were largely moderate to conservative, pragmatic and commercial-minded, pro-French, and based in the middle and southern states—and Lee's supporters, who were associated with the New England–based Adams-Lee wing of the early revolutionary movement, were suspicious of Benjamin Franklin and of the French, advocated "republican virtue," and opposed the self-interested and commercial activities of Deane's associates. The divisions influenced appointments to diplomatic posts, attitudes toward the French alliance, and stands taken in peace negotiations for many years.

Deane returned to Europe in 1780, where he became increasingly suspicious of French intentions. He espoused a peace that would guarantee U.S. rights but not independence. In 1781 his letters, which advised abandonment of independence and of the French alliance, were published, probably with his collusion, in the Loyalist press. Reviled as a traitor, nearly friendless and penniless, he retired to neutral Belgium and struggled unsuccessfully to settle his public accounts and recoup his funds. He moved to England after the preliminary peace treaty, where he may have contributed to Lord Sheffield's influential 1783 pamphlet opposing U.S. shipping access to the British West Indies.

When animosities had faded, Deane set sail for the United States in 1789 and died shortly after boarding ship. The historian Julian Boyd has attributed Deane's death to poisoning by his ostensible friend Edward Bancroft, who allegedly feared exposure of his activities as a double agent. Deane's accounts of his transactions on behalf of the United States were finally settled in 1842 and payment was made to his heirs.

ELIZABETH NUXOLL

See also American Revolution; Beaumarchais, Pierre Augustin, Caron de; Franklin, Benjamin

FURTHER READING

The Deane Papers. 5 vols. New York Historical Society, Collections for the Years 1886–1890. New York, 1887–1891.

Boyd, Julian. "Silas Deane: Death by a Kindly Teacher of Treason?" *William and Mary Quarterly*, 3rd ser., 16 (1959): 165–187, 319–342, 515–550.

Ferguson, E. James. *The Power of the Purse: A History of American Public Finance, 1776–1790.* Chapel Hill, N.C., 1961.

Smith, Paul, Gerald W. Gawalt, Rosemary Fry Plakas, Eugene R. Sheridan, and Ronald M. Gephart, eds. *Letters of Delegates to Congress, 1774–1789.* 22 vols. as of 1996. Washington, D. C., Library of Congress, 1976–.

DECLARATION OF INDEPENDENCE

The document, dated 4 July 1776, that justifies the decision of the Continental Congress to separate the thirteen colonies from the British Empire and declares the United States of America independent of Great Britain.

Aside from John and Samuel Adams and Richard Henry Lee, few colonists in British North America advocated independence prior to late 1775. Colonial protests against British policies explicitly denied any desire to break with Great Britain. Some colonies issued instructions to their delegates to the Continental Congress that required them to oppose measures toward independence. Many colonists, however, saw the Coercive Acts of 1774, fighting at Lexington and Concord, the Prohibitory Act of 1775, and other aggressive actions by the British and by Loyalists as tantamount to a declaration of war against them. Calls for independence gained support with each British action. In January 1776, the publication and wide circulation of Thomas Paine's *Common Sense* popularized the idea of independence and lent it greater emotional appeal. Paine urged colonists to separate from Great Britain and to champion liberty and human rights. He attacked hereditary monarchy and called for the establishment of a republic that would serve as a haven for the oppressed. He postulated the political advantages of independence, notably freedom from European wars, as well as the economic advantages, particularly freedom to trade with the entire world.

As Paine's word was being propagated, various colonies established state governments and the Continental Congress initiated actions equivalent to those of a sovereign government. Congress ordered the disarming of Loyalists, authorized the issuance of letters of marque and reprisal to privateers to attack British ships, and, in April 1776, opened American ports to all nations except Great Britain. In May 1776 the Continental Congress advised colonial assemblies that had not yet done so to adopt governments suitable to "the happiness and safety of their constituents in particular and America in general."

Many congressional delegates still opposed any resolution in favor of independence. Some objected in principle, and argued that the options of negotiation and compromise had not yet been exhausted. Others urged postponement of independence until aid was promised or obtained from other nations. John Dickinson, delegate from Pennsylvania, cautioned against a declaration before commercial negotiations with France began to prevent Congress from jeopardizing economic opportunities with France. Other delegates refused to act without specific authorization by their legislatures. Beginning with Massachusetts in January, South Carolina in March, Georgia and North Carolina in April, and Virginia in May 1776, states passed resolutions rescinding their bans on votes for independence or ordering their delegates to favor a declaration of independence.

A declaration of independence was tied to the quest for foreign aid. By 1776 Congress realized that, faced with a British naval blockade, the colonies could not obtain all the munitions they needed through ordinary commerce. Nor could they expect substantial support from Great Britain's rivals, France and Spain, or conduct trade with neutral nations while the possibility of reconciliation remained. As colonies, they lacked international legal standing: they were not eligible to enter into treaties or contracts because under international law they remained parts of Great Britain engaged in civil war. Nations were not willing to risk provoking Great Britain by conducting commerce with its colonies. The need for a clearer picture of European attitudes about independence contributed to the appointment of Silas Deane in March 1776 as the first American agent to France, the nation that would benefit most from dismemberment of the British empire. Deane was instructed to ascertain how France would respond to a declaration of independence, and surprisingly, he reported a pledge of support before independence was even declared. As Richard Henry Lee of Virginia proclaimed on 2 June, "It is not choice then but necessity that calls for independence as the only means by which foreign alliance can be obtained."

On 7 June 1776, Lee initiated the formal debate on independence in the second Continental Congress by introducing a three-part resolution: "That these United States are, and of right ought to be free and independent States, that they are absolved from all allegiance to the British Crown, and that all political connection between them and the State of Great Britain is, and ought to be, totally dissolved. That it is expedient forthwith to take the most effectual measures for forming foreign alliances. That a plan of confederation be prepared and transmitted to the respective colonies for their consideration and approbation." The proposals were interlocked: independence had to be declared to get foreign aid, and a league had to be formed to negotiate that aid.

Debate began on 8 June. The initial vote showed seven delegations in favor (New Hampshire, Rhode Island, Massachusetts, Connecticut, Virginia, North Carolina, and Georgia), and six opposed or undecided. Congress appointed a committee consisting of Thomas Jefferson of Virginia, Benjamin Franklin of Pennsylvania, John Adams of Massachusetts, Roger Sherman of Connecticut, and Robert R. Livingston of New York to prepare a formal draft of a declaration of independence that set forth the contents of the first section of Lee's resolution. Other committees were formed to draw up plans for treaties with foreign powers and for a confederation. Further debate on the resolution was postponed until 1 July.

Jefferson was chosen to write the first draft of the Declaration of Independence. He forwarded the completed text to John Adams and Benjamin Franklin for review and editing, then presented it to the entire committee, which reported the revised version to Congress on 28 June. Among significant changes made in Congress were a softening of attacks on the people of Great Britain so as not to offend potential supporters there and the deletion of a passage condemning British promotion of the African slave trade. According to Jefferson, the latter deletion was made in deference to South Carolina and Georgia, which wished to continue importing slaves. Jefferson stated that many Northerners had become uncomfortable with the censure of slavery because, though they held few slaves, many profited considerably by transporting them.

Opinion in favor of independence had advanced while the document was being drafted. The vote taken on 1 July counted nine states in favor, two opposed (Pennsylvania and South Carolina), one deadlocked (Delaware), and one abstaining (New York, whose delegates were awaiting revised instructions). The deadlock in the Delaware delegation was broken by the dramatic arrival of an additional delegate, Caesar Rodney, who, though ill, rode eighty miles in stormy weather to cast his vote. Once two Pennsylvania delegates, Robert Morris and John Dickinson, who considered the declaration premature but were unwilling to stand in its way, absented themselves, that state cast its vote three to two for independence. South Carolina decided not to go against the tide, and on 2 July, with New York still abstaining, Congress voted 12 to 1 in favor of Lee's resolution for independence. After further alterations, Congress approved the text of the revised declaration on 4 July, again by a vote of 12 to 1. The document was signed only by John Hancock as president and Charles Thomson as secretary of Congress. Dated 4 July, the text was first read publicly on 8 July, then to the Continental Army on 9 July, the day the New York legislature approved a vote for independence. When the news from New York reached Congress, it resolved that the declaration be embossed on parchment as the unanimous declaration of the thirteen United States of America. Most delegates signed the text on 2

August; six others not then present signed later. A few delegates refused to sign. Some of these, such as John Dickinson of Pennsylvania and James Duane, Robert R. Livingston, and John Jay of New York, nevertheless remained involved in the Revolution. Others left Congress, withdrew from the war effort, or became active or passive Loyalists (Thomas Willing of Pennsylvania, John Alsop of New York, Robert Alexander of Maryland). Though singled out for punishment by the British government, none of the signers ever recanted his decision.

The declaration is composed of three parts. The first two state political philosophy and list grievances directed at King George III rather than at Parliament. These were based on Jefferson's original draft. The third part and closing paragraph (the formal declaration of separation) was added by Congress and derived from Lee's original motion. Though partly designed to encourage popular domestic support, the declaration promptly sought primarily to persuade a foreign audience. The declaration was a manifesto, a propaganda piece proclaiming to the "candid world" the reasons for the decision to become independent. The declaration appealed to the "Laws of Nature and Nature's God" as its philosophical underpinnings, declaring that all men were created equal and endowed with rights that could not be set aside, including "life, liberty and the pursuit of happiness." Since governments derived their authority from the consent of the governed to secure their rights, they could be overturned if they failed to do so. According to John Adams, "there was not an idea in it, but what had been hackneyed in Congress for two years before."

Silas Deane reported that the declaration was well received by the French government. The text had little immediate popular impact abroad, though the Revolution itself was greeted with enthusiasm, especially in France. Even in the United States, the document did not become a national symbol and testament until the nineteenth century, though the Fourth of July soon became a national holiday.

Once independence was declared, the United States was free to send ministers to Europe to seek recognition and help. The declaration led to the appointment by Congress of commissioners to negotiate treaties of alliance and commerce, and brought about the promotion of the American cause by Benjamin Franklin in France. The United States had to win political and military independence before it could obtain treaties of alliance or commerce.

ELIZABETH NUXOLL

See also Adams, John; American Revolution; Deane, Silas; Franklin, Benjamin; Jefferson, Thomas; Loyalists; Morris, Robert; Paine, Thomas; Privateering; Slave Trade and Slavery

FURTHER READING

Becker, Carl L. *The Declaration of Independence: A Study in the History of Political Ideas.* New York, 1922.
Boyd, Julian P. *The Declaration of Independence: The Evolution of the Text.* Princeton, N.J., 1945.
Fliegelman, Jay. *Declaring Independence: Jefferson, Natural Language & the Culture of Performance.* Stanford, Calif., 1993.
Hawke, David Freeman. *In the Midst of a Revolution.* Philadelphia, Pa., 1961.
———. *A Transaction of Free Men: The Birth and Course of the Declaration of Independence.* New York, 1964.
Rakove, Jack N. *The Beginnings of National Politics: An Interpretive History of the Continental Congress.* New York, 1979.
Van Alstyne, Richard. *Empire and Independence: The International History of the American Revolution.* New York, 1965.
Wills, Garry. *Inventing America: Jefferson's Declaration of Independence.* Garden City, N.Y., 1978.

DEFENSE, U.S. DEPARTMENT OF

The federal executive agency embracing most of the military strength available to the U.S. government. Its primary components are the army, navy, air force, and Marine Corps. National Guard units, the Coast Guard, military reserves, and other security-enforcing agencies can be temporarily assigned in emergencies to augment the regular armed services as part of the Department of Defense. Specialized and largely civilian groups, such as the Defense Mapping Agency and the Defense Supply Agency, are also part of the Defense Department. The department's primary purpose is to guard against and possibly to fight armed outsiders perceived as threats to the interests, security, or sovereignty of the United States. Secondary purposes include the implementation of martial law if and as necessary, to assist local police forces when they are unable to cope with disruptions, and to provide humanitarian relief at home or abroad in the wake of natural and manmade disasters.

The head of the Defense Department is the secretary of defense, a cabinet officer appointed by the president with the advice and consent of the Senate. Consistent with the constitutional principle of civilian control of the military, the secretary of defense must be a civilian. A department of war had existed since the earliest days of the Republic, and there had been a separate Department of the Navy since 1798. Because of traditional American concerns about concentrating too much power in one office, the landmark National Security Act of 1947 did not absorb them into a consolidated military department; it provided only for the Office of the Secretary of Defense (OSD), initially staffed by just a small number of assistants and clerks. By 1949, however, it was clear that the secretary could not manage the vast responsibilities imposed on his office without a full-scale department. The 1949 amendments to the 1947 legislation therefore created the Department of Defense. Ironically, Secretary of the Navy James V. Forrestal, who had led the bitter fight to minimize any structural consolidations, was appointed by President Harry S. Truman the first secretary of defense. The National Security Act was further amended in 1953 and 1958, giving the secretary of defense additional new authority. The position continued to grow in influence and prestige.

New legislation stipulated that the secretary of defense stood third in order of presidential succession, behind the secretaries of state and the Treasury. For the populace and the media, the secretary of defense was at times the most prominent member of the cabinet. For example, in the 1960s Secretary of Defense Robert S. McNamara, rather than the secretary of state or a top presidential adviser, was perceived to be the cabinet figure most influential in setting overall foreign policy.

The Department of Defense is sometimes known by the initials DOD or the name of its headquarters building, the Pentagon, a massive five-sided and five-storied structure located in Virginia and designed to be able to withstand a direct bomb hit; it is the only cabinet-level department not headquartered in the District of Columbia. The DOD's proliferating subagencies occupy many other buildings in Washington, D.C., and its suburbs.

Historical Roots

The Department of Defense that emerged in 1945–1949 from the experience of World War II was the product of a much longer evolutionary process that began with the founding of the new nation. The founders of the nation recognized that the United States would occasionally need military force to assert and protect American interests. Because their European heritage taught them to beware of leaders backed by strong military forces, the framers of the Constitution ensured through checks and balances that neither the president nor Congress could carry out military action alone.

The Constitution makes the president "Commander in Chief of the Army and Navy of the United States, and of the Militia of the several States, when called into the actual Service of the United States," and gives him the unshared power to "receive Ambassadors and other public Ministers," making him the official point of contact between the United States and all other governments. The Constitution, on the other hand, gives Congress considerably more enumerated powers that limit the president's sole control of the military, including the power of the purse; that is, the president would have no forces to command if Congress did not first raise the revenue and appropriate the money to pay for military capabilities.

Article I, Section 8, of the Constitution stipulates many other congressional responsibilities either directly

SECRETARIES OF DEFENSE		
ADMINISTRATION	SECRETARY	PERIOD OF APPOINTMENT
Truman	James V. Forrestal	1947–1949
	Louis A. Johnson	1949–1950
	George C. Marshall	1950–1951
	Robert A. Lovett	1951–1953
Eisenhower	Charles E. Wilson	1953–1957
	Neil H. McElroy	1957–1959
	Thomas S. Gates, Jr.	1959–1961
Kennedy L. Johnson	Robert S. McNamara	1961–1968
	Clark M. Clifford	1968–1969
Nixon	Melvin R. Laird	1969–1973
	Elliot L. Richardson	1973
	James R. Schlesinger	1973–1975
Ford		
	Donald H. Rumsfeld	1975–1977
Carter	Harold Brown	1977–1981
Reagan	Caspar W. Weinberger	1981–1987
	Frank C. Carlucci III	1987–1989
Bush	Richard B. Cheney	1989–1993
Clinton	Leslie Aspin, Jr.	1993–1994
	William J. Perry	1994–Present

Source: U.S. Department of Defense

or indirectly bearing on the nature and use of U.S. military forces. One of these is the power to declare war, which rests solely with Congress. Another is the power to "raise and support Armies," with the stipulation that "no Appropriation of Money to that Use shall be for a longer Term than two Years," which suggested that any army could exist only for brief periods, when the need arose, and would then be demobilized. The framers of the Constitution clearly wanted to keep ground forces on a short leash, fearing a possible threat to civil authority posed by standing armies. They expressed less anxiety about naval forces, stipulating simply that Congress should "provide and maintain a Navy," which implied a recognition that navies historically represented far less usurpative dangers to civil governments than armies, an awareness that navies were hard to create and dismantle on short notice, and a suggestion that a navy of some sort should be kept in existence at all times.

These constitutional provisions laid the groundwork for many of the disputes leading to the creation of the Defense Department a century and a half later. The separation of powers between the president and Congress led to endless struggles between the White House and Capitol Hill for dominance in the decision-making process regarding the nature and use of U.S. military

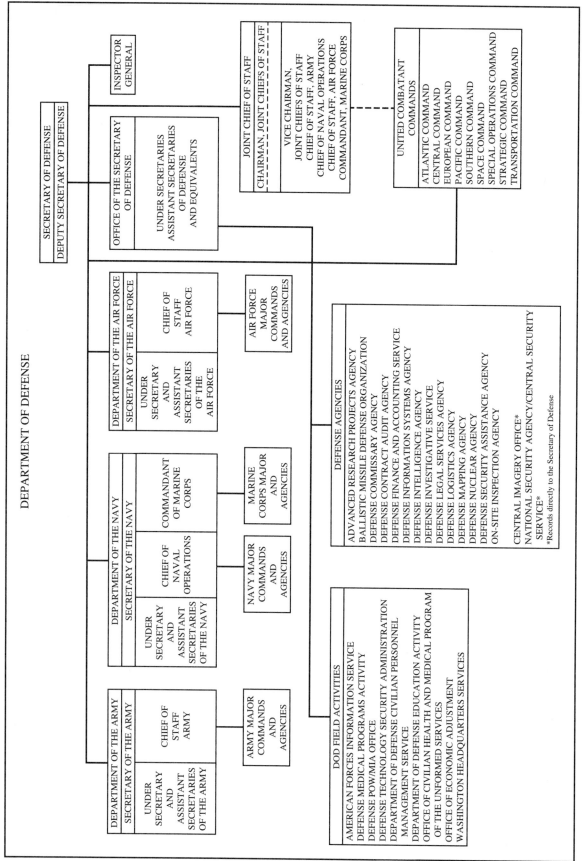

DEPARTMENT OF DEFENSE

Source: *The U.S. Government Manual*

force. This fragmented the attention and interests of senior admirals and generals, virtually preventing the overall cohesion that would ideally characterize any military establishment.

There were also more fundamental differences dividing the army and the navy, the result of the differentiation of the purposes of these two historic armed services in the very language of the Constitution and the differences between land and navy forces in accepted military thinking around the world. When Congress and the administration differed, army and naval leaders were often left without clear understanding as to which of their political masters to follow at any particular time, and they were commonly uninformed about any overarching strategic vision or purpose that might have existed. The determination of the Constitution's framers to avoid expensive and potentially dangerous standing armies led to great cycles of tardy mobilizations before wars and helter-skelter demobilization afterward.

Improvisation thereby became a useful word in describing the U.S. military establishment up until the twentieth century—and, in many respects, thereafter—but none of the fragmentations and confusions was perceived as a serious problem until the decade 1895–1905, when important developments aroused new concerns about U.S. military capabilities. First, the United States won its war with Spain in 1898, foreshadowing the growing role that the United States was to play on the world stage throughout the twentieth century, but the victory was anything but well organized. Japan, another non-European power, won a war with Russia in 1904–1905, further undermining European dominance of world politics, but providing the United States with a new rival.

Important developments were also taking place in science and engineering. The submarine, for example, was rapidly emerging by 1900 as a radically different kind of naval vessel that would soon transform many accepted rules of warfare. By far the most important technological innovation of that same decade was the invention of the airplane, calling into question the ancient principles that had governed the organization of all armed forces everywhere into armies and navies. Aviation zealots quickly began arguing that the airplane made land and sea forces obsolete and that appropriately designed kinds of aircraft would constitute an all-purpose military weapons system. The argument had great appeal in the United States, where Americans typically sought cheap and easy solutions to military problems. Indeed, it was an argument heard again as late as the final decade of the twentieth century.

Ever since the Spanish-American-Cuban-Filipino War of 1898, U.S. leaders have seen centralization as the solution to fragmentation, confusion, and improvisation. This process, still under way as the twentieth century drew to a close, involved consolidating previously autonomous pieces of organizational machinery, whether tightly or loosely, under a new umbrella structure. The first step was taken in 1900, when several older admirals were retained on active duty to serve as members of a navy committee dubbed the General Board. Although given little actual power, it was supposed to impose some coherence on the navy's fractured and contentious bureau system. In 1903 Congress created the army's General Staff system, which was different in approach but similar in purpose to the navy's General Board. In the same year, the Joint Army-Navy Board was created in an effort to generate for the first time some communication, cooperation, and maybe even cordiality between the two armed services, particularly in the area of strategic planning.

President Woodrow Wilson during the period preceding U.S. involvement in World War I, and then President Franklin D. Roosevelt before World War II, informally created senior civilian and mixed civilian-military advisory groups to help in making policy at the White House level. These committees were in the nature of "war cabinets" and succeeded in developing some ideas that were later incorporated in various war plans. On the whole, however, their work did not amount to much, largely because Wilson and Roosevelt were determined to have a free hand as their own defense ministers. As a consequence, when the Japanese attacked Pearl Harbor on 7 December 1941, the United States was not in substantially better shape in terms of organization structures and processes for decision-making for the defense establishment than it had been on 1 May 1898, when Admiral George Dewey somewhat inadvertently won the Battle of Manila Bay and opened the Spanish-American-Cuban-Filipino War.

The Cold War Era

By the end of World War II in 1945, centralization was perceived as unfinished business at best, and a failure at worst. The most difficult question was how to structure military aviation into the military establishment. The stage was set for a great struggle to produce an overall solution with a single omnibus piece of legislation—a struggle that preoccupied much of official Washington from 1945 to 1947. The outcome was the National Security Act of 1947, as amended in 1949, 1953, and 1958. It was the single most important package of legislation pertaining to the organization of the defense bureaucracies, and particularly the structure of the military establishment, in the history of the country. The Department of Defense was created and steadily strengthened while the formerly separate and autonomous cabinet-level Departments of War and the Navy were gradually downgraded. The air force, which had earlier come to enjoy virtual autonomy while technically remaining a part of the army, was set free as a new third service at the same time it was being captured within the new DOD structures. The Marine Corps remained a small component of the navy, but in later years was able to gain more autonomy, especially when its commandant was named a fully statutory rather than voluntarily advisory member of the Joint Chiefs of Staff (JCS).

The National Security Act gave the JCS and its chairman their first statutory recognition, creating a kind of dual chain-of-authority system extending downward from the president and the secretary of defense to the JCS on the uniformed side and to the secretariats on the civilian side. The OSD was the largest, most comprehensive, and powerful of the secretariats, eventually including not just a deputy secretary but also undersecretaries, assistant secretaries, and miscellaneous others with such numbing titles as "principal deputy assistant secretary." Each of the residual service departments (army, navy, and air force) tried to maintain its own duplicate copy of OSD in order to hold on to a shred of autonomy, but it was a losing battle. For the most part, service secretaries thereafter were little more than specialized assistants to and appendages of OSD.

Centralization proceeded along another important avenue. Standing entities called "joint unified and specified commands" emerged in World War II, in recognition that modern war required special mixtures of military capabilities concocted for the job at hand. A unified command was defined in terms of geographic territory—for example, the European theater or the Pacific Ocean arena. A specified command was defined in terms of a special function to be performed as ordered on a global basis—for example, the Strategic Air Command (SAC). Both the unified and specified varieties were called "joint," because they operated under the nominal directives of the JCS while under the ultimate command of the secretary of defense and the president. More than a dozen of these joint commands existed at one time or another during and after World War II. These were America's armed "forces," as contrasted to the traditional armed "services," which remained the army, navy, air force, and marines. Each joint command consisted largely of a brass-heavy headquarters group sitting on top of an empty shell ready to be filled up whenever the commander in chief wanted to deploy it for a particular task. The armed services were assigned to act as repositories of the trained personnel and equipment ready to transfer to whatever joint command might be designated.

This system, however elegant it might have looked in theory, never worked all that well in practice—at least, not until the early 1990s. The entrenched separate services, each with its preferred way of waging war in keeping with its favorite weapons systems, roles, and missions, fought shrewd political battles to avoid being completely enfolded in the centralized OSD and the joint systems. The uniformed and civilian careerists in the services were often easy winners over the politically appointed officials holding the key jobs in the civilian secretariats. Each joint command was largely captured by the traditional service capable of making what appeared to be a logical case. Top navy admirals, for example, always dominated the Atlantic and Pacific Commands; top army generals did the same with the European Command, while the air force hung on to the Strategic Air Command and later the Space Command. In the early 1990s the marines finally got a unified shell to call their own when a marine general was named to head the Central Command (designed mainly for Middle Eastern and Southwest Asian conflicts, such as the Persian Gulf War of 1990–1991). The assignment of a few individuals from the other nondominant services made any joint command look more joint than it actually was.

From the outbreak of World War II until the end of the Cold War, the traditional separate services and their allies both in and out of the government strongly tended to resist centralization measures. Both their executive and legislative masters ordinarily aided them in this resistance. Virtually all of their executive masters, primarily the secretaries of defense, wanted to play divide-and-conquer games, keeping the services off-balance so that they could never gang up on the secretary by developing a strong consensus contrary to official policy. Members of Congress played the same games, but largely because congressmen cultivated special relationships with the various armed services in order to enhance military spending in their districts.

In the early 1980s, however, a consensus began to build among knowledgeable civilians and even some top military officers that the rickety old system could not be made to work at an acceptable price. Embarrassing operational difficulties occurred in the 1983 invasion of Grenada and the 1982–1984 intervention in Lebanon, and procurement scandals became common. The emerging consensus held that the powers and responsibilities of the secretary of defense should be clarified and strengthened even further and that the uniformed side of the dual chain-of-authority system should be significantly strengthened. The result was passage of the Goldwater-Nichols Act of 1986, passed by Congress with almost unanimous support, which made the chairman of the JCS a far more powerful figure, supported by a far more capable staff. He was given authority to discipline the separate services if they did not delegate to him their best officers for joint duty, often known as "purple-suit jobs" in Pentagon parlance, because an officer in one of those positions was not supposed to exhibit loyalty to the uniform color of his or her parent service. It had occasionally happened that when an officer returned to his or her parent service following a "purple" tour, the officer was penalized in some way for having worked against that service's interest; the Goldwater-Nichols Act gave the JCS chairman powerful weapons for dealing with such incidents. The four-star officers who headed the joint specified and unified commands (known informally as the CINCs—for commanders in chief—and pronounced "sinks") were given new glories and responsibilities, although it was made clear to them that they were working for the defense secretary and the JCS chairman, not for their parent services.

Many knowledgeable observers gave much of the credit for the remarkably swift and successful operations in the Persian Gulf War in January-February 1991 to the Goldwater-Nichols Act. It was said that only three levels of authority existed, going from the president as commander in chief through the secretary of defense and the JCS chairman before reaching the operational commander in the field. That streamlined and efficient arrangement contrasted sharply with the almost thirty levels of authority before reaching the field operation commander that existed in October 1983, when the marine barracks in Beirut, Lebanon, were blown up and 241 marines were killed.

An old truism, that the president tends to dominate U.S. foreign relations in times of war or crisis while Congress dominates at all other times, was validated in the years after the Cold War ended. Key people in Congress felt that the White House and the Pentagon were taking entirely too long to recognize and prepare for small-scale military situations, the most likely form of U.S. military involvement in the new global configuration. In the late 1980s and early 1990s, therefore, Congress enacted a law directing the grudging Pentagon to create a new civilian position, the assistant secretary of defense for special operations and low-intensity conflict (abbreviated and sometimes pronounced as "SO/LIC"). The Pentagon was further directed to create a new joint command under a four-star officer who would in turn fall under the authority of this new assistant secretary—one more sign that the U.S. defense establishment was being driven in new directions by new realities.

After the Cold War

With little agreement on prospective external threats, but with a general sense that none of those threats could directly, seriously, or immediately jeopardize U.S. national interests, defense spending tumbled after the Gulf War. Defense spending, which, as a percentage of gross domestic product had peaked at 15 percent during the Korean War, and which had gone up and down in the course of the Cold War, was about 5 percent in 1993 and was forecast to continue down to less than 3 percent by 1998. Using another measure, by 1998 defense outlays as a percentage of total federal outlays were projected to bottom out at about 16 percent, the lowest such figure in more than fifty years.

The declining number of active-duty U.S. armed services personnel in uniform similarly reflected the end of the Cold War. In midsummer 1993 the total stood at just over 2 million, the smallest number since the eve of the Korean War (when it was about 1.5 million), in sharp contrast to a relatively steady figure of more than 3 million from the late 1950s to the early 1980s—and an even sharper contrast to the 12.5 million Americans in uniform at the peak of World War II. The army in the early 1990s projected that it was headed downward to a small size not experienced since the 1930s. All of this was predictable enough, given the historical American pattern of mobilization to meet a serious threat and rapid demobilization once it was believed to have passed. It was also consistent with the historical pattern that, with threats to U.S. security relatively diminished, congressional influence would not be as restrained as in times of crisis. In the first years of President Bill Clinton's administration (1993–1997), it was already clear that, while the interbranch conflict was not as intensely ideologized as it had been when different political parties controlled the different branches, the pulling and tugging for influence over the Department of Defense was still going on.

VINCENT DAVIS

See also Air Force, U.S. Department of; Army, U.S. Department of; Bureaucracy; Cheney, Richard Bruce; Defense Reorganization Act; Forrestal, James Vincent; Goldwater, Barry; Gulf War of 1990–1991; Joint Chiefs of Staff; Marine Corps, U.S.; McNamara, Robert Strange; Military-Industrial Complex; Navy, U.S. Department of; Strategic Air Command; Weinberger, Caspar Willard

FURTHER READING
International Institute for Strategic Studies. *Military Balance* (yearbook). London, 1992.
———. *Strategic Survey* (yearbook). London, 1993.
Kruzel, Joseph J., ed. *American Defense Annual.* New York, 1993.
Millis, Walter, Harvey C. Mansfield, and Harold Stein. *Arms and the State: Civil-Military Elements in National Policy.* New York, 1958.
Secretary of Defense. *Annual Report to the President and the Congress.* Washington, D.C.
U.S. House of Representatives. *United States Defense Policies Since World War II.* Washington, D.C., 1957.

DEFENSE INTELLIGENCE AGENCY
See Intelligence

DEFENSE REORGANIZATION ACT
(1986)

Also known as the Goldwater-Nichols Act, mandated an extensive restructuring of the U.S. military establishment, perhaps the most far-reaching such reorganization since the National Security Act of 1947. It is notable as a high-water mark in the pursuit of "jointness," the capacity of the military services to integrate their efforts on matters ranging from procurement to planning to fighting a war. Ever since 1898, when squabbling between Major General William R. Shafter and Admiral William T. Sampson off the coast of Santiago de Cuba had marred the conduct of the Spanish-American-Cuban-Filipino War, jointness had been a nagging issue, pitting advocates of integration against those devoted to preserving the autonomy and prerogatives of the individual services. Earlier reforms, such as the creation of the Joint Army-Navy Board in 1903, the broadening of the board's mandate during the interwar period, the formalization of the Joint Chiefs of Staff (JCS) in 1947, and subsequent efforts to increase the authority of joint commands, all had failed to satisfy reformers bent on eliminating the service parochialism that they viewed as an obstacle to genuine military effectiveness. The embarrassing failure of the U.S. effort in April 1980 to free its hostages in Iran—a failure largely attributed to the breakdown of coordination between the participating services—touched off yet another round of calls for reform. Likewise, the U. S. intervention in Grenada in 1983, although successful, exposed further deficiencies in joint operations, thereby bolstering the case of critics who insisted that only congressional action could force the military to take jointness seriously. It was in this environment that passage of Goldwater-Nichols was secured.

Sponsored by Senator Barry Goldwater, chairman of the Senate Armed Services Committee, and Representative Bill Nichols, chairman of the Investigations Subcommittee of the House Armed Services Committee, the legislation contained several important provisions. It designated the JCS chairman—rather than the Joint Chiefs as a corporate body—as the principal military adviser to the president, the secretary of defense, and the National Security Council. It assigned to the JCS chairman authority over joint commands and created the new position of JCS vice chairman to assist in directing the activities of that staff and to serve in the chairman's place in his or her absence. It enhanced the authority of the commanders in chief (CINCs) of each of the specified and unified commands, thereby reducing the influence of the individual service chiefs of staff within those commands. It gave the CINCs a more prominent voice in the budget process. Although emphasizing that the chain of command ran directly from the president and secretary of defense to senior commanders in the field, it directed that all operational communications from the president or secretary of defense to combatant commanders be routed through the JCS chairman. It also imposed on the services new requirements for officer education, requiring that service school curricula incorporate matters relating to joint operations, and established guidelines for personnel policies that created incentives for promising officers to seek out joint assignments and to protect officers assigned to joint staffs from being penalized with regard to subsequent opportunities for advancement.

For several years the military services resisted the changes contained in the Goldwater-Nichols Act. Evidence of improved performance in joint operations both in the 1989 invasion of Panama and in the Gulf War of 1990–1991 silenced most of the legislation's critics. By the mid-1990s jointness had been elevated to the level of conventional wisdom both within and without the uniformed services.

ANDREW J. BACEVICH

See also Defense, U.S. Department of; Goldwater, Barry; Joint Chiefs of Staff; National Security Act